THE
CAMBRIDGE
ECONOMIC HISTORY

GENERAL EDITORS: M. M. POSTAN, Late Professor Emeritus of Economic History in the University of Cambridge; D. C. COLEMAN, Professor Emeritus of Economic History in the University of Cambridge; and PETER MATHIAS, Master of Downing College, Cambridge

VOLUME VIII

THE
CAMBRIDGE
ECONOMIC HISTORY
OF EUROPE

VOLUME VIII
THE INDUSTRIAL ECONOMIES:
THE DEVELOPMENT OF
ECONOMIC AND SOCIAL POLICIES

EDITED BY

PETER MATHIAS
Master of Downing College, Cambridge

AND

SIDNEY POLLARD
Professor of Economic History, University of Bielefeld

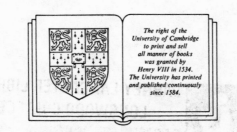

The right of the
University of Cambridge
to print and sell
all manner of books
was granted by
Henry VIII in 1534.
The University has printed
and published continuously
since 1584.

CAMBRIDGE UNIVERSITY PRESS

CAMBRIDGE

NEW YORK   NEW ROCHELLE

MELBOURNE   SYDNEY

Published by the Press Syndicate of the University of Cambridge
The Pitt Building, Trumpington Street, Cambridge CB2 IRP
32 East 57th Street, New York, NY 10022, USA
10 Stamford Road, Oakleigh, Melbourne 3166, Australia

© Cambridge University Press 1989

First published 1989

Printed in Great Britain at the University Press, Cambridge

British Library cataloguing in publication data

The Cambridge economic history of Europe.
Vol. 8: The industrial economies: the development
of economic and social policies.
1. Europe – Economic conditions
I. Mathias, Peter   II. Pollard, Sidney
330.94   HC240

Library of Congress cataloguing in publication data

The Cambridge economic history of Europe.
Include bibliography.
Contents: v. 1. The agrarian life of the Middle
Ages. – v. 2. Trade and industry in the Middle
Ages.–   – v. 8. The industrial economies.
1. Europe – Economic conditions.   2. Europe – History.
I. Mathias, Peter, ed.
II. Pollard, Sidney, ed.
HC240.C312   330.94   66–66029

ISBN 0 521 22504 3

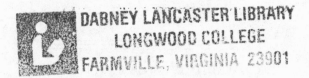

CONTENTS

v

CHAPTER III

International financial policy and the gold standard, 1870–1914

By A. G. FORD, Professor of Economics, University of Warwick

CHAPTER IV

The gold standard and national financial policies, 1913–39

By D. E. MOGGRIDGE, Professor of Economics, University of Toronto

CHAPTER V

Taxation and public finance: Britain, France, and Germany

By D. E. SCHREMMER, Professor of Economic and Social History, University of Heidelberg, and Director, Institute of Social and Economic History, Heidelberg
Translated by Walter Stern

CHAPTER VI

State policy toward labour and labour organizations, 1830–1939: Anglo-American union movements

By JOHN H. M. LASLETT, Professor of History, University of California, Los Angeles

CHAPTER VII

Labour and the state on the continent, 1800–1939

By G. V. RIMLINGER, Professor of Economics, Rice University

CHAPTER VIII

British public policy, 1776–1939

By S. G. CHECKLAND, late Professor Emeritus of Economic History, University of Glasgow

CHAPTER IX

American economic policy, 1865–1939   641

By WILLIAM LETWIN, Professor of Political Science, London School of
Economics and Political Science

CHAPTER X

Economic and social policy in France   691

By T. KEMP, former Reader in Economic History, University of Hull

CHAPTER XI

German economic and social policy, 1815–1939   752

By VOLKER HENTSCHEL, Professor of Economics, University of Mainz
Translated by Walter Stern

CHAPTER XII

Economic policy and economic development in
Austria–Hungary, 1867–1913   814

By SCOTT M. EDDIE, Professor of Economics, University of Toronto

CHAPTER XIII

East-central and south-east Europe, 1919–39   887

By ALICE TEICHOVA, Emeritus Professor of Economic History, University of
East Anglia

CHAPTER XIV

Economic and social policy in the USSR, 1917–41   984

By R. W. DAVIES, Professor of Soviet Economic Studies, Centre for Russian
and East European Studies, University of Birmingham

CHAPTER XV

Economic and social policy in Sweden, 1850–1939   1048

By LENNART JORBERG, Professor of Economic History, University of Lund, and
OLLE KRANZ, Professor of Economic History, University of Lund
Translated by Paul Britten Austin

CHAPTER XVI

Aspects of economic and social policy in Japan, 1868–1945   1106

By SEYMOUR A. BROADBRIDGE, Professorial Research Associate, Japan Research
Centre, School of Oriental and African Studies, University of London

Bibliographies

FIGURES

TABLES

CHAPTER XIII

CHAPTER I

European trade policy, 1815–1914

I. *General introduction*

The analysis of European trade policy in the nineteenth century is of particular interest. This was not only the century in which the various mechanisms, institutions, and theories of modern trade policy took shape, but also a time when the growth of foreign trade was not just extremely rapid, but actually exceeded the growth in production. It has perhaps not been sufficiently recognized that at the end of the nineteenth century (which we take to end in 1914, as is the usual practice) the relative importance of exports in relation to the Gross National Product reached a level in Europe that it has not equalled since (if one excepts the period of upheaval linked to the recent oil price increases).

The nineteenth century saw both the flourishing of liberalism in theories of international trade, and the development of modern protectionism. The nature and structures of tariff legislation changed considerably. Former prohibitions on imports and exports disappeared almost entirely, as did export duties and the very wide-ranging privileges granted to national shipping interests. But, at the same time, new networks of preference were set up, as a result of the creation of numerous colonial empires.

The rapid expansion of trade was the cause but also partly the result of these changes of policy. Between 1815 and 1914 the total volume of exports in Europe probably multiplied by nearly forty-fold, whereas during the previous century it had at the most doubled or trebled. In the 70 years after 1914 the volume of exports was only multiplied by a little below 12 times. In terms of annual growth rates, this works out at 3.9 per cent from 1830 to 1913 and 3.5 per cent from 1913 to 1986.[1] Whereas at the beginning of the nineteenth century exports represented only some 3 per cent of the Gross National Product, in 1913 this figure reached 14 per cent; in 1970, though, it was only 12 per cent (and only 6 per cent around 1938). It is clear that there have been considerable changes, and an

[1] The low rate for 1913 to 1986 is obviously largely explained by the effects of the two wars, the crisis period of the 1930s and the partial withdrawal from world trade of the economies of Eastern Europe. From 1953 to 1986 the volume of European exports increased by about 7.1 per cent per annum.

understanding of European economic policy in this period is therefore important.

In the first instance, the limits of this study must be defined, since the term 'trade policy' is currently used in a wider sense than will be employed in this chapter. Trade policy is dealt with at national level rather than at the level of individual firms and industries. Similarly, we are concerned with international commercial relations rather than with the admittedly very limited area of internal trade policies. Since, in the nineteenth century even more than today, international trade policy was very closely linked with tariff policies, which therefore have an important place in this study, all the more so since we do not have, at the moment, any general tariff history of nineteenth-century Europe which covers most countries.[2] It also goes without saying that the space given to each country depends on its commercial importance rather than on its demographic or even economic strength. As can be seen from Table 1, these various factors do not necessarily coincide. In 1840, for example, three countries (United Kingdom, France, and Germany) were responsible for 62 per cent of European exports, although their populations represented only 36 per cent. In 1910, Belgium, with 7 million inhabitants, exported more products than Russia with 153 million.

The chapter is not confined to a linear account of tariff policies in the various European states, but tariff history is integrated into the analysis of general economic development, in particular that of foreign trade and the theoretical debates. Certain aspects that go beyond tariff policy as such are also touched on, notably navigation policies and the organization of institutions connected with foreign trade. However, this chapter is neither a history of European foreign trade, nor an account of international trade theories, still less a study of the relations during the nineteenth century between foreign trade and economic growth – even though part of the material used was collected for a study which had precisely this aim.[3]

The next five sections of the chapter are based on changes in tariff policies, since these form the core of the analysis.[4] Section II centres on the movement towards free trade in the United Kingdom, and therefore covers the period from 1815 to 1846, a period which saw the establishment of British economic supremacy. The years 1846–60, essentially marked by the efforts of the United Kingdom and of national pressure groups to extend free trade policies to the European continent, are the subject of section III. Section IV is concerned with what may be called the

[2] The only exception as far as I know is the work of K. Graf, *Die zollpolitischen Zielsetzungen im Wandel der Geschichte* (St Gallen, 1970). But only about 80 pages are devoted to nineteenth-century Europe, and certain countries and problems are not discussed.

[3] P. Bairoch, *Commerce extérieur et développement économique de l'Europe au XIXe siècle* (Paris, 1976).

[4] I should like to acknowledge the indirect collaboration of the students in my seminars on foreign trade and tariff policy in Europe in the academic years 1972/3 and 1975/6.

Table 1. *Total population, Gross National Product, and exports of European countries in 1840 and 1910*

	1840			1910		
	Population[a]	Gross National Product[b]	Exports[c]	Population[a]	Gross National Product[b]	Exports[c]
Austria–Hungary	31.3	(8,100)	43	55.1	(24,600)	482
Belgium	4.1	(1,400)	29	7.4	5,700	629
Bulgaria	(2.7)	(530)	—	4.3	(1,300)	28
Denmark	1.3	(320)	7	2.8	2,100	131
Finland	1.4	(300)	2	3.1	1,400	55
France	34.2	10,700	150	39.5	26,100	1,160
Germany	31.2	(8,300)	(135)	64.6	47,700	1,760
Greece	1.0	(200)	1	2.8	940	25
Italy	22.0	(5,500)	(60)	34.4	14,700	396
Norway	1.2	(310)	(9)	2.4	(1,300)	71
Portugal	3.7	(1,000)	7	5.9	(1,900)	36
Romania	(3.8)	(760)	(13)	6.9	(2,300)	115
Russia	(66.0)	(12,200)	67	152.7	(46,000)	772
Serbia	(1.4)	(280)	—	2.5	(700)	20
Spain	(14.4)	(3,800)	(19)	19.8	7,900	186
Sweden	3.1	(780)	13	5.5	3,400	155
Switzerland	2.2	(600)	(40)	3.8	3,100	228
The Netherlands	2.9	(1,000)	(20)	5.9	(4,100)	349
United Kingdom	26.5	10,750	254	44.9	43,300	2,049
Europe	257.8	67,000	870	464.4	240,000	8,650
United States	17.1	(10,600)	116	92.4	117,800	1,790

Notes:
[a] In millions of persons.
[b] In millions of 1960 US dollars and prices (three-year annual averages).
[c] In millions of current dollars and prices (three-year annual averages).
The degree of rounding off of figures does not imply a correspondingly low margin of error. Figures in parentheses have a higher margin of error than other figures for the same periods.
— = Not available throughout tables.
Sources: Author's computations and estimates from material assembled for P. Bairoch, *Commerce extérieur et développement économique de l'Europe au XIXe siècle* (Paris, 1976); P. Bairoch: 'World's Gross National Product 1800–1985 (Computations Estimates and Guesses)'; to appear.

liberal period in Europe, which goes roughly from 1860 to 1879, and in the middle of which begins the 'great depression' of the European economy. The years 1879–92 were characterized by a return to protectionism in most countries on the European continent, and section V deals with this. The period 1892–1914, which saw an acceleration in the rate of trade and production, was also a time of increased protectionism in most continental countries; this forms the subject of section VI.

Following these five chronological sections – which divide the history of European trade policy into relatively homogenous periods – are four sections devoted to problems which straddle one or more of these periods. Section VII concerns the development of institutions for the promotion of foreign trade. European colonial trade policies form the subject of section VIII. Section IX considers the position of the socialist and labour parties with regard to trade policy. Finally, the last section deals mainly with the trade policies of independent (and semi-independent) countries outside Europe.

As can be seen from this summary, this study of trade policy is concerned more with the relations between European countries than with their links to the rest of the world, though the latter are not ignored (see sections VIII and IX). This is because of the primordial importance of intra-European trade in the past (and indeed today), when it represented an average of two-thirds of all European trade during the nineteenth century (see Table 2).

II. The movement towards liberalism in the United Kingdom, 1815–46

If, to simplify matters, the sixteenth and seventeenth centuries are described as an age of protectionism, then the eighteenth century is to be seen as a period of transition. Policy during the first half of the century was still closely linked with mercantilism, but after 1760 important changes took shape. First with the Physiocrats, then with the theories of Adam Smith, and above all with the Anglo-French commercial treaty of 1786, commercial liberalism, an integral part of *laissez-faire* economics, was established if not all over Europe, at least in the trade between two of its leading powers. But the unrealized hopes of the treaty of 1786, and above all war, caused the eighteenth century to end with a return to protectionism.

The wars which marked the period 1790–1815, and, in particular, the English and French blockades which began in 1806, reinforced the European tendencies towards protectionism at the level of government commercial policy. However, so far as economic thought was concerned, liberalism made progress. Book IV of Smith's *The Wealth of Nations* (which, together with book V, is the longest) is essentially a defence of free trade at the international level. Smith's book became the leading work in economics at the end of the eighteenth century. In England it went through eight editions before 1800 (1776, 1778, 1784, 1786, 1789, 1791, 1793, and 1796). The first French translation dates from

Table 2. *Share of intra-European[a] trade in total European trade (three-year annual averages, except for 1986)*

	Exports	Imports	Total foreign trade
1830	72.1	63.0	67.6
1860	67.5	61.0	64.2
1890	72.2	64.7	68.2
1900	71.1	60.7	65.5
1910	67.8	60.0	63.6
1970	72.7	71.7	72.1
1986	72.0	76.0	73.9

Note:
[a] Trade between European countries.
1970 and 1986 not strictly comparable with preceding data: derived from trade networks based on destinations and origin of exports (in f.o.b. values).
Sources: 1830–1910: P. Bairoch, 'Geographical Structure and Trade Balance of European Foreign Trade from 1800 to 1970', *Journal of European Economic History*, vol. III, no. 3 (Winter 1974), pp. 557–608. 1970–86: Derived from United Nations, *Statistical Yearbook*, various issues, and *Monthly Bulletin of Statistics* (June 1987; New York).

1779, and three more French translations were already made by 1802.[5] The first translation into German dates from 1776–80, into Danish from 1779–80, into Italian from 1780, into Spanish from 1792, and into Dutch from 1796.[6]

The direct or indirect successors of Smith all adopted a position favourable to liberalism in international trade. In France in 1803 Jean-Baptiste Say published his *Traité d'économie politique*, which was very largely inspired by Smith. In Britain as early as 1804 James Mill published a liberal pamphlet while David Ricardo published his first works in 1809.

But this supremacy of liberal economic thought in Europe did not eliminate the mercantilist type of protectionism, still less prevent the development of a new type of protectionism. This new-style protectionism was related to the rising nationalisms of the early nineteenth century, and still more important, it was the result of awareness of the process of economic development resulting from the industrial revolution, and of the advance of British industry. Frederic List's *National System of Political Economy* did not appear until 1841, but before this the works of the

---

[5] C. Gide and C. Rist, *Histoire des doctrines économiques depuis les Physiocrates jusqu'à nos jours*, 5th edn (Paris, 1926), pp. 122–3.
[6] Article 'Smith' in *The Dictionary of National Biography*, vol. XVIII (London, 1909), p. 418.

Table 3. *Summary of commercial policies in selected European countries around 1820*

	Imports of manufactured goods		Protection of agriculture	Export duties	Internal duties	Navigation laws
	Prohibitions	Average level of duties (%)[a]				
Austria–Hungary	Numerous	*b*	*c*	Yes	Yes	Liberal
Denmark	Rare	30	Moderate	*c*	Yes	Liberal
France	Numerous	*b*	Moderate	Rare	No	Protective
Portugal	No	15	Strict	Yes	*c*	Liberal
Prussia	No	10	Moderate	No	*c*	Liberal
Russia	Numerous	*b*	Moderate	Yes	Yes	*c*
Spain	Numerous	*b*	Strict	Yes	Yes	Protective
Sweden (Norway)	Numerous	*b*	*c*	Yes	Yes	*c*
Switzerland	Rare	10	Moderate	Yes	Yes	Liberal
The Netherlands (Belgium)	No	7	Moderate	Yes	No	Mildly protective
United Kingdom	Rare	50	Strict	Rare	No	Protective

Notes:
[a] Figures quoted are very approximate.
[b] Not at all significant in view of the importance of the prohibitions.
[c] Incomplete information or difficult to classify.
Sources: Author's estimates from various sources.

American Alexander Hamilton (1791), the German Adam Müller (1809) and the Frenchmen Jean Antoine Chaptal (1819) and Charles Dupin (1827) should be mentioned. Most important of all, liberal thought was attacked by a wider range of representatives of different sectors of the economy, who, rightly or wrongly, considered it harmful to their own particular areas of interest.

In the present state of research, it is impossible to establish accurately either the relative importance of foreign trade in Europe in 1815 compared with that of the period before the wars of 1792-1815, or the development between 1815 and 1835. There was probably a fairly rapid growth in the volume of European exports between 1815 and 1835: around 3 or 4 per cent per annum. This rapid growth can be explained in part in terms of a return to previous levels of trade, which was probably achieved around 1830. What is more certain is that between 1836-8 and 1844-6 the volume of exports continued to increase very rapidly (3.5 per cent per annum) compared to what probably happened in the eighteenth century.

The situation as regards trade policy in the various European states in 1815-20 can be described as that of an ocean of protectionism surrounding a few liberal islands. Table 3 gives a comparative outline of the state of trade policy in the main countries.

The three decades between 1815 and 1846 were essentially marked by the movement towards economic liberalism in Great Britain. This remained a very limited form of liberalism until the 1840s, and thus only became effective when this country had nearly a century of industrial development behind it and was some 40-60 years ahead of its neighbours. A few small countries, notably The Netherlands, also showed tendencies towards liberalism. But the rest of Europe developed a system of defensive, protectionist policies, directed especially against British manufactured goods. Of course, in addition to this geographical division, there were in varying degrees clashes of opinion within each country between those in favour of, and those against, liberal policies in foreign trade.

A.   THE CORN LAWS AND THE INDUSTRIALIZATION OF THE UNITED KINGDOM

In the United Kingdom the political struggle between the supporters of free trade and those in favour of protectionism began more or less at the end of the wars with France, in 1815; this was when the gentry voted in a new Corn Law aimed at protecting local agriculture against foreign grain imports. It should be noted that 'Corn Laws' were a quasi-permanent feature of tariff history in most European countries. They had always aimed at a precarious balance between protecting local agriculture and preventing the price of bread from rising too steeply. In England the first national laws of this kind date back to 1436. Until then imports had been totally prohibited. From 1436, in certain cases, exports were permitted and in 1463 certain small changes were made in the law. In 1663 the internal trade in grain was freed from restrictions and in 1670 an embryo sliding scale was introduced. But the first law which sought to reconcile the contradictory aims we have mentioned was Burke's Act of 1773. This allowed the import of wheat with minimal customs duties when the price of wheat on the home market exceeded 44 shillings per quarter (a quarter of wheat was 217.7 kg).[7]

The law of 1815 fixed the price level of wheat above which imports became free at 80 shillings, which meant that the price of food and therefore also wages would be kept at a relatively high level. This did not please the manufacturers who wanted to expand their exports still further, through the combination of mechanization and low wages. This marked the beginning of conflict between the interests of agriculture, whose relative importance in economic life was declining, and those of manufacturing industry, which was becoming the main sector of economic activity. The balance of power between these two sectors and the degree to which their interests converged was to determine the changes in tariff policy not only in Great Britain but in practically all European countries during the nineteenth century.

It is likely that pressure from industrialists, especially from the cotton manufacturers, would have been greater if the government had not abolished the East India Company's trading monopoly with India in 1813 (see section VIII). This change of policy opened up the huge Indian market to British cotton fabrics. From practically nothing before 1813, imports of British cotton reached 5 million yards per annum in 1816–18, rising 20 years later to 73 million yards, in addition to some 9 thousand million pounds of cotton thread.[8]

In the United Kingdom some of the most important and persuasive economists championed free trade and hence supported the interests of industry. In 1815 David Ricardo in his *Essay on the Influence of a Low Price of Corn on the Profits of Stock* attacked the Corn Laws by emphasizing the very high cost, to the economy as a whole, of too great a protection of agriculture. From 1820 pressure from the advocates of free trade increased, and was manifested in the so-called Merchants' Petition drawn up by the economist Thomas Tooke. This petition, whose real organizers were members of the Political Economy Club founded by Ricardo

---

[7] W. Smart, *Economic Annals of the Nineteenth Century* (London, 1910), p. 90; D.G. Barnes, *A History of the English Corn Laws from 1660 to 1846* (London, 1930).

[8] M. Desai, 'Demand for Cotton Textiles in Nineteenth Century India', *Indian Economic and Social History Review*, vol. VIII, no. 4 (December 1971), pp. 337–61 (especially pp. 347–8).

and his friends to promote the 'new' economic thought, was presented to the House of Commons by the influential banker, Baron Baring.

It was William Huskisson who, influenced, it seems, by the Physiocrats during his youth spent in Paris, introduced the first liberal measures in 1822. These led to the reduction of customs duties on raw materials and industrial products, the suppression of import prohibitions and above all the reform (mainly in favour of the colonies) of the notorious Navigation Acts introduced in the middle of the seventeenth century in order to give British shipping the monopoly of British foreign trade. In 1825 there was a complete reorganization of commercial legislation; the new tariff repealed more than 1,100 tariff acts, some of which went back to the thirteenth century. In 1828 the sliding-scale Corn Law, which reduced agricultural protection to a small extent, was passed. This sliding scale was a customs mechanism, used by certain countries, whereby import duties on corn varied in inverse relation to the level of grain prices on the home market, and thus tended to reduce imports to the minimum, but without provoking famines. On the other hand, when home prices passed a certain threshold, exports of grain were prohibited so as not to reduce the local supplies. As far as the United Kingdom was concerned, the adoption of a sliding scale amounted to a certain reduction in agricultural protectionism, since the lower limits of import duties were distinctly below the general level of the period before the Corn Laws.

It should be noted that in 1822 an act had already reduced the price level above which wheat imports (subject to customs duties, of course) were allowed to 70 shillings per quarter, and had set up a preferential system for Canadian wheat (allowing it to be imported whatever the price on the home market, but subject to duties ranging from 1 to 12 shillings according to its local price). This could not lead to massive imports because of the combination of very high transport costs and a fairly limited supply. In 1830 Canada's total cereal output was about 500,000 metric tons, in other words, about 4 per cent of the United Kingdom's output at the same period. Canadian exports to the United Kingdom in the quarter century up to 1830 amounted to a mere 25,000 tons per annum.[9]

The general sliding scale in 1828 was as follows: 23s. import duty when the home market price was 64s., 16s. 8d. when the price was 69s., and 1s. when the price reached or exceeded 73s. As the home price, though, averaged 56s. 9d. in the decade 1830–9, and 56s. 8d. in the years 1840–5, and only once reached 69s., British agriculture was still protected since imports were relatively unimportant. Even though the net balance of wheat and flour imports in the two years following the 1828 law more

---

[9] Production figures: from M. C. Urquhart and K. A. H. Buckley (eds.), *Historical Statistics of Canada* (Toronto, 1965), p. 384. Trade figures from M. G. Mulhall, *The Progress of the World* (London, 1880), p. 206.

than doubled compared to the five years leading up to it, it still only represented 290,000 metric tons, or 17 kg per capita; which amounted to only about 10 per cent of consumption.[10]

In other spheres, though, liberalism did make some progress. In 1833 certain reductions in import duties were introduced. As early as 1825, Parliament again authorized the emigration of skilled workers, which had been forbidden since 1719. On the other hand, the efforts of some engineers to remove the ban on the export of machinery were not successful at this time. They were opposed chiefly by the textile manu-facturers who feared the competition such exports might lead to. This did not, of course, prevent these same manufacturers from holding liberal views as far as agriculture was concerned (see this and section B).

During this time British industry was increasing its lead over its rivals, a lead which – since we are dealing with the first industrial nation – was already considerable. Even if calculations are made for the whole of the United Kingdom, which reduces the average level of industrialization, this lead was remarkable. The United Kingdom, which between 1800 and 1830 contained about 8–10 per cent of the population of Europe, produced in 1800 some 29 per cent of all pig iron in Europe, a proportion which reached 45 per cent in 1830. The United Kingdom's share of raw cotton consumption went from 55–60 per cent in 1800 to 66 per cent in 1830. For the whole of the manufacturing industry United Kingdom's share in Europe went up from 15 per cent in 1800 to 28 per cent in 1830. Even more important is the fact that the per capita level of industrializa-tion exceeded in 1830 that of the rest of Europe by 250 per cent, com-pared to 110 per cent in 1800.[11] From this we can understand the efforts of the industrial lobby to establish a more effective system of free trade.

B.   THE ANTI-CORN LAW LEAGUE AND THE ACHIEVEMENT OF LIBERALISM IN THE UNITED KINGDOM

The main obstacle to effective free trade, however, was still the substan-tial protection of agriculture. Since this aimed at high food prices and

[10] Table of annual averages of foreign trade in wheat (and flour) in Great Britain (in thousands of quarters):

	Exports	Imports	Balance of imports
1823–7	64.8	652.4	587.6
1828–32	108.8	1,985.5	1,876.7
1833–7	191.0	973.9	782.9
1838–42	77.4	2,716.5	2,639.1

Source: J. R. McCulloch, *A Dictionary of Commerce and Commercial Navigation* (London, 1844), p. 418. (Mulhall, *Progress of the World*, p. 134, estimates the proportion of wheat imported for the whole period 1831–50 at 13 per cent.)

[11] P. Bairoch, 'International Industrialization Levels from 1750 to 1980', *Journal of European Economic History*, vol. XI, no. 2. (Autumn 1982), pp. 269–333.

hence very low real wages, the strategy of the manufacturers, especially those in the cotton industry, was to use the poverty of the workers to strengthen their attack on the Corn Laws. The free traders also emphasized the point that by reducing the import of foreign foodstuffs from countries with an agricultural surplus, the Corn Laws were thus reducing the chances of exporting British manufactured goods to these countries. The famous Anti-Corn Law League was founded in September 1838 in Manchester.[12] Although it was a pressure group of manufacturers, the league was led by sincere men: John Bright, and in particular, Richard Cobden who was to be the true 'apostle' of free trade. The Anti-Corn Law League quickly became very active, building its headquarters, the Free Trade Hall, and launching into a vast programme of publications (weeklies and others) and lectures.

The social motivation of the Anti-Corn Law League – in particular its aim of reducing the price of bread to raise the standards of living of the workers – was energetically disputed by the Chartists, who believed that the campaign for cheap bread was merely an attempt on the part of the factory owners to justify wage cuts. It should be remembered that the years 1830–45 showed, on average, a very limited increase in real wages; probably less than 0.5 per cent per annum. This by no means excludes the probability of short periods when there was a drop in real wages, nor of an overall drop in certain sectors. The position of other working-class movements – or rather socialist movements in the widest sense of this term – to the Anti-Corn Law League and commercial liberalism in general, was more complex. As a general rule, the first socialist movements were favourable to free trade; for, as Comby notes, 'free trade appears to be the corollary of a universal vision based on the abolition of frontiers. National particularities and national conflicts are part of the past which is to be swept away. It is impossible to imagine tariff wars between Fourier's phalansteries.'[13] We shall return to these problems in more detail in section IX.

It goes without saying, however, that economic interests, and in particular those of the cotton industry, were at the root of the action of the Anti-Corn Law League. Bright, the son of a mill owner, went into the family business at the age of sixteen; Cobden was first a commercial

---

[12] There is often some confusion about the date of the foundation of the Anti-Corn Law League. Three alternative dates are usually quoted: 1836, 1838, and 1839. A first association against the Corn Laws was indeed founded in London in 1836 (the Anti-Corn Law Association). Most important radicals in London belonged to this, but it did not have much success. In September 1838 (a year of poor harvests) an Anti-Corn Law Association was formed in Manchester. Its initiator was John Benjamin Smith, and it quickly received the active support of Bright and Cobden. This group organized a conference in London in 1839 at which it was decided to form, in March, a permanent Anti-Corn Law League which would be based in Manchester. N. McCord, *The Anti-Corn Law League. 1838–1846* (London, 1958), pp. 16–53.

[13] J. M. Comby, *Les doctrines interventionnistes en politique commerciale du XVe au XIXe siècle;* (Paris, 1930), p. 110.

traveller and then in 1831 he became, with two associates, the owner of a calico printing plant. It was no accident that the Anti-Corn Law League was located in Manchester. Moreover, thanks to mechanization, cotton manufactured goods had become the major British export; whereas in the decade 1760–9 these products represented 2 per cent of total exports, in the decade 1800–9 they already accounted for 39 per cent, and 72 per cent in 1830–9.[14] In the 1830s, though, foreign markets began to level off. Cotton exports, which according to the estimates of Deane and Cole, accounted for 56.4 per cent of cotton production in 1829–31, fell to 50.4 per cent in 1834–6, and to 49.8 per cent in 1839–41.[15]

Next to these dominant socio-economic factors, we should not ignore the implications for international politics suggested by the Anti-Corn Law League, who saw free trade as an element in international peace, thanks to the resulting prosperity and mutual dependence of nations. Richard Cobden talked lyrically of this, and went as far as dreaming of the 'Commune'. However, we must not conclude that this undeniable idealism was the only motivation of the free traders. As Semmel underlines very well, this group was by no means free from imperialist aspirations.[16] Did not Joseph Hume declare that by extending her foreign trade, England could make all the world dependent on her?[17] There have been long debates over the reality and the extent and importance of the 'imperialist' aims of the free traders, but it is difficult to absolve them totally from this 'sin'.

In April 1842 the Prime Minister, Robert Peel, introduced a fairly liberal tariff reform which not only reduced import duties (even on wheat) appreciably but also abolished the export tax on wool and, most important, completely revoked the ban on exporting machinery which had been in force since 1774. For manufactured goods, customs duties were reduced to some 10 per cent for semi-finished products, and to 20 per cent for finished ones. These measures were part of a general reform of finance – to which Peel was committed – by the reintroduction of the income tax (abolished in 1815) which allowed the Treasury to compensate (then and later) for the income lost through tariff reform. But it must be said that Peel, despite his liberal economic views, had been elected in 1841 on a programme which included the commitment to maintaining the Corn Laws. It was only gradually that Peel, who had a strong interest in political economy, changed his opinion and not until December 1845 that he made his change of views public; he was then attacked by part of

---

[14] P. Mathias, *The First Industrial Nation: An Economic History of Britain, 1700–1914* (London, 1969), pp. 466 and 468.

[15] P. Deane and W. A. Cole, *A British Economic Growth, 1688–1959* (Cambridge, 1969), p. 187.

[16] B. Semmel, *The Rise of Free Trade Imperialism: Classical Political Economy, the Empire of Free Trade and Imperialism 1750–1850* (Cambridge, 1970).   [17] *Ibid.*, p. 148.

the Conservative Party, and in particular by Benjamin Disraeli, the leader of this faction, who accused him of having betrayed the principles of their party.

In 1845 a new series of liberal tariff reforms were introduced. Import duties on raw cotton and wool, which were already very low, were abolished. Duties on tropical foodstuffs, meat, and dairy products were greatly reduced. Grain imports, however, were still liable to a duty high enough to keep them at a relatively low level. In the three years up to 1846, net imports of wheat and flour were very low indeed: about 239,000 tons per annum for the United Kingdom, or just 9 kg per capita. In 1850–4 there were 1,030,000 tons per annum imported, and in 1880–4 3,530,000 tons.[18]

In short, the main obstacle to a complete system of free trade remained, although weakened, and it was because of the climatological conditions of 1845 (a very wet summer and autumn), together with the disastrous potato crop in Ireland, that the Corn Laws were repealed (law of 15 May, promulgated on 26 June 1846). As Morley wrote in his life of Cobden 'it was the rain that rained away the Corn Laws'.[19] This law also abolished duties on livestock and on nearly all meat; it reduced or abolished many duties on manufactured goods and led to a schism in the Conservative Party, and hence, a little later, to Peel's resignation (two-thirds of the party did not support his position on the Corn Laws).

It should be noted that, contrary to what is generally thought, grains remained liable to duties until 1869. These duties were, however, relatively low and, most important, imports were permitted whatever the price on the home market. In 1846 these duties varied between a minimum of 4 shillings and a maximum of 10 shillings per quarter (but there was still a preferential system of 1 shilling for British colonies). The home price of wheat at this period was around 55 shillings per quarter.

The date 15 May 1846 is rightly held to mark the beginning of the free trade era in the United Kingdom. And, by one of those common historical coincidences, that year (six months later, in November) was also that of the suicide of the ill and financially harassed Frederic List – the most influential exponent of protectionism in the nineteenth century. If the weather was the immediate cause of the repeal of the Corn Laws, it merely accelerated a trend in trade policy that was in any case inevitable. For if around 1810 agriculture's contribution to the Gross National Product in Britain still exceeded that of the secondary sector of the economy by 70 per cent, around 1840 it was industry that exceeded agriculture by 60 per cent.

[18] Calculated from B. R. Mitchell and P. Deane, *Abstract of British Historical Statistics* (Cambridge, 1962), pp. 8 and 98.
[19] J. Morley, *The Life of Richard Cobden* (London, 1882), p. 215.

C. THE RISE OF DEFENSIVE PROTECTIONISM ON THE
EUROPEAN CONTINENT

At the same time as Britain was becoming aware of its industrial lead and
drew the logical conclusions from this by adopting a free trade policy,
the rest of Europe was becoming conscious of its backwardness and was
seeking in a new form of mercantilism – more defensive than offensive,
in short in what was from the 1840s to be called protectionism – a way of
catching up. It should be noted, and this is important, that for the first
time in history people began to argue, as we have already seen, in terms of
levels of development to be reached more or less quickly, rather than in
terms of taking the biggest share of total wealth.

1. *France*

In France, the fall of the First Empire (April 1814) was followed by a very
ephemeral liberalization of the tariff system which lasted only a few
months; in December 1814 a set of relatively protectionist laws was
introduced. Under joint pressure from farmers and manufacturers, the
law of 17 December 1814 was reinforced several times in 1816 and 1817.
In 1819, after a succession of increases of import duties on grain, France
introduced (or rather, reintroduced) the sliding scale for grain, that
keystone of agricultural tariff policy. We should note that a law establishing a sliding scale for grain had already been issued in 1804 (and
abolished in 1814). This sliding scale was reinforced still further in 1821.
At the same time, the laws of 1820, 1822, and 1826 increased protectionist
legislation for agricultural products as well as for manufactured or
mining goods. 'A coalition of farmers and manufacturers imposed a strict
protectionism opposed strongly by a small proportion of manufacturers
of silk and printed cloth and merchants of the ports.'[20]

The tariff policy of the July monarchy (1830–48) at first showed a
slight relaxation of protectionism, in the sense that certain total prohibitions were replaced by very high duties and certain duties were reduced
(the laws of 1834 and 1836). With regard to these reductions, given that
an important proportion of the duties were 'specific', it should be noted
that the fall in prices between 1820–4 and 1830–4 resulted in real
reinforcement of protectionism.[21] There are, it should be remembered,
two main ways of fixing duty levels. The first, or *ad valorem*, system

[20] R. Schnerb, *Libre-échange et protectionnisme* (Paris, 1963), p. 50.
[21] Between these two periods, the price of manufactured goods on the home market had dropped
by about 20 per cent and the import prices by some 10 per cent. M. Levy-Leboyer, 'L'héritage
de Simiand; prix, profits et termes des échanges au XIXe siècle', *Revue Historique*, no. 493
(January–March 1970), pp. 108–9.

consists of duties expressed as a percentage of the value of the product. The second, or *specific*, system is calculated in terms of quantity (for example, $3 per ton).

Still for France, let us note that the law of 31 March 1841 'raised more tariffs than it lowered'.[22] All the same, some prohibitions were lifted. For the small percentage of manufactured articles which could be imported, the level of customs duties in the new tariff of 6 May 1841 were about 40–60 per cent.

The law of 19 June 1845, the last tariff law of this political regime, again increased the protection of industry (in particular that of the machinery industry). The protectionist nature of the legislation in force in 1846 can be illustrated by the fact that imports of manufactured goods accounted for only 6 per cent of total imports (but 70 per cent of exports).

2. Germany and the Zollverein

In Germany, List's native land, the period 1815–46 was that of the establishment of the *Zollverein*, whose basic economic philosophy was to create a free trade zone, large enough to foster conditions favourable to industrialization under the shelter of initially limited common tariff protection. The idea of a customs union had been debated since 1816. List was very active in this cause in 1819–20; especially in his encouragement of the creation of the German Trade and Industry Association (Deutscher Handels-und-Gewerbsverein).[23] In 1818, the union of the various Prussian provinces marked the beginnings of the *Zollverein*. We must not forget that Prussia – the biggest and most densely populated of the German states – accounted for about 60 per cent of the population of the *Zollverein* in 1846.

The abolition of internal customs duties in Prussia ·was one of the elements in the law of 26 May 1818 that established a new tariff system which was liberal (for the period). In spite of the opinion of the representatives of manufacturing industry, who sought a return to the restrictive, pre-1806 system, the government opted for a customs policy that excluded prohibitions and advocated a moderate protection of industry which would not eliminate foreign competition.[24]

This legislation irritated not only Prussian manufacturers but also those in the other German states. The petition drawn up by List in 1819 declared that this new law had plunged the whole of Germany

---

[22] E. Levasseur, *Histoire du Commerce de la France*, vol. II: *De 1789 à nos jours* (Paris, 1912), p. 170.

[23] A. H. Price, *The Evolution of the Zollverein: A Study of the Ideas and Institutions leading to the German Economic Unification between 1815 and 1833* (Ann Arbor, 1949), pp. 26–46.

[24] H. Richelot, *L'Association douanière allemande ou le Zollverein* (Paris, 1859), pp. 24–5.

into the deepest consternation, for it appears to be directed less against French and British trade than against that of Germany. It fixes duties according to weight. Since foreign countries today mostly export finished goods to Prussia whereas the neighbouring German states, whose industry had been held back by British competition, only export common, heavy goods, the duty paid by the foreigners works out at about 6 per cent, while the Germans generally pay around 25 to 30 or even 50 per cent which amounts to a prohibition.[25]

If the tariff unification of Prussia is, rightly, considered as the first stage of the Zollverein, the second stage was that of the customs union between Bavaria and Württemberg, which took effect on 1 July 1928. This was followed by other customs agreements linking various German states. One of these had been agreed between Prussia and Hesse–Darmstadt in February 1828, and in January 1832 this was extended to incorporate Hesse–Cassel. The real beginning of the Zollverein, however, was 1 January 1834, the date of the treaty bringing Bavaria and Württemberg under the Prussian tariff system. In less than two months Saxony and Thuringen also joined. At this point, the customs union represented, in terms of population, some 83 per cent of the final Zollverein.[26]

The next stages were the inclusion of Baden and Nassau in 1835 and of Frankfurt am Main at the beginning of 1836. At the end of 1841 the Duchy of Brunswick and a few other very small states joined, to be followed by Luxemburg in 1842. Of the large states, only Hanover waited till 1851 to complete what was already, for Europe, an enormous customs union, since in 1850 the Zollverein had 30 million inhabitants, compared with 27.5 million in the United Kingdom, 32.5 in Austria, 35.6 in France, 24.1 in Italy, 15.0 in Spain and 72.5 million in Russia.

While the Zollverein was expanding its territory, its tariff system was

[25] Ibid., p. 34.

[26] Population figures, in millions (for 1850), of the main states of the Zollverein. Frontiers are those of the period, and the figures in brackets give the date of joining the Zollverein:

(1818)	Prussia	16.6
(1828)	Hesse–Darmstadt	0.8
(1832)	Hesse–Cassel	0.7
(1834)	Bavaria	4.5
(1834)	Württemberg	1.7
(1834)	Saxony	1.9
(1834)	Thuringen	1.0
(1835)	Baden	1.4
(1835)	Nassau	0.4
(1836)	Frankfurt am Main	0.1
(1841)	Brunswick	0.2
(1842)	Luxemburg	0.2
(1851)	Hanover	1.8
	Others*	2.5
	Whole of Germany	33.8

* Partly in the Zollverein.

becoming more protectionist. In 1836 duties were increased on a series of manufactured articles (the specific duties on wrought iron were trebled and those on linen thread doubled). In 1842 new increases particularly affected woollen and mixed fibre cloth. One of the characteristics of German tariff policy was already emerging – a tendency to fix duties according to the degree of transformation of the production (we shall return to this later – see section VIA1). Despite the increase in duties, the tariff system remained relatively liberal, which can be explained by the importance of Prussian agricultural interests. Cereals were one of its major exports.[27] Moreover, in the first half of the nineteenth century this region was the main source of supply of grain to the United Kingdom.

3. Austria–Hungary

In Austria–Hungary the period between 1815 and 1848 shows a distinct unity, not only in internal and foreign affairs, but also in trade policy. Overall, this period was marked by a very strict mercantilist form of protectionism. There were numerous prohibitions on imports and exports, and duties on both were very high. We should obviously make allowance for the size of the Austro-Hungarian Empire, and for the fact that it had only one sea outlet, at Trieste. This was the reason Austria–Hungary was only the sixth largest country in Europe in terms of the total value of its exports, even though in 1840 (see Table 1) it had the third largest population and the fourth highest overall Gross National Product. It is true that because of the existence of customs barriers between Austria and Hungary (which were only abolished in 1851) one can in a sense regard exchanges between the two parts of the Empire as foreign trade. It should be noted here that Hungary's tariff autonomy was somewhat limited, for whereas Austrian products (especially manufactured goods) benefited from a preferential system in Hungary, the reverse was not true.

The tariff law which took effect in February 1838, and which was in force for most of the 1838–51 period, was considered more liberal than the previous measures. It provided for ad valorem duties of 60 per cent on most cotton, wool, iron, and earthenware manufactured goods, and very high specific duties on everything else, not to mention the many remaining prohibitions.

Prussia's success with the Zollverein was not, of course, a matter of indifference to Austria–Hungary, whose ambition was to take over the leadership of all the German states. But the real efforts towards this end took place after 1848, and will therefore be considered in section III.

[27] The quantity of cereals exported annually by the Zollverein was about 300,000 tons in 1840 and about 700,000 tons in 1860 (sources from various sets of foreign trade statistics).

4. Russia

After various vicissitudes in trade policy occasioned by wars, the new Russian tariff of 1816 can be seen as the starting point of nineteenth-century tariff history. This tariff was a step towards liberalization, given the regimes that had preceded it. Nevertheless, its measures were highly protectionist, there were numerous prohibitions and high taxes were added to customs duties. After the violent reactions provoked by the new tariff of 1819 (the most liberal in Russia in the whole of the nineteenth century) an extremely restrictive tariff was introduced in 1822. Numerous prohibitions affected nearly all locally produced manufactured goods.[28] This new legislation seriously restricted imports, which had risen from 119 million roubles (paper) per annum in 1814–16 to 210 millions in 1919–21, leading to the disappearance of the surplus generated by the favourable balance of trade which was running at 72 per cent of imports for 1814–16. During 1822–4, imports totalled 165 millions per annum; the 1819–21 level was not equalled again till 1833–5.[29]

The period 1823–44 was strongly influenced by the presence of Count Kankrin as the head of the Ministry of Finance (which controlled internal and foreign trade). His Ministry, as Portal observes,

was the very symbol of an industrial policy prompted by financial and social considerations and characterized by undisguised timidity. His Ministry, to use his own expression, was one of 'progressive amelioration'. His encouragement to industry, based chiefly on protective tariffs, was given in 'homeopathic doses', to avoid 'unduly accelerating the course of things'. Industry was in the first place a source of revenue for the budget; the protection granted to it was of course considered as a factor in its future development, but also – and primarily – as a means of safeguarding its existence in the present, and avoiding unemployment and its attendant disturbances.[30]

During these twenty years, the tariff system was amended some six times, always in the direction of more efficient protectionism.

5. Spain

The new tariffs of 1816, 1820 and 1825 took Spain from the mercantilist era of preceding centuries into the protectionism of the nineteenth

---

[28] It must be emphasized that the number of prohibitions is not in itself an indication of the prohibitive nature of a tariff. Indeed, a prohibition can affect either a very specific product (for example cotton threads of a certain thickness) or a wide range of products (for example all cotton manufactured goods).

[29] P. A. Khromov, *Ekonomischeskoye razvitiye Rossii v XIX-XX vekakh. 1800–1917* (Moscow, 1950), pp. 435–6.

[30] R. Portal, 'The Industrialization of Russia', in H. J. Habakkuk and M. Postan (eds.), *Cambridge Economic History of Europe*, vol. VI, part II (Cambridge, 1965), ch. IX, p. 804.

century. Tariff laws had to be adjusted to Spain's new situation as a metropolis at the centre of a greatly reduced colonial empire, following the independence of most Latin American countries. A very strict protectionism was in force. In the tariff of October 1825, import prohibitions were brought in on about 650 products (nearly all manufactured goods) and customs duties on everything else were very high. Besides this, strong preferential measures were taken to favour national maritime interests: surtaxes ranging from 50 per cent to 300 per cent were levied on goods imported in foreign ships. The decree of 30 April 1832 reinforced protectionism still further by suppressing a number of privileges which had facilitated the import of manufactured goods (notably cottons).

After the civil war (1833–9) the pressure of the free traders increased. As everywhere else in Europe, the free traders included economists, business, and agricultural groups whose products were exported (particularly wine-growers). Manufacturers were obviously protectionist and since they were concentrated in Catalonia the conflict of interests took on a regional connotation. The tariff of 1841 (like that of 1849) was in fact extremely protectionist, although it was presented as a concession. The prohibitions, although reduced to 93 items, affected virtually all manufactured consumer goods and grain. On products which were not prohibited, import duties ranged from 15 to 50 per cent *ad valorem*.

6. Portugal

The loss of the Brazilian market was evidently a severe blow to Portugal; and the first real attempt to adapt to the new situation took place in 1820 when the Liberals came to power. The main change in tariff policy was a move to protect agriculture, especially cereals, whereas grain imports had previously been encouraged.[31] Because of high wine exports, directed mostly to the United Kingdom,[32] Portuguese industry was not protected to the same extent.

In 1836 the Septembrists came to power, and this led to a radical change in economic policy. The Septembrists, who represented the manufacturers and artisans as well as the intellectuals, made changes to the tariff system in 1837 and 1841 in order to protect industry. But when the Chartists (representing the big merchants) came to power in 1842 there was a swing towards liberalism. In the same year a trade agreement

---

[31] S. Sideri, *Trade and Power: Informal Colonialism in Anglo-Portuguese Relations* (Rotterdam, 1970), pp. 134–5.

[32] Portuguese wine formed the bulk of British wine consumption, namely 75 per cent of the total in 1786–95, 56 per cent in 1814–24, but dropping to 40 per cent in 1839–41 and to 25 per cent in 1859–61. M. Halpern-Pereira, *Livre Câmbio e Desenvolvimento Economico: Portugal na Segunda metade do Seculo XIX* (Lisbon, 1971), p. 250.

was signed with the United Kingdom, which had become Portugal's main trading partner since the Methuen treaty of 1703. In the first half of the nineteenth century Portugal's exports to the United Kingdom accounted for 50–70 per cent of her total exports. Between 1842 and 1856 income from customs duties dropped from 24.5 per cent of the value of imports to 19.0 per cent.[33]

7. The Netherlands and Belgium

At the beginning of the nineteenth century, The Netherlands – which until 1830 also included Belgium – was probably the most liberal country in Europe. As far as import duties were concerned, the tariff of 1819 does not appear to have laid down any prohibitions, and duties were very low. *Ad valorem* duties on iron manufactured goods varied between 8 and 12 per cent (averaging somewhere about 9 per cent); for textiles, they varied between 1 and 12 per cent (averaging about 6 per cent). Specific duties also appear to have been very low.[34] The 1822 tariff reduced many of these duties still further, and export duties only affected a limited number of products. There were no duties on transit trade, which represented a high proportion of Netherlands trade throughout the nineteenth century.

In 1830 Belgium – the most industrialized part of The Netherlands – became a separate nation. This was probably an important factor in The Netherlands' pursuit of liberal policies. The southern provinces' decision to separate from the rest of The Netherlands was no doubt partly influenced by their awareness of their different economic interests, the south being rich in coal and having early established textile and iron industries, whereas the north depended on international trade. If the new Dutch tariff of 1845 was a landmark on the way to almost free trade (including the abolition of export duties), it must be said that there had been a certain strengthening of the small degree of agricultural protection in 1822 and in 1824 when grain duties were raised, and again in 1835 when a sliding grain scale was introduced.[35]

Belgium's independence led to a protectionist reaction in that country, due to three main factors. First, there were the traditionally protectionist tendencies of the Ghent cotton mill owners.[36] Secondly, independence resulted in the closure of the Dutch colonial markets to Belgian products.

---

[33] Sideri, *Trade and Power*, p. 133.
[34] H. R. C. Wright, *Free Trade and Protectionism in the Netherlands, 1816–30: A Study of the First Benelux* (Cambridge, Mass., 1955), pp. 226–30.
[35] A. Heringa, *Freetrade and Protectionism in Holland* (Haarlem, 1914), p. 5.
[36] Ghent manufacturers, annoyed by trade policy, refused to pay homage to King William during his visit in 1815. E. Mahaim, 'La politique commerciale de la Belgique', *Schriften des Vereins für Sozialpolitik*, vol. XLIX (Leipzig, 1892), pp. 195–238; p. 198.

Finally, the farmers demanded a greater degree of protection than that provided in the Dutch tariff of 1822, which provisionally applied to Belgian foreign trade. The law of 31 July 1834 introduced a sliding grain scale, and raised duties on cloth made from linen, hemp, and tow from 1.5 per cent to 15.0 per cent.

In addition to these increases in duties, the government took measures to encourage industrialization by means of subsidies aimed especially at the coal and cotton industries. Moreover, the law of 5 February 1834, backed up by that of 7 March 1837, refunded import duties on machinery and tools to all manufacturers who moved their factories to Belgium; and to any Belgian or foreigner who introduced new machinery and tools into Belgium, either for the purpose of setting up a new industry or to improve an existing one.[37]

It was not until 1842 that there were any real changes in the tariff system, successive governments having opposed any attempts at protectionism. This delay can partly be explained by the plans for a customs union between Belgium and France which were discussed seriously between 1836 and 1843. Between 1840 and 1842 an enquiry into trade and industry was held, and this came out in favour of protectionist measures. Nearly all manufactured goods and a wide range of agricultural products were hit by high duties. Many prohibitions (on both imports and exports) and export duties were introduced on a large number of products. In 1844 (Law of 21 July) a preferential tariff was brought in to benefit national shipping in order to promote direct trade. In 1840 Belgian merchant navy shipping totalled only 22,600 tons, or 0.4 per cent of the European total, while Belgian exports accounted for 3.2 per cent of the European total.

As far as railways were concerned, Belgium was ahead in two respects. It was the first country on the European continent to rapidly develop a railway network: in 1841 it already had in use 335 km of track, or 11.4 km per 1,000 km^2, as opposed to 1.1 km in Germany, 0.8 km in France, and only 4.3 km even in Great Britain. Moreover, Belgium was one of the few countries in which the railway network was built and run by the state right from the start, although there was also a private network which, in 1890, accounted for less than one-third of the whole system.

8. Sweden and Norway

In 1814 Sweden received Norway from Denmark, in exchange for Pomerania. Norway, however, retained some independence in internal affairs, including customs until 1827, when a system was introduced

37 W. Loridan, 'Esquisse de la politique douanière de la Belgique (1830–1844)', *Revue Economique Internationale*, vol IV, 30th year (November 1938), pp. 313–49; especially p. 318.

which led to the attenuation of the fiscal border between Norway and Sweden for a wide range of products.

Until 1857 Sweden's trade policy could be said to have been highly protectionist. The tariff law of 1816 was still of a mercantilist nature, since it contained 318 prohibitions on imports and 53 on exports. These prohibitions were reduced to 194 and 28 respectively by the law of 1824; but this modification, like a few others which followed later, did not noticeably reduce the degree of protectionism in Sweden's tariff policy, nor the preferential system for her navigation.[38] It was not until 1857 with the arrival of Baron Gripenberg at the Ministry of Finance that there was a movement towards a more liberal trade policy in Sweden (see section III).

Norway's trade laws were also extremely protectionist, but a slightly earlier movement developed towards liberalism, with a noticeable drop in import duties in 1842. This reduction applied particularly to manufactured goods, duties being fixed at 25 per cent for non-prohibited products.[39] From 1851 onwards, this movement towards liberalism became more pronounced.

9. Denmark

The break with mercantilism happened very early in Denmark. It can be dated from the edict of 1 February 1797, which removed all prohibitions and limited import duties to 10 per cent. There remained, however, an internal customs system which enabled the authorities to safeguard the industries specific to each region. Without going into the problems caused by war at the beginning of the century, we can consider the trade laws of 1838 and 1844 as remaining within the general framework of the provisions laid down in 1797.[40]

10. Finland

Although Finland had been ruled by the Russian czars since 1808, it retained a certain degree of internal autonomy which also applied to customs. However, this autonomy did not extend to relations with Russia, and the czars also had the power to intervene in tariff policy. From 1820, and almost continuously until 1917, nearly all Russian products (or those coming from Russia) passed freely into Finland, whereas only some Finnish goods benefited from a similar franchise. Finnish tariff legislation with regard to the rest of the world was very protectionist.[41]

---

[38] P. Drachmann, *The Industrial Development and Commercial Policies of the Three Scandinavian Countries* (Washington, DC, 1915), pp. 38–43.   [39] *Ibid.*, p. 87.   [40] *Ibid.*, pp. 12–14.

[41] N. C. Frederiksen, *La Finlande: Economie politique et privée* (Paris, 1902), especially pp. 240–50; L. Harmaja, *Die Einwirkung der Zollpolitik*, ed. Kansantaloudellinen Yndistys II (Helsinki, 1933), pamphlet issued by Volkswirtschaftliche Forschungen.

11. *The rest of Europe*

It is difficult to generalize about the tariff and trade policies of the other European countries, which form a very heterogeneous group. *Italy*, for example, did not develop either political unity or a unified tariff policy until the 1860s. Before then the trade policies of the various states were too divergent to be considered here. *Switzerland* only developed a federal tariff in 1850, and there again the tariff policies of the 22 cantons were very diverse. The period 1815–46 will therefore be discussed with that of 1846–60.

Of the *Balkan states*, Greece achieved total independence from the Ottoman Empire in 1830, Romania in 1856, Serbia and Bulgaria in 1878, and Albania in 1913. This does not mean that these countries showed no earlier signs of autonomy in trade policy. Even so, the Balkan states played a very minor role in European foreign trade, providing collectively only 1.6 per cent of European exports in 1880, two-thirds of the total coming from Romania. For this reason we deal only with Greece here and return to Romania and other Balkan states in section VI. The first Greek trade laws were fairly liberal, since import duties were fixed at 10 per cent *ad valorem* (with some even lower specific duties) and export duties at 6 per cent. On the other hand, there was a sliding grain scale, by means of which duties varied greatly according to the price level and the home market (for wheat, these duties ranged from 2 to 56 per cent of the domestic prices).

III. *The influence of British liberalism, 1846–60*

While liberalism was gaining a stronger hold in the United Kingdom, protectionism was being maintained on the continent, in spite of free trade propaganda. The fact that the British continued to advance economically was a great advantage to the supporters of free trade: the most highly developed country had become the most liberal, which made it easy to equate economic power with a free trade system, whereas in fact this causal link had been just the other way round. After 1846, moreover, the United Kingdom continued to pursue a liberal trade policy and her economy went through a period of marked expansion in trade and industry.

On the other hand, the period 1846–60 witnessed a number of phenomena, which, although partly exogenous to economic life in the strict sense, had important consequences for the economy, and especially on the flow of trade. These included the dramatic reduction in transport costs following the introduction of the steam engine to railways and shipping; the very rapid expansion of the stock of precious metals as a result of discoveries in North America and in Australia; and finally, the beginnings of the mechanization of agriculture in the United States.

A.   CHANGES IN THE CONTEXT OF THE EUROPEAN ECONOMY

Even if the first public railway line to use steam had been opened in 1825, the real development in this field only began in the 1840s. The period of most rapid expansion in Europe, as in the United States, took place between 1845–6 and 1873–4. In 1845 there were about 9,200 km of railways in Europe, and 7,500 km in the United States (20,500 in the world); in 1860 these figures had reached 51,900 km in Europe, and 49,200 in the United States (and 108,000 in the world). In 1874 they had increased to 136,000 km for Europe, 116,000 km for the United States and 282,000 for the world. In other words, in Europe between 1845 and 1874 the network increased by 6,700 km per annum, or by 15.2 per cent, whereas in the period 1874 to 1913 these figures were 5,800 km per annum, or 2.5 per cent. In 1874 Europe excluding Russia had an average of some 25 km of track per 1,000 km^2; or, in other words, on the hypothetical assumption that these tracks were uniformly distributed, no part of Europe would have been more than 10 km from a railway line.

Given that land transport costs were very high and that the railways were used more as a link between regions without waterways than as a complementary form of transport, the expansion of the railway network led to a marked reduction in land transport costs. It is likely that between 1840–5 and 1870–5 the average cost of land transport dropped in real terms by 75–85 per cent – a fourfold decline – and this is without taking into account a tenfold increase in speed.

The introduction of steam had begun to have an impact on maritime transport at about the same period. In 1840 steam ships made up only 4 per cent of the world fleet, or, in terms of carrying capacity (largely because of their greater speed), 14 per cent of the total stock. In 1860 this proportion had already reached 32 per cent, and in 1870 it was 49 per cent. What is more, by 1860 the carrying capacity of the steam ships alone was greater than that of the whole fleet in 1820. This, too, led to a drop in transport costs – a reduction which had already begun before the introduction of steam but accelerated afterwards. Between 1820 and 1840 the real cost of freight charges by sea fell by 1.5 per cent per annum. Between 1840 and 1860 this had become 2.3 per cent per annum, as opposed to 0.3 per cent between 1860 and 1880, and 2.0 per cent between 1880 and 1900. There was a further sharp drop of 3.3 per cent per annum between 1900 and 1910.

The discovery of very rich gold deposits in the United States in 1848 and in Australia in 1851, and of important silver deposits in the United States in 1859, led to a very rapid increase in the world production of precious metals. The average production of gold went from less than 20 tons per annum in 1700–1847 to 198 tons per annum in 1851–60, and to

206 tons per annum in 1861–70. Silver production went from 600 tons per annum in 1700–1850 to 1,200 tons in 1861–70, and to 2,200 tons per annum in 1871–80. In 1840 the value of precious metal production (gold and silver) amounted to about 2.9 per cent of world exports; by 1860 it was nearer to 5.3 per cent – and the value of these exports had meanwhile gone up from $1,410 million to $3,200 million (in current prices).

The mechanization of American agriculture may seem of secondary importance compared with the other factors mentioned. All the same, it had important consequences, given the role that cereal imports were to play in bringing about changes in tariff policies and in the general economic development of Europe. The reaping-machine was the major innovation, since harvesting demanded an enormous labour force. This determined the price of grain, especially since the country was short of labour. In the United States in 1840 one acre of wheat required 35 man-hours, including 23 for the harvest; in 1880 only 20 hours were needed, of which 12 were for the harvest. This was largely due to the use of reaping-machines, which began to spread from the early 1850s. The increase in investment in agricultural machinery in the United States was more pronounced between 1850 and 1860 (4.9 per cent per annum) than during the other decades from 1860 to 1900.[42] Between 1839 and 1859 wheat production increased by 100 per cent, whereas the population only increased by 84 per cent, a discrepancy which led to the beginnings of a vast export movement which developed after the civil war. Wheat exports – which had risen to some 50,000 tons per annum, between 1843 and 1851 – reached 240,000 tons per annum between 1852 and 1861, and 2,140,000 tons per annum between 1872 and 1881.

B. LIBERALISM AND ECONOMIC GROWTH IN THE UNITED KINGDOM

In 1849 the United Kingdom gave a supplementary proof of its liberalism. Parliament repealed (by a small majority: 173 for, 163 against) the notorious Navigation Acts with effect from the beginning of 1850. The various Navigation Acts, the first one dating from 1651, had reserved the bulk of foreign trade for British ships and largely contributed to the supremacy of the British fleet in the eighteenth century.[43] This maritime supremacy had much to do with British commercial supremacy and the success of colonial expansion.

The liberalism of British commercial policy continued during the

---

[42] US Bureau of the Census, *Historical Statistics of the United States: Colonial Times to 1957* (Washington, DC, 1960), pp. 281–5.

[43] A ship where the owner, the captain and three-quarters of the sailors were of British nationality counted as a British ship.

years 1846–60. Customs duties were reduced still more, and in many cases totally abolished. In the case of grains, duties were reduced to 1s. per quarter from 1849, that is about 2 per cent of the price of wheat on the home market (4s. 6d. for flour). After the reductions of 1846, a new tariff, introduced by a law of 20 August 1853, abolished a large number of customs duties, especially in the case of manufactured articles. The long list of duty-free imports included virtually all manufactured articles. Duties were extremely low on the articles not included in this list, 5 per cent *ad valorem* in general, sometimes 10 per cent, and more rarely 20 per cent. The list of duty-free imports was lengthened still further by the 1860 tariff.

All this naturally decreased the relative importance of customs revenue. In the years 1841–5 it brought in £23.2 million per annum, which represented 27.2 per cent of the value of imports (re-exports excluded); from 1855–9 the total revenue was much the same (£23.1 million), but it represented only 15.8 per cent of the value of the imports.[44] This stability in revenue was a further argument for liberalism (for 1895–9 the revenue was £21.2 million, but this was only 5.4 per cent of the value of imports). This revenue came above all from the duties on tea, sugar, tobacco, wine, and spirits; duties which, as Mathias notes, 'became the remaining contribution of the working class to indirect taxation by foreign trade'.[45] For 1849–51 these four groups of products provided 82 per cent of customs revenue; for 1859–61 this increased to 87 per cent.[46]

A supplementary but important question needs to be asked about liberal policies. One of the key arguments of the supporters of free trade, such as the Anti-Corn Law League, was that free trade would lower the cost of living in general and thus increase the standard of living for workers in particular. Did this happen? On looking at this question, the watershed is clearly 1846. In his first study on British wages, Bowley concluded that within the period 1790–1914, the years 1852–70 were the ones in which real wages increased most rapidly.[47] In any case, the available statistics reveal a noticeable acceleration in the rise of the average standard of living after 1846. Both direct and indirect evidence (Gross National Product and consumption per capita) indicate that growth was four to five times quicker from 1841–5 to 1851–5 than from 1831–5 to 1841–5. So as far as the income of the working class was concerned, progress was apparently less rapid. However, it is almost

[44] Calculated from Mitchell and Deane, *Abstract of British Historical Statistics*, pp. 283–4 and 393–4.
[45] P. Mathias, *The First Industrial Nation: An Economic History of Britain 1700–1914* (London, 1969), p. 301.
[46] Calculated from figures given by W. Page, *Commerce and Industry: A Historical Review of the Economic Conditions of the British Empire from the Peace of Paris in 1815 to 1914* (London, 1914), p. 62. Also Mitchell and Deane, *Abstract of British Historical Statistics*, p. 394.
[47] A. L. Bowley, *Wages in the U.K. in the Nineteenth Century* (Cambridge, 1900).

certain that real wages increased more quickly after the repeal of the Corn Laws than before. It is important to note that the rises in both the standard of living and of real wages were the result of more rapid economic growth rather than the result of a fall in prices. The general level of prices between 1841–5 and 1851–5 did not follow a very different curve to prices between 1831–5 and 1841–5. In the earlier period there was a very slight fall in prices, while there was a slight rise in prices in the later period. Even if the price of wheat fell after 1846, the fall was very slight and in any case considerably slighter than had been expected.[48] Thus in this important field, the repeal of the Corn Laws and the liberalization of trade achieved their aim in Britain, even if they did not lead to a fall in corn prices. This result implies that the British economy as a whole was advancing rapidly.

The analysis of annual statistics on exports and Gross National Product shows that this major change in tariff policy was accompanied not only by acceleration in the growth of foreign trade; but in the rate of growth of Gross National Product more generally.

The expansion of exports was already extremely rapid in the ten to fifteen years before 1846 (about 5 per cent per annum) and it accelerated further after that date. From 1843–7 to 1857–61 the volume of British exports increased by just over 6 per cent per annum. It is worth emphasizing that this growth was the most spectacular ever achieved for such a time-span in the whole of British economic history (at least between 1697 and 1986). It is also worth emphasizing that the rate of growth mentioned is not 'artificially' increased because we have chosen to divide up the periods in terms of tariff phases, for if we had looked at changes between 1846–8 and 1858–60 we would have found that the annual growth rate of the volume of exports was 7.3 per cent. It should, however, be noted that in other European countries in the nineteenth century similar growth rates, or even slightly higher ones, can be found. This was the case in France from 1850 to 1875, in Germany from 1898 to 1913, in Sweden from 1862 to 1874, and in Belgium from 1847 to 1864.

Economic growth was equally exceptional in this period. Between 1843–7 and 1857–61 the annual growth of the volume of Gross National Product was 2.4 per cent. Since this period was marked by a very slight demographic growth (0.2 per cent per annum) due to the fall in the population of Ireland, the per capita growth of Gross National Product was 2.2 per cent, which is the highest recorded for a period of this length, certainly between 1800 and 1945, and probably from the industrial revolution to 1945.

The share of British cotton sold abroad, which had begun to fall before

---

[48] S. Fairlie, 'The Corn Laws and British Wheat Production 1829–1876', *Economic History Review*, vol. XXXII, no. 1 (April 1969), pp. 88–116.

1846 as we have seen, now rose again. The proportion of cotton goods exported rose from 49.8 per cent of total production for 1839–41 to 60.8 per cent for 1849–51, and to 63.8 per cent for 1859–61. From the point of view of the international cotton trade, this meant a further rise in the importance of the United Kingdom, which was already predominant in this field. As far as iron was concerned, Britain's share of European production rose from 54.2 per cent for 1838–42 to 58.5 per cent for 1851–62.

Despite the fact that these British economic and commercial developments led to an increase in the trade of the other European countries, and despite the deterioration of British terms of trade, the share of Britain in European foreign trade increased during this period. The United Kingdom already provided 29.1 per cent of European exports for 1839–41, and this went up to 30.2 per cent for 1859–61. On the import side the respective percentages are 29.6 and 35.5.

It is clear that the global balance-sheet was extremely favourable to Britain. Because of the liberalization of trade, British industry, which had a technological lead, had found a much larger market. But this market was essentially to be found outside Europe, especially in Asia and Oceania. The value of exports to Europe increased by 4.5 per cent per annum between 1839–41 and 1859–61, while those to the rest of the world increased by 5.1 per cent. Exports to Asia increased by 6.1 per cent per annum, those to Oceania by 9.9 per cent (to North America by 4.2 per cent, to South America by 2.3 per cent and to Africa by 4.8 per cent per annum). This expansion of imperial trade reduced the importance of Europe. In 1830 exports to Europe accounted for about 48 per cent of British sales, in 1860 for no more than 34 per cent.

These last percentages highlight the fundamental difference between the geographical structure of British exports and that of the rest of Europe. Towards 1860 the continental European exports to other European countries represented 82 per cent of the total.[49] The relatively small proportion of British exports to Europe explains the attempts to convert the Europeans to liberalism in the 1850s and is itself explained by the protectionism of continental Europe.

C.   REACTIONS TO THE BRITISH ACHIEVEMENT: RESISTANCES AND SUCCESS ON THE CONTINENT

Already in August 1846, following the success of his ideas in his own country, Richard Cobden had begun his European tours. He virtually lived abroad till June 1859, carrying on the crusade he began in Manches-

[49] P. Bairoch, 'Geographical Structure and Trade Balance of European Foreign Trade from 1800 to 1970', *Journal of European Economic History*, vol. III, no. 3 (Winter 1974), pp. 557–608.

ter in October 1838. All over Europe pressure groups of manufacturers and economists were formed to fight against certain tariffs which were considered prohibitive. In France, the followers of Saint-Simon founded the Société d'Economie Politique and the *Journal des Economistes*; in Belgium, the Société Belge d'Economie Politique and *L'Economist Belge*. In Belgium in 1846 the Association Belge pour la Liberté Commerciale was also founded, under the aegis of which met (in Brussels in 1847) the Congrès des Economistes, which was in fact an international congress of free traders. In Germany a great number of associations favourable to liberalism were founded, notably the Freihandelsverein. It is interesting to note that the leader of these German associations was an Englishman, John Prince Smith, who had been living in that country since he was 21.[50]

The liberalization of British trade directly and indirectly fostered foreign trade in the rest of Europe. The continent's volume of exports – which had grown by 1.9 per cent per annum between 1837–9 and 1845–6 – increased by 6.1 per cent per annum between 1845–7 and 1857–9. In fact for this reason these years were one of the three most favourable periods for export growth in the nineteenth century. The second of these was from 1857–9 to 1870–2 (5.8 per cent per annum) and the last between 1893–5 and 1911–13 (4.2 per cent per annum). Between 1849–51 and 1859–61 Britain increased its imports from Europe by more than 85 per cent, but it is clear that this alone is not enough to explain the rapid growth in continental sales, since Britain around 1860 absorbed only 16 per cent of the continent's exports.

Besides this positive evolution of international trade the European supporters of free trade did not fail to draw attention to the British example itself. For example, the Association Belge pour la Réforme Douanière, which developed out of the Société Belge d'Economie Politique, published in 1855 a manifesto for tariff reform which started as follows, 'Inspired by the results of economic science and by the experience of real facts, especially that of England, where, since the introduction of Sir Robert Peel's reforms, agriculture, navigation and industry, far from declining, have flourished in force and energy in the most unexpected way . . .'[51] In France, Michel Chevalier – who as we shall see was responsible for the commercial treaty between Britain and France – wrote in 1852–3, 'Britain's adoption of the principle of the freedom of trade is one of the great events of the century. When such a powerful and enlightened nation not only puts such a great principle into practice but is

---

[50] W. O. Henderson, 'Prince Smith and the Free Trade in Germany', *Economic History Review*, vol. II, no. 3 (1950), pp. 295–302.
[51] *Congrès International de réformes douanières réuni à Bruxelles* (22–25 September 1856); Brussels, 1857.

also well known to have profited by it, how can its emulators fail to follow the same way?'[52]

It was generally at the instigation of these national pressure groups, and sometimes under the more direct influence of the British as well, that tariff reductions were made by the majority of great European states. However, they were not very important until 1860. They did only a little to weaken the thoroughly protectionist character of the tariff laws of the major powers of continental Europe. Let us now look at changes in commercial policy on the continent between 1846 and 1860.

1. The major continental European countries

In *France*, Napoleon III, who was in favour of free trade (see section IV), came to power in 1851. During the years 1853–5 there was a series of small changes brought about by means of decrees,[53] in the highly protectionist system. But if the Chamber of Deputies endorsed most of these decrees at the beginning of 1856, the bill of June 1856 was withdrawn in view of the emotion it aroused. Basically, it had aimed only at replacing prohibitions by import duties ranging from 30 to 50 per cent. This shows in effect that until 1860 the highly protectionist character of the tariff system remained almost intact. Prohibitions were in force on nearly all manufactured goods, which, moreover, in 1858–60 represented only 3.8 per cent of total imports as opposed to 6.0 per cent in 1846–7.

There was no more important change in the field of navigation. Between 1814 and 1816 a series of surtaxes replaced the very strict rules governing the use of foreign ships laid down in the Navigation Act of 21 September 1793. The system became slightly less rigid, however, as a result of navigation treaties with first the United States (1822) and then with Great Britain (1826).[54]

In *Germany*, the movement towards protectionism in the *Zollverein* continued at the end of the 1840s and through the 1850s. List, who had returned from the United States in 1832, worked actively in support of pressure groups – mostly of industrialists – demanding a more effective protectionism. Political and economic rivalries provoked several crises which almost broke up the *Zollverein* (notably in 1852). Prussia slowed down this movement towards protectionism, probably for two reasons. First of all, it was a less industrialized state;[55] and secondly, it wanted to

52 M. Chevalier, *Examen du système commercial connu sous le nom de système protecteur* (Paris, 1853), p. 205.
53 Under article 34 of the 1814 law, the head of state could, in an emergency, temporarily reduce duties on raw materials necessary for industry.
54 A. Arnauné, *Le commerce extérieur et les tarifs de douane* (Paris, 1911), pp. 171–8.
55 W. O. Henderson, *The Zollverein* (Cambridge, 1939), pp. 179–89.

retain the leadership of the *Zollverein*, which would have been challenged if Austria had joined. One of the obstacles to a customs union between Austria–Hungary and the *Zollverein* was the extremely protectionist trade policy of the Habsburg Empire. Plans for such a customs union, which had already been mooted in 1841, were put forward more seriously from 1848 on, when von Bruck became Minister of Finance in Austria. He was a rich shipowner from Trieste (although he originated from Bonn, in Germany). His business activities led him to favour free trade, and he worked towards this end during his time in government.

The tariffs of the *Zollverein* in force during the 1850s were distinctly protectionist. The tariff promulgated on 4 December 1853 (and which remained in force till 1865) provided for specific duties on cotton thread amounting to about 20 per cent of the value of the finished goods. For crude iron, duties were to be of the order of 25 per cent *ad valorem*, and some 80–100 per cent for non-highly manufactured iron goods.

As we have just seen, thanks to von Bruck, *Austria–Hungary* underwent a fairly thorough reorganization of trade policy, of which the most important feature was the tariff of 1851. Until this new tariff Austria–Hungary retained an extremely prohibitive tariff system. The 1843 proposals, which among other things included customs duties of 40 per cent on manufactured goods, had been rejected as too liberal. The new tariff, passed on 6 November 1851 (and which came into force on 1 February 1852) was the result of two years' study. Nearly all prohibitions were lifted and replaced by relatively low specific duties, which amounted to a tariff of about 20–30 per cent for manufactured goods. Export duties on nearly all products remained, however.

Even though von Bruck managed to conclude negotiations for a twelve-year trading agreement with the *Zollverein* (signed 19 February 1853, to take effect 1 January 1854), Austria–Hungary did not enter the *Zollverein* – and this despite the passing of a supplementary agreement by the monetary union in 1857. In this context it should be noted that the 1851 tariff applied to the whole of Austria–Hungary.

In the same period, another plan for customs union – that of the *Italian states* – suffered the same fate. The origins of this plan – which was clearly influenced by the *Zollverein* – can be found in a series of articles published in 1843 by Count Serristori. On 3 November 1847 the official *Gazette* of Turin published a joint declaration by the Holy See, Sardinia, and Tuscany announcing a customs association which it was hoped the other Italian states would join. Austria, however, also hoped to involve the Italian states in a customs union. In the end, the commercial unification of Italy did not take place until its political unification in 1861.

In *Russia*, the protectionist policies drawn up by Krankin (between 1823 and 1844) remained more or less unaltered till 1857. For example, under the 1851 tariff, import duties on non-prohibited manufactured goods were generally 50–75 per cent *ad valorem* (and there were also many specific duties). The defeat of Russia in the Crimean War appears to have been one of the factors which led in 1857 to reform in the direction of a liberalization of trade policy. The list of prohibitions was reduced (from nineteen to twelve), but those remaining affected very loosely defined categories of goods. Customs dues were reduced by about 30 per cent on a wide range of products, which meant that duties on manufactured goods were about 35–50 per cent.

In *Spain*, the timid liberalization of the highly protectionist system which had begun in 1841 was continued with the tariff of 1849. This reduced the number of prohibitions to seven, but increased duties on a large range of products.

The tariff in force after the law of 17 July 1849 (with modifications in 1849 and 1852) provided for differential duties according to the nationality of the ship. There was a surtax of 20 per cent for foreign ships. For non-prohibited manufactured goods carried by Spanish ships, duties averaged about 30 per cent. In 1856 a parliamentary commission was set up to enquire into tariff reform, and this eventually resulted in a tariff with liberal tendencies – but not until 1862. From the end of the 1850s, associations were formed to support both liberalism and protectionism.

2. The small countries of continental Europe

As just seen, the major European countries on the whole stayed with protectionist trade policies, but, in certain cases, eliminated what can be called the surviving traces of the mercantilist system. In the small countries, however, the movement towards liberalism was more pronounced.

The factors which encouraged these countries to favour free trade must be considered here. Their very size led most small countries into economic specialization. This affected their trade policy in two ways. First, they lacked certain sectors of production, so there was no need to protect these products by import duties. Specialization also meant that the share of exports from most sectors of industry in the small countries was higher than that from the same sectors in the big countries. The home market represented only a fraction of the outlets for these sectors, and hence the protection of the home market was less important than the expansion of overseas ones.

The most liberal of these small countries around 1846 was already *The Netherlands*. The period 1846–60 was marked in particular by a further liberalization stemming from the laws of 30 May 1847, 8 August 1850, and 1 September 1854. The law of 1850 again lowered customs duties and abolished the preferential system in favour of Dutch ships which had been introduced by the law of 1816. Nevertheless, until 1872 The Netherlands retained a preferential tariff for Dutch products in its colonies (see section VIII). In the 1854 tariff, customs duties – mostly *ad valorem* – were about 2–6 per cent for manufactured goods in general, and 1 per cent for almost all machinery. Duties on agricultural products were equally low – specific duties on cereals came to about 3 per cent of their value.

In *Belgium* from 1850 onwards a series of trade agreements (notably with the United Kingdom in 1851, with the *Zollverein* in 1852, and with France in 1854) led to a slight relaxation of the protectionism of the 1842–4 laws. At the same time, a series of laws adopted between 1850 and 1853 gave a more liberal slant to trade policy – especially the laws of 1852 which reduced some import duties, and of 1853 which abolished nearly all export prohibitions. The tariff then in force, however, could not be called liberal. Duties were about 20–35 per cent of the value for manufactured goods, though it is true that under the previous tariff they had averaged about 30–45 per cent.

Pressure against protectionism increased from 1856, when the Farmers' Association came out in favour of liberalism and joined forces with pressure groups dating back to 1846 and the creation of the Association Belge pour la Liberté Commerciale. A year earlier, in September 1855, another free trade association, the Société Belge d'Economie Politique, had been founded. On the protectionist side, an Association pour la Defense du travail National was set up in 1856; this association was the offspring of the iron, coal, and textile spinning industries.

The system of preferential duties for goods imported in Belgian ships was abolished by the law of 19 June 1856. Although this preferential system had not led to any very great expansion of the national merchant fleet (from 1840 to 1856 the tonnage rose from 23,000 to 42,000) it should be noted that its abolition was to lead to a recession, since in 1870 the tonnage was only 30,100 tons.[56] In terms of approximate carrying power, the Belgian fleet's share of the world total was 0.25 per cent in 1840, some 0.28 per cent in 1856, but only 0.19 per cent in 1870, whereas Belgium's share in world exports rose from 1.9 per cent to 3.0 per cent from 1840 to 1870. A series of laws in 1857–8 liberalized trade policy as much in the field of agriculture as in industry. All the same, it could be said that tariff policy strictly speaking remained relatively protectionist until the treaty with France in 1861. Import duties on manufactured

[56] B. R. Mitchell, *European Historical Statistics, 1750–1970* (London, 1975), pp. 614 and 619; and *Annuaire Statistique de la Belgique 1885* (Brussels, 1886), p. 380.

It should be noted that although the tonnage of sailing ships had fallen from 40,000 tons in 1846 to 21,000 in 1870, that of steam ships had risen from less than 2,000 tons to 9,500 tons.

goods were on average about 15–20 per cent *ad valorem*; but only about 4 per cent was charged on grain.

Switzerland's first federal tariff only came into force in 1850. However, we should not totally ignore the few measures taken and suggestions put forward before that date. Already in 1816 a federal border tax was introduced, with the sole aim of raising revenue. It was very low (1 *batz*, or about 14 centimes per 50 kg) and did not apply to the major foodstuffs. However, the cantons retained total customs autonomy, and since their economic structures varied considerably, so did their trade policies. On the whole, though, the trade policy of the cantons could be said to have been liberal; in England in the 1830s Switzerland was even held up as an example of liberalism.

After 1822, efforts to establish a true federal trade policy received a boost from the presence of the industrialist Zellweger, as Inspector General of Customs. He supported free trade. Many proposals about a possible customs union were put forward, but the only one to be acted on was that which linked 12 of the 22 Swiss cantons in 1847. The adoption of the federal constitution of 12 September 1849 was to provide the legal structure for the creation of a federal customs system. The preamble of the bill shows a spirit of compromise, taking into account 'a fair distribution of burdens, the protection of national employment and the principle of free trade'.[57] This tariff, passed on 16 May 1849 and coming into force on 1 February 1850, can be considered as more liberal than protectionist. The number of tariff items was limited to ten, and as for *ad valorem* duties, these varied from 2 to 10 per cent on imports and from 3 to 5 per cent on exports. By the law of 27 August 1851, which came into force on 1 January 1852, this tariff was altered to provide for a slight increase in duties. There was, moreover, a complete change and enlargement of tariff items (from then on, too, duties were expressed in francs and centimes rather than in *batz* as in the past).

The shift towards free trade was very noticeable in *Sweden*. Baron Gripenberg – who was Minister of Finance from 1856 – was entirely in favour of free trade. As Heckscher remarked, Gripenberg probably saw himself as Sweden's Napoleon III.[58] The changes introduced in 1857 were important: the abolition of prohibitions, and of duties on grain, the reduction of duties on manufactured goods, and the abolition of the preference previously given to Swedish ships.[59]

In *Norway*, the tendency towards liberalism which was first noticeable in 1842 became more marked between 1851 and 1857, when there was a series of cuts in duties on manufactured goods. Norway's lack of impor-

[57] R. M. W. Vogel, *Politique commerciale de la suisse* (Montreux, 1966), p. 73.
[58] E. F. Heckscher, *An Economic History of Sweden* (Cambridge, Mass., 1963), p. 237.
[59] Drachmann, *Industrial Development and Commercial Policies*, p. 44.

tant industry explains the complete reform of her tariff system with the aim of increasing revenue. This entailed an increase in duties on the traditionally highly taxed products, in other words, on products for which demand is not very elastic: coffee, tobacco, alcohol (and also sugar, which is not entirely in this category). Further slight reductions in the duties on manufactured articles partly compensated for these increases.

Denmark was also continuing to become more liberal. In 1853 internal customs duties were lifted. In 1857 the traditional sund toll (the payments made to the Danish authorities for every ship passing through the Sund Straits), which Denmark had levied ever since the fifteenth century, were abolished. After an international conference Denmark agreed to renounce her claim to these dues, in return for a single sum of 30.5 million rix-dollars – about twelve years' revenue – paid by the major maritime powers, and of which more than one-third was contributed by the United Kingdom.

Finland did not change its protectionist policy. A fairer system of trade with Russia operated from the czar's decree in 1859 until the tariff reform of 1869.

In *Portugal*, the period of 1846–60 was marked, on the whole, by the pursuit of liberal policies reintroduced after the victory of the Chartists in 1842. From 1851, however, the reconciliation of the Chartists and the Septembrists (reunited from 1852 in the Regeneradores Party) brought not only a period of more than 40 years of internal peace (or armistice) but led also to an economic policy with greater emphasis on development. Fontes Pereira de Melo, who was Minister of Finance from 1851 to 1852 and Prime Minister from 1852 to 1856, was responsible for this policy, which, we must stress, remained liberal in matters of foreign trade.

The tariff of 31 December 1852 provided for quite high import duties, but with little differentiation between various cotton manufactured goods – duties on thread were much the same as those on cloth and made-up garments. On cotton thread, these duties were around 20–40 per cent of the value; and on cloth and garments they were 10–20 per cent. Duties on iron manufactured goods, on the other hand, were progressive but very low (about 5–10 per cent).

From 1852 there was an active attempt to favour foreign trade through an improvement of the transportation network. The consequences of this opening-up of the country were a considerable worsening of the balance of trade and a decline in the importance of the fleet. The trade deficit, which around 1840 must have represented some 50 per cent of exports, reached some 85 per cent around 1860. Between 1842 and 1888 the fleet declined from 81,000 tons to 78,000 and furthermore contained very few steam ships. As a result the Portuguese share in world shipping declined from 0.9 per cent to 0.3 per cent.

IV. The phase of European free trade, 1860–79

As we have just seen, on the continent before 1860 only a few small countries had adopted a truly liberal trade policy. These were The Netherlands, Denmark, Portugal, Switzerland, to which we may add Sweden and Belgium (but only from 1856–7 on, and even then they maintained some degree of protectionism).

In spite of this success, which must not be exaggerated since the four small free trade countries accounted for only 4–5 per cent of the population of the continent, the true free trade period only began in 1860 with the Anglo-French trade treaty. The concentration of the efforts of the English free traders on France rather than on any other European country can largely be explained by the fact that France was not only one of the main European trading partners of the United Kingdom, but was also the country with whom Britain had the highest trade deficit. From 1854 to 1860, British exports to France rose to $25.6 million per annum, while imports from France reached $62.5 million, leaving a trade deficit of $36.9 million. British exports to Germany were worth $56.9 million per annum, but the deficit was only $6.9 million.

The beginning of the 1860s, during which liberalism reached the continent, was a time when the levels of economic development in the countries of Europe were very unequal, above all their levels of modern industrialization, but also of agricultural productivity. This was the time of Britain's greatest lead, but there were also important differences between countries on the continent (see Table 4).

This period can be divided into two distinct economic phases. From 1860 to 1868–73 (depending on the sector) there was a positive phase, which was to a large extent the continuation of the period of rapid growth which began about 1850. From 1868–70 (for domestic production) or 1873 (for trade) there began what may be called the great European depression. This depression, which began in the middle of the liberal period, lasted till the beginning of the 1890s. The problems which this depression posed for trade policies are discussed later (pp. 45–51). Meanwhile we shall examine the setting up of the Cobden treaties and the main aspects of the trade policies of the different countries of Europe from 1860 to 1879. If virtually the whole of Europe went over to liberalism, individual countries did so at different speeds.

Table 4. *Indicators of economic development of*
European countries around 1860

	Per capita level of industrialization[a]	Agricultural productivity[b]	GNP per capita (1960 US dollars and prices)
Austria–Hungary	11	6.2	295
Belgium	28	10.9	400
Bulgaria	5	6.0	215
Denmark	10	20.0	320
Finland	11	5.7	245
France	20	12.2	380
Germany	15	12.2	350
Greece	6	4.9	235
Italy	10	5.1	280
Norway	11	7.9	325
Portugal	8	4.0	290
Romania	6	6.7	215
Russia	8	5.9	200
Serbia	6	7.0	225
Spain	11	6.1	280
Sweden	15	8.3	300
Switzerland	26	9.1	415
The Netherlands	11	10.8	410
United Kingdom	64	18.0	575
Europe	17	7.9	315
Continental Europe	12	7.4	290
Great Britain[c]	80	23.0	630

Notes:
[a] 100 = United Kingdom in 1900.
[b] Net production of agriculture per male worker in agriculture (expressed in millions of calories).
[c] Figures derived from those of United Kingdom and less reliable data for Ireland.
Sources (with some complementary calculations): P. Bairoch, 'International Industrialization Levels from 1750 to 1980', *Journal of European Economic History*, vol. XI, no. 2 (Autumn 1982), pp. 269–333; P. Bairoch, 'Production yields and productivity of agriculture of developed countries: 1800–1985' to appear; P. Bairoch, 'World Gross National Product 1800–1985 (Computations Estimates and Guesses)'; to appear.

A. THE ANGLO-FRENCH TREATY AND THE NETWORK OF
COBDEN'S TREATIES IN EUROPE

What the supporters of protectionism of the period, that is the majority of deputies, called the new *coup d'état* was revealed by a letter of Napoleon III to the Minister of State. This letter, dated 5 January 1860 and published by the *Moniteur* on 15 January, presented a vast programme of liberal reforms, including a declaration of intent on the part of the Emperor to sign some commercial treaties. This letter made public the secret negotiations the origins of which go back to the meeting in Paris in 1846 between Richard Cobden and Michel Chevalier, a former disciple of Saint-Simon and professor of political economy at the College de France. When he became a member of the Council of State, Chevalier played an important part in the semi-official negotiations which began in October 1859 to bring about a commercial treaty between the United Kingdom and France.[60] It was signed on 23 January 1860, to last for ten years. A way was found of avoiding the passage of the bill through parliament, which would probably have been fatal to the project. Hence, a group of theorists succeeded in introducing free trade into France, and thus indirectly to the rest of the continent, although this was against the will of the majority of people in charge of the different sectors of the economy. The pro-free traders were strongly supported by Napoleon III who had been converted to free trade ideas during his long stays in Great Britain (first two and then six years) and who saw political implications in this treaty. This was a liberal victory. As Lutfalla notes, 'The free trade agitation was one of the great tasks of French liberals in the first half of the nineteenth century.'[61]

It took some time for the treaty to be put into practice in every field. For coal and coke, the crucial date was 1 July 1860, and for iron and steel (of the kind that was not prohibited before 1860) it was 1 October 1860. For iron manufactured goods the date was 31 December 1860, for linen and hemp thread, 1 June 1861, and for other manufactured articles, 1 October 1861.[62]

France abolished all prohibitions and replaced them with import duties not exceeding 30 per cent *ad valorem* (25 per cent from 1 October 1864). The United Kingdom allowed free entry to a large number of French products, and abolished export duty on coal. Duties on wine were reduced by more than 80 per cent; France had anticipated a significant increase in British wine consumption, but this did not fully materialize. The Anglo-French treaty contained the most-favoured-nation clause, which was to play an important part in tariff history in the second half of the nineteenth century. Indeed, we can talk of a return to the use of this most-favoured-nation clause after an interval of some 30–40 years, during which the reciprocity clause, or as it was also called, the American clause, had been dominant.

The most-favoured-nation clause is a formula by which each of the two signatories to a treaty agrees to grant the other any advantage,

[60] A. L. Dunham, *The Anglo-French Treaty of Commerce of 1860 and the Progress of Industrial Revolution in France* (Ann Arbor, 1930).

[61] M. Lutfalla, 'Aux origines de libéralisme économique en France. Le "Journal des Economistes". Analyse du contenu de la première série, 1841–1853', *Revue d'Histoire Economique et Sociale*, vol. L, no. 4 (1972), pp. 494–517.

[62] P. Boiteau, *Les Traités de Commerce. Textes de tous les traités en vigueur* . . . (Paris, 1863), p. 6.

favour, or privilege with regard to trade or navigation that it granted at the time of signing, or that it would grant in the future, to any other nation. Such a clause had already been used in a vague form very occasionally since the twelfth century. It became more frequent and better defined in the sixteenth and seventeenth centuries, but with certain limitations – the favoured countries were specifically named. The true most-favoured-nation clause began to be used from the beginning of the eighteenth century, notably in the treaties concluded by England. For example the treaty of October 1706 between England and the town of Danzig contained the following stipulation: 'For what remains, if any greater privileges, which any wise respect the persons, ships, or goods of foreigners at Danzig, shall be hereafter granted to any foreign nation, the British subjects shall in the like manner fully enjoy the same themselves, their ships and commerce.'[63] From the second half of the eighteenth century most European states included a most-favoured-nation clause in their treaties.

It was the United States – for whom tariff problems had been a major factor in their decision to become independent – who introduced the notion of reciprocity into the most-favoured-nation clause. This reciprocity clause implies that the most-favoured-nation clause only works automatically in cases where the new benefit which is to be shared has been obtained without a concession in return. If a state cannot obtain a new benefit without making a concession in a particular area, it is necessary for it to receive the same concession from the state enjoying the advantage of the most-favoured-nation clause. This reciprocity clause already figured in the first commercial treaty signed by the United States (on 6 February 1778, with France). According to article II, 'The Most Christian King and the United States engage mutually not to grant any particular favor to other nations in respect of commerce and navigation which shall not enjoy the same favor freely, if this concession was freely made or on allowing the same compensation if the concession was conditional.'[64]

Although the reciprocity clause was to be used systematically by the United States and also by most Latin American countries from the early nineteenth century, it did not reach Europe until about 1830. From the early 1840s such a clause was to be found in most treaties signed between European states.[65] The Anglo-French treaty of 1860 (and in particular the complementary agreement of 16 November 1860) reintroduced the previous form of most-favoured-nation clause, in other words, without restrictions.

---

[63] C. Poznanski, *La clause de la nation la plus favorisée. Etude historique et théorique* (Berne, 1917), p. 24.
[64] S. K. Hornbeck, *The Most Favoured Clause in Commercial Treaties: its Function in Theory and in Practice and its Relation to Tariff Policies* (Madison, Wis., 1910), p. 14.
[65] Poznanski, *La clause de la nation la plus favorisée*, pp. 46–63.

This Anglo-French treaty, which was very quickly followed by further treaties between France and a great many other countries, led to tariff 'disarmament' in continental Europe, mostly as a result of this most-favoured-nation clause. Already in May 1861 a treaty was signed between France and Belgium. In August 1862 Germany, or more precisely, Prussia (in the name of the *Zollverein*) ratified a treaty with France which led to a reduction in import duties of about 40–80 per cent on cotton goods, 25 per cent on crude iron, 80 per cent on manufactured iron goods, and 60–80 per cent on woollen clothes, etc. Between 1863 and 1866, by means of treaties with France, most European countries entered the free trade network, or what has been called the network of Cobden–Chevalier treaties. Italy did so in January 1863, followed by Switzerland in June 1864; Sweden and Norway in February 1865; the Hanseatic towns one month later; Spain in June 1865; The Netherlands in July of the same year; and, finally, by Austria in December 1866.[66] Portugal and Denmark were integrated into the free trade network by means of their commercial treaties with England. Only Russia remained outside the network of treaties, since she did not sign a commercial treaty with France until April 1874; in other words, as we shall see, only three years before taking protectionist measures. Earlier, though, and particularly in 1868, Russia did make liberal reforms in her tariff system.

B.   THE LIBERALIZATION OF TRADE POLICIES

Although the network of Cobden treaties played a crucial role in the liberalization of trade in continental Europe, we should not neglect the changes in trade policies that took place in most countries between 1860 and 1877. Of course, the general tariff (that applicable to countries not party to a treaty) has rather less impact when the network of treaties is as wide as that in force at the end of the 1860s. But we now look briefly at the most important changes in trade policy in the different countries.

In *France*, the law of 5 May 1860 (followed by a series of decrees in 1861 and 1862) abolished most import duties on the vast majority of raw materials. The law of 15 June 1861 abolished the sliding scale for grain and fixed import duties at a level of about 3 per cent of their value. The 1863 law removed a few prohibitions and nearly all export duties. Even more important was the new general tariff of 1869 which exempted nearly all agricultural products and raw materials from all customs duties. As for navigation, nearly all discriminatory practices were abolished between 1860 and 1872.

In *Germany*, the Austro-Prussian war in 1866 enabled Prussia to set up

[66] L. Amé, *Etude sur les tarifs de douanes et les traités de commerce*, vol. II (Paris, 1876), pp. 1–36; Arnauné, *Le commerce extérieur*, pp. 257–8.

a new organization of German states, from which Austria was excluded. This led to a reorganization of the *Zollverein*, and, in particular, of the general congress of this union. In 1867 the individual states' right to veto was abolished and decisions were taken by a majority vote. Out of a total of 58 votes, Prussia had 17, Bavaria six and the other 23 states from one to four each.[67] In 1868–70 this new Chamber of the *Zollverein* approved some measures to extend the liberalization of trade policy. However, it was after the foundation of the German Empire (18 January 1871) that the liberalization process became really effective. In 1873 and 1875 a certain number of import duties were reduced or completely abolished; and the law of 1 January 1877 abolished import duties on nearly all iron manufactured goods.[68] Germany had virtually become a free trade country, probably the most liberal of the major continental European countries. In 1875 the average import duty on manufactured goods was about 4–6 per cent, compared with 12–15 per cent in France (see Table 5).

As for agricultural products, the 1862 tariff made important changes in a liberal direction. Cereals were no longer taxed, and duties on a wide range of other agricultural products were considerably reduced.

Liberalization was much less obvious in *Austria–Hungary*, in spite of the fact that since the 1867 Austro-Hungarian 'Compromise', Hungary – more inclined towards free trade – had an equal share in decisions on trade policy. Austria–Hungary was, moreover, to be one of the first countries to revert to a protectionist system with the tariff of 27 June 1878. This tariff involved an increase of 80–100 per cent on average for manufactured goods. It also involved the payment of duties in gold, which meant an extra increase.

The unification of *Italy* in 1861 led to the application to the whole country of the Piedmontese tariff liberalized by Count Carnillo Cavour in 1851 and 1859. For certain states this involved a dramatic reduction in duties – especially in southern Italy, where it meant a drop of 80 per cent. This drop probably contributed to the industrial setback in this region. In January 1863 the signing of the treaty with France further

---

[67] Henderson, *The Zollverein*, pp. 315–16.
[68] To illustrate this, here are the figures for import duties on metallurgical goods (in marks per 1,000 kg):

	1845	1865	1870	1873	1875
Pig iron	20	15	5	0	0
Bar iron	90–180	50–70	35–70	20	0
Iron plates	180–240	70–150	50–70	20	0
Coarse cast-iron goods	60	24	24	20	0
Coarse iron goods	360	80–160	80	50	0
Fine iron goods	600–3,000	240–600	240–600	240–600	240–600

Source: P. Ashley, *Modern Tariff History: Germany–United States–France*, 3rd edn (London, 1920), p. 40.

Table 5. *Average levels^a of duties on manufactured products in 1875*

	Percentage
Austria–Hungary	15–20
Belgium	9–10
Denmark	15–20
France	12–15
Germany	4–6
Italy	8–10
Norway	2–4
Portugal	20–25
Russia	15–20
Spain	15–20
Sweden	3–5
Switzerland	4–6
The Netherlands	3–5
United Kingdom	0
Continental Europe^b	9–12
Europe^b	6–8

Notes:
^{a} Probable level of averages, but not extreme ranges.
^{b} Weighted averages (by value of 1869–71 imports).
Sources: Author's computations based on tariff duties and prices for 14 different manufactured products.

liberalized Italian trade policy. In the mid-1870s Italy had the second most liberal tariff of the major countries of continental Europe.

One of the consequences of the 1868 revolution in *Spain* was to bring into power in the government of the First Republic a group favourable to free trade. The 1869 tariff made trade policy considerably more liberal. Prohibitions were abolished and replaced by duties of 30–35 per cent which it was proposed to reduce, over a period of twelve years, to a maximum of 15 per cent. Differential duties were abolished and most other duties were sharply reduced. This liberalization was short-lived, however. The tariff reductions planned for 1875 did not take place and, after the change of government in 1876, the return to protectionism began (see section VCI).

Trade policy in *Russia* became noticeably more liberal with the 1868 tariff. It led, though, to a rapid increase in imports and hence to a deterioration in the balance of trade. From 1866–8 to 1877–9 imports rose by 8.9 per cent per annum, and the balance of trade slumped from a surplus of 5.3 per cent of the value of imports to a deficit of 15.2 per cent.

The two small, highly industrialized countries (Belgium and Switzerland) gradually achieved something close to a total free trade system. It should not be forgotten that these two countries – which in 1870 accounted for only 2.4 per cent of the population of Europe – provided 8.1 per cent of all European exports and probably about 11.0 per cent of European exports of manufactured goods.

In *Belgium*, because of the larger number of treaties, the special tariff had become more or less the rule and the general tariff the exception. The law of 14 August 1865 was to extend the provisions of the special tariff to the general tariff.[69] From 1873 (law of 3 January) there was free trade in foodstuffs, and the law of 27 April of the same year abolished, among others, the duties on linen, hemp, and jute thread. At the same period the tolls payable to The Netherlands for navigation on the Scheldt estuary were redeemed. These had been a serious handicap to the port of Antwerp. At the beginning of the 1860s, the tolls amounted to 2 million francs per annum (or about 0.5 per cent of the value of imports) and they were redeemed by the treaty of 16 July 1863 for 36.3 million francs, of which Belgium paid one-third and the United Kingdom a little over one-fifth.

Without really altering her general tariff (which was in any case fairly liberal) *Switzerland* liberalized her trade policy by means of numerous treaties containing the most-favoured-nation clause. Between November 1860 and August 1875 such treaties were signed with sixteen countries.

In *The Netherlands*, the new tariff of 1877 marked a further stage towards a completely free trade system. The Scandinavian countries and Portugal were also moving in the same direction. In *Scandinavia*, the law of 20 May 1874 (called Inter-Dominion) set up a free trade zone for local products between Sweden and Norway. *Denmark*, which, like Portugal, was linked to Great Britain by treaties containing the most-favoured-nation clause, was integrated into the network of Cobden treaties from 1860. *Finland* made some liberal reforms in the 1869 tariff, but this still remained highly protectionist. The liberal nature of *Portugal*'s trade policy further increased with the signing, in 1866, of a trade treaty with France and through two additional agreements with Great Britain (1876 and 1882).

To end this brief summary, we should note that in the *United Kingdom* the government further strengthened its liberal trade policy. The very

---

[69] For brief definitions of the different types of tariff, see section VA.

Table 6. *Annual rate of growth of different sectors according to tariff policies and economic periods (per cent)*

	Exports	GNP	Industry	Agriculture[a]	Population
Tariff policy periods (Europe)					
Protectionist 1830–1844/6	3.5	1.7	2.7	(0.8)	0.6
British liberalism 1844/6–1858/60	6.0	1.5	2.3	(0.9)	0.7
European liberalism 1858/60–1877/9	3.8	1.7	1.8	0.5	0.8
Shift to protectionism 1877/9–1890/2	2.9	1.2	2.2	0.9	0.9
Protectionism 1890/2–1913	3.5	2.4	3.2	1.8	1.0
Economic periods					
Europe					
Slow growth 1829/31–1842/4	3.5	1.6	2.5	(0.8)	0.6
More rapid growth 1842/4–1868/70	5.0	2.0	2.3	(0.9)	0.7
Depression 1868/70–1891/3	2.8	1.1	1.9	0.7	0.9
Rapid growth 1891/3–1911/13	3.8	2.4	3.4	1.7	1.0
Continental Europe					
Fairly rapid growth 1829/31–1868/70	4.3	1.8	2.0	(1.0)	0.7
Depression 1868/70–1891/3	2.9	1.0	2.0	0.8	0.9
Rapid growth 1891/3–1911/13	4.0	2.6	3.8	1.5	1.1

Note:

[a] For agriculture based on seven-year annual averages.

Figures in parentheses have a higher margin of error than other figures for the same periods.

The first starting dates have been chosen for reasons of availability of data.

Sources: P. Bairoch, *Commerce extérieur et développement économique de l'Europe au XIXe siècle* (Paris, 1976); and data assembled for this study.

low import duties on wheat (about 2 per cent of the value) were abolished in 1869. Duties on sugar, which had been reduced by half in 1870 and then by half again in 1873, were abolished in 1874. In 1875–7 import duties amounted to only 5.2 per cent of the value of imports, and out of the total customs revenue, 97 per cent came from tea, coffee, wine, spirits, and tobacco.

C.   FREE TRADE AND THE GREAT EUROPEAN DEPRESSION

The period when free trade reached its height in Europe (before, that is, the second free trade epoch in Europe of post-1962) was undoubtedly during the twelve years 1866–77. In the middle of this period (around 1870–2) began what has been called the great depression of the European economy.[70]

As far as the volume of European trade is concerned, the reversal of the trend began in 1873. Partly as a result of the rapid expansion of British foreign trade, the volume of European exports grew very rapidly in the period 1846–60: 5.6 per cent per annum from 1844–6 to 1858–60. The first decade of the free trade period had already been marked by a noticeable slackening in this growth (5.0 per cent from 1858–60 to 1870–2), but the decrease was much less obvious for continental Europe (5.7 per cent from 1844–6 to 1858–60 and 5.6 per cent for 1858–60 to 1870–2). From 1873, though, until 1893–4 there was a period in which the volume of European sales only grew by about 2.3 per cent per annum. For continental Europe this slowing down was even more pronounced. Whereas during the two decades up to 1873 there were many periods where the annual growth rates (calculated on three-year moving averages) exceeded 6.0 per cent (between 1848 and 1872 there were twelve such instances, including five which exceeded 8.0 per cent), from 1872–93 the maximum was 4.0 per cent, and only on seven occasions did this rate exceed 3.0 per cent.

This serious decline in the growth of trade is obviously only one aspect of the depression. In the case of growth rates of the economy as a whole, the turning-point came a little earlier, in 1868–70, with recovery in 1891–3. The per capita growth rate of Gross National Product declined from an annual rate of about 1.6 per cent for the 1850s and 1860s to 0.6 per cent for the next two decades. In other words, during this depressed phase, European economic growth was even lower than it had been even in 1830–40 (when it was about 1.0 per cent; see Table 6).

[70]   This term has been used particularly in relation to Great Britain, since until recently the statistics for the growth of production and trade for the whole of Europe were not available. For these statistics, see Bairoch, *Commerce extérieur et développement economique.* As we shall see, in the period from 1871–3 to 1889–91, the great depression affected continental Europe much more than Great Britain.

The important thing to notice here is that the depression ended around 1892–4, just when, as we shall see in section v, the return to protectionism in continental Europe had become really effective. This poses the important problem of the influence of tariff policy on economic development. How, and to what extent, could free trade have caused a depression in the European economy, and how could protectionism have led to a recovery?

A first clue to the role of trade policy can be found in the fact that the depression was less pronounced in Great Britain, and that the economic recovery mainly benefited those countries that had reverted to protectionism. Thus, from 1870–90, compared with 1850–70, the decrease in the growth rate of Gross National Product per capita was 30 per cent in Great Britain (or from 1.6 per cent to 1.1 per cent per annum) and 80 per cent for continental Europe (or from 1.1 per cent to 0.2 per cent per annum). Moreover, whereas during the protectionist phase the economy of continental Europe grew at an annual rate per capita of about 1.5 per cent, in Great Britain this growth rate continued to decline and was only about 0.7 per cent.[71] Because of the continuity of British trade policy from 1846 to 1913, concentration must be particularly on continental Europe.

The second clue, which tells much more about the impact of changes in trade policy on economic development, is to be found in the analysis of the causes of the decline in growth in Europe in general, and in continental Europe in particular. As can be seen from Table 6, for Europe as a whole, the slowing down in the growth of the Gross National Product was mostly the result of a decline in the growth rate of agricultural production. For continental Europe, growth in the volume of agricultural production slowed considerably after 1870; between 1870–4 and 1888–92 agricultural production increased by only 0.6 per cent per annum, whereas the population increased by 0.8 per cent. In other words, there was a drop in production per inhabitant of about 0.2 per cent per annum, compared with a growth of about 0.3–0.4 per cent during the previous decades. This crisis in agriculture in continental Europe can be almost completely explained by the influx of overseas grain, itself the result of the drop in transport costs, and of the total abolition of tariff protection which took place in continental Europe between 1866 and 1872.

It should be noted here that as far as agriculture was concerned, tariff 'disarmament' was all the more complete because in this respect the theories of the free traders and of the protectionists coincided. List did not envisage a protectionist 'learning' period for agriculture. As we have

---

[71] This analysis and these statistics are taken from Bairoch, *Commerce extérieur et développement economique*. Obviously, only the main elements can be put forward here.

seen, the influx of American grain began at the end of the civil war, and rapidly became very significant, even compared to total local European production. In France, imports of wheat which had amounted to 0.3 per cent of domestic production in the decade 1851–60, rose to 19.0 per cent in 1888–92. In Belgium, the level of imports rose from about 6 per cent around 1850 to more than 100 per cent around 1890. In the rest of Europe the figures were usually somewhere between these two extremes. The period of most rapid change was 1867–79. Imports of grain (and of flour expressed in terms of grain) into Germany, Belgium, and France increased from some 1.0 million tons per annum in 1862–6 to 2.7 millions in 1867–71, 6.6 millions in 1876–80 and to 7.5 millions in 1888–92. These imports represented about 3 per cent of local production in these countries in 1862–6, 20 per cent in 1876–80, and 22 per cent in 1888–92. Moreover, whereas these countries exported significant quantities of grain (about 5 per cent of production) in 1862–6, in 1888–92 these exports had seriously declined (2 per cent of production).

In 1860–80, grain accounted for some 35–40 per cent of all agricultural production in the industrialized countries of continental Europe. In such a system, the substitution of 22 per cent of grain production by imports in the space of 26 years represents in very simple terms a decrease of 0.33 per cent per annum in the volume of total agricultural production, assuming there was no exceptional increase in consumption due to the availability of supplies.[72] It does not seem that such an increase in consumption took place in these countries. In France, the country for which the most complete statistics are available, total consumption of grain per head (including animal consumption, but excluding seed-corn) increased by only 0.27 per cent per annum from 1855–64 to 1875–84,[73] whereas it had grown by 0.75 per cent per annum between 1825–34 and 1855–64. Thus the rapid influx of grain itself explains in large part the serious deceleration of growth in the total agricultural production of continental Europe.

This influx of grain particularly affected the farmers because the low price of the imports led to a drop in the domestic prices of grain and of agricultural products in general. On the other hand, it should be noted that the share of cereals in cash crops is more important than their share in total agricultural production. As a result, the standard of living of farmers in nearly all the countries of continental Europe remained static, or even fell. This question of farmers' standard of living is returned to in section v.

---

[72] If only the period 1862–6 to 1876–80 is taken the figure reached is close to 0.5 per cent per annum.

[73] On the basis of figures given by J. C. Toutain, 'Le produit de l'agriculture française de 1700 à 1958', *Cahiers de l'ISEA* (Histoire quantitative de l'économie française), series AF 2, suppl. no. 115 (July 1961), p. 238.

The decline in the farmers' standard of living clearly had important consequences not only within the agricultural sector but also outside it, because of the relative importance of this sector, which, at the time, accounted for some 60 per cent of total population in continental Europe. This decline affected the overall demand for industrial products, and for the building sector. Its consequences on the European economy were further aggravated by the fact that the United States had been the main supplier of grain to Europe from the 1870s to the 1890s. Because of the protectionist trade policies of the United States – which hardened after the victory of the North in the civil war (see section x) – additional grain sales to Europe did not lead to a corresponding increase in purchases of European manufactured goods, creating an unfavourable balance of trade between Europe and the United States. About 1870, continental Europe's imports from the United States were within 5–6 per cent of the value of its exports to that country; in 1880 these imports exceeded exports by 90 per cent.

The apparent contradiction between the negative effects of these increased imports of foodstuffs in continental Europe and the positive effects of this same policy in Great Britain some 25 years earlier is to be explained essentially in terms of the different stages of economic development reached by the two areas at the time this policy was adopted. In Great Britain, the active farming population represented only about 22 per cent of the total active population in 1846, whereas the active population engaged in manufacturing industry was about 37 per cent. For the whole of continental Europe in 1860–2 about 63 per cent were in the agricultural sector and some 18–20 per cent in manufacturing industry. Even in the industrialized countries of continental Europe[74] some 52 per cent of the active population were engaged in agriculture, and 19–21 per cent in industry. These striking differences suggest that the transfer of man-power from agriculture to industry should have taken place in continental Europe at a rate at least twice as fast as in Great Britain, and at a time when foreign outlets clearly could not play the same role as for Great Britain because of the latter's established economic lead. Two other structural differences emerge between the two types of economy and the two periods. In 1846 Great Britain already had a higher level of imports of foodstuffs than continental Europe (and even than industrialized continental Europe) had around 1860;[75] a situation – it is important to note – which was the result of a very slow process which had begun in 1770–80. This process had therefore already allowed a

---

[74] In other words, Germany, Belgium, France, Sweden, and Switzerland.

[75] Around 1840–5 Great Britain imported 530,000 tons of grain annually, which represented 4–5 per cent of its own production. Around 1860 continental Europe as a whole produced more grain that it required, and the same was true (though to a lesser extent) for industrialized Europe.

gradual shift in production factors (labour and capital) from agriculture to industry. Secondly, around 1846 non-European grain was not yet available in large quantities, and, moreover, the cost of transport made it less competitive.

Climate is the only factor which could have reduced the responsibility of the liberalization measures concerning food imports on the agricultural depression in continental Europe. However, it is evident that, even in such a case, it would not have meant much lower levels of food imports, but less negative effects of those imports. In other words, only an exceptional series of bad harvests could have reduced the responsibility of the trade measures for the slump. There are, however, no cases of outstandingly bad harvests, or even really unfavourable ones, especially of grain. In France, wheat yields – which had increased by 0.15 per cent per annum between 1842–51 and 1862–71 – rose by 0.46 per cent per annum between 1862–71 and 1882–91 (and by 0.75 per cent between 1882–91 and 1902–11). Between 1872 and 1891 there were ten years which showed a drop in yield over the previous year, but there had been twelve years like this between 1852 and 1871, and twelve again between 1832 and 1851, and there were nine between 1892 and 1911. The data are less good for other crops, but they appear to show similar trends.

If we move to Central Europe we see that in Germany wheat yields – which had increased by 0.70 per cent per annum between 1846–54 and 1862–71 – rose by 0.99 per cent per annum between 1862–71 and 1882–91 (and by 1.45 per cent between 1882–91 and 1902–11). Other cereals followed a similar pattern, with the exception of rye (which was the main cereal crop grown in Germany). This showed a less positive trend, since the increase in yields was only 0.45 per cent per annum between 1862–71 and 1882–91, as opposed to 0.81 per cent for the previous period. In Northern Europe an indicator exists for Sweden which is interesting because it excludes the effects of technical progress: an index of the overall level of yields on a scale of 0 to 5, with 3 representing the average harvest. This index is based on appreciations made in the period itself. For the years 1869–92 the annual average of this index is 3.28, compared with 2.88 for the preceding 24 years and 3.31 for the following 24 (and 3.13 for the 24 years between 1916 and 1939). On the other hand, in the South, in Italy, yields remained stagnant. This was a long-term stagnation linked to the country's difficulties and was not due to climatic conditions.

However, for Europe as a whole, it is likely that in the middle of this period the years 1875–81 were rather bad as far as the weather was concerned, particularly for wheat cultivation. Yields in this period were a little lower than those in the years before and after it. In France, for example, wheat yields were 10.42 quintals (1 quintal = 100 kg) per hectare in 1875–81, as opposed to 11.32 in 1868–74 and 11.88 in 1882–8. In Germany wheat yields which had been 13.33 quintals per hectare in 1868–74 rose to only 13.65 in 1875–81, but to 15.11 in 1882–8. In Sweden, where climatic variations had more influence, the yield was 13.14 quintals per hectare in 1875–81, compared with 15.22 in 1868–74 and 15.12 in 1882–8. The drop is less pronounced in the case of the indicator of the level of harvests: 3.17 for the period 1875–81, as opposed to 3.24 for the period before and after this. For Great Britain (where we do not have an annual series of yields before 1885) the year 1879 is usually considered to have had the worst harvest of the century. All the same, the relative impact of this factor is reduced by the extent of these decreases in yield (8 per cent for France, 14 per cent for Sweden, but almost zero not only for Germany, but also for Austria–Hungary and Russia) and by the fact that the phase was short-lived. Moreover, a similar phase is to be found in the United States during the years 1875–85: 8.24 quintals per hectare in 1875–85, compared with 8.37 in 1868–74 and 8.53 in 1886–92.[76]

As far as the climate of Europe in the nineteenth century is concerned, the only available data are those of the average temperatures. What is called the 'Little Ice Age' probably began in the fourteenth century and ended around 1850–60, after which there was a warmer period which apparently lasted until 1963. Within this cycle, though, in the years 1884–1889/97 there was a short cold spell, very probably caused by the volcanic eruption of Krakatoa, in 1883.[77] Almost the whole of the nineteenth century, then, was a period of climatic change. But it goes without saying that the influence of the climate on agriculture is not just a matter of average annual temperatures; much more important are the seasonal fluctuations in temperature, the annual and short-term variations in the amount of rainfall and its phasing over the year.

It is clear then, that as the figures for foreign trade allow clearly to be seen, the imports of grain were the basic cause of the agricultural crisis in 1870–90. Moreover, even if the climate had been responsible for the

---

[76] Figures for yields and harvests from *Annuaire statistique de la France* (retrospective sections); W. G. Hoffmann, *Das Wachstum der Deutschen Wirtschaft seit der Mitte des 19. Jahrhunderts* (Berlin, 1965), p. 278; Statistiska Centralbyran, *Historisk Statistik for Sverige* (Stockholm, 1959), pp. 44 and 60; G. Sundbarg, *Aperçus statistiques internationaux* (Stockholm, 1908), pp. 210, 211, and 233. For the whole of Europe, if one takes into account the long-term increases in wheat yields, the increase in 1876–81 was 3 per cent above 'normal'.

[77] Derived from H. H. Lamb, *Climate, Present, Past and Future*, vol. 1 (London, 1972), and especially vol. 11 (London, 1977); E. Le Roy Ladurie, *Histoire du climat depuis l'An Mil* (Paris, 1967); S. W. Matthews, 'What's Happening to Our Climate?', *National Geographic Magazine*, vol. cv, no. 5 (November 1976), pp. 578–615; E. V. Rudloff, *Die Schankungen und Pendelungen des Klimas in Europe seit dem Beginn der Regelmässigen Instrumenten-Beobachtungen (1670)* (Brunswick, 1967); T. M. L. Wigley, M. J. Ingram, and G. Farmer, *Climate and History: Studies in Past Climates and their Impact on Man* (New York, 1982).

flattening in the curve of agricultural production, the consequence of this for the agricultural sector would not have been so severe if free trade policies for grain had not been operating. In that case, there would have been a rise in the price of grain, and hence a more positive evolution of the purchasing power of the farmers. This would have led to a higher demand for manufactured goods. In 1875–81 – which, as we have seen, was not a good period as far as climate was concerned – the price of grain not only did not rise, but actually fell. In France and in Prussia the price for wheat paid to the producer fell by 9.5 per cent in relation to the period 1868–74, and in Belgium by 13.2 per cent. Let us remind ourselves that the increased imports of cereals were not balanced by increased exports of manufactured goods, mostly because of the protectionist policies of the United States.

As we shall see in section v, the politicians of the period eventually became aware of the consequences of the opening of the frontiers to agricultural products, and the first protectionist measures were designed for this sector. We shall also see, in sections v and vi, that as a general rule these measures facilitated a recovery not just in agriculture but in the whole economy of these countries.

V.   The return to protectionism on the continent, 1879–92

As we have seen, economic growth slowed down a great deal on the continent from 1870–2 on. This slowing down was caused by difficulties in the agricultural sector which were due essentially to the influx of foreign grain. Such a situation was bound to lead to a shift in trade policy, inducing a return to protectionism.

This return to protectionism coincided with three factors closely linked to trade policy. The most important of these in terms of its immediate and lasting consequences was the colonial expansion of the 1880s and 1890s. This led to a considerable increase in European trade with Asia and above all with Africa. The share of these two continents in European trade between 1880 and 1910 rose from 11.1 per cent to 14.6 per cent for exports, and from 10.8 per cent to 14.5 per cent for imports. More details on this and on colonial trade policies are given in section viii.

The second important factor was the rapid expansion of international capital movements which was at once cause and consequence of the expansion of international trade, but also in part a substitute for this trade. Between 1870 and 1913 the gross stock of European capital abroad passed from $8.8 to $40.0 thousand million.

The third factor was the rise of institutions for promoting trade, a rise which accelerated from the 1880s on (see section VII). The return to protectionism was thus accompanied by profound shifts in economic life, which obviously included more than the three factors just referred to.

Germany was the first important country to make serious changes to its customs policy, which it did with the new tariff of July 1879. This was an important event. Just as the Anglo-French treaty of 1860 marks the beginning of the free trade period, this new German tariff marks the end of the period and the gradual return to protectionism on the continent. It is true that in 1877 Russia (because of its new requirement that customs dues should be settled in gold, which meant increasing them by 32 per cent), Austria, and Spain (also in 1877) had all preceded Germany, but these countries played only a minor role in the international trade in manufactured goods. Besides, Austria had been led to this move by Germany's refusal to renew the trade treaty between them. It must also be said that in 1878 Italy, too, moved a little way towards protectionism, but this was not a serious modification of her policy. This modification did not take place till the beginning of 1888 when the new tariff law of 1887 was put into practice (see p. 63).

This modification of trade policy coincided with an increasing sophistication of tariffs. There are two main kinds of tariff. The first is called 'autonomous', or 'statutory', or sometimes 'single schedule', and it is a tariff which can only be established or modified by legislation. The second type is the 'conventional' or 'multi-schedule' tariff, which can be established and, still more important, modified as a result of treaties and agreements with other countries. In the case of the conventional tariff the term 'general' tariff is used in the case of dues paid by countries with no special treaty relationship, and the term 'special' tariff in the case of the countries where special treaties apply.[78] From the years 1877–92 a system of double tariffs spread, which was also known as the 'minimum and maximum' tariff, a combination of autonomous and conventional tariffs where the maximum tariff was paid by all states with which no special treaties existed, while the minimum tariff was only granted after negotiations for reciprocity.

It should also be noted here that nearly all tariffs which came into force in the period 1879–1914 provided for specific duties. This trend was partly because specific duties were much easier to collect (and there was less risk of fraud) since it was only necessary to establish the nature of the product in order to calculate the duties payable. Moreover a duty based

---

[78] For an analysis of the tariff system, see in particular: G. M. Fisk and P.S. Pierce, *International Commercial Policies with Special Reference to the United States* (New York, 1925); T. E. G. Gregory, *Tariffs: A Study in Method* (London, 1921); M. Moye and B. Nogaro, *Les régimes douaniers, législations douanières et traités de commerce* (Paris, 1910).

Table 7. *United Kingdom foreign trade of manufactured goods with industrial Europe[a] (annual averages in current £million)*

	1854–7	1871–9	1898–1901	1909–13
Imports	8.5	42.4	71.9	98.9
Exports	20.3	41.2	42.4	65.8
Gross trade balance	+11.8	−1.2	−29.5	−33.1
Trade balance corrected for transport cost[b]	+14.6	+3.7	−25.3	−26.5

Notes:

[a] Austria–Hungary, Belgium, France, Germany, Italy, Luxemburg, The Netherlands, Switzerland.

[b] F.o.b. exports have been (in part arbitrarily) increased by 14 per cent for 1854–7, by 12 per cent for 1877–9 and by 10 per cent for the last two periods.

Source: Derived from W. Schlote, *British Overseas Trade from 1700 to the 1930s* (Oxford, 1952).

on quantity increased the degree of protection when imported goods dropped in price. From 1874 until 1897–8 the international price level showed a falling trend, with a decline of about 35 per cent in export prices and about 40 per cent in import prices. This means therefore, that if specific duties remained stable during this period, there was an increase in the degree of effective protection of about 40 per cent. One other important characteristic of the tariffs drawn up at this time was the continual increase in the number of headings and subheadings in the tariff schedules.

In continental Europe, the triumph of protectionist ideas was very largely the result of the coalition between the interests of agriculture and those of industry. The farmers, who were disappointed by the slow growth of sales to Great Britain and seriously handicapped by the influx of grain and other foodstuffs from overseas, thus supported the manufacturers, who had never really been convinced of the advantages of free trade.

The arguments of the farmers carried all the more weight because in most of the industrialized countries industry had not, in fact, suffered from the tariff disarmament. The flood of British goods onto the continent had not been as serious as the protectionists had feared, and, in particular, the British market had been opened up to European manufacturers leading to increasing sales. On examination of the balance of British trade with the industrialized countries of continental Europe, one finds that although Great Britain did indeed double its sales of manufactured goods to industrialized Europe between 1854–7 and 1877–9, her imports of these same products from these countries increased fivefold (see Table 7).

If these figures are adjusted to take into account the cost of transport, Great Britain's trade surplus with industrialized Europe (so far as manufactures are concerned) decreases from some £15 million to about £4 million between 1854–7 and 1877–9. This seems at first sight paradoxical, given the British technological advance. It resulted essentially from a symmetry of tariff disarmament affecting manufactured goods, since manufactured goods moved freely into the United Kingdom whereas very often in continental Europe duties were still around 15–20 per cent (see Table 5). This trend was to continue and even accelerate, since after 1879 the asymmetry in tariffs became even more pronounced.

Despite this, we should not underestimate the impact of the liberalization of free trade on the influx of manufactured goods into certain continental countries, in particular those which were least industrialized. These countries faced unequal competition, not just from British industry but also from the more highly developed countries of continental Europe. Just before the liberalization of trade policies, for example, the gap between Austria–Hungary, Russia, and Spain on the one hand, and Germany, France, and Belgium on the other was greater than that between Germany, France and Belgium, and the United Kingdom (see Table 4).

As the title of this section indicates, the period 1879–92 saw a gradual return to protectionism. This means that if continental Europe as a whole is considered, a large part of this period can still be said to have been characterized by predominantly liberal trade policies, using this term in its nineteenth-century sense. The end of the liberal period can be dated from 1892 with the adoption of the so-called Méline tariff in France. That year was a watershed for tariff reform, since most treaties expired then (the majority in February). If one counts the number of treaties carrying an expiry date that were in force on Europe in 1889, out of a total of 53 treaties, 27 ran out in 1892 (21 of these in February), 3 in 1890, 9 in 1891, 3 in 1893, 1 in 1894, 5 in 1895 and 4 between 1896 and 1901 inclusively.[79]

We shall now consider how far the changes in tariff policy can be regarded as, in part, a compensation for the fall in transport costs, and then look at the trade policies themselves, with an analysis of the change of direction in Germany and of the main aspects of what can be called the tariff 'contagion' of continental Europe. Protectionist reaction in certain circles in Great Britain (which came to nothing) are dealt with in the following sub-section (section VI B).

---

[79] Figures derived from A. Eichmann, *Recueil des tarifs conventionnels des douanes de tous les pays et des traités de commerce suisses* (Berne, 1889), pp. x–xx.

It should be noted that, generally, even treaties drawn up with a fixed expiry date had to be revoked twelve months before that date, otherwise they remained in force until one year after the date on which one of the contracted parties revoked it.

A. THE DROP IN TRANSPORT COSTS AND TARIFF PROTECTION

In a sense, the tariff measures adopted in Europe can be seen partly as a means of compensating for the drop in transport costs. This is particularly true for agricultural products, but it also applies to some extent to manufactured consumer goods. In order to assess the real impact of this factor, we have tried to estimate the influence of changing transport costs on import prices of five representative products: wheat, two semi-finished manufactured goods (cotton thread and bar iron), and two manufactured goods (iron goods and cotton textiles).

Two sets of transport costs have been elaborated, one affecting overland transport and the other transport by sea. As far as land transport is concerned, the average cost per kilometric ton is estimated by examining three types of transport: roads, inland waterways, and railways. The cost per kilometric ton of each of these means of transport has been estimated for the following years: 1830, 1850, 1880, and 1910. These are average costs based on often-disparate data for the main developed countries. For each period the relative importance of the three forms of transport has been postulated on the basis of the fragmentary data available for some countries. For 1850, for example, we have assumed that road transport accounted for 55 per cent of transport, inland waterways for 40 per cent, and the railways for 5 per cent; whereas for 1910 the percentages were 5, 20 and 75 respectively. As far as maritime transport is concerned, calculations are based on the transatlantic crossing between the United States and England. The average length of land journeys involved in international trade is estimated at 800 km, which may seem too low, but it should be remembered that internal trade also necessitated transport. Here we are concerned only with transport directly connected to international trade.

The average transport costs assembled are considerably affected by the very low cost of transporting relatively heavy goods in bulk. The information available shows that transport costs in the nineteenth century, as is the case today, varied according to the density, value, nature, etc., of the goods concerned. In the first scale of freight rates of British railways, for example, the freight charges per kilometric ton varied from one to three (or even more) times as high for some goods as for others;[80] the lowest charges were for goods like coal, sand, etc.; and the highest for manufactured goods. In our calculations the average costs of transport are applied to wheat and bar iron. These average costs are then increased by 80 per cent for cotton thread and iron manufactured goods, and by 150 per cent for cotton textiles. Supplementary expenses such as insur-

[80] See for example C. E. R. Sherrington, *A Hundred Years of Inland Transport, 1830–1933* (London, 1934), pp. 31–5.

ance, which in many cases was a significant item are not included. These additional costs varied widely – for goods with a low specific value it might represent only about 5–10 per cent of the total transport costs, but it could reach or exceed 100 per cent for goods with a very high specific value.

The most representative series of prices have been used, whether they relate to production or export. For manufactured iron goods and cotton textiles the data are less complete and in certain cases these prices have been calculated on the basis of a ratio of about 1:6 between bar iron and iron manufactured goods; and from 1:2 between cotton thread and cotton textiles.[81]

Let us now look at the results of these calculations. As far as wheat is concerned, if one assumes a journey by both land and sea transport costs are arrived at amounting to the following percentages of the cost of production (in Europe): 1830, 76–82 per cent; 1850, 73–79 per cent; 1880, 39–43 per cent; and 1910, 25–30 per cent. Between 1850 and 1880, therefore, the decline in transport costs alone could have accounted for a fall of about 30 per cent in the price of imported wheat. It should be noted that between 1830 and 1880 the decrease was mainly due to a fall in land transport costs whereas after 1880 there was also a decrease in maritime freight charges.

For bar iron, assuming that only land transport was involved, the incidence of transport costs probably developed as follows: 1830, 89–94 per cent; 1850, 68–74 per cent; 1880, 31–35 per cent; and 1910, 18–20 per cent. If the cost of a transatlantic crossing is taken into account the figures are about 94–100 per cent in 1850, and 27–31 per cent in 1910. Transport costs for cotton thread were relatively much lower. The specific value of thread of average thickness and value was, on the whole, 15 to 20 times higher than that of bar iron. For overland journeys the following figures

[81] It is not possible here to give all the 50 or so references necessary to establish all the parameters of the present estimates (transport costs and prices of goods). However, the transport costs and the prices of select commodities are given below (costs and prices in current US dollars, and representing an average for all developed countries):

	1830	1850	1880	1910
Average cost of land transport (per ton and per 100 km)				
Roads	6.2	5.0	4.0	3.6
Rivers/canals	1.0	0.7	0.4	0.2
Railways	—	1.5	1.1	0.8
Average cost of maritime transport (per ton) on the crossing				
US/England	9.5	9.0	8.5	3.3
Reference price of commodities (per ton)				
Wheat	54	45	45	36
Bar iron	36	35	30	34
Manufactured iron	216	210	180	204
Cotton thread	550	530	580	780
Cotton textiles	1,100	1,030	1,110	1,450

are obtained: 1830, 9–13 per cent; 1850, 7–10 per cent; 1880, 3–4 per cent; and 1910, 2–3 per cent. If a sea voyage is taken into account, costs range from 10–13 per cent in 1850 to 2–3 per cent in 1910. In this case the decrease in transport costs did not have any very marked effect, but it should be remembered that we are only dealing here with transport costs as such, and have excluded a whole series of supplementary expenses which in this case would probably have doubled these percentages.

For iron manufactured goods the relative proportion of land transport costs developed as follows: 1830, 24–30 per cent; 1850, 19–23 per cent; 1880, 8–12 per cent; and 1910, 5–7 per cent. If a transatlantic crossing is included, these figures are 32–38 per cent in 1830, 27–31 per cent in 1850, 16–20 per cent in 1880 and 8–10 per cent in 1910. Finally, for manufactured cotton goods land transport costs probably represented no more than 6–9 per cent of their value in 1830, 5–7 per cent in 1850, only 2–3 per cent in 1880 and 1–2 per cent in 1910. Including a transatlantic crossing, these figures would be 8–11 per cent in 1830, 7–9 per cent in 1850, 4–5 per cent in 1880 and about 2 per cent in 1910. Here, the comments about additional expenses are even more relevant than for cotton thread.

Overall, it can be postulated that between 1850 and 1880 the introduction of a supplementary import duty of about 25–30 per cent *ad valorem* on agricultural products merely compensated for the effects of the drop in transport costs which occurred during this period. For manufactured goods, the degree of compensation is more difficult to estimate. For metal goods, one can surmise that the average increase ranged from 10 to 50 per cent *ad valorem* depending on the degree of sophistication of the product. For textiles, the corresponding figures are only 3 to 7 per cent.

Between 1880 and 1910 the fall in transport costs was about 60 per cent of that which had taken place between 1850 and 1880, and this ratio can be applied to the above-mentioned shares. All the same, it should be noted that as far as countries outside Europe are concerned, the fall in transport costs was greater after 1880. Similarly, in the peripheral countries of Europe (peripheral in relation to the most industrialized countries) the effects were greater than those estimated above. It should be remembered that these calculations were based on the assumption of a journey of 800 km. The distance from Paris to Bucharest or Paris to Athens, though, is about 2,200 km, and from London to Moscow it is about 3,000 km. These factors can partly, at least, explain the stronger protectionist reaction of the most peripheral countries.

It can be concluded that to a large extent the tariff barriers set up during the period 1880–1914 merely replaced the previous natural barriers provided by high transport costs. However, importantly, tariff barriers were more efficient than natural ones because they were adjusted to take into account the degree of sophistication of the goods (or in other words the share of value added) or other factors, while in the case of natural barriers (transport costs), their incidence decreases with the degree of elaboration of the product.

B.   THE CHANGE OF DIRECTION IN GERMANY

The liberalization of trade policy in Germany had led – as in nearly all continental European countries – to a very great increase in imports of grain. In 1861–70 760,000 tons were imported annually, but in 1873–7 the figure was 1,300,000 tons. In other words, Germany, which had traditionally exported more grain than it imported, now did the reverse, since in 1873–7 her exports were only 890,000 tons per annum. On the eve of the first protectionist measures annual imports were 3,070,000 tons (for 1877–9). If flour is included (expressed in its grain equivalent), the figure for this period is about 3,800,000 tons, or in other words, about 20–22 per cent of home production, as opposed to 4–5 per cent in 1861–70.

The growth of the volume of value added of the agricultural sector, which was 2.5 per cent per annum from 1850–6 to 1858–64, was reduced to 0.4 per cent per annum from 1858–64 to 1874–80.[82] The effect of these developments upon agricultural real incomes caused the farmers to change their mind about free trade, and they pressed for a protectionist system for agriculture. The landowners, together with the Agrarian Party, were a powerful political force. The elections of 30 July 1878 returned to the Reichstag more than 200 deputies opposed to free trade. In October 1878, 204 members of the Reichstag (out of a total of 397) signed a declaration in favour of a reform of trade policy.

Bismarck, faithful to his *Realpolitik*, rallied to the idea of a limited strengthening of customs barriers since, in addition to the economic arguments, there were financial reasons for increasing duties. In Germany, more than in other countries, customs duties were an important source of revenue for the central government (see Table 8). This is a situation peculiar to federal states. In 1872–4 these duties had provided 49 per cent of government revenue, but by 1877–8 this had dropped to only 41 per cent. The situation was aggravated by the fact that another source of revenue – the large sum (about 5,000 million francs) paid by France as reparations after the war – was coming to an end.

It should be remembered that of the major countries of continental Europe it was Germany which had adopted the most liberal tariff for

---

[82] Statistics for the period before 1850 are not available. Calculated from W. G. Hoffman (with the collaboration of F. Grumbach and H. Hesse), *Das Wachstum der Deutschen Wirtschaft seit der Mitte des 19. Jahrhunderts* (Berlin, 1965), pp. 204–5 and 321.

Table 8. *Share of customs revenues in total central (or federal) government revenue (in percentages) for selected countries*

	1850–2	1862–4	1876–8	1892–4	1911–13
Belgium	10.6	9.6	7.1	7.3	9.3[a]
France	10.0	7.9	7.3	12.6	15.2
Germany	—	—	42.2	35.8	43.9[a]
Italy	—	11.3	12.2	13.0	10.8
Russia	14.6	9.8	12.4	15.2	10.6
Spain	12.9	9.7	9.3	18.4	16.7
The Netherlands	8.8	7.4	5.8	5.1	9.8
United Kingdom	38.8	34.0	25.4	20.3	17.5
United States	91.5	94.2[b]	49.1	49.0	44.6
Canada	—	—	71.7	70.1	82.9

Notes:
[a] 1910–12.
[b] 1859–61.
Sources: Author's estimates derived from B. R. Mitchell, *European Historical Statistics 1750–1790* (London, 1975), pp. 698–726; US Bureau of the Census, *Historical Statistics of the United States: Colonial Times to 1957* (Washington, 1960), p. 712; M. C. Urquhart and K. A. H. Buckley (eds.), *Historical Statistics of Canada* (Toronto, 1965), p. 198.

manufactured goods. Around 1875 the average import duties on manufactured goods were about 4–6 per cent, compared with 12–15 per cent in France, and 15–20 per cent in Austria–Hungary, Spain, and Russia.

The new tariff was passed on 12 July 1879, and was implemented in stages until 1 January 1880. This tariff reintroduced import duties on agricultural products in general. For grain, they were 10 marks per ton (20 marks for flour), which was relatively low since this figure represented about 6 per cent of the import value of wheat, and about 8 per cent for other cereals. Import duties were also increased on manufactured goods; for textiles they were fixed at 15–30 per cent *ad valorem*, which was again fairly low.

The 1879 tariff (which was autonomous) was only one step towards protectionism. The period 1880–90 was characterized mainly by a steady reinforcement of duties on agricultural products. In 1885 (law of 15 May) import duties on wheat and rye (the two main cereals) were trebled, reaching 30 marks per ton. In 1887 (from 26 November on) they reached 50 marks, which represented about 33 per cent of the import price of wheat, and about 47 per cent for rye (consumption of rye per capita in Germany around 1890 was about 70 per cent higher than that of wheat).

One of the arguments put forward for increased production of agriculture was a military one – the risk of being dependent on foreign countries for foodstuffs. On the whole, the tariff reforms of 1885 and 1888 did not protect industry to anything like the same extent. Germany was thus able to pursue a policy of renewing commercial treaties with the majority of European countries which were little affected by this agricultural protectionism. The United States, on the other hand, felt its effects very keenly (see section x).

The protection of agriculture is the most striking feature of the shift in German trade policy, but we must not altogether ignore a tendency towards a return to the protection of industry too. Already in 1879, when plans for the 1879 tariff were being discussed, Bismarck insisted that German industry was being handicapped by the influx of foreign goods. After expressing doubts about the likelihood of an extension of free trade, he declared,

The only exception is England, and that will not last long. France and America have both completely forsaken that direction. Austria, instead of reducing its protective duties, has increased them. Russia has done the same, not only through the gold coinage, but in other ways. Therefore no-one can expect Germany to remain permanently the dupe of an honest conviction. Hitherto the wide-opened gates of our imports have made us the dumping-place [*Ablagerungsstatte*] of all the over-production of foreign countries. At present they can deposit everything with us, and their goods, when once in Germany, have always a somewhat higher value than in the land of origin – at least our people think so – and it is the surfeiting of Germany with the over-production of other lands which most depresses our prices and checks the development of our industry and the restoration of our economic condition. Let us once close the door and erect the somewhat higher barriers which are proposed, and let us see that we at any rate preserve the German market – that market which, thanks to our good nature, is not exploited by foreign lands – for German industry. The question of a great export trade is always exceedingly precarious. There are no longer any great countries to discover; the globe is circum-navigated, and we cannot find any new mercantile nations of any great extent to which we can export. The policy of commercial treaties is, I grant, under certain circumstances very favourable, though whenever such a treaty is concluded it is a question of Qui trompe-t-on ici? and it is only seen some years later who is really the victim.[83]

It was in particular the industrialists involved in the metal industries (and especially Krupp) who were demanding protectionist measures. Import duties on metals and on crude manufactured metal goods had been totally abolished (see pp. 40–1). In the 1879 tariff import duties on crude iron were fixed at 10 marks per ton, which was about 18 per cent of the import value; for wrought iron, duties ranged from 25 to 60 marks

[83] Quoted by W. H. Dawson, *Protection in Germany: A History of German Fiscal Policy during the Nineteenth Century* (London, 1904), pp. 71–2.

per ton. Duties were similarly increased for textiles. For cotton thread they were levied at 120–480 marks per ton, depending on the thickness of the thread (in 1878–80 the average value of cotton thread imported into Hamburg was 2,690 marks per ton). Although, on the whole, duties on manufactured articles remained relatively low, the 1879 tariff was an important step towards protectionism. The tariff reforms of 1885 and 1888 particularly affected agriculture (see p. 59) but they also made changes in some duties on manufactured goods.

Together these protectionist measures appear to have favoured a very rapid expansion of the German economy. Between 1877–81 and 1893–7 Gross National Product per capita grew by 1.9 per cent per annum, compared with only 1.4 per cent during the liberal period. During the same period the volume of agricultural production per worker increased by 1.6 per cent, while during the liberal period it remained stagnant. Even more significant is the fact that, in relative terms (relative, that is, to the rest of Europe) this growth was very swift. The production of pig iron per capita, which in 1878–82 was 33 per cent higher than the European average, was 79 per cent higher than this average in 1878–92 (in relation to Europe, excluding Germany, these figures are 40 and 102 per cent respectively). As regards foreign trade, though, the results were not nearly so good. Germany's share of European exports, which had been 18.2 per cent in 1879–81, dropped to 17.4 per cent in 1889–91. In addition, the trade deficit increased from 2.5 per cent to 17.4 per cent of imports between these two dates.

The fall of Bismarck (in March 1890) and his replacement by von Caprivi was to lead to changes in economic policy both at home (notably in relations with the working class) and in trade policy. These changes were provoked by the rather unsatisfactory development of foreign trade. However, the new trade policy should definitely not be seen as a return to liberalism. Indeed, it was more of a geographical reorientation of German foreign trade, and this was largely provoked by the protectionism of the United States. Germany turned more towards the countries of continental Europe and towards the East for the supply of raw materials and agricultural products, and she found here growing outlets for her industrial products. Von Caprivi remained in power from March 1890 to October 1894, and encouraged the signing of a series of commercial treaties, of which the first, and most important, was that of 6 December 1891 with Austria–Hungary. This took effect on 1 February 1892, and was to last for twelve years. It reduced duties on grain by about 30 per cent. Treaties with Italy, Switzerland, Romania, Belgium, and Russia followed in the next few years (see section VI). North America, which had taken 12 per cent of German exports in 1889–91, took only 9.3 per cent in 1899–1901, and 8.9 per cent in 1909–11.

C.   PROTECTIONISM SPREADS ACROSS THE CONTINENT

In the rest of continental Europe the same causes produced the same effects, modified by factors peculiar to each country. In the agricultural sector the effects of the influx of overseas grain were determined not only by the degree of liberalization in the importing countries, but also by the ease with which these goods could reach the countries concerned. In the industrial sector, the type of specialization and the level of economic development were clearly important elements. Finally, political factors should not be forgotten. Since in most countries changes in customs legislation reflected a change of opinion amongst the parliamentary representatives, the time-span between elections may have caused serious delays in adapting economic policies to new situations. But, as a growing number of countries modified their trade policies, resistance to such changes diminished in the remaining countries. It became increasingly easy to quote precedents, and even to point out the anachronism of remaining a liberal island in a sea of protectionism.

The first countries to modify their tariff policies were usually those where these changes did not have to be approved by parliament. Thus we find that amongst the major European countries in this movement towards protectionism Russia, Austria–Hungary, Spain, and Italy – besides Germany – were ahead of France.

1. The major countries of continental Europe

Russia, which had been the last country to adopt a liberal trade policy (and not such a liberal one at that), was the first to move towards protectionism. Following the law of 18 November 1877 requiring payment of customs duties in gold, which we have already noted in practice amounted to a tariff increase of about 32 per cent, on 3 June 1885 duties were increased by 20 per cent, and a further increase of 20 per cent was introduced in 1891. The new tariff of 1891, called the Mendeleyev tariff after the president of the commission that prepared it,[84] was firmly based on protectionist ideas specifically to promote industrialization. In 1892 subsidies were made available to encourage exports of manufactured cotton goods (especially to Asia).

Austria–Hungary in a way imitated the Russian example by requiring the payment of customs duties in gold under the tariff of 1878. It should be remembered that around 1880 some European countries, including Austria–Hungary, had not yet adopted the gold standard. From 1865–8 on, the relation between the price of gold and silver, which had remained

---

[84] Mendeleyev was the well-known chemist to whom we owe the periodic table of the chemical elements.

relatively stable since the end of the seventeenth century, fluctuated sharply. This resulted from a very different development in the relative volumes of production of these metals (a drop in production for gold, and a large increase for silver) over twenty years which led to the end of the silver standard and therefore of the bimetallic standard. The price ratio between the two precious metals rose from 15.4:1 in 1864–6 to 17.2:1 in 1874–6 (reaching 35.4:1 in 1911–13).

In 1882 the tariff was reformed in Austria–Hungary, but it was very limited in both the agricultural and industrial sectors. On the other hand, the tariff of 1887 (which came into force on 1 June), showed a more marked return to protectionism, especially for agriculture, where import duties on grain tripled, reaching 15 florins per ton (or about 18 per cent of the value).

In *Spain*, a new regime came to power in early 1876 under Alfonso XII, after the fall of the short-lived first Spanish Republic and the flight of Don Carlos. One of its first measures was to draft a reform of the tariff system. The new tariff of 11 July 1877 was the first example, in an international context, of a double tariff, although there was a fairly narrow gap between the maximum and minimum tariffs (in many cases zero, and on average less than 10 per cent). The increase in import duties in the maximum tariff compared with the old tariff was on the whole fairly low for manufactured goods (in general less than 10 per cent) but larger for agricultural products. In 1882 the tariff was revised to include a clause providing for a progressive reduction of duties (over a ten-year period) to 15 per cent *ad valorem*. In 1886, however, this reduction was revoked, as a result of hostile reaction from both farmers and manufacturers. The double tariff of 1 February 1892, which led to a very steep increase in duties, marked the real return to a severe form of protectionism. The gap between the maximum and minimum tariffs was still very small, but increases in the minimum tariff were around 80–100 per cent for textiles (and there were even cases of 200 and 300 per cent). For iron manufactured goods, duties increased three- or fourfold.

In *Italy*, the tariff of 30 May 1878 (which came into force on 1 July) is traditionally held to mark the end of the free trade era. But it should be pointed out that this tariff – which contained noticeably more items – was only moderately protectionist. Duties on cotton thread, for example, ranged from 180 to 600 lire per ton; which represented on average about 7 per cent of the value. For cotton cloths, duties were about 10–15 per cent, and for iron and steel about 30 per cent. The protection of agriculture remained very limited: duties on cereals were only 14 lire a ton (or about 5 per cent of the value).

As a result of pressure from manufacturers, and also the need for revenue, the law of 14 July 1887 (which came into force on 1 January

1888) increased almost all duties by about 15–20 per cent for cloth manufactured goods and about 40 per cent for metal goods, and it doubled the duties on agricultural products (though these still remained relatively low). The introduction of this new tariff led directly to a tariff war with France which was to last until January 1892 (see section VI).

The influx of American grain began later in Italy (thanks to the higher transport costs) but it greatly accelerated in the years 1884–7. Between these two dates, imports of grain rose from 355,000 tons to 1,016,000 tons per annum. This led the government to pass a decree on 10 February 1888 (confirmed on 10 July) raising the duties on wheat from 30 to 50 lire per ton, which brought them up to about 22 per cent of the value.

It is often wrongly thought that the new French tariff of 1881 marked an important step in the return to protectionism in *France*. In fact this tariff was intended to harmonize customs legislation by revising the general tariff. This had become necessary since the latter still contained a collection of disparate, antiquated provisions, some dating from 1791: 'full of anachronisms and inconsistencies, it was due for a complete overhaul'.[85] In particular, there were serious discrepancies between the general tariff and the conventional tariffs. Work on revising the general tariff began in April 1875, when the Minister of Agriculture and Commerce issued a circular to find out the views of the chamber of commerce and of the Chambres Consultatives des Arts et Métiers.

After long discussion and much modification, the new tariff was promulgated on 7 May 1881. Altogether, the general tariff was fixed at a level about 20 per cent higher than that of the conventional tariff. But, given that most treaties were renewed and that, in any case, there were very few changes in the agricultural sector, one can say that this tariff merely reorganized existing legislation. Besides, if we look at the trend in the amount of customs duties collected, we see how few changes were made. In 1878–80, customs duties represented 6.5 per cent of the value of imports. In 1882–4, they amounted to 7.1 per cent, or an increase of 8.7 per cent. By way of comparison, after the 1892 tariff the increase was 32.5 per cent. It should be noted that this kind of calculation tends to underestimate the magnitude of the increase of customs duties, since in nearly all cases a new duty would have an effect on imports. This happens in two ways. First, there would be a relative decrease in imports of highly taxed goods. Secondly – and more difficult to estimate – false declarations would be likely either about the nature of the products (especially with the same categories of goods) or about country of origin (where commercial treaties existed).

The law of 29 January 1881 also introduced a double system of

---

[85] Arnauné, *Le commerce extérieur et les tarifs de douane*, p. 288.

bounties for shipping. The first applied to shipbuilding, and bounties were graduated according to the size and type of the ship. The second applied to navigation in its true sense: bounties for long-distance voyages were granted to ships flying the French flag (for ships built abroad but flying the French flag this was reduced by half).

The lack of any real changes in the regulations for the import of foodstuffs meant that the influx of grain continued (1.2 million tons per annum in 1881–4, compared with 1.3 million tons in 1876–80, and 0.6 million in 1871–5). This, together with the loss of wine production caused by phylloxera, led to a drop in farm incomes. Whereas between 1845–54 and 1865–74 gross agricultural production (adjusting for self-consumption) per capita had increased by 0.9 per cent per annum, between 1865–74 and 1875–85 it decreased by 0.3 per cent per annum.[86]

Pressure for agricultural protectionism increased. Just before the elections of 1885, the government – so as not to lose too many votes – passed a law on 28 March altering import duties on a wide range of agricultural products. For example, duties on wheat rose from 6 to 12 francs per ton (and on wheat flour from 30 to 60 francs). Other grains, previously exempt from duties, were now taxed at 15 francs per ton. The increase in duties was sharp, but the level of protection remained relatively low, since for wheat, for example, the increased duties represented only about 6 per cent of the price on the home market. Strong pressure from farmers therefore continued, and on 29 March 1887 a new law was adopted. This dramatically increased import duties on a wide range of agricultural products – duties on wheat, for example, were fixed at 50 francs per ton, or about 22 per cent of the price on the home market.

Work on the revision of the tariff began in 1889. Under joint pressure from farmers and manufacturers, the majority of whom had never ceased to advocate protectionism, a new, distinctly protectionist tariff was passed. The tariff of 11 January 1892 (which came into force on 1 February) put an end (until the beginning of the 1960s) to the free trade interlude in France. The tariff problem had been one of the major issues in the 1889 general elections which returned a protectionist majority to the Chamber. The new tariff – the previously mentioned Méline tariff – retained the principle of the double tariff. Even the minimum tariff was distinctly protectionist. According to the calculations of the customs administrators, if the minimum tariff had applied to the imports of 1889 (which brought in 355.6 million francs in customs duties) customs revenue would have increased by 115.5 million francs. As for the general

[86] J. Marczewski, 'Le produit physique de l'économie française de 1789–1913 (comparaison avec la Grande-Bretagne)', *Cahiers de l'ISEA* (Histoire quantitative de l'économie française), series AF 4, no. 163 (July 1965), p. LXXXIII.

tariff, the surplus value would have been 212 million francs.[87] In other words, there would have been an increase of 32.5 per cent or 59.6 per cent respectively – which gives us some idea of the extent of the increase of tariff protection in France. France was thus the last of the major European countries to go back to protectionism.

Import duties on grain were considerably increased. It should be noted that the law of 2 July 1891 had reduced duties on grain, for example those on wheat fell from 50 to 30 francs per ton. The new tariff (which came into effect on 1 June 1982) restored the duties on wheat to 50 francs. A wide range of raw materials, which until then had been allowed free entry, became liable to duties. These included timber and related products, and a wide range of non-metallic minerals, iron oxide, etc.

In parallel with these increases in import duties, a series of measures aimed at protecting different sectors was introduced. In particular, bounties were offered for the cultivation of flax and hemp, as well as for the production and spinning of silk. A law (of 30 January 1893) even offered bounties for the production of shale-oil, in order to strengthen competition against petroleum!

2. The small European countries

As we have just seen, all the major continental European countries returned, sooner or later, to a fairly rigid form of protectionism. The small countries, however, did not all develop trade policies in uniform ways. The Netherlands, for example, persisted in her liberal policies. At the other extreme, Sweden returned to being one of the most highly protectionist of the small countries. The rest of the small nations came somewhere between these two extreme cases, but all eventually adopted some degree of protectionism. As already pointed out, it is not easy to calculate the degree of protectionism or liberalism of a small country, since it may be lacking in certain sectors, and hence in duties on certain products.

Belgium and Switzerland may be said to have been the first small countries to adopt protectionist measures in 1887. Sweden followed in 1888, and Norway in 1890. The Balkan countries did not do so until after 1892 (see section VI).

In *Belgium* the return to power of the Catholic Party in 1884 was to encourage the return to protectionism for agriculture, since this party gained most of its support from the countryside. The farmers based their arguments partly on an anomaly – the fact that there was completely free

---

[87] Arnauné, *Le commerce extérieur et les tarifs de douane*, p. 330. Levasseur gives an erroneous figure of 144 million francs for customs revenue in 1889. This exaggerates the protectionist tendencies of the law: *Histoire du commerce de la France*, vol. II (Paris, 1912), p. 585.

trade for agricultural products (since 1873 foodstuffs were allowed freely into Belgium) whereas a wide range of industrial goods were liable to duties of between 2 and 24 per cent (the average was about 10 per cent). A first law (promulgated on 18 June 1887) reintroduced import duties on most agricultural products from temperate climates, and increased duties on livestock and meat. This revision of the tariff, however, was relatively limited, as indeed was the more important one in 1895 (see section VI).

In *Sweden*, pressure for a return to protectionism intensified from the end of the 1870s. From 1885 the tariff problem became the main feature of political debate. In 1886 manufacturers and farmers in favour of protectionism even founded a political party. But the shift towards protectionism did not take place until the tariff reform of 1888. In this tariff it was mainly, but not exclusively, duties on agricultural products that were altered. They were sharply increased, duties on the main cereal crops being fixed at 25 crowns per ton (or about 18 per cent of the value).

In *Norway* pressure from protectionists took a more organized form with the 1879 petition drawn up by artisans and manufacturers. This petition led to the formation of a commission which was, however, dominated by free traders (8 out of 15 members). The tariff reform of 1881 therefore remained very limited and did not satisfy the manufacturers who gradually gained support from the farmers. This joint pressure resulted in the 1890 tariff which increased duties on both industrial and agricultural products.

At the same time, pressure grew form tariff reform: during the 1880s opposition grew to the Inter-Dominion law of 1874, which had set up a free trade zone for local products between Norway and Sweden. The law of 30 May 1890 modified the Inter-Dominion law, but not enough to satisfy the Norwegians, and because the two parties could not reach an agreement, this law in fact expired on 1 July 1897.

Denmark was the only country in continental Europe that really adapted to the new situation created by the influx of overseas grain. Specialization in butter, cheese and meat was very quickly increased. Cereals – which still represented 25 per cent of her exports of agricultural products in 1875–9 – fell to 2 per cent in 1900–9, whereas in the same period butter rose from 23 to 47 per cent, ham and bacon from 17 to 26 per cent, and eggs from 1 to 8 per cent. In addition, the proportion of agricultural products relative to total exports rose from 76 to a record 90 per cent during this period. It should be emphasized, however, that by concentrating on dairy products Denmark was not moving in a totally new direction but merely intensifying an existing trend.

This adaptation meant that Denmark did not need to make serious changes in her tariff system, particularly as far as agriculture was concerned. All the same, we should not be deceived by the traditional image of a very liberal Denmark, since this country had in fact retained fairly high duties on most manufactured goods (see Table 5).

Finland – which, like Russia, had never really gone over to liberalism – did not make any significant changes in trade policy in this period. In 1880 there was, however, an increase in duties on metal goods.

In *Switzerland*, in spite of a difficult period for industry during the great depression, the majority of manufacturers still supported liberalism. In 1878 plans for tariff reform were drawn up, but it was not until 26 June 1884 that a general tariff was promulgated. However, this tariff proved the possibility of reductions in duties as a result of trade agreements (the tariff commission of the National Council had envisaged a double tariff). This tariff (which came into force on 1 January 1885) moved towards a general increase in duties, but these duties could not by any means be called protectionist. Import duties on manufactured goods were only about 2–4 per cent.

From 1885 protectionist pressure from farmers increased in number and became more radical. This led to the additional tariff of 17 December 1887 (introduced on 1 May 1888) which provided for an increase in import duties of about 200–400 per cent on agricultural products, and about 50–100 per cent on industrial ones. This resulted in a fairly extensive protection for processed agricultural products (meat, butter) but only limited help for grain and manufactured goods. The lack of protection for grain can be explained by the fact that Switzerland traditionally imported more grain products than it exported. From the beginning of the nineteenth century, these imports had accounted for a significant proportion of consumption; and for the decade 1861–70 imports of grain (and of flour expressed in the equivalent amount of grain) rose to 71 kg per capita per annum, which probably represented one-third of total consumption.

Further changes were made in the tariff of 10 April 1891, which was the first to be subject to a popular referendum (18 October 1891). The initiative for this referendum had come from the League Against the Rising Cost of Living, created in 1890. This league was opposed to protectionism and included in particular representatives of the Grütli,[88] the Socialists and also the free trade members of the Radical Party (some of whose members supported protectionism). However, 58 per cent of the voters accepted the new tariff, which came into force on 1 February 1892, and led to a rise in import duties of 20–50 per cent on a wide range of products, especially agricultural ones.

In *Portugal* between 1861 and 1889 the Regenerators (Regeneradores) and the Progressives (Progessistas) agreed on a system of rotation of power. This led to the continuation of the 'fontist' policy, which was

---

[88] The Grütli was a cultural and political association (founded in 1838) which, from the 1880s, had distinctly socialist tendencies and played an important role in Swiss life.

based on economic development of foreign trade and was therefore liberal, delaying changes in trade policy until 1889. In spite, or more probably because of, this open policy the Portuguese share in European exports fell from 0.72 per cent for 1859–61 to 0.52 per cent for 1889–91 (the Portuguese share in the exports of the small countries of Europe fell from 5.1 per cent to 2.7 per cent).

But this liberalism does not imply the absence of a policy of industrialization based on protectionism in the case of the textile industry. However this was a moderate protectionism (with import duties of the order of 20–25 per cent). It appears that limited industrialization took place until the middle of the 1880s, when financial and, above all, agricultural problems were among the causes of the exhaustion of the industrialization process. The financial problems, which were due to a large foreign debt, came to a head in the crisis of 1892. They had been aggravated by a sharp increase in chronic trade deficit. This deficit, which amounted to 22 per cent, of imports for 1868–72, rose to 36 per cent in 1878–82 and 47 per cent in 1889–91. Agriculture was seriously affected by phylloxera from 1887 and from 1875–6 by the increase in grain imports (between 1870–4 and 1884–8 annual wheat imports rose from 24,000 to 110,000 tons). This evolution was made possible by a law of 11 April 1865 which greatly modified the previous very strict controls on grain imports. Pressure from farmers after 1889 led to restrictions on grain imports but the true shift towards protection of industry took place in 1892.

VI. *The strengthening of protectionism in continental Europe and the continuation of liberalism in Great Britain, 1892–1914*

The period 1892–1914 raises some difficult problems for liberal theories of foreign trade. The evolution of the European economy reveals a disturbing correlation. Grossly oversimplified this can be expressed in the following equations: protectionism = economic growth and expansion of trade; liberalism = stagnation in both.

This contradiction, expressed in simplistic but dramatic terms, has both a historical and a geographical dimension. In the first place, the return to protectionist trade policies undoubtedly coincided with a considerable change in the main economic trend, leading to a period of growth unprecedented in European history (see Table 6). In the spatial dimension, the expansion of production and trade in this period essentially affected the countries which had returned to protectionism. Hence, in spite of widespread European economic expansion, in the United Kingdom, which remained liberal, Gross National Product and trade grew much more slowly than it had done. Whereas for continental

Europe between 1889–91 and 1911–13 Gross National Product increased in real terms by 2.6 per cent per annum, for the United Kingdom the increase was only 1.8 per cent (or in terms of growth per capita 0.6 per cent and 0.9 per cent respectively). But perhaps even more significantly, foreign trade in the protectionist countries grew more rapidly than in the liberal countries: exports from the United Kingdom, which had represented 36.3 per cent of those from continental Europe in 1889–91, represented only 32.0 per cent in 1913.

This problem of expansion of foreign trade (and also of the economy) in spite of protectionism deserves analysis. This is considered at the end of this section. We must first look at the development of European trade policies, which were marked by an almost universal strengthening of protectionism in continental Europe, and by the continuation of liberalism in Great Britain. Increased protectionism was not confined to continental Europe. Among those important trading partners of Europe which increased protectionism were the United States, with the McKinley tariff of 1890, Australia with its 1906 measures, and Argentina with its 1891 tariff etc. (see section X). From 1898, and more extensively from 1903–7, a zone of unilateral preferences (see section VIII B3) was set up in the British self-governing dominions. It should be noted that, if many of these changes in tariffs made by non-European countries were justified by the same tendency in Europe, they were in turn invoked in Europe to justify a further turn of the screw over tariffs. In short, a vicious circle of protectionism had replaced that of liberalism.

Another important characteristic of the years 1892–1914 was the outbreak of numerous tariff wars, involving a large number of countries, usually during the period of renegotiation of treaties. One of the two partners, for reasons either directly connected with the negotiations or for more general considerations, would decide to increase import duties. These increases could apply either generally to the import of a range of products which would affect the partner's sales, or (and in this case there was very clear conflict) just to the import of certain goods coming from this partner. Reprisals generally followed, the trading partner adopting similar measures. In such a war, peace obviously took the form of a new trade treaty, more or less balanced, which would more or less reflect the relative strength of the two partners. In certain cases, however, the retaliatory measures could remain in force for quite a long time. Dietzel remarked about this period, 'As a matter of fact tariff policy is being considered by various countries at the present day from the point of view of "Retaliation".'[89]

The introduction of legislation designed to combat dumping, and especially bounties on exports, should also be emphasized here. The

---

[89] H. Dietzel, *Retaliatory Duties* (translated from German) (London, 1906), p. 10.

overseas countries of European settlement were the pioneers in this. In 1904, however, Switzerland and Serbia took some measures in this direction, followed by Spain in 1906, and by France in 1910.[90]

All the same, it should be noted that since nearly all import duties were specific,[91] the price increases which began in 1896–8 led to a reduction in their relative importance. Between 1896–8 and 1911–13, one can say that export prices in Europe increased by about 1.5 per cent per annum, or about 25 per cent over this time-span.

Before moving on to a rather more detailed analysis of these changes in trade policy and their consequences, it is useful to remind ourselves that this period also saw the first international convention whose aim was to adjust the production and trade in one agricultural product: sugar. Attempts to regularize international trade in sugar, which had been disturbed by the large export bounties in force in most continental European countries, date back to the European conference on sugar which met in Paris in 1862. Eight of these conferences were needed between 1862 and 1902 before there were any noticeable results. The London conference (in July 1887) drew up a convention which was not ratified, largely because of France's refusal to sign it on the grounds of the absence of the United States. The convention signed in Brussels on 5 March 1902 (which took effect at the beginning of 1903) aimed essentially at abolishing direct or indirect bounties for the production of, and trade in, sugar. The convention was ratified in February 1903 by the signatories (Germany, Austria–Hungary, Belgium, Spain, France, Great Britain, Italy, The Netherlands, and Sweden). In 1907 and again in 1912 this convention was renewed for five more years. Russia, an important producer, joined in 1907, following some other countries (notably Switzerland in 1905). This convention managed to prevent a fall in sugar prices. In France, for example, the import price of sugar (calculated in real terms and using a wholesale price index) actually rose by 3.9 per cent per annum between 1901–3 and 1911–13, whereas it had dropped by 3.3 per cent per annum between 1879–81 and 1901–3.[92]

---

[90] League of Nations (International Economic Conference, Geneva, May 1927), *Memorandum on the Legislation of Different States for the Prevention of Dumping with Special Reference to Exchange Dumping*, pp. 10–20.

[91] In the period 1892–1914 the only European countries where specific duties did not account for at least 90 per cent of all import duties were The Netherlands (where most duties were *ad valorem*) and Belgium (where a significant proportion of duties were *ad valorem*).

[92] Sugar is one of the foodstuffs which, in the very long term, probably showed the greatest real drop in price in relation to other agricultural products.

Between the thirteenth and fourteenth centuries and today the relative price drop is about 190 to 1 in relation to products like butter, cheese, and eggs. As an illustration, here are quantities of butter that could be purchased for the price of a kilo of sugar (at the retail price in Great Britain): in 1259–1400, 29 kg; in 1541–82, 7 kg; in 1583–1702, 5 kg; in 1937, 0.19 kg; in 1968–70, 0.20 kg; and in 1985, 0.23 kg. From P. Lyle, 'The Sugar Industry', *Journal of the Royal Statistical Society*, vol. CXIII, part 4 (1950), pp. 531–43 (p. 531), plus my calculations for 1968–70 and 1985, taken from the ILO *Bulletin of Labour Statistics*, Geneva (various versions).

Finally, it should be noted that the question of non-tariff barriers to trade, which is an important issue today, was not seen as a problem before 1914. This is due to the fact that non-tariff barriers were extremely rare (but not non-existent), and that tariff barriers were important and had not fallen into discredit.

A. THE STRENGTHENING OF PROTECTIONISM IN CONTINENTAL EUROPE

The years 1892–1914 can undoubtedly be described as a period of increased protectionism in continental Europe, but different countries did not all develop at the same rate, especially during the first ten years of this period. The two major trading powers on the continent showed a substantial contrast in their development between 1892 and 1902.

In Germany, Caprivi's policy, which had begun with the treaty concluded with Austria–Hungary in 1891, was to be continued. Treaties with Italy and Belgium were signed in the same year, followed by ones with Switzerland in 1892, Serbia and Romania in 1893, Russia in 1894, and Spain in 1896. These treaties led to a certain reduction in protectionism, especially with regard to agriculture. France, on the other hand, became more and more protectionist, first by the double tariff of 1892, and then by numerous tariff revisions in the next few years.

1. Germany

Germany played a crucial role in the return of continental Europe to protectionism, if only because of her commercial power which had consolidated considerably. Although Germany was still behind the United Kingdom as far as total trade was concerned, for intra-European trade she had become more important. In 1889–91 Germany's share in the total intra-European trade (the average of intra-European imports and exports) was 19.9 per cent, compared with 17.8 per cent for the United Kingdom (which was more oriented towards overseas trade), 13.4 per cent for France, and 8.6 per cent for Belgium. For continental Europe alone, Germany was responsible for almost one-quarter (24.3 per cent) of the total intra-European trade.

The new trade treaties were not concluded without problems. They provoked, in particular, two important tariff wars. The first, with Russia, was a grim battle lasting six months (September 1893–February 1894). It led to a serious drop in German exports to Russia (179 million marks annually in 1890–1 and 136 million in 1893). The tariff war with Spain lasted longer: from the summer of 1894 to that of 1896.

As a result of the treaties concluded between 1892 and 1896, the protection of agriculture in Germany had been weakened. For wheat and rye this meant in practice a drop of 30 per cent in duties, which had gone from 50 to 35 marks per ton. Imports of grain, which before the tariffs of 1879, 1885, and 1887 had been checked, now showed a new upward tendency.[93] Although this upward trend had in relative terms fewer negative effects than that of the 1870s, and the agricultural population was smaller – it had dropped from 50 per cent in 1870 to 43 per cent in 1890 – nevertheless, farmers reacted angrily and created, in February 1892, the Agrarian League (Bund der Landwirthe). This league was founded by Ruprecht, a small landowner, who aimed his propaganda at people of his own social group. It was supported by the great Prussian landowners and Junkers, and it very quickly attracted 200,000 members and became a very active pressure group, holding annual meetings in Berlin.

The action of the Agrarian League was strengthened by its amalgamation, in 1893, with the Deutscher Bauernbund (a league of peasants founded in 1885), and by an agreement it made with the group representing the manufacturers. Together, these two groups pressed for an increase in the level of the minimum tariff. This was one of the factors leading to the fall of Caprivi, who was forced to resign on 26 October 1894. He was succeeded by Prince Hohenlohe until 16 October 1900.

As far as trade is concerned, Chancellor Hohenlohe's most important action was perhaps what is held to be the first German navigation law voted on 26 March 1898. This was to encourage further rapid expansion of the fleet. Between 1898 and 1913 the tonnage of the steam ships in the German merchant fleet increased by 180 per cent, as opposed to 70 per cent for Great Britain and 97 per cent for France. The 1890s saw a distinct recovery in German foreign trade. Her share in European exports went from 17.4 per cent in 1889–91 to 19.6 per cent for 1899–1901. In 1913, with 22.8 per cent of European exports, Germany had nearly caught up with the United Kingdom (24.2 per cent). If the trends registered between 1890 and 1913 had continued, Germany would have overtaken Great Britain in 1917.

It was Chancellor Bernhard Heinrich Bülow who instigated a shift in German trade policy with the new tariff of 1902. The liberals, and in particular the French liberals, considered Bülow:

[93] Quantities of grain imported annually (in 1,000 tons):

1860–4:   570, before and around the liberalization of imports.
1875–9:   2740, before the first protectionist measures.
1886–90:   2200, before the period of treaties.
1901–5:   5630, before the 1902 tariff came into force.
1909–13:   7270, after the 1902 tariff came into force.

Calculated from statistics provided by Mitchell, *European Historical Statistics*, pp. 339 and 341.

one of the main creators of the complex political and economic situation that led to the first world war . . . Under the illusion of prosperity, this pretentious policy was to lead the country little by little to an impasse, at the end of which, in spite of the applause of the ruling classes, whose basest motives were constantly flattered by Bülow, there could only be war and ruin for Germany.[94]

The new tariff, which was passed on 25 December 1902, only came into force on 1 March 1906, in order to allow rearrangement to be made to a certain number of treaties. The 1902 tariff noticeably increased the general level of protection and extended the number of tariff headings which resulted in a distinct increase in effective protection. It was a general tariff, but contained a double tariff for wheat, rye, oats, and malt. For these four cereals, the minimum tariff was slightly higher than the general tariff of 1887 and nearly twice as high as the conventional tariffs agreed by Caprivi after 1892. This guaranteed farmers a sufficient level of protection.

As far as manufactured goods were concerned, import duties were to be increased according to the relative importance of the added value. This was made possible by an increase in the number of headings and subheadings, which rose from a total of 391 to 1,459. The increase in duties was around 40–80 per cent. Apart from the treaties which were signed with about ten countries,[95] especially in 1904–5, and which did not imply any great changes in the general tariff, German tariff policy remained the same until the war. But within this framework German manufacturers and businessmen were involved in some very aggressive trade policies, obviously supported by the government (see next section VII). In addition, Germany's policy of colonial expansion, to which she was a latecomer, was strengthened, especially in Africa (see section VIII). These two factors contributed to the very rapid expansion in the volume of German exports which characterized the period between 1902–4 and 1911–13. They increased at a rate of 6.5 per cent per annum:

2. France

In France, the new tariff of 1892 remained in force until 1910. In the meantime, however, it was subjected to numerous modifications. More than 40 new laws were passed, or an average of two a year, the most important on 27 February 1894 which again raised duties on wheat, this

---

[94] A. Robinet de Clery, *La politique douanière de l'Allemagne depuis l'avènement de Caprivi jusqu'à nos jours (1890–1925)* (Paris, 1935), pp. 126–7.

[95] Belgium (22 June 1904); Russia (28 July 1904); Romania (25 September 1904); Switzerland (12 November 1904); Serbia (29 November 1904); Italy (3 December 1904); Austria–Hungary (25 January 1905); Bulgaria (1 August 1905). In 1911 treaties were also signed with Sweden and Japan.

time to 70 francs per ton (or about 37 per cent of the domestic price). This increase in protectionism took place in spite of opposition from the liberals and in particular from the Anti-Protectionist League led by the economist Leon Say. Another relatively important law was that of 30 January 1893 which increased bounties awarded by the fleet for ship-building as well as for navigation.

It should be noted that, by means of negotiation, all the European countries (except Portugal) and a large number of countries outside Europe (including the United States and Japan) came to benefit wholly or partly from the minimum tariff. But this did not come about without tariff wars, of which the most important were those with Italy and Switzerland.

The conflict with Italy began, in fact, well before 1892 and originated from Italy's decision, in December 1886, to repudiate her treaty with France in order to make possible the revision of her tariff. The tariff war as such began at the end of February 1888, when Italy applied the general tariff to French goods and France retaliated with the law of 27 February 1888, bringing duties on a wide range of Italian goods up to the level of the Italian general tariff. By the decree of 29 February, Italy in turn levied a surcharge of 50 per cent of the duties for goods coming from France. This war lasted until January 1892, when France abolished her surtaxes (Italy had adopted a more flexible position in December 1889). During these five years, Franco-Italian trade dropped to less than half the level it had been in the years before this conflict.

The conflict with Switzerland really began in January 1893, when Switzerland decided to impose surcharges on some 200 French products because the minimum French tariff was notably higher than her own import duties. France retaliated by charging Swiss goods at the maximum tariff. The conflict lasted until August 1895, and led to a reduction in trade of about one-third between these two countries.

On the whole, the changes in French trade policy achieved their aims. Imports of grain fell sharply, from 1,490 thousand tons per annum in 1888–92 to 250 thousand tons in 1905–9.[96] Imports of manufactured articles had risen from 68 million francs per annum in 1856–60 to 606 million francs in 1887–91; which, taking into account the drop in prices, amounts to an increase of about 9.3 per cent per annum in the volume of these imports. Between 1887–91 and 1905–9, however, this increase was only 2.7 per cent.[97]

Work on the new tariff of 29 March 1910 (which came into force on 1

[96] This can, however, be partly attributed to the series of good harvests which occurred in 1898–1907.

[97] These volumes have been calculated with the help of the index of import prices of manufactured goods drawn up by Lévy-Leboyer, 'L'héritage de Simiand', pp. 108–12.

Table 9. *Some indicators of import tariff levels in 1913 (percentage of value)*

	Import duties as % of special total imports (1909–13)	League of Nations' indices — All products[b]	League of Nations' indices — Manufactures	Liepmann's indices[a] — All products[b]	Liepmann's indices[a] — Manufactures	British manufactures (1914)	Level of duties on wheat
Austria–Hungary	7.6	18	18	23	20	35[c]	35
Belgium	15.8	6	9	14	9	10	0
Bulgaria	15.1[d]	—	—	23	22	18[c]	3
Denmark	5.8	9	14	—	—	—	0
Finland	12.1[d]	—	—	35	28	22	—
France	8.7	18	20	24	21	17	38
Germany	7.9	12	13	17	13	19[c]	36
Greece	26.6	—	—	—	—	18	37[c]
Italy	9.7	17	18	25	20	12[c]	40
Norway	11.4	—	—	—	—	—	4
Portugal	23.7	—	—	—	—	—	Prohibitive
Romania	12.1[d]	—	—	30	28	14[c]	1
Russia	29.5[d]	—	—	73	84	131[c]	0
Serbia	14.8	—	—	22	20	—	27
Spain	14.3	33	41	37	34	42	43
Sweden	9.0	16	20	28	25	23	28
Switzerland	4.4	7	9	11	8	7[c]	2
The Netherlands	0.4	3	4	—	—	3	0
United Kingdom	5.6	0	0	0	0	—	0

Notes:

[a] Potential indices in the sense that those indices are calculated on a standard list of 144 goods imported (thus including some products normally not imported).

[b] Excluding alcoholic drinks, tobacco and mineral oils (in general very high duties).

[c] 1904, and not strictly comparable with 1914 figures; in general they have to be reduced by some 30 per cent to be more comparable.

[d] To general imports.

Sources: Import duties as percentage of imports (author's estimates derived from various sources); League of Nations, *Tariff Level Indices* (Geneva, 1927); H. Liepmann, *Tariff Levels and the Economic Unity of Europe* (London, 1938); British manufactures, 1914: Great Britain Committee on Industry and Trade, *Survey of Overseas Markets* (London, 1925), p. 543; 1904: Board of Trade, *British and Foreign Trade and Industrial Conditions* (London, 1905).

Level of duties on wheat: author's based on duties provided in Board of Trade, *Foreign Import Duties, 1913* (London, 1913), pp. 1,065–6. Assumed uniform import prices of wheat of $36 per ton (based on average import prices for selected European countries).

April 1910) had already begun in 1903. This tariff had become necessary more for technical than purely commercial reasons. It was necessary to adapt the tariff headings to new products. The minimum tariff was left much as it was, but the maximum tariff was increased. On the whole, this tariff increased the effective protection of manufactured goods, but did not alter the import duties on agricultural products. Since agricultural products rose in price from 1901–5 onwards, this amounted to a reduction in real protection, which, together with the very poor harvest of 1910 and the mediocre ones of 1911–13, led to a sharp increase in grain imports.

3. The other large continental European countries

There was a general trend towards increased protectionism in the other main European economies. *Russia*, in 1890–1913, was the fourth commercial power in Europe in terms of the total value of her exports (8 per cent of exports). Although in 1885–1901 her trade policy was already highly protectionist, this protectionism was steadily reinforced, especially in the industrial sector. Between 1893 and 1903 Count Witte, an ardent disciple of List, was in charge of the Ministry of Finance (which was responsible for foreign trade). He introduced the maximum and minimum tariff system, and encouraged expansion of the railways and the transfer of foreign capital to Russia. After Witte's departure, Russia did not significantly alter her trade policy, which, as far as industry was concerned, was probably the most highly protectionist in Europe before the First World War (see Table 9).

There is no doubt that from the 1890s, due particularly to these measures, Russia industrialized very rapidly, even if the rapid growth in population is taken into account. Thus, for example, the production of pig-iron per capita – which had been 26.6 per cent of the corresponding figure for continental Europe in 1888–92 – rose to 31.7 per cent in 1908–12 (and in relation to the whole of Europe the figures were 16.2 per cent and 25.7 per cent respectively).

Italy, who had already increased import duties in 1878 and in 1887, adopted a new tariff on 24 November 1895 (which came into force immediately). Almost all duties on manufactured goods remained as before. As these were specific duties, given the rise in prices, this meant an effective increase of about 8 per cent compared with 1887; but this increase was to be wiped out after 1896–8 when prices began to fall again. Import duties on agricultural products, though, were sharply increased. For grain, they rose to 75 lire per ton (or about 36 per cent of the value).

The low level of duties for industrial goods was the result of a deliberate policy aimed at increasing the outlets for Italian agricultural products. It is in this context that we should place the treaties of January 1889, April 1892, and July 1904 between Italy and Switzerland, which between 1888 and 1899 became Italy's main outlet (more important than France and Germany). Between 1888 and 1892 Switzerland took 20 per cent of all Italy's exports.

Various treaties signed during the period 1892–1904 resulted in a further reduction in import duties on manufactured goods, even though these were already relatively low. This, in the international context of increased protection, led to protests, particularly from manufacturers in the north. But there was no change of policy. Even the new tariff of 28 July 1910 hardly altered the level of duties. Italy thus retained a more liberal tariff than most other large countries of continental Europe in the period 1892–1914 (see Table 9).

In *Austria–Hungary* the adjustment of trade policies to the new conditions produced by the tariff reforms of her commercial partners took place with some difficulties. In this context the long tariff war with Romania (from 1886 to 1893) must be cited. However, without seriously modifying her tariff system Austria–Hungary succeeded, between 1892 and 1894, in renegotiating trade treaties with her main commercial partners (Germany, Italy, Switzerland, Belgium, Romania, and Russia). From the beginning of the twentieth century the pressure of the protectionists grew stronger, due to a progressive change in the attitudes of Hungarian farmers. But in fact Austria–Hungary did not join the ultra-protectionist camp. Her trade policy just before the First World War was midway between those of the most liberal and the most protectionist countries of Europe (see Table 9).

Added to these general problems was the delicate issue of the divergences of interest between Austria and Hungary themselves. Negotiations begun in 1895 ended at last in an agreement in October 1907 which provided for separate but identical customs tariffs for Austria and Hungary to last ten years. This was considered the first step towards an autonomous customs system for each of these two states.

Spain experienced difficulties in the renegotiation of new treaties after she had adopted a protectionist tariff in 1892 (which provoked a tariff war with France and Germany). The loss of her main remaining colonies (the Philippines, Cuba, and Puerto Rico) in 1898 resulted in a decline in exports to these countries from 350 million pesetas per annum in 1896–7 to 75 million in 1901–2 (or from 33 to 9 per cent of total exports). This in turn led to pressure for increased protectionism, which resulted in the double tariff of 1 July 1906. Import duties were sharply increased, and the number of tariff items liable to duty raised to 697 (as opposed to 410 in the 1892 tariff). The tariff was revised again in 1912 (and included a plan for periodic revision of import duties). Just before the First World War,

Spain had one of the most highly protectionist tariffs in Europe (see Table 9), with import duties on manufactured goods averaging about 40 per cent.

4. The small European countries

The development of trade policies in the smaller European countries was more uneven than in the large ones. It is true that the general trend was the same; but their protectionism took a less radical form, and there is also the case of *The Netherlands* which did not at all follow the same pattern, remaining faithful to a liberal policy. In 1895 the Dutch Second Chamber rejected by 52 votes to 33 a motion putting forward very limited protectionist measures. For the uncompromising liberals of Het Vreiye Ruilverkeer (a Dutch free trade association) the 5 per cent *ad valorem* duties affecting about 60 per cent of manufactured goods (the rest having free entry) were protectionist duties.[98] Even more significant is the fact that in 1897 the Dutch Committee for Agriculture (Nederlandsche Landbouw-Comite) declared itself opposed to any protection for grain.

The other predominantly agricultural small countries did not follow the same policy. Those of Southern and Eastern Europe (Bulgaria, Greece, Portugal, Romania, and Serbia) as well as those of the North (Denmark, Finland, and Norway) considerably increased their duties and widened their ranges of application. As in the large countries, the degree of effective protection increased more rapidly than the average level of duties.

In *Portugal*, the protectionist tariff of 1892 had very serious consequences on the country's industrialization and marked, after 189 years, the true end of the Methuen treaty between Portugal and England, a treaty which had prevented the creation of a mature local textile industry. The domestic consumption of raw cotton which fluctuated around 0.5 kg per capita (or 18 per cent of the average European level) in 1860–80 reached 2.2 kg (49 per cent of the European level) as early as 1893–7. The tariff was modified somewhat in 1908 to facilitate the export of greater quantities of wine. Wine still represented 33 per cent of total exports (compared with 52 per cent before 1892). In the agricultural sector tariff policy remained relatively liberal. The new measures taken in response to pressure from the farmers (notably in 1899) were not sufficient to reduce cereal imports.

When the Balkan states became independent they inherited a very liberal tariff system from the Ottoman Empire. Import duties were not only low but also very uniform, which meant that effective protection was in practice minimal. Gradually, however, during the 1880s, these

---

[98] A. Heringa, *Freetrade and Protectionism in Holland* (Haarlem, 1914), especially pp. 7–8.

countries adopted protectionist legislation, influenced by the trend in continental Europe. Each of the four Balkan states (excluding Albania which became independent in 1913) developed in different ways and at different speeds.

Bulgaria, which became independent in 1878, did not modify her tariff legislation until 1895, when import duties were increased from 8 to 11.5 per cent. In 1897 they were raised once more, but still remained relatively low. Numerous treaties also helped to keep the level down. In 1904, though, Bulgaria revoked all her treaties and replaced them with a distinctly protectionist tariff.

In *Greece*, which had been independent since 1830, liberal legislation remained in force a long time. In the years 1882–95 the almost uninterrupted presence of Trikoupes as head of the government meant an open-door policy, and particularly a call for foreign capital. However, in 1892 Greece adopted a double tariff which was revised in 1893, 1904, 1910, and 1911. On the whole this resulted in a progressive reinforcement of protectionism. By 1913 duties on manufactured articles averaged 25 to 30 per cent. Pressure by farmers against grain imports grew stronger in the first years of the twentieth century and led in 1904 to an increase in duties which brought them to about 30–40 per cent of the domestic price.

Although *Romania* remained under the suzerainty of the Ottoman Empire until 1877, from 1874 she developed an autonomous trade policy with a tariff which came into force with the law of 1 July 1876. The commercial treaty signed with Austria–Hungary on 22 June 1875 (which came into force on 19 June 1876 for a period of ten years) was even more important. This treaty in fact allowed Austro-Hungarian products free entry into Romania. It was followed by other treaties with Russia (3 December 1876), Switzerland (30 March 1878), Greece (6 April 1878), Germany (14 November 1877), and England (24 March 1880). From 1885 onwards the Romanian government introduced some protectionist measures, but these were fairly limited. The 1891 tariff contained about as many increases as reductions in import duties. However, the 1893 tariff strengthened protectionism, although it was not until 1904 that Romania adopted a tariff aimed to encourage industrialization. This tariff was drawn up by the Minister of Finance, Emile Ortinesco, who was a manufacturer. It was adopted in 1904, and took effect from 1 March 1906. Apart from minor modifications (in 1911 and 1912) it remained in force until May 1920. Between 1904 and 1914 Romania signed treaties with 15 countries.[99]

[99] G. D. Cioriceanu, *La Roumanie économique et ses rapports avec l'étranger de 1860 à 1915* (Paris, 1928), pp. 137–40, 266–70; C. B. Faust, *La politique douanière de la Roumanie des débuts jusqu' à nos jours* (Neuchâtel, 1934), pp. 13–24; V. T. Jordachescou, *L'évolution de la politique douanière de la Roumanie de l'époque Dacie-Trajane à nos jours* (Paris, 1925).

The shift towards protectionism in *Serbia* (which became completely independent in 1878) can be dated from the 1893 tariff, which was revised in 1899, 1900, and 1902. The 1904 tariff went one step further along the same road.

Between 1890 and 1913 the three non-industrialized Scandinavian countries (Denmark, Norway, and Finland) experienced a period of very rapid expansion of their economies and of their foreign trade. Their share in total European exports rose from 2.2 per cent in 1889–91 to 3.3 per cent in 1913, and the annual increase in their average Gross National Product per capita was during this period some 25 per cent higher than that of the rest of Europe.

In *Denmark*, the tariff introduced in 1863 remained in force until 1908, with only minor modifications. The new legislation was fairly liberal as far as agricultural products and raw materials were concerned, but it was quite severely protectionist with regard to certain sectors of industry which Denmark wanted to develop. This was particularly true for manufactured textiles, which were liable to duties of about 20–25 per cent.

In 1897, *Norway* adopted a less liberal double tariff which increased import duties on certain manufactured goods. In 1905 she took a more decisive step. On the initiative of the Minister of Finance, Gunnar Knudsen (who was a manufacturer in favour of protectionism), a tariff which protected industry as well as agriculture was established.

In *Finland* from 1893 onwards the czar intervened several times to ask the Finnish Senate to increase import duties so as to bring them into line with those in force in Russia. However, in spite of a few modifications (especially in 1906, 1908, and 1910) the gap remained; and just before the First World War the average level of duties in Finland was about half of that in force in Russia (see Table 9). This did not mean that Finland had a liberal tariff – on the contrary, it was one of the most highly protectionist of the small European countries.

Of the three small industrialized countries, Sweden remained undoubtedly the most protectionist. The trade policies of Belgium and Switzerland could be described as moderately protectionist.

It was probably in *Switzerland* that plans for tariff reform aroused most public interest. This was essentially because of a peculiarity of the political system in this country. If a petition against federal laws and decrees containing 30,000 signatures was presented, the government was practically forced to submit its plans to a popular vote. As already seen, this had already happened in the case of the 1891 tariff. This tariff was hardly modified at all until a new tariff, known as the 1902 tariff, came into force on 1 January 1906. It had taken a long time for this protectionist tariff to be drawn up and adopted, since as early as 1898 the Federal Council had instructed the Vorort (the organization of manufacturers and business-owners), the Swiss Union of Craftsmen (Union Suisse des Arts et Metiers) and the Swiss Union of Farmers (Union Suisse des Paysans) to prepare reports to serve as a basis for tariff reform. The federal bill, presented in February 1902, provoked lively discussion both inside and outside parliament. The Swiss Consumers' Union (the Union Suisse de Cooperatives de Consommation) formed a 'league against the customs tariff' which was supported by the Socialists. There were even several demonstrations. The movement against the tariff, however, was defeated on 15 March 1903 by 60 per cent of the voters (participation in the elections had been amongst the highest up to that date).

This tariff increased the number of tariff items from 476 to 1,112 and it was a single-schedule tariff. Compared with the previous tariff, it increased duties on livestock by about 80–100 per cent, on meat by about 200 per cent, and on wine by about 120 per cent, but it did not alter the duties on grain, which remained fixed at 3 francs per ton, or only about 2 per cent of the value, as opposed to 8–16 per cent for livestock (meat animals) and meat, and 10–30 per cent for wine. For finished manufactured goods, the increase in duties was about 30 per cent (essentially for textiles), whereas for semi-finished articles and iron manufactures the increase was lower, which meant there was a relatively low level of protection (see Table 9).

As in other countries, the adoption of this tariff (as had happened in 1891) necessitated the renegotiation of treaties with Switzerland's main trading partners. As was common at this period, there was a series of tariff wars, notably with France (see p. 75) and with Spain (lasting only two months, July–August 1906). The tariff was not altered until the 1921 reform (which came into force on 1 July). But the fairly large number of trade agreements, which all contained the most-favoured-nation clause, effectively extended the normal tariff to all countries.

In *Belgium*, the changes introduced by the 1895 tariff (law of 15 July) were of little importance. This tariff, which remained in force until the war, can be described as moderately protectionist. This was justified by the size of the country, and especially by the outward-looking nature of the main industries. As the preamble to the bill noted, the government did not consider itself to be protectionist. For this government, protectionism risked 'hindering' the exports of a country which cannot absorb one-half of its metal production, one-twentieth of its glass, or one-third of its linen.[100] Import duties on manufactured goods averaged about 9 per cent. In other words, together with the Swiss duties, they were the lowest of the industrialized countries of continental Europe (see Table 9).

From 1892 (the year in which most treaties ran out) *Sweden* strength-

---

[100] Quoted by M. Suetens, *Histoire de la politique commerciale de la Belgique depuis 1830 à nos jours* (Brussel, 1955), p. 127.

ened her protectionism by a series of partial changes in her commercial legislation. The most important change was that of 1895, which increased import duties on grain by 160 per cent. The tariff was not revised completely until the law of 9 July 1911 (the new tariff came into force on 1 December 1911). This tariff contained 1,325 items, and if the size of the country is taken into account, had a very high level of protectionism (see Table 9).

B.   THE TEMPTATIONS OF FAIR TRADE AND TARIFF REFORM IN THE UNITED KINGDOM

The reversal in the trends of commercial policy in continental Europe which began in 1877–9, and also that in Canada (see section x), brought inevitable repercussions in Great Britain, where the impact of these events was enhanced by the new trends in the economy: from 1875–7 British economic growth slowed down considerably. Whereas the volume of Gross National Product had increased by 2.2 per cent per annum between 1864–6 and 1874–6, between 1874–6 and 1882–4 it grew by only 1.4 per cent (or an annual increase in Gross National Product per capita of 1.3 and 0.4 per cent respectively). Between 1880 and 1884 there was a period of near-stagnation, and hence a decrease in Gross National Product per capita. At the same time, not accidentally, imports of manufactured goods increased rapidly. In terms of value, this increase was 4.4 per cent per annum between 1869–71 and 1879–81, which represented an increase in volume of 5.0–5.5 per cent per annum. Finally, and perhaps most importantly, during the 1870s the total value of exports to Europe and to the United States fell, whereas those to the rest of the world, and especially to the British Empire, noticeably increased. Imperial markets rose from 25 per cent of total export sales in 1868–72 to 34 per cent in 1878–82. This increase was even more pronounced in the case of manufactured goods. Empire markets for textiles, for example, rose from 27 to 37 per cent of total exports between 1870 and 1880, and crude iron and semi-finished iron goods from 22 to 31 per cent.[101]

1. The Fair Trade League [102]

The combination of the above factors inevitably created a climate of opinion which favoured a certain degree of protectionism and especially a retreat to the Empire. This reaction crystallized in 1881 with the

---

[101] W. Schlote, British Overseas Trade from 1700 to 1930s (Oxford, 1952), p. 166.

[102] In fact the official name was National Fair Trade League, but the word 'National' was dropped in use, perhaps to reduce confusion with the National League formed with similar aims in the same year.

creation of the Fair Trade League,[103] which, it should be acknowledged, did have a very strong influence on British public life. The Fair Trade League was led by Farrer Ecroyd, a textile manufacturer and former Member of Parliament. Its demands were fairly moderate and were designed to restructure commercial policies. The League wanted to impose retaliatory import duties as a prelude to negotiations for reciprocity. In particular, manufactured goods imported from countries which did not allow free entry to British manufactured goods would be liable to duties of 10–15 per cent. Imported products which competed with those coming from British colonies would also be taxed.

At the beginning of the 1880s the arguments put forward by those in favour of a realignment of commercial policy came up against a very convincing, because very simple, argument on the part of the Liberals. Thus Gladstone, in October 1881 at the beginning of his second term of office, could speak with pointed irony when he declared that,

An institution has been formed in the imposing name of the Fair Trade League. What in the world, you will ask, does that mean? Well, gentlemen, I must say it bears a suspicious likeness to our old friend Protection. (Cheers and laughter). Protection was dead and buried 30 years ago, but he has come out of the grave and is walking in the broad light of day, but after long experience of the atmosphere underground, he endeavours to look somewhat more attractive than he used to appear... and in consequence he found it convenient to assume a new name (Laughter)... can you strike the foreigner hard by retaliatory tariffs? What manufactures do you import from abroad? In all £45,000,000. What manufactures do you export? Nearer £200,000,000 (cheers) – over £200,000,000.[104]

Note here that Gladstone's figures apply more to the situation in the mid-1870s than in the early 1880s. Indeed, if the annual trade figures for the export of manufactured goods drawn up by Schlote are examined,[105] one sees that it was only around 1873–5 that the corresponding two figures and ratios (to be more precise, imports of £46 million a year in 1873–5, and exports of £205 million) can be found. Around 1880 (see Table 10) the balance between these two aggregates was already noticeably less favourable. But as nearly always happens (including today) such polemical arguments are more likely to be based on the situation prevailing five to ten, or even more, years earlier rather than on the current situation.

---

103 Note, however, that in 1871 a 'reciprocity Free Trade Association' was created which lasted until 1880. During the period 1879–81 other 'protectionist' organizations appeared and disappeared. B. H. Brown, *The Tariff Reform Movement in Great Britain 1881–1895* (New York, 1943), pp. 8–18.
104 Published in *The Times* of 8 October 1881. Quoted by N. McCord, *Free Trade: Theory and Practice from Adam Smith to Keynes* (London, 1970), p. 132.
105 Schlote, *British Overseas Trade*, pp. 121–5.

Table 10. *United Kingdom trade in manufactured goods*
(current £million; three-year annual averages)

	Imports	Exports	Excess of exports		Re-exports
			In value	In % of imports	
1855	11.2	88.5	77.4	693	2.2
1860	15.7	114.6	98.9	630	2.6
1870	35.9	178.8	142.9	398	3.7
1880	55.1	182.4	127.4	231	7.7
1890	71.3	206.5	135.1	189	10.0
1900	102.5	213.0	110.5	108	11.7
1910	126.4	320.3	193.9	153	18.7
1912	145.3	362.9	217.6	150	19.7
1924	221.2	565.5	344.4	156	22.7

Source: Derived from W. Schlote, *British Overseas Trade from 1700 to 1930s* (London, 1952).

The Free Trade League reached its peak in 1887. From 1888 it turned its attentions more towards the problems of the Empire. But its audience declined. The League lasted until the beginning of 1891 when most of its members joined the United Empire Trade League.[106]

It was not until the early twentieth century that a new pressure group in favour of a change in British commercial policy emerged. It is true that in the meantime Gladstone's calculations of a ratio of 5:1 in favour of British exports of manufactured goods had been replaced by a ratio of only 2:1. Moreover, even this situation was essentially the result of the large surplus of manufactured goods traded with the British Empire. As we have seen (Table 7), at the beginning of the twentieth century Britain had developed an unfavourable balance of trade with the industrialized countries of Europe, so far as manufactures were concerned. Even in extra-European markets, where British influence was very strong, British products faced serious competition from European rivals. If we look only at the ten countries outside Europe in which about 82 per cent of British capital was invested, we find that Great Britain's share in the total imports of these countries fell from 50 per cent in 1869–71 to 37 per cent in 1894–6, and to 29 per cent in 1913.[107]

In short, it began to look as though a theoretical impossibility had in fact happened – that an economic 'heresy' had proved fruitful. The

[106] Brown, *The Tariff Reform Movement in Great Britain*, pp. 137–9.
[107] Bairoch, *Commerce extérieur et développement économique*, pp. 215–16. The ten countries are: Argentina, Australia, Brazil, Canada, Chile, China, Egypt, the United States, India, and the Union of South Africa.

protectionist countries experienced rapid economic expansion not only in the home markets but also in their exports. On the other hand, the Empire had become increasingly important as an outlet for British industrial products, and especially for more sophisticated goods.

2. Chamberlain and the Tariff Reform League

It is in this context that Joseph Chamberlain's campaign for tariff reform should be seen. Paradoxically, when the Free Trade League was active, Chamberlain's task as president of the Board of Trade was to lead the counter-attack. As Amery points out:

his reply to Ritchie's motion in the House of Commons and his speeches in the country were generally regarded as masterly expositions of the Cobdenite doctrine. But his persecution of the Fair Traders proved to be the first step on his journey to Damascus. It was while preparing his speeches in defence of Free Trade that serious doubts first rose in his mind. Many years later, after the Tariff Reform campaign had begun he was asked by Herbert Maxwell when it was that he had first begun to doubt the application of Free-Trade doctrines. 'Well', he replied 'there is no reason why I should not tell you that it was in 1882 when, as President of the Board of Trade, I had to answer a motion of Ritchie's in favour of retaliatory tariff'.[108]

Already during the discussion of the 1901 budget the return of certain protectionist arguments may be detected from a small group led by Sir Howard Vincent and by Viscount Lowther. In 1902 there was an attempt to put forward an amendment in favour of protectionist measures for agriculture (on grounds of military security), linked with a preferential system for the colonies.[109] In this context it should be noted that the second colonial conference (known as the Ottawa conference) had adopted a resolution supporting the principle of unilateral preferences of 25 per cent for British products. Although the fourth colonial conference (London 1902) rejected the notion of imperial defence, it reiterated the consensus in favour of a preferential system (for further details see section VIII).

Given that the United Kingdom levied hardly any import duties, a real preferential trade zone incorporating the whole British Empire could not be set up unless the mother country introduced import duties. Such a policy was clearly incompatible with the free trade 'dogma'. Chamberlain, who did not succeed, during his time in office in various governments, in introducing a true preferential trade system with import duties on grain in particular,[110] gradually moved towards a more

---

[108] J. Amery, Joseph Chamberlain and the Tariff Reform Campaign, 2 vols. (London, 1969), vol. I, pp. 209–10.   [109] Ibid., pp. 20–21.

[110] In fact from 15 April 1902 to 30 June 1903 cereals became liable to duties again. While Chamberlain was away (on a mission to South Africa) the British cabinet reversed the decision to refund to the colonies the import duties collected.

protectionist position. His speech in Birmingham on 15 May 1903 marked the beginning of what was to be a real crusade for tariff reform. This reform was to further three aims: to increase revenue (in order to finance social policies); to give some protection to industry; and to set up a preferential system for the benefit of the Empire. This far-reaching speech made a big impact and was followed by others giving further details of what was to become the doctrine of the Tariff Reform League. The League was formed on 21 July 1903 and Chamberlain appointed the Duke of Sutherland as president, and Cyril Arthur Pearson as chairman. It was a well-organized body with adequate funds, and became a very powerful pressure group supporting Chamberlain's activities, who remained the key figure. Chamberlain stepped up his personal campaign after his resignation from the cabinet as Colonial Secretary, which, after being refused on 9 September 1903, was accepted seven days later.

Two propaganda campaigns for tariff reform are commonly distinguished, the first lasting from October 1903 to June 1904, and the second from July 1905 to January 1906. The Tariff Reform League was proposing only a limited form of protectionism: no import duties on raw materials, 2 shillings per quarter on wheat (i.e., about 7 per cent of the domestic price), 5 per cent on meat and dairy produce (with the exception of bacon, the food of the under-privileged classes), and 10 per cent on manufactured goods. In order to reduce the inflationary effect, appreciable reductions were proposed in the import duties on tea and sugar in particular. This, of course, was incorporated into a reciprocal preferential system for the Empire.

The Liberals' counter-attack took shape in 1903 in the report of the economist Alfred Marshall, in reply to a request from the Treasury for an analysis of the situation. He concluded:

The position, then, is this. On the one hand, England is not in a strong position for reprisals against hostile tariffs, because there are not important exports of hers, which other countries need so urgently as to be willing to take them from her at a considerably increased cost, and because none of her rivals would permanently suffer serious injury through the partial exclusion of any product of theirs with which England can afford to dispense. And, on the other hand, it is not merely expedient – it is absolutely essential – for England's hopes of retaining a high place in the world, that she should neglect no opportunity of increasing the alertness of her industrial population in general, and her manufacturers in particular; and for this purpose there is no device to be compared in efficiency with the plan of keeping her markets open to the new products of other nations, and especially to those of American inventive genius and of German systematic thought and scientific training.

Earlier, when discussing the substantial revenue from foreign trade and also from the profits of British capital invested abroad, he made a remark which sounds quite contemporary,

Her people think that these, taken together, are enough; and prefer expensive summer holidays to increasing still further above the German level their consumption of oranges or silk. Who shall say that they are wrong?[111]

Marshall was supported by most important English economists of the period, as can be seen from a letter to *The Times* of 15 August 1905 signed jointly by fourteen economists, including Arthur Cecil Pigou and, of course, Marshall himself.[112]

The economic stagnation – and even decrease in the volume of Gross National Product per capita; a noticeable drop in real wages; and a relative stagnation of exports – in the years 1900–4 lent support to those pressing for tariff reform. However, the events of the year 1905, which led up to the elections of 12 January 1906, were favourable to the Liberals. In this year the total value of exports rose by 9.7 per cent (9.9 per cent in terms of volume) and the volume of Gross National Product by 3.0 per cent (or 2.1 per cent per capita). The Liberals swept the board in the elections, gaining 377 seats out of a total of 670. The Unionists (who supported Chamberlain) gained only 157 seats and their defeat was all the more decisive since the election turn-out was the highest ever recorded: on average 92 per cent. Six months after the elections (on 11 July 1906) Chamberlain suffered a stroke (partial paralysis). Three days earlier he had turned 70. He never really returned to active politics, and died on 2 July 1914.

Although the Tariff Reform League no longer had the benefit of Chamberlain's great talent as an orator and organizer, it did not abandon its campaign. In the 1910 elections the Unionists made significant gains (increasing their number of seats to 277). These gains are generally attributed to the increase in the supporters of tariff reform. However, improvements in the economic climate allowed action to be delayed. It may be said that certain ideas of the Tariff Reform League began to be applied from 1916 on. But these were war measures, and 1932 was the real date of the abandonment of free trade (see p. 91).

C.   PROTECTIONISM AND THE EXPANSION OF FOREIGN TRADE

Despite what the title could lead one to believe, this section is not concerned with an explanation of the development of European foreign trade purely in terms of changes in commercial policy. Its primary aim is to present facts that constitute real paradoxes to diehard supporters of free trade: not only did the period of reinforcement of protectionism coincide with a more rapid expansion of trade, but also, and even more

[111] Quoted by W. H. B. Court, *British Economic History, 1870–1914: Commentary and Documents* (Cambridge, 1965), p. 467.   [112] McCord, *Free Trade*, pp. 144–7.

paradoxically, the most highly protectionist European countries experienced the most rapid expansion of their trade. Even if this cannot be taken as proof that protectionism generates international trade, it at least proves that protectionism does not always and necessarily hinder such trade.

On the other hand, expansion in trade is not an aim in itself but merely a way of achieving economic growth. It could even be argued that, if identical levels of production of goods and services could be obtained either with or without foreign trade, the quantity of goods and services available for effective consumption would be greater (all things being equal) without foreign trade, since in this case a reduced amount of transport and fewer services would be needed to distribute the goods.

The data presented in section IV C, and in particular Table 6, showed how far the protectionist period facilitated a recovery not only in the different sectors of the economy but also in trade: during the twenty years after the re-introduction of protectionist policies, the annual growth rate of volume of Gross National Product increased by more than 100 per cent and the volume of exports grew by more than 35 per cent (compared with the previous twenty years).

If the statistics from Table 11 show individual variations, according to country and period, it remains generally true that in all countries (except Italy) the introduction of protectionist measures resulted in a distinct acceleration in economic growth during the first ten years, and this took place no matter when the measures were introduced. In the next ten years, during which the protectionist measures were strengthened, there was usually a further acceleration in economic growth. The years 1909–13 – which fall outside this analysis – were marked in every country by an even higher growth rate. (In continental Europe the annual real growth rate of Gross National Product was 3.0 per cent in 1908–10 to 1911–13, as opposed to 2.3 per cent in 1897–9 to 1908–10. In the United Kingdom, on the other hand, there was first a period of stagnation, then a marked decline in the growth rate.) Furthermore, in continental Europe the rate of growth reached its peak from the moment all countries strengthened their protectionism.

As far as foreign trade was concerned, an almost universal slowing down of expansion is noticeable in the first ten years after the abandonment of free trade, but in the second ten years the rate of growth in the volume of exports in nearly all the protectionist countries was faster than it had been in the ten years before protectionism was adopted (see Table 11). Moreover, and this is important, during these two decades the expansion of trade was much faster in the countries which had adopted for protectionism than in the United Kingdom which remained liberal. Even if the unlikely possibility of a systematic bias in the calculations of

Table 11. *Annual rate of growth of exports and Gross National Product by countries and periods in relation to commercial policy change (based on three-year annual averages[a])*

| | Date of policy change | 10-year period preceding protectionist move | | Periods following protectionist move | | | |
| | | | | First 10 years | | Second 10 years | |
		Exports	GNP	Exports	GNP	Exports	GNP
Protectionist countries							
France	1892	2.1	1.2	1.9	1.3	2.7	1.5
Germany	1885	3.0	1.3	2.4	3.1	5.2	2.9
Italy	1887	0.4	0.7	1.7	0.5	4.5	2.7
Sweden	1888	3.4	1.5	2.8	3.5	2.4	3.3
Semi-protectionist countries							
Belgium	1887	4.9	1.2	2.3	2.0	2.7	2.8
Denmark	(1889)	1.4	3.3	4.3	3.8	4.1	3.0
Switzerland	1887	0.4	—	−0.6	—	3.8	—
Continental Europe	(1889)	3.0	1.1	2.6	2.3	3.7	2.3
United Kingdom	(1889)[b]	3.9	2.2	1.1	2.3	3.2	1.2
Europe	(1889)	3.4	1.3	2.2	2.3	3.6	1.9

Notes:
[a] Average of the three years preceeding the period, including the year when the policy change was made.
[b] No commercial policy change at this date, but year used in the calculations of annual growth rates.
Brackets indicate approximate dates.
Sources: See Table 6.

the volume of exports is taken into account, the value of Great Britain's exports represented only 31.1 per cent of those from continental Europe in 1909–11, whereas they had accounted for 36.3 per cent in 1889–91. As with economic growth, the expansion of trade became even greater when all countries increased their protectionism.

D.   A BRIEF OUTLINE OF THE TRENDS IN EUROPEAN TARIFF POLICY, 1914–50

To conclude this section a few words must be added about the main trends in tariff policies between 1914 and 1950. The First World War obviously caused an upheaval in trade which led to the adoption of emergency trade measures. The years 1920–9 are usually, but wrongly, described as a period of considerable reinforcement of protectionism in Europe. One of the reasons for this confusion is perhaps connected with the meeting in 1927 of the International Economic Conference, one of whose aims was to correct the tendencies of trade policies which were thought to be moving towards protectionism. In fact, the weighted average of customs duties in continental Europe came to 24.6 per cent for 1913 and 24.9 per cent for 1927.[113] It is true that this overall stability conceals divergent tendencies at the level of individual products and countries. Reductions (in decreasing order of importance) had been made in average import duties in Poland, Austria, Sweden, and Belgium; and increases (in increasing order) in Italy, Germany, Hungary, Spain, Czechoslovakia, Romania, Yugoslavia, Switzerland, and Bulgaria.

However, outside Europe the general trend was in the direction of an increase in protectionism. On the one hand, the tariff autonomy regained by certain semi-independent countries led to a radical change of policy in the direction of protectionism (see section x D). On the other hand, the tariff system set up in nearly all independent non-European countries after the war was more restrictive. The same applied to certain colonial possessions, in particular India. In addition, the increase in import duties on manufactured goods was greater than that affecting other products. During the 1920s Great Britain retained a series of import duties imposed during the war – even though she did not actually abandon her free trade policy until 1932. This was also one of the factors that helped to mask the real character of the 1920s: in the years 1919–25 a certain number of European countries retained restrictive measures (usually quotas) introduced during the war, but most of these were abolished between 1923 and 1929.[114]

In 1928 and 1929, partly due to the recommendations of the International Economic Conference of 1927, some reductions in import duties and some free trade measures were introduced. On the whole the period 1920–9 can be said to have been marked by a trend towards a liberalization of European trade policy. It was also a very positive period as far as international trade was concerned. The volume of world exports increased by about 7 per cent per annum between 1921 and 1929, and even by 6 per cent per annum between 1924 (the year in which the level of 1913 was reached again) and 1929. Such growth rates had never been achieved before.

[113] Calculated by adjusting the indices of H. Liepmann (*Tariff Levels and the Economic Unity of Europe* (London, 1938), p. 415) for the value of the imports of each country at each period (according to *Statistical Yearbook* of the League of Nations, Geneva, various editions). Great Britain is excluded from this calculation for lack of data. On the basis of the League of Nations' *Tariff Level Indices* (Geneva, 1927), the following trends may be observed:
General level: 1913, 13.2 per cent; 1925, 13.5 per cent (including Great Britain 10.2 per cent).
Manufactured goods: 1913, 15.0 per cent; 1925, 19.7 per cent (including Great Britain 14.5 per cent).

[114] For this, see League of Nations, *Commercial Policy in the Interwar Period: International Proposals and National Policies* (Geneva, 1942) and *Commercial Policy in the Post-War World* (Geneva, 1945).

In the United States, debates began in January 1929 about the possible revision of the current tariff, in order to increase the degree of protectionism (see section x). From this project the idea emerged of a new International Economic Conference on tariff problems. Invitations were issued by a resolution voted at the Assembly of the League of Nations on 23 September 1929 (before the first collapse of the stock market on 19 October). The aim of the conference was to conclude a 'tariff truce'..

The conference was held in Geneva between 17 February and 24 March 1930[115] in an economic climate very different from that of 1927. The abstention of the United States contributed to the failure of this meeting, which resulted in nothing but a rather general convention on trade and a few recommendations of which the first among the supplementary recommendations was a kind of draft of a 'North–South dialogue' between Europe and the countries exporting raw materials.[116]

The new American tariff was voted on 28 May 1930. By 1931 nearly all European countries (except Poland and Sweden) had already significantly raised their tariffs. In nearly all cases this was due to the prolonged economic crisis and also to the American attitude. The average level of import duties was about 39.5 per cent in 1931 (compared with 24.9 per cent in 1927). When the United Kingdom abandoned free trade in 1932 the way was opened for what are known as the Ottawa agreements concluded in August 1932, which established a reciprocal system of imperial preference.

The tendency to try to overcome the depression by isolating the national market increased in the following years, and the battery of protectionist trade measures (especially the fixing of quotas) grew considerably, in spite of attempts to draw up international agreements. The problem was aggravated by monetary instability, and quite a large

---

[115] The official title of this meeting was the Preliminary Conference with a View to Concerted Economic Action. It is often wrongly called the Second International Economic Conference, or the (Geneva) Tariff Conference.

[116] Draft recommendations:

Having regard to the importance of the markets of overseas countries for the economic life of Europe;

Considering that it is highly important for Europe to investigate all possible means of taking a larger place in these markets;

Considering that the majority of the overseas countries are producers of raw materials and foodstuffs of which Europe is one of the main consumers;

Considering that, in order that the future negotiations contemplated by the present Conference may give the fullest results, it would be valuable to associate the overseas countries with them to the greatest possible extent:

Recommends that the Economic Organisation of the League of Nations should undertake an objective investigation into the means of establishing close co-operation between Europe and the overseas countries and, in particular, consider in what respect the trade relations between Europe and the said countries might be improved to their mutual advantage.

League of Nations, *Proceedings of the Preliminary Conference with a View to Concerted Economic Action* (Geneva, 1930), p. 71.

proportion of trade took place through clearing agreements. The volume of European and world exports dropped by some 35–40 per cent between 1929 and 1933.

Changes of economic regimes also affected trade policies and foreign trade. In 1917 the Soviet revolution brought in its train the withdrawal of Russia from the network of international trade. In 1909–11 this country had accounted for 6.7 per cent of exports from the developed countries, but in 1928 the figure had dropped to 1.7 per cent (and 1.6 per cent in 1938). The autarkic policies of the Fascist (in Italy) and Nazi (in Germany) regimes had similar consequences, partly hidden by their economic expansion fed by rearmament.

Moreover, as Kindleberger has rightly pointed out,

the international economic and monetary system needs leadership, a country which is prepared, consciously or unconsciously, under some system of rules that it has internalized, to set standards of conduct for other countries; and to seek to get others to follow them, to take on an undue share of the burdens of the system, and in particular to take on its support in adversity by accepting its redundant commodities, maintaining a flow of investment capital and discounting its paper. Britain performed this role in the century to 1913 . . . part of the reason for the length, and most of the explanation for the depth of the world depression, was the inability of the British to continue their role of underwriter to the system and the reluctance of the United States to take it on until 1936.[117]

All this led to a reduction in international and European trade. In 1938 the volume of European exports was about 70 per cent of the level of 1929; and this 1929 level was itself probably only 3–8 per cent higher than that of 1913 (on a world scale, the level in 1938 was probably about 85 per cent of that of 1929).

In the middle of war (on 23 February 1942) an 'agreement on mutual aid' was signed at the instigation of the United States between that country and the United Kingdom. Article VII stipulated that they would adopt measures 'open to participation by all other countries of like mind, directed to the expansion, by appropriate international and domestic measures of production, employment, and the exchange and consumption of goods . . . to the elimination of all forms of discriminatory treatment in international commerce and to the reduction of tariffs and other trade barriers'.[118] And as soon as the war ended, the United States, which had become an economic super-power, even in international trade,[119] played an active part in the setting up of liberal trade policies.

After the failure of attempts to create an organization to liberalize

---

[117] C. P. Kindleberger, *The World in Depression, 1929–1939* (London, 1973), p. 28.

[118] Foreign Office, *British and Foreign State Papers, 1940–1942*, vol. CXLIV (London, 1952), p. 1,044.

[119] The United States' share in world exports rose from 14 per cent in 1938 to 22 per cent in 1948 (it was 13 per cent in 1913).

international trade, gradual liberalization of trade policies developed after 1948 for the advanced Western industrial economies in the framework of the General Agreement on Tariffs and Trade. In Western Europe real trade liberalization began after the 'Kennedy round' of 1962. The new situation created by movements towards economic integration and the spread of centralized economic planning, together with the unprecedented rate of economic growth which marked the three postwar decades (1945–74) make this period a separate and highly specific chapter in European commercial history which lies beyond the scope of the present volume.

VII. Protectionism and the development of institutions for the promotion of foreign trade

The return to protectionism played a significant part in the development and creation of a set of institutions aimed at promoting sales of national products abroad. These were private, public, or semi-public organizations which acted at national or regional level, or at the level of specific industries.

The increase in tariffs was certainly one of the main reasons these organizations sprang up but it was certainly not the only one. Amongst the other important reasons we should mention the increase in the range of products exported. In nearly all European countries involved in the process of industrialization the relative share of textile exports, which had been dominant until the 1870s, was reduced in favour of new products. Whereas in the 1840s manufactured textile goods accounted for some 59–63 per cent of total exports from the industrialized European countries (Belgium, France, Germany, Switzerland, Great Britain), this proportion was about 52–54 per cent in 1860, about 44–46 per cent around 1880, and only about 28 per cent around 1913. In countries like Great Britain and Switzerland, where textiles accounted for more than 70 per cent of total exports in 1840, this proportion dropped to 40 per cent, or even less, just before the First World War.[120]

The geographical diversification of trade was less marked than diversification in products. But it was far from being marginal, especially for the continental European countries, as Great Britain had had a diversified pattern of trade ever since the first half of the nineteenth century. For continental Europe as a whole, exports to non-European countries exceeded 15 per cent of the total in 1880, and reached 22 per cent in 1910. For Germany this proportion rose from 12 per cent to as high as 26 per

---

[120] Calculated from various national sources; the national series are not, however, strictly homogenous.

cent; and the proportion of exports to South America, Africa, Asia, and Oceania rose from 6 per cent to 17 per cent. For Belgium the relative proportion of exports to countries outside Europe (still between 1880 and 1910) increased from 7 per cent to 18 per cent, and for Switzerland from 19 per cent to 25 per cent.[121]

These rapid changes in the geographical patterns of trade in Europe and even more the diversification in the mix of products exported implied changes in the structure of industry and also in commercial organization. For obvious reasons we cannot deal here with alterations in the commercial departments of individual firms. We shall concentrate on institutions at the national level, or on those which were set up by collective organizations. This period saw the foundation and/or the rapid development of four types of institution. First, on the level of governmental organization, commercial attachés and ministries of foreign trade were set up. Secondly, chambers of commerce abroad were established, especially after 1880. International trade fairs were promoted. Finally, commercial museums and similar institutions were created. These four types of institution will be examined below. The very important problem of the organization of foreign trade from the point of view of export and import agents is not touched upon,[122] or the various policies of the different banks with regard to export credits considered, since state intervention in this field did not begin until after the First World War.

A.   COMMERCIAL ATTACHÉS AND MINISTRIES OF COMMERCE

In its first phase, the expansion and diversification of foreign trade simply led to an enlargement of the commercial functions of the consulates and an increase in the functions of the ministries or departments responsible for these problems. Gradually, however, it became necessary to create new frameworks within which these functions could be exercised. It is true that from their beginnings, and all through history, consulates had always had a commercial function but the facts available show that this function developed rapidly in the years 1880–90. In the United Kingdom, for example, commercial attachés began to be appointed to embassies and to legations from 1880. In 1886 embassies received instructions to pay more attention to commercial interests, since British manufacturers had complained that other countries were much more active in this role. In 1896 the Commercial Intelligence Branch of the Board of Trade[123]

---

[121] Bairoch, 'Geographical Structure', pp. 557–608; p. 573.

[122] For an account of the situation in this area at the end of the nineteenth century, see A. J. Wolfe, *Theory and Practice of International Commerce* (New York and London, 1919).

[123] 'Trade Organization', in *Encyclopaedia Britannica*, 13th edn, vol. XXVII, pp. 135–40, especially p. 136.

was created, under pressure from the chambers of commerce. The Board of Trade itself dated from as far back as 1786.

The number of commercial attachés did not increase greatly before the First World War when, according to statistics collected for twelve small European countries, only 21 attachés and commercial agents were in post.[124] But of course this does not mean that the consular staff did not increase their efforts to promote trade.

From 1880–90 ministries and/or departments responsible for foreign trade were set up in a great number of countries. As a general rule, these ministries were also concerned with other affairs – it was only after the First World War that greater specialization took place. In *France*, the Ministry for Commerce and Employment was created in 1881. Between 1869 and 1880 these functions were within the competence of the Ministry of Agriculture; and before that trade and agriculture had both been the responsibility of the Ministry of Public Works.[125] By a ministerial decree of 28 April 1883 a Bureau du Mouvement General et des Expositions was created. But it was not until 1898 (law of 4 March) that the National Office for Foreign Trade[126] was set up, thanks to the concerted efforts of the Paris Chamber of Commerce and the Ministry of Commerce.

In *Belgium* the Ministry of Trade was not established until 1895. Until then, its functions had been the responsibility of the Ministry of Foreign Affairs.[127] But expenditure on political and consular agents had risen from 0.6 million francs per annum at the beginning of the 1860s to 1.3 million in 1880 and to 1.5 million in 1890.[128]

In *The Netherlands* only in 1900 did a government commission draw 'the attention of the Minister for Foreign Trade Affairs to the need to use government organizations in foreign countries to meet the new requirements of foreign trade'.[129] This project was inspired by the English Commercial Intelligence Branch. It did not have much effect until 1907 when an autonomous section was created for trade within the Ministry of Agriculture, Industry and Commerce (set up in 1905). This commercial section included a central information service.

In *Austria–Hungary* the Ministry of Trade was established in 1853 (1867 in Hungary) but it was concerned essentially only with internal trade. In *Italy* a Ministry of Commerce was set up in 1876 and, later on, a

---

[124] A. Jacoby, *Les institutions d'expansion commerciale en tenant compte plus spécialement de la Suisse* (Neuchâtel, 1918), p. 22.

[125] *Annuaire statistique de la France*, vol. XLVII (Paris, 1932), p. 180.

[126] A. Serre, *L'Office National du commerce extérieur. Historique-fonctionnement* (Paris, 1927), pp. 16–17.   [127] 'Trade Organisation', in *Encyclopaedia Britannica*, 13th edn, p. 140.

[128] *Annuaire Statistique de la Belgique, 1885* (Brussels, 1886), pp. 268–9 and *1911* (Brussels, 1912), pp. 282–3.

[129] J. A. Wever, *Les institutions d'expansion commerciale des Pays-Bas* (Paris, 1927), p. 22.

consultative council was associated with it. The terms of reference of the council were not limited to matters of external trade but included industrial issues.

In *Finland*, a Department for Trade and Industry was set up in 1888, before which such activities had been the responsibility of the Ministry of Finance.[130] But it should be remembered that Finland was subordinate to the Russian czars.

Spain, Portugal, Sweden, Norway, and Switzerland were amongst those European countries which did not have a ministry or department for trade before 1914.[131]

Germany could also be included in this list. However, some of the individual German states did have ministries of trade, some of which had existed for a long time. That of Prussia, in particular, dated from 1848 and from 1880 onwards the Minister of Trade was advised by the Council for the National Economy (Volkswirthschaftsrath).

Finally, in the *United States* the Department of Commerce was only created in 1913. Foreign trade had previously been the responsibility of the Department of Commerce and Labour, established in 1888.[132] The *self-governing British colonies*, on the other hand, possessed boards of trade. Before 1914 about half of the independent countries outside Europe had either ministries or departments specially concerned with foreign trade.

B.   CHAMBERS OF COMMERCE ABROAD

Chambers of commerce were fairly long-established institutions (the first was that of Marseilles founded in 1599)[133] but the establishment of chambers of commerce abroad took place essentially in the period covered here. It is significant that in the 1844 edition of McCulloch's *A Dictionary of Commerce and Commercial Navigation* only four lines (in 1,378 pages of 66 lines each) are devoted to the article 'Chamber of Commerce'.

The first chamber of commerce abroad was that set up by Belgium in New York in 1867.[134] In 1870 the Austrian chamber of commerce in

---

[130] *Finland: The Country, its People and Institutions* (Helsinki, 1926), p. 398.

[131] According to an analysis of data presented in *The Statesman Yearbook, 1914* (London, 1914).

[132] 'Government Departments', in *Encyclopaedia Britannica*, 1947 edn, vol. X, pp. 571–9, especially p. 579.

[133] In 1599 an office for trade (*bureau du commerce*) was set up in Marseilles on the initiative of the town. This was made official by royal letter patent in 1600 and 1603. From 1650 this office became completely independent from the town and took the name chamber of commerce. B. Ippolito, *Les chambres de commerce dans l'économie française* (Bordeaux, 1945), p. 7.

[134] In fact we should also mention the chamber of commerce founded in 1868 in Yokohama. But this one included traders of various nations and this links it to similar institutions in countries outside Europe which only allowed the presence of a limited number of foreigners (a type of chamber of commerce which probably dates back to at least the sixteenth century).

Table 12. *Evolution of the numbers of active chambers of commerce abroad, by country of origin*

	1880	1890	1900	1910	1913
France	2	21	27	34	36
Germany	—	—	1	2	3
Italy	—	11	12	18	18
Spain	—	5	5	6	7
United Kingdom	1	2	5	7	8
The Netherlands	1	1	2	9	10
Other European countries	2	4	9	19	20
Europe (total)	6	44	61	95	102

Note:
The figures concern the number of chambers of commerce abroad in activity at the beginning of the date indicated, excluding those created during this year.
Source: Derived from C.G. Drossinis, *Les Chambres de commerce à l'étranger* (Paris, 1921); additional sources, see text.

Constantinople was founded, and in 1872 the British established one in Paris. Two years later the Italians set up their first chamber in Alexandria, and in 1878 the French followed suit with their first overseas chamber of commerce in New Orleans.[135]

During this first phase, these chambers of commerce (apart from the Italian chamber in Alexandria, which remained an isolated example until 1883) were the result of private enterprises. From the middle of the 1880s, however, the state took over, and the main development of these institutions dates from that period. The figures given in Table 12 are possibly too low as a result of the lack of accounts for some chambers which later disappeared, but the underestimate is probably not more than 5–10 per cent.

In Italy in April 1883 the Ministry of Agriculture, Industry and Trade issued a report recommending that the state establish a network of chambers of commerce abroad. This report was in a way the by-product of the work of a commission set up by royal decree (of 29 May 1870) to investigate the most satisfactory ways of encouraging the expansion of industry and trade.[136]

In France, in the same month (April 1883), a commission was set up to study ways of improving commercial representation abroad. It concluded that commercial attachés should be associated with embassies and consulates, a recommendation not followed until 1908. Also in 1883 another commission was set up to deal more specifically with chambers of commerce abroad; and, on 30 June 1884, a circular from the Ministry

[135] C. G. Drossinis, *Les Chambres de commerce a l'etranger* (Paris, 1921) pp. 17, 26, 55, 102–3.
[136] Drossinis, *Les Chambres de commerce à l'étranger*, pp. 101–2.

for Foreign Affairs to diplomatic and consular agents indicated that the measures proposed by the commission had been approved.[137] Because of the rapid development of French chambers of commerce abroad, and because of France's prestige in matters of legislation, France served as a model for a number of countries. This was particularly true for Spain in 1886.

Most other countries, though, left the establishment of these institutions to private enterprise. This was true for Great Britain as well as for Belgium, The Netherlands, and Switzerland – even though these countries were extremely dependent on exports. In such cases few overseas chambers of commerce were established except in the case of The Netherlands, where they developed quite rapidly, especially after 1900 (see Table 12). The three countries where the government played an important part in this field (France, Spain, and Italy) were responsible for 84 per cent of all Europe's chambers in 1890. In 1900 this proportion was about 79 per cent, and it was still 60 per cent in 1913.

Germany was a special case. She had forbidden the establishment of foreign chambers of commerce on her soil, and for a long time remained opposed to the development of German chambers of commerce abroad. Although a German chamber was set up in Brussels in 1894 (as a result of private initiative), numerous bills (put forward especially by the deputy Munch-Ferber) recommending this were rejected. One of the arguments put forward by the government for the rejection of a bill in 1900 was that 'as a result of reciprocity, the German government would find itself obliged to allow foreign chambers of commerce to be established in Germany, and would thus open the door to industrial espionage'.[138] In spite of a certain relaxation which came in 1904 as a result of a law authorizing the setting up of councils (*Beiräte*) under consular control, the government did not alter its position on this until after the war.

As far as the non-European industrialized countries were concerned, the United States did not open their first chamber of commerce abroad until 1894 (in Paris), and Japan opened its first in 1906 in Mukden in China. This delay on the part of the United States should be seen in the general context both of its foreign policy and also the type of products it exported. At this period, even more than today, manufactured goods were not the most important American exports. In 1879–81 manufactured and semi-manufactured articles (excluding foodstuffs) amounted to only 16.2 per cent of exports (in 1889–91 this rose to 21.8 per cent, but in 1909–11 it was already 43.7 per cent).[139]

---

[137] *Ibid.*, pp. 56–9; J. A. Pruniere, *Origines et rôles des chambres de commerce françaises à l'étranger* (pamphlet) (Paris, 1938), pp. 6–7.
[138] Drossinis, *Les Chambres de commerce à l'étranger*, p. 172.
[139] Derived from United States Bureau of the Census, *Historical Statistics of the United States: Colonial Times to 1957* (Washington, DC, 1960), pp. 544–5.

C.   UNIVERSAL OR INTERNATIONAL EXHIBITIONS[140]

The history of international exhibitions may be linked to the fairs of the Middle Ages, to go no further back. However, the essential difference between the fairs and the exhibitions is that at the latter no commercial transactions took place. There is a better case for linking them with national exhibitions. The first national exhibition was, apparently, that held in September 1798 in Paris, although an industrial exhibition had taken place earlier in London in 1756. Similar exhibitions were held in 1806 in Antwerp and in 1808 in Trieste. The process accelerated after 1820. Between 1800 and 1819 there were probably nine or ten national exhibitions; between 1820 and 1829 probably 20–25; between 1831 and 1839, 23–28; and between 1840 and 1849, 45–50.[141] More than 95 per cent of these exhibitions were held in European towns. In a few cases some foreign exhibitors were admitted, but the first really international exhibition was the Great Exhibition held in London in 1851.

This exhibition was explicitly part of the British policy of free trade. It was organized by the Prince Consort, Charles, who emphasized its international character. What was to have been a great national exhibition became the first universal one. Besides this, its scale was quite different from that of its predecessors. Whereas the number of exhibitors at national exhibitions reached a maximum of 4,500 (with an average of about 2,000) and the number of visitors did not exceed 500,000, at the Great Exhibition there were 14,000 exhibitors (some sources say 17,000) and more than 6 million visitors.

International exhibitions took place on a smaller scale in Dublin and in New York in 1853. However, the second truly international exhibition was that held in Paris in 1855 as part of Napoleon's free trade policies. The real expansion took place after 1880. From 1851 to 1879 the number of international exhibitions can be estimated at 12–15; about 25 were mounted between 1880 and 1889, and a further 25 between 1890 and 1898. The movement then slowed down noticeably with only about 10–12 international exhibitions between 1900 and 1913, but that held in Paris (in 1900) had 83,000 exhibitors and received about 50 million visitors – making it the biggest exhibition of the nineteenth century.

This type of exhibition almost disappeared after the First World War.[142] The trend has been, on the one hand, towards specialized, more

---

140   This section is based on the following sources: J. N. H. Huynem, *Trends in Trade Fairs* (Utrecht, 1973); K. W. Luckhurst, *The Story of Exhibitions* (London and New York, 1951); R. Poirier, *Des foires, des peuples, des expositions* (Paris, 1958); M. Tamir, *Les expositions internationales à travers les âges* (Paris, 1939).

141   Calculated from the sources listed in note 140 above (which often vary).

142   The exhibitions that received the most visitors during the inter-war period were those in Chicago in 1933 (39 million) and in New York in 1939–40 (45 million). After the Second World War the exhibition in Brussels in 1958 also had 45 million visitors; New York, 1964–5 (52 million), Montreal, 1967 (50 million), Osaka, 1970 (64 million), Tsukaba, 1985 (20 million).

directly commercial exhibitions and, on the other hand, towards export sample fairs, whose origins can be traced to the famous Leipzig fair. Ever since the 1830s this fair had gradually taken the form of a sample fair and this was made official in 1894. The Leipzig fair was the only fair to continue more or less uninterrupted since it began in the twelfth century.

There is no valid analysis of the effect of the expansion of international exhibitions in the period 1880–1900 on European foreign trade. This can be explained by the methodological difficulties of this type of study. It is certain that in most cases the exhibitions were organized for commercial reasons and they probably had a positive effect on trade, although we should not rule out the possibility that they were counter-productive; the flows of technical information encouraged by such means might have fostered the substitution of local production for imports.

D.   COMMERCIAL MUSEUMS, INFORMATION BUREAUX, AND EXPORT SAMPLE WAREHOUSES

It seems that the first commercial museum was that established in Vienna in 1873. As was to be the case for other museums of its kind, it was created as a direct result of the universal exhibition of Vienna, being at first called the Oriental Museum of Vienna and subsequently becoming the Austrian Museum of Trade in 1886.[143]

These institutions were primarily warehouses displaying samples of various products from different countries so as to allow manufacturers to adapt their products to the tastes and needs of foreign countries. Museums of commerce multiplied both inside and outside Europe, especially in Germany, in the United States, and in Japan. The Commercial Museum of Brussels was founded in 1881 (after the national exhibition) and this served as a model for numerous similar institutions. In addition to its exhibits, it had an information bureau and a library. As a general rule, from the 1880s on, central governments were responsible for the setting up of these museums. The Berlin museum was opened in 1883, and was followed by those of Stuttgart and Leipzig. The Budapest museum was established in 1885.

Just before the First World War there were some twenty commercial museums or similar institutions in Europe. They were distributed among ten countries – but France, Switzerland, and Russia did not have any.[144] In the United States the most important commercial museum (and probably the biggest in the world) was established in Philadelphia in 1894.[145] Apart from Turkey and Japan, no other country outside Europe appears to have had such institutions.

[143] Jacoby, *Les institutions d'expansion commerciale*, p. 90.
[144] From Jacoby, *Les institutions d'expansion commerciale*, pp. 90–2; and the article 'Trade Organisation' in *Encyclopaedia Britannica*, 10th edn.
[145] Fisk and Peirce, *International Commercial Policies*, p. 243.

Gradually these museums turned into what may be called information offices, providing details of the state of foreign markets, and, as such, were either wholly or partly public institutions. From the beginning of the twentieth century nearly all European countries had set up such offices, but in very different forms.

Export sample warehouses differed from commercial museums in that they were exhibitions designed to display the range of local products to potential customers, and were set up either in the home country or in the foreign countries to which it was hoped to increase exports. The first institution of this kind was opened in Stuttgart in 1881, being quickly followed by others elsewhere in Germany (in Berlin in 1897) and by bureaux established in foreign towns, notably in the Middle East.[146] Other European countries followed the German example.

Export sample warehouses should be distinguished from sample fairs. The main differences were the temporary nature of sample fairs, and their more directly commercial function. Besides as we have seen above, these sample fairs were only important between the two world wars.

This section cannot be concluded without stressing that, during the nineteenth century, private enterprise probably played a more important part in promoting foreign trade than all these sponsored institutions. For one thing, foreign trade was probably more the result than a cause of economic expansion. It is also certain that private enterprise – whether that of entrepreneurs or commercial agents – was a decisive element in each country's trade growth. The case of Germany is significant here. As we have seen, at this time Germany did not set up many institutions for promoting foreign trade, but her exports increased rapidly from the 1890s. This increase can be explained by the rapid growth of her home market and also by the dynamism of her commercial agents. As Wolfe noted:

The most casual observer of foreign trade conditions cannot fail to be impressed by the genius of organization, by the thoroughness, and by the adequate manner of meeting existing needs which distinguish the export trade of Germany. There is not a nook in the world without a German importer and trader. And wherever there is a German importer and trader there is also a very accurate knowledge of what the local customer wants and a striking spirit of accommodation in permitting these customers to pay as they can.[147]

---

[146] *Ibid.*, p. 245.
[147] A. J. Wolfe, *Foreign Credits: A Study of the Foreign Credit Problems with a Review of European Methods of Financing Export Shipments* (US Bureau of Foreign and Domestic Commerce, Washington, DC, 1913), p. 12.

VIII. *Colonial trade policies*

Colonization was not a phenomenon exclusive to the nineteenth century nor to Europe, but in the nineteenth century it did reach unprecedented proportions and took a specific form. Both of these characteristics were the direct result of the industrial revolution, which gave Europe the means and the military resources to ensure that it remained politically dominant, with technical progress and a high standard of living sufficient to encourage a dramatic expansion of trade.[148]

A.   FROM 'COLONIAL PACT' TO INDUSTRIAL COLONIZATION

1. *'Colonial pact'*

We shall not attempt to analyse here the different trade policies for the colonies before the nineteenth century. All we can do is pick out the main elements in what is generally known as the colonial pact. This pact can be summarized in simplified ideal terms in the following six rules:

1. Only goods coming from the mother country and, generally speaking, also produced there, to be imported into the colony.
2. Products from the colonies should be exported exclusively to the mother country, from which they could, of course, be re-exported. The mother country usually gave preference to products from her own colonies over those from other colonies, but not to the detriment of home-produced goods.
3. Goods should only be transported between the mother country and her colonies, and between the colonies themselves, in ships bearing the mother country's flag.
4. The production of manufactured goods (and also of certain agricultural products) likely to compete with those from the mother country would be forbidden in the colonies.
5. Immigration of Europeans into the colonies was normally restricted to citizens of the mother country.
6. Trade relations with the colonies were often restricted to companies enjoying a trading monopoly.

[148] This section is based essentially on the following sources (at the beginning of each subsection on individual countries a list of additional sources is given if necessary): various articles in *Encyclopaedia Britannica*, 11th edn (1910); McCulloch, *Dictionary of Commerce and Commercial Navigation* (1844 and 1877 edns); C. D. Newdegate, *A Collection of the Customs Tariffs of all Nations: based upon a Translation of the Work of M. Hübner* (London, 1855); J. W. Root, *Colonial Tariffs* (Liverpool, 1906); US Tariff Commission, *Colonial Tariff Policies* (Washington, DC, 1922) (a comprehensive study for the period 1890–1914); *Statistical Yearbooks* of the various colonial powers; *International Trade Statistics*, various edns, League of Nations (Geneva).

It is true that these rules were not applied with the same rigour by all colonizing countries to all colonies; they also varied during the period. The only rule to which there were hardly any exceptions was the one that summarizes the six listed above; namely, that the interests of the mother country override those of the colonies themselves.

2. Upheaval resulting from industrialization

Between 1770 and 1820 relations between Europe and the rest of the world experienced a complete upheaval. This was the result of two profound changes. First, there was the change in the political climate, as a result of the independence movement which affected almost the whole of America and transformed that continent – the most important European colony – into a set of independent states, one of which was to become the leading economic power in the world by the end of the nineteenth century. The second profound change which was to have important consequences for the rest of the world was technological; and included especially the mechanization of the textile industry and the development of iron industries based on coal. As a result of the mechanization of cotton spinning between 1770 and 1820 the gross productivity of labour was probably multiplied by 100–200 times and the real price of cotton thread dropped to one-fifteenth of previous levels. The consumption of raw cotton in Europe – which had probably been about 5,000 tons around 1770 – rose to 95,000 tons around 1820, and to 860,000 tons around 1870. The freedom from dependence on renewable resources (charcoal) and other technical advances allowed the European iron industry to develop very quickly. In broad terms, in 1770 Europe probably produced only 200,000 tons of pig-iron (of which 5 per cent was produced by coke) out of a world total of about 600,000 tons; in 1820 this had reached 1,000,000 tons (of which 50 per cent was produced by coke) out of a world total of 1,400,000 tons. In 1870 Europe produced 10,500,000 tons (about 95 per cent of which was produced by coke), the United States 1,850,000 tons and the rest of the world 20,000 tons (this last figure being very approximate).

These technological and economic changes allowed Europe both to extend her colonial empire and to modify radically the nature of her trade with the colonies. The expansion of the colonial empire particularly affected the industrialized mother countries, especially Great Britain (see Table 13). The colonial expansion should be measured in terms of numbers of inhabitants rather than of surface area since the possibilities of exploiting a colony depended on population. In 1750 the European colonial empire had about 22 million inhabitants (including about 15 million in North and South America). In 1826 this figure was

Table 13. *Evolution of the importance of colonies, 1826–1913*

Mother country	Area of colonies (in 1,000 km²)			Population of colonies (in millions)		
	1826[a]	1876	1913	1826[a]	1876	1913
United Kingdom	9,000	22,470	32,860	190	250	390
France	100	970	10,590	1	6	60
Netherlands	1,200	2,020	2,020	10	25	50
Portugal	500	600	2,080	2	2	9
Spain	400	430	350	6	8	1
Germany	—	—	2,940	—	—	12
Belgium	—	—	2,360	—	—	7
Italy	—	—	1,530	—	—	2
Europe[b]	11,200	26,500	54,800	210	300	530
United States	—	—	310	—	—	12
Japan	—	—	290	—	—	22
World	11,200	26,500	55,400	210	300	570

Notes:
[a] Effectively colonized, but very approximate data (probable margin of error: area 40 per cent, population 25 per cent).
[b] Excluding Iceland and Arctic possessions of Denmark and Asiatic possessions of Russia.
Sources: 1826 and 1876: derived from A. Supan, *Die territoriale Entwicklung der Europäischen Kolonien* (Gotha, 1906), especially p. 257. But, especially for 1826, some figures derived from map and population figures from other individual sources. For 1876, the figures for Portugal and Denmark have been corrected.
1913: US Tariff Commission, *Colonial Tariff Policies* (Washington, DC, 1922), p. 5.

about 210 million, and in 1913 about 530 million, without counting virtual 'informal' colonies like China, in which case the figure would have been 1,000 million.

From the beginning of the nineteenth century an ever-growing tide of manufactured goods was exported to the colonies in exchange at first for agricultural products, and then, increasingly, raw materials. Between 1800 and 1860 alone the volume of sales of manufactured goods to the colonies increased tenfold, and then again fivefold between 1860 and 1913; in other words the volume increased fifty- to sixty-fold between 1810 and 1913. The periods of most rapid expansion were 1820–60 and 1890–1913.

This very rapid expansion cannot be explained by technological advances alone; it is also necessary to consider the trade policies pursued by each of the European mother countries. The development of these policies will be examined in section VIII C, but it is convenient to look first at a few international measures concerning colonial trade policies.

3. International measures concerning colonial trade policies

One can say that only three series of international agreements had any significant influence on European colonial trade policies in the nineteenth century. These were the Congress of Vienna in 1814–15 (which prohibited the slave trade), the Berlin Conference of 1885 (which partitioned Africa), and the Brussels Conference of 1902 (on the sugar problem).

The provisions of the Congress of Vienna with regard to the slave trade followed a series of similar national measures. As early as 1792 a royal decree in Denmark fixed 1802 as the date on which the slave trade would end in Danish colonies. The British decision, taken in May 1807, to forbid the landing of any slave in a British colony after 1 March 1808 had more important consequences. Again, in January 1808 the United States forbade its subjects to participate in the slave trade and prohibited the landing of slaves in the United States. Sweden abolished slavery in 1813, and The Netherlands in 1814. In November 1814 it was decided at the Congress of Vienna that the slave trade should be abolished as quickly as possible but that the exact dates were to be negotiated with the countries concerned. In March 1818 slavery was finally abolished in the French colonies (slavery and the trade in slaves had been abolished and reintroduced several times between 1791 and 1815). Spain followed France in 1820. Portugal reacted more slowly and less wholeheartedly: not until February 1830 was the slave trade banned definitively and the import of slaves into Portuguese colonies was prohibited only in 1836. The Asburton treaty of 1842 whereby Great Britain, France, and the United States joined forces to keep a flotilla off the west coast of Africa dealt a crippling blow to the illegal European traffic in slaves (although this trade did not cease entirely).

The numerous international meetings concerned with the 'scramble' for Africa resulted in a series of resolutions which affected trade policy. The most important of these resulted from the Berlin Conference. Four of the six provisions of the declaration adopted by the conference (signed 26 February 1885) dealt with trade policies. The most important aspect was the 'Declaration concerning the freedom of trade in the Congo basin, its delta and the surrounding countries', which prohibited any differential treatment of goods or ships. Article 1 of this declaration was quite explicit, beginning, 'The trade of all nations shall enjoy complete freedom.' Two provisions dealt with free navigation on the Congo and Niger (with their tributaries) and another concerned the banning of the slave trade. In 1890 this treaty was modified to allow *ad valorem* duties of 10 per cent to be applied, with higher import duties on alcohol (and from 1910 on arms).

The Brussels Conference of 1902 was the outcome of a very long process of negotiation, begun in 1862, to try to solve the problem of sugar production and trade. The history of this agreement has already been examined briefly at the beginning of section VI, since during the nineteenth century sugar had, thanks to beet, gradually become a European product. As far as colonial trade policies were concerned, the conference of 1898 and the Brussels agreement of 1902 led to a whole series of adjustments in the various policies dealing with colonial sugar. At first (until 1898–1902) these measures, taken together, did something to halt the decline in the relative importance of cane sugar in the total production of sugar. In a second phase (from 1898–1902 onwards) they led to a reversal in growth rates; the production of cane sugar rose faster than that of beet sugar in this period.[149] This reversal was accompanied by a rise in prices (see section VI).

Altogether though, international measures had little effect on colonial trade policies in the nineteenth century. But more important is the fact that the trade policies of the individual countries developed in quite different ways. For this reason we now move on to the analysis of individual cases.

B. BRITISH COLONIAL TRADE POLICY[150]

The state of traditional British trade policy towards the colonies is summed up well by Holland:

The old 'colonial system' was based on the idea of a self-contained and self-dependent Empire, governed from London and regarded as an extension of Great Britain treated as much as possible as a single State, subject to such modifications as were made necessary by distance, varying circumstances, and varying needs of revenue for local purposes. This empire was to supply, as much as possible, all its own needs, the overseas dominions feeding the mother country with raw material and food products and the mother country supplying these dominions with manufactured goods. The Empire was to have its own commercial marine and it was to exclude from its intra-imperial trade all ships of the other Powers. That marine was supplied by Great Britain, and, if this monopoly were disadvantageous to the Colonies, it was considered that they received ample compensation in being freed from the whole burden of naval and military defence, which was borne by the British taxpayer.[151]

---

[149] From Food and Agriculture Organisation, *The World Sugar Economy in Figures, 1880–1959* (Rome, no date), pp. 21–2.

[150] In addition to the titles listed at the beginning of this section the following sources were used for Great Britain: Brown, *The Tariff Reform Movement in Great Britain*; B. Holland, *The Fall of Protection 1840–1850* (London, 1913); R. M. Martin, *History of the Colonies of the British Empire* (London, 1843); E. Porritt, *The Fiscal and Diplomatic Freedom of the British Overseas Dominions* (Oxford, 1922); R. L. Schuyler, *The Fall of the Old Colonial System: A Study in British Free Trade, 1770–1870* (New York, 1945); Smart, *Economic Annals of the Nineteenth Century*; J. B. Williams, *British Commerial Policy and Trade Expansion, 1750–1850* (Oxford, 1972).

[151] Holland, *The Fall of Protection*, pp. 53–4.

The loss of the American colonies proved to be very important in the history of British trade policy, especially in regard to the colonies of European settlement. It is true that one cannot talk of a sudden change in trade policy after 1776. Much more important were the longer-term effects this had on the autonomy of the white colonies.

The independence of the United States can, in fact, be attributed directly to trade policies and a tax system that were prejudicial to the interests of the white settlers. This fact largely explains the relative commercial independence granted fairly early on to what were to become the 'self-governing colonies' in the nineteenth century. This independence finds its origin in the 'Declaration Act' of 1778, passed in the middle of war, which provided for local administrations to be established in the North American colonies, and also for an independent financial system. By extension, this law was also taken later to apply to Australia and New Zealand.

Major changes in British colonial trade policy in the nineteenth century began in 1813, with the abolition of the East India Company's trade monopoly with Europe. (Its monopoly on trade between India and China survived until 1833.) The war in the United States (18 June 1812–24 December 1814) had led to a scarcity of raw cotton which had in turn led to increased pressure from the cotton manufacturers to abolish the East India Company's monopoly – which in practice meant that the Indian market was closed to British cotton manufacturers. It is true that already in 1700 the manufacturers had succeeded in banning imports of Indian cotton goods into England; but between 1769 and 1813 the English cotton industry had become mechanized. This led to an enormous increase in productivity in this sector, which was in turn induced after a complete reversal in the structure of trade: India was forced to switch from exporting manufactured goods (about 70 per cent of her sales) to importing English cotton goods in exchange for raw cotton and other agricultural products. As pointed out, this marked the real beginning of this new type of commercial relations between Europe, which was industrializing, and the rest of the world, especially the colonies, which were, as a result of this, to de-industrialize. Already in 1830 the Empire took 23 per cent of all British textile exports, and 30 per cent of iron manufactured goods.

The history of British colonial trade policy between 1813 and 1914 can be divided into two main phases. The first, which lasted until 1846–9, was characterized by a reciprocal preferential system, and a shipping monopoly. In 1846 the preferential tariff for colonial products in the United Kingdom was abolished; and on 13 August in the same year a law was voted allowing the colonies to abolish surtaxes on foreign goods. This law was gradually put into effect. Finally, the act of 26 June 1849 repealed the ancient Navigation Acts. The second phase lasted from 1846 to 1916, when a new preferential system was introduced. In 1898, though, Canada led the return to a preferential system based on unilateral concessions, by introducing a preferential tariff of 25 per cent for British goods (see section VIII C).

1. *The preferential system, 1813–46*

Although the really important changes did not take place until 1846, a noticeable liberalization of the system took place between 1822 and 1825. In 1822 the colonies were allowed to trade directly with countries other than the United Kingdom, and the Navigation Laws were made a little less strict. In 1823 the rules governing the colonial navigation system were further relaxed, notably by means of reciprocity treaties. Finally, in 1825 most of the prohibitive import duties on non-British manufactured goods were reduced; import duties on woollen manufactured goods, for example, dropped from 50 to 15 per cent; on glass from 80 to 20 per cent; on foreign iron from £6 10s. to £1 10s. per ton. The maximum tariff for foreign manufactured articles was fixed at 30 per cent.

British products, however, did not pass into the colonies entirely freely. To raise revenue, low import duties had been introduced in most colonies. These varied from one colony to another. In India, for example, by the tariff law of May 1836, import duties on cotton manufactured goods were 3.5 per cent for British products imported on British ships and 7.0 per cent for those imported on foreign ships, whereas for foreign products these duties were 7.0 and 14.0 per cent respectively, depending on the nationality of the ship. As a general rule, the preference for British products was 50 per cent of the duties applied to foreign products. In spite of the relatively low level of duties imposed on foreign products, the United Kingdom in fact monopolized the colonial market for manufactured goods. This monopoly was the result of a combination of the preferential system and the effects of British technical superiority. We must also take into account here, as in every colonial situation, the effects of 'indirect preference', which resulted from colonization itself. In the years 1833–5, only 0.02 per cent of goods imported into India came from continental European countries (and 0.01 per cent from North and South America); 47.5 per cent came from Great Britain and the rest from other British colonies and neighbouring regions.[152]

In return for the preferences which British goods enjoyed in the colonies, a certain number of products from the colonies received preferential treatment in Great Britain. In this context we should first of

[152] Martin, *History of the Colonies of the British Empire*, pp. 348–50.

all mention grain. For example, between 15 July 1828 and 28 August 1842 import duties on wheat from the colonies were 6d. per quarter when the price on the home market was higher than 67s. and 5s. per quarter if the price was below this level. For foreign wheat duties were from 1 to 18s. when the domestic price was above 67s., and 20 to 38s. when it was lower. The extent of the preference should, however, be seen in the context of the difference in transport costs, which at this period were very high. Amongst the numerous other products benefiting from a significant preference should be mentioned sugar. In the 1844 tariff, import duties on raw sugar were £3 5s. per cwt. (50.8 kg) for foreign sugar, and £1 6s. 8d. for sugar from the colonies (or about 10 and 3 per cent of the value).

2. The free trade period

Before we look at the fundamental changes which took place in 1846 and 1849 the reforms of 1842 deserve mention. On the one hand, in spite of the trend towards free trade, the preferential system for products from the colonies was retained (out of 825 items, 375 were subject to preferences).[153] On the other hand, the general level of duties on imports of British and foreign goods into the colonies was lowered, and a series of high duties on foreign products which were not in competition with British products was abolished.

The gradual abolition of the preferential system from 1846 onwards and the repeal of the Navigation Acts in 1849 imply an open-door policy in the British colonies. But from this date the differences in trade policy between the so-called Crown colonies and the self-governing colonies (Canada, Australia, New Zealand) became much more important. Most of these self-governing colonies did not follow the British road to liberalism and adopted relatively protectionist trade policies. Indeed, these countries should be considered as independent as far as trade policies are concerned. For this reason their commercial policy will be dealt with in section x. Here we concentrate on real colonial trade policies and the system of colonial preference.

The tariffs set up in the British colonies at the end of the 1840s were

---

[153] But the important changes should be noted in the case of one of the two colonial products, timber and sugar, which played an important role at the beginning of the nineteenth century. From the time of the Napoleonic wars, in order to make the import of Canadian timber possible, its cost of transport being about three times that of timber from traditional sources (the Baltic), extremely preferential tariffs were established in 1809: free for the colonies and 65 shillings a load (40 cubic feet of logs, or 50 cubic feet of planks) for foreign timber. In 1821 the preference was reduced to 45 shillings (55 shillings for foreign timber and 10 shillings for colonial timber). In 1842 this preference was fixed at 29 shillings (30 and 1), and in 1843 at 24 (25 and 1).

very low, but not uniform. The average *ad valorem* duties on manufactured articles varied between 2 and 6 per cent: as a rule they were 3 per cent for semi-finished manufactured articles and 6 per cent for finished products. In a great many cases, the surtax on foreign products was retained until the end of the 1850s. This was true for India in particular – preferential duties were not abolished there until 1859.

Even if occasionally, for financial reasons, import duties on manufactured goods were increased, the pressure from British manufacturers was strong enough to reverse this quickly. The most significant case is that of import duties on cotton goods in India. Under pressure from British manufacturers import duties on these goods had been abolished in 1882. In December 1894, for financial reasons, the Indian government decided to reintroduce import duties of 5 per cent, but pressure from these same manufacturers led to the introduction of a compensatory 5 per cent tax on textiles produced in Indian mills.

The gradual abandoning of the system of imperial preference proved the most difficult in the case of sugar. In 1846 the preference was still very high; with import prices 33 shillings per cwt. at the time, duties per cwt. were: 14 shillings for colonial sugar, 23 shillings for that from other countries, with 63 shillings for sugar produced by slaves. It was not until 1854 that the preferential system for the colonies disappeared altogether, but import duties remained relatively high: 10 shillings.

3. *The movement towards a new unilateral system of imperial preference*

This trend can be said to have become obvious at the end of the 1870s, both in the colonies and in Great Britain. In Britain it was part of a general movement towards a change in trade policy, of which the most important aspect at the beginning of the 1880s was the Fair Trade League (see section VI BI). In 1884 the Imperial Federation League was created. This remained active until 1893. The United Empire Trade League, set up in February 1891 (and revived in 1894 under the name of the British Empire League), was more important, but this was more a movement in support of the preferential system, as sought by the colonies.

In the self-governing colonies the first important sign of support for a preferential system was the informal offer of reciprocal preference made to the British government by the Canadian Prime Minister, John Mac-Donald, in 1879. In the second half of the 1880s branches of the Imperial Federation League were formed in several colonies. At this period the problem of imperial preference was linked to that of expenditure on imperial defence, the whole cost of which was borne by Great Britain alone. From this came the idea of a political federation. This problem of imperial defence[154] was one of the two subjects (together with that of promoting trade) discussed at what may be retrospectively called the 'first' colonial conference, which met in London from 4 April 1887, and which marked the end of what Porritt calls 'the second half of the era of indifference' of Great Britain with regard to her self-governing colonies.[155]

However, this first colonial conference, which already made clear the self-governing colonies' desire for a preferential system, did not result in any concrete achievements. The second colonial conference met in Ottawa from 22 June to 10 July 1894, at the suggestion of the Canadian government who were disappointed by the British lack of progress towards establishing a preferential system for the Empire. The suggestions put forward by the colonies with a view to such a system were rejected by Great Britain. The third colonial conference, held in London in 1897 (on the occasion of the fiftieth anniversary of Queen Victoria's accession), did not make any real progress either.

Because of the virtually non-existent import duties in Great Britain and the rise of protectionism in the self-governing colonies (see section x), practical measures towards establishing a new preferential system came from these colonies. The first concrete step was taken in 1898 by Canada.[156] From 1 August of that year, British goods and those from certain colonies benefited from a preference of 25 per cent. In 1900 this preference was increased to 33.3 per cent. These steps had an important influence on the debates at the fourth colonial conference, which met in London from 30 June to 11 August 1902. Politically it was a failure, since the proposal to create a Council for the Empire was ignored, and Chamberlain's request for a contribution from the colonies towards the defence of the Empire was rejected. However, as far as trade was concerned, the idea of a preferential system made progress. Canada, the prime mover, even offered to increase her import duties in order to reinforce the effect of the preference for British goods. The final resolution, though, recognized that 'in the present circumstances of the Colonies, it is not practicable to adopt a general system of Free Trade as between the Mother Country and the British Dominions beyond the

---

[154] This was a problem that greatly preoccupied contemporaries. The expenses for the maintenance of armed forces in the colonies represented about £4 million in 1858–60, of which about 10 per cent was paid by the colonies. (£3.5 million was about 6 per cent of total British government expenditure at the time.) From 1863–4 till 1871 more and more of these troops in the self-governing colonies were sent home and the military contribution of the self-governing colonies was increased.

[155] This is the title of the last part of Porritt's book, *Fiscal and Diplomatic Freedom*.

[156] Note, however, that a few very marginal preferences had been included in the Canadian tariff of 1870. The tariff of 22 April 1897 provided for preference of 12.5 per cent for British goods. Previously, though, Great Britain had had to give her approval.

Seas', but the first article declared, 'That this conference recognises that the principle of preferential trade between the United Kingdom and His Majesty's Dominions beyond the Seas would stimulate and facilitate mutual commercial intercourse, and would, by promoting the development of the resources and industries of the several parts, strengthen the Empire.'[157]

In Great Britain the failure of Chamberlain's crusade and of the Tariff Reform League (see section VI B) delayed the establishment of a preferential policy for the Empire until the First World War.

A fifth colonial conference was held in 1907. Of course, the victory of the free traders in the 1905 elections reduced the effect of the pressure from the colonies, and in response to British pressure, the question of imperial preferences was not even raised at the next conference of 1911. Only as a result of the economic exigencies of the First World War was it decided in 1916, and especially at the Imperial Conference in 1917, to establish a system of imperial preferences after the war. It should, however, be noted that under the influence of Chamberlain (who was Colonial Secretary from 1895 to 1903) some preferential measures had been introduced in certain Crown colonies, especially from 1903 onwards. These were not very important, and did not last long, except in the case of South Africa which in 1903 granted a preference of 25 per cent on British products, increased in 1906 in spite of growing opposition. Meanwhile, the movement towards a unilateral preferential system, which had begun in Canada, spread to the other self-governing colonies. New Zealand was the first to follow the Canadian example, in 1903. Her preferential system was established by means of two measures. On the one hand, as far as manufactured articles were concerned, import duties were reduced by 50 per cent on a wide range of articles coming from the United Kingdom. On the other hand, machinery which had previously entered freely, was taxed at 20 per cent if it came from outside the British Empire.

Australia joined the movement in 1907. Her preferential system was provisionally fixed to come into force on 9 August 1907, but in fact this did not happen until the tariff revision of 1908, when the general level of import duties was doubled. But it allowed a high proportion of British goods (about 68 per cent) to be subject to *ad valorem* duties 5 points lower than those levied on goods from other countries, which amounted to a preference of about 20 per cent. All the same, the level of import duties on British products was higher under the 1907 tariff than the general level in 1902. In 1911 new products were added to the list of goods entitled to preferential duties.

[157] Amery, *Joseph Chamberlain*, vol. I, p. 54.

C. OTHER COUNTRIES' COLONIAL TRADE POLICIES

1. *French colonial trade policy* [158]

After the revolt of Haiti (1792), and the cession of Louisiana to the United States in 1803 and of Mauritius to the British in 1814, the French colonial Empire in the period 1815–30 was limited essentially to the islands of Martinique, Guadeloupe, and Réunion. From 1830 Algeria was added, and this increased the French colonial Empire from less than 100,000 km^2 and fewer than 1 million inhabitants (in 1825) to some 600,000 km^2 and 4 million inhabitants. In the 1880s there was a new phase of colonization which resulted in the acquisition of Indochina, the black African territories, Tunisia and Morocco. This meant that in 1913 the French colonial Empire had some 60 million inhabitants spread over an area of 10,950,000 km^2.

French colonial trade policy between 1815 and 1914 falls into three quite different periods. The first, from 1815 to 1860, was marked by a return to the traditional colonial pact. The second period, which ended around 1884, saw the virtual abolition of this policy, with the colonies being now regarded as an extension of France. After 1884 there was a return to a new form of the colonial pact which was more subtle both in its principles and in its geographical application.

The colonial pact had already been substantially modified during the period of the revolution. The decree of 11 September 1793, which had abolished internal customs in France, also abolished all customs duties between the colonies and France, and in particular allowed the Assemblies in the colonies to fix local tariffs. At the same time, however, the Navigation Act of 21 September 1793, which restricted coastal trade to French ships, also applied to traffic between France and the colonies. With the return of the monarchy in 1815 came a virtual return to the colonial pact, with a few attenuations: in particular, a decree of 5 February 1826 allowed non-French goods to be imported into the Antilles, and the law of 12 July 1837 allowed the establishment of free warehouses in the Antilles and in Réunion.

The customs and navigation regulations affecting other colonies did not apply to Algeria. Until 1835 Algeria was considered a foreign country as far as trade was concerned. The main principles of the system established by the decree of 11 November 1835 were to remain in force until 1867. These were as follows: French goods were to be allowed free entry into Algeria, but partial exemptions only and only for certain

---

[158] In addition to titles cited at the beginning of this section, the following sources were used for France; Arnauné, *Le commerce extérieur*, A. Girault, *The Colonial Tariff Policy of France* (Washington, DC, 1916); B. Nogaro and M. Moye, *Le régime douanier de la France* (Paris, 1931).

Algerian goods into France, however those goods were freed from duties completely by 1851 (law of 11 January); a special tariff was to be drawn up for Algeria, and foreign ships were to be allowed to trade in Algerian ports on payment of a surtax. As a general rule, Algeria's tariff was more liberal than that of France: in particular, there were no prohibitions on specific manufactured goods.

As far as the other colonies were concerned, the law of 17 December 1814 reintroduced a preferential system for goods from the French colonies on the French market. This law applied essentially to sugar. But the law of 2 July 1843 put sugar from the colonies on the same footing as beet sugar produced locally.

The beginning of the 1860s was a turning-point in French colonial trade policy. By the law of 3 July 1861 the colonial pact was in practical terms abolished: the principal colonies (but not Algeria) became subject to French commercial law, and were considered as part of France. This implied, on the one hand, that foreign goods would be allowed entry on payment of the same duties as were in force in France, and on the other, that French products would continue to pass freely into the colonies. In return products from the colonies (but not all products) were allowed free entry into France. In 1869 (law of 9 July) all discriminatory measures against foreign ships were abolished, although these had already been greatly reduced in 1861 and in 1866.

For Algeria, the important date is that of the law of 17 July 1867 which introduced the free passage of goods with France. Until the law of 19 December 1884, however, Algeria retained her own customs tariff which remained on the whole slightly more liberal than the French tariff.

After 1884 and more clearly from 1892 onwards, there was a return to a form of colonial pact. By the law of 29 December 1884 Algeria was virtually assimilated into France as far as trade was concerned. The law of 2 April 1889, which did not come into force until 1893 because of existing treaties, reserved transport between France and Algeria for French ships alone in a trade which was more important than that between France and all the rest of her colonies. This remained the case until the early 1900s.

After the law of 11 January 1892 the system known as 'assimilation' was extended to cover an important part of the French colonial Empire. This meant that these colonies became subject to French commercial law. But not all colonies were included in this system, and even in the so-called assimilated colonies there were some tariff peculiarities. Although all French products could pass freely into the colonies, the reverse was not the case (except for Algeria). Most products from the colonies benefited from a preference of about 50 per cent, rather than being imported freely.

The main assimilated colonies were the Antilles, Réunion, Indochina, and Gabon. Algeria can be added and, from 1897, Madagascar. The main non-assimilated colonies were those in Africa (except Gabon), Tahiti, and the protectorates of Tunisia and Morocco.

Each non-assimilated colony thus operated a preferential tariff for French products (except in certain Black African colonies where, as a result of the Berlin agreements, a free trade policy was in force) and benefited from the application of the minimum tariff when their goods were imported into France. In the case of Tunisia, however, the general tariff of 1890 applied in principle to both foreign and French goods, but the decree of 2 May 1898 granted free entry to a large number of French products (nearly all manufactured goods and a large number of agricultural goods).

French colonial trade policy was hardly modified either by the law of 29 March 1910, or by that of 5 August 1913. Because of the political status of Morocco the tariff system in force there before 1914 did not grant any preference to French goods, which were liable to low *ad valorem* duties (either 5 or 10 per cent, plus a tax of 2.5 per cent).

2. Dutch colonial trade policy

We are essentially concerned here with Dutch policy with regard to what in the second half of the twentieth century became Indonesia (or Dutch East Indies) – the two main parts of which were known in the nineteenth century as Java and Sumatra. Dutch colonial trade policy was liberal to start with, and became increasingly so, with the law of 1858 and the tariffs of 1865 and 1872.

The tariffs set up after the Dutch return to power (1814 in Sumatra, 1816 in Java) provided for import duties of 12 per cent for foreign products and 6 per cent for those from the mother country. In 1819 the preferential system was strengthened, since Dutch goods imported in Dutch ships were allowed free entry into the Dutch East Indies. Between 1819 and 1858 the tariff system was modified several times, sometimes increased, sometimes reduced, but it always remained fairly liberal.

In 1858 a decree reduced the shipping monopoly by opening sixteen ports to general trade. But this did not abolish the preferential treatment for goods imported in Dutch ships. The tariff which was in force until the revision of 1862 only provided for some of the goods imported in Dutch ships to benefit from a preference. Cotton and woollen articles, in particular, were only liable to duties of 12.8 per cent when imported in Dutch ships, instead of 25 per cent in other cases (rising to 50 per cent for goods coming from countries with which The Netherlands did not have reciprocity treaties). A similar type of preference was in force for certain wines and spirits. On the whole, import duties were 6 per cent for machinery and equipment, 12 per cent for semi-manufactured articles, and 24 per cent for finished products. Export duties varied between 4 and 12 per cent (with a very high proportion at 4 per cent); these duties were reduced by half for all goods exported in Dutch ships.

Most of the duties in the 1862 tariff were *ad valorem*. For manufactured goods these were between 6 and 20 per cent, most goods being liable to either 6 or 10 per cent. In the few cases where Dutch products benefited from a preference, this was worth four points (in other words, 6 per cent instead of 10 per cent, for example).

However, the major step towards liberalization came in 1872. The new tariff which came into force on 1 January 1872 completely abolished the limited advantages granted to products from The Netherlands under the 1862 tariff. Import duties remained essentially *ad valorem*. For textiles (semi-manufactured and manufactured) these were 6 per cent, and for other manufactured goods either 6 or 10 per cent. The range of products allowed to enter freely included, in particular, rice, all machinery and equipment, all crude or semi-manufactured metals, and all materials for building and for shipbuilding. Specific duties, intended to raise revenue, affected wines, spirits, tobacco, opium, candles, and matches (this last product bringing in substantial sums).

The tariff system set up in 1872 underwent numerous modifications, but only in matter of detail. We should note, however, the new tariff promulgated in 1886 and that of 1895 which was concerned with the east coast of Sumatra, which had always benefited from a special tariff system as a result of its more important relations with the British colonies known as the Straits Settlements (Singapore, Malacca, and Penang). For example, duties which were 6 per cent in the rest of the East Indies were reduced in this case to 4 per cent and those of 10 per cent became 6 per cent.

Export duties disappeared only gradually (and not completely) after the end of the nineteenth century. Those on sugar, which had already been suspended on several occasions, were abolished in 1898, and those on coffee and indigo at the end of 1901. The basic reason for this was the downward trend of price.

3. *Portuguese colonial trade policies*

After the definitive loss of Brazil in 1822 (which as a result of British pressure had been opened up to international trade from 1808) the Portuguese colonial Empire remained very limited until the 1880s. From then on, Portugal acquired a new colonial Empire by extending her old African territories towards the interior of the continent. In 1913 this new Empire had a surface area of 2.1 million km², or about 22 times that of

Portugal itself, but a population of 9 million only, compared with 6 million for the mother country.

From 1809 the colonial pact system was relaxed in the sense that from that date all raw materials from the colonies could enter Portugal freely. But the other terms of the colonial pact were retained. From 1837 the import into her African colonies of foreign goods likely to compete with Portuguese products was allowed, on condition that this trade was carried on in Portuguese ships.

In 1844 and again in 1853 a fairly large number of colonial ports (about 30) were opened to foreign ships. But at the same time a preferential system was established through the tariff of 12 December 1852. In general, Portuguese products were liable to only one-tenth of the duties that applied to other countries, which were about 10 to 30 per cent for manufactured goods. The preference was even higher for certain Portuguese products.[159] The only exception concerned the import of machinery which was exempt from duty, in the case of both Portuguese and foreign products. Another exception was Guinea, which (because of her small size and situation) had a very liberal tariff throughout the nineteenth century (about 10 per cent *ad valorem*) and enjoyed no preferential duties until the decree of 21 April 1897, which increased duties on wine and set up a preferential system for this product. The preference granted to products from the colonies in Portugal was not so great: as a rule they paid one-fifth of the usual rates. This preference was gradually reduced, especially in 1861, 1870 and 1889.

This preferential system was also in force at the end of the nineteenth century when the African colonies became more important. In Mozambique (divided into three customs areas) the preferences for Portuguese goods, which were 50 per cent from 1877 to 1892, were increased by the tariff of 1892. But as a result of British pressure (especially during the negotiations in 1882–4) the general level of duties on both imports and exports was fixed at a very low level – about 5 per cent. The regime in force in Angola was more protectionist and more restrictive, with the exception of a free trade zone which, as a result of the treaty of Berlin, was to be found in the little enclave of Caminda (in the interior of the Congo). According to the tariff of 1892, Portuguese products paid only 10 per cent of the duties applied to other countries (and on the list of 24 products exempt from duty, eleven were exempt only if they came from Portugal). Duties were in theory about 6–10 per cent for most manufactured goods, but the majority operated as specific duties, which in many cases implied a higher degree of protection.

---

[159] In the African colonies, for example, leaf tobacco from Portugal was taxed at 25 *reis* per kilo, whereas foreign tobacco was liable to 1,800 *reis*.

4. *Spanish colonial trade policy*

Spanish colonial trade policy had already become a little less rigid during the eighteenth century. In 1774, in particular, several colonies in America regained the freedom to trade with other countries, but restrictions on the manufacture of goods liable to compete with those from the mother country remained in force.

The independence movement in Latin America considerably reduced the importance of the Spanish colonial Empire. Around 1820 this Empire consisted of only Cuba, Puerto Rico, the Philippines, the Canary Islands, and a few other very minor colonies. In 1898–1900 the three main colonies came under American rule; but at about the same period the Spanish Empire in Africa was expanding. To the islands of Fernando Po and Annobon, which had belonged to Spain since 1778, was added in 1885 the Rio de Oro region, and in 1900 part of Morocco. From the middle of the nineteenth century (1842) Spanish influence spread gradually from the island of Fernando Po to the Guinea coast.

As a general rule, Spanish colonial trade policy in the nineteenth century established preferential systems both for Spanish goods and for Spanish ships. All the same, the structure of import duties and the extent of preferences were not identical in the three main colonies left over from the vast Spanish Empire (Cuba, Philippines, and Puerto Rico).

In Cuba, the 1848 tariff (which remained in force until 1 July 1868) granted free entry to nearly all goods coming from Spain, apart from those imported in foreign ships, which were liable to *ad valorem* duties of between 17.3 and 21.5 per cent. Foreign goods were liable to the following *ad valorem* duties: 24.5 to 30.3 per cent for goods imported in foreign ships; 17.3 to 21.5 per cent for those imported in Spanish ships and taken on board in foreign ports; and 13.3 to 16.8 per cent for those taken on board in Spanish ports. On the other hand, machinery for making sugar was imported freely. Export duties varied as a rule from 2.5 to 6.5 per cent, according to the nationality of the ships and the ports of destination.

The Cuban tariff was revised three times before the loss of this colony; in 1868, 1879, and 1892. In the 1879 tariff, which was similar to that in force in the Philippines, import duties on foreign goods transported in foreign ships were on average four times as high as those affecting Spanish goods transported in Spanish ships.

In the Philippines, under the tariff of 14 December 1837, which remained in force until 1891, Spanish goods were liable to import duties, though these were low. For nearly all manufactured goods the *ad valorem* duties were as follows: 3 per cent for Spanish goods if imported in

Spanish ships, otherwise 8 per cent; 7 per cent for foreign goods if imported in Spanish ships, otherwise 14 per cent.[160] These import duties were higher on wines and spirits, ranging from 3 to 10 per cent for Spanish goods imported in Spanish ships to 14 to 60 per cent for foreign goods transported in foreign ships. Export duties were very low, and there was little or no differentiation according to nationality.

In Puerto Rico, Spanish goods transported in Spanish ships were liable to only one-quarter of the import duties imposed on foreign goods. Foreign manufactured goods were liable to import duties of about 14 to 20 per cent, depending on the nationality of the ship. For foodstuffs these duties were about 24–26 per cent. Export duties were from 1 to 3 per cent for goods carried by Spanish ships and from 2 to 5 per cent for those carried by other ships.

The customs system set up in the African colonies was broadly similar to that of the other colonies. In Guinea, for example, the 1893 tariff granted free entry to most Spanish goods brought in Spanish ships, whereas foreign goods and goods transported in foreign ships were liable to duties. In the case of textiles, for example, there were no import duties on Spanish goods transported in Spanish ships; foreign textiles transported in Spanish ships and Spanish textiles transported in foreign ships were liable to duties of 12 per cent; and foreign textiles transported in foreign ships were liable to duties of 15 per cent.[161] In addition to the preference granted to goods from the colonies exported in Spanish ships, exports from the colonies to Spain benefited from a significant preference. In most cases (apart from local taxes) these goods entered freely.

5. Belgian colonial trade policy

Although Belgium's colonial Empire was restricted to the Congo, we should not forget that this was a territory of about 2.4 million km² (or 78 times the size of Belgium) with a population (in 1913) of about 15 million (or twice that of Belgium). Between 1885 and October 1908, when the Congo was virtually a personal colony of the king of the Belgians, the application of the treaty of Berlin placed all countries on an equal footing. This did not prevent Belgium from gaining a *de facto* dominant position, since from 1896 to 1900 69.5 per cent of all imports came from Belgium, and 89.4 per cent of exports were sent to that country (for cocoa, coffee, and rubber this level reached 100 per cent). Although in

[160] Let us note that for *cambajas* (coloured cloth used by the native population) duties were 3 and 20 per cent and 8 and 30 per cent respectively.

[161] For alcohol other than wine import duties were 20–75 and 100 per cent respectively.

theory there was complete free trade, in fact certain administrative restrictions favoured Belgian traders and businesses so that in practice Belgium had a *de facto* monopoly of trade and transport.

When the Belgian government took over the colony they took on the obligations of the different international treaties. The customs system set up was designed to provide revenue, and differential duties were low – 10 per cent at the most for imports and even less for exports. Monopolies were gradually abolished between 1910 and 1912, but Belgium remained predominant until the war; in 1912, 66 per cent of imports into the Congo came from Belgium. Goods from the Congo did not receive preferential treatment in Belgium. Even so, 50 per cent of exports from the Congo were sent to Belgium in 1912. It was only after the war that this trade diversified geographically, but not drastically. By 1926, only 51 per cent of the Congo's imports came from Belgium, and only 45 per cent of the Congo's exports were sent to Belgium.

6. German colonial trade policy

We should remember that Germany was late developing a colonial Empire and that it was relatively small and short-lived. German colonization is traditionally held to have begun on 24 April 1884, which was the date of Bismarck's official announcement that part of South West Africa had come under German control. Just before the First World War, Germany's colonial Empire had the fifth or sixth highest population and was the third largest on the African continent, but it only amounted to 3–4 per cent of all colonized territories (see Table 13) and to 2 per cent of Germany's population. Germany lost all her colonies under the treaty of Versailles.

Germany's colonial trade policy contrasted with her national policy: the open-door principle was maintained throughout the period. It seems that the different tariffs set up did not even contain concealed preferences for German goods. Moreover, goods from the German colonies did not enjoy any preferential treatment in the mother country. As far as this was concerned, Germany's policy was thus close to that of the free trade countries such as Great Britain and The Netherlands. In addition to political reasons, it is easy to believe that this liberalism resulted from the fact that the German colonies represented only a limited market for German goods, whereas the colonies belonging to the other powers were important outlets. In 1913 German exports to British India and the Dutch East Indies alone accounted for 2.5 per cent of all German exports, while those to the German colonies accounted for only 0.5 per cent of this total.

7. Italian colonial trade policy

Italy was very late in acquiring a colonial Empire. Eritrea only really became an Italian colony from 1882 onwards. Although four ports in Somalia were leased to Italy in 1893, the interior was not significantly colonized until after 1910. The most important part of the Italian colonial Empire was Libya, where troops landed in Tripoli on 5 October 1911, but it took several years to conquer the whole country.

The governments of the various Italian colonies enjoyed a considerable measure of autonomy, and so the trade policy varied from one territory to another. On the other hand, the system was quite uniform as far as the treatment of goods from the colonies in Italy was concerned – there were virtually no preferences (except for 1904 in the case of some goods from Eritrea). One explanation for this absence of preference was that Italy (or at least certain parts of it) had a similar climate to that of the colonies.

The tariffs in the different colonies varied, but Italian goods enjoyed a high preference everywhere. In Eritrea this was about 90 per cent, in Somalia 70 per cent, and in Libya 50 per cent.[162] The average level of import duties on foreign manufactured goods was about 8 per cent in Eritrea, 12 per cent in Somalia, and 35 per cent in Libya (but most machinery entered freely into Eritrea and into Libya).

8. Colonial trade policies of the United States and Japan

The expression 'colonial power' might seem inappropriate to apply to the United States, whose constitution was opposed to all colonization in principle. In fact, however, a form of colonial status did exist. The Supreme Court in 1901, by a majority of five votes to four, decided that 'since, under the intent of the Constitution, the colonies were "unincorporated" territory, "appurtenant to" the United States, the clause regarding uniformity of duties does not apply to them. Congress, therefore, has the power to draw up distinct tariff schedules for the colonies, and to impose duties on their products entering the United States.'[163] Within three years the United States had begun to establish a kind of colonial rule in four important areas: Hawaii in 1897, Puerto Rico in 1898, Cuba in 1899, and the Philippines in 1900.

Since Hawaii had been completely annexed, it was considered part of the United States for commercial legislation. In Puerto Rico a tariff based on that of the United States, but a little less protectionist, was promulgated on 20 January 1899. But from 1 March 1902 a free trade system was

[162] These were often concealed preferences, taking the form of an underestimate of the value of Italian goods.   [163] US Tariff Commission, *Colonial Tariff Policies*, pp. 577–8.

set up between the two countries; as a first stage (from April 1900) while waiting for the establishment of an internal taxation system, import duties were fixed at 15 per cent of those normally collected by the two partners.

In Cuba, a new tariff very similar to that in force at first in Puerto Rico came into force as early as 15 June 1900. Import duties on manufactured goods were about 40–45 per cent *ad valorem*. From December 1903 a preferential system was established, on the basis of a reciprocal reduction of 20 per cent of import duties, but with reductions of as much as 40 per cent for certain American manufactured goods. America's direct administration of Cuba came to an end on 28 January 1909.

As soon as the American army had taken possession of Manila, the administration abolished the preferential system in favour of the Spanish. As early as 10 November 1898 a single-schedule tariff replaced the previous multiple tariff, but the level of duties remained the same. By the treaty of Paris, signed on 10 December 1898, Spain received the assurance that for ten years she would benefit from the same privileges as the United States. The tariff of 17 September 1901 (which came into force on 15 November 1901) was also modelled on the American tariff, but it contained more specific duties and, as in Cuba, a lower level of protection. In October 1903 the Payne–Aldrich Tariff authorized the free import into the United States of only limited quantities of sugar, tobacco, and hemp. No counterpart arrangements were introduced at this time for American products in the Philippines. One of the reasons for this was the clause in the treaty of Paris which would have extended any preferential system to Spain.

It was only the tariff law of 9 August 1909 which authorized the free import of American goods into the Philippines and of all Filipino goods into the United States, apart from rice (300,000 tons per year), tobacco and cigars (1 million lbs and 150 million cigars). Additional quantities were allowed in, but were subject to the general tariff. Similarly, goods from the Philippines containing more than 20 per cent non-local products were liable to the general tariff, which was an obstacle to the establishment in the Philippines of industry intending to export to the United States. A law of 8 March 1902 had already established a system reserving trade between the two countries for American shipping. But since the American fleet was not big enough, this law was suspended several times and was never applied during the period covered here.

No sooner had Japan regained her tariff independence from the 1897 legislation (implemented in 1899) than she established an embryo colonial system. In September 1909 Japan's colonies were assimilated into her tariff system. These colonies were Formosa (Taiwan), the Pescadores, and Sakhalin. A more informal free trade system existed between these colonies and Japan before 1909. The annexing of Korea in 1910 was followed by a pledge of an open-door policy to last for ten years. At the end of this period, the Korean tariff was assimilated to that of Japan.

D.   AN OVERVIEW OF THE COLONIAL TRADE POLICIES ON THE EVE OF THE FIRST WORLD WAR

The two tables (14 and 15) – one describing the policies in themselves, the other concerned with the consequences of these policies assessed by comparing the relative importance of colonial trade – reveal the position of colonial trade policies of European countries in 1914. The main commercial options can be grouped into three categories, as far as imports into the colonies are concerned. The most liberal system is that of the open door, with all countries having free access to the colonial market. Next comes the preferential system, in which products from the mother country benefit from varying degrees of advantage. Finally there is the system that can be said to be the most exclusive – assimilation, which implies a generalized and complete preferential system.

Table 14 gives an overall picture of the types of trade policy in force in the main colonies.[164] As can be seen, different tariff regimes were adopted not only by the different mother countries, but by different colonies of the same mother country. It it clear that within each of these three main types of tariff system there were important variations in the level of effective preference enjoyed by the mother country. As far as assimilation was concerned, the extent of preferential treatment depended essentially on the level of protection of the national tariff systems.[165] In practice, the degree of preference under the assimilation system was 100 per cent, but the effect of this preference depended on the level of import duties. For manufactured goods, for example, the average rate of import duties in assimilated French colonies was about 20 per cent, whereas in Puerto Rico (an American colony) it was about 44 per cent (see Table 9). In the case of preferential systems, the level of preference varied according to the mother country and the colonies, from a minimum of 33 per cent to a maximum of 95 per cent; with rates of about 50–80 per cent on the whole. But here, too, the effect of the preference depended on the level of import duties. Finally, even in the case of the open-door policies, concealed preferences or *de facto* preferences resulting from particular situations have to be taken into account. For all these reasons, it is important to examine the results of these policies and we shall do this below.

---

[164] The colonies not mentioned in Table 14 accounted for less than 1 per cent of all colonies in terms of population (or of trade).

[165] In some cases, however, import duties were not necessarily exactly the same.

Table 14. *Type of dominant import tariff system in the main colonies around 1913*

Mother country	Assimilated	Preferential	Open door
Belgium	—	—	All colonies
France	Algeria	West Africa	Morocco
	Indochina	Oceania	Somalia
	Tunisia	St Pierre and Miquelon	West Africa
	Madagascar		New Hebrides
	Guadeloupe		
	Gabon		
	Guinea		
	New Caledonia		
Germany	—	—	All colonies
Great Britain	—	Self-governing colonies:	All colonies
		Trinidad	except preferential
		Jamaica	
		Barbados	
		Leeward Islands	
		Windward Islands	
		Honduras	
		Bahamas	
		Cyprus	
		Fiji	
Italy	—	North Africa	Rhodes
Portugal	—	All colonies except	Macao
		open door	Congo
Spain	—	All colonies except	Canary
		open door	Morocco
The Netherlands	—	—	All colonies
Non-European countries			
Japan	Taiwan	—	Kwangtung
	Karafuto		Kiaochow
	Korea		
United States	Puerto Rico	Philippines	Samao
		Virgin Islands	Canal Zone
		Guam	

Sources: Derived from US Tariff Commission, *Colonial Tariff Policies* (Washington, DC, 1922), pp. 36–9.

As a general rule, in return for the preferences enjoyed by goods from the mother country in the colonies, exports from the colonies themselves benefited from preferential treatment on the markets of the mother countries practising either assimilation or preferential systems. Since the colonies exported mainly raw materials, the great majority of which passed freely into most countries, this preference was less important. In addition, however, a whole series of factors tended to encourage exports from the colonies to the mother countries, such as the nationality of the merchants and the owners of plantations and mines; shipping lines; navigation policies, and so on.

National policies for shipping with regard to the colonies can be divided into four types.[166] (1) The trade between the mother country and its colonies and the intercolonial trade could be open to all vessels without discrimination (this was the case with Great Britain, The Netherlands, Belgium, and Germany). (2) This trade could be open to vessels of all nationalities but with dutiable merchandise receiving the preferential tariff rates only when transported 'directly' from the country of origin (France and British dominions and colonies). (3) Preferential tariff rates might apply only where goods were carried in national vessels or might receive additional preferential reductions if so carried (Portugal). (4) Colonial trade might be restricted to national vessels independently of tariff regulations (Spain, and in part of the United States, Portugal, and Japan).

In short, the way in which trade was concentrated between the mother countries and the colonies (see Table 15) can serve as a relatively reliable indicator of the degree of effective preference, especially if one analyses the situation in the light of the four following factors: the size of the mother country and its level of economic development, the proximity of the colonies, and the size of the colonial empire. For obvious reasons, all these factors tended to increase the level of trade between the mother country and its colonies.

The pattern revealed is that, as far as the large countries are concerned, France and the United States imposed the most restrictive regime on their colonies; and Great Britain the most liberal. Germany, Italy, and Japan come quite close behind France and the United States. There were no very marked differences among the medium-sized or small countries: on the whole these countries are to be classed with the group of large countries following a restrictive policy.

The relative importance of the trade of the mother countries with their colonies varied much more than trade in the other direction. Whereas imports from the mother country varied between 31 per cent and 77.4 per cent (mean: 49.8 per cent; coefficient of variation: 31 per cent), exports from the mother country varied between 0.5 per cent and 37.2 per cent (mean: 8.2 per cent; coefficient of variation: 138 per cent). The essential difference lay in the situation of Great Britain compared to that of the other colonial powers. Whereas 37 per cent of Great Britain's exports went to her colonies (20 per cent to colonies in the strictest sense, and 18 per cent to the self-governing colonies) the proportion was no

[166] US Tariff Commission, *Colonial Tariff Policies*, p. 60.

Table 15. *Relative shares of colonial trade for mother countries and for colonies in 1913*

	Mother country's trade			Colonies' trade		
	Total exports (million US $)	Share of trade with colonies (%)		Total exports (million US $)	Share of trade with mother country (%)	
		Exports	Imports		Exports	Imports
United Kingdom	2,556	37.2	20.5	2,450	42.0	45.7
Self-governing[a]	—	17.6	12.0	950	57.8	38.4
Others	—	19.6	18.5	1,400	25.7	53.8
Continental Europe						
Belgium	702	0.7	1.0	11	90.4[b]	66.1[b]
France	1,328	13.0	9.5	320	50.0	61.8
Germany	2,403	0.5	0.4	57	20.7[b]	40.5[b]
Italy	485	1.8	0.2	3	42.8	43.0
Portugal	37	14.2	3.2	35	31.0[c]	31.0[c]
Spain	204	2.1	0.5	7	27.3	38.5
The Netherlands	413	5.3	13.5	275	28.1	33.3
Non-European countries						
United States[d]	356	5.2	6.6	70	58.8	62.7
Japan[e]	2,429	2.0	9.2	150	75.4	75.4

Notes:
[a] Australia, Canada (including Newfoundland), New Zealand, South Africa.
[b] 1912.
[c] Total of imports and exports.
[d] Including Hawaii as a colony.
[e] Korea and Taiwan only (but those represent over 95 per cent of this trade).
Sources: Author's estimates based on various national and international sources (mainly statistical yearbooks of individual countries).

more than 4.1 per cent (weighted average) in the case of the other colonial powers.

This section cannot be concluded without mentioning the importance of colonial trade policy in the process of de-industrializing the colonies in the nineteenth century. By opening up the ports to modern manufactured goods, these trade laws led first to the disappearance of existing crafts and later curbed the process of re-industrialization.

IX. *Labour movements and trade policies*

Labour movements in Europe did not show any consistent attitudes towards trade policies, which can easily be explained in theoretical terms as well as by the diversity and often contradictory nature of the interests involved. As far as theory was concerned, it is scarcely surprising to find that nearly all the workers' movements which claimed to be socialist should have neglected this aspect of a society they were hoping to reform radically and in such a way as to set the problem of international trade in a very different (if undefined) context. At the level of practical short-term action, the choice between free trade and protectionism involved something of a dilemma. Free trade, which promised lower food prices, involved a risk of unemployment. Protectionism, which promised employment, risked increasing food prices. It also threatened to result in an influx of foreign labour, although this did not seem to be perceived as a direct consequence of protectionism.

On the whole, European labour movements, and in particular the various socialist parties, opted in practice for free trade, adopting a more liberal position for agriculture than for industry. However, despite this general trend, fairly radical protectionist views were sometimes adopted in certain areas and certain sectors. In the developed countries outside Europe, especially in the United States and Australia, by contrast, workers' movements clearly favoured protectionism.

Only the main trends at the most critical periods in the most representative labour movements can be mentioned here. The term labour movement is used here in a very wide sense to include parties, groups or individual theorists concerned with the working class and viewing themselves as closely associated with the working class.

A. THE CHARTISTS AND THE CORN LAWS

In Great Britain the labour movements' attention to trade matters in the period of the Anti-Corn Law League were dominated by the Chartists. It appears that the Grand National Consolidated Trade Union, which was set up in 1834 but only lasted a few months, did not concern itself with the problems of trade policies. On the other hand, the Chartist movement (which was particularly active between 1838 and 1843) did take up this important problem.

It appears that before 1832 there was a frequent convergence of opinion between the political representatives of the working classes (who later formed the Chartist movement) and the groups which opposed the Corn Laws. The disillusionment caused by the 1832 Reform Bill (which in the counties, for example, only gave the right to vote to those paying £10 per annum in rent, a large sum which amounted to about 40 per cent of national income per capita) led directly to the founding of the Chartist movement, and also marked the beginning of a certain class division with regard to trade policies. The Chartists were not originally opposed to the Anti-Corn Law League, but from 1842 marked hostility developed between these two groups. It should be noted that the Anti-Corn Law

League was not against the working classes in principle, indeed its proposals were designed to benefit all consumers through cheaper food, even though it disapproved of the methods adopted by the Chartists. On the other hands, Brown has argued that 'The attitude of the Chartists to the League was more complex. Unlike the members of the League, with their centralized organisation and their remarkable consistency of propaganda, Chartists had not even the appearance of unanimity. The basis of their hostility to the League was the class antagonism.'[167]

One of the main factors in the Chartists' opposition to the Anti-Corn Law League stemmed from their purely protectionist attitude. Moreover, as a general rule, but not systematically, the editorials of the *Northern Star* – the mouthpiece of the Chartists – were protectionist in tone, revolving round the theme of protecting local employment. 'Chartist audiences were looking for a system which would ensure them full and steady employment, and it was not clear to them how free trade would do this.'[168]

However, it seems that the Chartists did not come out against the repeal of the Corn Laws on the eve of repeal. All the same, some of those opposed to repeal, even outside the ranks of the Chartists, argued that it would have a harmful effect on employment. Disraeli, in particular, declared that, 'the price of wheat . . . is not a question of rent, but it is a question of displacing the labour of England that produces corn, in order, on an extensive and even universal scale, to permit the entrance into this country of foreign corn produced by foreign labour. Will that displaced labour find new employment?'[169] After 1846 the Chartist movement declined, just when the problem of trade policy ceased to be a major preoccupation for them, or for the other workers' movements in Britain (see section IX D).

B. MARX, ENGELS, AND FREE TRADE

Before we consider the attitude of the nineteenth-century Marxists to free trade it should be recalled that the socialist writers who preceded Marx did not hold uniform views on this matter. Fourier's advocacy of free trade for his utopian 'phalanstery' system cannot be regarded as normative with regard to the existing economic system. The followers of Saint-Simon were won over to liberalism and as we have seen (sections III and IV), in the 1850s and the 1860s their disciples played a decisive role in the militant movements in favour of free trade on the European

---

[167] L. Brown, 'The Chartists and the Anti-Corn Law League', in A. Briggs (ed.), *Chartist Studies* (London, 1959; new edn 1965), pp. 342–71; especially p. 348.   [168] *Ibid.*, p. 352.
[169] G. M. Young and W. K. Hancock (eds.), *English Historical Documents, 1833–1874*, vol. XII(I) (London, 1956), p. 466.

continent. Proudhon, on the other hand, was inclined towards protectionism – although inspired by the ideas of Saint-Simon. Robert Owen declared himself in favour of free trade for cereals and cotton, if not for free trade in general.

As far as Marx, Engels, and their followers in general are concerned, their comments on these matters must be seen, of course, in the context of the analyses of an economic system which they predicted, and hoped, would disappear. Since the disappearance of the capitalist system would not only resolve all contradictions within the state, but also cause the state itself to wither away, the question of the place of foreign trade in the socialist system of the future was not one which concerned the nineteenth-century Marxists.

Marx's own position is set out in essence in his famous speech on free trade delivered in Brussels on 7 January 1848. This speech severely criticized the arguments put forward by the supporters of free trade, concluding:

if the free traders cannot understand how one country may become rich at the expense of another, we should not be surprised, for these same gentlemen do not want to understand how, within a given country, one class can enrich itself at the expense of another class. But do not think, gentlemen, that in criticizing free trade we have any intention of defending the protectionist system.

Then, having emphasized that protectionism in fact led to free trade within a given country, Marx finished his speech with this often quoted passage:

in general, in our time, the system of free trade is destructive. It dissolves the old national groups and sharpens the antagonism between the bourgeoisie and the proletariat. In a word, the system of free trade accelerates social revolution. It is only in this revolutionary sense, gentlemen, that I vote for free trade.[170]

This relative ambiguity of Marx's attitude is the obvious explanation for the absence of true socialist doctrines concerning trade policy in the second half of the nineteenth century. However, this did not prevent Marx from taking up a more definite position when proposing solutions to concrete issues. For example, in a letter to Engels written twenty years after the speech on free trade, Marx noted that Ireland needed not only independence from England and an agricultural revolution, but also a protectionist policy directed against English goods in particular. In this connection Marx recalled that the union of Ireland with Great Britain had led to Irish deindustrialization.[171] However, these remarks were

---

[170] K. Marx, *Discours sur la question du libre-échange*, a pamphlet published by the Association Démocratique de Bruxelles (Brussels, 1848), reprinted in K. Marx, *Misère de la philosophie* (Paris, 1946), pp. 148–64, especially pp. 160–1.

[171] Letter from Marx to Engels, dated 30 November 1867 in 'K. Marx, P. Engels', *Werke*, vol. XXXI (Berlin, 1965), pp. 398–400 (especially p. 400).

exceptional. Marx and Engels were only rarely concerned with trade policies and the problem is not raised in *Das Kapital*.

This relative lack of interest in the problems of trade policy can be found throughout nineteenth-century socialist thought. It is significant that in the index to the five volumes of Cole's history of socialist thought the terms 'commerce', 'trade', and 'international trade' are absent, while the term 'free trade' occurs only four times.[172] Of these four references, two are to Henry George, and a third has nothing to do with socialist thought. In fact the entire area of international trade problems is completely neglected. However, the limited role played by commercial issues in socialist thought in no way implies that the socialists abstained from political debates on trade policy and, because free traders and protectionists were very often equally balanced, the votes of the members of socialist parties could be decisive. This is the justification for the analysis that follows.

C.   SOCIALIST PARTIES AND TRADE POLICIES IN CONTINENTAL EUROPE, 1880–1914

In continental Europe we can disregard the attitudes and actions of the labour movements before the first years of the 1880s as far as trade policies were concerned. In any case, these movements had developed much later than in the United Kingdom. In most countries, the various laws preventing workers from associating were not repealed until 1860–70. It was quite natural that, in this first phase, they should have concentrated on the more specific problems which directly concerned the working classes.

In *France*, the few socialist members of parliament did not take any part in the discussion of the 1881 tariff. On the whole, the few occasions on which the representatives of workers became involved in tariff problems between 1880 and 1890 were when they opposed potential protectionist measures for agriculture.[173] This tendency towards liberalism may have been reinforced by the translation in 1888 of the free trade ideas of the American publicist Henry George, who tended towards socialism.[174] On the other hand, French-speaking socialist thinkers such as Jules Guesde in 1887 and Emile Vandervelde in 1892 declared themselves against protectionism, which they saw as a form of nationalism which conflicted with the international character of socialism.[175] Also, we should not forget that the protectionist measures planned or intro-

---

[172] G. D. H. Cole, *A History of Socialist Thought*, 5 vols. (London, 1960–2).

[173] M. Hollande, *La défense ouvrière contre le travail étranger. Vers un protectionnisme ouvrier* (Paris, 1913), pp. 79ff.

[174] H. George, *Protection or Free Trade: An Examination of the Tariff Question with Special Regard to the Interest of Labor* (New York, 1886).   [175] Hollande, *La défense ouvrière*, pp. 83 and 84.

duced during this period applied above all to agriculture, and thus implied the risk of raising the cost of living, especially for the workers, but without prejudicing directly the level of employment. In 1885 the whole socialist press supported a demonstration in Paris organized by the Popular League Against Import Duties on Wheat. At the time of the discussion of the 1892 tariff law, the socialist deputies declared themselves almost unanimously against the new protectionist tariff. Occasionally, though, certain groups adopted protectionist positions, even as far as agriculture was concerned. For example, at a local socialist congress held in Nîmes in 1886 a motion was voted according to which it was unacceptable for 'the state to take no interest in the fare of millions of French farmers and leave them at the mercy of speculators in American, Indian or Australian wheat'.[176]

Although the socialist deputies scarcely intervened during the discussion of the 1892 law, they acted quite differently with regard to a bill in February 1894 (concerned with an increase in import duties on grain) and the tariff reform of 1909. In 1894, when presenting a counter-project, Jean Jaurès declared that 'it is the first time that a socialist solution to a tariff problem has been proposed'.[177] This solution consisted of a state monopoly of grain imports in order to fix prices on the home market at a level allowing the reconciliation of the interests of both farmers and consumers. This opposition bill was attacked by free traders as well as protectionists. We should note that Jaurès' position was tied to that of the Marxists, for in his speech presenting this socialist opposition bill Jaurès declared that 'protectionism and liberalism, like society itself (of which we prepare the extinction), are relative and temporary phenomena'.[178]

During the discussion of the 1909 tariff, the most active man in the Socialist Party was Eduard Vaillant. On this occasion the party took a free trade position. On 9 July, Jaurès, the last speaker, even managed to have carried by 521 votes to 1 a motion inviting the government 'to organize an international conference of all the interested powers, with the aim of gradually and simultaneously reducing import duties'.[179] Jaurès' main idea was that French agriculture could become an export industry – 'the greatest export industry'.[180]

It should be noted, however, that the doctrinal position of the French Socialists was less clear than that of the German Social Democrats (see below, p. 133). In the years 1907–14, especially in certain occupations prone to unemployment (cabinet makers, glass makers, weavers, glove makers, and miners), the trade unions adopted a distinctly protectionist position. This protectionism as part of a major trend amongst certain

---

[176] Hollande, *La défense ouvrière*, p. 97, from *Revue Socialiste* (1886), vol. I.
[177] Quoted by Hollande, *La défense ouvrière*, p. 120.   [178] *Ibid.*, p. 123.
[179] *Ibid.*, p. 134.   [180] Arnauné, *Le commerce extérieur*, p. 344.

labour movements, especially in Australia and America. They resisted competition from foreign workers, whose acceptance of less favourable working conditions could provoke a reduction in real wages in the country importing their manufactured goods, or in the country which welcomed such workers as immigrants. Albert Thomas (a member of the Socialist Party and the future founder of the International Labour Office) wrote an article in *L'Humanité* of 15 June 1907 called 'Protectionism or Free Trade' in which he declared in particular that 'There is no theory that can persuade us to allow ourselves to be suppressed without protest.'[181]

In France, as in Europe in general, this protectionist movement towards 'foreign labour' applied to goods rather than men and did not lead (before 1914) to restrictions on immigration of the kind to be found in overseas countries of European settlement. In those countries, such restrictions at first applied only to non-white immigrants, as in 1855 when a tax of £10 was introduced on each Chinese passenger disembarking in Victoria. The United States adopted similar measures in 1888. Towards the end of the nineteenth century this form of 'protectionism' was supported and even instigated by labour movements in Australia and America. From the beginning of the twentieth century these restrictions were extended to European immigrants, especially those coming from the Mediterranean basin.[182]

From the 1900s there was an increased tendency towards xenophobia among local workers' organizations (especially trade unions) in most European countries, even if it did not take quite the same form. This xenophobia was in no way shared by the political leaders of the European workers' parties, who were dedicated to the internationalism of the socialist movement. Apart from the notorious British Aliens Act (1905) no restrictions were placed on immigration as such into Europe, but in a great many European countries administrative procedures discriminated against foreigners; these were very often supported and sometimes instigated by local trade unions.

In *Germany*, the Socialists at first kept their distance from the controversy over trade. The socialist congress of Gotha (1876) declared that: 'The Socialists of Germany are indifferent to the controversy raging in the proprietary classes as to Protection and Free Trade; the problem is a practical one, and must be so considered in each particular case.'[183] Gradually, though, the trend towards free trade became stronger. The founding of the Social Democrat Party in 1890 accelerated this trend. At the Stuttgart congress (1898) the question of tariff policy was widely

[181] Quoted by Hollande, *La défense ouvrière*, p. 214.
[182] G. Prato, *Le protectionnisme ouvrier (l'exclusion des travailleurs étrangers)*, trans. from Italian (Paris, 1912). [183] Quoted by P. Ashley, *Modern Tariff History*, p. 47.

discussed and Karl Kautsky's[184] very liberal views were adopted, with the minor reservation that, in exceptional cases, the principle of 'strict' free trade could be relaxed. Later, the trend towards free trade was stengthened still further.

In *Switzerland*, as we have seen (section vi), the 'socialist' party had taken part in 1890 in the creation of a League Against Increases in the Cost of Living. This league fought against an increase in import duties on agricultural products. Similarly, in 1902, the socialists supported the League Against the Customs Tariff which was opposed to a reform of commercial legislation. In 1914, Jacob Lorenz (assistant secretary of the Swiss labour movement) declared to the Swiss workers' congress at Lucerne, 'We want neither an agriculture nor a handicrafts industry which are parasitic plants . . . what we do want are agriculture and handicrafts industries that justify their existence in terms of their intrinsic economic worth and the international division of labour.'[185] It is true that he added that, up till then, the Swiss working class had taken little interest in problems of tariff policy.

In *Italy*, the socialist movement held extremely liberal attitudes towards trade policy and migration. The classical economists, like Einaudi, collaborated with the socialist journal *Critica Sociale*. The attitude of the Italian socialist movement to trade policies was influenced (at least until 1914) by the doctrines of liberal economists like Pareto, Pantaleoni, Einaudi, etc.[186]

In *Belgium*, Emile Vandervelde, who was one of the most influential theorists of the Belgian Workers' Party, held, as we have seen, liberal views. In 1892 he declared, 'the protectionist ideal is one in which every nation is self-sufficient and turned in on itself; the socialist ideal is the abolition of frontiers and international understanding assuring a guaranteed minimum to all producers'.[187] In practice, the problems of trade policy did not greatly interest the Belgian labour movement, or its representatives in parliament. In general then, liberalism persisted, especially in the agricultural sector. The report of the parliamentary socialist group to the 1913 congress of the Workers' Party noted that, 'the high cost of food had made itself felt everywhere, but the protectionist countries, including Belgium, have suffered the most . . . the protectionist measures which have been taken in our country are to the advantage of the landowners alone and the closing of the frontiers against imports of

[184] Karl Kautsky even published, in 1901, a book on tariff problems, *Handelspolitik und Sozialdemokratie* (Berlin, 1901), which went through several editions.

[185] Jacob Lorenz, 'La classe ouvrière suisse et la politique douanière', in *Rapports annuels du Comité directeur de la Federation ouvrière suisse et du Secrétariat ouvrier suisse pour les années 1912 et 1913* (Geneva, 1914), p. 79.

[186] G. Busino, *L'Italia di Pareto* (Milan, 1988).

[187] Speech given at the Antwerp international Congress on tariff legislation and employment regulations, 1892. Quoted by Hollande, *La défense ouvrière*, p. 83.

foreign cattle also prevents the working classes from eating adequately.'[188]

As a transition to section D below, let us note that at the International Socialist Congress in Amsterdam (1904) the English Labour Party tabled a resolution that was clearly in favour of free trade, stating:

That in view of the policy of the capitalist classes and the imperialist governments to divide the workers of the world from each other by tariff walls, and to protect the economic interest of the landlords, the richer classes and the monopolists by imposing import duties upon the workers' food and by creating market conditions under which trusts and cartels can derive exorbitant profit from the home consumers, this Congress, representing the wage-earners of all nations, declares that protection does not benefit the wage-earner and that it is a barrier to international disarmament and peace.[189]

D. THE 'LIBERALISM' OF THE BRITISH LABOUR PARTY

For more than half a century British labour movements were absent in the discussions of trade policies. This is the period between the decline of the Chartists and the founding of the Labour Party – between the end of the 1840s and 1900.[190] This absence can be explained by the distinct improvement in the standard of living which benefited the working class after 1846; by the lack of results from attempts at tariff reform before 1903; and also by the struggles within the various labour movements, especially after 1886. It should be noted that, on the whole, the workers' movements of this period tended towards free trade, unlike the Chartists (see section IX A above).

In September 1903 the annual Trades Union Congress adopted, with only two votes against, a motion disapproving of Chamberlain's plans for tariff reform. In February 1904 the Labour Representation Committee adopted, by an overwhelming majority, a motion condemning protectionism.[191] This was the beginning of an attachment to free trade that was to characterize the Labour Party for at least 30 years.

In formal terms the Labour Party had no commitment to the doctrine of free trade as such. However, its position was not far removed from this, and the arguments put forward appear to come straight from a breviary of free trade. In a pamphlet about tariff problems at the time of the 1906 elections, the Labour Party, after having stressed the negative

---

[188] Parti Ouvrier Belge, Rapports présentés au XXVIII Congrès annuel, 23–25 March 1913 (Brussels, 1913), p. 75.

[189] Congrès Socialiste International (International Social Congress) Amsterdam 1904: Resolutions (Brussels, 1904), p. 54. We have replaced the terms 'trusts en Kartels' by 'trusts and cartels'.

[190] In fact the Labour Party was only founded in 1906 but in February 1900 the Labour Representation Committee was created. This united the trade unions and socialist workers' groups, as the Labour Party was to do.   [191] Hollande, La défense ouvrière, pp. 271–2.

aspects of protectionism, declared, under the title *We Are More Than Free Traders*, that:

We do not, however, regard Free Trade as in any way offering a solution to the problem of poverty. It is economically sound, and so we support it at the present crisis. It is right so far as it goes. Free Trade has enabled us to accumulate National Wealth; a Labour Party must now supplement Free Trade to enable us to distribute that wealth equitably.[192]

In another pamphlet published by the Labour Party at the beginning of the First World War, the conclusions to the examination of the tariff problems were presented in six points. We give here the first, the third, and the fifth:

Though neither Free Trade nor Protection will solve the unemployed problem, all experience goes to show that, other things being equal, employment is steadier and better under Free Trade.

Tariffs tend directly to reduce the quantity of employment by raising prices and this limiting the effective demand for goods and the labour embodied in them.

Protection is not really designed to provide employment, but to raise prices. This it effectively does, to the advantage of the 'protected' capitalist, but to the injury of the worker.[193]

Even after the war, when the Labour Party came to power for the first time (January 1924), among the measures taken during its brief period of eleven months in office were the repeal of certain import duties. But from then on this policy began to be contested within the Labour Party. Penty wrote in 1926 that 'Perhaps the most important of recent political developments in this country is the revolt of Mr. Wheatley and certain other members of the Labour Party against the Free Trade policy of their party.'[194] However, the change of direction did not occur until after the 1929 crisis. In June 1930 an American business weekly observed that 'Britain's Free Trade labor is turning protectionist.'[195] Even then only a fraction of the Labour Party was involved. The official line remained firmly in favour of free trade during the Labour Party's second term of office, June 1929–August 1931. Snowden's speech as the Labour Party's Chancellor of the Exchequer in reply to a motion of censure on the tariff question was even published by the Labour Party under the title *The Truth about Protection: The Worker Pays*. In addition to the classic arguments for free trade, Snowden stressed the fact that the increase in prices which would result from protectionism would particularly affect the

[192] McCord, *Free Trade*, p. 141.
[193] B. Villiers, *Tariffs and the Worker*, publication of the Labour Party (London; undated, but given the reference to 1913 as the last year of peace and the absence of certain statistical figures for 1913, it is presumably 1914 or 1915), p. 8.
[194] A. J. Penty, *Protection and the Social Problem* (London, 1926), p. 1.
[195] *Business Week*, 18 June 1930, pp. 31–2.

low income groups. When a series of protectionist laws imposing a general tariff (in particular the new Corn Laws) – which in effect marked the end of free trade in Britain – were adopted in February 1932, they were only approved by a minority, break-away group of the Labour Party known as the National Labour Group.

X. Trade policies of the rest of the world

The history of the trade policies of European states, including their colonies, is in fact the history of an economic unit which accounted for about 75 per cent of world trade in the nineteenth century. This is the justification for the phrase in the title 'the rest of the world'. This justifies the inclusion of this section – it makes it possible to give an overall view of world trade policies in the nineteenth century without extending this study too much.

In this overall view the United States will obviously have a privileged place, for it not only became the greatest economic power in the world at the end of the nineteenth century but also, despite the rather inward-looking nature of its economy, accounted for some 10–12 per cent of world trade (or 42–46 per cent of the trade of the rest of the world). Apart from the United States, the other countries can be divided into two groups. On the one hand, there are the countries where economic policy was made de jure or de facto by the population of European origin. These included Argentina, Australia, Canada, Chile, New Zealand, Uruguay, and also the rest of Latin America (apart from a few isolated colonies which continued to exist after 1825; see section VIII). The other group is made up of African and Asian countries that were not formally colonized but were nearly all subject to one form or another of imposed commercial policies.

As far as trade policy was concerned, these three groups had their own specific characteristics which can be schematized by the degree of protectionism, ranging from the almost total liberalism of the semi-independent African and Asian countries to the very strict form of protectionism characterizing the United States. The countries of European settlement came between these two, though this intermediate system was nevertheless extremely protectionist, relative to European policies. Table 16 shows the approximate degree of protectionism of the tariff systems in these different countries at the end of the period which concerns us.

Section A concerns the United States, and Section B examines the 'European settlement' countries of the British Empire. Section C deals with the independent countries of Latin America, and section D with those countries that were not formally colonized but did not have true commercial autonomy. Because they include China and Japan, these latter countries accounted for about 30 per cent of world population, but only some 4–5 per cent of world trade.[196]

A. THE UNITED STATES: FROM HAMILTON'S PROTECTIONIST THEORIES TO THE PROTECTIONISM OF THE HAWLEY–SMOOT TARIFF[197]

At the end of the nineteenth century, Callender could write, with no exaggeration, that

Next to currency problems no purely economic subject has aroused so much interest in the United States, and played so great a part in political discussion both in and out of Congress as the tariff policy of the federal government. From the first measure of 1789 until the present time no generation of the American people has escaped the tariff controversy.[198]

A legislator in the state of Pennsylvania suggested that man should be redifined as 'An animal that makes tariff speeches.'[199] What is more, there is no exaggeration to say that the tariff question was one of the causes of the American revolution.

The first tariff of 1789 (4 July) is often described as moderately protectionist; in fact, an analysis of the levels of import duties shows it to be one of the liberal tariffs. It is true that, compared with the previous situation, this tariff was a step towards protectionism, and, in addition,

[196] To illustrate this, here are figures showing how world exports were divided in 1913 (the situation was obviously different at other periods):

	$ million (current prices)	% of total world exports
Europe	10,500	56.8
European colonies	2,300(*)	12.6
United States	2,430	13.1
British self-governing colonies	950	5.1
Independent Latin American countries	1,400	7.6
Others(**)	910	4.9
World	18,560	100.0

(*)Including the American and Japanese colonies (total 220).
(**)Semi-independent countries (especially China and Turkey) and Japan.
Sources: estimates and calculations from various national sources. The degree of rounding off of the figures does not imply a correspondingly low margin of error.

[197] In addition to certain titles mentioned in the notes, the following sources have been used here: Ashley, Modern Tariff History, R. Mayo–Smith and E. R. A. Seligman, 'The Commercial Policy of the United States, 1860–1890', Schriften des Vereins für Sozialpolitik, vol. XLIX, no. 3 (Leipzig, 1892), pp. 3–74, F. W. Taussig, The Tariff History of the United States, 7th edn (New York, 1923); US Tariff Commission, The Tariff and its History (Washington, DC, 1934).

[198] G. S. Callender, Selection from the Economic History of the United States, 1765–1860 (Boston, 1909); quoted by G. R. Taylor in G. R. Taylor (ed.), The Great Tariff Debate, 1820–1830 (Boston, 1968), p. v.

[199] M. R. Eiselen, The Rise of Pennsylvania Protectionism (Philadelphia, 1932), p. 7.

Table 16. *Indicators of tariff levels in 1913 in different types of country*

	Import duties as % of special total imports (1908–12)	Approximate average level of import duties on manufactures	Level of duties on wheat
Developed countries			
Continental Europe	10.4	19	25
United Kingdom	5.7	0	0
Australia	18.2	16	22
Canada	18.7	26	
Japan	9.1	25–30	18
New Zealand	16.6	15–20	3
United States	21.4	44	0[d]
Non-developed countries			
Selected independent (in 1913) countries			
Argentina	21.6	28	0
Brazil	37.4	50–70	—
Colombia	49.1[b]	40–60	20
Mexico	33.7[b]	40–50[c]	42
Selected semi-independent (in 1913) countries			
China	3.3	4–5	0
Iran	8.0[b]	3–4	0
Siam	2.7[d]	2–3	3
Turkey	—	5–10	11

Notes:
[a] With 10 per cent for wheat originating from countries where US wheat is imposed.
[b] To total imports.
[c] 1910.
[d] 1910–13.
Sources: Percentages of import duties: author's computations based on various national sources.
Average level for manufactures:
Ranges: author's estimates on basis of individual tariffs.
Other figures: see Table 9 and national sources.
Level of duties on wheat: see Table 9 for method of calculation. Additional sources were used for this table.

the remoteness of the United States constituted a natural, protective barrier. Whatever the circumstances, this first American tariff, which, according to its preamble, was aimed at protecting local industry, did not further Alexander Hamilton's much more radical project; a project which was to remain in the background of most plans for trade policy for much of the nineteenth century.

In this first tariff most of the import duties were *ad valorem* duties for manufactured goods averaging about 7.5–10 per cent. After two successive revisions (10 August 1790 and 2–3 March 1791) the tariff of 2 May 1792 increased duties on most categories of goods by 50 per cent. Further slight increases were introduced in 1795, 1800, and 1808. Then, as a result of the 1812 war, duties were doubled for financial reasons and they did not, in fact, return to their previous levels. This meant that under the 1816 tariff import duties were about 35 per cent for nearly all manufactured goods, but, and this is important, there were no prohibitions.

The opposition between the South, which, as an exporter of agricultural products (cotton, tobacco), was liberal, and the North, which was industrializing and hence protectionist, emerged already during this period. The protectionist movement – supported by economists like Daniel Raymond and, later, Henry C. Carey – was encouraged by pockets of unemployment and by cyclical crises. From 1819 on associations were formed to press for industrialization to be achieved as a result of protectionism. This movement was also well supported by publications.[200]

From then on it is possible to divide nineteenth-century American commercial history into three relatively distinct periods. The first, which can be labelled a protectionist phase, lasted from 1816 to 1846. From 1846 till 1861 came a period which is sometimes said to have been liberal, but should more accurately be described as one of very modest protectionism. The last phase, which lasted from 1861 to the end of our period (and in fact to the end of the Second World War), was one of strict protectionism.

After a few parliamentary vicissitudes, a series of modifications adopted between 1824 and 1832 (especially in 1828 tariff) further strengthened the protectionist nature of the 1816 tariff. Import duties on woollen manufactured goods were 40–45 per cent, and those for clothing 50 per cent; but import duties on all manufactured goods averaged

---

[200] Among these publications should be mentioned in particular the weekly *Nile's Register* (in Baltimore), which was founded in 1811 and was a semi-official mouthpiece of protectionism during the 1820s and the 1830s. It had a very wide audience throughout the country. Another important centre of protectionism was neighbouring Pennsylvania, where, in 1819, two new protectionist societies were formed (*ibid.*, p. 52).

As far as contemporary opinions on this period are concerned, till very recently the dogma of free trade was so strong that I have not seen any paper published in an 'orthodox' periodical showing a positive impact of protectionism on American industry in the first half of the nineteenth century. The first of those type of papers is, to my knowledge, that of Mark Bils whose main conclusion is that 'My finding could hardly conflict more with the consensus view on the economic importance of the tariff. The calculations above demonstrate that, as of 1833, removing protection would have eliminated the vast majority of value added in the cotton textile industry' (M. Bils, 'Tariff Protection and Production in the Early U.S. Cotton Textile Industry', *Journal of Economic History*, vol. XLIV, no. 4 (December 1984), pp. 1,033–45).

Table 17. *Ratio of import duties to imports in the United States for significant policy periods*

	Ratio of duties calculated to imports (%)	
	Total imports (free and dutiable)	Dutiable imports
1821–4	43.4	45.8
1829–31	50.8	54.4
1842–6	25.3	31.9
1857–61	16.3	20.6
1867–71	44.3	46.7
1891–4	22.9	48.9
1908–13	20.1	41.3
1914	14.9	37.6
1923–7	14.1	37.7
1931–3	19.0	55.3
1935–8	16.4	39.8
1944–6	9.5	28.3
1968–72	6.5	10.1
1978–82	3.5	5.8

Sources: US Bureau of the Census, *Historical Statistics of the United States. Colonial Times to 1970* (Washington, DC, 1975), p. 888; US Bureau of the Census, *Statistical Abstract of the United States, 1974* (Washington, DC, 1975), p. 801; and *ibid.* (1985), p. 823.

about 40 per cent. Several specific duties on agricultural products were also increased: on many of these products duties amounted to more than 60 per cent of their value. On the basis of the importance of import duties relative to import values – not a very reliable indicator – the tariff in force after 1829 shows American protectionism at its height (see Table 17).

This development led to a fairly serious crisis, because of the opposition from the South: certain states declared the federal laws on these matters null and void. The crisis was resolved by the adoption of the Compromise Bill (which came into force on 2 March 1832). This provided for a progressive reduction of the highest import duties, leading up to a relatively unified level of 20 per cent in 1842. This liberalization of trade policy reached its peak with the tariff of 30 June 1842 which reduced import duties on manufactured goods to an average of about 25 per cent and increased the number of products that could enter freely. However – and this was characteristic of American tariff history – this tariff remained in force for a short period only: two months. The emergence of the 'whig' party (which was highly protectionist) and the crisis of 1841–2 led to the tariff of 30 August 1842, which more or less restored the tariff levels of 1832.

The return of the Democrats in 1844 led to the tariff of 30 July 1846 which reduced import duties by about 10–20 per cent and generalized the system of *ad valorem* duties. The average *ad valorem* duty on the 51 most important categories of goods was 27 per cent (coefficient of variation 45 per cent).

There were scarcely any modifications until the tariff of 3 March 1857. According to contemporary observers this policy, which was half-way between a very relative form of protectionism and moderate liberalism, did not have any noticeable effect on economic life. 'The critics of the tariff legislation of 1846 cannot profess that it did more than slightly retard the industrial process in the United States; whilst its warmest supporters do not pretend that it did much to hasten the development. In fact, its effect in either direction was probably only small.'[201] The data available to us today do not enable us to be much more positive; the statistics for the 1840s and the 1850s are unreliable enough, but those for the period before 1840 belong to what has been called the 'Statistical Dark Age'.[202] The data available on the volume of Gross National Product per capita shows an annual growth rate of about 1.9–2.3 per cent from 1820 to 1840, and about 1.7 per cent from 1840 to 1860. It is thus probable that economic growth slowed down, but this growth was still fairly rapid if one sees the 1.7 per cent per annum in relation to the growth rates of other countries at this period (the rate in Europe from 1840 to 1860 was about 0.9 per cent).

It is during the period 1860–90 that the contrast between European and American trade policies became most marked. Although the tariff of 3 March 1857 implied a liberalization of trade policy, that of 2 March 1861 marked the beginning of the policy which was to be followed in the United States until the end of the Second World War. Import duties were to be increased again during the civil war, and the victory of the North brought increased protectionism. The tariff in force from 1866 to 1883 provided for import duties averaging 45 per cent for manufactured goods (the lowest rates of duty were about 25 per cent and the highest about 60 per cent). In 1867–71 import duties amounted to 44 per cent of the total value of imports (see Table 17).

Without linking the two things, it is important to note that the period 1870–90, which was a time of serious economic depression in Europe, was a phase of prosperity in the United States. In these twenty years the growth of the American Gross National Product reached an average of 2.1 per cent per annum; that is to say a level which had not only never

---

[201] Ashley, *Modern Tariff History*, p. 175.
[202] P. A. David, 'New Light on a Statistical Dark Age: US Real Product Growth Before 1840', *American Economic Review*, Papers and Proceedings LVII (1967), pp. 294–306.

been reached before, but was never to be exceeded again for a period of this length.[203]

The way in which the United States caught up with, and even overtook, European industry[204] rendered obsolete the 'infant industries' argument for United States protectionism. The Republicans therefore based their case for introducing the celebrated McKinley tariff (named after the president of the commission responsible for drawing it up) on the need to safeguard the wage levels of American workers and to give the agricultural sector more protection. This tariff (of 1 October 1890 which came into force five days later) implied a distinct increase in effective protection, thanks to a general increase in import duties, a combination of specific and *ad valorem* duties (with sliding scales) and an enlargement of the number of tariff items. It should be noted that duties were increased even on grains (intended to help the struggle against Canadian competition).

Changes in the structure of imports as a result of tariff reform masks the protectionist nature of the McKinley tariff documented in Table 17. But a look at the import figures reveals that the previous slow increase in the volume of manufactured goods imported changed to a decline. Taking 1913 as a base (= 100) the volume of imports of finished manufactured goods, which had risen from 50.9 to 64.1 between 1879–83 and 1886–90, was only 61.3 in 1891–5 (and 69.3 in 1896–1900).

During the period 1890–1913 there was a series of tariff modifications which alternately reduced and increased import duties by small amounts, according to the election results. At the same time the tariff items of goods liable to duty became more complex. The sophisticated system of 'drawbacks' (the sum paid back by a government for certain goods exported on which duty had already been paid) introduced under the McKinley tariff was retained. So was the principle of reciprocity, which

[203] These are the average annual growth rates of GNP per capita for the following medium-term periods:

| 1890–1913 | 1.9 per cent | 1928–53 | 1.7 per cent | 1973–86 | 1.5 per cent |
| 1913–28 | 0.9 per cent | 1953–73 | 2.1 per cent | | |

[204] The per capita level of industrialization (UK in 1900 = 100) evolved as indicated below:

	1860	1880	1900	1913
United States	21	38	69	126
Europe (excluding Russia)	19	29	41	58
United Kingdom	64	87	100	115
Belgium	28	43	56	88
Switzerland	26	39	67	87
France	20	28	39	59
Germany	15	25	52	85

Sources: Bairoch, 'International Industrialization Levels', pp. 269–333.

was always central to United States trade policy. In his message to Congress in 1901, Roosevelt wrote 'Reciprocity must be treated as the handmaiden of Protection. Our first duty is to see that the protection granted by the tariff in every case where it is needed is maintained, and that reciprocity be sought for so far as it can be safely done without injury to our home industries.'[205]

The two most important modifications in this period (1890–1913) were the so-called Dingley tariff of 1896 (which came into force on 24 July 1897) which annulled certain small reductions in duties, and especially the Payne–Aldrich tariff (5 August 1909, coming into force on 6 August) which introduced the double tariff system. This double tariff, however, only remained in force until 4 October 1913, when a serious, but temporary, break with previous policy occurred. This change of direction was made possible by the recent victory of the Democratic Party in the 1912 elections. The so-called Underwood tariff of 4 October 1913 (which came into force the same day) led to a big increase in the categories of goods allowed free entry and to a substantial drop in average import duties. According to the calculations of the League of Nations, the average duty on imports fell from 33 to 16 per cent, and the average duty on manufactured goods from 44 to 25 per cent.[206] This still remained one of the highest tariff rates in the world (see Table 16).

This interlude of moderation in the protectionist policies of the United States did not last long. The war prevented the tariff of October 1913 from having any important role, and in May 1921, with the return to power of the Republican Party, new 'emergency' tariff legislation (known as the Fordney–McCumber tariff) came into force on 22 September 1922. This involved a distinct increase in protectionism compared with the 1913 tariff. Although import duties did not return to the high levels of the tariffs in force in 1861–1913, the percentage effectively paid on manufactured goods rose by 30 per cent. The tariff which came into force on 19 June 1930 (known as the Hawley–Smoot tariff)[207] involved even greater increases in import duties. This tariff should not be seen as a measure taken to deal with the 1929 crisis. The law was in fact discussed from January 1929 onwards and the final vote in the Senate and in Congress took place on 13 and 14 June 1929, whereas the crisis dates at the earliest from the collapse of the stock market in October 1929 (industrial production in October 1929 was 3 per cent higher than in the same month of the previous year). The fact that Herbert Hoover signed

[205] Ashley, Modern Tariff History, p. 238.
[206] League of Nations, Tariff Level Indices.
[207] In 1932 the revenue raised from goods liable to import duty amounted to 59.1 per cent of their value. This was the highest level in the history of the United States, the previous record being in 1829, when this percentage was 54.2

the law on 17 June 1930 (in spite of a petition signed by more than 1,000 economists) adds a specific character to it. But if the crisis had not occurred, the president would probably still not have opposed a law which had been passed by a fairly large majority in Congress (222 votes to 153), even if it had only just squeezed through the Senate (44 votes to 42).

The tariff of June 1930 raised import duties to the highest level in the history of American protectionism. This was especially true for manufactured goods, on which import duties in many cases exceeded 60 per cent and averaged about 45–50 per cent. Before the end of 1931 25 countries had increased their import duties on American products as a form of reprisal. This process was, however, largely a result of the depression. Moreover, in the United States quantitative import restrictions were later introduced, largely under the provisions of the National Industrial Recovery Act voted on 16 June 1933 as part of the New Deal.

It is generally considered that the Reciprocity Act signed on 2 June 1934 marks a change of direction in trade policy. Certainly a change of direction took place in the sense that from then on the power of the executive was strengthened, but protectionism was not abandoned. Thanks to this act reciprocity treaties were signed with 20 countries; but just before the Second World War the effective level of import duties was even higher than that in force from 1923 to 1929 (see Table 17). Indeed, the United States did not radically change this trade policy in favour of liberalism until the end of the Second World War. This was exactly one century after Great Britain, but it came at a time when the economic and technical development of the United States (as in the case of Great Britain) were virtually at their height. From then on, the United States was to play a crucial role in the liberalization of international trade, largely through its participation in the General Agreement on Tariffs and Trade (see section VI D).

B. BRITISH COLONIES OF EUROPEAN SETTLEMENT: TARIFF INDEPENDENCE LEADING TO PROTECTIONISM

We have seen (section VIII B1) how the revolt of the American colonies was an important factor in the granting of a large measure of tariff independence to what were later to become the self-governing colonies – in other words, essentially the colonies with a large 'European' population (Canada, Australia, New Zealand, South Africa). Until the 1850s the differences between the self-governing colonies and the other colonies were less important (for this period, see section VIII. An account of the system of unilateral imperial preferences may also be found in subsection VIII B3). The trade policies of these countries after 1860 and their relations with countries outside the British Empire are concentrated on here. Since the British did not control the whole of the Union of South Africa until quite late (1902), only the other three countries will be dealt with here.

The history of trade policies in these countries in the nineteenth century went through two main phases. The first phase, which, depending on the country, lasted until 1867–88, was a period of liberal policies justified mainly by the good export opportunities for agricultural products favoured until the early 1850s by the British preferential system. During this second phase, all these countries sought, in some degree and with varying degrees of success, to foster their industrial sectors through protectionist tariff policies. The geographical position of these countries was an important influence on policies: the isolation of Australia and New Zealand contrasted with the proximity of the United States to Canada.

1. *Australia*[208]

Australia, or more precisely, the colony of Victoria (accounting for about 46 per cent of the population of the six colonies which, from 1 January 1901, came together in the Commonwealth of Australia) was the first British colony to introduce a trade policy intended to promote industry by means of a protectionist tariff. This policy, which dates from 1867, can be largely explained by the unemployment and the underemployment in this region at the beginning of the 1860s. This underemployment was itself the result of the extremely rapid influx of population[209] resulting from the discovery of rich gold seams in 1851. After 1856 gold production began to drop, thus liberating a large labour force composed mainly of townspeople.

From the mid-1850s there is evidence – not only in Victoria – of pressure for the modification of the tariff system. From 1860 on pressure increased, thanks to Syme and his Melbourne newspaper *The Age*. The 1867 tariff which resulted provided for import duties aimed at protecting local industry. This change of trade policy made it even harder to achieve any degree of standardization in the economic policies of the different Australian colonies, most of which still supported free trade; between

---

208   The main sources for Australia are: C. D. Allin, *A History of the Tariff Relations of the Australian Colonies* (Minneapolis, 1918); *Cambridge History of the British Empire*, vol. VII, part 1, 'Australia' (Cambridge, 1933); A. T. Carmody, 'The Level of the Australian Tariff: A Study in Method', *Yorkshire Bulletin of Economic and Social Research*, vol. IV., no. 1 (January 1952), pp. 51–65; W. M. Corden, 'The Tariff', in A. Hunter (ed.), *the Economics of Australian Industry* (Melbourne, 1962), pp. 174–214; E. Shann, *An Economic History of Australia* (Cambridge, 1930), especially pp. 260–80 and 386–447; W. A. Sinclair, 'The Tariff and Manufacturing Employment in Victoria', *Economic Record*, vol. XXXI, no. 60 (May 1955), pp. 100–4; US Bureau of the Census, *Historical Statistics of the United States; Colonial Times to 1957* (Washington, DC, 1960), pp. 779–809.

209   In 1850 Victoria had 76,000 inhabitants, but by 1860 there were 538,000. (This represents an annual growth rate of 22 per cent.)

1867 and 1873 alone four conferences took place on this problem. The only area in which an agreement was reached was in the standardization of measures prohibiting the employment of Chinese labour. On this issue the Australian workers' parties adopted an extremely protectionist position. It was during the period when the Labour Party was in power that very strict laws limiting immigration were drawn up and adopted (the 1901 and the 1905 acts).

The Victorian tariff of 1867 was relatively moderate. Of course, in the case of Australia one must take into account 'the tyranny of distance',[210] which, at this period, must have involved a natural protection of about 10–20 per cent for Australian manufactured goods. However, import duties were noticeably increased in 1871 and in 1877 and it is generally agreed that this trade policy played a substantial role in the industrialization of the colony.

The first federal tariff in 1902 represented a compromise between the protectionism of Victoria and the liberalism of the other states. On the whole, however, it tended more towards protectionism. Import duties ranged from 5 to 25 per cent. This truce did not last long: the 1906 elections returned a protectionist majority due notably to the support given to such a policy by the Labour Party. In 1906 the Australian Industries Preservation Act was passed; this was an anti-dumping law. The new tariff of 3 June 1908 aimed at protection and provided for a doubling of import duties on most categories of goods, while retaining preferences for British products (see section VIII B3). On the whole, the degree of protection in 1913 (see Table 16) was lower than that prevailing in Canada, and lower even than the average level in continental Europe. But, once again, Australia's remoteness must be taken into account (even with the transport costs current at this period this implied an additional protection of between 5 and 10 per cent); and, on the other hand, the tariff reform of 3 December 1914 provided for an increase in import duties on manufactured goods of about 25 per cent. Even though this increase was a result of the war, it should be noted that the tariff measures adopted after the war reinforced protectionist tendencies.

2. Canada[211]

The repeal of the Corn Laws in Britain and the abolition of other preferences on Canadian goods led to the necessity of a drastic reorgani-

[210] G. Blainey, The Tyranny of Distance: How Distance shaped Australia's History (London, 1968).

[211] The main sources used for Canada are: H. G. J. Aitken, 'Defensive Expansion: The State and Economic Growth in Canada', in W. T. Easterbrook and M. H. Watkins (eds.), Approaches to Canadian Economic History (Toronto and Montreal, 1969), pp. 183–221; O. J. McDiarmid, Commercial Policy in the Canadian Economy (Cambridge, Mass., 1946).

   I should also like to thank the students in my seminars in 1970–1 in the graduate Area Studies at Sir George Williams University (now Concordia University, Montreal). These seminars were concerned with trade policy and the economic development of Canada.

zation of Canadian trade policy, since in 1840–6 some 60–70 per cent of Canadian exports went to the United Kingdom. The Canadians naturally turned towards their southern neighbours. This led to the reciprocity treaty of 1854 with the United States which resulted in free trade in agricultural products between the two countries in exchange for fishing and navigation rights for the Americans. This treaty remained in force until 1866 when it was revoked by the United States. Another solution was to protect Canadian industry, but this was not, in fact, done until 1879. From the 1840s, however, and more noticeably in 1857–8, pressure built up for a tariff policy that would encourage industrialization. At the instigation of Isaac Buchanan an Association for the Promotion of Canadian Industry was established in 1858 and the tariffs of 1858 and 1859 did increase import duties considerably but these were not yet expressly designed to protect industry.

The major turning point came when the Conservatives adopted a 'National Policy' based on protectionism as their election platform in October 1878. The new tariff legislation of 1879 protected both agriculture and industry. For agricultural goods, average import duties were between 20 and 50 per cent *ad valorem*, and manufactured goods about 20–30 per cent. In 1878 import duties had amounted to 14.3 per cent of the value of imports, whereas in 1880 they increased to 26.3 per cent.[212] This was only the beginning of a series of rises in duties which continued to 1887, increasing the degree of effective protection in most sectors of industry. By 1887 the average import duties on manufactured goods were around 25–35 per cent.

As Aitken remarks, 'The question is not why Canada turned to protectionism, but why protectionism came so late.'[213] In 1846, when Canada turned towards its southern neighbour, the American economy was still scarcely industrialized and had a moderately protectionist trade policy, but by 1878 this had all changed. Moreover – and here Aitken has the benefit of hindsight – although the National Policy did indeed have a positive effect on the process of industrialization in Canada, this industrialization depended heavily on foreign capital and entrepreneurs. This could perhaps have been avoided if measures had been taken earlier.

The National Policy, which also included plans for the development of an internal transport system, was so successful that after 1896 – when the Liberals came to power – there was no really significant change in trade policy. 'Vociferous though the Liberals were in criticism of high tariffs and in extolling the theoretical principles of free trade, they failed to tear down the protective walls when they came to power.'[214] The tariff of 22 April 1897 even increased import duties in certain cases.

212 Urquhart and Buckley, *Historical Statistics of Canada*, pp. 173 and 198.
213 Aitken, 'Defensive Expansion', p. 208.
214 McDiarmid, *Commercial Policy in the Canadian Economy*, p. 203.

The only significant changes before the First World War were the introduction after 1898 of unilateral preferences of 25 per cent for British goods (see section VIII B3) and the reciprocity treaty with the United States in 1911. On 30 July 1897 Canada revoked treaties containing the most-favoured-nation clause, so as to be able to offer unilateral preferences. Similarly there were few serious changes in trade policy during the 1920s. Not until the so-called Duning tariff, which came into force on 2 May 1930, were there any new, noticeable increases in protectionism. This tariff was introduced partly in response to the American Hawley–Smoot tariff.

3. New Zealand[215]

Throughout the nineteenth century New Zealand was a more liberal tariff than either Australia or Canada. This can be explained by the size of the country (fewer than 500,000 inhabitants in 1880, as opposed to 2,500,000 in Australia and 4,300,000 in Canada) and by the dominating importance of agriculture in the New Zealand economy. However, even in New Zealand the depression of the 1880s brought about a change of attitude towards the tariff system, which had up till then been regarded purely as a means of raising revenue. Part of this revenue, moreover, came from export duties, notably on gold. In much the same way as had happened in Australia, the drop in gold production and the end of what is called the 'Vogel' boom[216] resulted in the strengthening of a protectionist trend which was already noticeable in 1873. In 1884 the New Zealand Protection Association was formed. Again, as in Australia, the workers' parties strongly supported the protectionist movement.

This pressure came to a head in 1888, and the tariff adopted in that year not only provided for average import duties to be doubled to about 20 per cent, but also involved a policy based in principle on the protection of certain sectors of industry. Certain specific duties were replaced by *ad valorem* ones. A series of tariff revisions (in 1895, 1900, and 1907 – particularly that of 1895) then led to an overall increase in protectionism. However, it should be noted that this protection was still fairly limited, since the average import duty on manufactured goods was about 15–20 per cent.

---

[215] The main sources used for New Zealand are: *The Cambridge History of the British Empire*, vol. VII, part 2, 'New Zealand' (Cambridge, 1933); *New Zealand Official Year-Book, 1915* (Wellington, 1915), section XI D, 'Tariff and Revenue', pp. 447–63.

[216] Julius Vogel (Colonial Treasurer, then Prime Minister) carried out, in the period 1869–76, a policy of stimulating economic development and immigration by means of public borrowing. This caused the population to rise from 218,700 in 1867 to 414,400 in 1878.

C.   THE INDEPENDENT LATIN AMERICAN COUNTRIES: A
DEFENCE AGAINST A NEW FORM OF COMMERCIAL
DOMINATION[217]

The political independence of most Latin American countries (which took place mainly between 1804 and 1822) had been largely helped by British intervention. The result was that, as far as trade policies were concerned, the first measures tended towards liberalism. This trend was also fostered by the new elites, dominated by plantation owners and merchants engaged in exports of tropical products. On the other hand, the abolition of the colonial system tended to encourage more or less everywhere the development of local handicrafts and industries, which had obviously been held back till then by the provisions of the 'colonial pact'. However, very soon, from 1830–40 onwards, competition from European, and especially from British goods, caused these industries to decline. As a result, and also under the influence of North American trade policy, most of these countries radically altered their own policies during the period 1870–90, introducing protectionist tariffs intended to promote industrialization. In the case of Mexico this shift took place much earlier, in the 1830s.

Needless to say, these policies were not uniform everywhere, and their results also varied. Their main tendencies were determined by factors like the size of the country and, in particular, by the balance of power between the great landowners (producers of tropical goods) and the manufacturers and artisans. It would thus be difficult to give a coherent account, however brief, of the development of the twenty independent states of Latin America in the nineteenth century. Here we shall consider only Argentina, Brazil, and Mexico, three countries which in 1913 together accounted for 56 per cent of exports from Latin America, and also 56 per cent of its population. The lack of research on some of the other countries makes an overall view extremely difficult.

1. *Argentina*[218]

The history of trade policy in Argentina is, for the first half century of her independence (1810–59), the history of the conflicting interests of

[217] In addition to the titles given at the beginning of each of the sections on Argentina, Brazil and Mexico, the following sources have been used for Latin America: O. Hubner, *A Collection of the Customs Tariffs of all Nations* (London, 1855); US Federal Trade Commission, *Report on Trade and Tariffs in Brazil, Uruguay, Argentina, Chile, Bolivia and Peru* (Washington, DC, 1916).

[218] This section is based on the following sources (in addition to those mentioned in the previous note): C. F. Diaz Alejandro, 'The Argentine Tariff, 1906–1940', *Oxford Economic Papers*, vol. XIX, no. 1 (March 1967), pp. 75–98; A. Ferrer, *The Argentine Economy* (Berkeley, 1967); V. Vázquez-Presedo, *El Caso Argentino. Migración de factores, comercio exterior y desarrollo, 1875–1914* (Buenos Aires, 1971).

Buenos Aires and the other provinces. Buenos Aires – which was mainly a trading centre – remained in favour of a very liberal policy, whereas other provinces – especially those in the north and the west, which had had a significant industrial sector since the eighteenth century – supported protectionism. Buenos Aires even tried to secede from the Federal Union several times before 1880, and from 1853 to 1859 she was an independent state. On the whole, from the second half of the nineteenth century, trade policies tilted towards protectionism.

The tariff which was adopted in 1854 (and which did not affect Buenos Aires) already contained protectionist elements. The tariff schedule was a very rudimentary one, containing only 60 items, but there were fairly progressive *ad valorem* import duties: 5 per cent for raw materials and semi-manufactured goods; and 15–20 per cent for manufactured goods (apart from machinery, which was taxed at 5 per cent). This protection also affected agricultural products, most of which were liable to duties of 20 per cent. A certain number of specific duties were levied on exports, especially for products derived from animals which, until the 1880s, formed the major part of Argentina's exports.

The real shift towards a protectionism aimed at industrialization took place during the 1870s. From 1873–5 bounties were offered to the first companies to develop particular industries. Three reasons explained the tariff reform of 1876: the need to protect infant industries, the desire to reduce imports, and the fiscal imperative of increasing federal revenue. Manufactured goods were liable to *ad valorem* duties of 40 per cent; semi-manufactured goods to either 10 or 20 per cent. Most machinery and equipment, however, was exempt from duty; and most raw materials were taxed at 20 per cent. In 1880 Argentina experienced one of those shifts in economic policy which have remained characteristic until the present time. The effective protection of the tariff system was reduced by increasing import duties on raw materials and by reducing certain duties on manufactured goods. In 1889, however, the trend was reversed, and the new protectionism was strengthened by the tariff reform of 1891. The effective protection of manufactured goods was then very high (except for machinery), since the scale of import duties ranged from 5 to 15 per cent for semi-manufactured goods; 40 per cent for semi-finished goods; and 60 per cent for fully manufactured goods.

In the case of Argentina, as for the other Latin American countries, the analysis of trade policies is complicated by the monetary problem. In most of these countries a wide, fluctuating gap existed between paper money and gold. In the 1905 tariff reform in Argentina this led to the adoption of a system whereby even *ad valorem* duties became in effect specific duties as a result of legislation fixing the value of products to which those duties were applied in terms of gold. The 1905 tariff –

which, with only minor modifications, remained in force until the beginning of the Second World War – implied a liberalization of the import system. On the whole, there was a return to the position in 1880, but with lower import duties on raw materials. This liberalization, however, did not imply a free trade policy. The system in force could be described as a form of protectionism half-way between the moderate protectionism for the Western European countries and the strict protectionism of the United States and of Brazil.

2. Brazil[219]

When the Prince Regent of Portugal fled to Brazil with his court in 1808 one of the first steps he took was to abolish the old system of trade regulation dating back to the colonial pact. A fairly liberal system was established through a series of decrees. As a result of the commercial treaty signed in 1810 with Great Britain, British products even enjoyed a slight preference in relation to Portuguese products: import duties were 15 per cent for British goods, and 16 per cent for Portuguese ones, with an average level of 20 per cent for goods from other countries. Machinery and raw materials for industry were exempted from duty in order to encourage industrialization which remained a more or less constant feature of Brazilian trade policy. Not until 1818 were Portuguese products afforded the same treatment as British ones. In 1828 came a further step towards liberalization: all goods were liable to import duties of 15 per cent, regardless of their country of origin or the nationality of the ships transporting them.

The abolition of the colonial pact had allowed the rise of a fairly wide range of industries, but liberalization had a harmful effect on them. In reaction, what may be called the first true Brazilian tariff was established on 12 August 1844. This tariff had 2,919 items, with predominantly *ad valorem* duties and, in certain cases, the possibility of a choice between *ad valorem* and specific duties. The average import duty was about 20–30 per cent for agricultural products, and 30–40 per cent for manufactured goods. There were no export duties. As a result of pressure from the influential import interests, the 1844 tariff was made more liberal for the next few years; and the 1857 tariff implied a further step towards liberalism.

In the context of Latin America, however, this was not a particularly liberal tariff. At the beginning of the 1850s, *ad valorem* duties on goods 'not elsewhere' classified (quite a good indicator of the degree of average protection hoped for) were 30 per cent in Brazil, that is about the same as

---

[219] This section on Brazil is based essentially on the following source (in addition to those already mentioned): A. Bandeira de Mello, *Politique commerciale du Brésil* (Rio de Janeiro, 1936).

in Mexico and Venezuela, compared with 28 per cent in Bolivia, 25 per cent in Chile and Peru, 15 per cent in Argentina, 10 per cent in Uruguay, and 5 per cent in Haiti.

The shift towards a strict form of industrial protectionism began in 1874 when a uniform duty of 40 per cent was applied to all imports. This obviously led to a very limited degree of effective protection. The first real tariff principally aimed at economic rather than revenue objectives was that of 1879 (which came into force in 1880). This was openly protectionist. Its creator claimed that 'Protectionist measures are never wrong for new countries like ours, where industry is not yet strong enough to face foreign competition.'[220] Import duties on manufactured goods were about 50–60 per cent. Brazil thus became one of the three to five most highly protectionist countries in the world. It should be added that export duties were also in force, and these were, in fact, the main source of revenue for most states in the Brazilian Federation.

A series of tariff revisions and other changes made only fairly minor modifications to this trade policy, which continued to be based on the development of industry by protectionist means until the tariff of 5 June 1934. This policy clearly owed as much to the example of the United States as to that of continental Europe. As far as industry was concerned, it was certainly successful. Between 1882 and 1915 the output of cloth in Brazil multiplied twenty-threefold, reaching 470 million metres (or 18 metres per capita). Between 1878 and 1913 the number of spindles for spinning cotton increased eightyfold. In 1913, too, the foundations of a metal industry were already established.[221]

3. Mexico[222]

In contrast to the majority of the countries of Latin America, Mexico's independence was achieved only after a long and bloody conflict in which social conflicts were as important as the political. Independence was achieved only in 1821. The first tariff of 15 December 1821 was

[220] Quoted by Bandeiro de Mello, *Politique commerciale du Brésil*, p. 66.
[221] According to S. J. Stein, *The Brazilian Cotton Manufacture* (Cambridge, Mass., 1957); N. H. Leff, *Underdevelopment and Development in Brazil* (London, 1982); W. Baer, *The Development of Brazilian Steel Industry* (Nashville, 1970).
[222] This section on Mexico is based on the following sources: M. Bitar Letayf, *La vida económica de México de 1824 a 1867 y sus proyecciones* (Mexico, 1964); D. Cosio Villegas, *Historia de la Política aduanal mexicana* (Mexico, 1932); Lerdo de Tejada, *Commercio exterior de México desde la Conquista hasta hoy* (Mexico, 1953); D. G. Lopez Rosado, *Historia y pensamiento económico de México*, vol. IV: *Commercio interior y exterior. Sistema monetario y del crédito* (Mexico, 1971); R. A. Potash, *El banco de Avio de México y el fomento de la industria 1821–1846* (Mexico, 1959); L. Randall, *A Comparative Economic History of Latin America, 1500–1914*, vol. I, *Mexico* (Ann Arbor, 1977); G. Tardiff, *Historia general del comercio exterior mexicano* (Mexico, 1968).
    I wish to thank Mr P. Luban for his help in collecting data.

liberal. But, very soon, the shift towards protectionism was felt, the tariff of 1824 being already less liberal, and that of 1827 implied high protection of goods produced locally, especially cotton fabrics, imports of which faced a 49 per cent *ad valorem* duty.

The real turning-point came in 1829, clearly expressed in a speech of the newly elected president, Vincente Guerrero:

industry, agriculture and manufacture, not only can be improved, but also extended to entirely new fields. The alien application of liberal economic principles and the ill-considered amplitude given to foreign commerce aggravated our problems . . . For the nation to prosper, it is essential that her workers be distributed in all the branches of industry, and particularly that manufactured goods be protected by wisely calculated import prohibitions.[223]

The very strict tariff of 1829 had to be amended in 1830, largely in order to provide more revenue specifically intended for the Banco de Avio Para Fomento de la Industria Nacional (National Industrial Development Bank) which was founded in the same year to foster Mexico's industrialization. It appears that the effects of this bank together with those of the very protectionist elements in the tariff of 1837 (somewhat attenuated in the 1842 tariff) allowed a rapid development of Mexico's industry and especially of its textile production. Around 1850, Mexico was certainly the most industrialized country of the future Third World. Its local industry was able to provide for the entire local consumption of textiles and in terms of the number of cotton spindles per capita, Mexico was then ahead of countries like Russia, Italy, or Spain. Besides textiles, there was also a more or less advanced embryo of other industries: paper, glass, and especially iron, whose production was the most important among the future less-developed countries.

The *de facto* alliance of the industrial group with the local raw cotton producers became looser in the 1840s when local production of cotton became unable to supply the demands of industry. The prohibition of raw cotton imports was lifted in 1846. Two other factors led to a reduction in the extent of the prohibitions: the fiscal needs of the government and the development of smuggling. The tariff of 1856 did not involve major changes, but that of 1872 implied a total reorganization – all prohibitions were abolished and, as a rule, *ad valorem* duties were replaced by specific ones. But this did not imply any real change in trade policy which remained protectionist, and designed to shelter the local industries.

No real break occurred in the years when Porfirio Diaz was in power (1876–1910). The new tariff of 1887 was designed more to adapt the classifications than to change commercial policies. Some modifications were incorporated in the 1891 tariff which tried to yield to some liberal

---

[223] Randall, *Comparative Economic History*, vol. I, p. 137.

demands, but without really abandoning protection for local industries. This and other measures in favour of industrialization enabled a further development of local industries which had stagnated during the troubled quarter of a century that preceded the Porfirio period. In 1910, the eve of the revolutionary period, the local cotton industry had over 700,000 spindles, and iron production amounted to some 50,000 tons. However, in relative terms, the success of Mexican industrialization policy through tariff protection was less great in 1910 than around 1850. The textile industries of the less-advanced European countries had largely overtaken Mexico by 1910 and so had Brazil.

The fall of Diaz did not lead to a change in the tariff system until 1930, but, in order to raise revenue, a surtax of 5 per cent was introduced in 1912 which was raised to 10 per cent on 16 February 1913, and to 65 per cent on 28 October of the same year.

D. THE SEMI-INDEPENDENT COUNTRIES OUTSIDE EUROPE: AN ENFORCED LIBERALISM

The commercial history of these countries is by no means uniform, but nearly all ten or so of the states in this category[224] shared one important characteristic. This was the fact that the European powers obliged them, directly or indirectly, to open up their national markets. This could be described as an enforced commercial liberalism. These countries thus found themselves among the few liberal countries, along with the United Kingdom and The Netherlands (see Tables 9 and 16). We cannot here examine the history of trade policies in all these countries, so we shall look at just the most important and significant ones: China, Japan, Turkey, and Iran. These four represented around 1913 some 90 per cent of the trade of this entire group of countries and some 94 per cent of its population.

1. China[225]

After a period of commercial freedom which had begun at the end of the seventeenth century,[226] the imperial edict of 1757 marked the beginning

---

[224] The following countries in Asia and Africa were not formal colonies in the nineteenth century (the independent Latin American countries are not included here; see the preceding section): Abyssinia, Afghanistan, China, the states of the Arab peninsula, Iran, Japan (until 1899), Liberia, Siam, and Turkey (or the Ottoman Empire).

[225] Based on the following sources: (Chin) Chu, *The Tariff Problem in China* (New York, 1916); (Hon-Chun) Hou, *Histoire dounaière de la Chine de 1842 à 1911* (Paris, 1929); Stephane Siao, *Les régimes douaniers de la Chine* (Paris, 1931); S. F. Wright, *China's Struggle for Tariff Autonomy 1843–1938* (Shanghai, 1938).

[226] In 1685 Chinese ships were allowed to leave the mainland and the ports were open to foreign trade. In 1690 a general tariff common to all ports provided for duties of 4 per cent to be paid by ships coming into port and of 1.6 per cent to be paid by those going out. This was in addition to taxes based on the tonnage of foreign ships.

of a very restrictive phase. This edict confined maritime trade to the two ports of Canton and Macao, and increased various import duties which resulted in a very low level of trade. Around 1840, just before China was forced to open up her market, Chinese exports were probably worth only about $20–30 million per annum, or about $7 per 100 inhabitants, as opposed to 43 for the rest of Asia, 460 for Latin America, and 420 for Europe excluding Russia (and 960 for the United Kingdom).

The opium war (1839–42), which was in fact aimed at making the vast Chinese territory available to British trade by military action, ended with the treaty of Nanking signed on 29 August 1842. The most important clauses of this treaty concerned trade and involved the opening up of five ports[227] to British trade and the establishment of 'a fair and consistent tariff of import duties'. This 'fair' tariff was set up by supplementary agreements signed in 1843, which provided for specific duties calculated on the basis of 5 per cent *ad valorem* of both imports and exports. They also included the most-favoured-nation clause (which was to remain a feature of the tariff history of this type of country) and the opening up of the five ports to all foreign ships. In addition, treaties were signed with the United States (1844), France (1844), Belgium (1845), Sweden (1847), and Russia (1851).

This was the beginning of China's loss of tariff independence, which was to last until 1929. The next stage in this process was the signing of the treaties of Tientsin in June 1858, drawn up after the joint military intervention of France and Great Britain. These treaties opened up ten more ports to foreign trade and explicitly authorized the import of opium. Furthermore, the administration of duties gradually came under the control of British officials; among other posts, the British took over that of inspector general of customs.[228] Finally, a set of measures gave European traders certain advantages over local traders.

The adjusting of specific duties to the principle of 5 per cent *ad valorem* duties, the further opening up of the Chinese market and the thorny problem of internal taxes resulted in numerous modifications to commercial legislation – modifications which were nearly always made in the interests of the Europeans. The only positive development was the agreement with Great Britain in December 1906 providing for an annual reduction of 10 per cent (based on the 1907 volume) in imports of opium, from 1908 on. This agreement at first covered the period 1908–10 but was prolonged until 1917 (by which time there was a complete ban on opium imports).

From 1906 efforts to achieve tariff autonomy intensified. The first step was taken at the Special Tariff Conference held in Peking from 26 October 1925 to 9 April 1926 when the great powers recognized in

---

[227] These were Canton, Amoy, Foochow, Ning-Pong, and Shanghai.
[228] The second Inspector General, R. Hart, remained in office from 1863 to 1908.

principle China's right to fix her own autonomous tariff from 1 January 1929, the first autonomous tariff passed on 30 December 1930. From then onwards her autonomy gradually became effective. However, the political problems which marked this period delayed this process so that in practical terms its effects were negligible. In 1913 China (excluding Manchuria) provided 1.6 per cent of world exports, but in 1932–4 this had fallen to 0.97 per cent and was only 1 per cent in 1934–6, on the eve of the Japanese attack.

2. Japan[229]

For Japan, the military expedition of Commodore Perry's four American ships in 1853 marked the end of three centuries of severe restrictions on trade with the rest of the world. These restrictions were even more severe than those in China, since, around 1840, it is likely that Japanese exports were less than one-fifteenth or one-twentieth of those from China, whose population was ten times that of Japan. The extent to which the Japanese economy was cut off from the rest of the world is also revealed by the ratio between the prices of gold and silver which around 1850 differed by a factor of eight times in Japan, compared with a ratio of 16:1 in the West. The treaty of Kangawa (31 March 1854), which resulted from Perry's American military expedition, opened up two ports for trade. Other countries pressed for and obtained similar advantages for themselves; but Japan really relinquished her commercial sovereignty on 29 July 1858 when she signed a formal trade agreement with the United States granting substantial advantages, which were then extended to nearly all the other trading powers by a series of similar treaties. These treaties involved rights of extra-territoriality for Europeans (who monopolized foreign trade), and very low import duties. In fact, as in China, the 5 per cent rule was applied for both imports and exports.

Efforts to achieve commercial independence began with the Meiji revolution (1868), but only began to show results in 1899. Between 1894 and 1897 treaties were renegotiated with the major trading powers. These treaties, which came into force simultaneously in July and August 1899, allowed an increase in import duties and provided for complete tariff autonomy in 1911. Import duties, which in 1889–91 amounted to 3.9 per cent of the value of imports, rose to 9.9 per cent in 1906–9.[230] The first autonomous tariff of 1910 (which came into force in 1911) was protectionist. Import duties (most of them specific) on manufactured

[229] Based essentially on the following sources (but see also the notes): K. Takahashi, *The Rise and Development of Japan's Modern Economy: The Basis for 'Miraculous' Growth* (Tokyo, 1967), pp. 303–7; US Tariff Commission, *The Tariff and its History*, pp. 44–7.

[230] From *Oriental Economist: Foreign Trade of Japan: A Statistical Survey* (Tokyo, 1935), pp. 452 and 454.

goods varied between 15 and 50 per cent. In 1913 the average duties in force were about 20–30 per cent for semi-manufactured goods and about 30–40 per cent for manufactured goods (except for machinery and equipment, where duties averaged some 20–25 per cent).[231]

3. Turkey[232]

The great paradox of Turkish trade policy in the nineteenth century is the fact that its whole tariff system depended on treaties signed in the sixteenth and seventeenth centuries; treaties which, at the time, were essentially favours granted by a powerful Empire to partners rightly held to be her political and military inferiors. These concessions concerned tariff policies amongst other things, and in particular they contained the most-favoured-nation clause. According to the capitulations signed with France in 1673 (the first one dates from 1535) import duties could not exceed 3 per cent *ad valorem*. In fact, most duties were specific, but they were revised every 14 years to keep them in line with this level of incidence.

The treaty signed with Great Britain on 16 August 1838 allowed import duties to rise from 3 to 5 per cent, but abolished all monopolies and prohibitions. Again, most of these duties were converted to specific duties which brought the rate, on average, nearer to 3 than 5 per cent. This treaty contained the most-favoured-nation clause. In addition to the uniformity and the low level of port duties (which gave virtually no effective protection), local industry was further handicapped by high taxes and export duties. As the Austrian ambassador to Odessa remarked at the time, 'Now that a Belgian merchant pays five per cent on goods sold in Turkey; a Turkish merchant pays twelve per cent for exports or even for transport from one of the Ottoman States to another.'[233]

There is no doubt that the extreme liberalism of her commercial regulations, which made McCulloch declare Turkey entitled 'to read a lesson to the most civilised European powers',[234] was one of the fundamental causes of the deindustrialization of the Ottoman Empire. In 1846 Disraeli noted, in connection with the discussion of the British tariff, 'There has been free trade in Turkey and what has it produced? It has destroyed some of the finest manufacturers in the world. As late as 1812 these manufacturers existed; but they have been destroyed.'[235]

---

[231] Calculated from data provided by the Board of Trade, *Foreign Import Duties 1913* (Parliamentary Paper by Command No. 7180) (London, 1913).

[232] Based on the following sources: C. Issawi (ed.), *The Economic History of the Middle East, 1800–1914* (Chicago, 1966), especially pp. 38–40; V. J. Puryear, *International Economics and Diplomacy in the Near East: A Study of British Commercial Policy in the Levant, 1834–1853* (Stamford, 1935); US Tariff Commission, *The Tariff and its History*.

[233] Puryear, *International Economics*, p. 127.

[234] J. R. McCulloch, *Dictionary of Commerce and Commercial Navigation* (1844 edn), p. 374.

[235] Quoted by B. Holland, *The Fall of Protection*, p. 265.

From 1861 Abdul Aziz attempted to carry out a policy of economic development, but this was seriously hampered by his lack of freedom to manoeuvre. The creation of an industrial sector proved almost impossible with new import duties, which could only be raised to 8 per cent, resulting from a series of treaties signed in 1861–2. The attempts to encourage reindustrialization were no more successful than those to promote foreign trade. In spite of Aziz's efforts to promote the sale of semi-tropical goods, exports did not fulfil their promise (probably for climatic reasons). Between 1865–9 and 1908–12 imports from the Ottoman Empire into Great Britain only rose by some 20 per cent, declining from 8.1 to 4.5 per cent of all British imports.[236]

From the beginning of the twentieth century pressure for tariff independence increased. In 1911 Turkey was allowed to increase her import duties to a new maximum of 11 per cent. In September 1914, benefiting from the war, the concessions were abolished, allowing the tariff system to be modified. Real tariff autonomy, however, only began with the treaty of Lausanne (24 July 1923) by which the European powers accepted the total repeal of the concessions.

4. Iran[237]

Russia played the same role in relation to Iran as England did for China and the United States for Japan. The Russo-Iranian peace treaty of Golestan (12 October 1813) marked the beginning of Iran's loss of commercial autonomy. This treaty contained commercial clauses which, in particular, fixed import duties on trade between Russia and Iran at 5 per cent *ad valorem*. It should be noted that since the sixteenth century Iran had maintained a liberal trade policy with very low import duties. The treaty of Torkamantchai (22 February 1828) was even more one-sided and, as a result of the most-favoured-nation clause, was to lead to the loss of tariff autonomy. Not only were import duties fixed at a uniform 5 per cent, but foreign goods were exempted from internal customs duties.

The tariff agreement signed with Russia on 13 December 1902 and the commercial convention of 9 February 1903 with England meant an additional loss of commercial autonomy. As far as imports were concerned, the new tariff resulting from these agreements exempted 34 items out of 42 from duties, and the specific duties affecting the remaining goods were generally lower than the previous 5 per cent (about 3.5 per cent for manufactured goods).

---

[236] Figures adjusted to take into account changes of territory.
[237] Based essentially on H. Korassani, *Le régime douanier de l'Iran* (Paris, 1937).

Iran recovered her tariff independence only in 1928 as a result, on the one hand, of the International Economic Conference of 1927, and on the other hand, of the change of regime in Russia, which renounced in 1928 her previous privileges. The first autonomous tariff was voted on 4 May 1928, being a double tariff intended to raise revenue rather than increase protection (it also provided for export duties). Import duties averaged about 15 per cent.

CHAPTER II

Commercial policy between the wars*

I. *War and post-war reconstruction*

The First World War marked the end of an era in the history of commercial relations among countries. New boundaries set in the peace treaties, especially with Austria and Hungary, converted pre-1914 internal trade to international trade. Trade relations interrupted by war could not always be restored. Extended fighting and disruption of peacetime economic intercourse produced substantial changes in the economic capacities and interests of major trading nations. Monetary disturbance evoked responses in trade policy, especially increases in tariffs, to offset effects of exchange depreciation abroad. A loosely concerted attempt was made after the war to patch up the fabric of trade relationships, but with nothing like the fervour exhibited after the Second World War. There was virtually no planning of post-war trade policies, despite President Wilson's third of the fourteen points that called for 'removal, as far as possible, of all economic barriers and the establishment of an equality of trade conditions among all nations consenting to the peace and associating themselves with its maintenance'.

Exigencies of war led to changes in commercial policy. The McKenna budget in Britain in 1915 imposed duties of $33\frac{1}{3}$ per cent on motor cars and parts, musical instruments, clocks, watches, and cinematographic film in an effort to reduce imports of luxuries and to save shipping space – although the point has been made that the shipping space taken by watches is minimal (Kreider, 1943, p. 13). Unlike previous luxury taxes in Britain, these duties on imports were not matched by domestic excises to eliminate the protective effect. The tariffs, moreover, made it possible for the United Kingdom to discriminate in trade in favour of the British Empire, something it could not do under the regime of free trade which had prevailed since the 1850s. Canada had granted preferential tariff treatment to Britain on a unilateral and non-reciprocal basis since 1898 – Britain assenting to the extent that it denounced the trade treaties with Germany and Belgium going back to the 1860s under which those

---

* I am grateful for the comments on the original draft of Barry Eichengreen, Jonathan Hughes, and Donald Moggridge.

countries had the right to claim concessions made by one part of the Empire to another on a most-favoured-nation basis. The Finance Act of 1919 further reduced excise taxes on Empire tea, cocoa, coffee, chicory, currants, and certain dried fruits by one-sixth, and on Empire wines by one-third. The Key Industries Act of 1919 designed to strengthen defence industries equally contained preferences for the Empire, as did the Safeguarding of Industries Act of 1921. If the McKenna duties were designed to economize shipping and foreign exchange, the Finance Act of 1919 to raise revenue, and the Key Industries Act of 1919 to serve national defence, the Safeguarding of Industries Act levying tariffs on imports of gloves, domestic glassware, gas mantles – a list extended in 1925 to include leather, lace, cutlery, pottery, packing paper, and enamelled hollow ware – represented straightforward protection of industries hurt by foreign competition.

A number of countries increased tariff coverage and raised rates to gain revenue. French minimum tariff rates had been raised by 1918 from 5 to 20 per cent, and maximum rates from 10 to 40 per cent. The use of import quotas in France dates from 1919, rather than the depression in 1930, although export and import prohibitions were a widespread feature of Colbert's mercantilism two and a half centuries earlier. In countries where the principal fiscal instrument was the tariff, such as Canada, tariff duties were increased early after the outbreak of war.

Fitful attention was given to commodity problems by Britain. Long concerned about the prospect of interruption of cotton supplies from the Southern United States as a result either of boll weevil or black rebellion, she had contemplated an Empire scheme for producing cotton. The planting of Gezira in the Sudan was started in 1914 with the decision to irrigate 300,000 acres, but the Empire Cotton Growing Corporation was not chartered until November 1921, sometime after the acute shortage of cotton fibre during the war and early post-war period. An Empire Resources Development Committee proposed in 1915 a scheme for producing palm kernel in West Africa and processing it in the United Kingdom, foreshadowing the East African groundnut scheme after the Second World War. The technique envisaged was an export tax of £2 per ton to be continued for five years after the war, but that was to be rebated in favour of British processors. The scheme was started in October 1919 but met sharp Gold Coast resistance. When the price of palm kernel fell, the project became untenable and the duty was withdrawn in July 1922 (Hancock, 1940, pp. 113–18).

Limited as it was, post-war planning took place along lines of military alliance. France took the lead in an Allied economic conference in June 1916 that produced a resolution committing the Allies to take first temporary and then permanent steps to make themselves independent of enemy countries in matters of raw-material supply, essential manufactures, and the organization of trade, finance and shipping (Drummond, 1972, p. 56). Neutral reaction, including that of the United States neutral at that time, was hostile. When the United States entered the war, the notion was dropped despite French efforts to revive it at Versailles (Viner, 1950, pp. 24–5). On the other side, Germany and Austria concluded a treaty before the Armistice in 1918, providing for customs union after the war; the arrangement was not for complete free trade within the union, but permitted Austria–Hungary to retain protection at a preferential level in certain weak industries (*ibid.*, pp. 105–6). In defeat it proved academic, except perhaps as a precedent to the 1931 proposal for *Zollunion* (customs union) between Austria and Germany, and the 1937 *Anschluss*.

Commercial-policy features of the treaties ending the First World War were minimal. Germany was required to agree to apply the tariff nomenclature worked out at The Hague in 1913 (as well as to accept the international conventions of 1904 and 1910 suppressing the white slave trade, the conventions of 16 and 19 November 1885 regarding the establishment of a concert pitch (the wavelength of the musical note of A) and a host of others). The principal effect of these measures seems to have been to stiffen German resistance to subscribing to the agreements. More significantly, Germany was required by the treaty of Versailles to grant the Allies unilateral and unconditional most-favoured-nation treatment for five years. On 10 January 1925 when the five years elapsed and Germany was free to negotiate trade agreements on her own, the post-war period of reconstruction may be said to have come to an end – at least in the area of trade. The lapse of these provisions helped Germany but posed a problem for France which now had to negotiate to obtain outlets for Alsatian textiles and Lorraine minette iron ore which earlier had been marketed in Germany without payment of duties (Schuker, 1976, pp. 219–27).

These five years, however, constituted a period of considerable disorder in fluctuations of business and of exchange rates, and, in consequence, in policies relating to international trade. Anti-dumping legislation was enacted in Japan in 1920, in Australia, Britain, New Zealand and the United States in 1921, when also earlier legislation dating from 1904 in Canada was amended; the anti-dumping provisions of the Fordney–McCumber tariff took effect in 1922 (Viner, 1923, repr. 1966, pp. 192, 219, 227, 231, 246, 258). The United Kingdom further authorized $33\frac{1}{3}$ per cent duties against countries devaluing their currencies, although these were never imposed and were allowed to lapse in 1930. With the franc free to fluctuate, France initiated a system of tariff coefficients which could be adjusted to compensate for inflation at home or revaluations of the exchange rate. The Fordney–McCumber Act of 1922 in the United States not only extended anti-dumping provisions but raised tariffs on a variety of materials which had fallen in price in the sharp recession of 1920–1. Insult was added to injury from this and from the wartime enactment of Prohibition in the United States that cut off imports of wine, beer, and spirits, when the United States took sanitary measures against Spanish grapes and oranges to limit the danger of entry of fruit flies, without giving consideration to the possibility of refrigeration which kills the fruit fly (Jones, 1934, p. 35).

In Eastern Europe, new countries struggled with inflation, depreciation and inadequate sources of revenue, and were forced to levy heavy taxes on trade in a vain effort to restore financial balance. Export taxes were imposed along with import duties, despite a variety of international resolutions urging strongly against prohibitions of exports, and taxation, on the basis of equal access to materials (Bergsten, 1974, pp. 23–4). The finances of Austria and Hungary were supervized by experts under programmes of the Finance Committee of the League of Nations – Austria in 1922, Hungary in 1924 – which experts exerted strenuous efforts to liberalize trade.

As the world economy slowly settled down, the pre-war system of trade treaties was resumed, with extension of the principle of high legislative tariffs – so-called 'bargaining' or 'fighting' tariffs – which would be reduced through mutual tariff concessions agreed in bilateral treaties, and extended through the most-favoured-nation clause. To a degree, the initial increases in tariff rates succeeded better than the subsequent reduction through negotiation, especially as not all countries were prepared to subscribe to the unconditional version of the most-favoured-nation clause (League of Nations (W. T. Page), 1927). The United States especially, with its high Fordney–McCumber tariff, stood aloof from the system. Except in the period from 1890 to 1909 the United States Administration was not empowered to enter into tariff treaties; under the Dingley tariff from 1897 to 1919, no tariff treaties came into force since Senate approval was required but not forthcoming. The Fordney–McCumber tariff of 1922, however, changed United States policy from conditional most-favoured-nation to unconditional treatment. Under the conditional version, concessions offered to one country were made available to others only in exchange for a reciprocal concession. The Tariff Act of 1922's provision for retaliation by the United States against countries which discriminated against American exports was judged to require the more general form of the non-discrimination clause (US Department of State, *Foreign Relations of the United States*, 1923, I, pp. 131–3). Exceptions to the unconditional most-favoured-nation clause were recognized for specific countries, such as Cuba and the

Philippines insofar as the United States was concerned, and regional arrangements, in which 'propinquity' was a usual characteristic (Viner, 1950, p. 19). The British position, opposed by the United States, was that a further exception could be based on 'historical associations, such as were generally recognized'. This referred to Empire preference.

As a policy, Empire preference meant more the relations of the United Kingdom with the Dominions than those with the colonies, including India. 'Tariff reformers' at the turn of the century would have welcomed an imperial *Zollverein*, eliminating all tariffs between the mother country and the rest of the Empire. This was opposed not only by British free traders, who viewed free-trade areas and preferences both as disguises for protectionism, but also by the Dominions that regarded tariffs as a symbol of sovereignty and were unwilling to remove all vestiges of protection for their manufactures against British products. Preferences in the Dominions meant largely tariffs to be levied in Britain against non-Empire foodstuffs, and higher domestic tariffs on foreign manufactures, rather than reductions in existing duties on British goods. Resistance to Empire preference in Britain came not only from free traders, but from those who wanted to hold down the price of food on the one hand, and on the other, those who sought protection against Empire as well as against foreign food producers.

The slogan of Empire visionaries in Britain and the Dominions after the war was 'men, money, and markets'. 'Men' meant assisted settlement of British workers in the Dominions; 'money' help for Empire borrowers in various ways, ranging from preferences in the queue to guaranteed interest; 'markets' referred to Empire preference, to a considerable degree in new products that especially Australia wished to have produced for export by immigrants settled on new farms – particularly dried fruit and frozen beef – rather than the traditional wheat, butter, wool, apples, bacon, cheese.

The Imperial Economic Conference of 1923 made little progress toward tariff preferences: the election called by Stanley Baldwin in 1924 to provide tariffs that could be used for the purpose ended in a Labour victory and even repeal of the McKenna duties and the preferences granted under them. The return of Baldwin to power eleven months later restored the McKenna duties, with lorries added to motor cars, but the Conservatives stopped short of extending tariff discrimination. Feeble efforts were made to undertake non-tariff discrimination through an Empire Marketing Board which was to perform research and promotion. Empire settlement fizzled gently. Empire preference was postponed.

The reconstruction period to 1925 or so was characterized by instability. Rapidly changing exchange rates required rapidly changing tariffs through countervailing charges, or the application of coefficients. Trade agreements were frequently contracted for only three months. Where changes in tariff rates did not occur, administrative regulation was applied. The League of Nations Economic Committee worked to improve the position through such actions as the International Convention Relating to the Simplification of Custom Formalities of 1923, although this soon proved inadequate as far as worst practices were concerned (Winslow, 1936, p. 182).

II. *Normalization of world trade*

The end of the reconstruction period about the middle of the decade was marked by the opening up of capital markets, following the success of the Dawes Loan in 1924 that primed the resumption of German reparations after the hyperinflation of 1923, by the restoration of the pound sterling to par on the gold standard in 1925, or perhaps by the expiration of the Versailles restriction on Germany's right to conclude commercial treaties, and with it the rapid extension of trade agreements in Europe. Whatever the event, it marked the initiation of increased efforts for trade normalization. A minor effort was represented by the International Convention for the Protection of Industrial Property of 1925 (Brown, 1950, p. 34). Of greater weight were the convention for the Abolition of Import and Export Prohibitions and Restrictions, with which was associated a special agreement on hides, skins and bones, and a World Economic Conference on trade expansion, all in 1927. In 1929 a special conference produced a convention calling for national treatment for foreign nationals and enterprises. A modernized tariff nomenclature to replace the 1913 Hague list was started in the 1920s, produced a first draft in 1931, and a final one in 1937 (League of Nations, 1942, p. 45).

A number of these conventions failed to be ratified. That on the treatment of foreign nationals fell through because some states were unwilling to liberalize, and the liberal states were unwilling to sign an agreement which would have weakened the force of the principle of national treatment (League of Nations, 1942, p. 27). The Convention on Imports and Exports prohibitions finally lapsed when the Poles refused to sign, because of an exception made for Germany, which reduced the value of the treaty in their eyes. Agreement on a tariff truce and subsequent reductions in rates was reached at the 1927 World Economic Conference, but this meeting was attended by delegations in their individual capacities and did not bind governments. Governments agreed on the necessity of reducing tariffs but did nothing about it. The League of Nations review of commercial policies in the inter-war period called it a striking paradox that conferences unanimously adopted recommendations, and governments proclaimed their intentions to lower tariffs, but did nothing (League of Nations, 1942, p. 101), asking why governments made such recommendations if they did not propose to carry them out (*ibid.*, p. 109). The answer furnished by one economist who had served on the economic secretariat of the League was that 'the pseudo-internationalism of the nineteenth century was clearly an out-growth of British financial leadership and trading enterprise, backed by the economic supremacy of London and by the British Navy' (Condliffe, 1940, p. 118). With British hegemony lost and nothing to take its place, international relations lapsed into anarchy. Britain lost the will and lacked the power to enforce international cooperation as she had done in the nineteenth century (*ibid.*, p. 145).

Discouragement over the failure of tariffs to come down despite agreement to lower them led to an attempt at a commodity-by-commodity approach, foreshadowing the free trade for iron and steel undertaken in the European Coal and Steel Community on Robert Schuman's initiative in May 1950. The Economic Committee of the League of Nations reported in March 1928 that there was no prospect of a general tariff reduction by means of standard cuts or the setting of a maximum scale of duties. Cement and aluminium were chosen for a case-by-case approach. A year of negotiation, however, produced no result. The League's account of the attempt cites as reasons (1) that reductions in duties in single products would upset national industrial structures; (2) that it would increase the protection of finished goods – implying the so-called effective-rate-of-protection argument which was more fully developed in the 1960s; and (3) that among the limited groups of commodities and countries concerned, compensatory reductions were hard to find (League of Nations, 1942, pp. 128–9).

While governments were agreeing to the necessity to lower tariffs but doing nothing about it, action was taken directly on a number of commodity fronts. Most conspicuous was the Stevenson rubber plan of 1923–4 which raised the price of rubber by 1926 to almost four times its 1923 level. To American protests, the British replied that it was 'impossible to argue that the present high price is attributable solely or even mainly to the operation of the rubber restriction scheme. It is due to the great expansion of the demand for rubber. Only one half of the supply comes from the restricted area' (*Foreign Relations of the United States*, 1926, vol. II, p. 359). The fact that the other half – the Netherlands East Indies – had been left out of the scheme contributed to its early breakdown (Knorr, 1946).

More cartels were formed in a variety of commodities, that Mason divides into three groups: (1) industrial raw materials and foodstuffs, like tin, oil, wheat, sugar, etc.; (2) standardized processed and semi-fabricated goods such as steel rails, cement, tinplate, plate glass, dyes, etc.; and (3) highly fabricated, specialized, and frequently patented items such as electrical equipment, pharmaceuticals, glass, etc. (Mason, 1946, p. 16). Mason notes that the Soviet Union was a party to at least three international control schemes and eight cartel arrangements, despite its hostility to capitalism (*ibid.*, p. 14n.). Most of the commodity agreements begun in the 1920s broke down in the depression of the 1930s. The rubber scheme collapsed in 1928. Prices of agricultural commodities levelled off in 1925 and declined thereafter, faster after 1928, as European reconstruction crowded the extra-European supplies expanded to fill the gap left by war and post-war shortages, and demand shrank with such changes as the replacement of oats for horses by gasoline for motor cars.

Two of the most durable agreements were in oil: the As–Is Agreement concluded at Achnacarry, Scotland in 1928 between Sir Henry Detering of the Shell Oil Company and Walter Teagle of the Standard Oil Company of New Jersey, that provided that no oil company would seek to penetrate into markets where it was not already distributing, so that everything would stay 'as is'; and in the same year the Red-Line Agreement, among members of the Turkish Petroleum Company, that drew a line across the Middle East (through what is now Kuwait) and limited exploration by partners below that line, thereby ultimately making it possible for the Standard Oil Company of California, which was not a partner, to discover oil in Saudi Arabia (Federal Trade Commission, 1952, pp. 199ff., 63).

National programmes further affected world markets in wheat and sugar. The Italian 'battle for grain' begun by Mussolini in 1925 was of limited economic significance, since Italy could not escape dependence on foreign supplies, but provided a disturbing symptom of the troubles of the 1930s. Great Britain expanded production of beet sugar through a bounty; Japan undertook sugar production in Formosa (Taiwan) and ceased to buy from Java. As the price of wheat declined, Germany raised tariffs in 1928 to slow down the movement of labour off the farm. From 1927 to 1931, German tariffs on foodstuffs were broadly doubled. France raised tariffs in 1928 and 1929 before resorting to quotas. Mixing provisions, under which foreign grain had to be mixed with domestic, were undertaken from 1929 on, patterned after the practice in motion pictures which allowed exhibitors to show foreign films only in fixed proportions to those domestically produced. In the United States, help for agriculture took the form of proposals for export subsidies, but President Coolidge's veto of the McNary–Haugen bill in 1928 led presidential candidate Herbert Hoover to seek other means of agricultural relief, and to promise help for farmers in his campaign speeches in the summer and autumn of that year. The League of Nations commented in 1942 that 'before the end of 1928 it was evident that the United States tariff was going to be raised above the formidable level of 1922' (League of Nations, 1942, p. 126).

Grain exporters of Eastern Europe were especially affected by the world decline in price and sought solutions in meetings at Warsaw in August 1930, Bucharest in October 1930, Belgrade in November 1930, and Warsaw again in the same month. They tried on the one hand to limit exports of grain to improve the terms of trade, and on the other to obtain preferences in import markets of Western Europe. The first proposal was never adopted. After the 1932 Stresa meeting, some reciprocal preferences were worked out between Austria and Hungary on one side and Italy on the other, but with poor results.

A strenuous effort was made to halt tariff increases. The World Economic Conference of 1927 recognized that general demobilization of tariffs would be slow, and the Economic Committee of the League of Nations in March 1928 saw no prospect of general reduction. The September 1929 General Assembly of the League moved from attempts at reduction to an effort to halt increases. It called for a conference to stabilize rates for two or three years and then to lower them. The Preliminary Conference with a View to Concerted Action met in February 1930, but too late. It proposed extending existing agreements to 1 April 1931 and to provide opportunities for negotiation before tariffs were raised. By this time, however, retaliation against the forthcoming Hawley–Smoot tariff bill was far along. A second Conference with a View to Concerted Economic Action in November 1930 failed equally. The Netherlands, which, along with Britain, had pressed for the tariff truce, turned to a smaller group and organized the Oslo group. On 22 December, Norway, Sweden, Holland, and Belgium signed an agreement undertaking not to raise tariffs without giving notice to other members. It was a brave example without much impact.

Quite unrelated to the fortunes of world incomes, prices, or trade, a highly original argument for tariffs emerged in Australia at the end of the prosperity of the 1920s. It bore resemblance to an earlier argument put forward by Alvin S. Johnson in 1908 that tariffs could add to capital formation by reallocating income from spenders to savers – an argument which went unnoticed until Harvey Leibenstein introduced similar notions into the discussion of economic growth in the 1960s. J. B. Brigden published an article in the *Economic Record* of November 1925 on 'The Australian Tariff and the Standard of Living'. He concluded that whereas the tariff on wheat in Britain favoured the landed classes, that on manufactured goods in Australia would redound to the standard of living of wage-earners, and increase the population of the country. Subsequently the Australian government appointed a committee of experts, including Brigden, D. B. Copland, E. C. Dyason, L. F. Giblin, and Wickens, which in 1929 produced *The Australian Tariff: An Economic Enquiry* that supported Brigden's conclusion. The analysis remained to be worked out by W. F. Stolper and P. A. Samuelson in their classic article of 1941, 'Protection and Real Wages', and was to be rediscovered for Canada in the post-war period by C. L. Barber. It was heatedly debated during the 1930s both in Australia and in Anglo-Saxon economic literature. What was clear, however, was that Australia chose not to be guided by the neo-classical static maximizing calculus of foreign-trade theory, but rather to introduce into the discussion dynamic considerations of economic growth, migration, as well as income redistribution.

III. *The disintegration of world trade*

A. THE HAWLEY–SMOOT TARIFF

The origins of the Hawley-Smoot tariff, as already noted, reach back to the autumn of 1928 when Herbert Hoover, campaigning for the presidency, promised to do something to help farmers suffering under the weight of declining agricultural prices. A special session of the Congress was called in January 1929, long in advance of the stock-market crash of October of that year, and began to prepare a tariff bill. Its scope was widened from agriculture to include industry; Democrats joined Republicans in their support for tariffs for all who sought them; and both Republicans and Democrats were ultimately pushed from the committee room as lobbyists took over the task of setting the rates (Schattschneider, 1935). A groundswell of resentment spread around the world and quickly led to retaliation. Italy objected to duties on hats and bonnets of straw, wool-felt hats, and olive oil; Spain reacted sharply to increases on cork and onions; Canada took umbrage at increases on maple sugar and syrup, potatoes, cream, butter, buttermilk, and skimmed milk. Switzerland was moved to boycott American typewriters, fountain pens, motor cars, and films because of increased duties on watches, clocks, embroidery, cheese, and shoes (Jones, 1934). Retaliation was begun long before the bill was enacted into law in June 1930. As it passed the House of Representatives in May 1929, boycotts broke out and foreign governments moved to raise rates against United States products, even though rates could be moved up or down in the Senate or by the conference committee. In all, 34 formal protests were lodged with the Department of State from foreign countries. One thousand and twenty-eight economists in the United States, organized by Paul Douglas, Irving Fisher, Frank Graham, Ernest Patterson, Henry Seager, Frank Taussig, and Clair Wilcox, and representing the 'Who's Who' of the profession, asked

President Hoover to veto the legislation (*New York Times*, 5 May 1930). A weak defence was offered contemporaneously by President Hoover as he signed the bill, saying 'No tariff act is perfect' (Hoover, 1952, p. 291), and another 45 years later by Joseph S. Davis, who claimed that the Senate got out of hand, but that Hoover had won two key points: inclusion of the flexible provisions permitting the Tariff Commission to consider complaints and recommend to the president higher or lower rates, and exclusion of an export-debenture plan along the lines of the McNary–Haugen bill (Davis, 1975, p. 239). Both views were in the minority.

The high tariffs of 1921, 1922, and *a fortiori* 1930 were generally attacked on the grounds that the United States was a creditor nation, and that creditor nations were required to maintain low tariffs or free trade in order that their debtors might earn the foreign exchange to pay their debt service. This view is now regarded as fallacious since the macroeconomic impacts effects of tariffs on the balance of payments are typically reversed, wholly or in large part, by the income changes which they generate. Under the post-Second World War General Agreement on Tariffs and Trade, balance of payments considerations are ignored in settling on tariff reductions in bilateral or multilateral bargaining. In addition, a careful study for the Department of Commerce by Hal. B. Lary states that the effect of the tariff increases of 1922 and 1930, and those of the reductions after 1930, cannot be detected in the import statistics. This was partly perhaps because tariffs were already close to prohibitive and early reductions were minimal, but mainly for the reason that wide fluctuations in world economic activity and prices overwhelmed any lasting impact of tariffs on trade (Lary, 1943, pp. 53–4).

The significance of the Hawley–Smoot tariff goes far beyond its effect on American imports and the balance of payments to the core of the question of the stability of the world economy. President Hoover let Congress get out of hand and failed to govern (Schattschneider, 1935, p. 293); by taking national action and continuing on its own course through the early stages of the depression, the United States served notice on the world that it was unwilling to take responsibility for world economic stability. Sir Arthur Salter's view (1932, pp. 172–3) that Hawley–Smoot marked a turning point in world history is excessive if it was meant in causal terms, apposite if taken symbolically.

Retaliation and business decline wound down the volume and value of world trade. The earliest retaliations were taken by France and Italy in 1929. In Canada the Liberal government kept parliament in session during the final days when the conference committee was completing the bill, and then put through increases in tariff rates affecting one-quarter of Canadian imports from the United States. Despite this resistance to its neighbour, the government lost the August 1930 election to the Conservatives, who then raised tariffs in September 1930, June 1931, and again in connection with the 1932 Ottawa agreements (McDiarmid, 1946, p. 273). The action in May under the Liberal, W. L. Mackenzie King involved both increases and decreases in duties, with Empire preference extended through raising and lowering about one-half each of general and intermediate rates, but lowering the bulk of those applicable to Empire goods. Subsequent measures typically raised Empire rates, but general and intermediate rates more. In September 1930, anti-dumping rates were increased from 15 to 50 per cent.

B.   DEEPENING DEPRESSION

The Hawley–Smoot tariff began as a response to the decline in agricultural prices and was signed into law as the decline in business picked up speed. For a time during the second quarter of 1930, it looked as though the world economy might recover from the deflationary shock of the New York stock-market crash in October 1929, which had come on the heels of the failure in London of the Clarence Hatry conglomerate after the discovery of fraudulent collateral used to support bank loans in September and the failure of the Frankfurt Insurance Company in Germany in August. This is not the place to set forth the causes of the depression in agricultural overproduction, the halt to foreign lending by the United States in 1928, the end of the housing boom, the stock-market crash, frightened short-term capital movements, United States monetary policy and the like. It is sufficient to observe that the chance of recovery was seen to fade at the end of June 1930 with the signing of the Hawley–Smoot tariff, the outbreak of retaliatory cuts in international trade, and the near-failure of the Young loan (to reprime German reparations) in international capital markets. Events thereafter were uniformly depressing from Nazi gains in German elections in September 1930, the collapse of the Creditanstalt in Vienna in May 1931, the run on German banks in June and July, until the Standstill Agreement that blocked repayment of all German bank credits shifted the attack to sterling, which went off the gold standard in September 1931, followed by the yen in December.

One item of commercial policy contributed to the spreading deflation. In the autumn of 1930, Austria and Germany announced an intention to form a customs union. The proposal had its proximate origin in a working paper prepared by the German Foreign Ministry for the World Economic Conference in 1927. It was discussed on the side by Austrian and German Foreign Ministers at the August 1929 meeting on the Young Plan at The Hague. Germany took it up seriously, however, only after the September 1930 elections which recorded alarming gains for the National Socialists, and Brüning, the Chancellor, felt a strong need for a foreign-policy success. The French immediately objected on the grounds that customs union between Austria and Germany violated the provision of the treaty of Trianon which required Austria to uphold her political independence. France took the case to the International Court of Justice at The Hague for an interpretation of the treaty. Other French and British and Czechoslovak objections on the grounds of violation of the most-favoured-nation clause were laid before the League of Nations Council (Viner, 1950, p. 10). The International Court ultimately ruled in favour of the French position in the summer of 1931. By this time, however, the Austrian Creditanstalt had collapsed – barely possible because of French action in pulling credits out of Austria, though the evidence is scanty – the Austrian government responsible for the proposal of customs union had long since fallen, and the run against banks and currencies had moved on from Austria to Germany and Britain.

In the autumn of 1931, appreciation of the mark, the dollar and the gold-bloc currencies as a consequence of the depreciation of sterling and the currencies associated with it, applied strenuous deflation to Germany, the United States and to Western Europe from September 1931 to June 1932. Depreciation of the yen in December 1931 marked the start of a drive of Japanese exports into British and Dutch colonies in Asia and Africa, and of colonial and metropolitan steps to hold them down. June 1932 was the bottom of the depression for most of the world. The United States economy registered a double bottom, in June 1932 and again in March 1933, when spreading collapse of the system of many small separate banks climaxed in the closing of all banks for a time, and recovery thereafter. German recovery started in 1932 after the resignation of Brüning, who had hoped to throw off reparations by deflation to demonstrate the impossibility of paying them, the succession of von Papen as Chancellor, and finally the takeover of the chancellorship by Hitler in February 1933. The gold-bloc countries remained depressed until they abandoned the gold parities of the 1920s, first Belgium in 1935, and the remaining countries in September 1936.

In these circumstances, there was little if any room for expansive commercial policy. Virtually every step taken was restrictive.

C.   OTTAWA

The Hawley–Smoot Tariff Act occupied most of the time of the Congress for a year and a half (Smith, 1936, p. 177). Empire preference was the major issue in Canadian politics for more than half a century (Drummond, 1975, p. 378). The Imperial Economic Policy Cabinet worried more about tariffs than about any other issue (*ibid.*, p. 426), though much of it dealt with objectively insignificant goods (Drummond, 1972, p. 25). Drummond several times expresses the opinion that the Ottawa discussions in the summer of 1932 should have abandoned the question of tariff preferences and focused on monetary policy, and especially exchange rate policy. In fact Prime Minister Bennett of Canada sought to raise the issue of the sterling exchange rate prior to Ottawa only to be rebuffed by Neville Chamberlain with the statement that the Treasury could not admit the Dominions to the management of sterling. Canada did succeed in getting exchange rates put on the Ottawa agenda, but the Treasury insisted that the question was minor and nothing came of it (Drummond, 1975, pp. 214–16).

Monetary policy and tariff policy were occasionally complements, occasionally substitutes. The Macmillan Committee report contained an addendum, no. 1, by Ernest Bevin, J. M. Keynes, R. McKenna and three others recommending import duties, and, insofar as existing treaties permitted, a bounty on exports, the combination being put forward as a substitute for devaluation of sterling (Committee on Finance and Industry, 1931). In the event, Britain undertook both depreciation of sterling and the imposition of import duties.

Sterling left the gold standard on 21 September 1931 and depreciated rapidly from \$4.86 to a low of \$3.25 in December, a depreciation of 30 per cent. Canada and South Africa adopted anti-dumping duties against British goods. On its side, Britain enacted an Abnormal Importations Act on 20 November 1931 that gave the Board of Trade the right to impose duties up to 100 per cent as a means of stopping a short-run scramble to ship goods to Britain before the exchange rate depreciated further. While 100 per cent tariffs were authorized, only 50 per cent were imposed. This act was followed in a few weeks by a similar Horticultural Products Act. Both the Abnormal Importations Act and the Horticultural Products Act exempted the Empire from their provisions (Kreider, 1943, p. 20).

In the Christmas recess of parliament, Lord Runciman, President of the Board of Trade, persuaded Chamberlain to take up protection as a long-run policy, as had been recommended by Keynes and the Macmillan Committee, prior to the September depreciation, and opposed by Beveridge (1931), since without tariffs, Britain had nothing to exchange with the Dominions for preferences in their markets. The resultant Import Duties Act of February 1932 established a 10 per cent duty on a wide number of imported products – but not copper, wheat, or meat – and created an Import Duties Advisory board, charged with recommending increases in particular duties above the flat 10 per cent level. At the last minute a concession was made to the Dominions and colonies.

The latter were entirely exempted from the increase, and the former were granted exemption until November 1932, by which time it was expected that mutually satisfactory arrangements for preferences would have been reached. Eighteen countries responded to the Import Duties Act by asking Britain to undertake negotiations for mutual reductions. The reply was universally negative on the grounds that it was first necessary to arrive at understandings with the Empire (Condliffe, 1940, pp. 300–8). In the spring of 1932, the Import Duties Advisory Board was hard at work raising duties above the 10 per cent level, with the notable increase in iron and steel products to $33\frac{1}{3}$ per cent. Three years later in March 1935 the iron and steel duties were increased to 50 per cent in order to assist the British industry in negotiating a satisfactory basis with the European iron and steel cartel (Hexner, 1946, p. 118).

Imperial economic conferences held in 1923, 1926, and 1930 had all broken down on the failure of Britain to raise tariffs which would have put her in a position to extend preferences to the Empire. Substitute assistance in the form of arrangements for Empire settlement or Empire marketing boards failed to produce significant effects on either migration or trade. British bulk-purchase schemes sought especially by Australia had been halted as early as 1922 and had not been resumed. Hopes were high for the Imperial Economic Conference of 1932 in Ottawa which now had British tariffs to work with.

Canada cared about wheat, butter, cheese, bacon, lamb, and apples; Australia about wheat, chilled meat, butter, cheese, currants, dried fruits, canned fruits; South Africa about wine and dried and canned fruits; New Zealand, butter and mutton. The position differed in those commodities that the Dominions produced in greater amounts than Britain could absorb, like wheat, in which diversion of Dominion supplies to Britain from third markets would produce an offsetting increase in non-Dominion sales in non-British markets, and leave Dominion export prices overall unchanged, from those in which Britain depended upon both Dominion and foreign sources of supply, among the latter notably Argentina in meat, Denmark in butter, Greece in dried currants and raisins, and, it would like to think, the United States in apples. Trade diversion from foreign to Dominion sources was possible in this latter group, but only at some cost in British goodwill in the indicated import markets. On this score, the United Kingdom was obliged to negotiate at Ottawa with an uneasy glance over its shoulder.

A significant Dominion manufacture, as opposed to agricultural product, which had earlier received preference in the British market, in 1919 under the McKenna duties, was motor cars. This preference had led to the establishment of tariff factories in Canada, owned and operated by United States manufacturers. Its extension in the Ottawa agreement led to the unhappy necessity of defining more precisely what a Canadian manufactured motor car consisted of, and whether United States-made motor parts merely assembled in Canada qualified as Canadian motor cars.

In exchange for concessions in primary products in the British market, the United Kingdom expected to get reductions in Dominion duties on her manufactures. But it proved impossible at Ottawa to fix levels of Dominion tariffs on British goods. Instead, the Dominions undertook to instruct their respective tariff boards to adjust the British preference tariff to that level which would make British producers competitive with domestic industry. Resting on the notion of horizontal supply curves, rather than the more usually hypothesized and far more realistic upward-sloping curves, the concept was clearly unworkable and gave rise to unending contention. It was abandoned in 1936.

Argentina, Denmark, Greece, Norway, and Sweden were not content to yield their positions in the British market without a struggle. Even before the Import Duties Act had taken effect, Denmark in January 1932 legislated preferences favouring Britain, and on raw materials used in manufactured exports. By June 1932, total imports had been reduced 30 to 40 per cent, but import permits issued for British goods allowed for a 15 per cent increase (Gordon, 1941, p. 80). In similar fashion Uruguay undertook to discriminate in the allocation of import licences in favour of countries that bought from her. The threat to discriminate against Britain was clear. Quickly after Ottawa British customers pressed to take up negotiations postponed from early 1932 and to settle the extent to which Ottawa would be allowed to squeeze them out of the British market.

In the Roca–Runciman Agreement of 1 May 1933, Britain agreed not to cut back imports of chilled beef from Argentina by more than 10 per cent of the volume imported in the year ended 30 June 1932, unless at the same time it reduced imports from the Dominions below 90 per cent of the same base year. This was disagreeable to Australia which was seeking through the Ottawa agreements to break into the chilled-beef market in Britain in which it had previously not been strong (Drummond, 1975, p. 310). Three-year agreements with Denmark, Norway, and Sweden, running from various dates of ratification about mid-1933, provided minimum butter quotas to Denmark and (much smaller) to Sweden, a minimum bacon quota to Denmark amounting to 62 per cent of the market, and agreement not to regulate the small and irregular shipments of bacon, ham, butter, and cheese by Norway. But guarantees to these producers left it necessary, if domestic British producers of, say, butter were to be protected, to go back on the Ottawa agreements which guaranteed unlimited free entry into the British market. The position was complicated by New Zealand's backward-bending supply curve which increased butter production and shipments as the price declined, and Australian policy, which evoked the most profound distrust from New Zealand, of subsidizing the export of butter to solve a domestic disposal problem (Drummond, 1975, pp. 320ff., 475). The problems of the Dominions and of the major foreign suppliers of the British markets for foodstuffs compounded the difficulties of British agriculture. In defence of the lost interest, the British agricultural authorities developed a levy-subsidy scheme under which tariffs imposed on imports were segregated to create a fund to be used to provide subsidies to domestic producers. The levy-subsidy scheme was first applied in Britain on wheat in 1932; strong voices inside the British cabinet urged its application to beef, dairy products, and bacon and ham. Wrangling over these proposals went on between British and Commonwealth negotiators for the next several years as Britain tried to modify the Ottawa agreements, with Dominion and foreign-supplier consent, in order to limit imports. In the background, dispute deepened within the British cabinet between the Agricultural Minister, Walter Elliott, who wanted subsidies, and the Chancellor of the Exchequer, Neville Chamberlain, who feared their effect on the budget and consistently favoured raising prices and farm incomes, in Britain and abroad, by cutting production and limiting imports.

In its agreements in Scandinavia, Britain sought to bind its trading partners to give preferences to British exports, and especially to guarantee a percentage share of the market to British suppliers in that sorely afflicted export industry, coal. In eight trade agreements, British coal exporters were guaranteed generally the major share of import volume, with quotas as follows: Denmark, 90 per cent; Estonia, 85 per cent; Lithuania, 80 per cent; Iceland, 77 per cent; Finland, 75 per cent; Norway, 70 per cent; Sweden, 47 per cent. In addition, Denmark agreed that all bacon and ham exported to the United Kingdom should be wrapped in jute cloth woven in the United Kingdom from jute yarn spun in the United Kingdom (Kreider, 1943, pp. 61–2). The Danish government gave British firms a 10 per cent preference for government purchases, and undertook to urge private Danish firms to buy their iron and steel in the United Kingdom wherever possible. Kreider notes that these agreements constrained British trade into a bilateral mode: British agreements with Finland lifted the unfavourable import balance from 1 to 5 against Britain in 1931 to 1 to 2 in 1935. The agreement with Russia called for the import/export ratio to go from 1 to 1.7 against Britain in 1934 to 1 to 1.5 in 1935, 1 to 1.4 in 1936 and 1 to 1.2 in 1937 and thereafter. Argentina agreed to allocate the sterling earned by its exports to Britain to purchases from Britain.

The Ottawa agreement dominated British commercial policy from 1932 to the Anglo-American Commercial Agreement of 1938, and to a lesser extent thereafter. It was continuously under attack from foreign suppliers other than the United States that entered into trade and financial agreements with the United Kingdom, and from the United States which undertook to attack it as early as the World Economic Conference of 1933. But at no time could the agreement have been regarded as a great success for the Empire. It produced endless discussion, frequently bitter in character, and dissatisfaction on both sides that each felt they had given too much and gained too little. By 1936 and 1937, there was a general disposition to give up the attempt, or at least to' downgrade its priority.

D.   THE NETHERLANDS

The United Kingdom embraced free trade, broadly speaking, with the repeal of the Corn Laws in 1846, and gave it up with the McKenna duties in 1916. The Netherlands' support goes back at least to the sixteenth century, and lasted until 1931. A faithful supporter of attempts to spread freer trade throughout the world from the World Economic Conference in 1927 until the Convention on Import and Export Prohibitions and the Conference with a View to Concerted Economic Action, The Netherlands ultimately turned to the smaller arena of the Oslo agreement of Scandinavia and the Low Countries. The pressure from declining wheat prices, however, proved too severe. In 1931 The Netherlands undertook to regulate farm prices and marketing. The Wheat Act of 1931 set the domestic price at 12 florins per 100 kg at a time when the world price had fallen to 5 florins, necessitating the first major break with the policy of free trade in nearly three centuries. There followed in 1932 as a response to the depreciation of sterling, first an emergency fiscal measure establishing 25 per cent duties generally, and then in agriculture the Dairy Crisis Act and the Hog Crisis Act, which were generalized in the following year as the Agricultural Crisis Act of 1933 (Gordon, 1941, p. 307). The freer-trade tradition of the Oslo group continued, however. At the depth of the depression in June 1932, the Oslo group concluded an agreement to reduce tariffs among themselves on a mutual basis by 10 per cent per annum for five years. Though it was already blocking out the discrimination to be achieved at Ottawa two months later, the United Kingdom objected on the grounds that the arrangement would violate the most-favoured-nation clause. After dissolution of the gold bloc in 1936, the Oslo group resumed its example-setting work in reducing trade barriers, agreeing first to impose no new tariffs and then to eliminate quotas applied to one another's trade on a mutual basis. Since the most-favoured-nation clause applied only to tariffs and not to quotas, there was no basis for an objection or to claim extension of the concession.

During the period of restricted trade, The Netherlands licensed not only imports, but in some cases exports. The latter practice was followed where quotas in foreign import markets left open the question whether the difference between the domestic price and the world price would go to importers or exporters. A law of 24 December 1931 established a system of licensing exports in instances of foreign import quotas, with permits distributed among exporters in accordance with the volumes of some historical base period. Licence fees were then imposed, in the amount of 70–100 per cent of the difference between the world price and the domestic price in the import market, with the collected proceeds distributed to Dutch producers. The purpose of the fees was to divert the scarcity rents available from import restriction, first to the exporting country as a whole, and then, within the exporting country, from exporting firms to agricultural producers (Gordon, 1941, p. 356).

E.   FRANCE

The French are often given the credit in commercial policy between the wars for the invention of the quota, a protective device which was to flourish until well into the 1950s, and even then to experience revival in various forms in the 1970s. While its origins go well back in time, the proximate causes of the quota in 1930 were the limitation on France's freedom of action imposed by the network of trade treaties it had fashioned, beginning with that with Germany in 1927, and the difficulty of ensuring a restriction of imports sufficient to raise domestic prices – the object of the exercise – in the face of inelastic excess supplies abroad. Like the Hawley–Smoot tariff increases in committee, quotas spread from agricultural produce to goods in general.

Under an old law of December 1897 – the so-called *loi de cadenas* – the French government had authority in emergency to change the rate of duty on any one of 46 agricultural items. The emergency of falling agricultural prices after 1928 caused the laws of 1929 and 1931 which extended the list. With especially wheat in excess supply overseas in regions of recent settlement like Australia and Canada, the French decided that raising the tariff under their authority would not only pose questions about their obligations under trade treaties, but might well not limit imports, serving only to reduce world prices and improve the terms of trade. Australia, in particular, lacked adequate storage capacity for its wheat and had no choice but to sell, no matter how high the price obstacles erected abroad. The decision was accordingly taken to restrict quantity rather than to levy a customs duty (Haight, 1941, p. 145). The device was effective. As the depression deepened, and as imports grew with the overvaluation of the franc, it was extended to industrial goods. Other countries followed suit, especially Germany with its foreign exchange control. In 1931, Brüning and Pierre Laval, the then French premier reached an agreement establishing industrial understandings to coordinate production and trade between German and French industries. One such understanding in electrical materials developed into a cartel. The rest were concerned primarily with restricting German exports to France. When they failed to do so, they were replaced by French quotas (Hexner, 1946, pp. 119, 136). After a time, the French undertook bilateral bargaining over quotas, which led in time to reducing quotas below desired limits in order to have room to make concessions during negotiations.

F. GERMANY

Less by design than by a series of evolutionary steps, Germany developed the most elaborate and thorough-going system of control of foreign trade and payments. Foreign claims on Germany were blocked on 15 July 1931, when Germany could no longer pay out gold and foreign exchange to meet the demands of foreign lenders withdrawing funds. This default was followed by a negotiated Standstill Agreement between creditors and Germany, involving a six-month moratorium on withdrawals, subsequently renewed. The decision not to adjust the value of the Reichsmark after the depreciation of sterling in September 1931 made it necessary to establish foreign exchange control, and to prevent the free purchase and sale of foreign currencies in the private market. The proceeds of exports were collected and allocated to claimants of foreign exchange seeking to purchase imports. Clearing agreements developed under which German importers paid Reichsmarks into special accounts at the Reichsbank in favour of foreign central banks, which then allocated them to their national importers of German goods. The foreign central bank faced a particular problem whether or not to pay out local currency to the exporter in advance of its receipts of local currency from national importers of German goods. Some central banks did pay off local exporters against claims on the German clearing, following what was later called the 'payments principle', and experienced inflation through the resultant credit expansion. Other central banks made their exporters wait for payment which both avoided monetary expansion and held down the incentive to export to Germany (Andersen, 1946).

A number of countries with large financial claims on Germany, such as Switzerland, insisted that the proceeds of German exports be used in part to pay off creditors abroad, thus converting 'clearing' into 'payments' agreements. These payments agreements were also used in a few cases to require Germany to continue spending on non-essential imports of importance to the exporter, such as tourism in Austria.

Germany set limits on the use of foreign-owned marks within Germany as well as against their conversion into foreign exchange. They were not permitted to be used for many classes of exports, capable of earning new foreign exchange, but only for incremental exports which could be sold only at implicit depreciated exchange rates, for travel within Germany – the so-called Reisemark – and under certain limitations for investment in Germany. Foreshadowing some post-war limitations on foreign direct investment, permission was granted for investment by foreigners in Germany with outstanding mark balances only when the investment was considered generally beneficial to the German economy, was made for at least five years, did not involve a foreign controlling interest in a German enterprise, and did not exceed a stipulated rate of interest (Gordon, 1941, pp. 92–3).

In August 1934, the New Plan was adopted under the leadership of the German Minister for Economics, Hjalmar Schacht. In the words of Emil Puhl, an associate of Dr Schacht's at the Reichsbank, it provided totalitarian control over commodities and foreign exchange, with stringent controls on imports and on foreign travel, administered through supervisory boards for a long list of commodities and foreign exchange boards in the Reichsbank (Office of the Chief Council for Prosecution of Nazi Criminality, *Nazi Conspiracy and Aggression*, vol. VII, 1946, p. 496). Along with trade and clearing agreements, designed especially to ensure German access to food and raw materials, and to promote exports, the Reichsbank developed a series of special marks for particular purposes. In addition to the Reisemarks for travel, there were special-account (*Auslands-Sonder-Konto*, or 'Aski') marks which came into existence through imports of raw materials, especially from Latin America, and which were sold by the recipients at a discount and used by the buyers on a bilateral basis for purchases of incremental German goods. The incremental aspect of the exports was of course difficult to police. Because Aski-marks would be sold only at a discount, the raw-material supplies against them tended to raise their prices in the bilateral trade (Gordon, 1941, p. 180). On the German side, Schacht established a price-control agency in 1935 in each export group – amounting to 25 in all – to prevent German exporters from competing with one another for export orders and to assure that all exporters sold at the highest possible price (*Nazi Conspiracy*, vol. VII, 1946, p. 383).

Beginning in 1934, German foreign-trade plans were intended particularly to ensure access to imported food and raw materials. The New

Plan, and especially the Four Year Plan which succeeded it in the fall of 1936, were designed to produce synthetic materials, especially Buna-S (synthetic rubber) and gasoline from coal, where foreign supplies for wartime needs could not be assured. Particular problems were encountered in non-ferrous metals, in iron ore, for which the low-grade Salzgitter project was developed in the Four Year Plan, and in synthetic fertilizer required for self-sufficiency in food. Schacht at the Reichsbank, Goering as Schacht's successor in the Economics Ministry and as the head of the Four Year Plan, the War and Food Ministries wrangled among themselves over policies, including especially whether to export wheat against foreign exchange following the bumper crops of 1933 and 1934 or conserve it as a war reserve; whether to hoard Germany's meagre free foreign exchange reserves or to spend them for crucially short raw materials; the mobilization of privately owned foreign securities and their conversion to cash for buying materials; the pricing of exports; the purchase of unnecessary imports like frozen meat from Argentina, for lack of which Schacht was unable to conclude a favourable trade treaty, etc. (*Nazi Conspiracy*, vol. VII, 1946). The documents published by the prosecution at the Nuremberg post-war trials reveal considerable internal dissension, especially in the exchanges between Schacht and Goering that lasted through 1937 and ended in Schacht's defeat and resignation.

German sentiment had continuously decried the loss of the country's African colonies in the Versailles treaty. Schacht continuously referred to the loss in Young Plan discussions of the late 1920s and was still harping on the issue in an article in *Foreign Affairs* in 1937. In a conversation with the American ambassador, Bullitt, in the autumn of 1937, Goering noted that Germany's demand for a return of the German colonies which had been taken away by the Versailles treaty was just, adding immediately that Germany had no right to demand anything but these colonies. Particularly sought were the Cameroons which could be developed by German energy (*Nazi Conspiracy*, vol. VII, 1946, pp. 890, 898). Three weeks earlier, however, in a private conference, Hitler had stated that it made more sense for Germany to seek material-producing territory adjoining the Reich and not overseas (*ibid.*, vol. I, 1946, p. 380). And at a final war-preparatory briefing in May 1939, he went further to explain the need for living space in the East to secure Germany's food supplies. It was necessary to beware of gifts of colonial territory which did not solve the food problem: 'Remember blockade' (*ibid.*, vol. I, 1946, p. 392). The directive to the Economic Staff Group on 23 May 1941 just before the attack on the Soviet Union stated that the offensive was designed to produce food in the East on a permanent basis.

It was widely claimed that Germany squeezed the countries of Southeast Europe through charging high prices for non-essential exports, while not permitting them to purchase the goods they needed, at the same time delaying payment for imports through piling up large debit balances in clearing arrangements. In a speech at Königsberg in August 1935, Schacht expressed regret that Germany had defaulted on debts to numerous pro-German peoples abroad, indicated confidence that Germany could obtain the raw materials it needed, acknowledged that the trade relations of Germany with different countries had changed a great deal, but insisted that these new relations had created for a number of countries new possibilities of exporting to Germany which had helped relieve them from the rigours of the world depression (*Nazi Conspiracy*, vol. VII, 1946, p. 486). In a polemical exchange in 1941, Einzig insisted that Benham was in error in holding that South-east European countries had improved their terms of trade in dealing with Germany, which paid higher prices than Western Europe was able to pay, and sold German goods competitively in the area. A post-war analysis of the matter tended to show that Benham and Schacht had been right (Kindleberger, 1956, pp. 120ff.).

An intellectual defence of the Benham–Schacht position had been offered in a somewhat different context as early as 1931 by Manoilesco who expressed the view that the theory of comparative advantage had to be qualified if the alternative to tariff protection for an industry were either unemployment, or employment at a wage below the going rate. His statement of this position in *The Theory of Protection and International Trade* (1931) was strongly attacked on analytical grounds by the leading international-trade theorists of the day – Habeler, Ohlin, and Viner, each in extended treatment – but was resurrected after the war by Hagen, and then generalized into a second-best argument for interference with free trade, e.g. by tariffs. When the conditions for a first-best solution under free trade do not exist, protection may be superior in welfare for a country to free trade. By the same token, export sales at less than optimal terms of trade may be superior to no exports and unemployment.

G. THE UNION OF SOVIET SOCIALIST REPUBLICS

During the 1920s, commercial policy in the Soviet Union had been the subject of a great debate under the New Economic Plan, between the Right that advocated expansion of agriculture, and of other traditional exports, plus domestic production of manufactured consumer goods to provide incentives for farmers, and the Left that favoured development of domestic heavy industry and the relative neglect of agriculture. Under the proposals of the Right, exports of agricultural products would be expanded to obtain imports of machinery, metals, raw materials, and exotic foodstuffs such as coffee and tea. This was the trade-dependent strategy. The Left, on the other hand, sought to increase trade in order to achieve autarky as rapidly as possible, as it feared dependence on a hostile capitalist world. With Stalin's achievement of power, the Left strategy was adopted in the First and subsequent Five Year Plans. Strong efforts were made to reduce dependence on imports to a minimum. Territorial losses during the First World War, land reform which divided large estates, and the inherent bias of planning which favoured domestic users over foreign markets helped reduce the ratio of exports to national income, which fell from a figure variously estimated within the range of 7–12 per cent in 1913 to 3.5 at the inter-war peak in 1931. Estimates of the volume of Soviet exports vary, depending upon the weights chosen, but on the basis of 1927/8 weights, exports fell from 242 in 1913 to 53 in 1924/5 before recovering to 100 in 1929. Thereafter they rose sharply to 150 in 1930 and 164 in 1931 with disastrous consequences for the Russian peoples (Dohan and Hewett, 1973, p. 24).

In 1930 and 1931, Soviet exports conformed to the model of the backward-bending supply curve in which volume increases, rather than decreases, as price falls. Declines in the prices of grain, timber and oil, starting as early as 1925, had threatened the Soviet Union's capacity to pay for the machinery and materials necessary to complete its Five Year Plans, and threatened as well its capacity to service a small amount of foreign debt contracted in the 1920s. To counter this threat, the Soviet authorities diverted supplies of foodgrains from domestic consumption to export markets, shipping it from grain-surplus areas to export ports and leaving internal grain-deficit areas unsupplied. The result was starvation and death for an unknown number of the Russian people numbering in millions. The world price of wheat fell by half between June 1929 and December 1930, and more than half again by December 1932. So hard did the Soviet Union push exports that supplies of pulp wood, woodpulp, timber, lumber, and even coal, asbestos, and furs threatened to enter the Canadian market, a notable exporter of these products in ordinary times, and led the Canadian government in February 1932 to prohibit the import of these commodities from the Soviet Union (Drummond, 1975, p. 205). Similar discriminatory restrictions were taken in many other markets. The dysfunctional character of forcing exports on the world market became clear and the volume of Soviet exports levelled off and started downward in 1932. As primary-product prices rose after 1936, moreover, the export volume declined sharply below the 1929 level.

H. JAPAN

Japan had not participated fully in the boom of the 1920s, but the fact that it had restored the yen to par after the First World War as late as January

1930 made it highly vulnerable to the liquidity crisis of 1930 and 1931. It was vulnerable, too, because of heavy dependence on silk, a luxury product, about to experience both a sharp decline in its income-elastic demand and severe competition from rayon and later from nylon. In 1929 silk was responsible for 36 per cent of Japanese exports by value, and produced 20 per cent of Japanese farm income. The price of silk fell by about half from September 1929 to December 1930. With the help of the depreciation of the yen after December 1931, it reached a level of $1.25 a pound in March 1933, compared with $5.20 in September 1929.

The combination of sharp exchange depreciation and the collapse of the American market in silk produced a drastic reorientation in Japanese export trade, away from North America and Europe and toward Asia, Africa, and Latin America. Export drives were especially intense in British and Dutch colonies, and in the so-called 'yen bloc' of Korea, Formosa, Kwantung, and Manchuria. The Japanese share of the Netherlands East Indies market, for example, rose from 10 per cent in the 1920s to 32 per cent in 1934 before restrictive measures were applied under the Crisis Act of 1933. (Furnival, 1939, p. 431; Van Gelderen, 1939, p. 24). Japanese exports to the yen bloc rose from 24 per cent in 1929 to 55 per cent in 1938, with imports rising from 20 to 41 per cent over the same period (Gordon, 1941, p. 473). Within Asia, Japan developed sugar production in Formosa and stopped buying it in Java in the Netherlands East Indies. The British and Dutch Empires imposed quantitative restrictions on Japanese imports, especially in textiles. Foreshadowing a technique extensively used by the United States after the war, at one stage the British asked the Japanese to impose export controls on shipments to India or face abrogation of the Indo-Japanese Commercial Convention of 1904 (Drummond, 1973, p. 133). By 1938 Netherlands East Indies imports from Japan were down to 14 per cent of the total from a high of 30 per cent in 1935 (Van Gelderen, 1935, p. 17). Japanese fear of reprisals led them to amend the Export Association Act of 1925, which had been enacted to promote exports, so as to control exports in accordance with restrictions imposed by importing countries (Gordon, 1941, p. 360).

I.   THE WORLD ECONOMIC CONFERENCE OF 1933

Sir Arthur Salter termed the Hawley–Smoot tariff a turning-point in world history. Lewis Douglas thought the Thomas amendment under which the dollar was devalued in March 1933 marked 'the end of Western civilization as we know it' (Kindleberger, 1973, p. 202). W. Arthur Lewis regarded the failure of the World Economic Conference of 1933 as 'the end of an era' (Lewis, 1950, p. 68). Each characterization contained an element of hyperbole. The World Economic Conference offered only the slightest of chances to reverse the avalanche of restrictions on world trade and to stabilize exchange rates. The reversal in tariffs came the next year with the June 1934 Reciprocal Trade Agreements Act in the United States. More stability in exchange rates took root with the Tripartite Monetary Agreement of September 1936 among, initially, the United Kingdom, France, and the United States.

The inspiration for a new world economic conference after 1927 went back to the early years of deflation and to a suggestion of Chancellor Brüning of Germany to treat disarmament, reparations, war debts and loans as a single package to be settled on a political basis, rather than separately in each case by economic experts. A preparatory commission of economic experts under the auspices of the League of Nations fashioned a package of somewhat different ingredients, in which the United States would lower the Hawley–Smoot tariff, France would reduce quota restrictions, Germany relax foreign exchange control and the United Kingdom would stabilize the pound. War debts were excluded from the agenda by the United States, and consequently reparations by France and Britain. Pending the convening of the conference, delayed first by the November 1932 elections in the United States and then by domestic preoccupations of the newly elected President Roosevelt, Secretary of State Cordell Hull tried to work out a new tariff truce, but ran into blocks. The United States desired new tariffs on farm products subject to processing taxes under the new Agricultural Adjustment Act; Britain had some pending obligations under the Ottawa agreements; France reserved her position until she could see what would happen to United States' prices as a response to the depreciation of the dollar initiated in April 1933. Only eight countries in all finally agreed to a truce on 12 May 1933, many with explicit reservations. In the final preparations for the conference, commercial-policy measures seemed secondary to all but Cordell Hull, as contrasted with the problem of raising international commodity prices and international public-works schemes, for neither of which could general solutions be found. In the end the United States broke up the conference by refusing to stabilize the exchange rate of the dollar (only to reverse its position seven months later in February 1934), the British felt moderately comfortable with their Empire solution in trade with the vast volume of wrangles still to come, and the gold bloc battened down to ride out the storm. The only positive results were an agreement on silver negotiated by Senator Key Pitman of the US delegation, and bases laid for subsequent international agreements in sugar and wheat. Perhaps a negative result was the de facto constitution of the sterling bloc with most of the Commonwealth, save Canada and the subsequent withdrawal of the Union of South Africa, plus foreign adherents such as Sweden, Argentina, and a number of countries in the Middle East.

J.   COMMODITY AGREEMENTS

From the decline in commodity prices in the mid-1920s, one after another attempt had been made to devise schemes for raising prices. Some were private, like aluminium, copper, mercury, diamonds, nickel, iron and steel; some were governmental. Of the governmental, some were under the control of a single government – Brazil in coffee, Chile in nitrates, the United States in cotton, the Netherlands East Indies in cinchona bark; others, especially in sugar and wheat, were world-wide. Some of the private/government agreements in iron and steel, petroleum, and aluminium were regional, especially European (Gordon, 1941, pp. 430ff.).

The Chadbourne Plan in sugar was reached in May 1931 among leading export countries – Belgium, Cuba, Czechoslovakia, Germany, Hungary, Java, Peru, and Poland – later joined by Yugoslavia. But British India, France, and United Kingdom, and the United States – important consumers that also maintained substantial production – remained outside the agreement. The United States formulated its own legislation, the Jones–Costigan Act of 1934, which assigned rigid quotas to imports from abroad and discriminated in favour of Cuba. Under the Chadbourne Plan, production declined among the signatories but rose almost as much outside. Particularly hard hit was Java which lost both the Japanese and the Indian markets, the former to Formosan production, the latter to domestic production. Unsold stocks in Java reached $2\frac{1}{2}$ million tons in 1932, and the government took over in January 1933 as the single seller. The failure of the Chadbourne scheme led the World Economic Conference to push for a new agreement, which was finally reached under League of Nations auspices only in May 1937 at the height of the recovery of primary-product prices.

The World Economic Conference was the twentieth international meeting on the subject of wheat after 1928 when the price of wheat started to plummet – two on imperial preference, seven limited to Eastern Europe as already mentioned, and eleven general. The agreement that emerged after the World Economic Conference achieved a system of export quotas for major producers, but no agreement on acreage controls to limit production (Malenbaum, 1953).

Tea was regulated in this period by an international committee which met in London. In March 1931 the four leading producers of tin – Malaya, Bolivia, Nigeria, and the Netherlands East Indies – cooperated in the Joint Tin Committee. In May 1934 nine countries in South-east Asia producing 95 per cent of the world's rubber supply undertook to impose export quotas to reconstitute the Stevenson rubber plan which had broken down in 1928 (Van Gelderen, 1939, pp. 51ff.). Their problem was complicated by sharply differing supply elasticities in the plantation and the native sectors, the latter characterized in many countries by backward-bending responses. As rubber prices rose in the 1936/7 inventory boom, a number of governments sought to tax away the price increase from the producers, but until the price collapse of September 1937 succeeded mainly in raising the price to buyers in a sellers' market. With the eventual decline in prices, the incidence of the export taxes shifted back from the foreign consumer to the domestic producer and in most instances they were quickly removed.

K.   SANCTIONS

In December 1934 a border incident occurred between Italian Somalia and Ethiopia. Italy demand an apology; Ethiopia refused. With tension rising, the League of Nations sought to arbitrate but received no help from Italy. After further border clashes, Italian troops invaded Ethiopia on 3 October 1935 without a declaration of war. Later in the month, the League of Nations declared Italy the aggressor and voted sanctions to be applied to her in arms supply, finance, and export–import restrictions. The League did not, however, decree sanctions in the critical item, oil. Germany refused to comply with the League vote; the United States, though not a member of the League of Nations, was strongly sympathetic. Oil sanctions were discussed again in March 1936. At this time an attempt was made to apply them informally through major world oil companies. These companies stopped selling to Italy, but the increase in oil prices thereby brought about encouraged a vast number of small shippers to enter the business for the first time and to deliver oil to Italian troops at Red Sea ports in the full quantities required. With the fall of Addis Ababa, the Italians proclaimed empire over Ethiopia and withdrew from the League. League members continued to apply sanctions with increasing resolution until 15 July 1936 when sanctions were abandoned (Feis, 1946, vol. III).

IV.   The disintegration of the world economy

In a few countries – notably France and the United States – foreign trade fell by the same proportion as national income from 1929 to 1938. In others trade fell more than output. Thus the ratio of imports to industrial production declined by 10 per cent in the United Kingdom, nearly 20 per cent in Canada, 30 per cent in Germany, and 40 per cent in Italy. Crop failures in the United States in 1934 and 1936, and in Germany in 1937 and 1938, prevented the decline in the proportion of imports from being wider (League of Nations (Meade), 1939, pp. 107–8). Buy-British and Buy-American campaigns, involving government discrimination

Table 18. *Proportions of world trade balanced bilaterally and multilaterally (in percentage of total)*

	By non-merchandise	Multilaterally	Bilaterally
1928	11.1	21.2	67.7
1938	14.3	16.9	68.8

Source: Thorbecke (1960), p. 82.

against foreign as against domestic suppliers with margins of initially 10 per cent, increased to 25 per cent, in the United States, and 100 per cent for items under $100, were often supported by programmes affecting state governments, and campaigns to persuade the general public to discriminate as well (Bidwell, 1939, pp. 70–1 and Appendix A). The major influences to be sure were higher tariffs, quotas, clearing and payments agreements, and preferential trade agreements.

What trade remained was distorted, as compared with the freer market system of the 1920s, both in commodity and in country terms. The index of German imports for 1937 with a base of 100 in 1929 strongly reflected *Wehrwirtschaft*, and especially rearmament: 'other ores' 153, manganese ore 142, iron ore 122, iron and steel 121, copper 100, cotton 73, wool 62, coal 59, oil seeds 57, timber 28 (League of Nations (Meade), 1938, p. 128). The share of Germany in Turkish, Greek, and Italian imports rose between 1928 and 1939 respectively from 13 to 43 per cent, 8 to 29 per cent, and 10 to 24 per cent; the same percentages of national exports to Germany rose from 13 to 43 per cent, 27 to 39 per cent and 13 to 17 per cent for the same countries in the same order (Thorbecke, 1960, p. 100). By 1937, bilateral clearings amounted to 12 per cent of total world trade and 50 per cent of the trade of Bulgaria, Germany, Greece, Hungary, Romania, Turkey, and Yugoslavia (League of Nations, 1942, p. 70). Pioneering estimates of the shrinkage of multilaterally as opposed to bilaterally balanced trade were made for the League of Nations Economic and Financial Department by Folke Hilgerdt. In 1928, bilateral balancing of export and import values between pairs of countries on the average covered 70 per cent of merchandise trade, with about 5 per cent more covered by exports or imports of services or capital movements, and 25 per cent balanced multilaterally (League of Nations (Hilgerdt), 1941). Hilgerdt's two studies emphasized the shrinkage of the proportion of the trade balanced multilaterally during the depression years, without furnishing a precise estimate for the end of the 1930s (League of Nations (Hilgerdt), 1941 and League of Nations (Hilgerdt), 1942). A post-war study on a somewhat different basis furnished a comparison for 1938 with 1928, shown in Table 18.

Major changes occurred both world-wide and within Europe. On a world basis, the largest change shown in the Hilgerdt analysis derived from the fact that the developing countries of the tropics no longer earned large surpluses in merchandise trade with the United States to pay their interest on debts owed to Europe, and especially to the United Kingdom. Regionally, within Europe, the most important change was the failure of Germany to earn an export surplus in Europe, largely Britain, to enable her to pay for her net imports of raw materials from overseas. Another striking feature was the shift by Britain of procurement from Europe to the sterling area. France, The Netherlands, and especially Britain diverted trade from the rest of Europe to their colonial empires, a trend which would be reversed after the Second World War, and especially after the formation of the European Economic Community in 1957 and Britain's accession to it in 1973. In 1913 22 per cent of British exports went to the Empire. By 1938 the figure had more than doubled to 47 per cent. In imports, the proportion rose over the same period from 22.3 to close to 40 per cent. As noted earlier, the figures might have risen further had it not been for what has been called 'Imperial Insufficiency' (Hancock, 1940, p. 232; see also Drummond, 1972).

V.   World trading systems

Recovery of raw-material prices from 1933 to 1937 was followed by some considerable reduction in tariffs, and relaxation of quota restrictions. The renewed, though less far-reaching, decline of these prices in September 1937, outside the fields dominated by European rearmament, set back the movement towards freer trade. The last five years of the inter-war period were most clearly characterized by what have been called disparate 'world trading systems' (Tasca, 1939). At the limits were the system of German trade, locked into a network of bilateral clearing and payments agreements, and practising autarky for the sake of war economy (Petzina, 1968), and at the other extreme, the United States, which stood aloof from all payments and clearing agreements, with few quota restrictions, largely in agriculture, some subsidies to export in agricultural commodities, plus government credit through the Export–Import Bank for export promotion. Within Europe, the Balkan countries were nearer to the German model, the Oslo group to the American. Midway between was the Empire preference scheme of Britain, the Dominions, India, and the dependent colonies. Latin America had been hard hit by declines in raw-material prices and the decline in foreign lending, but was hopeful of trade expansion under the Roosevelt 'Good Neighbor' policy. The Soviet Union went its own way. Anxious to join a system, but largely orphaned outside them were the Middle East and

Japan, the latter of which carved out its own Greater East Asia Co-Prosperity Sphere.

There were limited attempts at achieving a single unified world trading system. The League of Nations Committee for the Study of the Problem of Raw Materials reported in September 1937 at a time when payments difficulties had eased but the position was on the point of reversal (League of Nations (Meade), 1938, p. 162). It found few problems of supply or access to materials, and argued in favour of valorization schemes to raise prices provided that consumers' interests were safeguarded. The report went to the League of Nations Assembly where it was pigeonholed as a consequence of the sharp check to commodity prices and deterioration in payment balances.

Before that time, the British and French governments had asked Paul Van Zeeland, a former Belgian Prime Minister, to prepare a programme for world action in the commercial-policy field. In January 1938, the Van Zeeland report was presented to the public, equally an inopportune time. It called for reciprocal reductions of tariffs, generalized by the most-favoured-nation clause, replacement of industrial quotas by tariffs or by tariff quotas, removal of foreign exchange control, clearing agreements, and the ban on new lending in London; and, as a final step when all else was in operation, six-months agreements on foreign-exchange rates leading ultimately to the establishment of fixed rates under the gold standard (League of Nations (Meade), 1938, p. 159). The report was received with universal agreement that the restoration of trade was needed, but equally universal reluctance on the part of all governments to take any decisive initiative in the matter (Condliffe, 1940, p. 47).

The 1937–9 recession in fact led to increases in tariffs in Belgium, France, Greece, Italy, the Netherlands East Indies, Norway, Sweden, Switzerland, and Yugoslavia in 1938, and in that stronghold of free-trade sentiment, The Netherlands, in March 1939. Rubber and copper quotas which had been freed in 1937 under their commodity schemes were tightened down again. Brazil, Colombia, and Japan extended their foreign exchange restrictions. Germany and Italy introduced the death penalty for violations of foreign exchange regulations in December 1936 and June 1939, respectively. Italy also constituted a Supreme Autarky Commission in October 1937 (League of Nations (Meade), 1939, p. 197). In all, the number of clearing and payments agreements rose from 131 on 1 June 1936 to 171 by 1 January 1939 (Gordon, 1941, p. 131).

Meanwhile some considerable relaxation of commercial policy was underway in the United States, led by Cordell Hull, whom Herbert Feis, his economic adviser in the Department of State, called a monomaniac on the subject of tariff reductions (Feis, 1966, p. 262). Hull had long been a Congressman from eastern Tennessee, which specialized in tobacco for export, before becoming Secretary of State, and had been in opposition to the Fordney–McCumber and Hawley–Smoot tariff increases in 1922 and 1930 as a member of the House of Representatives Committee on Ways and Means. As early as the World Economic Conference of 1927, as a Congressman, he had been thought to believe that the tariff of the United States was the key to the entire world situation (US Department of State, *Foreign Relations of the United States*, vol. 1, 1928, p. 239). As Secretary of State and leader of the United States delegation to the World Economic Conference of 1933, he had been frustrated in his attempts to get world tariffs reduced by the repudiation of President Roosevelt which prevented him from encountering the profound disinterest of the other countries. The tariff truce of May 1933 lapsed when the conference failed, but Secretary Hull persevered. At the Seventh Conference of American States at Montevideo in November 1933 – the first having been held in 1889 – he had tariffs put on the agenda for the first time and induced President Roosevelt to offer the Latin American republics tariff reductions (Gordon, 1941, p. 464). The main business accomplished at Montevideo was the strengthening of the most-favoured-nation clause, as Hull had tried to do at London, by government agreement not to invoke the clause in order to prevent the consummation of multilateral tariff reductions in agreements to which a government was not a party. The full agreement provided for no tariff reductions, and was signed by eight countries, though ratified only by the United States and Cuba (Viner, 1950, p. 37).

Upon his return from Montevideo, Secretary Hull found that the President had established an Executive Committee on Commercial Policy under the chairmanship of George Peek, agricultural expert and opponent of trade liberalization, and that the committee had already drafted a bill providing for trade treaties to be subject to Senate ratification. This was unsatisfactory to Hull. The Department of State had already been negotiating with Argentina, Brazil, Colombia, Portugal, and Sweden in the summer of 1933, had signed an agreement only with Colombia, but had not submitted it to the Senate for ratification. In early 1934 new legislation was drawn up that delegated authority from the Congress to the Executive branch of government to conclude reciprocal trade agreements on its own authority. The draft legislation was completed on 24 February, approved by President Roosevelt on 28 February, passed the House of Representatives on 20 March, the Senate on 4 June, and was signed into law on 13 June 1934 as the Reciprocal Trade Agreements Act. The initial delegation of authority was for a period of three years. The legislation was renewed in 1937 and 1940. It provided for mutual bilateral reductions in tariff duties, generalized by the most-favoured-nation clause, limited to 50 per cent of the existing (largely Hawley–Smoot) tariff levels.

Even before the legislation had been drafted, further talks were going forward to reduce tariffs, with Belgium and Denmark in January 1934, and with Canada. Canada and the United States each made official public statements on the subject in February 1934, emphasizing the importance of their mutual trade relations. A request for negotiations was made by the Canadian government in November 1934 and an agreement was achieved a year later to the effect on 1 January 1936. Canada received concessions on 88 items, largely primary products, including along with Hawley–Smoot items the lumber and copper affected by the US Revenue Act of 1932. United States concessions obtained from Canada were largely in manufactured goods.

The first agreement under the Reciprocal Trade Agreements Act, however, was that concluded with Cuba in August 1934. By November 1939, agreements had been reached with twenty countries, eleven of them in Latin America. A second agreement was concluded with Canada in November 1938, but the most important was the British agreement concluded simultaneously with the revision of the Canadian agreement.

In the British and Canadian agreements, the United States hoped to break down Empire preference. This was beginning to happen of its own accord. In a British–Canadian trade agreement of 1937, five years following the Ottawa agreements of 1932, the British persuaded the Canadians to abolish the doctrine of equalizing competition and to substitute fixed tariff rates and fixed preferential margins in the agreements (McDiarmid, 1946, p. 295). New Zealand was ready to abandon the Ottawa agreements, and started to conclude agreements outside them with Sweden (1935), Greece (1936), Germany (1937), and was negotiating a dozen others (Hancock, 1940, p. 278). Britain meanwhile was highly critical of Australian performance under Ottawa, on the ground that Australia had persistently violated its commitments. Australian Tariff Board studies were limited, and even when the Tariff Board recommended reductions on British goods, the government often failed to introduce them in parliament (Drummond, 1975, pp. 392ff.). British and Australian interests were only partly complementary. Accordingly the United Kingdom, Canada, and the other Dominions as well were ready in their agreements with the United States to sacrifice advantages in each other's markets in return for significant compensation in the market in the United States (Hancock, 1940, p. 265).

To an extent, the Anglo-American trade agreement was more symbolic than effective. Two years of hard bargaining went into it, and it lasted only eight months, from 1 January 1939 until British wartime controls were imposed on the outbreak of war with Germany in September 1939. Reductions were agreed on nine items in which trade amounted to no more than $350 per annum. Important concessions, as in cotton textiles, were prevented from being generalized to Japan and other competitors through reclassification. Full 50 per cent reductions in the United States were made on 96 items but the total trade involved was only $14 million. Under all twenty agreements, the unweighted (equal weights) United States *ad valorem* duties were reduced from 57 per cent on products subject to the tariff to 35 per cent, a reduction of 39 per cent, whereas the reduction under the British agreement, from 42 to 30 per cent on the same basis, amounted only to a reduction of 28 per cent. The 35 per cent level achieved on 1 January 1939 was somewhat lower than the Fordney–McCumber average of 38.5 per cent and the Payne–Aldrich tariff (1909) of 40.8 per cent, and well below the Hawley–Smoot average of 51.5 per cent. It was nevertheless still well above the 1913 Underwood level of 27 per cent (Kreider, 1943, pp. 170ff.).

Moreover, the trade agreements applied largely to industrial products and materials. United States opposition to Empire preference had export concerns in view, especially in competition with Canada in pork and apples. The reductions in tariffs under the agreements, however, went side by side with continued US protection against agricultural imports and subsidies on agricultural exports. Protection was required under those domestic programmes which raised prices in the United States and would, without new restrictions, have attracted further supplies from abroad; and subsidies were deemed necessary to offset the price disadvantage this imposed on American producers in their traditional markets. The trade agreements reduced tariffs on a few items, such as maple sugar from Canada, which had been a particular irritant under the Hawley–Smoot Act, and altered the arbitrary valuations on fresh fruits and vegetables early in the season that had hitherto been kept out of Canada by this device. A sanitary agreement between the United States and Argentina on the regulation of foot-and-mouth disease was not ratified by the Congress (Bidwell, 1939, pp. 217–18); and independence for the Philippines was accelerated to push its sugar production outside the tariff borders of the United States. On the whole, the trade agreements marked the beginning of regarding liberal commercial policies as appropriate only for manufactures, and their inputs, and leaving agricultural trade largely to special arrangements.

A small beginning was made by the United States on what was to be a major post-war issue, East–West trade. The United States was unwilling to recognize the government of the Soviet Union all through the 1920s. With President Roosevelt's New Deal, this was changed and recognition was accorded in 1933. In the mid-thirties, the United States and the Soviet Union undertook a series of trade agreements. In 1935, the Soviet Union contracted to purchase at least $30 million worth of US goods in the following year; in return, the United States accorded the Soviet Union most-favoured-nation treatment. In August 1937 under a new pact, the Soviet Union agreed to step up its purchases from the United States to $40 million (Gordon, 1941, p. 407).

British adherence to the more liberal trade policies pursued by Cordell Hull was highly ambiguous. Kreider claims that the British concessions were not spectacular but represented a reversal of policy (1943, p. 240). At the same time, the British government was unwilling to repudiate the principle of Ottawa, despite its effects, as Mackenzie King claimed, in destroying the principle of imperial harmony (Drummond, 1975, p. 316).

Moreover, British ministers were experimenting with a new technique quite at variance with the American professed principle of increased reliance on the international market. Mention was made above of the special tariff assistance given to the iron and steel industry to assist in its negotiations with the International Steel Cartel. At the depth of the depression, in October 1933, the British had encouraged negotiations between Lancashire and Indian cotton-textile mill owners. The resultant Lees–Mody pact of October 1933 provided that India would lower her tariffs on British textiles to 20 per cent while holding those against other (i.e., Japanese) goods at 75, to which they had been raised from $31\frac{1}{2}$ per cent in August 1932 in several steps. As part of the negotiation, involving governments and business groups on both sides, the British agreed to take one and a half million bales of cotton that had piled up as a result of a Japanese retaliatory boycott. At the time Lord Runciman stated, 'The work of the Delegation has gone some way in justifying the Government in their belief that the best approach to the problem of international industrial cooperation is by the method of discussion between industrialists' (Drummond, 1972, p. 316).

In early 1939, immediately after signing the Anglo–American Reciprocal Trade Agreement in November 1938, and as part of an export drive, the British Board of Trade encouraged the visit to Düsseldorf of a delegation of the Federation of British Industry to meet with the Reichsgruppe Industrie, its institutional counterpart, and to fix quantitative relationships between the exports of the two countries in each commodity and market. In prospect, The Economist after some qualifications expressed itself as approving (CXXXIV, no. 4585 (February 1939), p. 383). The agreement was concluded on 16 March 1939, one day after the German invasion of Czechoslovakia (text in Hexner, 1946, Appendix III, pp. 402–4). The British government repudiated the agreement on political grounds, but not before The Economist had denounced it on the grounds that it involved cartelization of domestic industry as well as of trade, that it would extend Anglo-German subsidies to exports, and that it might involve joint action against competitors who refused to join the arrangement, including possible American firms (March 1939, p. 607).

In Eastern Europe the German bloc was strengthened in ways to guarantee German access to raw materials and foodstuffs in short supply. An agreement with Hungary in 1934 provided for a shift of Hungarian agriculture from wheat to oilseeds with an assured outlet in Germany. German treaties with Romania in March 1935 and again four years later fostered the expansion of Romanian agriculture in oil seeds, feedgrains, vegetable fibres, as well as industrial and financial cooperation, including the development of Romanian transport and petroleum under German–Romanian companies supervized by joint government commissions (Gordon, 1941, pp. 425–6). In 1937, the proportion of German exports sold through clearing agreements amounted to 57 per cent, while 53 per cent of her imports came through clearings. The comparable figures for Turkey were 74 and 72 per cent respectively, for Romania 67 and 75 per cent, for Switzerland 28 and 36 per cent, for Sweden 17 and 24 per cent, and for the United Kingdom 2 and 2 per cent (Gordon, 1941, Table 7, p. 133).

The disintegration of world trade thus proceeded, despite the attempts of the United States, the Oslo group, Premier Van Zeeland under Anglo-French auspices and the economists of the Economic and Financial Department of the League of Nations. With some prescience Condliffe concluded his book written at the outbreak of the Second World War (1940, p. 394), 'If an international system is to be restored, it must be an American-dominated system, based on *Pax Americana*.'

CHAPTER III

International financial policy and the gold standard, 1870–1914[1]

I. Introduction

The last quarter of the nineteenth century saw the spread of an international monetary system based on gold, linking the major countries of the world with fixed international exchange rates for their domestic currencies, a system more stable perhaps than anything seen since. The system evolved; it presented many institutional contrasts; yet all monetary authorities had a common policy aim – the preservation of specie payments or of convertibility of their currencies, to which all other aims were subordinated. *Why* the gold standard worked successfully in the sense of eliminating balance of payments imbalances without exchange rate changes in a rapidly changing world economy has proved a challenging question for economists and economic historians. Myths, indeed, have grown up about gold and its discipline before 1914 such that in later years they have at times dominated and even perverted international economic policies. Even now gold refuses to lie down and accept its role as a barbarous relic. Besides describing and analysing the institutional and structural arrangements underlying the gilt facade, this chapter will seek to explain why and how the gold standard worked, especially for Britain, and will emphasize the importance of the particular and peculiar economic relationships of this period in providing a favourable environment within which the gold standard could flourish.

II. Basic gold standard elements

By the middle of the nineteenth century most countries had sought to define their domestic currencies in terms of a metallic base of silver or gold, with silver or gold coins of the appropriate weight as the basic money substance. In addition, they sought to provide that any banknotes issued should be freely exchangeable at face value into gold or silver as a matter of domestic convertibility. At this stage, whether silver or gold had been chosen as the base was related to the past history, politics and

[1] I am indebted to Professors L. S. Pressnell, D. Moggridge, P. Mathias and G. E. Wood for helpful comments on an earlier version.

preferences of the countries concerned. However, so long as the ratio between the price of silver and the price of gold remained steady, fixed international exchange rates could prevail amongst all such countries whether they had adopted silver or gold, and indeed some countries could hold comfortably to a dual or bimetallic standard, so avoiding the explicit choice of gold or silver. In the second half of the nineteenth century the gold/silver ratio came under pressure to the detriment of silver as the sterling price of silver fell relatively to the (fixed) sterling price of gold, and more countries followed the British example of choosing gold as the metallic base. For Britain, and its associated monetary area in the Empire except for India, had been since 1821 the only major European country which had consistently linked its domestic currency to a gold metallic base.

Indeed, the evolution of the international monetary system in the last quarter of the nineteenth century can be seen in terms of the abandonment of silver by more and more countries as their metallic standard and the choice of gold as the basis of their domestic currency for a variety of motives, both economic and non-economic.[2] For example, the German Empire adopted gold in 1871 followed by The Netherlands in 1873 and Switzerland and Belgium in 1878, while France moved closely towards gold but still retained a form of bimetallism. The United States of America fixed the value of the dollar in terms of gold in 1879, while Russia and Japan had adhered to gold by 1897 as had the Austro-Hungarian Empire in a *de facto* way. The gold standard, as this form of international monetary system became known, had spread world-wide by 1900. However, it was not consciously planned – as with the International Monetary Fund (IMF) at Bretton Woods in 1944 – but grew from this deliberate choice of metallic standards on the part of countries, and is best thought of as a particular system of international monetary arrangements and balance of payments adjustment.[3]

Once a country had chosen gold, then it became the overriding policy of its monetary authority (central bank, or Treasury, or commercial banks) to maintain specie payments or convertibility of notes for gold in the face of demands for gold, whether for domestic or international purposes, bearing on its limited gold holdings. The monetary authority had to rely on its own efforts in the main to preserve convertibility with little willing cooperation from other monetary authorities. International monetary policy in the period 1870–1914 must thus be defined in terms of the sum of individual monetary authorities' efforts to maintain the fixity of the link between their domestic currency and gold.

---

[2] For an interesting and revealing discussion, see M. de Cecco, *Money and Empire* (Oxford, 1975), ch. 3.

[3] Compare, for example, W. M. Scammell, 'The Working of the Gold Standard', *Yorkshire Bulletin of Economic and Social Research*, vol. xvii, no. 1 (May 1965), pp. 32 and 34.

Let us consider more analytically what was essentially involved in joining the international gold standard. To become a member of this international fixed exchange rate system, a country had to undertake three basic measures:

1. It had to define by law its national currency unit in terms of weight of gold.
2. If notes were used domestically in addition to gold coinage, then it had to see that they were freely convertible at face value into gold on demand.
3. It had to permit the free export and import of gold.

Measures (1) and (2), besides providing for domestic convertibility, fixed the *mint par* rate of exchange of one national currency for another in terms of the ratio of weights of gold for each currency unit. For example one pound or one sovereign was defined as 113.0016 grains of fine gold, while one US dollar was defined as 23.22 grains of fine gold.

Hence the mint par rate of exchange was

$$\pounds 1 = \frac{113.0016}{23.22} \text{ US \$} = 4.8665 \text{ US \$}$$

From this came a system of international fixed exchange rates with orderly cross rates. Measure (3) was needed to ensure the maintenance of these fixed exchange rates between national currencies in the face of imbalances in international payments. For in the nineteenth century international exchanges of goods and services were financed mainly by the use of bills of exchange rather than by gold coin, and we might regard this financing as approximating to the mutual exchange of national currencies in foreign exchange markets.

To provide a crude example, which is phrased in such a way as to reflect the important feature that, as most British international transactions were conducted in sterling, foreign exchange business was small in London and the exchanges of sterling for other currencies took place in foreign exchange markets *outside* Britain: suppose that the United States spent less on imports from Britain than she received for her exports thence, so that America had a balance of payments surplus with Britain or that Britain had a deficit with America. American exporters, not wanting to keep the pounds received thus, would seek to sell them for dollars to American importers who required the sterling to pay for British goods. In the above circumstances the importers would be demanding less sterling than was being offered, or the American exporters would be demanding more dollars than the importers were offering. At the current sterling–dollar exchange rate there would be an excess demand for dollars – or an excess supply of pounds – so that the price of dollars in sterling would rise or the price of sterling would fall in terms of dollars and the exchange rate would diverge from the mint par. Clearly it would become cheaper for an American merchant (or banker) with sterling, but wanting dollars, to use the sterling to buy gold in London and to ship it to America for conversion into the desired dollars at the American Treasury.

Yet gold was not immediately taken as soon as the exchange rate depreciated from the mint par because gold movements were not costless. Freightage and insurance costs had to be paid, while interest was lost during passage, and there was the inconvenience of the operation. Once the sterling exchange rate had depreciated sufficiently to cover these costs, it became cheaper to ship gold: this position was known as the gold export point for sterling at which the outflow of gold stabilized the exchange rate. In the circumstances above the British gold export point was the American gold import point, or the limit to the appreciation of dollars in terms of pounds, and vice versa. For the pound–dollar exchange rate *The Economist* cited the British gold export point as £1 = $4.827 for the period 1877–1914, while the gold import point was £1 = $4.890. It does seem that these are average figures and their stability over time seems somewhat suspicious, for costs of freight and insurance varied and individual bankers could evaluate differently the costs and advantages of shipping gold. Indeed, Morgenstern quotes estimates of the gold export point as high as $4.857 and of the gold import point as low as $4.872.[4] The free international movement of gold was thus crucial in keeping the exchange rate fluctuations of national currencies within narrow bounds about the mint par, as was the profit-seeking behaviour of merchants and bankers who shipped gold regardless of any other considerations.

An additional view of the gold-point mechanism relying on arbitrage in gold may be suggested. Suppose the pound depreciates from the mint par against some other currency: it will then become profitable for bankers to buy gold for sterling in London, ship it to the foreign monetary centre where it can be exchanged at the appropriate mint par for foreign currency. This foreign currency may then be converted into pounds at the prevailing market rate and afford sufficient extra pounds to cover the costs of the transactions. (For example, £10,000 would purchase sufficient gold at mint par to convert into US $48,665. This could be converted at the gold export point of $4.827 to yield £10,082 – a gross gain of £82 before settling transaction costs.) Such transactions would increase the demand for pounds in foreign exchange markets and prevent any further decline in the sterling exchange rate. Arbitrage in gold, which was cheap to transport and generally acceptable, would limit the

⁴ O. Morgenstern, *International Financial Transactions and Business Cycles* (Princeton, 1959), p. 177.

degree to which a currency could diverge from its mint part in international currency markets.[5]

Monetary authorities could thus be confronted with both internal and external demands for gold, the former being associated with the needs of home trade and even with loss of confidence in banknotes or bank deposits as compared with gold coins. The latter demands were linked directly to balance of payments deficits which could be seasonal, cyclical, or random. Hence the monetary authorities needed to deploy some of their assets into non-remunerative gold holdings, ample to meet such demands immediately without question and thus to maintain convertibility of their national currencies. Such reserves might be replenished from the internal reflux of gold and from the import of gold whether from other monetary authorities or from the mines. Indeed, the size of gold reserves held would be influenced by the speed at which gold losses could be reversed, the ease with which they could be replenished and the individual variability of foreign currency receipts and payments, while of importance, would be the institutional position of the country and its monetary authority's attitude to the holding of idle, unremunerative reserves of gold.

Yet it was not enough that the above measures should be adopted and that the monetary authorities should hold gold reserves and hope for the best. It was necessary for there to be mechanisms and devices and for discretionary policies to be available to monetary authorities by which gold losses could be choked off before reserves were exhausted. Certainly they must have existed and operated effectively, for balance of payments imbalances and gold movements occurred frequently but most gold standard members were successful in preserving convertibility in this period, as such imbalances and movements were reversed. Later we shall suggest what they might have been and how they operated, but first we must consider the pattern of international monetary arrangements as they evolved in the fifty years before 1914.

III.   *Institutional arrangements*

Although the new members who joined the gold standard in this period put into force the essentials of the three measures earlier mentioned, they did not adopt any standard legal or institutional arrangements. Much variety and diversity were to be found in institutional practice and in legal provisions: Britain, Germany, and the United States had a full gold standard with gold coin circulating, while France, amongst others,

---

[5] See D. N. McCloskey and J. R. Zecher, 'How the Gold Standard Worked 1880–1913', in J. A. Frenkel and H. G. Johnson (eds.), *The Monetary Approach to the Balance of Payments* (London, 1976), pp. 365–6.

retained a 'limping' gold standard under which the Bank of France had a choice of converting notes into gold or into full legal-tender (but depreciated) silver coins. Other countries, notably Russia, Japan, and much of the British Empire, embraced a gold exchange standard, under which they held much of their international reserves in the form of foreign currency, itself convertible into gold, in balances of pounds, French francs, and marks. In some countries the principal form of internal money was provided by gold coin, in others banknotes were preferred, while Britain led the way in the wide use of cheques. The regulation of the domestic money supply varied from country to country: in some note issue was rigidly linked to gold reserves held, in others more discretion was permitted to the monetary authorities, while in the former case the effectiveness of such a link was weakened, as in Britain, by the existence of a banking system with no minimum legal cash-deposit ratio, thus giving greater elasticity to the money supply (defined as notes, coin, and bank deposits).

As various countries were at different stages in their economic development and in their degrees of industrialization, likewise some were more developed than others in their domestic and international financial arrangements. Some possessed effective central banks working within developed capital and money markets with international business and contacts; others had weak or ineffective central banks. Some, again, had no central bank, but were served by commercial banking systems which might be independent of, or dependent on, foreign monetary centres. Despite this confused picture of monetary institutions, nevertheless all had the same policy objective, the maintenance of the convertibility of their currency into gold, even though the responsibility for this could lie with a central bank, a Treasury or an official conversion office, a domestically based commercial banking system or a foreign-based banking system, each with their attendant political problems. This diversity should warn us against accepting too easily some of the facile stereotypes which have been applied to gold standard provisions regardless of individual circumstances.

Different sizes of economy, different stages of development, elements of political and economic dominance and dependence within and without Empire help to explain the emergence of dominant and dependent relations, or a centre–periphery pattern, in international monetary arrangements, confused though they seem. Indeed as we look further into the substance of the system a more coherent picture results if the international monetary and payments system is regarded as a form of solar system with London at the centre, although this analogy should not be pressed too far since Paris and Berlin were providing other (minor) suns as they developed their international banking. Nevertheless, London and the pound sterling were dominant within the system.

In the first place the various multilateral settlement patterns in the network of trade pivoted on London[6] where the various international banks could make the requisite residual settlements in the world's only truly international financial centre. The bill on London served as the world currency, such was its convenience and usefulness in settlements, and so great was the confidence of holders of sterling that gold would always be freely available on demand in London: indeed, sterling was better than gold since interest could be earned. London possessed the world's main short-term and long-term capital markets together with the world gold market and produce markets while the role of sterling was further enhanced by the steady development of British overseas banking. The spread of Anglo-imperial and Anglo-foreign banks not only encouraged the use of sterling internationally but also facilitated the Bank of England's task in meeting strain on its reserves. For these banks, which held sizeable balances in London as their cash reserves (and the foreign exchange reserves of territories which they served), were usually prepared to see them rise in settlement of a British payments deficit with their territories rather than take gold, particularly if it was made worth their while with higher short-term interest rates in London. Furthermore, this transfer of ownership of London balances meant that the London money market would not suffer any loss of resources. London thus had a privileged position in that a rise in sterling balances provided an alternative to a gold loss in the face of a balance of payments deficit.

London, indeed, before 1914 was not greatly concerned with foreign exchange dealings, since the British export and import trade was essentially conducted in sterling – cash against documents. British merchants and traders made and received payment in sterling and did not concern themselves much with foreign exchanges – that was for the foreigner. This was natural enough when London was the world's clearing centre and sterling was the international currency for settlements. Hence, while British merchants did not worry about the exchanges, foreigners were very much concerned with keeping their rates on London steady in their foreign exchange markets and by their dealings the various sterling exchange rates were kept steady. In this way they helped to make the gold standard approximate to a sterling standard or rather a bill on London standard.[7]

From this brief survey there emerges the special position of sterling and London which had developed under the gold standard, not only because of the size of international transactions financed in sterling but also through the international institutional dominance of London and

---

[6] S. B. Saul, *Studies in British Overseas Trade 1870–1914* (Liverpool, 1960), chs. 3 and 4.

[7] See in particular W. A. Brown, Jr, *The International Gold Standard Reinterpreted, 1914–34* (New York, 1940), pp. 637–41; and P. Einzig, *The History of Foreign Exchange* (London, 1962), pp. 182–3.

Table 19. *Official gold, silver, and foreign exchange reserves, 1913*
(£ million, 35 countries)

	Gold	Silver	Foreign exchange	Total
Great Britain: Bank of England	34	0	0	34
France: Bank of France	139	25	1	165
Germany: Reichsbank	57	14	10	81
Other Europe	361	63	126	550
N. and S. America	363	108	13	484
Africa, Asia, Australia	41	23	83	147
Total	995	233	233	1461

Converted into pounds at 1913 parities.
Source: Lindert, 'Key Currencies and Gold 1900–13', *Princeton Studies in International Finance*, no. 24 (August 1969), pp. 10–12.

the supreme confidence in sterling which the Bank of England had won by always supplying gold on demand. It is important to recognize that by 1900 the international gold standard was very much a sterling standard based on London, when considering its actual operations. Yet the early twentieth century sees some crumbling of the role of sterling, particularly in respect of the rise of the international business of Paris and Berlin.

Official reserves of gold in the world are estimated to have grown from some £205 million in 1880 through £535 million in 1903 to £1,010 million in 1913, the bulk of this fivefold increase being concentrated in the last decade before 1914.[8] Gold discoveries and their exploitation, particularly in South Africa, underlie this rate of expansion. In the same period Bloomfield has estimated that official holdings of foreign exchange for 18 countries grew from £13 million in 1880 to £185 million in 1913,[9] thereby forming a growing proportion of world international reserve assets, but remaining a minor part. This impression is confirmed by Lindert's estimates for 1913 which are presented in Table 19. Official holdings of silver are also included, although nearly half were held by the American Treasury and their size overstated their relative importance and use. It is clear that gold remained the major international reserve asset, and it is interesting to note that the Bank of England, which was very much at the centre, held a mere 3.4 per cent of the total official holdings of gold.

[8] P. H. Lindert, 'Key Currencies and Gold 1900–13', *Princeton Studies in International Finance*, no. 24 (1969), p. 25, who points out the roughness of the estimates, which are in US dollars at 1913 parities and have been converted into pounds at the 1913 mint par.
[9] A. I. Bloomfield, 'Short-Term Capital Movements under the pre-1914 Gold Standard', *Princeton Studies in International Finance*, no. 11, (1963), pp. 96–7.

Table 20. *Official holdings of foreign exchange, 1913 (£ million)*

Where held	Total	European holdings	Rest of world holdings
Great Britain	89	16	73
France	57	54	3
Germany	31	24	7
Other	13	9	4
Unspecified	43	34	9
Total	233	137	96

Source: Lindert, 'Key Currencies', pp. 10–12, 19.

Of the official holdings of foreign exchange in 1913 nearly 60 per cent was held by three countries, Russia with £63 million, Japan with £48 million, and India with £28 million. Furthermore, while the greatest reported single holding of foreign exchange reserves was in the United Kingdom (38 per cent), this holding was matched by the combined holdings in France and Germany. Indeed, European countries clearly preferred to hold their official foreign exchange reserves in francs and marks rather than in sterling, while the position was reversed for the non-European countries, who strongly preferred London. It is more difficult to obtain as complete coverage for private holdings of foreign exchange but Lindert's estimates indicated a figure of some £120 million for 1913 with a similar relative division between Britain, France and Germany.[10] Again, it should be noted that official holdings of foreign exchange grew from £51 million in 1899 to £233 million in 1913 at an annual rate of 10.8 per cent, while official holdings of gold grew at an annual rate of 6.3 per cent between 1903 and 1913.[11] This build-up in balances (three-quarters of which were reported as being in pounds, or marks, or francs) would also indicate a collective excess of payments over receipts in the British, French, and German balances of payments after allowing for all other transactions including gold movements.

Although the compilers of these statistical estimates properly urge caution. nevertheless they do provide a broad picture of the rise of the gold exchange standard, the growth of rival centres to London, and the extent to which the Bank of England chose to keep its gold reserves so low, both relatively and absolutely. Not only do they indicate some modest crumbling of the pure gold standard (quite apart from the issue of its sterling underlay) after 1900 but also of the relative British position within it, a decline which had parallels in other spheres of British economic activity.

[10] Lindert, 'Key Currencies', pp. 18–19.   [11] *Ibid.*, p. 22.

IV.   *Mechanisms of adjustment*

Within this framework how did monetary authorities cope with balance of payments deficits and their associated gold losses? How were they reversed? Let us consider the economic implications of an external gold loss or a fall in foreign exchange holdings, before we discuss the policy-induced reactions of monetary authorities.

When a country experienced a balance of payments deficit and an associated gold loss, might there be equilibrating forces set in motion by the disturbing factors causing the gold loss? Consider the case where a country's export proceeds fall because of a loss of foreign markets or a fall in export prices. Foreign currency receipts fall relatively to foreign currency payments and there is an immediate loss of gold. However, the fall in export values, the disturbing factor, will reduce incomes and output in a multiplier process and hence will reduce import purchases so that the immediate balance of payments deficit is narrowed as the process works itself out (assuming other categories of autonomous spending remain unchanged initially). Similar equilibrating forces would operate when the disturbing factor was a rise in lending abroad *at the expense* of home spending, or when from a given income there was a switch from spending on home goods to spending on imports, or when there was a fall in the proceeds of foreign borrowing which were being used to finance home (investment) spending. In all cases contractionary income movements would cause import payments to fall and the deficit to narrow.

Not all disturbing forces would have such consequences. Suppose gold was being lost because a domestically financed boom had increased imports sharply, or because lending abroad had risen by the use of idle deposits, or because there was a switch in non-resident balances from one monetary centre to another, as holders adjusted their portfolios to a more preferred choice of assets. (Here, in the case of a once-and-for-all transaction the gold flow would cease as holders completed the desired readjustment of their stocks of assets, but would persist so long as asset-holders continued to unwind their position to which there was a clear limit eventually set.) In all these circumstances there would be no direct effect on incomes and imports as earlier outlined.

The importance of these factors would depend on how frequently deficits occurred for reasons which had equilibrating tendencies as outlined above. Secondly, the strength of such effects would depend very much on the nature and structure of the economy, being more powerful in an economy with a low marginal propensity to save and a high marginal propensity to import (for example, developing economies such as Australia, Argentina, South Africa) and less where the marginal propensity to save was higher and the marginal propensity to import lower (for example, France, United States).

Consider where the marginal propensity to save is 0.1 and the marginal propensity to import is 0.4 and governmental transactions are assumed away. The multiplier would then be 2. A fall in exports of 100 would immediately worsen the balance of payments by 100, but then incomes would fall by 200 and imports by 80 so that the ultimate worsening is limited to 20. Reverse the propensity values. The unchanged multiplier still produces the same fall in incomes of 200, but imports only fall by 20 so that the ultimate balance of payments worsening merely declines to 80.

Again, it might be expected that these equilibrating effects would operate more speedily than, say, money supply effects since the disturbing factor affected spending and incomes directly. Experience bears this out. Likewise these effects would exert deflationary pressure on prices unless they were very sticky and this could further promote adjustment. All these effects would apply equally in the specified cases with a gold gain as the balance of payments moved into surplus. Where applicable, the disturbing factor would serve to reduce the surplus imbalance by expansionary income movements.

It is important to take explicit account of repercussion effects of one country's actions on the rest of the world and back to itself, but at the same time to recall that the strength of these effects would be directly related to the sizes of the countries and of their involvement in trade. Suppose a large country, which previously was not losing gold, is stimulated to boom conditions as a result of *internal* factors (for example, Britain in the first half of the nineteenth century). Activity rises, its imports rise and the balance of payments deteriorates so that gold is lost. The rest of the world's exports thus rise, and their incomes and imports, including purchases from the large country. Some limited balance of payments relief thus would be provided, as well as a further stimulus to its boom. These repercussion effects could prove particularly important for countries with strong bilateral trading links where they took a large proportion of their traded goods from each other. They also illustrate the potential role of the gold standard in transmitting boom and slump internationally.

The second adjustment force is provided by monetary factors. The loss of gold or the fall in, say, London balances would cause a reduction in the cash base of the country's monetary system and a reduction in its money supply, which would tend to be magnified where fractional reserve banking prevailed – unless offsetting tactics were pursued. Deflationary effects would follow as the fall in the stock of money brought a rise in interest rates and hence checks to spending, and more directly insofar as economic units sought to restore their cash balances by cutting their spending. The consequent decline in incomes and output would reduce import purchases and increase the availability of goods for exports, thereby bringing a fall in foreign currency payments relatively to foreign currency receipts. This improvement in the balance of payments might be reinforced insofar as the prices of exportables and import-competing goods were reduced (assuming favourable price elasticities of demand), while this might also alleviate the growing unemployment associated with the former effects. As long as the deficit persisted, the money supply would continue to fall and to induce the corrective deflationary effects until the imbalance was eliminated.

If we now recall that one country's deficit is someone else's surplus, we can introduce actions by the gold gainers into the adjustment process. Other countries would move into balance of payments surplus and import gold, and would experience a rise in the money supply, expansionary effects on spending, incomes and output. Imports would rise, the supply of exportables would be checked, while the price level might rise, thereby causing foreign currency payments to rise relatively to foreign currency receipts and lessening the surplus imbalance. Such actions would assist the deficit country to reduce its imbalance more easily as the surplus country tended to buy more of the former's goods.

This monetary analysis would indicate a two-way process of adjustment which would come about automatically and might thus provide the answers to our initial questions. However, doubts must be expressed about this analysis on its own: economic experience has indicated that the above monetary processes tend to be slow-moving with time-lags of up to twelve months or more, so that gold reserves could easily have been exhausted before the sluggish adjustment had been completed. Monetary authorities appear to have behaved with more discretion and gold losses were reversed more quickly than the above monetary processes would allow. Hence, although the above analysis provides one possible strand of explanation, we must lay much emphasis on the earlier automatic income adjustment mechanisms, but recall that the monetary effects would always work in the same direction as the income effects for the economy in question.

Despite the possibilities of eventual adjustment to gold losses from the operation of these various automatic effects, monetary authorities reacted to declines in their gold and foreign exchange holdings with various policy-induced measures to protect their ability to maintain specie payments. These measures could be classified into interest rate policies, money supply policies, and gold and other devices.

When confronted with a serious decline in its reserves, a central bank might increase its rate of rediscount with the intention of increasing the interest-rate structure in its financial markets – in other words the increase in its rediscount rate had to be 'effective' – and it might have to undertake money supply policies to achieve this. Secondly, it might react to a gold loss by reducing the money supply (by open-market operations) to deflate the economy and vice versa in the case of a gold gain in accordance with the well-known interpretation of the 'rules of the game' doctrine of later years (gold in, inflate the stock of money; gold out, deflate it), although it must be said that there is little evidence of this behaviour on the part of central banks.[12] Indeed, this interpretation has been persuasively challenged by Michaely and will be discussed later.[13] Thirdly, it could seek to discourage the export of gold by placing obstacles, legal and otherwise, in the path of those seeking gold, or it could enhance its ability to acquire gold by raising its buying price of bar gold or *foreign* gold coins. Equally it could raise its selling price of such gold. Finally, as a separate device those central banks which held foreign exchange could protect their gold holdings by supporting the foreign exchange market thus above the gold export point. How many of these policies were used, and by whom, depended on particular circumstances and this will be discussed later.

In those economies with no central bank, commercial banks could react in similar ways by raising their lending and borrowing interest rates, by increasing their desired cash-deposit ratios, and by reducing their willingness to lend. Such institutions had less discretion than central banks and, indeed, were more wholehearted followers of the rules of the game, as popularly interpreted.

How might the interest rate and money supply policies help to reduce balance of payments deficits and gold losses? As the interest rate structure rose and particularly the market rate of discount, alterations in international capital movements could be expected. Funds employed abroad could be repatriated to now more profitable home use; fresh foreign funds could be attracted, while higher rates could help to retain existing non-resident balances; those seeking short- or long-term loans for use abroad might defer their transactions or even seek loans in another cheaper monetary centre. These quick effects may be interpreted as stock adjustments by the various holders of portfolios of financial assets to a given change in interest rate differentials amongst various monetary centres. In these circumstances a given change in differentials would produce a limited effect which would cease when the most preferred holding had been achieved. To produce a continuing net inflow of funds further widenings of the interest rate differentials would be required to induce further stock adjustments.

These quick effects, whose operation would clearly be confined to

[12] A. I. Bloomfield, *Monetary Policy under the International Gold Standard 1880–1914* (New York, 1959), pp. 47–51.
[13] Michael Michaely, *Balance of Payments Adjustment Policies* (New York, 1968), pp. 11–18.

developed monetary centres, would afford valuable, but *temporary*, help to monetary authorities seeking to reverse gold losses, for there would be limits to their continuance over time. They would depend for their efficacy on perfect confidence felt by profit-seeking bankers in the stability of mint par rates of exchange, and on the comparative lack of reaction of other monetary authorities when one sought to establish an interest rate differential in its favour to reverse its gold losses.

The longer-run effects of higher interest rates and reduced money supply would bear on spending plans in the economy: investment activity might fall, while consumers might seek to replenish their cash balances by reducing consumption expenditure out of a given income. These deflationary effects would reduce incomes, output and import purchases, thereby reinforcing the adjusting forces already noted but only after a substantial lag, and could further promote adjustment if they brought a fall in the price level.

Insofar as gold-gaining monetary authorities pursued opposite discretionary policies to gold losers – lower interest rates and an increased stock of money – they would tend to check their gold-gaining tendencies and ease the size of the adjustment problems for the gold losers. This point is made with clarity in *The Report of the Committee on Finance and Industry* – the Macmillan Report – Cmnd 3897 of 1931:

The nineteenth century philosophy of the gold standard was based on the assumptions that (a) an increase or decrease of gold in the vaults of Central Banks would imply respectively a 'cheap' or a 'dear' money policy, and (b) that a 'cheap' or a 'dear' money policy would affect the entire price structure and the level of money incomes in the country concerned (para. 43).

and as a result of following such policies when gaining or losing gold,

Gold standard countries were indeed supposed to meet each other halfway, each altering its conditions sufficiently to bring about the desired equilibrium (para. 185).

This *Report* was indeed sceptical whether things had actually worked like this (para. 295) as indeed we shall be.

Our analysis has concerned itself with *external* drains of gold, but monetary authorities who were responsible for a gold coin circulation faced also the possibility of an *internal* drain on its reserves as rising activity brought an increased domestic transactions demand for gold coin, or because of a panic demand for liquidity. The above policy measures would help to restore gold reserves after such an internal drain by attracting gold from abroad, by making it more costly to take gold internally, and by checking home activity to produce an internal reflux. Such countries in a period of steady growth would need to ensure favourable balances of payments to produce net imports of gold to meet internal coinage demands: for this the output of new-mined gold and gold discoveries were essential. Nevertheless, Triffin's estimates indicate that over 90 per cent of the increasing total domestic money supply in the major countries of the world between 1885 and 1913 was accounted for by increases in credit money (currency *plus* bank deposits).[14] Financial innovations formed a vital element in meeting growing domestic monetary demands – pyramiding on a small, but growing gold base.

From these features other views of international gold movements can arise. As Barrett Whale said, 'Our theory must also take account of the possibility that gold movements, instead of being the determinants of the supply of money, may themselves be determined by monetary requirements.'[15] This was the precursor of an alternative analytical approach to the gold standard which, relying on the recently developed monetary theory of the balance of payments, regards gold movements and central bank operations in a very different light. Gold movements are not viewed as disturbing factors which provoke (in the manner suggested above) with lags and difficulty income and price adjustments, but as reflecting domestic monetary requirements. If the demand for money rises in an economy and cannot be satisfied from domestic sources of monetary expansion, then this excess demand for money will be met by the import of gold which thus equilibrates the demand and supply of money. Likewise, an excess supply of money is eliminated by the export of gold.[16]

It is fundamental to this view that the world commodity markets especially, and also the capital markets, are unified, with the world's economy determining prices and interest rates prevailing in each economy. Individual countries do not have individual control over their prices and interest rates, for through arbitrage between commodity and capital markets they have to accept ruling world prices and interest rates so that domestic deflation, say, cannot influence their prices and interest rates relatively to prices and rates prevailing in other countries. Under such a system central banks lack power, the rules of the game lose their importance, gold flows cannot transmit price changes and the 'gritty' adjustment mechanisms are not required. Rather, arbitrage serves to ensure impressive parallelism in price behaviour in the world, and smooth responses without heavy strain.

How, then, could gold flow into an economy which was experiencing

---

[14] R. Triffin, 'The Evolution of the International Monetary System', *Princeton Studies in International Finance*, no. 12 (1964), pp. 51–63.

[15] P. Barrett Whale, 'The Working of the Pre-War Gold Standard', *Economica*, NS, vol. IV (February, 1937), pp. 25–6.

[16] See McCloskey and Zecher, 'How the Gold Standard Worked', pp. 357–85. For a more cautiously worded view see Whale 'Pre-War Gold Standard', pp. 18–32. There are distinct Ricardian overtones here.

an excess demand for money? How could the exchanges become favourable and reach the gold import point? This theory assumes that real output is determined by supply-side factors so that 'full employment' output is maintained but that economic units reduce their absorption or spending in an effort to achieve their desired money holdings. This releases home output for exports (readily sold in perfect international markets) and reduces import purchases. Hence the balance of payments improves, the exchange rate reaches the gold import point and gold flows in to expand the domestic money stock and to eliminate the excess demand for money. Absorption then matches output, the balance of payments is restored to equilibrium and the gold inflow ceases. (And similarly for an economy with an excess supply of money which would lose gold until monetary equilibrium was restored.) Further, insofar as the excess demand for money tended to put upward pressure on domestic interest rates, funds might flow in from abroad in the context of perfect capital markets to assist in the above process.

In this account one does not ask what repercussions will follow from international gold movements: they are responding to excess demand for money positions (gold imports) or to excess supply positions (gold exports) to produce equilibrium. In this way McCloskey and Zecher explain the conjuncture (for Britain and America) of boom and gold imports, slump and gold exports, and the smoothness of gold standard operations (regardless of central bankers) with no need for painful relative price and wage adjustments which have no place in this perfectly arbitraged world. Gold enters because it is wanted: gold leaves because it is redundant.

However, this simple and attractive approach must be questioned. In the first place, were markets for goods so unified in reality? Certainly, the great commodity markets of the world ensured common behaviour for primary product prices – allowing for transport costs and tariffs – but there was surely less unity for tradable manufactures where differentiated products and monopolistic competition lessened the power of arbitrage, especially in the short run, and even less unity for non-tradable goods and services. Indeed, the marked cyclical parallelism of prices in this period might reflect booms or slumps in activity occurring roughly together in the major countries of the world, rather than the power of arbitrage.

Secondly, were the various capital markets of the world so unified? It does seem that they were less closely connected than for commodities and that relationships of dominance and dependence prevailed. It would be better to regard world capital markets as in various stages of development, with Britain almost in a market leader position to which others would accommodate. Discussion later in this chapter will attempt to substantiate London's drawing power. Indeed, gritty capital markets would not permit the capital flows envisaged in this view. Nevertheless, certain securities were quoted on the world's main stock exchanges so that arbitrage in these could happen.

Again, could all countries acquire their desired gold imports in a world characterized by cyclical parallelism, even with new-mined gold production? Evidence to be presented later will suggest that at boom times the British and American appetite for gold was satisfied by the reluctant willingness of France and Germany to forgo their normal import purchases on the London gold market. Barrett Whale, after noting the possibility that gold movements may be determined by monetary requirements and instancing the inflows of gold to Britain and America in booms and outflows in slumps, states in this respect 'Further evidence . . . confirms the view that it was the monetary requirements determined by a given price level which provided the underlying cause of the international gold movements.' However, he goes on to say 'Presumably the countries which acted as the counter-parties to Britain and America in these movements were in a position to allow a considerable fluctuation in their reserves.'[17]

Any simple application of this equilibrium type of analysis must be treated with caution, especially the supply-side determination of output in the short run. Our earlier economic analysis is surely more useful for explaining how situations of disequilibrium were corrected in the short run when the scope for arbitrage was limited, while in the longer run the monetary analysis may have more value in explaining common trends in prices and interest rates and in suggesting an underlying equilibrium for economies, although it does ignore the specific institutional positions to which we shall attach importance. It also has value in suggesting that countries and their central banks had less control over their individual price levels than classical theories had supposed, and in indicating how the flow of new-mined gold might be distributed according to need.

To decide how much of our earlier general analysis is applicable to particular countries, it is necessary to examine their financial, commercial and political structures in these gold standard years. While this enquiry might lay low any hopes of a general explanation such as the rules of the game model, nevertheless it might well indicate why the gold standard worked so well in some countries and so poorly in others.

Certain key points may be distinguished. Given imperfections in world capital markets and different credit ratings, it was easier for a lending economy such as Britain, France, or Germany to stop a gold loss by lending less abroad than for a borrowing economy such as Australia or Argentina to achieve the same by borrowing more.

---

[17] Whale, 'Pre-War Gold Standard', pp. 25–7.

Whether an economy was a lender or a borrower would have implications for the operation of the 'quick' effects of short-term international capital movements.

Secondly, whether an economy was a primary producer or industrialized had a bearing on the adjustment process. For in primary producers such as Canada, Australia, Chile, New Zealand, Argentina, and South Africa the prices of their exportable products were determined in world commodity markets and the prices of their imports were determined by their major suppliers so that much of their price levels lay outside their control and was insensitive to domestic monetary policies. On the other hand, in industrialized countries such as Germany or Britain, prices of their manufactured products were determined on a 'cost-plus' basis and clearly monetary policies could have more influence on such price-makers.

Different balance of payments patterns resulted if a country's economic activity was influenced mainly by variations in export sales as in Britain, Argentina, Canada, and other major primary producing 'export' economies, or by variations in home investment as in the United States. For in the former export-induced booms brought balance of payments current account surpluses and monetary ease, other things equal, as gold flowed in and exaggerated the boom: in the latter home-induced booms would be accompanied by current account deficits, gold outflows, and monetary stringency so that the boom was checked: and vice versa in slumps. Gold standard adjustments in the 'export' economy case meant exaggerating booms and slumps (assuming no capital movement changes), while it meant mitigating booms and slumps for the 'investment' economy.

The stage of development of a country's financial system had important influences on adjustment reactions. In countries with central banks (particularly Britain, France, and Germany) more discretion was available in reacting to gold gains and losses, whereas in countries with no central bank the commercial banks on occasion reacted more sharply. This was more noticeable in those economies with predominantly overseas-based banks, such as Australia, New Zealand, South Africa in the embryo sterling area, than in those countries where domestic banking facilities were provided in the main by home-based banks who, at least in Latin America, tended to look more to domestic conditions and were less committed to deflation for the sake of the exchange rate parity.

The nature of a country's social and political system and the priorities accorded to various economic aims shaped a country's reactions to crisis conditions. In countries where *rentier* interests were dominant, there would be a greater attachment to the stability of the gold standard and the enforcement of 'discipline', than in countries where debtors were politically dominant and the attractions of a depreciating exchange rate were strong. Again, the political features of empire and the colonial systems imposed by Britain, France and Germany, made for greater priorities for maintaining specie payments.

This is not intended to be an exhaustive list but to suggest that a variety of patterns existed and that in some environments a fixed exchange rate system such as the gold standard worked better than in others. Indeed, it will be contended that the 'success' of the system in Britain before 1914 resulted from the conjuncture of some highly specific circumstances at a particular phase of world economic development rather than from the masochistic willingness to undergo the 'discipline' of gold.

V. Behaviour of monetary authorities

This section is concerned with the actual behaviour patterns of monetary authorities – especially central banks – and will examine in some detail the position of the Bank of England. It will attempt to assess the strength of the various adjustment effects associated with such monetary policies and will suggest that we may have to look elsewhere for an explanation of the speedy, sustained adjustment which was such a feature of the gold standard before 1914.

The avowed objective of central banks was to maintain convertibility and the guide to their policy actions was provided by the state of their reserves relative to their liabilities, although it has been suggested that policy reactions would not of necessity follow rigidly from changes in the reserve ratio but would involve the use of judgment in individual situations. How far did events bear this out? In his careful examination of the relationship between central bank discount rates and reserve ratios from 1880 to 1913, Bloomfield found a good inverse correlation – discount rates rising as reserve ratios fell, and conversely – for Britain, Germany, Austria–Hungary, Belgium, Holland, and Russia, while the inverse correlation was less marked for France, and non-existent for Denmark, Finland, Norway, and Switzerland.[18]

On the other hand, when the behaviour of annual average discount rates over time was compared for twelve European central banks (the eleven mentioned plus Sweden), they tended to rise and fall together, particularly for their larger movements, and the resultant cyclical pattern to have peaks and troughs much in line with the European trade cycle.[19] Morgenstern's investigation of the financial interrelationships of London, Paris, Berlin, and New York confirms in detail this pattern and reveals that the three European short-term interest rates moved together

---

[18] Bloomfield, *Monetary Policy*, pp. 30–5.   [19] *Ibid.*, pp. 35–7.

in 60.6 per cent of all months between 1879 and 1914, while the addition of New York reduced this phase agreement to 48.6 per cent with the British rate the most volatile and the French the most stable.[20] Indeed, the Bank of France preferred a stable discount rate and allowed its ample reserves to fluctuate, while it frequently allowed a gold premium to develop to discourage demands for gold. In contrast, the Bank of England chose to keep low reserves, to maintain a free gold market, and to employ sharp changes in Bank Rate to protect its reserves from strain. For example, it chose to meet the seasonal fluctuations in the British balance of payments – the 'autumnal drain' – by seasonal fluctuations in short-term interest rates right through the period, rather than by holding higher (non-remunerative) reserves.

This common cyclical pattern in discount rates is to be explained partly by other central banks' defensive reactions to the Bank of England's use of Bank Rate, for London occupied a dominant position, and, as the Macmillan Report says, 'other countries had, therefore, in the main to adjust their conditions to hers' (para. 295), while for certain central banks, European cyclical parallelism in activity helped to cause reserve ratios to fall or rise together as the central banks experienced internal drains and refluxes, unless swamped by external gold movements. (Given the monetary arrangements and institutions of varying development and influence it does seem preferable to explain the cyclical pattern more in terms of defensive reactions and less in terms of arbitrage amongst various capital markets.) Certainly this pattern of high discount rates in booms and low rates in slumps should not be taken as evidence of a conscious anti-cyclical policy on the part of central banks, although on occasions they did temper their policies somewhat in the face of domestic hardship. That will be illustrated later in the dominant case of Britain and the Bank of England.

How did equilibrating short-term international capital movements come about when this marked parallelism of discount rates implied that any differential, which a central bank might obtain by increasing its rediscount rate, was speedily eroded by similar (defensive) actions by other central banks? The analysis underlying this question is assuming that there was no asymmetry in effects when the rise of 1 per cent in the rate of one central bank was offset by the rise of 1 per cent of another, whereas much of the literature on the gold standard has always stressed the drawing power or dominance of London. Despite the paucity of data, Lindert's careful statistical investigation of the influence of discount rates of pairs of countries on the bilateral exchange rate between them for the period 1899–1913 bears out the importance of these asymmetries in relation to the drawing power of central banks.[21]

[20] Morgenstern, *Financial Transactions*, p. 118.
[21] Lindert, *Key Currencies*, pp. 48–57, and especially figure 3 (p. 51).

His results indicate that the Bank of England possessed short-run command over most of the sterling exchanges even without changes in international interest rate differentials. London enjoyed supremacy among the three main centres as a result of confidence in sterling, more attractive and useful financial assets and perhaps a lively fear of what might happen if Bank Rate had to rise yet more, with a clearer edge over Berlin than Paris, while Paris appeared to have greater influence over the franc–mark exchange rate, so that London gained when all discount rates went up by one percentage point and Paris gained from Berlin. How did Berlin react when losing funds to both London and Paris? Lindert's analysis shows that Berlin had drawing power over smaller European centres, so that her reserves were replenished from the more peripheral countries when a London-initiated squeeze occurred.

He also points out that in every case where there exists a significant inequality in influence over an exchange, the country with the greater leverage appears in the role of a bill lender and deposit debtor as compared with the other country.[22] In times of rising rates of discount foreign borrowers on bill finance could well liquidate these transactions rather than renew, while higher rates could reduce the demand for bill finance from abroad; on the other hand, the deposits were held as reserve assets and would remain. Given this explanation, it does seem unnecessary to insist in the British case on the key importance of the alleged net short-term creditor position of London internationally, particularly when the available evidence casts doubt on this assertion.[23] As Lindert says:

It is thus on manipulation of short-term flows of capital that the impressive ability of major centres to adjust exchange rates and gold flows in the short-run seems to have rested. Quantification of the influence of different countries' discount rates over exchange rates reveals that larger financial centers tended to have greater command over each exchange rate than each smaller center, the Bank of England controlling the sterling–mark exchanges more effectively than the Reichsbank, while the latter had greater power than peripheral continental countries over their mark rates. Through this hierarchy, the impact of monetary tightness in London was promptly shifted to . . . peripheral countries.[24]

Some have attributed the successful operation of the gold standard before 1914 to the fact that central banks behaved in accordance with the rules of the game, that as a central bank's international assets rose or fell, so it should increase or decrease its domestic assets (by open-market operations) to reinforce the effects of international gold movements on the domestic monetary situation. Bloomfield's findings indicate that these items moved in *opposite* directions in 60 per cent of all observations

[22] *Ibid.*, p. 56.
[23] Bloomfield, *Monetary Policy*, p. 42, and 'Short-Term Capital Movements', pp. 73–4.
[24] Lindert, *Key Currencies*, p. 57.

(annual figures), so that doubt may be cast on this doctrine thus interpreted.[25] However, this test must be approached with caution: not only could the changes which are based on annual information mask different movements within any year, but it should be questioned whether the above is the appropriate interpretation of the rules of the game. Michaely has persuasively argued that the rules of the game require 'that the quantity of money decrease in the reserve-losing country and interest rates rise, and *vice versa* in the gold gaining country'.[26] With this interpretation the quantity of money could well fall without the central bank's undertaking any open-market sales and still fall even if the central bank attempted offsetting open-market purchases. In this light such admittedly crude tests have to be viewed.

On the other hand, overseas banks, based on London and operating a gold exchange standard for their territories, exhibited greater conformity to the former interpretation. For their external assets (resources in Britain) formed part of their cash reserves so that a fall in the former would dictate a fall in their domestic assets as a matter of commercial banking prudence, and vice versa.[27] Again commercial banks in countries with no central banks reacted in similar ways when international gold movements affected their cash position.[28] Central bankers had more discretion, while they might alter their views as to the desirable reserve ratio.

In addition to their use of discount rates, all central banks used other devices to protect their gold reserves.[29] Gold might be attracted by raising the buying price of *bar* gold or *foreign* gold coins, equivalent to lowering the gold import point, or a gold drain checked by raising the selling price of bar gold or foreign gold coins, thereby lowering the gold export point. These measures reduced the profits of the central banks and some central banks deterred demands for gold by redeeming (legally) notes for silver rather than gold (for example, in France, Belgium, and Switzerland), while obstacles were also placed in the way of gold seekers. These ranged from having only one clerk paying out gold, to the German doctrine that it was unpatriotic to seek profit by exporting gold, while heavy hints were dropped that in future the central bank might not accommodate the offenders. These devices and obstacles help to explain why exchange rates frequently exceeded the normal gold points and in

[25] Bloomfield, *Monetary Policy*, pp. 48–50.
[26] Michaely, *Balance of Payments*, p. 18.
[27] C. G. F. Simkin, *The Instability of a Dependent Economy* (Oxford, 1951), for a discussion of the New Zealand case.
[28] A. G. Ford, *The Gold Standard 1880–1914: Britain and Argentina* (Oxford, 1962), pp. 106–7, for the Argentinian case.
[29] For a fuller discussion, see R. S. Sayers, *Bank of England Operations 1890–1914* (London, 1936); and Bloomfield, *Monetary Policy*, pp. 52–7.

the short run gold did not move. British bankers were somewhat contemptuous of these continental obstacles and took great pride in their free gold market, made possible by London's superior drawing power. In general, central bank reactions to each other, especially in times of crisis, tended to be defensive rather than cooperative.

As Bloomfield says, 'inter-central bank cooperation before 1914 was definitely the exception rather than the rule',[30] yet some occasions arose when central banks helped each other in times of crisis. For example, the Bank of England borrowed 75 million francs in gold from the Bank of France in 1890, while the Bank of France on several occasions (notably, 1906, 1907, 1909, 1910) discounted British bills and made gold available to London. Certainly some of these actions were designed to prevent the London discount rate from having to rise more and thereby necessitating a defensive rise in the French rate.

Let us examine in more detail the operations of the key central bank, the Bank of England, and attempt to assess where the effects of changes in Bank Rate actually made themselves felt. The Bank of England's paramount objective was the maintenance of convertibility, yet it reacted with discretion rather than automatically to strain on its reserve, being aware of the sometimes conflicting needs of external stability and internal activity. To protect its reserve it employed two main weapons, namely Bank Rate, and 'gold devices', and its Bank Rate policy was succinctly enunciated to the United States National Monetary Commission of 1910:

Q. When is the Bank Rate raised and when lowered?
A. The Bank Rate is raised with the object of either preventing gold leaving the country or of attracting gold to the country, and lowered when it is completely out of touch with market rate and circumstances do not render it necesssary to induce the import of gold.[31]

This confident position nevertheless had been built up hesitantly and tentatively from 1870 as the Bank and the London financial markets came to learn the business of central banking. Note that the second half should be interpreted as a joint condition. The Bank was mindful of earlier years when Bank Rate was out of touch with market rate but circumstances *did* render it necessary to import gold.

As Scammell and others have pointed out, in 1870 the Bank was still of the opinion that Bank Rate should follow the London market rate of discount, and that it should not initiate changes.[32] However, improving international financial arrangements and information together with the

---

[30] Bloomfield, *Monetary Policy*, p. 56.
[31] US National Monetary Commission of 1910, *Interviews*, pp. 26–7.
[32] W. M. Scammell, 'Working of the Gold Standard', pp. 36–41. See also E. V. Morgan, *The Theory and Practice of Central Banking 1797–1913* (repr. London, 1965), pp. 173–99.

growth of the gold standard brought pressure to bear on the Bank, which began hesitantly to use Bank Rate more positively to protect its reserve from the 1870s onwards. The next two decades saw the Bank struggling to make Bank Rate effective and to gain ascendancy over the market at a time when its own relative position and size were declining. Gradually the Bank was becoming more ready to take on the role of lender of last resort to the market and the market to accept and recognize this so that by the end of the century 'Bank Rate became a swiftly variable and effective means of adjusting the interest rate structure and of influencing capital movements and the balance of payments.'[33]

An increase in Bank Rate had to be made 'effective', if it was to bring relief to the Bank's reserve by influencing gold movements. It had to bring a rise in the market rate of discount and other (short-term) interest rates to set in motion the quickly adjusting forces analysed earlier. Since the demand and supply of funds in the market determined the market rate of discount, the Bank had to be ready to diminish the supply of funds by its primitive open-market operations of directly borrowing from institutions or by selling (temporarily) its British Governmental stock (Consols). Sometimes this action was not necessary when the market was short of funds relative to demand, say when the balance of payments was in deficit along with high home activity. Yet it must be recognized that it was only in the last years of the nineteenth century that the Bank had gained the requisite control over the market rate whenever the foreign balance required it.

Within this pattern of development it is easy to see the attraction to the Bank of 'gold devices' which were especially developed in the 1880s as an adjunct or even substitute for Bank Rate changes.[34] By increasing its buying price for foreign coin or bar gold or by offering interest-free loans to gold importers the Bank was able to influence international gold movements in London's favour and to replenish its reserve somewhat without having to place pressure on home activity and without having to incur the very real cost of trying to force market rate up. These gold devices were less used after 1907, when the power of Bank Rate was so successfully demonstrated in the November crisis of 1907.

Whenever the Bank's reserve was threatened, swift action was necessary, so low was the reserve relative to British financial transactions (unremunerative gold holdings were disliked by profit-seeking British bankers), and an effective rise in Bank Rate was the main method of protecting the reserve. Given the particular institutional position of London and its drawing power and confidence in sterling, a rise in the market rate and other short rates speedily influenced international capital

[33] Scammell, 'Working of the Gold Standard', p. 40.
[34] See R. S. Sayers, *Bank of England Operations 1891-1914* (London, 1936), pp. 71-101.

movements, improved the exchanges, and induced the *net* import of gold into Britain which the Bank could tap.

Particular channels may be distinguished. Some of the British funds employed abroad were promptly repatriated to now more lucrative home uses as the overseas transactions they supported were unwound daily; overseas-owned sterling balances received an added inducement to stay in London, while new overseas money was attracted to London, both with the interest rate differential (where applicable), the drawing power of London, and with a zero exchange risk at the gold export point. Goodhart concludes indeed that in periods where British booms and high Bank Rate coincided, British domestic funds moved towards domestic advances and bill finance shifted to the foreign funds attracted thus.[35] Some foreign bills were diverted for discounting to other (cheaper) markets, while on occasions high Bank Rate led to the postponement of long-term overseas issues on the London Stock Exchange.

These quick effects lifted the sterling exchanges from their gold export points so that the gold loss was staunched, and they enabled more of the regular influx of new-mined gold to the London bullion market to be acquired by the Bank rather than being passed on abroad. Indeed, if the exchanges rose to the gold import point, gold might even be attracted from other monetary authorities, although the European central banks were reluctant releasers.[36] The net import of gold into Britain did bear some positive relationship to Bank Rate changes and the trade cycle,[37] and when that was decomposed into net imports from geographical areas, it was only the European net imports which displayed a *general* and marked similarity with Bank Rate movements.[38] It, indeed, seemed more a matter of European central banks' desisting from making their normal purchases of gold on the London bullion market when Bank Rate was high, for on average after 1890 net imports of gold from Europe were negative, as the London gold market played its part in allocating part of the flow of new-mined gold to Europe. Help also came at times from the United States and South America.

As a result of this Bank Rate policy and mechanisms, distinct patterns emerge for Bank Rate and short-term rates in London. Within any year Bank Rate tended to rise in the early autumn and to fall away in the early spring, reflecting the distinct seasonal patterns in home trade and in the British balance of trade, which moved adversely in the autumn and

---

[35] C. A. E. Goodhart, *The Business of Banking 1891–1914* (London, 1972), p. 218.

[36] Ford, *Gold Standard*, pp. 23, 33–4.

[37] *Ibid.*, pp. 34–5, and especially, W. E. Beach, *British International Gold Movements and Banking Policy, 1881–1913* (Cambridge, Mass., 1935), ch. 2.

[38] Ford, *Gold Standard*, pp. 39–40.

provoked the autumnal drain. The Bank of England chose to cope with this by the use of Bank Rate to avert strain on its scant reserve, rather than by holding more ample reserves to withstand this seasonal movement. From year to year a distinct cyclical pattern can be traced: annual average Bank Rate and market rate tended to be high in booms and low in slumps, thereby providing some mild anti-cyclical stabilization by accident rather than design. One reason why the reserve was subjected to strain in booms was provided by the higher internal drain of gold to finance increased domestic transactions, while in slumps this drain lessened or even became a reflux.[39] As will be shown later, another reason lay in the tendency of the British 'basic' balance of payments to move into deficit in an upswing, and into surplus in a downswing, despite that the current account for Britain as an export economy tended to improve in booms and deteriorate in slumps. As noted earlier, other European central banks tended to match Bank Rate changes in a defensive way, as well as finding themselves facing similar internally caused strains at the same time because of the European tendency towards cyclical parallelism.

From their very nature these quick effects were temporary, for there were distinct limits to short-term capital movements and to the willingness of financiers to continue them. They provided a breathing space during which more fundamental adjustments must have taken place because after a period of strain the subsequent fall in Bank Rate did not provoke a renewed gold loss. Our theoretical analysis and the classical theory suggested that such adjustments *could* have been promoted by monetary effects. Here the automatic effects of the gold loss in reducing the money supply and in increasing interest rates would be reinforced by the Bank's Bank Rate policy and by any action to reduce bankers' cash reserves so that this deflation would reduce spending, output and imports, and perhaps prices would decline also to effect further adjustment.

Nevertheless, there is little evidence of any of these processes taking place in Britain in the period 1870–1914. Spending appears insensitive to Bank Rate changes; the domestic money supply accommodated itself to the needs of domestic activity, while the Bank did not pursue the rules of the game in the manner later envisaged.

In more detail, Bloomfield's findings which first cast doubt on the adherence by central banks to the rules of the game have already been noted, while Sayers has remarked, 'that a movement of Bank Rate would probably be accompanied by some change in the availability of bank credit, though the absence of traders' complaints suggests that the latter effect cannot have been marked'.[40] Lindert has commented, 'The main

---

[39] *Ibid.*, pp. 34–5; and Beach, *Gold Movements*, where these marked cyclical relationships are demonstrated.   [40] R. S. Sayers, *Central Banking after Bagehot* (Oxford, 1957), p. 64.

argument against emphasizing this adjustment mechanism is simply that it operated only with lags too great and too uncertain to account for the remarkable smoothness and rapidity with which exchange rates, international gold flows, and the gold reserves of central banks seem to have been altered.'[41]

Recent work by Goodhart has demonstrated the lack of any close positive association between the cash base of the commercial banks, as represented by bankers' balances at the Bank of England, and the reserve position of the Bank, which adherence to the rules of the game doctrine (old interpretation) would require.[42] In other words the Bank did not reinforce the liquidity pressures on the banks during periods of domestic expansion when its own reserve was under strain. In periods of rising activity and increased demands for cash, the Bank allowed the proportion of reserves to liabilities to fall and earning assets to liabilities in its banking department to rise so that increased demands for cash could be met at the expense of a higher Bank Rate. Commercial bankers increased their balances at the Bank of England to support their increased business at the expense of call money, thereby forcing the discount market to seek accommodation at the Bank, which granted the requisite accommodation at the now higher Bank Rate.

In this way can be explained the marked statistical associations of rising activity, rising bankers' balances and Bank Rate but falling reserve and proportion of reserve to liabilities at the Bank, which would negate rules of the game activity on the part of the Bank. Goodhart concludes that, 'these results suggest that domestic credit expansion, and the money supply, generally varied in such a way as to accommodate changes in the level of activity. Movements of income and of the money supply were quite closely associated, but this association was owing to variations in the money supply being adapted to the fluctuations in money incomes.'[43]

While it is not possible to show a stable relationship between bankers' balances and their deposits because of lack of suitable and accurate information about deposits, nevertheless individual banks appear to have maintained their chosen cash-ratios quite steadily, although these did vary widely between banks. It can be reasonably supposed that increases in banks' reserves would be accompanied by rises in deposits and advances. Indeed, deposits and advances do exhibit a strong cyclical pattern,[44] while the ratio of advances and discounts to deposits is associated positively with Bank Rate fluctuations and variations in

[41] Lindert, *Key Currencies*, pp. 43–4. See also Ford, *Gold Standard*, ch. 3.
[42] Goodhart, *The Business of Banking*, pp. 195–220.
[43] *Ibid.*, p. 219.
[44] Ford, *Gold Standard*, p. 42.

activity, particularly before 1893.[45] In booms then bankers met increased demands for accommodation by becoming less liquid, while in slumps they became more liquid as demand fell away.

Although the money supply effects had this accommodating character in Britain, we must consider whether the associated interest rate changes affected spending in the ways economic analysis (and the rules of the game) might suggest to promote longer-term adjustments by influencing spending, output, and import purchases, and prices. It is useful here to distinguish between the higher costs of borrowing resulting from higher interest rates and the effects on confidence and profit expectations from higher rates. The so-called 'liquidity' effects of higher rates whereby financiers were unwilling to sell securities (now depreciated in price) at a loss to provide extra loans to finance extra spending are ignored here as are the 'crisis' effects where people and banks so desired liquidity after a rise in rates that a dearth of loanable funds resulted, as happened in the first half of the nineteenth century.

It is very doubtful whether high short-term rates in Britain directly had any significant cost effects on investment decisions since they were rarely high enough for long enough: rather one would expect higher long-term rates to bring significant cost effects. On the other hand, in so far as Bank Rate had become regarded as an index of economic prospects – a rise in Bank Rate signifying possible (international) difficulties and indicating caution – then a sharp rise in Bank Rate could lead to a reappraisal of profit forecasts and a postponing or abandoning of a project, thus setting in motion corrective forces.

Certainly Bank Rate affected (sometimes after a struggle) the short-term interest rate structure in London (bill rates, deposit and advance rates) and thus altered the cost of short-term borrowing, but the *short-period* connection between changes in Bank Rate and in the long-term rate of interest as represented by the actual yield on Consols was quite insignificant, although the rising trend of Bank Rate after the 1890s was accompanied by a rising yield on Consols.[46] However, we have suggested that it was the long rates which would have the more significant cost effects, but they were insensitive immediately to Bank Rate changes.

In his statistical work on the British economy Tinbergen concluded, 'We have already observed that the influence of interest rates on the course of investment activity – which is the chief influence interest rates exert, according to our results – is only moderate. A rise in interest rates depresses investment activity, but only to a modest extent.'[47] Supporting

[45] A. G. Ford, 'British Economic Fluctuations, 1870–1914', *The Manchester School*, vol. 37, no. 2 (June 1969).   [46] R. Hawtrey, *A Century of Bank Rate* (London, 1938), ch. 5.

[47] J. Tinbergen, *Business Cycles in the United Kingdom 1870–1914* (Amsterdam, 1951), p. 133: 'The elasticity of investment activity with respect to short-term rates was estimated to be −0.08 and with respect to long-term rates to be −0.50' (p. 96).

evidence is provided by Pesmazoglu's study of British home investment fluctuations which states, 'But it seems that variations . . . in the long-term rate of interest did not have an important influence on fluctuations in British home investment between 1870 and 1913'.[48]

The Economist conducted a survey late in 1907 into interest rate effects on investment activity at a time when short rates had been high for a year but the American crisis of 1907 had broken.[49] It emerges from the replies that Bank Rate was but one factor influencing businessmen and in this case its cost effects were less important than declining American purchases and shocks to confidence. Nevertheless, respondents strongly believed that middlemen would be squeezed and expected prices of raw materials to fall in this gloomy atmosphere.

In short, the influences of Bank Rate and associated rates alone on home activity and investment decisions were weak, but when a rise in rates was associated with an international crisis, which might coincide with a boom in Britain as in 1890 or 1907, then the combined effects were more powerful, and it did seem that merchants were more severely affected than manufacturers.[50]

It has been suggested that the use of Bank Rate shifted the burden of readjustment onto other countries (in particular the primary producers).[51] On the one hand, higher Bank Rate forced suppliers of imports to Britain to liquidate their stocks at lower prices, thereby providing better terms of trade for Britain and bringing relief to the British balance of payments at the expense of the primary producers. However, the monthly and annual movements of British import prices and the terms of trade do not support this suggestion.[52] On the other hand, there does seem more support for the view that higher Bank Rate and difficult monetary conditions in London could on occasions postpone new overseas issues, and thus improve the British balance of payments at the expense of diminishing supplies of sterling for the borrowers, who would also be adversely affected if the higher Bank Rate attracted short-term funds from their monetary systems. The primary producers, it was argued, would thus face deflationary pressures and adjustment burdens thrust on them from Britain, the centre country. Yet the costs were shared. For as their activity declined, these primary producers returned the burdens onto British export industries in terms of

[48] J. S. Pesmazoglu, 'A Note on the Cyclical Fluctuations of British Home Investment 1870–1913', *Oxford Economic Papers*, NS, vol. III, no. 1 (February 1951), p. 61.

[49] *The Economist*, 23 and 30 November 1907, 'Inquiry into the Effects of Dear Money on Home Trade'. For a discussion see Ford, *Gold Standard*, pp. 44–6.

[50] Ford, *Gold Standard*, p. 46.

[51] R. Triffin, 'National Central Banking and the International Monetary System', *Review of Economic Studies*, vol. XIV (1946–7), p. 61; and P. B. Kenen, *British Monetary Policy and the Balance of Payments 1951–7* (Cambridge, Mass., 1960), pp. 61–2.

[52] Lindert, *Key Currencies*, pp. 44–6.

lower purchases and growing unemployment there, although the City of London remained unscathed.[53]

In summary, then, the major influence of Bank Rate lay in promoting equilibrating (short-term) international capital flows into London, while the longer-run influence on domestic activity must be considered as weak on its own. Rules of the game behaviour by the Bank of England appears non-existent and the money supply accommodated itself to the needs of domestic trade. The longer-run forces, which enabled specie payments to be maintained by the Bank, must be sought elsewhere than in the monetary mechanism, which provided relief while other forces eliminated more persistent imbalances. A caution must be issued: these monetary sector conclusions refer to Britain. It would be dangerous to think that they were typical and that behaviour elsewhere was similar without more detailed work.

VI. Stabilizing elements and British experience

The monetary arrangements of the gold standard survived in this period only because they were not subjected to persistent strain. British arrangements, in particular, have been examined and this revealed that fundamental adjustment forces had to be sought elsewhere, while the behaviour patterns of other central banks did not accord well with the rules of the game mechanism. However, there were particular features of the developing international economic environment which made for stability or prevented excessive imbalances from developing and swamping the monetary arrangements.

One major source of assistance was provided by the tendency of the four main trading countries of the world – Britain, France, Germany, and the United States, collectively accounting for roughly one-half of world trade – to display similar cyclical fluctuations in economic activity. All four were in the same phase of their reference cycles in 53.5 per cent of all months between 1879 and 1914, while the three European countries were in the same phase in 83.1 per cent of all months.[54] The interlinking of these countries with others by means of trade and capital flows, together with contagious changes in business confidence, ensured that broadly similar changes in activity took place in most other countries.[55] This cyclical parallelism tended to ease the problems of balance of payments adjustment. As one country experienced rising incomes and

[53] A. G. Ford, 'Bank Rate, The British Balance of Payments, and the Burdens of Adjustment, 1870–1914', *Oxford Economic Papers*, NS, vol. XVI, no. 1 (February 1964), pp. 24–39.

[54] Morgenstern, *Financial Transactions*, p. 43.

[55] See also W. Ashworth, *A Short History of the International Economy since 1850*, 3rd edn (London, 1975), p. 219.

imports and a worsening balance of payments, the parallel expansion of incomes and import purchases elsewhere brought it rising exports and an easing of its balance of payments difficulties.

Again, the cyclical parallelism in the movement of prices diminished the scope for expenditure – switching effects which might have occurred if one country was booming or slumping on its own and which would have exaggerated its imbalances. This also would imply that if a country had succeeded in reducing its general price level, as in the classical model of the Cunliffe Report, to stop a loss of gold by improving its balance of trade, it would have been confronted in practice by similarly falling prices in its main markets and of its main rivals. Scope for adjustment by (relative) price changes was limited.

Noteworthy also besides the cyclical parallelism in prices in major countries were the similar secular or trend movements in prices in these countries, which became particularly marked after 1880, so that major changes in relative prices of various countries did not occur over time to provoke payments imbalances.[56] Clearly the common input of raw material and food prices, determined on world commodity markets, provided one important ingredient, but differential movements in productivity, money wage rates, or in profit margins could have caused price trends to move out of alignment. Perhaps, then, gold standard mechanisms helped to keep them in line?

The monetary theorist's stress on arbitrage between unified commodity markets is certainly relevant and important here, but other forces can be invoked. Suppose that a country's prices moved out of line from others in an upward trend: falling export sales and sales of import-competing goods could be expected together with tighter monetary policies induced by the worsening balance of payments, all of which would lower incomes, output and employment. In an environment of weak trade unions, competitive firms, and a relative absence of price-fixing, the growing unemployment would apply a corrective by restraining the growth in money wage rates until prices were realigned more competitively with other countries.[57] This case is consonant with cyclical parallelism in that the country would suffer more severe slumps and weaker booms until realigned.

A second source of stability was provided by the links between Britain and the borrowing primary producers on the periphery of the gold standard, in that they prevented large imbalances from developing.

[56] See E. H. Phelps Brown and Margaret H. Browne, *A Century of Pay* (London, 1968), pp. 110–15, where cost of living indices and GNP deflators are compared for Britain, Germany, Sweden, France, United States. Also, A.C. Pigou, *Industrial Fluctuations*, 2nd edn (London, 1929), p. 12.

[57] Note the historical references and calculations in A. W. Phillips, 'The Relation Between Unemployment and the Rate of Change of Money Wage Rates in the United Kingdom, 1861–1957', *Economica*, NS, vol. XXV, no. 100 (November 1958).

British loans to overseas countries tended to stimulate, both directly and indirectly, purchases of British exports and their debt-service payments (both interest and dividends) to Britain. Increased lending by Britain thus did not increase their foreign exchange reserves – indeed, frequently the loans until used were held as London balances – nor diminish British reserves appreciably for any length of time. With the completion of the projects financed in this way, production of exportables rose for which free trade Britain provided a growing market. The primary producers' exports rose so that they could meet their foreign debt-service obligations and make dividend remittances to British lenders easily and purchase extra goods from Britain, without balance of payments strain. Such trade flows contributed to the economic growth of both partners and provided a basis for stability, while it should be noted that the settlement patterns underlying these trade flows had a multilateral character.

Such is the long-run picture which contributed to mutual growth and stability, but short-run difficulties and crises did occur. The flow of lending abroad at times exceeded the British current account surplus and had to be checked by Bank Rate, with ensuing harmful repercussions on the borrowers; frequently, borrowers had to make debt-service payments immediately while it took time (up to five years) for their export earnings to expand, and in the meantime the flow of loans had declined. In difficult times borrowers seeking to avert balance of payments problems might well find access to short-term credit in London very limited or even impossible so that these imbalances were eliminated by the (automatic) mechanism of falling incomes and imports, with consequent repercussions on British export sales. Indeed, one element in the British trade cycle is to be found here, and it is important not to underrate these short-run problems.

In those not infrequent cases of imbalance where the factors causing the initial gold gain or loss brought automatic equilibrating income movements, the forces acted speedily and without governmental offsets to affect the balance of payments, indeed being reinforced by monetary institutions' actions in certain cases, particularly in those countries without central banks. The actions here of gold-gaining countries in reducing their surpluses thus (and through the slower-working money supply effects) were particularly helpful to the gold losers, since one country's surplus imbalance was the counterpart of others' deficits and adjustment was thereby eased for deficit countries. Severe imbalances were thus less likely to persist. Furthermore, under the conditions of economic growth and development in this period, adjustment for deficit countries implied rather a temporary check to their growth rates than an absolute decline in incomes.

The growth in international economic transactions was fortunately matched by a corresponding growth in gold reserves in the hands of monetary authorities, which came from the various and spectacular gold discoveries. Erratic though they were, they served to increase the cash basis of the expanding gold standard and to ensure that the growth in world payments and trade was never permanently checked by liquidity problems and rising interest rates. This is allotting a permissive role to gold discoveries. Their influence on the behaviour of prices before 1914 is debatable, while factors such as innovation, population growth, the extension of areas of supply, and the growth of money substitutes must be reckoned with. Gold discoveries also helped to ensure for deficit countries that adjustment was not so much a matter of competing for an existing stock of gold from other monetary authorities, but rather trying to acquire a larger share of the currently new-mined gold. The growth in international reserve assets was further helped by the willingness of some to hold increased currency balances in London, Paris, and Berlin, especially after 1900. This also enabled Britain, France, and Germany to amass more monetary gold, although otherwise their balance of payments positions would not have permitted this. Adjustments were immediately eased for these centres, although the increased balances would become a potential source of strain.

Within this framework in the 50 years before 1914, Britain received a steady net import of gold, without having her interest rate structure permanently higher than elsewhere; indeed the long rate on average was lower than in other monetary centres. Her balance of payments was not protected by any import restrictions, the London financial and gold markets were far freer than elsewhere, while unemployment did not seem to be greater than in other countries. From this it must be concluded that Britain enjoyed over the period a favourable balance of payments, which enabled her to claim a share of the growing output of gold without having to impose severer deflationary forces or restrictions than elsewhere. How was this achieved, since doubt has earlier been cast on the efficacy of the monetary forces as operated in Britain?[58]

In the first place, many of the occasions when Britain experienced balance of payments imbalances and gold tended to move (until Bank Rate took charge), promoted automatic equilibrating forces which brought partial relief. In particular for a deficit imbalance may be specified:

1. An autonomous fall in export sales, other things being equal.
2. An increase in lending abroad at the expense of spending on home goods.

[58] For a full discussion, see Ford, *Gold Standard*, ch. 4.

3. An increase in import purchases at the expense of spending on home goods.

4. An increase in cereal import purchases, necessitated by a bad home harvest, this bringing an immediate fall in domestic output as well as a switch from home goods to imports.

In all these cases incomes fell and so did import purchases to lessen the deficit imbalance, and vice versa for a surplus imbalance. The size of such relief may be instanced by estimating roughly the size of the British multiplier from the likely values of the marginal propensities. With a marginal propensity to save of 0.15, to import of 0.30, and a marginal tax leak of 0.10, all with reference to national income at factor cost, the multiplier is 1.8. Hence a fall in export values of 100 brought a fall in national income of 180, and a fall in imports of 54. This relief was increased on those occasions when home investment spending declined along with exports. These relationships have been cast crudely in current price terms rather than in real terms. Money value terms are important for the balance of payments although this approach compounds price and income effects together. Perhaps no great harm is done in the absence of spectacular changes in prices and where cyclical parallelism limited the scope for substitution effects.

However, where the balance of payments moved into deficit because of short-term or long-term lending abroad from idle balances, then no such relief was present, although the gold loss would cease where the international capital movement was an unrepeated portfolio adjustment by asset holders to reach a more preferred composition of assets. If it was desired to replenish gold reserves or if the international capital flow persisted, then we must look to Bank Rate effects alone in reversing these flows. While these cases were not infrequent, there do seem to be fewer occasions when a domestic investment boom increased imports sharply and provoked a deficit with no relieving mechanism except cyclical parallelism.

The longer-run position of the British economy and its balance of payments noted earlier becomes remarkable when it is recalled that British overseas lending at times exceeded 8 per cent of her national income during the eighteen- to twenty-year long swings in investment abroad which could have formed a serious disruptive force. For it was not a case of Britain lending abroad an existing and otherwise uncommitted current account surplus and of avoiding accumulating too much gold. It was rather that the act of lending abroad (a main vehicle being overseas new issues on the London Stock Exchange) tended to create after a lag of a year or so an increased current account surplus needed to bring about the transfer of this lending without permanent loss of gold.[59]

[59] *Ibid.*, pp. 62–7; and A. G. Ford, 'The Transfer of British Foreign Lending 1870–1913', *Economic History Review*, 2nd series, vol. XI, no. 2 (1958).

Of central importance in these economic processes were the sensitivity of British exports to British lending abroad, and the long-swing alternation of home and overseas investment. For the use made of the funds by the developing borrowers of the funds – to buy directly extra imports from Britain, or to finance increased domestic spending which increased import purchases – served to increase British exports directly and indirectly. The expansionary effects of such increased exports did not communicate themselves fully to British incomes and imports because the trend of home investment was falling at the same time as the trend of overseas investment was rising. Hence, export values rose relatively to import values, and, with the help of increased interest and dividend remittances from abroad as a result of extra lending, created a current account improvement sufficient to cover the overseas lending transfer without loss of gold. It must be stressed that the argument has been cast in terms of trends and in the long run, whereas changes in overseas lending did give rise to balance of payments problems in short-run cyclical terms.[60]

Why these opposite trend patterns should have developed is a complex matter which remains somewhat unsettled.[61] At times, the pull of overseas ventures attracted men and finance away from home enterprises, causing home investment to decline. On other occasions, the drying up of profitable opportunities at home increased the relative attractiveness of overseas ventures, whose promoters then met with a more favourable reception in London, and men and finance were pushed abroad. Gradually, however, matters reversed themselves as the more profitable projects abroad were undertaken and at home the number of attractive possibilities grew. Underlying, and related to, these movements in relative profitability and attractiveness were the inverse courses of the building cycles in North America and in Britain. While the behaviour of the terms of trade can be incorporated into the above framework, allowance must be made for random factors. Nevertheless, the consequences of this inverse pattern are highly important for long-run stability of the British balance of payments in that they explain, along with the sensitivity of British exports to overseas investment, why such large waves of overseas lending did not disrupt British adherence to the gold standard and why the long swings in home investment did not bring periods of heavy unemployment or of inflationary pressure.

Given that the British balance of payments exhibited this long-run stability, how did the economy cope with the short-run fluctuations in such variables as exports, imports, overseas lending, home investment,

---

[60] See A. G. Ford, 'Overseas Lending and Internal Fluctuations 1870–1914', *Yorkshire Bulletin of Economic and Social Research*, vol. XVII, no. 1 (May 1965).

[61] P. L. Cottrell, *British Overseas Investment in the Nineteenth Century* (London, 1975), provides a useful survey.

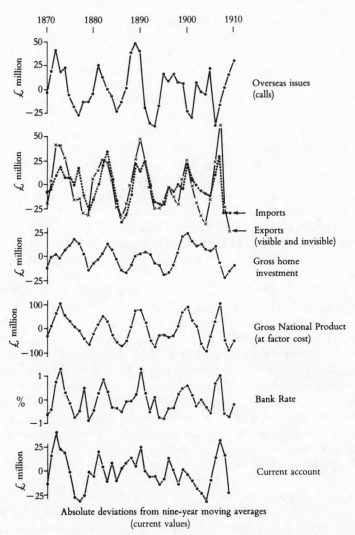

Fig. 1. Great Britain: economic fluctuations, 1870–1914

all of which impinged on the balance of payments to produce imbalances and gold movements? Movements in these variables have been set out in Figure 1 in terms of absolute deviations from nine-year moving averages.

Deviations in exports (visible and invisible, including net income from abroad), national income, and imports were closely and positively associated, thereby providing evidence of the working of the automatic adjusting mechanisms previously specified, as well as of the immediate causes of the British trade cycle. As British imports rose, so this stimu-lated activity in the rest of the world and led to yet further increased export sales, although damping factors were strong. This mechanism ensured thus that imbalances between exports and imports were speedily reduced, while the current account balance of payments tended to improve relatively to trend in booms and worsen in slumps as a product of this process. It was, indeed, important that it behaved thus, for overseas lending (as measured by deviations in overseas new issues) rose prior to exports and incomes in their upswings, and fell away before them in their downswings, the lead being of the order of one or two years. Hence the balance of payments strain in upswings through extra lending abroad was somewhat offset by the subsequent current account improvement, while in the downswings the worsening current account could be tolerated because overseas lending had fallen away.

Fluctuations in home investment, of smaller amplitude than those in exports, were less closely associated with fluctuations in exports and incomes. This association between investment and exports was more noticeable in the period 1879–1902, in which the influence of variations in exports on incomes and imports were reinforced by like variations in investment so that fluctuations in the current account balance of pay-ments were damped down and the transfer of overseas lending in upswings was made more difficult; on the other hand, before 1879 and after 1902 investment deviations tended to be negatively related to exports so that variations in income and imports were less than otherwise and current account fluctuations were widened, thereby making the transfer of overseas lending easier in upswings.

Bank Rate deviations were positively associated with deviations in exports, incomes, and the current account balance of payments. In upswings strain was thrust on the Bank's reserve from home demands for gold (as noted earlier) and from the external drain brought about by the tendency for overseas lending expansion to exceed the current account improvement so that Bank Rate was moved up to bring relief by short-term capital flows and perhaps by influencing the pace of overseas issues, which tended to fall after successive annual rises in Bank Rate.[62] In slumps the reserve position was eased by the internal reflux and by a more comfortable external position as overseas lending declined more rapidly than the current account position.

The British terms of trade deviations (export prices divided by import prices) exhibited varied cyclical responses, improving in most booms and in few slumps, and worsening in few booms and in most slumps. This behaviour was a product of deviations in export and import prices

[62] Compare J. S. Pesmazoglu, 'Some International Aspects of British Cyclical Fluctuations, 1870–1913', *Review of Economic Studies*, 16 (1949–50), pp. 117–45.

moving up together in booms and down in slumps, as did retail prices and money wage rates, and so all were positively associated with fluctuations in Bank Rate. In general, the behaviour of these prices does not offer support for the classic price–specie flow mechanism of adjustment.[63]

Particular circumstances and institutions underlay Britain's success in operating the gold standard for herself, yet within this success there were to be discerned, after 1900, growing signs of difficulties to come as Britain's economic and financial position was crumbling relatively to other countries. Indeed, the overall economic mechanisms presented above may mislead somewhat unless it is recalled that they operated within a changing institutional and economic environment.

The Bank of England had evolved its policies and weapons after 1870 and had gradually gained control over London's financial markets by 1900, so that its power and position were more secure then than in 1870, despite a much larger gold standard world. However, rivalry of alternative supply and a relative decline in technology amongst other things had brought difficulties for British exporters who reacted by seeking new markets for old products. Undoubtedly they were helped in this search by British overseas lending to the newer, developing primary producers and the latter's subsequent development, by commercial ties and by the economic and political power exerted by Britain in these markets to facilitate sales of (less competitive) goods. It is noteworthy that British goods claimed a larger share of total imports into such markets as Australia, South Africa, New Zealand, India, than into Argentina, Brazil, Chile, where Germany and the United States had penetrated more. While the sensitivity of British export sales to British overseas lending assisted very much the maintenance of convertibility by the Bank of England, nevertheless the process did help to preserve in profitability an old-fashioned industrial structure and thus to delay the necessary adjustments if Britain was to remedy her technical backwardness.

Again, the dominance of London as the world financial centre and the very great confidence in sterling, the key currency, encouraged the build-up of sterling balances by non-residents in London, more especially after 1900. The counterpart of this build-up of balances was a British balance of payments deficit after allowing for the net import of gold so that these features permitted Britain to postpone, or even avoid, some of the adjustment discipline which others faced. In this way the relative decline of the British export share, the rise in imports, and the desire to lend abroad could be accommodated, when otherwise keener

[63] See Ford, *Gold Standard 1880–1914*, pp. 76–8.

adjustment, in the form of lower growth than actually occurred, would have been entailed.[64] Lindert even states 'Britain's position just before World War One in fact provides the classic example of the "deficit without tears".'[65]

The above analysis of the operations of the gold standard in Britain, the main central country, has laid stress on the particular favourable circumstances facilitating the Bank of England's maintenance of convertibility. Besides the institutional and financial arrangements centring on London, the sterling system and the confidence in sterling as the world currency, cyclical parallelism, the long-term alternation of British home and overseas investment, and the sensitivity of British exports to this overseas lending played important parts in lessening or averting potential imbalances in the British international accounts. Furthermore, automatic adjusting mechanisms consequent upon factors causing gold movements had a notable role in speedily lessening imbalances so that all in all the monetary mechanism associated with Bank Rate had to cope with relatively slight *long-run* difficulties. This, indeed, was as well since its weakness in affecting spending has been demonstrated, as has the Bank's lack of adherence to the rules of the game doctrine for influencing the money supply. On the other hand, Bank Rate, when made effective, contributed vitally in the short run by promoting swift international capital movement reactions to staunch gold losses from the Bank's reserve. While Britain thus avoided persistent deficits unmatched by a willing build-up of London balances, equally large surplus imbalances were avoided and the pound was never a scarce currency for the rest of the world so that, when in deficit, other countries found balance of payments adjustment easier. Yet, in the early twentieth century, as has been indicated briefly, seeds of future difficulties for Britain were being sown by certain elements which had contributed to her successful maintenance of specie payments.

VII. *Experiences elsewhere – France, Germany, Canada, and Argentina*

The previous section has concentrated on the behaviour of the Bank of England and on Britain as the central country under the gold standard, and the balance needs redressing by more detailed examination of other countries' experiences in addition to the brief remarks earlier. First, French and German experiences will be examined, to be followed by a discussion of two 'periphery' countries, Canada and Argentina.

[64] Lindert, *Key Currencies*, pp. 74–5. See also de Cecco, *Money and Empire* for a more impressionistic treatment.   [65] Lindert, *Key Currencies*, p. 75.

Table 21. *Changes in Bank Rates*

	1871–1890			1880–1913		
	Low %	High %	Number of changes	Low %	High %	Number of changes
Bank of England	2	9	176	2	7	194
Bank of France	2	7	28	2	4	30
Reichsbank	3	6	72	3	$7\frac{1}{2}$	116

Sources: 1871–1890: *Bankers Magazine*, vol. LI, (1891), p. 971; 1880–1913: H. D. White, *The French International Accounts 1880–1914* (Cambridge, Mass., 1933), p. 189.

Both France and Germany possessed central banks and were building up international monetary business particularly with other European countries with long-term overseas lending and the discounting of bills and with the growth of non-resident owned balances in Paris and Berlin. The Bank of France and the Reichsbank were each committed to maintaining their gold standard parities and employed Bank Rate policies and gold devices like the Bank of England but used in addition more 'questionable' devices to deflect pressures on their gold reserves. Table 21, which presents evidence of the range and frequency of Bank Rate changes for the three major central banks, indicates that those two used their Bank Rates less frequently to protect their reserves than the Bank of England, even though they were victims of London's drawing power (see above pp. 216–17), some of which strain they could pass on to others.

The Bank of France had a strong preference for stability of interest rates, which it believed was to the benefit of home trade, and was able to maintain such stability partly by keeping large gold reserves so that it did not have to react to a gold loss as precipitately as the Bank of England. Secondly, the Bank of France which had the legal option of redeeming notes with legal tender silver (though depreciated in terms of gold), used a gold premium policy to deter demands for gold by charging up to 1 per cent more if gold was requested. Hence it could protect its reserves by partially suspending free payments in gold rather than by manipulating its rediscount rate. Such a policy was used regularly, and indeed as late as November 1912, and quite sharply at that.[66]

In Germany, since the Reichsbank's reserves were not high enough to enable it to behave as the Bank of France, it reinforced its Bank Rate policy, which was modelled on the Bank of England pattern, by unseen pressure on 'difficult' bankers who sought gold (for export) at inconve-

---

[66] See, for example, J. M. Keynes, *Indian Currency and Finance* (London, 1913), p. 20. *The Economist* and other British financial journals of the period make frequent and 'superior' references to this French 'practice'.

Table 22. *Annual changes in international and domestic assets, 1880–1913*

	Similar	Opposite	No change
Bank of England	16	17	1
Bank of France	9	25	0
Reichsbank	10	22	2

Source: A. I. Bloomfield, *Monetary Policy under the International Gold Standard, 1880–1914* (New York, 1958), p. 49.

nient times, and by occasional and covert use of a gold premium policy (for example, in November 1912). Indeed, while British bankers could be profit-seekers on all occasions, German bankers were compelled at times to be 'patriots' and not seek gold for export. Furthermore, as an additional measure, after 1900 the Reichsbank built up its holdings of foreign bills which it used to support the mark exchange-rates at difficult times.

Passing 'to other countries of less financial strength, we find the dependence of their Central Banks on holdings of foreign bills and on foreign credits, their willingness to permit a premium on gold, and the inadequacy of their bank rates taken by themselves, to be increasingly marked'.[67] There seems little reason to disturb this verdict of Keynes.

Table 22 indicates that the Reichsbank and the Bank of France appear to have ignored the so-called rules of the game even more than the Bank of England, when these rules are interpreted as implying that the central bank should change its domestic assets in the same way as its international assets have changed to reinforce the effects of gold movements on the domestic money supply. Indeed, it would seem that in both France and Germany international gold movements did not, at least in the short run, affect the domestic money supply – rather the domestic money reaction to gold movements was very much a (muted) short-term interest rate reaction. As White has put it for France, 'Fluctuations in these (*sc.* specie) reserves exerted only a slight influence on the volume of credit or note circulation. There was no trace of the gold-reserve–discount-rate–volume-of-credit sequence held by the neo-classical theory to be the necessary chain connecting disequilibrium in the balance of payments with sectional price changes.'[68]

International transactions are less well and less reliably documented for France and Germany than for Britain, but reference to Figures 2 and 3 indicates the parallel movements of merchandise export and import values for each country. This would suggest that some of the automatic

[67] *Ibid.*, p. 23.
[68] H. D. White, *The French International Accounts 1880–1914* (Cambridge, Mass., 1933), p. 303.

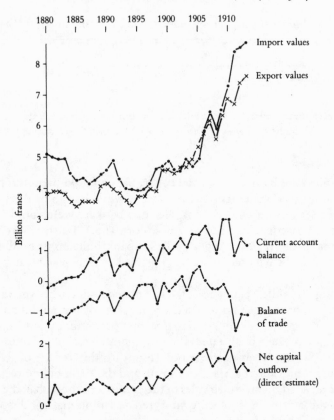

Fig. 2. France: balance of payments components, 1880–1914

effects noted earlier were operative together with the forces of cyclical parallelism. It is interesting to note for France that export values behaved relatively to imports in such a way that the balance of trade and hence the balance of payments on current account moved in the long run to offset the outflow of French foreign lending (from direct estimates), and thus to prevent balance of payments strain. Given the character of French foreign lending and export composition, it does seem less likely that these movements were achieved by lending stimulating French exports directly as happened in the British case. Rather it would seem that rising French exports stimulated rises in incomes, savings and imports, and an improving current account balance of payments; some portion of the increased French savings were then lent abroad and thereby lessened the net import of gold into France which would otherwise have followed the current account improvement.

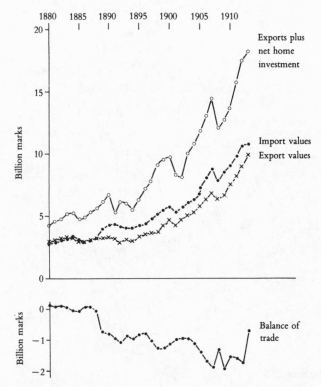

Fig. 3. Germany: balance of payments and investment, 1880–1914

Less can be said about German activities since annual estimates of German foreign investment are unavailable. The course of import purchases follows closely the path of, and fluctuations in, export sales, and likewise when estimates of net home investment are added to export values. The German balance of trade shows a tendency to deteriorate over time, and exhibits an opposite long-run trend as compared with the French, while neither show the pronounced eighteen- to twenty-year swings which are such a feature of the British balance of trade and current account behaviour.

In Figure 4 are presented annual changes in merchandise export and import values so that we can see in more detail whether they are closely related together in each of the French and German cases, and thus lend more support for the 'automatic' adjustment forces discussed earlier. The degree of agreement is certainly less close than in the British case, but there are periods of reasonable agreement, particularly in the 1880s and after 1900. The French import value fluctuations from year to year are distorted by abnormal imports in the bad harvest years of 1891, 1894,

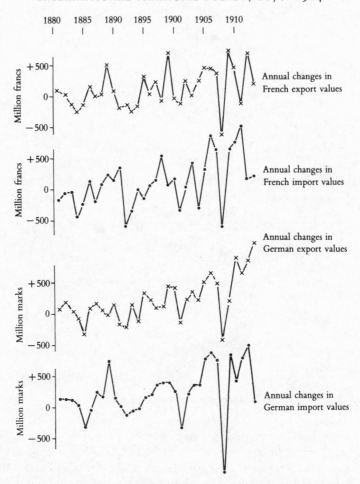

Fig. 4. Germany and France: fluctuations in exports and imports, 1880–1914

1898, 1903, and 1911,[69] while German incomes and imports were strongly influenced by the fluctuating behaviour of German home investment, which did not always match the behaviour of exports, notably in the 1890s. Although more detailed work needs to be done on these cases, it does seem reasonable to suggest that imbalances from fluctuations in exports on some occasions were narrowed by similar fluctuations in imports, while in the long term parallel movements in exports and imports prevented the emergence of serious balance of payments problems for France and Germany.

[69] *Ibid.*, p. 139.

The working of the gold standard for a periphery country may be illustrated by the experiences of Canada in the period 1900–13 when the Canadian economy grew rapidly with a marked expansion in capital formation, output of primary products, and a large immigration of labour and capital funds. This episode has been the subject of much interest – in particular the important studies by Viner and Cairncross.[70] The account here draws on the statistical material presented in Cairncross and, although using it for somewhat different purposes, is in broad agreement with his analysis.

At this stage Canada did not possess a central bank, no gold coins circulated, and the note issue comprised Dominion notes and the issues of the chartered banks. The former were issued to a certain limit ($9 million in 1870 and raised to reach $50 million by 1914), backed by 25 per cent gold and 75 per cent government bonds, above which limit 100 per cent gold backing was required. The chartered banks were permitted to issue notes of $5 denomination or more but no legal reserve ratio was required, save that 40 per cent of a bank's reserves must be held in Dominion notes. Thus the latter were linked to gold holdings while the banks were permitted some elasticity in their issuing policy, although the expansion of 1900–13 brought further modifications to ease strain.[71]

The Canadian banks conducted their transactions in foreign exchange and in monetary gold almost entirely by way of New York, where they held large reserves either at call or on deposit while smaller reserves were held in London. These reserves they used to meet balance of payments imbalances, to steady the price of foreign exchange, and in times of need to supplement domestic cash reserves so that the cash ratio might be maintained at what seemed the lowest safe point. Indeed, these 'outside' or 'secondary' reserves (as distinct from *cash* reserves) 'took the place of gold as the residual item in the balance of payments'[72] and fluctuated in the same way as gold reserves of 'gold' countries. If extra notes were required domestically, some of the 'outside' reserves would be converted into gold, transmitted to Canada as monetary gold and the demand for extra currency thus was met.

Viner has claimed that the total demand liabilities of Canadian banks were determined by financial conditions in Canada, and that the banks maintained their cash ratios by deliberately adjusting their cash reserves to total demand liabilities and not vice versa.[73] Certainly there was a close positive relation between money stock and economic activity, and

---

[70] J. Viner, *Canada's Balance of International Indebtedness, 1900–1913* (Cambridge, Mass., 1924); and A. K. Cairncross, *Home and Foreign Investment 1870–1913* (Cambridge, 1953), pp. 37–64.

[71] See J. W. O'Brien, *Canadian Money and Banking* (New York, 1965), pp. 176–80.

[72] Cairncross, *Home and Foreign Investment*, p. 50.

[73] Viner, *Canada's Balance of International Indebtedness*, pp. 176–7.

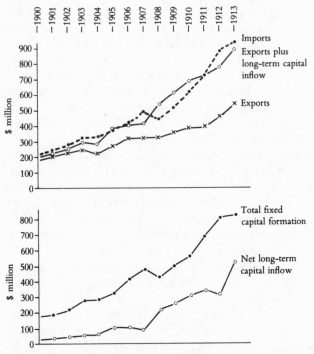

Fig. 5. Canada: trade and capital formation, 1900–13

reserve ratios fell in upswings and rose in slumps, but this could imply more than accommodation: such behaviour by banks could have reinforced upswings and downswings initially caused by external factors. It would appear that the banks followed loan policies which kept the ratio of their secondary reserves to demand liabilities within fairly wide limits, but subject to an apparent working minimum of some 10 per cent. Indeed, Rich has suggested that, as upswings continued and external and banking reserves became depleted, the banks did seek to raise short-term rates of interest and check advances.[74]

In Figure 5 are presented the behaviour over the period of export and import values (visibles and invisibles) as well as total home capital formation and the net long-term capital inflow. It is noteworthy how closely imports matched the behaviour of exports plus net long-term capital inflow, with the imbalance in the basic balance kept within bounds despite the large and variable capital inflow and the sharply

[74] Cairncross, *Home and Foreign Investment*, pp. 51–3, 55, and his Figure 7. See G. Rich, 'External Disturbances, Bank Reserve Management and the Canadian Business Cycle under the Gold Standard 1868–1913', mimeo., Carleton University, 1977, p. 39.

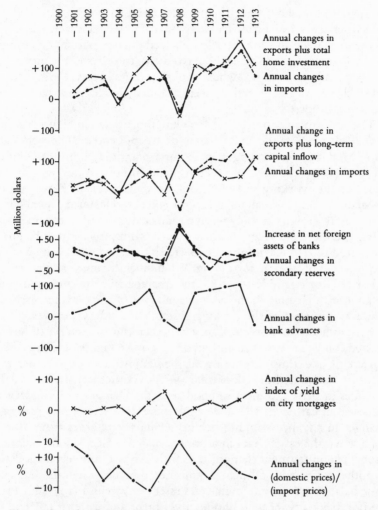

Fig. 6. Canada: fluctuations in balance of payments components and
monetary responses, 1900–13

expanding investment activity as a whole. The basic balance clearly
exhibited sharp deficits in 1907 and 1912–13 while it was in considerable
surplus in 1908–10. These movements are reflected in the banks' secondary reserve changes and in the increase in their net foreign assets (the latter
depicted in Fig. 6).

Clearly, rising exports and long-term capital inflow (when eventually
used by the borrowers for spending on investment projects) increased
economic activity, incomes, and import purchases, and thus narrowed

the surplus imbalance which might otherwise have been expected – as our earlier analytical section had suggested. These effects were reinforced by the increase in the domestically financed portion of total investment, so much so that the basic balance of payments moved sharply into deficit in 1907 and in 1912–13 when banks' foreign assets were reduced: nevertheless, persistent deficits were avoided, while likewise surpluses remained modest.

The adjustment processes are shown in more detail in Figure 6, where annual changes in the main variables are presented. The very close association between changes in exports *plus* total home investment (injections into the flow of spending) and imports is noteworthy evidence of the working of the income-flow mechanism. However, the association between changes in exports *plus* net long-term capital inflow (changes in foreign currency receipts) and changes in import values is less close, and there does seem some evidence of imports lagging behind in the period 1904–11, as might be expected if there were delays in spending the proceeds of foreign borrowing. Where such changes are markedly at variance – for example 1905–8 – the discrepancies are mirrored in the behaviour of changes in the net foreign assets of banks which formed a major component of the banking system's secondary reserves.

It is difficult to discern clearly whether the monetary authorities reacted consistently to such inflows or outflows by increasing or decreasing credit and thus promoting further adjustment or whether they accommodated to the needs of trade. While Cairncross has observed that 'changes in bank advances responded to the changes in secondary reserves at an earlier date'[75] and while there does seem some pattern of changes in advances lagging behind secondary reserves from 1902 to 1910, nevertheless changes in advances match closely the behaviour of export *plus* investment changes, thus fitting in with the accommodation hypothesis. On both of the occasions noted earlier when the Canadian basic balance moved into deficit and reserves were lost (1907 and 1912), we find bank advances and home investment and imports fallen in the following year, thereby bringing a marked recovery in foreign assets and liquidity of the banks, and Rich has indicated this as deliberate policy on the part of banks as their liquidity position tightened. Again, changes in mortgage yields display an inverse pattern with changes in net foreign assets and in secondary reserves, particularly for 1905–12, so that such interest rates tended to rise with a balance of payments deficit, and to fall with a surplus.

For Canada, then, at this period of rapid development the income-flow adjustment mechanisms seem well borne out, although the analysis

---

[75] Cairncross, *Home and Foreign Investment*, p. 52.

has been in terms of values and has compounded real income and price effects, while the monetary mechanisms and monetary policy reactions of the banking system seem less clear cut, but of importance. The behaviour of domestic prices relatively to import prices did not seem to promote adjustment on their own account: as domestic prices rose relative to import prices (or as import prices fell relative to domestic prices), a rise in import values might be expected, but the reverse occurred, for the annual changes in these two variables seem inversely related. Perhaps it should be concluded that any possible price effects were swamped by other forces operating simultaneously.

Argentina provides another example of a primary producer which experienced rapid economic growth in the early twentieth century under the stimulus of an upsurge in foreign investment activity (bringing overseas-owned capital assets there to some £650 million in 1913). However, as distinct from Canada, Argentina had a chequered monetary history in the nineteenth century of attempts to institute the gold standard, periods of depreciation and flexible exchange rates and later efforts to stabilize the exchange rate.[76] Secondly, one major element in Argentina's national government's decisions to forsake or embrace gold was provided by the tendency for exchange rate depreciation to shift the domestic distribution of income in favour of the primary-producing, exporting, and landowning groups, who were in fact the ruling oligarchy, and for exchange rate appreciation to shift the income distribution against them.[77] Hence in bad times of balance of payments deficit, gold was readily abandoned (for example, in 1876 or 1885) and difficulties were eased for the oligarchy at the expense of wage-earners and the urban middle class, while in good times of rising exports, balance of payments surplus and exchange rate appeciation, the gold standard was rapidly rejoined (for example, in 1900) to prevent further income-distribution deterioration for the exporter and landowner.

The gold standard arrangements adopted in 1900 accepted the degree of depreciation since 1884 and stabilized the exchange rates at 5 gold pesos to the pound and 227.27 paper pesos to 100 gold pesos. The issue of notes, over and above the existing issue and circulation, was tied pro rata to the deposit of gold in the Conversion Bureau (*Caja de Conversion*), which received gold and emitted notes or redeemed notes for gold at the above official rate. Banking facilities were provided by both overseas-based and domestic banks, with the Bank of the Nation dominating in size and, although not formally a central bank, undertaking *some* of a

---

[76] Argentina has been the subject of a detailed case study in Ford, *Gold Standard*, and this treatment draws heavily on that work. It has not been thought necessary to present similar statistical treatment to that offered in the Canadian case. The subsequent page references in this section can be taken up by the interested reader.   [77] *Ibid.*, pp. 90–2.

central bank's functions.[78] Notes formed the main medium of exchange, with cheques being used sparingly. Under these arrangements the note issue, and with the addition of bank deposits, the money supply, were strongly influenced by the import and export of gold,[79] while the bulk of the new inflow of gold in 1900–13 – some 88 per cent – found its way into the holdings of the *Caja* as counterpart to the issue of notes.

A very distinct pattern emerged of a gold inflow, a rise in notes issued and in bank deposits together with some tendency for the cash–deposit ratio of banks to fall, while gold exports brought declines to, or checks in the growth of, notes issued, bank deposits and some tendency for the cash–deposit ratio to rise (for example in 1913–14).[80] Operations, indeed, were very much like the rules of the game, but the Bank of the Nation pursued some offsetting tactics with its stabilization fund of some £6 million in gold and foreign currency, which it used to lessen the 'excessive' effects on the money supply of a gold export, and which it replenished by mitigating the expansionary effects of a gold import.[81] Nevertheless, the main conclusion holds that under these monetary arrangements international gold movements reflecting balance of payments imbalances affected the domestic money and credit supply directly and with some reinforcing on occasions.

The principal causes of imbalances in Argentina's balance of payments lay in changes in foreign currency receipts, stemming from the variability of merchandise export values of primary products together with the uneven inflow of foreign investment funds. Net imports of gold into Argentina were positively related to such annual changes in foreign currency receipts.[82] The automatic equilibrating mechanisms noted earlier can, indeed, be demonstrated.

A rise in foreign currency receipts as a result of a rise in export values brought a rise in domestic incomes and import purchases, thereby narrowing the initial surplus imbalance, while an increase in the inflow of foreign investment funds had a twofold effect.[83] Some portion of the increased borrowing was spent directly on investment good imports, such as locomotives, carriages, wagons, rails, while the remaining portion was used to finance increased (investment) spending so that incomes and import values rose and lessened the surplus. In similar fashion the impact deficit of a fall in foreign currency receipts was lessened.[84] The residual gold movement, after the initial imbalance had been thus reduced, affected Argentina's note issue, deposits, and advances so that monetary forces stimulated further the booming incomes and imports

---

[78] *Ibid.*, pp. 95–6, 102.   [79] *Ibid.*, pp. 106–7.   [80] *Ibid.*, pp. 101, 106–7.
[81] *Ibid.*, p. 104.   [82] *Ibid.*, pp. 164–5.   [83] *Ibid.*, pp. 157–8.
[84] See *ibid.*, pp. 165–7 for an empirical justification of these mechanisms in Argentina.

after the rise in exports and consequent gold imports, and, in the case of falling foreign currency receipts and consequent gold exports, aggravated the slumping incomes and imports. Thus further adjustment was promoted.

Given the monetary institutions and history of Argentina, little help could be expected from short-term international capital movements to offset gold losses, while changes in import values had to take the main force of adjustment since the income paid abroad included a large inflexible core of fixed interest payments. Furthermore, the scope for relative price adjustments stemming from gold movements was limited since the prices of exportables and imports, comprising a large section of the price level, were determined in world commodity markets or by suppliers quite outside Argentina's control. Argentina's terms of trade were thus insensitive to domestic monetary policy, which did have some effect on the prices of non-traded goods such as land and real estate, but here the elasticity of substitution between non-traded goods and traded goods did seem low.

Hence, in Argentina the monetary rules of the game effects promoted further reduction of imbalances in the balance of payments after the automatic income effects at the cost of exaggerating the fluctuations in domestic activity brought about by the initial changes in foreign currency receipts. Adjustment aggravated such export-induced booms and slumps and this finding is of wider interest than Argentina for potential application to (borrowing) export economies on a gold standard or a sterling-exchange standard – for example, Australia, New Zealand, South Africa, Chile, and colonial dependencies. Clearly such gold standard arrangements were very acceptable in good times of surplus, but in bad times of deficit they enhanced the temptation for Argentinian governments to leave the gold standard and thus to avoid the 'discipline' of credit contraction. In such difficult circumstances:

these economic difficulties which might have sufficed in themselves to render adherence to the gold standard impossible in a severe crisis, were supplemented by political and social factors which in the last resort in Argentina could prove decisive. The domestic convertibility of notes for gold, which was the prime object for Britain and certain other economies and from which the international gold standard sprang, was not such a point of honour. Other primary producers, such as Australia and New Zealand, maintained exchange-rate stability, which is to be explained by different administrative and political systems with different social structures and by their banking systems being based on London. However, in Argentina before 1914, the landed and export-producing oligarchy, aided by the particular economic and political structure, willingly abandoned or adopted the gold standard whenever it was to their benefit and profit.[85]

[85] *Ibid.*, p. 169.

VIII. *Conclusions*

The above account of the international financial system and policy has described the varied and evolving patterns of institutional arrangements in the pre-1914 gold standard under which all participant monetary authorities were pursuing individually a common objective – the maintenance of convertibility of their currencies. It has indicated the dangers of uncritically applying to gold standard behaviour stereotypes such as the rules of the game. Equally, although much of the system did amount to a sterling standard, centred on London with great confidence in sterling and with the concentration of financial markets and settlement patterns as well as London's 'drawing power', nevertheless there were other small, but growing monetary centres in Paris and Berlin with distinct European interests.

For these three monetary centres together with New York, where interest rates tended to move up and down together, short-term international capital movements were very important in the quick adjustment to imbalances and gold movements, but more generally central banks did not seem to operate in accordance with the rules of the game to provide more permanent adjustment. Traditional emphasis here seems misplaced. Certainly, detailed study of the British monetary arrangements and the Bank of England's activities as the pivotal bank of the gold standard bear out these contentions with the powerful quick Bank Rate mechanism contrasting with the weaker longer-run influences.

The brief discussion of French and German monetary arrangements, while showing some similar features, nevertheless makes it clear that the monetary findings in the British case should not be transferred uncritically to other countries, and the Canadian and Argentinian experiences reinforce this view. Central banks had more scope for discretionary actions than commercial banks, and used it, while it is evident that some commercial banks in certain territories without central banks pursued rules of the game policies more vigorously in response to gold and foreign exchange movements which affected their cash-reserve positions.

Various features have been stressed in this centre–periphery system as making for stability and as averting persistent large imbalances – cyclical parallelism, similar longer-run price trends in industrial countries, links between Britain and the primary producers, and gold discoveries which ensured growing supplies of monetary gold to avoid any liquidity difficulties. It was suggested that factors which provoked gold losses or gains frequently activated automatic income-adjusting mechanisms to reduce imbalances speedily, while monetary influences from gold movements to promote adjustment worked more slowly and uncertainly, but that under each of these mechanisms reactions were taking place in both gold gainers and gold losers to reduce imbalances in a mutually helpful way.

The monetary theory of the balance of payments which has been developed recently may well be valuable in explaining why there should be such similar price movements in the long run. However, the analysis presented in this chapter seems more appropriate for handling the (short-run) disequilibrium situations which occurred so frequently under the gold standard.

For one country in surplus implies another in deficit and the above reactions might be expected to narrow such imbalances in a symmetric way. However, in the centre–periphery system, outlined above, with a strong underlying sterling standard based on London, it is not surprising to find asymmetric reactions with unequal distribution of adjustment costs and burdens. It has indeed been claimed that Britain, in its pivotal role, was able to exploit its particular position and to thrust the burden of readjustment onto other shoulders, when losing gold, by reducing the supply of sterling to the rest of the world and thus to remain unscathed. This surely exaggerates an undoubted asymmetry.

It is true that, if Britain lost gold, the use of Bank Rate via London's drawing power shifted the immediate burden onto others, particularly France and Germany, as short-term capital flowed into London; that London's unique position and leverage favoured 'quick' effects; that long-term capital flows to primary producers might well be checked, although there seems little evidence that the use of Bank Rate alone caused British import prices of primary products to fall; that periphery countries were denied the second line of defence (from European central banks) available to Britain, even though Europe, and especially Britain, acted as lender of last resort to the United States. Nevertheless, the ensuing cuts in foreign currency receipts accruing to periphery countries brought reductions in their spending, incomes, and imports and in particular reacted on British exports to return some of the burden of adjustment as slump and unemployment for British industry, if not for the City of London. Furthermore, it should not be forgotten that certain major upper turning points in the British trade cycle were associated with crises and difficulties abroad – consider 1873, 1890, 1907 – although it should be mentioned that fluctuations in British overseas lending had a role in some of these difficulties. Britain was, indeed, favourably placed for adjustment at the centre, but was not unscathed from repercussions.

In conclusion, particular circumstances were highly important in providing a favourable environment within which various (automatic) mechanisms could operate to narrow imbalances and the gold standard could flourish. It is not surprising to find that with vastly changed circumstances and a far less favourable environment after 1918 it no longer flourished.

CHAPTER IV

The gold standard and national financial policies, 1919–39[1]

The inter-war gold standard, along with most other aspects of economic experience for that period, has a relatively bad name in the literature. In part, this bad name has been a product of the myth-making about the 'bad old days' which accompanied the birth of such post-1930s institutions as the International Monetary Fund.[2] In part, inter-war gold standard experience acquired its reputation through a process of guilt by association which suggested that it must have played a significant role in the economic difficulties of the period, most notably in the years after 1928–9. This guilt-by-association view of the standard is perhaps strongest in Great Britain, where references to the return to gold in 1925 or subsequent, related events recur in articles or letters in the press to this day.

The purpose of this chapter is to examine the construction, operation and disintegration of the inter-war gold standard system. In doing so, I shall pay particular attention to the interrelationships between the system as a whole and its constituent countries. The focus throughout will be predominantly European, but events in overseas economies will enter the story where appropriate and, of course, the United States remains omnipresent.

I. *The war*

The inter-war gold standard had its origins in the effects of the First World War on the pre-war gold standard regime. Although 'no simple

---

[1] This chapter was completed and submitted to the editors in the autumn of 1978. It reflects the state of the literature at that time, although foreknowledge of those forthcoming publications of my colleagues Ian Drummond and Susan Howson mentioned in the supplementary bibliography influenced my drafting. Given other commitments, the two months allowed for final revision in December 1985 and January 1986 did not permit alterations to take account of all the subsequent literature. Rather than make revisions where this has caused me to alter my views, as for example, in the discussion of the relative importance of the early 1919 explosion in British unit wage costs and the overvaluation of sterling in 1924–5 in Matthews, Feinstein and Odling-Smee's *British Economic Growth 1856–1963* (Stanford, 1982), pp. 314–15, 470–2, I have left the text unchanged and added a supplementary bibliography of useful subsequent publications.

[2] See, for example, R. N. Gardner, *Sterling–Dollar Diplomacy: The Origins and Prospects of Our International Economic Order*, rev. edn (New York, 1969), especially chs. 1 and 2.

statement with respect to the breakdown of the gold standard during the war can be true',[3] it is clear that in most countries the forms of the pre-war system were sufficiently altered that significant changes in the bases of the old system were possible. Moreover, the changes that did occur were sufficiently great that it was, and is, reasonable to refer to the reconstruction of the gold standard system, and for that matter of the international economy, in the years following 1918.

Although during the war the gold standard ceased to work as a system of international economic adjustment, the authorities in various countries kept many vestiges of the old regime intact. These were to be important in shaping the post-war world. Thus legal forms often remained largely intact with minimal alterations in substance. For example, the gold content of the British sovereign remained unchanged, as did the obligation of the Bank of England to buy all gold offered to it at £3.17s.9d. per standard ounce. The right to import gold remained legally unimpaired, although the Bank of England's purchase of all Empire-produced gold overseas at a fixed price, the requirement that all other importers sell gold to the Bank at its statutory buying price and, later, the May 1918 regulation making it illegal to buy and sell gold at a premium, effectively limited imports and destroyed the London gold market at a time when sterling was well below the pre-war gold export point. Similarly, legal restrictions on the export of gold did not come until 29 March 1919 – a step confirmed by the Gold and Silver (Export Control) Act, 1920 – although moral suasion, the post-1916 prohibition on the melting of gold coin or its use otherwise than as currency, and the refusal of the authorities to include gold under the war risks insurance scheme allowed a substantial lowering of the gold export point. The behaviour of other belligerent (and neutral) countries differed in detail with prohibitions of gold exports (or imports[4]), suspensions of specie payments at central banks and moral suasion to concentrate all gold in official reserves and limit the demand for hand-to-hand coinage being most common. However, as in Britain most of the legal provisions of the pre-war regime remained, especially those relating to the role of gold in each national monetary system.

Not only did many legal trappings of the old order survive the war: despite the disruption of pre-war patterns of trade and investment, not to mention the pressures accompanying the large intersectoral shifts in resources resulting from the demands of total war, most exchange rates remained near their pre-war gold standard parities. An examination of

---

[3] W. A. Brown, Jr, *The International Gold Standard Reinterpreted, 1914–1934*, 2 vols. (New York, 1940), vol. 1, p. 27.

[4] Several neutrals, such as Argentina, Denmark, The Netherlands, Norway, Spain, and Sweden placed obstacles in the way of gold imports in order to reduce the domestic rate of inflation.

the November 1918 Allied and neutral exchange rates on New York revealed that sterling and the franc had depreciated from par by less than 4 per cent, while most neutrals had seen their exchange rates appreciate by less than 10 per cent.[5] Even the German mark had only started to fall significantly away from pre-war par in July 1918, although it had experienced difficult periods during 1917, and in October 1918 it still stood at almost 40 per cent of pre-war par.[6] These rates were, however, artificial in that the various authorities concerned had constrained the range of possible movement through pegging operations financed by gold shipments, sales of overseas assets and foreign borrowing, as well as various rudimentary exchange and import controls. Nevertheless, along with the preservation of many of the legal external forms of the pre-war regime, the 1918 pattern of exchange rates forged important psychological links with the pre-war world, even if it bore little relation to post-war realities.

For the war had shattered many of the elements underlying the pre-war system of exchange rates. Before 1914 the price experience of major members of the international monetary system had been similar;[7] the war period brought marked disparities in experience which were heightened in many cases in the immediate post-war period. Table 23 provides a rough indication of the position, although one must also allow for the differential incidence of price controls, rationing, subsidies, etc.[8] In addition, government finances in the core countries of the international economy were in varying degrees of disarray. By themselves, these factors would have made an early return to exchange stability, not to mention pre-war exchange rates, difficult. But the war had also altered many of the 'fundamentals' underlying the pre-war exchange rate system. The war disrupted many pre-war trading relationships – some of them permanently. As the belligerents devoted more resources to war, or were subject to blockade, exports fell off. Shipping difficulties and blockades also disrupted the belligerents' import patterns. Neutrals and others, unable to obtain goods from traditional sources of supply, turned to other suppliers or produced the goods themselves. After the war, they

---

[5] The Italian lira had, however, depreciated by 19 per cent.

[6] C. Bresciani-Turroni, *The Economics of Inflation: A Study of Currency Depreciation in Post-war Germany, 1914–1923*, trans. E. M. Sayers (London, 1937), Appendix Table v(a). Austrian depreciation had gone further (*ibid.*, p. 161). Sterling had also experienced severe difficulties in 1917 prior to American entry into the war.

[7] D. N. McCloskey and J. R. Zecher, 'How the Gold Standard Worked 1880–1913' in J. A. Frenkel and H. G. Johnson (eds.), *The Monetary Approach to the Balance of Payments* (Toronto, 1976), pp. 378–80; E. H. Phelps Brown and M. H. Browne, *A Century of Pay: The Course of Pay and Production in France, Germany, Sweden, the United Kingdom and the United States of America 1860–1960* (London, 1968), p. 111.

[8] For an indication of the British position in this respect, see A. C. Pigou, *Aspects of British Economic History 1918–1925* (London, 1947), part 4.

Table 23. *Price changes, 1913/14–1920 (end of year, 1913/14[a] = 100)*

	Wholesale prices			Cost of living		
	1918	1919	1920	1918	1919	1920
United States	195[b]	226	173	—	—	—
United Kingdom	246	297	264	230	236	278
France	335	432	444	248	285	424
Germany	260[c]	803[c]	1,440[c]	—	—	1,158
Italy	296	416	596	260[d]	323[d]	455[d]
Sweden	335	317	267	238	263	271
Switzerland	—	—	—	211	245	243
The Netherlands	—	286	235	184	205	222

Notes:

[a] Wholesale prices, 1913 average = 100; cost of living, mainly July 1914 = 100.

[b] January 1919.

[c] End of year price indices for imported goods in 1918–20 were 289, 1,508 and 2,023; those for domestic products alone were 250, 633 and 1,323.

[d] Average of two indices of retail prices for food in Rome and Milan.

— = Not available, throughout tables.

Sources: League of Nations, *The Course and Control of Inflation: A Review of Monetary Experience in Europe after World War I* (New York, 1946), p. 88; E. V. Morgan, *Studies in British Financial Policy 1914–1925* (London, 1952), p. 362.

frequently continued to rely on these new suppliers, or in the case of new import-substituting domestic industries protected them with tariffs. Protection was also applied to the war-stimulated manufacturing industries of such countries as Australia, Canada, and India. Post-war boundary changes in Europe also brought increased protection. The result was often a permanent loss of traditional export markets by the European belligerents. Those most seriously affected were the large pre-war international traders, Britain and Germany. The largest beneficiaries were Japan and the United States.

The war also altered the invisible account positions of many countries, most particularly as a result of changes on investment account, although in the cases of Britain and Germany shipping losses were also important.[9] To finance the volume of imports necessary for the war effort and to peg the exchanges in the pattern mentioned above, normally in the face of declining export earnings, the belligerents realized existing foreign assets and issued new overseas liabilities. As well, revolution made previous Russian investments worthless, while defeat for Germany brought

[9] D. E. Moggridge, *British Monetary Policy 1924–1931: The Norman Conquest of $4.86* (Cambridge, 1972), p. 32. The Germans had ceded most of their surviving merchant navy to the Allies under the Treaty of Versailles; J. M. Keynes, *The Economic Consequences of the Peace* (London, 1971), pp. 41–2.

Table 24. *Changes in international investment positions, 1914–19*
(£ million[a])

	United States	United Kingdom	France	Germany
Loss through default[b]	—	150	900	165
Sales of assets	—	500	140	150
Repurchases of liabilities	800	—	—	—
Issues of new debt	80	1,340	1,350	—
Purchases of new debt	2,000	2,085	700	—
Seizures		6	—	585
Change in short-term position	−200	−250 to 300	—	—

Notes:
[a] All conversions have been done at pre-war pars of exchange.
[b] Excluding war loans to Russia, which in the British case ran to £568 million.
Sources: D. E. Moggridge, *British Monetary Policy 1924–1931: The Norman Conquest of $4.86* (Cambridge, 1972), pp. 31, 33; Royal Institute of International Affairs (ed.), *The Problem of International Investment* (London, 1937), pp. 129–31; C. P. Kindleberger, *The World in Depression 1929–1939* (London, 1973), p. 40; D. Landes, *The Unbound Prometheus: Technological Change and Industrial Development in Western Europe from 1750 to the Present* (Cambridge, 1969), pp. 362–3.

confiscation of her overseas assets. The results of these changes appear in Table 24. Of course, this table does not set out the position in all its detail, for the quality of the assets and liabilities under the various heads differed markedly as the subsequent writings down of inter-allied war debts was to indicate. Also, it does not allow for the stream of reparation payments imposed by the Allies on Germany and the other central powers – a stream whose magnitude was unknown at the end of 1919.[10] Nevertheless, the result was clear. The large invisible earnings that had characterized the pre-war balances of payments of Britain, France and Germany were sharply diminished, while America's position was strengthened. Moreover, in Europe the balance of payments support provided by such earnings as remained had often been eroded by the rise in the world price level during the war.

As well as differentially affecting the trade and invisible earnings positions of the pre-war participants in the international economy, the war also affected their stocks of international liquidity. As the internal use of gold coin and commercial bank holdings of gold declined under the influence of gold centralization policies, the figures for the levels of reserves in central banks and treasuries after the war do not accurately

[10] However, informed observers were able to guess the ultimate sums involved relatively accurately (*ibid.*, ch. 5; J. M. Keynes, *A Revision of the Treaty: Being a Sequel to the Economic Consequences of the Peace* (London, 1972), p. 24).

reflect the changes that had actually occurred.[11] Also, before 1914 many countries' official reserves contained significant amounts of silver and foreign exchange. These were often dissipated in financing wartime overseas imbalances. However, Table 25 gives some indication of the redistribution of reserve assets that occurred during the war. Further redistributions were to occur during the period of post-war reconstruction, although exchange fluctuations with their induced capital flows took over much of the task of financing and removing international imbalances. The redistribution of gold reserves, the dissipation of stocks of other means of international settlement and the decline in the purchasing power of gold with its consequential effect on gold production left the world at the beginning of the inter-war period with a potential international liquidity problem.

The war also affected many of the institutional bases of the pre-war system. Most importantly it reduced the international economic and financial predominance of London – a centre whose institutions and financial practices had evolved, albeit often accidentally, to meet the 'needs' and effect the 'management' of the pre-war gold standard system.[12] (It also adversely affected, as a result of changes in financial instruments and patterns of trade finance, the ability of the British authorities to manage Britain's international position with pre-war policy instruments.[13]) The balance of international economic and financial predominance shifted towards the United States, in particular New York, a centre whose institutions and practices were not as well attuned towards international 'responsibilities'. The American authorities made some efforts to alter the situation and develop new institutional forms,[14] but, compared with London, New York financial market conditions tended to be dominated by the domestic needs (and enthusiasm) of the American economy while international considerations remained residual. On the other hand, London market institutions remained heavily internationally orientated, perhaps too much so, for the changed position of Britain in the international economy.[15]

---

[11] Thus in Britain between June 1914 and June 1918 £45.8 million in gold was withdrawn from circulation. In the years 1918–22 another £55.6 million was withdrawn. In June 1914, the banks and the public had held £123 million in gold coin; E. V. Morgan, *Studies in British Financial Policy 1914–1925* (London, 1952), pp. 218–19.

[12] See, for example, R. S. Sayers, *The Bank of England 1891–1944*, 3 vols. (Cambridge, 1976), vol. I, ch. 3.

[13] Brown, *International Gold Standard*, vol. I, pp. 144–6, 154–7; Sayers, *Bank of England*, vol. I, pp. 275–9, 298–9; Moggridge, *British Monetary Policy*, pp. 34–6.

[14] Brown, *International Gold Standard*, vol. I, ch. 7; L. V. Chandler, *Benjamin Strong: Central Banker* (Washington, DC, 1958), pp. 87–93; F. C. Costigliola, 'Anglo-American Financial Rivalry in the 1920s', *Journal of Economic History*, vol. XXXVII, part 4 (December 1977), especially pp. 911–20.

[15] See, for example, A. E. Kahn, *Great Britain in the World Economy* (New York, 1946), especially ch. 2; Moggridge, *British Monetary Policy*, pp. 199–201; Brown, *International Gold Standard*, vol. I, ch. 19 and vol. II, ch. 21; C. P. Kindleberger, *The World in Depression 1929–1939* (London, 1973), ch. 14.

Table 25. International reserves, selected countries, 1913, 1918, 1925[a] ($ million[b])

	1913				1918	1925			
	Central gold[c]	Central other[d]	Other gold[e]	Total gold	Central gold	Central gold	Central other	Other gold	Total gold
United States	1,290	0	634	1,924	2,658	3,985	0	414	4,399
United Kingdom	165	—	605	770	521	695	24	8	703
France	679	127	1,021	1,827	664	711	13	355	1,066
Germany	279	115	699	978	539	288	243	0	288
Belgium	48	89	20	68	51	53	6	0	53
Netherlands	61	10	11	72	278	178	99	11	189
Sweden	27	45	1	28	77	62	54	0	62
Switzerland	33	13	20	53	80	90	43	51	141
Total	2,582	399	3,011	5,593	4,868	6,062	482	839	6,901
World total	4,859		3,828	8,687	6,816	8,997		1,158	10,155

Notes:

[a] Other countries with over $100 million in total gold:

1913 – Austria, Italy, Russia, Canada, Argentina, India, Turkey, Australia. Total gold = $2,553 million, Central gold = $1,873 million.

1918 – Italy, Canada, Argentina, Japan, Australia, Spain. Central gold = $1,398 million.

1925 – Italy, Canada, Argentina, India, Japan, Australia, Spain. Total gold = $2,360 million. Central gold = $2,186 million.

In 1913 Russia, India, and Japan also had large foreign exchange holdings totalling $678 million.

[b] Gold valued at $20.67 per ounce, foreign exchange, and silver (1913) converted at current exchange rates.

[c] Central gold: gold holdings of central banks and governments.

[d] Central other: for 1913 includes both silver and foreign exchange; for 1925 includes only foreign exchange.

[e] Other gold: normally includes gold in circulation, including gold reserves of commercial banks, etc. For detailed notes see League of Nations, Interim Report.

Sources: US Federal Reserve Board, Banking and Monetary Statistics (Washington, DC, 1943), Table 169; League of Nations, Interim Report of the Gold Delegation of the Financial Committee (Geneva, 1930), Appendix II; League of Nations, International Currency Experience (Princeton, 1944), Appendix IV; P. H. Lindert, 'Key Currencies and Gold, 1900–1913', Princeton Studies in International Finance, no. 24 (Princeton, 1969), Table I; R. S. Sayers, The Bank of England 1891–1944 (Cambridge, 1976), vol. III, Appendix 37.

The above changes in the international economy and its institutions provided the backcloth against which the inter-war international financial system evolved. However, one final element is also important. The European aspects of the inter-war international monetary regime took shape in the context of American economic events. The American economy, by far the dominant element in the international economy, remained to a considerable extent apart from events elsewhere as regards the important determinants of its own behaviour. This is not to say that European or overseas events had no effect on the American economy, or on the thinking or behaviour of American policymakers.[16] Rather it is to emphasize that the primary orientation in Europe (and elsewhere) towards the United States was often reflexive. Foreigners reacted to American events and tried, where possible, to influence American behaviour in certain directions, but they could do little by themselves to shape the basic course of American affairs. The discussion that follows will attempt to maintain a similar perspective. The American economy and American economic policy will always be in the background and sometimes in the foreground, but the discussion will devote little space to explaining American behaviour or its dynamics.

II. Reconstruction

The reconstruction of the international monetary system after 1918 was shaped by the ultimate goal of almost all post-war policymakers – the return to some sort of a gold standard system of fixed exchange rates.[17] Throughout the reconstruction period as well, the pre-war pattern of exchange rates played an important role of shaping the behaviour of economic actors and policymakers. At the end of the war, however, the methods and processes of international reconstruction were unclear, even in many cases in their broadest outlines. True, the United States, which had experienced the lowest degree of price inflation and the least wartime disruption amongst major belligerents, returned to gold convertibility in June 1919. But the 'full' reconstruction of the system was to

---

[16] See, for example, American involvement in post-war monetary reconstruction as recorded by Chandler, *Benjamin Strong*, chs. 7–11; R. H. Meyer, *Bankers' Diplomacy: Monetary Stabilisation in the Twenties* (New York, 1970); S. V. O. Clarke, *Central Bank Cooperation 1924–1931* (New York, 1967); S. V. O. Clarke, 'The Reconstruction of the International Monetary System: The Attempts of 1922 and 1933', *Princeton Studies in International Finance*, no. 33 (November 1973).

[17] Prior to 1922 one might think of the goal as being a gold coinage or a gold bullion standard. After that date, i.e., after the Genoa Conference with its resolutions on currency, the gold exchange standard under which countries held reserves in claims denominated in the currency of some gold standard centre became more important as a goal and as an influence on the behaviour of the system.

take another decade.[18] By that time, the reconstructed system had started to disintegrate.

Reconstruction took place against the background of wartime changes discussed above and the large swings in incomes, prices and production in the United States, which made the price level of gold something of a moving target and had a major impact on balance of payments positions.[19] In all cases except the American, before rejoining a fixed exchange rate system the nations involved had to regain a degree of financial and balance of payments stability and to devise new or restore old institutions and mechanisms of international adjustment. This meant that they had to clear away much of the financial debris of war (and, in many cases, of reconstruction): to adjust levels of government expenditure and taxation, to come to terms with the national debts resulting from previous policies and to contain such potential sources of instability as unknown reparations and war debt payments.[20]

Inevitably the course and pace of events varied across countries. Shaped in part by the desire to return to a gold standard type of system, it also affected the form of the system that emerged. The variations in events and policies were considerable as the ultimate reconstructed pattern of fixed exchange rates suggests, but in Europe four classes of solutions emerged:[21]

1. Stabilization at pre-war par with gold (and the US dollar): United Kingdom, Denmark, Netherlands, Norway, Sweden, Switzerland;

2. Stabilization at between 1/4 and 1/8 of pre-war par: France, Belgium, Czechoslovakia, Finland, Italy;

3. Stabilization at between 1/11 and 1/33 of pre-war par: Bulgaria, Greece, Portugal, Romania, Yugoslavia;

4. New currency introduced after hyperinflation: Germany, Austria, Hungary, Poland.

Coupled with the wide range of rates chosen was a considerable range of dates of stabilization. Looking at the same countries discussed above in terms of the dates of effective *de facto* stabilization, the point is clear:[22]

---

[18] It might be said to have been completed amongst major trading nations with the return of Japan in January 1930.

[19] H. B. Lary and associates, *The United States in the World Economy: The International Transactions of the United States during the Interwar Period* (Washington, DC, 1943); Brown, *International Gold Standard*, vol. I, p. 287.

[20] This formulation follows Brown, *International Gold Standard*, vol. I, ch. 9.

[21] This classification ignores cases of new national currencies in the successor states to pre-war regimes. League of Nations, *The Course and Control of Inflation: A Review of Monetary Experience in Europe after World War I* (New York, 1946), p. 93.

[22] *Ibid.*, p. 92.

1922 (or earlier)	Sweden, Austria
1923	Germany, Finland, Czechoslovakia
1924	Hungary, Bulgaria, Netherlands, Switzerland
1925	United Kingdom, Yugoslavia
1926	Denmark, Belgium, Poland, France
1927	Italy, Romania
1928	Norway, Greece
1929	Portugal

This range of dates and rates of stabilization necessarily presents problems of organization. An examination of each stabilization in context would take us well beyond the limits of a single chapter. It is probably best to take an example from each of cases (1), (2) and (4), each of which provides us with the experience of a major gold standard centre, and provide brief comments where appropriate on the others. Such an approach provides good examples of the interaction between international considerations and domestic policies. The countries involved are Britain, France and Germany.

Perhaps the best documented inter-war stabilization experience is Britain's return to the gold standard in 1925.[23] From the end of the war, the Bank of England 'had no doubt where it wanted to go and no doubt what were the lions in its path'.[24] Politicians were somewhat less certain as to the goal and the methods of achieving it, particularly given their commitments to a post-war 'land fit for heroes' and fears of unrest, but the available evidence indicates that they soon came under Bank and Treasury officials' tutelage, even if they were occasionally unruly pupils.[25] The execution of a policy of a return to gold at pre-war par required that the authorities establish a basis for calculating the distance from their target, that they establish an index of sterling's depreciation from the target level and that they develop policies to remove that depreciation. The very first task was therefore the reopening of the London gold market and the making of international, especially Far Eastern, demand in order to discover the current world price of gold. This occurred in the course of 1919 and early 1920.[26] The establishment

---

[23] Sir Henry Clay, *Lord Norman* (London, 1957), ch. 4; Chandler, *Benjamin Strong*, chs. 6 and 7; Clarke, *Central Bank Cooperation*, ch. 5; A. Boyle, *Montagu Norman: A Biography* (London, 1967), 6–8; Moggridge, *British Monetary Policy*, chs. 2–4; S. Howson, *Domestic Monetary Management in Britain 1919–38* (Cambridge, 1975), chs. 2 and 3; Sayers, *Bank of England*, vol. I, chs. 6 and 7; Costigliola, 'Anglo-American Financial Rivalry', pp. 920–8; L. S. Pressnell, '1925: The Burden of Sterling', *Economic History Review*, 2nd series, vol. XXXI, part I (February 1978).

[24] Sayers, *Bank of England*, vol. I, p. 111.

[25] See, for example, S. Howson, 'The Origins of Dear Money, 1919–20', *Economic History Review*, 2nd series, vol. XXVII, part I (February 1974), pp. 90–6. Compare Brown, *International Gold Standard*, vol. I, pp. 221–2.

[26] Brown, *International Gold Standard*, vol. I, pp. 185–8.

of an index of depreciation, assuming no massive immediate post-war deflation along the lines advocated by the Bank of England in 1918 and early 1919,[27] necessitated the unpegging of the exchanges, supported at $4.76 $\frac{7}{16}$ since 1915, the end of government borrowing to support the exchange rate and the end of controls on domestic prices, consumption and many international transactions. Once these steps had occurred, the sterling exchange rate could reflect 'normal' market forces. This process of unpegging and decontrol took approximately two years.[28] The restoration of 'normal' conditions in other areas directly affecting the exchange rate, given London's role as an international exchange centre for the continent and America, took somewhat longer. It also made the Bank and the Treasury strong supporters of the financial internationalism of the early 1920s.[29] Parallel to these developments went efforts to revive and restore the machinery of monetary control. In their essentials, these involved a restoration of the Bank Rate mechanism, a shorthand phrase for the Bank's control of London short-term interest rates, which carried with it changes in government financial policy and in the relationships among the Bank, the Treasury and financial markets. For without a balancing of government revenue and expenditure, an increase in the average term to maturity and/or a reduction in the size of the outstanding national debt, and an end to the seemingly endless discussions and consultations prior to any change in monetary policy, the Bank believed it had too little room for manoeuvre.[30] By the summer of 1920 the Bank had moved quite far towards its goals, although a full restoration of its control over the markets was to take somewhat longer.[31]

While the Bank attempted to restore its control at home, Britain, along with the rest of the international economy, experienced a strong restocking boom which (along with exchange depreciation) carried wholesale prices up by 44 per cent in the year from April 1919.[32] During the same boom American wholesale prices rose by 21 per cent. This boom ended in the spring of 1920, at the same time as the authorities in Britain and America administered a stiff dose of dear money which they thought might have to be (and was) maintained for a long time.[33] The

[27] See Howson, 'Origins of Dear Money', pp. 90–5; Sayers, Bank of England, pp. 111–17.

[28] Sayers, Bank of England, p. 190.   [29] Ibid., ch. 8.   [30] Ibid., pp. 110–15, 119.

[31] Howson, Domestic Monetary Management, pp. 25–7. In the case of capital markets the process of post-war de-control was really never complete as the Bank found new methods necessary to maintain a semblance of influence. See J. M. Atkin, 'Official Regulation of British Overseas Investment, 1914–1931', Economic History Review, 2nd series, vol. XXIII, part 2 (August 1970), pp. 324–35; and Moggridge, British Monetary Policy, pp. 200–19.

[32] Pigou, Aspects, p. 234, col. 2. During the same period, the exchange rate against the dollar depreciated by 16 per cent.

[33] Sayers, Bank of England, vol. I, pp. 110–19; Howson, 'Origins of Dear Money', pp. 90–107; Howson, Domestic Monetary Management, pp. 11–24; Chandler, Benjamin Strong, ch. 5 (2); M. Friedman and A. J. Schwartz, A Monetary History of the United States, 1867–1960 (Princeton, 1963), pp. 221–40; E. R. Wicker, Federal Reserve Monetary Policy, 1917–1933 (New York, 1966), chs. 2 and 3.

ensuing slump brought sharp falls in prices and costs. British wholesale prices fell by almost one-half, while the cost of living and money wage rates fell by over one-third and two-fifths respectively. However, American prices fell almost as far, so that the deflation did little to bring sterling closer to par with the dollar.

The need for further, differential deflation in the United Kingdom after the slump of 1920–2, if Britain was successfully to return to gold at pre-war par, left the authorities in a dilemma. During the slump and afterwards, Treasury policy maintained a deflationary stance with a tight rein on public expenditure and continued funding of the national debt.[34] However, the continuously high level of post-slump unemployment and the increasing tendency to associate high unemployment with a restrictive monetary policy resulted in increasing constraints on Bank Rate policy – constraints that continuous Treasury pressures for easier money, owing to the political difficulties associated with high levels of unemployment, did much to tighten.[35] As a result, with occasional discussions of possible alternative methods of hastening the movement towards gold, the authorities waited upon events abroad.[36]

While the Bank (and, to a lesser extent, the Treasury) was regaining control at home, it took unprecedented steps abroad. An international programme of consultation and coordination with the Federal Reserve Bank of New York and cooperation with other European central banks and the Financial Committee of the League of Nations formed a part of the process of restoring an international gold standard system. Thus, as far as possible within their respective domestic constraints and perceptions of national advantage, Montagu Norman of the Bank of England and Benjamin Strong of the Federal Reserve Bank of New York attempted to coordinate policies to break the 1919–20 boom, to encourage stability abroad, and, later, to reduce the dilemmas on Britain's path towards gold through relatively easier American financial conditions.[37] Similarly, through the international financial conferences at Brussels (1920) and Genoa (1922), the League's Financial Committee, the Dawes Committee and the widening web of contacts amongst central bankers, the Bank, with Treasury assistance, attempted to increase the potential stability of the post-war international economy and prospective gold standard environment by means of an agreed gospel of central bank practice,[38] exchange stabilization schemes and the de-politicization,

---

[34] Howson, *Domestic Monetary Management*, pp. 21–9. For a useful discussion of the meanings of deflation see *ibid.*, pp. 32–3.

[35] *Ibid.*, pp. 28, 34–6; Sayers, *Bank of England*, vol. I, pp. 124–5, 1929–32; Clay, *Lord Norman*, pp. 133, 139, 145, 148.

[36] Sayers, *Bank of England*, vol. I, p. 122.

[37] Clarke, *Central Bank Cooperation*, ch. 3; Chandler, *Benjamin Strong*, ch. 7; Sayers, *Bank of England*, vol. I, chs. 6(c) and 8(b).

[38] Sayers, *Bank of England*, vol. I, pp. 157–60; vol. III, Appendix 10.

wherever possible, of international financial affairs. By the late spring and early summer of 1924, events had gone so far that the British authorities felt able again to begin consideration of the formal details of a return to gold.

Such consideration did not remove the need for an ultimate decision on the matter. The timing of the ultimate political decision – for in the end it was a matter for the politicians – was, to some extent, the result of a series of accidents. The date chosen for the expiry of the Gold and Silver (Export Control) Act, 1920 concentrated attention on 1925 as the year of decision.[39] This concentration was heightened by the steady, speculative rise in sterling, based on market expectations of an early return to gold following the Conservative Party's victory in the election of October 1924.[40] Both strengthened the authorities' resolve to act. In the end, the final decision for gold at pre-war par was a product of several consider-ations best summarized under three headings: the rejection of alternative long-term policies, perceptions as to timing and alternative adjustment mechanisms and beliefs concerning Britain's international economic position.[41] Though set in the context of Britain's position in 1924-5, they were handled in a manner characteristic of most international financial decisions of the period and are worth examination.

The two contemporaneously discussed long-term alternatives to a British return to gold at pre-war par were a return to gold at a devalued exchange rate and managed money, a policy aiming at domestic price stability with exchange rate flexibility providing the buffer from exter-nal price developments. In the official discussions of 1924-5, devaluation never received any serious consideration, despite Keynes's last ditch advocacy of the policy in the spring of 1925: those involved either rejected it out of hand or considered it unnecessary given the rise in sterling after October 1924. It only really came up after the event in official reactions to Keynes' *The Economic Consequences of Mr. Churchill* and Sir Josiah Stamp's Addendum to the *Report* of the Court of Inquiry into the ensuing coal dispute.[42] Managed money, which had been the object of much more discussion in various forums including the Genoa Conference, received somewhat more attention.[43] Some rejected the

---

[39] The act was to lapse after 31 December 1925. For the origins of this particular date see *ibid.*, vol. III, Appendix 6.

[40] *Ibid.*, vol. I, pp. 140-1; Moggridge, *British Monetary Policy*, pp. 59, 87; R. Z. Aliber, 'Speculation in the Foreign Exchanges: The European Experience, 1919-1926', *Yale Economic Essays*, vol. II, part 1 (Spring 1966), pp. 194, 196-8.

[41] On the whole episode see Moggridge, *British Monetary Policy*, ch. 3; Sayers, *Bank of England*, vol. I, ch. 7 and Clay, *Lord Norman*, ch. 4.

[42] J. M. Keynes, *The Economic Consequences of Mr. Churchill* (London, 1925); UK, Court of Inquiry Concerning the Coal Mining Dispute, *Report*, Cmd 2478 (London, 1925), pp. 21ff.

[43] The English classics of the period are R. G. Hawtrey, *Currency and Credit* (London, 1919); and J. M. Keynes, *A Tract on Monetary Reform* (London, 1923). For Keynes' and Hawtrey's

idea because it was impracticable, given the state of economic theory or contemporary policy instruments and indicators; others thought it would not bring greater stability for Britain than a gold standard regime, which might of course eventually operate along the line proposed at Genoa and stabilize the purchasing power of gold. But the most influential arguments against management without gold appear to have been those which made it synonymous with inflation, or, more generally, currency instability. This pairing was largely a product of the period after 1914,[44] when, to a generation which at worst had experienced short slumps amidst the gently rising prices of the gold standard years 1896–1914, the wide swings in prices and activity after 1914 and the inflationary or hyperinflationary experiences of post-war continental Europe hardly seemed effective advertisements for management.[45] The resulting distaste for 'management' in many cases took the form of distrust of anything that seemed to lack automaticity – a feeling shared by other central bankers such as Strong[46] – and with a lack of analysis of the origin of post-1914 problems, or for that matter of the pre-1914 gold standard's bases of success, limited exploration of this alternative to gold in 1925.

Thus in Britain in 1925 the rate of exchange and the regime for monetary management were not really important issues to officials or politicians. Rather, given the desire to return to one gold standard rate of exchange, the important question was one of timing. The speculative improvement in sterling in the autumn and winter of 1924–5 left the authorities with a dilemma: either they could ratify speculative anticipations and stabilize the exchange at what many regarded as an overvalued rate, or they could disappoint expectations by refusing to stabilize for the time being and face the prospect of a fall in the exchange as speculators withdrew their commitments.[47] The pressures for ratifying speculative anticipations were strong as other countries within and without the Empire moved towards gold, as the Dawes Plan negotiations suggested possible reductions in Britain's influence from not being on gold, as an extension of the 1920 legislation would bring with it public discussion of

involvement at Genoa, see S. Howson, 'Monetary Theory and Policy in the 20th Century: The Career of R. G. Hawtrey', in M. Flinn (ed.), *Proceedings of the Seventh International Economic History Congress* (Edinburgh, 1978); Sayers, *Bank of England*, p. 156; *The Collected Writing of John Maynard Keynes*, vol. XVII, ed. E. Johnson (London, 1978), pp. 369, 384.

[44] For an indication of the abnormality of the post-1914 period to the contemporary period see Keynes, *Tract*, ch. 1. One also must remember the pre-1914 attitude towards paper standards in 'banana republics' as expressed, for example, by R. G. Hawtrey in *Good and Bad Trade* (London, 1913), pp. 6–7.

[45] See D. Winch, *Economics and Policy: A Historical Study* (London, 1972), pp. 97–8 for a good, brief discussion of this point.   [46] Chandler, *Benjamin Strong*, p. 329.

[47] At the time, these balances were estimated at £100 million. A disappointment of market expectations would also have weakened the existing informal official controls on overseas lending, for these depended for their success on the expectation that sterling would rise. See Moggridge, *British Monetary Policy*, pp. 87, 218–19.

financial policy in any case, and as there were beliefs within the Treasury that the Bank would in any event try to hold the exchange rate at its existing level.[48] Nevertheless, much still depended on contemporary views as to the amount of adjustment necessary to make the new exchange rate viable and the nature of the adjustment mechanism that would be operative.

The size of the adjustments envisaged in the return to gold as compared to not doing so was, given Treasury assumptions as to Bank policy, somewhat conditioned by the exchange rate ruling at the time of the discussions. In the final stages of the 1924–5 examination of the issue, this conditioning had narrowed the issue to that required to raise the rate from $4.80 to $4.86. Other conventions in official thinking tended to minimize the problem. In 1924–5 relative purchasing-power parity calculations were common in official circles.[49] There were, it is true, frequent, if formal, disclaimers as to the accuracy of particular estimates, but such calculations had a powerful impact on all thinking about the extent of the adjustment problem. However, these calculations tended to use 1913 or 1914 as the base year for the inevitable Anglo-American comparisons used and wholesale prices as the most common index. The choice of the base year without compensating adjustments, took no account of any changes that might have occurred in Britain's underlying relative international economic position since that time. The use of wholesale price indices, dominated by the prices of the staple commodities of international trade which in Britain moved inversely with the sterling exchange rate, also tended to conceal rather than provide additional information.[50] In fact, the use of this very influential method of measuring over- and undervaluations tended to underestimate sharply any problems involved in returning to gold at $4.86.

Despite these tendencies to underestimate the possible adjustments involved, most of those concerned with the decision still saw the need for some further relative decline in British prices. But they were very imprecise as to the nature of the processes involved. Two not mutually exclusive schools of thought existed: one expected inflation abroad; another expected deflation at home. The expectation that American inflation resulting from past gold inflows would ease the path to $4.86, despite American official assurances to the contrary, played a significant, but not decisive, role in the final decision to return. As for any domestic deflation that might prove necessary if American inflation did not occur

[48] Pressnell, '1925: The Burden of Sterling', pp. 71–80; Clarke, *Central Bank Cooperation*, pp. 58–63; Sayers, *Bank of England*, vol. I, p. 146, n. 2; Moggridge, *British Monetary Policy*, pp. 87–8, 231.

[49] Sayers, *Bank of England*, pp. 142, 151–2.

[50] For a full discussion of the problems of purchasing-power parity calculations, see L. H. Officer, 'The Purchasing-Power-Parity Theory of Exchange Rates: A Review Article', *IMF Staff Papers*, vol. XXIII, part I (March 1976). See also, Moggridge, *British Monetary Policy*, pp. 101–6.

or was insufficient, discussions of the processes involved were brief and euphemistic. There were the usual references to the 'discomforts' and 'extra sacrifices' that might precede or accompany such deflation-induced reductions in British costs as might prove necessary, but the expectation was that these would prove temporary, since most people involved believed that British money wages would be flexible, as they had been in 1920–2. Many saw a return to gold as increasing British trade and employment. Exchange stabilization at pre-war par was seen as part of the employment policy *par excellence* for the open British economy.[51]

Similar lack of consideration was given to the international position of Britain and the effects of a return to gold at $4.86 thereon. It was assumed that the return would be a 'good thing' for the City of London and the international economy and that stabilization would aid the revival of international trade. However, there was no discussion of the effects of exchange appreciation on Britain's balance of payments position beyond sentiments to the effect that everything would be satisfactory if everything turned out satisfactorily. In addition, the discussions, centred on the dollar–sterling rate, completely ignored the possible implications of past or prospective stabilization decisions elsewhere for Britain. Moreover, those involved assumed repeatedly that the traditional Bank Rate mechanism could handle any problems that might arise quickly and almost automatically.

In the end, partially on the basis of the advice received at the time, but more importantly because of the perceived political costs of not acting in accordance with the professions of successive governments and informed opinions, and a deep faith in the mechanisms of the pre-war gold standard, Britain returned to gold in April 1925. At the time, Keynes suggested that sterling was overvalued by 10 per cent, given the authorities' goals regarding employment, tariff and overseas lending policies.[52] Some authors have disputed this figure, as well as the present author's very crude 'back of the envelope' calculations suggesting that sterling was overvalued in 1925 by *at least* 10 per cent, if not more.[53] On the whole, I am inclined to think that if anything, both figures are unduly conservative in that either lower elasticities or, more correctly, a fuller consideration of repercussions effects would necessitate a larger depreciation to generate the foreign exchange flows necessary for the authorities

[51] Howson, *Domestic Monetary Management*, pp. 140–1; R. S. Sayers, 'The Return to Gold, 1925' in S. Pollard (ed.), *The Gold Standard and Employment Policies between the Wars* (London, 1970), pp. 89–91.   [52] Keynes, *Economic Consequences of Mr. Churchill*, especially part 1.
[53] Moggridge, *British Monetary Policy*, Appendix 1 is a slight reworking of Appendix 1 in my *The Return to Gold, 1925: The Formulation of Economic Policy and its Critics* (Cambridge, 1969). The most notable critics have been D. H. Aldcroft, *The Inter-war Economy: Britain 1919–1939* (London, 1970), especially pp. 250–2; and B. W. Alford, *Depression and Recovery? British Economic Growth 1918–1939* (London, 1972), pp. 34–6.

to meet their policy goals.[54] Separable from the degree of overvaluation of sterling in 1925 is, to some extent at least, its importance. Some authors, believing that the major problems of the British economy were structural, play down the importance of overvaluation on the grounds that the higher level of aggregate demand resulting from a more realistic exchange rate would have done little to help ease these problems.[55] If the issues were completely separable, this might be the case, but decades of experience with regional policies in the United Kingdom and elsewhere suggest that structural changes are easier to effect at higher rather than lower levels of aggregate demand and certainly at levels of unemployment below 10 per cent characteristic of Britain in the 1920s.[56] In other words although an exchange rate below $4.86 would not have solved all the problems facing the British economy of the 1920s it would have made many of the necessary adjustments easier.

[54] This point was made in British Monetary Policy, p. 245, n. 2. Some of the discussants of the exercise undertaken there have missed its purpose, which was primarily concerned with the balance of payments implications of alternative exchange rate policies in relation to the authorities' policy goals. A suggestion, therefore, that the elasticities used in the 'back of the envelope' calculations were too high, as made by Alford (Depression and Recovery, p. 36), carries with it the implication that to achieve a given current account improvement, to allow, say, a higher level of activity, the authorities would have had to depreciate from $4.86 by a larger amount. Thus lower elasticities would, in the context of the authorities' policy goals and the circumstances of the 1920s, mean a greater overvaluation of sterling at $4.86, unless, of course, the elasticities were so low as to suggest appreciation above $4.86 as the appropriate policy, a suggestion that has not yet appeared in the literature.

A factor which might also affect the outcome would be any monopoly power in export markets or monopsony power as an importer enjoyed by Britain. The possibility as regard imports in particular has been raised by C. P. Kindleberger in his The Terms of Trade: A European Case Study (New York, 1956), pp. 97–8. His results have been picked up and misunderstood by both Alford (pp. 35, 37) and Aldcroft (The Inter-War Economy, p. 251), who, in the tradition of Treasury knights of the 1920s (and probably more recently), have failed to work consistently in either foreign currency or sterling when discussing the effects of exchange rate changes. Kindleberger noted in the course of his discussion of the appreciation of sterling between 1924 and 1925 that the dollar unit values of British exports and imports rose by 5.8 per cent and 9.2 per cent respectively between the two years. He then went on to suggest that Britain's bargaining power as regards imports was stronger than for exports. If Britain's bargaining power in import markets was sufficiently great that the sterling prices of imports on average remained unchanged as the exchange rate fell, one would need a smaller depreciation than suggested in British Monetary Policy to improve the current account by a given amount, for both the volume and value of imports would remain unchanged (excluding repercussion effects resulting from higher import demand resulting from higher export volumes or domestic incomes). This compares with the rise in the value of imports that occurs so long as imports are price inelastic (i.e., a demand elasticity in terms of price of less than minus one). However, such a behaviour pattern for import prices would have had dramatic implications for export prices and incomes abroad, which would feed back on British exports. Moreover, the case under discussion is a polar case – lower levels of monopsony power would have much smaller effects – and these would be similar to higher demand price elasticities for imports in their impact effects on the trade balance.   [55] See, for example, Aldcroft, The Inter-War Economy, p. 322.

[56] See, for example, A. J. Brown, The Framework of Regional Economics in the United Kingdom (Cambridge, 1972), pp. 120–2, 184–5; C. D. Hoover, 'Old and New Issues in Regional Development', in E. A. G. Robinson (ed.), Backward Areas in Advanced Countries (London, 1969), pp. 345–6.

Britain was the only European belligerent to return to gold at pre-war par. All the other European countries that managed to do likewise had been neutrals. Their experience can be briefly summarized. As in Britain, a return to gold at pre-war par had strong moral overtones.[57] All the countries involved experienced the sharp post-war boom and slump, although prices in the slump fell by less in Norway and Denmark than elsewhere in the group. Again, most of them experienced some further deflation between the end of the slump and the restoration of gold convertibility. The deflation was relatively mild in Switzerland and The Netherlands, slightly more substantial in Sweden and much more substantial in Denmark and Norway. The differential degrees of deflation show up amongst other problems in the unemployment statistics with the Scandinavian countries experiencing rates as high as Britain's in the case of Sweden and much higher than Britain's in Norway and Denmark, while Dutch experience brought lower than British levels of unemployment and Switzerland something like full employment.[58] As to whether pre-war par brought under- or overvaluations to the currencies involved, the evidence is more mixed than in Britain's case. In Denmark and Norway, all available price and employment statistics clearly point to overvaluation. The statistics for retail prices and unemployment for Sweden would also suggest some overvaluation, but the evolution of unit wage costs and the very rapid structural changes occurring in the economy cloud matters somewhat.[59] At worst, they suggest that any overvaluation was relatively temporary. The Dutch statistics also point both ways with some series suggesting overvaluation and others the opposite. In the end, perhaps only the Swiss seem to have managed the return to gold more or less satisfactorily.[60]

The stabilization experiences of Britain's major western European allies, France, Belgium and Italy, were similar in many respects, despite the differences that occurred in the final stages of inconvertibility prior to the date of stabilization itself. Before the war, all three countries, along with Switzerland, had been members of the Latin Monetary Union and had kept their exchange rates at par and their basic unit of currency equal to one French franc.[61] This pre-war experience was to be important in

---

[57] See, for example, R. A. Lester, *Monetary Experiments: Early American and Recent Scandinavian* (Princeton, 1939), pp. 195–205.

[58] I. Svennilson, *Growth and Stagnation in the European Economy* (Geneva, 1954), Tables 3 and A2; B. R. Mitchell, *European Historical Statistics 1750–1970* (London, 1975), Table C2.

[59] Phelps Brown and Browne, *A Century of Pay*, ch. 2A, especially Figure 38.

[60] For the Dutch and Swiss cases see Aliber, 'Speculation in the Foreign Exchanges', pp. 229–38. See also Mitchell, *European Historical Statistics*, tables 11 and 12.

[61] Italy, although a member of the Union, had stabilized her rate not through gold convertibility at a fixed ratio but through the operations of the Bank of Italy and the Ministry of Finance. France and Belgium were, along with Switzerland, on a 'limping gold standard' under which notes were convertible not only into gold but also into legal tender silver coin.

the course of post-war exchange fluctuations, for the three currencies, unlike the Swiss franc, often tended to be regarded by the market as one and their course was often dominated by movements of the French franc.[62] All three countries had suspended gold convertibility during the war and had seen considerable fighting on their soil, although the areas occupied and the extent of damage varied. At the end of the war, during which the French franc was pegged with British and American assistance within 10 per cent of pre-war par and the Italian rate pegged at various levels close to par until it fell away after the reverses of 1917, the pattern of exchange rates was relatively close to par with the French franc at 91 per cent, the Belgian franc at 91 per cent and the Italian lira at 82 per cent of pre-war parity.

The subsequent course of these three exchange rates reflected both the experiences of war as well as the problems and basic decisions of reconstruction. All three countries ended the war with substantial budgetary imbalances; all had experienced considerable wartime inflation; and all had suffered extensive wartime dislocations. Also, in many cases the war had exacerbated pre-war social tensions to a greater extent than in, say, Britain, thus hampering decision-taking and 'quick' solutions.[63] In themselves, these factors would have resulted in a period of post-war exchange difficulties, but the possibility was heightened by early post-war decisions associated with reconstruction. A major assumption of post-war policy in France and Belgium was that German reparations would cover wartime damage. This assumption not only provided a basis for reconstruction expenditures financed by borrowing in anticipation of future interest and amortization coming from reparations receipts, but it also meant that the public sector bore more of the cost and that reconstruction was probably more extravagant than would otherwise have been the case.[64] This put substantial additional pressures on budgets already strained by war finance. Nevertheless, the resolution of the legacies of war and reconstruction were to vary significantly across the three countries by the date of stabilization. However, taking the French case we can see the general character of the problems that emerged and their resolution.

Discussions of the French experience between the end of the war and stabilization normally divide the period into three or four blocks. The first, covering the post-war boom and slump, was dominated by the

[62] Aliber, 'Speculation in the Foreign Exchanges', pp. 219–29; J. S. Cohen, 'The 1927 Revaluation of the Lira: A Study in Political Economy', *Economic History Review*, 2nd series, vol. XXV, part 4 (November 1972), p. 645.

[63] C. S. Maier, *Recasting Bourgeois Europe: Stabilisation in France, Germany and Italy in the Decade after World War I* (Princeton, 1975).

[64] S. A. Schuker, *The End of French Predominance in Europe: The Financial Crisis of 1924 and the Adoption of the Dawes Plan* (Chapel Hill, NC, 1976), pp. 42–3.

financial legacies of the war and the early stages of reconstruction. The second, running from the spring of 1922 to mid-1924, was dominated by struggles over reparations ultimately 'resolved' by the Dawes Plan. In the third period, from mid-1924 to the accession of Raymond Poincaré in June 1926, speculative factors were dominant, for by this stage the budget had approached a rough balance and the basic balance of payments position was strong. The final block covered the two stabilizations, *de facto* then *de jure*.

The first phase of the franc's post-war history saw it fall from its wartime peg of 5.425 to the dollar to a low of just over 17 to the dollar at the end of 1920 before recovering to a level of just over 11 to the dollar in the spring of 1922. Around these trends there were sizeable fluctuations: in both 1920 and 1921 the range of fluctuations exceeded 25 per cent. The broad trends in the exchange rate were determined primarily by economic factors: the adjustment to the relatively higher rate of wartime inflation in France than elsewhere, the large budget deficits on both ordinary and reconstruction accounts, and the post-war restocking boom and subsequent slump. During 1919 and 1920 the current account of the balance of payments was heavily in deficit, but thereafter it moved into surplus, a position maintained until 1931.[65] During the same period the Treasury began to regain some control over its financial position and to reduce by agreed stages its debt to the Bank of France. It cut its deficit by over two-thirds and reduced other elements of the floating debt. In fact, the position had improved sufficiently by the end of this phase so that J. P. Morgan and Company, the French government's New York agents, believed that the authorities could stabilize the currency at existing rates. The authorities scotched the idea: they still believed that the franc would ultimately return to gold at pre-war par.[66]

From June 1922, when France broke with Britain and her other former allies over the flexibility of the schedule for German reparations laid down at the London Conference of May 1921, political factors became more important in determining the course of the exchange. As it became more and more apparent that reparations on the London Conference scale were unattainable, the French economic position, with its reconstruction finance predicated on the receipt of such a scale of payments, looked more uncertain. In the course of the remainder of the year the franc fell by over 30 per cent before recovering at year's end to 80 per cent of the June level. The invasion of the Ruhr, the German policy of passive resistance and the collapse of the German mark towards nothingness resulted in further pressure on the franc and took it beyond its 1922 low to a level in November 1923 almost 40 per cent below that of June

[65] M. Wolfe, *The French Franc Between the Wars, 1919–1939* (New York, 1951), Appendix III.
[66] Schuker, *End of French Predominance*, p. 37.

1922. At that stage, strong speculative forces appear to have taken over and carried the franc to a low of 28.65 to the dollar on 8 March 1924.[67] The fall in the franc during this period gave a sharp upward twist to the domestic price level.[68] At the same time, despite the slow, if halting, improvement in the budgetary position, the finances of the Treasury became more precarious, for the authorities began to have problems financing such deficits as remained and keeping the outstanding debt firmly held. In 1922 and 1923 the Treasury was unable to meet its commitment to repay part of its outstanding debt to the Bank of France and on more than one occasion in 1923 it only avoided exceeding the legal upper limit to such debt by devious expedients. From January 1924 such expedients became commonplace.[69]

However, the speculative drop in the exchange after the end of 1923 did strengthen the prospective financial position of the authorities. As a condition of an international loan for J. P. Morgan and Company and Lazards, the London merchant bankers, to stem the depreciation of the franc, the government agreed to push a substantial tax increase through the Senate, to bring expenditures into line with revenues, to make no new appeals to domestic capital markets except to fund existing short-term debt and to abstain from subsequent new issues, even for recon-struction, unless the normal income from taxation could provide the necessary servicing.[70] The assistance, $100 million and £4 million, halted the speculative slide and dramatically reversed the position: with official support the franc rose to 14.9 to the dollar on 22 April. During the rest of 1924 it fluctuated between this level and 20 to the dollar with a tendency towards the lower rate. The foreign financial assistance proved expensive in a political sense, however, for its renewal six months later proved to be an important factor in weakening the French negotiating position on the implementation of the Dawes Plan.[71]

May 1924 brought a change in French politics as the left-wing Cartel des Gauches came to power. The first Cartel government lasted until April 1925, but thereafter continuous change was the order of the day – there were five finance ministers in the last eight months of 1925. The various Cartel governments all had difficulties in getting their financial proposals through the Senate, even those agreed with the foreign bankers in March 1924. Initially the deficit grew smaller, but the problems of debt management were becoming acute. As the exchange rate began to fall again, rising prices complicated the budgetary position given the

[67] *Ibid.*, pp. 52–3; Aliber, 'Speculation in the Foreign Exchanges', pp. 199–200; Brown, *International Gold Standard*, pp. 434–5.

[68] Aliber, 'Speculation in the Foreign Exchanges', p. 210; Schuker, *End of French Predominance*, p. 53.   [69] Schuker, *End of French Predominance*, pp. 50–2.   [70] *Ibid.*, pp. 108–15.

[71] *Ibid.*, pp. 140–68 and part II.

regressivity of the tax system.[72] The debt management problem loomed particularly large because in the course of 1925 the authorities had to refinance 22 billion francs of non-floating debt, keep over 54 billion in short-term *bons de la defense nationale* in circulation and stay within its borrowing limits at the Bank of France, yet finance any deficit that arose – a deficit that would rise with inflation.[73] At the same time, rising prices and rising activity increased the demand for cash balances, making it harder to keep the *bons* outstanding firmly held and pushing the authorities against yet another constraint, the ceiling on the Bank of France note issue.

Cornered by these various constraints and subject to 'the daily plebiscite of the bondholder',[74] the authorities attempted to secure budget balance and maintain confidence through higher taxes and economies. But the political system, suspicious of the left, moved slowly and the government attempted to meet its needs with advances from the Bank, hidden as usual in its balance sheet to avoid exeeding the statutory limit. However, the authorities also ran up against the ceiling on the note issue. Faced with this problem, the Treasury induced the Bank to falsify its balance sheet further by understating the note issue, a stratagem which became public knowledge in April 1925 and brought down the government.[75] The revelations of balance sheet rigging hardly increased confidence. Nor did many of the proposals to reduce the floating debt, most notably a capital levy. Even bonds with their rate of interest tied to the sterling exchange rate were not a success. Four times during the year the authorities managed to raise the ceiling on Bank of France advances to the government; three times they managed to raise the limit on the note issue. The results appeared in the exchange market, despite periods of official intervention, particularly after May 1925 when the franc broke out of the range of 18 to 19.9 to the dollar and fell to beyond 27 to the dollar in December.

Early 1926 was but a sequel to 1925. The struggles over taxation and economies continued, as did the 'waltz of the portfolios' with a new finance minister every thirty-seven days between October 1925 and July 1926.[76] The franc continued to fall, going beyond 50 to the dollar. The final collapse brought Poincaré to power on 24 July as the head of the third government within a month.

[72] Aliber, 'Speculation in the Foreign Exchanges', p. 211.

[73] *Ibid.*, pp. 212–15; Brown, *International Gold Standard*, vol. I, p. 437.

[74] A. Sauvy, *Histoire économique de la France entre les deux guerres*, vol. I: *de l'armistice a la devaluation de la livre* (Paris, 1955), p. 61.

[75] E. L. Dulles, *The French Franc, 1914–1928: The Facts and their Interpretation* (New York, 1929), p. 240; E. Moreau, *Souvenirs d'un gouverneur de la Banque de France: histoire de la stabilisation du franc (1926–1928)* (Paris, 1954), p. 7.

[76] L. B. Yeager, *International Monetary Relations: Theory, History, and Policy*, 2nd edn (New York, 1976), p. 327.

The Poincaré stabilization programme, devised by a committee of experts (the Sergent Committee) was very simple. There were no changes in taxation beyond a slight increase in the turnover tax and improved methods of collection. More dramatic changes involved the note issue and the floating debt. The management of the floating debt was transformed by the solemn procedure of a constitution amendment. This created a Caisse Autonome d'Amortissement, a recipient of certain assigned tax receipts sufficient not only to service the debt but also to reduce it at a regular rate. The note issue reform gave the Bank of France the power to issue notes over and above the legal limit if backed franc for franc by foreign exchange or gold, which the Bank could buy at a premium above pre-war par. Such a regime could prevent the appreciation of the franc beyond an agreed limit, but, unless supplemented by other resources such as the remnants of the Morgan loan or France's limited gold reserves, it could not prevent further depreciation.

There was no need to worry about the eventuality of depreciation. On 20 July, as Heriot failed to form a lasting government, the franc fell to 49.2 to the dollar. The average for the next ten days was 41.9. Thereafter, with slight fluctuations the rate improved and the authorities faced the problem of choosing a possible target range of rates for stabilization. At this stage, opinions varied considerably, from a return to pre-war par of just over 5 to the dollar to something closer to the existing market rate of 34–36 to the dollar around which the rate fluctuated until September, when it began to appreciate further.[77] When the exchange rate broke out of its August–September range, the question of future policy became more urgent as pressure from industrialists adversely affected by appreciation became less a theoretical possibility and more a day-to-day reality.[78] As a result, at the urging of the Bank of France, aware of the British mistake of 1925, the authorities decided on 20 December to peg the rate at around 25 to the dollar or 122 to the pound.[79] There the rate remained, with the Bank accepting massive inflow of foreign exchange, as a strong underlying balance of payments position was supplemented by the repatriation of fugitive balances and speculation on further appreciation, until *de jure* stabilization in June 1928 at a par of 124.21 francs to the pound or 25.52 to the dollar. This rate certainly undervalued the franc. The question is by how much and here, of course, the answers vary with the base year chosen, the price indices compared and the adjustments made for the effects of the war on the underlying position.[80]

[77] Moreau, *Souvenirs*, pp. 73–4.   [78] *Ibid.*, pp. 162–3, 177.

[79] *Ibid.*, pp. 182–3. On the whole process of stabilization in France see G. C. Schmid, 'The Politics of Currency Stabilisation: The French Franc, 1926', *Journal of European Economic History*, vol. III, no. 2 (Autumn 1974), pp. 359–77.

[80] See, for example, Phelps Brown and Browne, *A Century of Pay*, pp. 229–33; Wolfe, *The French Franc*, p. 58.

The consensus is certainly towards a rather substantial undervaluation, which, with the additional factor of the mechanics of the French monetary system was to make the positions of countries with overvalued currencies more difficult in the ensuing years.

The Belgian experience paralleled the French in many respects. There as well, the war, plus a post-war reconstruction programme based on the presumption that Germany would pay for the costs of the war and reconstruction, left the public finances in some disarray and the economy subject to substantial inflationary pressure. This pressure was easily accommodated by the monetary system, given its extremely liquid condition following the unfortunate method chosen for the redemption of outstanding mark notes in the formerly German-occupied zone in the course of 1918–19.[81] With the exception of the periods of the Ruhr occupation, which affected Belgian economic life more severely than French, and the attempted stabilization of the Belgian franc between the autumn of 1925 and mid-March 1926, the Belgian and French exchange rates move closely together until the Belgian stabilization of October 1926. The reasons for this parallelism have not been fully sorted out. It seems reasonably clear, however, that there were substantial underlying similarities in the experiences of the two economies, closely linked by trade, which were emphasized by the similarities in the growth of their post-war public debts and their money supplies, and that the speculative belief, based on the pre-war Latin Monetary Union, that the two currencies should exchange at par was important.[82] The attempt to stabilize the Belgian franc in the autumn of 1925 represented, amongst other things, a deliberate attempt to break the link with the French franc.[83] Despite extensive exchange market intervention by the authorities, the attempt came to nought in the face of a lack of international banking support, opposition from the domestic financial community and the sharp depreciation of the French franc during the stabilization period.[84] The failure of this attempt made all the parties involved that much more cautious in October 1926, when a second stabilization attempt occurred. This time the target rate was 175 instead of 107 to the pound. Both Norman and Strong encouraged the Belgians to adopt this

---

[81] The problem here lay less with the act of redemption itself (although it could have been financed with a long-term bond issue) than with the long period during which redemption was possible and the exchange rate chosen – pre-war par or double the market rate of the period. Both of these factors encouraged the smuggling of mark notes into Belgium and over-expanded the base for the note issue. See H. L. Shepherd, *The Monetary Experience of Belgium, 1914–1936* (Princeton, 1936), chs. 3 and 4; H. van der Wee and K. Tavernier, *La Banque Nationale de Belgique et l'histoire monetaire entre les deux guerres mondiales* (Brussels, 1975), pp. 37–48.

[82] Shepherd, *Monetary Experience of Belgium*, pp. 96–100; Aliber, 'Speculation in the Foreign Exchanges', pp. 221–7.

[83] Van der Wee and Tavernier, *Banque Nationale*, pp. 111–12.

[84] *Ibid.*, ch. 3; Meyer, *Bankers' Diplomacy*, pp. 20–4.

undervalued rate to avoid future difficulties,[85] even though this rate aggravated Britain's problems at $4.86.[86] The procedure for dealing with the floating debt by enforced conversions into securities of the Belgian National Railway Company suggested caution, as did the specific provisions for the retirement of the debt through a sinking fund administration endowed with the proceeds of assigned taxes. The stabilization programme, backed by an international loan and central bank credits, was a success.

Italy's experience had both parallels with and sharp differences from that of France and Belgium. As in France and Belgium, the war and early post-war periods were characterized by inflationary public finance and eventual exchange depreciation. Similarly, the extent of the depreciation was such that a return to pre-war par for the lira was impossible. Also, as in Belgium and France, post-war Italy experienced political and social disorder, but of a more sinister sort, which culminated in the March on Rome in October 1922. Even prior to that date, financial reconstruction had started: the Fascists simply accelerated the process.[87] The budget deficit fell by 50 per cent in 1921–2, and, thereafter, the position improved until the budget was in surplus in 1924–5. The exchange rate and the price level remained roughly stable from mid-1921 to late 1924. After September 1924, however, wholesale prices began to rise (by 11 per cent in the last quarter of the year) and the lira came under pressure by the end of the year and depreciated sharply in the three months after May 1925 following the failure of official exchange support.[88] In August 1925 the authorities imposed informal exchange controls and in September they began to support the exchange with owned and, later, borrowed reserves, pegging it at 25 to the dollar until April 1926, when the sharp fall in the French franc and, perhaps, the backwash of the British general strike, made the peg untenable.[89] The exchange rate depreciated by almost 25 per cent in the next few months. Thereafter, the official response was a vigorous policy of deflation that raised the exchange rate from 30.5 to the dollar in August 1926 to an eventual stabilization level of 19 to the dollar in December 1927, at the cost of substantial unemployment. The rate chosen for stabilization was the product of Mussolini's desire for political prestige and advantage, despite its anticipated adverse economic consequences. The central banks assisting the stabilization programme with credits were unhappy with the rate chosen but they

[85] Sayers, *Bank of England*, vol. 1, p. 192; Meyer, *Bankers' Diplomacy*, p. 37.

[86] Sayers, 'The Return to Gold', pp. 93–5; Meyer, *Bankers' Diplomacy*, pp. 33–7.

[87] Meyer, *Bankers' Diplomacy*, p. 43.

[88] Cohen, 'The 1927 Revaluation of the Lira', p. 644.

[89] *Ibid.*, p. 645; Meyer, *Bankers' Diplomacy*, p. 44; Brown, *International Gold Standard*, vol. 1, pp. 428–9.

accepted the Italian decision, given the adequacy of the supporting policy of deflation.[90]

It remains for us to consider a case of hyperinflation, the best documented being Germany's.[91] Germany's post-war currency problems impinged significantly on events and policies in other countries. Insofar as they were related to reparations possibilities, they obviously played a role in the already-discussed French and Belgian situations. Also, given the destabilizing effects of mark fluctuations and their associated speculative capital flows on other European currencies, the stabilization of the mark becomes a necessary, if not a sufficient, condition for stability elsewhere in the eyes of central bankers such as Norman and Strong.[92] Moreover, the spectre of the German hyperinflation, not to mention inflations elsewhere, had a profound effect on the way in which economists, politicians and the general public, both in Germany and elsewhere, thought about and reacted to monetary affairs and exerted an important influence on later occasions.[93]

At the end of the hostilities in 1918, although she had suffered a defeat, Germany's financial position did not seem that much worse than that of many of the better-off Allies. The wartime expansion in Germany's money supply, the rise in prices and the end of war size (if not the maturity structure) in her national debt were broadly similar to those of the principal European Allies.[94] Moreover, unlike Britain and France, Germany ended the war without any long-term overseas debts.[95] However, the post-war German situation was complicated by not only social and political difficulties, which bore a family resemblance to those in France and Italy,[96] but also by the terms of the peace treaty. For the treaty of Versailles with its territorial changes and transfers of assets altered Germany's underlying international economic position for the worse, especially in the short run, while the requirement that she pay reparations in cash and kind added new short- and long-run burdens. The reparations payments, although far from the sole cause of Germany's post-war

[90] Cohen, 'The 1927 Revaluation of the Lira', pp. 651–4; Meyer, *Bankers' Diplomacy*, pp. 52–5; Sayers, *Bank of England*, vol. I, p. 194. For an argument similar to Cohen's see R. Sarti, 'Mussolini and the Italian Industrial Leadership in the Battle of the Lira, 1925–1927', *Past and Present*, no. 47 (May 1970), pp. 97–112.

[91] See, in particular, Bresciani-Turroni, *Economics of Inflation*; F. D. Graham, *Exchange, Prices and Production in Hyperinflation: Germany, 1920–1923* (Princeton, 1930); K. Laursen and J. Pedersen, *The German Inflation, 1918–1923* (Amsterdam, 1964).

[92] Clay, *Lord Norman*, ch. 5(iii); Sayers, *Bank of England*, vol. I, pp. 174–83; Chandler, *Benjamin Strong*, pp. 273–7, 294, 295.

[93] See, for example, Winch, *Economics and Policy*, p. 89; S. Howson and D. Winch, *The Economic Advisory Council, 1930–1939: A Study of Economic Advice During Depression and Recovery* (Cambridge, 1977), pp. 91–2, 95.

[94] Graham, *Exchange, Prices and Production*, pp. 5–6.

[95] *Ibid.*, p. 7.   [96] Maier, *Recasting Bourgeois Europe*.

currency difficulties, proved extremely important in the events that followed. Not only did they add yet another complication to the finances of the Reich but they also worsened Germany's international prospects. As an uncertain sum, in that the Reparations Commission did not, in conjunction with the Allies, fix a total until May 1921, reparations effectively destroyed Germany's international credit immediately after the war. Thus, more so than the European Allies, Germany had to make the transition to peace in her external accounts without external credits. This meant that exchange depreciation was likely to be greater than it otherwise would have been. Even when the relevant sums and payments schedules were imposed in 1921, further problems faced Germany. For she had to make large foreign payments at a time when her balance of payments position, although improving, could not stand the strain without further depreciation in the short term. As this occurred, the current account deficit widened and the problems of the fisc, never that robust, became more severe. Both of these fed back on the exchange rate, which also affected the domestic price level and resulted in further problems for public finance, further balance of payments difficulties, and so on. However, Germany was able to make few such payments in foreign currency before difficulties brought further negotiations, reductions in payments, eventual default and the occupation of the Ruhr. This ended almost all reparation payments in cash or kind and pushed Germany firmly over the precipice into hyperinflation.

None of the above is meant to imply that the outcome might not have been different. Certainly a more spartan budgetary policy, greater economic literacy amongst those in authority (and more generally) as to the underlying mechanisms at work, less willingness to accept inflation as, perhaps, a lesser evil than reparations payments, especially if the former would prove that the latter were impossible, and more time and assistance to make the adjustments necessary to the post-war world and the peace treaties all might have made some difference to the final outcome with its stabilization on the basis of one unit of the new currency being equal to one trillion units of the old. Be that as it may, Germany's hyperinflationary experience added to the alterations in her underlying economic position resulting from the war. Inflation had destroyed the long-term capital market, wiped out most of the capital and loss reserves of the banking system and denuded firms of working capital. These changes had significant effects on the future stability of the banking system, which could no longer float off industrial loans as long-term issues and yet faced almost insatiable demands for credit from German business. The results were high domestic interest rates and strong incentives for overseas borrowing by German banks and their customers. In addition, the inflation and the other changes wrought by the war and the terms of the peace make it almost impossible to assess the appropriateness of Germany's exchange rate of 4.2 to the dollar at stabilization. The available evidence adds to the difficulty. The rapid rise in money wage rates, unit wage costs and the behaviour of export prices all suggest an element of undervaluation.[97] However, the underlying balance of payments position, sustained as it was by substantial unemployment and heavy foreign borrowing, points the other way. But then in Germany more than elsewhere other things had not remained equal.

If one looks back at the process of international monetary reconstruction after 1918, the strongest impression that remains is, despite international consultations, the relatively isolated, case-by-case nature of decision making, even in the later stages. The pattern of exchange rates that emerged was hardly consistent in the sense of allowing the constituent parts of the world economy to experience normal rates of growth at reasonably high levels of employment without balance of payments difficulties. Over- and undervaluations were common, and frequently, if often inadequately, recognized, but there was no common perception or agreement as to how the adjustments, the mixture of inflation and deflation, necessary to remove the resulting imbalances would occur. Moreover, many of the legacies of the reconstruction period itself might sharply constrain the possible patterns of adjustment to the new regime. Differential pre-stabilization price experiences left behind possible divergences between actual and desired private portfolios which might affect the balance of payments adjustment process in the post-stabilization period. In some cases, institutional arrangements, often the accompaniment of stabilization programmes, might also affect adjustment patterns. Patterns of holdings of international reserves at the time of stabilization might also not persist, especially if these were the product of external circumstances such as League of Nations or central bank stabilization schemes, rather than experience and evolving national preferences. If the finally desired patterns of reserve asset holdings differed markedly from those existing at the time of stabilization, the resulting attempts at shifting might affect both the stability of the system as a whole and the adjustment problems of particular countries within it. Finally, the operation of the reconstructed gold standard system and the possible paths of adjustment for individual countries in it were constrained by changes in attitudes on the part of the system's managers. The goals of national monetary management were changing, partly as a result of changing ideas. However much policymakers in the 1920s may have disliked the notion of monetary management, they were taking a much

[97] Phelps Brown and Browne, *A Century of Pay*, pp. 221–34; A. Maddison, 'Growth and Fluctuations in the World Economy, 1870–1960', *Banca Nazionale del Lavoro Quarterly Review*, no. 61 (June 1962), Table 29.

wider range of considerations into account in the course of policy making than their pre-war predecessors.[98] For example, they were much more likely to take internal domestic considerations such as unemployment and, in the case of stabilizations such as the French, the burden of the national debt into account. Also, the period of reconstruction had left behind resentments over past slights and hopes of regaining lost or gaining potential national power and prestige lying very close to the surface, especially in the case of France.[99] Thus, although central bankers might talk of cooperation, and even cooperate on occasion, the possibilities of conflict between national and systemic needs was greater than before 1914 – this at a time when the process of reconstruction had produced systemic problems that were more complex and demanding than those of an earlier age.

III.   *The operation of the reconstructed system*

The first thing that strikes the observer is how little the reconstructed system successfully removed the disparities that were implicit in the initial pattern of costs, prices and exchange rates before a major part of the system collapsed in 1931. An indication of what took place appears in Table 26 and Figure 7. From the figures available in that table and additional material available for France,[100] it is clear that the trend in unit wage costs was downwards in Britain, Sweden, and the United States as money wages remained broadly unchanged or rose slightly in the face of rising productivity, whilst the trend for France and Germany was upwards as money wage increases outstripped productivity gains until the slump. In France, however, much of the rise was offset by the pre-stabilization fall in the exchange rate which left unit wage costs in foreign currency during the period to 1931 at or below the level of 1924. In fact, Britain's relative cost position over the period to 1931 tended to deteriorate in comparison with all her major competitors bar Germany (and towards the end of the period France), while the German position grew particularly difficult after 1928. Looking at export prices, which may be less sensitive indicators of competitiveness because exporters, in the face of higher domestic costs, rather than exceed world prices, may reduce quantities or profit margins so that pressures on prices may not be caught in the statistics, one finds Britain's position somewhat more hopeful. It did not change much in the aggregate, although there were variations amongst individual competitors over the years. The French advantage

[98] See, for example, Clarke, *Central Bank Cooperation*, pp. 27–33; Sayers, *Bank of England*, vol. I, pp. 130–2, 331–5.
[99] Sayers, *Bank of England*, vol. I, pp. 184–8; Moreau, *Souvenirs*, pp. 24, 49, 488–9, 505–7.
[100] Phelps Brown and Browne, *A Century of Pay*, pp. 229–33.

Table 26. *Indices of prices and costs for selected European countries and the United States, 1925–32 (1925 = 100)*

	1925	1926	1927	1928	1929	1930	1931	1932
A. Unit wage costs in industry (in national currency)								
Germany	100	102	101	106	112	113	108	91
Sweden	100	90	87	88	80	72	70	69
United Kingdom	100	100	97	97	95	92	90	89
United States	100	98	96	93	90	88	79	72
B. Export unit values (in current dollars)								
Belgium	100	90	81	84	87	83	72	59
France	100	82	83	77	76	72	60	51
Germany	100	100	101	101	99	93	81	71
Italy	100	108	114	107	99	83	68	55
Sweden	100	103	95	94	92	86	71	49
The Netherlands	100	92	89	89	88	80	65	51
United Kingdom	100	95	90	89	87	83	69	50
United States	100	92	86	88	87	78	60	51

Sources: E. H. Phelps Brown and M. H. Browne, *A Century of Pay: The Course of Pay and Production in France, Germany, Sweden, the United Kingdom and the United States of America 1860–1960* (London, 1968), Appendix III; A. Maddison, 'Growth and Fluctuations in the World Economy, 1870–1960', *Banca Nazionale del Lavoro Quarterly Review*, no. 61 (June 1962), Table 29.

remains clear throughout the period, as does the Belgian up to 1929, while Germany's deteriorating position is also apparent. The story told by the wholesale price statistics in Figure 7 is similar, if sometimes more complex on occasion. Overall, there seem to have been some elements of adjustment, most notably in Sweden, Belgium and Italy, but it was relatively slight as compared with the initial disparities.

The question then arises as to why adjustment was so limited. If one were to believe the orthodox statements of the period concerning the working of the gold standard (as well as modern economic theory), countries whose price and cost structures were high in relation to the exchange rates chosen should have experienced deflationary pressures, both directly in traded goods markets and indirectly through the effects of weakened trade, invisible and probably capital account positions on balances of payments, exchange rates, central bank reserves, and domestic credit policies. In countries with relatively low cost and price structures the reverse would be true. To some extent, the differential experiences of the countries concerned are in accord with these expectations. For example, despite differences in coverage and definition which might blur comparisons, the unemployment statistics of the period suggest differential pressures, as do the statistics for exchange rates and

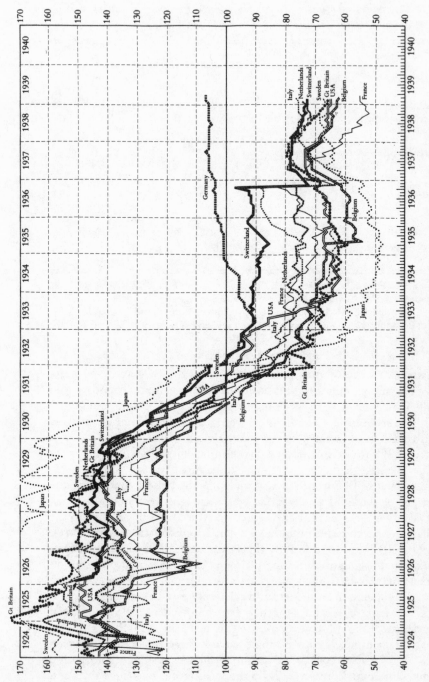

Fig. 7. Indices of wholesale prices for industrialized countries, 1924–38 (1913–14 = 100)

Source: Bank for International Settlements (ed.), *Annual Report for 1938–9* (Basle, May 1939), p. 52.

interest differentials.[101] However, these statistics reflect the interaction of the pattern of parities and official polices after stabilization. Therefore let us turn to policy and its contribution to adjustment.

The post-1918 period saw policymakers and economists much more conscious of balance of payments policies. Rather than simply accept or describe the working out of 'automatic' forces, as set out in, say, the Cunliffe Report,[102] they began to consider codes of good conduct that would contribute to systemic stability. In other words, they began to formulate appropriate 'rules of the game', a process that their successors have also experienced on several occasions since the 1920s.[103] In the existing literature there seem to be three possible interpretations of the rules applicable to the inter-war gold standard. The first, associated with Ragnar Nurkse, might be called the active formulation, in that to stay within the rules central bankers must take active steps to reinforce the effects of changes in a country's international reserves on the credit base. Thus, for example, a decline in international reserves should lead the authorities to undertake open-market operations to reduce the credit base further.[104] The second interpretation might be called the passive formulation. Here the authorities follow the rules of the game if they avoid deliberately offsetting the effects of reserve losses on the credit base.[105] The third approach, suggested by Michaely, has the authorities following the rules if the money supply falls and interest rates rise in the reserve-losing country and vice versa in the reserve-gaining country.[106] All of these formulations have the disadvantage of being set in a rather static context in the sense that in a growing economy with, say, stable prices one would expect the money supply, appropriately defined, to be rising over the medium term roughly in line with the growth of output. Thus a concentration on changes from given levels, as indicators of adherence to a set of rules, may be misleading.

[101] Mitchell, *European Historical Statistics*, Table C2; O. Morgenstern, *International Financial Transactions and Business Cycles* (Princeton, 1959), especially chs. 4 and 5.

[102] I.e., UK Committee on Currency and Foreign Exchanges after the War, *First Interim Report*, Cd 9182 (London, 1918).

[103] See A. I. Bloomfield, 'Rules of the Game of International Adjustment', in C. R. Whittlesey and J. S. G. Wilson (eds.), *Essays in Money and Banking in Honour of R. S. Sayers* (Oxford, 1968). Bloomfield (p. 27) attributes the phrase to J. M. Keynes in the early 1920s. However, there is no published reference by him to the term before his 'private evidence' to the Macmillan Committee on 20 February 1930 (D. E. Moggridge (ed.), *The Collected Writings of John Maynard Keynes*, vol. xx: *Activities 1929–1931: Rethinking Employment and Unemployment Policies* (London and New York, 1981), p. 42. There Keynes credits Sir Robert Kindersley with originating the term. Kindersley had given evidence to the Committee on 6 February 1930. See UK Committee on Finance and Industry, *Minutes of Evidence* (London, 1931), Q.1595. See also Keynes' *A Treatise on Money* (London, 1930), vol. II, p. 306, and UK Committee on Finance and Industry, *Report* (London, 1931), Cmd 3897, paras. 46–7 (drafted by Keynes).

[104] League of Nations, *International Currency Experience: Lessons of the Inter-War Period* (Princeton, 1944), pp. 6–7.   [105] Bloomfield, 'Rules of the Game', p. 28.

[106] M. Michaely, *Balance-of-Payments Adjustment Policies* (New York, 1968), p. 18.

The most comprehensive study of inter-war experience is Nurkse's own examination of the experience of 26 countries between 1922 and 1938.[107] Using his own active formulation of the rules of the game in examining the 382 available annual observations, he found that 60 per cent of the observations ran contrary to the rules. (If one stuck to the period 1925–31 the number of contrary observations would be even higher. Interestingly enough, though, the proportion of contrary observations fell as the gold standard system became widespread.) Nurkse qualified the implications of his findings by allowing that reaction lags, short-term neutralization resulting from the responses of domestic money market institutions, capital mobility in response to interest rate differentials and destabilizing capital movements might explain the contrariness of the results. Nevertheless, he still concluded that the deliberate neutralization of reserve movements was more often than not the case during the inter-war period.

An examination of the details of particular cases suggests that the story was perhaps more complex than Nurkse's mechanical exercise with its caveats allows. Thus while he suggested that the United Kingdom followed 'a systematic policy of neutralisation',[108] a more detailed examination of the case suggests that the authorities were at least pushing in the direction of underlying adjustment, despite shortages of appropriate assets for open-market operations.[109] If one looks at quarterly averages of weekly observations for the 26 quarters of Britain's inter-war gold standard experience, one finds the Bank gaining reserves (gold plus foreign exchange) in eighteen quarters and losing them in eight. In periods of reserve gain, the Bank did on average offset most of the inflow. In periods of reserve loss, the Bank allowed much less offsetting and it even reinforced reserve losses when they occurred in the first quarter of the year, normally a time of seasonal strength for sterling. On average, periods of reserve loss saw a decline in the Bank's domestic assets and rising interest rates. Periods of reserve gains saw falls in interest rates, although the Bank was, on average, less willing to let rates fall away in periods of reserve gain than it was to raise them when losing reserves.[110] The evidence suggests a system to the Bank's operations, but it was a system with a difference. Given the overvaluation of sterling in 1925 and the consequential general weakness of sterling on the exchanges throughout the period, it was only sensible for the Bank to maintain a restrictive stance and not let reserve gains relax policy substantially. Such a policy reduced the stock of high-powered money (or potential reserve assets for the banking system) by 2 per cent between 1925 and 1929, and

---

[107] League of Nations, *Currency Experience*, pp. 68–73.   [108] *Ibid.*, p. 75.
[109] Moggridge, *British Monetary Policy*, pp. 219–20, 257; Sayers, *Bank of England*, vol. I, pp. 306–8.
[110] Moggridge, *British Monetary Policy*, pp. 146–53.

another 1 per cent in 1930–1.[111] Whether the Bank's policy was sufficiently restrictive is another matter, for despite the fall in high-powered money the growth of the money stock slightly exceeded the growth of domestic output between 1925 and 1929, as the banks and the public adjusted their portfolio behaviour to conditions where accommodation was both expensive and difficult to obtain.[112] Nevertheless, the overall stance of policy was probably more appropriate for adjustment than Nurkse suggested. Perhaps it would have even proved enough but for developments elsewhere.

The French case is even more complex. Nurkse refers to it as a striking, but in many respects peculiar, example of neutralization. From the *de facto* stabilization of 1926 to the end of the gold standard as the only significant international system in 1931, the trend in France's stock of international reserve assets was strongly upwards as they more than quadrupled. Over the same period, the Bank's note issue and private deposits also rose, by 62 and 370 per cent respectively, but their combined total less than doubled. The explanation for these differences in behaviour lies in changes in other items in the Bank's balance sheet. Most important was the decline in the Bank's advances to the government from 36 billion francs to zero as a result of revaluation profits, budget surpluses and sales of securities. In addition, the cash management policies of the savings banks and the debt management policies of the Treasury and other agencies effectively immobilized much of the rise in the Bank's liabilities in terms of the private sector.[113] The result was the same as if the Bank had undertaken substantial open market operations to neutralize the reserve inflows, but the causes of these changes lay beyond the Bank's control. Moreover, the Bank could do little to offset this 'automatic' neutralization given the limitations of its statutes.[114] However, this institutional neutralization in the context of a rising demand for money in France after the end of the period of post-war inflation, plus the existence of substantial overseas balances in private French hands, resulted in still further rises in the reserves as French banks and individuals realized their foreign assets to finance domestic transactions.[115] Thus the institutional underpinning of the gold standard in France produced problems for other members of the international monetary system: to an undervalued exchange rate, large private overseas balances and rising demand for money balances after an inflation was added a peculiarly inelastic financial system. The result was that adjustment in France was

---

[111] Howson, *Domestic Monetary Management*, Appendix 1, Table 1.
[112] *Ibid.*, pp. 43–7, Appendix 1, Tables 1 and 5.
[113] T. Balogh, 'The Import of Gold into France: An Analysis of the Technical Position', *Economic Journal*, vol. XL, no. 159 (September 1930), pp. 449–51.
[114] *Ibid.*, pp. 456–7; R. G. Hawtrey, *The Art of Central Banking* (London, 1932), pp. 30–2.
[115] Balogh, 'The Import of Gold', pp. 449–50.

slower than it otherwise would have been and that France became a 'reserve sink' into which gold flowed with little prospect of its returning to the system, albeit a somewhat cooperative one as far as Britain was concerned, with important effects on the operation of the standard.[116]

The German case differed yet again, although she too often violated Nurkse's rules. After stabilization, the German authorities faced a dilemma. Hyperinflation had left the economy short of working capital, had distorted the allocation of fixed capital and had deranged traditional patterns of holding cash. The banking system and domestic capital markets were in some disarray. These factors tended to keep German interest rates above those abroad and to make access to foreign capital attractive to German residents. Foreign borrowing also seemed desirable to finance reparations payments while the economy returned to normal and adjusted to the post-war world. However, there was the risk that over time the servicing of heavy foreign borrowing might impede the transfer of reparations. In this situation, though, the Reichsbank's ability to shape the course of events was limited, for it lacked access to many of the orthodox instruments of monetary policy.[117] The Bank's 1924 statutes gave it very restricted possibilities for open-market operations and the 1926 revisions to the statutes only eased the position in a limited way. Also, the Bank's statutes left it basically passive in the commercial bill market and did not give it full control over the placement of government deposits, another possible policy instrument. True, the Reichsbank's ownership of the Gold Discount Bank offered some escape from the constraints of its own statutes, but the possibilities for control were limited, especially in a system where banks' reserve ratios were very flexible! Shorn of many of the means of making its discount rate effective in the market, the Bank of necessity, more often than not, had to follow market conditions rather than lead, although on occasion it could move actively if conditions played into its hands. Thus, if the money market and the banks affected by gold outflows sought to replenish their reserves by bringing in the appropriate securities for discount, the Bank could force the pace towards higher interest rates and tighter conditions. However, this rediscounting would lead to offsetting in Nurkse's scheme. On other occasions the Bank might conduct open-market operations with foreign exchange, which although useful for control purposes also would not lead to Nurkse's desired signals, so as to limit the expansion of the note issue. But these opportunities for control were

---

[116] Sayers, *Bank of England*, vol. I, p. 220; Moggridge, *British Monetary Policy*, pp. 239–42; Clarke, *Central Bank Cooperation*, pp. 134–8, 164–8.

[117] The most useful discussion in English of the German banking system in this period is M. B. Northrop, *The Control Policies of the Reichsbank, 1924–1933* (New York, 1938). Also useful are the discussions in Brown, *International Gold Standard*, vol. I, especially ch. 16 and M. Palyi, *The Twilight of Gold, 1914–1936: Myths and Realities* (Chicago, 1972), especially chs. 5 and 6 *passim*.

limited, as were those for controlling capital outflows or domestic developments through credit rationing, or for affecting institutional behaviour through moral suasion, especially as the economy became more open. Given their basic decision to depend on foreign capital, as evidenced by Germany's markedly higher discount rate for all but three months of the period, the monetary authorities found themselves in the position of those in a small open economy, accepting such foreign capital as current interest rate configurations would bring them and with little independent control of the domestic economy. This decision certainly contributed to the deterioration of Germany's competitive position after 1925 and increased potential instability when overseas conditions became less favourable.

In the 1920s, the United States was in such a strong position that the Federal Reserve System could ignore gold movements in determining its policy. Throughout the decade, the authorities' only concern with respect to the reserve ratio centred on its reduction by means other than monetary expansion. Throughout the period of the gold standard as a general international system, there was no relationship between gold movements and the stock of high-powered money as the monetary authorities pursued largely domestic ends. Foreign considerations were rarely, if ever, important in themselves in the determination of policy, except when a coincidence of foreign and domestic needs provided an additional justification for the pursuit of policies already decided on domestic grounds.[118] Moreover, the policy pursued was relatively restrictive in terms of the rate of growth of the money supply, especially during 1928–9.[119] American sterilization aided adjustment in periods of reserve loss, but the generally conservative stance of policy in general shifted the burden of balance of payments adjustment firmly overseas.[120] However, it is far from clear whether the stability of the American economy, and indirectly of the gold standard system as a whole would have been enhanced by a more expansive stance on the part of the Federal Reserve.

[118] For discussions of American policy in the 1920s see, in particular, Friedman and Schwartz, *Monetary History*, ch. 6; Wicker, *Federal Reserve Monetary Policy*, chs. 4–10; L. V. Chandler, *American Monetary Policy 1928–1941* (New York, 1971), part 1. Most of the discussion as to the role of international considerations in the formulation of American monetary policy centre on the easing of policy in 1927 with Friedman and Schwartz (*Monetary History*, p. 269), as usual taking a polar position. Chandler (*Benjamin Strong*, p. 440) takes a somewhat more internationalist line, but is taken to task by Wicker (*Federal Reserve Monetary Policy*, pp. 110–16) for underestimating the strength of international considerations. More recently, Clarke (*Central Bank Co-operation*, pp. 124–7) and Sayers (*Bank of England*, vol. 1, pp. 340–1) return towards the Chandler position. Given the available evidence, including recollections, it is not clear that the appropriate balance to the argument will ever be found, but one suspects that the consensus will fall towards the Chandler–Clarke–Sayers middle ground.

[119] Friedman and Schwartz, *Monetary History*, pp. 290, 298.

[120] In the sense that overseas prices and monetary developments would have to broadly conform to American if the fixed rate regime was to survive.

The variations in national willingness or ability to follow the rules of the game in Nurkse's sense, or indeed in the other senses discussed above should now be apparent. It should also be clear, however, that a short-term, mechanical application of the rules was probably inappropriate, given the longer-term stances of policy 'necessary' for successful adjustment to the post-war pattern of exchange rates. Thus in Britain, where adjustment to gold at $4.86 required relative deflation over a fairly considerable period, the sterilization of reserve inflows was probably appropriate, whilst in the American case the Federal Reserve's offsetting of reserve losses again met the 'needs' of the system. True, both countries might have been more vigorous in their pursuit of policies appropriate for international adjustment, but this would not have meant that they would have been more likely to follow the rules. In the German case, it is not clear that a Reichsbank willing and able to follow the rules would necessarily have improved matters, given the underlying policy dilemma. As for France, whose undervaluation caused considerable problems for others, particularly the British, despite official attempts to reduce the pull of the franc over the exchanges, a more expansive policy would have made overall adjustment easier.[121] Instead the policies actually followed in the second half of the 1920s made more difficult the adjustment to the pattern of exchange rates that had emerged from a series of national decisions.

The pattern of exchange rates and subsequent national policies almost inevitably resulted in policy problems for individual members of the system. These were perhaps most pronounced in Britain, where the authorities' gold standard expectations of 1924–5 were almost uniformly disappointed. Instead of rising, American prices fell slowly after 1925. At the same time money wages proved inflexible downwards, other countries undervalued their exchange rates, and strong domestic political constraints emerged on the overt use of policy instruments, particularly Bank rate, in a deflationary direction.[122] As a result the authorities, particularly the Bank of England, found themselves driven to the use of a succession of temporizing palliatives to meet the almost continuous difficulties facing sterling and to make gold at $4.86 to some extent tolerable. These palliatives had no impact on the fundamental disequilibrium at the heart of sterling's problems, but they allowed the authorities to live from hand to mouth, hoping for something better to run up while maintaining a modicum of deflationary pressure on the economy.[123] Instead of the non-interventionist, pre-1914 simplicity expected in 1924–5, the authorities found themselves using moral suasion to control

---

[121] For an indication of French attempts see Brown, *International Gold Standard*, vol. II, pp. 992–4.
[122] For a discussion of the constraints see Moggridge, *British Monetary Policy*, ch. 7; Sayers, *Bank of England*, vol. I, ch. 9.   [123] Moggridge, *British Monetary Policy*, pp. 236–8.

new overseas issues of securities, to squeeze the last drop of international pull over short-term capital flows out of a given level of Bank Rate and to impede gold exports, whilst actively intervening in the gold and foreign exchange markets.[124] They depended on central bank cooperation with the Americans, French and Germans to ease the position if possible at times of acute stress and to make changes in national policy relatively less painful for Britain.[125] As well, however, they attempted through cooperation and consultation to develop a 'workable' international system. However, international cooperation and assistance became more reluctant as the period progressed and as the intractability of Britain's problems became even clearer, thus forcing the authorities towards a policy of self-help.[126] By then it was probably too late to save sterling.

But Britain was not the only country facing dilemmas as to the best balance between domestic and international considerations. Although in 1924 and 1927 domestic considerations allowed an easing of American monetary policy with beneficial results for Europe and most particularly for Britain,[127] in 1928–9 matters were much less easy to resolve. The dispute within the Federal Reserve System over the best way to contain the stock market boom is well known.[128] To some extent, it reflected a disagreement over the relative importance of the System's domestic and international responsibilities, although one cannot push this too far because the New York Reserve Bank saw them as both pointing in the same direction as regards policy.[129] The Federal Reserve Board in Washington's view of matters was more complex, but reflected the priority it gave to domestic considerations. The soaring stock market prices and high money market rates that emerged from the policy of drift had major repercussions overseas. American long-term overseas lending declined dramatically after mid-1928, whilst foreign funds flowed towards New York.[130] Some countries were able to offset the decline in long-term lending and shifts in balances through short-term lending and shifts in balances through short-term borrowing, either in New York or elsewhere, but only at the cost of some domestic credit stringency which

---

[124] *Ibid.*, chs. 8 and 9; Sayers, *Bank of England*, vol. I, chs. 9 and 15A.
[125] Clarke, *Central Bank Cooperation*, pp. 119–20, 130–3, 161–4, 174–6.
[126] *Ibid.*, p. 176; Sayers, *Bank of England*, vol. I, p. 233, vol. II, pp. 389–91; Moggridge, *British Monetary Policy*, pp. 192–3, 195; Howson, *Domestic Monetary Management*, pp. 69–71; Howson and Winch, *Economic Advisory Council*, pp. 82ff.
[127] Clarke, *Central Bank Cooperation*, pp. 75–8, 85–8; Wicker, *Federal Reserve Monetary Policy*, ch. 6; above, fn. 118.
[128] For the American view of 1928–9 see Clarke, *Central Bank Cooperation*, pp. 147–64; Wicker, *Federal Reserve Monetary Policy*, chs. 9 and 10; Friedman and Schwartz, *Monetary History*, pp. 254–66; Chandler, *American Monetary Policy*, chs. 3 and 4. For a British view, see Clay, *Lord Norman*, pp. 238–55; Sayers, *Bank of England*, vol. I, pp. 222–30.
[129] See, for example, Clarke, *Central Bank Cooperation*, pp. 152–5.
[130] See Kindleberger, *The World in Depression*, pp. 70–6.

produced further upward pressures on international interest rates. With
the added complications of declining raw material prices, continued rises
in French gold reserves, partially for balance of payments reasons and
partially for purposes of portfolio diversification, and flows of hot
money surrounding the Young Plan for reparations negotiations, the
position remained deadlocked as the international economy slid into the
recession that shattered the gold standard system. Whilst American
handling of the dilemma of 1928–9 did not by itself push the British and
German economies into recession, for other forces were also at work, it
hardly made matters easier by reinforcing these forces.[131]

As a result of the constraints imposed on it by national policy preferences and institutions, the adjustment mechanism underlying the inter-
war gold standard was more or less jammed for much of the period under
consideration. This is not to say that tendencies towards adjustment did
not exist: rather it is to suggest that such tendencies were much less
powerful and pervasive than one might expect. The jamming of the
mechanism naturally affected flows of reserve assets and the answers one
might give to the question of the adequacy of international reserves
during the period.

The international monetary system of the 1920s had three main
reserve assets – gold, sterling and dollars.[132] The pre-1914 period had
known the use of reserve currencies, largely sterling, francs and marks,
and such holdings had been both widespread and a significant proportion
of total owned international liquidity.[133] However, reserve currencies
were a relatively unanalysed phenomenon – hence the significance of
Keynes' *Indian Currency and Finance*.[134] The inter-war period saw the
spread of the reserve currency system to Western Europe. In addition to
the standard economic reasons why countries might desire to hold some
of their international reserves in the form of balances in a gold standard
centre, this spread of the gold exchange standard had other causes.[135] As

[131] On the British recession see Howson, *Domestic Monetary Management*, pp. 64–6. On the German
recession, there has been a recent controversy in the literature which was, to some extent at least,
unnecessary given earlier discussions. See P. Temin, 'The Beginning of the Depression in
Germany', *Economic History Review*, 2nd series, vol. XXIV, part 2 (May 1971); M. E. Falkus, 'The
German Business Cycle in the 1920s', *Economic History Review*, 2nd series, vol. XXVIII, part 3
(August 1975); 'The German Business Cycle in the 1920s: T. Balderston, A Comment; P.
Temin, A Comment and Reply; M. E. Falkus, A Reply', *Economic History Review*, 2nd series,
vol. XXX, part 1 (February 1977) and the sources cited therein.

[132] There were also some holdings of francs.

[133] See P. H. Lindert, 'Key Currencies and Gold 1900–1913', *Princeton Studies in International
Finance*, no. 24 (August 1969), chs. 1 and 2.   [134] London, 1913.

[135] For modern surveys of the standard theory of the demand for reserves see J. Williamson,
'International Liquidity: A Survey', *Economic Journal*, vol. LXXXIII, no. 331 (September 1973),
pp. 688–97; H. G. Grubel, *The International Monetary System*, 3rd edn (Harmondsworth,
Middx., 1977), chs. 2 and 3. For an earlier exposition see League of Nations, *Currency Experience*,
especially pp. 9–16.

a response to fears that the combination of a falling gold output due to higher post-war prices and costs and a general post-war return to gold might lead to a deflationary scramble for the available reserve assets, the Genoa conference, largely in response to a British initiative, emphasized the potential of the gold exchange standard as a gold economizing device and as a possible means of stabilizing the purchasing power of gold – i.e., the world price level.[136] (British advocacy of such a set of arrangements was not completely disinterested or purely internationalist, for the gold exchange standard with sterling as a widely held reserve asset would help re-establish London as a centre of the European and international financial system and protect the position of sterling by increasing the demand for it, especially after the return to gold.[137]) The gold exchange standard, largely as a result of British influence, was an important facet of the League of Nations' financial reconstruction schemes for Austria, Hungary, Greece, Bulgaria and Estonia, where the currency authorities were empowered to hold all their reserves in gold-convertible currencies. The Italians took similar powers, whilst a number of other central bank laws went part way with some gold required within a reserve of gold and foreign exchange – e.g., Germany, Albania, Belgium and Poland.

In the late 1920s the gold exchange standard became somewhat less popular. This was partially the result of a shift in the balance of international financial power, especially towards France, whose authorities opposed the standard British-influenced League of Nations reconstruction schemes and were an important factor in the Polish and Romanian stabilizations.[138] It was also partially a result of the belief that the gold exchange standard was a second-class system owing to its British and League origins and the company the adoption of the regime forced one to keep. Sir Otto Niemeyer, an advocate of the system, made the point with characteristic bluntness in 1930:[139]

I feel that the prospects are rather dubious. It seems to me that the gold exchange standard has rather fallen from the high estate which it had in Genoa . . . Further, many eminent bankers have referred to the gold exchange standard as a transitory measure which had its uses at certain times, but which could hardly be regarded as a permanent state of blessedness . . . It has come for good or evil to be regarded as a British fad, and in some quarters on the continent even as a nefarious plan to put Europe under the financial heel of London; in other quarters as a cry of despair from a Great Britain harassed by unemployment, which other countries not in that position need not heed.

[136] R. G. Hawtrey, 'The Genoa Resolutions on Currency', Economic Journal, vol. xxxi (September 1922), pp. 290–304.
[137] Sayers, Bank of England, vol. I, p. 158; PRO T208/28 Genoa Conference, Mr Hawtrey's Memoranda 1922. I am grateful to Dr S. Howson for the document.
[138] Meyer, Bankers' Diplomacy, chs. 4 and 5.
[139] Royal Institute of International Affairs, The International Gold Problem (London, 1931), pp. 90–1, see also the remarks by R. G. Hawtrey and Charles Rist, in ibid., pp. 110, 220.

Some countries such as France moved away from the system for other reasons as well. For France, after placing a substantial portion of her rising foreign assets in sterling during 1926–7, found herself severely constrained in any attempt to shift into other reserve assets because of the repercussions of such a shift on sterling.[140] Consequently, after 1927 she altered her policy on future accruals to her reserves so as to take only gold, and unwound some previous forward exchange commitments into gold. Her willingness to hold reserves in sterling after 1927, plus the relative stability of her holdings up to September 1931,[141] played an important role in keeping sterling on gold, even if movements of French private and Treasury balances caused problems for London.[142] Nevertheless, the change in French policy over reserve composition proved important in terms of the pressures it exerted on the system as a whole, as is clear from Table 27. Several other countries also shifted the composition of their reserves away from foreign exchange, most notably Germany (from 1925), Italy and Poland (1928). Nevertheless, the ratio of foreign exchange to total reserves for 23 European central banks, excluding France, remained remarkably stable between 1924 and 1930 at between 35 and 40 per cent.[143] Only in 1931 did it fall dramatically. Then some central banks switched out of sterling before 21 September to avoid risk in the face of declining yields and, after Britain left gold, most gold standard central banks switched out of foreign exchange almost completely.[144] The changes in reserve holding patterns away from the gold exchange standard and some of their implications for the world as a whole are apparent from Table 27. However, before discussing them more fully, it is necessary to face the question of whether global reserve supplies were adequate for the successful operation of the system.

Central banks and other official agencies in the 1920s, as before and afterwards, held reserves of internationally acceptable means of payment for a variety of reasons. Reserves could be held to finance payments imbalances, to show financial strength (including under this head the 'backing' of domestic currencies and banking systems), and to provide insurance against the breakdown of the existing international monetary

---

[140] Clarke, *Central Bank Cooperation*, pp. 110–23, 136–8, 166–8, 214–15.

[141] At the time sterling left gold the Bank of France held £80 million in London, within its £70–80 million limit agreed in 1927, but below the £97 million of October 1929. Sayers, *Bank of England*, vol. II, p. 414; Clarke, *Central Bank Cooperation*, pp. 119, 167–8. On the Bank of France's freedom to purchase foreign exchange after stabilization see Moggridge, *British Monetary Policy*, Appendix 3.   [142] *Ibid.*, pp. 138, 164, 240.

[143] League of Nations, *Currency Experience*, p. 41.

[144] Van der Wee and Tavernier, *Banque Nationale*, pp. 239–41; Clarke, *Central Bank Cooperation*, p. 214; Sayers, *Bank of England*, vol. II, pp. 414–15; Moggridge, *British Monetary Policy*, p. 196; League of Nations, *Currency Experience*, pp. 39–41.

Table 27. *Changes in reserves for selected countries, 1925–31ᵃ ($ million)*

	Changes during					
	1925–8		1928–30		1931	
	Total	Of which gold	Total	Of which gold	Total	Of which gold
United Kingdom	112	49	−5	−29	−155	−131
United States	−239	−239	479	479	−133	−133
Belgium	146	73	121	65	28	163
France	1,817	543	585	845	415	600
Germany	245	362	−66	−122	−505	−294
Italy	298	45	−76	13	−97	17
Sweden	5	1	49	2	−102	−10
Switzerland	18	13	71	35	250	315
The Netherlands	−14	−3	7	−4	122	186
Total	2,388	844	1,165	1,284	−177	713

Reference statistics	1925–8	1928–30	1931
New supply of monetary gold	1,060	887	379
Rest of world supply of monetary gold	216	−397	−334
Total world gold reserves at start of period	8,997	10,057	10,944
Rest of world gold reserves at start of period	2,714	2,930	2,533

Note:
ᵃ All figures for end of year.
Sources: US Federal Reserve Board, *Banking and Monetary Statistics* (Washington, DC, 1943), Table 169; League of Nations, *International Currency Experience*, Appendix IV; R. S. Sayers, *The Bank of England 1891–1944* (Cambridge, 1976), vol. III, Appendix 37.

regime (including under this head the traditional war chest).[145] To decide whether the supply of international liquidity required to meet these general needs in the 1920s was greater or less than the actual supply of the 1920s is, however, more difficult than simply stating the determinants of the need for reserves. Contemporaries discussed the problem extensively without reaching any agreement before the collapse of the system and the depreciations against gold of the 1930s so raised mine output and stimulated dishoarding in the Far East as to make the issue of reserve adequacy academic.[146]

[145] This organization follows R. N. Cooper, 'International Liquidity and Balance of Payments Adjustment', in International Monetary Fund, *International Reserves: Needs and Availability* (Washington, DC, 1970), pp. 126–8.

[146] For a sample of the discussions, see Royal Institute of International Affairs, *International Gold Problem*; League of Nations, Gold Delegation of the Financial Committee, *First Interim Report* (Geneva, 1930); *Second Interim Report* (Geneva, 1931); *Final Report* (Geneva, 1932) plus accompanying documents.

Perhaps the best way to approach the issue in the context of the 1920s is to begin, as usual, by looking at the effect of the war and reconstruction on the demand for reserves and the supply of reserve assets. To begin with the supply side, the rise in the world price level after 1914 affected the production of gold which reached a peak in 1915, declined by 42 per cent between 1915 and 1922 and then stabilized at a level of about 80 per cent of the 1915 level. At the same time, however, the removal of gold coins from circulation and the centralization of bankers' gold holdings in central bank reserves increased the proportion of current supplies readily available to central bankers. As well, the better recognition of the alternative of the gold exchange standard offered the possibility of increased supplies of international liquidity, although the possible direct gains here were probably not all that great, except in cases where Genoa made changes in central bank statutes easier, given the incentives towards diversification in this direction that did exist.[147] Finally, central bank cooperation, private market loans and the existence of bodies such as the Bank for International Settlements resulted in an increase in the availability of borrowed reserves, to some extent a substitute for owned reserves.

On the other side, several factors were working to increase the need, and often the demand, for international reserves.[148] One result of the post-war inflations and currency difficulties was an increased emphasis on 'confidence'. This led to a general rise in statutory cover requirements for note issues and other central bank liabilities in countries outside North America.[149] These same experiences also increased the potential for destabilizing hot money movements insofar as they decreased confidence in institutions and exchange rates, thus raising the size of potential balance of payments imbalances and hence the demand for reserves. Again, the increase in the number of separate national monetary authorities probably raised the demand for reserves as potential balance of payments variability increased when economies became less diversified and as economies of pooling disappeared. Finally, the great post-war concern for domestic economic stability increased the desirability of buffer stocks of international assets which would allow the authorities to buy time and ride out potentially reversible balance of payments difficulties without altering domestic policies, especially as the decreased cyclical parallelism amongst the major countries in the system increased the possibilities of dilemmas between internal and external balance. (Insofar as countries placed differing values on the need for internal stability, the

---

[147] League of Nations, *Currency Experience*, pp. 17, 30–1. On the determinants of the composition of reserves from a later perspective, see Williamson, 'International Liquidity', pp. 697–703.

[148] As in most cases in economics, it is important to keep the concepts of need and effective demand separate. See B. J. Cohen, 'International Reserves and Liquidity', in P. B. Kennen (ed.), *International Trade and Finance: Frontiers for Research* (Cambridge, 1975), pp. 415ff.

[149] League of Nations, Gold Delegation, *First Interim Report*, Annex XIII, p. 96.

need for reserves might increase further.) All in all, despite some favourable changes on the supply side, the shift in circumstances after the First World War was such that it shifted the balance more in favour of demand than supply.

With these general considerations in mind, one can begin to assess the situation as revealed in the various statistical series available. Historically, the most commonly used index or reserve adequacy at both the national and international level has been the ratio of owned international reserves to imports. Such a measure has also been subject to numerous theoretical objections.[150] For an individual country or central bank, an analogy with that version of the quantity theory which postulates a stable relationship between the demand for money and the value of transactions may be inappropriate. For monetary reserves are not held for transactions purposes; they are held for precautionary reasons, largely to finance discrepancies between streams of payments and receipts reflecting private transactions. Moreover, it is not clear that even if a quantity theory type of approach held for individual countries in the system it would, given the possible externalities involved, necessarily prove a useful guide to global requirements. Nor, of course, would the reverse be true. Nevertheless, in the literature there is some agreement that the need for reserves would grow with the value of trade, even if there are numerous doubts as to proportionality.

If one compared reserves/import ratios for the 1920s with those for 1913 using the central gold reserve figures underlying Tables 25 and 27 as the appropriate index of reserves, one would find that the ratio rose from 23 per cent in 1913 to an average of 28 per cent between 1925 and 1929.[151] If one gave some weight to the existence of gold stocks outside central banks in 1913, this initial increase of over 20 per cent would decline, given that a substantial proportion of the rise in central bank gold stocks reflected wartime and post-war centralization policies. If one allowed for holdings of foreign exchange reserves the ratio of reserves to imports would again lie above the pre-war level as the ratio of foreign exchange reserves to gold reserves rose above the pre-war level after 1925.[152] Overall, it is clear that the ratio of reserves to imports probably rose between 1913 and the late 1920s. Thus, at least at first glance, it hardly seems appropriate to speak of a shortage of international liquidity in the 1920s.

The global level of reserves might not, however, have seemed ade-

---

[150] J. Niehans, 'The Need for Reserves of a Single Country' in International Monetary Fund, *International Reserves*, pp. 58–60; Williamson, 'International Liquidity', pp. 688–90.

[151] The trade figures come from W. S. Woytinsky and E. S. Woytinsky, *World Commerce and Governments: Trends and Outlook* (New York, 1955), Table 14.

[152] Lindert, 'Key Currencies', pp. 14–15.

quate to most members of the system unless the distribution of reserves tended to match national needs.[153] During the period under discussion, there were large changes in the distribution of reserves. From 1914–24, most particularly between 1921 and 1924, the aggregate share of central gold reserves held by the United States doubled. The rise in American gold reserves over this period exceeded the world output of new gold available for monetary purposes, and only the withdrawal of gold coin from circulation and other measures of reserve centralization allowed other countries' central gold reserves to rise. Outside the United States over this period reserve/import ratios fell. Between 1925 and 1928, the position stabilized somewhat, as indicated in Table 27. The gold stock of the United States remained relatively constant, as did those of the other creditor countries, Britain, Sweden, Switzerland, and The Netherlands. This stability amongst creditors, plus the spread of the gold exchange standard, allowed a wider dispersion of reserve assets, both in Europe and overseas. However, from 1927 in terms of foreign exchange and 1928 in terms of gold, France began to accumulate reserve assets on a large scale. These accumulations were large in terms of new supplies of such assets and in the case of gold were to last until the early 1930s. This accumulation, plus a smaller flow into the United States, put substantial pressure on the reserve positions of other countries in the international economy, even before the slump further complicated matters, with important effects on policy. Thus, although at the time the global level of reserves may have been adequate, they were not distributed in a manner which left all the participants in the system secure in the knowledge that in general individual countries' supplies were over the medium term likely to be so. The resulting international discussions of the reserve issue were not unrelated to this.

The image that remains of the international gold standard system prior to the downturn of 1929, at least at the centre, is one that hardly encourages a belief that it could deal successfully with severe stresses. It was a system that saw Britain in almost perpetual difficulties, Germany dependent on foreign borrowing, often at short term, to finance its way, the United States largely preoccupied with domestic concerns, and France and Belgium incompletely adjusted to the post-war pattern of exchange rates. At the same time patterns of reserve asset holdings were potentially unstable, yet any change would have important effects on sterling, as advocates of a move away from the gold exchange standard such as Strong and Moreau (Governor of the Bank of France) recognized. While prosperity lasted, a modicum of central bank cooperation held things together, although even this cooperation was becoming

---

[153] Cooper, 'International Liquidity and Balance of Payments Adjustment', pp. 132–5.

subject to greater strains as time passed. The end of prosperity produced new pressures and, ultimately, disintegration.

IV. The slump

At the centre of the international economy, the downturn in economic activity came in the course of 1929 (or 1930 in the case of France). At the periphery, however, the downturn came earlier, as did the beginnings of the disintegration of the inter-war gold standard system.[154] In the course of 1928–9, primary producers faced a variety of problems – primary product prices were weak, stocks were rising, levels of overseas borrowing had been high for several years, and debt servicing requirements loomed large. Exacerbating these underlying problems were various attempts at price control through schemes designed to restrict output and/or to hold stocks back from the market. These schemes were commonly financed by overseas borrowing. During 1928–9 this borrowing became more difficult as a result of the decline in American overseas lending and its repercussions on European capital markets.[155] The upshot of weakening prices and reduced overseas borrowing was balance of payments difficulties. In part, peripheral countries met these by financing – by the use of official reserves and short-term borrowing – but they also turned to other policies – deflation, increased protection and exchange depreciation. The problem of primary producers and their reactions to them had repercussions at the centre of the system, for declining incomes, increased protection, and exchange depreciation affected the exports of manufactures from the industrialized countries and had, for example, an important role in initiating the recession in Britain.[156] So too did their methods of balance of payments financing affect the centre, for large gold movements from the periphery eased London's position in 1930, whilst the running down of sterling balances by proto-sterling area countries, plus their demands for short-term accommodation, made Britain's position more difficult.

Although economic activity in many peripheral countries, as well as in Britain and Germany, had turned down before the United States went into recession in the summer of 1929, the American recession and subsequent stock market crash exacerbated matters even further. Falling

---

[154] H. Fleisig, 'The United States and the Non-European Periphery during the Early Years of the Great Depression', in H. van der Wee (ed.), *The Great Depression Revisited* (The Hague, 1972), pp. 151–7; D. Williams, 'The 1931 Financial Crisis', *Yorkshire Bulletin of Economic and Social Research*, vol. xv, no. 2 (November 1963), pp. 92, 96, 98.

[155] D. Williams, 'London and the 1931 Financial Crisis', *Economic History Review*, 2nd series, vol. xv, part 3 (April 1963), pp. 518–19, 521–4; Pressnell, '1925: The Burden of Sterling', pp. 81–2.

[156] Palyi, *The Twilight of Gold*, pp. 229–31; Brown, *International Gold Standard*, ch. 25; H. S. Ellis, *Exchange Control in Central Europe* (Cambridge, Mass., 1941), pp. 158–64.

incomes and industrial production at the centre resulted in declines in the demand for primary products, which, with the large stock overhangs and the collapse of some restriction schemes, led to further sharp declines in prices and further difficulties for producers. Also, declining incomes at the centre brought falls in trade amongst the industrial countries. At the centre, the initial stages of the international decline in activity had their most marked effects in the United Kingdom and Germany. In the former case, these were masked to some extent initially by the continued buoyancy of domestic demand. In the latter, the decline in foreign borrowings had marked deflationary effects as the authorities attempted to meet reparations commitments and capital outflows with domestic expenditure reductions and a restrictive monetary policy. The depression of domestic demand was remarkably successful, as the fall in imports and the rise in unemployment indicated, for the German current account deficit (exclusive of reparations payments) of 1928 became a growing surplus in 1929 and 1930. The strains in this adjustment were great, not only for the political system but also for the financial system, dependent as it was on foreign short-term capital and bank loans to industry.

The British position was more complex. Between 1929 and 1931, despite the decline in exports, the deterioration in the balance of trade was minimal, of the order of £5 million in September 1931, given sharp falls in import prices.[157] The slump, however, reduced the invisibles surplus by over 40 per cent, as earnings from overseas investments, shipping and short interest and commissions all declined.[158] Moreover, as long as the slump continued, the prospects for an improvement were slight. At the same time the capital account was a source of pressure, as some long-term lending continued, despite official controls, albeit at a diminished rate; foreign holders of sterling reduced their balances to meet balance of payments deficits, to improve liquidity positions (something encouraged by low interest rates in London and uncertainty as to the future of sterling) and to meet budget deficits (France); and as distress borrowers, particularly from the sterling area, turned to London for short-term assistance.[159]

The obverse of the balance of payments problems at the periphery and the problems of countries such as Britain and Germany, were the strong positions of certain international creditors, most notably the United States and France. In the United States, the sharp decline in economic

---

[157] D. E. Moggridge, 'The 1931 Financial Crisis: A New View', *The Banker*, vol. cxx, no. 534 (August 1970), pp. 833–5; Moggridge, *British Monetary Policy*, pp. 121–2.

[158] Sayers, *The Bank of England*, vol. iii, Appendix 32, Table c and Chart 1.

[159] Moggridge, *British Monetary Policy*, Table 16, pp. 212–13; Wolfe, *The French Franc*, p. 98; Williams, 'London and the 1931 Financial Crisis', pp. 521–2; Williams, 'The 1931 Financial Crisis', pp. 100–5; van der Wee and Tavernier, *Banque Nationale*, pp. 239–40.

activity, a decline sharper than in most countries, and the continued weakness of overseas lending resulted in a marked fall in the supply of dollars available for payments to the United States.[160] This fall in supply was not matched, either *ex ante* or *ex post*, by a fall in demand, especially given foreigners' large fixed payments due to the United States, with the result that the dollar exerted a strong pull over the exchanges. Moreover, the pull of the dollar was exceeded by that of the franc, for despite a declining current account surplus as France moved into recession more slowly than any other member of the international economy, the repatriation of overseas assets by Frenchmen, partially in response to the workings of French domestic monetary arrangements and partially in response to falling overseas yields and increased uncertainty, meant that Paris received gold continuously during the first year of the slump. To the pressures from these sources were added those from smaller European creditors – Belgium, Switzerland and the Netherlands – all of whom were in recession but gaining gold. By late 1930 the pressure on debtor and deficit countries had in many cases become severe, as was clear from the growing number of departures from gold and rumours of difficulties elsewhere. Nevertheless, despite isolated episodes of central bank support and cooperation in 1930, the few attempts at longer-term solutions to strengthen sterling, the mark, or debtor currencies came to nothing.[161] In fact, in some circles there was a distinct hardening of attitudes towards those in difficulty: they would have to find their own salvation through domestic deflation.[162]

The late winter and early spring of 1931 saw some relaxation of the pressure on sterling and the mark. It was not until the months following 11 May that the system came apart. The spark necessary for the explosion could have come from a number of places, as banking difficulties had been widespread for some time.[163] However, with the collapse of the Credit-Anstalt, the largest bank in Austria, events quickly took a more serious turn. The Austrian authorities and the international central banking community moved to pick up the pieces and limit the repercussions of the collapse. But the international community moved slowly and hesitantly, impeded by caution, domestic worries, political considerations and a lack of sense of the real magnitude of the problem.[164] In the interval, foreign creditors ran down their Austrian assets until a standstill agreement, later backed by exchange controls, led them to try and improve the average quality of their remaining assets by withdrawing

[160] Lary and associates, *The United States in the World Economy*, pp. 5–7.
[161] Clarke, *Central Bank Cooperation*, pp. 173–81.   [162] See fn. 126.
[163] See, for example, Kindleberger, *World in Depression*, pp. 146–8; Ellis, *Exchange Control*, p. 75.
[164] Clarke, *Central Bank Cooperation*, pp. 183–9; Clay, *Lord Norman*, 375–7. On the whole problem of Austria and Germany see E. W. Bennett, *Germany and the Diplomacy of the Financial Crisis, 1931* (Cambridge, Mass., 1962).

them from other centres, starting with the weakest. The crisis spread to other countries in Central Europe and to Germany, accompanied by further spectacular financial failures, further restrictions on the withdrawal of foreign balances and moratoria on longer-term inter-governmental debts and reparations. Again the necessary international support operations were delayed by lengthy negotiations, largely the result of French attempts to use the crisis to win political concessions from Germany.[165] Again, delays intensified the ultimate crisis and made international support measures inadequate for the tasks at hand.

Ultimately, on 13 July, the crisis spread to London, the premier money market of Europe. By this time, sterling had been under a cloud for some months, given the by-then widespread acceptance that sterling was overvalued at $4.86, the seeming intractability of the balance of payments position, and continuing budgetary difficulties, but the authorities had, as yet, done nothing but appoint an expert committee on the budgetary problem. It was the conjuncture of these underlying circumstances with the freezing of substantial British short-term assets in Germany and Central Europe and the publication of the Macmillan Report, which revealed, albeit incompletely, the magnitude of Britain's net foreign short-term debtor position, that made the British crisis so difficult to deal with.[166]

As in previous cases on the continent, international financial cooperation came into play as both the Bank of England and the government raised credits in New York and Paris, initially to hold the exchange rate while discussing a programme of fiscal retrenchment and then to put the programme into operation. However, the assistance merely prolonged the crisis, while certain misunderstandings and mistakes probably shortened it, until reports of unrest in the Royal Navy over pay cuts resulting from the retrenchment programme, political uncertainties and fresh financial difficulties on the continent, this time in Amsterdam, drove Britain from gold on 21 September.[167] In Britain, the inter-war international gold standard had lasted a week under 77 months.

V.   Disintegration

With Britain's departure from gold on 21 September 1931, the focus of the crisis again shifted. Several countries, such as Sweden, Norway, Denmark and Finland, experienced heavy speculative pressure and fol-

---

[165] Ibid., especially chs. 6–8; Clarke, Central Bank Cooperation, pp. 189–201; Clay, Lord Norman, pp. 377–83.   [166] Sayers, Bank of England, vol. II, pp. 389–91.

[167] Ibid., pp. 404–5; W. Hurst, 'Holland, Switzerland, and Belgium, and the English Gold Crisis of 1931', Journal of Political Economy, vol. XL, no. 3 (October 1932), pp. 655–9.

lowed sterling off gold. The United States also came under heavy pressure as individuals and firms tried to improve the quality of their assets, and as gold exchange standard countries, who were incurring capital losses on their holdings of sterling balances, moved from foreign exchange to gold. This pressure towards liquidation was heightened by the fact that for some months prior to September the Bank of France had earned a negative nominal rate of return on its dollar balances.[168] In September and October the US gold stock fell by over $700 million.[169] The Federal Reserve responded orthodoxly with sharp rises in its discount rates on 9 and 16 October, which took the New York Bank's rate from $1\frac{1}{2}$ to $3\frac{1}{2}$ per cent. This rise in rates, plus reassuring political statements on America's continued commitment to gold, stemmed the gold losses until the turn of the year, when renewed rumours and uncertainties affected the exchanges. From April 1932 the gold losses increased as the Federal Reserve asked France and other gold standard countries to liquidate their dollar portfolios, which they did at a cost of another $500 million to the reserves.[170]

The 1931 crisis also affected American domestic finance, for the external drain was accompanied by a renewal of domestic banking difficulties. The Federal Reserve met the internal drain by discounting freely at its increased rates and the stock of high-powered money actually rose. It did not rise by enough, however, to meet the increased public demand for currency, so that the stock of money fell sharply.[171]

Britain's departure from gold split the international monetary system into two broad groups of countries: those who followed sterling and those who followed gold. With the exceptions of India and the dependent Empire, adherence to sterling was not imposed by Britain, although it might be assisted by credits, loans and, later, trade concessions.[172] In their discussions as to a suitable target rate for sterling after September 1931, however, the British authorities did take some account of the potential effects of their decisions on possible adherents to the sterling area.[173] The countries who followed sterling did not necessarily maintain their pre-1931 parities with it, but the trend in their exchange rates tracked that of sterling when compared with currencies still on gold. Most of the members of the sterling area joined it soon after 21 Septem-

---

[168] The income on the Bank's holdings of foreign securities were subject to a French tax equal to one-half the discount rate of the Bank of France. With its discount rate at 2 per cent and New York bill rates at $\frac{1}{2}$ to $\frac{4}{5}$ per cent the Bank's loss was $\frac{1}{2}$ to $\frac{1}{2}$ per cent. Chandler, *American Monetary Policy*, p. 169; Federal Reserve Board, *Banking and Monetary Statistics*, Tables 121 and 122.
[169] US Federal Reserve Board, *Banking and Monetary Statistics*, Table 156.
[170] Chandler, *American Monetary Policy*, pp. 171-3.
[171] Friedman and Schwartz, *Monetary History*, pp. 345-6.
[172] Clay, *Lord Norman*, pp. 411, 412-13; Brown, *International Gold Standard*, vol. II, pp. 1165-9.
[173] Howson, *Domestic Monetary Management*, pp. 79-86; Appendix 4.

ber 1931, but the area subsequently gained more adherents such as South Africa in December 1932 and the Scandinavian countries in 1933.[174]

The gold standard group of countries after 1931 consisted of three sub-groups: those who remained on a gold standard with few impediments to gold flows (the United States, France, The Netherlands, Belgium and Switzerland); those who kept themselves pegged to gold with the assistance of various types of formal and informal exchange controls (Italy, Austria, Germany, Poland, Czechoslovakia, Romania); and those who altered their pre-depression exchange rates against gold but whose rates on London thereafter followed the course of those of the gold standard countries (Argentina, Brazil, Chile, Greece, Hungary, Yugoslavia). Membership of these categories was not, however, constant. Moreover, all of the European countries in these groups reacted to the depreciation of sterling with increases in tariff rates, quantitative restrictions on imports, non–tariff barriers such as the milling restrictions in France, or intensified exchange controls. Most countries which introduced or intensified exchange controls did so rather than follow sterling because of fears of the inflationary expectations depreciation would arouse and worries as to the consequences of depreciation against gold on their foreign debt burdens.[175] In the German case the reparations settlement and the Standstill Agreements also inhibited depreciation.[176] Throughout the period after 1931 these controls were intensified, as were many of the impediments to trade in more orthodox gold standard countries. As well, as the international deflationary pressure spread, partly as a result of the backwash effects of the 1931 exhange depreciations and trade policies overseas, those governments subject to balance of payments pressures, such as Germany, continued to deflate. However, in Germany from mid-1932 attempts at further deflation were halted and thereafter exchange controls were developed into an elaborate regime for containing a growing international disequilibrium.[177]

[174] The exchange rates of the Scandinavian countries after September 1931 had moved more with sterling than with the gold-standard currencies but until 1933 the links with sterling were much less tight than those of, say, Australia, New Zealand and Portugal. Brown, *International Gold Standard*, vol. II, pp. 1,078–9; League of Nations, *International Currency Experience*, p. 47; Bank for International Settlements, Monetary and Economic Department, *The Sterling Area* (Basle, 1953), p. 15.

[175] The logic of the debt-burden argument for not depreciating is far from obvious. True depreciation would raise the domestic currency costs of debt service, but the balance of payments effects of depreciation, unless circumstances were perverse, would make debt service easier by increasing foreign exchange earnings. For the original arguments against depreciation see, for example, Brown, *International Gold Standard*, vol. II, pp. 1201–2, 1203–5; and Ellis, *Exchange Control*, pp. 33–4, 174.

[176] Brown, *International Gold Standard*, vol. II, p. 1204; Ellis, *Exchange Control*, p. 174.

[177] On the later evolution of German exchange controls see Ellis, *Exchange Control*, ch. 4; F. C. Child, *The Theory and Practice of Exchange Control in Germany* (The Hague, 1958). A good summary exists in Yeager, *International Monetary Relations*, pp. 366–71.

At the time Britain left gold, Bank Rate was raised to 6 per cent and some rudimentary controls were placed on some international transactions.[178] At first, except for a successful attempt to push the exhange rate downwards between 24 and 28 September,[179] the authorities were constrained in their policy choices by the low level of the free reserves and the need to repay the central bank and market credits expended in the futile defence of sterling during the summer, but over the ensuing weeks and months a profound reorientation of British policy began. Almost from the moment of departure from gold, policymakers had a sense of liberation from the constraints of many old myths and a fixed exchange rate, and they began to discuss, coldly and dispassionately, the possible courses of action before them. If one compares the breadth and sophistication of these discussions with those of 1925 or earlier, one cannot escape the conclusion that a revolution was taking place.[180] The authorities' target exchange rate was affected by other changes in policy: the introduction of extensive protection in November 1931, after the National Government's overwhelming electoral victory, and the long-desired move in the first half of 1932 towards cheap money culminating in the reduction of Bank Rate to 2 per cent and the conversion of 5 per cent War Loan 1929–47 to a $3\frac{1}{2}$ per cent basis, announced on 30 June 1932.[181] This final operation was supported by an embargo on new overseas issues which was later relaxed but never abandoned in the course of the decade.[182] It was in the context of these policy decisions that the authorities conducted their foreign exchange policy, at first through the Bank of England and an old Treasury account and later through a new Treasury instrumentality, the Exchange Equalisation Account.[183] Initially, the target rate for the Account's day-to-day managers was $3.40, a 30 per cent depreciation from $4.86. The authorities hoped to keep in the region of that rate until British prices had risen by one-quarter. But the target was somewhat elastic – the Account only had resources to smooth a sustained slide in the rate rather than halt it – and, except in the spring of 1932, the flow of funds was away from London until early 1933.

The package of cheap money, depreciation and protection was associ-

---

[178] For the details of the controls see Sayers, *Bank of England*, vol. III, Appendix 30, Document 15.   [179] *Ibid.*, vol. II, p. 419.

[180] *Ibid.*, vol. II, ch. 18A; Howson, *Domestic Monetary Management*, pp. 79–86, Appendix 4; Howson and Winch, *Economic Advisory Council*, pp. 100–5.

[181] On the introduction of cheap money, see E. T. Nevin, *The Mechanism of Cheap Money: A Study of British Monetary Policy 1931–1939* (Cardiff, 1955), ch. 3; Sayers, *Bank of England*, vol. II, pp. 424–5, 429–45; Howson, *Domestic Monetary Management*, pp. 71–4, 86–9.

[182] Howson and Winch, *Economic Advisory Council*, pp. 111–13; R. B. Stewart, 'Great Britain's Foreign Loan Policy', *Economica*, NS, vol. V, no. 17 (February 1938), pp. 45–60.

[183] On the origins of the account see Sayers, *Bank of England*, vol. II, pp. 425–30; S. Howson, 'The Managed Floating Pound 1932–9', *The Banker*, vol. CXXVI, no. 601 (March 1976), pp. 249–50.

ated with a recovery in British economic activity which began in the third quarter of 1932 and continued until 1937. Although there is a substantial variation of opinion in the literature as regards the causes of recovery, it is generally agreed that protection played a small role in the story.[184] As for the effect of depreciation the situation is more obscure. Depreciation certainly removed the competitive disadvantage British exporters had suffered as a result of overvaluation.[185] It provided a breathing space in that the volume of British exports did not fall as did world trade; whereas, before 1931, British export volumes had been declining more rapidly than world exports.[186] However, export volumes did not rise substantially. Producers of import-competing goods as a result of depreciation also felt some relief from foreign competition, but the major decline in the volume of imports did not occur until recovery was underway. In sum, depreciation, or more correctly depreciation and the removal of a commitment to a fixed exchange rate, did allow the authorities to commit themselves to a sustained period of cheap money *and* to ignore short-term exchange difficulties. Moreover, cheap money played an important role in the initiation of the subsequent rise in housing investment which began in the last few months of 1932. This rise moved Britain into recovery earlier than the other major economies.[187] Many of the economies which had depreciated with sterling also began to recover in the course of 1932.[188]

Many of the advantages that depreciation gave Britain and the countries that moved with her in 1931-2 were not sustained. For in 1933 the advent of a new administration in Washington changed the rules of the game. In the first few months of 1933 sterling had, for a change, been stronger on the exchanges and the authorities enjoyed a sharp increase in the reserves as they tried to moderate the rise in the rate.[189] The upward pressures on sterling largely reflected market uncertainties as to the future course of American policy. The uncertainty was justified by events. When the new administration proclaimed a national banking

---

[184] The best extensive, recent treatment is H. W. Richardson, *Economic Recovery in Britain 1932-9* (London, 1967) ch. 10. The theoretical underpinnings of Richardson's approach with its failure to consider levels of effective rather than nominal protection – i.e., to consider the margin of protection on value added in the production process rather than that on product prices – have rightly been questioned, but as yet nobody has done the necessary job of estimating the full implications of the correct approach. See F. Capie, 'The British Tariff and Industrial Protection in the 1930s', *Economic History Review*, 2nd series, vol. XXXI, part 3 (August 1978), pp. 399–409.

[185] See Table 26 on p. 279 and Table 28 on p. 306.

[186] Maddison, 'Growth and Fluctuations', Table 24.

[187] See Howson, *Domestic Monetary Management*, pp. 108–17 and the sources cited therein.

[188] See, for example, A. E. Safarian, *The Canadian Economy in the Great Depression* (Toronto, 1959), ch. 4; C. B. Schedvin, *Australia and the Great Depression: A Study of Economic Development and Policy in the 1920s and 1930s* (Sydney, 1970), ch. 12.

[189] UK, HM Treasury, *Reserves and Liabilities 1931–1945*, Cmd 8354 (London, 1951), Table 1; Howson, 'Managed Floating Pound', p. 251; Sayers, *Bank of England*, vol. II, p. 454.

holiday on 6 March, it also prohibited foreign exchange operations and the export of gold or gold certificates. Four days later it proclaimed that all future gold exports would require Treasury permission. With the Thomas Amendment to the Agricultural Adjustment Act, which became law on 12 May, the Executive gained the power to devalue the dollar against gold by up to 50 per cent and to undertake a large credit expansion. Meanwhile, the Executive acted on 20 April by ending the limited gold exports it had allowed under the regime of 10 March. In effect, therefore, from early March until the end of August 1933 the dollar floated on the world's exchange markets with very limited official support, buffeted by rumours, Executive pronouncements and Congressional resolutions. During this period there were efforts to reach a stabilization agreement between the French, British and American authorities, but these came to nought with President Roosevelt's 3 July veto, which also wrecked the World Economic Conference. The result was a further fall in the dollar and manifestos of group solidarity by members of the other two currency areas, the European gold bloc and the sterling area. With the autumn came an American policy of deliberate depreciation against gold until, under the Gold Reserve Act of January 1934, the dollar price of gold was pegged at \$35 per fine ounce, a depreciation of just under 41 per cent from the old peg of \$20.67.[190] The American authorities had designed the policy of depreciation to raise American commodity prices and, given that in most commodities the United States was neither a dominant supplier or purchaser, it was largely successful. The devaluation, perhaps the clearest example of competitive depreciation in the 1930s, markedly undervalued the dollar and, with sterling above its pre-1931 dollar parity, it removed some of Britain's competitive advantage on international markets. But it did not remove it all, given the existence of the gold bloc.[191]

The depreciation of sterling and the devaluation of the dollar, with sympathetic exchange movements by members of their currency areas had by 1934 put severe strains on those countries remaining on the gold standard at their pre-1931 parities. In some cases, as in Germany, these strains were masked by elaborate systems of exchange control, and domestic recovery proceeded, inhibited only by the inefficiencies and the decline in the volume of international trade associated with the overvaluation and controls. In the case of the gold bloc countries, attempting to maintain their exchange rates without substantial controls,

---

[190] On the tangled events of this period see Sayers, *Bank of England*, vol. II, ch. 18(D); vol. III, Appendix 27; Clarke, 'The Reconstruction of the International Monetary System', ch. 3; Chandler, *American Monetary Policy*, ch. 18; Friedman and Schwartz, *Monetary History*, ch. 8(2); Howson, 'Managed Floating Pound', pp. 251–2; H. Feis, *1933: Characters in Crisis* (Boston, 1966).   [191] See Table 28, p. 306.

their currencies came under increasing pressure, despite the attempts of the British authorities to ease the strains.[192] The difficulties of the gold bloc showed themselves not only in continued weakness of their exchange rates and, except in France in 1934, reserve losses, but also in renewed attempts at domestic deflation and further trade restrictions. Belgium, perhaps the weakest member of the gold bloc, suffered most severely from these pressures and survived 1934 only with foreign assistance.

Early in 1935 renewed weakness in sterling, whose origins were not readily obvious although difficulties in London commodity markets[193] and political rumours played a part, increased the pressure on Belgium, as did a rise in British duties on iron and steel. The result was a political crisis, a National Government and a devaluation of the belga by 28 per cent on 1 April.[194] The Belgian devaluation, despite the attempts made to limit its direct economic effects on Belgium's gold bloc partners, did increase the pressure on them. The 42 per cent Latvian devaluation of 2 May 1935 increased the strain and the French franc, Dutch guilder and Swiss franc experienced severe pressure – the forward discount on the French franc reached the equivalent of 40 per cent per annum. All three countries, as well as Italy, experienced large reserve losses. Some indication of the severity of the pressures faced comes from the discount rate changes in their countries, which often occurred in 2 per cent steps – the first such occasions for such large movement in France and The Netherlands in a century – and were much more frequent than previously,[195] with pressures of this magnitude following on several attempts at domestic deflation. They continued into 1936, especially in France. Devaluations on the part of the gold bloc were simply a matter of time. However, in the case of a gold bloc devaluation, there was the problem that no major outside currency could be assumed as fixed: sterling was clearly managed but not pegged and the dollar price of gold was subject to change under the American legislation of 1934. During 1935 there had been tentative American feelers concerning an Anglo-American stabilization agreement, but these had come to nothing. With the French difficulties of 1936 such discussions took on a new urgency, especially

[192] Sayers, *Bank of England*, vol. II, ch. 19 (B and C); Howson, 'Managed Floating Pound', p. 252.
[193] Sayers, *Bank of England*, vol. II, pp. 544–6.
[194] Van der Wee and Tavernier, *Banque Nationale*, pp. 268–85.

[195]

Number of changes in Bank Rate	In the 20 years before the war	In the 20 years before 1935	In the year to 31 March 1936
France	15	19	14
The Netherlands	36	24	17
United Kingdom	90	38	0

Source: Bank for International Settlements, *Sixth Annual Report* (Basle, 1936), p. 46.

after French gold losses of $570 million in April and May and the election of a Popular Front government pledged to economic reform, public works and the Poincaré franc. Pledges to maintain the 1928 gold parity ended the reserve losses and even brought some gains in July, but they did nothing to resolve the underlying problems, further heightened by a rapid rise in French labour costs.[196] After inconclusive attempts at negotiations during June and July, there was a lull in August before, after a flurry of cables and conversations, the American, British and French governments were able to issue broadly similar declarations on 25 September 1936. The declarations themselves accepted a devaluation of the franc, agreed to minimize the exchange market disturbances surrounding the change, abjured unreasonable, competitive exchange depreciation and agreed to work towards improved conditions for international trade.[197] The declarations did not contain agreements as to the opening exchange rates after the French devaluation[198] or on day-to-day operating procedures under the new regime, especially as regards the gold convertibility of the foreign exchange balances acquired by national exchange funds during their operations. In the end, the negotiators agreed on an opening rate of 105 francs to the pound. The British did not commit themselves to any particular rate or range of rates against the dollar. The parties agreed on twenty-four hour gold convertibility for official exchange balances – hence the name twenty-four hour gold standard. The declarations and surrounding agreements were an improvement over the previous regime, but they did *not* represent a long-term commitment to exchange stability. They did, however, represent an acceptance of the notion that rates of exchange were a matter for multilateral consideration.[199] In the weeks after 25 September several other countries acceded to the Tripartite arrangements.

With the French devaluation into a wide band in September 1936 and the subsequent exchange rate adjustments by the Dutch, Swiss, Italians, Latvians and Czechs, the exchange rate relationships amongst the countries with relatively freely convertible currencies differed remarkably little from those of six years earlier.[200] Moreover, the remaining peace-

---

[196] In the first nine months of the regime, wage increases, reduced hours and paid holidays raised hourly wage earnings by 60 per cent (Phelps Brown and Browne, *A Century of Pay*, p. 238).

[197] The declarations appear in Bank for International Settlements, *Seventh Annual Report* (Basle, 1937), Annex VII.

[198] The French devaluation allowed a range of possible rates, as the gold price for the franc could by law lie between 49 and 43 milligrams of gold 900/1,000 fine instead of the 65.5 milligrams of the Poincaré franc. Sterling, of course, was not pegged.

[199] Sayers, *Bank of England*, vol. II, ch. 19 D; S. V. O. Clarke, 'Exchange-Rate Stabilization in the Mid-1930s: Negotiating the Tripartite Agreement', *Princeton Studies in International Finance*, no. 41 (September 1977).

[200] See, for example, League of Nations, *Currency Experience*, p. 129, n. 1. The only currency to survive the 1930s at its old pre-1931 parity without exchange controls was the Albanian franc – which only succumbed after the Italian occupation when it was devalued and pegged to the lira.

Table 28. *Indices of prices and costs for selected European countries and the United States, 1931–8 (1931 = 100)*

	1931	1932	1933	1934	1935	1936	1937	1938
A. Unit wage costs in industry (in national currency)								
Germany	100	84	77	78	74	74	73	75
Sweden	100	99	99	94	91	92	99	88
United Kingdom	100	99	97	93	89	88	90	96
United States	100	92	82	95	92	90	101	104
B. Export unit values (current dollars)								
Belgium	100	82	97	118	97	99	113	104
France	100	85	100	121	118	114	109	91
Germany	100	88	102	126	122	124	132	139
Italy	100	80	89	108	105	104	95	97
Sweden	100	69	78	94	91	95	106	115
The Netherlands	100	79	91	113	110	110	118	117
United Kingdom	100	72	87	105	103	107	115	117
United States	100	85	89	104	108	110	116	108

Sources: As for Table 25.

time years of the decade were to see little further alteration in the pattern of rates beyond the step-like movements in the French franc in the light of Popular Front policies and the social strains of previous years of deflation to a level of 179 to the pound by May 1938. Thereafter it remained pegged at this level. After May 1938, sterling in the face of capital outflows, initially back to France, but increasingly elsewhere as well, slid slowly to $4.68 at a cost of over £250 million to the reserves, carrying with it the exchange rates of those countries which pegged to sterling, which by this time included France. There it remained until 24 August 1939, when under great pressure the authorities let it drop to $4.03, where it remained for a decade.[201]

The exchange rate movements of the 1930s amongst the centre countries were substantial, as Table 29 makes clear. What the table also shows is that the advantages or disadvantages gained or lost by depreciations were not sustained and that at the end of the decade rates were not, except in the case of Germany and France, substantially different from what they had been at the beginning. Moreover, it is not clear from Table 28 and Figure 1, that in the case of those countries that continued to leave transactions uncontrolled either substantial depreciation, as in the case of France, or the lack thereof, in the cases of Belgium or The Netherlands, left the relevant exchange rates out of line with evolving prices and costs.[202] In fact, despite the sharp fall in the French franc between 1936

[201] Sayers, *Bank of England*, vol. II, pp. 571–2.
[202] See also Phelps Brown and Browne, *Century of Pay*, Figure 38.

Table 29. *Indices of December exchange rates in dollars for selected European currencies, 1930–8 (no. of US cents per unit of foreign currency in December 1930 = 100[a])*

United Kingdom	1930	1931	1932	1933	1934	1935	1936	1937	1938
Belgium	100	99	99	155	167	120	121	121	120
France	100	100	99	155	167	167	118	86	66
Germany	100	99	99	156	168	168	168	169	168
Italy	100	97	97	157	163	154[b]	100	100	96
Sweden	100	69	66	98	95	94	94	99	93
The Netherlands	100	99	99	156	167	168	135	138	134
United Kingdom	100	69	67	105	101	101	101	102	96

Notes:
[a] Monthly averages of daily rates.
[b] Nominal for at least five days during month.
Source: US Federal Reserve Board, *Banking and Monetary Statistics* (Washington, DC, 1943), Table 173.

and 1938, perhaps the only clear cut case of competitive depreciation during the decade was that of the United States, although it is arguable that on some occasions British exchange management may have come close to the line.[203]

What the devaluation cycle of the 1930s did, more than anything else, was to raise the price of gold and hence the value of international reserves. It did so, not only by providing central banks and treasuries with capital gains but also by further encouraging Eastern dishoarding of existing stocks and increased production.[204] Despite a deliberate mine conservation policy and higher taxes on gold mining profits in South Africa, gold output rose substantially. The quantity of new gold mined in 1938 was double that of a decade earlier. The value of this larger quantity was even greater, for the devaluation cycle had raised the market price by 70 per cent on average.[205] However, this rise in output and price was not the result of an attempt to secure an appropriate balance between the need for and the supply of international liquidity. The 70 per cent rise in the price of gold was fortuitous in that it was determined largely by the extent of the British and American depreciations of 1931–2 and 1933–4, neither of which was undertaken with very much, if any,

[203] Howson, 'Managed Floating Pound'. However, the high level of domestic demand in the UK during the decade left the British balance of payments relatively weak. See Bank for International Settlements, *Sterling Area*, pp. 24–5; Sayers, *Bank of England*, vol. II, Appendix 32.
[204] Both had already been encouraged by economic distress and the fact that gold prices remained constant while the prices of other commodities fell in the early years of the depression.
[205] League of Nations, *Currency Experience*, p. 18.

Table 30. *Changes in gold reserves for selected European countries, 1931–8^a ($ million^b)*

	Changes during	
	1931–3	1933–8
United Kingdom	628	483
United States	−40	4,558
Belgium	26	−37
France	323	−1,587
Germany	−142	−75
Italy	77	−259
Sweden	44	90
Switzerland	−68	26
The Netherlands	14	217
Total	867	3,416
Reference statistics	1931–3	1933–8
New supply of monetary gold	653	3,324
Rest of world supply of monetary gold	−214	−92
Total world gold reserves at start of period	11,323	11,976
Rest of world gold reserves at start of period	2,237	2,023

Notes:
^{a} All figures for end of year.
^{b} Gold valued at $20.67 per fine ounce.
Sources: US Federal Reserve Board, *Banking and Monetary Statistics* (Washington, DC, 1943), Table 167; League of Nations, *International Currency Experience*, Appendix 1; UK, HM Treasury, *Reserves and Liabilities 1931 to 1945*, Cmd 8354 (London, 1951).

thought of their effects on the liquidity problem of previous years.[206]
Moreover, as Table 30 indicates, this rise in the supply of international liquidity, a rise which swamped any changes in the value or volume of world trade, was very unequally distributed.[207] For countries outside the centre countries listed in Table 29 physical gold stocks actually

---

[206] This is not to say that Britain's exchange-rate policy was not uninfluenced by Britain's need to rebuild her reserves after the 1931 crisis. See Howson, *Domestic Monetary Management*, Appendix 4.

[207] At their peak in 1937 the value of world exports was 4 per cent below that of 1929, while the volume of world exports was 23 per cent below that of 1929. See Maddison, 'Growth and Fluctuations', Tables 20 and 25.

continued the fall which had started in 1928–9 and only the rise in gold prices provided any relief. In the centre itself, the large reserve redistributions were towards Britain and the United States. By the end of 1938 the latter held 60 per cent of world gold stocks while the United Kingdom held another 12 per cent.[208] Most of the redistribution had come from France, Germany, Italy and Japan. True the United Kingdom had a need to rebuild her reserves after 1931 and the centre countries, especially Britain and the United States, may have had more 'need' for reserves given the huge hot money movements of the 1930s, but the existence of higher trade and exchange restrictions in the 1930s in Britain and elsewhere suggests that all was not well with most members of the system as regards overall reserve adequacy.

In the 1930s, however, gold was not the only reserve asset in the system. Sterling continued to play an important role as a reserve currency, although after the unwinding of the gold exchange standard amongst many European countries in 1931–2, the geographical extent of its role was more limited. The sterling area of the 1930s or that group of countries who for all or some part of the period after September 1931 kept their exchange rates pegged to the pound, consisted of the dependent Empire, the independent members of the Commonwealth except Canada,[209] the Scandinavian countries, Iraq, Egypt, Portugal, Thailand, Argentina, Greece, Iran, Japan and, after May 1938, France. In the case of the rest of the Empire and Commonwealth countries, most foreign reserves were kept in sterling, or, where gold was held, gold holdings remained constant. Only Sweden and South Africa markedly increased their gold reserves in the years to 1937.[210] In 1938 there was a more marked shift towards gold on the part of Sweden, Eire, Norway, and Latvia.[211] However, the existence of a reserve currency standard over such a wide area had less effect on global supplies of liquidity during the years after 1931 than before, for Britain's reserves grew more rapidly than her liabilities.[212] Nevertheless, despite the facts that it did not provide a substantial increase in international liquidity and that it presented Britain's economic managers with more difficult problems than

---

[208] For further changes during 1939, see League of Nations, *Currency Experience*, p. 90.

[209] Newfoundland, which started the decade a Dominion and ended it a colony, remained part of the dollar area during the decade.

[210] League of Nations, *Currency Experience*, p. 55.   [211] *Ibid.*, p. 56.

[212] Some of Britain's reserve growth after 1931 reflected the abnormally low levels to which the net reserves had fallen during the crisis, while some obviously was a counterpart to the hot money movements of the period against which the authorities wished to insulate domestic economic policy. Thus there was some room for an overall increase in supplies of international liquidity in the sterling area. But it was much smaller than in the 1920s or before 1914. See Howson, 'Managed Floating Pound', pp. 251–2; Sayers, *Bank of England*, vol. II, especially ch. 19B; UK, HM Treasury, *Reserves and Liabilities, 1931 to 1945*, Cmd 8354; Bank for International Settlements, *Sterling Area*, p. 68.

otherwise, the sterling area did provide a wide area of exchange stability during a rather disturbed period.[213]

Looking back over the two inter-war decades of monetary experience, is it possible to draw any conclusions? In some cases one can whilst in other the position is less clear. Certainly the period as a whole is replete with stories of the consequences of a lack of international coordination in international monetary affairs. For despite some attempts at international reconstruction in Europe in the 1920s and the negotiated depreciation of the franc in 1936, countries tended to act in a relatively uncoordinated manner in their choice of exchange rates. True, after initial national choices of a target or actual rates of exchange, members of the international community did tend – according to their lights – to help the achievement of these rates, but this international validation of frequently inappropriate exchange rates of the 1920s was hardly the best route to long-term systemic stability. In the 1930s, with the exception of 1936 and, perhaps, to a lesser extent in 1934–5, cooperation was less in evidence. Even the much heralded Tripartite Agreement did little to increase coordination, as the circumstances surrounding the 1937–8 slide in the franc indicate,[214] although day-to-day technical coordination probably increased. The upshot was larger exchange rate movements than were necessary for the countries involved to achieve their domestic goals, larger international imbalance and probably larger movements of hot money and refugee capital than would otherwise have been the case.

The inter-war period has often provided a focus for discussions of the usefulness or otherwise of flexible exchange rates. Generally speaking, the *locus classicus* for the modern focus on the inter-war period has been Nurkse's negative League of Nations discussion of inter-war experience.[215] This soon came under fire from Friedman,[216] and the issue took on a life of its own in economists' debates of the 1950s and 1960s over the relative merits of the two regimes.[217] Much of the ensuing

[213] League of Nations, *Currency Experience*, pp. 60–5; Bank for International Settlements, *Sterling Area*, p. 29.   [214] Sayers, *Bank of England*, vol. II, pp. 482–3, 562.

[215] League of Nations, *Currency Experience*, ch. 5.

[216] M. Friedman, 'The Case for Flexible Exchange Rates', in his *Essays in Positive Economics* (Chicago, 1953), especially p. 176.

[217] The classic articles here are W. Stolper, 'Purchasing Power Parity and the Pound Sterling from 1919–1925', *Kyklos*, vol. II, part 3 (1948), pp. 240–59; S. C. Tsiang, 'Fluctuating Exchange Rates in Countries with Relatively Stable Economies: Some European Experiences after World War I', *International Monetary Fund Staff Papers*, vol. VII, no. 3 (October 1959), pp. 244–73; Aliber, 'Speculation in the Foreign Exchanges', pp. 171–245. There is a useful summary of the discussions from the point of view of a supporter of flexible rates in Yeager, *International Monetary Relations*, especially pp. 319–21, 328–9, 344–6, 353–4, 364–6. More recently, interest in the subject has revived with further work by Yeager's pupils and by those committed to the monetary theory of the balance of payments. See, for example, J. S. Hodgson, 'An Analysis of

discussion has not been terribly helpful as authors have tended to explain away what are from their point of view difficult or contrary cases with appeals to unique political circumstances or other such events external to the exchange market. However, given that most floats of the 1930s were far from the simple clean floats of pure theory or even analogous to the managed Canadian float of the 1950s with the authorities smoothing day-to-day fluctuations but not interfering with the trend in the rate,[218] most of the attention has been concentrated on the early 1920s. Here the tests have been bedevilled by disagreements as to the proximate determinants of exchange rates in the short-to-medium term. Some, working with wholesale price purchasing-power parities, have found changes in relative prices strong determinants of exchange rate movements and have tended to suggest that speculation was relatively unimportant, which others, following Keynes,[219] have seen as not surprising given the nature of the index number used. Others, using other indices of purchasing-power parity, have found more examples of other factors acting as important determinants of exchange rate changes and have, on occasion, seen speculation as playing a destabilizing role. At present, the vogue of the monetary approach to the balance of payments is leading to further exercises on the determinants of exchange rates and wholesale price purchasing-power parity seems back in fashion. At present, it would probably be fair to say that the balance of opinion is running away from Nurkse, but not as far as Friedman.

Another issue which has also risen in inter-war discussions is the role of financial centres in the stability or instability of the international monetary system as a whole. In his monumental study of the inter-war gold standard, Brown in comparing the success of the pre-1914 regime as compared with the problems of its successor placed considerable emphasis on the differential effects of the single-centred pre-war system with London dominant as compared with the competition among London, New York, and, to a lesser extent, Paris after 1918.[220] Kindleberger, drawing on Brown's analysis and on the relative stability of the American-dominated 1950s and 1960s, has echoed and reinforced Brown's view.[221] Kindleberger's work has stimulated discussion on the

---

Floating Exchange Rates: The Dollar–Sterling Rate, 1919–1925', *Southern Economic Journal*, vol. xxxix, part 3 (October 1972), pp. 249–57 and J. A. Frenkel, 'Purchasing Power Parity: Doctrinal Perspective and Evidence from the 1920s', *Journal of International Economics*, vol. viii, part 2 (May 1978), pp. 169–92.

[218] The classic study of the Canadian experience in the 1950s is P. Wonnacott, *The Canadian Dollar, 1948–1962* (Toronto, 1965). As yet, recent concerns with 'dirty' or aggressively managed floats have yet to reach back into the historical literature on the 1930s, but doubtless work is underway.   [219] Keynes, *Treatise on Money*, vol. i, pp. 73–4.

[220] Brown, *International Gold Standard*, vol. i, especially ch. 17.

[221] Kindleberger, *World in Depression*, especially pp. 292–307; C. P. Kindleberger, *Manias, Panics, and Crashes: A History of Financial Crises* (New York, 1978), especially ch. 10.

role of hegemonic centres in the promotion of international economic stability.[222] At present, the discussion is inconclusive, partially owing to disputes as to the extent of London's international dominance before 1914, especially with respect to Western European centres, but also more generally. Also relevant to the discussion are questions as to London's consciousness of its pre-war role and the associated responsibilities, especially given the rudimentary nature of pre-war management as compared with those of later years.[223] It is generally agreed that Britain after 1918 was in international economic terms weaker than she had been pre-war, even though her leaders had greater pretensions of influence and a more coherent systemic view than their predecessors. It is also agreed that the United States was stronger internationally after 1918, even if less integrated into international economic affairs and less conscious of any international responsibilities than, say, Britain, while the French role was more problematic. However, even by the late 1930s it is not clear that any new hegemonic system had emerged: France was weakened by years of deflation; Britain had withdrawn to tend her own garden;[224] and American policy was confused and confusing. It is certainly arguable that the policies resulting from these changed circumstances either lengthened or increased the depth of the depression of the 1930s, but the exact extent of their effects as compared with other forces at work is far from clear.

Any discussion of hegemony often naturally leads one on to discussions of relations between the centre and the periphery in the international economy. In discussions of the pre-1914 gold standard, it has often been suggested that much of the process of balance of payments was shifted from the centre countries to the fringes of the system, either through changes in the terms of trade[225] or through the effects of interest rates on capital flows.[226] These mechanisms are themselves subjects of dispute in discussions of the pre-1914 system,[227] but in the inter-war system the question still arises as to whether the pressures on the periphery were greater than previously. As usual it is probably more helpful to take the question in more than one stage. First, were countries at the periphery more subject to fluctuations resulting from changes at the

[222] See, for example, B. M. Rowland (ed.), *Balance of Power or Hegemony: The Interwar Monetary System* (New York, 1976).
[223] The evolution of conscious central banking is the major theme of Sayers' *Bank of England*.
[224] The phrase is Brown's (*International Gold Standard*, vol. II, p. 1092).
[225] The strongest proponent of this view has been Robert Triffin. See, for example, his 'The Evolution of the International Monetary System: Historical Reappraisal and Future Perspectives', *Princeton Studies in International Finance*, no. 12 (June 1964), p. 6.
[226] *Ibid.*, p. 8. See also Lindert, 'Key Currencies', p. 57; Moggridge, *British Monetary Policy*, p. 67.
[227] See, for example, Lindert, 'Key Currencies', pp. 44–6 on the Triffin hypothesis, and D. Williams, 'The Evolution of the Sterling System' in Whittlesey and Wilson (eds.), *Essays in Money and Banking*, pp. 274–80.

Table 31. *Changes in capital flows over two slumps (millions of units of national currency)*

	Recession	Measure of capital flow	Two years' average before slump	Three years' average after slump	Per cent change
United Kingdom	1890	Long-term capital	121	42	−65
United Kingdom	1890	Current account plus gold	86	60	−30
United Kingdom	1929	Long-term capital	101	27	−73
United Kingdom	1929	Current account plus gold	91	−56	−162
United States	1929	Long-term capital	942	127	−87
United States	1929	Current account plus gold	1,087	295	−73

Sources: M. Simon, 'The Pattern of New British Portfolio Investment 1865–1914', in A. R. Hall (ed.), *The Export of Capital 1870–1914* (London, 1968), Table II; R. S. Sayers, *The Bank of England 1891–1944*, vol. III (Cambridge, 1976), Appendix 32, Table C; H. B. Lary and associates, *United States in World Economy*, (Washington, DC, 1943), Table I.

centre than previously? Secondly, even granting a change or no change, were any difficulties that did occur exacerbated, as compared to pre-war, by changes in the working of the international monetary system. Table 31 presents some summary measures for the worst fluctuations in lending for each period, those surrounding the dates 1890 and 1929. The figures indicate clearly that the fluctuations on the second occasion were, by all measures, larger over the inter-war than the pre-war slump. So too were the corresponding changes in such real variables as the terms of trade,[228] although countries on the periphery eventually gave back to the centre more real, if not monetary, destabilization than they received.[229] Although in both cases it might be argued that some of the declines in lending were reactions to 'excesses' at the periphery, in the case of the 1929 slump the initial drying up of lending had more to do with changes at the centre completely unrelated to foreign events than previously. Moreover, the current account plus gold figures make clear that there was much less accommodation for the periphery in other elements of the balance of payments after 1929 than previously – in fact in the United Kingdom case after 1929 her current account plus reserve behaviour exacerbated the strains caused by the decline in lending. In neither case was there a lender of last resort in the formal sense to prop up the system,

[228] Maddison, 'Growth and Fluctuations', Chart III.   [229] *Ibid.*, p. 147.

but after 1890 the London institutions, despite their difficulties, did more to ease the transition than their successors in either London or New York did after 1929. But in their area, as in others, there is a need for more, and in this case comparative, research.

In fact, perhaps the strongest statements we can make about our understanding of the inter-war gold standard experience is how much we have learned since, say, the publication of the biographies of Montagu Norman and Benjamin Strong almost a quarter century ago. But as should also be clear, we are still heavily dependent on even earlier work for much of our understanding. Doubtless, the years to come will continue the processes of understanding and reassessment.

CHAPTER V

Taxation and public finance:
Britain, France, and Germany

Note on currency (units)

Britain		£1	= 20s. (shillings)
		sovereign	= 240d. (pence)
France	up to 1795:	1 *livre tournois*	= 20 sous
			= 240 denier
	after 1795:	1 franc	= 20 sous
			= 100 centimes
		1 franc	= 1.00125 *livres tournois*
Prussia	1764–1821:	1 taler	= 24 groschen
			= 288 pfennig
	from 1821:	1 taler	= 30 groschen
			= 360 pfennig
		1 taler (of 1820)	= 1.00223 taler (of 1822)
German Reich	from 1871–5:	1 mark	= 100 pfennig
		1 mark	= ⅓ Prussian taler

Rates of exchange of gold standard currencies, 1900

Britain	£1	=	gr. 7.98806 gross weight net content: 916 ⅔‰
		=	gr. 7.32239 net weight
France	100 francs	=	gr. 32.25806 gross weight net content: 900‰
		=	gr. 29.03225 net weight
German Reich	10 marks	=	gr. 3.98248 gross weight net content: 900‰
		=	gr. 3.58423 net weight

£1 = 25.222 francs = 20.429 marks

I. *Tax system and national budget in Britain*

A. HISTORICAL BASIS: THE DEVELOPMENT OF PUBLIC FINANCE UP TO THE NAPOLEONIC WARS

1. *The system of public revenues* ★

(i) *Parliament's prerogative to grant taxes*

Early establishment of a unitary public administration in Britain led to a close connection between public law, tax law and the national budget. From Magna Carta in 1215 onwards, parliament possessed an enshrined prerogative *vis-à-vis* the crown to grant taxes, confirmed and amplified in 1297; it was buttressed by the Bill of Rights of 1689, declaratory of the

---

★ If not otherwise stated 'public' means 'national' resp. 'states' throughout the chapter.

rights of parliament. The prerogative to grant taxes related to direct capitation, property and revenue taxes, also to the levying of the so-called direct taxes and (import) duties on domestic consumption of goods. 'The Commons taxed the whole, and built on that eternal rock their power'[1] (Dowell). This contributes to explaining the liability to taxes of the aristocracy and clergy. Hence, Britain had no problem in rendering liability to tax universal, a problem which afflicted countries on the European continent far into the nineteenth century.

(ii) Revenues from crown lands and stamp duties

Parliamentary prerogative to grant taxes possibly helps to explain why the British state by the nineteenth century had practically ceased to draw revenue from crown lands which parliament had difficulty in ascertaining. The Stuarts (1603–1714) had begun the process of selling off the public lands accumulated by the Tudors (1485–1603); the last wholesale disposal of public lands occurred in 1670 under Charles II (1660–85). Not even the '1422 manors or lordships besides lands and farms' quoted in the Domesday book of 1086 were retained. Revenue from public lands fell to a level so low that it was no longer a separate budget item, but in time became a constituent of 'minor revenues'. Public lands around 1800 comprised approximately 130 estates of 52,000 acres of arable, pasture, and meadows, 1,800 buildings in London and Westminster and, besides royal forests, 450 houses, mills and cottages in the remainder of Britain.[2]

Income derived from crown lands amounted in 1888 to a mere 0.43 per cent, in 1913 to 0.28 per cent, of total public revenue. There is a striking contrast between the diminution of British public lands, to which neither in the eighteenth nor in the nineteenth century were added any productive enterprises, and the efforts of German states to increase their public lands and the rights enshrined in princely monopolies and to safeguard the revenues flowing from them as one of the most substantial and reliable sources of revenue. Nor is this contradicted by Britain treating the new technical services rendered by the postal, telegraphic, and telephone systems as fiscal monopolies and securing thereby a good source of revenue, owing to their world-wide ramifications. The only substantial new property acquired by the British state, producing revenue and itemized separately in the budget, was the takeover of Suez Canal shares in 1875; in conjunction with 'sundry loans', their yield accounted in 1913 for about 0.75 per cent of public revenue.[3]

---

[1] Dowell (1965), vol. I, p. xix. For the fiscal economy from 1688 to 1756, see Dickson (1967), for the period from 1774 to 1792, see Binney (1958); for differences in the development of Britain and Prussia, Braun (1975), pp. 243ff.

[2] Vocke (1866), pp. 151, 156; Madge (1938), pp. 29ff., 32.   [3] Mallet (1913), pp. 353, 404.

The strong entrenchment of the British parliament presumably accounts for the remarkably retarded development of a second kind of revenue difficult to control, the stamp duties. On the continent on the other hand, especially in France, a whole system of highly productive fee-like taxes or tax-like fees developed out of stamp duties. Though levied in each instance for a separate service rendered by authority, the state determined the volume of such compulsory services which it commanded its citizens to receive, and the prices (fees) to be paid therefor.

Stamp duty is a tax on legal transactions, above all on documents which derive from the tax on official authentication, thus becoming acceptable proof in courts of law. The origin of stamp duties may be sought in Holland around 1624; they reached France as early as 1651. Britain, after some experimenting around 1671, introduced the general stamp tax in 1694 – one of the novel forms of tax introduced by Britain subsequent to the revolution and the war against France.

Though 'various deeds, instruments and law proceedings' liable to tax were somewhat extended in scope and stamp duties charged at six different rates tended on the whole towards an increase in tax burden, revenues from stamp duties during the eighteenth century remained small. The yield from stamp duties amounted to £117,000 in 1714, £160,000 in 1727, £290,000 in 1760, £366,000 in 1770, £442,000 in 1778, representing about 2–4 per cent of total revenue. Only after bills of exchange and promissory notes became liable to stamp duty in 1782, after Pitt almost doubled the duties in 1797 and after the *ad valorem* principle had been entrenched for the authentication of conveyances, did stamp revenues show an increase in the nineteenth century, but even then their proportion of the budget stagnated at 4–5 per cent, though at a higher total level. This does not include death duties.[4]

British stamp duties – in the sense of the subsequent 'general stamp' – were not fashioned into a fiscal instrument. However, it was a British peculiarity to include among stamp revenues those which on the continent at times arose from death duties, this is, property taxes falling due at irregular intervals. This happened because Britain levied death duties in the form of a stamp authenticating the transfer of the estate. These transaction taxes were extended in 1779 and 1796 and their yield increased in the nineteenth century. In the 1880s, the British legislature adopted the new continental system: from then onwards, stamp duties became subdivided into something like 'death duties' and 'general stamp duties', from 1894 onwards into 'stamp duties' and 'estate etc., duties'.

---

[4] Dowell (1965), vol. III, pp. 290, 296ff. The share of stamp duties, including inheritance taxes, in the budget during the nineteenth century at times exceeded 10 per cent; see budgets in Table 13.

(iii) Government loans

As Britain derived hardly any public revenue from public lands and little more from stamp duties levied in the shape of the 'general stamp', the British fiscal system rested on two substantial pillars: government loans and taxes, especially excise and import duties. It is therefore not surprising that Britain, contrary to continental practice, carefully developed the government loan as a source of revenue. Never after 1689, the glorious revolution and the parliamentry guarantee of the public debt, did Britain reduce the public debt by means of state bankruptcy, a practice adopted by so many European states which turned unredeemed loans into delayed property taxes levied on their creditors. The Bank of England, established in 1694, became the institutional cornerstone of government loan policy. It was the public loan, not the tax, which at least up to the introduction of income tax in 1842 provided the decisive variable element in British public revenue.[5]

Part of the care bestowed on the public debt was the principle, carefully implemented, that a public debt must be a funded debt: the indebtedness of the state matched the claims of private creditors. This represents a transfer of purchasing power to the state out of the total volume of purchasing power (money), but not an increase in purchasing power via new money creation by banks. The British state reinforced its creditworthiness by a remarkable monetary discipline which – after temporary suspension of convertibility of bank notes into legal tender from 1797 to 1819 and the appointment of the bullion committee by parliament in 1810 – became institutionalized by Peel's Bank Charter Act of 1844; thereafter, as before, currency increase conformed to the restrictive currency theory principles laid down by David Ricardo (1772–1823).[6]

Meanwhile the legal bimetallic gold–silver standard had been turned in 1821 into a legal single gold standard. Starting in the eighteenth century, public debt and monetary orthodoxy throughout the nineteenth century were closely linked. Both were rendered feasible and easier to sustain by a balance of trade favourable in the long term and – interacting with these factors in the total context – the remarkable stability of the value of the pound sterling throughout the period.[7]

The long-run strategy of British governments in the field of the public

---

[5] For early forms of British state debt in international comparison, Landmann (1958), pp. 14ff., 18ff., 22–3, also Dickson (1967), with indications of foreign loan creditors pp. 304ff.; the costs of Britain's various wars between 1688 and 1869 and the state indebtedness caused by them is tabulated in Dowell (1965), vol. II, pp. 534–5, supplemented on p. 453; further Grellier (1810); for the size of the British armed forces during the various wars, Rostow (1975), p. 236.

[6] See Fetter (1965), pp. 26ff., 165ff.; Cannan, 1919.

[7] See Deane and Cole (1969), pp. 12ff., 17, 33ff., Table 11 on p. 34, Figure 7 pull-out at end of book.

debt was guided by considerations of inter-generation equity, aiming at allocating the debt burden fairly among different generations of taxpayers. Whether this resulted simultaneously in a fair distribution of burdens among beneficiaries of the public expenditure financed by these loans – corresponding to a 'pay-as-you-use' system – is difficult to determine.[8] Simultaneous inter-dependence of formation, use, and distribution of the national product requires a cost–benefit analysis sufficiently detailed to relate to individual people or groups; empirical historical science is hardly able to provide it. Hence, all that can be said about the British system of public finance, public debt and economic performance in the eighteenth and nineteenth centuries is that it worked. How to match closely relative benefits with justice can probably be discussed only in the framework (not here considered) of a fundamental social philosophy, because this determines the economic system.[9]

At the end of the *ancien régime*, the British national debt in 1792 amounted to about £244.4 million, roughly 13 times annual budget revenue. Such a relation of revenue to debt was almost unthinkable for continental countries, short of state bankruptcy. The great volume of public debt was overwhelmingly caused by war expenditure, coupled with the determination not to finance wars out of taxation (see Table 32).

Comparison of long-term development of public expenditure with public debt shows the history of British public finance to be as much a history of voluntarily advanced public loans as of taxes levied by the state. Though it is not possible to apportion total indebtedness unequivocally between home and foreign loans, it is reasonable to assume that the overwhelming amount of money flowed to the state Treasury through voluntary transfers out of its own citizens' incomes, less from abroad (e.g. Holland) and from colonial possessions. There is in fact a particularly striking historical link between the development of the public debt and the growth of the British economy. Already in the eighteenth, more strongly in the nineteenth century, there existed among the British population a wealthy section capable and willing to invest part of its income in state bonds. Between 1761 and 1820 about 30.5 per cent of British public expenditure was financed from this source; between 1689 and 1820 the proportion did not fall as low as 29.5 per cent. This section of the population derived from these loans an income in the form of annual interest which grew to a substantial independent source of incomes within the total economy. Interest due to the wealthier section of the population was defrayed via the budget mainly from revenues derived from indirect taxes, paid overwhelmingly by sections of the population in receipt of lower incomes. The growth of the British

---

[8] For both systems see Musgrave (1958), pp. 72ff. [9] Schremmer (1976), pp. 122ff.

Table 32. *Financing of British public expenditure by loans, taxes, etc., 1689–1820 (in £000)*

Period	No. of years	Total expenditure	From taxes, etc.	From taken-up loans (national debt increase)	Foreign policy events	% expenditure financed by loans	Repayment of indebtedness
				Total revenue		$(5) = (3):(1)$	
	(0)	(1)	(2)	(3)	(4)	(5)	(6)
William III (1689–1702)	13	71,229.1	55,498.7	15,730.4	Revolution in Ireland, war with France	22.1	0
Anne (1702–14)	13	100,271.0	62,520.4	37,750.7	War of Spanish Succession, 1702–13	37.6	0
George I (1714–27)	13	77,000.1	77,000.1	0	War with Spain, 1718–21	0	2,053.1
George II (1727–60)	33	303,990.5	217,217.3	86,773.2	War of Austrian Succession, 1739–48, Seven Years War, 1756–63	28.5	0
George III (1760–1820)					Seven Years War, 1756–63		
1761–75	15	141,940.4	141,940.4	0		0	10,281.8
1776–86	11	256,201.3	134,933.3	121,268.0	War of American Independence, 1776–85	47.3	0
1787–93	7	118,274.1	118,274.1	0		0	5,411.3
1794–1817	24	1,712,525.6	1,108,683.4	603,842.2	Wars with France, 1793–1815	35.3	0
1818–20	3	146,275.5	146,275.5	0		0	0
1761–1820	60	2,375,216.9	1,650,106.7	725,110.2		30.5	15,693.1
1689–1820	132	2,927,707.6	2,062,342.2	865,364.5		29.6	17,746.2

Calculation of balance of national debt (in £000):

State of debt 1689	664.3
+ Loans raised 1689–1820	865,364.5 (3)
− Repayments 1689–1820	17,746.2 (6)
State of debt 1820	848,282.6

Source: Calculated from Vocke, 1866, pp. 82f, 90; see also Dowell, 1965, vol. II, p. 453.

economy was thus accompanied by an invisible transfer of revenues from poorer to partly the middling, partly the richer sections of the population. It is therefore not surprising that Pitt, when introducing income tax in 1799, tried to tax these revenues, nor is it surprising that Pitt's first attempt was frustrated by parliament. In the event, income from capital remained tax free until 1842.

There was a close connection between wars, their finance and the public debt. Without an extension and carefully elaborated system of public loans, wars would presumably have been shorter, periods of peace longer.

(iv) Taxes

Direct taxes

The main direct tax was the land tax,[10] introduced in 1688 as an extraordinary impost, but within a few years turned into an annual tax. The land tax replaced a poll tax imposed from time to time, modelled on French precedents in 1380 and repealed in 1698; it had been graded according to taxpayers' origin, status, position of life, and other circumstances. Assessment for land tax took as its basis a fairly crude estimate of land value, derived from a registration system which often failed either to measure the extent or to establish the quality of the land, nor did it take account of agricultural capital or household inventories. It calculated a ground rent of 6 per cent of land value, on which a 20 per cent tax was payable; this resulted in the so-called quota of 4 shillings. Surprisingly modern in its establishment of a quota, this tax proved unproductive, owing to widespread evasion; it was difficult to estimate its yield. From 1697 onwards the land tax therefore reverted to the old-established system of allocation to the various counties, parishes, and towns, whose administrations sub-allocated them while remaining liable for payment. The change to an allocation system – the government determining total yield *ex ante* – led to tax rates of 2 and 3 shillings in the pound. Sub-allocation by local authorities was – again a very forward-looking idea – to extend the incidence of the tax from owners of immovable to owners of movable property, such as craftsmen, traders, and unearned income recipients, 6 per cent of their property or income to be the basis for the assessment to tax. Even the revenues of certain categories of officials and other income recipients were to be subjected to the tax. Owing to the inadequacies of assessment of non-agrarian property and incomes, however, in the end land rents remained the only source taxed, and very unequally at that. Objectively this arose from the imperfection of land

---

[10] Ward (1953); for the detailed history of British taxes and the fiscal system to about 1880, Dowell (1965), 4 vols.

registration, subjectively from the arbitrariness of sub-allocating local authorities, but this was true of all contemporary land taxes based on land registers; it was not a British peculiarity. Though planned on modern lines, British land tax *de facto* resembled the old continental land taxes, even though it possessed from the outset elements of a general property and income tax. When after 1798 taxpayers took advantage of the opportunity to compound for the tax by means of 3 per cent Consols, land tax ceased to bear the characteristics of a tax and became a charge on land. In the nineteenth century, land tax remained a subsidiary tax on immovable property, of little importance compared to the new income tax.

Taxes on houses and establishments replaced the old hearth tax. In 1696 they were embodied in a graded window tax. In 1747 this was split into a fixed tax of 2 shillings per dwelling house and a tax on the windows of other buildings of every conceivable kind, the rate per window rising for every window beyond the tenth. This was an attempt, though made without adequate effort and thought, to levy tax on the establishments in these buildings, based on the simple technical equation: the larger the establishment, the larger the building; hence the larger the number of taxable windows belonging to the establishment to be taxed.

Indirect taxes

Introduction and refinement of excise duties took place following Dutch examples from 1643 onwards. The excise – the new impost – had made its victorious entry into Britain in order to help finance rapidly growing state requirements. To begin with, it fell mainly on consumer goods, such as beverages and foodstuffs, above all beer, alcohol, salt, meat, and a few colonial imports, such as tea, sugar, and subsequently tobacco; in the eighteenth century, the incidence of excise extended ever more to goods employed in industry, comprising raw materials, inter-mediate and finished goods. The excise grew into an entire set of increases in commodity prices, becoming by far the most important form of public revenue in the eighteenth and nineteenth centuries. Already in 1649, parliament had proclaimed the excise to represent 'the most equal and indifferent levy that could be laid on the people'.[11] Peculiar to the British version of excise was its link with a licensing system. Publicans, traders, and producers dealing in goods subject to excise had to register with the authorities and pay an annual licence. From this beginning, liability to license was extended to a number of other business activities, for instance advocates and banks.

Domestic consumption taxes corresponded to customs on goods in overseas trade (tonnage and poundage duties).[12] Whether customs tariffs

---

[11] The quotation is attributed to Josiah Child (1630–99); see Mann (1937), p. 64.
[12] Hoon (1968).

were levied on goods imported for domestic consumption and/or for the export and entrepôt trades depended on whether policies aimed at revenue or protection. Specific and *ad valorem* duties existed side by side. To achieve a better system of control and to separate the flow of goods split by the Navigation Laws of 1651, a network of specialized warehouses was developed in ports from 1711 onwards, first for silk, then, among others, for pepper, tea, and coffee. Deposit of goods in warehouses was partly voluntary, partly compulsory. Britain, similarly to Venice in the fifteenth and sixteenth centuries, became a large bonded warehouse, benefiting from all the port and storage revenues arising therefrom. These supplemented consumption duties, especially since export duties, apart from those on a few raw materials, had been abolished under Walpole in 1700. It is as difficult to distinguish semantically between excise and customs as to determine their economic effects. Both forms of tax were therefore often lumped together as indirect taxes or simply as taxes on food and on non-food articles.

Taxes on expenditure and luxuries

The prehistory of these taxes had a stronger influence on British political history than almost any other event in the late eighteenth century. The extraordinary multiplicity and ramifications of the British tax system at the end of the eighteenth century were decisively determined in the 1770s. The Seven Years War against France (1756–63) cost about £82 million. Taxes had been raised to a pitch where the costs of the war could be financed only by an increase of about £60 million in the public debt. The British government, unable to increase the incidence of domestic taxes, formed the ill-fated plan to levy taxes on the North American colonies, hitherto untrammelled by British taxes. Up to that time, British customs duties on goods exported to the colonies and British port dues had been regarded, even by the colonists, as economic charges required to control and regulate commerce, not as fiscal imposts contributed by the colonies to the British budget. The difference was a subtle one, legal, political and parliamentary rather than one of economic incidence. Grenville, Chancellor of the Exchequer, believed that he could play on this subtle difference – and made a mistake. He aimed in 1764 at increasing British public revenues at the colonies' expense in two ways: (1) raising customs duties in British export ports on entrepôt goods in transit in Britain, among others wine, coffee, sugar, tea, and linen; (2) introducing a tax in the colonies, to be paid into the British Treasury, resembling the mother country's stamp duties. Stamp duties were introduced in America in 1765. The sense of justice of a colonial population of overwhelmingly British origin caused immediate rebellion: parliament in London, in which colonists were not represented, had no right to impose a colonial tax. Thereupon the American Stamp Act was repealed.

The conflict between mother country and colonies about the right in principle of a parliament at Westminster to impose taxes was, however, greatly exacerbated when simultaneously the British parliament passed a declaratory act which 'asserts the right and authority of the parliament of Great Britain to make laws and statutes of sufficient force and validity to bind the colonies of America, subjects to the Crown of Great Britain, in all cases whatsoever'.[13]

This once again raised doubts in the colonies whether customs duties were really no more than fees needed to regulate commerce or whether they represented fiscal revenue drawn by Britain from the colonies. When in 1767 the British parliament introduced new duties, among others on British manufactures exported to the colonies, open resistance broke out: the colonies refused to import British goods. Thereupon, Britain in 1770 renounced the new tariffs – all except one, the tariff on tea. This insignificant impost of threepence in the pound, not likely to yield revenue of any substance, was maintained as a matter of political principle, to implement the act which declared parliament's right to impose taxes on the colonies. Open rupture resulted: in 1773, colonists invaded British ships in Boston harbour and threw overboard the cargoes of tea chests. War began between America and Britain, and the British colonies in 1776 declared their independence of the mother country. For the sake of a 'peppercorn rent', Britain had violated her very own principle, 'no taxation without representation', thus losing her American colonies.

The unexpected colonial war, escalating into a European war against France and Holland, cost Britain £97 million. It swelled the public debt and the British tax system in a manner hitherto unknown. However insubstantial, no old nor new tax was too insignificant to be exploited to an increasing extent, none to be renounced.[14] The system of indirect taxes was fully utilized, wherever possible at higher tax rates. Fiscal ingenuity regarding direct and similar taxes knew practically no limit; there were even so-called taxes on domestic establishments employing carriages (1747–1885), men servants (1777–1885), women servants (1785–92), horses (1784–1885), racehorses (1784–1874), sporting licences (1784–1885), hair powder (1795–1869), dogs (1796–1874), clocks and watches (1797–8), armorial bearings (1798–1885); also taxes on property insured, fire insurance (1782–1869), marine insurance (1795–1885); further taxes on particular professions and businesses, for example auctioneers (1777 +), pawn brokers (1784 +), attorneys and

[13] Dowell (1965), vol. II, pp. 160, 162.
[14] On the British fiscal system and its management between the American War of Independence and the Napoleonic wars, Binney (1958), pp. 20ff.; on the ramifications of indirect taxes, Dowell (1965), vol. IV.

solicitors (1785 +); finally taxes on transport entrepreneurs, for instance coaches and cabs (1694–1870), caravans (1779–1869) and post horses (1779–1869). Many of these new taxes followed the precedent of Holland, considered '*la terre classique de la fiscalité*' (de Parieu, *Traité desimpôts*, cited by Dowell).

The mixture of business, expenditure, luxury and property taxes exceeded the capacity of tax collectors. Pitt therefore, for the better assessment and policing of taxes, in 1785 picked out of this system, difficult to survey, a few taxes which constituted a rather heterogeneous and open-ended group of so-called assessed taxes. These were a set of taxes, partly direct, partly indirect, meant to bear especially on the wealthy. They attached to particular objects, luxuries, or services, for instance maintenance of carriages, men servants, pack, carriage or race horses, dogs, use of hats, gloves, clocks, silver plate, or armorial bearings. Taxes on dwellings also counted as assessed taxes. Thus, even in the field of luxury taxes, British legislation expanded unmethodical enumeration for taxation employing indicators of consumption.

The British fiscal apparatus, obviously extended to the utmost limit of productivity by the War of American Independence, necessarily required reform. This was advanced by Adam Smith's views (*Wealth of Nations* (1776)) on tax policy: tax yield could be substantially raised by more equal and just tax incidence, without increasing the burden on the majority of the population.[15] An urgent request for a higher tax yield by means of more equal and just tax incidence led to the first concept of a modern direct income tax, as we understand it today. Assessed taxes formed a transition, the first step in this direction being Pitt's *Triple Assessment* of 1799. The extraordinarily heavy costs of the war against Napoleon's France provided the external impetus to eventual reform.

2. *Structure of public budgets*

So far as public budgets reflect state activity,[16] Britain was mainly preoccupied in the eighteenth century with conducting wars in order to safeguard national security and to expand and protect its external sphere of influence. Given the causal connection between increasing public debt and war, budget debt charges hid mainly delayed war costs. On a long-term average of the eighteenth century, current and funded military expenditure jointly accounted for 80–90 per cent of total public expenditure, the former percentage applying more to the beginning, the latter more to the end of the century (see Table 33). This spelt out the arid budgetary consequence of the sentence contained in almost all history books: England became a world power.

[15] Smith (1776, 1937 edn), pp. 777ff. [16] For budget structure, Binney (1958), pp. 244ff.

Table 33. *Key figures of (net) Great Britain budget, 1705–92[a] (£000)*

	1705	1739	1755	1775	1792
Expenditure approx.					
Debt service	1,220	2,000	2,600	4,600	9,300
Army and navy	1,300[b]	1,850	2,000[c]	3,810	6,250[d]
Civil Service and administration[e]	703	950	1,000	1,200	1,230
Totals	3,223	4,800	5,600	9,610	16,780
Revenue from taxes, etc., approx.					
Land tax	1,000	1,000	1,000	1,750	2,000
Window and public pension taxes		135	235	—	—
Excise		3,000	3,660	5,100	8,740
Customs duties		1,400	1,780	2,750	4,100
Stamps		150	137	—	952
Other taxes and revenues	3,250				2,215
Totals	4,250	5,685	6,812	9,600	18,007
Population approx. in millions[f]					
England and Wales	5.8		6.1	7.1	8.2
Scotland	1.0		1.2	1.4	1.5
Ireland (part of the United Kingdom after 1800)	(2.5)		(3.1)	(4.8)	(4.8)
Totals	6.8		7.3	8.5	9.7
Revenue per head of Great Britain population approx. (£)	0.62		0.93	1.13	1.86

Notes:
[a] Dowell (1965), vol. II, pp. 68, 109, 128, 163, 206. 1775 and 1792 supplemented from Mitchell (1975), pp. 697, 706; see further Vocke (1866), p. 48.
[b] Average of 1698–1700.
[c] Average of 1753–5.
[d] Average of 1790–2.
[e] Royal household, civil administration, including judges, foreign office personnel, other civil servants, public pensions.
[f] Deane and Cole (1969), p. 6.

To provide military protection was perhaps the government's most important contribution to British industrialization. 'In so far as the state was important, its main role was . . . to provide security at home and abroad within which market and economic forces . . . would operate.'[17] This security was expensive, and the expanding scope of the market and economy required more and more – thus market expansion and state security were mutually reinforcing. Tax burden per head of population

[17] Mathias (1969), p. 32.

therefore roughly trebled in the eighteenth century, doubling in the second half of the century alone.

Public expenditure, taking the century as a whole, was financed to an extent of 25–30 per cent by the public debt, the remainder by taxation. The emphasis among taxes unequivocally fell on the so-called indirect taxes, that is excise and customs duties. Their share of total tax revenue varied regularly between 75 and 80 per cent. Imposts on domestic consumption (including a few capital investments) formed the dominant source of fiscal revenue.

To show types of commodities taxed and their tax burden at different times, we reproduce the revenue half of the 1792/3 budget on the eve of the French wars. By far the largest single source of tax revenue was domestic alcohol consumption (see Table 34).

B.   PUBLIC FINANCE DURING THE PERIOD OF
INDUSTRIALIZATION

1. *The system of finance during the period of breakthrough, 1798–1815*

The high costs of the Anglo-French wars, 1793–1802 and 1803–15, formed the immediate cause of the great public revenue reforms which ushered in the nineteenth century. Britain's war expenditure amounted to £831 million, of which a mere £209 million could be defrayed from tax revenues.[18] The heavy increase in public debt required a modification of the existing tax system, especially an expansion in direct taxation. A modern income tax formed the fiscal answer to the state emergency. It followed upon the assessed taxes of the eighteenth century; Pitt's triple assessment of 1798 was a transitional form of taxation.

(i) A premature innovation: income tax

Pitt's triple assessment of 1798
The principle underlying this emergency tax was an increase in tax levied on the wealthy part of the population. The tax consisted of a multiple of the previous year's assessment to the assessed taxes. The decisive development of the old expenditure and property taxes (assessed taxes) towards an income tax consisted in the manner of calculating the 'multiple'.

People liable to assessed taxes were divided in the first place into a presumably wealthy group of persons (those keeping a taxable establishment of carriages, men servants, etc.) and a presumably less wealthy group (those not keeping any such establishment, but chargeable in

---

[18] The expenses of particular wars are in Dowell (1965), vol. II, p. 209; for the early forms of British income tax see Seligman (1921), pp. 57ff.; international comparison of income tax development in Popitz (1926), pp. 437ff., specifically on Britain pp. 464ff.

Table 34. *Approximate yield of some principal taxes, 1792–3*

	£000	£000	%
I. Direct taxes			
Land tax	2,000		
Houses and establishments	1,300		
Property insured against fire	185		
Property sold at auction	75		
Post horses, coaches, hackney coaches	277	3,837	22.1
II. Taxes on articles of consumption			
(a) Foodstuffs:			
Salt	377		
Sugar	1,316	1,693	9.8
(b) Beverages:			
Beer	2,224		
Malt	1,203		
Hops	151		
Wine	1,016		
Spirits	1,532		
Tea	650		
(c) Tobacco		6,776	39.1
		567	3.3
(d) Commodities not foodstuffs, drink or tobacco:			
Coal exported or coastwise	700		
Raw and thrown silk	300		
Iron, bars	150		
Hemp (rough)	103		
Muslins	118		
Calicos	96	1,467	8.4
(e) Manufactures:			
Candles	256		
Leather	281		
Soap	403		
Printed goods	265		
Newspapers	140		
Glass	183		
Bricks and tiles	128	1,656	9.6
III. Stamp duties			
Bill and Notes	156		
Receipts	48		
Consolidated duties	748	952	5.5
Net receipts from the business of the Post Office		378	2.2
Totals I–III		17,326	100

Source: Dowell (1965), vol. II, pp. 206–7.

respect of their houses, dogs, clocks and such-like). Both groups were then subdivided into at least five sub-groups or classes each, according to the amount of the previous year's assessment to the assessed taxes. Those in the highest class of taxpayers, with an assessment of £50 or more for the previous year, in both groups paid the quintuple of the previous year's tax (quintuple assessment), whereas taxpayers in the lowest class of the first group – assessed up to £25 – paid treble the previous year's tax: hence the name 'triple assessment' – a simple and early form of progressive taxation. The amount of tax was not to exceed a maximum of 10 per cent of incomes of those drawing incomes above £200.

Two decisive features of the subsequent income tax had thus been introduced in a most original manner and interrelated:

1. A slightly progressive tax through the formation of classes of income liable to different fixed amounts of tax, the effect within each level being regressive;
2. The possibility of a personal income declaration: a taxpayer considering himself taxed in excess of the maximum rate of 10 per cent was at liberty to provide proof by submitting a 'form of general declaration of income', listing his total income from all sources. If successful, he benefited from a corresponding tax reduction. This ingenious idea of a voluntary income declaration for purposes of tax reduction pervaded Britain's entire income tax history in the nineteenth century.

The triple assessment was a fiscal failure. The tax proved almost impossible to collect. Pitt therefore developed his concept of an income tax further and in 1799 replaced the triple assessment by a 'property and income tax' – not without safeguarding public revenues against a shortfall by raising customs duties and consumption taxes.

Pitt's property and income tax, 1799–1802

Pitt by a general calculation estimated Britain's total taxable income at about £102 million (see Table 35). On these assessments, he based his income tax. The detailed income estimates – even considering the deductions and the minimum cost of living – provide early evidence on the level and structure of British national income, especially as regards contributions to total national income made by different sources. Comparison can also be made with calculations on the composition of taxable income based on the income statistics of 1801 and 1811.[19]

Calculations assuming a 10 per cent tax rate on net total income resulted in a tax yield of £10 million, on which Pitt based one of his great

[19] Deane and Cole (1969), pp. 323ff. in conjunction with Hope-Jones (1939), pp. 26ff.

Table 35. *Estimated incomes around 1798*

Type of income	Income (£000)
The land rental, after deducting one-fifth	20,000
The tenants' rental of land, deducting two-thirds of the rack rent	6,000
The amount of tithes, deducting one-fifth	4,000
The produce of mines, canal navigation, etc., deducting one-fifth	3,000
The rental of houses, deducting one-fifth	5,000
The profit of professions	2,000
The rental of Scotland, taking it as one-eighth of that of England	5,000
The income of persons resident in Great Britain, drawn from possessions beyond the seas	5,000
The amount of the annuities from the public funds, after deducting one-fifth for exemptions and modifications	12,000
The profits on the capital employed in our foreign commerce	12,000
The profits on the capital employed in domestic trade, and the profits of skill and industry	28,000
in all	£102,000

Source: Dowell (1965), vol. II, pp. 224–5.

speeches in parliament. Maximum justice was to be done to taxpayers by spreading the burden; that was possible only if individual taxpayers' incomes could be exactly ascertained. For this purpose, Pitt designed a form universally applicable to a general income statement. The form, to be filled by those chargeable, specified 19 separate sources of income and of income-yielding property, derived from the four following heads of income:

1. Income from land and houses;
2. Income from personal property, trades, professions, offices, pensions, stipends, employment, vocations;
3. Income arising out of Great Britain;
4. Income not falling under (1)–(3).

The fundamental principle laid down by Pitt is applied today in the income tax laws of every twentieth-century industrialized country. So revolutionary in finance and tax history was Pitt's form of income tax declaration that the birth certificate of income tax is reprinted here (Fig. 8).[20]

Incomes declared by the taxpayer under the different headings are aggregated into total income, reduced by some legally fixed deductions in respect of certain relevant expenditures and by some abatements

---

[20] Dowell (1965), vol. III, pp. 96ff.

related to family status; the resulting chargeable income is then subject to a differential tax rate, but a standard level for total income:

Chargeable income	Tax rate
below £60	exempt from tax
£60–£199 (in steps)	0.8–5.5 per cent (in steps)
£200 and above	10 per cent (2s. in the £)

So novel was this fundamental principle comprising an obligation to declare total personal income, a minimum necessary to existence remaining exempt, legally permitted abatements so as to ascertain net revenues, tax differentiation based on family circumstances, deduction at source and for debts, but above all taxation of income derived from capital, that this type of taxation did not take final root in Europe until the late nineteenth and early twentieth centuries. For the first time in European tax history a tax had been thus matched to the personal incomes of individual taxpayers. It signifies the entry of the liberal principle of individualization into the system of public finance. But property-owning citizens fought against it.

People liable to tax around 1800 refused to disclose their incomes on the grounds of tax rates seeming extraordinarily high and on the pretext of the state conducting unwarranted inquisitions into taxable capacity. Tax revenues remained so unsatisfactory, only £5.6 million in 1801, that Pitt resigned office in 1801 and the property and income tax was repealed in 1802 – partly owing to the peace of Amiens, after which a war tax no longer appeared expedient. However, war resumed, and with it the necessity for a further war tax – the question was only of what kind. Pitt's successor, Addington, found a pragmatic answer in the year during which Napoleon declared the continental blockade against Britain.[21]

Addington's property and income tax, 1803–6, and that of Petty, 1806–15

Addington adapted Pitt's ingenious concept to practical reality. To mitigate state inquisition into personal circumstances, so unpopular among taxpayers, Addington waived declaration of the individual's total income, replacing the general income statement by five partial tax declarations, relating to income under five different heads (separate returns of income from particular sources, schedules), thus converting a single tax of total income into a set of five partial income taxes, to be declared and taxed separately. The government resigned itself to the greater ease with which taxpayers could obfuscate their total incomes. This was one aspect of solving in practice the conflict between greater protection of individual privacy and adequate fiscal income. The other

---

[21] Crouzet (1958); Kisselbach (1850).

332

Fig. 8. *Pitt's form of general statement of income, 1799*

No.	DESCRIPTION OF PROPERTY FROM WHICH INCOME ARISES.	£	s.	d.	ANNUAL VALUE.
1	Land occupied by me as owner . . . . . { Rent / Annual value				
2	Houses and buildings occupied by me as owner				
3	Lands, tenements, or hereditaments in occupation of tenants at rack rent . . .				
4	Land, tenements, or hereditaments demised to tenants in consideration of a fine paid and rent reserved . . . . . { Amount of fines on an average of years' amount of rent.				
5	Lands, tenements, or hereditaments demised to tenants in consideration of a fine without any rent reserved, or nominal rent only . . . . . { Amount of fines received upon an average of years . . .				
6	Houses demised to tenants at rack rent . . .				
7	Houses demised to tenants in consideration of rent reserved and fine				
8	Houses demised to tenants in consideration of a fine without rent, or a nominal rent only				
9	Tithes received in kind, or composition reserved for the same. . . . . { Amount of average receipt for three years				
10	Profits of { Manors—average receipt for years / Timber— ,, ,, ,, / Woods— ,, ,, ,, / Mines— ,, not exceeding five years / Other profits of uncertain amount ,, ,, for years				

		£	s.	d.
11	Lands or hereditaments demised to me as tenant at rack rent			
12	Profits of { Manors / Timber / Woods } Demised to me, average the same as the 10th case, deducting the rent payable . .			
	Other hereditaments of uncertain amount . .			
	Tithes { taken in kind / compounded for } as in the 9th case, deducting the rent			
13	Lands or tenements demised to me in consideration of a fine, whether with or without a rent reserved; annual value			
14	Lands or tenements demised to me in consideration of fine, with or without a rent, and underlet to a tenant			
15	Lands demised to me at rent, and underlet to a tenant at an improved rent . .			
16	From professions, offices, pensions, stipends, employments, trade, or vocation, being of uncertain annual amount			
17	From offices, pensions, stipends, annuities, interest of money, rent charge, and other payments, being of certain annual amount and allowances applied to my use, including the income of the wife, if any, for which she or her trustee or trustees shall not be charged living with husband, though separately secured			
18	From foreign possessions			
19	From money arising from foreign securities . . .			
	From any income not falling under any of the above heads, or within the rules prescribed by the Act . .			
	Nature of the income and grounds on which the amount thereof is estimated . . .			
	Total amount of income	£		
	Deduction from above			
	Income chargeable	£		

DEDUCTIONS.

	£	s.	d.	For one year preceding the delivery of the schedule.			£	s.	d.
Land tax payable on the several properties mentioned under Nos. on the other side, from the day of to the day of last post									
Fines paid upon an average of years on the other side				.	.	.			
Fee farm rents, payable out of Nos.				.	.	.			
Quit rents, payable out of Nos. ,,				.	.	.			
Rent charges, payable out of Nos. ,,				.	.	.			
Ground rent, payable out of Nos. ,,				.	.	.			
Other rents, payable out of Nos. ,,				.	.	.			
Tenths				.	.	.			
Procurations, synodals, payable (by ecclesiastical persons) out of Nos. upon an average of seven years				.	.	.			
Repairs { Of farm, with principal messuage, under Nos.				.	.	.			
Of farm-buildings, without principal messuage, under Nos.				.	.	.			
Of drainage lands, under Nos. { by rate / for improvement of lands				.	.	.			
Of embankments under Nos.				.	.	.			
Of houses and buildings not occupied with a farm, under Nos.				.	.	.			
Of chancels of churches, by rectors, vicars, and others bound to repair the same, upon an average of 21 years				.	.	.			
Tithes { Expenses in collecting the same, upon an average of three years				.	.	.			
Value thereof paid in kind, upon an average of three years				.	.	.			
Value of composition for the same, upon an average of three years				.	.	.			
Annual interest for debts { Personal / Charged on Nos.				.	.	.			
Allowances to children, or other relations, viz. [ ]				.	.	.			
Assesed taxes under Acts 38 Geo. III. c. 40 & 41				.	.	.			
Annuities				.	.	.			
Land tax on personal estates, offices, pensions, &c.				.	.	.			
Premiums of insurance on life				.	.	.			
Total amount of deductions				£					

Witness my hand
this day of

Source: Stephen Dowell, *A History of Taxation and Taxes in England*, 1884, vol. III; *Direct Taxes and Stamp Duties.* 3rd edn, rep. (London, 1965), pp. 96, 97, 98.

aspect resulted from the manner in which incomes in the various schedules were ascertained. This caused the income tax to assume partially the character of the more traditional tax on revenues, relying on external indicators for average incomes.

The following is an abbreviated pattern characteristic of the British income tax system until the twentieth century, based on five income categories; the fundamental structure was reproduced in the French taxation of parts of income in 1914–17.

Schedule A: land and house owner's tax, taxed 'rent' or 'annual value' arising from ownership of lands, houses, manors, tenements, tithes (not commuted), fines, etc. With these were taxed – partly by subsequent addition – revenues derived from working mines, iron, gas and water works, docks, canals, and railways – large-scale industries which a feudal view of the world linked with immovable property. After 1866, these large-scale industrial categories of income were transferred to Schedule D. Mixture of agricultural and industrial revenues and the changing of categories within schedules render statistical use of tax revenues within particular schedules difficult. Through Schedule A, income tax acquired the character of a property tax tending to a tax on objects, because land was chargeable to tax as property even if temporarily not cultivated.

Schedule B: land occupier's and farmer's tax, again taxed 'rent' or 'annual value' from occupation of land, tenements or hereditaments. Revenue from the cultivation of land could be derived by a tenant or by the owner-occupier. Separation of Schedules A and B, so closely linked, is explained by greater frequency in Britain than on the continent of letting agricultural land to tenants.

Schedule C: fund holder's tax, taxed income from capital, represented by British (Indian, colonial) and foreign government securities. Revenues from other capital and interest fall under Schedule D.

Schedule D: the sweeping-clauses tax, taxed all other gains from any business concern, trade, profession, employment (except in the public service), certain interests and revenues from any sources which did not fall under other schedules. Where revenues were drawn from several sources, gains and losses could be set off against each other under Schedule D. Only from 1890 onwards could gains and losses also be balanced across schedules.

Schedule E: the public employee's tax, taxed all salaries, pensions, etc., of government, corporation, and public company officials. From 1922 onwards, this also included the incomes of private employees, until that time allocated to Schedule D.

The exemption limit remained at £60. The principle of allowable deductions was retained, modified for different types of income; abatements for family circumstances were limited. The rate of tax varied at different income levels between £60 (where the lowest rate began) and upwards of £150 (highest rate). The lowest rate of tax in 1803 amounted to 3d. in the pound, the highest, representing 5 per cent, to 1s. in the pound, in 1806 10 per cent of chargeable income. Throughout the nineteenth century, 10 per cent was regarded as the absolute upper limit of taxation.

Petty in 1806 modified assessment of chargeable income in a few details, but left Addington's income tax structure in principle unchanged. For the first time in tax history, taxation at source was firmly anchored in the legal framework. To make deduction at source possible and easy, a simple rate of tax – the proportional standard rate – was introduced. A proportional rate of tax could be understood in principle and as an idea and defended in parliament, whereas differential tax lacked a ready and easily understood test justifying the degree of differentiation; thus progression smacked of arbitrariness – which here as everywhere was objectionable.

This income tax provided the answer to public expenditure which since 1793 had risen from £24.2 million to £65.5 million (in 1800) and to £106.3 million (in 1814), producing every year a budget deficit and an increase in the public debt.[22]

(ii) Structure of public revenues, 1815

The pragmatic treatment adopted by Addington and Petty, renouncing state inquisition into details of citizens' property and income, was psychologically correct. After Pitt's failure, the new five-schedule income tax proved a great fiscal success. In the year of the hitherto heaviest tax burden, that is 1815, it accounted for 57 per cent of direct taxes and 21 per cent of total public revenue. At the same time, the British tax system at the moment of highest political and military effort reached probably the greatest diversification in its history, as is shown by the structure of public revenue (see Table 36).

2. The fiscal system between restoration and rationalization, 1816–42

(i) Abolition of property and income tax

After the second peace of Paris in 1815, the unloved income tax was repealed and the documentation recording assessments destroyed (as

22 Total budgets and annual deficits in Gayer, Rostow and Schwartz (1953), pp. 44, 76, 103, 131, with figures on the issue of paper money; also Rees (1921), pp. 24ff.; for paper money especially, Cannan (1919); also Silberling (1919).

regards preservation of duplicate files, see Hope-Jones, *Income Tax* (1939)). The tax had fully partaken of the character of an extraordinary war tax, a temporary special emergency tax. The British parliament did not yet possess a majority devoted to the principle of individualism inherent in the income tax – precisely the principle which, in pursuit of a liberal economy, it vehemently advocated in other fields. The idea that that government was best that taxed least, linked to the liberal concept of the nightwatchman state, retained the upper hand, allied to anti-tax agitation by interest groups. Parliament was equally unable to discern in 1815 that, in the light of rapidly progressing industrialization and an increasing disparity in the distribution of incomes and property among different sectors, the concept of fairness and justice in taxation – always liable to controversy and to different interpretations – was increasingly violated. 'Proportionate to ability to pay' need not always be 'proportionate to revenue received'; and then there was also 'proportionate to their respective interests'. It was difficult to accept that somebody ought to pay more merely because he was able to pay more. Nor could parliament foresee the conveniently high elasticity of income tax yield consequent upon growing national income.

(ii) Rationalization measures in indirect taxes and tariffs

Traditional taxes, particularly indirect consumption imposts and customs duties, filled the gap left by the repeal of income tax at a time of diminishing public expenditure. To this extent, Britain on retreating from taxation of incomes enjoyed a period of fiscal restoration. During this period, a number of reforms considerably tightened up the tax system inherited from the eighteenth century: repeal of unremunerative petty taxes, difficult to collect and police, but above all reduction of import duties. It was fortunate that that reduction conformed to two principles, that of economic liberalism and that of tax efficiency in the sense of reducing collection costs.

The first phase of tax rationalization during the 1830s saw a lowering of many indirect consumption taxes, partly on British, partly on imported manufactures and on some consumption goods: salt (1825), leather (1830), candles, coal, stone, and slate, printed silk, calico, linen, and cotton (all in 1831), tiles (1833), bottles, starch, almanacs, and calendars (all in 1834).

After reintroduction of income tax in 1842, the trend towards dismantling the traditional eighteenth-century system of indirect taxes was reinforced: by 1846, iron, wool, silk, flax, hemp, cotton, indigo, and glass were free from duties, followed by bricks (1850), soap and advertisements (1853), newspapers (1855), paper (1861), finally playing cards

Table 36. *Structure of tax revenues, 1815*

	£000	%	£000	%
I. Direct taxes				
on Income	14,600	21.4		
Houses and establishments	6,500	9.5		
Succession to property	1,297	1.9		
Land	1,196	1.7		
Property insured	918	1.3		
Property sold at auction	284	0.4		
Passenger, postal and hackney carriages	471	0.7		
Shipping tonnage	172	0.3	25,438	37
II. Taxes on articles of consumption				
(a) Foodstuffs:				
Sugar	2,957	4.3		
Salt	1,616	2.4		
Currants, raisins, pepper, vinegar	542	0.8	5,116	8
(b) Beverages:				
Beer, malt, hops	9,596	14.0		
Spirits	6,700	9.8		
Wine	1,901	2.8		
Tea	3,591	5.3		
Coffee	277	0.4	22,065	32
(c) Tobacco			2,026	3
(d) Commodities not foodstuffs, beverages or tobacco, i.e. coal and raw materials for manufacture, building, ship building and other trades:				
Timber	1,802	2.6		
Coal and slate	916	1.3		
Raw cotton	760	1.1		
Raw and thrown silk	450	0.7		
Barilla, indigo, potash, bar iron, furs	297	0.4		
Hemp	285	0.4		
Export duties	364	0.5		
Other customs duties	1,188	1.7	6,062	9
(e) Manufactures:				
Leather	698	1.0		
Soap	748	1.1		
Paper	476	0.7		
Glass	425	0.6		
Printed goods	388	0.6		
Newspapers	383	0.6		
Candles	354	0.5		
Bricks and tiles	269	0.4		
Minor taxes	132	0.2		
Advertisements	125	0.2		
Plate	82	0.1	4,081	6

Table 36. *(cont.)*

	£000	%	£000	%
(f) Excise licences			753	1
III. Stamp duties				
Bills and notes	841	1.2		
Receipts	210	0.3		
Other documents	1,692	2.5	2,743	4
IV. Other revenue (mostly minor taxes)			63	–
Total revenue			68,347	100

Sources: Dowell (1965), vol. II, pp. 258–9; total revenue from Mitchell (1975), p. 75; £79 million, referring to gross receipts; small differences throughout. Discrepancies in figures due to rounding.

and dice (1885). While reintroduction of income tax eased the trendy liberalization of overseas trade, the fate of customs duties after 1815 belongs to the history of British commercial and economic policy rather than of its public finance system. The controversy of protection versus free trade was decided in favour of free trade, particularly during the periods 1824/5 and 1841–53: repeal of the Navigation Acts, first reduction, then repeal of customs duties on raw materials, agricultural and food tariffs and of duties protecting industries, simplification of the tariff and concentration of revenue duties on a few commodities: tobacco, tea, sugar, wine, spirits, coffee, cocoa, Mediterranean fruit. Of the approximately 1,200 imported commodities chargeable up to 1842, duties were reduced on about 750, repealed on 450. After the British–French Cobden treaty of 1860, import duties remained on a mere 48 commodities. The 1838 Anti-Corn Law League achieved a substantial reduction of duties on cereals in 1849; their final repeal occurred in 1869. All surviving export duties disappeared in 1842.

Germany carefully watched Britain's progressive transition to free trade, admiring the implementation of a theory resulting in a unified system. At the same time, there was little understanding abroad for the neglect of agricultural interests and of small and medium farmers – a section of the population and of the economy which Germany traditionally cherished. In addition, foreign observers had considerable doubts how far the emphasis on British trading and commercial interests was well judged, given the growing emancipation of continental and American industries and their deliberate attempt to rid themselves of British supremacy.[23]

[23] Wagner (1889), part 3, pp. 301–2.

Table 37. *Change in the base of indirect taxation, excise, and customs duties (selected examples), 1825–1913*

	1825	1850	1870	1913
Domestic consumption:				
Beer (barrels)	8,000	15,250	25,750	33,325
Spirits (gallons)	20,250	26,000	31,500	31,794
Tobacco (lbs)	16,750	27,500	41,500	94,079
Tea (lbs)	29,700	51,100	117,500	305,490
Sugar (cwt)	3,000	6,000	13,750	33,919
Imports (in £000)	37,500	105,750	303,250	768,735
Exports (in £000)	59,000	190,000	244,000	634,820
Shipping Inwards } in	3,000	7,000	18,000	49,064
Outwards } 1,000 tons	2,500	7,500	18,500	67,820
United Kingdom population (millions)	22	27	31	45.6

Sources: 1825, 1850, 1870: Dowell (1965), vol. II, p. 386.
1913: *Statistical Abstract for the UK, 1911–1925* (1927), pp. 4, 154, 260–1, 280–1, 318.
Mallet (1913), pp. 480–1, giving fiscal revenue for the years 1888–1912.

British free trade policy did not reduce customs revenue receipts. In spite of considerable reductions in rates and items of tariff gross customs revenue remained unchanged at about £22–23 million.[24] This was due to the increase in the volume of goods passing through ports and in imports consequent upon the growing prosperity of the British population in the course of industrialization. That is the paradox described by Pitt when he referred to the most famous trade treaty of the period of protection, the Methuen treaty between Britain and Portugal in 1703, as an 'increase by means of reduction' (see Table 37).

This paradox applies to all indirect consumption dues, that is customs duties as well as excise. Growth of population and of per capita income increased popular consumption, especially of beer, alcohol, tobacco and sugar to such an extent ('An Englishman will fairly drink as much as will maintain two families of Dutch' (Defoe, *True-born Englishman*, cited by Dowell)) that indirect taxation of domestic consumption remained by far the largest and most productive source of public revenue up to the First World War.

Nevertheless, revenue derived from the traditional direct taxes which after 1816 either stagnated or partly fell off, and from the increased yield of consumption taxes sufficed to offset the absence of income tax at a

[24] See figures for years from 1835 to 1856 in Dowell (1965), vol. II, appendix.

period of reduced need for public income, but the British tax system lacked its most elastic component. After 1837 the budget could no longer be balanced without increasing public debt. At the same time, increasing industrialization meant that a revenue system rationalized, but traditionally relying on indirect taxes did not achieve an even approximately fair – that is, proportionate to income – distribution of the tax burden. Especially incomes from capital business concerns, trade, professions, and private employment, falling up to 1815 under Schedules c and d, remained very inadequately taxed, often even exempt.

In the end, the two fundamental rules, those of the income elasticity of tax yield and of fair, even just, distribution of tax burden, were bound to necessitate a reintroduction of income taxation; the only question was when. The immediate cause was once more the need for finance of a government involved in military expenditure. One point was clear: there was no hope of increasing taxation on the wealthier section of the population by means of the so-called luxury and expenditure taxes, as had been attempted in the eighteenth century. Remnants of traditional assessed taxes and petty taxation linked to them could not possibly survive: the tax on inhabited houses had already been repealed in 1834, the window tax in 1851. The only subsidiary taxes on property extant, poor in yield, were land tax and house duty.

(iii) Structure of public budgets, 1816–42

The period without income tax witnessed a perceptible shrinking of budget totals, made possible by the drop in military expenditure after the end of the war. The contraction cannot therefore be attributed unreservedly to the prevalence of the 'liberal nightwatchman state'. While the existence of a nightwatchman state is the citizen's day dream as regards the state's domestic activities, it never represents the reality applying to a state furthering expansion abroad. Yet tax burden per head of population fell perceptibly (see Table 38).

The proportion of the budget earmarked to pay interest on the public debt remained at an unchanged level of about 54 per cent, while the public debt could be slightly reduced (see Table 43).

3. The modern fiscal system of the first industrial nation

(i) Breakthrough to a regular property and income tax from Peel onwards, 1842

Britain's world-wide activities and the Afghan war led to Peel's reintroduction of income tax in 1842. From that date onwards, income tax in the shape of Addington's set of taxes on five categories of income

Table 38. *Revenue and expenditure of the United Kingdom,*
1816–42 (£000)

	1816	1822	1826	1832	1836	1842
Expenditure						
Public debt interest	32,000	31,900	29,229	28,324	29,244	29,428
Army and navy	56,500	16,600	16,708	13,805	12,113	16,159
Tax collection costs			5,387	4,534	4,247	4,278
Civil administration etc. }	10,800	9,900	2,384	1,848	2,937	2,398
Sundries }			2,567	2,397	2,279	2,960
Total expenditure	99,300	58,400	56,275	50,908	50,819	55,224
Total revenue	79,100	61,600	55,629	51,523	52,949	51,244
of which						
excise and customs	43,800	42,600	40,000	37,000	39,000	37,000
income tax	14,600	—	repealed up to 1842			
other revenue	20,700	19,000	15,600	14,500	13,900	14,200
Population (millions)	19	20.9	22.5	24	25.6	26.7
		(1821)		(1831)		(1841)
Approximate per capita revenue (£)	4.16	2.95	2.47	2.15	2.07	1.92

Sources: Acworth (1925), p. 137 for 1816 and 1822; Vocke (1866), p. 101, for remaining
years; Dowell (1965), vol. II, pp. 281, 323, gives slightly different figures for 1826 and
1842. Budgets are net; gross budgets from 1854 onwards, according to Vocke (1866), p.
126 n. and Rees (1921), p. 110 n. Discrepancies in figures due to rounding.
Population figures: Acworth (1925), p. 135; supplemented from Mitchell (1975), p. 708.

had been firmly integrated into the British tax system.[25] Parliament after
1842 no longer discussed repeal or reintroduction of the tax, but merely
the level of the tax rate and modifications of (a) exemptions: the lower
exemption limit being raised to £150 in 1842, lowered to £100 in 1852,
raised to £160 in 1894; and (b) allowances: mainly in favour of lower-
income groups, even though Peel in 1842 removed exemptions for
children (until 1909) and for insurance premiums (until 1853) on grounds
of excessive administrative costs, and did not at the time permit income
to be assessed net of debts.

The new tax was extended to the English and Scottish populations.
Ireland could be included in the income taxation in 1853, when the
bureaucratic apparatus for administration and assessment had been established. The yield of income tax was high as expected.

To begin with, the rate of tax was a simple standard rate of 7*d*. in the
pound, applicable to all kinds of income. At the lowering of the
exemption limit in 1852, a graduated rate was introduced, reduced for

[25] Seligman (1921), pp. 128ff., 167ff.; on Gladstonian finance, Sabine (1966), pp. 75ff. For the fight
of the Liberals against income tax, using the current objections of inequality, inquisition,
oppression and fraud, see Mann (1937), pp. 230ff.; introduction of income tax was a Conservative
victory; Popitz (1926), pp. 464ff.

Table 39. *Abatements and allowances from actual incomes, 1913*

| Total actual income | | | Allowances from actual income in respect of | | |
Exceeding £	Not exceeding £	Abatements £	Children £	Wife £	Life insurance premiums £
130	160	Exempt	Exempt	Exempt	Exempt
160	400	160	10	0	
400	500	150	10	0	Various; Maximum one-sixth of income
500	600	120	0	0	
600	700	70	0	0	
700	—	0	0	0	

Source: Mallet and George (1929), p. 359.

incomes between £100 and £150; it remains surprising that it took so long for progression to become part of income tax, in spite of its early antecedents (Pitt, 1798). Social thinking left little mark on the British tax system. The relative tax disadvantages suffered by the lower-income classes reflected the interests of the wealthier groups represented in parliament, but also the encouragement of capital accumulation necessary for industrialization, achieved by gentle taxation of revenues from capital.

Though it was occasionally argued that taxation of estimated average revenues of groups of taxpayers with identical types of incomes rewarded hard work among individuals and capital accumulation among taxpayers for the public benefit,[26] governments from the 1860s onwards intensified efforts to ascertain the actual taxable incomes of individuals by requiring individual income declarations. The demand for protection of privacy was slowly but progressively pushed back. The government recalled Pitt's ingenious 'trick' of 1798: it 'rewarded' declaration of income, where appropriate, by tax reduction. This was rendered possible from 1863 onwards by the introduction, elaboration, and refinement of a system of multiple allowances, consisting of exemptions, abatements, and graduations. To these was added in 1907 differentiation, taxing earned income, especially of the lower and middle income earners up to £2,000, at a rate lower than unearned income.[27] After 1898, the rates, abatements and allowances relating to income tax were as in Tables 39 and 40.

[26] Actual revenues exceeding average achievable revenues remain tax free; that provides a tax incentive to increased hard work; actual revenues falling short of average achievable revenues are taxed as though they had reached the level of average achievable revenues; this represents tax punishment for economic supineness.

[27] For the system of abatements, see Harzendorf (1914), pp. 167ff.; for the differentiation of 1907 and the graduation of 1910, see Seligman (1921), pp. 202ff., 207ff.

Table 40. *Normal and reduced rates of income tax chargeable on taxable income, 1913*

Total taxable income from all sources		Normal rate 1s.2d. on income	
Exceeding £	Not exceeding £	Earned s. d.	Unearned s. d.
130	160	Exempt	Exempt
160	2,000	0 9	Normal rate
2,000	3,000	1 0	Normal rate
3,000	—	Normal rate	Normal rate

Source: As Table 39.

A taxpayer wanting to benefit from tax deductions by way of tax refund had to declare his total income after the end of the income tax year. Thus the state offered its citizens a choice between 'preservation of privacy' and 'tax refunds'. The number of tax declarations increased substantially, citizens' aversion against the inquisitorial state diminished; by a process of indirect pressure, gradual education of taxpayers to declare their income to tax proved successful – and taxation at source, convenient for tax collection, remained in being.

By introducing graduation, by differential tax exemptions and by a rate differentiating between earned and unearned income, the state had introduced a threefold social modulation into taxation; earned incomes were burdened less than other incomes; determining the level of chargeable income caused a chiefly hidden, graduating subsequently an overtly, progressive tax, though very modestly so *in toto*. Later continental systems of income tax – with the exception of France – preferred in contrast a more steeply graduated progression of rising tax rates. Further considerations of social policy were ingrafted in the tax system by Lloyd George's reforms. Introduction of 'super tax' in 1910, a progressively structured additional tax on high incomes exceeding £5,000 per annum, subsequently in 1927 incorporated as surtax in the income tax, patently displayed open progression in the British tax system. In 1912/13, 11,800 people were assessed to super tax.[28]

From 1863 onwards, the early income tax of classical finance, upholding three principles reminiscent of revenue tax:

Protection of citizens against state inquisition
A proportional tax rate

[28] Mallet (1913), p. 486; on p. 484, details on the repeated alterations in income tax rates since 1887, the abatements, taxable income and the produce of each penny of the tax.

Far-reaching unconcern with personal conditions (e.g., number of children) and behaviour (hard work, laziness) of taxpayers,

was finally converted to the present-day income tax, bearing the stamp of financial interventionism and abandoning those three principles. Income tax was thus converted to a first-class tool of social and economic policy without thereby sacrificing tax yield.

Income tax served the ends of an interventionist economic policy by that part of the system of allowances which determined different levels of chargeable incomes among five different categories of income, taxing differently revenues from work, capital and land within the schedules.[29] In addition, different tax treatment could be meted out to each type of income, for example, according to type of work performed, purpose of investment, land use, or geographical location of taxpayers' activities. Income tax took account of social policy by the second part, a system of abatements, the personal allowances (relief in respect of children, wife, age, etc.). A taxpayer's chargeable income thus resulted from a concatenation of income-related allowances and person-related abatements.

Viewed from the continent in the second half of the nineteenth century, the British income tax system was distinguished above all by two widely admired characteristics which in the end made it the prototype of all subsequent European income taxes:

1. An efficient and pragmatic method of assessment and collection;
2. High elasticity of tax revenue, varying with changes in national income and fiscal needs.

An efficient and pragmatic method of assessment and collection
The method of annual assessment and collection was regarded as an example of British pragmatism. A triple formula embodied in an abbreviated form the compromise between what the purity of the theoretical concept required and what practical politics could achieve:

Collection at source, where possible; assessment plus declaration, where necessary;
Taxation of actual (net) income, where possible; taxation of estimated total (gross or net) revenue, where necessary;
Assessment of general commissioners locally, where possible, but by special commissioners if the taxpayer preferred this more anonymous form of assessment by officials at a distance from his locality.

Where collection took place at source, the recipient received merely his net income, tax having been previously deducted, so no unpopular

[29] Details in Mallet (1913), p. 485.

assessment was required. It made private persons and institutions render ancillary services – usually free of charge – to the state fiscal administration; the value of this part of fiscal infrastructure can hardly be overestimated. Deduction at source also served state interest by largely obviating fraud on the taxpayer's part. The purest form of tax deduction was possible in the income categories taxed under Schedules C and E. Salaries and wages were paid to public employees net of tax charged on incomes from employment; public paymasters or private banks made interest payments after deducting tax due on income derived from capital revenues. Under Schedule A the tenant discharged to the collector's office tax due for the proprietor under the title of income from ground or building rents, paying to the proprietor a net rent.

Assessment to tax by means of an income declaration which not only touches on the taxpayer's area of privacy, but also facilitates tax evasion, applied mainly to people charged under Schedules B and D. The problem consisted of ascertaining net income in full, while preserving individual privacy – a mixture of bank and income confidentiality. The compromise in practice permitted, according to category of income, a declaration of total presumed average revenue in lieu of actual net income, consisting partly of gross revenue calculated on a standard basis, partly of approximate net revenue, mostly an amount midway between the two. Especially for large-scale trading or manufacturing enterprises, assessment for several years meant the negotiation of agreed tax amounts. The difference between actual higher and tax-chargeable lower incomes presumably increased with the growth of total income. Only after 1927 were business incomes taxed according to the previous year's actual revenue. According to continental terminology, British income tax thus represented a mixture of income and revenue taxation.[30]

The normal rate of tax after deduction of the abatements constituted a burden proportional to income. This did not satisfy the principles of ability to pay and justice inherent in contemporary tax theories. On the other hand, strengthening the social policy component, high exemption limits and abatements meant that the mass of wage-earners, craftsmen, traders, small industrialists, and farmers did not pay income tax; these constituted the manual labour classes, in contradistinction to the class of income tax payers (over £160 per annum). Within the class of income tax payers again, in the last pre-First World War tax year, 1913/14, of 1,200,000 people assessed for income tax, 70,000 remained exempt on

[30] Income tax is based on the principle that the taxpayer's contribution to state requirements is proportional to his individual actual total income. Revenue tax is based on the principle of the taxpayer being charged according to estimated average achievable revenue, mainly determined by external indicators. The estimate does not necessarily relate to the individual, but to a group of taxpayers having identical types of revenue. For more details on revenue taxes see pp. 378ff., 390f., 483f.

grounds of abatements and allowances claimed.[31] Exemption of a large circle of people lowered costs of collection attributable to income tax substantially, thus implementing the principle of efficiency in the tax system.

High elasticity of tax revenues

There are two aspects to the elasticity of tax revenues. One means that tax revenues increase as national income rises without involving changes in tax rates. That was a decisive advantage, compared to continental allocated taxes whose total yield had to be fixed *ex ante* by governments for each revenue period. Even when there was a business upswing, any plans to raise total tax revenue – even with incidence on taxpayers remaining unchanged – regularly provoked resistance to taxation in continental parliaments. Behind this stood the underlying continental concept which differed from the British and may be represented, much simplified but correct in substance, as follows: the increment arising from growing national income should remain in people's pockets and no part of it should be automatically transferred to the state. There should be no increase in public revenue, unless first granted by parliament. If, on the other hand, national income fell in the depression periods, it was the state's duty to take its share by tax remissions. The British government enjoyed the comfortable and frictionless proceeds of a tax linked to national income during the long-term increase of the national produce throughout the nineteenth century. The British Treasury benefited extraordinarily from the economic upswing of the second half of the nineteenth century without having to change tax rates or seek parliamentary sanction. A few examples are given here:[32]

Year	Rate of tax	Tax yield
1866	4*d*. in the £	5,750,000
1867	4*d*. in the £	6,000,000
1871	4*d*. in the £	6,250,000
1873	4*d*. in the £	7,500,000

The tax yield of 1*d*. in the pound produced £867,000 in 1850, £1,500,000 in 1870 and as a rule of thumb £2,000,000 in 1880–5.

The second aspect of tax elasticity concerns the variability of the tax rate. It can be changed relatively quickly – given parliament's agreement and willingness of the population to pay taxes – and adjusted to changed

---

[31] Mallet and George (1929), p. 398. Mallet (1913), pp. 430ff. gives a number of estimates for the incomes of the three following classes of the population for 1903: income of income tax payers £750 million, of manual labour classes £700 million, of the intermediate class outside the manual labour class, but not liable to income tax £205 million.

[32] Dowell (1965), vol. III, pp. 110f.

state requirements without modifying collection procedure. The rate of continental revenue taxes could be changed equally expeditiously, but not so the clumsy registers for land, houses and industrial establishments which complemented the tax system. The British income tax automatically adapted itself to structural changes in the economy. Continental revenue taxes did not. That was the second main reason for the superiority of the British tax.

To give a few examples of the variability of the tax rate: between 1842 and 1912 the rate moved between 2d. (minimum, 1875/6) and 16d. (maximum, first occasion 1856/7, Crimean War, second occasion 1903, in Boer War) in the pound of chargeable income; usually it remained between 4d. and 7d. This corresponded to a moderate tax incidence of 2 to 3 per cent, if measured by the decimal system usual on the continent (1d. = 0.417 per cent). Income tax incidence of 10 per cent constituted, as before, the 'natural limit of the tax'. It was never reached. Increased rearmament in 1910–13 saw the rate raised to 1s.2d.

Full of admiration, Schmoller wrote in 1909: 'How jubilant would the German people be, had it so adaptable a factor of revenue as to make it vary between £2.4 million (48 million marks) and £24 million (480 million marks), such as Britain has in the shape of its income tax.'[33] Schmoller admired the 'political and patriotic sense' and the 'feeling of justice among the wealthy in Britain' which made possible that elasticity, thus underpinning the state by so secure a fiscal foundation.

Attempt at using income tax statistics to estimate the level of different types of income

Repeated attempts have been made to use the yields of the separate income tax schedules developed in an early phase of industrialization to measure changes in taxable income and its distribution among different types of income – a problem congenial to classical British political economy. While Adam Smith was mainly concerned with the wealth of nations, that is with production, David Ricardo in his principal work, *The Principles of Political Economy and Taxation*, published in 1817, enquired into production and distribution of national income, trying to establish laws governing the distribution over time of total income as between rent, interest and profits, and labour. National income distribution is one of the fundamental questions of European industrialization in the nineteenth century; it links the interdependent and simultaneously arising problems of economic growth, capital accumulation and pauperism. No industrial nation in the world had a tax system focused on the taxation of individual incomes from the three factors of production as

---

[33] Schmoller (1909), p. 37. A comparison of the British 'mobile' tariff system with continental regulations in Laufer (1911), pp. 20ff. For the Reich see pp. 466ff.

early as did Britain – 'classical British economics'. It can hardly be assumed that the last word has been said on this, but two results are presented here, one derived directly from the tax statistics from 1866 to 1895, using mostly uncorrected (see Table 41), the other corrected figures (see Table 42). We also refer to Pitt's estimates of income distribution around 1798 (see Table 35) and during the Napoleonic period, 1803–15.[34]

The new 1972 estimates of corrected taxable income differ considerably from the uncorrected figures. They are reproduced here without entering more closely into the reasons for the differences. Taxable income was calculated, as follows:[35]

1. Gross income brought under review, less
    incomes remaining below exemption limit,
    incomes of charities, hospitals, friendly societies, etc.,
    foreign dividends accruing to residents abroad;
2. Gross income of persons liable to tax, less allowances for
    repairs to land and buildings,
    vacant property,
    wear and tear of machinery,
    other allowances, reductions and discharges;
3. = Taxable income.

According to this correction of figures, taxable income from the different sources changes as in Table 41. A rough interpretation of changes in different types of income indicates that the greatest growth by far took place in incomes of government officials (E), followed by incomes from industry and trade (D), agrarian incomes from land and houses (A, B) and incomes from public loans (C). We must, however, remember that in the course of decades different types of income were switched between schedules (see p. 335 above, Schedule A).

In absolute figures, the importance of types of incomes shifts, taxable income from 'profits of trades and professions' (D) constituting by far the largest amount, followed by agrarian income from land and houses (A, B), salaries and wages of predominantly public loans. Essentially, these proportions of 1865 to 1895 remain the same in the enquiry of 1972. However, nobody has yet weighted these types of income according to the number of their different recipients.

The structural shifts clearly reflect Britain's change to a mature industrial economy up to the First World War. According to the 1972 enquiry, the proportions of total taxable income derived from land and houses and from trade and industry were approximately equal at 38 per

---

[34] As described, commented on and expanded by their own estimates by Deane and Cole (1969), pp. 323ff.   [35] Feinstein (1972), pp. 159f., 169.

Table 41. *Income assessed to, and receipts from, income tax, 1842–95 (£000)*

| | Peel's estimate of income from different sources (GB) and yield of income tax on reintroduction in 1842, compared to actual yield in 1843 | | 1860 | 1865 | 1865* | 1882 | 1895 |
	1842 Estimated income	1843 Ascertained income					
1. Income or annual value schedules							
Schedule A							
Rent of land	39,400	45,754					
Rent of houses	25,000	38,476					
Tithes	3,500	1,960					
Dividends of railway companies, canals and similar properties	3,429	6,454					
Mines and iron works	1,500	2,641					
Total Schedule A	72,829	95,285	126,057	150,765	161,397	190,532	208,125
Schedule B: Rent from occupation of land	26,000	46,770	49,238	57,120	56,181	68,799	55,722
Schedule C: Income from public funds, etc.	30,000	27,910	28,343	32,013	32,044	39,993	38,645
Schedule D: Profits of trades and professions	56,000	71,330	90,547	110,081	124,076	267,402	336,720
Schedule E: Incomes of public and private employees	7,000	9,718	18,040	20,602	22,131	34,725	51,040
Total	191,829	251,013	312,225	370,581	395,829	601,451	690,252

2. Tax receipts

	Estimate	Actual receipts				
Schedule A	1,600	2,501	4,817	3,769	3,563	4,752
B	150	335	574	428	331	189
C	646	813	1,114	800	851	1,258
D	1,220	1,682	3,247	2,752	4,675	8,352
E	155	278	674	515	585	1,098
Total	3,771	5,609	10,425	8,264	10,005	15,649
Standard rate in the £	7d.	7d.	10d.	6d.	5d.	8d.

Sources: 1842 and 1843: Dowell (1965), vol. III, p. 311, appendix; 1860 and 1865: Vocke (1866), pp. 589–90: income here is 'taxable income'. For years up to 1860 Great Britain, from 1865 onwards United Kingdom; 1865★: *Statistical Abstract for the United Kingdom 1866–80* (1881), p. 27: income here is gross income. Error in addition of receipts from the various schedules in the sources remains unexplained; 1882 and 1895: *Statistical Abstract for the United Kingdom, 1881–1895* (1896), pp. 17, 34: income here is gross income.

Table 42. *Calendar year estimates of taxable income under each schedule,*
1855–1914 (£ million)

| | Schedule | | | | | |
	A	B	C	D	E	Total
1855	80.0	12.5	25.0	85.6	13.0	216.1
1860	87.8	12.3	27.8	103.4	14.8	246.1
1865	98.2	14.2	32.6	147.3	18.9	311.2
1870	107.8	14.2	37.2	192.1	21.7	373.1
1875	121.4	15.1	41.6	244.5	26.8	449.4
1880	131.1	15.0	38.9	266.1	30.4	481.5
1885	133.5	12.4	40.2	258.7	35.3	480.1
1890	134.9	9.3	39.6	340.2	43.6	567.6
1895	146.0	7.9	37.2	365.6	51.4	608.1
1900	159.8	6.1	39.1	459.4	71.5	735.9
1905	168.0	5.4	44.2	462.0	88.7	768.3
1910	172.8	5.4	46.0	540.5	113.5	878.2
1914	178.5	5.4	49.4	576.0	147.5	956.8
Index of change 1914 (1855 = 1)	2.2	0.4	2.0	6.7	11.3	4.4

Source: See fn. 35.

cent in 1855; by 1914, the share of landed income had fallen to 18 per cent, whereas that of trade and industry predominated with 60 per cent. Though figures for 1865 to 1895 confirm this trend, landed income during that period remained relatively higher. However, the concept of 'income' and the level of revenues under different schedules have by now become so dependent on tax legislation that a comparison of taxable income, tax incidence, and rates of tax in the same country at different periods of time – or between different countries at the same point in time – is valid only if the tax laws in force at the time are exactly known.

(ii) Public debt and Gross National Product

The item of 'debt service' on the expenditure side of the budget clearly indicates that the state, over the period under review as a whole, had to take up loans in order to defray expenses not otherwise covered. Yet so flexibly was income tax handled after 1842 that there were instances when debt was either not incurred at all or at least remained within limits. Indeed in this period of high total indebtedness, it was even possible to reduce somewhat the national debt, as shown in Table 43.

The patent reduction in public per capita debt is paralleled by an even greater reduction relative to public revenue: in 1856, debt amounted to 10.7 times, in 1913 to only 3.5 times annual public revenue. France in a long-term comparison shows the opposite development: its continuously increasing public debt in 1913 reached 7 times public revenue and an indebtedness of about 841 fr. (£33.3) per head of population (£1 = 25.22 fr.).

Whether British citizens lent more of their savings to their own government or invested more capital abroad, either in the form of foreign (state) loans or of direct investment, cannot be established in absolute figures, but there is reason to believe that capital exports clearly had the edge.[36]

There is no complete parallel in the development of indebtedness and debt service. This results from changes in interest rates on new issues effected during the period (invariably between 3 and 5 per cent), from loan conversions and from the laws in force at various times, regarding the level of amortization. In spite of increasing loans, Britain's tax system rested on so solid a foundation that it enabled the country to finance a large part of First World War expenditure by taxation, thus reducing the pressure of inflation, compared to Germany (see the survey on p. 470).

(iii) Structure of public budgets, 1843–1919/20

Long-term comparison of macro-economic data are risky, above all for the nineteenth century with its large-scale structural changes in the course of the industrial revolution. If the following paragraphs attempt such comparisons, the results can only be treated as a first approximation.[37] The statistics are suspect, base years of comparison not invariably the same.

In the 120 years from the beginning of the French wars to the beginning of the First World War, the total budget increased roughly 11-fold in money value, public indebtedness 3-fold, population 4-fold; the dubious index of industrial output roughly increased 15-fold, that of industrial money wages 1.5-fold, whereas the index of wholesale prices fell by about 10 per cent.[38]

Limiting the review to the years from 1856 to 1913 causes different relationships to emerge: the *total budget* increased 2.7 times, public indebtedness fell by 16 per cent, *population* increased to 160 per cent. Gross National Product increased 4.5-fold, industrial production 3.6-fold, industrial money wages 1.5-fold, as also did wages in agriculture. Increase of per capita tax burden is estimated at about 1.7-fold, reaching

[36] See details in Kuznets (1966), p. 322; Feis (1965), pp. 11, 14, 23, 81ff.

[37] For the following figures Mitchell (1975), pp. 24, 184ff., 190ff., 355ff., 697ff., 706ff., 736ff.

[38] O'Brien and Keyder (1979), p. 1,301 give the following values for the 'production de biens aux prix courant' (decadel averages of output of goods at current prices) – 1701–10, £37 million; 1781–90, £65 million; 1905–13, £863 million, always for Great Britain. More detail in O'Brien and Keyder (1978), p. 58; 'commodity output' excluding services for 1845–54 amounts to an annual average of £283 million.

Table 43. *Public debt and Gross National Product, 1820–1913*

	Total indebtedness		Population (UK millions)	Gross National Product (£ million)	Events
	In £ million	£ per head of population			
1820	848	40.5	21.0	c. 341	
1829	796	33.2	23.9	c. 438	
1842	791	29.6	26.7	461	
1854	775	28.5	27.2	680 }	Crimean War
1857	808	28.4	28.4	660 }	
1859	824	28.5	28.9	677	
1868	749	24.9	30.1	856	
1870	798	25.3	31.5	953	
1884	654	18.4	35.5	1,403	
1899	599	14.6	41.0	1,963 }	Boer War
1903	743	17.7	42.0	2,109 }	
1910	733	16.2	45.2	2,403	
1914	678	15.0	45.2	2,743 }	First World War
(1919	7,460	167.3		5,751 }	
Index of change 1914 (1820=1)	0.8	0.4	2.2	8.0	

Sources: Total indebtedness: Calculated from Vocke (1866), pp. 82, 90; Dowell (1888), vol. II, p. 453; Eheberg (1927), p. 63; *The Statesman's Year Book* (1892), pp. 50–1, *ibid.* (1912), pp. 33ff., *ibid.* (1921), pp. 48–9; *ibid.* (1923), pp. 45–6. Figures in the various publications differ slightly on occasions. Indebtedness does not include capital value of terminable annuities; these insignificant amounts are documented separately in *The Statesman's Yearbook* (1923), p. 46, with increments to 1914.
Population: Deane and Cole (1968), p. 8.
GNP: Mitchell (1975), pp. 782, 790, 797, up to 1870 at factor cost, thereafter at market price.

Table 44. *Tax burden per capita of United Kingdom population, 1912/13*

	£	s.	d.	£	s.	d.
1. Consumption taxes on food		4	6			
drink		16	2			
tobacco		7	6			
	1	8	2			
2. Direct taxes	1	14	4			
3. Taxes on transactions: gross total		19	7			
net total		9	2			
4. Total revenue: gross				4	2	1
net				3	11	8

Source: Mallet (1913), p. 444.

in 1912/13 the level indicated in Table 44. Tax burden per head of population had increased, compared to the middle of the nineteenth century, but remained at or even below the level reached at the end of the Napoleonic wars.[39] Taking into account the long-term development of incomes, we may conclude that the share of tax burden in citizens' incomes diminished; it would presumably diminish more, were we to base our calculation on the long-term change in price levels instead of on nominal money values.[40] The index of wholesale prices fell from 1821–5 (= 100) to 73.5 in 1850; on the changed base of 1913 = 100, it moved between 91 (in 1851) up to 130 (in 1872, maximum), down to 76 (1896, minimum), up to 100 (1913). Real national income per capita rose from £18.3 in 1855 to £44.3 in 1913 – a 2.4-fold increase.[41] These rough macro-economic approximations give little information on the relative tax incidence on recipients of either different totals or different types of incomes.

The overall impression remains that of the state in the late nineteenth century absorbing by taxation a portion of Gross National Product noticeably smaller than after the Napoleonic wars. This may also be the result of Britain's rapid industrial development and the fast increase of the volume of trade of the British Empire. Overseas trade formed the cornerstone of the country's economic growth. Annual increments of the volume of overseas trade during the nineteenth century considerably exceeded those of real national income; between 1831 and 1870, incre-

[39] See also Pollard and Crossley (1969), survey of economic development, including consideration of changes in standards of living, pp. 174ff.; figures on per capita consumption and corresponding per capita tax burden, pp. 206, 217ff.; on changes of taxable income, pp. 212f.; also O'Brien and Keyder (1978) on change of living standard and per capita income.

[40] Mitchell (1975), pp. 736ff.

[41] Net national income at 1900 prices from Kindleberger (1964), pp. 387f.; similar values at 1913 prices in Deane and Cole (1969), p. 283.

ments of exports and of total overseas trade were twice as high as those of total volume of output.[42]

Wagner's famous law of increasing government activity can certainly not be corroborated from domestic budget figures alone. This may be due to some of Britain's expenses as a world power falling upon the colonial population of the British Empire.

A comparison of income and expenditure structures of the British budget at the end of the eighteenth with those at the end of the nineteenth century shows the following – in general trends rather than exact proportions:

Expenditure: Military expenditure and debt service throughout absorbed the largest amount of expenditure, though the percentage, 93 in 1792, had fallen to 58 in 1913/14. However, the two items changed place: while debt service outranked military expenses in 1792 (at 55 per cent the largest expenditure item), military expenditure at just over 40 per cent occupied first place in 1913. The main effect of the British state therefore continued to lie in the 'external' sphere, administratively speaking in the ministries of war or defence (see Table 45). However, in that respect Dowell's words, looking back upon the Crimean War in the retrospect of 1884, must be taken into account: 'It cost us ten millions a year more to live as part of that armed camp into which the Western World has resolved its system.'[43]

The strong growth of expenditure on civil service and administration, including the rather insignificant civil list, is remarkable. Between 1792 and 1873 it increased from 7 to 16 per cent, by 1883 to 22 per cent, reaching 27 per cent of total expenditure in 1913; by 1919/20 it amounted to almost 35 per cent. The state turned more and more to 'domestic' tasks. Civil expenditure up to the middle of the nineteenth century consisted above all of the salaries paid to government administrative staff and the expenses of justice and police; from the 1880s onwards, even more strongly after the 1890s, expenditure on public education, science and art occupied the foreground; to these must be added before the outbreak of the First World War transfer payments for old age pensions and expenditure in the health field.

The three largest civil expenditure items aggregated, public education, old age pensions, and Ministry of Health and health insurance, with

---

[42] Deane and Cole (1969), p. 311; a few details on capital exports, *ibid.*, pp. 259ff., 352f., Table 91; see also Feis (1965), pp. 3ff., 83ff. Different and cautious regarding direct furtherance of economic growth, Kindleberger (1961–2), pp. 289ff.; on this O'Brien and Keyder (1978), p. 76: 'the impetus to economic growth seems to flow from the international sector to the domestic economy'; then qualifying, 'it is perhaps easier to see Britain's paramount position in international services as being more closely linked to stable government, to a well-ordered system of public finance and above all to superior naval power directed by statesmen with a sharp perception for the nation's long-run economic interests'.   [43] Dowell (1965), vol. II, p. 355.

£36.9 million accounted for 67 per cent of civil expenditure, thus exceeding the costs of the army and equalling 43 per cent of the military budget. In the light of the British tradition, that was an enormous move towards a state active in civic matters.

The Elementary Education Act of 1870 and supplementary legislation caused a very strong increase in the number of masters and pupils in publicly financed and publicly assisted schools[44] (see Table 46).

Under the item of 'civil expenditure', the state undertook duties towards four categories of people outside productive life: children – free education; the aged – old age pensions; the poor and unemployed – relief for poor and unemployed workers; finally the sick – hospitals, medical inspection and treatment of schoolchildren. The state thereby assumed tasks which – insofar as they formed part of public domain at all – had traditionally been incumbent on local authorities. This signifies the increased importance of those four problem areas and the people involved in them.[45]

Revenue: Throughout the nineteenth century, the main type of taxes without doubt were the indirect taxes and customs duties. As in the previous century, domestic consumers bore the chief weight of public expenditure by the higher prices paid, above all for tobacco, beer, spirits, tea, and sugar. Gladstone's pragmatic attitude of 1862, subsequently famous, remained dominant throughout the industrial revolution; he gave greater weight to considerations of financial than of primary social and distributional policy:

We are faced . . . by the old controversy between direct and indirect taxation. I take some credit to myself for never having entered, in this House, into any disquisition upon such a subject. I have always thought it idle for a person holding the position of finance minister to trouble himself with what to him is necessarily an abstract question, namely the question between direct and indirect taxation, each considered upon its own merits . . . I never can think of direct and indirect taxation except as I should think of two attractive sisters . . . both having the same parentage (. . . necessity and invention).[46]

However, the high share in total revenue of consumption taxes and customs duties dropped from about 64 per cent in 1843 to 58 in 1863, to 49 in 1893; in 1913, at barely 38 per cent, it fell below the share of direct taxes, which was 39 per cent (income tax, land and house tax, etc.,

---

[44] Private schools, only partially supported by the state, played a much larger part in Britain than in the German states. Of £15.5 million state expenditure for all schools in the last pre-war years, £10 million went to local authority schools, £3.9 million to private schools, the remainder to central school administration; see Statistisches Reichsamt (1927), p. 254.

[45] Figures for the whole state and local authorities from around 1900 – with transition to post-1918 period – in Feinstein (1972), pp. 66–104.

[46] Quoted from Dowell (1965), vol. II, pp. 365, 369.

Table 45. *Revenue and expenditure of the United Kingdom, 1843–1913/20 budgets (£000)*

	1843	1853	1856	1863	1873	1883	1893	1903/4	1913/14	1919/20
Revenue										
Customs duties	21,034	20,903	23,321	23,421	21,033	19,657	19,715	34,433	35,450	149,360
Excise	12,878	15,338	18,165	17,745	25,785	26,930	25,360	32,100	39,590	133,663
Income tax	5,249	5,588	16,090[a]	9,806	7,500	11,900	13,470	38,800[b]	47,249	359,099[c]
Land, house, and other taxes	4,190	3,154	3,116	3,208	2,337	2,800	2,450	2,650	2,700	2,640
Stamp duties	}6,948	}6,975	}7,372	}9,252	}9,947	}11,841	}13,805	8,200	9,966	22,586
Inheritance taxes[d]								13,850	27,359	40,904
Post (including from 1870 telegrams, from 1908 telephones)	595	1,104	2,886	3,800	4,820	9,010	10,400	18,380	30,800	44,150
Sundries	1,689	1,368	1,384	3,202	5,187	5,249	5,195	3,139	5,129	587,169[e]
Total	52,583	54,430	72,334	70,434	76,609	87,387	90,395	151,552	198,243	1,339,571
Expenditure										
Debt service	29,268	27,805	28,681	26,218	26,805	29,004	25,200	30,071	37,323	348,205
Army, navy, air force	14,515	16,326	29,211[a]	27,407	24,956	29,903	33,423	100,610[b]	77,179	604,028[c]
Civil Service and administration	7,356	7,044	8,400	9,869	11,750	18,878	19,303	39,240	53,901	569,054
Sundries	0	0	9,297	4,317	7,203	9,503	12,449	14,563	29,090	144,486
Total	51,139	51,175	75,589	67,811	70,714	87,288	90,375	184,484	197,493	1,665,773
UK population (millions)	26.7 (1841)	27.4 (1851)	c.28.5 —	28.9 (1861)	31.5 (1871)	34.9 (1881)	37.7 (1891)	41.5 (1901)	45.2 (1911)	44.6
Approx. revenue per head of population (£ per head)	1.97	1.99	2.54	2.45	2.43	2.50	2.40	3.65	4.38	30.04

Notes:

[a] Increase because of Crimean War.

[b] Increase because of Boer War.

[c] Increase because of the First World War.

[d] Death duties: probate, legacy, succession, corporation, estate duties, according to the law valid at the time.

[e] Including excess profit duties, etc., amounting to £290,045.

Sources: 1843, 1853, 1856 and 1863: Vocke (1866), pp. 126–7. Budget values net up to 1853. Additional figures for total revenues and expenditures in Rees (1921), pp. 82, 110, 137–8, 166ff. Total expenditure in Rees differs substantially from Vocke 1856 at £93.1 million; there is no budgetary explanation for the difference. For all years, Mitchell (1975), pp. 697ff. gives slightly different figures. 1873: *Statistical Abstract for the United Kingdom, 1866–1880* (1881), pp. 8ff.

1883 and 1893: *Statistical Abstract for the United Kingdom, 1881–1895* (1896), pp. 9ff.

1903/4: Mallet (1913), pp. 474ff.

1913/14 and 1919/20: Mallet and George (1929), pp. 390–1.

Statistical Abstract for the United Kingdom, 1911–1925 (1927), pp. 4–5.

inheritance tax). This is another pointer to the increasing penetration of the budget by considerations of justice and social concern, because the growing share of direct taxes in practice achieved greater justice[47] (see Table 44).

A decisive part of this shift was embodied in the reform of British inheritance taxation, a particular type of property taxation. Almost 17 per cent of total tax revenue in 1913/14 was drawn from inheritance taxes. They developed out of the eighteenth-century stamp duties (see above, p. 317). Probate and legacy duty were charged on personal property; taxation of real property by means of succession duty followed in 1853, supplemented after 1881 by account duty; above all, after 1889 the state levied by far the most productive kind of inheritance tax, namely estate duty. The reforms were completed in 1894. From a continental point of view, the yield of inheritance taxes was very high.

With the rapid increase in revenues from post, telegraphy and telephone from the turn of the twentieth century onwards, the share of taxes in total revenue fell from 97 per cent in 1826 to about 82 per cent in 1913/14. However, international comparisons of public trading revenues are exceedingly hazardous, because of the difference in the methods of profit calculations.

4. *Secular percentage of state's share in national income: international comparisons*

Adolph Wagner proclaimed in 1892 the law of increasing government activity, subsequently named after him, conjuring up the all-pervading government of the future. The law was reflected in the literature as a theorem of the rising state share in national expenditure.[48] It predicted that public expenditure in the long run would rise absolutely and relatively to national product (state quota), the reason being in the last resort a gradual transition from a *laissez-faire* to a more socially motivated system; this system allocated more duties to the state, above all as

---

[47] Distinction between direct and indirect taxes varies. Mallet and George (1933), Appendix Table 18 define for the period under review, 1874–1914: 'Indirect taxes represent all taxes which are levied in respect of consumable articles. They include all customs duties and all excise duties, excepting licences and railway duty (and in 1874–5 the racehorse duty).' Direct taxes represent 1874–1914 all other taxes. They include excise licences, railway passenger duty (in 1874–5 racehorse duty), death duties, land tax, house duty, property and income tax including super-tax, land value duties, and stamps.

[48] Timm (1961); according to Timm, the law was first formulated by Wagner in 1863; Peacock and Wiseman (1961); Recktenwald (1977); Weitzel (1967); Fabricant (1952); Andic and Veverka (1963).

Table 46. *Teachers and pupils (000, United Kingdom)*

	Teachers	Pupils	Teacher/pupil ratio
1850	?	282	?
1860	?	920	?
1870	16.8	1,432	1:85
1880	50.7	3,274	1:64
1890	86.6	4,288	1:50
1900	132.9	5,383	1:40
1913	186.8	6,121	1:33

Source: Mitchell (1975), pp. 750ff.

regards public production of goods and services; the state assumed entrepreneurial functions at the expense of a private sector working with excessive frictional losses.[49]

Wagner's theorem has been repeatedly tested empirically and by and large confirmed during the period when statistically more reliable evidence is available, approximately from the last quarter of the nineteenth to the middle of the twentieth century. In the course of these calculations, many traditional data have been corrected; public activity has been disaggregated either among different localized public bodies or according to functional or economic areas; varying indices converted nominal into real values. The causation of the long-term trend of increasing governmental activity departed somewhat from Wagner's view, being seen in a concatenation of a number of causes pointing to a change in the tasks (the function) of the state: social security, education, urbanization in the course of industrialization, but also military security and expansion up to empire status; all this has been supplemented by the concept of a productivity lag – the productivity of governmental activities lagged behind that of the private sector – and occasionally also by the assumption of an unremitting Keynesian policy of deficit spending.

It is hardly possible to determine a precise state quota for the entire nineteenth century, especially when combined with the attempt to link it historically to the eighteenth century. Traditional rudimentary data and estimates cannot be improved by refining statistical methods. The figures used in this account show changes in the state quota in the long run in

[49] Wagner here anticipated part of Schumpeter's ideas; see Schumpeter (1950): technology and science render creative productive activity of the individual entrepreneur ever more complicated – until individual is replaced by collective creativity.

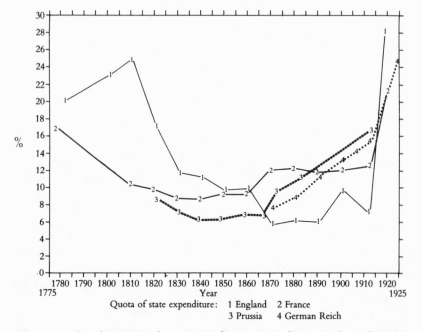

Quota of state expenditure: 1 England   2 France
                               3 Prussia   4 German Reich

Fig. 9. Secular changes in the quotas of state expenditure in Great Britain,
France, Prussia, and the German Reich

international comparison, as illustrated in Figure 9.[50] The typical state
quota in the middle of the twentieth century amounts to between 30 and
40 per cent; compared to it, the nineteenth-century state quota at less
than 10 per cent, particularly in the middle of the century, was very low.
This small state share accorded well with the ideas of a liberal social order
to the effect that the natural upper limit of citizens' tax burden was
around 10 per cent and that the smallest budget was the best. It fitted the
model picture of the desirable nightwatchman state, though if this meant
to indicate a passive state, it never existed; however, under Liberalism,
state activity remained indeed small, as indicated by the state quota.

The curve marking the secular state quota in the nineteenth century

[50] *For Britain*: figures from Table 43, government expenditure from Mitchell (1975), pp. 697, 699.
The base is up to 1870 Gross National Product at factor cost, after 1871 at market price. The state
is 'central government'. In Peacock and Wiseman (1961), the state is 'total government', thus
resulting in somewhat higher state quotas, though the trend does not change. Rostow (1961), pp.
37, 42, gives estimates for Great Britain in the eighteenth century of state quotas from 'total net
public expenditure' and 'GNP': 1711 – 25 per cent; 1749 – 15 per cent; 1761 – 20 per cent; 1782 –
20 per cent.
For Germany: Andic and Veverka (1963), p. 183. The state is 'total government' (Reich, federal
states, local authorities); base is the Gross National Product.
For Prussia: figures from Tables 67, 68, 78, 80. Base is the net national product, state means central
government.

was V-shaped. Starting at a relatively high level of public expenditure during late mercantilism and then during the French wars, the quota dropped to below one-half of those years. Roughly in the last third or quarter of the century, the quota rose again and resumed in the first third of the twentieth century a mercantilist level of state activity. The uniform trend of this secular process in all countries investigated is astonishing, particularly as state functions differed between countries and the data from which national quotas had to be calculated were hardly homogeneous. The striking uniformity of the trends may be a sign that in Europe social order, social value systems, industrialization, and fiscal administration moved more uniformly than is indicated by the partial analyses devoted to national sectors which emphasize differences. The following sections will show even more uniformities within national peculiarities. Perhaps there was even a European indigenous type of modernization through industrialization within a fundamental philo-sophical framework of liberal individualism. From this angle, the indus-trial revolution of Europe can be regarded as a uniform phenomenon.[51]

Nevertheless, an empirical discovery does not constitute a law of social development. It is difficult to predict which image comes closer to reality, 'an old age pensioner relying on his insurance policy to finance a round trip by a competitive travel agency or an old age pensioner on a free trip round the world organized by the State Holiday Association'.[52] Furthermore, a social law is not a prognosis. A thesis requires an antithesis; the relative strength of both – hence the course of develop-ment – can hardly be prophesied.[53] It is even a matter of controversy whether laws of social development exist.

For France: figures from Tables 52 and 54, supplemented for 1920 from Mitchell (1975), p. 700; the base is Gross National Product, the state is central government. Rostow (1975), p. 238, gives estimates of state quotas for the eighteenth century, related to gross physical product: 1701–10 – 13 per cent: 1758 – 10 per cent; 1774 – 12 per cent; 1777–9 – 17 per cent; for the nineteenth century, Rostow (1971), p. 108, gives quotas higher than those indicated here, because his base is 'gross physical output' (exclusive of services) at constant prices. Relating it to 'gross product of agriculture and industry in current francs', Ardant (1975), p. 221, writes about decadal averages from 1803 to 1913: 'production increased a little less than state expenditures', giving the state quota as 13.6 per cent for 1803–12, 14.7 per cent for 1905–13; in between a minimum of 11.5 and a maximum of 18.8 per cent; figures calculated from Marczewski (1965). Juxtaposition of the development of the *produit physique en valeur* and government expenditure both in total and for particular items of budget from 1815 to 1969 in Fontvieille (1978), pp. 242f., supplemented by André and Delorme (1978), pp. 256ff., with figures from 1872 to 1970.

A comparison of quotas of government expenditure, using a simple public choice model, for USA, Germany, France and Britain in the period 1872/90–1972 in Blankart (1977), pp. 74ff. The position of the figures in Figure 9 indicates the years for which quotas were calculated. Quotas which can be deduced from linear connections are uncertain.

[51] See Pollard's (1976) reflections to see the industrialization of Europe as a single process, and contributions to the discussion of this subject in Büsch (1976), pp. 4, 17ff.; pp. 636ff.; see Otsuka (1982), for a Japanese angle.   [52] Andic and Veverka (1963), p. 222.

[53] Kuczynski (1970), p. 31.

5. *Consolidated balance sheet for the British Empire 1910/11; some indications*

The history of United Kingdom public finance is incomplete without a history of public finance of the British colonies – irrespective of the different legal status of particular areas – and without considering the interrelationship of public finance systems within the British Empire as a whole. United Kingdom budgets alone could hardly reflect the political and economic activities of 45 million inhabitants of an island covering 121,000 square miles, given that at that moment, i.e., 1910, that kingdom was situated at the centre of an economically closely interlinked empire of 419 million people, who existed and worked on a surface area of 11.4 million square miles.[54] A kind of officially consolidated balance sheet of public state budgets of territories forming part of the Empire, such as was published in London shortly before the outbreak of the First World War, may give an approximate idea of what is commonly called 'Britain, the World of Power' (see Table 47). It was during this period that the British state reached almost the apogee of its political, military, economic and financial power.

II.   *Tax system and national budget in France*

A.   HISTORICAL BASIS: THE FISCAL SYSTEM AT THE END OF THE ANCIEN RÉGIME

France, a country centrally governed and covering a large surface area, became Europe's leading power between 1500 and 1789, breaking Spain's world domination and cutting Austria's strength; in the nineteenth century, it had to yield precedence to Britain. In the seventeenth and eighteenth centuries, France had developed an extensive and productive fiscal system, linked to the names of Turgot (1727–81) and Necker (1733–1804), which served – as in the rest of Europe – to finance three large items of expenditure: public debt, military, and civil (justice and administration) services.[1]

1. *The structure of the budget*

Necker's estimates for the beginning of the 1780s showed a budget structure for the French state as in Table 48.[2]

---

[54] Keith (1924); survey in Statistisches Reichsamt (1927), pp. 121ff.

[1] Vuitry (1883); Wolfe (1972).
[2] A. Wagner (1910), pp. 176f.; more detailed division of revenues for the years 1718, 1781 and 1789 in Marion, *Histoire*, vol. 1 (1914), Appendix.

The French state had so heavy a debt – public debt already in 1721 was said to amount to 2.06 milliard *livres*[3] – that in the 1780s 43 per cent of total expenditure was required for the debt service – a percentage rising to 50.5 in 1788.[4] Next to Britain, France was the most heavily indebted of the European great powers. The next largest item of expenditure – in line with that of Europe's other great powers – was almost 25 per cent for army and navy, while public and fiscal administration absorbed slightly more than 21 per cent of expenditure. Compared to Britain and Prussia, the military share of the French budget was perceptibly smaller, that for public administration of a centrally governed country noticeably larger. The function of the court as an instrument of power, whether *vis-à-vis* the subjects or the nobility, is difficult to assess, and the same applies to court expenditure: in absolute figures, at almost 34 million *livres*, it was very high. The same might be said about its proportion of the budget, compared with the Vienna court, the only one in Europe measuring up to it in rank, pretension, and splendour. In middle-sized and above all in smaller German territories, on the other hand, the relative burden of maintaining a court was several times larger, with the significant exception of the admittedly rather frugal Prussian court and the court of the British monarchy which conformed to a quite different constitutional tradition.[5] Expenditure was covered to the extent of 55 per cent by taxes which were mainly indirect, and of 45 per cent by mainly direct taxes.

2. The tax system[6]

It is striking that France – like Britain – drew hardly any revenue from public lands. In the budget of 1773, revenues attributed to public lands and forests amounted to a mere 6.4 million *livres* or 1.6 per cent of total revenue. Hence the French government had to levy comparatively considerably higher taxes on its subjects than the German states. Pressure of taxation in France before the great revolution was considered especially heavy; beyond that, if we identify justice with equality, taxes were distributed very unequally and thus unjustly.

(i) Indirect taxes

Consumption taxes and customs and duties: Indirect consumption dues[7] and customs duties represented more than one-half of tax revenues. Their practical application differed almost from province to province, because their collection was incumbent upon five large tax farming companies (*fermes générales*). The state determined the indirect tax total *ex ante*,

---

[3] Thus Gaettens (1955), p. 121.   [4] Guéry (1978), p. 228.
[5] Kruedener (1973), figures on pp. 13ff.   [6] Marion, *Histoire* (1914–28).
[7] Sestier (1889), pp. 1229ff.; he also gives a survey of indirect taxes in the nineteenth century.

Table 47. *The British Empire, 1910–11: public budgets, debts, area, and population*

	Area sq. miles	Population	Revenue £	Expenditure £	Debt £
1. United Kingdom	121,391	45,365,599	203,850,588	171,995,667	733,072,610
2. India–British	1,097,821	244,126,512	80,326,000	76,936,000	299,338,899
Feudatory States	675,267	70,828,723	—	—	—
Total India	1,773,088	314,955,240	80,326,000	76,936,000	299,338,899
3. Europe:					
Gibraltar	2	19,596	80,930	76,410	—
Malta	117	228,442	441,444	467,372	79,115
Total Europe	119	248,038	522,374	543,782	79,115
4. Asia:					
Cyprus	3,584	273,857	286,848	251,520	280,926
Aden Perim, Socotra	10,387	57,859	—	—	—
Ceylon	25,332	4,109,054	2,852,629	2,380,552	6,196,256
Straits Settlements	1,600	707,523	1,089,238	878,762	7,943,431
Labuan	30	6,546	—	—	—
Fed. Malay States	27,700	1,035,933	3,097,851	2,753,171	—
Other Malay States	23,450	920,000	—	—	—
Borneo and Sarawak	73,106	700,000	411,779	252,297	—
Hong Kong and Territory	405	366,145	609,076	604,372	1,485,733
Wei-hai-wei	285	147,133	6,586	12,689	—
Total Asia (except India)	165,879	8,324,050	8,354,007	7,133,363	15,906,346

5. Australia and the Pacific:					
N.S. Wales	310,372	1,648,210	17,209,575	15,742,265	90,365,758
Victoria	87,884	1,315,551	10,730,475	10,659,830	49,219,865
Queensland	670,500	605,813	6,192,531	6,217,814	43,146,067
S. Australia	380,070	403,558 }	4,712,381	4,879,456	27,552,020
Northern Territory	523,620	3,310			
Western Australia	975,920	282,114	4,246,515	4,060,850	22,570,453
Tasmania	26,215	191,211	1,318,253	1,312,555	10,511,660
Papua	90,540	272,000	34,322	64,874	—
Total Australia	3,065,121	4,727,005	44,444,552	42,937,644	243,365,823
New Zealand	104,751	1,071,428	10,394,195	9,442,474	81,078,122
Fiji	7,740	139,541	211,952	236,661	104,115
Tonga, Solomon, and Gilbert Islands	12,556	210,000	61,100	57,000	—
Total Australia and Pacific	3,190,168	6,147,974	55,111,799	52,673,779	324,548,060
6. Africa:					
Ascension	34	400	—	—	—
St Helena	47	3,477	5,806	9,596	—
W. Africa:					
N. Nigeria and Prot.	256,400	8,069,071	304,000	586,951	—
S. Nigeria and Prot.	77,260	7,836,189	1,933,235	1,592,282	5,000,000
Gold Coast and Prot.	80,000	1,502,898	1,006,633	924,862	2,514,118
Sierra Leone and Prot.	30,000	1,400,000	424,215	361,222	1,262,501
Gambia and Prot.	3,619	160,807	82,880	63,384	—
Total West Africa	447,279	18,968,965	3,750,963	3,528,701	3,776,619

Table 47. (cont.)

	Area sq. miles	Population	Revenue £	Expenditure £	Debt £
Mauritius and dependencies	850	374,625	719,982	629,951	1,300,390
Seychelles	156	22,620	36,243	32,773	15,039
Somaliland	68,000	302,859	30,842	99,224	—
East Africa Prot.	202,000	2,295,336	605,986	682,041	—
Uganda Prot.	223,500	3,503,564	287,094	276,157	—
Zanzibar	1,020	197,199	181,705	192,925	75,573
Nyasaland	39,801	970,430	94,980	112,368	—
Union of South Africa					
Cape of Good Hope	276,995	2,563,024	7,747,332[a]	7,611,298[a]	48,240,891
Natal	35,371	1,191,958	4,293,728[a]	3,530,349[a]	20,895,943
Transvaal	110,426	1,676,611	5,585,537[a]	5,909,811[a]	40,000,000
Orange Free State	50,392	526,906	952,860[a]	957,741[a]	1,250,000
Total Union	473,194	5,958,499	19,579,557[a]	18,009,199[a]	110,386,334
Rhodesia	439,575	1,770,871	882,383	797,768	—
Swaziland	6,536	99,959	58,722	52,257	100,000
Basutoland	10,293	405,932	119,974	111,444	—
Bechuanaland	275,000	125,350	52,067	64,790	—
Total Africa	2,187,275	34,999,986	25,407,304	24,609,194	120,654,955

369

7. America:					
Canada	3,729,665	7,081,869	24,210,418	18,042,474	97,626,861
Newfoundland and Labrador	162,734	241,607	708,753	642,932	4,716,102
British Honduras	8,598	40,510	94,252	76,327	34,736
British Guiana	90,500	296,041	563,100	542,757	887,115
Bermuda	19	18,994	78,593	68,392	45,500
West Indies:					
Bahamas	4,404	55,944	84,391	85,314	97,659
Turks and Caicos Islands	166	5,615	8,646	6,827	—
Jamaica	4,207	831,123	1,160,310	1,159,969	3,909,593
Windward Islands	672	320,246	389,902	385,108	695,300
Leeward Islands	701	127,189	164,390	159,263	273,250
Trinidad and Tobago	1,868	330,074	948,383	927,034	1,051,093
Total West Indies	12,021	1,679,191	2,756,022	2,723,515	6,026,895
Falkland Islands	6,500	2,272	18,535	17,405	—
Total America	4,010,034	9,360,484	28,430,473	22,113,802	109,337,209
8. Total all five continents	11,447,954	419,401,371	402,002,545	356,005,587	1,602,937,194

Note:
a Eleven months ended 30 May 1910.
Source: The Statesman's Year Book (London, 1912), pp. xxxii-xxxv.

Table 48. *The French budget around 1780[a]*

		Million *livres*	%
Revenues			
1. Mainly direct taxes, of which		242.56	41
Taille	91.0		
Twentieth	55.0		
3rd twentieth	21.5		
Capitation	41.5		
Taxes on clergy	11.0		
2. Mainly indirect taxes, of which		319.04	55
Fermes générales, including the *gabelle*	166.0		
Régie générale	51.5		
Tax-type revenues (mostly on transactions)			
Timbres, etc.	41.0		
Octrois	27.0		
3. Other revenues, of which	23.4		4
Lotteries	11.5		
Postage, coinage	10.8		
Total revenues		585.0	100
Expenditures			
1. Debt service, of which		262.5	43.0
Interest on debt	207.0		
Repayment of debt	27.5		
Pension payments	28.0		
2. War department, of which		150.8	24.7
Army	105.6		
Navy	45.2		
3. Fiscal administration, of which		66.38	10.9
Tax collection expenditure	58.0		
4. Civil administration, of which		62.12	10.2
Economic administration, roads, bridges	30.2		
Domestic administration, justice	28.45		
Arts and education	3.47		
5. External affairs		8.5	1.4
6. Court		33.7	5.5
7. Sundries		26.0	4.3
Total expenditure		610.0	100

Note:
[a] The value of the *livre* in precious metal around 1773 was almost identical with that of the franc (1 *livre* = 1.02 fr.).
Deficit: *livres* 25 million.
Population (Necker's estimate) 24.8 million. Nicoles (1883), p. 327, estimates population at 26.5 million.

allocating it among the individual provinces, and received from the *fermes générales* responsible for the provinces a sum corresponding to the tax, leaving tax farmers to sub-allocate the amount plus the farmers' profits among the provinces – a process carried out very arbitrarily. The farming companies were further charged with collecting on the state's behalf – by way of service – other indirect dues (*régie générale*), potentially further exacerbating inequality of collection and incidence.

The tax yielding the highest revenue among the farmed indirect taxes was the salt tax (*gabelle*) felt to be particularly oppressive: it consisted of an obligation to purchase a fixed volume of salt at a prescribed price which included an element of tax. The *aides* were a set of consumption taxes, especially on wine, oil, and tallow; tobacco alternated between a state monopoly and a tax. Indirect dues mainly paid by towns were *octrois*, a type of entry or gate due paid mainly on agricultural produce.

The timbres: The *timbres*, also described sometimes as *droits de contrôle*, *droits d'insinuation*, *centième dernier* or in other terms, are related to the British stamp duties and the German/Austrian stamps. In France in the nineteenth century above all, *timbres* were extended far more widely than anywhere else in Europe; they could be regarded as a French speciality. The eighteenth-century *timbres* were the immediate forerunners of the nineteenth-century French *enregistrements*, that mixture of fees levied on controls, of dues on compulsory administrative transactions and of taxes. They could be described as taxes on legal transactions.

(ii) Direct taxes[8]

Direct taxes were structured as a mixture of revenue and capitation taxes, forming a system of three categories, the older *taille*, the newer *capitation* and the twentieth.

The 'taille': The *taille* dates back to 1445, being considered a tax levied in the countryside and small towns. Louis XVI (1774–92) converted it to a *taille personnelle* and a *taille réelle*. In the larger part of France, *taille personnelle* was levied in the form of a general property, revenue, and personal tax; its overwhelming incidence was on feudally restricted landed property. The *taille réelle* was levied in some provinces on land and house property in the form of a household or hearth tax. Allocation of the *taille*, imposed as a total sum, was the duty of local authorities. There was no well-conceived land registration on identical lines for the whole country. Local communities bore collective responsibility for their tax quotas. Many forms of privilege, among others the purchase of

---

[8] Marion (1910); Vignes (1889), p. 1211; he also gives a survey of direct taxes in the nineteenth century.

offices, rendered more and more people exempt, in addition to the nobility and the clergy. This worsened the tax inequality, imparting to the tax system a further element of arbitrariness which was resented.

The capitation: *Capitation*, like the *taille*, originated in an extraordinary war tax (1695) which during the eighteenth century was converted to a regular general personal capitation tax. The clergy discharged its tax duty by an annual lump sum (*don gratuit*). The nobility, civil servants, and privileged citizens were taxed by means of a tariff of fixed rates, varying from 20 *sols* to 2,000 *livres*, depending on rank, status, occupation and property. There were 22 (tax) classes. All other taxpayers shared in the total quota in proportion to their liability to *taille*.

The twentieth: In 1710, during the War of the Spanish Succession, France introduced a third direct tax in the shape of a universal proportional tax – a rudimentary forerunner of income tax. The law originally required all incomes and salaries to be declared and taxed at a standard rate of income amounting, according to type, to one-tenth, one-twentieth up to one-fiftieth; from 1749 onwards, one-twentieth became the normal standard rate. This tells us little about how much individual taxpayers really paid, because the twentieth could be imposed several times a year (extraordinary assessments). The clergy again successfully defeated the taxation, buying itself off by an extraordinary *don gratuit*. Similarly there were corporations, provinces and cities which compounded their tax liabilities by lump sums. Again, it proved impossible to allocate the twentieth evenly and to administer it on an equal basis in all provinces, mainly because of the inadequate administrative infrastructure.

Peasants and most income recipients in towns regarded the strongly felt burden of direct taxes, especially the cumulative injustice which violated the subsequently formulated principles of equality and justice, increasingly as arbitrary impositions. In addition, several collectors of taxes and dues co-existed, above all the tax farmers. This eventually contributed to the outbreak of the French revolution of 1789.

Around that time Adam Smith (1723–90), essaying a rough comparison between Britain and France, mused: wealthy France had almost three times the population of Britain;

the soil and climate of France are better than those of Great Britain. The country has been much longer in a state of improvement and cultivation, and is, on that account, better stocked with all those things which it requires a long time to raise up and accumulate, such as great towns, and convenient and well-built houses, both in town and country.[9]

---

[9] Smith (1937 edn), p. 856; more recent comparisons between the two countries for the eighteenth century in Crouzet (1966); Rostow (1975), p. 168; O'Brien and Keyder (1979), p. 1301, Appendix; *ibid* (1978), with chronological link to the nineteenth century.

The British population, he continued to reflect, sustained its state in the 1760s with about £10 million annually; it might be expected that France would experience 'as little inconveniency' in raising about three times that amount in tax revenue, whereas in fact it produced in 1765/6 only 308 to 325 million *livres*, that is not even £15 million. Smith's judgment was acute, his reasoning thought-provoking:

The French system of taxation seems, in every respect, inferior to the British,

which he followed up with the apparently contradictory argument that

the people of France, however, it is generally acknowledged, are much more oppressed by taxes than the people of Great Britain.

What he meant was an unequal distribution of the tax burden, felt to be unjust, and therefore unproductive. Even revolutions are not a thunderbolt out of a clear sky.

B. PUBLIC FINANCE DURING THE PERIOD OF INDUSTRIALIZATION

1. *The initial balance sheet of 1813/14*

At the first blow, the French revolution swept away, together with the feudal order, the traditional system of taxes and imposts. Apart from customs duties at national frontiers, all direct and indirect taxes, including government financial monopolies, were abolished without putting anything else in their place. Ideally, the new concept wanted to limit public revenue to a single new direct tax to be levied on real estate and buildings, supplemented merely by customs duties serving purposes partly fiscal, partly agrarian, partly protectionist for industry. Church property was expropriated and in 1790 proclaimed to be national property (public lands), such public lands declared to be free from debt and available for sale.[10] In spite of John Law's inglorious experiments around 1720, the public deficit was to be financed by printing paper money; public lands not yet sold were to be used as security for Mirabeau's (1749–91) *assignats*. The issue of paper money, reaching in 1796 the fantastic level of 45.6 milliard *livres*, led from the second half of 1791 onwards to the first great paper money inflation in economic history, when *assignats* changed hands at 0.5 per cent.[11] This amounted to state bankruptcy. Nevertheless, current budgets continued in deficit.

The monetary tributes and services in kind imposed on vanquished countries by France in the subsequent war years did not remotely suffice

---

[10] Marion (1908).
[11] Gaettens (1955), pp. 184ff.; details in Thiers (1828–9), vol. I, pp. 233f., 237; vol. III, p. 152; vol. V, pp. 146f., 153f., 196f.; vol. VI, pp. 312f.; vol. VII, pp. 40ff., 238–46, 368–80, 424–8; vol. VIII, pp. 183f., 187, 103–19.

to keep the disrupted French public finances afloat, or at least until the planned new and revolutionary tax system could be introduced. Taxes and imposts initially abolished had therefore to be reimposed, though notably modified and improved; neither could Napoleon afford to do without the financial monopolies. Napoleon thus contributed to equipping France with a tax and impost system lasting into the twentieth century, which in comparison with Britain and from a twentieth-century point of view was somewhat conservative and backward-looking.[12] France itself and some European states on the other hand regarded the system as modern, particularly the direct taxes which – given the alleged objectivity of assessment by means of external indicators – appeared to conform especially well to the liberal principles of generality and equality.

(i) The system of post-revolutionary taxes

The system of state taxes consisted of three categories of taxes, direct, indirect and registration taxes.[13] Details were as follows:

1. *Direct taxes*
    Land tax (*contribution foncière*), since 1790; to begin with, linked with a building tax (*contribution des propriétés bâties*), the latter becoming an independent tax in 1881–3
    Trading or business tax (*contribution des patentes*) since 1791, 1795
    Personal and movable property tax (*contribution personnelle et mobilière*) since 1791, 1798
    Door and window tax (*contributions des portes et des fenêtres*) since 1798, 1802
    A few minor supplementary taxes (*taxes assimilées*): taxes on billiards, private luxury carriages and horses, convivial associations since 1871
    Tax on the yield of securities (*taxes sur le revenu des valeurs mobilières*) since 1872.

Taxes on real estates and buildings, doors and windows, and on persons and movable property were allocated, the trading or business tax was a proportional tax. Allocated taxes – total tax yield being fixed *ex ante* by the government – from the yield point of view, formed the foundation of the direct tax system down to their abolition as national taxes in 1916.

Apart from the indirect *octrois*, departmental and local authority taxes consisted almost exclusively of percentages surcharged on national direct taxes.

---

[12] Arnould (1806); Nervo (1865); Stourm (1885).
[13] Summary in d'Audifret (1863–70); Clamagérand (1873); Cailloux, Touchard and Privat-Deschanel (1896, 1904); Mallez (1927); Trotabas (1937); Formery (1946); Wolff (1977).

2. *Indirect taxes*

Taxes on domestic consumption, above all on wine, spirituous liquors, beer (from 1804), tobacco (from 1781, reverting to monopoly in 1802), gunpowder (monopoly from 1797), salt (from 1806), sugar (from 1837), matches (monopoly from 1871, 1872)

Customs duties (from 1796), limited to duties on imports from 1882

Taxes on public transport by horse and carriage (from 1794), by railway (from 1838, 1855)

Licences (from 1816)

3. *Registration taxes*

A set of registration fees (from 1790, 1798): *droits d'enregistrement* (registration fees), *de greffe* (court register fees), *d'hypothèque* (mortgage fees), also taxes and fees on gifts among the living and inheritances

A set of stamp duties (from 1791, 1798)

The dividing line between direct and indirect taxes is not clear. The constitutive assembly established in 1790 a legal definition which became of practical importance in the nineteenth century: direct taxes were taxes imposed 'direct' on the individual and his property, relying on tax registers (*rôles nominatifs*) and land registers; indirect taxes were levied on the import, production, sale and transport of commodities and objects of trade, hence paid 'indirectly' by consumers.[14]

The development outlined in the 1790s influenced the French fiscal system down to the twentieth century in three ways:

1. Taxes were redesignated by no longer being described as imposts (*impositions*), but as contributions (*contributions*), to reflect the transformation of feudal subjects into free citizens.

2. French state revenue from public lands and other public property diminished substantively, both in absolute and relative terms. The revenue item 'public lands and forests' yielded on an average of the years

1801–14	12	
1848–51	3	per cent of total ordinary revenue.
1871–83	1.7	
1910	0.7	

---

[14] Wagner (1889), part 3, p. 373. Revenues from public monopolies are thus to be counted as indirect taxes; this lowers the calculated share of French entrepreneurial revenues. For public enterprises, see Carvallo (1894); also Chaumard (1889). Registration taxes, though an independent category of revenue, are often included in indirect taxes.

The high percentage of 12 per cent reflected the sale of public property.[15]

3. From the outset, the nature and level of taxes were such that they could not finance total government expenditure. As in the remainder of Europe, the principle was for regular taxes to defray only current public expenditure, whereas once-and-for-all expenditure was to be covered by loans, supplemented by extraordinary temporary taxes. However, neither in France nor in the remainder of Europe was this interrelation between categories of income and expenditure strictly observed. After the revolutionary years, the public debt once again slowly grew. During the Third Republic (around 1886), after wars in Crimea, in Mexico and against Germany, budget expenditure for the debt service, at about 44 per cent of total public expenditure, reached almost the same proportion as just before the revolution. In the long view, the 'century of revolution' had changed this percentage as little as the long-term proportion of military expenditure at about 25 to 30 per cent.

As in Britain, the French fiscal system during the industrialization period in the nineteenth century rested on two strong pillars: taxes and voluntary transfers of citizens' incomes to the state. Increasing state indebtedness, as in Britain, signified a steady growth of the French economy, growing incomes accruing to a wealthy sector of citizens able and willing to save. At the turn of the twentieth century, people on the continent knew from experience that nowhere were loans easier to obtain than in France.

(ii) The structure of the post-revolutionary budget

The effect of the new tax system on the structural base of the revenue side of the budget was so minimal, compared to the pre-revolutionary period, that it could hardly be discerned, as illustrated by a comparison of Napoleon's last budget with that of Necker. The vision of a single direct tax had vanished. The share of indirect (including registration) taxes in 1813 amounted to about 53.2 per cent, having been about 55 per cent in the 1780s. The proportion of direct taxes rose slightly from about 41 to about 43.2 per cent, but declined during the nineteenth century and in 1913 amounted to a mere 14.2 per cent (see Tables 49, 54).

Comparison of the expenditure side on the contrary shows obvious shifts (see Table 50), shaped by the particular events of the two decades preceding 1814: the expenses of the large French military forces, in conjunction with the waning extraordinary revenues from occupied territories, caused the military share to rise to almost 62 per cent, compared to 25 per cent in the 1780s. Surprising and completely unex-

[15] A. Wagner (1889), part 3, p. 373.

Table 49. *Public revenue, 1813 (Napoleon's last budget)*

Ordinary revenue	Fr. million	%
1. Direct taxes: 1. Land tax	242	30.7
2. Tax on persons and movable property	37	4.7
3. Additions to 1 and 2	22	2.8
4. Tax on trade or business	20	2.5
5. Door and window tax	20	2.5
Total of direct taxes	341	43.2
2. Indirect taxes: 1. Consumption taxes	150	19.0
2. Customs duties	100	12.7
Total of indirect taxes	250	31.7
3. Registration taxes	170	21.5
4. Other revenues (e.g., lottery, postal, coinage)	28	3.6
Total ordinary revenue	789	100

Source: Collated from Bruguières (1969), pp. 13ff., see also pp. 25ff., 75ff. Slightly higher amounts through a different accounting method in Nicolas (1883), p. 15. Currency units were changed between 1795 and 1803 from 1 *livre* = 20 *sols* to 1 franc = 100 centimes; 5 fr. = L.5 1/16th, according to Klimpert (1896).

Table 50. *Public expenditure, 1814 (Louis XVIII's first budget)*

	Fr. million	%
1. Public debt	120	14.4
2. War, military expenditure, etc. of which	516	61.9
1. Navy	70	8.4
3. Administration, etc. of which	173	21.4
1. Internal affairs and police	94	11.3
2. Crown and chambers	27	3.5
3. Financial	27	2.9
4. External affairs	9	1.3
4. Sundries	18	2.3
Total expenditure	827	100

Source: Bruguières (1969), pp. 77, 80; see the reports of the Minister of Finance on the budget, *ibid.*, Appendix, pp. 243–56.

pected is the heavy reduction of expenditure on the debt service from 43 per cent in the budget of 1780 to a mere 14.4 per cent at the end of the Napoleonic period: though militarily the loser of the European wars, France emerged from the war years bearing a considerably smaller financial burden than Britain, the great victorious rival. The explanations are that the French public debt, linked to the issue of *assignats*, was wiped out by state bankruptcy, that France conducted its wars to a large extent at the expense of vanquished countries and that only a moderate reparation payment was imposed upon France in the peace treaties of 1814 and 1815: 700 million fr. war reparations due to the allies; financing an army of occupation of 150,000 men, quartered on seventeen French fortresses for five years, calculated to cost 150 million fr. per annum; and finally compensation to emigrants which in the course of subsequent settlements resulted in an annuity of 26 million fr.[16]

The French public debt was shown in 1815 to amount to 1,267 million fr., corresponding to no more than 1.4 times annual budget revenue (see p. 398). Much more unfavourable was the relationship in Britain around 1820–2 at about 13:1 (see p. 354) and in Prussia around 1820 at about 9:1 (see p. 454). State bankruptcy, the means by which France rid itself of its debt and solved its financial problems, was taboo in Britain, but not very unusual on the continent. It corresponds to a once-and-for-all extraordinary property tax levied on contemporary debenture holders, that is, presumably on a group of higher income recipients. Britain, on the other hand, distributed the war burden over future generations. This helps to explain why Britain, under heavy financial pressure, developed a modern system of efficient income taxation already during the Napoleonic wars (1806, then definitely 1842). France, moving into post-Napoleonic times astonishingly burden-free, did not join the process of modernization until 1914–17, when weighed down by the costs of the First World War.

To complement these ordinary revenues, the law provided for extraordinary revenues, foreseen in the bill of 20 March 1813 to amount to 190 million fr., in the bill of 26 November 1813 to 228 million fr.[17] The revenue budget gives some points of reference for the French fiscal system. For public expenditure in 1814, the details are in Table 49.

2. The fiscal system

(i) Direct taxes[18]

The basic principle of a just direct tax – the revenue tax
French revolution proclamations of liberty, equality and justice guided development of the French tax system down to the smallest details.

Liberty was interpreted as unconditional protection of the privacy of the individual from official arbitrariness. The integrity of the private

---

[16] Bray (1894), pp. 380f. for clarification of reparations of 1815; on reparations of 1870–1, see pp. 382ff.   [17] Bruguières (1969), p. 26.
[18] Parieu (1866–7); Vignes (1889), pp. 1,210ff.; additionally Martel (1894), pp. 663ff. and Arnoux (1894), pp. 1334ff. On the early switch from the ideal of an excise to the ideal of a direct tax see Mann (1937), pp. 50ff., 123ff.

sphere in the tax system was considered to be best guarded by granting financial authorities no rights whatsoever to ascertain the citizens' actual 'internal' incomes and property. Thus understood, liberty was the overriding consideration which shaped the new tax system, leading to the development of the essentially traditional type of revenue taxes proportioned strictly and as exclusively as possible on a basis of external indicators of average achievable ability of citizens to bear taxes. Such external indicators were – by definition – ascertainable in type and volume; by means of the exclusion of subjective elements, they offered the best guarantee of objective equality uninfluenced by arbitrary elements; thus tax justice. The principle of taxation on the basis of indicators was backed by a mixture of hope, faith, and certainty that there existed enough external indicators reflecting with sufficient accuracy the protected private incomes and fortunes to make indicative taxation a just taxation in terms of average productivity of chargeable assets in the citizens' possession – thus also of the citizens' average ability to pay. It was one hundred years before the error inherent in objective indicators came to be corrected.

Levying tax in proportion to the differential productivity of chargeable assets achieved equality of relative tax burdens among citizens. Equality was seen simply as tax burden equal in relation to income and property. This led to proportional taxation: distribution of incomes remained the same before and after taxation, thus excluding implicitly any tax progression. Equality and justice added up to the principle of generality, meaning taxability of all citizens; nobility and clergy lost their traditional tax privileges. Liberty and justice, equality and generality thus merged into a single concept, while largely recognizing the unequal distribution of incomes and property arising partly from historical tradition, partly from future events; this led to unequal tax demands on individuals, if measured in monetary amounts. Thus the abolition of the feudal, nominally equal capitation tax – and the notion of a leave-them-as-you-find-them rule.

The *locus classicus* linking the principle of relative equality, that is evenhandedness, to the theorem of ability to pay, is found in article XIII of the Declaration of Human Rights of 1789:

Pour l'entretien de la force publique et pour les dépenses d'administration une contribution commune est indispensable; elle doit être également répartie entre tous les citoyens en raison de leurs facultés.

Article 15 of the French constitution of 1814 added a brief description of evenhandedness:

L'égalité de proportion dans l'impôt est le droit.

There is probably no other European country which lavished as much logic, consistency and administrative exertion on the concept of object-ive indicators as did France. To give concrete expression to principles such as liberty, equality, and justice was the lawyers' delicate task. Starting from the *Code Napoléon*, they elaborated an ever narrowing web of rules and administrative regulations to comprise, categorize, and classify as completely as possible all objective indicators. Essentially these were laws to control and limit governmental activity and to safeguard citizens' individual rights. This was one of the most important principles of liberalism.

The School of French Inspecteures des Finances developed and became the model for that part of Europe which admired French perfection in administration, the brilliance and elegance of French legal thought, and accepted as inevitable the increasing complication of the system arising from it. Continental thinking based on codified law, decisively influ-enced by the *Code Napoléon*, developed in a different direction from the British legal system, based on common law and precedents, each influ-encing the tax system belonging to it. The continental constitutional state thus was codified, formalized, and lashed down in every detail, remaining fettered at the same time by those restrictions designed to guarantee liberty; the pragmatic British way to a personal income tax with a duty to declare and a fiscal check on individual circumstances of taxpayers' incomes was blocked for a long period. The exceedingly strong emphasis on the legal and formal side in the French tax system is presumably also responsible for the virtual absence of any really pro-found theoretical publication on economic or scientific aspects of fiscal problems in France in the nineteenth century – in contradistinction to Italy and Britain, but also to Germany.

French direct taxes were the earliest and most important 'modern' examples of indicative taxes in Europe. They acted as pacemakers for, among others, the direct tax systems of Austria and the south German states, where this type of tax was brought to even higher perfection in detail. The Württemberg revenue taxes of 1821, in the form of allocated revenue taxes, presumably reached the maximum of what indicative taxes of this kind were capable of achieving in a total tax system, supplemented by dues on personal income. They also exemplified the failure of objective revenue taxes in a growing and industrializing economy, because of their immobility at the turn of the twentieth century, when they had to give way to an income tax on British lines. Allowing for chronological differences, this was true of all of Europe.

Objective revenue taxes
Land tax: Land tax was to be levied on average achievable net revenue from real estate. Napoleon ordered in 1807 the compilation of new land

registers showing net revenue, to list every single plot of land. In 1815, one-quarter of French surface area had been trigonometrically surveyed and one-eighth of the land registered. By 1850, the enormous administrative task was (almost) completed: 52, 153, 150 ha of land were registered, split into 126,079,962 separate plots belonging to 11,036,601 proprietors.[19]

Two types of objective indicators determined the registered net revenue. The land was divided according to utilization, such as arable, meadows, vineyards, pasture, forest, waste land, subdivided according to the usual crop cultivated on each plot (such as wheat, barley). A quality class, based on geographical situation and quality of soil, was laid down for every type of cultivation. That was the first group of objective indicators circumscribing the factor of production land as a source of revenue. The calculation of average net revenue of a plot according to the quality class of cultivation and the produce cultivated resulting therefrom was the cornerstone of this tax system. Net revenue was arrived at by deducting from the average achievable gross revenue the legally authorized costs of cultivation, of seed, harvesting and mainte nance, determined by a multitude of detailed regulations. All this presupposed a set of objective quantities (such as average relationship of seed to crop) and a set of objective prices (such as average prices of produce, equipment, wages). That was the second group of objective indicators. Personal exemptions were not permitted; by virtue of the system, subjective elements were excluded from consideration.

Estimated net revenues were recorded in the community land register for individual plots and served as a means of allocating their share of the total tax bill, plus additions to be levied as determined *ex ante* by the annual finance laws. Such aggregate assessment was allocated proportionately via sub-assessments on individual *départements*, on *arrondissements*, on local authorities and finally on individual plots.

The land tax was originally designed to become the main pillar of the new tax system. The ordinary principal yield was therefore fixed in 1790 at a correspondingly high level of 240 million *livres*, calculated on the basis of an estimated net revenue for all French lands amounting to 1,200 million *livres* and a desired tax incidence not exceeding 20 per cent of that net revenue. Both the yield and the desired dominance of the land tax proved utopian. The principal yield had to be drastically scaled down: to 150 million fr. in 1821, slowly rising thereafter to 163 million fr. in 1851, 181.4 million fr. in 1885, reaching 107 million fr. in 1914 — in other words, barely 16 per cent of direct taxes, or 2.3 per cent of total

[19] According to the enquiries of landed property; A. Wagner (1889), part 3, pp. 440ff., 446f.; with many detailed facts, Arnoux (1889), p. 743; *ibid., Foncière* (1894), pp. 232ff.; Kaufmann (1882), pp. 152ff., 165ff.; Hock (1857); then Dreux (1933), Herbin and Pebereau (1956).

revenue.[20] That was less than envisaged in 1790, even without taking into consideration the nineteenth-century price rises. It is difficult to establish the effective tax incidence on land revenue. Three great enquiries, in 1818–21, 1851–4 and 1879–83, aimed at making *inter alia* this information available: according to the methods of calculating productivity adopted by the law, the average taxation of net revenue appears to have fallen from a maximum of 20 per cent to 16.67, then 10.7 and in the early 1880s to 4–5 per cent. Such average figures disguise the wide scatter of individual incidence: taxation of net revenue varied from *département* to *département* in a ratio of 1:2 and 1:3, within a local authority and according to land utilization up to 1:10. Even extreme figures of 0.19 per cent and 30 per cent are on record. To the general clumsiness of land registration in respect of changes in productivity, prices and utilization, was added the specific regional variation in initial registration, containing a calculation of net revenue according to the rules in force at the time. Though individuals were taxed according to objective indicators, both the first and the second group of indicators changed over time, thus doing away with the evenhandedness of tax burden as between different taxpayers. The principle of justice was infringed. Revision of registration, though provided for, hardly ever took place, mostly because of the enormous labour involved; the hostility of land registries to innovation became proverbial. A system of land tax based on registration and suitable for a stationary economy could not serve as a main financial support: it remained what it had been from the beginning, an eighteenth-century tax system inelastic in the face of any kind of structural change.

The trading or business tax: The trading or business tax was the second limb of the revenue tax system.[21] The dual tax applied to craft establishments, workshops, factories, traders, banks, transport, and service occupations and some professions. From the point of view of fiscal history, the business tax constitutes the most interesting of direct indicative taxes. The basic principle of taxation remained unchanged down to the First World War: the level of taxation was determined by the productivity of the business, measured by objective indicators. In order to adapt the tax somewhat to the structural changes experienced by the general economy in the process of quick industrialization, it was elaborated by an ever subtler application of external indicators. The French example shows what a business revenue tax of this type could achieve.

---

[20] Statistisches Reichsamt (1927), p. 198. Revenues from building tax, shown separately in 1914 at 113 million fr. were insignificantly higher than land tax. On the very large variation of incidence in the *départements* and local authorities, Köbner (1889), pp. 1f.

[21] Hennebique, 'Contribution' (1894), pp. 740ff.; *ibid.*, 'Rôles' (1894); Kaufmann (1882), pp. 215ff., with a table on pp. 236ff. showing occupations and professions taxed according to location and *droit proportionnel*.

The *patent* was the registration, subject to fee, of a business; this was the basis of taxability and recorded the establishment by authoritative entry in the tax registers and thereby in the list of taxpayers. The establishment was – like a farm – fitted into a scheme of several classes and groups, circumscribed by a network of four indicators. The establishment was (1) allocated to a type of trade: there were four chief classes of trades, each with subsections, their number increasing as new branches of such occupations emerged. Each group of trades was (2) subdivided according to the establishment's location, the indicators being determined by the size of the place in terms of resident population. The indicators of type of trade and location jointly determined the 'fixed rate' (*droit fixe*) of the tax. Its second part, the 'variable rate' (*droit proportionnel*), resulted from the (3) estimated rentable value of the premises occupied and (4) the size of the establishment, in terms of type and number of people employed, number and type of machinery used, furnaces, vats, and whatever other equipment was specific to the nature of the trade. The growth or decline of an establishment could be measured by indicators (3) and (4) and resulted in a change in the variable rate.

The highly diversified set of indicators determining type of trade, location, rentable value, and size of establishment was finally combined with revenue figures, expressed in francs, and entered in the tax list. It is not possible today to be absolutely certain how tax inspectors used an establishment's different indicators to assess its productivity, hence what determined the figures entered in the tax list. They must at least have given different weights to various indicators, treating indicators as variables of a production function considered typical for a particular trade. Revenue estimates presumably represented index numbers indicating the interrelationship of different establishments from the point of view of their average achievable productivity rather than the desired absolute average achievable productivity of each individual establishment. Yet the latter was required for a proportional tax, such as the business tax, aiming at an even incidence of tax burden by means of a percentage of revenue, whereas an allocated tax could make do with the interrelationship of average achievable revenues. Thus, the acid test of the business tax is the assessment of the presumed revenue of a taxable asset. It does not appear that the problem was solved; it is thus extremely difficult to make statements regarding the actual tax incidence on business revenue.

The French roster of classifications, the list of tables, and the scheme of tax rates were excellently structured in detail. On the assumption of adequately sound principles in assessing individual taxes, the government fixed annual rates of tax accordingly; they were changed from time to time. Around 1885, the 'fixed rate' of the location and type of trade

384 PUBLIC FINANCE IN BRITAIN, FRANCE, AND GERMANY

tariff varied from 2 fr. for the smallest taxable asset in the countryside to 400 fr. for the largest Paris establishment. The 'variable rate' was originally meant to be a standard levy of 10 per cent on registered gross revenue, but was subsequently reduced, after 1880 being levied at rates of 5, 3.33, and 2 per cent. Small businesses enjoyed tax reductions beyond these rates. The mass of ordinary taxpayers – *les commerciants ordinaires et artisans occupants des ouvriers* – formed the main body of those lightly taxed, amounting around 1885 to about 1.4 million taxpayers or 85 per cent of all people liable to business tax.[22] Not liable to business tax were wage labourers, salaried employees and officials, unless they carried on a taxable business as a sideline. A yield of 198 million fr. made the business tax in 1914 the most productive direct tax, which at 29 per cent of direct taxes accounted for 4.2 per cent of total revenue.[23]

Personal and movable property tax: Personal and movable property tax, the third limb of the revenue tax system, was designed as a supplementary tax to cover income from movable property and from professions. Here too, concern for the citizen's privacy overrode ascertainment of the taxpayer's actual personal income. Personal tax affected every domestic and foreign citizen in France, provided he was 'not notoriously poor' and 'in full possession of his rights'. It was a kind of capitation tax, graded according to the value of the taxpayer's working day. The value of an individual's working day was fixed according to external indicators and outward appearance within legal limits of 0.5 fr. to 1.5 fr.; the 'treble value of the working day' was the amount of tax to be paid monthly. The yield to the Treasury was rather uncertain, owing to the difficulty of actually locating all taxpayers. In order nevertheless to retain the character of an allocated tax with a yield calculated *ex ante*, personal tax was linked to a tax on movable property. If the sum of personal taxes did not reach the aggregate tax demand determined *ex ante*, the shortfall, the residuum, was imposed in the form of a tax on movable property. The external objective indicator of income to bear the tax on movable property was expenditure on the dwelling, reflected by the estimated capital value of the dwelling (*valeur locative*) or its rentable value. Tax on movable property was allocated as a proportion of capital or rent values of dwellings, particular rules applying to buildings used commercially and let.

The aggregate yield of the allocated tax amounted to 30 million fr. in 1798, achieving after modifications 27 million in 1815, 34 million in 1832, 55.5 million in 1870 and 70 million in 1885. According to censuses around 1885, there were 8.2 million taxpayers; personal capitation tax

[22] A. Wagner (1889), part 3, pp. 468ff., to be read with Hennebique, 'Contribution' (1894), pp. 740ff.

[23] Statistisches Reichsamt (1927), p. 198 for the year 1914.

had in fact turned into a family tax.[24] Its total yield in 1914 amounted to 114 million fr. – at 17 per cent of direct tax revenue or 2.4 per cent of all tax revenue only a little more than the yield of the land tax.[25]

The door and window tax: The door and window tax was introduced during Napoleon's campaign in northern Italy in 1798. It was a kind of house revenue tax, meant to supplement the tax on movable property and to be levied above all on tenants of dwellings. It was originally to be paid by the dwelling's owner, who passed it on to his tenants by means of a surcharge on rent. *De facto* the tax developed into an impost on the proprietor. Indicators were openings in dwellings, workshops and factories, criteria being mainly the number and type of such openings (such as gates, doors, windows with balcony railings, small attic windows), their position within the building (which storey, whether to the street, to the courtyard, to gardens, facing factories), and the location of the building itself, again graded according to the size of the place. Linked to this catalogue of indicators was a tariff of different classes – for the taxation of 'light and air', as it was occasionally put. The tax, originally allocated among local authorities, was changed in 1831 into a tax fixing a sum in francs for each opening classified, in accordance with the current finance law.

The high cost of collecting the tax is illustrated by the following figures: in 1885 it covered 8,975,176 buildings, houses, factories, etc., of which

248,362		1 opening
1,827,104		2 openings
1,624,516	buildings had	3 openings
1,165,902		4 openings
849,961		5 openings
3,259,331		6 or more openings.[26]

Architects with an eye to taxation designed buildings with smaller and fewer windows so as to reduce their tax incidence.

Altogether 37,245,507 openings were registered in the cause of tax equality and justice and in the same year charged with an aggregate tax of 47.2 million fr.; it had been 16 million fr. in 1802.[27] The levy varied in 1885 from 0.3 fr. for the smallest cottage in the country with a single opening to 18.8 fr. for the gate of a department store in a large Paris edifice. The tax yield in 1914 amounted to almost 73 million fr., that is 11 per cent of direct taxes or 1.5 per cent of total revenue.[28]

[24] Hennebique, 'Contribution' (1894), pp. 845ff.; A. Wagner (1889), part 3, pp. 458ff.; Kaufmann (1882), pp 195ff.   [25] Statistisches Reichsamt (1927), p. 198.

[26] Arnoux, 'Contribution' (1894), pp. 896ff.; Kaufmann (1882), pp. 209ff.

[27] A. Wagner (1889), part 3, pp. 465ff.   [28] Statistisches Reichsamt (1927), p. 198.

The door and window tax points to British origins; with its extremely simple mechanical form of assessment by external indicators, it remained methodically speaking the weakest link in a set of revenue taxes which no effort had been spared to make precise. As a method of taxing income from movable property and professional activities, it was most unsuitable; even a combination of indicators as different as the values of the working day, of dwellings, doors and windows provided no remedy.

The tax on income from securities: The tax on incomes from securities, introduced in 1872, initiated in France the direct taxation of income in the shape of a partial tax on unearned income from capital.[29] Yields from domestic and foreign shares, bonds, and partnerships in companies were taxed at 3, from 1890 at 4 per cent, interest on home and foreign government bonds and domestic mortgages remaining exempt. This was to preserve the credit of the state and of landed property and to direct private lenders preferentially to these investment opportunities. The state, perennially in debt and in need of loans, could in this manner offer its creditors a *de facto* higher rate of return or alternatively increase its own receipts by issuing new bonds at a higher emission price. Tax on unearned income from capital was deducted at source by the interest-paying agency. Similarly foreign private debtors had to remit the tax to the French Treasury before paying the net income to the creditors; only on that condition were foreign securities admitted to the French capital market. The tax on unearned income from capital also served to strengthen the French capital market in favour of French seekers of capital – a particular form of protection for capital. The revenue tax on securities in 1914 was recorded as part of general income tax.

(ii) Indirect taxes

Having established his central authority, Napoleon reintroduced the indirect consumption taxes outlawed during the revolutionary period.[30] It appears that the principles of justice and equality, while very weighty in shaping French direct taxes, received little consideration in indirect taxation. Easy to levy, indirect taxes served only to bring to the Treasury funds on which the state depended. Experience showed that consumption duties, accruing mostly day by day and in small amounts, were much less noticed by taxpayers than direct taxes levied at regular intervals; hence neither post-revolutionary France nor the other European states would do without indirect taxation. Indirect taxes notori-

[29] Dumaine, Neymarck and Salefranque (1894), pp. 1467ff.; Swarte (1894).
[30] Sestier (1884), pp. 1226ff.; Kaufmann (1882), pp. 263ff., especially pp. 320ff. (consumption taxes), pp. 460ff. (customs duties); Hock (1857), on indirect taxes pp. 138ff., *enregistrements* pp. 177ff., consumption taxes pp. 319ff.

ously constituted a relatively heavier burden on recipients of smaller than of higher incomes – an injustice inherent in an impost on consumption, but the state acquiesced in it. By the time of Napoleon's abdication the system of French indirect taxes – admittedly with numerous administrative improvements – once again resembled rather closely what it had been under the *ancien régime*.

Consumption taxes, customs duties, and licence fees

The first to be reintroduced was tobacco tax in 1791, only a little later the transport tax, and equally the *octrois* revived in several towns. Reconstruction of a large indirect internal tax system on beverages and salt followed in the course of the years from 1804 to 1808 – the period of the war of the third coalition with France. Consumption dues, including revenue from the tobacco and match monopolies, at 1,996 million fr. in 1914 accounted for about 42 per cent of public revenue.[31]

Customs duties: An old scheme of Colbert's, 1619–83, found its fulfilment in 1791: the abolition of internal customs established a free internal market, surrounded by a barrier of external customs. The external customs tariff was all-embracing and on the moderate side at the time. Napoleon raised the duties and used them as an instrument of deliberate economic policy – to supplement the continental blockade against Britain. Up to around 1860, French tariffs remained protectionist, partly at a prohibitive level; agriculture (cereals, livestock, wool) and industry (textiles, iron) were to be shielded, above all from British competition. The revenue purpose of the duties was only of secondary importance.

French industry having gained strength, Napoleon III introduced a system of liberal trade treaties and moderate (protective) tariffs, beginning with the French–British Cobden–Chevalier trade treaty of 1860. This had a historical link with the Eden treaty of 1786, by which Britain and France had conceded to each other low standard customs duties, but the 1860 treaty had decisive novel features: a most-favoured-nation clause and the principle of reciprocity. Both have ever since played a crucial part in the political implications of international trade treaties. The Cobden treaty was soon followed by a large network of trade treaties between Western and Central European countries, in which the contracting parties conceded low duties to each other, while collectively protecting themselves by 'general' customs duties, usually higher, against outsiders, meaning America, Asia, and Africa; the system entailed preferences given by metropolitan powers to their colonies. A domestic market free from internal dues in a single country had developed into a domestic market with low internal duties for a whole group of countries.

---

[31] Statistisches Reichsamt (1927), p. 198, where there are also customs revenues.

More than that, liberal trade doctrine could not achieve – and even that did not last very long. The revenue purpose of customs duties was not lost sight of, compared to their economic and trade policy aspects, but it clearly took second place.

From 1872 onwards, French customs duties became more protectionist, above all as regarded agriculture (protective agrarian duties on cereals and livestock). At the same time, the payment of France's war reparations to Germany after the 1870–1 war also stimulated a growing fiscal concern with customs duties: duties were raised on colonial goods, such as coffee, tea, cocoa, and pepper. Customs revenue amounted to 672 million fr. in 1914, equal to 14.3 per cent of public revenue.

Even during its liberal phase, the French customs tariff remained far more complicated, judged by the number of dutiable commodities and situations, than the British tariff, as well as more voluminous than the German. Added to this, there existed a system of export duties up to 1882, with which was associated a set of customs drawbacks and export subsidies.

Licence fees: These fees were regarded as an appendage of indirect taxes. They were levied above all on drink publicly consumed, because a victualler had to take out a licence. Similarly, transport contracting was liable to licence – the charge to be shifted to the goods transported. The yield from licences was insignificant.

Registration taxes (taxes on legal transactions)

The group of quasi-tax fees (*timbres*) extant during the *ancien régime* survived the revolutionary period without experiencing excessive opposition. A type of taxation very difficult to legislate for and collect, it was elaborated greatly in the 1790s, taking the form of registration fees (*enregistrements*) and stamp duties (official stamps, *timbres*, tax stamps) and on this basis remained a central component of French finances in the nineteenth century.[32]

There is probably no other branch of tax legislation which links the principles of taxation so closely to those of civil law governing property, usufruct, rent, and tenancy to the law as it affects shares, debentures and securities, and to the law of contract and inheritance, of commerce and of litigation. The typically French 'codes', such as the *Code Civil*, the *Code de Commerce*, and their commentaries and legal decisions, had a permanent influence on this group of taxes. High French public and fiscal officials were first and foremost lawyers. A multitude of contracts, documents, and documentary changes (*mutations*) were subject to registration, hence liable to registration and official stamp fees; the amount of

[32] Dumaine (1894), pp. 88ff., Salefranque (1894), pp. 1390ff.; Kaufmann (1882), pp. 277ff.

detail in this field of taxation was almost beyond comprehension.

The resulting systematic elaboration of these imposts, setting very complicated tasks in the field of tax technique and collection, aroused distinct admiration among German teachers of fiscal science.[33] Above all, it caused some astonishment that the system proved surprisingly capable of development, as well as fiscally productive and elastic in response to changes in government financial needs. The high yield resulted from numerous increases by which the government raised the original levels of various types of dues, such as a war surcharge of 10 per cent in 1799, a further 10 per cent surcharge in 1855, or a 20–25 per cent surcharge after the lost war of 1871 which burdened France with reparations.

The proportion of total tax revenue in the state budget raised by *enregistrements* and *timbres* thus remained surprisingly stable during the nineteenth century at about 20 per cent; in absolute figures, *enregistrements* rose from 118.1 million fr. in 1816 to 519.11 million fr. in 1886, while *timbres* over the same period increased from 24.94 million fr. to 156.14 million fr. Totalling jointly 1,330 million fr. in 1914, they accounted for 28 per cent of public revenue at that date.[34]

Nevertheless, neither politicians responsible for finance in individual German states nor German academics teaching fiscal science fully adopted this unadulterated French speciality of the tax system. As little as the admired and rather simple British form of income tax could satisfy the 'pure doctrine' of German tax theory on account of its pragmatism and elements of revenue tax, were the Germans prepared to stomach the admired French rather complicated transaction taxes: these went too far in mixing up inextricably the 'pure fee' payable for specific public services (above all attestations) with the 'pure tax' used to finance the government's general business. French *enregistrement* and *timbre* contained elements of a tax supplementary to the direct taxes; inasmuch as they were levied on capitalized income, they acted as a property tax; at the same time, they were inheritance taxes and partook of the character of special transaction taxes. Systematic German tax doctrine required all these elements to be neatly separated.

Thus it remained: from the outset, France by her indicative revenue taxes provided a model for the south German states and Austria, Britain, considerably later, for the Saxon–Prussian, subsequently the German Reich universal income tax. However, both precedents were – or so it was believed – refined in terms of theory, and thus modified to suit German requirements.

---

[33] For instance A. Wagner (1889), part 3, p. 545.

[34] A. Wagner (1889), part 3, pp. 395, 567; Statistisches Reichsamt (1927), p. 199.

(iii) Characteristics of state taxes at the turn of the twentieth century

Between the revolution and the First World War, the French tax system remained dominated by an emphatic dislike of inquisitorial tax investigation. Given a choice between more accurate criteria of tax distribution which involved declaring full incomes – the British method – and safeguarding maximum privacy, French legislation invariably and unhesitatingly chose the method which protected individuals from any possible arbitrariness on the part of the state and the tax inspectorate – though it was expensive and administratively cumbersome, yet ingeniously designed in many details. This French legislation is based on the fundamental lessons drawn from French history, of the arbitrariness considered inherent in the pre-revolutionary tax system. That the principle of justice in the sense of equality of incidence was increasingly infringed *de facto*, though ever more strongly entrenched *de jure*, is one of those contradictions accepted by the government up to the early twentieth century. In the last resort, this also was a kind of political pragmatism.

Probably in no other European country was the principle of the inviolability of privacy of income maintained for so long, but it accorded well with the interests of a property-owning bourgeoisie in an industrializing country, leading to a *system of indicative revenue taxes*, based on external indicators within an excellent legal structure. What was lacking for a long time to complete the system was the direct taxation of monetary capital – again in agreement with the interests of a property-owning bourgeoisie which had acquired an additional source of income in the form of bonds issued by a government deeply in debt. Only at a late stage, in 1872, was a tax on parts of interest from capital, held in the form of certain types of securities, embodied in the direct taxes. Direct taxation of individual earned income, such as wages, salaries, pensions, was inadequately achieved by the personal and movable property tax. Seen as a whole, the direct tax system, in spite of the ever-expanding trading or business tax, remained rather unresponsive in its elasticity of yield. It lacked a 'flexible element' in the pattern of taxation which would have adapted to changes in the structure and growth of the economy – the element Britain possessed in its income tax.

It is presumably for that reason that France – in complete contradiction to what had originally been intended immediately after the revolution – developed the indirect consumption and transaction taxes to an unparalleled degree of perfection and productivity. However, their multiplicity and ramifications subjected taxpayers to much annoyance and – again contrary to revolutionary plans – to relatively higher burdens on the lower income groups. The elastic element in the tax system from the middle of the century onwards consisted, alongside the transaction taxes, of the consumption tax, its yield augmenting in proportion to increasing population, growing national income and mass consumption; jointly with the raising of a few tax rates, it covered such part of increasing state requirements as could not be financed from loans and direct taxes.

In contradistinction to Britain, growing state taxation heavily shifted the proportion of direct and indirect tax yields towards the latter. At the end of Napoleon I's regime, direct taxes had accounted for 42.4 per cent of total tax revenue; under Napoleon III, their share fell to 23 per cent, eventually in 1913 bottoming out at 14 per cent. Even at that time, this was considered ominous and undesirable from the point of view of social policy. Britain took a different course: the system of income tax schedules devised in 1803 and more fully after 1842 shifted the tax burden more towards the higher income classes by having a high exemption threshold, in spite of the insignificance of the progressive tax element. France on the other hand emphasized indirect taxation and laid more of the tax burden on the group of low income recipients, incidentally by such fiscal action diminishing substantially private purchasing power.

The conspicuously inferior importance of direct taxation is, however, somewhat corrected and amended by taking into account taxation on the part of subordinate local authorities, that is, *départements* and communes, which consisted overwhelmingly of additions to direct taxes. Table 51 indicates the magnitude and the structure of such revenues in some detail for a year fiscally not in the least untypical, that is, 1885, adding by way of supplementary information taxation by *départements* and communes.

From a twentieth-century point of view, it is difficult to credit the immense exertion in money, labour, and intelligence necessary to establish and maintain the land register and lists tabulating objective indicators for an objectively just assessment to revenue taxes of each individual, given the comparatively poor yield of these taxes and the eventual failure of this whole tax concept. However, such a judgement, based on Adam Smith's fourth tax canon of economy of collection, manifests incomplete understanding: the immense exertion constitutes the costs devoted to the attempt to realize the highly esteemed principle of justice, requiring both general liability to tax and equality of tax incidence. This was a central component of the new philosophical principles which the French revolution had helped to establish.

(iv) Late breakthrough: the new system of income tax of 1914–17

The idea of income taxation accords entirely with the principles of the French revolution to burden each individual *en raison de ses facultés*. Yet its introduction remained unachieved until 1914, when financial pressure of

Table 51. *Tax revenue (gross), 1885*

		Fr. million	% of state taxation
I. State taxation			
1. Direct taxes, of which		446	16.6
1. Land tax	177		
2. Personal and movable property tax	67		
3. Door and window tax	46		
4. Trading or business tax	105		
5. Supplementary tax	1		
6. Tax on the yield of securities	50		
2. Registration taxes, of which		708	26.3
1. *Enregistrements* (incl. inheritance tax)	553		
2. Stamps	154		
3. Indirect taxes, of which		1,538	57.1
1. Customs duties	291		
2. Salt tax	33		
3. Tax on beverages	455		
4. Sugar tax	151		
5. Tobacco monopoly	379		
6. Lesser taxes (e.g., transportation tax) (92.8)	228		
Total of state taxation		2,692	100
II. Taxation by départements and communes			
1. Additions to the direct taxes	349		
2. Local commune *octrois*	277		
Total of *département* and commune taxation		626	23.2
III. Total tax burden (I and II)		3,318	

Source: A. Wagner (1889), part 3, p. 395. Discrepancies in figures due to rounding.

war is likely to have played an important part.[35] Up to that time, the liberal bourgeoisie resisted income taxation – parallels occur in other countries – using and formulating for its own purposes time and again two demands from the revolutionary days:

the idea of liberty, allegedly precluding inquisitorial incursion by authority into the citizens's private affairs,
the idea of equality, allegedly precluding progressive taxation.

A first comprehensive legislative bill in 1896 embodying the duty of income declaration and a progressive tax led to the fall of the government. However, in 1901 and 1902 a progressive element was successfully embodied in the substantially increased inheritance tax. After bills of

[35] On the different concepts of the equality principle, see Mann (1937), pp. 112ff.

1907, parliamentary battles achieved piecemeal introduction of a new system of direct taxes – including income tax – between 1914 and 1917 (Cailloux reforms). The fiscal historian sees this mixed system as an exemplary illustration of the different principles of direct taxation in nineteenth-century European industrial countries.[36]

The new system of direct taxes combines three sub-systems:

1. The restructured traditional 'objective revenue taxes' of 29 March 1914;
2. Newly introduced partial income taxes according to schedules of 15 July 1914 and 31 July 1917, taxing actual income, but continuing to rely on a few external indicators;
3. A newly introduced general income tax of 15 July 1914, a modern tax on the individual.

Thus the shape of the entire system:

The (new) general tax on total income (*impôt général sur le revenu*), law of 15 July 1914

The three (traditional) revenue taxes, law of 29 March 1914	The five (new) partial income taxes (*impôts cedulairs sur les revenus*), law of 31 July 1917
1. Building tax (*contribution foncière des propriétés bâties*)	Taxes on (*impôts sur les*)
	1. Income from business (*bénéfices industriels et commerciaux*)
2. Land tax (*contribution foncière des propriétés non bâties*)	2. Agricultural incomes (*bénéfices de l'exploitation agricole*)
	3. Earned incomes (*traitements publics et privés, les indemnités et émoluments, les salaires, les pensions et les rentes viagères*)
3. Tax on income from securities (*taxes sur le revenu des valeurs mobilières*)	4. Incomes from professions (*bénéfices des professions non commerciales*)
	5. Particular revenues from capital (*impôt sur les revenus des créances, dépôts et cautionnements*)

The five taxes on partial incomes

By relating particular types of income to their sources, France adopted the pattern of the British income and property tax designed by Pitt and Peel. Different types of income were assessed according to differential

---

[36] Popitz (1926), pp. 478ff.; Oualid (1929), pp. 130ff.

methods and taxed at differential rates, thus aiming at differentiating the incidence on incomes from land, capital, and labour. However, the new taxes on partial incomes retained a recognizably French element of objective taxes: a proportional rate, absence of subjective personal elements in the assessment of taxable income and absence of any offset of profits and losses between different types of income, that is partial incomes. If several types of income accrued to the same taxpayer, losses in one category could not be counted against profits in another. The somewhat biased slogan of 'privatizing gains' and 'socializing losses' by means of shifting losses to the state by means of taxation did not yet apply. Only from 1920 onwards did laws introduce, by way of *discrimination sociale*, a social differentiation of tax burden by taking account of individual circumstances, such as family status.

It was a further characteristic of traditional French thinking on taxation that even in 1914–17 no unconditional duty to declare income existed, with the exception of professional incomes. Taxpayers in other categories had the right to declare, but did not have to exercise it, if prepared to accept the permissible alternative of letting the authorities estimate total incomes and deductions by which net taxable income was calculated.

Taxation of *business incomes* comprehended the preceding year's inland *bénéfit net*, derived from carrying on a craft, industry, trade, bank, or transport undertaking. Profits from foreign business establishments remained tax free. The law determining taxable profits in the declaration regulated the volume and level of expenses and depreciation deductible. The rate of tax was (in 1917) around 4.5 per cent. Assessment was based on turnover (*chiffre d'affaires*); regulations fixed the percentages of taxable profit.

Tax on *agricultural income* amounted (in 1917) to 3.75 per cent of profit, in addition to the land tax of March 1914. Profit was deemed to be 50 per cent of the capitalized value of annual rent determining land tax, unless the taxpayer could in an individual instance prove a different (lesser) profit figure. Even the seasoned French tax legislators and administrators had little success in integrating agricultural taxation in a modernized tax system; other countries have not solved that problem satisfactorily even in our own day. The reason was, on the one hand, the imperfection of farmers' accounting practice, as they could not be required to keep books, on the other hand, the often violent fluctuations in their incomes. In parallel to traditional revenue taxes, recourse had eventually to be had to average values and estimates.

Tax on workers' and employees' earned incomes began above a tax-free income of 1,500 fr. (exemption threshold) and deductions for consorts and children. The exemption limit was fixed at a level high enough to keep workers, certainly if married, free from tax. At 3.75 per cent, the rate of tax (in 1917) was the same as for income from agricultural establishments. There was no deduction at source, as practised in Germany and Britain.

Professional income was treated like wages and salaries, as far as rate of tax and exemption threshold were concerned, but with fewer deductions permitted in assessing net taxable income. The tax on revenues from particular investments was deducted at source by means of stamps; it constituted an extension of the tax on income from capital to several revenues from movable capital not hitherto caught in the net, such as arising from private notes of hand, deposit accounts, fees paid for guarantees and sureties.

The traditional building and land revenue taxes, combined through new regulations in a single system with the taxes on partial incomes, remained in essence typical revenue taxes, recognizing neither exemption limits nor consideration of personal circumstances. Ideally, tax was levied on net revenue, determined by capitalized non-individual deductions from gross revenue: 25 per cent for dwelling houses, 40 per cent for buildings used for business, 20 per cent for land not built on. That land revenue tax was retained alongside the tax schedule on agricultural income, can be explained only on historical, hardly on logical tax grounds. Perhaps land and building taxes took the place of a kind of property tax additionally levied on invested income. The tax rate amounted to 4 per cent of net revenue. At least the coexistence side by side of the 4 per cent income tax on capital of 1872 in its 1914 version, and the tax on income from particular kinds of capital of 1917 could have been avoided.

The general comprehensive income tax
The comprehensive income tax approximated fairly closely to the Prussian income tax. In addition to the taxpayers' partial incomes, it was levied on their total incomes, if in excess of 7,000 fr. per annum. Available was an alternative analogous to the tried and proved British model of 1863, very cleverly designed by the legislature: the taxpayer could submit for assessment, and pay tax on, a figure representing the sum of the figures declared in all the other schedules. But he could equally – and this, beneficial in tax terms, was an incentive to that individual declaration which the state favoured, but could not yet enforce – declare his total income as a single figure; only then was he allowed to set off profits against losses incurred under different heads of income. Subjective personal circumstances were taken into account. The standard nominal tax rate amounted to 2 per cent in 1914, rising to 10 per cent in 1916 and 12.5 per cent in 1917. A further 10 per cent war surcharge was

added in 1914. However, the maximum rate of 22.5 per cent (in 1917) was not attained, because the tax progression introduced only for the *impôt général* operated 'in reverse': in the first instance, through family-related deductions from total income permitted for consorts, children, and aged relatives, the remaining income was divided into steps, and only a fraction, growing with every step, counted as taxable income (*progression par tranche*). Differences in taxing particular accruals to income produced a progressive tax in spite of the nominally unchanged tax rate.

By using this combination of income taxes, France rediscovered Montesquieu (1689–1755). He had written in book XIII, chapter VII of *Esprit des Lois* in 1748 that a quantum of personal tax burden kept strictly proportional to personal fortune was unjust, recommending an exemption threshold for a minimum of existence and a moderate progressive tax:

La taxe étoit juste, quoiqu'elle ne fût point proportionnelle; si elle ne suivoit pas la proportion des biens, elle suivoit la proportion des besoins. On jugea que chacun avoit un nécessaire physique égal; que ce nécessaire physique ne devoit point être taxe; que l'utile venoit ensuite, et qu'il devoit être taxe, mais moins que le superflu; que la grandeur de la taxe sur le superflu empêchoit le superflu.

This links with traditional French thinking of the Enlightenment, somewhere between Voltaire's (1694–1778) rather ironical definition: '*Le superflu, chose si nécessaire*', and Rousseau's (1712–78) complete annihilation of superfluous fortunes by way of taxation in pursuit of his ascetic ideal: '*Il faut que tout le monde vive et que personne ne s'enrichisse.*'[37]

After the introduction of the general comprehensive income tax in July 1917, door and window, personal and movable property, business and trade taxes to the Treasury were abolished and transferred to the local authorities. There were no longer any local authority surcharges on income tax. This did away with the traditional tax system of the 1790s and completed the most comprehensive fiscal reform since the days of the French revolution, placing France into the mainstream of what was then considered a modern system of taxation suitable for a developed industrial country.

Prospect
The system of new income taxes made available to the French government a highly productive source of revenue. In a volume of total tax revenue which between 1913 and 1925 had multiplied 6.7 times, the new

---

[37] Quoted from Mann (1937), p. 163. The dual form of French income taxes: objective tax character in partial income taxes, personal tax character in the general comprehensive income tax was difficult to operate in practice; modifications of the law became necessary and complicated the network of taxes; see for this Coulbois (1958), p. 249.

Table 52. *Structure of French tax revenue, 1913 and 1925*

| Type of tax | Revenue | | | |
| | 1913 | | 1925 | |
	Fr. million	%	Fr. million	%
1. Direct taxes				
1. General income tax and schedule taxes	—	—	5,683	20.4
2. Capital revenue tax	138	3.3	1,939	6.9
3. Other direct taxes	634	15.4	390	1.4
Total direct taxes	772	18.7	8,012	28.7
2. Registration taxes	1,085	26.2	6,343	22.7
3. Indirect consumption taxes of which	2,278	55.1	13,545	48.6
1. General turnover tax	—	—	3,865	13.6
2. Customs duties	756	18.3	1,486	5.3
3. Other consumption taxes of which: Tobacco	542	13.1	2,337	8.4
Brandy	399	9.6	1,738	6.2
Salt, sugar	191	4.6	500	1.8
Luxury articles	—	—	688	2.5
Mineral waters	82	2.0	715	2.6
Railway transport	91	2.0	730	2.6
Motor car tax	—	2.0	313	1.1
Total tax revenues 1–3	4,135	100	27,900	100

Source: Calculated from Oualid (1929), pp. 138–9. A detailed subdivision of revenues, comparing 1914 with 1925 and taking account of changes in purchasing power and administrative categorization in Statistisches Reichsamt (1927), pp. 198–9.

income taxes achieved a high absolute yield and accounted for 20.4 per cent. However, the traditional dominance of indirect taxes remained inviolate – above all, owing to excise introduced in 1921 in its modern form of a turnover tax. This distribution of total tax yield persisted even after the appearance of new types of transaction taxation which blurred the separation of direct and indirect taxes usual in the nineteenth century. Once again, the high elasticity of French registration and stamp dues remained astonishing, apparently confirming a general rule born from centuries of fiscal revenue experience: a tax of long-standing – to which taxpayers are accustomed – is a good tax (see Table 52).

(v) Public debt and Gross National Product

Public revenue originating from taxes, dues, and small service fees of various kinds fell far short of satisfying government requirements. On a

Table 53. *Public debt and Gross National Product, 1800–1913*

Events	Public debt Fr. milliard	Fr. per head of population	Population (millions)	Gross National Product (fr. milliard)	Capital exports cumulative (fr. milliard)
1800 Napoleonic Wars	714	26.2	27.3	8	
1815	1,267	43.5	29.1	10.5	
1820	3,456	113.7	30.4	10.5	
1830	4,627	142.4	32.5	12.6	0.5
1839	4,458	130.7	34.1	14.9	
1841	4,613	134.9	34.2	14.9	
1850	4,886	136.9	35.7	17.4	
1851 Crimean War, 1854–6	5,012	140.0	35.8	17.4	2.4
1869 Mexican Expedition, 1864	11,179	296.6	38.2	26.5	
1871 German–French War, 1870–1	14,014	388.2	36.1	26.5	1870: 12.9
1887	23,723	626.0	37.9	27.3	
1913	32,976	841.1	39.2	38.0	45.8
Index of change 1913 (1815=1)	2.6	19.3	1.3	3.6	

Sources: Funded debt calculated from Oualid (1929), pp. 106–7, 109, 111–12; *The Statesman's Year Book* (1890), p. 471, (1910), p. 760, (1921), p. 853; population figures from Mitchell (1975), p. 20.

GNP from Markovitch (1966), p. 93: *produit national brut* given for decadal averages.

Capital exports from Cameron (1961), p. 61; excluding indemnities: 705 million fr. 1817–18; 4,350 million fr. 1871–2; see also Feis (1965), pp. 44, 47–8, 188ff. and Kuznets (1966), p. 322.

calculation covering the period from 1801 to 1880–2, only in four years, 1826, 1875, 1876, and 1877, did ordinary revenue exceed total expenditure.[38] The chronic budget deficit had to be covered by loans. They became a source of income for the expanding state, indispensable, systematically exploited, and favoured by taxation, hence by the savers among the citizens, to whom purchase of state bonds secured an income out of the interest which for practical purposes remained tax free. In this respect, government creditors were highly satisfied with the tax system (see Table 53).

Between 1800 and 1913, public indebtedness rose from about 0.7 milliard fr. to about 33 milliard fr. This total is considerably higher than the amount flowing into the Treasury through loans, as most of these loans were issued via banks at a discount. During the Restoration period, the July monarchy and the Second Republic (1815–51), the state received funds amounting to a mere 2,566 million fr. in return for assuming nominal debts of an aggregate of 3,326 million fr. corresponding to an issue price for bonds calculated to be 77 per cent. The increase in debt of 6,442 million during the Second Empire (1852–70) brought into the state coffers only 4,312 million fr. in cash, giving an issue price of 70 per cent.[39]

At the end of the first decade of the twentieth century, French public debt, both in total and per head of population, was considered the highest in the world,[40] testifying to the prosperity, the patriotism, and the confidence in the government of the bourgeoisie undeterred by the incidence of income tax from acquiring claims to annuities. French governments occasionally turned loan issues into political and national manifestations, describing loan subscription as a general election or a plebiscite of capital. Saving was accounted a virtue, and the nineteenth century was rightly described on occasion as 'l'âge des petits rentiers'.[41]

(vi) Structure of public budgets, 1801/14–1913

Expenditures and revenues of the French budget – ordinary, extraordinary and for particular accounts as well as the multiple forms of incurring debt – can hardly be presented as a simple continuous chronological series because of the profound changes in budget structure. Among the basic rules of budget formation, that of the single annual budget enjoyed little

---

[38] Nicolas (1883), p. 7.
[39] Oualid (1929), p. 109; see also Neymarck (1889), pp. 1418ff.; Bray (1894).
[40] For population development see also Walle (1979), pp. 123ff. Hirschfeld (1875), pp. 26f., 32ff., has figures showing how war finances and the reparation total of 5 milliard fr. were composed and defrayed by public debts and taxes.
[41] On the virtues of saving and small annuitants, Goffin's contribution on 'Les valeurs mobilières' in Morrisson and Goffin (1967).

respect: 1833 saw a supplementary budget, 1837 an extraordinary budget which disappeared in 1840, re-emerging in 1860–3, heavily criticized by the opposition. A special budget was compiled in 1871 for the overlapping periods 1872–6 and 1875–8. Special accounts, *ressources spéciales*, existing since 1863, were *de facto* independent budgets. Ordinary budgets between 1870 and 1913 contained in part extraordinary expenditure on military and public services.[42]

Principles of budget clarity and continuity, truth and transparency were observed only very incompletely in the other European countries, partly because they were unwelcome to governments, partly because the technique of ordinary fiscal bookkeeping changed over time. This as well as the transfer of tasks between government departments makes it difficult to compare budgets over long periods, even more between nations. On a long-term comparison, the French budget grew much more rapidly than the British, as did public indebtedness and taxation by the local authorities. The scissors of this trend open farther if the increase in population between 1800 and 1913 is taken into account: France grew from 27 to 39 million only, the United Kingdom from about 16 to 45 million. The volume of the French budget expanded between 1810 and 1913 nominally almost fivefold. To this increase corresponds the estimated rise in real income and in industrial production. Taking *revenu national réel global* in 1913 as 100, the index figure for 1810 is 21,[43] whereas the *revenu national en francs-or* of 4 milliard in 1789 reached 16 milliard in 1859 and 33 milliard in 1914.[44] The *produit national brut* at current prices grew, taking 1803–12 as 100, to an index figure of 390 for the annual average of 1905–13.[45] Industrial production grew continuously in index figures from 19.2 in 1815 to 100 in 1913.[46] Per capita figures are a little lower. Estimates appear to suggest that the long-term share of the state varied within relatively narrow limits, whereas that in Britain noticeably diminished. This constitutes perhaps the background for the statement occasionally encountered that the 'state' in Britain grew 'small' during the industrial revolution while it grew 'large' in France.

[42] See Cluseau (1952), p. 370; Oualid (1929), pp. 112f.; further the presentation of the various budgets in Nicolas (1883), pp. 14ff.; Boiteau (1889), pp. 501ff.; Stourm (1889), Kaufmann (1882), pp. 685ff.; comprehensive, partly comparing with Britain, Jèze (1922), pp. 13ff.

[43] Lesourd and Gérard (1963), vol. I, p. 130.

[44] Colin Clark's estimate adopted by Lesourd in *ibid.*, p. 130.

[45] Markovitch (1966), pp. 93, 97, 99.

[46] Mitchell (1975), pp. 355f. O'Brien and Keyder (1979), p. 1,301 calculate the following annual average values of *production de biens au prix courant* (output of commodities at current prices) in £ million – 1701–10: 89; 1781–90: 232; 1905–13: 878; converting French francs to pounds sterling at a medium purchasing power parity. In O'Brien and Keyder (1978), p. 58, decadal average annual values for 'commodity output' in million francs are 1781–90: 5,097; 1803–12: 7,012; 1815–24: 7,674; 1845–54: 12,586; 1905–13: 25,814. Commodity output means 'physical commodities; services are excluded', *ibid.*, p. 29; calculations of purchasing power and exchange rate see pp. 34ff., pp. 40ff.

The structure and long-term development of public expenditure, on an international comparison of the great powers, showed fewer peculiarities than in the field of revenues. States require revenue chiefly for three purposes: the armed forces, the debt service, and general public administration. In the course of the century, armed forces and colonies absorbed almost one-third of expenditure, as did the debt service, one occasionally exceeding that of the other, mostly the debt service. The remainder was divided among the various branches of general public administration, including justice, culture, the arts, public education and public works, plus collection costs. Such a division of expenditure corresponded fairly accurately to the function of the state as seen by the late eighteenth and again the nineteenth century, as Adam Smith summarized it very precisely in 1776:

The first duty of the sovereign, that of protecting the society from the violence and invasion of other independent societies, can be performed only by means of military forces . . . the second duty of the sovereign, that of protecting . . . every member of the society from the injustice or oppression of every other member of it, requires . . . expense . . . the third and last duty of the sovereign . . . is that of erecting and maintaining those public institutions and those public works which, though they may be in the highest degree advantageous to a great society, are however of such a nature that the profit could never repay the expense to any individual . . . and which it therefore cannot be expected that any individual . . . should erect or maintain.[47]

The public tasks mentioned third manifested themselves among others in expenditure items devoted to culture, arts, public education, and public works, to which, in the aggregate, the state at the beginning of the twentieth century applied about one-eighteenth of its expenditure; it had been about one-twentieth a century earlier (see Table 55).

The comprehensive concept attributed to this third public duty is illustrated for the last pre-war year in a comparison with Britain. France, reaching neither absolutely nor per capita of population the level of British national income, spent less in total on this third duty (see Tables 56 and 57). However, proportionally to national product, French public expenditure on art and science was higher than the British, whereas that on public works, roads, canals, port installations, etc., remained noticeably below that of the island kingdom.

In assessing the above state activities relating to the infrastructure,[48] it has to be remembered that there is a long historical tradition in France and the European countries of having horizontally stratified public authorities. The highest public authority was 'the state', the lowest local authority 'the parish', with regional authorities of different kinds and

[47] Smith (1937 edn), pp. 653, 669, 681. On Smith's treatment of public finance see Peacock (1979), pp. 37–51.   [48] Fontaine (1894).

Table 54. French public revenue (résultats généraux des budgets), 1801–1913

| | Annual averages for regnal periods | | | | | | | | | | | | | Particular years | | | | | |
| | Consulate and First Empire 1801–14 | | Restoration period 1815–29 | | July monarchy 1830–47 | | Second Republic 1848–51 | | Second Empire 1852–69 | | Third Republic 1870–5 | | 1876–80 | | 1890* | | 1900* | | 1913* | |
	frs. million	% of (6)	frs. million	% of (6)	frs. million	% of (6)	frs. million	% of (6)	frs. million	% of (6)	frs. million	% of (6)	frs. million	% of (6)	frs. million	% of (6)	frs. million	% of (6)	frs. million	% of (6)
1. Direct taxes[a]	369	42.5	357	38.3	386	33.9	429	34.1	489	27.6	633	24.6	696	22.6	478[b]	15.9	516	15.1	622	14.2
2. Indirect taxes[a]	217	24.9	347	37.3	454	39.9	497	39.5	751	42.4	1,127	43.8	1,445	47.1	1,816	60.1	2,092	61.1	2,595	59.3
3. Stamp and registration fees	147	16.9	163	17.5	220	19.3	224	17.8	365	20.5	517	20.1	613	19.9	669	22.2	718	21.0	1,022	23.3
4. Public lands and forests	103	11.9	35	3.8	37	3.3	37	2.9	41	2.3	52	2.0	53	1.7	43	1.4	53	1.5	68	1.6
5. Other revenues	33	3.8	29	3.1	41	3.6	72	5.7	121	6.8	243	9.5	267	8.7	17	0.4	46	1.3	71[c]	1.6
6. Total ordinary revenue (1 + 2 + 3 + 4 + 5)	870	100	931	100	1,138	100	1,259	100	1,777	100	2,572	100	3,074	100	3,023[d]	100	3,425[d]	100	4,378[d]	100
7. Extraordinary revenue	102		97		83		239		282		576		246		62[d]		69[d]		361	
8. Total revenue (6 + 7)	972		1,028		1,221		1,498		2,059		3,148		3,220		3,085		3,494		4,739	
9. Extraordinary (7) as % of total (8) revenue	10.5		9.4		6.8		15.9		13.7		18.3		7.4							

Notes:
a Includes customs duties, fiscal monopolies, post, telephone and telegraph.
b Includes 9.1 million frs. from Algeria.
c Includes 2.6 million frs. from Algeria.
d Figures calculated; total revenue minus exceptional revenues and loans, receipts d'ordre. The state must have received further extraordinary revenue; Mitchell (1975), pp. 710, 719, shows higher revenues for these three years, frs. 3.2, frs. 3.8, frs. 5.1.

Sources: Years 1801–80 according to Nicolas (1883), pp. 34–5; particular years ibid., pp. 14ff. Total revenues include some income from Algeria which in the budget was treated as part of France (see ibid., p. 2). Specification of budgetary items (*) in The Statesman's Year Book (1891), pp. 472–3: (1901), pp. 500–1; (1914), pp. 822–3; see also (1893), p. 482 and (1905), p. 610. Owing to different bookings of some budgetary items from those for the period 1801–80, a comparative illustration is difficult.

Table 55. French public expenditure (résultats généraux des budgets), 1801–1913

| | Annual average for regnal periods | | | | | | | | | | | | | | Particular years | | | | | |
| | 1801–14 | | 1815–29 | | 1830–47 | | 1848–51 | | 1852–69 | | 1870–5 | | 1876–80 | | 1890 | | 1900 | | 1913 | |
	frs. million	%	frs. million	%	frs. million	%	frs. million	%	frs. million	%	frs. million	%	frs. million	%	frs. million	%	frs. million	%	frs. million	%
Total expenditure of which	1,003	100	1,020	100	1,277	100	1,588	100	2,089	100	3,148	100	3,316	100	3,237[a]	100	3,497	100	4,739	100
1. Debt service	121	12.1	301	29.6	348	27.2	410	25.8	531	25.4	993	31.5	1,176	35.5	1,318	40.7	1,253	35.8	1,286	27.1
2. Army, navy, colonies	506	50.4	302	29.6	404	31.6	480	30.2	691	33.1	932	29.6	846	25.5	966	29.8	1,078	30.8	1,557	32.9
3. General civil administration	91	9.1	144	14.1	288	22.5	420	26.4	480	23.0	732	23.2	804	24.2						
of which culture, arts, public																				
education	18	1.8	31	3.0	52	4.1	67	4.2	81	3.9	106	3.4	126	3.8	183	5.7	228	6.5	331	7.0
Public works	28	2.8	29	2.8	104	8.1	166	10.5	153	7.3	215	6.8	312	9.4	171	5.3	215	6.1	341	7.2
4. Collection expenses (trais de régie)	110	10.9	127	12.4	131	10.3	149	9.4	198	9.5	232	7.4	258	7.8	334	10.3	205	5.9	?	?
Expenditure in excess of revenue	31	3.1			56	4.4	90	5.7	30	1.4										
Population (millions)	1802	28.2	1821	30.5	1846	35.4	1851	35.4	1866	39.2	1871	36.1	1881	37.3	1891	38.1	1901	38.5	1913	39.2
Surface area (km²)	1802	626	1821	530	1846	530	1851	530	1866	543	1871	528	1881		1891	530	1901		1913	

Notes:

[a] In addition to this, extraordinary expenditure amounting to $39.9 million frs.

[b] Additional expenditure must have been incurred; according to Mitchell (1975), pp. 698, 700, total expenditure in 1900 amounted to 3.7 million frs, in 1913 to 5.1 million frs.

Sources: Years 1801–80 according to Nicolas (1883), pp. 34–5; see particular years in Eheberg (1892), p. 456. Particular years 1890–1913 see *the Statesman's Year Book*: (1891), pp. 472–3; (1901) pp. 550–1; (1914), pp. 822–3, each showing ordinary budgets, incorporating some extraordinary expenditure (military, public works). Owing to slightly different bookkeeping methods, a comparison of particular years from 1890 onwards with annual averages (up to 1880) is difficult. After 1890, expenses of the general government of Algeria and of colonial administration in general (excluding colonial armed forces) are included in item 3 above, before 1890 in item 2 above. Residual surpluses in the money and percentage figures are not separately shown. Population figures from Mitchell (1975), p. 20.

Table 56. *State expenditure on public works in France and Great Britain (millions of respective currency units)*

Head of expenditure	France 1914	Great Britain 1912/13
1. General civil administration	10.5	—
2. Maintenance		
Roads	40.5	15.9
Coastal shipping routes, canals	13.8	0.1
Port installations, lighthouses, etc.	9.5	0.9
3. New construction		
Roads	12.4	8.0
Coastal shipping routes, canals	17.0	—
Port installations, lighthouses, etc.	15.8	1.1
4. Sundries	0.3	—
Total	119.8	26.0
per head of population	3.1 fr.	£0.57
National income per head of population (estimate)	920 fr.	£48
National income (estimate, millions)	36,000 (for 1911)	2,200 (for 1913)

Source: Statistisches Reichsamt (1927), pp. 389, 443, 449. £1 = 25.22 fr.

Table 57. *State expenditure on education, arts, and science in France and Great Britain (for each in the last pre-war budget, millions of respective currency units)*

Head of expenditure	France		Great Britain
1. Central administration		8.2	0.7
2. General education of which		341.4	16.6
Elementary schools	255.7		15.2
Secondary schools	45.7		1.0
Joint expenditure	40.0		0.3
3. Technical schools		19.2	0.8
4. Teacher training		11.3	0.8
5. Universities		19.3	0.5
6. Science and research		6.7	0.4
7. Arts		10.7	0.5
Total		416.8	20.2
Per head of population		10.6 fr.	£0.5

Source: Statistisches Reichsamt (1927), pp. 256ff., 449. £1 = 25.22 fr. Discrepancies in figures due to rounding.

Table 58. *Expenditure of state and inferior local authorities in France and Great Britain (millions of respective currency units)*

	France 1913	Great Britain 1913/14
Expenditure of the state	5,067[a]	146[a]
Expenditure of local authorities	1,569[b]	126[c]
Total public expenditure	6,636	272
Local as % of total public expenditure	23.6	46.3

Notes:
[a] Includes net expenditure of state enterprises.
[b] Includes net expenditure of local public enterprises; transfers from state funds deducted.
[c] Includes net expenditure of local public enterprises; transfers from state funds deducted.
Source: Statistisches Reichsamt (1927), p. 483. All inferior authorities are here described as local authorities.

sizes between them: in France, *départements* and *arrondissements*,[49] in Prussia provinces, official regions and districts, in Württemberg magistratures and superior magistratures, in England counties and county boroughs. It was a common characteristic of these inferior public authorities to assume a substantial part of the duties which Adam Smith describes as 'the sovereign's' third task. If we take 'the sovereign' to mean the totality of all public authorities at every administrative level, all European state budgets were characterized by a distortion of structure similar in principle: military allocations too high, allocations for civil activities within the country too low. A complete picture of the functions and achievements of the state, including all its inferior authorities, could emerge only from a consolidated budget comprising all public and public auxiliary bodies – a task still to be attempted.

The following brief survey can give no more than an indication of the order of magnitude of the relevant finances – it needs to be remembered that the competence of local authorities within the entirety of public administration varied from country to country. Both limitations render international comparisons of fiscal practices very difficult. A comparison with Britain (see Tables 58 and 59) shows the preponderance of the state *vis-à-vis* local authorities to be palpably greater in France than in Britain – an indicator of the stronger French centralization of government. A corresponding comparison with Germany would be meaningless, because of the threefold division of public authorities into Reich, federal states and their local authorities.

[49] On the budgets of inferior local authorities, Crisenoy, 'communal' (1889); *ibid.*, 'départemental'(1889); further Kaufmann (1882), pp. 725ff.

Table 59. *Tax revenue of state and inferior local authorities in France and Great Britain (millions of respective currency units)*

	France 1912	Great Britain 1913/14
Revenue of the state	3,316	163
Revenue of local authorities	1,021	71
Total public revenue	4,337	234
Local as % of total public revenue	23.5	30.3

Source: Statistisches Reichsamt (1927), pp. 483–4. All inferior authorities are here described as local authorities. £1 = 25.22 fr.

3. *Consolidated balance sheet for the French Empire, 1912–14: some indications*

The following survey, summarizing the position for the French Empire, will demonstrate that the French state budget was affected both directly and indirectly by the financial relations between France and her colonies and dependencies. There is as yet no consolidated balance sheet showing the totality of payments.

The Assemblée Constituante in 1790 decreed that colonies should be part of the French Empire, but not of the French kingdom; the constitution applied only to the kingdom.[50] The *charte coloniale* of 1830, supplemented in 1833, fixed the extent of the Paris legislative authority over the colonies. Different colonies were granted limited self-government to a different degree, in each case including local and communal budgets. Colonies had to defray their public expenditure from their public revenue, unless it resulted from direct financial relations between the colony and the French state. In accordance with decrees of 1855 and subsequently of 1882, these direct financial relations concerned on the revenue side of the French state budget:[51] (1) a legally fixed annual payment by the colony to the French Treasury (in the 1880s only Cochin China, amounting to 2 million fr.); (2) a payment from India, roughly of 1 million fr., to be raised by Britain in exchange for French rights to the opium trade and the production of salt; (3) salary deductions in respect of subsequent superannuation payments to colonial officials; (4) proceeds from the sale of produce from French publicly owned properties in the colonies. The expenditure side of the *service colonial* concerned: (1) expenses of central administration and military defence of the colonies; (2) contributions towards the expense of public education;

[50] Goldscheider (1889), pp. 1090f.
[51] *Ibid.*, pp. 1094f., and on p. 1102 total of finance for local authorities and communes in selected colonies in 1886; Merly (1926).

(3) particular types of expenditure fixed annually by law. Such expenditures were part of the state budget, especially under the heading of war, navy, and colonies. This resulted in a typically colonial fiscal structure: one side concerned with the domestic finances of the colonial government, the other external for relations between colonial government and mother country.[52] The survey in Table 60 for the period around 1913 includes Algeria, a country at the time considered by the French government no longer as a colony, but as integral part of France, with three Algerian *départements*.[53] In 1870, administrative responsibility for Algeria changed from the Ministry of War to that of the Interior; a little later, direct relations between Paris and Algeria were assigned to the relevant ministries; thus, fiscal revenues from Algeria appear in the French budget scattered under different headings.[54] In addition, there was a civil budget of the Algerian general government (*Budget du Gouvernement général de l'Algérie*) and local government budgets. The French system of taxation was only partially imposed upon Algeria, in order to take account of local conditions by special taxes; *inter alia*, a fourfold system of direct Arab taxes (*impôts directs arabs*) was developed, including a palm tree tax (*lezma sur les palmiers*). Tunisia enjoyed the status of a protectorate, regarded from the French point of view as a modern form of colonization.[55] The same status was conferred on some other possessions, for instance Madagascar, parts of Indochina and from 1912 onwards a region of Morocco.

At the end of the nineteenth century, France was second only to Britain as a European colonial power, measured by the surface area of overseas possessions and the population resident there.

III. *Tax system and state budget in Prussia*

A. HISTORICAL BASIS: THE DEVELOPMENT OF PUBLIC FINANCE UP TO THE NAPOLEONIC WARS

After 1806, government, administration, and army were reformed and the feudal economic relationships were abolished step by step. This necessarily affected the system of public finances – more obviously on the

---

[52] Ganiage (1968), shows the state of the colonial empire in 1914, divided according to separate governmental areas; survey of colonial development and industrialization in Henderson (1968), pp. 189ff.

[53] On the phases of integrating Algeria into the mother country and the changes in fiscal relationships caused thereby, Charton (1889), pp. 99ff.

[54] Details in Nicolas (1883), pp. 2, 184f., 238ff.

[55] Thus J. Durant de Saint-André, 'Protectorats' (1894), p. 1,010; for the different relationships of public and administrative law between France and the areas it ruled see Statistisches Reichsamt (1927), pp. 121f., 125ff.

Table 60. *The French Empire around 1913**

	Year of acquisition	Surface area (km 1,000²)	Population (000)	Budget of colony (frs. million)	Subsidy from French budget (frs. million)	Debt (frs. million)	Comments
Asia							
1. India	1679	0.5	273	2.9^a (1913)	0.2 (1914)	0.5 (1913)	
2. Indo-China	1861			126.0^b (1913)	19.3 (1914)	345.9 (1913)	Total budget for Indo-China; additional individual budgets for colonial countries
Cochin-China	1861			27.3 (1914)			
Cambodia	1862			17.6 (1914)			
Tonkin	1884	803	14,500	31.7 (1914)			
Annam	1884			15.4 (1914)			
Laos	1892			3.5 (1914)			
3. Kwangchou-Wan	1900	0.5	150	1.1 (1914)			
Total Asia		804	14,923	225.5			
Africa							
1. Northern Algeria	1830–1902	208	5,070	157.2 (1913)			
1. Southern Algeria		367	494	6.7 (1913)			
3. Tunisia	1881	119	1,879	85.0 (1914)		232.2 (1906)	
4. Congo (Equatorial Africa)	1884			5.5 (1913)	10.4 (1914)	6.5 (1913)	Total budget for Congo; additional individual budgets for colonial countries
Gabon				2.1 (1913)			
Central Congo		1,432	3,900	2.4 (1913)			
Ubangi				1.7 (1913)			
Chad				1.0 (1913)			
5. West Africa and Sahara	1637–1889			20.9 (1911)	24.5 (1914)	156.3 (1912)	Total budget for West Africa and Sahara; additional individual budgets for colonial countries; small local budgets existing only in West Africa have been added to the budgets of the respective colonial countries
Senegal			1,250	7.2 (1912)			
Upper Senegal and Niger	1893		5,100	9.0 (1912)			
Guinea	1843	4,107	1,900	8.8 (1912)			
Ivory Coast	1843		1,400	7.3 (1914)			
Dahomey	1893		900	4.3 (1912)			
Mauretania	1893		250	1.7 (1914)			
Sahara		3,999	800				

6. Reunion	1649	2.5	174	5.1 (1912)	2.4 (1914)	6.7 (1913)
7. Madagascar	1643–1896	585	3,258	30.7 (1912)		98.2 (1912)
8. Mayotte Comoro Isles	1843	2.2	94	0.8 (1913)		
9. Somalia Coast	1864	15	14	1.6 (1912)	0.7 (1914)	
Total Africa		10,837	25,681[c]	(359.0)	57.5	
America						
1. Guiana	1626	88	48	3.6 (1912)	6.5 (1914)	
2. Guadeloupe	1634	1.8	213	4.5 (1913)	0.3 (1914)	3.8 (1913)
3. Martinique	1635	1	185	5.4 (1913)	1.4 (1914)	4.2 (1913)
4. St Pierre et Miquelon	1635	0.2	4	0.020 (1913)	0.3 (1914)	5.0 (1912)
Total America		91	450	(13.5)	8.5	
Pacific						
1. Tahiti and islands	1841–81	4	31	1.7 (1910)	0.2 (1914)	
2. New Caledonia	1854–87	19	50	4.3 (1913)	2.6 (1914)	
Total Pacific		23	81	(6.0)	2.7	
Total colonial empire 1912–14		11,755	41.1	604.0	68.8	859.3
France, 1913		536	39.2	budgetary expenditure (1913) 4,738.6		32,976 (1913)

Notes:

For international comparison 100 frs. = £3.96 = mark 81.

[a] Currency unit is the rupee; rate of exchange based on precious metal content: R1 = 1.5973 frs. (R1 = mark 1.972, 1 fr. = mark 0.81).

[b] Currency unit is the piastre (de commerce); rate of exchange based on precious metal content: Pi 1 = 3.54294 fr. (Pi 1 = mark 4.374).

[c] A difference in the total amounting to 1.2 million remains unexplained.

Source: Calculated from The Statesman's Year Book (1914), pp. 843–83; individual budgets for colonial countries were normally balanced; the budget column shows revenue; expenditure occasionally differs insignificantly from revenue, in which case the higher figure is shown.

revenue than on the expenditure side, though a comparison of systems before and after reform discloses manifold continuities.[1]

1. The system of public revenues

(i) Revenues from public property

A glance at the revenue side of the budget reveals the magnitude and importance of Prussian revenue from public property, especially public lands and forests, in covering state requirements. As an approximation, at the death of Elector Frederick-William (1688), about one-third, at the accession of Frederick II (1740) one-half of net public revenue derived from public property. Such income-yielding public properties included mills, inns, smithies, sheep-rearing establishments, bakeries, ponds, buildings, brickworks, and other utilities, subsequently also mines, smelters, salt works, and some manufactures, and in the nineteenth century the trinity of railway, postal, and telegraphic services. The state was concerned that public property should be productively exploited; on occasion, it can be seen to have been the focus of (agrarian) economic progress. Prussia's laborious climb to the status of a European great power rested on the side of public finance, largely on continuous acquisitions of productive public finance, largely on continuous acquisitions of productive public properties from 1640 onwards, there being no clear distinction between government property and the property of the monarch throughout.

Although Frederick II (1740–86) ceded some agricultural public lands, especially in southern Prussia, in 1800 public lands still accounted for about 2 per cent, public forests for almost 9 per cent of total productive surface.[2] Forests apart, public property was usually let for six to twelve years, exploitation by the state itself and public lands held in hereditary tenure being in a minority. The old feudal concept – though hardly ever implemented – that the king should live on his own[3] retained enough vitality for it to be considered at the beginning of the nineteenth century, whether Prussia should renounce taxation altogether and increase the volume of its public properties instead. However, a calculation around 1803–5 revealed that the government would in that case have to own almost 22 per cent of productive land surface[4] – a proportion which

---

[1] On the early Prussian fiscal economy up to the Napoleonic wars see Bergmann (1901); A. Wagner (1889), part 3, pp. 106ff., Schmoller (1898), pp. 104ff.; Klein (1974), pp. 41ff.; references to literature also in Borchard (1968), pp. 304ff.   [2] Krug (1805), part 2, p. 471.

[3] According to Mann (1937), pp. 39, 44, this was the political basis in a patrimonial fiscal system. The basis lasted in a diluted version into the nineteenth century: according to the constitution of the Kingdom of Württemberg of 1819, public expenditure was to be defrayed from the revenues of publicly owned entrepreneurial establishments; taxes were to be levied only to cover a financial shortfall (which regularly occurred).   [4] Krug (1805), part 2, p. 472.

it seemed neither possible nor expedient to reclaim from the aristocracy and the peasantry respectively; so the idea was dropped, as were concepts of an *impôt unique* imposed only on agriculture which, launched by Quesnay, had confused many heads throughout Europe. However, even when at its most liberal in the nineteenth century, the government never dispensed with the notion that public property constituted an indispensable part of a country's wealth, public property and traditional state monopolies forming part of the same train of thought. Substantial public property was particularly desirable because it guaranteed public loans and enhanced the government's creditworthiness.

(ii) Taxes

The reforms of the Great Elector (1640–88) introduced into the structure of the Prussian tax system during the years 1641 and 1667 a characteristic principle surviving even the Stein–Hardenberg reforms of 1807–12 and retained until 1873: different tax treatment for urban and rural residents. Tax reforms were prompted by the introduction of a standing army in the Prussian military system. Permanent contributions (direct taxes) and an increase in excise (indirect consumption taxes) were needed to cover the costs, but which sectors of the population should bear them?

The feudal aristocracy was capable of shifting to its serfs and smallholders a direct, but hardly an indirect tax imposed upon it; the resistance of the rural aristocracy to an excise was therefore so powerful that the Elector in 1667 succeeded in imposing it only in towns, and not equally in town and countryside, as had been intended. Thus the main tax in towns was the (indirect) excise, in the countryside the direct contribution. The attack on aristocratic tax privileges by means of the excise had been defeated.

The excise consisted of a set of consumption taxes, levied on most products in general use required by the urban population, in particular beverages, brandy, cereals, meat, other foodstuffs, and so-called merchandise, such as spices, coffee, tobacco, textiles, building materials. The principle of collection combined extension to the maximum number of commodities with the lowest possible rate of tax. Domestic tolls on roads and internal waterways, at bridges and town gates bore close similarities to excise duties and varied from province to province. Delimitation of excise and toll was imprecise, as also in other states: a rural resident purchasing goods in a town *de facto* paid both duties. The *contribution*, occasionally referred to simply as 'the tax', was a land tax bearing different descriptions in various provinces, e.g., tax on holdings, impost on gables, on general holdings, land tax. It was levied by allocation. Land registers used for sub-allocation were in some instances incomplete and out of date, based sometimes on yield, sometimes on the quantity of seed, on head of livestock, on size of holding or of hearths, rendering differences in assessment substantial both within and between provinces. Neither the land registration of Frederick William I (1713–40) nor that of Frederick II (1740–86) introduced even approximately equal standards of assessment to tax. Public and aristocratic estates remained exempt, for the most part also ecclesiastic estates – according to the traditional rule: aristocracy serves the country by its blood, clergy by its prayer, the lowest estate by its labour,[5] from which tax is derived. Insignificant public revenues under headings like knight horse fees, feudal horse fees, and riding horse fees related to aristocratic services commuted to money, due from aristocratic estates. Contribution payers were the 'contributing estate' of the countryside: above all peasants, smallholders, day labourers, and village craftsmen.

Among the indirect taxes of the period were the stamp duties. In Prussia, they dated back to 1682, augmented in 1701 and 1776, without however reaching the extent and the precision of the French stamp system. But French influence is unmistakable; it was partly on account of stamp duties that Frederick II brought French fiscal officials to Prussia in order to approximate the Prussian fiscal and tax system closer to the higher French standard. Both towns and countryside were liable to stamp duties, and to customs and internal dues, every province having its own customs system. In the period of absolute sovereignty, there was nothing like a unitary Prussian state.

(iii) Public loans

Revenue from public property and taxes did not suffice to cover state requirements. As a third source of revenue, the government needed loans. Raising public loans was much harder for poor Prussia than for wealthy Britain. An agrarian country, Prussia lacked a broad and growing bourgeois sector deriving income from industry and trade and able to save and provide money for the purchase of state bonds. The Prussian government, rarely able to resort to voluntarily proffered portions of middle class, aristocratic and clerical income, lacked a decisive element of budgetary elasticity. This forced upon the government certain rules of behaviour:

> Revenue from public property and taxes being limited, a verily proverbial state frugality, considered a virtue in Prussia;
> Constant attempts at expanding and augmenting state taxes, ever and

---

[5] This was the Archbishop of Sens' reply to Cardinal Richelieu when the clergy was asked to pay taxes; from ancient times it was accepted 'que le peuple contribuât par ses biens, la noblesse par son sang et le clergé par ses prières'; clerical tax privilege derived partly from canon, partly from Roman law; details in Mann (1937), pp. 67f.

again against resistance from the rural, manorial, and estate aristocracy 'protecting' its peasants from the fiscal onslaught of the state, so as not to impair the scope of its own exactions; the sovereign had invariably to 'purchase' tax grants from the estates by delegating rights of authority to the lower aristocracy, which thus became the public authority for residents on its estates;

Acceptance of subsidies from foreign countries for consideration given, especially in the political–military field. Hiring out of mercenaries was a particular instance;

Attempts by the sovereign to abstract dishonestly products and services out of the country's economic circulation. The almost classical method was payment in devalued coin from the sovereign's mints, a forerunner of paper money and central bank notes. Thus for instance Frederick the Great financed a large part of his Seven Years War expenditure by silver coins which were below weight, thus producing one of the great coin inflations in European history.[6] State bankruptcy, whether by government debts remaining unpaid or government-induced inflation, were both dishonest appropriations of private incomes and fortunes by the state, though affecting different groups of persons;

Attempts to make public revenue in 'normal years' exceed public expenditure so as to establish out of the surplus an immediately realizable public reserve for times of emergency, i.e. war. The formation of public monetary reserves for subsequent wars continued to the First World War: the Reich treasure in the Spandau Tower in Berlin, amounting to 120 million marks, sufficed to finance several days of war. This hoarding of funds has a present-day parallel in the hoards of metal and foreign currency reserves held by central banks against the emergency of balance of trade or payments deficits;

Floating loans abroad.

The significance of public indebtedness for Prussia's finance is apparent from Table 77. The level of debts has to be seen in relation to the application of public revenue: part of public expenditure served to secure, maintain and increase public landed and productive property. 'State' indebtedness in this sense included 'productive' indebtedness, that is, entrepreneurial investment financed by raising foreign loans in the capital market. Economically, debts incurred to finance productive investment differ substantially from those which finance military action. Different concepts of government functions, as for instance between Britain and Prussia, and the budgets derived therefrom render a direct comparison of both types of public debts difficult.

[6] Minting during the war estimated at 75 million taler; Gaettens (1955), p. 166.

While the British budget was based on loans and tax revenue, the Prussian budget, like that of other German states, rested on the yield of productive public establishments and on taxes, supplemented by taking loans. The Prussian state was entrepreneurial to an incomparably higher degree than the British or the French. The fiscal economy of German states was to a substantial extent entrepreneurial activity in the agricultural, industrial, and mining sectors as well as in the realm of trade and services. This changed by no means during the nineteenth century.

2. Structure of public budgets

Prussia's budgets can no longer be reconstructed to a satisfactory degree of precision. Principles of completeness, standardization, clarity and precision of the budget,[7] let alone periodical regularity of budgetary publication remained alien to the contemporary system of public accounting. Little would be gained from attempting to harmonize and summarize existing fragments of information, drawn up for different purposes along different lines of classification. A long-period survey of indicators for 1688–1806 (see Table 61) at least enables clarification of the general budget of 1740 specifically, drawn up on the occasion of Frederick II's assumption of government. Up to the French revolution, there remained a gap. From the confusion of the subsequent war period emerge two informative tables of revenue for 1800 and 1812, serving as a bridge between the eighteenth and the early nineteenth century in what follows. For the beginning of fiscal economy in the new Prussia, there is a survey of tax revenues in 1816 – and subsequently the first budget of 1821. This provides a framework which enables at least a sketchy indication of the final balance sheet of the old and of the opening balance sheet of the new Prussia.[8]

Public expenditure in 1740 was overwhelmingly military expenditure; Prussia in this respect differed little from other European powers. The desire for national power and the build-up of a military apparatus were inseparable (see Table 62). In clear distinction to Britain and France, public revenue to finance the army, the court, the administration, and the financial reserve showed a very high proportion of total income derived from public productive establishments. The strict tax separation of town (indirect taxes) and country (direct taxes) further necessitated – again in clear distinction to Britain and France – a high proportion of direct taxes compared to consumption dues.

In addition to recorded ordinary revenue and expenditure, there was extraordinary revenue and expenditure, only fragments of which are

---

[7] On these modern principles see Neumark (1952), pp. 554ff.

[8] A collection of further financial figures for Prussia in 1601, 1688–1807 in Behre (1905), pp. 71–109; Riedel (1866), supplements 1–20; Borchard (1968), pp. 22, 158ff., 166.

Table 61. *Indicators of Prussian state finances, 1688–1806*

	1688	1713	1740	1786	1806
1. Surface area in 1,000 km²	111	113	119	195	347
2. Population (millions)	1.5	1.6	2.2	5.4	10.7
3. Army (000 men)	30	38	72	195	250
4. Total net revenue approx. in million taler of which	3	4	7.4	19–20	27–31
4.1 Taxes, etc.	1.6	2.4	4	10–11	16–20
4.2 Income from state property	0.9	1.6	3.4	6–7	8
Income as % of 4	(30)	(40)	(46)	(33)	(28)
5. Military expenditure approx. in million taler		2.5	6	12–13	16–17
as % of 4		(62)	(81)	(64)	(57)
6. Public treasure approx. in million taler			8.7	72	17
7. Public debt approx. in million taler				48.1	53.5
				(1794)	(1807)

Sources: Surface and population from *Meyer's Grosses Konversationslexikon* (1908), survey and maps on p. 316; public treasure and public debt from Reden (1856), vol. II, pp. 5ff., 73, 76, 80, 620ff., 629ff., 666ff., and Heckel (1911) p. 494f.; state finance from Mayer (1952), p. 259 and Eheberg (1892), p. 446; slightly different, Borchard (1968), pp. 78f., 156ff.

Table 62. *General budget of the Prussian treasury, around 1740*

Revenue	in 000 taler	in %	Expenditure	in 000 taler	in %
I. War fund			I. Army,		
Contribution	2,440	33.1	fortications,		
Licences, customs			etc.	5,977	81
duties, excises	1,400	19.0	II. Administration		
Riding horse money	70	1.0	and court	740	10
Feudal and knight			III. Formation of		
horse monies	60	0.8	state reserve	650	9
Stamp duties	35	0.5			
Total I	4,005	54.4			
II. Public property fund					
Public lands	2,615	35.5			
Salt monopoly	544	7.4			
Postal monopoly	180	2.4			
Jews protection money	15	0.2			
Recruits' fund	8	0.1			
Total II	3,362	45.6			
Totals	7,367	100		7,367	100

Source: Reden (1856), pp. 73, 76f.

Table 63. *Structure of Prussian budget revenue, 1800 and 1812*

	c. 1800		c. 1812	
	in 000 taler	in %	in 000 taler	in %
I. Income from public property				
public lands	7,446	25.2	4,360	25.6
forests	1,234	4.2		
Salt monopoly	4,500	15.2	1,679	9.8
Total I	13,200	44.6	6,039	35.4
II. Taxes and other revenues				
Excise	7,889	26.6	6,020[a]	35.0
Contribution	5,615	18.9	2,984[b]	17.6
Customs revenue	1,611	5.4	760	4.4
Lottery	700	2.4	—	—
Stamp duties	594	2.0	701	4.1
Feudal and knight horse monies	58	0.2	—	—
Business tax	—	—	681	3.6
Total II	16,467	55.5	11,146	64.7
Total I and II	29,667	100	17,185	100

Notes:
[a] Composed of excise 4,669, rural consumption tax 1,351.
[b] Composed of contribution and land tax.
Source: Reden (1856), p. 80.

known. Frederick–William I during his reign up to 1740 is supposed to have disbursed 'extraordinary expenditure' of almost 30 million taler, among it 7 million in the purchase of estates for the crown and the royal family, 8.7 million for the formation of a state treasure, 1.5 million for silver equipment and table ware, without evidence of the (extraordinary) financing of such expenditure having survived.[9]

The basic structure of ordinary public revenue changed during the Napoleonic wars.[10] Losses of territories and income caused the volume of revenues to shrink to almost half between 1800 and 1812, revenue from public property falling noticeably more than from taxes. The remarkably small absolute reduction in excise which proportionally increased its share indicates that Prussia – like France and Britain – materially tightened the screw on consumption. Once again, indirect tax proved a practicable form of war taxation; experiments in direct income taxation failed in Prussia, much as in Britain and France (see Table 63). Public expenditure probably substantially exceeded ordinary revenue, the deficit being covered by British subsidies and loans.[11] From 1794 to

[9] Reden (1856), vol. II, p. 77.
[10] For the Prussian fiscal economy in the early nineteenth century, Mamroth (1890); Grabower (1932).
[11] British subsidies to Prussia given for 1813 as 7.3 million taler in cash and 5.2 million taler in credit

Table 64. *Prussia's surface area and population*

	Surface area in 1,000km^2	Population in millions
1786	195	5.4
1797	299	8.7
1806	335	10.7
1807	158	4.9
1815	272	10.3
1867	348	23.9

Source: See fn. 13.

1807 and to 1815, the public debt swelled from 48.1 million to 53.5 million and to 287.6 million taler (see Table 77).

B. PUBLIC FINANCE DURING THE PERIOD OF INDUSTRIALIZATION

1. *The political breakthrough*

The Napoleonic wars, the wars of liberation (1796–1815), and the outcome of the Congress of Vienna in 1815 brought considerable territorial changes in Central Europe. The old German Reich had in 1791 comprised 570 'lands' directly under the Reich (territories, confederations) belonging to 334 'states' on a surface area of about 655,000 km^2. The 304 so-called splinter-states had a surface area of 65,520 km^2, an average of 250 km^2 per state. Subdivision, political and consequently also fiscal, was illustrated particularly clearly by the example of the Swabian Reich district: distributed over 32,820 km^2 were 49 lands of electors or imperial princes, 48 imperial charitable foundations and monasteries, 24 lands belonging to imperial counts, 33 imperial cities and imperial villages and 9 imperial knights' federations or dominions.[12]

After 1815, the German Federation consisted of a mere 39 sovereign individual states, four being free cities. The five states with the largest surface areas, excluding Austria which withdrew in 1866, were Prussia, Bavaria, Württemberg, Baden, and Saxony, not counting Hanover which had been in personal union with England since 1714 and fell to Prussia in 1866. After 1806, every state developed its own system of taxes.

Within three decades against the background of these territorial shifts, the size and population of Prussia changed repeatedly and drastically.[13] This is also reflected in the budgets (see Tables 63 and 64). From 1806

instruments; British subsidies to Austria between 1800 and 1808 documented at 31.3 million gulden, according to Klein (1974), pp. 95, 111. On Austrian loans in London during the Napoleonic period, Helleiner (1965).   [12] A. Wagner (1910), pp. 257f.
[13] A. Wagner (1867), vol. xix, pp. 544. 547; (1869), vol. xxi, pp. 299, 386; Viebahn (1862), vol. i, pp. 29, 32, 103; complementary population details in Hohorst (1977), p. 125.

onwards, Prussia began to reorganize its territory for the time being: 1807 abolition of serfdom, 1808 constitution of towns, 1810 and 1811 first finance edicts and regulation of peasant conditions, 1812 introduction of freedom of occupation, reorganization of taxes and public finances, 1814 reorganization of the army. Thus fragmented Prussia, in one of the weakest periods of its history, laid decisive foundations for its subsequent hegemony in Germany. In 1815, the new state consisted of 117 originally separate parts which had hitherto belonged to different territorial states with differing administrative and financial institutions. The difficult and lengthy processes of administrative incorporation of these components into the central state absorbed much governmental energy, especially as the process of integration was overshadowed by the dissolution of the feudal order, which had shown great regional differences, and the introduction of the nineteenth-century liberal social and economic system. The predicament of a multiplicity of inherited state taxes – while at the same time feudal dues and services were being abolished in principle – caused in the short run the rule: leave everything temporarily as it is, as long as existing state taxes and dues can be collected in the customary manner; even that was a considerable achievement. *Ad hoc* harmonization of such variegated, historically developed tax systems could not be contemplated, especially as Prussia in 1815 was not a territorially compact state, but had acquired a separate territorial area in the form of the Rhineland provinces which had up to 1813 been part of the Rhineland Federation under Napoleon's protectorate. Compared to the traditional agrarian Eastern provinces, these areas had more industry and agricultural smallholdings; and during the French regime, they had progressively introduced a new tax system on the French Napoleonic model. Many regulations intended as provisional in the short term later proved hard to change. Prussia's reorientation towards the West, militarily enforced, was a time-consuming process. After 1815, Prussia was more 'German' than it had ever been. Thus began patriotism which around 1871 spilled over into nationalism.

2. The fiscal system

(i) Survey

A survey of the Prussian fiscal system in the nineteenth century in the light of tax systems and budgets focuses attention on five points:

1. As before, the modern Prussian state remained a large-scale business entrepreneur drawing considerable productive income. The substantial public property dating from the seventeenth and eighteenth centuries was continually augmented thereafter; to public lands and forests were added above all heavy industry and railways. The state's productive

income alone from 1875 to 1913 increased from 57.9 to 75.4 per cent gross of all ordinary revenue, whereas the share of direct taxes during that period fell from 22.0 to 10.4 per cent, that of indirect taxes (excluding matricular contributions) from 6.9 to 2.8 per cent. No wonder that public expenditure was considerably affected by productive state establishments; expenditure devoted to their administration claimed in 1875 39.8, in 1913 58.5 per cent of ordinary public expenditure. The extraordinary budget, designed in principle to record unique or at least not regularly recurring items of revenue and expenditure, showed a corresponding alignment: extraordinary income from, and extraordinary expenditure on, productive activities, including the debt service, above all for railway construction, determined the shape of these budgets.[14]

2. The tax system remained mainly on traditional lines up to the introduction of the general income tax in 1891; compared to Britain and from a twentieth-century point of view, it bore a distinct conservative modernist character:

(a) The tax dualism as between town and country, dating back to at least 1667, continued with modifications up to 1873;

(b) The second tax dualism, that between taxable and exempt population, continued far into the nineteenth century. Though tax exemptions were to be abolished in 1811, general liability of landed aristocracy was not achieved until 1861, of former princes not until 1891;

(c) Prussia did not engage in modernization of its tax system either in the direction of the British individual income tax or by increasing the precision of objective revenue taxation on the basis of external indicators along French lines. Half a step towards partial personal income taxation and half a step towards objective revenue taxes surprisingly sufficed to stabilize the Prussian tax system throughout the nineteenth century.

3. Though the Prussian state sought elasticity for its revenue in the realm of entrepreneurial rather than tax income, thus avoiding to some extent a solution to the clash of tax interests among different sectors of the population, Prussian tax legislation in two complex areas shaped the tax constitutions of German member states and eventually of the German Reich:

(a) The early Prussian customs law of 1818, abolishing internal tolls and introducing customs duties at the frontiers, became funda-

---

[14] Budget details for 1821–50, see Tables 68 and 69, for 1847/57–1870 see Tables 77 and 78, and for 1875 to 1913 see Tables 79 and 80. Comparisons are rendered difficult, *inter alia* by the change from net to gross budget values in 1857 and by enlargements of Prussia's territory, *inter alia* by the addition of Hanover in 1866.

mental for the German customs union *Zollverein* in 1833, for the
German Reich after 1871;

(b) The Prussian income tax of 1891, late in coming, eventually led to
the abolition of revenue tax systems inspired by France, above all
in the south German states, and became the model of the imperial
German standard general income tax of 1920.

4. Prussian tax reforms between the two outstanding decisions of 1818
and 1891 were evidence of stabilization and subsequent very slow
changes in tax systems not yet fully harmonized.

1820   Confirmation and elaboration of status quo regarding differential taxation of town and country; emphasis on revenue and
consumption taxes; introduction of personal graduated taxes
for country dwellers.

1851   After the revolution of 1848/9: partial abolition of differential
taxation of town and country by introducing a superregional
graduated income tax for part of the affluent population.

1861   Assimilations and modifications in revenue taxes, partly following former French examples encountered in Prussia's
western provinces; traditional tripartite revenue tax system
for the entire state area – without capital revenue tax.

1873   After the establishment of the Reich in 1871: abolition of the
tax dualism between town and country; changes in the two
personal graduated taxes, the harbingers of the general income
tax of 1891.

Throughout all these reforms, the tax system showed, as in Britain and
France, one dominant principle: promotion of capital accumulation and
thus of economic growth. Promotion in this sense implied partly positive
action, but even more passive toleration of development tending in that
direction. A high rate of investment presupposes a high rate of saving.
This affects the burden of growth and its distribution among different
sectors of the population. It relates to the connection between
industrialization and savings, the right to property and disposal of
commodities, a market economy along liberal lines and distribution of
income and fortunes. Tax legislation took account of social welfare
policy only late and gave it a low priority.

5. In the long run, the state turned from 'external activities' more and
more to 'internal concerns'. The development of domestic administration and jurisdiction, combined with the production and
institutionalized supply of public property and services, made a decisive
contribution to the preconditions and complementary needs of industrial
development. This can be understood in the material sense, for instance
when building schools, or in the creation of the appropriate atmosphere:

the security embodied in the codified law, the predictability of executive action, of due process, of legal protection – whatever pitfalls in detail remained for one or the other sector of the population – can hardly be overestimated as motivating activities; they determined manners of thought and conduct down to everyday details. The security provided by keeping consistently to general rules, noticeably improved since the seventeenth and eighteenth centuries, represents a voluntary discipline on the largest possible scale, without which neither civilized action nor industrial activity is conceivable. This constituted one of the central functions of the state – in its multiple ramifications.

(ii) The compromise on fiscal principles, 1810–20

Prussia, almost halved in surface area and population, and under the pressure of war expenditure, post-war expenditure and public debt, tried to reorganize its fiscal economy immediately after the peace of Tilsit in 1807.[15] It passed a series of measures and declarations of intentions, largely embodied in the financial edict of 1810.

The short-term goal was the levy of an extraordinary direct emergency tax on personal incomes in 1808; a second attempt was made in 1812. The long-term goal, proclaimed in the edict of 1810, was a just and equal distribution of land tax, needing reform along principles of universality (abolition of tax exemptions) and equality of tax incidence. A general business tax to be newly introduced was to solve the problem, inherited from the previous period, how to assess and tax crafts, trade, and industry, including the professions. Neither aim, mainly affecting direct taxation, was achieved. What resulted in 1810–20 was rather a kind of fiscal compromise on principles.[16] The laws of 1820 bore all the marks of a provisional nature in a period of transition. Another 70 years were needed to construct a tax system along unitary principles. Attempts at reform in the meantime constituted a series of partial compromises, resulting in an aggregate mixture of much that was traditional with a few modern sectoral measures – a compromise, however, mostly to the disadvantage (in general) of the mass of agrarian compared to those of industrial income recipients. Beneficiary of the compromise, alongside the aristocracy with its agrarian income exempt from land tax, was the rising bourgeoisie. Both sectors used their influence in the formation of the compromise and offered resistance to tax burdens being placed on their members.

[15] A comprehensive description of the Prussian fiscal economy in the nineteenth century in Schwarz and Strutz (1900–4); on direct and indirect taxes, *ibid.* (1902), vol. I, section 4 (by G. Strutz).   [16] Benzenberg (1820); Kanitz and Schönbrodt (1822); Dieterici (1875).

Changes in the field of indirect taxes were somewhat simpler in comparison; above all, they could be carried through faster.

Indirect taxes
General consumption taxes levied throughout the state territories: 1810 saw the first effort at reorganizing indirect taxes on the principle: increase of dues on consumption and luxuries, while limiting tax to the minimum number of commodities – very much the opposite of the guidelines followed by the Prussian fiscal bureaucracy ever since the introduction of the general excise in 1667 which had sought to submit the largest number of commodities to tax. That old guideline had led to 57 customs and excise tariffs existing in the old provinces alone as late as 1815, affecting 2,775 types of commodities.[17] Within barely ten years (1810–20), the indirect tax system was so tightened up that it continued without significant upheavals beyond the establishment of the Reich in 1871.

Taxation of luxuries was abandoned as impracticable and unprofitable after unsuccessful attempts in 1810. Neither riding nor carriage horses nor servants, dogs, etc., could usefully be taxed under the heading of 'luxury consumption'.

Of the multiplicity of excise duties on articles of mass consumption, there were left in 1820 consumption taxes on brandy, brewers' malt, new wine (until 1865), tobacco leaves, and salt (the salt monopoly). Apart from customs duties not here included, the highest yield came from taxes on beverages. The tax on sugar became more profitable only in the 1850s and 1860s, when the sugar beet industry developed.

The milling and slaughter tax in towns: The endeavour pursued in 1811 to equate town and country in tax treatment could not be put into practice, owing to resistance from the landed aristocracy. The old principle of the feudal agrarian state of 1667 persisted, leaving countryside residents to pay mainly direct taxes, urban residents mainly indirect consumption dues, corresponding to the traditional division of labour between town and country; town being the location for industrial, countryside for agrarian production and the two categories of goods being exchanged in towns. The tax legislation in 1820 formulated these concepts, renouncing pragmatically the introduction of a universal income tax:

> The countryside to bear the new direct graduated tax, supplemented by a land (and building) tax;
> Towns to pay special indirect consumption taxes on bread and meat, separate from, and additional to, general consumption taxes.

Thus a milling and slaughter tax[18] as a levy on consumption was

---

[17] Ohnishi (1980), p. 267.   [18] Bergius (1853).

introduced in 132 named large and medium towns of Prussia – ranging in size from about 155,000 (Berlin) and 56,000 (Königsberg) down to little towns of approximately 2,700 inhabitants. Settlements smaller than the latter were treated as countryside by taxation, irrespective of their legal status. Bread and bakery products were taxed in the shape of milled products of every kind of grain, as were meat and legumes as well as slaughtered animals required for urban consumption, irrespective of whether the commodities had arisen in, or were imported into, the towns.

The indirect state tax on basic foodstuffs bore on poorer people relatively harder than on the affluent, especially as town surcharges on milling and slaughter taxes – up to 50 per cent – aggravated the disproportion. Partial extension of the personal graduated tax in 1851 reduced the number of towns liable to milling and slaughter taxes to 83, in 1867 to 75, but not until 1873 were these taxes entirely abolished.

Taxation of urban consumption was an emergency device also inasmuch as, after the failure to introduce income tax in 1808 and 1812, no practicable way existed of taxing with approximate accuracy urban industrial producers' incomes; traditional business tax did not solve the problem. Thus the milling and slaughter tax was thought of as a kind of indirect 'business' tax complementary to the direct 'agrarian' graduated tax introduced at the same time for countryside residents.

The extent of consumers' burden imposed by consumption dues depended on consumers' behaviour and household consumption totals. No major micro-economic enquiries of this kind cover the period under review. It is moreover in practice impossible to measure the incidence of customs duties down to the ultimate consumer.[19]

Customs duties: The old Prussian customs duties were indirect dues, collected within the country, on traffic in commodities (transit dues, import and export dues) and on purchases and sales in markets (market dues). After the establishment of the German Confederation, Prussia issued its famous trade and customs law of 1818. A single tariff at a moderately high rate, based on weight of goods, replaced 60 customs tariffs on different commodities hitherto in force. Prussian territory, though geographically separate, became a single customs area, free from internal dues, with an external customs line along the frontiers. Though Prussia had never since 1818 lost sight of the considerable fiscal value of customs duties, it gave clear priority to economic development and foreign policies which eventually resulted in the formation of the German customs union of 1833/4. Its members adopted the Prussian customs tariff. The customs union members jointly levied customs

---

[19] See the enquiries with very small random samples in Table 76.

duties, distributing the revenue among themselves in proportion to their population.[20]

The use of customs duties and customs union treaties as instruments of Prussia's foreign policy was repeated at the establishment of the North German Federation of 1867 and its customs union treaty with the south German states, and was instrumental in the political and economic exclusion of Austria and the foundation of the German Reich in 1871. The link between customs duties and consumption taxes on the one hand, and between member states, customs union and the Reich on the other hand resulted in a delicate network of relations, both between different German states and between the totality of the states and the Reich.

Stamp duties: From 1822 onwards, documents and receipts of every kind, bills of exchange, share certificates, calendars, playing cards and newspapers were liable to stamp duties, partly fixed, partly *ad valorem*. As inheritance had to be validated by legal process, an inheritance stamp replaced – as originally also in Britain – a separate inheritance tax. The inheritance stamp was considered moderate; it was not levied where the heirs were children of the deceased; the surviving spouse paid only 1 per cent of the inherited fortune, the rate rising to 4 per cent for distant relatives, up to 8 per cent in all other instances. German fiscal literature of the late nineteenth century repeated regrets that this traditional French method of inheritance taxation had been adopted in preference to the modern British method of direct inheritance taxes from the 1880s, which complemented income tax as a kind of capital impost, thus bearing more heavily on invested income.

Direct taxes
Up to the introduction of the universal income tax in 1891, the system of direct taxes consisted substantially of two groups of taxes:

(1) The three traditional revenue taxes (*Ertragsteuern*) on land, buildings and business in the countryside and in towns;
(2) The graduated tax (*Klassensteuer*)in the countryside, introduced in 1820, and its subsidiary of 1851, a graduated income tax (*klassifizierte Einkommensteuer*) on higher income earners in the countryside and in towns.

Objective revenue taxes: Revenue taxes, above all the land tax, in the eighteenth century had formed the backbone of Prussian direct taxes.[21]

[20] Henderson (1959), pp. 138ff.
[21] On the difference in principle between revenue taxes based on objective indicators and income taxes determined by subjective individual incomes, see p. 346, n. 30; details for the German federal states in Eheberg (1908), pp. 204ff.

In the nineteenth century, they underwent a curious shift of position. Looking at fiscal yield, they remained of considerable importance down to the 1890s (Tables 69, 78 and 79); from the point of view of their conceptual position in the total tax system, they were banished to the periphery of interest in fiscal and financial policy. Revenue taxes were considered mere supplementary taxes: the tax on land and buildings became an inadequate supplement to the rural direct graduated tax, that on business an equally inadequate supplement to the urban milling and slaughter taxes. Being supplementary, Prussian revenue taxes received far less attentive and thorough treatment at the hands of the law than in south German states and in Austria, where revenue taxes as a type were developed into the modern direct form of tax. Prussian revenue taxes were old fashioned in concept and unjust in their unequal incidence on taxpayers – though the latter was true generally for this type of direct tax.

Land tax: Land tax had been developed as an allocated tax and even after 1810 was assessed on the basis of inadequate land registers prepared in the eighteenth century. The principle established by the tax law of 1820 was the maintenance of the historically determined tax yield from each province, whereas sub-allocation of tax in the various regions of each province was to be made more equitable, if possible. The maximum rate of tax was not to exceed 20 per cent of the taxpayer's net average revenue. The thankless task of sub-allocation, not regulated by adequate instructions valid for the whole of the monarchy, fell on local authorities. No wonder that there was no question of even approximately equal tax incidence or of a standard system of collection. The 25 government districts after 1815 pursued 33 different systems of land tax,[22] 23 of them in the six eastern provinces alone, using 114 special varieties of the tax.[23] The law of 1820 was resigned to their continuance. The Berlin government did not resort to an even approximately consistent standard development of revenue tax systems for the whole country, though it inherited in the western provinces (Rhineland, Westphalia) fairly modern land registers from the French period. At least, land registers there were continued and in 1839 used as a basis of a separate land tax law for the western provinces.[24] The differential land tax systems of the western and eastern provinces justify the description of a third dualism in the Prussian tax system.

A very belated attempt to establish a standard net revenue land registration for the whole state by the land tax ordnance of 1861[25] remained a half-hearted experiment. The superficial procedure re-

22 Schwarz and Strutz (1902), vol. I, section 4, p. 1,101; more generally for direct taxes Schimmelpfennig, *Direkte Steuern*, 3rd edn (1859).
23 S. Wagner (1980), p. 28. 24 *Ibid.* (1980), pp. 58ff., 259ff.
25 H. A. Mascher, *Grundsteuer-Regelung von 1861*, 1862.

mained technically and organizationally imperfect, especially as it proved impossible to dispense with differential regulations in different provinces. Entry into the new land registers – every commune had its registration book – took place according to categories of cultivation specific to each province (e.g., ploughed fields, gardens, meadows, etc.), every method of cultivation being subdivided into eight quality grades. The revenue estimate was arrived at on the now customary basis of assessment: net revenue being what remained from gross after deduction of costs, provided that this was substantially attainable on average over a number of normal years. The land tax continued on the allocation principle, the national aggregate for the state fixed at 10 million talers.

At best, approximate values can be calculated for the effective tax incidence on land. The legal maximum limit of nominal 20 per cent (law of 1820) was probably not nearly reached, probably not even the reduced limit (law of 1839 for the western provinces) of nominal 11 to 12 per cent of land register revenues. A calculation *ex post* of the development of new revenues and its relation to the amounts allocated shows on average a falling real incidence within the limits of 5–8 per cent (around 1816) rising for a short period to a peak somewhere between 8 and 11 per cent (around 1885). Both in weight and long-term trends, this incidence fits into the indicators we have for the remainder of Germany. Surcharges made by local authorities varied chronologically and regionally between 100 and 200 per cent of the national tax.[26]

Buildings tax: Buildings tax was encoded with land tax until in 1869 the land tax ordinance produced a separate buildings tax. It was intended to afford relief to peasants. Developed as a kind of net revenue tax, it remained from the outset a still-born limb within the Prussian tax body. The allocated tax was to be levied on dwellings at no more than 4 per cent of assessed annual value, and 2 per cent of the assessed annual value of buildings used commercially, especially workshops and factories. Small dwellings were subject to a minimum tariff of 1.6 per cent, above which it rose to the maximum rate in a series of steps.[27] The effective rate of tax probably remained below the nominal, because as a rule the actual yield of buildings lay above that assessed.

Business tax: After the abolition of the guilds and the introduction of freedom of occupation in 1810, anyone wishing to pursue a craft as a rule needed merely to take out a craft licence and pay a fee. Such a rudimentary once-and-for-all 'business-tax-like fee' gave so little satisfaction that an attempt was made in 1820 to introduce a business revenue

---

[26] Incidence according to S. Wagner (1980), pp. 66, 183ff., 187; for local government finances, Schimmelpfennig, *Kommunalabgaben* (1859).   [27] S. Wagner (1980), pp. 72ff.

System of business tax

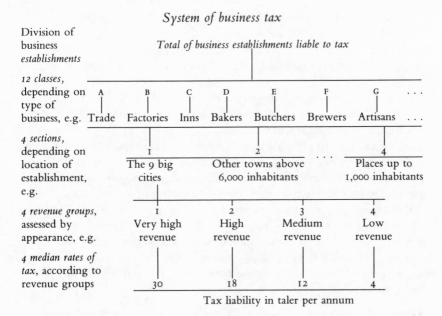

Division of business establishments	Total of business establishments liable to tax						
12 classes, depending on type of business, e.g.	A — Trade	B — Factories	C — Inns	D — Bakers	E — Butchers	F — Brewers	G — Artisans ...
4 sections, depending on location of establishment, e.g.	1 — The 9 big cities		2 — Other towns above 6,000 inhabitants		...		4 — Places up to 1,000 inhabitants
4 revenue groups, assessed by appearance, e.g.	1 — Very high revenue		2 — High revenue		3 — Medium revenue		4 — Low revenue
4 median rates of tax, according to revenue groups	30		18		12		4

Tax liability in taler per annum

tax assessed by external indicators.[28] Business tax was regarded as a surcharge on graduated, milling and slaughter taxes; that alone prevented it from occupying a central position in the tax system. It was to be levied only on those businesses which were regarded as particularly profitable.

Occupations liable to tax were divided into 12 classes of 'types of business' (criterion 1); into four sections according to 'location' (criterion 2); into four revenue groups according to 'estimated average revenue' (criterion 3). The survey above illustrates the basis of classification adopted until 1891. Every revenue group was allocated by law a 'median rate of tax' – not identical with the actual tax incidence, but used only to calculate the total business tax falling on the group: multiplication of total establishments in each revenue group and section, using the 'median rate of tax', yielded the annual quota to be raised from all members of a group in a particular location. How this 'taxpayers' association' allocated the tax quota imposed among its individual members, thus fixing the actual tax incidence falling on each establishment, remained at the 'association's' discretion. The government believed members of an occupation to be best qualified by business experience to know real incomes and to make 'equitable' assessments accordingly, seeing in this procedure the nearest approach to the demand for tax justice. It was

[28] Benda (1817); H. A. Mascher, *Gewerbesteuergesetzgebung* (1868); Oesfeld (1877).

intended that the highest tax levied on any establishment should be 30 taler, the lowest 1 taler or less per annum.

In spite of modifications of the tax in 1861 (diversification of business classes) and further changes in 1872, 1874 and 1876 with special regulations for millers, bakers, butchers, and hawkers, the Prussian business tax, owing to its piecemeal development and its standard classification, remained hardly more than an unsatisfactory patchwork – unsatisfactory both as regards system and yield, though probably highly satisfactory to business men subject to only light burdens. The tax system was in no way adapted to the rise of large industrial enterprises, of factories and new branches of industry and to the ensuing and permanent obliteration of the traditional locational categories of town (industry) and countryside (agriculture), in short, to industrial development and the rise of Prussia to an industrial state. The youthful industry grew in the shelter of an antiquated tax system which gave it some protection. After the introduction of income tax in 1891, a modified version of the business tax – in common with the other revenue taxes – was transferred in 1893 to the local authorities.

Graduated tax: in quest of an income tax: Overcoming the town–countryside tax dualism was almost identical with introducing universal income tax. The history of the Prussian income tax in many aspects of its elaboration and development showed striking similarity with British experience.[29]

Frustrated attempts, 1808–20: A personal universal income tax was introduced in 1808, experimentally in the first instance, in East and West Prussia, Lithuania and in the cities of Königsberg and Danzig. The ministers responsible, von Stein and von Schrötter, took over from Pitt's income tax (1799) the principle of assessing total income accruing to an individual and self-assessment by the taxpayer, and from Addington's income tax (1803) the principle of dividing total income into different types of income. British pragmatism in the form of five schedules was, however, abandoned in favour of Adam Smith's pure doctrine. Types of income were rigidly separated according to three sources associated with the three factors of production of land, capital and labour: landed income, capital income, income from work. From this resulted a twofold division distinguishing landed and invested from uninvested income, the former from profitable and independent occupations, the latter for subordinate work remunerated by salary or wage. The linkage of objective production factors with corresponding personal income factors was achieved by means of the new legal device of private

---

[29] See Grätzer (1884); Fuisting (1894); Grabower (1932), pp. 195–253; Mauz (1935); Popitz (1926), pp. 439f.

property in material means of production. Thus was transition from a feudal economic and social to a liberal and capitalist order reflected in tax legislation.

In order to achieve equality, the three types of income, considered unequally secure, received unequal tax treatment both as regards assessment of taxable income – deduction of debts being permitted only to land and building proprietors, not to salary and wage-earners – and as regards rate of tax: agricultural land revenue was taxed at 4 per cent, capital revenue at 3, salaries and wages on a scale from 0.16 per cent to 3 per cent (with numerous exceptions in East Prussia).

Such a modern concept of a personal income tax was well ahead of its time; there existed neither the administrative infrastructure necessary for its collection nor could the 'universality' of tax liability be enforced; tax yield therefore fell well below expectation. The tax failed for the same reason as did British attempts in 1799 and 1803; it was abolished in 1811. The first attempt had foundered.

The second attempt was the introduction in 1812 of a graduated extraordinary income tax, by character a capitation tax, for the whole kingdom. The heavily controversial duty to declare income (self-assessment) applied only to recipients of incomes in excess of 1,000 taler; the remaining taxpayers were assessed by a graduation commission according to presumed incomes and allocated in the first instance to one of nine income classes. As laid down in the class tariff in 1812, uninvested incomes were taxed, if in excess of 300 taler at 3, from 100 to 300 taler at 1 per cent; of those with incomes below 100 taler, artisans paid 18, day labourers and servants 12 groschen.

Taxpayers refused to pay; the inadequate collection apparatus could not enforce the tax. Graduated income tax, linked to an extraordinary 3 per cent tax on capital and bonded interest – again a very modern concept – remained a failure once more at the second attempt, yielding a mere 4.5 million taler in lieu of the 20 million taler, the minimum expected.[30] Moreover, collection caused so much unrest that it was suspended in 1814 and abolished in 1820; the introduction of universal personal income tax in town and countryside on British lines had been frustrated.

As in Britain, a period without income taxation followed the failed attempts; after new starts in 1851, success eventually came in 1891. While Britain had in the interval resorted to a combination of consumption taxes and loans, Prussia after 1820 developed a fairly substantial tax system which entrenched the inequality of taxation between town and country. This reorganized dual tax system was supplemented by the long-standing objective revenue tax; whereas customs tariffs were sub-

[30] Schwarz and Strutz (1902), vol. 1, section 4, p. 1079.

The graduated tax system of 1820

Status, occupation, tax class	Tax liability per month	
	Household	Individual
1st class: aristocracy and higher bourgeoisie e.g., Estate owners, manufacturers, bankers, very wealthy and rich residents	4 taler	2 taler
2nd class: medium bourgeoisie e.g., Landowners, merchants, wealthy residents	2 taler	1 taler
3rd class: medium bourgeoisie e.g., Landowners, merchants, also wealthy residents	1 taler	12 groschen
4th class: low bourgeoisie Peasants and artisans	8 groschen	4 groschen
5th class: working class Wage-workers, servants, day labourers, generally people without capital	1 groschen per person, but no more than 3 persons in any household liable to tax	

ject equally to fiscal and non-fiscal considerations, the Prussian revenue system retained its elastic element in the shape of income from public property.

Graduated tax in the countryside: Compared to the failed attempts at a universal income tax in 1808 and 1812, the eventually introduced graduated tax of 1820 represented a relapse into a fairly antiquated, graduated capitation tax favouring the wealthier sectors of the rural population.[31] That was all that was politically feasible at the time. The 'universality' of the rural graduated tax cannot conceal the fact that the landed aristocracy and the former manorial lords continued to be exempt from land tax. The graduated tax rested on a division of rural taxable population into five tax classes according to social status. The reasoning was fairly simple, relating function to tax liability: from a citizen's 'status' derives his 'occupation', from his occupation his 'affluence', from his affluence his 'ability to bear tax', and from this in turn, his 'tax liability'. With the exception of tax-exempt landed classes, military and clerical personnel, teachers and midwives, additionally from 1827 onwards also people above 60 years of age, and from 1828 people below 16 years, every person or every household was allocated to a tax class by the local authorities and had to pay the amount of tax fixed by law for the particular class. The assessment of a taxpayer's liability took into consideration neither the composition of his income from one or several sources nor the actual

---

[31] On graduated taxes in general, Heckel (1907), vol. I, pp. 345ff.; on Prussia specifically Fischer (1878); Beckerath (1912).

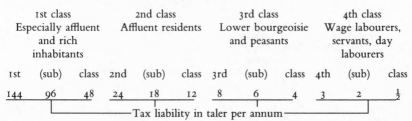

The graduated tax system of 1821
4 (main) classes

1st class	2nd class	3rd class	4th class
Especially affluent and rich inhabitants	Affluent residents	Lower bourgeoisie and peasants	Wage labourers, servants, day labourers

1st	(sub)	class	2nd	(sub)	class	3rd	(sub)	class	4th	(sub)	class
144	96	48	24	18	12	8	6	4	3	2	½

Tax liability in taler per annum

level of his income within his class. Adjustment of individual tax liability to individual ability to pay in accordance with the elsewhere greatly emphasized demands for 'equality' and 'justice' was grossly neglected. Nor was there a lower exemption threshold, but certainly an upper limit in money terms.

Combination of status membership and presumed income level in assessing tax caused much dissatisfaction, above all in the Rhineland, industrially more fully developed and differentiated than the eastern provinces; unjust distribution of tax burden apparently was considered more oppressive than absolute tax levels. For this reason, the (main) classes were subdivided in 1821 into three (sub)classes or steps each, while the 5th class of 1820, representative of the working class, was integrated into the 4th class of 1821. Thus workers 'officially' became 'the fourth estate', distinct taxwise from 'lords', 'bourgeois' and 'peasants'. In this tariff of twelve steps, the highest tax payment per month in monetary terms was 12 taler, thereby retaining what was in fact a regressive tax. Allocation of taxpayers to one of the twelve classes was by subjective estimates of possessions, type of property, revenue, occupation, status, affluence. Local authorities made the assessment, with the taxpayer entitled to make representations.

In spite of subsequent modifications, the graduated tax of 1821 remained unsatisfactory from the social policy point of view: recipients of low incomes were at a disadvantage; wealthy rural inhabitants could escape graduated tax completely by residing for more than six months of every year in a town liable to milling and slaughter tax.

Graduated tax levied on households also had an outstanding fiscal defect: the tax yield was very inelastic. Contrary to income tax, it could bear no surcharge in times of emergency. The state's tax revenues increased mainly through increase in the number of taxpayers by virtue of population growth, but not through growth in individual taxpayers' incomes. Any change in tax rates or introduction of additional tax (sub)classes encountered resistance in parliament.

Table 65. *Yield of graduated tax, 1822–47*

	1822	1837	1847
Population (millions)	11.57	14.02	16.12
Resident taxpayers (million persons)	9.85	12.05	?
Yield of graduated tax (in million taler)	6.29	7.10	7.3

Table 66. *Contribution of the four classes to graduated tax yield, 1821–38*

	% for average of years	
Class	1821–6	1833–8
1st	3.6	3.5
2nd	16.8	16.2
3rd	36.2	33.7
4th	43.4	46.6

The yield of graduated tax fell below expectation, above all below population growth, with 4th-class taxpayers having to bear the main tax burden (see Tables 65 and 66).[32] As late as 1846, no more than 676 families in the first class were taxed at the maximum rate.

The classification of population liable to tax in the countryside was extended after the 1848 revolution to the entire monarchy (town and country) on a political basis, when Prussia introduced its universal, yet unequal 3-class voting system, of 1849 for indirect elections to the house of deputies (representation of the bourgeois estate), subsequently also to the Reichstag; individual voters' rights depended on the level of individual tax payments. The total yield of direct tax in a constituency was divided into three equal parts. Beginning with the taxpayer paying the highest tax in the constituency, as many further taxpayers, in descending order of tax contributions imposed upon them, were included in the first class of taxed voters as made their aggregate tax payments one-third of total yield – usually a small number of taxed voters. The second and third classes of taxed voters were similarly constituted; most taxed and exempt voters were in these. Members of each of the three taxed-voters' classes then elected one-third each of the electors and thus of the parliamentarians. This led to the intended result: representation of the interests of wealthier, more highly taxed citizens by a larger number of deputies in

[32] Details in Schwarz and Strutz (1902), vol. 1, section 4, p. 1089; population from Hohorst (1977), p. 131.

parliament than those of the poorer, lightly, or not at all taxed ones. Votes were not counted on the one-man-one-vote basis, but weighted by voters' tax payments. (Saxony (1896) and Austria (1873, 1882, 1896) had a similar electoral system based on classes.) When the Prussian tax system was fundamentally changed in 1891 with the introduction of universal income tax, the three-class voting rights were modified in favour of small taxpayers (see p. 447f.).

(iii) Fiscal results and structure of state budgets, 1821–50

A comparison of tax revenues in 1816 with 1821 shows the fiscal results of the tax reforms:[33] manifest growth of direct and surprising stability of indirect taxes, new types of tax replacing the old in both groups. The emphasis on differential taxation of town and countryside led to a palpably greater burden on rural in favour of urban population – a result cumulatively achieved by newly introducing graduated tax, continuing milling and slaughter taxes and abolishing urban excises.

The state made heavy work of the four classical tax principles propounded by Adam Smith and well known in Prussia: equality, certainty, convenience of payment, and economy of collection.[34] Certainty and to a lesser degree convenience of payment were possible, but equality and economy of collection were difficult to achieve. The concept of universal liability to tax in an impoverished country was pushed so far into the lowly paid sectors down to day labourers that high collection costs resulted. Neither social considerations nor rationalization of collection methods suggested an exemption threshold until 1873. The grip of the administration, backed by disciplinary measures, thus reached via the tax collectors even to the remotest villages.

A view of total tax revenues within the framework of the 1821 budget (see Tables 67 and 68) discloses, with all due reservations, two striking changes in structure, compared to budgets of the middle eighteenth century: on the revenue side, the share of total public property income, especially from public lands, forests, etc., had fallen, probably due to the cessation of feudal dues and services, to price fluctuations, and even more to loss of property during the territorial reorganization of the state area. In spite of the seized secularized clerical property, the gap thus opened could be closed only by the rising incomes from mines and smelters, and finally by the railways. On the expenditure side, the share of domestic purposes had risen to over 30 per cent, compared to the earlier budgets.

---

[33] Ohnishi (1980), p. 281; for 1816 amounts realized, for 1821 amounts assessed; there are unexplained differences.

[34] Smith (1937 edn), pp. 777ff.; for principles of taxation, Hasbach (1891), pp. 291f., Mann (1937), pp. 144ff.

Table 67. *Structure of Prussia's tax revenue, 1816 and 1821*

	1816		1821	
Types of tax	000 taler	%	000 taler	%
I. Direct taxes				
1. Land tax	9,802	31.4	9,326	26.6
2. Business tax	1,362	4.3	1,600	4.6
3. Graduated tax	—	—	6,321	18.0
4. Personal taxes in eastern provinces and Westphalia	1,387	4.4	—	—
5. Furniture, door and window tax etc. in western provinces	868	2.8		
Total of I	13,419	42.9	17,247	49.2
II. Indirect taxes				
1. Customs duties	3,865	12.4	3,600	10.3
2. Consumption tax on foreign goods	—	—	4,300	12.3
3. Consumption tax on consumables	—	—	5,000	14.2
4. Milling and slaughter tax	—	—	2,000	5.7
5. Urban excise in old provinces	8,681	27.8	—	—
6. Rural consumption tax in old provinces	816	2.6	—	—
7. Consumption dues	2,406	7.7	—	—
Unexplained difference	2,090	6.6	2,910	8.3
Total of II	17,858	57.1	17,810	50.8
Totals of I and II	31,277	100	35,057	100

Source: Ohnishi (1980), p. 281; the unexplained differences probably arise from stamp duties; partly different figures in A. Wagner (1901), part 4, pp. 50f. and Reden (1856), vol. II, p. 88.

The setting up of an administrative apparatus for a new, territorially not yet compact state was expensive – and time-consuming. Prussian officialdom emerged.

The changes in the budget structure of 1821 are confirmed by a glance at the subsequent budget development from 1821 to 1850. Amounts can only be approximate, as changes in budget technique cannot be fully allowed for. Though from 1821 onwards budgets showing modifications of categories were published in the collections of Prussian laws at irregular intervals, there are more detailed annual budgets only from the state constitution of 1850 onwards.[35] Budget totals grew more slowly than population, civil expenditure showing fastest growth, reaching a budget proportion of 47.3 per cent by 1850. The two expenditure items of civil and military changed place, presumably for the first time in

[35] Greater detail in A. Wagner (1901), part 4, pp. 49ff.

Table 68. *Prussia's state budget, 1821 (net values)*

Revenue	000 taler	%	Expenditure	000 taler	%
1. Public property, of which	11,777	23.6	1. War Department	22,800	45.6
Public lands, forests, mines, smelters, salt refineries,			2. Debt service: interest and repayment	11,300	22.6
workshops	7,177		3. Department of the Interior, includes	10,200	20.4
Salt monopoly	3,800		central		
Post Office	800		administration,		
2. Taxes and similar			provincial		
imposts, of which	36,365	72.7	governments,		
Excise, customs,			church,		
tolls, etc.	15,700	31.4	superannuations,		
Direct taxes, of which	17,247	34.5	police, education, medicine		
Land tax	9,326		4. Department of		
Graduated tax	6,321		Justice	1,720	3.5
Business tax	1,600		5. Department of		
Stamp duties	2,910	5.8	Industry and		
Lottery	508	1.0	Trade	1,574	3.2
3. Miscellaneous and			6. Department of		
extraordinary			Foreign Affairs	600	1.2
revenue	1,858	3.7	7. Miscellaneous	1,766	3.5
Total revenue, approx.	50,000	100	Total expenditure, approx.	50,000	100

Source: Reden (1856), pp. 88ff. Revenues and expenditures reveal minor differences which could not be eliminated.

Prussian history.[36] The state consolidated internally, with a tighter bureaucracy, which developed into an increasingly weighty power factor, whose independent importance in Prussia's economic and political development – as in the other major German states – has probably hitherto been underestimated.

All this was financed by the yield of indirect taxes, increasing once again in the face of strikingly poor elasticity of the direct tax yield. It even proved possible to reduce the level of the public debt *vis-à-vis* 1821 to 73 per cent and once more to accumulate a public treasure to the tune of 19.4 million taler. The state began a more effective adaptation to early

---

[36] On public expenditure Borchard (1968), pp. 156ff., with a concluding detailed presentation of areas of expenditure in 1850, pp. 179f. The largest expenditure items within civil administration were public security with 17 per cent, traffic with 9 and central administration with 6 per cent, related each to total net expenditure.

industrial development by shifting the weight of its entrepreneurial interests from agriculture to heavy industry, predominantly coal, though also to some extent to iron and steel. In the process of shifting productive capital, a few agricultural properties were sold, though up to the First World War acquisitions predominated in this category.[37] Introduced in these decades, the long-term and thoroughgoing restructuring of public entrepreneurial capital completely changed the proportions of the productive revenues of the Prussian state which by 1901 exhibited the following relationships, reflecting the transition from an agrarian to an industrial state:

Prussia's productive revenues (in million marks)[1]

1. Railways	271.9 (net)[2]
2. Mines, smelters, salt refineries	282.8 (gross)
3. Forests	135.8 (gross)
4. Public lands	35.8 (gross)

1. Heckel (1911), vol. II, pp. 320, 354.
2. Gross revenues 2,040.5 million marks; administrative expenses, 1,768 million marks, *ibid.*, p. 354.

However highly it esteemed private entrepreneurship, the liberal state had recalled its own mercantilist entrepreneurial tradition. It invested in heavy industry and, after initial hesitation, turned the new rail transport system into a public monopoly 'for the benefit of its Treasury'. For a long period, the state had no reason to repent its investment policy from the point of view of profits; at the same time the penetration of the railway system by the Prussian government was gradual and carefully calculated. Up to 1849, a private railway system existed, from 1850 a mixed system of early public railways, private railways both publicly and privately managed, until finally from the 1880s onwards the system of public railways was completed.[38]

Macro-economic estimates for the period from 1821 to 1850, to be interpreted with care, show an unexpected result (Tables 69, 70 and 77): while public expenditure grew at the same rate as per capita national income, the government's share (gross public expenditure as percentage of national income) fell perceptibly, requiring 8.6 per cent in 1822, and 6.2 per cent in 1850. Even in 1867, the last budget year before Prussia's territorial increase, its share was low at 6.7 per cent. Figures for budgetarily recognizable government activities after 1871 can be compared with pre-1867 values only with reservations, owing to the division

---

[37] Cultivable surface of public lands in 1903 was 347,700 ha, of which 51,700 ha came from territories acquired in 1866; the area had grown to 441,800 ha by 1910; Heckel (1911), vol. II, pp. 310f.   [38] Schwarz and Strutz (1901), vol. I, section 3, railway administration.

Table 69. *Prussia's state expenditure (net budget values), 1821–50*

	Total expenditure in million taler		Of which % of total net expenditure on			
	Net	Gross	Court	Internal	Military	Treasury and debt service
1821	52.57	70.09	4.9	30.2	43.4	21.5
1829	53.37	71.15	4.8	33.2	41.5	20.5
1841	59.44	76.92	4.3	41.2	39.9	14.6
1850	68.10	90.97	3.8	47.3	37.8	11.1
Index of change 1850 (1821 = 1)		1.3	1.0	2.0	1.1	0.5

Source: From Karl Borchard, 'Staatsverbrauch' (1968), p. 158; further budget details in W. Gerloff, 'Staatshaushalt' (1929), pp. 4ff. Index of change calculated from absolute (gross) expenditure figures.

of functions between Reich and member states and to the very high productive revenues, with the double counting which these presumably involved. Bearing these reservations in mind, the government's share rose rapidly from 9.4 per cent (1873), and 11 per cent (1903) to 16.5 per cent in 1913. Indicators of development in similar nations show the same trend. However, any international comparison of state proportions has to take account of different budget structures reflecting different government functions.[39]

(iv) Subsequent fiscal compromises

The revolution of 1848/9 and the modifications of the tax system after 1851

Dissatisfaction with the graduated tax grew in the 1840s; proposals for modification or even a new concept of a graduated tax multiplied, caused by the example of Peel's reintroduction of income and property tax in Britain in 1842 and the good results it produced there, but also by increasing concern with the 'social question'.

Accelerated industrialization increased the number of wage-earners and the grievance of small artisans and farmers. Combined with unequal tax incidence, these produced a curious combination of a mildly philanthropic reform movement with recognition by part of the well-to-do bourgeoisie that the (later so-called) proletariat might one day constitute a danger to it. Readiness for compromise increased after the 1848/9 revolution. Its first indication was the lowering of the milling and

[39] On international comparisons of government shares, see pp. 405 and 475.

Table 70. *Prussia's state revenue (net budget values), 1821–50*

	Total revenue in million taler	of which % of total revenue from				Public debt in		Population (millions)	Income per head (taler)
		Productive income	Direct taxes	Indirect taxes and customs dues	Miscellaneous	Million taler	Taler per head		
1821	52.57	28.3	32.8	35.4	3.5	c.217	c.19.2	11.3	70.7
1829	53.37	29.4	36.2	33.3	1.1			12.8	77.3
1841	61.94	27.2	30.3	36.4	6.6	c.175	c.11.6	15.0	84.0
1850	68.15	24.5	28.6	37.0	9.9	158.5 (1948)	9.8	16.4	90.7
Index of change 1850 (1821 = 1)	1.3	1.1	1.1	1.4	3.6	—	—	1.5	1.3

Sources: Public revenue: from Borchard (1968), pp. 33, 131, 158.
Public debt: does not include paper money issue; Gerloff (1929), pp. 6ff., Heckel (1911), vol. II, pp. 49ff., Reden (1856), vol. II, pp. 5ff., 80, 620ff., 629ff., 666ff. In 1848, a state reserve of 19.4 million taler is shown. Index of change calculated from absolute revenue figures.
Income per head: from Hohorst (1977), p. 276, converted into taler; his data refer to 1822, 1831, 1840, 1849. For the base year of 1816, he calculates a per capita income of 66 taler.

slaughter tax rate in 1848 by one-third, which was to benefit above all urban lower income recipients. The financial reform of 1851 represented a compromise: heavier tax burdens on the affluent bourgeois wherever he resided – but not yet a definite breakthrough to a universal income tax.

More tax justice and a first and partial abolition of the tax dualism between town and country came about in 1851, when the graduated tax of 1820 was split into two partial taxes:[40]

the new graduated income tax on people with an income of 1,000 taler or over in the country *and* in towns subject to milling and slaughter tax, that is, throughout the state;
the modified old graduated tax of 1820 for people with incomes below 1,000 taler in the countryside, including as before places not liable to milling and slaughter tax.

Assessment to the new income tax (people of and above 1,000 taler income), undertaken by local authorities according to external indicators and after recording land charges and mortgages in registers, was by 30 classes or income steps, authorities being explicitly prohibited from investigating personal incomes and fortunes in depth. Fixed tax payments, related to class, ranged from 2 taler 15 groschen to 600 taler per month, the rate of tax calculated for each class amounting to 3 per cent.[41] The highest income class was limited to 240,000 taler, producing a maximum tax burden of 7,200 taler per annum. Overall, tax rates were linear, but regressive as regards income steps. For the first time, the law defined more exactly the different sources of revenue liable to tax: from landed and investment property, trade, industry, the pursuit of other profitable occupations as well as the receipt of periodical payments, including pensions. Interest owed, charges on land and certain insurance premiums were deductible. In a population of 16.6 million in 1851/2, only 45,000 taxpayers were assessed to graduated income tax. The new tax was a taxation on wealth, clearly favourable to the highest income earners. Legal persons (corporations) were made liable to tax in towns from 1852, in rural communities from 1885.

For purposes of the modified old graduated tax, taxpayers with incomes below 1,000 taler were divided, according to presumed income,

[40] On this, see Kletke (1865); *ibid.* (1877); Fischer (1878); Kautz (1889); Teschemacher (1912); Mauz (1935); Popitz (1926), pp. 400f.
[41] Heckel (1907), vol. I, pp. 345ff. In turning the monetary total stipulated in the tax law in taler per income class into a rate of tax payable per class, different percentages result within each income class, depending on whether the highest or lowest base is used for reference. Occasionally the base is taken minus the minimum of existence, thus resulting in a slightly lower percentage. This explains the differences in the literature in quoting tax incidence in terms of percentage of taxable income.

The combined system of graduated tax and graduated income tax of 1851

Graduated tax	Graduated income tax

3 main classes			Groups in steps 100, 150 and 350 taler, the width growing with increasing incomes. Altogether 30 tax steps with a rate of 3 per cent on the minimum amount in each step
(Highest) 1st class	(Medium) 2nd class	(Lower) 3rd class	
4 sub-classes	5 sub-classes	4 sub-classes	
24 20 16 12	10 8 6 5 4	3 2 1 ½	

Tax liability in taler per annum

into 3 classes each with sub-classes, producing 13 steps altogether, on which monthly taxes were levied, ranging from 2 taler on small landowners and artisans without additional earnings to 1 groschen for wage and day labourers, servants and journeymen. All those liable to graduated tax in Prussia would have remained exempt in Britain, where the lower limit lay in 1842 at £150, converted into 1,011 taler (1 taler = 3 marks; £1 = 20.43 marks), and was lowered to £100 (681 taler) between 1852 and 1894.

The concept of 'class' in *Klassensteuer* had now largely lost its original alignment with the concept of 'status' or 'estate' and in fiscal science now acquired the meaning of 'income level', hence 'tax level'.

Graduated tax was now considered the tax on the poor, graduated income tax that on the wealthier parts of the population.

By means of this combined system, parliament believed it had introduced the principle of taxation according to taxable capacity. Yet assessment of income by external indicators in 43 steps remained inexact, varying from district to district and remaining inferior to the British achievement. Neither tax implemented the principles of taxation according to capacity to pay.

Reduction of tax dualism between town and country was also diminished by somewhat expanding the regional application of the graduated tax; the number of towns liable to milling and slaughter tax was reduced to 83 in 1851, to 75 in 1867. The wealthier inhabitants of these towns, made liable to the new direct graduated income tax and thus considered subject to double taxation, were on that account granted a tax remission of a lump sum of 20 taler.

Lack of reform between 1851 and 1891 had the effect that there was no substantive increase in yield of direct personal taxation. Supplementation of revenue taxes by a tax on revenues from capital failed to materialize. This was a 'fault of political omission';[42] a graduated income tax not fortified by the duty to declare income could not fill the gap. From the

[42] A. Wagner (1901), part 4, p. 27.

social policy point of view, Prussia thus became a backwater, compared for instance with Württemberg – which had taxes on revenues from capital and on income from services, professions and independent sources since 1820[43] – or Saxony which introduced a modern income tax in 1878.[44] Prussia's priorities were different. It retained a direct tax system unchanged in its main characteristics, (a) subsidizing capital accumulation by private entrepreneurs and companies at the expense of the lower income sector, (b) giving preference to industry, trade and services over the agrarian sector, at a time when industrialization came to fruition in Prussia and made it take its place among the most industrial countries in Europe, overtaking Saxony which had for a time been the pioneer of industrialization in Germany.[45]

Discussion of the organization of a Prussian tax system adapted to industrialization – on the one hand, direct graduated tax and graduated income tax, on the other, indirect, above all milling and slaughter taxes – has a qualitative and a quantitative aspect; both are clearly separate. Qualitative considerations point to the importance in principle of taxation of all incomes from different sources flowing into the same pocket and concern the principle of personal taxation in an industrializing society – the weakest point in the Prussian nineteenth-century tax system. Quantitative consideration – as a glance at the budget reveals – shows up the comparatively low fiscal significance of existing personal taxes. Graduated tax, up to the 1851 reform, produced only 8.7 per cent (1847), after the reform 5.9 per cent of total revenue, the new graduated income tax a mere 2.2 per cent (1867). Milling and slaughter tax reached in 1847 a proportion of 3.6, in 1867 of 2.1 per cent. The centre of fiscal interest and initiative was unmistakeably occupied by the income from state enterprises, which after inclusion of railway revenue leapt from 31.2 per cent (1847) to 47.3 per cent (1867) of total revenues.[46] There was no great pressure from the point of view of the total fiscal income to find a solution for the qualitative tax problem. In parliament, moreover, a conservative bourgeois attitude persisted.

The events of 1866 pointed in the same direction. Prussia, victorious in the German war, acquired as new provinces Hanover, Electorial Hesse, Nassau, Hesse-Homburg, the city of Frankfurt, Schleswig-Holstein and smaller territorial areas of Hesse-Darmstadt and of Bavaria. Prussia consolidated its political territory, bisected since 1815; the surface of the

---

43 Anon. (C. Schütz) (1835); Riecke (1887); Schremmer (1974), pp. 679ff., on the chronologically earlier tax order of Swabian–Austrian landed estates, Schremmer (1966), pp. 377ff.

44 Conrad (1879); Löbe (1889).   45 Forberger (1982), vol. 1, part 1, pp. 101ff.

46 Calculated from the budgets in A. Wagner (1901), part 4, pp. 50ff.; the figures for 1867 still refer to the older area of the country in 1866 without the acquisitions of 1866–7, hence can be compared with 1847 values. Through changes in accounting methods, Wagner shows higher figures than those given in Tables 78 and 79.

state increased by more than 25 per cent, the population by just 23 per cent. This entailed problems of administrative and tax integration of the new areas; the economic structure of the newly acquired lands strengthened the agrarian, or at least the non-industrial, component of Prussia as a whole. Reinforced by the above-mentioned quantitative aspect, these influences were on the side of continuing the status quo in taxation rather than going in for a fundamental modification and modernization of the entire tax system; thus such a fundamental reorganization of the entire tax system once again failed to materialize. Further modifications of the tax system were brought about predominantly not by domestic circumstances, as after the 1848/9 revolution, but by the foundation of the Reich in 1871.

The establishment of the Reich in 1871 and the modifications of the tax system after 1873

Once a delimitation in principle between the functions of the German Reich, founded in 1871, and its member states had been achieved, the fundamental fiscal rule of the Empire was as follows: the Reich received from the states the indirect taxes, whereas direct taxes and revenues from state enterprises remained with individual states. This division of taxes led Prussia to pursue the extension of direct at the expense of indirect taxes. Moreover, a tidying up of direct taxes had been overdue after 1851–6; if this tended at the same time to a degree of harmonization among the indirect taxes of different member states, so much the better.

In 1873, the milling and slaughter tax was abolished as a state tax, slaughter tax being assigned to local authorities, thus ending the century-long tax differentiation between town and country. However, differential treatment arising from taxation depending on income level, now valid throughout the state, either by virtue of the graduated or of the graduated income tax, was confirmed for the last time.

Graduated tax in 1873 contained for the first time (a) a low exemption threshold of 420 marks (140 taler), (b) a progressive element in simultaneously reduced tax rates: 12 income steps, tax rates ranging from 3 to 27 marks, or in terms of percentage 0.7 to 2.7 on assessed income, (c) reductions given in respect of taxpayers' personal circumstances (e.g., children). Surprisingly, however, graduated tax remained an allocation tax, the annual total of between 11 and 14 million taler being proclaimed *ex ante*; if total assessed *ex post* differed from total proclaimed, it was adjusted by surcharges on, or abatements from, standard tax rates. This was the minister of finance's scheme to avoid the risk of deficient revenues drawn from the lower income groups in the population.

Graduated income tax was reorganized in 40 steps, instead of 30 as hitherto, of taxable income, ranging from 1,000 to 240,000 taler, being charged, as it had been from 1851 onwards, at the rate of 3 per cent of each step. The maximum tax charge in money terms maintained hitherto lapsed through the opening of the top step, thus removing the proportional regression of taxation for recipients of income exceeding 240,000 taler. Total tax receipts were not fixed *ex ante*, so that rising (falling) incomes correspondingly increased (reduced) the tax incidence on well-to-do citizens – a decisive step in the direction of a modern tax varying with income.

Both taxes were felt to be oppressive and inequitable, owing to local authority surcharges, frequently high and occasionally reaching 300 per cent, and to unequal assessments. To obviate large numbers of tax reminders and sequestrations affecting lower-income recipients, the exemption threshold from graduated tax was raised in 1883 from 420 to 900 marks; though this saved collection costs, the exemption threshold still remained noticeably below the British limit of £100 (2,040 marks).

Payers of graduated tax and graduated income tax, as before, had to pay in addition land, building and business taxes so far as the law applied to them. Inequalities of tax in respect of all these taxes showed the same tendency, the disadvantage to the sectors least capable of bearing tax increasing if all these taxes happened to fall on the same taxpayer. In 1891/2, the year prior to the levy of the new universal income tax, a mere 5.91 per cent of population paid graduated income tax, 44.57 per cent graduated tax.

(v) The fiscal breakthrough of 1891–3

Introduction by Miquel of the general Prussian income tax removed the last traces of Prussian tax dualism: it terminated the coexistence of graduated tax and graduated income tax, caused by differential tax treatment of town and countryside, by amalgamating both taxes with their different catchment areas of taxpayers into a universal standard income tax.[47]

The general income tax of 1891 and its complementary property tax of 1893
The Prussian income tax of 1891, in its day considered the most modern of its kind in Europe, has connections with both the Prussian financial reforms of 1891–3 and the financial relationships between the Reich and its member states.

The new income tax represented a mixture of British pragmatism, French precision of legal–bureaucratic detail and German desire for the

---

[47] A. Wagner (1891), pp. 551ff; A. Wagner (1894), pp. 1ff.; Gerlach (1893); Fuisting (1905), vol. II, 1902, vol. IV, pp. 107ff., 1915, 1916, vol. I (8th edn) in two halves; Popitz (1926); Mauz (1935).

greatest possible abstract and theoretical purity of concept, taking account of the stage of progress of fiscal science and the historical continuity with previous taxes. The Prussian general income tax was characterized by several traits which, considered in isolation, certainly had historical precedents and were, thus, not pioneer achievements. However, their combination and concrete structuring established the basis and the original version of what twentieth-century slogans have described as 'fiscal state interventionism' or 'a state tool for the management of economic policy within the framework of a free market economy'.

The new tax implied:

1. General tax liability. All citizens and legal corporations were in principle liable to tax. The last few feudal tax exemptions of erstwhile princes were removed against compensation amounting to $13\frac{1}{2}$ times the income tax contribution due from them for the first time in 1893/4. The only sectors remaining exempt were explicitly enumerated in the law, e.g., private soldiers and non-commissioned ranks;

2. The duty to disclose business accounts to public authorities, to declare private income and property and to permit their detailed investigation by fiscal officials. Protection of citizens no longer implied a guarantee of their privacy, as in 1851, but of due process of law by complaint, action, appeal, on the part of anyone who felt unjustly treated. The rule of law was strengthened, the scope of individuals' and authorities' discretion palpably reduced; untruthful tax declarations leading to tax evasion were punished by fines, indiscretions of the tax inspectorate in the discharge of their duties by fines or imprisonment of the officials. This represented the *quid pro quo* of the taxpayers' duty to declare their cirumstances;

3. Enumeration of all sources from which revenues accrued to taxpayers:
    invested capital (interest)
    landed property (ground and building rents)
    trade, industry, mining operations (profits)
    other 'remunerated employment' (wages, salaries), including the enjoyment of profitable rights (interest, annuities, profits).
    In principle, all types of revenue were liable to tax, exempt were only those explicitly mentioned in the law (usually non-recurring), e.g., life insurance payments, lottery winnings;

4. Introduction of a detailed and complicated system of abatements, deductions and exemptions, differing according to revenue type

(e.g., development costs). These determined the taxable level of the four types of revenue in individual instances;

5. Aggregation of the four taxable types of income, from which a number of further abatements, for special expenditure, could be made, usually relating to taxpayers' personal circumstances, such as family status, number of children, contributions to compulsory social insurance. This diminished aggregate income liable to tax even beyond the amount of development costs. As legally defined, aggregate (net) taxable income differed from gross revenue and gross income chiefly by the abatements permitted for developing, safeguarding and maintaining income and for depreciation on buildings and capital investments in balance sheets, for interest owed etc. The balance sheet of an enterprise drawn up to establish 'true economic profit' (so-called trading accounts) was no longer identical with that establishing 'taxable' profits (so-called tax balance sheet for the Inland Revenue);

6. The individual's aggregate taxable income was taxed at a standard rate; this did not prevent revenue from different sources being unequally taxed (effect of differentiation in development costs). Cumulation of development and special expenses, in combination with a progressive tax rate, enabled fine tuning of individual taxation;

7. The actual taxable revenue of the previous tax year served as the basis for taxation. Erstwhile principles of taxing the 'average achievable profits' (particularly in the case of revenue taxes) and the *ex ante* fixing of total tax yield were abolished.

Thus, income tax contained all those features which enabled it to become alongside 'budget policy' an outstanding instrument of 'fiscal policy', complementing 'monetary policy' and the remaining armoury of economic policy. Modifications of abatements, development and special expenses could be introduced almost 'noiselessly', for instance to achieve targets, immanent in the economic system, of sectoral and regional capital accumulation in particular branches of industry, to cope with business fluctuations, to redistribute income and property and to correct the outcome of a market economy where this was considered politically necessary.

Apart from abatements, the rate of tax strengthened the element of social policy. The exemption limit amounted to 900 marks; progression of tax began at 1.13 per cent, ending at 3.95 per cent of taxable income. In comparison with the former graduated income tax, this graduation somewhat relieved recipients of low and middling, considerably increas-

Table 71. *Average tax incidence on taxable aggregate income, 1890, 1893*

Aggregate taxable annual income (marks)	According to	
	Graduated income tax of 1890 (%)	General income tax of 1893 (%)
Below 900	Exempt	Exempt
900– 2,999	1.18	1.13
3,000– 5,999	2.56	2.25
6,000– 9,499	2.76	2.73
9,500–30,499	2.79	3.00
30,500–99,999	2.80	3.46
100,000 +	2.82	3.95

Source: Strutz (1902), vol. I, section 4, p. 1212.

Table 72. *Distribution of taxable incomes, 1900*

Taxable incomes in steps of tax rates (marks)		Number of persons assessed, including family members	
		Totals	% of population
Assessed by tax inspectorate	Exempt incomes below tax threshold	20,890,000	62.4
	900– 2,999	9,692,000	28.9
Individual duty to declare	3,000– 5,999	909,800	2.7
	6,000– 9,499	240,200	0.7
	9,500–30,499	200,700	0.6
	30,500–99,999	41,480	0.12
	100,000 +	8,678	0.03

Source: Strutz (1902), vol. I, section 4, p. 1216.

ing the incidence on those of higher incomes[48] (see Table 71). Wherever possible, collection took place at source. In order to lower further the high costs of collecting income tax and to facilitate collection in practice, only people with incomes exceeding 3,000 marks had to make a personal annual declaration of income; tax due from other taxpayers was determined by the tax inspectorate, rights of appeal remaining undiminished.

The general income tax actually raised permits as for the first time to delineate at least approximately the *income distribution* in Prussia and the *sources of income* (see Tables 72 and 73). Taxpayers required to declare individually incomes of 3,000 marks and more received their revenues in

[48] The tax law stipulates for a monetary tax total in mark per income class; possible differences in converting it to a percentual incidence discussed in n. 41. Survey on rates of tax and tax thresholds in the other German states as in 1910 in Laufer (1911), pp. 82ff., Tables 1–3.

Table 73. *Sources of taxable income, 1901*

Sources of taxable income	Income declared	
	In million marks	As %
Invested capital	1,208	26
Landed property	968	20
Trade, industry, mining	1,497	32
Remunerated employment	1,037	22
Total taxable income	4,710	100

Source: Strutz (1902), vol. I, section 4, p. 1,216.

1901 from the sources shown in Table 73. Undeclared incomes assessed by the inspectorate (below 3,000 marks per taxpayer) in that year amounted to 3,666 million marks. The aggregate sum of 8,376 million marks taxable income was derived as to 67 per cent from towns and 30 per cent from the countryside; the remainder cannot be allocated.

Increasing public requirements caused a state tax surcharge on taxable incomes above 1,200 marks, graduated from 5 to 25 per cent of the rate of tax, to be levied from 1909 onwards along the British super tax model. Taking into account the additional local government surcharges fluctuating between 100 and 300 (average in 1914: 190) per cent on state rates of tax, the incidence of income tax on the highest incomes was about 15 per cent.

Property tax: the general attitude of the period required landed and invested income to bear higher tax rates than uninvested; thus income tax needed to be supplemented, for which purpose a property tax was chosen in 1893. In Britain also, income tax, though otherwise constructed, was entitled 'income and property tax'. Property consisted of capital claims, fixed and working capital, immovable property, cash, precious metals, and certain capitalized rents and periodical claims; debts owed could be deducted. Tax fell on the 'general value' of the property, to be established by the tax inspectorate, if possible in conjunction with the income tax assessment. Full taxability commenced at property exceeding 20,000 marks, the rate of tax being 0.5 per mille. In 1895, 1.152 million taxpayers were assessed to property tax, that is, 3.7 per cent of total population; they declared taxable property aggregating 63,918 million marks.[49]

Introduction of universal income tax and local authority reform in 1893 had repercussions in the 3-class voting system of 1849, which had been linked to tax payments. It was modified: while the basis remained

[49] More detailed explanation in Schwarz and Strutz (1902), vol. I, section 4, pp. 1223ff.; Strutz (1912).

the same, people exempt from taxes were deemed to have paid a tax of 3 marks. This increased the aggregate tax raised in a constituency by a fictional amount, augmenting also the number of people in the second and third classes of 'tax voters', reducing somewhat the under-representation of the poorer sectors in parliament. From 1893, taxes collected by local authorities and provinces were added to the tax total which had to be divided into three.

Transfer to local authorities of land, building, and business taxes, 1893
Reform of income tax in 1891 necessitated modification of the business tax, originally designed as a supplement to the milling and slaughter tax now abolished.[50] Parliament, not anticipating a substantial burden on taxpayers, passed the bill of 1891 without controversy. It was designed to tax all existing productive enterprises, as long as annual income exceeded 1,500 marks and fixed and working capital 3,000 marks. This exempted more than 50 per cent of previous taxpayers from the new business tax. The remaining artisan, trade, and industrial establishments were divided into four classes, according to mixed criteria of revenue and business capital:

Tax class	Annual income (marks)		Fixed and variable capital (marks)
I	50,000+	or	1,000,000+
II	20,000–50,000	or	150,000–1,000,000
III	4,000–19,999	or	30,000–149,999
IV	1,500–3,999	or	3,000–29,999

The duty of owners of establishments was, not to declare details, but merely to state officially to which tax class they belonged; they could refuse to answer more detailed enquiries. The highest rate of tax in tax class I amounted to 1 per cent of self-assessed income.

As part of the reorganization of local authority taxation in 1893, the state transferred the modified business tax along with the two older land and building taxes to the local authorities which thereupon reorganized the three taxes in many different ways individual to each local authority.[51] Above all in the Rhineland, business tax took as the basis of assessment the number of people employed per establishment; in other regions, it was total wages paid, or aggregate capital invested, in each establishment; in 1913, 1,380 local authorities levied 139 differently constituted business taxes. Land and building tax showed similarly regional variety of actual organization. The transfer of revenue taxes to local authorities led to a peculiarity regarding the originally approximately 16,000 independent (manorial) estates of the eastern provinces:[52]

---

[50] Fuisting (1893); Fuisting (1906), vol. III; Gerlach (1893).
[51] Lohmann (1913); on the period before 1893, see Schimmelpfennig (1859).
[52] A. Wagner (1901), part 4, pp. 64ff.

local authorities are corporations somewhere between the individual and the state, with limited authoritative functions in the provision of public amenities and services (local authority duties) and corresponding rights (*inter alia* revenues from landed property, productive property, fees), including executive power. Within the widely ramified apparatus of local authorities, there existed in the old Prussian provinces the independent estates which had grown out of seventeenth- and eighteenth-century manors, resembling local authorities in their functions. On such independent estates – as for instance also in the kingdom of Saxony – the head of the estate was vested with the headship of local and police authority inherent in the estate ownership. 'Ownership' meant that such an estate (*patrimonium manor*) could be bought and sold by aristocratic or bourgeois individuals, local authority public rights and duties attaching to ownership – remnants of traditional *nobilitas realis*. 'Police authority' meant executive rather than judicial authority. In 1877, an act of the imperial German legal system removed the last remnants of manorial or private jurisdiction (patrimonial jurisdiction), formerly forming part of estate ownership, for the whole of Germany, such removal having been undertaken in principle in 1848, but not fully carried through.

Within the fiscal system, local authorities depended for their revenues on surcharges on state taxes in supplementing their own incomes. When in 1893 revenue taxes were assigned to local authorities and thus also to independent estates for the finance of local authority–estate functions, independent estates received both public and private revenues (independent estate self-finance), not always in detail strictly separate, to defray public and private duties and expenditure. This was an enduring survival from the confusion, usual in the eighteenth century, of public-authority and private aristocratic competence and criss-crossing of interests resulting therefrom. However, the dual flow of funds in both directions, particularly evident after 1893, must not be simplified into the conclusion that estate owners' exemption from land tax, cancelled in 1861, had been restored by the local authority finance reform of 1893; even less can we conclude that landowners had to pay for local authority–estate public duties out of privately earned income.

The tax incidence on incomes
The completely new organization of the system of direct taxes after the establishment of the Reich changed the incidence on taxpayers. The aims of the reform were an increase in tax burden, a shift in its incidence in the direction of a higher yield from those earning more and a higher taxation of unearned (= funded) compared to earned (= unfunded) income. Together with the perceived long-term rise in taxable income, these three aims were to increase public revenue from direct taxes. Assuming families otherwise similar, but receiving either only earned or only

Table 74. *Incidence of direct taxes as percentage of earned and unearned incomes, 1874 and 1914*

Annual income (marks)	Incidence on earned income[a] (% p.a.)		Change of cash amount of tax (%) 1874–1914	Incidence on unearned income[b] (% per annum)		Change of cash amount of tax (%) 1874–1914
	1874	1914		1874	1914	
500	(6)[c]	—		(6)[c]	—	—
3,000	2.4	1.8	− 24.2	2.4	3.4	+ 39.7
5,000	2.9	2.6	− 9.9	2.9	4.2	+ 45.0
12,000	2.7	3.5	+ 27.8	2.7	5.0	+ 84.6
25,000	2.6	3.6	+ 38.9	2.6	5.2	+ 101.8
50,000	2.9	4.2	+ 45.8	2.9	5.8	+ 102.4
100,000	2.9	4.9	+ 69.3	2.9	6.5	+ 125.9

Notes:
[a] Of graduated tax, graduated income tax or universal income tax.
[b] As in note (a) plus property tax, but without revenue tax.
[c] Abolished 1883.
Source: Calculated from Gerloff (1916), p. 40.

Table 75. *Earned and unearned incomes in the German Reich, 1874 and 1914*

	Net domestic national income	Earned income	Unearned income	Average annual earned income (in marks)
	in million marks			
1874	14,709	11,285	3,424	559
1914	48,236	34,112	14,124	1,084
Index of change 1914 (1874 = 1)	3.3	3.0	4.1	1.9

Source: Hoffmann (1965), pp. 492ff., 506ff. Data for Prussia not available.

unearned income, the consequences on incidence are illustrated in Table 74.

The surcharge made by the towns and larger countryside local authorities on the income tax reached an average of 187 per cent in 1913.[53] The trend of tax reforms thus achieved the intended shifts in tax incidence, additionally relieving from tax the lower classes of earned

[53] Gerloff (1916), p. 42, Appendix.

Table 76. *Incidence of state and local authority taxation as percentage of income, 1900–8*

Income class (marks)	Total incidence according to		Incidence attributable to customs duties and consumption dues only, according to	
	Gerloff	Conrad	Gerloff	Conrad
Below 800	5.6–7.7		4.4–6.5	
Below 900		4.72–6.05		3.56–5.12
800–1,200	6.2–8.1		4.4–6.3	
900–1,200		5.38–8.1		3.68–5.08
1,200–1,500		5.38–6.63		2.98
1,500–2,000		8.07–10.07		4.07
1,200–2,000	7.4–8.9		3.6–5.1	
2,000–3,000		6.67–10.12		1.82–2.17
2,000–4,000	7.0–8.0		2.2–3.2	
4,000–6,000	8.1–8.7		1.3–1.9	
3,000–10,000		10.22– 13.94		1.11–1.33

Sources: Gerloff (1909), p. 456; sample surveyed 180 households of urban workers' families and middle-class families during 1900–5; places of sample in German Empire not known; not counting revenue taxes. Mistakes in addition in original.
Conrad (1908): sample surveyed presumably 30 households with supplements from around 1901–8; place of sample Halle an der Saale, Prussia; includes revenue taxes. Mistakes in addition in original. See also Cohn (1899), pp. 172f.

income recipients by the level of tax rate. Presumably the proportional incidence on other groups of earned and unearned income recipients also dropped, as Table 75 appears to indicate: incomes rose faster than direct taxes. At 900 marks in 1913, the lower tax exemption threshold was close to average annual earned income.

Linking tax statistics to macro-economic data is difficult, not so much perhaps because of the different territorial catchment areas to which they refer, but because definitions of earned and unearned incomes differ in tax assessment and national income calculations.

Progression in direct taxes contrasted with regression in indirect taxes.[54] An indication of total tax burden is given by sample enquiries in private household budgets (see Table 76).

[54] The care required in delimiting direct from indirect taxes is shown by the example of Saxony. The Royal Saxon Statistical Office in 1913 enumerated pragmatically as direct taxes: income tax, land tax, capitation tax, rent tax, liquor and restaurant licences, wholesale to retail sales, retail liquor sales and itinerant trading establishments; indirect taxes: fees on change of hands of property, capital gains tax, dog licences, entertainment fees, surcharges on slaughter tax and brewing malt tax, tax on ale, other dues on articles of use or consumption and all other fees expressed in money; from Gerloff (1916), p. 15, n. 1.

Retrospect

The reforms of 1891 and 1893 represented a great step forward in three directions:

1. The almost complete elimination of antiquated direct 'objective' revenue taxes on the basis of objective indicators for which was substituted a universal income tax system, consisting of income tax and an independent new supplementary tax, the property tax. To a degree, the inheritance tax of 1873, levied independently, formed part of it, but remained insignificant even after minor modifications in 1891 and cannot be compared with the substantial elaboration of this special type of property tax in Britain and France.

2. The tentative approach of the state tax system to the 'social question'. The incompatibility between Bismarck's social legislation on the one hand and state taxation – which rather ignored social considerations and favoured capital accumulation and growth – on the other hand, was diminished. Well-to-do and richer recipients of income, of revenue from capital and entrepreneurial profits which had arisen in the course of industrial growth throughout the long period of peace were taxed somewhat more heavily and thus more fairly than before. This change, which affected various private interests, was facilitated by reinterpreting the demand for justice which continued to enjoy high esteem: the tax burden should now reflect individual economic capacity to pay, and need thus no longer necessarily exclude an infringement of horizontal justice, that is, a redistribution of incomes through taxation.

It became evident that taxation of revenue from capital did not inhibit accumulation of private capital, so important for the industrial development in the nineteenth century; such accumulation was no longer to remain tax-privileged to the previous extent – which often enough had meant having been exempt altogether.

However, in the long view, at the heart of the foundation of income tax in the new tax system was not the social welfare component, but the state's claim on the growing mass income of an ever increasing part of the population in an industrial country. This led in the twentieth century both to the financial foundation of the so-called 'welfare' or 'interventionist state' – intervening for varying purposes in economic policy – and to the fiscal technical tool used by such a state for intervention by taxation in the process of social budgeting. The mercantilist sovereign's direct decree found a parallel, adapted to a market system, in the instruments of economic intervention in pursuit of the new fiscal and monetary policy. The 'nightwatchman state' had never been more than a fiction; now even that fiction no longer existed.

3. The third step forward was the attempt to establish a workable and reasonably flexible new financial order for local authorities. Conflicts between the interests of government and local fiscal authorities, hitherto caused *inter alia* by local authorities' surcharges on state taxes, were noticeably reduced. Local authorities were given local rates, fees, and contributions to administer largely in their own ways: modified land and building taxes, newly organized business tax, and mining royalties. Local authority decrees regulated the type and level of fees and contributions chargeable for goods and services provided by them. The local authorities' far-reaching independence in regulating their revenues corresponded to their multiple functions in the education system (elementary, middle, and higher schools, institutions for sport and culture), in welfare (health care and support of the unemployed), in infra-structure (roads, paths, short-distance transport; public utilities, such as gas, water, electricity, canalization) and in local aspects of administration (from registers of birth to cemetery maintenance).

Wise as was the step forward, it proved too short in subsequent years: the local authorities' tasks and expenditure grew faster than the income-inelastic former revenue taxes. Much as in the relation of Reich to member states, so in that of member states to local authorities, the financial settlement was the sensitive Achilles' heel as between delegation of functions and centralization of revenues. Local authorities after 1893 once again levied surcharges which in the last pre-war years averaged around 190 per cent of income tax.[55] However, the level of surcharges on state tax now was tied by law to the rise in the local authority's own taxes. No longer could a local authority spare local landowners via surcharges on state taxes at the expense of their landless neighbours who paid only state taxes. That was one of the detailed problems of tax incidence.

(vi) State indebtedness and national income, 1794–1913

The expenditure item of 'debt service' in the budget increased in money terms throughout the period under review, but as a proportion of total it fluctuated between extremes of 6.4 per cent (in 1875, reduction of debt by use of French reparation monies) and 18.4 per cent (in 1895, investment in the railway sector). As the item of debt service comprises both interest and capital repayment at levels subject to change by legislation, an indication of public debt in total and per head of population is more informative than in relation to total budget. It can also advantageously

[55] See n. 53 above.

Table 77. *Public debt and national income, 1794–1913*

	National income		Public debt		
	In million marks	Per head (marks)	In million marks	Per head (marks)	Population (millions)
1794	?	?	144	16.8	8.6
1807	?	?	160	32.7	4.9
1815	2,031	197	863	83.7	10.3
1820	2,333	210	652	58.5	11.1
1841	3,788	252	525	34.8	15.0
1848	4,382	270	475	29.4	16.2
1856	4,742	274	743	42.9	17.3
1866	5,923	303	870	44.4	19.5
1869	7,849	324	1,302	53.8	24.2
1872	8,804	355	1,248	50.3	24.8
1882	10,054	364	2,686	97	27.6
1892	12,940	422	6,240	204	30.6
1902	17,691	499	6,721	189	35.4
1913	30,184	725	9,421	226	41.6
Index of change 1913 (1815 = 1)	14.9	3.7	10.9	2.7	4.0

Sources: National income: net national income at factor cost; Hoffman and Müller (1959), p. 86 for figures from 1856; previous years calculated from Hohorst (1977), pp. 133, 276f. 1 taler = 3 marks.
Public debt: Funded debt: Reden (1856), vol. II, pp. 5ff., 80, 620ff., 629ff., 666ff. Heckel (1911), vol. II, pp. 494ff.; slightly different Strutz (1902), vol. I, section 3, appendix V, pp. 20ff.; Gerloff (1929), pp. 38f.
Population: from Hohorst (1977), pp. 127, 131f.

cover a longer period[56] (see Table 77). The violent changes in debt around 1815 are accounted for by wars, territorial changes and transfers of reparations, those around 1866 by the assumption of the debts of territories annexed after the German–Austrian war and again by transfers of reparations. Debts between 1882 and 1902 were predominantly on account of railways, 96.6 per cent in 1882, 89 in 1892, 62 in 1902, then falling to 33.9 per cent in 1908.[57]

The inclusion in the public debt of substantial sums incurred as debt by state productive enterprises makes it difficult to draw an international comparison with countries where the equivalant enterprises were in private hands. Further neither in Prussia nor in the other German federal states did the state budgets from 1871/2 onwards include military expen-

---

[56] On state indebtedness see Krug (1861); Sattler (1893); Schwarz and Strutz (1904), vol. III; Borchard (1968), pp. 78ff.; Klein (1974), pp. 112f., 119ff.; division of Reich debt up to 1908 in Reichschatsamt Treasury Office (1908), pp. 28ff. [57] Heckel (1911), vol. II, p. 500.

diture, so that once-and-for-all expenditure on armed forces could no longer be shown as part of state indebtedness; this makes a comparison with other nations, such as Britain or France, fairly meaningless; we therefore abstain from such a comparison.

(vii) Structure of state budgets, 1847–1913

A comparison of Prussian budgets[58] for the long period from 1848–57 to 1913 is difficult for two reasons: in the first place, the territorial change of 1866 constituted a discontinuity, Prussian budget structure being influenced by the budget structures of the regions incorporated. In the second place, the establishment of the German Reich in 1871 and the division of functions and revenues between Reich and member states led to a reduction in all member states' budgets, Prussia included; on the revenue side, indirect taxes largely disappeared, on the expenditure side the military item. Up to 1871, both had been such important budget components that a comparison of budgets is meaningful only up to 1870 and subsequently from 1872 onwards. A little less troublesome is the change from net to gross budgets after 1850, as its effect can be calculated, as well as the change of the currency unit from taler to mark (1 taler = 3 marks), in conjunction with the decimalization of 1871–3.

Period before the establishment of the Reich, 1847–70

The 2.5-fold increase of the budget total between 1847 and 1870 is due chiefly to the 3.2-fold increase of revenues from state properties. By far the leading sector within these revenues consisted of mines, smelters, and salt refineries with a 13.3-fold growth – a remarkable result, which explains the view, based on the self-interest of the state, that all basic raw material industries ought to be nationalized. Revenue from state enterprises accounted for more than 44 per cent of total revenue. In second place was the increase in the budget total derived from a 2.7-fold rise in indirect taxes. Below this growth remained the income from public lands and forests, now relatively insignificant, though rising 2.1-fold as the result of a long-term upswing in agriculture. Taken all in all, the state was evidently a successful entrepreneur during this period. Figures of gross expenditure correspondingly showed the greatest increase (3.3-fold) in entrepreneurial expenditure and debt service (2.9-fold). Clearly continuing a trend exhibited since 1821, the share of military expenditure fell to 25.4 per cent in 1867, whereas the residual of civil (with debt service) grew to 74.6 per cent. This again shows continuation of internal

---

[58] Herrfurth (1905); Kaufmann (1900).

Table 78. Prussia's state revenue, 1847–70 (gross budget values)^a (1 taler = 3 marks)

Type of revenue	1847 Million taler	%	1857 Million taler	%	1867 Million taler	%	1870 Million taler	%	Index of change 1870 (1847 = 1)
1. Entrepreneurial revenue, of which	29.5	34.7	55.6	45.3	87.2	50.8	94.6	44.4	3.2
public lands and forests	11.4	13.4	12.0	9.8	15.8	9.2	24.2	11.4	2.1
smelters, salt refineries	1.7	2.0	13.7	11.2	17.8	10.4	22.6	10.6	13.3
railways	—	—	6.5	5.3	19.6	11.4	35.3	16.6	—
2. Taxes	34.8	41.0	41.1	33.5	56.8	33.1	81.7	38.4	2.4
Direct taxes of which	20.3	23.9	24.7	20.1	32.7	19.1	42.8	20.1	2.1
graduated tax	7.4	8.7	11.0	9.0	13.4	7.8	18.2	8.5	2.5
revenue tax	12.9	15.2	13.7	11.2	19.3	11.3	24.6	11.6	1.9
Indirect taxes of which	14.5	17.1	16.4	13.4	24.1	14.1	38.9^b	18.3	2.7
stamps	4.2	4.9	3.6	2.9	5.5	3.2	6.7	3.1	1.6
consumption tax	9.6	11.3	12.8	10.4	18.6	10.8	32.2^b	15.1	3.4
3. Customs duties	13.8	16.3	12.3	10.0	11.2	6.5	19.4^c	9.1	1.4
4. Miscellaneous^d	6.8	8.0	13.8	11.2	16.3	9.5	17.2	8.1	2.5
Sum total 1–4: ordinary revenue^a	84.9	100	122.8	100	171.5	100	212.9^b,c (170.1)	100	2.5

Notes:
^a The distinction between 'gross' and 'net' varies; even the so-called gross budget contained some net revenue items, e.g. stamp and legal fees, revenues from the Seehandlung (State Bank) and salt monopoly; see Wagner (1901), part 4, pp. 5off., and the attempt there made to contrast gross and net budgets for 1821, 1838, 1847, 1867; Borchard's (1968) juxtaposition, pp. 33, 39, 42.
^b Consumption tax revenues of 25.12 million taler of these transferred to North German Federation.
^c Customs duties of 17.68 million taler of these transferred to North German Federation.
^d Mainly general administrative revenue and fees.

Sources: Gesetz-Sammlung für die Königlichen Preussischen Staaten 1847, 1857, 1866, 1869; territories: old Prussia budgets 1847–67, including new territories, Hanover, etc., after 1868.

consolidation. In 1870, military expenditure was part of the budget of the North German Federation.[59] (See Tables 78 and 79.)

The period after the establishment of the Reich, 1875–1913

The reduction of the size of the budget after the establishment of the Reich after 1871 was less significant than might have been expected, because of the incidence of matricular contributions and transfers. The total budget increased six-fold at an accelerating pace, again supported by the growth of the income of productive enterprises which remained well above average. While the leading sector in the previous period had been heavy industry, now it was railway services. Income from state enterprises in 1913 accounted for 75.4 per cent of ordinary public revenue.[60] This brought the public budget close to the business balance sheet of a large-scale entrepreneur. To assess it correctly would require the application of business criteria, above all depreciation, valuations, terminal balances, and profit-and-loss accounts; this has not hitherto been done. All other revenue items clearly grew more slowly than the budget total, tax revenue in fact only at half its rate. This is explained by the low tax burden imposed on the entire Prussian population, whatever the inequality in individual tax incidence. To put it in a nutshell, the population financed state expenditure by the purchase of railway tickets rather than by tax payments (see Table 80).

A large-scale entrepreneurial state differs from a state without experience in business activity. On the supply side, the state was perhaps a monopolist; on the demand side, it invariably competed with private entrepreneurs. Alongside particular private interests which influenced the state 'from the outside', there must have been economic interests originating 'on the inside' of the state itself, represented by the closely interlinked state administrative and state entrepreneurial bureaucracies. Further, the immediate and direct contact of the state with the actual material situation requiring economic action must have differed from a merely indirect contact filtered through groups of varying attitudes represented in parliament. It is not unreasonable to surmise that such direct economic influence on the state, exercised upward from below – and the reciprocal state influence on the economy downward from above – must have been more intensive than those indicated by slogans

---

[59] Shares in expenditure as in 1870 can be compared to those of previous years only by remembering that there was no longer any military expenditure. The share of civil expenditure is a residual, including the debt service, which contains some military elements which cannot be precisely indicated.

[60] The Prussian property in heavy industry was, however, substantial. Among state establishments in 1899 were 17 coal, 8 lignite, 7 ore, 4 salt, 4 copper, silver and other mines, 10 smelters, 6 salt refineries; see for this with fiscal details, Schwarz and Strutz (1900), section 2; on public lands and forests, *ibid.*, section 1.

Table 79. Prussia's state expenditure, 1847–70 (gross budget values) (1 taler = 3 marks)

Type of expenditure	1847		1857		1867		1870		Index of change 1870 (1847 = 1)
	Million taler	% of III	Million taler	% of III	Million taler	% of III	Million taler	% of III	
1. Defence	25.7	30.3	29.5	24.0	43.4	25.4	—ᵃ	—	—
2. Administration of enterprises	16.1	19.0	36.3	29.6	44.4	26.0	52.9	24.9	3.3
3. Debt service	9.3	11.0	13.2	10.8	16.3	9.5	26.6	12.5	2.9
4. Central administration	2.8	3.3	1.2	1.0	1.6	0.9	0.7	0.3	0.3
5. Central fiscal administration	0.1	0.1	3.0	2.4	4.8	2.8	25.8ᵇ	12.1	258.0
6. Domestic administration	11.5	13.5	12.9	10.5	14.7	8.6	21.1	9.9	1.8
of which economy and traffic	8.3	9.8	6.9	5.6	8.1	4.7	11.0	5.2	1.3
7. Jurisdiction	6.5	7.7	10.7	8.7	12.1	7.1	17.1	8.0	2.6
8. Culture and education	2.9	3.4	3.2	2.6	4.2	2.5	5.7	2.7	2.0
9. Miscellaneousᶜ	10.0	11.8	7.7	6.3	14.2	8.3	14.9	7.0	1.5
I. Sum total 1–9: ordinary expenditure	84.9	100	117.7	95.9	155.7	91.1	164.8	77.4	1.9
II. Total extraordinary expenditure	—	—	5.1	4.2	15.3	9.0	5.8 42.8ᵈ	20.1	—
III. Total expenditure I and II	84.9	100	122.8	100	171.0	100	212.9 (170.6)	100	2.5

459

Notes:

[a] Defence no longer shown, forms part of North German Federation expenditure; see note [d].

[b] Contribution from this item to North German Federation expenditure 18.8 million taler.

[c] Mainly fiscal administration and pensions.

[d] 42.8 million taler shown are consumption taxes and duties remitted to the North German Federation; see notes [b] and [c] to Table 77. Allocation of these items to extraordinary expenditure is the author's. The original Prussian budget omits this amount both on the revenue and expenditure side, in addition to an annual remittance of about 2.5 million taler to the crown property trust fund. The North German Federation probably used the 42.8 million taler for military purposes. The author therefore, in extending the comparison of Prussian budget balances down to 1870, does not take into account the allocation of that amount to any particular expenditure items, but includes it in its entirety in extraordinary expenditure. Percentages for 1870 are calculated accordingly.

Source: Gesetz-Sammlung für die Königlichen Preussischen Staaten 1847, 1857, 1866, 1869.

Table 80. *Prussia's state revenue (gross budget values), 1875–1913*

| | (1) Total ordinary revenue (million marks) | (2) Of which as % of (1) | | | | | (3) Total extra-ordinary revenue (million marks) | (4) of which as % of (3) | | | (5) Total (1) + (3) = total revenue (million marks) |
| | | Entrepreneurial revenue | | Direct tax | Indirect tax | Transfers from Reich | | Surpluses | Entrepreneurial revenue | Debt increase | |
		Total	Railway only								
1875	664.9	57.9	24.7	22.0	6.9	—	306.7	42.0	26.6	1.5	971.6
1882	1,000.0	62.2	43.3	14.7	5.0	5.1	213.8	30.4	56.7	1.4	1,213.8
1892	1,815.6	67.1	50.8	9.9	3.9	12.0	262.8	42.2	40.6	17.2	2,078.4
1902	2,685.1	66.5	52.4	8.4	3.4	12.7	373.7	54.9	45.1	—	3,058.8
1913	4,418.0	75.4	57.2	10.4	2.8	3.4	1,678.0	18.3	81.7	—	6,096.1
Index of change 1913 (1875=1)[a]	6.6	8.7	15.4	3.1	2.7	—	5.5	2.4	16.8	6.3	6.3

Notes:

1 taler = 3 marks.

[a] Index of change calculated from absolute revenue figures.

Sources: Jahrbuch für die amtliche Statistik des Preussischen Staates (1883), vol. v; *Statistical Handbook for the Prussian State* (1888), vol. i; (1898), vol. iii; *Statistisches Jahrbuch für den Preussischen Staat* (1903 and relevant years).

relating to important sectors, such as 'policy of agrarian and industrial interests' and 'state orders placed with the private sector'. The subject matter here alluded to, involving a constellation of *three* poles of power and interest – agrarian interests, industrial interests, and the interests of the state administrative and state entrepreneurial bureaucracies, without even including the military power – is so largely unknown that we cannot even as yet formulate questions which would separate out the problems raised.

Entrepreneurial expenditure and debt service between them in 1913 required 69.6 per cent of ordinary expenditure. Of the remainder, 'culture and education' took up slightly more than 7 per cent; this was the item which, after entrepreneurial revenues and debt service, grew fastest (see Table 81). The omnibus description of 'culture and education' covered *inter alia* the state's *de facto* educational and training monopoly, 'the state' in this instance because of the stratification of authorities standing for all public authorities. The expansion of schooling and training, of the personal infrastructure, the production of 'human capital', was a priority. By 1860–70, illiteracy had practically disappeared. However, far more 'striking, even singular'[61] in international comparison was the very high proportion of each cohort from the early nineteenth century onwards passing through the full eight years of elementary schooling (see Table 82). As against the 3.5-fold population increase between 1822 and 1911, there was a higher increase in the number of students in all educational institutions. Especially high was the growth of pupils attending the secondary (grammar) schools and technical colleges. The systematic increase of these technical colleges, concerned specifically with occupational training for middle and higher management, above all in the agricultural, mining and industrial sectors, was considered a veritable Prusso-German speciality. Without this mass production of knowledge, which the government either enforced, or furthered, the entire economy of Prussia and Germany could not have grown so fast in the nineteenth century, especially in the industrial sector (see Table 83). Public expenditure on education is specified in Table 84.

Behind these amounts of cash, there looms something (in part) still visible today: the typically 'imperial' (elementary) school building, a fairly standardized design by Prussian state architects during the building boom of the 1870s and after. There are – slightly earlier – parallels in the shape of (rural) railway stations and imperial railway buildings, centrally designed and built by similar state architects.

[61] Lundgreen (1973), p. 93; on expenditure for art see Feldenkirchen (1892).

Table 81. *Prussia's state expenditure (gross budget values), 1875–1913*

	(1) Total ordinary expenditure (million marks)	(2) of which as % of (1)					Total (3) extra-ordinary expenditure (million marks)	(4) of which as % of (3)		(5) Total (1) + (3) = total expenditure (million marks)
		Entrepreneurial administration	Administration and jurisdiction[a]	Debt service	Culture and education	Matricular contribution to Reich		Debt service	Entrepreneurial administration	
1875	605.4	39.8	33.6	6.1	6.5	5.3	207.2	41.0	8.1	812.6
1882	953.8	44.3	24.7	13.1	5.0	5.5	184.1	73.0	2.7	1,137.9
1892	1,802.1	43.7	19.1	15.2	5.6	10.7	191.6	55.2	6.6	1,993.6
1902	2,519.6	45.3	15.4	11.7	5.9	14.1	358.4	—	69.6	2,878.0
1913	4,172.2	58.5	14.5	11.1	7.0	3.8	1,745.7	45.6	41.9	5,917.9
Index of change 1913 (1875 = 1)[b]	6.9	10.1	3.0	12.6	7.5	5.0	8.4	9.4	43.4	7.3

Notes:
[a] Administration includes central, domestic, and revenue administration.
[b] Index of change calculated from absolute expenditure figures.
Source: As Table 79.

Table 82. *Percentage distribution of male population in Prussia with no schooling (illiterates) and with eight years of schooling (full elementary schooling), 1800–76*

Years of birth	Elementary school attendance	
	No schooling	8 years at school
	as % of cohort	
1800–9	18.08	78.83
1830–9	4.73	91.47
1857–66	2.72	90.51
1867–76	0.0	93.27

Source: Lundgreen (1973), p. 92. Shortfall from 100 per cent represents pupils attending school for more than eight years.

Table 83. *Male students in Prussia, 1822–1911, according to educational institutions (thousands)*

	Public elementary schools	Secondary schools, grammar schools	Universities	Technical and higher training colleges[a]
1822	743	24	4	3
1855	1,323	62	5	5
1873	1,925	127	7	11
1891	2,467	157	13	16
1911	3,293	267	27	32
Index of change 1911 (1822 = 1)	4.4	11.1	6.7	10.6

Note:
[a] Teacher training colleges, technical high schools, academies of mining and forestry, agricultural and veterinary high schools, schools for machinery construction and textiles.
Source: Lundgreen (1973), p. 152. Leaves out of account middle and private schools and high schools for girls.

Table 84. *Public expenditure on education, 1864–1911, according to educational institutions (million marks)*

	Public elementary schools	Boys' secondary and grammar schools	Universities	Technical and higher training colleges[a]
1864	33.0	7.7	?	?
1873	?	20.4	6.8	?
1891	129.0	30.9	13.5	8.2
1901	227.6	54.0	17.3	14.7
1911	420.9	90.0	23.4	25.2

Note:
[a] Teacher training colleges, technical high schools, academies of mining and forestry, agricultural and veterinary colleges, schools for machinery construction and textiles.
Source: Lundgreen (1973), p. 111. Leaves out of account middle schools and high schools for girls.

IV. *The fiscal economy of the German Reich and the relationship between Reich and member states*[1]

1. *The federal structure of the German Federation of States*

Francis II, Habsburg emperor, renounced the imperial crown on 6 August 1806. The Holy Roman Empire of the German Nation existed no longer. The Congress of Vienna in 1815 achieved the metamorphosis of the erstwhile empire into a German Federation – a federation of princes from 35 almost sovereign federal states (monarchies) and four imperial cities. The insignificant functions of the German Federation, a weak central body, did not warrant the development of a fiscal system. Thus, the customs union of 1833/4 and the North German Federation of 1866 were the forerunners of the establishment of the German Reich in 1871 – and simultaneously steps towards a federal and ultimately imperial fiscal system.[2] The process of territorial concentration continued after 1866. The Reich in 1871 comprised 26 member states, including Alsace-Lorraine. After 1815, each member state had worked out its own tax system. Individual state parliaments had exclusive rights to grant taxes; the system of public budgets was institutionalized. The growing econ-

[1] The research for this section was generously supported by the Volkswagen Foundation.
[2] Details on fiscal systems of the North German Federation and the German Reich in Gerloff (1913); Cohn (1899); Eheberg (1908); Zimmermann (1916); Witt (1970), with a detailed list of sources and literature.

omic integration of the federal states after 1833, necessitating the regulation of their fiscal relationships with the relevant central organization. Allowing for fiscal continuity, these relationships were finalized in principle by the imperial constitution of 1871, reflecting the distinctly federal structure of the German Reich.

2. Functions and sources of finance of Reich and member states

The fiscal systems of Reich and member states were conditioned by their respective functions which determined the expenditure of the Reich and the states. Consequently, the expenditures had to have certain revenues assigned to them.

According to the constitution, the Reich's functions were to

1. safeguard the external interests of the German Reich: armed forces, defence, diplomatic representation;
2. take care of supra-state internal common interests: rule of law, traffic (supervision, coordination), post and telegraphy, patent protection – above all, maintenance of economic unity through tariff and commercial legislation, the central banking system, standardization of weights and measures. From the 1880s onwards were added obligations arising from the social welfare legislation.

To fulfil these functions, the Reich received authority to legislate on, and draw revenue from (1) customs duties, (2) indirect consumption taxes on salt, tobacco, liquor, sugar, and beer; there were some special arrangements and special lump sum payments (equalization contributions) in relation to the south German states of Baden, Württemberg, and Bavaria; (3) some indirect transaction taxes (*inter alia* bills of exchange stamps). The states raised and administered customs duties and indirect taxes, paying over to the Reich net revenue after deducting a moderate administration fee. Finally, the Reich received (4) the working surpluses from the postal and telegraph system, plus the railway system of Alsace-Lorraine taken over from France in 1871, and a few minor surpluses from central institutions, such as the imperial printing works. If these revenues proved insufficient to defray current imperial expenditure, the states had to cover the deficit with (5) matricular contributions from the member states proportional to their population. Given analogous functions, this represented substantially the provision of ways and means as it had existed in the North German Federation.[3]

As the Reichstag was inclined to increase total imperial expenditure,

---

[3] Compilation of the North German Federation budget in Gerloff (1913), pp. 34ff.

above all the military budget, beyond the matricular contributions of member states, the Reich had to obtain additional revenue through (6) floating imperial loans. This complied in the first place formally with the traditional budgetary principle requiring current expenditure to be defrayed from ordinary revenue, non-recurrent expenditure from extra-ordinary revenue, the latter including incurring debt. In fact, the problem of imperial revenue involved the power of the Reichstag, jealously guarded, but not entirely unambiguously regulated by the constitution of 1871, to authorize revenue and control the budget.

Corresponding to the functions of the Reich, as limited by the imperial constitution, member states enjoyed a wide field of exclusive responsibility in the realms of jurisdiction and police, economy, transport, culture and education, public health, welfare and infrastructure. Member states' revenues were the direct taxes, stamps and working surpluses from the management of public lands, forests, mines and smelters, railways, and other public enterprises, supplemented by state loans. The structuring of the tax systems and fiscal administration were a matter for individual states; in principle, there were as many different tax systems as member states. North German states, guided by Prussia and Saxony, tended more towards the British system of personal taxes, South German states and Austria more towards French revenue taxes.

3. Financial settlement between Reich and member states – and consequent Reich indebtedness

(i) Financial settlement [4]

Monetary payments of matricular contributions from member states to the Reich were the primary part of the financial settlement between these two types of territorial authorities. This unidirectional flow of payments determined the financial settlement from 1872 to 1878. This changed in 1879 when – in a second phase of the financial settlement – a flow of payments not originally foreseen was siphoned back from the Reich to the member states, entitled remittances. This was the result of the Reich's newly designed protectionist policy. After a short spell of free trade–liberal commercial and tariff policy on the part of the Reich until 1878, there was a return to revenue and protective tariffs which accorded with agrarian and iron-making interests as well as with Bismarck's wishes. Member states managed to slow down the Reich's expected surplus revenue and its resulting gain in financial strength; the states' financial interests and their endeavour not to let the Reich become too wealthy and financially independent led to the famous Frankenstein clause of

---

[4] Popitz (1926); Popitz (1927); Stumpp (1964); Albers (1961).

1879: any yield of customs duties and tobacco taxes in excess of 130 million marks was to be refunded by the Reich to member states in proportion to their populations (this limit to remittances being raised to 143 million marks in 1896, 180 million marks in 1897). In this manner, the Reichstag secured for itself, alongside the right of authorizing expenditure, in fact also the right to authorize revenue.

Bismarck's plan to disentangle Reich from state finances, to strengthen the Reich's financial power by means of an undiminished increase and development of customs duties and indirect taxes accruing to the Reich, and if possible to render the Reich financially independent of member states by means of Reich-originated taxes, thus foundered as did his attempt in 1877 to amalgamate the railways of the member states into one imperial railway, which would have secured to the Reich a large and profitable business asset. Bismarck's preference for indirect taxes grew out of his preference for strong central government; already in 1872 he had asserted the need for German superiority over all second-rate maritime powers.[5] Emphasis on indirect taxation, inherent in the establishment of the Reich, ran counter to the trend of general European tax discussion which stressed direct income taxation, whereas strong central government was wholly in harmony with contemporary trends. Bismarck was unable to resolve this contradictory element in the Reich constitution. In spite of further attempts at reform, the Reich remained what it had been from the beginning: a pensioner of the member states, a beggar at their doors. The Reich remained tied fast to the network of interests of the individual states.

The flows of funds deriving from the financial settlement, from member states to Reich and then back from Reich to states, are summarized in Table 85 so as to show for each period the net recipient (Reich or states). The rapidly rising volume of financial flows from the 1890s onwards and the persistent balance in favour of member states caused the Reich to desire a fundamental fiscal reform. Between 1896 and 1898, the details of the Frankenstein clause were changed in the Reich's favour on several occasions – and immediately afterwards the first navy law passed the Reichstag (April 1898). In spite of hold-ups by resistance from the ranks of the Reichstag, a major financial reform (lex Sydow)[6] eventually resulted in 1909 by way of the small lex Stengel (1904) and the large lex Stengel (1906). The indirect taxes due to the Reich were increased; an inheritance tax was introduced for the first time; distribution of monetary flows arising from the financial settlement was changed so as noticeably to reduce the volume of payments. But the situation did not change in principle: the Reich remained a pensioner of the member states

---

[5] From Gerloff (1913), p. 79.
[6] For the individual reforms, Witt (1970), pp. 8off., 94ff., 199ff.; Wolf (1909).

Table 85. *Financial settlement between Reich and member states,*
1872–1913/19 (million marks)

	Flow of funds					
	From states to Reich: matricular contributions[a]		From Reich to states: remittances		Balance in favour of	
	Total	Annual average	Total	Annual average	Reich	Member states
1872–78	183.9	26.27	—	—	183.9	
1879–87	1,003.7	111.52	817.4	90.82	186.3	
1888–98	3,836.4	348.76	4,191.1	381.0		354.7
1899–1911	4,454.3	342.64	4,084.1	314.16	370.2	
1912–13	103.8	51.9	398.6	199.3		294.8
1914–19	278	46.3	1,016.5	169.42		738.5

Note:
[a] Includes settlement payments of the South German states arising from their rights of reserving some indirect taxes; excludes lump sums (aversa) from some customs enclaves outside the Reich boundaries
Source: Stumpp (1964), Appendix.

– and its military budget continued to rely on imperial loans. Insufficient current revenue led to a delimitation, not always unambiguously drawn, between ordinary and extraordinary revenue and expenditure.[7]

(ii) Reich indebtedness

The situation from the later 1880s onwards was thus almost grotesque: a financially rather weak Reich remitting funds to financially rather strong member states and thus rapidly incurring more and more debt so as to defray its expenditure. That alone can explain why, while between 1872/4 and 1910–13 the sum of all customs duties and imperial taxes rose from 228 to 1,624 million marks, the Reich's indebtedness increased substantially.[8] At its establishment in 1871 the Reich had been free from debt; up to 1876/7, it had paid its non-recurring military expenditure (army and navy) mainly out of the French war indemnity, which totalled 4,207 million marks[9] (see Table 86). The concept of matricular contributions was as inappropriate as possible for lump-sum financing of military expenditure. The first imperial loan had to be issued in 1877.[10]

---

[7] Gerloff (1929), p. 16.
[8] Division of total debt according to types of debt and purpose of expenditure in Reichsschatsamt (1908), pp. 28ff.   [9] Gerloff (1913), pp. 82ff.
[10] Reichsschatsamt (1908), p. 76.

Table 86. *The Reich debt, 1877–1914*

	Reich indebtedness		Population (millions)
	Million marks	Marks per head of population	
1877	16	0.37	43.6
1880	218	4.8	45.1
1885	410	8.8	46.7
1890	1,118	22.7	49.2
1895	2,081	40.0	52.0
1900	2,298	41.0	56.0
1905	3,203	53.1	60.3
1910	4,844	75.0	64.6
April 1914	5,200	77.6	c. 67.0
Index of change 1914 (1877 = 1)	319	209	1.5

Sources: Funded debt: Gerloff (1913), p. 521; Deutsche Bundesbank (1976), p. 153. Population: Hoffman (1965), pp..172ff.

In the face of the rapid increase in debt, a law (1st *lex* Lieber) was passed in 1896 designed to lay down a rate of debt redemption. This financial technique, prescribed by budget law and the Reichstag for defraying the officially extraordinary once-and-for-all expenditure by means of loans, was used by the Reich in attempting in 1914 to finance the war: war expenditure was to be part of the extraordinary imperial budget, to be financed by extraordinary means.

This relationship of imperial loans and creation of money by the Reichsbank and loan banks provided a basis for the great inflation of 1923. There is still controversy today whether it would have been preferable to equip the central power with better tax provisions and to finance the war to a greater extent by means of (Reich) taxes.[11] A comparison of the indebtedness of the three principal Western European belligerent powers clearly illustrates this weakness in Reich fiscal methods – and the subsequent debt cancellation by public bankruptcy via inflation and currency devaluation (see Table 87).

'Reich' indebtedness is not identical with 'Germany's' indebtedness. Though member states had in 1871 transferred their military commitments to the Reich budget and welfare expenditure was chiefly a charge on local authority budgets, in 1914 member states' indebtedness still accounted for 57 per cent of total public debt; this was due mainly to using the capital market to finance productive public enterprises. The

[11] Holtfrerich (1980), pp. 97ff., 104ff., the share of war expenses financed by taxes is estimated for Britain at 20 to 28 per cent, for Germany at 0 to 6 per cent; see pp. 105, 101, n. 10.

Table 87. *Indebtedness of major countries, 1914–18: international comparison[a] (milliards of respective currency units)*

	State of indebtedness			State of indebtedness, 1924
	1914	1919	–fold growth	
France	33.54	245.44	7.3	418.08
Great Britain	0.70	7.88	11.2	7.64
German Reich	4.92	156.09	31.7	2.68[b]

Notes:

[a] Excludes loans floated abroad. Terhalle (1948), p. 256; detailed division of public debt into types of debt for Great Britain and France in Statistisches Reichsamt (ed.) (1927), pp. 214ff., 221ff.; on foreign debts, pp. 230ff.

[b] Escape from debt by Reich through inflation; conversion of mark currency unit (1873–1924) to Reichsmark (1924–48). 1914: £1 = 25.22 fr. = 20.43 marks.

Table 88. *Indebtedness of all territorial authorities in the German Reich, 1914 and 1919 (milliard marks)*

Territorial authorities	Indebtedness		
	1914	1919	–fold growth
Reich	4.92	156.09[a]	31.7
Member states	16.84	18.67	1.1
Local authorities	7.78	21.00	2.6
Hanse towns	—	2.23	—
Total	29.54	197.99	6.7

Note:

[a] Of this, 63.7 milliard marks floating debt, including 29.9 milliard marks borrowed from the Reichsbank, Deutsche Bundesbank (1976), p. 154. Floating debt and debt owed to the Reichsbank shown only from 1915 onwards.
Source: Terhalle (1948), p. 257.

war fundamentally changed this structure, the share of member states falling to 10.5 per cent, that of the Reich rising to 79 per cent of total public debt (see Table 88).

4. Structure of Reich budgets, 1872–1913

The Reich budgets, both on the income and expenditure sides, have to be seen as continuing the budgets of the North German Federation (see Tables 89 and 90). Owing to the allocation of the Franco–German war

Table 89. *Last pre-war budget of the North German Federation, 1870 (net budget; 1 taler = 3 marks)*

Expenditure	Million taler		%
1. Current expenditure, of which		75.1	91.5
Army administration	69.0		84.0
Navy administration	3.1		3.8
2. Once-and-for-all expenditure, of which		7.3	8.5
Army administration	1.8		2.2
Navy administration	4.8		5.8
Total expenditure		82.4	100
Revenue			
1. Ordinary revenue, of which		76.2	41.8
Customs duties and consumption taxes	49.8		27.3
Matricular contributions	23.1		12.7
2. Extraordinary revenue, loans		105.9	58.2
Total revenue		182.1	100

Source: Calculated from Gerloff (1913), pp. 34ff. Net budget: free of revenue collection costs.

Table 90. *First Reich budget, 1872 (net budget; 1 taler = 3 marks)*

Expenditure	Million taler	%
1. Current expenditure	97.9	83.8
2. Once-and-for-all and extraordinary expenditure	18.9	16.2
Total expenditure	116.8	100
Revenue		
1. Ordinary revenue		
Customs duties and consumption taxes	62.6	53.6
of which import and export duties	25.1	
Bill of exchange stamps	1.3	1.1
Post, telegraph, newspapers	3.0	2.6
Alsace-Lorraine Imperial Railway	2.9	2.5
Matricular contributions from member states	32.1	27.5
Miscellaneous revenues	0.1	0.1
2. Extraordinary revenue		
Reich's share of French indemnity	14.8	12.6
	116.8	100

Source: A. Wagner (1901), vol. IV, p. 652.

expenses and the distribution of the French indemnity, the transition from the budget of the North German Federation to that of the German Reich is not completely transparent. This is due also to the Reich remitting part of the French indemnity to the following extra-budgetary imperial funds:

1. General Fund at the Reich Office of the Interior
2. General Fund at the Imperial Treasury
3. General Pension Fund
4. Imperial Fund for Disabled Persons
5. Imperial Building Fund for Fortifications
6. Reichstag Building Fund
7. Imperial War Treasure
8. Management Fund for the Iron Reserve.

From the initial balance sheet of the German Reich, there were some changes in the structure and aggregates of revenue and expenditure up to the First World War without, however, changing the main features, in accordance with the unchanged allocation of functions between Reich and member states: Reich expenditure was dominated by armaments, Reich revenue by customs duties and indirect taxes, supplemented by loans, once the financial effect of the contributions from the French indemnity had been spent.

The formal structure of the imperial budget also changed.[12] At the foundation of the Reich, only expenditure (but not revenue) had been shown separately for continuing and once-and-for-all items. From 1889/90 onwards, the budget was officially divided into an ordinary and an extraordinary budget, though even then the ordinary expenditure retained the division into current and non-recurrent items. Thus total expenditure was shown in three, total revenue in two divisions. Budget calculation adopted the gross-value principle, which will be used hereafter in illustrating imperial expenditure. However, the gross-value principle must be understood within limits: the costs of collection of indirect taxes, customs duties and contributions paid to the Reich fell to a large extent on the member states which remitted imperial taxes 'net'.[13] In contradistinction to imperial expenditure, imperial revenues hereafter will be shown 'ordinary, net', so as to document the 'actually extant own revenues' (thus *Denkschriftenband* (1908), p. 4). This omits items arising above all from the two-directional flow of funds between Reich and

---

[12] Survey of the format of the Reich fiscal system, see Cohn (1899), pp. 160ff.

[13] The concepts 'gross' and 'net' are often imprecise. Though the Reich budget was presented 'gross', only surpluses were shown for the entrepreneurial establishments; Cohn (1899), pp. 160ff.; for the costs of collecting Reich taxes and customs duties, not accounted for in the Reich budget, see pp. 101ff.

member states (see Table 85) and from productive enterprises. Revenue from loans (see Table 86) almost alone constituted the extraordinary budget.

International comparison of budgets of central governments is rendered difficult as much by the countries' different political structure as by the different meanings attributed to non-recurrent and current, ordinary and extraordinary, gross and net.

(i) Reich expenditure[14]

Roughly one-half of total imperial expenditure was for military purposes. In the years from the establishment of the Reich to around 1885, armament expenditure dominated, as it did again from 1910 to the First World War. In the intervening years, expenditure on civilian objectives dominated (see Table 91).

Armament expenditure

Expenditure on the army: The Reich constitution fixed the peacetime strength of the army for 1871 at 1 per cent of the population of 1867; the percentage changed in subsequent years. The planned strength of the army was 401,000 men in 1881, 492,000 in 1890, 601,000 in 1900, 791,000 in 1913. Total expenditure on the army rose by 165 per cent, or substantially faster than army strength at 92 per cent. This was due to the more than proportionally strong growth of expenditure on military administration, the updating of armaments, above all in the artillery, the (re-)construction of fortifications and barracks as well as to price rises.[15]

Expenditure on the navy: At the time of the North German Federation (1867), a scheme for the construction of a fleet was published, and after the establishment of the Reich a first memorial in 1873 on the future development of a fighting navy allotted the following three functions to the ships:[16] (1) protection of German merchant shipping in all oceans; (2) defence of the mother country's coasts; (3) developing of an offensive naval potential. In accordance with quickly changing technique and new methods of warfare, the emphasis of naval armaments rested on the construction of a battle fleet consisting of ships of the line and cruisers. The state of British armaments served as a point of reference. Naval laws in 1898 and 1900 led to a large lump sum expenditure on the navy in the last two decades before the First World War. Lacking experience in the management of a fighting navy, the Reich considered this means of

---

[14] Current and once-and-for-all, ordinary and extraordinary expenditure gross, the various types of expenditure and per capita figures 1872 to 1908 from Reichschatsamt (1908), pp. 5f., 119.

[15] Development of numerical strength of army and navy from 1875 to 1914 in Witt (1970), p. 387.

[16] The three tasks of the navy, formulated already in 1867, in Gerloff (1913), pp. 8off.

Table 91. *Total Reich expenditure, 1876–1913 (million marks)*

Average of years	Total expenditure*	Armament expenditure Army	Armament expenditure Navy	Civil expenditure miscellaneous	Population[a] (millions)
1876–80	717.6	435.1	40.6	232.9	44.1
% of*	100	60.6	6.9	32.5	
Marks per head	16.27	9.86	1.12	5.28	
1881–5	775.5	419.1	43.4	313.0	46.0
% of*	100	54.0	5.6	40.4	
Marks per head	16.85	9.11	0.94	6.80	
1886–90	1,372.6	598.9	57.1	716.6	48.2
% of*	100	43.6	4.2	52.2	
Marks per head	28.47	12.42	1.18	14.86	
1891–5	1,553.0	650.5	86.1	816.4	50.8
% of*	100	41.9	5.5	52.6	
Marks per head	30.57	12.80	1.69	16.07	
1896–1900	1,877.7	702.7	133.9	1,041.1	54.4
% of*	100	37.4	7.1	55.5	
Marks per head	34.51	12.91	2.46	19.33	
1901–5	2,253.1	781.6	228.2	1,243.3	58.6
% of*	100	34.7	10.1	55.2	
Marks per head	38.44	13.33	3.89	21.21	
1906–10	2,872.4	958.1	362.1	1,552.1	62.9
% of*	100	33.4	12.6	54.0	
Marks per head	45.66	15.23	5.75	24.67	
1911–13	3,103.8	1,147.7	478.1	1,478.0	66.2
% of*	100	37.0	15.4	47.6	
Marks per head	46.88	17.33	7.22	22.32	
Index of change 1911–13 (1876–80 = 1)	4.3	2.6	9.6	1.5	1.5

Note:

[a] Up to 1910 in each instance five-year averages, 1911–13 three-year average. Figures from Hoffmann (1965), pp. 172ff.

Source: Assembled from Gerloff (1929), p. 18. After 1872, the army received a first investment amounting to 2.6 milliard marks from the French war indemnity. Insignificant differences of figures due to rounding.

achieving great power status so important that total expenditure on navy and army in the years from 1911 to 1913 was in the proportion 1:2.4. What the proportion of armament to total public expenditure amounted to can be calculated approximately by reference to the federal structure of the German Reich. The imperial government assumed orders of magnitude for 1907 as in Table 92.

Calculating the amount of ordinary and extraordinary armament

Table 92. *Expenditure of Reich, member states, and local authorities, 1907*

Fiscal requirements in 1907	Million marks	In %
1. Reich fiscal requirements		
Ordinary expenditure	2,679.8	22.7
Extraordinary expenditure	388.4	3.3
Total 1	3,068.2	26.0
2. Member states' fiscal requirements		
Ordinary expenditure	5,100.1	43.2
Extraordinary expenditure	503.8	4.2
Total 2	5,603.9	47.4
3. Total local authorities' fiscal requirements	3,138.0	26.6
Totals 1–3	11,810.1	100

Source: Denkschriftenband (1908), as interpreted by Gerloff (1929), pp. 19ff.

expenditure for 1907 as 1,264.2 million marks,[17] the proportion for armaments is 41.2 per cent relative to imperial expenditure, 10.7 per cent relative to the total expenditure of all public authorities. Rectifying total public expenditure of 11.81 milliard marks by deduction of items in transit (matricular contributions and remittances so far as they cancel out) and of expenditure devoted to public productive establishments, the armament proportion is 18 per cent relative to the rectified total imperial expenditure, that of member states and local authorities jointly, which amounts to 7.04 milliard marks, or 26.9 per cent, of the rectified total expenditure of Reich and member states, which amounts to 4.70 milliard marks.

So far as a comparison with the budgets of Britain and France makes sense at all, the appropriate proportion of armaments would be 26.9 per cent, clearly lower than that of the two European great powers. This is explained by their high military costs in safeguarding their colonial empires.

Civil expenditure: Though military and civil expenditure cannot be separated unambiguously in all sectors, this division, usual also in other European countries, was adopted in the budget structure of the German

---

[17] Thus Gerloff (1929), p. 22; the budget in 1907 showed for army and navy 1,112 million marks. Unambiguous separation of military from civil expenditure is hardly possible; Witt (1970) calculates military expenditure in 1907 as 1,631 million marks, including in that amount *inter alia* military pensions, provision for the disabled from the Imperial Disabled Persons Fund, part payments of the debt service, part of the costs of widening the North Sea–Baltic canal and for strategic railways. This illustrates the problems of allocation.

Table 93. *Reich expenditure for civil purposes, 1872–1912 (million marks)*

| | Administration | Judiciary | Ordinary and extraordinary expenditure | | | | |
			Social welfare expenditure	Administration of productive enterprises	Remittances to member states	Debt service	Totals*
1872	6.3	0.2	22.2	105.7	—	0.5	134.9
% of*	4.7	0.1	16.4	78.4	—	0.4	100
Marks per head	0.14	0.01	0.54	2.57	—	0.03	3.29
1890	55.1	2.1	63.3	252.6	378.9	48.2	800.2
% of*	6.9	0.3	7.9	31.6	47.3	6.0	100
Marks per head	1.13	0.04	1.29	5.15	7.73	0.99	16.33
1912	231.4	3.0	147.8	868.8	—	231.2	1,482.2
% of*	15.6	0.2	10.0	58.6	—	15.6	100
Marks per head	3.51	0.05	2.24	13.16	—	3.50	22.46
Index of change 1912 (1872=1)	36.7	15	6.6	8.2	—	462.4	10.9

Source: Calculated from imperial budgets in *Statistisches Jahrbuch* (1880), sections XIV, XV, XVI.

Reich. The development of civil expenditure here is shown in Table 93. By far the largest item of civil expenditure was the administration of productive enterprises,[18] above all the administrative expenditure on public enterprises yielding productive revenue to the Reich: the imperial railway in Alsace-Lorraine, the imperial post and telegraphy, the imperial printing works, and the Reichsbank. 'Administration' in this context included expenditure on staff and material expenses as well as investment.

The increase in expenditure on central administration in the domestic and external service is striking.[19] Social welfare expenditure from 1890/1 onwards referred mainly to imperial contributions to age and invalidity pensions due under compulsory social insurance. The imperial Treasury and the insurance reserve funds were linked in this financing. Expenditure on debt service is difficult to interpret and needs some care. From the point of view of budgetary structure, it formed part of civil expenditure, but objectively military expenditure predominated. In spite of the rapid increase of indebtedness, the total debt at 2.5 times ordinary annual revenue in 1914 remained small, compared to Britain and France; this applied even more to the rate of debt service which even in 1904 barely exceeded 5 per cent of total expenditure and after some fluctuations reached 8 per cent in 1911–13.

This low indebtedness in comparison with the two world powers Britain and France also applied over the long term of 1815 to 1914 to the local authorities, the member states and the German and North German Federation. Neither the reforms instituted to end the feudal order (peasant liberation, freedom of occupation) nor the political movements of 1848 nor the events leading to national unity and the accompanying wars of 1864, 1866 and 1870/1 produced unusually high indebtedness or unusually high rates of tax. Public indebtedness, debt service and tax burden did not pull each other upward. Perhaps the capacity for indebtedness (relative poverty of population) and the inclination to incur debts (the German states' relatively high propensity to save) were still small; added to this, there was the continuous attention to and increase of public productive property and the once-and-for-all financial injection of French indemnity, as allocated between Reich and states. Also, expenditure on the military remained relatively low up to the 1890s: the small member states acquired no empires and hardly maintained a fighting navy. The Reich possessed no colonies before 1884, constructing its

[18] For the administration of productive enterprises and the Reich property see Cohn (1899), pp. 104ff.
[19] The development of Reich bureaux and administration, of the civil service, the military and the pay scales in Cohn (1899), pp. 6ff.

fighting navy only after that date. What was later to be called the vain 'grasp for world power' manifested itself relatively belatedly.

However, the share of the debt service exhibits the same phenomenon as was observed of military expenditure: the federal structure of the Empire and the budget structures of the territorial authorities distorted the military share of the Reich upward and the debt service share downward.

(ii) Reich revenues[20]

The development of revenues from tariffs and indirect taxes displayed the pattern known already from Britain: a continuous rise in conjunction with the continuous growth of mass incomes used for consumption (see Table 94).

Customs receipts in the 1870s accounted for about 25 per cent of ordinary revenue, from the beginning of the 1880s to the end of the 1890s for about 40–50 per cent, dropping by 1913 to about 35 per cent. Within this category of customs, the yield from agrarian tariffs clearly predominated (inter alia on cereals, fats, meat) over the revenue tariffs (inter alia on coffee, tea, cocoa, rice, Mediterranean fruit) and the small revenue from industrial tariffs (inter alia on iron and iron goods, yarns and textiles, dyes).[21]

Indirect consumption taxes fell on mass consumption of liquor, sugar, beer, salt and tobacco, listed in order of yield. Their share in 1913 represented about 35 per cent. Indirect taxes on legal transactions (stamps) accounted in 1913 for at least something over 11 per cent of total ordinary revenue. These stamp duties fell inter alia on bills of exchange, cheques, lottery tickets, certain authentications by notaries public, insurance contracts and the issue of securities and bills of lading.

Matricular contributions were originally the third large income category of the Reich. Though these monetary payments reached the Reich with annual regularity from the member states, there resulted on balance strongly fluctuating 'net' Reich receipts, once they had been set off against the remittances to be paid from the Reich to the states. During the years from 1888 to 1898, and again from 1912 onwards, remittances in favour of member states were indeed higher than matricular contributions (see Table 85). Such negative matricular contributions were

---

[20] Ordinary revenue net; for the concept of 'net', see Gerloff (1926), p. 26, explanations; structure of tax revenue for Reich and member states for 1914 compared in O. Schwarz, Finanzpolitik (1919), p. 105; Gerloff (1916), pp. 6ff.

[21] Comprehensive treatment in Wiesinger (1912), including the Reich's tariff and commercial treaties with foreign countries, pp. 393ff.; Reichsschatsamt (1908), pp. 56ff., including details of the tariffs imposed on important commodities; enumeration of agrarian industrial and revenue duties in Gerloff (1926), p. 28, explanations.

termed 'uncovered' matricular contributions. For the Reich fisc, the (net) matricular contributions were of quantitative importance only during the 1870s, but they had considerable political–functional significance in the mutual dependence of Reich and member states.

The Reich inheritance duty (with states participating) introduced in 1906 was a low direct property tax. As the federal fiscal principle – indirect taxes to the Reich, direct to the member states – could not be infringed, owing to the Reichstag's constitutional sensitivity, the inheritance tax was simply labelled an indirect tax, contrary to all internationally current usage. Its share in 1913 was around 2 per cent. The Reich did not possess any other substantial direct taxes.[22]

The Reich's productive revenue at an average of 8–9 per cent was below the average reached in the larger member states – but probably of a magnitude comparable to productive revenue in Britain and France, if their state monopoly revenues are counted as productive revenue. The only substantial productive Reich property was the imperial Alsace-Lorraine railway. As an abstract juridical concept, the Reich – excepting the Alsace-Lorraine imperial land – possessed no territory of its own, as did the member states, and thus could not have any public lands, forests, mines or enterprises requiring territorial ownership.

Extraordinary revenues: Setting ordinary imperial revenue against total imperial expenditure resulted in a recurring revenue deficit. After 1877, this deficit was covered from receipts obtained by Reich debt creation (see Table 86), before that from the imperial share of the French war indemnity.

The question posed for Britain and France whether at the outbreak of the First World War direct or indirect taxation predominated can be answered only for both types of territorial authorities jointly, on account of the specific allocation of indirect taxes to the Reich and direct taxes to member states.[23] To make the answer complete, local authorities' revenue is taken into account separately. In 1913/14, direct taxes clearly predominated with 35.6 per cent (new income and old revenue taxes), compared to indirect taxes at 30.1 per cent (consumption and transaction taxes, tariffs). This accorded with the British, clearly contrasting with the French structural pattern. The comparison is not fully valid, owing to different lines of demarcation between the two types of tax (see Table 95). Thus, general income tax was put also in Germany ahead of all taxes raised by the Reich, the states and local authorities. Rightly, by virtue of its concept and its yield, it passed as the queen of taxes. But its

---

[22] In 1913, a once-and-for-all property tax, defence contribution, was imposed in the Reich's favour and allocated, at one-third per annum, to the budgets of 1913 to 1915; Terhalle (1930), p. 342.

[23] Division of direct and indirect taxes by enumeration in Gerloff (1916), p. 15, n. 1.

Table 94. Ordinary Reich revenue, 1872–1913 (million marks)

Average of years*	Customs, taxes aversa[a]	Matricular contributions less remittances	Settlement payments[b]	Productive revenue[c]	Disability fund[d]	Miscellaneous	Total ordinary revenue**	Population (millions)[e]	Net national income at factor costs[f]
1872–4	228.4	+78.4	—	15.1	20.9	2.1	344.9	42.0	14,718
% of**	66.2	22.7	—	4.4	6.1	0.6	100		
Marks per head	5.44	1.87	—	0.36	0.50	0.05	8.21		350.42
1875–9	253.6	+77.7	—	35.4	39.5	11.5	417.7	44.6	13,746
% of**	60.7	18.6		8.5	9.5	2.7	100		
Marks per head	5.69	1.74		0.79	0.89	0.26	9.36		308.20
1880–4	350.9	+17.1		43.3	33.4	7.8	452.5	46.3	15,778
% of**	77.5	3.8		9.6	7.4	1.7	100		
Marks per head	7.58	0.37		0.93	0.72	0.17	9.77		340.77
1885–9	462.3	−33.2		52.9	28.4	10.6	521.0	48.7	19,158
% of**g									
Marks per head	9.49			1.09	0.58	0.22	10.70		393.38
1890–4	663.2	−19.8		55.7	26.3	12.2	737.6	51.3	21,297
% of**g									
Marks per head	12.93			1.09	0.51	0.24	14.38		415.14
1895–9	801.7	−6.4	12.2	82.9	28.9	17.4	936.7	55.2	27,475
% of**g									
Marks per head	14.52			1.50	0.52	0.31	16.97		497.73
1900–4	906.4	+21.4	15.5	92.3	43.2	36.3	1,115.1	59.4	32,023
% of**	81.3	1.9	1.4	8.3	3.9	3.2	100		
Marks per head	15.26	0.36	0.26	1.55	0.73	0.61	18.77		539.10
1905–9	1,163.3	+30.6	17.5	126.9	35.9	58.3	1,432.5	63.7	39,508
% of**	81.2	2.1	1.2	8.9	2.5	4.1	100		
Marks per head	18.26	0.48	0.27	1.99	0.56	0.91	22.49		620.21

481

1910–13	1,624.3	+50.2	48.9	180.9	17.5	83.4	2,005.3	66.9	48,806
% of**	81.0	2.5	2.4	9.0	0.9	4.2	100		
Marks per head	24.28	0.75	0.73	2.70	0.26	1.25	29.97	729.53	
Index of change									
1910–13 (1872–4 = 1)	7.1			12.0	0.8	39.7	5.8	1.6	3.3

Notes:

a Aversa are payments from territories outside the Reich customs area.

b Settlement payments are remittances from south German states for reserved rights to levy indirect taxes.

c Net balance.

d Interest from the earmarked fund established in 1873 from the French war indemnity. Spent by 1911.

e The figures are for the last year in column marked * in each instance, drawn from Hoffmann (1965), pp. 172ff.

f Corresponding to national income at current prices in million marks; figures for the last year in column marked * in each instance, drawn from Hoffmann (1965), pp. 506ff.

g Percentages omitted as unrealistic for periods during which matricular contributions are negative.

Source: Calculated from Gerloff (1929), p. 26. On extraordinary revenue from loans see p. 469.

Table 95. *Structure of public revenues of Reich, member states, and local authorities, 1913 (million marks)*

Type of revenue	Reich	States	Local authorities	Total	%
1. Taxes on income and property					
(a) Income tax	—	609	781	1,390	22.6
(b) Property tax	41	155	430	626	10.1
(c) Business tax	—	18	162	179	2.9
	41	782	1,373	2,195	35.6
2. Tariffs and consumption taxes					
(a) Tariffs	641	—	—	641	10.4
(b) Consumption taxes	655	62	64	781	12.7
	1,296	62	64	1,422	23.1
3. Transaction taxes (stamps, etc.)	247	112	76	434	7.0
Total taxes	1,586	958	1,511	4,054	65.8
4. Revenues from public enterprises	176	538	279	993	16.1
5. Fees, contributions, miscellaneous	84	388	642	1,133	18.1
Total 1–5	1,846	1,883	2,432	6,160	
as %	30.0	30.6	39.4		100

Sources: Zorn (1976), Table 3, p. 184; Terhalle (1948), pp. 142ff.; Terhalle (1930), pp. 140ff.

position did not remain uncontested for long. The fast-growing need for finance of Reich, states, and local authorities – in fact, of all modern industrial states – led rapidly back to the principles of taxation in the seventeenth and eighteenth centuries, that is, the convenience, ease and productivity of indirect consumption taxes, in other words, the excise. Thus, after the First World War, once again a new impost developed, covering popular consumption in a manner more comprehensive than a mercantilist absolute sovereign of pre-industrial times could have conceived of: the general turnover tax, younger sister of the traditional indirect consumption taxes.

5. Possible effects of the federal fiscal systems in the German Reich

The economic and political development in individual member states and in the German Reich altogether is the result of a multitude of internal and external determinants which affected one another. One of these determinants was the fiscal system. A precise attribution of effects isolating this one determinant is difficult, but three probable effects promoting industrialization will be sketched here.

(i) Tax systems promoting industrialization

The tax and fiscal systems of German member states and of the Reich were favourable to industrialization. While not likely to act as triggers, they constituted stimulants, accelerating a growth process in progress up to the point of industrialization. Tax systems designed in the first two decades of the nineteenth century were essentially systems of impost appropriate to an agrarian and craft economy of the late eighteenth century. Consequently, the main incidence of taxation was on the agrarian sectors and on consumers of goods in daily use. There is a general impression that at least until well into the last quarter of the nineteenth century, manufacture and the young industry, born after the structure of the early tax system had been completed, enjoyed preferential tax treatment. This applied to entrepreneurial profits in establishments of all sizes, the degree of preference probably growing with increasing profits. This relates to the capital accumulation necessary to industrialization.

It appears that even the employed recipients of medium and higher occupational incomes enjoyed preferential tax treatment, owing to the inadequately developed personal taxation. Such individuals had an opportunity of participating in private and public investment, thus securing for themselves an additional income from interest on capital, which was taxed lightly or not at all. On the other hand, the tax incidence on recipients of low incomes remained higher, because of taxation of indirect consumption, even though a minimum of existence remained exempt. The combined effect of all this favoured private and public accumulation of capital in the sectors of manufacture, industry, commerce, and infrastructure. The unequal distribution of income and property which resulted therefrom attracted hardly any criticism at the time. However, the social costs created a serious burden. Only the state bankruptcy in 1923 proved after the event to have been a drastic kind of property tax, above all on movable property, but that did not constitute 'retrospective justice'.

Favouring capital accumulation specific to sectors or groups of persons or occupations, there was also a feature, difficult to relate to individuals, implicit in revenue tax systems. Individual tax incidence was assessed according to the level of achievable output of the taxable object, averaged over a number of periods. In the last resort, average achievable output of an enterprise was assessed by taking an indicator of the objectively ascertainable quantity of input of factors of production – according to the concept of a production function typical of the sector and line of production. The underlying thought was convincing: equal actual input and equal production time should result in equal output, hence equal tax incidence.[24] If an individual achieved an effective output above that achievable on average, the surplus output remained exempt from tax. This was a tax incentive, a tax premium awarded to above-average effort and ability. The classical liberal slogan 'clear the road for the efficient' was embodied in a tax-exempt reality. The obverse applied equally: an individual producing a return below average nevertheless paid tax as though he had obtained the average-achievable returns; this represented a kind of tax penalty on entrepreneurs' economic sloth.[25] Only income tax, introduced belatedly in states already largely industrialized, treated the returns individually achieved (profit, taxable income) over a short period as the basis for individual assessment to tax. The principle of liberalization, pervading the whole of the nineteenth century, did not penetrate into the tax system until the turn of the twentieth century.

(ii) The federal structure of the whole German state promoting industrialization

The politically, hence also geographically decentralized structure of the German Federation and the German Reich, given the historical situation, was rather favourable to catching up and achieving industrialization. The sovereign federal states, coming into existence only in 1815 and insisting on their strongly federal rights, endeavoured to safeguard and increase the economic potential within each state in a spirit of national state egoism – true to mercantilist tradition, even though linked to considerably greater elbow room for the entrepreneurial individual. The target of a 'powerful state' had not changed, only the route, the method by which to achieve it. Gustav Schmoller's interpretation of eighteenth-century mercantilism in its continental-German version as 'simultaneous growth of state and economy' has undertones of truth for the German member states until far into the nineteenth century. Thus, the whole surface of the Reich was covered with political territorial state centres of unequal size, consciously using their administrations to press authoritatively for development of their economies within their regional space. The governments of member states were able to concentrate predominantly on internal and economic policies, without having to divert scarce managerial or planning resources to the exacting requirements of army and (subsequently) navy and colonies, which were removed from their competence after 1866–71. The states – to put it pointedly – bought

---

24 Demand was at least hinted at by using the revenue indicator of 'geographical location'.
25 Details illustrated by Württemberg revenue taxes in Schremmer (1974), pp. 679ff. The tax laws put a premium on substituting capital for labour; this was a way of favouring by taxation technical progress linked to the introduction of machinery.

themselves free from these state functions by paying matricular contributions and partially renouncing customs duties and indirect tax.

There were therefore links between member states and the economy – affording mutual strengthening and support. One link were the public productive enterprises, and still more the provision of public services to the private sector of the economy at the expense of the entire population. This consisted above all in the construction and maintenance of an intricate network of institutions servicing in multifarious ways the material, personal, and institutional infrastructure – a precondition of industrialization. There were (public) railways and (public) roads as well as (public) universities and colleges, public elementary and trade schools, places for occupational training and further education, (public) libraries and (public) note-issuing banks, multifarious measures, adapted by each state to its regional peculiarity, devised to publicize and spread new techniques, linked to rewards for special achievements within the home-based economy; there was construction of regional and local means of communications, the provision of public power and water supplies, public social, fire, and building insurance; there were cultural and social institutions, such as (public) theatres, museums, (public) hospitals, sometimes children's and homes for the elderly, orphanages, and asylums for the blind. All these fell to the duty of the public authorities, clearly limiting the scope of private entrepreneurs. Added to this, there were a number of semi-authoritarian institutions midway between state and citizen, for instance chambers of industry and trade, trade associations, craft guilds, to some extent also savings banks and local friendly societies. Everywhere in these examples, the state faced the individual citizen – sometimes directly, sometimes indirectly – in a very peculiar relationship combining disciplinary authority with partial partnership.

Thus, from the territorial–political point of view, neither the German Federation nor the German Reich knew the typically French pattern of 'capital and provinces', characterizing the proverbial topheaviness of Paris, nor the pattern of 'distant' or even 'state-less' areas, to which one could well apply the epigram that 'Russia is large and the czar far away'. It seems as if an equilibrium had existed between the size of the state space (territory) and the intensity of political and economic activity within this space, determined by the state of technique, legislation, and administration; this implies that there are such intangibles as a 'spatial equilibrium' and an 'optimal size'. It is possible that the chequered structural pattern of this member state network of centres of economic growth, decentralized from the imperial point of view, linked in a unified internal market and belonging to a protective overall association, was an important reason for Germany's quick breakthrough into the ranks of great European industrial states in the last two or three decades before the First World War, in spite of the relatively late and slow initial phase of industrialization: the combination of member state economies into an increasingly interlinked total economy. Changes in technology, organization and administration, in production and sales obviously required a new and larger state space provided by the German Reich under the hegemony of Prussia, the largest of the member states.

In the short run, it may be true to argue that the member states, having tax authority, autonomous fiscal power and monarchic ambition, had produced at least temporarily an excess capacity of infrastructural institutions, thereby wasting resources from the point of view of the economy as a whole, but not in the long run. The picture here is the growth of the economy to fill out a generously carved framework of infrastructural institutions. It is perhaps possible to apply to different German territories considerations of an optimal state size which varies over time, and this could perhaps explain in part the lower degree of industrialization of Prussia's eastern provinces, compared with the west.

Given the conditions of decentralization, tax and fiscal systems of member states made possible and facilitated the construction of an intricate network of public infrastructural institutions, suggesting the idea of a fruitful joint blend of territorial size, infrastructure and industrialization. This connotes the importance of spatial structure.

(iii) Trend towards a wider spatial–economic political unit promoting industrialization

Inherent in the fiscal systems of member states and of the Reich was a tendency to change the existing federal structure in the direction of more centralized relationships – towards the next-larger political–economic territorial unit adapted to the level of economic and industrial development achieved, at the same time envisaging new potential growth. Three circumstances implicit in the system achieved this:

1. The more the tariffs and indirect consumption taxes in the individual federal states were standardized through inter-state agreements – from the customs union of 1834 via the North German Federation of 1866 to the German Reich of 1871 – the more noticeable were the remaining differences among member states in taxing the output of land, capital, and labour. This had disadvantages for the flow of factors of production, because the internal Reich market, free from customs boundaries, became a single area of traffic and economy, hence also of competition. The desire to standardize the member states' taxation systems originated both with entrepreneurs and with governments.[26]

---

[26] See for instance Glässing (1900), p. 188.

2. Because of the growing need of the Reich for finance and the strong political and constitutional position of member states, the financial settlement, with its matricular contributions and remittances, imposed a clear element of poll tax upon the total fiscal system. Using population numbers to calculate the shares of matricular contributions and remittances pertaining to individual member states had – in spite of the outward appearance of a method of equal allocation – on balance noticeably redistributive effects. Owing to the differences in the tax yield accruing to individual states (depending on economic structure, economic growth, and the tax system), a charge of matricular contributions and a discharge of remittances, both based solely on population numbers, had a distinctly unequal effect. Among the states, there were net payers (to the Reich) and net recipients (from the Reich), though these positions could change more than once in the course of time, the redistributive effect of the financial settlement contributing to its destabilization.

3. Presumably the strongest incentive to changing the tax systems came from the continually growing financial needs of the member states themselves. In the years after the establishment of the Reich, it was recognized ever more clearly, with reference to British experience, that a budget based on revenue taxes had the advantage of lower vulnerability to loss of income in periods of economic stagnation than a fiscal system relying on income tax, but that this advantage was balanced by the disadvantage of lower revenue growth at times of economic upswings. Member states, with their inelastic direct objective taxes, incurred debt in order to finance their productive enterprises and infrastructural institutions, above all their railways. As long-term economic development was conceived to be upward and income tax moreover was viewed as 'equitable' and 'modern', the way to standardized harmonization of member states' direct tax systems lay open.

Local authorities – without adequate original sources of income – met growing financial needs by ever-increasing surcharges on direct state taxes. One could almost describe it as surcharge financing of these bodies.[27] This considerably accentuated the peculiarities of the state tax systems, their preferential treatment of industrial production and their inelasticity.

The participation of the public sector in the increasing income of an industrial society in progress of formation appeared ever more inadequate, while the obligations of local authorities to render services simultaneously increased. A horizontal financial settlement might achieve equalization; it could not produce additional revenue. Thought of reform once again pointed to taxation of subjects in the form of an

[27] For local authority finance, Birnbaum (1914); Bolenz (1965).

income tax depending on individual incomes. Thus it was precisely in the field of fiscal administration that the imperial period was a period of reaching uniformity by gradual steps through the separate decisions of member states on a federal basis.[28] After a timid attempt in Hesse in 1869,[29] it was the early industrializer, Saxony, which is considered to have been the first member state reorienting its tax system from the old 'objective' revenue taxes to the new 'subjective' income tax, pointing the way for the other member states.[30] A provisional income tax law appeared in 1874, the definitive version in 1878. It included a limited obligation to declare income, a small progression from 0.5 to 3 per cent and a maximum limit at an annual income as low as 5,400 marks. The land tax was reduced, and the existing rudimentary personal taxes were repealed. Baden adopted its income tax in 1884. Only subsequently in 1892 did Prussia introduce an income tax, with a property tax to supplement it, relinquishing all revenue from land, business and building taxes to the local authorities. This clear-cut system acted as a model for the other member states. Württemberg followed suit in 1903, Bavaria eventually in 1912. All member states nevertheless persisted in the preindustrial principle of maintaining and, if possible, increasing, public productive properties. As before, entrepreneurial incomes remained one of the most important sources of revenue. The different taxation systems of the member states in 1908 are shown in Table 96.

The large state of Prussia and the medium states of Bavaria, Württemberg, Baden, and Saxony comprised in 1910 between them 87.7 per cent of the surface of the German imperial territory, containing 86.6 per cent of the population.[31] The combined budget of these five member states accounted for 91 per cent of the budget total of all 27 member states of the Reich, including Alsace-Lorraine.[32]

Standardization of tariffs and trade was followed by economic and infrastructural, then political, finally in principle also tax standardization. The standardization of monetary and currency systems had occurred during 1871 to 1873, linked to a harmonization of weights and measures.

A thorough fiscal reform carried through in several stages immediately after the Weimar constitution of 1919[33] led to an unambiguous centralization of fiscal authority in the Reich: the direct taxes were now allotted to it, and it achieved an income tax standardized for the entire Reich territory. The severely reduced tax prerogatives of the states and

[28] Presentation of tax systems of the 26 member states, showing budget years, in Reichschatsamt (1908), pp. 153ff.; abridged survey in Zimmermann (1916), pp. 222ff.
[29] Glässing (1900).   [30] Nostitz (1903); Conrad (1879).
[31] *Statistisches Jahrbuch für das Deutsche Reich* (1913), p. 1.
[32] Explanation in Zahn (1927), p. 125.
[33] The new Reich constitution of 1919; in conjunction with it the fiscal reforms of Erzberger in 1919/20 and of Popitz in 1925.

local authorities were limited essentially to revenue taxes on business enterprises, land, and buildings, now standardized for the Reich, which had shrunk in importance. The situation was now completely reversed, compared to the previous century: the states, and thus also local authorities, had become pensioners of the Reich.

The price paid for thus achieving strong central Reich power *vis-à-vis* the clearly weakened state powers can only be conjectured. To be sure, there had been a trend, justifiable in the first place by economic considerations, running from the customs union all the way to the Weimar Republic, continuing with renewed force in 1934. In this year legislation decreed the sole and all-embracing fiscal power of the Reich: remainders of sovereign rights of the states passed to the Reich; state governments became subordinate to the Reich government. Nothing was left of the old states' independence. Possibly a less drastic weakening of federal elements within the Weimar Republic, forming a counterweight to the combination of Prussia and the Reich – a combination amounting almost to identity – would have counteracted this development. This is a speculative hypothesis, but it led after 1948 to a reconstruction of Germany on more federally conceived, decentralized lines within the boundaries of the Federal Republic of Germany.

6. *The failed attempt to achieve a German Empire: some indications*

The official beginning of colonial ambitions on the part of the German Reich dates from 1884, when Bismarck's imperial government took under its protection the acquisitions of a private merchant in South-West Africa. In this field, the Reich copied mainly British methods of procedure: establishment of societies for the acquisition of colonies, imperial protection for trading settlements abroad, expansion of protectorates until these ultimately came – under more or less partial self-government, supervized by a governor – to be looked upon as foreign administrative areas of the Reich. Declarations of protection, assumptions of possession, international treaties, and the occasional lease for a term of years (Kiaochow) merged into a colonial policy. In 1890, a colonial department was established in the foreign office; from 1907, the newly founded independent Reich Colonial Office became responsible for the protectorates. A protectorate budget law was passed in order to obtain a more precise supervision of public finance (budgets) of individual colonies. Current administrative expenditure was to be defrayed from the territories' own current revenues: direct consumption taxes, above all on alcohol, tobacco, luxury articles, administrative fees and direct poll, house and hut taxes; in East Africa, the indigenous taxpayer could commute his money payment into labour services. The small recurring

490

Table 96. Taxation systems of the German member states: revenue according to the budgets of 1908

Characteristics of taxation system	Prussia: General progressive income tax. Property tax fall on entire capital consumption tax and stamp duties		Saxony: General progressive income tax. Land tax as remainder of former revenue taxes. Property tax not falling on landed property. Consumption tax and stamp duties		Hesse: General progressive income tax. Property tax falling on entire capital. Consumption tax and stamp duties		Württemberg: General progressive income tax. Land, building and business tax as remainders of former revenue taxes. Capital annuities tax, consumption tax and stamp duties in the form of a tax on conveyance of land		Baden: General progressive income tax. Property tax falling on entire capital, consumption tax in the form of a tax on conveyance of land		Bavaria: Revenue tax system on revenues from land, houses and commercial establishments; special progressive income tax; capital annuities tax; consumption tax	
Type of tax yield	Gross revenue as % of total tax revenue	Burden per head (marks)	Gross revenue as % of total tax revenue	Burden per head (marks)	Gross revenue as % of total tax revenue	Burden per head (marks)	Gross revenue as % of total tax revenue	Burden per head (marks)	Gross revenue as % of total tax revenue	Burden per head (marks)	Gross revenue as % of total tax revenue	Burden per head (marks)
Direct taxes												
Income taxes												
General income tax	70.22	6.44	73.31	11.4	54.37	8.98	43.56	7.82	35.90	7.76	0	0
Special income tax	0	0	0	0	0	0	0	0	0	0	5.30[a]	0.76
Capital annuities tax	0	0	0	0	0	0	8.11[b]	1.46	0	0	7.95[c]	1.13
Property tax	12.87	1.18	5.69	0.89	16.80	2.77	0	0	21.21	4.58	0	0
Land register taxes												
Land tax	0	0	6.79	1.06	0	0	3.73	0.66	0	0	11.15	1.59
Building tax	0	0	0	0	0	0	4.57	0.83	0	0	10.40[d]	1.49
Business tax	0	0	0	0	0	0	4.96	0.89	0	0	14.39	2.05
Indirect taxes												
Wine tax	0	0	0	0	0	0	6.05	1.09	5.76	1.25	0	0
Beer tax	0	0	0	0	0	0	20.84	3.74	18.25	3.95	44.72	6.38
Slaughter tax	0	0	8.37	1.30	0	0	0	0	1.77	0.38	0	0
Luxury tax	0	0	0	0	0[e]	0	0	0	0	0	0	0

Stamp duties	15.21	3.07	22.06	7.86	11.68	0.06
	1.39	0.48	3.64	1.41	2.52	0.01
Conveyance tax on landed property	Part of stamp duties	Part of stamp duties	Part of stamp duties	Part of stamp duties	Part of stamp duties	Part of stamp duties
Inheritance and gift tax	0	0	0	0	0	0
Total tax burden per head (marks)	9.10	15.22	15.76	17.94	20.87	13.78
Population (million)	40.16	4.81	1.28	2.44	2.14	6.89

Notes:

[a] Liable to tax is income from professional activities, fees, superannuation, the monetary part of remunerations, etc.

[b] Liable to tax are interest, dividends, annuities and other revenues from capital.

[c] Liable to tax are interest, dividends, annuities and other revenues from capital.

[d] Tax on buildings and rents.

[e] 8 marks for each nightingale.

Sources: Denkschriftenband (1908), pp. 357ff. Population figures from *Statistisches Jahrbuch für das Deutsche Reich* (1913), p. 1, for the year 1910.

Table 97. *Cumulative budget for the African colonies, 1893–1913*
(million marks)

Territory	Total expenditure	Total revenue		
		Own revenues	Reich subsidies	Protectorate loans and loans from Reich
South-West Africa	992.9	346.9	587.9	58.1
East Africa	349.7	118.8	95.3	135.6
Cameroon	129.5	57.1	38.4	34.0
Togo	52.7	29.8	3.5	19.4
Total	1,524.8	552.6	725.1	247.1
As % of total	100	36.2	47.6	16.2

Sources: 1894–9 calculated from the *Statistisches Jahrbücher für das Deutsche Reich*; 1900–13 from Schnee (1920), pp. 618ff. There are no exact figures for the years from 1891–3; for the period up to 1890, expenditure was defrayed by the colonial companies.

revenue did not suffice for current expenditure, so that protectorate budget deficits had to be met continuously by considerable subsidies from the Reich. Public expenditure considered once-and-for-all was financed by the Reich by means of extraordinary revenue via the extraordinary budget. To this end, the Reich provided in the first instance loans – above all, to improve the infrastructure, railways, and port installations. After the establishment of the Reich Colonial Office in 1908, this extraordinary system of finance was largely replaced by the so-called combined colonial loan system: floating protectorate loans on the private capital market, covered by collective liability of all colonies and the assumption of a Reich guarantee.

The consolidated public balance sheet for the *African territories* from 1893 to 1913 is given in Table 97. The share of the total financed by subsidy, amounting to about 48 per cent of all budgetary expenditure of colonies in Africa, is high. This resulted partly from the high starting costs of administration and infrastructure, partly from a method of budgeting military costs with somewhat unusual features in international comparison: the German Reich made its current military expenditure (army and navy) part of the respective colonial budgets, while in Britain and France for instance they formed part of the budget of the metropolitan power (there were exceptions). This made for high imperial subsidies. In the same vein, the substantial costs of the colonial war in South West Africa in 1904–7, amounting to about 400 million marks, appeared in the colony's budget and accounted for this territory's high budget total. Table 98 shows financial data for the entire German

Table 98. Budgets of the German protectorates, 1914

Territory	Years of taking possession or of protective titles	Area (000 km²)	Indigenous population (millions)	Revenue in million marks						Expenditure in million marks			
				Own revenues[a]		Savings from previous years	Reich subsidies	Extraordinary revenue[c]	Total revenue	Current expenditure		Once-and-for-all and extraordinary expenditure[c]	Total expenditure
				Total	Of which taxes[b]					Total	Of which civil administration		
East Africa	1885–90	995	7.6	16.5	6.2	4.0	3.3	37.5	61.3	20.5	10.2	40.8	61.3
Cameroon	1884	790	2.6	11.3	3.6	2.8	3.2	15.2	32.5	13.0	7.8	19.5	32.5
Togo	1884	87	1.0	3.5	0.8	0.7	—	0.03	4.2	3.5	2.1	0.6	4.1
South-West Africa	1884–90	835	0.08	23.5	14.3	4.7	12.1	7.5	47.8	30.1	6.3	17.7	47.8
New Guinea	1884–6	240											
Caroline Islands	1899	2.5	0.6	2.1	0.4	0.2	1.7	—	4.0	3.1	2.6	—	3.1
Pelew													
Marianas													
Marshall Islands													
Samoa	1900	2.5	0.04	1.2	0.3	0.2	—	—	1.4	1.0	1.0	—	1.0
Kiaochow	1897	0.6	0.2	8.1	—	1.4	9.0	—	18.5	14.6	4.5	—	14.6
Total		2,952.6	12.1[d]	66.2	25.6	14.0	29.3	60.5	169.7	85.8	34.5	78.6	164.4

Notes:

[a] Taxes, customs duties, administrative revenues.

[b] By far the most important tax was the diamond tax in South-West Africa; otherwise mainly indirect consumption taxes and direct poll, house and hut taxes.

[c] Extraordinary revenue to defray extraordinary expenditure came almost exclusively from loans floated by the protectorates on the capital market, only occasionally from loans by the Reich.

[d] Among them approximately 24,000 white inhabitants.

Source: Last pre-war budget estimates; *Statistisches Jahrbuch für das Deutsche Reich* (1914), p. 454.

Table 99. *Colonial possessions of European powers, 1914*

	Metropolitan power		Colonial territory	
	Surface in 000 km²	Population (millions)	Surface in 000 km²	Population (millions)
Great Britain	314	45.4	33,000	400
France	536	40.0	11,500	41
The Netherlands	33	6	2,000	38
Belgium	30	7.5	2,400	15.5
Germany	541	66	2,950	12
Portugal	91	5.3	2,100	7
Italy	287	35	1,500	1.6
Spain	497	20	250	0.7
Total	2,329	225.2	55,700	530.8

Source: Leutwein (1923), p. 799. Figures for colonial territories are approximate.

colonial territories, indicating how strongly the Reich looked to Africa. Table 99 compares the colonial position of the German Reich with that of the remaining European colonial powers in 1914.

Measured by surface of colonial territory, the Reich had become within the lifetime of one generation the third-largest, by population numbers the fifth-largest European colonial power. Although economic criteria would show its shortfall *vis-à-vis* the great colonial powers to be much greater – there are as yet no comprehensive comparative enquiries – imperial colonial policy after 1884 caused considerable friction in the relationships between European countries. The traditional 'balance of power' – however difficult it may be to give concrete shape to this concept – had become even more precarious (see Table 99).

Section 119 of the Versailles treaty of 28 June 1919 reads:

Germany renounces in favour of the Principal Allied and Associated Powers all her rights and titles over her overseas possessions.

That brought it to an end.

European countries had subjected to their colonial rule in one form or another slightly more than one-third of the inhabitable surface of the earth (taken as lying between 80 degrees north and 70 degrees south), containing slightly more than one-third of world population (estimated at 1,500 million inhabitants). Europe's industrialization and the development of the fiscal systems of European countries must be seen in this context.

State policy towards labour and labour organizations, 1830–1939: Anglo-American union movements

I. *Introduction*

When considering the industrial revolution in Europe and the labour movements to which it gave rise, it is customary to think in Anglo-European, or more precisely Anglo-French terms. Britain was master of the first industrial revolution based on coal and cotton, so tradition has it, while French thinkers such as Proudhon, Saint-Simon, and Louis Blanc provided the intellectual analysis upon which the first rational critiques of the new industrialism were built. Yet an equally suggestive – if less orthodox – way of approaching the history of the labour movement, at least in the English-speaking world, can be obtained through an Anglo-American rather than through an Anglo-European form of analysis. This is partly for reasons to do with similarities in language, customs, and law. Anglo-American traditions with regard to the legality of strikes, picketing, and other trade-union practices, which differed markedly between Great Britain and the French Napoleonic Code on which most continental labour law was based, were similar on both sides of the Atlantic.

This approach is also plausible because, although quite different in other regions, the process of American industrialization as it occurred between 1815 and 1840 in New England, in the Ohio valley and to some extent in the mid-Atlantic states, was quite similar to that which had taken place in Lancashire, in Yorkshire and the English Midlands not many years before. As a result, it has been argued by one scholar that the growth and character of the American labour movement can best be seen as developing along similar lines to those adopted in Great Britain, save that major advances in the American movement followed along approximately one generation behind the British.[1] Thus the American Knights of Labour (K. of L.) of the 1870s and 1880s pursued many of the same interests in cooperative experiments and Utopian politics that the

---

[1] H. Pelling, 'The American Labour Movement: A British View', *Political Studies*, vol. II, no. 3 (October 1954), pp. 227–41.

Owenites had done in England in the 1830s; and the American Federation of Labor's (A.F. of L.) benefit systems and craft union policies, which triumphed over the anti-monopolist traditions of the K. of L. in the late 1880s, followed consciously in the tradition of skilled unionism which had first been developed in the 1850s by the Amalgamated Society of Engineers (1851), and by the English Trades Union Congress (1868). Important similarities along these lines also existed between the British labour movement and those which grew up in Canada, Australia, and other English dependencies, although they cannot be gone into in any detail here.

Finally, there is the fact that an Anglo-Saxon rather than an Anglo-European comparative approach can be more readily fitted into the overall framework which has been chosen for this chapter: namely, a discussion of the policies taken up by the state in its relations with labour organizations during and since the industrial revolution. At the suggestion of the editors, I will be going beyond this somewhat narrow compass, and will include brief discussions on the nature and recruitment of the labour force and the role of labour political action in Britain and America, as well as analysing the Anglo-Saxon labour movement's ambivalent attitude towards state power. This is because neither of these first two topics, particularly in the case of the United States, was more than briefly referred to in the relevant chapters of volume VII of *The Cambridge Economic History Of Europe*. Because of the institutional approach which has been mandated by the editors, however, the reader should be aware that this chapter does not contain an extended analysis of the social and cultural history of the Anglo-American working class, which has recently engaged the interest of historians on both sides of the Atlantic. For that he must look elsewhere.

Nevertheless, the issue of state power in relation to the labour movement is important to a proper understanding of Anglo-American trade unionism and we will return to it often. For, in the early years at least, perhaps the most fundamental characteristic which all Anglo-Saxon labour movements shared in common – including at least to some extent, those of New Zealand and Australia, as well as the trade union movements of the United States and Great Britain –was a belief in anti-mercantilism, and a sensitivity towards any effort which government might make towards controlling the labour movement though the use of state power. This view was even manifested at the end of our period. At the Trade Union Congress held in Southport in 1943 Ernest Bevin, then Minister of Labour, made a characteristic remark concerning the desirability of a guaranteed working week, 'Do not rely on the government only to maintain it. Why not weave it into your collective agreements at the earliest opportunity; we are not anxious to have the duty of enforcing it by law.'[2]

The strength of this anti-mercantilist tradition in the Anglo-Saxon countries depended partly upon the prior history of class relations. More particularly, as Adolf Sturmthal among others has pointed out[3], the character and intensity of the feudal heritage present in any given society may be one of the most important factors determining the attitude of its labour movement towards revolutionary political action. Thus in countries like tsarist Russia in which mercantilism, characterized by a strong central government and the granting of subsidies and state monopolies to particular merchants and businessmen, remained strong, the labour movement's first goal was to try to secure political power in the state. In Britain and the United States, on the other hand, where the tradition of mercantilism was weak, where the power of the state was more limited, and where the economic strength of the labour movement was considerable, there was less emphasis on political action.

This argument can be taken one step further. For if, as was in fact the case, the anti-statist traditions of America's political heritage were even stronger than were Britain's, then the American labour movement can be seen as standing at the extreme liberal pole of the *laissez-faire*/non *laissez-faire* spectrum of economic development. The British labour movement, being somewhat more inclined towards independent labour politics than the American, comes next in this liberal–absolutist continuum. At the other extreme lay the labour movements of Prussia or tsarist Russia, countries in which the mercantilist, or politically absolutist tradition was at its strongest. Hence it was in these two countries – as manifested in the Russian revolution of 1917 and the abortive German revolution of 1918–19 – that the labour movement was most inclined towards politics, and where it went furthest in its efforts to secure state power.

There are some difficulties with this mercantilist/anti-mercantilist argument, difficulties to which we shall return at the end of this chapter. But it certainly provides a plausible framework within which to examine the overall development of the labour movement in the United States and Great Britain. First, however, a general distinction should be made. In the early period anti-mercantilism was used primarily by employers as a weapon to prevent trade unions from interfering with the free movement of goods and capital in a *laissez-faire* economy, rather than as an internal deterrent to independent politics on the part of the labour

[2] A. Sturmthal, *Unity and Diversity in European Labour: An Introduction to Contemporary Labour Movements* (Glencoe, Ill., 1953), p. 30. [3] *Ibid.*, pp. 26–33.

movement itself. Thus at the beginning of the nineteenth century law and custom on both sides of the Atlantic emphasized the sanctity of private property, defined not simply as the physical plant or output of a factory, but also as the property rights which individuals or corporations held in the profits which resulted from economic enterprise. Natural law, not legal provisions, determined the market value of most economic entities. Hence strikes, boycotts, or other union activities designed to interfere with this broad definition of employers' property rights were nearly always defined as unacceptable infringements on the free flow of goods and services, and frequently brought down the agencies of the state upon both English and American workers' heads.

With the passage of time the greater residual strength of the feudal tradition in Britain led both to the establishment of powerful trade unions to protect the economic interests of the working class, and to the founding and political acceptance of the Labour Party. In America, on the other hand, where the anti-mercantilist tradition was even stronger, not only were most efforts at independent socialist or labour politics rejected as alien, or unnecessary: trade unions as such had dubious legality until a much later date in the nineteenth century than they did in England; and employers were able to use far more than simple legal precedent, or American traditions of *laissez-faire* economics, in order to inhibit the growth of labour organizations. They employed Pinkerton detectives, company spies, and state and federal militia to defeat strikes and destroy existing unions in the coal, steel and other major American industries with much greater impunity than their counterparts in the United Kingdom were able to do. Hence, in some ways paradoxically, whilst being much less favourably disposed towards taking independent political action than their English counterparts, in the nineteenth and early twentieth centuries American labour leaders sometimes found themselves embroiled in labour disputes with employers which were characterized by a greater degree of violence and overt class conflict.

Thus despite obvious similarities between the British and American labour movements, at least as far as independent politics and the building of mass unions were concerned, the history of the labour movement in each country was in many ways quite different. It is to an exploration of these similarities and differences that this chapter is devoted.

II.   *The character of the labour force*

All students of economic history are aware that it was as a result of the availability of coal, iron, and water power, and technological advances such as Watt's steam-engine (1781), Hargreaves' Spinning Jenny (1790), and Arkwright's water frame and rollers that industrial methods of production first arose in Great Britain, and then fanned out across the Western world. But it is important to recognize, also, that in the 1820s and 1830s the availability of similar resources in and around such towns as Boston and Fall River, Massachusetts, or Portsmouth, New Hampshire, made it possible to develop American textile mills and an industrial infrastructure which did not differ greatly from that which had been established in Leeds, Manchester and other Lancashire towns a few years before. In the United States two methods of textile production were used, one being the so-called Slater system in which whole families, including men, women, and children, were used to prepare yarn which was then sent out to handloom weavers to be finished. The other model was provided by the celebrated Lowell system in Waltham, Massachusetts. Initially, this made heavy use of young, unmarried Yankee farm girls from the surrounding countryside, an attempt being made to protect them from the worst effects of industrialization by providing dormitories, educational facilities, and food. Without consciously modelling themselves on New Lanark (1818), the managers at Waltham sought to take further the attempts which Robert Owen had earlier made to mitigate the effects of factory life at his textile establishment in western Scotland.

Only a few thousand worked under the Waltham system, however. And with the important exception of higher wages, conditions for the majority of New England cotton operators, faced as they were with growing mechanization, inadequate housing, and a 'sun-up-to-sundown' workday, did not differ very much from those of their fellow workers in Great Britain.[4] In heavier industries such as coalmining, railway construction, or the later production of steel in the Ohio valley and the Midwest, the industrialization process also followed a similar path on both sides of the Atlantic. Had a visiting cutler or iron puddler from Sheffield or from Birmingham walked through the steel mills of Pittsburgh at the time of the Civil War, for example, he would have found much that was familiar: company paternalism, skill differentiation, a rapidly growing labour force, and the recently introduced Bessemer smelting process which had first been used in England in 1864, and was introduced into America the following year.

Had our English visitor applied for a skilled job in any of the northern or midwestern cities which he visited he would also, as like as not, have found among his fellow workers somebody from his own country, or even from his native town. For in its formative years before the Civil War American industry relied heavily upon skilled English workers, and to a lesser extent those from Germany and Scandinavia too, to develop its

---

[4] R. T. Berthoff, *British Immigrants in Industrial America* (Cambridge, Mass., 1953), p. 7.

basic infrastructure. In 1850, for example, of the 2,244,602 foreign-born workers employed in the United States 961,719 were Irish, 278,675 were English, 70,550 were Scottish, and 29,868 were Welsh. Welshmen from Cardiff and Swansea established a high reputation as iron-puddlers; Cornish tin miners were imported to work the same metal in Wisconsin that they had at home; Yeovil glovemakers migrated to Connecticut; and Staffordshire potters found enough suitable clay on the banks of the Ohio River to help set up an equivalent American industry there.

In coalmining the similarities were even greater. In the decades immediately before the Civil War, and still more in the massive expansion which took place after it, Anglo-Saxon miners including Scots, Yorkshiremen and Welshmen, as well as men from Durham and Northumberland, predominated in both the anthracite and the soft coal fields in Pennsylvania, and also as in the bituminous fields of Ohio, Indiana, and Illinois. John L. Lewis, who in the 1930s became president of the Congress of Industrial Organizations (CIO), was born the son of a Welsh miner in 1880 in Lucas, Iowa. In skilled hand trades such as cigarmaking, typography, bespoke tailoring and cabinetmaking German artisans came second after the British, these two elements being the largest and most influential of the various 'old' immigrant groups which came to work in American industry from Northern and from Western Europe between 1830 and 1885. Samuel Gompers, president of the American Federation of Labor from its founding in 1886 almost uninterruptedly until his death in 1924, learned his trade as a cigarmaker in his father's Bishopsgate shop in London before migrating to New York at the age of 13. So important were old world ties to many of these occupations, indeed, that they sometimes began by setting up city-wide labour organizations based as much on ethnic loyalties as upon those of class. The United German Trades of Philadelphia, established in 1886, was a good example of this. Save for the Irish, and a scattering of Jews and other Eastern European elements in Manchester or the East End of London later on in the century, these ethnic differences were rarely significant in Great Britain.

From our point of view, the most important fact about these Anglo-Saxon immigrant workers was that a significant minority of them had already had experience of trade unionism in their country of origin. John Jarrett, president of the Amalgamated Association of Iron, Steel and Tin Workers (1876), was a Welshman who had led an Iron Workers' Union in Britain before emigrating to the United States. The early leaders of two of the oldest American national unions, the International Typographical Union (1852) and the Cigarmakers' International Union (CMIU, 1863), were German immigrant radicals. And in the 1860s and

1870s the number of English engineers and building tradesmen in northern American cities became great enough to warrant the establishment of separate American lodges for the Amalgamated Society of Engineers (ASE, 1852), and the Amalgamated Society of Carpenters and Joiners (1860).

III. *First efforts at organization*

Despite emerging differences in scale, therefore, and the persistence of a much larger agrarian sector in the American compared to the British economy, by the time of the Civil War the industrialization process had created a form of capitalism in New England and in the old Midwest which was recognizably similar to that of Great Britain at the same developmental stage. As a consequence, even before the influx of former English trade unionists that we have just described the first, small efforts at trade organization which the American labour movement threw up were not very different from those of their English counterparts, either. By the end of the eighteenth century, several groups of London compositors had successfully petitioned their master printers for an increase in piece-rates, or 'price of work' and journeymen leaders were encouraging the formation of trade associations, or combinations, among printers, blacksmiths, shoemakers, sailmakers and other tradesmen. In the United States, too, the earliest attempts at long-range organization took place in similar skilled trades, with city-wide groups of printers, carpenters, tailors and shoemakers taking the lead. The first continuous American trade organization appears to have been a Society of Shoemakers organized in Philadelphia in 1792. In both countries, moreover, these combinations were initially intended as much to provide social advantages and friendly benefits (e.g., some kind of unemployment or sickness insurance) as they were to conduct industrial disputes. Nevertheless, by 1800 strikes, or 'turnouts' as they were first called, were being used as a means of expressing discontent on both sides of the Atlantic.

But even at this early stage it is possible to discern some differences between the emerging British and American movements. To begin with, although skilled workers on both sides of the Atlantic were concerned with defending hand crafts against the threat of mechanization, with the passage of time American artisans showed even greater anxiety about this question than their English counterparts. This was partly because of the relative weakness in America of pre-industrial guilds, which in England had been charged with the responsibility of maintaining standards in long-established crafts such as harness-making, brass-turning, or silversmiths' work. It was partly because the greater scarcity, and hence the higher cost, of skilled workers in a number of

American trades gave American manufacturers an added incentive to replace artisans with labour-saving machinery. But it was also because, once the stream of poor Irish and other European immigrants had begun to cross the Atlantic in truly large numbers in the 1840s and 1850s, American employers were able to threaten those among their employees who attempted to form unions with discharge and replacement to an even greater degree than was possible in Great Britain. In turn, the availability of this larger pool of reserve labour constitutes one of the most important reasons for the greater size and strength of the British trade-union movement, when compared to the American, right up to the 1930s, if not to the present day.

As early as 1828, for example, a group of New York typographers complained to the Master Printers Association about its practice of 'taking full-grown men [meaning here foreigners] as apprentices for some twelve or fifteen months, when they are to be turned into [that is, given] the situations of men who are masters of their business, which men are turned out of their places by miserable botchers because they will work for what they can get'.[5] In this dispute lay the seeds of a widespread nativist attitude on the part of second generation, or 'old' experienced American artisans towards the ex-peasant, 'new' immigrant workers from southern and from eastern Europe who provided the bulk of factory labour at the end of the nineteenth century. In the 1880s and 1890s, indeed, this prejudice was to partially cut the skilled element off from widespread contact with the majority of American factory workers, and to widen the gap between the labour aristocracy and the factory proletariat to an even greater extent than occurred in Great Britain.

A second difference between the early labour movement in Britain and America, stemming this time from much greater regional differences which existed in the American economy when compared to the British, concerns the much earlier date at which consideration was given in England to national, rather than purely regional, forms of labour movement. Thus in December 1829, a young Irish cotton operative from Manchester named John Doherty launched the Grand General Union of Operative Spinners of Great Britain and Ireland, which attempted to organize textile workers throughout the entire country, instead of just in Lancashire and Yorkshire, at widely varying levels of skill. The following year Doherty helped establish an even more ambitious organization, the National Association for the Protection of Labour (NAPL), which enrolled not only a wide range of textile workers, including calico printers, silk weavers, wool workers, and hosiery makers as well as cotton operatives, but local societies of molders, colliers, potters, and other tradesmen as well.

[5] Quoted in H. Pelling, *American Labor* (Chicago, 1960), p. 27.

In 1831 NAPL broke up over the failure of spinners in other parts of Britain to support it in a strike over wage levels in Ashton-under-Lyne. But it was followed three years later by the creation of the nation-wide Grand National Consolidated Trades Union (GNCTU) which sought to systematize the internal structure of individual trades unions, assert general control over movements to secure higher wages, and coordinate assistance for strikes. Given the social turmoil then sweeping England over the minimal additions to the franchise sanctioned by the 1832 Reform Act, as well as over the newly enacted and much hated Poor Law Amendment Act (1834), the GNCTU at first grew with phenomenal rapidity. According to some reports, it even reached half a million members in the summer of 1834. It was also strongly influenced by the radical, cooperative doctrines of Robert Owen who in the 1820s, as we shall see later, spent much time and money attempting to establish socialist communes in the United States.

In addition, the more militant temper of the English labour movement compared to the American at this time stemmed from the atmosphere of political crisis and repression which lasted from the Napoleonic period right up to the mid-1830s, but which was not present in the United States on anything like the same scale. Starting with the anti-union Combination Acts of 1799 and 1800 these repressive measures included suppression of Luddite attacks upon hosiery knitting machines in 1812–14, the Peterloo massacre of 1819, and the 1830 deportation of Dorset agricultural labourers (better known as the Tolpuddle martyrs) for allegedly seditious behaviour. Angered and embittered by these events, many urban artisans, along with larger numbers of cotton operatives and of other northern workers, put great weight on the relief they hoped to secure from the extension of the parliamentary franchise.

In the event, as we have already suggested, the 1832 Reform Act failed to enfranchise more than a handful of property-owning English artisans, a result which points up a further significant difference which was beginning to emerge between the British and the American movements at this point in time. This concerned a conflict in strategy over how each labour movement could best secure its political demands. For the failure of the 1832 Reform Act to enfranchise the English working class had profound consequences for the growth of class consciousness among English workers. It added a political dimension to the economic one which was already separating elements of the manufacturing middle class from the poorer members of society. It reinforced the legitimacy of independent political action as a major component of labour's strategy. And it increased, albeit to a lesser degree than on the European continent, the appeal of wholly different forms of society as alternatives to the rapidly maturing capitalist system.

Another way of demonstrating this difference is to compare the

fortunes of the English Chartist movement with those of the independent Workingmen's Parties which came briefly into being in New York
and in other American East Coast cities in the 1820s and 1830s. In many
respects, the two movements were quite different. The American
Workingmen's Parties were largely composed of artisans, small masters
and petty-bourgeois reformers concerned to secure free public education, an end to monopolistic control over the banking system, and the
implementation of various other demands in what was known as the
Workingmen's Platform, in addition to extending the franchise. Chartism, by contrast, although it too started out as a vehicle for securing
political reform, soon acquired the characteristics of a mass working-
class movement which was concerned as much to vent anger against the
unemployment and economic hardships occasioned by the 'Hungry
Forties' as it was to bring about suffrage reform. Hence, despite the
relatively moderate nature of the Chartists' practical demands (universal
male suffrage, equal electoral districts, annual parliaments, payment of
Members of Parliament, secret ballots, and no property qualification for
Members of Parliament) the rejection of the petitions which they presented to parliament on several different occasions led the more radical
among them to suggest in 1838 that the Chartists' convention itself
should become an alternative legislative body to the House of Commons. Moreover in Birmingham, Manchester, Glasgow and several
other northern cities in which the Chartists secured support, there
emerged a 'physical force' school, led by men such as George Julian
Harney and Feargus O'Connor, which contemplated violence as a
legitimate means of bringing about reform. After the collapse of Chartism in 1848, quite a few of this 'physical force' element emigrated to
America.

In the United States, on the other hand, by the 1830s large numbers of
workers already had the vote. Hence they did not need to launch out into
independent political action except when one or the other of the two
major parties appeared unwilling to enact legislation favourable to
labour's interests. In 1829, for example, when bankers and merchant
capitalists became more influential within the Jacksonian Democratic
Party than working-class voters could tolerate, independent
Workingmen's Parties appeared in New York, Boston, and elsewhere
seeking to pressure the New York City Democratic Party – often known
as Tammany Hall – as well as other regular party organizations into
supporting various planks of what we have just described as the
Workingmen's Platform.

Then in 1835, when the New York Democrats again reneged on a
promise to support anti-bank legislation, a Locofoco Workingmen's
Party was established which nominated a partially separate ticket

of its own for the state legislature in the autumn elections. But it did not break entirely with Tammany; and when in the late 1830s the Jacksonian Democrats returned to a more acceptable stance, the Workingmen's Party disappeared. In addition, successful lobbying on the part of artisanal groups in various states secured quite a few working-class demands relatively quickly, in ways which in England took somewhat longer to obtain. Workers' imprisonment for debt, for example, was ended in 1838 in Vermont and Ohio; Rhode Island and Connecticut brought in universal male suffrage in the 1840s; and several other states introduced free public education during the course of the same decade.

It should be added that these measures were not 'free gifts' to the American working class, granted as an automatic concomitant of the development of popular democracy. They had to be fought for by means of petitions, mass demonstrations, and other manifestations of popular discontent.[6] Nevertheless it remains true that, unlike English labour at this time, by the 1840s organized elements in the American working class had already successfully demonstrated their ability to influence the political behaviour of one or both of the two major parties without having to launch out into a permanent political party of their own. This held important implications for the developing political moderation of the American labour movement.

Up to this point in our analysis it would be possible to conclude that industrially, if not politically, the similarities between the American and the British labour movements easily outweighed the differences, at least as far as comparisons between England and the north-eastern and mid-western United States were concerned. Such a degree of similarity cannot, however, be found between British developments and those which occurred in the other two great regions of the American economy, namely the slave South and the frontier West. In both of these areas the character of the American industrialization process differed markedly from what it had been in New England and the Midwest, again bringing with it highly important consequences for the different development of the labour movement in the United Kingdom and the United States.

IV. *Developments in the American South and West*

Following the American revolution and for a short period at the beginning of the nineteenth century, slavery played a relatively minor role in American economic development. At times, indeed, owing to soil

---

[6] For a discussion of this point, see Edward Pessen, *Most Uncommon Jacksonians: The Radical Leaders of the Early Labor Movement* (Albany, 1967), ch. 2.

exhaustion in the southern tidewater states and to its apparently limited value as a system of labour, it appeared as though the slave system might even die a natural death. But with the economies of scale brought about by the invention of the cotton gin in 1793, the institution took on a new lease of life. In addition, in the 1830s and 1840s a small but growing number of southern planters began to train their house slaves as skilled carpenters, teamsters (wagon drivers) or blacksmiths, and to lease them out for hire instead of keeping them on the plantations. This development created enmity among skilled white workers who had always thought of themselves as superior to black slaves but who now found themselves competing indirectly with them for jobs. After the Civil War this white racial enmity towards black workers tended to increase, rather than diminish. In the South this was because of the unsuccessful efforts of the Radical Republicans to elevate blacks over whites in the Reconstruction period, and the partial flooding of the labour market with ex-slaves looking for employment. As a result, the period between 1865 and 1890 saw the systematic exclusion of black artisans from local trades unions and from occupations where they had earlier been quite strongly represented, such as bricklaying, cooperage, cigarmaking, or printing. In 1879, for example, there were an estimated 21,409 skilled Negro printers in various parts of the South. By 1920, there were hardly 2,000.[7]

These developments did not, of course, mean that all southern blacks, or all poor whites, for that matter – for there were plenty of them in the South also – were turned overnight into unskilled labourers, sharecroppers, or tenants working the land. Nor did it mean that there were no instances of multi-racial unionism developing in both the North and the South in this period, still less that freed blacks did not develop some unions of their own. In 1867, for example, Charleston's black dockers formed a successful Longshoremen's Protective Union, which acquired almost a thousand members. In Virginia black coaltrimmers organized themselves. So, too, did black miners, waiters, teamsters, and other occupational groups. And in 1869, 160 black delegates under the leadership of a black radical shipcaulker named Isaac Myers met in Washington, DC, to establish what was to be the first of a series of autonomous black national organizations, the Colored Labor National Union. This group was not, however, permitted to affiliate with the National Labor Union, which was the dominant white labour federation at that time.

What these economic developments do show, however, is two things. First, that white racism and black resentment against their exclusion from white unions was a powerful divisive force with the American

---

[7] P. S. Foner, *History of the Labor Movement of the United States*, 6 vols. (New York, 1947–82), vol. 1, p. 389.

labour movement from the very beginning, in ways which were simply not present in Britain. And secondly, that for reasons partly deriving from its own ecological character, and partly from the failure of North American or European capitalists to inject sufficient investment capital into the region after the ending of Reconstruction in 1877, the South remained largely non-industrialized until the period following the First World War. This seriously retarded the growth of trade unions in that region, besides depriving much of the black labouring population of the industrial experience necessary for its rapid integration into the urban working class. There is a minor parallel between these black–white divisions in the United States, and Anglo–Irish conflicts in Britain. In 1838, for example, armed conflict broke out between English and Irish navvies working together on the North Union Railway; and in 1854, a number of employers imported Irish labourers to break a strike of Lancashire handloom weavers. But these incidents were relatively insignificant when compared to the major racial and ethnic divisions which had already begun to characterize the American working class by the 1850s and which continued to plague it up to the Immigration Restriction Act of 1924 and beyond.

Turning now to the frontier West, this region had two kinds of significance, neither of which were present in Great Britain to any more than a marginal degree. The first, after the Appalachian barrier had been surmounted, concerned the adoption, and then the promulgation throughout the West of the Jeffersonian ideal of the moral superiority of the independent yeoman farmer. This ideal had been depicted in English pastoral romances, but it had little practical economic application there. Politically speaking, however, the yeoman ideal had major negative implications for the future of independent labour politics in America. By contrast with the situation in Great Britain, it meant that if any independent working-class party was to have a chance of becoming a force to be reckoned with, it would have to secure the loyalty not only of a majority of the urban workers – many of whom were themselves divided ethnically between each of the two major political parties – but also of a significant proportion of the millions of homesteading ranchers, many of whom had become imbued with the petty-bourgeois aspirations of the single-family farm. Secondly, and more important, there was the impact of the Western frontier as a moving line of settlement, which is said to have inhibited the growth of political class consciousness by providing a safety-valve for discontented urban workers who in times of depression supposedly moved West in order to make a living from the land. In the period between 1820 and 1860 between three and five million people moved out West from the eastern seaboard, or came directly from Europe (and to a more limited extent from the Orient) to settle in the trans-Appalachian West.

In recent years this safety-valve theory has come under increasing attack, particularly for the post-Civil War period. Fred A. Shannon, for instance, has argued that even if the cost of American public land was minimal, the expense of seed, tools and transportation was too high for most working-class immigrants; that census returns indicate that migration westward was lower in periods of depression, not higher; and that major strikes and confrontations with employers occurred in both the East and the West, despite the presence of the frontier.[8] In response, other scholars have suggested that focusing on Eastern workers becoming Western farmers interprets the theory too narrowly, and that it ignores Eastern workers who remained working class but who may still have moved West. They also assert that the simple act of moving West kept wages higher and unemployment lower in the eastern states than they would otherwise have become. Faced with this scholarly disagreement, the wisest course for the general reader is to withhold judgment until further research on the topic has been carried out.[9] It should be remembered, though, that whatever the validity of the safety-valve theory in practical terms, *belief* in the upward mobility potential of moving West remained strong for a considerable period of time after the frontier itself was physically closed, in approximately 1890. In turn, this belief powerfully reinforced the exceptionalist myth in American popular culture, as well as in working-class thought.

The limited class-conflict potential of the American frontier can also be suggested by comparing it with the history of the frontier in other Anglo-Saxon countries, in particular in Canada and Australia. Canadian settlers in this period tended to be *habitants*, preferring to cultivate a limited number of fields rather than moving out into the open prairie like their American counterparts. When overpopulation fostered urban discontent, most French-Canadians moved to New England, or back east to the industrial provinces, instead of persisting with the isolated, single-family, type of frontier farming which helped to reinforce American bourgeois values. In Australia, other factors were at work. The first outbackers there tended to be wealthy sheep farmers, with a wage-earning labour force composed partly of English convicts, or of immigrant Chartists who had brought their radical beliefs with them to the new country, not single-family farmers with a relatively small homesteading claim. Even vaster open spaces, and a more meagre labour supply than was available in America also encouraged the emergence of the wage-working shepherd, not the yeoman farmer, as the central

---

[8] F. A. Shannon, 'A Post-Mortem on the Labor-Safety-Valve Theory', *Agricultural History*, vol. XIX (January 1945), pp. 31–7.

[9] For further discussion of the safety-valve theory, see R. Hofstadter and S. N. Lipset (eds.), *Turner and the Sociology of the Frontier* (New York, 1968).

agrarian figure. Thus, unlike his American counterpart, the typical Australian frontiersman in the second half of the nineteenth century tended to be a wage-worker who did not expect to become anything else.[10]

V. *Utopian socialism and other reform movements*

Earlier, we referred to the role of manufacturer–philanthropist Robert Owen in trying to mitigate the effects of industrialization by improving conditions of work in his New Lanark textile mill in Scotland, and also by helping to lead the short-lived English Grand National Consolidated Trade Union. However, American interest in Owen stemmed largely from the influence which he exerted in the New World in the period between 1825 and 1829, when he committed much of his time and fortune to trying to establish small Utopian communes in various places in the United States, based upon the principles of voluntary association and the collective ownership of property. The most famous of these communes was set up in 1825 at New Harmony, Indiana, to which Robert Dale Owen (Owen's son) and other well-known American reformers such as the Scots-born Fanny Wright gave their support. In addition, several communes based upon the principles of the French Utopian theorist Charles Fourier were also founded, the most famous of these being Brook Farm, Massachusetts (1841–6). This settlement was patronized at one time or another by such well-known literary and reform figures as Horace Greeley, Henry David Thoreau, and Ralph Waldo Emerson.

Interestingly also, for a country without any significant socialist tradition, was the fact that these communes appeared to prosper more in the United States than they did in the countries of their origin. One reason for this stemmed from the time-honoured American tradition of social experimentation, which went back to the Plymouth colony and other religious settlements in the colonial period. A second reason was the previously mentioned fact that in the America of the 1830s and 1840s land was still readily available, having been made even cheaper by the recent opening up of the trans-Appalachian frontier. In addition, there was the deeply held Enlightenment belief on the part of many American intellectuals (of which in practice the communes were very largely composed), in the power of reason to shape man's destiny. This can clearly be seen in the American (as well as in the French) Utopians'

---

[10] R. A. McKirdy, 'Conflict of Loyalties: The Problem of Assimilating the Far West into the Canadian and Australian Federations', *Canadian Historical Review*, vol. xxxii (December 1951), pp. 337–55.

assumption that all men could ultimately be convinced of the superiority of the communal way of life by the power of example.

None of these communes, with the exception of the religious ones, lasted for very long. Nevertheless, they indicated the presence in America of a tenaciously held desire for social progress, and of an antipathy towards industrialism which was, in its own way, just as deep as the one that had been manifested by the supporters of Chartist Feargus O'Connor's Land Scheme in Britain. Reworked under the name of the producer ethic, and associated also with the moral virtues of a citizens' republic, this tradition exerted considerable influence over the first two national labour federations to be founded in America. These were the National Labor Union (1866–72), and the much more important Knights of Labor. Founded by Uriah Stephens and other members of a collapsing cutters' benefit society in Philadelphia in 1869, the Knights of Labor had little success during the early and mid-1870s, which were marked by severe economic depression.

But with the return of prosperity in the late 1870s the K. of L. flourished like no other American labour organization had before it. Organizing unskilled, semi-skilled, and skilled workers alike, and including over 60,000 blacks as well as several thousand women from the shoemaking and textile trades, the Knights enrolled its members either into Mixed Assemblies, incorporating different trades in a given geographical area, or into Trades Assemblies which were defined occupationally. By the summer of 1886 the K. of L. reached a peak membership of more than 750,000, before dropping off rapidly in the 1890s. This was a higher figure than the 635,000 workers who had been organized by the English Trades Union Congress (1868) at this time, and it temporarily made the Knights of Labor the largest single federation of workers in the industrialized world.

Land and currency reform, temperance, third-party politics (particularly in support of the agrarian Populists between 1892 and 1896), and an ongoing hostility towards the wage system were the key elements in the K. of L.'s philosophy. But this philosophy had no Marxism in it. The Knights' most important leader, grand master Workman Terence V. Powderly, disapproved of strikes, favoured arbitration of industrial disputes, and upheld producers' and consumers' cooperatives rather than the class struggle as the proper way to reassert the dignity and independence of the individual worker. 'The aim of the Knights of Labor', Powderly observed in 1886, 'is to make each man his own employer.'[11]

Given this predisposition, earlier historians tended to look upon the Knights of Labor as backward-looking and Utopian in their philosophy,

---

[11] Quoted in G. N. Grob, *Workers and Utopia: A Study of Ideological Conflict in the American Labor Movement, 1865–1900* (Evanston, 1961), p. 44.

and to regard their anti-monopolist platform as little more than a hangover from pre-Civil War Jacksonian democracy.[12] It is true that in their predilection for secrecy and for Masonic rituals, in their admiration for the values of the early American republic, and in their disastrous handling of the 1886 Gould railway and other major strikes, the national leaders of the Knights showed poor judgment, as well as a limited understanding of the anti-union outlook of most modern industrial corporations. On the other hand, as Leon Fink has pointed out, the K. of L.'s ability to unify the working class around such issues as railway regulation, or the eight-hour day were very far from being backward-looking.[13] The fact is, too, that many of its members became influential in unions such as the Western Federation of Miners (1893) or Eugene Debs' American Railway Union (also 1893), which contained within them the seeds of modern industrial unionism.

Besides being a domestic American organization, the Knights of Labor also enrolled several thousand members in Canada, Australia, Belgium, England, and elsewhere. Curiously enough, it was in its brief period of influence in Great Britain, that the industrial union aspects of the K. of L.'s philosophy became most clear. In the mid-1880s K. of L. Local Assembly 300 of Pittsburgh, which constituted virtually a national union of the 3,000 or so glassworkers then employed in the United States, helped establish new Knights' Assemblies in the same trade in Smethwick, Sunderland, and various other northern English towns. These included St Helens, where Pilkington's glass works had become the largest such establishment in the world. The Knights' immediate purpose in organizing these glass Assemblies, as well as their efforts to establish Trades Assemblies among Liverpool dockers and Midlands coal miners a little later on, was to try to control the flow of English workers into American industry, drawn abroad as they sometimes were under false pretences to act as strikebreakers for American firms. But, directly in the case of the dockers, and indirectly in other trades, the influence of the K. of L. also helped to develop the English 'new' union movement, which was to appear in full measure after the great London dock strike of August 1889.

Indeed, this brief period at the end of the 1880s was one of only two occasions, the other significant one being the heyday of the CIO in 1936–8, in which the American labour movement appeared to be clearly in advance of the one in Britain, and in which new initiatives travelled across the Atlantic from the United States to the United Kingdom, instead of the other way around. Besides the activities of the Knights of Labor, there were Henry George's tours of Great Britain on behalf of the

[12] The leading exponent of this view is G. N. Grob in *Workers and Utopia*.
[13] Leon Fink, *Workingmen's Democracy. The Knights of Labor and American Politics* (Urbana, 1983).

Single Tax (a land tax whose purpose was to redistribute wealth); the influence exerted by Edward Bellamy's *Looking Backward* on the founding of the English Fabian Society (1884), and the subsequent establishment of the Labour Party (1901); and the recognition of May Day as the annual date for celebrating international working-class solidarity, which derived in 1886 from the labour movement in Chicago, not from the supposedly more radical labour federations on the continent of Europe.

VI.   *The growth of craft unionism on both sides of the Atlantic*

Of course only a very small minority of English trade unionists were in any way influenced by the Knights of Labor. In the 1870s and even throughout most of the 1880s, the most characteristic form of labour organization in Great Britain were still the so-called 'new model' unions. These were the relatively small, socially respectable unions composed of skilled workers which had first arisen during the early years of mid Victorian prosperity. The most seminal of them was the Amalgamated Society of Engineers (1851) which had the taciturn but able Scot, William Allan, for its general secretary. The new model unions were really a mixture of trade unions and friendly societies. Between 1851 and 1859, for example, the Amalgamated Society of Engineers spent £2,987,993 on friendly benefits, and only £86,664 on the settlement of industrial disputes. The benefit function of these unions was financed through high weekly or monthly dues, and the provision of a wide range of financial aids to the membership, ranging from strike and unemployment pay to sickness and pension provisions. The new model unions were also the first ones on either side of the Atlantic to appoint full-time officials to supervize the organizing of new members and to exercise strict central control over the funds of their respective organizations, and over the authorization of strikes. Probably the most important innovation of the ASE was to initiate the periodic 'equalization of funds' principle between local lodges, so as to ensure strike and other monies being available at short notice where they were most needed.

Care must be taken not to exaggerate either the novelty or the typicality of the new model unions in the British labour movement of the 1850s and 1860s, or even their conservatism. Several of their financial benefit principles could already be found in the Journeymen Steam Engine and Machine Makers' Society, which was the ASE's predecessor. In addition, socialists like Tom Mann of the ASE, as well as radicals at various levels in a number of other craft unions, were later to give their

support to legislative activities which ultimately resulted in the formation of the Labour Party, thereby belying the assumption that skilled
artisans were always likely to be politically more conservative than their
more poorly paid, unskilled counterparts. Nor was any consistent attempt made to follow these high-dues–high-benefit schemes in mining,
cotton, bootmaking, or metal manufacture. In these trades a looser form
of organization known as 'amalgamations' remained dominant. They
were typified by the Spinners and Weavers' Association, and were
characterized by district rather than national control over collective
bargaining.

Nevertheless, it was in the period of high Victorian prosperity in the
1850s and 1860s that the new model organizations enjoyed their highest
prestige in England, spreading from the engineers to the ironfounders,
and then on to the building trades. Probably the most characteristic
union here was Robert Applegarth's Amalgamated Society of Carpenters and Joiners (1860). 'New model' unionism also dominated the
outlook of the so-called Junta in London, where skilled journeymen such
as William Allan of the Engineers, Applegarth of the Carpenters, Edwin
Coulson of the Bricklayers, and George Odger of the London Trades
Council controlled the movement.

Something of the same kind of debate has emerged between historians
over the origins and character of the 'pure and simple' unions which
came to the surface in America about fifteen years after the 'new model'
unions had developed in Britain, and for which they served as a rough
equivalent. Philip Taft, for example, has argued that a preoccupation
with friendly benefits, with reducing work hours, with conditions in the
factory or workshop, and with dividing up control over the terms of
employment with the employers could be found in the Journeymen's
Tailors' Union in Philadelphia as far back as the beginning of the
nineteenth century.[14] It was these kinds of preoccupations which formed
the basis of the so-called 'job-conscious' model of the American labour
movement promulgated by University of Wisconsin labour theorist
Selig Perlman when he wrote his influential *A Theory of the Labor
Movement* in 1928. Yet there is also evidence to suggest that the A.F. of
L.'s job-conscious, or pure-and-simple, brand of trade unionism as it was
also called, owed a lot to the new model system which originated in
England. First, in newly emerging American craft unions of the mid-
century decades such as the Amalgamated Association of Iron, Steel and
Tin Workers, there were frequently demands for the same kinds of
financial benefits and internal union structure as had been present in
England. Secondly, in the 1860s and 1870s two of the largest and most

[14] P. Taft, 'On the Origins of Business Unionism', *Industrial and Labor Relations Review*, vol. VII,
no. 1 (October 1963), pp. 20–38.

powerful English new model unions – the Amalgamated Society of Engineers, and the Amalgamated Society of Carpenters and Joiners – established their own branches in the USA, in order to provide these same benefits for immigrant English workmen who wished to retain their old union associations.

Thirdly, both among A.F. of L. leaders generally, and in the Cigarmakers' International Union in particular (Local Union 144 of which in New York became the home base of A.F. of L. president Samuel Gompers) the principles of English new model unionism were not only looked up to; they were openly copied. In 1879, after a period of instability and strike defeats for the union, president Adolph Strasser of the CMIU and Gompers himself centralized much of the Cigarmakers' internal form of government, raised its weekly dues, made provision for strike, death, and unemployment benefits, and adopted the English principle of 'equalization of union funds'. At a Senate hearing on trade unionism held in 1883, William McLelland, representing the US branch of the English Amalgamated Society of Engineers, described the benefit system his organization had been using for years, and which had now taken hold in the United States. 'Mr Gompers informed me', McLelland stated, 'that he took the idea from our society and engrafted it onto the organization of Cigarmakers.'[15]

In the previous section we pointed out that by the summer of 1886 the Knights of Labor reached a peak of more than three-quarters of a million members, before dropping off rapidly in the 1890s. It is important that we take note of the reasons for this sudden decline, since the victory of the A.F. of L. over the K. of L. had profound consequences, both political and industrial, for the future of the American labour movement, which served to differentiate it further from that of Great Britain. Although the immediate cause of the break was allegations that New York District Assembly 49 of the Knights had helped to break a strike conducted by Local 144 of the Cigarmakers' International Union in the early part of 1886, longer-range reasons – both external and internal to the labour movement – were also involved.

As to the internal reasons for the defeat of the K. of L., or those resulting from at least partially avoidable errors of judgment or tactics, these encompassed organizational and leadership weaknesses, and disagreements over issues of policy. Grand master workman Terence V. Powderly, who headed the K. of L. in its most influential years, believed somewhat naively that all disputes between labour and capital could be settled peacefully by arbitration, and showed little tactical sense. In this he differed markedly from president Samuel Gompers of the A.F. of L.,

[15] Quoted in C. K. Yearley, *Britons in American Labor: A History of the Influence of the United Kingdom Immigrants on American Labor, 1830–1914* (Baltimore, 1957), p. 288.

who despite his political conservatism was a good organizer and union administrator. By organizational weaknesses is intended the poorly articulated chains of command in the Knights of Labor; its instability resulting from rapid mushroom growth; and increasing demands from skilled workers in the organization for the establishment of National Trades Assemblies consisting solely of one type of employee instead of the occupationally Mixed Assemblies that were favoured by Powderly and the National Executive Board.

The external, or socially induced, reasons for the decline of the Knights of Labor included disapproval of its secrecy by the powerful north American branches of the Roman Catholic church – a policy which was in fact modified in 1881 – and the hostility of both employers and government agencies towards its organizing activities. In order to check the Knights' growth, like that of more conventional unions later on, employers would blacklist K. of L. organizers, refuse to allow them access to workers on factory premises, and make use of federal or state militia to break up strikes. During an 1886 railway strike at Fort Worth, Texas, for example, over a hundred vigilantes and an even larger number of state militiamen used violence to force a train through K. of L. pickets. A gun battle resulted in which half-a-dozen strikers were killed and over 30 wounded. This was a prime example of the greater degree of violence and of overt class conflict that was present in the American compared to the British labour movement, to which we referred at the beginning of this chapter. An even more memorable example occurred in Haymarket Square, Chicago, on 4 May 1886, when after a bomb was thrown into a labour demonstration by an unknown assailant, the local police opened fire. One policeman was killed; many were injured; and of the eight anarchists subsequently condemned to death, the four among them who were actually hanged became international labour martyrs.

Politically, the K. of L.'s demise brought a repudiation of third-party, or even incipiently socialist forms of electoral activity in the American labour movement which the Knights themselves had been pursuing through local branches of the Greenback Labor Party, through the more radical elements of the Populists, and through the 1886 New York Labor Party movement – policies which the A.F. of L. leadership adamantly refused to continue. Instead, it adhered to a political policy of 'reward your friends, punish your enemies' under which it urged its members to vote for candidates of either the Republican or the Democratic parties who supported favourable legislation, and to vote against those who opposed it. Industrially the Knights' defeat, followed as it was by the loss of the Homestead steel strike of 1892, and of the even more important Pullman railway strike in July 1894, brought a virtual halt to efforts which more radical leaders like Eugene Debs were making to draw black, recent immigrant, and unskilled factory workers into the American labour movement. Partially as a result of this, the A.F. of L.'s narrow, job-conscious form of trade unionism remained dominant within the American labour movement until the rise of the CIO in the 1930s. In Britain, on the other hand, the TUC's craft unionism was to some extent successfully challenged in the early 1890s by the 'new unionism' of the dockers, the gas workers, and the Miners Federation of Great Britain.

VII. *Trade unions and the role of the state*

Mention in the previous section of the use of state militiamen in suppressing Knights of Labor strikes leads us, by extension, to confront directly the more general question of state policy towards labour and labour institutions, as it is specified in the title to this chapter.

At first, there seemed to be little to choose between the behaviour of America and Great Britain in this regard. Until the middle of the nineteenth century both statute and common law doctrines in England and America – and of British dependencies such as Australia and New Zealand as well – largely followed the Smithian principles of *laissez-faire* economic theory. These held that in most of their activities trade unions were illegal conspiracies in restraint of trade. This meant that efforts on the part of unions to influence conditions of employment improperly interfered with the employer's right to employ workers on whatever terms he saw fit; and that, in attempting to secure the closed shop, for example, unions improperly interfered with the employee's right to work for whomsoever he wished, also. In keeping with this economic doctrine, in 1798 and 1799 the British Parliament passed the Combination Acts, which declared all forms of trade-union activity to be illegal. Similar statutes were enacted in America, at both the state and federal levels. Some relief from this policy was afforded in England by the repeal of these same Combination Acts in 1824, after the period of crisis associated with the Napoleonic wars, and in America by the decision of the Massachusetts state Supreme Court in *Commonwealth* v. *Hunt* (1842). This declared that it was the legality or otherwise of specific acts undertaken by trade unions which determined whether they were conspiratorial or not, not the existence of unions as such. The doctrine of conspiracy was relaxed still further in England when the Court of Queen's Bench, in *Hornby* v. *Close* (1867), laid down that although the activities of unions could usually be considered as in restraint of trade, membership in them should no longer constitute a criminal offence. An additional effect of that case, however, was to nullify a prior protection which English unions had enjoyed by holding that the Friendly Societies Act (1855) did not protect these societies' ability to proceed against their own officers (in this case the Boilermakers' Society against its Bradford secretary) for embezzling union funds.

It was in the period between the 1870s and 1890s that the main divergence between the legal protection afforded by the state to trade unions in Britain and America became clear. In England the crucial step was taken by the Trade Unions Act (1871), which laid down that unions should no longer be considered outside the law merely because they interfered with the conduct of trade; that all unions which did not infringe upon the criminal law were to register under the Friendly Societies Act, thereby securing legal protection for their funds; and that no union could be sued or otherwise interfered with by outside bodies in the conduct of its internal affairs. In the United States, by contrast, both statute and common law persisted with the restraint of trade doctrine for considerably longer than they did in Great Britain. They did this by defining the right to do business as a property right in itself, thereby stretching the definition of property considerably further than was done by the English courts; and by sanctioning the issuing of legal injunctions to prohibit unions from carrying out such of their functions as would interfere with the exercise of that right.

Ironically it was the Sherman Anti-Trust Act (1890), which had initially been intended as a measure to break up corporate trusts, that became the main vehicle for this method of dealing with labour disputes. In the extensive Pullman railway strike of 1894, for example, the federal government secured a court injunction asserting that the American Railway Union's boycott of Pullman cars was an illegal conspiracy restricting the proper flow of interstate commerce, and that Eugene Debs' activities as a union officer attempting to enforce the boycott were in violation of the Sherman Act. It was the issuing of this injunction, in Debs' own opinion, more than the use of federal troops or the failure of the A.F. of L. to offer any financial support, which was the main reason for the defeat of this critical strike.

This brief review does not, of course, cover more than a fraction of the legal history of trade unionism either in Britain or America. Nor is it intended to suggest that as of 1871 English unions had complete freedom of manoeuvre, whereas American unions did not. In that same year a Criminal Law Amendment Act was passed by Parliament which included penal clauses against picketing, as well as against acts of obstruction or intimidation carried out by unions against employers or their non-striking employees, which were not rescinded for some years. Nevertheless, when the Conspiracy and Protection of Property Act (1875) legalized peaceful picketing, and withdrew the formerly threatening phrases about 'obstruction' and 'intimidation', it became clear, on the English side at least, that considerable progress had been made.

Along with the Employers' and Workmens' Act (also 1875), English law now appeared to give unions both adequate legal status and immunity from prosecution for damages in the conduct of industrial disputes. In the Taff Vale case (1900), however, in which a Welsh railway company successfully sued the Amalgamated Society of Railway Servants for loss of income, it seemed as though unions in the United Kingdom were once more to become liable to prosecution for damages resulting from a strike. But this tendency was reversed by the Trades Disputes Act of 1906; and although some political difficulties arose as a result of the Osborne Judgment (1909), which questioned the right of unions to use their money to help fund political organizations such as the Labour Party, in general the legal position of unions was now considerably better protected in the United Kingdom than it was in the United States. In both American state and federal courts unsympathetic to strikes, for example, picketing by strangers, boycotts (as in the Danbury Hatters case, 1902–8), and secondary boycotts (as in the Duplex Printing Press case, 1921), continued to be declared illegal. Indeed, in some ways it was not until the New Deal of the 1930s that American unions secured the kind of full legal recognition that British unions had for the most part secured by 1914.

A number of reasons can be cited to account for the greater reluctance of the American courts to grant full recognition to the activities of trades unions. The most plausible of them derive, once more, from the greater strength of the anti-mercantilist tradition in the United States, which remained suspicious of any form of activity that interfered with the free flow of goods and services. In addition to labour law, an equally important manifestation of the same phenomenon can be seen in the greater reluctance of American state and federal governments, when compared to government agencies in Great Britain, to adopt social legislation which would interfere with the workings of the free enterprise system, this time in order to protect workers against excessive exploitation by their employers. In England the history of protective legislation began as early as the Factory Act of 1833, which laid down that no child under nine years of age be employed in the textile mills, and that children under thirteen could work no more than nine hours a day. Subsequent acts in 1844 and 1847 extended the law to women, and also exerted some control over the use of dangerous machinery. After 1842, no women or children could be employed underground in coal mines. In 1867 a number of other industries were brought within the scope of the law. New legislation was later enacted providing for workmen's compensation in industrial accidents – ineffectively in 1880, more effectively in the acts of 1897 and 1906. The Trades Board Acts of 1909 brought many of the remaining sweated trades such as chainmaking, paper-box production, and various sections of the garment industry, within the laws providing for minimum wages and hours.

In the United States, especially at the state level, there was a comparable effort to secure the same protective legislation as in England. But it did not begin in earnest until after 1890, when reformers in both of the major political parties advocated child labour laws, the protection of women and other social legislation in states like Wisconsin, Illinois, and New York. In addition, there was the brief sally into third-party politics which was undertaken by ex-President Theodore Roosevelt in the short-lived Progressive Party of 1912. The rise of the progressive movement was due partly to the efforts of social gospel advocates and middle-class reformers like Jane Addams and Henry Demarest Lloyd – the circle around Jane Addams playing very much the same kind of role on this issue, as the circle of Fabians around Sidney and Beatrice Webb did in England – and partly to intense political lobbying carried out by representatives of the American Federation of Labor at both the state and federal levels. For the most part, however, the legislative results from this type of agitation proved considerably more difficult to secure in the United States than they were in Great Britain, some American legislation coming as much as 15 or 20 years after the comparable English enactments. It was not until 1917, for example, that a majority of northern industrial states had child labour laws comparable to the English legislation which had been enacted over a generation before.

At the federal level, President Woodrow Wilson's first administration did take some significant steps forward, particularly with the Clayton Act (1914), the LaFollette Seamen's Act (1915), and the establishment of a Department of Labor. But nothing directly comparable to three further pieces of social legislation which were enacted by the English Liberal government between 1906 and 1911 was passed in America until the time of the New Deal. These were the Workmen's Compensation Act (1906), the Old Age Pensions Act (1908), and the National Insurance Act (1911). Nor was this all. Virtually all of the social legislation adopted in Britain before 1914 remained on the statute books after the First World War to help provide the foundations for the modern welfare state. In the United States, on the other hand, during the conservative social and political climate which prevailed in the 1920s the Supreme Court once more intervened – as in *Hammer* v. *Dagenhart* (1918) concerning child labour, for example – to strike down legislation that had been enacted by Congress in the years before 1917. Indeed, in the language of *Adkins* v. *Children's Hospital* (1923) one can still find, virtually undimmed, a justification for classic *laissez-faire* economic doctrines which in the United Kingdom by this time had been largely abandoned. 'That the right to contract one's affairs is part of the liberty of the

individual . . . is no longer open to question', the court stated. And it
went on to show that it still clung to the notion that the company and the
individual worker were co-equals in the market-place, despite all the
evidence that had been accumulated by social reformers to show that
without the protection afforded by trade unions, the bargaining position
of the individual worker was far weaker than that of the modern
corporation. 'In making such contracts', the Supreme Court concluded,
'the parties have an equal right to obtain from each other the best terms
they can get as the result of private bargaining.'[16]

VIII. *Socialism and syndicalism: the Socialist Party of America, the Labour Party, and the Industrial Workers of the World*

It is clear, therefore, that at the turn of the century neither the American
courts, nor the federal government were yet willing to endorse legislation which would have provided the kind of legal protection and benefits
for the American worker which had already been gained in Germany
and Britain a number of years before. Faced with this situation, it might
have been thought that a significant number of American workers
would have turned towards radical, third-party politics in the manner of
the Labour Party in Britain, or perhaps towards syndicalism as ways of
registering their protest. Save for a relatively small minority of workers
in the period between 1900 and 1917, however, and a number of others
who joined the Communist Party in the 1930s, neither of these tendencies triumphed. Part of the reason for this derived from the greater social
and ideological flexibility of the two major political parties in America
which permitted them, as we saw in the case of the Progressives, to satisfy
the legislative demands of the working class without necessitating the
establishment of a separate labour party. And part of it derived from a
well-established tradition of voluntarism, descended in turn from anti-
mercantilism, which made the conservative leaders of the A.F. of L.
fearful of the state taking over the friendly benefit functions of the trade-
union movement, as well. This section describes the fortunes of both
syndicalists and socialists in Britain and America.

Taking syndicalism first, it might seem, on the face of it, that the anti-
statist assumptions that lay behind the Anglo-American political tradition would be more likely to throw up a radical working-class
movement based upon the decentralizing, localistic assumptions of
syndicalism than one committed to the statist doctrines of Marxism. Yet

---

[16] Quoted in M. Derber, *The American Idea of Industrial Democracy, 1865–1965* (Urbana, 1970), p. 25.

such small degree of sympathy as existed in the British and American labour movements for syndicalist ideas derived more from demands for industrial unionism, and for greater workers' control within the factory, than it did from the revolutionary doctrines of Proudhon and Sorel that were influential on the continent.[17] In 1901, in response to pressure from the United Mine Workers of America (U.M.W. of A.), the A.F. of L. permitted the U.M.W. of A. to organize all of the workers 'in and around the mines', because of the geographical autonomy of the coalmining camps. Also, between 1907 and 1912 the federation permitted the establishment of what were called Trade Departments in the Building Trades, the Metal Trades, and among the Railway Employees and some other groups of workers at various levels of skill. But these concessions were made to permit the easier resolution of jurisdictional disputes between unions in contiguous trades, or to coordinate collective bargaining strategies, not to unite all of the workers in a given industry behind a revolutionary trade union movement with syndicalist intent. For the most part, little encouragement was given to A.F. of L. affiliates to experiment with the kind of 'amalgamation' policy which led in England to the development of the National Transport Federation of 1912, or to the National Union of Railwaymen of 1913, and which in turn made possible the neo-syndicalist Triple Alliance of railwaymen, coalminers, and transport workers which appeared the following year.

What the American labour movement produced, instead, was the Industrial Workers of the World (IWW). This was a small industrially oriented, revolutionary trade-union body which was established in Chicago in June 1905, by a mixture of Debsites, disaffected A.F. of L. socialists, Daniel DeLeon's Socialist Trades and Labor Alliance (1895), and the 27,000 member Western Federation of Miners (1893). The IWW was not syndicalist at first; indeed, it never repudiated the parliamentary road to power as decisively as the European syndicalists did, including, at times, even the small British contingent. In 1906 its most famous leader, Secretary-Treasurer William D. Haywood of the Western Federation of Miners, even ran for the governorship of Colorado on a Socialist ticket. But in 1908 the Wobblies, as members of the IWW were sometimes called, did incorporate a statement of syndicalist principles into their constitution which placed industrial action above politics as its most immediate aim.

Organizationally speaking, the IWW never had a great deal of success. From the beginning it was seen as a dual union, which set itself up as a

---

[17] For a discussion of demands for workers' control in the factory and shop floor in Britain and America, see James Hinton, *The First Shops Stewards Movement* (London, 1973), and David Montgomery, *Workers' Control in America, Studies in the History of Work, Technology, and Labor Struggles* (Cambridge, 1979).

rival to the existing craft unions, and which sought to draw unskilled and semi-skilled as well as skilled workers into its ranks. The dual-unionist, or hostile stance which the IWW took up towards the conservative craft unionism of the A.F. of L. marked it off clearly from the syndicalist movements in Europe, including the one in Great Britain which almost universally collaborated with or worked inside of existing unions. Hence the IWW immediately drew down the wrath of the conservative A.F. of L. leadership on its head. The IWW, president Gompers declared in July 1905, only a few weeks after the Wobblies had been founded, had set out 'to direct, pervert, and disrupt the whole labor movement'.[18] Yet at various times between 1905 and 1917 the Industrial Workers of the World acquired between 50,000 and 75,000 members among hardrock miners, lumbermen, textile and railway workers, as well as among transients and recent immigrants from Southern and from Eastern Europe, which the A.F. of L. had ignored. Equally interesting for our purposes, is the fact that in addition to its organizing efforts in the United States the IWW also sought to enroll workers in various other countries, including Great Britain, as well as Canada, Australia, South Africa, and parts of Latin America. Numerically speaking, in Britain itself the IWW never enrolled more than a few thousand members, its biggest strike being one staged by engineers in 1911 against the Singer Sewing Machine Company at Kilbowie, Clydebank, involving about 4,000 men.

Nevertheless, in the years of general labour unrest which preceded the First World War the Industrial Workers of Great Britain (as the Wobblies were called in England) managed to exert a certain degree of influence in other industries as well. In 1912, for example, a group of young coal miners in the South Wales Miners' Federation led by Noah Ablett (formerly of the Plebs Club, which had earlier been influenced by DeLeon and the American Socialist Labor Party (SLP)) published *The Miners Next Step*, demanding that rank-and-file miners 'fight to gain control of, and then to administer that industry',[19] a proposal which contained more than a little IWW syndicalism in it. Partly as a result of this influence, moreover, when the three great national strikes occurred in Britain among the miners, the railwaymen, and the transport workers in the period 1911–12, radical English trade-union leaders such as Tom Mann and Ben Tillett were able to press, with a considerable degree of success, for increased militancy within and collaboration between each of these three major unions. In turn, as we have already mentioned, this policy was partially responsible for the formation of the Triple Alliance

[18] *American Federationist*, vol. II (August 1905), p. 43.
[19] Quoted in H. Pelling, *A History of British Trade Unionism* (Harmondsworth, Middx., 1965), p. 140.

SOCIALISM AND SYNDICALISM

just before the outbreak of war in August 1914. The American IWW, by contrast, remained largely isolated from the mainstream of the American labour movement. This was partly because its more obviously revolutionary opinions made it anathema to the bulk of American middle-class opinion, and partly because some of its members upheld a neo-anarchist 'propaganda of the deed' approach to organizing which made the establishment of stable trade unions difficult.

To a considerable extent the same fate lay in store for the Socialist Party of America (S.P. of A.), which was founded in July 1901, as an American counterpart to the social democratic parties which by then had sprung up in most of Western Europe. The S.P. of A. never secured the support of more than a minority of the A.F. of L.'s trade unions, which meant that it was unable to acquire the kind of mass labour base that enabled most Western European socialist parties to become a force to be reckoned with. This was probably the most important reason for the S.P. of A.'s long-range lack of success. Yet at the beginning it was by no means clear that this was going to be the case. In the 1901–17 period, for example, something close to a majority of members in the Boot and Shoe Workers Union, the International Association of Machinists, the International Ladies Garment Union, and several other major unions gave the S.P. of A. their political support. At the same time the party managed to elect more than a thousand of its members to public office, including two Congressmen – Victor Berger of Milwaukee and Meyer London, from New York's garment district – over thirty members of state legislatures, and several hundred mayors, city councillors and other municipal officers in towns as far apart as Schenectady, New York, Milwaukee, Wisconsin, and Berkeley, California.

Recent scholarship has also shown that contrary to previous opinions the members in the Socialist Party of America were not confined to German and Jewish refugees, or to other immigrants.[20] At its height in 1912 well over half of the S.P. of A.'s membership was native-born. It also secured a wide-ranging regional constituency of its own, some of the elements in which were quite similar to those which were attracted to the British Labour Party. Among these were the New England Bellamyite Nationalists, a group of middle-class municipal reformers similar to the English Fabians; Christian Socialists, such as Rev. W. P. D. Bliss and Rev. George D. Herron, whose Christian Social Union (1892) was modelled after a similar organization in Great Britain; and the followers of Eugene Debs, whose evangelical socialism bore a strong resemblance to the ethical–religious beliefs espoused by Keir Hardie and many members of the English Independent Labour Party (ILP) (1893).

[20] See, for example, J. Weinstein, *The Decline of Socialism in America, 1912–1925* (New York, 1967).

The absence of a major American radical working-class party also cannot be explained simply by reference to the structural difficulties which all third parties have to confront in the context of the American separation of powers political system. The British Labour Party, like the S.P. of A., had to force its way into an already established two-party structure. Neither was the British party necessarily secure by the early years of the twentieth century, when it elected a number of Lib/Lab MPs to Parliament. One historian, for example, commenting on the massive victory which the Liberal Party secured in the general election of 1906, has argued that the 29 Labour MPs who were elected in that election constituted no more than 'a cork floating on the Liberal tide'.[21] In fact, a strong case can be made for the view that the Labour Party only acquired a permanent position in British politics after a series of events had occurred during and after the First World War which were by no means pre-ordained. These events included the Asquith–Lloyd George split within the Liberal Party which took place in 1915–16; the difficulties which Liberals encountered in accommodating their individualist beliefs to the collectivist assumptions necessitated by total war; and the labour insurgencies which occurred after the war had come to an end.

Nevertheless, there were special reasons for the greater difficulties which the socialist movement encountered in attempting to establish itself in the United States. Some of these difficulties were of the movement's own making; and some of them stemmed from differences which existed between European and American society as a whole. As to internal difficulties, one critical difference appears to have lain in the greater moderation and tactical shrewdness displayed by the ILP leader Keir Hardie and his supporters in their efforts to persuade the Trades Union Congress to support establishment of the Labour Representation Committee, on the one hand; and the more dogmatic, and far less successful, tactics pursued by the emigré-dominated American SLP on the other. In December 1893, an English-born engineer named Thomas J. Morgan introduced a Political Programme at the Chicago convention of the A.F. of L. urging it to undertake political action along the same lines as the English Independent Labour Party, which had been founded at a conference held in Bradford only a few months before. Besides requesting the A.F. of L. to support independent political action, however, in its Plank Ten Morgan's Political Programme also sought to commit the US labour movement to a central tenet in Marxist philosophy, namely the collectivization of the means of production, distribution, and exchange.

There is evidence to suggest that by the time of the 1894 A.F. of L.

---

[21] Quoted in H. Pelling, *A Short History of the Labour Party* (London, 1974 edn), p. 16.

convention a majority, or near majority, of the affiliated unions of the federation had endorsed the Political Programme by means of referendum or some other action.[22] Nevertheless, at the convention itself the Morgan Programme was soundly defeated. Part of the reason for this was the overtly revolutionary implications of the call for nationalization in Plank Ten. And another part was the bitter attacks that were being levelled against the craft union policies of the A.F. of L by the national leader of the SLP, Daniel DeLeon, in *The People* at the same time the Programme was under debate.

Given the similar origins and philosophy of the A.F. of L. and the Trades Union Congress, it is not surprising to find that in the early 1890s Henry Broadhurst and the more conservative leaders of the English trade-union movement expressed the same reservations about independent labour political action as Samuel Gompers had done in the United States. In 1893 and 1894, for example, the Parliamentary Committee of the TUC found reasons for ignoring resolutions adopted earlier by the Congress calling upon it to initiate steps which would lead towards the collective ownership of property. And in 1895 the committee even succeeded in unconstitutionally revising the TUC's Standing Orders in an attempt to limit the influence of the socialists, without consulting Congress as a whole. The critical decision, however, was taken at the 1899 Trades Union Congress, at which a resolution proposed by P. Vogel of the Waiters' Union and James O'Grady of the Furnishing Trades' Association was carried committing the Parliamentary Committee to collaborate with the ILP, the Fabians, and other radical bodies in the establishment of a Labour Representation Committee for the sole purpose of securing the election (and paying the salaries) of working-class candidates for Parliament.

Of course, many other factors contributed to the founding of the Labour Party (as the Labour Representation Committee was called after 1906). These included the impact of the Taff Vale case, the seeming indifference of the prior Conservative government to social questions, and strength of English new unionism. But from the tactical point of view, the fact that the request for independent political action was put forward in the relatively innocuous form of a request for financial aid to labour candidates for Parliament played a critical role in carrying the day. There was an English equivalent to the DeLeonite faction in the American SLP, in the shape of H. H. Hyndman's overtly Marxist Social Democratic Federation (SDF), which was also highly critical of the TUC. During the critical years of the mid-1890s, however, when Keir Hardie and the ILP socialists were wooing the English trade unions, the

---

[22] On this point, see Foner, *History*, vol. II, pp. 289–90.

Hyndmanite Marxists in the SDF never went as far as the extremists did in the American SLP when, in December 1895, Daniel DeLeon took the fateful step of establishing the Socialist Trades and Labor Alliance as a rival trade-union federation to the A.F. of L. President Gompers and other A.F. of L. leaders immediately denounced this group as a dual-unionist organization which was out to destroy the A.F. of L.; and in subsequent years they repeatedly, and successfully, used that same weapon against any and all socialist attempts to commit the federation to independent labour politics.

Among the difficulties which the American socialists encountered which stemmed from the overall character of American society was opposition of the American Catholic church to the growth of Marxist ideas. This was an important matter when one remembers that the proportion of Catholics in the American labour force was considerably greater than it was in Great Britain. Besides this there was the division of the American working class into a wide range of different racial and ethnic groups, each of which had its own cultural and political traditions; and the repressive tactics of the employers which, as we have already seen, were widely used to defeat any signs of radical or prosocialist activity at the workplace. Behind these lie other, equally important but less tangible deterrents to the growth of socialism in America, such as the largely agrarian character of the American economy until the end of the nineteenth century, and the persistence of immigrant working-class beliefs in superior rates of upward American social mobility.

Space does not permit us to treat any of these factors in more detail here. But there was one additional societal factor in the United States which is too important to be ignored. This was the pre-existing commitment of most American workers to one or another of the two major parties, in particular to the Democrats, which by the turn of the century had already secured the allegiance of large numbers of working-class voters. It is, of course, also true that most English workers who could vote at this time gave their support to the Liberals. Some of them maintained their loyalty to that party right up to the First World War and beyond. But it must be pointed out that until the Third Reform Act of 1884, only the most skilled workers were eligible to vote in England. In the United States by that date, as we saw earlier on in this chapter, significant numbers of workers already had the vote. Some of the immigrants among them were also receiving patronage jobs and an indirect form of welfare service from the old party political machines, like the Tammany Hall Democrats in New York, for which there was virtually no equivalent in Britain. A similar comment can be made about the lack of any English analogue for the time-honoured tradition of most black workers in continuing to vote Republican, which was the party of former abolitionist president, Abraham Lincoln.

IX. *The First World War and the 1920s*

By the time of the First World War, with the exception of the political variable, several of the differences between the British and American labour movements which we noted in earlier sections appeared to be receding. In 1850 the American economy had been predominantly concerned with primary goods production, and over 60 per cent of its labour force was engaged in agriculture. By 1910 the proportion in agriculture had fallen to 30 per cent while the number of those employed in manufacturing, mining, and building had risen to approximately 30 per cent also. During this period the United States easily surpassed Great Britain in overall output, becoming by 1890 the greatest industrial power in the world. Between 1870 and 1920, for example, United States manufacturing output rose over tenfold, while the corresponding figure for the United Kingdom was less than three. And in those industries which had led Britain to industrial supremacy earlier on in the century – cotton, iron and steel, and coal – the processes of obsolescence and relative economic decline, which were to have such a significant impact on English labour relations as the twentieth century wore on, had already begun to make their mark.

The most obvious initial consequence of this US catching-up process was greater equality in the overall numerical strength of the British and American trade unions. If we compare membership figures for the movements in the two countries for the 1900–14 period, we find that the American unions, which in 1900 still possessed less than one million members, had broadened their basis of support considerably. If we add in the Railroad Brotherhoods and the IWW membership to the unions of the A.F. of L., by 1910 the American movement had organized as many as 2,141,000 workers. This compared with 2,565,000 in the English Trades Union Congress and the General Federation of Trades Unions (GFTU) in Great Britain in the same year, which in absolute terms was not a significant difference. (The GFTU was an offshoot of the TUC, with a partly overlapping membership.) Although the A.F. of L. had dropped behind again by 1914, and its figures represented a smaller proportion of the American labour force considered as a whole, it had by now become a force to be reckoned with in coalmining, in the garment industry, in engineering, in transportation, and in most of the building trades.

There was also a quite similar mix of cooperation and resistance to be observed in relations between government and labour in both countries during the actual course of the First World War. From the beginning both President Wilson and Prime Minister Asquith, as well as Lloyd George as English Chancellor of the Exchequer, sought to secure the cooperation of the British and American unions in the war effort by offering them some degree of official recognition in return for their relaxing customary trade practices at the workplace. The result, in England, was the various 1915 Treasury Agreements limiting the use of the strike, and permitting job dilution whereby unskilled workers, including women, could be employed in formerly male-dominated trades. In return for this the government promised to limit war profits and to return to normal collective bargaining procedures after the end of the war. In America, which entered the conflict in April 1917, nearly three years after it had begun in Europe, the result was the establishment of the National War Labor Board, which had five representatives from industry and five from the unions, to help increase war production. This was in return for a no-strike pledge, recognition of the right of collective bargaining, the eight-hour day in a wide range of federal employment areas, and equal pay for women. The latter promise, however, was rarely observed.

At the same time, in both countries considerable rank-and-file dissatisfaction was expressed with the results of these restrictions. There were also similar protests against military conscription, war inflation, and what many ordinary trade-union members considered to be excessive class collaboration with both business and government on the part of the official labour leadership. On the American West Coast, IWW strike action briefly impeded the supply of spruce lumber, which was important in the production of fighter aircraft. Strikes also closed down mining of copper in Michigan at various points in 1917, which was another vital war material. Overall, the war years of 1917–18 in America saw 2.4 times as many workers out on strike as there had been in 1914–15. But across the Atlantic in the South Wales coal industry, and most important of all in the Clydeside engineering industry, British outbursts against these same kinds of restrictions tended to be larger, better organized, and more effective than they were in the United States. This was due partly to the greater militancy of the shops stewards movement in the United Kingdom, which did not exist in America. It was also due to the fact that in America, the most important of these unofficial strikes were conducted by the explicitly anti-war IWW, not by the strongly patriotic A.F. of L.

Politically speaking, the position of the labour movements in the two countries was far less similar. The British Labour Party, like the German Social Democrats and most other affiliates of the socialist Second International, was at first bitterly divided over whether to support the war. Arthur Henderson and the majority of trade unionists supported it, while Ramsay MacDonald, Keir Hardie, and the ILP element were opposed. Although the anti-war minority was much criticized, the fact that Henderson accepted office in Asquith's first coalition government in May 1915 brought the Labour Party a measure of acceptance and respectability that was to stand it in good stead when the war was over. In the case of the Socialist Party of America, however, almost the opposite process occurred, with disastrous consequences for its standing in the country. At an emergency conference held in March 1917, when President Wilson was on the point of committing the United States to the conflict, the overwhelming majority of the Socialist Party delegates voted to oppose American entry. The S.P. of A. was one of very few socialist parties in the Second International to do so. Some scholars argue that this was only possible because it had so little support within the generally patriotic trade-union movement.[23]

Whatever the truth of this, opposition to the war placed the S.P. of A. entirely beyond the pale of respectability, as far as much of middle-class opinion was concerned; and this was one of the acts that helped to precipitate the 1919 Red Scare which had far more serious consequences for the American Left than did the anti-Bolshevik movement in Britain in the immediate post-war period.

Nevertheless, even during the war certain parallels between the British and American labour movements persisted. For example, recent scholarship suggests that despite the wave of hysterical patriotism that swept up most trade-union members once the US had entered the war in April 1917, the S.P. of A.'s opposition to American participation – like that of the Independent Labour Party, the British Socialist Party, and some other rank-and-file workers in Britain – struck a sympathetic cord amongst several segments of the US working class.[24] This was not only true of German-American skilled artisans, or of Irish-American labourers who, particularly after the crushing of the Easter Rebellion in Dublin, in April 1916, hated the idea of an alliance with Great Britain. It was also true of thousands of native-born working-class militants whose traditional distaste for standing armies and for the dangers of increased state power which war brought along with it, was even more deeply rooted than these same sentiments were among British workers.

Yet the overall effect of the social and political upheavals created by the First World War was to widen once more the developmental gap that had existed previously between the British and American labour movements, not to diminish it. To begin with, Arthur Henderson's further promotion to the War Cabinet in Lloyd George's coalition government of December 1916, together with the entry of John Hodge, secretary of the Steel Smelters, and George Barnes, former secretary of the ASE, into the government markedly increased public acceptance of

[23] See, for example, Daniel Bell, *Marxian Socialism in the United States* (Princeton, 1967), p. 102.

[24] For evidence on this point, see James Weinstein, *The Decline of American Socialism, 1912–1924* (New York, 1967), ch. 1; D. Shannon, *The Socialist Party of America: A History* (New York, 1955), ch. 1; and J. H. M. Laslett and S. M. Lipset (eds.), *Failure of a Dream? Essays in the History of American Socialism* (New York, 1974), ch. 3.

the Labour Party as a legitimate political entity. In America, by contrast, not even the relatively conservative A.F. of L. was to acquire this degree of acceptance until the New Deal period of the 1930s.

The long-standing independent political path along which British labour had been travelling since the turn of the century also reached its logical conclusion in January 1924, when the Labour Party took office briefly on its own. Despite its minority status, which made it dependent on Liberal support in the House of Commons, Britain's first Labour government was able to enact some beneficial social legislation. Its most notable achievements were John Wheatley's Housing Act, an act to raise pensions, and an amendment to the unemployment insurance system which extended benefits to the long-term unemployed. In America, on the other hand, not only did the A.F. of L.'s voluntaristic outlook mean that this kind of social legislation was delayed until the time of the New Deal. The impact of the 1918–19 Red Scare was so severe that even president Gompers and the other leaders of the trade-union movement were relegated for a time to the category of social pariahs and outcasts, even though they were strongly anti-Communist, and hostile towards any form of public disorder.

Lying behind many of these difficulties, and implicit in what we have already said, was a differential response on the part of the British and American movements not only to the First World War, but also to the Russian revolution and to issues of post-war reconstruction. In 1917 Lloyd George's government sent Arthur Henderson to visit the Kerensky regime in Russia in order to see if it could be prevailed upon to stay in the war. Henderson returned advocating a negotiated peace, and the sending of Labour Party delegates to a proposed Stockholm International Socialist Congress at which discussions might begin with German delegates on how to negotiate an end to the conflict. Reprimanded by his cabinet colleagues, Henderson resigned from the government. He and his colleagues then set about developing an independent foreign policy which advocated a League of Nations, mediation of international disputes, and international trusteeship for African colonies, proposals which were to play an important role in the foreign policy of future Labour governments. Ironically, these same demands formed part of the plan for post-war reconstruction which President Wilson took with him to the Versailles peace conference. But not only did the A.F. of L. not devise a foreign policy of its own which might under certain circumstances have conflicted with the American administration's position. It willingly cooperated in the American government's campaign against socialists and other opponents of the war, and even supported many of the repressive acts undertaken against the IWW, the S.P. of A., and the fledgling Communist Party by agents of the Department of Justice during the period of the Red Scare. In doing this, president Gompers and his colleagues laid the foundation for the generally cooperative, and usually conservative, attitude towards US foreign policy on the part of the American trade-union movement which has lasted to this day.

The A.F. of L.'s acquiescence in Woodrow Wilson's post-war foreign policy symbolized what was to become a decade of retreat and relative acquiescence on the part of the American labour movement in the 1920s, compared to one of greater militancy in Great Britain, at least up to the period of the 1926 General Strike. Between 1920 and 1930 overall membership figures in both the A.F. of L. and the TUC declined quite markedly, with the American total dropping from 4,298,000 to 2,834,000 during the decade, and the English dropping from 6,417,000 to 3,729,000. Yet these figures concealed an even greater weakness on the American side than at first appears, both as regards state policy towards the trade unions, and in the labour movement's relation with employers. In 1922 the Supreme Court declared unconstitutional the Owen–Keatings Act (1916), which had outlawed child labour; and, as we have already seen, in 1923 in *Adkins* v. *Children's Hospital* the court also struck down a law providing for minimum wages for women working in the District of Colombia, a decision which cast doubt on the validity of minimum wage laws in general. Other pre-1917 pieces of labour legislation enacted by the Progressives were also struck down. But the most serious setback took place in 1921, when in *Duplex* v. *Deering* the Supreme Court invalidated several provisions of the Clayton Act of 1914, which labour had assumed gave it permanent immunity from the issuance of injunctions against trade-union activity that was considered injurious to property rights in labour disputes.

As to relations with employers, the conservative political mood of the 1920s in America made it possible for the employers to mount an effective open-shop campaign under the name 'American plan'. This played upon US traditions of individualism by asserting what it called the 'inalienable' privilege of every American worker to enter any trade or business he chose without having to join an independent trade union. In addition to this, company unions increased both in number and in scope. Employers made use of profit-sharing schemes, scientific management to increase efficiency, and 'yellow-dog' contracts which made it a condition of employment that workers would not join a non-company union or go out on strike.

A number of scholars have argued that the relative apathy of the US labour movement in the 1920s resulted primarily from high wages, and a 'return to normalcy' (i.e. to an unrestricted form of free enterprise) as well as from the repressive measures cited above. Real wages in a number of manufacturing industries did rise during the decade, notably in car manufacture, meatpacking, and the building trades. But recent evidence has thrown doubt upon these conclusions by citing increased frictional unemployment resulting from the growth of the more modern electrical, mass-production, or oil and chemical industries; the poor conditions under which large numbers of black workers who had just arrived from the South had to work; and serious strike and union-organizing defeats in many industries, the most prominent of them being coal.[25]

There were three other general reasons for the greater ideological moderation of the American compared with the British labour movement in the 1920s. One was the greater success, as well as the greater virulence, of the aforementioned Red Scare tactics which both the American government and the employers used to defeat the political and industrial unrest which swept across the United States at the war's end, even though the true strength of the radical element in America by this time was probably less than it was in Great Britain.

In January and February 1919, unofficial strikes in the Clyde and Belfast engineering trades were beaten back with police batons, and the Anti-Socialist Union, the British Empire League, and other small right-wing propaganda organizations fulminated against the dangers of revolution in the United Kingdom. In 1920 Parliament adopted an Emergency Powers Act which gave the government legal authority to break any strike that threatened the public services. When looked at comparatively, however, these English acts of repression pale into insignificance when they are compared with Attorney General Palmer's 'raids' in the United States on Wobbly, S.P. of A. and Communist offices; with the emasculation of these organizations that resulted from the arrest and conviction of almost their entire national leadership, including Haywood and Debs; and with the campaign of extra-legal and indiscriminate violence and intimidation which was launched by Pinkerton detectives, armed company guards, and state and federal troops against American strikers or disturbers of the peace wherever they were to be found.

The most grisly example of the use of violence against American workers in this period is to be found in the brutal suppression of the September 1919–January 1920 national steel strike, which left 43 strikers dead, over 400 injured and a virtual reign of terror in Pittsburgh, Pennsylvania, Gary, Indiana, and other steel towns. By labelling the strike, without any demonstrable evidence, as Bolshevik-inspired, the United States Steel Corporation, along with other steel companies, were able to avoid negotiating with the workers, rally government support to their side, and set back the cause of industrial unionism in America for yet another decade.

[25] For this point, see Frank Stricker, 'Affluence for Whom? – Another Look at Prosperity and the Working Classes in the 1920's', *Labor History*, vol. XXIV, no. 1 (Winter 1983), pp. 5–33.

British capitalists did not, of course, like mass strike action any more than American ones did. However, given the renewed threat of Triple Alliance action by about one and a half million miners, railwaymen, and transport workers in the autumn of 1920, English employers were somewhat more hesitant to follow the same repressive line that their American counterparts did. They may also have been somewhat mollified by the collapse of the Triple Alliance which took place after the railwaymen and transport workers' unions failed to support the miners in a strike action in April 1921. Nevertheless, there was some truth to the remark which Walter Hines Page, the American ambassador in London, made as early as January 1918, when he said that the British labour movement would soon be in a position where it could be 'playing for supremacy'.[26] Although considerably exaggerated, this was not a judgment which could plausibly be advanced with respect to the American labour movement either at that time or since.

The second and third reasons for the greater weakness of the American labour movement in the 1920s are corollaries of the one just discussed. These were, that despite the opportunities for organizing presented by the First World War, unlike the British labour movement the American trades unions still had not put deep roots down into the factory working class, especially among unskilled immigrants and blacks; and that in an overall sense, British capitalism as an economic system had been weakened by the experience of the war whereas American capitalism was strengthened by it. This meant that any major episode of industrial strife in Britain could much more readily acquire the characteristics of a social crisis than it could in the United States.

The former point can best be illustrated by referring again to the steel strike of 1919. Before the First World War thousands of 'new' Italian, Polish, and East European peasant immigrants had entered the steel industry; during and immediately after it, a smaller but significant number of southern blacks. When in late 1919 the National Committee for Organizing Iron and Steel Workers, which was to conduct the steel strike, was formed under the direction of the future Communist leader William Z. Foster, it was these 'new' immigrants who were among the first to join the new body; and it was they who were among the most tenacious supporters of the strike. Yet most of these Southern and Eastern European workers, being unskilled, were not permitted to join the Amalgamated Association of Iron, Steel and Tin Workers, which, though tiny, had since the 1890s been the main craft union in the trade. Nor were blacks able to join. Instead, they were divided up by the A.F. of L. executive among a number of so-called federal unions, to await apportionment among the existing skilled unions in the trade. This pointed up even more clearly the need for industrial or general unions in

[26] Quoted in H. Pelling, *America and the British Left: From Bright to Bevan* (London, 1956), p. 121.

the American labour movement along the lines which had already been set down in Britain.

The latter point – concerning the impact of Britain's declining competitive position or her deteriorating industrial relations – can be made by referring to the United Kingdom's coal industry.

Before 1914 when pick-and-shovel methods were still the preferred way of mining coal, the British coal industry was the largest in the world. It was also still reasonably profitable. But by 1920 its relative output per-man-shift had fallen behind that of both Germany and the United States, principally because of its backwardness in employing coal-cutting machines, and its failure to rationalize the structure of ownership. Only 8 per cent of the record output of 187 million tons of coal raised in the United Kingdom in 1913, for example, was mechanically cut. By 1921 the proportion has risen to 14 per cent, and by 1930 to 31 per cent; but in the meantime the proportion of American coal mechanically cut had risen from 60.7 per cent in 1920, to 78.4 per cent in 1929. Much the same kind of obsolescence became apparent in the British cotton, shipbuilding, and textile industries at this time. But it was the declining profitability of the coal industry, coupled with the Lloyd George government's duplicity over the Sankey Commission's 1919 recommendation concerning mine nationalization, which lay at the root of the industrial turmoil of the 1920s in Britain, and which resulted ultimately in the 1926 General Strike.

The General Strike which took place in the United Kingdom on 4–12 May 1926 was, of course, in no sense a revolutionary act. In fact it was not a general strike in the syndicalist sense at all. Instead, it represented a withdrawal of labour under the direction of the General Council of the TUC by some two and a half million miners, transport workers, iron and steel employees, and by some others, in support of the refusal of the Miners' Federation of Great Britain to accept the Samuel Commission's recommendation for a further cut in mining wages.

Other, more extensive categories of workers were only called out after a week had elapsed. But the TUC leaders did not want the strike. They only called it because of what they considered to be the coal owners' and the Tory government's intransigence towards their cause, and perhaps also to make up for the lack of solidarity which had been displayed by the trade-union movement, on Black Friday in April 1921. Once out the strikers remained solid and disciplined, and there was very little violence, despite the government's use of troops to move essential supplies. However, far from redeeming the Triple Alliance's collapse of five years earlier, fear of the social turmoil which might have ensued if the strike had gone on for longer, coupled with the coal owners' continuing refusal to make concessions, brought the TUC to call the whole thing off after ten days without gaining a single one of the miners' demands. Embittered, the miners carried on alone until they were compelled to give in in the autumn of 1926.

In industrial terms, therefore, the British General Strike was a disaster for the labour movement in England, as humiliating a defeat as any suffered by the American unions in the same decade. Nevertheless, the strike did demonstrate the ability of the British unions to bring the whole operation of the economy to a standstill. Again, this was something which could not have been done by the A.F. of L. It also raised the issue of what the British government would do, or might do when faced with the prospect – however remote in this instance – of an insurrectionary act undertaken by the labour movement against the state. In practice, the Trades and Trade Union Act of 1927, which Baldwin's Conservative government passed as a direct response to the strike, made no significant additions to the body of labour law. Nor was it so destructive of trade-union effectiveness as was the cumulative effect of the Supreme Court decisions on the freedom to operate of American unions, which we examined above.

The British Trades and Trade Union Act of 1927 simply outlawed sympathetic stoppages except within the confines of the trade in which a strike originally broke out; made minor adjustments to the law of picketing; and substituted the politically motivated 'contracting-out' clause (terminating the prior automatic wage deductions as a political levy for the Labour Party) with a 'contracting-in' one. The immediate effect of this last provision was to reduce the Labour Party's income from its affiliated unions by approximately one-third. However resentment at this enactment, which was repealed in 1946, coupled with continuing high unemployment after Britain's return to the gold standard, appeared to increase trade-union support for the Labour Party rather than weaken it. In the May 1929 general election the party was returned to office with 287 MPs, for the first time becoming the largest, although not yet the majority, party in the House of Commons.

X.   The great depression, the New Deal, and British consolidation

There was, of course, much of drama and importance for the overall development of the British labour movement in the political events which followed two years after the 1929 election, in August 1931: the collapse of the second Labour government over Ramsay MacDonald's determination to stay on the gold standard; the Labour Party's disastrous split over the issue of a National Coalition; the party's humiliating defeat in the election that followed in October of the same year; and an important reassertion of the TUC's influence and control over the temporarily weakened Labour Party, until it had recovered its strength.

Nevertheless, the most interesting developments of the 1930s do not concern the British labour movement, which despite generally depressed economic conditions continued, if somewhat more gingerly, to follow the same broad industrial and political path which it had adopted during the previous decade. They concern instead the American labour movement, and the rise of the Congress of Industrial Organizations in the period from 1936 to 1939. For it was this organization, which was established by United Mine Workers' leader John L. Lewis and by other supporters of industrial unionism in the A.F. of L., that at last enabled the American movement as a whole to expand beyond the narrow, craft-union framework which had characterized it for so long. This meant that, with more than three million members each by the outbreak of the Second World War, the A.F. of L. and the CIO, when taken together, could take their places for the first time alongside the British and other European trade-union federations as genuinely mass organizations.

The rapid growth of the American labour movement coincided with, and was in part predicated upon, the final breakdown of the old voluntarist policy of opposition to any attempt by the state to interfere in the internal affairs of the trade-union movement and to the growth of state power in general. Thus the founding of the CIO also coincided with the development of a far more militant and socially progressive attitude on the part of American unions towards the building of what was to become the welfare state; as well as by a far more obvious and open commitment to partisan politics on the side of the Democratic Party. These changes did not happen all at once. Hostility towards the enactment of state or federal legislation providing for unemployment insurance and minimum wage laws persisted in the building trades unions and in other conservative A.F. of L. bodies until as late as 1938. But from the first the CIO, if not the A.F. of L., gave strong support to New Deal social legislation which ranged from the Tennessee Valley Authority (1933), through the Social Security Act (1935) to the Fair Labor Standards Act (1938). As a result, much of the labour movement, although still publicly maintaining its 'reward-your-friends, punish-your-enemies' political policy, in practice made an overt commitment to the Democratic Party to a degree that had never happened before. In the 1936 presidential campaign, CIO president John. L. Lewis committed half a million dollars from the U.M.W. of A.'s treasury to help elect pro-labour Democrats in various parts of the country. In addition, Labor's Nonpartisan League, which was later to become known as the CIO's

Political Action Committee, campaigned actively on behalf of a wide variety of Democratic candidates in New York, Michigan, Pennsylvania, New Jersey, Massachusetts, and elsewhere. This inaugurated a policy of support for economic and social reform on the part of the American unions which went considerably beyond their members' own relatively narrow constituency, and made them accept at least partial responsibility for the well-being of the lower classes in society as a whole. This, in turn, brought the American unions closer to the Western European tradition of social-welfare unionism than they had ever been before.

Ironically, this transformation of the trade-union movement in the USA occurred at a time when the British workers, temporarily at least, were following a policy of acquiescence, even of passivity, towards a number of major changes that were taking place in the society around them. Among these were the growth of the motor car, electrical, and other consumer goods industries in much the same manner as in the United States. Yet British industrial relations proceeded in much the same manner as before. Only miners' leaders such as A. J. Cook, and a minority of militants in the Amalgamated Engineering Union, objected to the Mond–Turner employer–employee conciliation talks of 1928–9. Ten years earlier, a much larger group would have condemned these meetings as an example of class collaboration. In addition, English efforts to proceed further down the path to more sophisticated forms of general, or industrial unionism were also stalled. At least some of this relative caution can be put down to the ongoing after-effects of defeat in the 1926 General Strike. Nevertheless, it presents a significant contrast to what was then happening in the United States.

The rise of the CIO becomes all the more intriguing when we remember that the great depression of the 1930s was even more severe in its consequences for working people in the United States than it was in Great Britain. After falling from an output peak of 46.4 in 1929 to 41.4 in 1931 (1958 = 100), the index of manufacturing production in Britain already showed signs of recovering in 1932. Unemployment, too, was less severe in the United Kingdom than it was in the United States. The number of jobless persons in America rose from one and a half million in 1929 to approximately 13 million in 1933, when one in every four persons in the labour force was out of work. This pattern of contraction, and the loss of income to the unions which it entailed, may have been partially responsible for the failure of the A.F. of L. leadership to take advantage of the early New Deal legislation which provided a much more secure legal framework in which to organize than had ever existed in America before.

The early measures of the New Deal were prompted largely by the need to cope with the massive unemployment occasioned by the depression, as seen, for example, in the financial support which was given to state unemployment agencies. But they also included legislation which intimately affected the relationship between the worker and the state. For example, the Norris–La Guardia Act of 1930 reversed the constraints which had been placed on the labour movement by the Supreme Court decisions of the 1920s. This act declared yellow–dog contracts illegal, and restored the immunity of trade unions from prosecution under the antitrust laws. Thenceforth, for the next four years, social reform measures of profound importance both for the restructuring of the American economy, and for the rapid growth of the labour movement, poured forth from Congress. First came Section 7a of the National Industrial Recovery Act (NRA) of June 1933, which gave all industrial workers the 'right to organize and bargain collectively through representatives of their own choosing';[27] and prohibited employers' efforts to undermine this right by coercion or by requiring their employees to join company unions.

In May 1935 the Supreme Court, in the Schecter case, declared the NRA unconstitutional on the ground that Congress had improperly extended its authority over inter-state commerce to include intra-state business. Hence in July 1935 the Roosevelt administration replaced the NRA with the Wagner Act, otherwise known as the National Labor Relations Act (NLRA), which was the most important piece of legislation enacted by the New Deal as far as labour organizing was concerned. Among other things, this law established a National Labor Relations Board (NLRB) to supervize union elections at the workplace, through which workers could choose whether they wanted to be organized, and by which union. The Board's authority was later extended by making its decisions legally binding; and this time, despite its even more sweeping provisions, the NLRA's constitutionality was upheld by the Supreme Court in the *National Labor Relations Board* v. *Jones and Laughlin Steel Company* case of April 1937. Another permanent piece of reform legislation was the Social Security Act of August 1935, which built upon pre-existing old age and unemployment laws that had been enacted at the state level by providing comprehensive pension, unemployment, and other benefits to the aged, to those out of work, and to others with medical disabilities. The law caused a furore, since its opponents used this act more than any other to attack F. D. R. as a 'pinko', if not an outright communist. But in a series of decisions handed down in May 1937 – in the *Steward Machine Co.* v. *Davis* case; in *Helvering* v. *Davis*; and in *Carmi-*

---

[27] Quoted in J. H. M. Laslett, *The Workingman in American Life* (Boston, 1968), p. 114.

chael v. *Southern Coal Company* – the Supreme Court also held the Social Security Act to be in accordance with the American Constitution.

The A.F. of L.'s initial response to the New Deal legislation which gave federal sanction to trade-union organizing, and in particular to Section 7a of the NRA, was disappointing. Even when it did begin organizing semi-skilled and unskilled factory workers, instead of estab-lishing new, industry-wide unions, it again divided its new enrollees into federal unions, intending to distribute them among existing craft unions once the organizing drives were over. It was the repudiation of this tactic, as well as the defeat of a resolution favouring industry-wide organizing at the A.F. of L. convention of November 1935, that brought the Committee on Industrial Organization (as it was initially called) into being. Led by John L. Lewis, Philip Murray, Sidney Hillman and a number of other progressive trade-union leaders, it immediately em-barked on an independent mass organizing campaign in manufacturing industry. The result was the series of bitterly fought sit-down strikes of 1936–7, which resulted in bringing more than 80,000 rubber workers, 400,000 car workers, 375,000 steelmen, 175,000 new textile workers, and numerous other categories into the framework of the American labour movement.

It should be made clear that these sit-down strikes, along with the other militant labour demonstrations that took place in America in the first half of the 1930s, were not political or syndicalist acts undertaken to acquire direct control over the means of production, any more than the English General Strike of 1926 had been. Instead, they were tactical devices on the part of factory workers to force the employers, for the first time in manufacturing industry on any truly large scale, into recognizing their organizations and negotiating acceptable contracts. Despite their lack of revolutionary purpose, however, the sit-ins were fought with immense enthusiasm and tenacity, bringing in blacks and other minority elements, and making full use of wives and daughters on the picket lines, many of them for the first time. As a result, they gave to the American labour movement a sense of purpose and of militancy which had not been seen on the same scale since the organized campaigns of the Knights of Labor in 1886. In March 1937, when the smaller rivals of the United States Steel Corporation began to recognize the Steel Workers' Organiz-ing Committee (which was soon to become the United Steel Workers of America) the back of the opposition was broken. The Congress of Industrial Organizations had come to stay. By 1939 the CIO and the A.F. of L., which had been galvanized into renewed activity by the example of its rival, had approximately three and a half million members each.

This sudden, militant expansion of the United States labour move-ment cannot be explained by arguing that the old A.F. of L. leadership had at last come to recognize the anachronistic nature of its organizing methods. Nor can the rise of the CIO be explained by the infusion of young blood into the trade-union leadership. New organizers were certainly appointed to help conduct the sit-ins. But most of those who led the actual breakaway from the A.F. of L., and took senior positions in the CIO hierarchy were seasoned and experienced men like John Brophy, Sidney Hillman, and Philip Murray, who had worked in the labour movement for years. Even John. L. Lewis, for all of his charisma and brilliance as a national labour strategist, was a tough-minded trade-union boss who had ruled his own union, the United Mine Workers of America, with a rod of iron, and until 1932 had always been a Republican.

Other factors besides the nature of the union leadership were clearly at work, too. Important examples were set by the unemployment demonstrations that took place in numerous American cities during the early 1930s, as well as by rank-and-file strikes that were undertaken by Longshoremen (dockers), by Auto-Lite Company employees, and by Teamsters in San Francisco, Toledo, and Minneapolis in the summer of 1933 and in the spring and summer of 1934. These stoppages, coupled with the even larger textile strike which took place all along the East Coast in September 1934, had no direct bearing on the sit-down strikes as such, which occurred in Michigan, Ohio, and other industrial states more than two years later. But they are important testimony to the grassroots character of much of the organizing that was carried out in the 1930s, and suggest strongly that the CIO came into being as much because of pressure from below as it did from plans made by the national leadership from above.

Finally, there was the role of the Communists. In neither Britain nor America, nor in any other Anglo-Saxon country for that matter, did the Communist Party have any real political success. At various points during the 1930s the Communist Party of the United States of America elected a municipal councillor here and there, as for example in Harlem, in New York; and they made a particular point of championing the cause of the blacks. In Britain, the Communists became politically strong only in Glasgow, the East End of London, and in other enclaves where radical intellectuals and militant rank-and-file workers were concentrated in sufficient numbers to affect the vote. Metal tradesman Willie Gallagher, for instance, was elected to Parliament as a Communist MP for West Fife in 1935.

Industrially speaking, however, the story was different. Taking advantage of the major industrial unrest that had occurred at the end of the First World War, the British Communist Party's trade-union arm, the

National Minority Movement (1924), secured considerable influence among coal miners, seamen, and in other occupations during the late 1920s and early 1930s. This influence spread, albeit for somewhat different reasons, to electricians, foundry workers, and fire workers after the beginning of the Second World War. After that, beginning in the late 1940s a determined, but only partially successful effort was made to prevent Communists from holding office in British unions at all. In the United States, the circumstances of the CIO's birth during the Popular Front period gave the Communists an even better chance of acquiring major influence in the unions than it had in Great Britain. This was because, due to the craft union orientation of the A.F. of L., when the CIO came into being there was a dearth of experienced trade-union organizers who could take advantage of the new opportunities for organizing industrial unions which had been opened up by the labour legislation of the New Deal. As a result, at both the national and the local levels experienced Communist trade-union organizers such as Harry Bridges, Len DeCaux, James Matles, Wyndham Mortimer, and Bob Travis were hired by the CIO leadership to partake in the main organizing campaigns. Hence by 1939 no fewer than 11 important US industrial unions were under effective Communist control. Altogether, the membership of these unions accounted for between one-quarter and one-third of the CIO's entire membership.

　None of this meant that president John L. Lewis of the CIO, or the other American trade-union leaders, had much sympathy for communism as a political ideology, any more than the leaders of the British Trade Union Congress did. To the contrary, by the late 1940s when the political pendulum had swung the other way, with the beginning of the Cold War, most American unions cooperated willingly with the American government's campaign to remove all traces of Communist influence from the labour movement. The result was that by 1950, first the A.F. of L., and then the CIO expelled all of their unions known to be Communist influenced, the immediate catalyst for this being the rapid deterioration of US–Soviet relations in the 1946–52 period, and the growth of the McCarthyite Red Scare. In Britain, on the other hand, where Cold War sentiments were not quite so widespread, the Communists managed to maintain their influence in unions such as the National Union of Mineworkers for a considerably longer period of time.

Summing up the relative position of the British and American labour movements on the eve of the Second World War, two general points can be made. The first is that, by succeeding at last in unionizing a significant proportion of the workers in heavy industry, the United States movement once more narrowed the numerical gap that had previously existed between it and the British movement. In 1940, for example, the overall figure for American trade-union membership was 6,542,000, compared to 8,717,000 for the British. This did not mean that there were no longer any major ideological or structural differences between the two movements. Relatively speaking, for example, still only about 25 per cent of the United States labour force was organized into unions in 1940, compared to 32 per cent in the United Kingdom. This factor continued to inhibit the degree of influence which the American movement could exert in its relations with both business and government. In Britain, on the other hand, where the Labour Party had now become the main opposition party, the trade-union movement was in a much stronger long-term position.

What is more, racial, if no longer so much ethnic, divisions continued to plague the American movement in a manner which had never been the case in England. This was the case even though the CIO had made its historic shift from the 'exclusive' organizing philosophy of the American Federation of Labor back to the 'inclusive' one which had earlier characterized the Knights of Labor. As we have seen, this enabled the CIO to enroll several hundred thousand black and other minority workers into its ranks. Yet it would be misleading to suggest that by 1939 the American labour movement had entirely overcome the culture of racism which had for so long been endemic in American society. The degree of effective democracy within American unions also continued to be somewhat less than it was in Britain, and the incidence of corruption somewhat higher. Thus, despite the social idealism which marked the early years of the CIO, by 1939 the new industrial unions were showing signs of returning to the same bureaucratic methods which had earlier characterized the A.F. of L. These include higher salaries than would be paid to elected officials in the British labour movement, less frequent submission of contracts for rank-and-file approval, and more extensive employment of statisticians and labour relations experts.

The second general point to be made is that politically speaking, by allying themselves openly with the Democratic Party during the 1930s, the American unions finally abandoned their traditional policy of refusing to become directly involved in partisan politics. This decision appeared to give the final *coup de grâce* to any lingering hopes that the much smaller American political Left may have had of persuading either the A.F. of L. or CIO to join with it in establishing an independent labour party. Nevertheless, if we ignore the independent character of the Labour Party for a moment, and compare instead the legislative results that were secured by the British and American trade-union movements as a consequence of their political activities, the presence of a separate political party of labour in one country and its absence in the other loses some of its significance. This was because, by virtue of their leading role in the New Deal coalition, in heavily industrialized states like Michigan, Pennsylvania, and New York, the Political Action Committees of major unions such as the United Auto Workers or the United Steel Workers had moved beyond seeking to influence the Democratic Party from the outside by the donation of money, or by urging their members to vote for a particular set of candidates. Instead, by having their unions represented on local party platform committees, and by influencing the choice of Democratic candidates for political office, they had begun to influence the party from the inside.

And yet, in 1939 at least, it would be going too far to suggest, as one commentator has done, that the Democrats had by then become 'a functional substitute for, or were performing many [of the] functions of a labour party which were carried out in Europe by social democratic groups'.[28] For one thing, the A.F. of L. leadership refused to join in the activities of the CIO's Labor Nonpartisan League until most of the way through the Second World War. For another, despite its major influence in the northern industrial states, elsewhere organized labour was still only one among a number of other constituent elements within the Democratic Party, some of which (immigrants, middle-class voters, or the black vote from the 'solid south') were its equals in strength. In Britain, on the other hand, the unions, as co-founders of the Labour Party, played an equal if not dominant role from the very beginning. To put it another way, without trade-union financial support the Labour Party could not have been established, or continued to exist. In the case of the US Democratic Party, by contrast, although a withdrawal of support by the unions would have dealt a serious blow to its political prospects in the industrial states just mentioned, it would not have destroyed it altogether. The subsequent history of the relationship of the A.F.L.–CIO to the Democratic Party confirms the view that organized labour in the United States has never been able to play the same indispensable financial and policy-making role in relation to the Democratic Party that the unions have always played in relation to the Labour Party in Great Britain.

XI. *Conclusions*

Beyond these general remarks concerning the industrial and political status of the British and American labour movements on the eve of the Second World War, what more can be said by way of conclusion? This chapter has not examined enough of the evidence concerning the Austra-

[28] J. Seidman, 'Organized Labor in Political Campaigns', *Public Opinion Quarterly*, vol. III, no. 4 (October 1939), p. 648.

lian, Canadian or other English-speaking labour movements to be able to speak with any authority about the character and history of Anglo-Saxon labour movements considered as a whole. Nevertheless, a number of alternative models of different labour movements in the West can be briefly mentioned, in order to see where the American labour movement might be placed among them, if it can be placed anywhere at all.

It is generally accepted that during the nineteenth century at least three different types of labour movement were established in Western Europe, each of which acquired considerable influence beyond the country of its birth. The first, and the oldest model was created by the British trade-union movement, which for most of its career was moderate and non-revolutionary in its orientation. It was also a model in which the unions may be said to have created an independent party of labour, rather – as was the case in many countries on the European continent – than the other way around. The Australian, New Zealand, and to a lesser extent the Canadian labour movements have all tended to follow the British example. Secondly, there is the model provided by the German labour movement, which was in many respects the opposite of that in Britain, since most of its important unions were not founded until after the establishment of the German Social Democratic Party (SPD) which took place in 1875. As a result, the SPD exercised a greater, although diminishing, amount of control over the German unions than did the socialists in Great Britain. The German model was also followed in Austria, Switzerland, Poland and in several other European countries as well. France provides a third, and somewhat more complex model since for much of its history the French movement was divided between Marxists, moderate reformers, and anarchists or anarcho-syndicalists. The latter elements also became influential – although not necessarily dominant – in Italy, Spain, and the Iberian peninsula.

If we put the American labour movement alongside each of these three types of European organization, it seems at first obvious that the American movement had most in common with the British one. And in terms of their common pragmatism, their early attachment to craft unionism, and their Lib/Lab rather than Marxist form of labour politics, it is clear that the British and the American labour movements did indeed develop along similar lines. Yet if we look a little more closely at the evidence, some reservations to this conclusion have to be made. From the point of view of working-class politics, the most important defining characteristic of a labour party, as opposed to a social democratic party, is that it is either heavily influenced, or actually controlled by, the trade-union movement to which it is attached. This was true both of the Labour Parties in England, Australia, New Zealand, and in a number of other British dominions and colonies. But the Socialist Party of America never secured the same degree of support from the American unions that the British Labour Party did from the English unions; and the higher proportion of German, Jewish, and other continental immigrants to be found in both the American Socialist and Communist parties meant that, the American Left (although not most American trade unions), adhered more closely to the continental, social democratic model than it did to the Anglo-Saxon, labourist one.

More importantly, as we found at several points in this chapter, the American labour movement was faced with a degree of ethnic and racial heterogeneity in its workforce, as well as with a much larger agrarian sector, than was its counterpart in Great Britain. From this point of view it may well be that detailed comparisons between the American, and the Canadian or Australian labour movements – both of which had a frontier tradition, as well as a partially immigrant labour force – would prove just as rewarding as an Anglo-American form of approach. To give one example of how fruitful American–Canadian comparisons can be, an illuminating study was written some years ago which compared the political fortunes of the radical farmers' Nonpartisan League in North Dakota during and after the First World War with those of the Saskatch-ewan-based Canadian Cooperative Commonwealth Federation, just the other side of the American–Canadian frontier. The economies of the two areas were almost identical, since both relied upon prairie wheat as their main source of income. Yet in the Canadian case the wheat farmers sought to resolve their economic distress by forming a permanent political alliance with an independent party of labour, whereas on the American side the Nonpartisan League had only a brief third-party career. As a result, the author was able to conclude that it was differences between the Canadian and American electoral systems – and particularly between the use of the party primary system and the direct election of the executive in America, as opposed to the much stricter national control of politics exercised by the two major parties in Canada – that largely accounted for the difference between the labour movement in the two countries.[29]

One-to-one comparisons such as these can be illuminating. But they run the risk of assuming that region-to-region, or industry-to-industry, comparisons are more representative of their respective national labour movements as a whole than they often are. In addition, although there is a considerable literature which explores the similarities and differences between the labour movements in various European countries, very little of an analytic or theoretical nature has been written that can encompass the American, or Anglo-Saxon form of labour movement within a

[29] The reference here is to S. M. Lipset, *Agrarian Socialism, The Cooperative Commonwealth Federation in Saskatchewan: A Study in Political Sociology* (Garden City, 1968).

common Euro-American framework. Even the mercantilist/anti-mer-
cantilist model which we have employed in this chapter has its
weaknesses, since it focuses primarily upon the relations between the
labour movement and the state. This may be appropriate in this particular chapter. But in doing so it runs the risk of slighting other significant
trans-national points of comparison, such as levels of economic development, the changing balance between class forces, or the degree of
commitment of different elements in a labour force to a common, pre-
industrial heritage.

Some might argue – basing themselves ultimately on a Marxist model
– that the presence or absence of a feudal heritage in any given society is a
more fruitful framework within which to examine the comparative
development of labour movements, since it leads to a richer form of
social analysis than the mercantilist/anti-mercantilist approach. The
most compelling American example of the use of this model was the one
put forward in the early 1960s by the political scientist Louis Hartz, who
argued that the historical circumstances under which a new society
comes into being exert the most important influence over the future
character of its labour movement. Thus French Canada and Spain's Latin
American colonies, founded as they were by conservative, backward-
looking, imperial elites in the fifteenth and sixteenth centuries, retained
important elements of pre-capitalist feudalism (Catholicism,
corporatism, and a deep respect for social hierarchy) which enabled them
to generate counter-impulses which could then become radical, or even
revolutionary. According to this view, Britain generated a radical labour
movement because it had gone through all of the historical stages
required by the Marxist dialectic, whereas the United States and English-
speaking Canada, lacking a fully fledged feudal heritage, did so only in
part. In addition, the Australian labour movement, being a 'proletarian
fragment' of the metropolitan country's political past, became radical –
although only in a Lib/Lab sort of way – because of the large number of
ex-Chartists and other British political emigrés who participated in its
founding.[30]

Hartz' theory is attractive because it helps to explain several of the
national differences between labour movements which we have examined in this chapter. But it also has serious weaknesses, of which the reader
should be made aware. Like the overly simple mercantilist/anti-mercan-
tilist argument, for example, Hartz' view represents a static and
unsatisfying model because it places the locus of historical change within
the dynamics of a class struggle which has already taken place within the
society of origin, thereby ignoring any class conflict that may have

[30] L. Hartz, *The Founding of New Societies: Studies in the History of the United States, Latin America,
South Africa, Canada, and Australia* (New York, 1964).

occurred in the new country itself. Thus his theory is unable to explain the extensive instances of social unrest which took place in America after its founding, some of which we have discussed in this chapter. Taken literally as a piece of social history, Hartz' theory would lead one to suppose that Americans have always lived in an unchanging and beneficient form of liberal capitalist society, which derived its ideas and much of its economic apparatus from the Enlightenment period. In fact, of course, since that time American society has clearly changed in ways which have had a major impact on the prospects and character of its labour movement: from rural to urban, from frontier to non-frontier, from agrarian to commercial, and from slave to free. Many of these factors, as well as comparable but somewhat different ones on the other side of the Atlantic, have had a profound effect in determining the character of both the American and the British labour movements. However, Hartz' theory does not permit us to take them into account.

The last, and until recent years, much the most influential American labour theoretician to address the issues we have taken up here – although not limiting his argument to the Anglo-Saxon labour movement – is Perlman, whose *A Theory of the Labor Movement* (1928) we have already mentioned in the text, and which has also exercised some influence in Great Britain. All workingmen, Perlman argued, whatever their historical background, if left alone by interfering intellectuals, tend to develop what he called an 'organic philosophy of labor', which leads them to confine their activities to dividing up control over limited job opportunities between themselves and their employers. They do this because of an inherent (although Perlman also regards it as historically induced) 'psychology of scarcity', according to which the individual worker accepts inherent limitations in his ability to manipulate the economic world, i.e. accepts his inability to become an entrepreneur. As a result, the manual labourer confines his efforts to the establishment of a job-conscious, instead of class-conscious labour movement, which concerns itself solely with bread-and-butter issues.[31]

In his book Perlman makes some further interesting remarks about the labour movement in various European countries, which the reader of this chapter should also find interesting. Nevertheless, like Hartz' work Perlman's *Theory* has serious faults, which disqualify it as a model for explaining the differences and similarities between the British and the American labour movements. Among other things, like Lenin in *What Is To Be Done?* (1902) Perlman exaggerates the role of intellectuals as the sole source of radicalism in the labour movement; he gives us no reason for believing that, when faced with scarcity, workers will retreat into a defensive form of job-conscious trade unionism instead of becoming

[31] S. Perlman, *A Theory of the Labor Movement* (New York, 1928).

revolutionaries; and he fails to take account of other elements – such as the impact of ethnicity and race or the significance of cultural, pre-industrial, or other non-workplace influences – which must be considered if one is to successfully analyse the Anglo-American or indeed any other form of labour movement.[32] Above all, Perlman like Hartz ignores the long history of class conflict which took place at the workplace, as well as between trade unionists and state authorities in America, which we have referred to in this chapter. This history, even though it was not politicized in the same way in America as it was in Great Britain, nevertheless bespoke a far more militant tradition of labour activism in the United States than his narrow, job-conscious model would have us believe. It should be evident, therefore, that much work remains to be done before we can construct a theory of the European and American labour movements that is both loose enough to take proper account of variations between different countries, but at the same time be sophisticated enough to compel whole-hearted belief.

---

[32] For a discussion of the role of ethnic, racial, and cultural influences on the behaviour of the American working class, as well as a critique of the excessively institutional character of the kind of labour history to which my brief in writing this chapter has largely confined me here, see Herbert Gutman, *Work, Culture and Society in Industrializing America; Essays in American Working-Class and Social History* (New York, 1976).

CHAPTER VII

Labour and the state on the continent, 1800–1939

I. *Introduction*

Industrialization requires major adaptations and readjustments of the labouring population. The workers drawn into industry must learn not only new skills and techniques, they must also become accustomed to new rhythms and hours of work and submit to new forms of discipline and control. Typically, they must also change their habitual styles of life and their customary environments. All of these changes tend to involve considerable economic and psychological hardships, against which the workers seek to protect themselves. The present chapter is an historical survey of the responses of governments in the major industrial countries of the continent to the problems faced by industrial labour and to the workers' organized efforts to improve their situation. If industrialization created a need for workers to combine for the defence of their interests, it also improved their capability to create common-interest organizations. But the collective actions of workers in the form of strikes, trade unions, and political movements represented an economic threat to employers as well as a challenge to the prevailing system of power and authority. In a broader sense, the inevitable strife was a threat to economic efficiency and to social stability. The basic historical task of labour policy was therefore to provide the means and institutions which would meet the essential demands of the workers and at the same time promote efficiency and preserve law and order. Over time, labour policy necessarily mirrored the changing balance of economic and social forces and was articulated in ways which reflected the ideological commitments of the engaged parties.

The second section of the chapter covers the beginnings of industrialization, which saw the early attempts at labour organization and the repressive governmental reactions as well as the first attempts by the state to protect some of the victims of industry, particularly children. This period extends to the 1860s in both France and Germany, which was the time when the governments in these two countries finally recognized the right to strike and granted freedom of organization. Section III traces the developments of labour and labour policy from the 1860s to the First

World War. This was the period of industrial transformation during which the fundamental principles of labour and industrial relations, the rights of organized labour and the role of the state were debated and fought out. The First World War marked a major break in continental labour history. During the inter-war period, which is the subject of section IV, the rights of labour were no longer fought over in terms of principles. The issues of principle were by and large settled, and conflict was over practical policies. Nevertheless the labour movements and the workers' gains faced new threats, this time from the state rather than recalcitrant employers. These first four sections concentrate almost exclusively on France and Germany. In section V, the broad historical patterns of these two countries are compared with developments in other continental countries, with particular emphasis on Russia.

II.   *Labour in early industrialization*

A.   FRANCE TO THE 1860s

It was not until the 1860s that labour organizations and labour policy in France began to take on modern forms associated with industrialism. Until then, the workers and institutions relating to labour continued to be dominated by a pre-industrial outlook and conceptions. While the frame of reference remained rural and artisanal, the historic fact of the 'Great Revolution' of 1789 was a major factor shaping French labour history. The legacy of the revolution consisted not only in ideas and ideals, but also in legal institutions and a restructuring of political forces. Although on the political level the bourgeoisie had to wait until after 1830 to play a significant role, the revolution and the First Empire had provided the basic legal framework for the development of modern capitalism. If the revolution had established institutions based on individualism and private property, thus favouring the ruling classes, it had also planted the seeds of egalitarianism and challenge of authority. The revolution had done much of the work of liberating the working classes from the traditional subordination to authority which the gradual process of industrialization had to do elsewhere. On the other hand, the revolution also bequeathed France highly centralized governmental institutions and an *étatist* tradition that was even older than the revolution. The combination of this *étatisme* and of the individualism of the revolution, as Virton has observed, strongly worked to check the development of collective action among French workers.[1]

Other factors which tended to retard the emergence of the labour movement in early nineteenth-century France were the slow pace of

---

[1] P. Virton, *Histoire et politique du droit du travail* (Paris, 1968), p. 188.

industrialization and the widespread peasant landownership. In contrast to England and eastern Germany, where a pattern of capitalistic farming based on large holdings emerged, the French revolution consolidated a widespread pattern of peasant landownership. Instead of a class of landless labourers who were pushed or pulled into urban industrial jobs, France inherited a class of peasants with a strong attachment to the soil they owned. Interacting with the slow pace of industrialization, this characteristic of the work-force contributed to a decided rural character of French industry during most of the nineteenth century, especially before 1850. By the middle of the century about 66 per cent of the population was still employed in agriculture, forestry, and fishing, and 75 per cent lived in rural areas. Only 15 per cent of the population lived in towns with 10,000 or more people.[2] The census of 1872 revealed that even then nearly 70 per cent of the population still lived in rural areas, in spite of the acceleration of industrialization between 1850 and 1870. The census indicated also that slightly over 60 per cent of the active population were owners of some form of property.

The labour organizations which developed under these circumstances bore for a long time a strong imprint of pre-industrial structures. In the early decades of the century, there was a revival of the *compagnonage*, the societies of skilled journeymen that flourished in pre-revolutionary times. Their sectarian spirit, secret symbols, mystical rites, and bitter rivalries hailed from an older era and contrasted sharply with the class consciousness and spirit of solidarity of the modern labour movement. The forms of economic self-protection of the *compagnons* were also pre-industrial: the black list was much more common than the strike. The *compagnonage* reached its high point during the Restoration (1815–30) and declined thereafter, but there are no membership figures available. The mutual aid societies were another form of labour organization with deep roots in the past. Although there are again no overall figures available, and many societies were short-lived, Paris is reported to have had 40 of them in 1819 and 123 in 1823, with 11,000 members in the latter year.[3] In the years of depressed trade between 1826 and 1831 many of the mutual aid societies seemed to have taken on the character of *sociétés de résistance*. In the first great strike of the period, the strike of the Lyon silk weavers in 1831, mutual aid societies played the central organizing role. The strike itself was really more in the nature of an old-fashioned insurrection, pitting workers and sub-contractors against merchant capitalists, but it was a signal of political awakening among the working class. After 1831, many new resistance societies sprang up in the industrial cities, especially during the 1840s. To evade official suppression they

[2] Roger Price, *The French Second Republic* (Ithaca, NY, 1972), p. 11.
[3] Jean Bron, *Histoire du mouvement ouvrier français*, 3 vols. (Paris, 1968–73), vol. I, pp. 50–1.

continued to disguise themselves as mutual aid societies. They played an active and open role in the 1848 revolution, but thereafter they returned to their mutual aid cover.

Certainly one of the major factors in the slow development of the French labour movement was the official policy of repression, supported by a highly constrictive legal framework. With the short-lived exception of 1848 the prohibition of labour combinations remained unchanged until 1864. Successive political regimes maintained and enforced the principle of the free market and the 'freedom to work' proclaimed by the revolution in the famous decree of Allarde (2–17 March 1791). This decree clearly abolished all guilds and trade associations, thus carrying out the liberal reforms which had been attempted by Turgot in 1776. The Le Chapelier law (14–17 June 1791) prohibited all coalitions of workers aiming at higher wages, as well as coalitions of employers seeking to lower wages. All deliberations and agreements to fix wages by persons in the same trade were declared in violation of freedom and of the Declaration of the Rights of Man. The prohibitions included also mutual aid societies, on the grounds that under the regime of liberty, no intermediate bodies between the individual and the state were to be recognized. The state was therefore left with the ultimate responsibility for the welfare of the individual, at least in the eyes of the more radical revolutionaries. The preamble of the 1793 constitution stated, 'Public assistance is a sacred debt. Society owes subsistence to unfortunate citizens, either by furnishing them work or by providing the means of subsistence for those unable to work.' This lofty ideal of the 'right to work' did not have much impact at the time, but it became more than a slogan in the 1848 revolution.

The legislation of the Napoleonic years (1799–1814) reflected the paradoxical combination of individualism and *étatisme* of the revolution. The law of 12 April 1803 reaffirmed the revolution's prohibition of labour and employer combinations, but at the same time it generalized the requirement, introduced before the revolution, of the *livret* as a condition of employment. The *livret* was a kind of labour passport which was found useful by both employers and the police to monitor the conduct of individual workers. Under an ordinance of 1 December 1803, a worker travelling without a *livret* could be arrested as a vagrant. Workers came to resent the *livret*, yet the requirement was not finally abolished until 1890, long after it had lost its policing function. Another aspect of the labour policy of the First Empire was a strong judicial bias in favour of the employers. The famous article 1781 of the Civil Code (1804) stated explicitly that in wage questions the master will be taken at his word. The word of the worker had no legal standing. Article 416 of the Penal Code (1810) prescribed harsh punishments for workers guilty of blackmail and intimidation, without providing comparable penalties for employers. All worker coalitions were illegal, but employer coalitions were illegal only if they sought to lower wages in an 'unjust and abusive manner'. For any legal violations, penalties stipulated for workers were always harsher than penalties for employers.

French law prohibited not only combinations of people in a given trade. Under article 291 of the Penal Code, associations of any kind – religious, political, literary – with more than twenty persons were illegal, except with governmental permission and under governmental regulation. This distrust of private groups was further heightened by the strike wave of the early 1830s, especially after the big Lyon strike had demonstrated the subversive potential of mutual aid societies. All of these prohibitions and related punishments failed to prevent worker associations and a rising strike movement. According to a recent study, the average annual number of strikes was 53 for the 1830s, 68 for the 1840s, and 77 for the 1850s.[4] Most of these strikes were of short duration and involved relatively few workers. There was one provision with regard to labour disputes which may be noted. In 1806 the government authorized the city of Lyon to establish a *conseil de prud'hommes*, a kind of labour court composed of trade representatives, to deal with worker grievances. Although the workers were not represented until 1848, the courts became quite popular. By 1844, when the first court was instituted in Paris, they existed already in 66 cities.

Beyond repressing labour combinations, the government essentially followed a policy of *laissez-faire* in industrial relations. The only exceptions to this policy were found in certain regulated industries, such as mining. In 1810 and 1813 laws were passed for the mining industry which regulated the safety of working conditions, required the provision of medical care, and prohibited child labour. The first real breach of the *laissez-faire* policy did not occur until the passage of the Child Labour Law of 1841. With respect to this kind of legislation France lagged behind not only England but even other continental countries such as Prussia and Switzerland. In France as elsewhere the demand for child labour legislation did not come from workers but from public-minded individuals and government officials, who were often supported by landed interests. Some of the larger employers, whose capital equipment often made child labour unprofitable, and related organizations, like the Société Industrielle de Mulhouse, supported the principle of legal restriction of child labour in France.

The proponents of state intervention found strong support in the report on the deplorable conditions of industrial workers published in

---

[4] Charles Tilly and Edward Shorter, *Strikes in France 1830–1968* (Cambridge, 1974), p. 360.

1840 by a physician named Villermé who had undertaken a careful investigation at the request of the Academy of Moral and Political Sciences. Louis René Villermé made a strong plea for the protection of children. Opponents of the legislation stressed its violation of the principle of economic liberty and the rights of parents. Workers generally did not wish to see any curtailment of the earnings of their children. Most manufacturers argued that the kind of legislative regulation envisaged was simply not feasible and a threat to the prosperity of the country. The outcome of the debate was a very limited law, which was doomed to failure. It prohibited employment of children under age 8 and imposed various restrictions on employment of children between the ages of 8 and 16. The two major weaknesses of the law were its limited coverage, probably only one-tenth of working children were covered, and the lack of adequate enforcement provisions. Under pressure from industrial interests, no paid inspectorate was created. Inspection was left to unpaid industrialists and local notables appointed by the prefects. Not surprisingly, this approach proved to be a nearly total failure and after mild initial attempts at enforcement, the law was generally ignored.

The revolutionary months of 1848 marked a brief interlude in the regime of industrial *laissez-faire* and organizational repression. The political consciousness of urban workers had been aroused during the 1840s by socialist ideas and a growing working-class press. In 1848, the Parisian workers succeeded in forcing their demands upon the government. Under the threat of an armed mob, the provisional government hastily accepted a vaguely worded decree which guaranteed 'work for all citizens' and recognized the workers' 'right of association to secure the legitimate fruits of their labour'. These concessions, as well as the creation of national work shops and the Luxemburg Commission to consider the workers' problems, were temporary measures designed to prevent a civil war. Judged on the basis of their petitions to the Luxemburg Commission, the mood of the workers was more pragmatic than revolutionary. They wanted greater economic security, better working conditions, elimination of abuses, higher wages, shorter hours, greater equality between masters and workers, and state aid to producers' associations.

The 1848 revolution did not have a lasting impact on labour policy. A decree of 2 March reduced the working day to 10 hours in Paris and 12 in the provinces. By September this decree was abrogated, and the 12-hour day was accepted for the whole country. As a concession to the spirit of equality, the workers achieved equal representation with the employers on the *conseils de prud'hommes* by a decree of 27 May. An interesting piece of legislation was the law of 5 July which established a loan fund of three million francs in order to encourage producers' cooperatives. This law is interesting because it appealed to both socialists and moderate republicans. The socialists saw in the cooperatives a means of liberating the workers from the wage system, and the republicans saw a means of spreading ownership of small enterprises. It was highly indicative of the important role of small-scale enterprise in French industrialization that the emerging labour movement should attach great significance to producers' associations as a means of liberating the wage worker. According to Moss, 'the Revolution of 1848 stirred tremendous hopes for emancipation through association'.[5] Hundreds of associations with thousands of members, in all kinds of trades, sprang up, but most were short-lived.

After the ill-fated national workshops were closed (June 1848), the right to work, which had been promised in 1793 and proclaimed in February 1848, remained a subject of passionate debate in the National Assembly. But by the time the new constitution was adopted (4 November 1848), the concept of right to work had been seriously mutilated. The preamble to the constitution stressed individual self-help as a duty of the citizen, and article 13 guaranteed the 'freedom to work'. The same article, however, noted also that 'society favours and encourages the development of labour through free primary education, professional education, equality between workers and employers, welfare and credit institutions, agricultural institutions, voluntary associations, and the creation . . . of public works for the unemployed; furthermore, it provides relief for abandoned children, and for the sick and the aged without means and without family resources'. Had these aspirations been realized, the Second Republic might have been an early welfare state, but the experiment never got started.

A decade of silence for the labour movement followed the year of revolution. Already before the *coup d'état* of December 1851, a legislative reaction had set in against the workers. The laws of 1849–51 on coalitions, the *livret*, and apprenticeship reflect a distrust of labour, and 'were conceived with the intent of subjecting the working class to a régime of police surveillance'.[6] The 1850s are nevertheless interesting, not because they marked a return to the policy of repression, but because for the first time repression was combined with seduction. The Napoleonic labour policy of the 1850s was inspired by paternalistic attempts to gain favour with the working masses while at the same time keeping a tight rein on their freedom of action.

Napoleon III had appealed to the working classes in his rise to power and had flirted with socialistic ideas and leaders. In 1852 he told a

---

[5] Bernard H. Moss, *The Origins of the French Labor Movement 1830–1914* (Berkeley, 1976), p. 41.
[6] Georges Bourgin, 'La législation ouvrière du Second Empire', *Revue des études napoléoniennes*, vol. IV, p. 222. All passages quoted from foreign language sources are the author's own translations.

delegation of workers, 'Those who work and those who suffer can count on me.'[7] While he sought to reassure the propertied classes through a policy of law and order, he was always concerned with maintaining the support of the working classes. Until the end of the 1850s he relied on the police and paternalism. The government used every available opportunity to parade the Emperor's solicitude toward the lower classes. Relief measures for disaster victims, the unemployed, and the poor were laced with heavy propaganda. The bureaucracy and the official press were constantly reminding the workers of the Emperor's deep concern for their welfare. And in 1857 the Minister of the Interior expressed the hope that the workers would reciprocate 'in affection and gratitude all the benefits which the paternal solicitude of the Emperor' had bestowed upon them.[8] The legislation of the 1850s was less promising than the propaganda. The government enacted a law in 1852 to encourage mutual aid societies but at the same time introduced regulations which kept these associations under the watchful eyes of the authorities. Each society had to have local notables as honorary members, and the president had to be named by the chief of state. The *conseils de prud'hommes* were reformed in 1853 to give stronger representation to the employers, and in addition the government appointed the chairman and vice-chairman of each court. As Levasseur noted, 'These measures changed the character of the courts and gave them the imprint of administrative subordination.'[9]

Until the 1860s, labour organization and policy in France had not yet taken on the hues of modern industrialism. The workers were still looking backward to associationist means of avoiding the wage system; mutual assistance societies and a declining *compagnonage* were survivals of an earlier age. The authoritarian paternalism which characterized the labour policy of the 1850s was in the tradition of royal absolutism, but it was also an early manifestation of the more modern concept of skilful use of welfare measures in the service of plebiscitary dictatorship.

B.   GERMANY TO THE 1860s

The German setting differed vastly from the French. Reforms from above rather than revolution from below marked the transition to industrialism. Strong feudal survivals checked the forces of political and economic liberalism. Germany was neither economically nor politically unified for a good part of the century. Prussia was the most important of the 39 states which constituted Germany in 1815, and in many ways

[7] David I. Kulstein, *Napoleon III and the Working Class: A Study of Government Propaganda under the Second Empire* (Sacramento, 1969), p. 97.   [8] Quoted in *ibid.*, p. 99.

[9] E. Levasseur, *Histoire des classes ouvrières et de l'industrie en France de 1789 a 1870*, second edn, 2 vols. (Paris, 1904), vol. II, pp. 282–3.

epitomized the German experience. Prussia took the leadership at the beginning of the century in the abolition of serfdom and compulsory guilds, but during the following decades official policies kept vacillating between promotion of more liberal reforms and conservation of inherited hierarchical social structures. Policies which appealed to the liberal forces of the industrialized western parts were likely to be opposed by the conservative elements of the agrarian east. The free labour market, which industrialists considered essential for the growth of industry, was seen as a force of social disintegration by conservative agrarians. The first stirring of a labour movement did not come until 1848, although strikes were not unknown before then in spite of strong paternalistic legacies. The labour unrest with the greatest impact on national consciousness was the riots of the Silesian weavers in 1844. These riots of displaced artisans are a reminder that the chief labour problems of the first half of the century in Germany were still primarily artisan problems. Industry had achieved importance only in a few scattered areas.

For Germany as a whole, the old regulatory spirit, including the prohibition of combinations and strikes, remained the basis of public policy regarding artisans until the 1860s, but actual policies varied considerably. In the parts of Prussia to which the reforms of 1811 abolishing compulsory guilds applied, journeymen were free to practise their trade as they wished, and technically they were presumably also free to form combinations and to strike. This technicality was not of much practical significance and in any case was formally removed in 1845. In the Palatinate and in parts of Prussia which had been occupied by Napoleon, the French revolutionary legislation prohibiting guilds, combinations, and strikes remained in effect after 1815. In some other areas, like in Kuhrhessen, Oldenburg, Bremen, and Hanover, the legislation introduced by the French during the Napoleonic years was abandoned after 1815 for a return to the old guild regulations.

The issue of protection of industrial labour was appropriately enough first raised in Prussia and with regard to child labour. In the more industrialized parts of Prussia, the Rhineland and Westphalia, there were old textile districts where child labour in factories was becoming important in the early nineteenth century. It was characteristic for Prussia that the labour protection issue should first be raised by senior government officials. Long before Bismarck, the higher Prussian bureaucracy had taken upon itself the role of interpreter of the national welfare and skilfully combined policy-making with administration. The first officials to call attention to the social problems of industrial workers were liberal reformers and disciples of Adam Smith. They apparently knew what Smith had said about the dangers inherent in the progressive extension of the division of labour for the personal development of the worker. Among these officials was Karl August Hardenberg, the great Prussian reformer and chancellor. In 1817 he addressed a circular to the *Oberpräsidenten* of the industrial provinces asking for their advice on the means to prevent the degradation of the industrial workers during years of depressed trade. His main concern was with the fate of factory children, whose mental and physical development he saw threatened. Hardenberg's circular did not go beyond raising the child labour problem, and the responses to it were generally against government intervention. The mood for intervention became more favourable when a Prussian investigation in 1824–5 revealed the shocking conditions of child labour, but no action was taken. Similarly, a report by General von Horn in 1828 calling attention to the medical unfitness of military recruits in industrial regions failed to yield any regulation of child labour. As in France, social, educational, and military considerations were intermingled in the demand for child labour protection.

It was finally in 1839, after many years of pressure by interested officials, that a child labour law was enacted in Prussia. This law prohibited all factory labour by children under 9 years of age and required evidence of 3 years of completed schooling. It prohibited also a working day in excess of 10 hours (including 2 hours of rest) as well as night work and work on Sundays and holidays for juveniles between the ages of 9 and 16. Unfortunately, as in the case of the French law, the Prussian law was easily evaded because no inspection system was created. Nevertheless, the 1839 law may properly be considered the beginning of the protection of industrial labour in private industry in Germany.

In industries which were regulated by the state or where the state was the employer, the official *laissez-faire* policy adopted toward labour in private industry was not followed. A good illustration of how the state acted as an industrial employer may be found in the enterprises of the Prussian *Seehandlung*. In these enterprises the state instituted comprehensive welfare programmes, including health care and cash sickness benefits, housing and saving schemes, training progammes, and profit sharing. The programmes were consciously designed for both income protection and promotion of productivity through higher morale, stronger discipline, and lower turnover. This approach, known as *Erziehung zur Tätigkeit*, contained the germs of many aspects of later policies toward industry in general. Similarly, one could look to the state regulated mining industry where the mutual assistance programme of the *Knappschaften* (miners' guilds, dating from the thirteenth century) set precedents which later influenced the shaping of state social insurance.

Demands for state intervention on behalf of the labour classes were widely heard during the depressed years of the middle 1840s. Such demands came from both conservatives as well as from prominent progressive industrialists like Friedrich Harkort and Gustav Mevissen. The Prussian king, Friedrich Wilhem IV, was responsive to the somewhat romantic ideas of a 'welfare monarchy' advocated by conservative writers. Official policy kept wavering between *laissez-faire* and interventionist tendencies, a hesitation which was reflected in the Prussian industrial code of 1845. The code had been in preparation for ten years and was an attempt to unify the country's handicraft legislation. It maintained the liberal principle of the free labour contract, but at the same time gave renewed strength to the guild system. For the first time since 1811 new guilds could be formed in Prussia. Compulsory guild membership was not reinstated, but the guilds were restored certain exclusive rights over apprenticeship and assigned industrial conciliation responsibilities. Even more important, however, the 1845 code reintroduced an explicit prohibition of 'coalitions' (strikes) and specified new fines and prison terms for strikes, inducements to strike, and picketing. Worker associations as such were not prohibited, but the police and local authorities kept a watchful eye over the mutual assistance and other worker societies, lest the workers became exposed to subversive ideas and developed notions beyond their proper state in life. Political clubs, of course, were forbidden. On the other hand, the 1845 code marked a first step towards the introduction of social insurance. It authorized cities to issue regulations which, with ministerial approval, could compel all locally employed artisans, helpers, and apprentices to join welfare funds. Factory workers were not included.

The Prussian law against coalitions and similar laws in other states could not prevent the emergence of the labour movement in 1848. This was, however, primarily a movement of skilled craftsmen, not of factory workers. These craftsmen had previous organizational experience, not only with guilds and the associated funds, but also in workers' education societies (*Arbeiterbildungsvereine*) and craftsmen associations (*Handwerkervereine*). The revolutionary fervour of 1847–8 evoked strong but conservative responses from the handicraftsmen, who saw their interests in sharp conflict with the economic liberalism of the rising industrialists. Within the crafts, the separate interests of masters and journeymen also came to the fore, even though both rejected *laissez-faire* policies. The masters assembled at their own national congress in 1848 in Frankfurt, from which they initially excluded the journeymen and demanded an integral return to the guild system. The journeymen also assembled a congress in Frankfurt and demanded state protection against unbridled competition and worker participation on decision-making committees. The workers' demands were formulated by the highly articulate printer Stephan Born, who became the leader of the first general German national workers' organization, the Arbeiterverbrüderung (Worker

Brotherhood), founded in the summer of 1848 at a worker's congress in Berlin. Born, who had lived in France, rejected the return to the guild system and offered instead to the German workers the ideal of workers' productive associations which was so popular in France in 1848.

The Arbeiterverbrüderung was a national federation. At the local level it consisted of workers' educational and other craftsmen societies, many of which sprung into existence in 1847–8. While factory workers were not excluded, the membership consisted mainly of artisans. Two national craft unions came into existence in 1848: a printers' union and a cigarmakers' union, both based on local craft societies. The fundamental orientation of these national organizations was towards political rather than direct economic action. They looked to the state for enactment of economic reforms to protect their livelihood, particularly for the provision of credit to establish production associations. By the beginning of 1849, the Arbeiterverbrüderung had decided on more wage-worker-oriented demands, such as higher wages, shorter hours, labour courts, regulation of child labour, election of supervisors, and the right to strike.[10]

The bloody ending of the revolutionary movement in 1849 heralded the end of the young labour movement. With the onset of political reaction, laws were enacted to curb the freedom of political expression. The police were given new powers to regulate and prohibit meetings dealing with political subjects. In 1850 a law was enacted in Prussia prohibiting communications and organizational links among similar associations. On the basis of this law the local branches of the Arbeiterverbrüderung were closed. The printers' union was prohibited in 1850 and the cigarmakers' union the following year. The reconstituted Diet of the German Confederation passed a resolution in 1854 urging all member states to require official approval of any association dealing with public issues and to dissolve immediately any failing to meet the requirement. Even where this resolution was not passed into law, the reactionary political climate of the 1850s imposed a dormant decade upon the German labour movement.

In spite of all the grandiose demands and pronouncements of the revolutionary assemblies and congresses, there was little legislative output. The economic committee of the Frankfurt Parliament produced an interesting draft for a national industrial relations code which called for worker participation in factory councils and welfare institutions as well as in regional industrial councils.[11] This forward-looking document, which failed to win general approval, contrasts sharply with the amendment to the Prussian industrial code enacted in 1849. The new code was

[10] Hedwig Wachenheim, *Die deutsche Arbeiterbewegung 1844 bis 1914* (Cologne, 1967), p. 49.
[11] Hans J. Teuteberg, *Geschichte der industriellen Mitbestimmung in Deutschland* (Tübingen, 1961), pp. 109ff.

rather backward looking, aimed towards strengthening the role of guilds and guild masters. Nevertheless, the new code provided also some protection for labour. It included a prohibition of the truck system of paying wages in goods instead of cash, which had been debated for a long time. The prohibition had first been considered by the Prussian government in 1831, and no doubt the final enactment owed something to the labour unrest of 1847–8. The 1849 law allowed also for the creation of local trade councils with elected members, but these councils never became important. The code further promoted the creation of welfare funds by allowing local ordinances to make participation compulsory for factory workers and to require industrial employers to contribute.

After 1850 the German economy began a period of rapid expansion, but politically the fifties were a decade of conservative reaction. It was hardly a period for new directions in labour policy. Strikes and trade unions remained on the prohibited list, although at least in Prussia the bureaucratic officialdom did not seem overly eager to prosecute strikers.[12] There was still much ambiguity in the official attitude with regard to the proper roles of *laissez-faire* and state intervention in industrial relations. The general tendency toward liberalism in economic matters was never fully reconciled with the surviving feudal authority structure in social relations. This authority structure had always implied acceptance of protection from above and deference from below. It is thus not surprising to find an extension in the fifties of protective labour policies initiated earlier. In 1853, the 1839 Prussian Child Labour Law was amended to raise the minimum age from 9 to 12 and to reduce the working hours for children between the ages of 12 and 14 to 6 hours a day. These children were also subject to compulsory school attendance for 3 hours daily. Perhaps even more important was the institution of an inspection system. There is no doubt that the government had become more serious about the protection of children. Prussian laws in 1854, 1855, and 1856 further facilitated the creation of worker health and welfare funds. Outside of Prussia similar laws were passed in Hanover, Oldenburg, Saxony, and Thuringia, but without the compulsory participation features of the Prussian laws. In southern Germany no such laws were enacted, but in that part of the country there was an established system of municipal assistance.

By the end of the 1850s, Germany was undergoing rapid industrialization. Policies with regard to the labour movement were still in the repressive stage, and the laws concerning craftsmen were still burdened with guild restrictions, but with regard to laws on labour protection, Germany had already moved ahead of most of the continent.

[12] Wolfgang Köllmann, 'Die Anfänge der staatlichen Sozialpolitik in Preussen bis 1869', *Vierteljahrschrift für Sozial- und Wirtschaftsgeschichte*, vol. LIII, no. 1 (March 1966), pp. 47–8.

III. *Struggles over principles and ideologies*

A.   FRANCE, 1860–1914

By the end of the 1850s the French labour movement began to stir again. Even in the surviving *compagnonages* there was a new spirit. Leaders of mutual aid societies took the initiative in a petition to the Emperor which resulted in sending 200 worker delegates to the London Exposition in 1862. The contact with British trade unions had an important psychological impact on the French workers. Upon their return they issued a series of reports contrasting the position of workers in the two countries and calling among other things for the right to strike and the right to organize. In 1864 a group of the new labour leaders issued the 'Manifesto of the Sixty' which contained a long list of demands. A growing boldness and class consciousness among the workers were in evidence. A workers' commission meeting between 1867 and 1869 produced a long list of complaints and reform demands. The 1860s were also a fertile decade for organizational activity. The cooperative and mutual aid movement experienced a strong revival, especially in Paris. A French bureau of the International was created in 1865. But for most of the 1860s, trade unions, in the scattered trades where they existed, still led a secret, camouflaged life. It was not until 1868 that a change in governmental policy allowed them to come out in the open. Then, in the last two years of the Empire, the union movement spread rapidly, reaching some 70,000 members in Paris and a like number in the provinces.[13] These numbers were still small when compared to the nearly 800,000 members of mutual aid societies, but there is no question that trade unionism had finally taken roots.

The labour policy of the Second Empire became more tolerant and more flexible from 1859 onward, but it remained unpredictable. Following the unfavourable election of 1863, the Emperor was prepared to move further in the direction of tolerance which he began by authorizing the sending of worker delegates to London in 1862. He pardoned nine printers condemned to prison terms for leading a peaceful walk-out for higher wages and then announced that the law on coalitions would be revised. This historic step was taken by the law of 25 May 1864. Two features of this law, which consisted in a modification of articles 414, 415, and 416 of the Penal Code, are of particular interest. First, the law abolished the prohibition of strikes, but it did not establish the freedom of association. Secondly, while authorizing strikes, it seriously increased the penalties for any kind of violence, intimidation, or 'fraudulent acts' committed in connection with a labour dispute. The government thus

[13] Val R. Lorwin, *The French Labor Movement* (Cambridge, Mass., 1954), p. 12.

granted a significant formal right, but the police and the courts kept a great deal of latitude on how to apply it. Because of the practical difficulties in distinguishing between 'coalition' and 'association', and between 'demands' and 'intimidation', there was much arbitrariness in practice. Bourgin has noted that 'it is absolutely impossible to determine the criteria of legality and illegality' applied with regard to strikes.[14]

The government's search for a demarcation line between the new liberalism and the old authoritarianism was evident also with regard to cooperative associations and trade unions. The problem was one of responding to the workers' demands for greater freedom of organization without surrendering governmental control of the emerging labour movement. The creation of an imperial fund of one million francs for cooperatives in 1865 was an attempt to promote an approved form of labour organization under official tutelage. When the cooperative movement showed too much independence, its publication, *L'Association*, was suppressed in 1866. The following year, an international cooperative congress was prohibited. Despite the law of 1864 there was renewed vigour in the prosecution of strikes in 1867, yet at the same time there were clear indications that the government was prepared to enlarge the freedom of organization and make more concessions to the workers. For instance, in 1867 the government announced its intention to create a salaried inspectorate to enforce the Child Labour Law of 1841; furthermore, it introduced a bill to establish the freedom of assembly which became law the following year. Other worker demands were granted in 1868; the irritating article 1781 of the Civil Code, which stipulated acceptance of the employer's word in wage disputes, was abolished, and insurance funds were established for employment-related deaths and accidents. But the freedom to organize labour unions was not legally granted. In response to a petition from workers' delegates, the government indicated that unions would be tolerated, although they were technically still illegal.

Governmental policy during the last decade of the Empire was both too restrictive to satisfy the demands of the emerging labour movement and too liberal to keep it completely under official control. Official propaganda and paternalistic gestures failed to placate the workers. The French labour movement was beginning to seek its independence from both the government and the propertied classes.

The momentum of the closing years of the Empire was severely checked by the Franco-Prussian war and the Paris Commune. If the Commune temporarily raised the hopes of the Parisian workers to overcome wage labour through cooperative socialism, the reaction

[14] Bourgin, 'La législation ouvrière', p. 229.

which followed was a serious setback for the labour movement of the whole country. 'Under the state of siege that lasted until 1876, the government exercised arbitrary authority over rights of assembly, association, and the press, dissolving assemblies and unions and suspending newspapers at its discretion.'[15] With the leadership and the ranks of labour activists decimated, it was not until the second half of the decade that the trade unions regained their pre-war strength. Although the government banned federations of unions, and by the Dufaure law of 14 March 1872 prohibited affiliation with the International, it did tolerate the reorganization of unions in specific trades after 1872. By 1876 the labour movement had picked up enough momentum to hold the country's first national workers' congress, which brought together representatives of both unions and cooperatives. This congress and the one which followed in 1878 were marked by a rather conservative atmosphere, emphasizing worker self-help, and independence from the government and the bourgeoisie. At the 1879 congress, on the other hand, a strong collectivist line emerged; it was decided there to create a socialist workers' party based on the class struggle. This development reflected a change in the country's political climate after the Republicans' show of strength in the 1877 election. By this time hundreds of local unions had been formed throughout the country, and the first national federations (hatters, typographers) were emerging.

Even before the labour movement revived, the government had returned to the question of protective labour legislation. While distrustful of labour organizations, the National Assembly shared the paternalistic sentiments of some industrialists towards the workers, which led to renewed attempts at regulating child labour. The law of 18 May 1874 for the first time established an inspectorate and in that sense marks the beginning of effective protective labour legislation in France. It regulated the hours of work and days of rest for children and young girls, and prohibited underground work for women. But it was not until the 1880s that both workers and employers came to accept the new regulations and the state was able to enforce them.

In the second half of the seventies the labour movement was gathering strength and pressing for full freedom of association, not merely administrative tolerance. Labour organizations were losing their predominantly artisan character as factory workers began to participate after 1875. The leftward shift marked by the creation of a labour party with a revolutionary programme in 1879 was taken as a sign by the government that some conciliatory gestures were needed to counteract the influence of the radical wing. Thus, the government assisted in the organization in

[15] Moss, *The Origins of the French Labor Movement*, p. 63.

1881 of a reformist labour federation, the Union des Chambres Syndicales, which called for 'legalization of unions, formation of mixed arbitration boards, a ten-hour day, state pensions and aid to associations'.[16] While the radical majority of the labour leaders had already decided against cooperation with the bourgeois government the Union des Chambres Syndicales was active in lobbying for the legalization of trade unions. After four years of debate and with the final active intervention of Waldeck-Rousseau, the law was enacted in 1884. Waldeck-Rousseau and other Republican politicians had hopes that the law would contribute to industrial peace and promote the peaceful development of trade unionism. The law itself did not have much of an impact, although it did give some legal standing to labour unions. Its requirement that statutes and names of officers be filed with the authorities, although consistent with civil law practice, was bitterly denounced by the workers as a police surveillance measure. The half-hearted labour policies of the government and the workers' hostile reactions were unmistakable signs of a growing mistrust between organized labour and the bourgeois republic. It was probably in the early 1880s that the last chance for effective cooperation between the social classes before the First World War was missed.

After 1880 the labour movement was rapidly growing in numbers and radical temper. By 1886 union membership probably passed the 100,000 mark; the 500,000 mark was reached by the turn of the century, and the pre-war peak of 1,064,000 was achieved in 1912.[17] A very important aspect of French labour organization was the formation from 1886 onward of federations of trades at the local level. These *bourses du travail* were concerned mainly with placement and training. As in other countries, local unions in given trades combined also into national unions and national federations. The first national trade-union federation was created in 1886; by 1894 it had fallen victim to internal political and ideological dissension. In 1892 a national federation of *bourses du travail* came into existence, and in 1895 a new trade-union federation, the Confédération Générale du Travail (CGT), was founded. These two national federations fused in 1902 and carried forward under the CGT banner of revolutionary syndicalism.

In the early days of French unionism there was a close link between trade unions and socialist parties. Inevitably, however, the tendency of French socialists toward factionalism spilled over into trade unionism. Under the influence of revolutionary syndicalism, the trade-union movement officially came to reject not only parliamentary socialism but all legislative reform efforts. Belief in the efficacy of 'direct action'

---

[16] *Ibid.*, p. 96.   [17] Lorwin, *The French Labor Movement*, p. 23.

hardened into dogma for the revolutionary syndicalists. They looked to the general strike as the basic strategy for achieving the socialist revolution and abolishing the wage system. When the first socialist, Alexandre Millerand, joined the cabinet of the Waldeck-Rousseau government in 1899, he was scathingly denounced by both socialists and trade-union leaders. The labour reforms which Millerand so valiantly sought to bring about were roundly condemned as attempts to entrap and mislead the working class. Only gains achieved by the workers themselves in fierce combat with the ruling class were deemed dependable. Some of the more extreme anarchistic labour leaders counselled electoral abstention, industrial sabotage, and anti-patriotism. Even after the unification of the most important socialist factions into one party in 1905, the CGT solemnly reiterated its independence of political groupings in the celebrated Charter of Amiens in 1906. While the charter recognized the need for some labour reforms and pledged cooperation with the socialist party to that end, it reaffirmed the fundamental tenet that the general strike was the chief instrument of worker emancipation.

It is very difficult to assess the impact which revolutionary syndicalism and revolutionary socialism had on the development of governmental labour policy. No doubt the verbal assaults of the CGT leaders frightened some elements of the bourgeoisie, but on the other hand, the patent weaknesses of French trade unions, their factionalism, low number of adherents, and even lower dues paying membership, were hardly causes for genuine alarm. Careful observers were aware of the ideological differences between the syndicalist leaders and the much more conservative majority of the workers. At the plant level French unionists were much more pragmatic than the syndicalist ideologies would lead one to expect. They were more often willing to negotiate than the employers. The anti-parliamentary sentiments did not keep local trade-union leaders from appealing to the authorities to intervene with employers on the workers' behalf. On the other hand, one could hardly conclude that the syndicalists' revolutionary strategy was conducive to the enactment of favourable labour legislation. They neither sufficiently frightened nor sufficiently cooperated with the dominant political forces to aid their cause through legislative enactments. When the CGT made legislative demands, it was usually more guided by the hope to arouse revolutionary fervour in its followers than by the hope of legislative success. The eight-hour day campaign from 1904 to 1906 was an apposite case in point.

Given a political party structure which was more geared to stalemate than to accomplishment, and the fact that at the eve of the First World War more than one-half of the French population was still rural, it is not surprising that industrial labour legislation was slow in developing. In fact, one could argue that in the light of these circumstances and the *laissez-faire* tradition, a remarkable amount of industrial legislation was enacted. The principle of government regulation of the work of children, women, and in some cases even adult men became well established. The law of 1874 mentioned earlier was extended in 1892 and 1900. A law of 2 November 1892 strengthened the provisions regarding hours of work of children and young women and introduced new provisions regarding adult women. A law of 30 March 1900 reduced the working day for young people (under eighteen) and women, and for men working with them, to 11 and after 2 years to 10 hours. In 1905 the 8-hour day for minors was enacted and the following year a legal weekly day of rest was made compulsory. Until the 1890s there was only very limited legislation concerning industrial safety and hygiene. A law of 12 June 1893 broadened this regulation and inspection from a few unhealthy and particularly dangerous industries to all industrial establishments and construction sites except those operated on a family basis.

On the other hand, in the area of industrial relations and trade-union rights there was not much significant legislation in the quarter century preceding the First World War. The law of 2 July 1890 which abolished the *livret* had more symbolic than practical importance. The dominant attitude of French employers, even those who sympathized politically with republican radicalism, was that they were perfectly capable of handling relations with 'their' workers, knowing that in case of trouble they could count on the police, the army, and a conservatively inclined magistrature. Nevertheless, following several major strikes, the Chamber of Deputies took up debate in 1891 on a law to regulate industrial conflicts. The idea had been discussed as early as 1864 but had been dormant since then. The debate led to the passage of the law of 27 December 1892 on conciliation and arbitration. Because recourse to the services provided under this law was voluntary, its role remained limited and in fact diminished over time. During the first ten years of the 1892 law, it was involved in 23.4 per cent of the strikes; during the second decade the percentage fell to 20, and during the last two years before the war to 15 per cent.[18] The declining role of the law may be due to the fact that it did not officially recognize either workers' or employers' organizations, but probably more significant was the rigid attitude of the employers. It is significant that recourse to the law was sought far more frequently by workers (1,350 times) than by employers (73 times) between 1893 and 1909. During the same period employers refused to participate in conciliation 859 times against 57 times for the workers.[19]

The workers' willingness to use governmental conciliation services

[18] David J. Saposs, *The Labor Movement in Post-War France* (New York, 1931), p. 213.
[19] *Ibid.*, p. 213.

contradicts the negative attitude towards the bourgeois state expressed in syndicalist propaganda. In fact, the workers appealed for ordinary administrative intervention about as often as they sought to invoke the 1892 law. This is not meant to indicate that there was a cordial relationship between the authorities and industrial workers. There were numerous violent confrontations between strikers and the forces of public order. There were also a number of attempts in the pre-war era to introduce compulsory arbitration, but none of them succeeded. After the turn of the century, the unions were noticeably cool towards arbitration and even conciliation.

The internal conflicts and tendencies towards stalemate were nowhere more in evidence than in the discussions surrounding the beginnings of welfare legislation. Fundamentally, the issue in this area involved the extent to which the individual was to be held responsible for his own welfare and the degree to which society accepted that responsibility. This issue was particularly susceptible to the influence of conflicting interests and ideologies. So long as the question was merely one improving the system of public assistance, no new principle of social rights was involved. A number of laws in this category were enacted after 1890 which provided medical care for indigents and other relief for aged and disabled poor. More or less in the same category was a law of 1894 which provided subsidies for low-cost housing and a law of 1905 which provided state subsidies to local unemployment assistance funds.

It was in the debate over compensation for industrial accidents where the new concept of a right to socially guaranteed compensation and a corresponding legal obligation was confronted for the first time in the industrial labour context. It took 18 years of debate before the principle was accepted, in the workmen's compensation law of 9 April 1898, that an injured worker was entitled to compensation regardless of whose fault the injury was. The initial law was restricted to factories and shops with power-driven machinery, but amendments in subsequent years made the protection more or less universal. Actually, the 1898 law was readily accepted by industry, especially by the larger companies, which in most instances had already insured themselves against accident-related damage suits. But liberally oriented senators raised many objections during the parliamentary debate. As liberals elsewhere, they objected to the 'collectivist principle' of the no-fault concept and to a centralized insurance fund. They argued that workers would be hurt by having to give up the right to sue employers over accidents. The idea that damages suffered by a worker should be determined by some arbitrary schedule rather than by the majesty of a court was repugnant to them. On the other hand, even though the compensation rates were only partial replacement of lost earnings, the liberals feared that they would set up adverse incentives for the lazy, shiftless, and improvident.

Although workmen's compensation embodied some of the elements of social solidarity, and therefore a rejection of individualistic solutions, the real test of a social approach to economic insecurity came with the debate over a compulsory national old age pension system. Sooner or later an industrial society must face the problem of how to provide a minimum of economic security for those of its citizens who are no longer able to earn a living through the market mechanism. Work-related pensions were not new in France. Colbert had instituted a programme to protect sailors in old age, sickness, and disability as early as 1673. Similarly, there was a system of pensions for government functionaries which antedated the revolution. Special retirement systems were created for miners (1894) and railway workers (1909) without undue difficulties. The creation of a general old age pension system was first suggested in 1879, and during the 1890s a whole series of projects was presented to the Chamber. It was not until 1905 that the matter received serious attention in parliament and not until 1910, after more than 20 years of discussion, that an ineffective law was passed.

The reasons for this long gestation period deserve brief attention. The only people who really pushed for the programme were individual reformers. Large-scale industry was in favour or at least acquiesced, while the elements representing the middle class, the broad spectrum of medium and small industry and the professionals, as well as organized labour, were in opposition. The reasons for these attitudes are historically interesting. As has been shown in other countries, the managers and owners of large-scale industry usually find that welfare programmes are productive investments in human capital. They promote efficiency through improved stamina, morale, discipline, recruitment, and stability. Although such employers may take pride in their own in-house welfare programmes, they usually do not find it difficult to appreciate the role and value of state social security. Certainly this kind of reasoning seems to be applicable to certain larger industries in France. For medium- and small-scale industry and the professions, the step toward acceptance of compulsory state social insurance was much more difficult. As Henri Hatzfeld has noted, 'To opt for social security was to question a certain order founded on the middle classes.'[20] The argument was not merely that compulsory insurance would destroy individual initiative and enterprise, as liberal economists like Leroy-Beaulieu maintained, but that it would prevent the salaried classes from using their limited saving capacity for acquiring property or small enterprises. Compulsory social insurance was seen as a barrier to the access to enterprise ownership. It would eliminate a major road of social ascent by removing a bridge between the lower and the upper classes. The prevalence of such views

[20] Henri Hatzfeld, *Du paupérisme à la sécurité sociale* (Paris, 1971), p. 308.

was consistent with the prestige of property and the predominance of small enterprises in France. As late as 1911, there were two employers or self-employed persons for every five workers in industry.

The hostile attitude of socialists and labour leaders toward social security had a different basis. The socialists in the Chamber of Deputies were divided: while none of them were satisfied with the legislative proposals, they disagreed over whether an imperfect law which at least established the principle of compulsory insurance was better than no law at all. In part this division of opinion involved different views of the possible impact of social insurance. Reform-oriented socialists like Jean Jaurès believed that it would strengthen the labour movement, but those with more revolutionary inclinations feared that it would appease the workers and undermine their will to fight. In the end, 25 socialist deputies voted for the 1910 law and 27 voted against, while others abstained.

In the trade unions there was also division of opinion. The miners and railway workers had favoured compulsory pensions in their own industries, and the printing trades were strong supporters of the concept of nationwide compulsory old age pensions. Most labour leaders objected to the low level of the planned pension, the contributions from workers, the late retirement age at 65, and the exclusion of women from coverage. For the leadership of the CGT, which had hardly much flair for reform, these weaknesses totally invalidated the proposed pension system. The CGT carried on a vigorous campaign against the project, labelling it 'a pension for the dead'. The capitalist state had already exploited the workers, they argued, and now it was going to rob them a second time by forcing them to contribute towards their maintenance once their physical strength had been exhausted. Even the pension stamp books to record contributions were attacked as a revival of the hated *livret*. With so much opposition and so few determined defenders, it is a wonder that even an inadequate law saw the light of day. In 1911 and in 1912 the courts ruled that if workers refused to contribute, employers could not withhold contributions. These rulings sounded the death knell for the principle of obligatory participation and for the pension plan which had been so passionately debated for so long. At the eve of the war, the French worker lost a major battle in the achievement of modern social rights, mostly with the aid of his own leaders. The struggle over principles and ideologies suitable for French labour institutions was still raging, but the coming war soon radically changed the perspectives.

B.   GERMANY, 1860–1914

The German labour movement came back to life during the 1860s after a decade of obscurity. In cities like Berlin and Leipzig, artisans' clubs and workers' educational societies renewed their activities, often under the sponsorship of middle-class liberals. In 1863 the General German Workers' Association (Allgemeiner deutscher Arbeiterverein) was founded in Leipzig. Under the leadership of Ferdinand Lassalle, this organization began to steer the workers away from the apolitical, self-help course that middle-class progressives like Schulze-Delitzsch had advocated. Lassalle advocated political action to secure assistance from the state for the organization of producers' cooperatives, but to achieve this objective the workers had to press first for universal equal suffrage. In the trades, the General German Cigarmakers' Union (Allgemeiner Deutscher Zigarrenarbeiterverein) was founded in 1865, and in 1866 the printers organized a national union. The tailors and woodworkers followed in 1868. During the same period, August Bebel and Wilhelm Liebknecht, both followers of Karl Marx, were promoting the development of a Marxist-oriented labour movement. The socialism they advocated was in competition not only with Lassallean cooperative socialism but also with the British-style trade unions led by Max Hirsch and Franz Duncker and the Christian Social movement under Roman Catholic sponsorship. In 1869 Bebel and Liebknecht founded the Social Democratic Labour Party, which meant that for a while there were two socialist parties in the country. In 1875 they combined their forces on the basis of the inevitability of the class struggle and the overthrow of capitalism.

These mighty stirrings in the labour ranks did not take place without responses in government policy. The central issue at the time was the freedom of combination, but there was also still debate over the elimination of guild survivals in the crafts. The move towards freedom of combination in Prussia was part, as it was in France, of an effort to capture the political support of the emerging industrial working class. In practice the 1845 prohibition of combinations had not been enforced very vigorously by Prussia. When strikes broke out the authorities usually intervened, but more with the aim of settling the conflict than with punishing the strikers. This situation was brought to light in an investigation in 1865 by the Prussian Ministry of Commerce. The investigation revealed a very widespread opposition to the strike prohibition among the higher Prussian bureaucracy. In fact, as Professor Born has noted, 'freedom of combination for workers was demanded by all factions of the Prussian Chamber of Deputies in the 1860s'.[21] Each of the parties sought favour with the workers for its own ends. For the liberals freedom to strike was part of the freedom of contract, just as it had been for the English liberals in 1825. And like the English liberals, the Germans believed that freedom to strike would soon teach the workers that strikes

---

[21] Kark E. Born, 'Sozialpolitische Probleme und Bestremungen in Deutschland von 1848 bis zur Bismarckschen Sozialgesetzgebung', *Vierteljahrschrift für Sozial- und Wirtschaftsgeschichte*, vol. XLV, p. 36.

are useless against the law of supply and demand. The Centre Party (Catholic) supported worker combinations for the opposite reason: they wanted labour organizations to be a countervailing force against the market for the sake of greater social justice. The agrarian conservatives similarly expected labour organizations to become a countervailing force, but mainly for the sake of stemming the power of the rising industrial bourgeoisie. The socialists, on the other hand, did not press any demands for freedom to strike and to organize unions: they had little faith in this kind of action.

The initiative for freedom of combinations came from Bismarck, who needed allies in his constitutional struggle with the liberal bourgeoisie in the 1860s. Before he became Prussian Minister-President, Bismarck had been ambassador in Paris and had become familiar with the labour policies of Napoleon III. For Bismarck the freedom of combinations was a tactical policy which temporarily suited his purposes. He expected that freedom to organize and to strike would convince the workers of the fairness of the state and would undercut the radical propaganda. He also hoped that management of their own organizations, including the management of collected funds, would make labour leaders more businesslike. He was always confident that he could deal with people who understood their vested material interests.

The freedom to strike and to unionize became part of the industrial code adopted by the North German Federation in 1869. It followed the French model in that it included prison terms for anyone who coerced, threatened, ostracized, or vilified non-strikers. These exceptional penalties, applicable specifically to labour conflicts, reflected the widespread view that most workers would not strike except when coerced or intimidated by radical agitators. It is noteworthy that by 1869 the liberals, who had opposed these exceptional provisions in an 1866 bill, were now overwhelmingly in favour of them. Bismarck also favoured these punitive provisions after 1867, the year when the first socialist deputies were elected to the North German Reichstag. The radicalization of the labour movement had already begun to influence labour policy.

In other respects the 1869 industrial code basically combined the existing laws of member states on child labour, Sunday and holiday work, and education. The general tenor of the code, however, was in the spirit of industrial freedom. Conditions of work were to be settled by free contract without state interference. The policy of leaving the internal order of the factory beyond the reach of the state was one that Bismarck pursued consistently during his career.

It was not until the 1870s that Bismarck definitely turned against the labour movement. In his view, the socialists had made themselves into enemies of the Empire and had to be checked by all means. The Social

Democratic Party was rapidly gaining in popular support. From one seat and 124,000 votes in the Reichstag elections in 1870, the socialists went to nine seats and 493,000 votes in 1877.[22] Although the absolute numbers were still small, for Bismarck they were alarming, especially in the aftermath of the Paris Commune. The socialists were subjected to police harassment; some of the leaders were imprisoned, and in 1876 the newly unified Social Democratic Party was suspended in Prussia. An opportunity to strike at the labour movement arose when two attempts were made on the Kaiser's life in 1878. Even though the would-be assassins were not Social Democrats, Bismarck took advantage of the inflamed situation to secure the passage of a federal law against the growing menace of socialism. The law was initially enacted for three years, as a concession to the liberals, but it was subsequently extended four times. It was not until 1890 that disagreements over new terms caused it to lapse.

The anti-socialist law prohibited all Social Democratic organizations and suppressed most socialist papers. The police were given the authority to exile Social Democratic officials from their places of residence. In all some 1,500 persons were imprisoned and 900 forced to move.[23] Oddly enough, in spite of this repression, the Social Democrats were allowed to continue electoral campaigning shortly before elections and were allowed to be elected. Most socialist trade unions temporarily fell by the wayside, but in the early 1880s local unions began to reappear. Although the government sought to suppress these unions, their right to existence was upheld by the courts, so long as they did not engage in political activity. The policy of oppression was thus tempered somewhat by an independent judiciary, which contrasts with modern totalitarianism. The German labour movement from 1878 to 1890 was severely curtailed but never totally annihilated.

Repression was only one aspect of governmental policy. At the same time that Bismarck was gearing up for his fight with the Social Democrats, he warned his ministers that a one-sided policy would not do. As early as the autumn of 1871, he stressed to his ministerial colleagues that the state must meet those socialist demands which were legitimate and compatible with the existing order. He noted specifically that the 'burning questions of working hours, wages, lack of dwelling accommodations, etc., must not be omitted'.[24] Bismarck believed strongly in welfare policies as a means to achieve his political objectives, but he was never willing to go very far in regulating working conditions. The various laws passed in the 1870s, such as the Employers' Liability Act of 1871 and

[22] Helga Grebing, *Geschichte der deutschen Arbeiterbewegung*, 4th edn (Munich, 1973), p. 91.
[23] *Ibid.*, p. 90.
[24] Quoted in Hans Rothfels, 'Bismarck's Social Policy and the Problem of State Socialism in Germany, Part II', *Sociological Review*, vol. xxx (1938), p. 291.

amendments to the industrial code to strengthen the protection of women and children, still indicated a commitment to *laissez-faire* in this area. The higher bureaucracy was known to prefer a non-interventionist policy, and by 1876 Bismarck himself strongly opposed any further extension of factory legislation.

From about 1877 on, Bismarck was thinking of a comprehensive social insurance scheme as the central part of the solution to the problem of labour discontent. His fundamental goal was to make welfare legislation into a pillar of the Empire. Theodor Lohmann, one of his closest collaborators in social insurance, put the Bismarckian view thus, 'social legislation must serve the purpose of anchoring an awareness of the state and of the authority of the state in the social order'.[25] This particular perspective of social legislation as a political instrument shaped the legislative programme as well as opposition to it. After encountering initial opposition, Bismarck had the Kaiser present an outline of his insurance proposals to the Reichstag at its opening on 7 November 1881. The message stressed that 'the cure of social ills must not be sought exclusively in the repression of Social Democratic excesses, but simultaneously in the positive advancement in the welfare of the working classes'.[26] All three programmes called for in the message were enacted: workingmen's health insurance in 1883, industrial accident insurance in 1884, and old age and invalidity insurance in 1889.

The first bill discussed was the one concerned with industrial accidents. Bismarck wanted a scheme that made the state a highly visible benefactor to the worker. He insisted therefore that the scheme be highly centralized, under an imperial insurance office, that private insurance companies be excluded from providing coverage, that it be compulsory, and that the bulk of the cost be borne by the employers and the state. He believed that if the worker had to pay for it himself, 'the effect on him would be lost'.[27] Another feature which Bismarck favoured was joint participation by workers and employers in administration through corporative associations. He still cherished an old hope to create vocationally based corporative bodies that might someday supplant the Reichstag politicians. By the time the law was enacted, Bismarck had given way on most of his special features. The political parties objected to his highly centralized system aiming at tying the worker to the state. Similarly, the majority opinion in all the parties rejected the state subsidy, and in the end the workers were left out of any meaningful administrative participation. The employer had to bear the cost of industrial accident insurance

---

[25] Otto Quandt, *Die Anfänge der Bismarckschen Sozialgesetzgebung und die Haltung der Parteien,* Historische Studien no. 344 (Berlin, 1938), p. 16.

[26] Quoted in William H. Dawson, *Social Insurance in Germany 1883–1911* (London, 1912), pp. 16–17.   [27] Quoted in Quandt, *Die Anfänge der Bismarckschen Sozialgesetzgebung*, p. 25.

alone and controlled the programme through membership in trade associations. The industrial injuries benefits provided included pensions for partial and total disability as well as compensation in the case of death.

With regard to the health insurance programme, Bismarck was less determined to shape it to meet his political ends. In health insurance there were long-standing precedents of a highly decentralized system based on autonomous funds. The workers had been paying two-thirds of the cost. Under the 1883 law, which made coverage compulsory for the majority of manual workers in industrial and commercial establishments, the workers continued to pay two-thirds and employers one-third of the cost. Representation on administrative councils was in proportion to cost sharing, which gave the workers a majority voice. It has been said that one of the reasons Bismarck was not much interested in using health insurance for political purposes was that he saw the short-term benefits not really suitable for creating effective ties to the state.[28]

In the old age and invalidity pension scheme, however, Bismarck saw a real potential for capturing the workers' loyalty to the state. He argued before the Reichstag that one of the reasons Frenchmen generally supported their government, no matter how unsatisfactory it may have been, was that so many of them were drawing small annuities from the state.[29] The chancellor hoped to make the old age and invalidity programme the centre-piece of his scheme to entice the workers away from socialism. It was important to him, therefore, that the system did not present a financial burden on the workers and that they would become involved in administering it through corporative bodies. He succeeded only partly in these objectives. Again, the political parties refused to tie the worker to state benevolence in the manner Bismarck wanted. The pension programme was made contributory on an equal basis for workers and employers, but the state contributed a flat base amount to each pension. The administrative mechanism turned out to be essentially bureaucratic, against Bismarck's hopes for extensive worker participation.

It is not possible to review here the complex interplay between Bismarck, the political parties, and other interest groups, but two significant points deserve to be noted. First, in Germany, as in France, large-scale industry was basically in favour of the emerging welfare state. Secondly, in both countries the labour movement was mainly in opposition to it. While there was a great deal of traditional paternalism in the attitude of big German industrialists like the coal king von Stumm-

---

[28] Friedrich Lütge, 'Die Grundprinzipien der Bismarckschen Sozialpolitik', *Jahrbücher für Nationalökonomie und Statistik*, vol. CXXXIV (1931), p. 592.

[29] Reichstag speech of 18 May 1889, in Otto Fürst von Bismarck, *Die Gesammelten Werke*, 15 vols. (Berlin, 1924–35), vol. XIII, p. 403.

Halberg and the steel magnate Ludwig Baare, these ardent supporters of social insurance were undoubtedly aware of its productivity implications. The German Social Democrats, on the other hand, anticipated most of the hostile arguments used later by the French socialists. Fundamentally, they rejected the very notion of meaningful social reform without radical change of the social order; they accused the state of trickery, trying to undermine the workers' will to independent thought and action; and finally, they deplored the limited protection provided, for which the workers moreover had to pay through contributions. This hostile attitude toward legislation to improve the workers' welfare could be explained partially in Marxist ideological terms according to which effective social insurance cannot exist in a bourgeois state. It also has to be taken into consideration that the whole idea of social insurance in Germany was part of the state's anti-socialist arsenal. When a labour movement is isolated and insecure, one cannot expect it to support measures by the state which are in direct competition with its own efforts to gain the workers' loyalty.

In its objective of wooing the workers away from Social Democracy, the Bismarckian social legislation was no more successful than the Bismarckian repression. By the time he had pushed through the old age and invalidity pensions, Bismarck decided that the labour welfare measures of the state had reached their limit. Even though there was still no protection for widows and orphans, and the retirement age at 70 was very high, while benefits were low, Bismarck feared that any further measures would threaten the competitiveness of German industry. He had also come to realize that social legislation, at least the kind that could be passed by the Reichstag, would not have the desired political effects. This left him with few alternatives, except renewed emphasis on repression. When the anti-socialist law came up for renewal in 1890, he pressed hard to keep it from being watered down. However, he lost the struggle, and the law was allowed to lapse.

The struggle over labour policy became inextricably involved in the antagonism between Bismarck and the young Kaiser, Wilhelm II, who ascended the throne in 1888. At the time it seemed that the new Kaiser wanted to follow a more interventionist policy in industrial relations in order to show the workers his deep paternal concerns. In February 1890, he issued a directive which stated in part, 'it is one of the duties of the state to regulate the timing, duration, and nature of work in a manner that will satisfy the maintenance of health, the commandments of morality, the economic needs of the workers and their right to equality before the law'.[30] The directive referred also to the need for legal provisions to

[30] Quoted in Karl E. Born, *Staat und Sozialpolitik seit Bismarcks Sturz* (Wiesbaden, 1957), p. 9.

assure the workers representation in dealing with employers in matters of mutual interest and give the workers a means of 'free and peaceful expression'. The Social Democrats acclaimed the directive as a great moral victory for their principles. It seemed to promise important new departures, but in reality the intentions of the Kaiser were much more modest. The extent to which he was willing to go in the matter of factory legislation came out in the proposals to amend the industrial code. Perhaps most significant was the attempt by the government to narrow substantially the right to strike by increasing the penalties provided in 1869 for 'coercing' workers into strikes. This attempt was rebuffed by the Reichstag. In the end, the law of 1 June 1891 added very little that was novel in a policy sense. It mainly broadened already-existing laws with regard to work on Sundays and holidays, child labour, underground and night work for women, and regulations concerning dangerous and unhealthy working conditions. With regard to the suggested measures to assure the workers a voice in the determination of working conditions, the law simply provided that in the relevant industries all enterprises must publicize internal regulations. These regulations had to be approved by the local police, after the workers had been given an opportunity to express their views. An expression of views, with no need to pay heed to such views, was the extent of worker participation in the establishment of the internal order that the law required. It was only in the mining industry, through a separate law enacted in 1892, that workers' views had to be officially reported and workers could elect delegates to verify fines related to production. Since coal-mines had always been closely identified with the state, the Kaiser wanted them to be model enterprises.

As noted before, government labour policy seemed to have little effect on the growth of the labour movement. If the young Kaiser had any illusions on that score they were probably shattered by the Reichstag elections of February 1890, two weeks after his directive on labour policy. After 12 years of repression, the Social Democrats received nearly 20 per cent of the votes cast, more than any other party in the country. From then on the Social Democratic Party kept on growing into a real mass party. In the last election before the First World War (1912), it received over 4 million votes (34.8 per cent of the total) and 110 seats out of a total of 397. In the setting of imperial Germany, however, this electoral success was not commensurate with political power. The Social Democrats remained an isolated party in an autocratic society which treated them as outcasts in their own land. They were always considered people of doubtful loyalty, without a fatherland.

The trade-union wing of the labour movement also made remarkable progress in the quarter of a century before the First World War. In spite of twelve years of anti-socialist legislation and considerable harassment by the police, the trade unions survived and even expanded during the 1880s. It is true that the repressive policy did not aim at eliminating trade unions. Its aim was to keep them out of politics and concerned only with narrow economic issues. In fact, German labour leaders, even the socialists, were quite pragmatic, even though they professed revolutionary doctrines. Trade unions in Germany remained split along ideological lines, with the socialist or 'free' unions having by far the largest membership, although the whole movement grew rapidly after the demise of the anti-socialist laws in 1890. It was mainly medium- and small-scale industries employing a high percentage of skilled workers that were organized. In heavy industry only mining was organized.

At the level of national labour policy, the hopes raised by the Kaiser's statements in February 1890 and the limited improvements in the industrial code in 1891 were followed by a period of renewed legislative attempts at suppressing the labour movement. In the minds of Wilhelm II and many of the higher officials, the labour movement and socialism were identical, and both were incompatible with monarchical authority. By 1893–4, big business and right-wing parties were pressing for a renewal of anti-socialist legislation. The Kaiser demanded an intensified struggle against the forces of revolution. These pressures led to a bill on 'subversive activities' (*Umsturzvorlage*), but it failed to muster the required parliamentary support. Although existing laws provided many opportunities to curtail socialist activities, the Kaiser and some of his senior officials complained that the courts were too lenient. Senior military officers reinforced the Kaiser's fears by claiming that socialist propaganda was undermining the martial ardour of working-class recruits. Having failed in the imperial parliament, the government tried to pass an anti-labour law at least in Prussia. The Prussian chamber was much more conservative than the Reichstag, but it refused to pass a law granting broader powers to the police.

Government officials still generally held that most workers would not participate in strikes or belong to unions if it were not for the terror tactics used by labour leaders. Preparatory work was continuing on new repressive legislation. On 8 September 1898, the Kaiser bluntly announced that soon a bill would be presented under which anyone 'who interferes with a worker willing to work or attempts to induce him to participate in strikes will be sent to the penitentiary'.[31] As presented to the Reichstag in May 1899, this so-called penitentiary bill (*Zuchthausvorlage*) sharply increased the penalties for coercion, threats, and vilification in connection with industrial disputes. It included picket-

[31] Quoted in *ibid.*, p. 147.

Table 100. *Trade-union membership in Germany, 1892–1913*

Unions	1892	1900	1913
Socialist	237,094	680,427	2,573,718
Christian	—	76,744	342,785
Liberal	45,154	91,661	106,618
Others	—	—	356,653

Note:
— = Not known.
Source: K. E. Born, H. J. Henning and M. Sohick (eds.), *Quellensammlung zur Geschichte der deutschen Sozialpolitik 1867–1914*, Introductory volume (Wiesbaden, 1966), pp. 154–61.

ing as a punishable form of threat, and made material damages subject to prosecution without action by the offended party. If strikes or lock-outs posed a threat to the security of the state or created a public hazard (*gemeine Gefahr*), the punishment was three to five years in the penitentiary. Although the bill had the outward appearance of restricting the activities of both workers and employers, its practical impact would have been mainly on workers. If it had been accepted by the Reichstag, the right to strike would have been severely curtailed in a country where the legal hazards connected with strikes were already very high.

After the failure during the 1890s to renew the exceptional anti-labour laws, there followed a period of about ten years of constructive labour policy. An important unresolved issue was the legal status of trade unions. They had to be tolerated because the law said worker combinations were not illegal, but they had no legal existence in either administrative or civil law. In fact, the old Prussian law (1854) prohibiting correspondence among unions was still valid, although not enforced. It was finally repealed in December 1899. Giving the unions a legal status was a very touchy issue. The Kaiser, big business, and all the right-wing parties were adamantly against any measure that would publicly recognize unions and thereby presumably strengthen the socialists. After much debate a federal law on associations was passed in 1908 which provided for official registration but still did not give protection to the property rights of unions.

More success was achieved with regard to regulation of working conditions. In 1901 the industrial courts, introduced on a voluntary basis in 1891, were made obligatory for all cities with more than 20,000 inhabitants; during the same year the federal government made funds available for the building of worker housing. In 1903 the child labour laws were extended to cottage industry, and 5 years later the 10-hour day for women in factories introduced in 1891 was extended to cover all enterprises employing more than 10 workers. Of greater strategic importance for labour, however, was the Prussian mining law of 1905. Its importance lies in the fact that it represented the first instance in modern German industrial history of a major improvement through legal enactment following almost directly from the pressure of a strike. In response to the strikers' demands, the law changed the piece-rate method of wage calculation, regulated the length of the working day and the system of fines, and prescribed the creation of works councils in all Prussian mines employing more than 100 workers. Since it applied to a major industry in the largest state, this law has been called the 'high point of state social policy before the First World War'.[32] In no other instance had the state been willing to go so far towards conciliating a group of strikers.

In the social insurance area there was also a number of improvements enacted. The most important were those of 1911, particularly the introduction of survivorship pensions, the extension of social insurance to salaried employees, and the extension of health insurance to agricultural labourers. All of these laws were consolidated in the imperial insurance code (Reichsversicherungsordnung) of 1911.

It is fair to say that by the eve of the First World War no other industrial nation had shown as much solicitude for the welfare of its workers as Germany had, and no other Western country had tried so hard to limit the freedom of organized labour. It would be hard to evaluate fully the implications of such a paradoxical policy. The least that can be said is that it gave the workers some stake in their fatherland. If in spite of all the revolutionary propaganda the French workers in 1914 felt they had their republican liberties to defend, the German workers could also feel that they had gains worth preserving. In 1914, notes Born, 'the German Social Democrats did not see the "exploiter state" but their own fatherland in danger'.[33]

IV. *Advanced industrialization*

A.   FRANCE SINCE 1914

The First World War was an important turning point for the French labour movement and for industrial relations. Until then, the clash of ideologies had dominated the scene, revolutionary syndicalism on the one hand and an unyielding *laissez-faire* liberalism on the other. The reality of everyday relations was somewhat more accommodating, but

---

[32] Hans J. Teuteberg, *Geschichte der industriellen Mitbestimmung in Deutschland* (Tübingen, 1961), p. 468.   [33] Born, *Staat und Sozialpolitik*, p. 251.

there is no question that the impression had been created of a wide and unbridgeable gulf between organized labour and the rest of society. August 1914 was a rude awakening for the militants of the labour movement. When the French workers revealed that their patriotic sentiments ran much deeper than their sense of class antagonism, the militants realized that their concept of French society and of the vitality of French capitalism was based largely on illusions. The leadership of CGT recognized the facts of life and joined the rest of the nation in the *union sacrée*. The secretary-general of the CGT, Léon Jouhaux, became *commissaire à la nation*, and many other labour leaders became members of governmental commissions dealing with national problems. This collaboration was not without dissidents and cooled off considerably after 1917, but it could not help but influence the development of labour policy.

The wartime labour policy was naturally mainly concerned with the war effort. From August 1915 onward joint commissions with labour and management representation were functioning all over France handling wage and working conditions issues. This arrangement was not totally effective in preventing strikes; industrial unrest became increasingly serious as the war dragged on. The government was forced to play a more active role. By a decree of 17 March 1917, it banned strikes and instituted compulsory conciliation and arbitration in all industries related to the war effort. In the application of this decree, the authorities often found themselves in the position of fixing wages and regulating working conditions. Another innovation of the war period was the institution in 1917 of a system of shop delegates. This was a significant sign of change in a country known for its industrial absolutism and its revolutionary labour movement. In the area of factory and welfare legislation there were no important innovations, although one could mention the law of 10 July 1915 which set minimum wages for women in cottage industry, which had importance as a precedent.

Conditions immediately after the war were highly propitious for new departures in labour policy. There was a widely shared yearning for a new order based on social justice. The French workers, who had rallied to the nation in its hour of danger and endured untold sacrifices, were surely deserving of the nation's gratitude. At the same time their economic and political strength reached a new peak. Wartime industrial expansion and concentration and the return of the demobilized soldiers lifted union membership to record levels. From 600,000 in 1914, membership had fallen to 35,000 in 1915 when the workers had left for the front. By 1919 it passed the one million mark and rose to around two million the following year. Another major factor favouring reform was of course the switch from a revolutionary to a reformist attitude on the part of the leading labour spokesmen. Furthermore, it was clear that in Europe French social legislation lagged behind that of other industrialized and even less industrialized countries.

Widespread unrest in 1919 forced the government to proceed without delay in meeting some of labour's demands. By a law of 25 March 1919, collective agreements were given legal standing and enforceability. Before the war the CGT would have opposed such a law, but now it supported it. The main effect of the law was to put the government's stamp of approval on the principle of collective bargaining. The immediate result was a rapid expansion in collective agreements, but it was short-lived. Another law, which was passed almost at the same time, established the principle of the eight-hour day. In effect this law provided for a 48-hour week, which could be arranged according to local conditions, with no reduction in earnings. The historic demand for an 8-hour day was met rather hurriedly in order to defuse mounting labour tensions as the 1 May demonstrations approached. The application of the law, however, left many problems to be resolved. Following the war experience, there was considerable debate over compulsory arbitration, but no law was enacted in this area until 1936. As part of this initial legislative effort, another law was passed, in 1920, to strengthen the civil rights of trade unions. It was then of limited usefulness, since the unions were already facing collapse over internal dissensions.

The dramatic conversion of the labour leadership from revolution to reform was never without its critics. As the war dragged on, the radical elements in the labour movement began to reassert themselves. Two disastrous strikes, the Paris metalworkers' strike of 1919 and the general strike of 1920, further inflamed the ideological conflict through mutual recriminations and accusations. But beyond all these factors, and the declining union membership, was the fact of the Bolshevik revolution, which put the old conflict of revolution versus reform into a new perspective. When the leftists were expelled from the CGT in 1922, they formed the Confédération Générale du Travail Unitaire (CGTU) and affiliated with the French Communist Party, which had been formed by a group that had split off the Socialist Party in 1920. Adding just a little more division to the house of labour, the Catholic unions had formed their own national federation in 1919, the Confédération Française des Travailleurs Chrétiens (CFTC).

With so much internal division, the French labour movement was in a weak position to be much of a constructive influence on social reform. Pressures came from elsewhere, particularly from Alsace-Lorraine, where the French lag behind German social legislation stood out in critical fashion. It was an Alsatian minister of labour who pressed for social security legislation as early as 1919. After many compromises, a social insurance bill introduced in the Chamber of Deputies in 1921 finally became law in 1928. It provided for old age and disability pensions, comprehensive medical insurance, and both short- and long-run disability insurance. The only major social insurance benefits excluded were unemployment and maternity benefits. The latter were added a short time later, but unemployment insurance was rejected as economically unsound and too expensive. During the years of debate over the 1928 programme, the unions worked at cross purposes. Contrary to its pre-war doctrinal position, the CGT now favoured social insurance, in spite of reservations about details. The communist CGTU, on the other hand, persisted in the old revolutionary attitude against reformist social legislation. It engaged in bitter attacks against the CGT and the Catholic unions, which were actively engaged in propaganda for the social insurance bill. When the law became operative in August 1930, the communists organized strikes and protests against it. With the exception of a partial success in northern France, the protest call went largely unheeded, but this does not mean that workers were generally enthusiastic about their new social benefits. There were few real defenders of the new social programme in France, outside of the leadership of the CGT, the CFTC, and some members of parliament.

Foremost among the opponents were the traditional groups of bourgeois France who were not part of the industrial labour class, the small entrepreneurs, artisans, shop keepers, professional people, and farmers. Many of these self-employed people were already covered in voluntary programmes of their own. They wanted to have nothing to do with a state bureaucratic system, nor with the taxes required to finance the state subsidy. Very strong opposition was put forward by the medical doctors, who feared the inevitable interference with the free exercise of their profession. The small employers resented mainly the increased financial and administrative burden. Even the large employers joined in the opposition, mainly on administrative grounds. They objected to worker participation in administrative matters, which in their opinion required managerial expertise and judgment.

Before the 1928 law went into effect it was modified in important respects by a law of 30 April 1930. Under the amended law, the contribution rates for employers and employees were reduced while the state subsidy was increased. Furthermore, the amended law increased the physicians' freedom to set their own fees for medical services and allowed them to collect direct from their patients. The latter were reimbursed from social insurance at the rate of 75 per cent of standardized fees, an approach which considerably weakened the level of protection originally envisaged. The increased freedom of the doctors to control fees was a tribute to their effective organizational activity during the development of the law.

Family allowances were another important social insurance area that was debated during the 1920s. Such wage supplements, based on the size of the worker's family, were paid on a voluntary basis by a handful of larger enterprises since the end of the nineteenth century. They had expanded considerably during the war, in response to inflation and wage control, and continued to grow during the 1920s. By 1930 some 32,000 enterprises paid allowances to nearly half a million families.[34] The system was not universally favoured. Small employers found the allowances financially burdensome. Among labour organizations, only the Catholic unions, following the recommendations of the papal encyclical *Rerum Novarum* of 1891, supported family allowances but often criticized them for their paternalistic character. The CGT and the CGTU looked upon family allowances as interference with the private lives of workers and a means to keep down the general level of wages. There were instances where company rules specified that allowances could be denied if the parents did not spend the money wisely. For competitive reasons, those employers who had established family allowances on their own were in favour of making them compulsory for all employers. At the same time, however, they wanted to maintain control over allowance funds. These considerations were taken into account by the law of 11 March 1932 which established a system of compulsory family allowances for all industrial and commercial employers. The law established only a minimum benefit level and left employers free to choose the fund in which they wished to participate. During the 1930s the family allowance system continued to expand rapidly with the effect that by 1937 more than three times as many families were drawing allowances than in 1930, in spite of the depression. In 1938 agricultural workers were included in the system, and the family code of July 1939 foresaw a universal system of family allowances as well as higher minimum benefits. The application of the latter laws was prevented by the outbreak of the war. Their inspiration must be traced to conservative sources, rather than to the great social reform upheaval of the Popular Front.

By the mid-1930s France had enacted a fairly comprehensive social security programme, although the depression prevented it from becoming fully operative. In the industrial relations field, no comparable developments had taken place. The percentage of unionized wage-earners in private industry in 1931 was lower than in 1911, and by 1936, just before the great membership surge, only 6.3 per cent of wage-earners in private industry were union members.[35] By 1933 only 7.5 per cent of all wage-earners in industry and commerce were covered by collective agreements. It is evident that the laws enacted in the past on freedom to unionize and on collective agreements had had very little impact on the pattern of industrial relations.

[34] Hatzfeld, *Du paupérisme*, p. 179.
[35] Henry W. Ehrmann, *French Labor from Popular Front to Liberation* (New York, 1947), pp. 25–6.

But in the 1930s forces were gathering that would soon bring about radical changes in the industrial relations setting. The dual threat of the great depression on the one hand and the rise of fascism on the other galvanized and unified the labour movement and brought about a *rapprochement* between labour and middle classes. Fascism threatened the republican institutions and was therefore the common enemy. In February 1934 the CGT and the CGTU were able to overcome their mutual hostility to combine in a successful anti-fascist general strike. Two years later these two federations were reunited. The Catholic unions remained separated but were prepared for limited cooperation with the main trade-union body. At the political level, the French Socialist and Communist Parties concluded a 'unity of action' pact in July 1934. This alliance was further strengthened by the adherence of the Radical Socialists and several minor groupings, thus creating the Popular Front which emerged victorious in the May 1936 national elections. When Léon Blum took over the first socialist government in French history (4 June 1936), the country was in the midst of massive sit-down strikes over which the unions had no control. The workers demanded higher wages, a shorter working week, and collective agreements. Blum promised quick action on a series of reform bills, but his immediate problem was to restore a measure of industrial peace.

On 7 June he summoned the leaders of the Confédération Générale du Patronat Francais (CGPF), as representatives of employers, and the leaders of the CGT, as representatives of labour, to the Matignon palace, where he in effect arbitrated a general settlement known as the Matignon Agreement. Although the CGPF had no mandate from its members and was not representative of French employers as a whole, its delegates 'agreed' under pressure to 'the immediate negotiation of collective agreements'. The employer delegates further agreed, among other things, to recognize trade-union rights, avoid discrimination against union members, raise wages from 7 to 15 per cent, allow for worker delegates in plants, and avoid sanctions against the strikers. The CGT delegates agreed mainly to ask the strikers to return to work in enterprises where the general agreement was accepted. Many employers resented the way in which their delegates were treated and denounced the agreement, which did not bode well for peaceful industrial relations.

Within two weeks after accession to power, the Blum government began to deliver on its labour reform pledges. The law of 20 June created the legal annual two-week holiday with pay. By the law of 21 June, the 40-hour week was established, with a proviso against reduced wages on account of the reduction in hours. The most important reform, which inaugurated a new era in French industrial relations, was the law of 24 June on collective agreements. The government, in effect, became a partner in collective agreements in both a procedural and a substantive sense. Collective negotiation meetings were convoked by officials of the Ministry of Labour upon request of one of the interested parties. According to the law, the 'most representative' organization was considered the bargaining agent for all workers in an industry or locality. The provision greatly benefited the CGT, which was the majority organization in most cases. When an issue of representation arose, it was the government, rather than the workers, that decided on which was the most representative organization. The law specified also a number of substantive issues which had to be included in each agreement. An indication of the semi-public nature of French collective agreements was the provision that an agreement negotiated by a group of workers and employers could be extended by official ordinance to a whole region or industry, even though the workers and employers affected by the extension were not party to the initial bargaining. In this manner many non-unionized enterprises could be covered. Another important provision enabled the government to extend the life of an agreement beyond its expiry date. The government could thus avoid what it considered 'inappropriate' timing of new collective negotiations.

The original bill on collective agreements had included a compulsory arbitration clause, which was dropped after heated opposition. Nevertheless, since neither the Matignon Agreement nor the new legislation brought the strike movement to a halt, the Blum government was forced to become involved in conciliation and arbitration. Many of the most important strikes were settled by government arbitration. The government was thus more or less forced to develop arbitration procedures in the summer and autumn of 1936. In a reversal of its historical position, the CGT now pronounced itself in favour of compulsory arbitration, which is understandable since for the first time it had a friendly government in power. Although the principle of compulsory arbitration was introduced in October, the system which the CGT wanted was created in December 1936. This system was operating on a temporary basis until 1938, when it was made permanent, only to be suspended with the outbreak of the Second World War.

Both the Matignon Agreement and the Collective Agreements Law of 1936 provided for the institution of shop stewards (*délégués du personnel*), but neither defined their duties and responsibilities. This lack of clarity hindered the development of the institution and helped to make it a highly contentious issue which led to many strikes. In 1937 the CGT called for new legislation to define the duties and responsibilities of shop stewards, and a measure to that effect was included in the 'modern labour code' proposed by the Camille Chautemps government in 1938. But it was left to the conservative Finance Minister Paul Reynaud to decide the issue by a decree-law in November 1938. By then public opinion and the government had turned against the labour unions. The decree-law restricted the shop stewards to a very narrow role.

This development was a signal that the great social reform era was over. The government modified the forty-hour week in spite of a general strike in November 1938. Labour apparently exhausted itself; from then until the war, the labour scene was remarkably calm. The great reforms had not yet been fully accepted by the country as a whole when the war broke out, but they were to provide the foundation for the reconstruction of industrial legislation after the war. The dominant role of the French government in industrial relations introduced in the 1930s remained a prominent feature of the French industrial scene.

B. GERMANY SINCE 1914

When the war broke out, the Social Democratic leader in the Reichstag declared: 'Now we demonstrate what we have always maintained; in the hour of danger we do not abandon the fatherland.'[36] In spite of the socialist anti-militarist posture in the past, the German workers and their leaders rallied to the national cause, just like their French counterparts. Trade-union leaders agreed to avoid strikes and became active on joint governmental boards. With each year the war continued, however, the same difficulties arose that surfaced in France. The strain began to show as early as 1915, as wages lagged behind prices, food shortages appeared, and promised electoral reform failed to materialize. Both the trade unions and the Social Democratic Party split into radical minorities and more conservative majorities, which made cooperation with the government increasingly difficult as economic conditions worsened.

In the area of industrial relations, the most important law of the war was the Auxiliary Service Act of 1916, which aimed at the mobilization of labour resources for an all-out war effort. While the law introduced restrictions on the workers' freedom, it set an important precedent by requiring the creation of compulsory works councils and employer–worker conciliation committees. Meanwhile, the workers were agitating for a long list of reforms, including greater freedom to organize and to strike, legal status for collective agreements, and improved legal regulations of hours and working conditions. The Kaiser announced a number of reforms at Easter 1917 but was slow to act. There was still strong resistance in the country, especially on the part of big business, to the idea of giving the labour movement greater freedom of action. The severe constraints on the right to strike imposed by the 1891 code were finally lifted in April 1918, thus granting one of the workers' long-

[36] Quoted in Ludwig Preller, *Sozialpolitik in der Weimarer Republik* (Stuttgart, 1949), p. 18.

standing demands. But it was not until military defeat and the end of the old order were in sight that a *rapprochement* between trade unions and big industry became possible. The outcome was an agreement on 15 November 1918 to set up a Central Joint Council (Zentralarbeitsgemein-schaft) of employers and unions. The agreement included reforms which anticipated a radically new era in industrial relations, but by then the storms of revolution were taking over the course of events. The Kaiser had abdicated, and socialists were in control of the government. For the first time, government labour policy was to be labour's policy.

The wartime split in the labour movement now became a policy problem. Various leftist groups, including the Spartakusbund led by Karl Liebknecht and Rosa Luxemburg, demanded the creation of a socialist society based on workers' and soldiers' councils, a Bolshevik-type dictatorship of the proletariat. The Majority Social Democrats, who controlled the official government through the self-styled 'Council of the Peoples' Commissaries', wanted to build a socialist society in a gradual manner and on the basis of parliamentary democracy. With the support of the military and the majority of political opinion, the Council was able to prevail against pressure from the radicals. Following a public proclamation of 12 November, it proceeded with a series of decrees to restructure labour and industrial relations. On 23 November 1918, the government decreed the eight-hour day for industrial workers, thus meeting an historic demand of the socialist labour movement in its first labour decree. This was but a provisional measure and was conditioned by the need to share available work during demobilization. Subsequent regulation of the working day became a source of considerable friction.

The most important labour decree of this early period, issued on 23 December 1918, concerned collective agreements and industrial conciliation. Like the eight-hour day, it was in line with the reforms envisaged by the Zentralarbeitsgemeinschaft in November. With regard to collective agreements the decree established three fundamental princi-ples. First, it stipulated that only bona fide trade unions could conclude valid collective agreements, thus excluding 'yellow' or company-domi-nated unions. The second principle was that of 'non-deviation' (*Unabdingbarkeit*), which meant that employers could not deviate from an agreement unless it favoured the workers, but unions were not liable for breach of contract. The third principle concerned extension of agreements. The Minister of Labour could extend an agreement to third parties in the same geographic area or industry. The decree established also joint employer–worker conciliation committees. In effect, it reconstituted the wartime joint conciliation committees, the main differ-ence being that the chairman of the committee was no longer a military officer but a person chosen by the parties. This person could also act as arbitrator, but his decisions were not binding. The works councils provisions of the decree were soon superseded by other legislation.

Government labour policy was following a highly pragmatic course. It sought to meet long-standing trade-union type demands on hours, collective agreements, joint committees, and greater equality of rights. With regard to the objective of creating a socialist society, the Majority Socialists were very cautious, in spite of pressures from the left. Commissions were created and manifestos were issued, and in 1919 nationalization was decreed for several industries (coal, potash, electricity), but these measures fell far short of the demands of the radicals.

The legal foundations of post-war labour policy were laid in the first half of 1919 by the socialist-controlled Constituent Assembly and embodied in the Weimar Constitution (August 1919). Article 156 of the constitution declares the labourer to be subject of special protection by the national government. The freedom of combination for the maintenance and improvement of economic and working conditions is guaranteed (article 159) for everyone, regardless of occupation. The social responsibility of the worker is expressed in article 163, which establishes for every German 'the moral duty to use his mental and physical capacities in a manner which will promote the welfare of the entire community'. Corresponding to this duty the same article states that every German is entitled to an opportunity to earn a living or to receive assistance if there is no work. Article 165 establishes equal rights for employers and workers 'to cooperate in the regulation of wage and working conditions'. In other articles the constitution stipulates the development of a comprehensive system of social legislation, including worker participation in economic decisions through joint committees and councils.

The fact the constitution clearly provided for the right of worker participation in decisions affecting labour did not settle the raging debate over how this right should be implemented, specifically, what the role of works councils should be. The radical elements were still pressing for broad powers to be given to these councils, while the Majority Socialists remained divided on the issue. The trade unions were in favour of works councils, provided they could control and use them to their own ends. The employers argued vehemently against any measure that might seriously limit their executive authority. Out of these conflicting pressures and interests came the Works Council Act of 4 February 1920, which made the creation of works councils obligatory in all establishments with 20 or more employees and required elected shop stewards in smaller places. The councils were charged with the supervision of working conditions, monitoring of collective agreements, handling of grievances, and promotion of labour productivity. They were to assist employers in the establishment of standing orders for the enterprise (*Arbeitsordnung*) and the development of service regulations (*Dienstvorschriften*), as well as in the formulation of safety rules and the administration of welfare schemes. Their general task was to promote good industrial relations, but they were given very little power to act. The works councils were explicitly prohibited from interfering in any way with the employers' executive authority. The employers had managed to defeat an earlier version of the bill, which would have given the councils considerable power in connection with hiring. The unions, on their part, succeeded in limiting the powers of the councils by the insertion of a series of clauses which assigned priority to any union-negotiated agreement over decisions by the councils. The law stipulated that the councils' power to determine or amend working conditions could be exercised only within the terms of existing collective agreements.

The works councils were thus from the beginning dependent on the unions if they were to exercise any power. This dependence was galling to the left-wing socialists who had always hoped to find a broad power base in works councils. During the 1920s the unions further strengthened their control through election of active union members to the councils. The employers also managed to come to terms with the councils much better than they had feared originally. For the most part they successfully neutralized the requirement to furnish operational information and to appoint council members to their supervisory boards.

In the important area of collective agreements, no substantive legal changes were introduced after December 1918. During the period of 1919–21 the Ministry of Labour worked on drafts for a new unified code on collective agreements to round out the 1918 decree, but the complexities involved in trying to define mutual rights and responsibilities and the pressing need to devise more effective machinery for settling the widespread industrial disputes of those years prevented the drafts from becoming bills. The law on collective agreements enacted in 1928 did not introduce any change in policy. In the meantime collective agreements had become generally accepted in the country. In 1914 there were 143,650 enterprises with 1,395,723 employees covered by agreements; by 1919 the numbers had risen to 272,251 enterprises with 5,986,475 employees and by 1930 to 1,067,500 enterprises with 11,950,000 employees.[37] This significant growth in collective agreements does not mean that the government stayed aloof from industrial relations. The extension provision of the 1918 decree had already assured an active role for the government, and the high level of industrial unrest in the early 1920s

---

[37] Pierre Waline, *Cinquante ans de rapports entre patrons et ouvriers en Allemagne*, 2 vols. (Paris, 1968–70), vol. I, p. 166.

almost assured further intervention. In both 1920 and 1922 the government invoked the national emergency provisions of the constitution to restrict the right to strike in public utilities and railways. During the state of emergency declared in the autumn of 1923 a decree was issued which established the principle of compulsory arbitration in German industrial relations. There was much opposition from employers to compulsory arbitration, and their resistance increased as their economic and political position became stronger in the late 1920s.

The growth of labour legislation since 1918 and the concurrent expansion of labour rights considerably increased the complexity of industrial relations. The feeling became widespread that the available mechanisms for handling contractual grievances, the industrial and commercial courts, and the guild and mining courts, were no longer adequate. There were overlapping jurisdictions as well as important gaps. After lengthy debates, the Reichstag created a system of labour courts in 1926 which replaced all previous special courts dealing with labour issues.

One of the labour gains of 1918 which proved difficult to sustain during the 1920s was the 8-hour day, the very symbol of labour's triumph. Already in 1920 there were collective agreements in mining which called for 2 extra shifts per week. Under pressure from the employers, the number of agreements which violated the 8-hour day increased between 1921 and 1923. The argument was that the impoverished state of the country and the burden of reparations made longer working hours imperative, especially in coalmining where the legal working day was 7 hours. A decree issued during the emergency of 1923 (hyperinflation and French occupation of the Ruhr territory) allowed for many deviations from the legal hours. This situation was rectified, after considerable agitation, by a law of 24 April 1928, which required official approval of collective agreements involving deviations. The state had taken a further step toward participation in collective agreements.

The promise of assistance in case of unemployment contained in the 1919 constitution was not fully realized until 16 July 1927, when the law on unemployment exchanges and unemployment insurance was approved. Unemployment insurance had been discussed in the Reichstag as early as 1902 but was repeatedly rejected as 'impractical', even after England introduced it in 1911. In 1918 an unemployment relief scheme was created, to which both employers and workers were required to contribute from 1923 onwards. The programme established in 1927 was an insurance rather than a needs-based relief scheme. It covered most wage-workers (all those covered by health insurance) as well as salaried employees subject to an earnings ceiling. Benefits were wage related and paid on condition that the beneficiary was able and willing to work.

Under certain circumstances beneficiaries had to be willing to accept retraining, and no benefits were payed to persons involved in strikes or lock-outs. The programme was financed entirely through equal employer and worker contributions, without subsidies from the state.

By the time this last major piece of Weimar social legislation had been enacted, strong doubts were voiced about the viability of the post-war reforms. German employers generally professed to support the concept of the welfare state, but their spokesman insisted that the feasible limits had been exceeded. The welfare programmes were said to undermine capital formation and the willingness to work. The National Association of German Industry (Reichsverband der deutschen Industrie) attributed the economic woes of Germany in 1929 to government intervention, excessive taxes, and excessive welfare costs. In the Reichstag the issue of financing unemployment insurance torpedoed (March 1930) the 'great coalition' of left, centre, and right that had governed for two years. The great depression was putting a tremendous financial strain on the unemployment insurance system. There were but two choices: either additional funds had to be provided, or benefits had to be cut. The employers and their political spokesmen (Deutsche Volkspartei) adamantly opposed both higher contributions and state subsidies. The trade unions and the Social Democrats were equally adamant in refusing to consider any reduction in benefits. As Timm has noted, 'The coalition collapsed, in effect, over the reform of unemployment insurance. The latter stood for the symbol of modern social policy, and disagreements over social policy had been narrowed to issues of principle.'[38] The collapse led to government by emergency decree under which some of labour's cherished gains were sacrificed. Both unemployment benefits and collectively negotiated wages were reduced by decree. The crisis paved the road for the Nazi takeover.

When Hitler came to power in January 1933, Germany had the largest labour movement and the most developed social legislation on the continent. Total union membership was of the order of six million, about five-sixths of them being organized in the socialist unions. The official Nazi party line was that the workers' social gains would be protected and that trade unions would play an important role in the new order, but the Nazis insisted from the beginning that the ideologically split labour movement had to be unified. In a pathetic gesture, the socialist trade-union leaders informed the government on 9 April 1933 that their national federation, the Allgemeine Deutscher Gewerkschaftsbund, 'would gladly cooperate with the new state to realize this unification and place its experience at the state's disposal'.[39] With a keen sense of

---

[38] Helga Timm, *Die deutsche Sozialpolitik und der Bruch der grossen Koalition im März 1930* (Düsseldorf, 1952), p. 66.

[39] Hans-Gerd Schumann, *Nazionalsozialismus und Gewerkschaftsbewegung* (Hanover, 1958), p. 166.

the workers' attachment to the historic symbols of their movement, the government declared 1 May, the international socialist labour day since 1889, to be from now on a paid legal 'Holiday of National Labour'. The last echo from Dr Goebbels' first May Day speech, *'Ehret die Arbeit und achtet den Arbeiter'*, had barely faded out, when the storm-troopers on the morning of 2 May invaded the facilities of the socialist trade unions, arrested the leaders, confiscated the unions' property, and blocked their bank accounts. Within a few days the other unions placed themselves 'voluntarily' under Nazi administration, and thus, without resistance, the independence of the mightiest labour movement in Europe came to an inglorious end.

For a while the unions maintained their identity and their lower echelon administrators within the Deutsche Arbeitsfront (DAF), which was begun in March 1933 and was seen then as an umbrella organization. Towards the end of the year the Nazis indicated that the time had come to eliminate the survivals of the old labour movement. A public declaration in November announced that 'The German Labour Front is the organization for all working people without reference to their economic and social position. Within it workers will stand side by side with employers, no longer separated into groups and associations which serve to maintain special economic or social distinctions or interests.'[40] The old trade unions were dissolved and the membership transferred to the DAF. There was no legal obligation for a worker to become a member of the DAF, but in practice it was extremely inconvenient to avoid membership. Employers also became members of the DAF while their associations dissolved themselves under official pressure.

The restructuring of industrial relations was initiated by the law of 20 January 1934 on the organization of national labour. Employers and employees became an enterprise community (*Betriebsgemeinschaft*), with the employer as enterprise leader (*Betriebsführer*), and the employees the *Gefolgschaft*, a feudal term which conveys a feudal retinue with a sense of martial loyalty and discipline. The law abolished the works councils and conciliation committees, and in a nominal sense it increased the power of the employer. Within the existing legal constraints, he was given complete authority over the internal order of the enterprise, including wages and working conditions. The old works councils were replaced by a mutual trust council (*Vertrauensrat*) which had only an advisory role, although not all *Vertrauensräte* were mere rubber stamps. The main restrictions on the power of the enterprise leader now came from above, from the state through the trustee of labour (*Treuhänder der Arbeit*). As a watchdog for the interests of the state, the *Treuhänder* issued guidelines

---

[40] Jeremy Noakes and Geoffrey Pridham (eds.), *Documents on Nazism, 1919–1945* (London, 1974), p. 434.

for wages and working conditions, as well as for internal rules. He was the arbiter who took the place of the former conciliation and arbitration committees, and he had ultimate control over the enterprise *Vertrauensräte*.

The law of 20 January 1934 established also a system of 'social honour courts'. In the feudalized Nazi perspective of industrial relations, the concept of social honour played an important ideological role, but it was defined only in terms of practices and forms of conduct which violated it. Violations included abuses of power, malevolent exploitation, injury to the honour of an employee, breach of industrial peace, unwarranted interference with the *Vertrauensrat*, disobedience of the orders of the trustee, trivial complaints to the trustee, and disclosure of industrial secrets. Employers were arraigned more often than employees before honour courts, but the brunt seems to have fallen on small employers.

In social security the leader of the DAF, Dr Robert Ley, envisaged radical reforms leading to comprehensive but equal benefits for all Germans who fulfilled their duty to the country. His system never materialized. Only in unemployment insurance were radical but backwards reforms introduced. A decree of 5 September 1939 substituted unemployment assistance for insurance and made it subject to a means test and to the requirement that the worker be willing to accept any job offered. During the 1930s some minor improvements were made in survivorship pensions, and in sickness and accident coverage. The most characteristic feature was the efforts of the Nazis to make social welfare programmes serve the ideological interests of the state. The traditional participatory approach to administration was abolished in favour of the leadership principle, carried out by trusted Nazi functionaries.

Perhaps the most distinctive Nazi labour welfare scheme was the 'Strength Through Joy' (Kraft durch Freude) programme, copied from the Italian 'after work' (Dopolavoro). It offered a wide range of recreational activities, including organized travel, orchestras during lunch hours, theatre nights, factory libraries, and sports. In 1938, some 10 million persons participated in vacation trips, with 180,000 going on cruises.[41] The DAF was in charge of this programme, as well as the related 'Beauty of Work' Schönheit der Arbeit programme, which was concerned with beautification of factories, and the provision of such amenities as rest-rooms, canteens and factory gardens. All of these schemes aimed at improving both welfare and productivity. Another approach pursued by the DAF for higher productivity was competition among enterprises as well as skills competitions among craftsmen which were carried through from the local to the national level.

[41] Richard Grunberger, *The 12-Year Reich* (New York, 1971), p. 198.

The aspects of labour policy which became increasingly prominent after 1935 were control over labour allocation, regulation of wages, and increases in the length of the working day. The individual employment book (*Arbeitsbuch*), introduced in 1935, carried detailed information on each individual's training and employment record, which enabled the authorities to keep track of the work-force. Although many decrees on training, placement, and movement were issued, it was not until 1938 that the workers' freedom to change jobs was seriously curtailed. Wage controls were in effect for a number of years, but again were not vigorously enforced until 1937. A decree which became effective in 1939 allowed for a longer working day and reduction in overtime pay. By the time the war broke out the 10-hour day had become widespread; in important industries like mining, metalworking, and construction, working days of 12 to 14 hours had become common.

The fundamental aim of Nazi labour policy was to mobilize all available human resources towards preparation for war. In spite of some pockets of resistance, the policy was highly successful. The Nazis demonstrated how modern methods of control and mass manipulation, when combined with solid economic achievement such as the elimination of mass unemployment, can be made to serve the purposes of a totalitarian state, notwithstanding the democratic traditions of three generations of organized labour.

V. *Developments in other countries*

There is a general historical pattern in the labour policies of France and Germany which is more or less repeated in other continental countries in the course of industrial development. The earliest labour laws were almost everywhere concerned with the prohibition of the right to strike and to organize. Usually before workers were given the right of organized self-protection, the state initiated some labour protective legislation. The first to be protected were children, then women, and finally other adult workers. The extension of protection to adult workers most often followed the granting of the right to strike and to organize, but this was not the case in Russia. Social security legislation generally came after legislation regulating hours and working conditions. The extensive state regulation of industrial relations did not come about until after the First World War, although measures concerned with the settlement of labour disputes had their beginnings in the pre-war era.

The prohibition of strikes and combinations was based either on the traditional prohibitions of workers to combine against their masters or on the more modern concept of freedom to work. The latter approach, which dominated in France, was also widely adopted in territories once occupied by Napoleonic troops, such as part of Germany and Belgium. Austria followed the more general German pattern of codifying the traditional prohibition. Where serfdom still existed, as in Russia, the codification of the traditional prohibition was bound to be expressed in harsh terms. Article 1791 of the revised Russian penal code of 1845 made 'manifest insubordination' by groups of workers 'liable to the legally prescribed penalties for acts of rebellion against state authority'.[42] The conception of resistance to the master as somehow equivalent to resistance to the state must be understood in the autocratic context of Russian society as well as in the light of the fact that most factory workers at the time were serfs. But there were not many prosecutions of strikers in pre-reform Russia.

The right to strike and to organize was granted in most Western European countries in the 1860s or early 1870s. Belgium followed France in 1867 by amending her criminal code on strikes, while Austria followed Germany with legislation authorizing trade unions in 1867 and amendments to her criminal code regarding strikes in 1870. In The Netherlands, the right to unionize was regulated in 1872, although technically it existed since 1848. In Spain the right of assembly and combination was included in the constitution of 1876. In Italy this legal change came about much more slowly and more indirectly; the right to strike and to organize was recognized only indirectly in the criminal code amendments of 1890 in connection with penalties for the use of violence and threats. But it was in Russia where the right of combination was delayed the longest. It took the revolution and general strike of 1905 to move Tsar Nicholas II to issue his proclamation of 17 October[43] of that year in which he promised 'full freedom of conscience, assembly and organization'. Following this promise, a law of 2 December 1905 legalized strikes for economic purposes, and a law of 4 March 1906 legalized trade unions. This legal recognition of the labour movement in Russia came after three decades of a rising strike movement which the government had been unable to prevent or suppress in spite of harsh policies. Between 1901 and 1905 the government had even tried to capture the labour movement through 'police socialism', trade unions and strikes organized and led by the political police. This concept, which had been suggested by the political police as early as 1871, ended a dismal failure. Under the policy initiated in 1906, trade unions had to be officially approved and remained under close police surveillance.

In the area of factory legislation the role of pioneer on the continent belongs to Switzerland, or rather the German-speaking Swiss cantons,

---

[42] Michael I. Tugan-Baranovsky, *The Russian Factory in the 19th Century*, 3rd edn, trans. A. Levin and C. S. Levin (Homewood, Ill., 1970), p. 139.

[43] All Russian dates before February 1918 follow the old-style calendar.

which were the most industrialized. Canton Zürich regulated the factory employment of children as early as 1815, although the regulation was largely ignored. A second child labour ordinance passed in 1837, two years ahead of Prussia, was much better enforced. It raised the factory employment age from 9 to 12, tightened school requirements, regulated hours, and prohibited work at night, on Sundays and holidays by children and juveniles. Two other cantons, Thurgau and Glarus, enacted similar regulations during the 1840s. Switzerland was also in the lead in regulating hours and working conditions for adults. Canton Glarus, which introduced the 14-hour day in 1848 in the textile industry, in 1864 established the 12-hour day for all factories, and at the same time prohibited night work and work by women 6 weeks before and after child birth. The same ordinance imposed upon factory owners the duty to look after the safety, health, and morals of the workers. Attempts to extend these regulations to other cantons were not very successful, but the federal Factory Act of 1877 and its subsequent amendments gave the country the most progressive factory legislation on the continent. Besides raising the employment age to 14, the act regulated the employment of women, established the 11-hour working day, prohibited work on Sundays, required at least 8 annual holidays, and imposed written internal factory rules. The workers had to be given an opportunity to express their views on these rules before they were presented to the authorities for approval.

From the 1840s onward, child labour laws were introduced in a number of countries, including Austria in 1842, Russia in 1845, Venice and Lombardy in 1843, Italy in 1865, and the Netherlands in 1874. Most of the laws passed before the 1870s were not enforced. It was not until the 1880s that most countries began seriously to regulate factories with regard to hours, safety, and other conditions of work. In a country like Austria, where German precedents were important, the regulatory principle was more readily accepted than in countries like Belgium or Italy, where economic liberalism and French influence were strong. In Belgium the legislative debate over regulating child labour began in the 1840s, but it was not until the 1880s that a combination of Christian social and socialist forces managed to push through such legislation against very strong spokesmen for economic liberalism. Both Belgium and Italy did take over the French institution of *conseils de prud'hommes*. In Belgium they were introduced in 1859 but spread very slowly. In Italy the *Collegi dei probiviri* were enacted in 1893; their impact is hard to judge, since the period from then until the First World War was one of sharply increasing labour unrest.

It is interesting that along with Switzerland, a country with strong democratic yet paternalistic traditions, it was Russia, the country with

the strongest autocratic traditions, that introduced the most comprehensive factory legislation in nineteenth-century Europe. The Tsar and the
higher bureaucracy saw the regulation of factory work as a natural object
of state control. They were not going to tolerate power contests between
disgruntled workers and intransigent employers. As early as 1835 the
state created a statute which tried to define the duties of factory workers
and the rights of employers, but that statute, like the Child Labour Law
of 1845, was largely ignored. In 1859 and again during the 1870s several
commissions were established to study factory conditions and make
proposals for regulation. Finally, during the 1880s a whole series of
factory laws were enacted; the law of 1 June 1882 regulated the employment of children and instituted an inspection system; the law of 12 June
1884 established school requirements and regulated the working day for
juveniles; and the law of 3 June 1885 prohibited night work for women
and juveniles in textile mills. The most important piece of legislation,
however, was the law of 3 June 1886, which, according to no less an
authority than Tugan-Baranovsky, 'fundamentally altered employment
conditions and the very position of the worker in the factory'.[44]

The guiding notion of the 1886 law, as explained by another leading
Russian authority, was that 'the hiring of factory labour is not merely a
civil contract, similar to any other private contract, but a matter of public
interest intimately related to public order and peace'.[45] In this spirit the
Russian lawmakers tried to define and circumscribe the contractual
relationship in a set of rules which could be controlled by the state. The
rules specified the contract period, during which the employer could not
reduce wages nor workers demand an increase. Wages had to be paid at
regular intervals and in cash. Workers had to have wage-books or
written contracts. Factory rules had to be written out and posted. The
nature of fines and related conditions had to be specified. Conditions of
contract terminations had to be specified in advance. The aim was not to
establish any kind of equality in labour relations, but rather a basis for
legality. There was no alteration in the civil code, which stated that
'workers have to be faithful, obedient, and respectful toward their master
and his family, and strive through good conduct to maintain peace and
harmony'.

While official objectives were clear enough, practical realization
would have been difficult under nearly any circumstances. It was practically impossible under Russian conditions of inequality and illiteracy.
The factory inspectors, on whom the enforcement burden fell, often
found themselves in the position of conciliators and abitrators. The rising
tide of industrial unrest during the 1890s testifies to the fact that the

[44] Tugan-Baranovsky, *The Russian Factory*, p. 136.
[45] S. N. Prokopovich, *K. Rabochemu Voprosu v Rossii* (St Petersburg, 1905), p. 87.

Table 101. *First social insurance laws in continental Europe*

	Workmen's compensation	Old age and/or invalidity	Sickness	Unemployment
Austria	1887	1906	1888	1920
Belgium	1903	1924	1894	1920
Bulgaria	1924	1924	1918	1925
France	1898	1910	1928	1940
Germany	1884	1889	1883	1927
Greece	1914	1934	1922	1945
Italy	1898	1919	1943	1919
Luxembourg	1902	1911	1901	1921
Portugal	1913	1935	1935	1975
Romania	1912	1912	1912	—
Russia	1903	1922	1912	1922
Spain	1900	1919	1942	1919
Switzerland	1911	1946	1911	1924
The Netherlands	1901	1913	1913	1916

Source: US Department of Health, Education, and Welfare, *Social Security Programs Throughout the World, 1975* (Washington, DC, 1976), *passim.*

regulatory approach to industrial relations was a failure. The government had to make more concessions to the workers. Under heavy pressure, it passed the law of 2 June 1897, which introduced the $11\frac{1}{2}$-hour working day, established Sunday as a legal day of rest, and provided for 18 annual holidays. Although the law was widely disregarded, the employers argued that it harmed the workers by reducing their earnings and kept them out of factories which were a lot healthier than workers' homes! Another concession without much practical significance was the 1903 law on factory councils (*starosty*). The councils, which were optional for employers, could deal only with contract interpretations, not with alterations of wages and working conditions. By the time of the 1905 revolution, only about three dozen such councils had come into existence in the whole country.[46]

In the area of social security legislation before the First World War Germany had the commanding lead, and none of the other countries was a close follower. There is a general pattern in the emergence of social security programmes. The right to compensation for industrial injuries regardless of fault almost everywhere preceded any other form of income protection. Most European countries guaranteed this right before 1914, as can be seen in Table 101. The next programme introduced was usually sickness insurance or pensions in case of disability or old age. Six of the 14 countries listed in Table 101 introduced such pensions

[46] Peisach Meschewetski, *Die Fabrikgesetzgebung in Russland* (Tübingen, 1911), p. 118.

before the war, but sometimes, as in the case of France, they were not operational. Not counted here are the much more prevalent pension programmes for special groups such as civil servants, miners, railway workers and seamen. Seven countries introduced sickness insurance programmes, not counting the maternity insurance programme introduced in Italy in 1912. The only form of unemployment insurance introduced on the continent before the war was in the form of subsidies to trade unions or other local funds. France introduced such a system in 1905. It developed also at the city level in Belgium, from where it spread to cities in other countries. National schemes of unemployment insurance developed after the First World War.

In the two decades between the world wars, as was noted earlier, the most important feature of labour and social policy was a growing participation of the state in industrial relations and in the determination of working conditions. Aside from Germany, the two countries where this trend was most pronounced were Italy and the Soviet Union. In each of these countries the trade unions lost their independence and became instruments of state labour policy. Italy began the post-war period with a weak labour movement that had long suffered from ferocious internal dissensions and excessive reliance on the general strike. The Italian record on social and labour legislation was relatively meagre, but programmes of old age and disability insurance as well as unemployment insurance were introduced in 1919. The workers were demanding the eight-hour day, holidays with pay and higher wages, while radical groups inspired by the Bolshevik revolution were insisting on worker control of the factories and peasant ownership of the land. In this troubled setting the Italian Combat Bands (Fasci Italiani di Combattimento) launched by Benito Mussolini began to appear to the frightened middle classes as a bulwark against Bolshevism. When Mussolini came to power in October 1922, he temporarily maintained some of the trappings of democracy but proceeded quickly to eliminate any potential sources of resistance, especially from the left.

While gaining control over the labour movement through Fascist-controlled unions, Mussolini appealed to the workers' interests by securing the passage of the 8-hour day and 48-hour week in 1923. He declared his labour policy to be based on the principle of 'class collaboration in the national interest'. In pursuance of this policy, he engineered the Vidoni Palace Declaration of 2 October 1925, where the representatives of the General Confederation of Italian Industry (Confederazione Generale dell'Industria Italiana) officially recognized the National Confederation of Fascist Syndical Unions (Confederazione Nazionale delle Corporazioni Sindicali Fasciste) as the sole representatives of Italian workers. The Fascist unions in return recognized Confindustria as the sole employer representative. This agreement and the principle of class collaboration became embodied in the law of 3 April 1926 and subsequent administrative regulations. Only Fascist employer and worker organizations were officially recognized, and each had exclusive jurisdiction in a given industrial branch or region. Worker membership was optional but contribution was compulsory. Collective agreements signed by officially recognized organizations were binding on all establishments in a given jurisdiction, regardless of membership or participation. Strikes and lock-outs were prohibited and treated as criminal offences. To resolve industrial disputes and contractual disagreements, new labour courts and an expanded conciliation machinery were created.

This new industrial order was consecrated in the Charter of Labour proclaimed by the Fascist Grand Council in 1927. As in Germany and in the Soviet Union, labour was declared to be a 'moral duty' and the labourer entitled to protection by the state. The charter enumerated the benefits to which the worker was entitled, including education, health and welfare programmes, paid holidays, training, and placement. A characteristic programme was the National Institution for After-work Activities (Opera Nazionale Dopolavoro), which seems to have served as a model for the Nazi 'Strength Through Joy' activities. The Fascist labour organizations kept the old dual structure of industrial unions and regional multi-trade chambers. Each type of organization was part of a national federation; federations were combined into confederations; and confederations were united under Fascist corporations. The corporations were ostensibly representative of the combined interests of employers, workers, and consumers, but all officials were appointed by the government. The whole organization was extremely unwieldy, but it did not prevent the state from exercising far-reaching control over wages and working conditions.

The Fascists brought industrial peace and order to Italy and extended the welfare state. In 1935 they introduced the half-day on Saturday and in 1936 the 40-hour week. Family allowances were established in 1936. But in terms of freedom and wages the workers lost. The real wage index (1913 = 100), which stood at 120.79 in 1927, sank to a low of 100.53 in 1938, and reached only 105.68 in 1939.[47] It remains unclear to what extent the decline in wages was compensated by other material advantages.

In contrast to Nazi Germany and Fascist Italy, in the Soviet Union those in power considered themselves to be ruling in the name of and for the proletariat. This circumstance determined two basic features of early

[47] Maurice F. Neufeld, *Italy: School for Awakening Countries* (Ithaca, NY, 1961), p. 316.

labour policy. First, every effort had to be made to enact into law all the traditional demands of the labour movement with regard to hours, working conditions, minimum wages, and social security. Secondly, the role of labour organizations and their relationship to those in authority in industry and the state had to be settled. Was there any room or indeed any need in the workers' state for organizations devoted specifically to the defence of worker interests?

Immediately upon seizing power the Bolsheviks began to proclaim the new rights of labour and to issue appropriate decrees. A decree of 27 October 1917 established the 8-hour working day, abolished night, underground, and overtime work for women and juveniles; employment of children under 14 was forbidden and overtime for male adults was restricted; official holidays were recognized, including Sundays and holy days. A decree of 11 December 1917 introduced unemployment insurance, and a further decree of 27 December promised cash sickness benefits, birth and burial grants, and free medical care. Under the prevailing chaotic economic and administrative circumstances, these decrees were little more than declarations of intention. Mainly also of ideological significance was the labour code published in December 1918, which laid down comprehensive rules for employment, dismissals, transfers, remuneration, and labour protection. The code proclaimed the right and duty to work for all citizens. All able-bodied persons between the ages of 16 and 50 became eligible to be drafted for labour service, and all citizens were entitled to work in their profession or trade at going rates.

With regard to labour organization, the early months of the Bolshevik regime were marked by a contest for power between trade unions and factory committees supported by local soviets. The outcome of the contest was settled in favour of the trade unions by early 1918, but with the coming of the civil war the unions themselves were transformed from independent organizations into agencies of state economic administration. Under the pressures of War Communism (1918–21), the trade unions became instruments of coercion in the militarization of the workforce. Some Bolshevik leaders, Trotsky, for instance, elevated the complete submission of organized labour to the state to the level of 'proletarian principle'. The appearance of forced labour camps during this period testifies that the Bolsheviks did not shrink back from harsh measures, but for many of them, including probably Lenin, such measures were a matter of expediency dictated by the civil war.

As the civil war ended in November 1920, the debate over the role of trade unions in the new society gained momentum. At the tenth party congress in March 1921, Lenin took a middle-of-the-road position between those who wanted more union independence and those who wanted complete 'statification' of the unions. The congress adopted his solution, under which unions became an instrument of government policy without being a formal part of the state apparatus. Acting as a major link between the party vanguard and the masses, the unions were to be 'schools for communism' and 'schools for discipline and production'. This solution left the trade unions with neither much autonomy nor much authority. But it became part of Leninist orthodoxy that unions should not be a formal part of the state apparatus, no matter how little autonomy they may have in practice.

The corner-stone of Soviet labour policy under the post-civil war New Economic Policy (NEP) was the labour code of 1922. Consolidating previous legislation, the code regulated recruitment, hiring, collective agreements, work contracts, work rules, output norms, earnings, hours, rent periods, women, minors, labour protection, trade unions, settlement of disputes, and social insurance. In terms of industrial legislation, the code of 1922 and amendments to it during the 1920s were highly progressive, but trade unions were 'reduced to the role of executors of production plans decided upon . . . without their participation; they were threatened by unemployment and in the struggle for higher wages they were handicapped by political loyalties and by the law'.[48] Strikes were frowned upon but not illegal. The trade unions were to work through the assessment-conflict commissions, on which they were represented, for the execution of collective contracts, settlement of disputes, and elaboration of internal factory rules. To assure compliance of the unions with party guidelines, the party resolved in 1922 that all chairmen and secretaries of trade-union central committees must be party members of long standing. With the help of the party cells within the trade unions, strict control of the party over the union was thus assured. During the remaining five years of the NEP, the unions increasingly became bureaucratic extensions of the party, although technically they were supposed to resist the bureaucratic excesses of the official state apparatus. It was evident by the mid-1920s that they had lost much of their influence over the workers. Unauthorized strikes were becoming increasingly frequent, which exposed the union leaders to criticism for failure to keep in touch with the masses. But the union leaders' dilemma had arisen from the fact that they were trying to follow the productionist guidelines of the party. Clearly, their role of linking the party and the masses was a very difficult one.

During the years 1925–7 when Soviet leaders debated the controversial issues of central planning and the speed of industrialization, the trade-union leaders for the last time rose in opposition to the dominant

---

[48] Margaret Dewar, *Labour Policy in the USSR 1917–1928* (London, 1956), p. 99.

will of the party. The union leaders understood what the case for rapid industrialization implied for the workers in terms of hardships, coercion, and ruthless discipline. By the time the dust had settled over the controversies, the ranks of the labour leaders had been drastically purged, and the unions had surrendered their last shred of autonomy. The inauguration of the first Five Year Plan in 1928 marked the beginning of a new era not only for the Soviet economy but also for Soviet labour relations. The next ten years witnessed the most massive creation of an industrial workforce in history. The overwhelming task of labour policy became the transformation of a mass of unskilled peasants into a skilled and disciplined industrial work-force. Such a task could not be performed in less than half a generation without almost boundless ruthlessness.

The task had essentially two parts: the first was to move the labour from the land into the factories and mines; the second was to impart skills and discipline. In many ways the first part was much easier than the second. Between 1926 and 1939 some 24 million people were shifted from the country to the city.[49] During the 1920s this movement was more or less spontaneous, but in 1930 Stalin decided that the 'spontaneous influx' was too slow and what was needed was 'organized recruitment'. The system that evolved was never highly coordinated. It relied on material inducements as well as a good deal of pressure, but it did not fall back on the forcible recruitment methods of War Communism. The pressure was put mainly on collective farms, which were expected to deliver stated numbers of bodies under contract with industrial enterprises. In theory, at least, freedom of movement was maintained, with important exceptions. From 1930 onward, skilled workers could be transferred obligatorily to essential jobs and industries, 'in agreement' with the trade union involved. A more serious infringement of the freedom to select one's own job was the vast expansion of forced labour camps. Women began to play an increasingly important role as industrial workers. By 1939 some 41.6 per cent of all industrial employees were women.[50]

A major concern of official policy during the 1930s was the combating of absenteeism and labour turnover, and the promotion of discipline. Since the workers were not allowed to strike, absenteeism and turnover were in the main expressions of protest over working and living conditions. Aside from the pressures exerted on the job against such protests, the government resorted to increasingly drastic measures. By 1932, even one day's absence from the job made a worker liable to instant dismissal,

---

[49] Isaac Deutscher, 'Russia', in Walter Galenson (ed.), *Comparative Labor Movements* (New York, 1952), p. 537.
[50] Solomon M. Schwarz, *Labor in the Soviet Union* (New York, 1952).

deprivation of ration cards, and eviction from housing allotted by the enterprise. In 1930 the labour exchanges were ordered to deal severely with workers who refused a job or retraining, and the unemployment benefit programme was eliminated. Social security and other social programmes were reshaped to make benefits contingent upon length of employment at a particular job. In 1933 the trade unions were given an expanded role in the administration of welfare programmes. Since benefits were often contingent upon trade-union membership, the threat of expulsion from the union gave union leaders a new weapon in the enforcement of discipline. As the threat of war appeared on the horizon in 1938, new measures were taken to tighten labour discipline, including the introduction of increased penalties for idleness, lateness, and violations of work rules.

The government undertook also major efforts to stimulate the incentive to work. In 1931 the wage structure was reformed to make rewards more contingent upon performance. Stalin denounced the tendencies toward wage egalitarianism that many socialists had supported. His pronouncements were the signal for the widest possible application of wages based on piece-rates. Non-material work incentives did not lose their importance. The title of 'Hero of Labour', introduced in 1927, and the 'Order of the Red Banner of Labour of the USSR', created in 1928, involved also significant material advantages for the recipient. Among the recipients in the 1930s were the leaders of the Stakhanovite movement. They were the models of the kind of 'socialist emulation' that the party sought to promote. From the point of view of many workers socialist emulation was primarily a means of raising the work norms to ever higher levels.

The Soviet experience represents the culmination of the central historical trend traced in this chapter, the long-term transformation of the employment contract from a private arrangement between employer and worker into a relationship which is heavily regulated by the state. In the individualistic setting of French economic liberalism with which the chapter began, the aim of the state was to keep the employment contract a private, individual matter between the two partners. While in theory each was free to maximize his welfare within this framework, in practice, even if the labour market had been perfect, the relationship of employer to worker was necessarily an authority relationship and therefore unequal if unrestricted. If the organizational logic of modern industry requires that a few command and many obey, the history of the labour movement has been a long series of efforts to limit the power and authority of the employer. The aim has been not only to change the distribution of economic rewards, but also to influence the exercise of discipline and control. The main weapons the workers have used have been the trade unions and the strike on the one hand, and the political weapon on the other. In the setting of the totalitarian state, however, the political weapon has turned against the workers. While they kept many of their welfare gains, a major aim of governmental labour policy turned out to be the elimination of the power of organized labour.

CHAPTER VIII

British public policy, 1776–1939

I. *The four transitions*

British public policy in the century and a half or so before the Second World War was characterized by four simultaneous transitions. The first was from landed rule in the eighteenth century, via dominance by the middle classes in the high Victorian age, to an uneasy and sometimes tense confusion between middle and working classes in the 1920s and 1930s. The second carried economic policy from the British form of mercantilism, via a period of state abdication unique among industrial nations, to the sudden adoption of an elaborate system of macro-controls in the 1930s. The third moved social policy from a provision that was minimal and local, via a complex set of struggles over particular issues between philanthropists and workers on the one hand, and cost- and profit-conscious business men on the other (mediated by parliament, the bureaucrats and the intellectuals), to a far-reaching commitment to welfare. The fourth was the elaboration of a system of implementation and control such that policy-making came to be shared between parliament and the senior members of the bureaucracy. The circumstances governing these four concurrent evolutions, their timing, and the relationships between them, provide the outline agenda for a consideration of the course of state action on the economy and society. So complex a pattern is best viewed in terms of successive time spans, five in all.

II. *Policy, industrialization, and war, 1776–1815*

In the 40 years between the publication of Adam Smith's *The Wealth of Nations* in 1776 and Waterloo in 1815 Britain gestated the first industrial society. But no obvious and systematic policy shift is perceptible. Policy did, of course, change in significant ways, but it did so mainly by a mixture of inadvertence and wartime improvization. For in spite of the emergence of new forms in the economy and society, a longer-term continuity in terms of power was present.

The Britain that underwent the industrial revolution was ruled by the landed men in the House of Lords and the House of Commons. As late as 1831 the electorate of England was less than half a million in a population of 14 millions; it was highly susceptible to electoral management through patronage and privilege. But the explicit power wielded from the centre was slight, certainly if measured on the European scale. Indeed a landed parliament, having wrested the weapon of taxation from a centralizing monarchy by 1688, intended not to wield it, but rather to protect property from it. Such central intervention as there was principally took the British form of mercantilism, namely trying to operate on the terms of foreign trade. Most government affecting the countryman was exercised at the level of England's 15,000 parishes, and at the quarter sessions, the places where poor relief and justice respectively were administered; in the towns power lay with unreformed corporations and parish vestries in which self-perpetuating oligarchies (derived largely from the middle classes) were powerful.

The landed class had, of course, its interests to defend. Its general bias was toward some sort of continuance of the social bond which had always been an ideal and had sometimes been a reality. Seen in retrospect the coming of industrialization posed for the landed interest the problem, to what extent and in what forms should it be controlled or even resisted? But such men did not ask themselves such a question explicitly, for that was not how tradition-formed minds operated. Yet in an *ad hoc* sense they did so: they insisted on the Corn Laws, giving protection to rents and farm incomes. Also, the landed men used the state through acts of parliament to carry out the enclosure of the land in the late eighteenth and early nineteenth centuries. Though a good many of such men were developing an interest in industrial and urban matters through coal-mining, canal building, and rising land values, the focus of their lives lay in agriculture and their place in it.

With such an outlook at the top of society the middle classes were more or less content. They shared with their betters the state-created security of property and freedom from royal taxation that the Whigs had achieved. Indeed this was a basic condition for their own emergence. Moreover, though largely unenfranchised, they had their own ways of exercising political power. The men of commerce and finance, according to Adam Smith, were largely responsible for British commercial policy, and through it, foreign policy: throughout the eighteenth century they had much to do with the chronic French and Dutch wars and with the terms of settlement which determined the shape of the expanding Empire. The emergent manufacturers, by the later eighteenth century, also knew how to organize to bring pressure to bear on the state, as they demonstrated over the abortive Irish treaty of 1785 and the Eden treaty with France of 1786. But whereas the traders and financiers of the City of London could enjoy an increasing share in the franchise by becoming landed, the industrialists had no effective direct participation in politics until the first Reform Act of 1832.

The mass of the people had no part whatever in the decisions of the state, except when the level of unrest among them was such as to induce caution in their masters. The long course of history, with its relatively static technological base, had given rise to no expectation on the part of labouring men that they should share in the state. And yet a small minority of them were prepared to challenge their employers by organizing trade unions. In so doing they encountered the state, both in terms of the judiciary (which held unions to be in restraint of trade), and of statute (the Combination Laws of 1799 and 1800 were passed in wartime to prevent sudden withdrawals of labour). A landed parliament thus acceded to the industrialists' wishes to restrain collective action by the labour force. Resentment at the illegality of unions could not be generalized among the population, especially as the war against the traditional enemy, France, resumed in 1793, generated a considerable sentiment of national unity.

In the 1700s Britain had to reconstitute her Empire after the loss of one of its largest components in the American War of Independence: this was done by seeking new areas of expansion, especially in the Pacific and the Indian sub-continent, and by reasserting the principles of the Navigation Acts which sought to confine British overseas trade to British merchants and their ships. In the 1790s France overthrew her monarchy and undertook to spread revolutionary ideas over much of Europe. The inevitable response from Britain, concerned with the prospect of a gross continental imbalance, was war, almost continuously from 1793 to 1815. But Britain was now exposed to strong republican and democratic sentiments, first from the new United States and, especially, from France, prompting a significant element of society, among whom middle-class intellectuals affected by the ideas of the Enlightenment were prominent, to question the basis of the British state. The state where necessary contained these pressures, partly by constraints on civil liberties.

But there were domestic changes at work of a yet more profound kind, to which policy had, in one way or another, to respond. These arose from that medley of atomistic actions by individuals or groups which comprised the agricultural and industrial revolutions. By means of many hundreds of Enclosure Acts the state was used to push through a major land reform, which raised output, sustained the upward trend of population, made possible a transfer of labour from agriculture to industry, commercialized the countryside, and confirmed the landed class in possession. But it also dispossessed many of the weaker members of the rural community.

In terms of commerce and industry there was no way in which the state could be used, as in agriculture, as a renovating agent. Moreover, even if there had been, the landed interest would not have employed it. Indeed much control in the old manner was continued. The Navigation Acts were confirmed. The attempts made by William Pitt's government to free trade with France and Ireland were abandoned: indeed the war with France put back the cause of free trade and the opening of world markets for a generation. There was a wide range of control on exports, including coal and wool, and on machinery (together with a prohibition on the emigration of artisans who could install and operate it). Elaborate import controls were continued, especially on timber and sugar, intended to assist Empire producers. The Corn Law, that great defence of the landed interest, remained inviolate. Behind each of these restrictions on freedom of action stood a vested interest operating upon policy.

But there were interests no longer strong enough to maintain their position; state policy turned against them. The East India Company in 1812 lost its monopoly of trade to India, though it continued to be immensely powerful, both in the City of London and as the administrator of a sub-empire. The slave traders found their business declared illegal from 1807, though slave owners continued in possession of their human property on the plantations until 1833.

The attitude of the state to the money and credit supply was a curious compound. By and large entry into banking in England and Scotland was free to individuals, together with the right of note issue. Both countries could thus proliferate banks on a scale such as to amaze continentals. But in the English case the Bank of England had enjoyed a monopoly of large-scale banking (over six partners) since 1709, thus arresting the growth of joint-stock banks on the Scottish models. The state had no wish to meddle beyond this – it left the money supply to market forces, subject to the Bank's control through curtailment of its willingness to rediscount bills of exchange. In 1797 the convertibility of the Bank's notes was suspended, so that the discipline of the gold standard was removed. Far from resisting this, a parliament at war welcomed the easier credit conditions thus made possible. It also continued in operation the traditional usury laws, setting a maximum rate of interest of 5 per cent.

The fiscal system was largely traditional, relying heavily upon the taxation of consumption through customs and excise duties. But by 1799 the war needs of the state forced the adoption of a tax on incomes. There was profound resentment at so inquisitorial a tax, shared by landed and middle classes alike.

In the consumer markets of the nation, official control had been lapsing steadily, so that in 1815 the last relic of a once-elaborate price control system, the Assize of Bread, was ended. The consumer was now fully exposed to the rule *caveat emptor*. In part this passing of paternalism was due to an easing of conditions, especially the ending of subsistence crises.

At the same time that the state was denying to the workers the right to combine to press wages upwards it withdrew its own traditional presence from wage determination, first by letting the Elizabethan labour statute go into disuse, and then by repealing it in 1813–14. The price of labour thus became market governed, with the workers still forbidden to act collectively. The state abdicated also from control of the training of apprentices and of the entry into crafts. This state withdrawal from wage and recruitment regulation reflected, in part, the official inability to continue to supervise such matters as they became more complex.

Down to 1802 the workers were wholly in the hands of their employers so far as conditions of work were concerned. The Health and Morals of Apprentices Act of that year was the first tentative and limited step in imposing humane standards on market-oriented manufacturers, beginning with children. Parliament responded to the plea, made by mill owner Sir Robert Peel, that in the name of decency the state should begin to prescribe minima.

With the care of the poor the central state had nothing to do, except that it had by statute fixed duties on the parishes. In England since Tudor times the labourer, though he was in large measure tied to the parish of his birth where he had a 'settlement', was there entitled to relief (in Scotland there was no such statutory requirement that made provision for the able-bodied). In the parishes the Poor Law officers and the local philanthropists, in a complementary relationship, struggled, over the generations, with the problem of the indigent. Since 1795, under the 'Speenhamland system', the conditions on which relief was given to the poor had been greatly eased, generating alarm in some quarters.

Public policy as formulated by parliament was a kind of continuous improvisation. It was the outcome of a basic landed reality, but one that was obliged to give scope to new emergent commercial and industrial interests which could not be flatly resisted. Nor was there any clear reason why they should be. Indeed, they had become indispensable parts of the economy and society, including its potential for war. Nor was there any suggestion that they should be deprived of the sanction of the courts and of statute in resisting attempts among their work-force to combine. Commercial policy was a more complex matter: some diminution of monopoly, as with the East India Company, was appropriate, but corn was inviolate, and so was the apparatus of an imperial economic system as embodied in the Navigation Acts and in colonial preferences. The challenges of industrial and social amelioration were not yet such as to become matters of policy on any significant scale: the Health and

Morals of Apprentices Act of 1802 was minimal and without effective enforcement, and the Poor Law continued in its traditional way, exposing the mass of the population to the threat of indignity.

III. *Assimilating the industrial revolution, 1815–51*

In the generation or so between Waterloo and the Great Exhibition of 1851 the industrialization of Britain accelerated and extended. The configuration of power changed accordingly. The landed class received its first great challenge in the Reform Act of 1832. Through it the new business world gained its first effective footing in the Commons. But businessmen remained a minority there, not to speak of the House of Lords. The business class was not yet ready to challenge in terms of the legislature (though it did so outside parliament through the agitation for repeal of the Corn Laws).

The Whig administration taking office in 1832, still largely landed based, implemented a wide range of new policies. These reflected a curious mixture of Benthamite demands for more effective and efficient government, together with a dual humanitarianism (deriving in part from evangelical urgings), that was much concerned with human debasement at home and plantation slavery overseas. The economy and society showed renewed stress in the later thirties and early forties, producing a new range of protests and challenges to parliament, including the Grand National Consolidated Trades Union of 1833–4 and Chartism. But these, like the war and post-war disturbances, also passed, so that the Great Exhibition of 1851 could be something of an assertion of new confidence and stability.

The general trend of economic policy is clear. It was toward commitment to the market system and economic abdication by the state. But in each aspect of action there was a strong element of pragmatism. The complex of politicians in parliament sought to deal, on a largely *ad hoc* basis, with a range of evolving problems. This they corporately did by balancing, in a series of specific situations, their concept of the common good against the configuration that seemed to be emerging from the relative strengths of interested power groups. The resolution of each such challenge to government had its own complexities and requires its own study.

Markets were progressively freed. The tariff had proliferated over the years, generating paper and engrossing manpower. As William Huskisson, Sir Robert Peel, and William Gladstone put the system under scrutiny, one protective device after another was seen as pointlessly inhibitive, reflecting past realities, if any at all, and as such was abandoned. With them disappeared much of the apparatus of imperial preference. The East India Company lost the last great element in its trading monopoly with the opening of trade to China in 1833. The Navigation Laws as they affected foreign trade were ended in 1849. The export of machinery was freed in 1842.

In 1846 even the great centre-piece of protection, the Corn Law, succumbed. The protection of cereal agriculture had been powerfully reasserted by the Corn Law Act of 1815. Successive governments thereafter had tried formulae that would maintain agriculture at something like its traditional level in the economy and society; at the same time however it was necessary to avoid excessive burdens on urban-industrial consumers of food, with a consequent rise in money wages. But by 1846 the sliding scale as a compromise device had run out. Peel finally opted to allow Britain to draw freely on world grain supplies. He used the sovereignty of parliament to subvert the most powerful interest in the land, depriving it of its most sanctified support, and leaving the Conservative Party in confusion for a decade.

Peel's impact on the system of domestic taxation, though less dramatic, was hardly less radical. His great simplification of the tariff in 1842 left him short of revenue. The income tax had been cast off in 1816 amid the enthusiasm of all parties. Peel brought it back in 1842: he and Gladstone hoped it would be a mere bridging device until the revenue recovered, but it was never to be abandoned again. The state had once more assumed the power to investigate private incomes, and to levy upon them: in short, it had put all incomes ultimately at its own disposal in the manner of feudal kings.

The money supply was a politically neutral issue, once the new post-war price level had been established after the resumption of cash payments in 1819. In times of commercial crisis the government could indeed be subjected to strong pressure to suspend the gold standard, but this was seen as a commercial and technical matter rather than one to be regulated by political philosophy. In spite of some soft-money campaigners like Thomas Attwood, successive governments clung to the idea of a market-determined money and credit supply based on gold.

But following the commercial crisis of 1825 the government was obliged to enter upon a course of legislation to restructure the banking system. To the Bank of England, still dependent for its continued existence upon the periodic renewal of its charter by the state, the government continued to delegate such regulative power as existed. The Bank was expected, in the light of its readings of various indicators (chiefly the course of the exchanges and the relationship between its own gold holdings and its demand obligations, together with 'opinion' in the

City of London), to vary the money supply. To make the Bank more effective in this role it was necessary to begin to concentrate the note issue in its hands (in England), and to set out new rules for the Bank itself and for the banking companies. The Bank Act of 1826 removed the six-partner rule and so made it possible for England to follow the Scottish lead into joint-stock banking, provided such banks stayed 65 miles out of London. The 1833 act made the Bank of England's notes legal tender everywhere but at the Bank itself, or its branches; moreover the 65 mile rule was removed, but all banks entering London had to give up their issue, to be replaced by that of the Bank of England. The act of 1844 was the basic British banking statute right up to 1931. No new banks of issue were to be permitted. The Bank of England was to be allowed a fiduciary issue of £14 millions, backed by securities, the whole of the rest was to be backed by gold. England was thus to have, when the transition was complete, a note issue confined to the Bank of England, and subject to regulations that would cause it to be varied in a manner strictly analogous to that of a metallic circulation. Consistent with the principle of an automatic money supply, the government repealed the usury laws as affecting bills of exchange in 1833; the short-term price of money was now free.

There were no direct government measures intended to stabilize the decennial trade cycle, or to sponsor long-term growth. There were some advocates of action against unemployment, by monetary manipulation or public works, but they failed to gain official support.

The most difficult decision in a sense centred round the question: what freedoms to combine should be conceded to the workers? The Trade Union Act of 1824, passed by a Commons scarcely aware of what it was doing, made industrial combination a free right. In the following year, with unions and their demands proliferating, parliament partially reimposed constraint. Combination remained a legal right, but it was subjected to various legal doctrines, including that of conspiracy. Organized workers could, for the first time, exercise organized pressure at the industrial level, but subject to a good many pitfalls.

Such social policy as came into being stemmed from particular needs, abuses and defaults. The law of necessary deterioration required that specific social challenges had to mature to the point at which pressure for action was able to overcome the prevailing obstacles to it. The market system had failed to function to the satisfaction of the community (or perhaps to certain groups of activist policy-makers) in three social aspects. These were concerned with the conditions of work, the conditions of urban living, and the treatment of the dependent poor. But the responses were not uniform: in the first two cases the state acceded in modest terms to campaigns for amelioration, but in the third it was pushed in the direction of rigour.

An embryonic labour code for factories and mines had been brought into being by 1851. The first effective Factory Act was that of 1833, affecting the textile trades, limiting the hours of work for children and providing for their schooling. An inspectorate was set up, with powers to make rules about ventilation, temperatures, work times, and the like. The 1844 act extended protection to women, the Ten Hours Act of 1847 carried matters yet further. Such controls for children and women obliged factory owners to adjust their total working. The Mines and Collieries Act of 1842 at a stroke excluded women and children from underground labour. In 1850 inspection was imposed, covering safety, lighting, and ventilation. Over all this there were, of course, long and bitter battles, of which Lord Ashley (from 1851 the Earl of Shaftesbury) and his middle-class supporters were the heroes.

The government, in spite of cholera, typhus, and the general condition of the expanding cities, was unwilling to undertake centralist action affecting the conditions of living. Nor was it willing to give too great a range of powers to local government. The Municipal Reform Act of 1835 required the reorganization of existing English civic corporations, and made it possible for the unchartered places like Birmingham to seek incorporation. It thus gave the cities an important range of explicit powers, but it excluded others. For fear of the doctrine of *ultra vires* the cities had, therefore, to proceed by cumbersome private acts of parliament. But in 1848, under pressure from Sir Edwin Chadwick and others, the Public Health Act was passed (1867 in Scotland). The corporate boroughs were empowered to set up local boards of health to combat bad sanitation and the sickness it generated. But the municipal response was slow: by 1853 only some two million people in England lived under boards of health. Chadwick and his colleagues pressed forward on other fronts, sponsoring acts on drainage, waterworks, burials, and common lodging-houses, challenging a wide range of vested interests.

Whereas industrial and health reform were urban based in terms of thinking, the Poor Law Act of 1834 was conceived in rural terms, arising from the burden of the poor rates in the countryside. Both the act and the report on which it was based took a moral rather than an environmental view of the poor, regarding them as having failed in their responses. The most important change was to reverse the easing of provision that had been going on since the 1780s. This was done by denying relief to the able-bodied outside of the workhouse, and by subjecting those within it to conditions inferior to those of the least well-off wage-earners outside it, the famous principle of 'less eligibility'. The parishes were to be merged into larger, and it was hoped more viable units, known as unions.

But a simple reversal from relaxation to rigour was not possible, especially in the industrial north. There the new Poor Law Guardians, chosen by election, had to employ the traditional kind of pragmatic adjustment to circumstances. They paid outdoor relief where local opinion, the fear of civil unrest, or simple humanitarianism, made it impossible to do otherwise. Though relief was indeed tightened up, and there was much harshness, crude less eligibility was impossible. The centralist principle had been embodied in the Poor Law Commission with Chadwick as its secretary, but the standardizing intention of national legislators was in significant measure frustrated.

IV. *The Victorian apogée, 1851–74*

Between the 1850s and the 1870s Britain reached its world apogée economically and politically. Half-way through the period the working classes made their first entry into the constitution via the second Reform Act of 1867. It increased the British electorate from about 717,000 males in 1832 to 2,226,000. The political parties had now to adjust their policies to an electorate with a new and powerful component. Indeed new forms of party organization emerged, with programmes, caucuses, and professional organizers. Yet concurrently with the introduction of popular politics British governments reduced the role of the state in the economy to the smallest compass it was ever to have. Moreover, both domestic and foreign trade were to be free to a degree unique in British or any other industrial history.

The money supply continued to be market determined within the rules of the gold standard game and the Bank Act of 1844 (suspended on occasion for a matter of days or weeks). The concentration of the English note issue in the Bank of England proceeded. Because there were no tariffs or subsidies, there was no manipulation of government on trade matters, either by political pressure or corruption. The income tax reached a minimum level (2*d.* in the pound in 1874, or 0.8 per cent). The tax structure had become increasingly regressive. The public sector was minimal in size and scope, its only commercial activities being those of the Post Office and the new electric telegraph.

But the market mechanism was intruded upon by the state in one important respect, namely concessions to the unions. It was now clear that it was unrealistic and perhaps hypocritical to argue that each worker and his employer were linked by simple contract between equal partners. Moreover, the skilled artisans had learned after 1851 to organize in a highly effective way, forming the 'new model' unions, pursuing limited objectives, conserving their funds, and in many cases reassuring employers. It was largely these men who entered into the franchise from 1867. They used their new power to secure the Master and Servant Act of the same year, which put master and man on the same footing in civil actions.

But there were two much more important issues: those of picketing and the closed shop, the two great means of inducing workers' solidarity. The Molestation of Workmen Act of 1859 had left it to the courts to decide what was legal in terms of picketing or any other mode of persuasion. Acts of violence against non-unionists were, of course, illegal, but an outburst of such actions led to a Royal Commission on Trade Unions which sat from 1867 to 1869.

The great question was, what should parliament concede in terms of modes of trade-union persuasion, the objects of which were to extend membership and induce concerted action against employers? Could the movement towards natural justice and effective action by the workers find an equilibrium, placing workers and employers on equal terms so that bargaining on such a basis would resolve differences, or would concessions by parliament prepare the way for irreducible conflict? The outcome of the debate was the Trade Union Act and the Criminal Law Amendment Act, both of 1871. The former finally recognized the unions as legitimate and legal bodies, entitled to register as friendly societies: their identity and status were now wholly secure. But the Criminal Law Amendment Act conceded nothing in terms of the techniques of inducing workers' solidarity; indeed it prohibited picketing. Gladstone's government thus deprived the unions of their most effective means of mass persuasion and of direct action at the scene of conflict. This was done in the liberal belief that only persuasion that was wholly peaceful and without threat was permissible. But the courts pushed the matter further: they interpreted a refusal to work as a threat, and hence a possible breach of the act; once more the unions felt denied the right to withdraw labour.

The code of control affecting conditions of work was much extended. In 1867 a new Factory Act brought a wide range of trades within inspection and protection; the Workshops Act of the same year covered children, young persons, and women in smaller establishments. The first safety code of General Rules was introduced in 1855; the Coal Mines Act of 1860 strengthened the Rules and excluded all boys under 12 from mining operations. The Regulation Act of 1872 made the position of the miners' check-weightmen secure. Though each change involved a struggle of interests, in general such controls were no longer a divisive issue on a national scale, being accepted by parliament and the public as a legitimate and indeed necessary role of the state.

At the same time public health similarly became a systematic and continuing public concern. Sanitation on the new scale now demanded vast, indivisible investment in terms of sewage systems, involving local authorities in engineering and financial problems. The Board of Health ceased in 1854 (partly as a reaction by local authorities to centralization), but in 1858 a Health Department was set up in the Home Office, with the remarkable John Simon as its head. An impressive number of acts were passed, in the tradition of Chadwick, extending or creating powers to deal with sanitation, epidemics, burials, venereal disease, and food defilement and adulteration. Each such step can be seen both as part of a general trend, but also in its own highly specific terms of the reconciliation of conflicting views and interests.

Meanwhile the Poor Law continued to be the only official safety net for economic and social casualties. The general governing rules as set out in the act of 1834 continued largely unchanged; so too did the variety of practice of the Guardians. A belief in the inhumanity and degradation of the workhouse was now securely established in working-class minds. Certainly there were bad cases, but these seem to have occurred less in the purpose-built workhouses put up by the active Poor Law unions, but in the decaying tail of obsolete institutions. A measure of greater freedom was conceded to the poor: the Irremoveable Poor Act of 1861 gave a pauper with a three-year residence in a parish a settlement there. In the early 1870s the Local Government Board (to which the Poor Law had passed in 1871), fearing that expenditure, especially on the able-bodied, might be getting out of hand, embarked on something of a campaign from the centre to rehabilitate the spirit of the 1834 act. But the principle of locality continued strong, especially because to the function of relief had been added growing educational and health roles associated with the Poor Law.

Whereas the Poor Law was the oldest area of official social provision, two further concerns now moved to the fore, namely education and housing. Elementary education for the masses first became the subject of serious national enquiry under the Newcastle Commission, reporting in 1861. The parliamentary grant for school building begun in 1833 had now reached £1 million. It was administered by the Committee on Education of the Privy Council, with Kay Shuttleworth its most creative civil servant. The Committee operated a system of school inspectors; these men (of whom Matthew Arnold was one), together with the Newcastle Report, revealed the sad deficiencies of the system. The Education Code of 1862 was a new beginning in the attack on general illiteracy. But it had to deal with two sets of deeply ingrained notions. One was religious: the hostility between the Church of England and the Nonconformists meant that a unified national secular system was impossible. William Forster's Education Act of 1870 accepted the 'voluntary' principle held by the Church of England, which allowed the continuation of its schools. But in addition, elected school boards were set up to establish board schools wherever the elementary education provision was inadequate. The dissenters through their National Education League (founded 1869), rallied to the school boards which taught an undenominational protestantism. The religious issue was so compelling that there was little real debate about the nature of secular education. The second governing notion was the belief in cost-effectiveness, or payment by results. Grants to schools were tied to satisfactory examination performance by the children, under the eye of the inspector; this had a serious effect on the system, committing it in a painful way to emulation and formal public tests.

In the housing of the working classes there was an even stronger adherence to voluntarism than in education, though for quite different reasons. The provision of housing by the state was even more dubious, for it was a major area of property owning and economic activity. But it was also, with education, a great area of default. The slums grew as the cities did, accumulating concentrated masses of decayed and congested houses. Lord Shaftesbury, that great hunter of social abuses or omissions, began the participation of British governments in the problem of homes and houses in the acts of 1851. These acts were concerned with the very worst end of the scale: they permitted local authorities to provide common lodging-houses for the homeless. In 1866 a more general measure came, though it treated housing as a problem in sanitation: this was the Torrens Act which put local authorities in a position to compel owners of insanitary houses to remedy their defects. This was the extent of state housing action until 1875.

V.   The challenge of maturity, 1874–1914

A further general widening of the franchise took place in 1884, including its extension to rural and mining areas: the electorate increased from some 2.2 millions in 1867 to just under 5 millions, so that two in three of the adult male population of England had the vote. The women with their suffragette movement fought for it but failed. The landed interest, though gradually diminishing in political potency, and economically threatened by the fall in cereal prices and farm rents, retained a good deal of influence. The industrialists increased in number, generating new sectors, and adopting monopolistic or semi-monopolistic tactics where markets made this necessary and possible. Some were showing an increasing concern with welfare, and with arbitration and conciliation. Britain was losing her high Victorian dominance over trade rivals, especially Germany and the USA; there were also the problems of diplomacy and potential war (with Germany replacing France as the great threat). The government of the elements of the Empire was an additional concern, especially that of India (prompting the Morley–Minto reforms of 1909, intended to carry India towards self-rule). At home there came a revival of working-class unrest in the 1890s, reaching a frightening peak in 1911–12. To all these threatening circumstances the state had to respond.

The monetary and banking system continued to operate under the traditional 'automatic' rules, together with an immense confidence in the effectiveness of manipulations of short-term interest rates. The Bank Rate was seen as a technical affair of bankers, with no serious implications for the level of trade, and remote from the structural problems of industry. The continuance of the official view that the money supply was outside politics was made possible by three circumstances: Britain's continued strength in exports (visible and invisible), new injections into the world's gold supply from South Africa, and the state's relatively modest borrowing requirements. Though there were misgivings about the adequacy of the City of London's liquidity position in terms of gold resources, and though there was a tortuous discussion of the alternative formula of bimetallism (the use of both the silver and the gold standards), Britain's monetary system continued under the terms of the act of 1844. But its basis was being eroded, partly by failure of other countries to honour the rules of the gold standard game when it demanded domestic contraction, and partly because the assumption was becoming unreal that British prices were flexible downwards, especially the price of labour.

Foreign trade, in contrast with the monetary system, became the centre of one of the most vigorous economic controversies in British history, brought to a dramatic, though negative, conclusion. A great national campaign was mounted between 1903 and 1906 under Joseph Chamberlain, then Chancellor of the Exchequer, to restore to the state the great policy weapon of the tariff. Chamberlain, beginning with protection as a device for promoting imperial unity, passed quickly to protection as the means of remedy for the ills of the British economy, placing it in a retaliatory position against high tariff rivals, especially Germany and the USA. At the same time there was much stress on the benefits to be enjoyed by working men through the promotion of incomes and employment by the exclusion or penalizing of foreign products. The Liberals replied with the classic free trade arguments, especially the British need for tax-free imports of foodstuffs and raw materials, the necessity that industry be subject to the goad of competitive efficiency, and the dangers of bringing the state back into trade. Chamberlain, having split the Liberals in 1886 by rejecting Gladstone's first Home Rule Bill, now split the Conservatives over free trade, placing Arthur Balfour, the Prime Minister, in the position of trying to find a compromise within his party. The Conservatives went down to devastating defeat in the election of 1905–6, with the Liberals triumphant, reasserting free trade and embracing a far-reaching social programme.

The fiscal system began to assume a new role, increasingly so after

1906. Chamberlain in his Radical Programme of 1885 had wished, on a fairly modest scale, to use the income tax as an instrument of social reform, to redistribute incomes and to finance welfare provisions. He was not alone in this or in urging that income tax rates should be made progressive. There was also the question of inheritance. Gladstone had remade the death duties in 1853, but their burden and yield were light. The Chancellor of the Exchequer, Viscount Goschen, in 1889–90 began a new tax on estates over £18,000; but it was William Harcourt with his death duties of 1894 who extended the progressive principle to estates. Though the highest rate was 8 per cent on estates of £1 million or more, this was a radical new beginning, both in practice and in social philosophy: the fiscal axe could now be taken effectively for the first time to the tree of inheritance, whether landed, commercial, or industrial.

The income tax too was brought under the progressive principle in consequence of the new age of expenditure, brought in by the Boer War and the continued demands thereafter for war preparations, together with the cost of the Liberal welfare programme from 1906. Herbert Asquith in that year took the first step in graduating the income tax, but it was David Lloyd George's budget of 1909 that marked the new fiscal age. Taxation of earned incomes between £2,000 and £3,000 was increased from 9d. to 1 shilling in the pound; those with earned incomes over £5,000 paid 1s.6d. in the pound on the amount by which the income exceeded £5,000. In addition the death duties were raised to new levels. There were two altogether new departures, a tax taking 20 per cent of the rise in land values, and a capital tax of $\frac{1}{2}d$. in the pound on lands or mineral resources left undeveloped. Partly because of assessment difficulties the land and capital taxes were more important as reflecting government hostility to unearned increments and idle resources than as revenue raisers: they were the result of growing concern in the country with the pattern of land ownership.

The Lords consistently blocked the Liberal measures; the 1909 budget became the crisis point. The Lords (still under landed dominance) tried to reject it outright. A whole set of questions affecting state power suddenly became explicit. There was the constitutional one, namely how far could parliament go in taxation, and, in particular, what powers of restraint did the hereditary chamber have? There was the question of classes as groups of wealth holders and income recipients. Was the landed class to be made vulnerable to being taxed out of existence? Were the Liberals acting as the party of the bourgeoisie; were they now, at long last, ready to consolidate their victory over the landed class? Were they doing so because of the necessity to protect themselves from the now-rising challenge of the working classes, by undertaking expensive new social programmes? Was parliament to prepare the way for a policy of populist redistribution?

Only when in 1911 (after two general elections), the new king, George V, agreed to swamp the House of Lords by creating hundreds of new peers on the nomination of Asquith, the Liberal Prime Minister, did the Lords capitulate. They were stripped of all say in money matters and their general delaying powers were reduced to two years. The whole of the wealth and income of the population were thus placed at the disposal of the elected chamber.

So it was that in the years 1874–1914 the state could continue outside the monetary and trading systems, but was drawn into the pattern of wealth and income distribution. Other matters it left to the market: the growth and stability of the economy, its structure and locational form continued to be no concern of government. Few people argued otherwise, except perhaps for Chamberlain and other Tory-collectivists, Sidney and Beatrice Webb and the Fabians, and the emergent Labour Party. But there were signs of a new governmental outlook here also, as in the Unemployed Workmen's Act of 1905 (authorizing local authorities to undertake a measure of job creation), and the first census of production of 1907 sponsored by Lloyd George.

Before 1874 the points of stress between labour and capital had been seen largely in terms of the particular firm, or of the industry; by 1914 it was becoming plain that the matter was assuming an aggregative, national aspect. The argument could now be seen, constantly by some and occasionally by many, as lying between two great orders of society, capital and labour, concerned with the distribution of incomes, and with the power relations involved therein. Socialist and syndicalist formulae were made available, rationalizing the hypothesis of conflict, and sustaining the new militancy arising from industrial unionism. To these great changes the state reacted in two ways – by concessions to organized labour, and by sponsoring conciliation.

The Tories coming to power under Benjamin Disraeli in 1874 passed two relevant acts: the Conspiracy and Protection of Property Act, and the Employers' and Workmen's Act, both of 1875. Henceforth the unions had all the rights, freedoms and identity of unincorporated bodies; any action that was legal for an individual was legal for a union. Picketing was made legal, so long as it was peaceful, both for those favouring industrial action and those opposed to it. The London dockers by strike action in 1889 won a famous victory in achieving the 'Dockers' Tanner' (a wage of 6d. per hour). A great impetus was thereby given to union organization among the unskilled. Under the Conciliation Act of 1896 the Board of Trade was empowered to investigate trade disputes, offer mediation, and provide for the voluntary registration of arbitration and conciliation boards. Llewellyn Smith, the gifted civil servant placed in charge, was concerned to stop labour militancy from driving on to a general polarization of society, but he and his colleagues had no powers of compulsion over either capital or labour. The socialist press inevitably attacked the Labour Department.

The Trades Union Congress (TUC, founded 1868) became increasingly important as the central forum for labour. The Labour Representation League (founded 1869) worked to promote the election of workers as Members of Parliament. In 1893 the Independent Labour Party was founded, with a comprehensive economic programme, including nationalization of the land and the basic industries. But there was a good deal of reservation in the TUC, especially from the craft unions, about such socialist objectives and their implications for class warfare. The Labour Representation Committee (the immediate antecedent of the Labour Party) was formed in 1900 with Ramsay MacDonald as its secretary.

Meanwhile the judges had been handing down verdicts on trade-union law. Were unions exempt from damages done to third parties in the course of disputes with employers? The courts said yes in 1893 and 1896, but the House of Lords in 1898 decided that the general public, like the employers, had no recourse against the unions. In 1901 the House of Lords in the Taff Vale case decided that damages could indeed be awarded against a union in certain circumstances. Under powerful union pressure, and after a Royal Commission on Trades Disputes and Combinations, the Trades Disputes Act of 1906 was passed: the unions henceforth were under no circumstances to be held responsible for torts, that is, for civil wrongs for which damages might be claimed. Legal decisions handed down in 1896–8 seemed to threaten picketing; the 1906 act reasserted the right to peaceful persuasion by this means. Finally, there was the question of using union funds for political purposes: the right to do so was granted under the Trade Union Act of 1913; unions might collect a political levy, though members had the right to contract out.

But the labour movement also wanted statutory support for minimum wages. In the case of the 'sweated' trades the Trades Boards Act of 1909 set up statutory bodies in a number of occupations, empowered to regulate wages. More important in scale was the Coal Mines (Minimum Wage) Act of 1912. After a national coal strike for a minimum wage the Liberal government conceded the principle, but on a district basis only (the miners wanted a national system). Such wage rates were to be set by local boards with independent chairmen. The state had withdrawn from the setting of wages in 1813–14; it resumed this function in 1909 and 1913, acting on behalf of the sweated workers and the coal-miners.

There was a third labour demand made in parliament. The Labour Representation Committee, having won 29 seats in the 1906 election (and having changed its name to the Labour Party), took up the question of unemployment. Dissatisfied with the Tory Unemployed Workmen's

Act of 1905, the Labour Party sponsored the 'Right to Work Bill', which proposed that either work should be generated by local authorities under government aegis, or adequate maintenance for the unemployed should be provided. The Liberal government was frightened that to accept an obligation to provide either work or maintenance would be to find itself moving deep into the economy and society, and so rejected the plea. It did, however, seek to improve the labour market by the Labour Exchanges Act of 1909, under which the country was quickly covered with 'exchanges' where jobs and workers were brought together. But the substantive problem of unemployment remained unsolved.

In this situation the government turned to the insurance principle in order to generate a fund out of which payments to the unemployed could be made. This would keep the state out of the economy, it would keep the strain on the tax system at a tolerable level, and it would leave the Poor Law for separate treatment. Part II of the National Insurance Act of 1911 provided a weekly benefit of 7s. for 15 weeks (a good deal less than 'full maintenance'). Some 2.25 million workers were covered. Workers and employers were each to provide 2½d. per week, with the state adding 25 per cent to the sum thus contributed. The state, in this guarded fashion, had begun to accept responsibility for the maintenance of the unemployed.

But these various actions by the state could not curb labour militancy. Between 1911 and 1913 there was profound labour unrest, highlighted by strikes by railwaymen, seamen, and the miners. Syndicalist activists offered an alternative leadership to that of trade-union officials, seeking not only industrial ends, but a new society. To the syndicalists the principles of conciliation and arbitration were invitations to self-betrayal. Nevertheless the government introduced a new scheme in 1911 to improve the operation of the conciliation and arbitration service.

The 'social problem' was, in a sense, discovered in the 1880s and 1890s. The Tories had never rejected a degree of collectivist action; the more active-minded Liberals were realizing that the age of minimal government was passing. The two great parties, and the emergent Labour Party, were being increasingly pressed toward the adoption of a consistent and to some degree comprehensive view of the welfare responsibilities of the state. Each party was impelled by its own internal dynamics, and each necessarily responded to the bids made to the electorate by the others.

London was, of course, the most pressing case of the social problem. It was a mass of contained concentration, especially in its East End; there was indeed something approaching crisis in the inner city of the metropolis. But the large industrial cities of the north of the country had also generated enormous challenges, each in its own terms. How far was it possible to redeem such areas by local initiatives? Could the tax burden be met by the local rates, or should they be augmented by government grants?

Concern with public health continued to focus upon sanitation, health regulation, and the provision of medical facilities. The last of these was still largely in the hands of the medical practitioners and the philanthropists, and so was in a sense outside social policy. The Public Health Act of 1875 consolidated the law and confirmed the division of the country into sanitary districts, each with its medical officer of health and inspector of nuisances. Local authorities were now required to maintain, pave and light the streets, and to provide drainage. A further act of 1907 confirmed the hygienic revolution. But sewage systems were costly, and by putting pressure on the rates raised the cost of house space, thus aggravating the problem of working-class shelter. No new houses might henceforth be built without running water and drainage, a further cost factor. Local authorities were given powers to acquire land for parks. In 1906 they were authorized to provide school meals on the rates, and in 1907 a school medical inspection was established.

By the 1880s the local authorities had assumed two great sets of duties, namely those imposed upon them by the Public Health Acts (chiefly 1848 and 1875), and those undertaken spontaneously, having to do with the provision of local public utilities. The growth of civic consciousness from the 1860s onwards meant that the municipalities pushed forward with a wide range of functions including the provision of water, gas, electricity, and tramways. By 1914 there were over 300 municipal boroughs, all with some sort of trading function, and most with several. All this was done without generalized statutory surveillance by the state. The initiative for each project came from the localities; parliament responded by dealing with each specific private bill as it was promoted. The result was a quite dramatic, but largely haphazard, growth of public utilities. There was much debate about the propriety of the intrusion of local authorities into such activities, generating a 'municipal socialism', but the increasing acceptance of such functions as appropriate to local government was inherent in local need.

The concern for working conditions continued, with the factory inspectors busier than ever in their unending fight against deterioration. A consolidating statute, the Factories and Workshops Act of 1878, prescribed a standard 10-hour day, with $6\frac{1}{2}$ on Saturday, that is, a $56\frac{1}{2}$-hour week. In the same year the lives of seamen were brought into protection by Samuel Plimsoll and his Merchant Shipping Act; in 1906 came a further advance. In 1886 hours of work for children and young persons in retail trade were limited. Working conditions were further improved by the Factory and Workshops Amendment Act of 1901. The Employment of Women Act came in 1906, following an international conference; in 1909 the Trades Board Act against sweating was passed. Meanwhile there had been a vigorous Eight-Hour Movement: its first fruit was the Coal Mines Act of 1908, limiting shifts below ground to that figure. In passing this measure the Liberal government breached the long-sacred principle that adult males should be left to settle their own terms with their employers.

Two new topics of workers' concern were added in the 1880s, namely compensation for injury, and pensions when work was no longer possible. Compensation was governed by Lord Campbell's Act of 1846 which defined the common law position. In 1880 the Employers' Liability Act laid down the principle that compensation must be paid by employers, but only where the injury was due to the employer's negligence, a difficult matter to prove. Chamberlain's act of 1897 made the employer responsible whether or not employer or worker or both were guilty of negligence; accidents were thus made a charge upon industry. But only a limited range of industries was covered. In 1900 the new principles were applied to agriculture labourers, and under the Workmen's Compensation Act of 1906 the law was generalized to all workers. In addition industrial diseases were brought within the scope of the act.

The state made no move to enforce any system of retirement pensions upon industry. But in 1908, for the first time, it relieved the working classes of a part of the burden of self-maintenance, providing, under the Old Age Pensions Act, payments of a standard size (5 shillings per week) as of right and without contributions, upon attaining a certain age (70 years). There were indeed reservations (the 'undeserving' could be excluded and those with incomes over 8 shillings per week could have their pensions reduced). Such qualifications reflected the fear that the incentive for workers to save from their earnings during their active lives might be damaged.

From Forster's Education Act of 1870 for England and Wales (the Scottish act came in 1872), it was inevitable that the nation would move progressively toward a comprehensive state system, superseding the voluntary principle. Mundella's Education Act of 1880 made elementary schooling compulsory to the age of thirteen, but children over ten, if they had gained a certificate of proficiency, needed only to attend half-time. This half-time minimum age was raised to eleven in 1893 and twelve in 1899; local authorities were empowered in 1900 to raise the basic leaving age to fourteen. In 1891 such schooling was effectively made free. It was time for a stronger organizational form: the Board of Education was set up in 1899, with Sir Robert Morant as its outstanding Permanent Secretary from 1903 to 1912.

It was Morant who largely prepared the Education Act of 1902 for Balfour's government. The 2,500 schools boards were replaced by 315 local education authorities (the county and county borough councils, each of which set up its local education committee). The local education authorities took over both the board schools and the voluntary (Church of England) schools, thus making an integrated policy possible. The Nonconformists were bitterly hostile, some indulging in passive resistance in the form of a refusal to pay rates that might be used to support the surviving religious education in Church of England schools. The 1902 act also brought elementary and secondary education together under the Board. The local education authorities were to take over many existing foundations, but in most areas they built entirely new schools. A broader band of pupils could thus enjoy a 'liberal' (e.g., a non-vocational) education, and could make themselves eligible for the universities. But no corresponding advance was made in terms of technical, scientific, and commercial education, a defeat for the national efficiency advocates. The Technical Instruction Act of 1889 (authorizing a penny rate for such purposes), and the allocation in 1890 of the proceeds of the wine and spirit duties, were not built upon in the act of 1902.

Housing was a matter of mounting concern in the generation before 1914. A succession of inquiries and debates made the short-fall of provision for the working classes ever more apparent. But policy recommendations were slight, not to say feeble, perhaps because of the very perception of the scale and intricacy of the problems involved. Fundamentally the cost of house space exceeded the income capacity of a large part of the population. Short of a radical alteration of incomes, only subsidy could induce the supply of the necessary houses. But the subsidy barrier was not to be broken, though there was a Conservative attempt to do so in 1911. The Liberals, in spite of their other welfare measures, were not prepared to commit the state to expenditure on the scale required. Instead, successive governments sought to press the local authorities into self-financing action. The Artisans' Dwellings Act of 1875 (the Cross Act) gave local authorities powers to undertake clearance schemes by the compulsory purchase of houses and land. There were some six Torrens and Cross Acts between 1868 and 1890, culminating in the Housing of the Working Classes Act of 1890, all aimed at enforcing higher standards and encouraging slum demolition programmes. But the dishoused simply crowded into the remaining properties, creating ever-denser rookeries. This immense failure of supply continued almost unrelieved.

A similar lack of effective action was present in the Poor Law: no new statute was passed regulating the care of social casualties. This, too, was not for lack of discussion: the Royal Commission on the Poor Laws (1905–9) published two remarkable reports. Their content and conflicts reflect the fundamental difficulties. The majority wished to preserve, as a basic element, the principles of rigour and less eligibility of 1834, remodelling and renaming the Poor Law so as to embrace all that was needful in terms of justifiable action within these assumptions. The minority, under the powerful influence of Beatrice and Sidney Webb, proposed to remove the stigma of pauperism, treating it as a misfortune. They urged, too, the 'break-up' of the Poor Law, each aspect of social need in each local authority to have its own separate committee. At the centre appropriate ministries or departments would be created or re-formed to coordinate and guide. The Liberal government, confronted by two such conflicting documents, felt it could extract no strong lead from its commissioners so no action was taken to reorganize the Poor Law. But old age pensions and unemployment insurance, initiatives taken quite outside the framework of the Poor Law, did serve to ease the problem.

VI.   *War and the troubled peace, 1914–39*

The war of 1914–18 cut across the policy debate of late Victorian and Edwardian times, overwhelming it with an experience of traumatic depth. It brought the greatest state manipulation of society that the nation had ever known, involving all available techniques from persuasion to conscription and civilian coercion. At the very outset the gold standard was abandoned, giving the government the means of control over real resources without limit. Once at war those in charge of the state could see no course but to go on. All punctilio about intruding into the realm of private enterprise was set aside almost without discussion: ministries meddled in every industry. Prices rose; the national debt grew relentlessly. Blockade by the Germans brought into being a Ministry of Food (1917). The unions, having agreed to the dilution of skilled labour, were left with the problem of containing radical action, especially by the shop stewards. But they made real gains, including a Ministry of Labour (1917), moving into the position of autonomous bodies that had to be listened to with respect by governments. The Representation of the People Act of February 1918 opened the vote to all males over the age of 21 and to women over 30; in this way the electorate multiplied by three, to some 20 millions, as well as changing in its composition.

In December 1916 Lloyd George took over from Asquith as Prime Minister. The war was going badly; as a contribution to morale the cabinet set up a Reconstruction Committee under Christopher Addison. To it passed practically the whole agenda of unsettled pre-war problems, together with some new ones. Elaborate inquiries were conducted into many of them. But before the war ended in November 1918 the public had become more interested in retribution against the Germans than in

British reconstruction. Moreover, both capital and labour regarded themselves as having made concessions that were temporary and which must be ended with the peace. By 1921 there had been, over a large part of the economy, a return to the position of 1914: the Ministry of Munitions (the setter of industrial priorities) had been wound up, the wartime tariff in the form of the McKenna duties was ended, the Corn Production Act was repealed (exposing the countryside once more to dereliction), the coal-mines had reverted to their former owners. Though victory had been the fruit of shared efforts and sacrifices, the gulf between capital and labour was now wider than ever.

But reconstruction was not a total failure. A Ministry of Health (with Robert Morant as Permanent Secretary), and a Ministry of Pensions were set up in 1919. The Old Age Pensions Act of that year raised the payment to 10 shillings per person: more far-reaching was the removal of the pauper disqualification so that the Guardians could augment the pension. The Education Act of 1918 was carried through the Commons by H. A. L. Fisher, inspired by the vision of a state system of education from primary school to university. It improved secondary education and made provision to make it free. The school-leaving age was raised to fourteen and Local Education Authorities were encouraged to set up day-continuation schools so that learning could continue beyond school into life. The Minister of Labour approved the suggestion of joint industrial councils (named after J. H. Whitely, Speaker of the House of Commons), in trades composed of small firms. Finally, the subsidy barrier was finally broken by the Housing Act of 1919, promoted by Addison as Minister of Health.

The Britain over which inter-war governments presided was a country much changed, bewildering to those who lived in it and tried to understand it. While the old landed families were being sapped by taxation, new men of wealth and power asserted themselves. As the Liberal Party split between the Lloyd George and Asquith factions, and as its prospects faded, a polarization of political allegiance took place between the Conservative and Labour Parties. Big business could no longer choose between two non-socialist parties. Accordingly, its representatives consolidated themselves within the Conservative ranks; in the course of the inter-war years the old landed Toryism with its continued ideal of a social bond was increasingly displaced by a business Conservatism. And yet the landed paternalist strain was never to be wholly lost in these years, but was to reappear in Harold Macmillan and those who thought like him in the later thirties. At the same time a good many middle-class men of radical intellectual bent deserted the Liberals for the Labour Party, it being for them the only remaining spiritual home and the only source of an effective political career.

Yet another order of men was moving forward in the contest for power. These were the Labour Members of Parliament and the trade-union leaders. A long and arduous learning process had to be undergone so that such men could move beyond the relatively easy posture of protest, to think in terms of the constructive action they would take when national power was theirs. Finally, there was the tragic hiatus left in British society by the lost generation of men from all classes killed or irreparably damaged by the war.

As for the electorate who were to adjudicate between the politicians and the parties, from 1923 men and women were entitled on equal terms to vote, to enter parliament, and to hold office.

The policy choices made in the inter-war years were dominated on the one hand by short-term configurations of electoral power generated by the parliamentary system, and on the other by emergencies arising both within the domestic economy and externally from the world economy within which it operated. Yet beneath this extemporization there moved value systems, ideologies, and long-term goals which in some sense represented the basic views of individuals, groups, and parties. More-over, there was the long British tradition of pragmatism, trying partial expedients in one direction or another, in the hope that the long-term course of action would clarify itself.

But one thing is clear: the choice from the inter-war policy menu was made, in the most general sense, in two phases, with 1931–2 as the divider. From 1918 to the beginning of the thirties there was a sustained attempt to return to pre-war economic arrangements. This effort to revert to the great days of Victoria and Edward having collapsed, Britain at last began to face the realities of a changing world and her diminished and embattled place within it.

Monetary and trade policy exemplified these two phases in dramatic terms. In large measure by 1918 the fundamental dilemma of the gold standard had faded from men's minds, namely the conflict inherent in it between the case for stable exchange rates and the domestic needs of the economy in terms of employment and incomes. Not only should the money supply be self-adjusting: free trade was the complementary principle to be preserved. The third in a trinity of canons of right policy was the balanced budget. This three-part liberal economic creed, derived from the nineteenth century, was the fundamental faith of the failing Liberal Party: it had a profound effect on its Labour successors. It was Phillip Snowden as the first Labour Chancellor of the Exchequer who in 1924 repealed the McKenna duties and who later fought to preserve the gold standard, free trade, and the balanced budget. It was the Conserva-tive Party, on the other hand, which was much less averse to the use of macro-controls for the economy: indeed Stanley Baldwin lost the general election of 1924 to the Labour Party, fighting for a return to protection in the form of a scientific tariff.

In spite of this it was the Conservatives, with Winston Churchill as their Chancellor, who carried through the return to gold in 1925 at the old parity of $4.85. It was too high, to a degree which is much disputed, perhaps by as much as 10 per cent. The result was to damage Britain's export capacity. The government was thus left with three choices: lower the parity, let the pound float (and thus determine its own level), or enter upon a struggle to lower costs in British industry far enough to compensate for the overvaluation. The third course was chosen. The largest element in costs was, of course, wages. Hence employers were forced by the state into a struggle with their workers and the unions in an effort to bring money wages down.

The stresses showed both in terms of the economy as a whole, and of its component sectors. The high sterling exchange rate deprived Britain of the power to respond to the modest growth in world trade. There were strikes on the railways and in the mines, culminating in the General Strike in 1926. The monetary policy of 1925 was the central action in the last attempt by the British state to exempt itself from macro-control of the economy. Its consequences were lowered working-class incomes, rising interest rates, generalized unemployment protest, and a further polarization of society along class lines.

The General Strike lasted nine days, from 4 to 12 May. The frightening question was asked, was the state being challenged by extra-parliamentary means? Though the miners stayed out until December, Mr Baldwin's government had won. The gold standard and its implications remained intact.

But the curious post-battle affinity sometimes seen between enemies, with its urge for mutual embrace, manifested itself. Certain unions and certain industrialists turned to one another in the Mond–Turner talks. They sought a means of lowering costs not through wage reduction, but through increased efficiency based upon rationalizing whole sectors of the old, export-based industries, concentrating production on the most efficient units. Though the Mond–Turner talks were overtaken by major crisis in 1929–31, they represented two great estates of the realm coming together to arrive at policies with which to confront the state. But the fissures within the Labour movement and within industry made such an attempt premature.

The second Labour government, a minority one as in 1924, took office in May 1929, elected largely as a response to heavy unemployment. In spite of its origins and expressed ideas, it fell under the constraints of responsible government, reinforced by the need to propitiate the Liberals. Revenues shrank, with expenditure, especially on the unemployed, mounting. The May committee report of August 1931 urged heavy retrenchment, including the social services. To the strait-jacket of gold was added that of fiscal soundness, as embodied in the Economy Act. Meanwhile a global upheaval was taking place, with world trade, the earlier basis of Britain's prosperity, shrinking fast. In the summer of 1931 there was heavy selling of sterling; the Bank of England's gold reserve drained away. The Labour cabinet split on the question of cutting unemployment benefits. A snap election in October confirmed the position of the National Government, mostly of Conservatives, but with Ramsey MacDonald still Prime Minister. The gold standard was abandoned. The result was an immense relief to the balance of payments.

The currency could now be 'managed' in terms of domestic need, making possible a policy of cheap money (Bank Rate stayed at 2 per cent for seven years, and much of the state debt was converted from 5 per cent to 3.5 per cent). The Exchange Equalisation Account was set up to stabilize sterling in the short run by purchases and sales. But managed currencies landed the trading nations on the other horn of the dilemma: how were currencies to be valued, and how were national price levels to be related to one another?

Moreover, the Import Duties Act of 1932 marked the resumption of protection as a general policy, carrying Britain back to her early industrial age. The Import Duties Advisory Committee was set up to recommend tariff rates. Britain could now bargain with other states as in Huskisson's time. She negotiated a range of bilateral treaties. The Ottawa Conference of 1932 brought in a system of imperial preference, but only after bitter wrangling.

But though the gold standard and free trade were gone, the third element of traditional policy, that of the balanced budget, survived. From 1936 the rival of welfare, namely warfare, made increasing demands. On the other hand, rearmament reduced unemployment payments and raised incomes; at the same time interest rates began to rise.

It is hardly surprising that within the Labour movement there was confusion. The movement contained a highly diverse set of components, with chronic tension between those seeking wage settlements and those disrupting them, and between the coolly rational and the emotively millenarian. But something of a common denominator did emerge. The movement was anti-capitalist, though sometimes without much conviction: there was ritual denigration of unreformed capitalism, together with a welcoming of the prospect of capitalist collapse (accompanied by a fear of the outcome if it should occur). There was an insistence upon trade-union freedom of action, with no inhibitions about union power in relation to employers, consumers, or the state. It was believed that large sectors of the economy should be nationalized in the interests of efficiency, the removal of political advantage, and the promotion of industrial democracy through worker participation. The poor were not responsible for their condition and so should not suffer penalties arising from it. There should be provided, through the state, a national minimum for all; this meant, of course, a policy of greater egalitarianism, brought about by redistributive taxation. Taxes on incomes should be steeply progressive, and on unearned incomes and inherited wealth almost confiscatory. There should be minimum wages prescribed by law in at least some sectors, and wage formulae should be on a national rather than a local basis. Such a programme was the result of starting from the conditions of the people (both in terms of their employment and incomes), and from their fulfilment while at work. No serious consideration was given to the question whether adequate scope would be left for the operation of market forces, and if they were rendered insufficient, what should replace them.

The ending of the General Strike was, at least in the short and medium terms, a defeat for organized labour, marking the end of a phase of militancy begun during the war, and the beginning of a phase of relative industrial quietism. This was confirmed by the Trade Disputes and Trade Union Act of 1927. All strikes and lock-outs 'designed or calculated to coerce the Government either directly or by inflicting hardship on the community' were declared illegal. The principle of contracting out of the unions' political funds was replaced by that of contracting in, thus requiring active and positive assent on the part of each union member. No public employee could strike to the injury of the community. The restrictions on the actions of pickets were tightened. The act was bitterly resented throughout its lifetime (1926–45): it reduced Labour Party funds and discouraged union membership. Yet though there were no further major strikes from 1926 to 1939, a concerted and sustained policy challenge of a kind came from the Labour side.

The union response to the post-1927 situation was partly organizational, combining, like the employers, into larger units: the Transport and General Workers Union under Ernest Bevin had by 1939 assimilated some 47 units and acquired 600,000 members. The Trades Union Congress pressed for a National Industrial Council, a kind of industrial parliament from both sides of industry, with a joint Conciliation Board, to the virtual exclusion of the parliamentary state. In this sense many labour leaders, with their deep distrust of state participation in wage bargaining, based their hopes on the industrial rather than the political side of the movement, insisting on 'free' bargaining between labour and capital.

The Trades Union Congress at its conference in 1927 debated the choice between a war of attrition against capitalism versus trying to make the system work by helping to promote efficiency and prosperity while at the same time seeking to bring about fundamental alterations. In spite of the sustaining anti-capitalist myths of the movement, and because of the bleakness of the prospect of a war of attrition, the unions chose participation combined with renovation. But it was to be on the basis of hard bargaining. Moreover there was to be planned industry, rather than a scramble for profits. The official union programme was thus to work for the modification of capitalism while at the same time keeping it going. The radicals and revolutionaries in the party and outside it never, of course, accepted this approach and exerted themselves to disrupt it.

A major area for the application of modifications to capitalism lay in the decaying basic industries. The newer and prosperous industries could look after themselves: for example four large companies combined in 1926 to form Imperial Chemical Industries. But for coal, steel, the railways, shipbuilding, and cotton manufacture the choice lay between nationalization and rationalization. At the parliamentary level there was still a powerful distrust of state ownership and operation, inherited from the prosperous and flexible past. Moreover, the business classes were in possession and were not willing to surrender industry to state bureaucrats. Though the unions urged nationalization of coal and the railways, as part of 'commanding heights' of the economy, parliament would take no such action.

Rationalization and market control were, however, adopted in many industries, in varying degrees and forms, especially in the traditional basic sectors, together with agriculture. In one after another, the state either acting directly, or through the Bank of England, encouraged industrialists to remake their own industries. Much redundant capacity was thus cut out, though as rearmament was undertaken in the later thirties there was sometimes a renewed need for what had been superfluous. In agriculture an elaborate set of marketing boards was brought into being. At no time was there a generalized statement of government policy in terms of rationalization and market control; instead each such industry was taken up on its own terms when its difficulties could no longer be ignored. In this way a wide range of new agencies was brought into being, concerned with renovating and running industry. But ownership and direct production were largely undisturbed, and there was no attempt at generalized coordination of the economy.

In addition to attempting to restructure industry in sectoral terms, the state in the inter-war years operated on the geographical pattern through regional policy. The Special Areas Act of 1934 provided incentives to bring work to the workers in the classic industrial revolution regions, now especially depressed. But success was limited: firms could not be offered inducements sufficient to cause them to relocate themselves on any significant scale, contrary to their commercial judgment.

Four sets of social issues demanded action in the inter-war years: health, education, housing, and relief for the unemployed and the impotent. Of these it was housing and relief that were politically imperative.

In the field of health two aspects required attention, the insurance provision and the hospital service. The realization was growing that the insurance scheme of 1911 with its distinction between the insured and the non-insured was inhibitive and harmful; it also needed improvement in other respects. But in spite of a Royal Commission on National Health Insurance in 1926 no effective action was taken. The hospital service, with its three main elements, the philanthropically funded, the Poor Law provided, and the municipal, was also seriously lacking in coherence, but little was done. The local authorities were given power under the Local Government Act of 1929 to take over the voluntary general hospitals, but were slow to do so.

The chief concern in education was with its secondary aspect. There was an anxiety to extend provision, especially for the mass of the population. This raised the question of the nature of education for older children. Following the Hadlow report (1926) and the Spens report (1938) England was committed to the streaming principle. The '11 plus' examination distinguished those children who after the age of 11 were to join the secondary (grammar) school stream of more academic children, and the others, who would attend secondary central (modern) schools for students suited to more directly vocational subjects. The two kinds of school were to be different, but equal. Though much was achieved, the distinction between the grammar schools (with their potential entrée to the extending university system) and the modern schools (with their much more limited prospects), had the effect of confirming the differences in life chances between social classes.

It was these years that saw the first real attack by the British state on the problems of rent levels and housing supply. Rent restriction (begun in 1915), though amended from time to time, was continued, and indeed for working-class housing in effect became a permanent feature. Though newly built houses were not affected, this price freeze on housing space did damage to the willingness of landlords to maintain their properties, thus deteriorating and reducing the housing stock. More positive action was called for. Addison's Housing and Town Planning Act of 1919 placed upon each local authority the duty of meeting housing need within its jurisdiction. The standards set by the act were well above those normal for working-class houses; moreover, the new houses were to be provided at rents comparable to those controlled under the Rent Restriction Acts. How was the inevitable deficit met? The local authorities were to pay to the extent of the yield of a penny on the rates. All the rest was to come from the Treasury. On the basis of this open-ended

BRITISH PUBLIC POLICY, 1776-1939

commitment the British state embarked upon the age of the council house. The subsidy barrier had been broken in a most dramatic way. Some 170,000 houses were built under the act. This generated a violent sectoral inflation in the building trades. The extraordinary financial burdens incurred outraged the Treasury and the Bank of England. The Geddes economy axe of 1921 fell upon the housing programme and the subsidy principle was repudiated.

But the state could not now extricate itself from housing. Neville Chamberlain as Conservative Minister of Health introduced a new Housing Act in 1923. It revived the subsidy principle, but brought it under the control of a limiting formula per house. In addition private builders were also made eligible for subsidy; indeed they were given preference. Slum clearance received state aid for the first time, with government and local authorities dividing the losses equally. The Labour government in 1924 restored the initiative to the local authorities under its Housing Act of that year, promoted by John Wheatley. Private builders were eligible for subsidy only if they provided houses for letting. The act raised both standards and grants. But there was to be no return to open-ended state finance. This made necessary the adoption of a more flexible rent policy, allowing rent increases where the losses were beyond the fixed Exchequer subsidies plus the contribution from the rates.

Between 1919 and 1939 some 1.3 million council houses were built, all involving subsidy. More than 3 million had been built for owner-occupation or rental, some 470,000 of them state assisted. Thus over 40 per cent of all new houses had received state aid. The principle of housing subsidy had become embedded in the national life, alongside rent restriction. The local authorities had become giant landlords. But the housing shortfall, chronic since the industrial revolution, had been greatly eased.

The support of economic and social casualties was the largest category of social welfare, the most diverse, and the most difficult to deal with. In 1919 the provision was of three kinds. The state had set up old age pensions (1908), together with unemployment insurance (1911), both administered from the centre. There remained the third and residual element, the Poor Law, run by the Poor Law Unions in the localities and financed from the rates; it was still the final point of relief.

Under the 1920 Unemployment Insurance Act of Lloyd George's coalition government the 1911 scheme was extended so that it included almost all industrial workers, both manual and non-manual, earning not more than £250 per annum. This increased its coverage from 4 to some 12 million workers. Both benefits and contributions were raised. With the Unemployment Insurance Fund in a very healthy condition it seemed that unemployment could continue to be entrusted to the insurance principle. But there was still much distress about; in 1921 benefits were extended so as to provide for dependants. With the ending of the post-war boom unemployment rose steeply. The Ministry of Labour was given authority to pay benefits in excess of the entitlement of 26 weeks prescribed. This was a radical and irreversible step, analogous to the adoption of the subsidy principle in housing. To such payments the press and the public gave the name of the 'dole'. In 1925 yet further scope was found for the insurance principle; provision was made for widows and orphans within the National Health scheme, together with contributory old age pensions between the ages of 65 and 70.

The second Baldwin administration was unwilling to throw the many thousands of workers whose standard benefits had expired back onto the hated Poor Law. Instead it passed the Unemployment Insurance Act of 1927, which continued and extended the extra benefits. Henceforth, also, such benefits were to be a statutory right. The government had to borrow heavily to sustain the fund: by 1931 the fund was in deficit to the extent of £115 millions. The second Labour government in its brief tenure relieved the fund of the cost of the additional benefits, making them a charge on the Treasury; the onus was laid upon the officials to prove that an applicant was *not* genuinely seeking work.

Meanwhile the Poor Law, though relieved of much of the burdens of unemployment and old age, was also in difficulties. Neville Chamberlain's Local Government Act of 1929 ended the 600 Poor Law Unions and passed their functions to appropriate specialized local government bodies as reorganized under the act. Relief to those not covered by unemployment insurance and its extended benefits, or to those who had needs not otherwise met, was to be paid out by new public assistance committees to be set up by local councils.

It was with the national insurance fund in deep deficit, and with unemployment of 2.6 millions, that the Labour government encountered the economic breakdown of 1931. Foreign lenders required a cut in government spending. This was acceded to: under the Economy Act of 1931 insurance benefits were cut by 10 per cent. Additional benefits continued, but they were now made subject to a family means test. This was to become a source of endless trouble and bitterness, replacing the workhouse as an object of working-class detestation.

The 1931 arrangements were soon seen to be in need of reform. The Unemployment Act of 1934 at long last sought to rest the system on some sort of principle. Part I reorganized the insurance scheme, adjusting the contributions and benefits. Part II set up a new and independent body, the Unemployment Assistance Board, charged with providing for the able-bodied who were out of work and out of benefit financed by the Treasury. Over 300 offices were set up throughout the country to administer the scheme. After some 400 years the localities were now finally relieved of all responsibility for the able-bodied unemployed. But provision continued to be subject to a test of means and of willingness to work.

The Poor Law was a continuously diminishing residuum. But it was still important, and indeed essential, with no less than 1,600,000 people in 1936 in receipt of its aid, now renamed public assistance and administered by the local authorities' Public Assistance Committees. Indoor relief catered for a changing mass of the sick, the infirm, and the incapable, deserted children, abandoned wives, and so on, placed in a wide range of local authority institutions. Outdoor or domiciliary relief was much larger, comprising 87 per cent of all public assistance, in the form of cash aid to the family in its own home. Public relief of these kinds was the nation's ultimate safeguard against starvation.

The system of support was by 1939 of a comprehensive nature, providing for the unemployed in terms of insurance and additional benefits, for the aged, widowed, and orphaned through insurance (with additional non-contributory benefits for the old), and for the impotent through local public assistance committees. But two questions remained. Were the ethical principles governing eligibility for the main uncovenanted benefits, as enforced through the means test, right? Secondly, were the *levels* of provision correct, in terms of the needs of the recipients, in terms of national equity, and in terms of the transfer payments between rich and poor such as might be necessary to sustain aggregate demand?

VII. *The policy pattern in 1939*

By 1939 Britain had universal adult suffrage, trade unions free of all legal restraint and seeking to make themselves a kind of parallel parliament, and what was effectively a two-party political system. The Conservatives were seeking a formula of accommodation with the labour force both in terms of the wages share of Gross National Product, and in terms of the transfer payments inherent in the welfare services. The Labour Party, too, wanted accommodation, not revolution. But it would go a good deal further in improving the labour share, and was much less solicitous about the continued viability of capitalism. The trade unions were committed to encroachment upon capitalism in the interests of labour, but with the proviso that the state should be excluded from wage bargaining, leaving such confrontations 'free' as between employers and unions. At the same time, however, the unions were vulnerable to radical revolutionaries in their own ranks and outside them, whose tactical strength and appeal to working-class solidarity gave them power far beyond their relative numbers.

As a reflection of this general configuration, public policy in both the economic and social sectors (and indeed between them) was characterized by an uncoordinated pragmatism. There was a powerful preference for the *ad hoc*, or, conversely, an aversion to trying to solve the leading problems in terms of a generalized simultaneous relationship.

In the case of macro-economic controls the state had found no direct and consistent policy to stabilize the economy; indeed thought, even in 1939, hardly proceeded in such terms. One great reason for this was the absence of a theoretical apparatus that was sufficiently comprehensive and which carried sufficient conviction. Much less had the state accepted responsibility for long-term growth. But there were fragments of policy with implications in both of these directions. The currency was subject to management of a kind, so that the domestic economy was not dominated by the imperatives of the gold standard. Monetary matters were not, indeed, direct state concerns, but were left with a private institution, the Bank of England, which made its independent judgment of the appropriate parity for sterling. There was an elaborate tariff, regulated in terms of the sectoral needs of industry. Redistributive taxation was operating on a considerable scale, but was varied on a marginal–incremental basis and not in pursuit of any optimal view of wealth and income distribution. A beginning had been made on a policy of regional development, but it was concerned with alleviating pockets of unemployment rather than with structural change. Nationalization and its consequent direct state involvement in industry had been rejected. But the state had sought to encourage industry to purge itself of redundant capacity and to promote greater efficiency through rationalization. Indeed such a policy had been directly enforced by statute in the cases of the railways (1921) and of coal (1930).

Social provision in all its many aspects exemplified the law of necessary deterioration, such that ameliorative measures were undertaken only when the need for them had become urgent and capable of expressing itself with political effect. This led, in turn, to a tendency to see each aspect of welfare in its own specific terms, rather than as part of a generalized policy of social improvement. Moreover, the implementation aspect was always important; indeed much of the concern in such matters was with how a policy could be carried out effectively in relation to existing or new administrative machinery. The provision for health care suffered from the inadequacies of the insurance scheme and of the hospital services. Education had been extended and improved, especially in the secondary sector, but had been unable to break with the past in terms of class configuration. In housing a new situation had been created by the entry of the state into the picture on a large scale with its rent control and subsidies, making itself the great arbiter of working-class

housing supply and price, and helping the local authorities, quite suddenly, to become landlords on a massive scale. With the spectre of large-scale
unemployment providing a continuous threat to stability, the state, after
long resistance, had accepted far-reaching support responsibilities.
Everyone in need in Britain had a claim upon the state for maintenance.
But the greater part of it was subject to two divisive questions, namely
the terms on which benefit was payable, and the amount.

CHAPTER IX

American economic policy, 1865–1939

I. *The general character of American economic policy*

A. 'LAISSEZ-FAIRE' AND THE WELFARE STATE

Many historians have said that the whole history of American economic policy is a movement from *laissez-faire* to the welfare state or alternatively from capitalism to a mixed economy, the turn having been briskly executed by the New Deal between 1933 and 1939. As the raw material for this history consists of a mass of evidence, overabundant yet fragmentary, much of it dubious and more contradictory, it is no wonder that historians try to extract from it a compact digestible capsule. But the necessary work of distillation can go too far, as it has in this instance.

The critical terms used in the common summary of American economic policy are misleading because they were alien to American experience. 'Capitalism' and '*laissez-faire*' do not appear in the Constitution of the United States, nor do any even remote synonyms, contrary to the suggestion by Charles Beard and others that the Constitution was chiefly intended to guarantee a capitalist economic order. It is not surprising, in any event, that those particular terms are absent from the Constitution. Capitalism, as the name for one kind of economic order, was not invented until the middle of the nineteenth century. *Laissez-faire*, to be sure, was available for use by the founders of American economic policy, but there was no strong reason why Americans should reach out for a French term, or that French term, when Adam Smith had supplied a perfectly good English one, 'the system of natural liberty', to go with the economic policy worked out in *The Wealth of Nations*, published, as it happened, in the same year as the Declaration of Independence. 'Economic freedom' might have been a still handier expression and 'free trade', commonly used anytime after 1700, had come by the end of the century to describe a freedom broader than it originally denoted. Yet none of these phrases appears in the Constitution nor does anything like them. As the founders of economic policy in the United States could not have spoken of their intentions as capitalist and did not choose to describe them as according with *laissez-faire* or anything equivalent, it is entirely gratuitous to graft those terms onto their behaviour, as some historians persist in doing.

A stronger reason for dismissing the usual formula is that it misrepresents the underlying facts. If by capitalism and *laissez-faire* we are to understand economic liberalism, a doctrine imperfectly expressed by the maxim, 'that government governs best which governs least', then the founders of American economic policy did not believe in capitalism and *laissez-faire*; some of them at times echoed some views of Adam Smith, but many others asserted that he was fundamentally mistaken. Evidence is often cited that Thomas Jefferson, John Adams, and their colleagues approved of Adam Smith's teachings and that some read his writings. But for each one who expressed himself as favouring Smith, it is possible to find another who strongly disagreed. Alexander Hamilton's *Report on Manufactures* (1791) is a striking and explicit denial of Smith's views on tariff protection for infant industries, and much of the tariff history of the United States amounts to a reiterated contradiction of free trade.

The making of American economic policy was seldom guided by any comprehensive doctrine, dogma, or ideology. Such doctrinaire advocates as appeared on the scene were counterbalanced by devotees of opposite views. The policies which prevailed at various times between 1776 and 1933 differed too substantially to permit of their all bearing the same name. Although the historian's reconstruction of history may be thought of as a search for continuity amidst change, historians are professionally compelled (and some are constitutionally prone) to cut the seamless web of history into neat pieces; the destruction inherent in doing so is not minimized, nor is the resulting illumination intensified, by cutting pieces that are too sharp-edged.

Similar objections apply to the part of the formula which has it that after 1933 American capitalism was superseded by the welfare state or a mixed economy. Many, perhaps most, makers of economic policy during the 1930s did not mean fundamentally to alter the old order. Much of what they did was inspired by their belief that an economic emergency, of unprecedented depth and length, required urgent action – and many New Deal measures were abandoned as soon as the emergency ended, or sooner. Even those who wanted to make permanent reforms in the relations of government to the economy did not wish to bring about a 'welfare state', as they had never heard of such a thing. The scope of their reforms was far too narrow to bring forth a new hybrid, the 'mixed economy'. If mixed economy means an economy in which government generates a substantial fraction of the national income, a fraction let us say tending toward half, then certainly nothing like a leap toward a mixed economy took place during the 1930s. The total number of employees of all American governments, federal, state, and local, rose by 34 per cent between 1930 and 1940 – which may seem momentous, until one notes that the number had risen by 40 per cent between 1900 and 1910, by 50 per cent between 1910 and 1920, and by 26 per cent even during the 1920s, one of the heydays of so-called 'rugged individualism'. During the whole period from 1900 to 1940, the number of government employees increased twice as fast as the population at large; this goes far towards showing that if a mixed economy was being created, it was not a creation uniquely of the New Deal. But as even by 1940 only about one in ten of all persons employed in the United States worked for government, and all governments together spent only one-tenth of the national income, the economy was as yet reasonably 'unmixed'.

For all these reasons, then, we should reject the familiar view that American economic policy was founded on *laissez-faire* and suddenly transmuted into that of a welfare state. Rejecting it does not require us to insist that nothing changed. Many things did change at many different times and in many irregular ways. There was no simple pattern; and even the most delicate and tactful of patterns will cast as much shadow as light on the history that we wish to trace.

It is astounding that anyone should think of describing early American economic policy in terms of *laissez-faire*, if *laissez-faire* is supposed to describe a commitment by government to refrain from intervening directly in economic affairs. The record shows that American governments, local and national, intervened heavily.

One illustration among many is the history of laws to fix prices. For instance, the New England states passed a series of parallel 'regulating acts' in 1777, which set the wages of farm workers, mechanics, and tradesmen, as well as the prices of agricultural goods, manufactured products, and services such as 'horsekeeping' and 'teaming'. The Continental Congress recommended that all 13 states emulate these models, and the next year a number did. Not everyone approved. John Adams was quoted as saying, 'it is as plain as any demonstration in Euclid that trade cannot be regulated, it must regulate itself'. On the other side it was said:

We are told by the whole posse of traders and sharpers, that the affair of commerce must regulate itself; and that it would, if suffered to take its course without governmental restraint, naturally operate to the advantage of the public . . . [But] trade by regulating itself has brought us into as deplorable bad a condition as ever any people were in.

And it was these sceptics about free trade rather than Adams who chiefly carried that day.

Nor was this a unique exercise of intervention, an exceptional departure to deal with wartime emergency. Controls on the prices of some
commodities and services continued far into the nineteenth century.
Such was the testimony of Chief Justice Waite, who declared from the
bench in 1876 that 'it has been customary . . . in this country from its first
colonization, to regulate ferries, common carriers, hackmen, bakers,
millers, wharfingers, inn-keepers, etc., and in so doing to fix a maximum
of charge . . . To this day statutes are to be found in many of the States
upon some or all of these subjects.'

Statutory regulation of prices was only a small part of intervention by
state governments before 1860. Hours of work were regulated and child
labour prohibited by a number of states. Enterprises were restricted by
licensing and inspection laws and by special provisions written into the
charters of corporations. Municipal ordinances, about which too little is
known, aimed at similar results.

Nor was intervention by state governments confined to regulation;
they did as much or more by way of subsidy and encouragement.
Pennsylvania invested $100 million in various firms and appointed
directors to over 150 mixed corporations. Governments of southern
states supplied more than half the capital invested in southern railways.
Various governments – principally those of New York, Pennsylvania,
and Ohio – provided nearly three-quarters of the considerable capital
invested in canals. And various subsidies, such as remission of taxes and
monopoly privileges, were granted to companies thought to be offering
public services.

The federal government, for its part, engaged in a similar array of
activities. It subsidized roads, canals, and railways by direct investment of
funds, by gift of public lands, and by lending public credit. It gave
bounties to fishermen. It licensed and bonded fur-traders. It established
sailors' hospitals, financed by a compulsory insurance scheme. Above all
it used protective tariffs to promote the development of various manufacturing industries and branches of agriculture and mining.

Laissez-faire has been interpreted in other ways, of course. One is that it
requires government to take whatever steps may be necessary to preserve
competitive private enterprise, among which steps are frequently mentioned the maintenance of stable price levels and the prohibition of
monopolies and cartels. On this view of the doctrine, it would have to be
said that American economic policy did not follow *laissez-faire* at the
beginning but began to do so after the Sherman Anti-trust Act was
passed in 1890 and the Federal Reserve Act in 1913.

Again, *laissez-faire* is sometimes interpreted merely as a loose preference for private enterprise, as a synonym in effect for capitalism. But read
in that sense, *laissez-faire* has prevailed throughout American history.

Interventionist though American government always has been, it has never practised centralized economic planning – even though many observers confuse the government's inescapable functions as a monetary and fiscal authority with 'planning'. Neither has American interventionism ever gone so far as to practise enforced nationalization of industry, notwithstanding the municipalization of certain public utilities and rare federal experiments such as the Tennessee Valley Authority. Taken all in all, the United States has remained a stronghold of private enterprise.

But of course many elements of economic policy, and therefore the character of the whole, did change between 1865 and 1939. At the risk of oversimplifying, the changes can be summarized under a number of distinct headings. As to the extent of government intervention in economic life, it certainly increased, though not so momentously as is usually supposed. As to the mechanisms of intervention, shifts took place from state and local towards federal control; within federal government, from congress to the executive branch; and from congress and courts toward independent regulatory commissions. As to the spirit animating economic policy, the earlier, more common, view, that governments (especially the federal government) ought not to take substantial responsibility for relieving poverty, gave way to the view that redistribution, insurance, and relief are essential functions of government. These changes came about slowly, sporadically, and often by way of dealing practically with particular emergencies, rather than as a concerted and coordinated revolution dictated by a massive change in opinion.

B. CHANGES RESULTING FROM THE CIVIL WAR

This being so, it is idle to look for a single great turning-point. One can identify, more or less sharply, the moments at which certain large changes began to be clearly visible.

The Civil War, for instance, certainly led to an alteration in the balance between the federal government on the one hand and state governments on the other. This change in balance came about partly because the defeat of the seceded states implied a higher degree of supremacy in the federal government than had previously been given general assent; and this was underscored by the adoption of the Thirteenth, Fourteenth, and Fifteenth Amendments (1865–70), which among other things made citizenship a national rather than local fact and put control of constitutional rights more nearly into the hands of federal government. It came about also by a rise in the federal government's general level of activity. During the post-war decade, 1866–75, federal civil spending (expenditures on all purposes other than defence, veterans' benefits, and interest payments on the national debt) was twice as high in real terms as during the pre-war decade, 1851–60, which amounted to a real rise per capita of about one-third. Comparable changes took place in the number of federal officials. Staff of the patent office increased eightfold from 1848 to 1876, of the New York customs office threefold from 1848 to 1867, and the total (excepting civilian employees of defence departments) rose from 25,000 to 49,000 between 1851 and 1871. But the rate of this overall expansion does not mean that the federal government was spreading into many new fields of activity: two-thirds of the increase in federal employment between 1851 and 1871 was accounted for by expansion of postal services, and even by 1871 three-quarters of all federal civilian employees still worked for the Post Office.

Neither does the record of federal legislation justify the view that 'one could easily call Lincoln's presidency the "New Deal" of the 1860s'. In proposing this interpretation, Elazar calls notice especially to the National Banking Acts of 1863–5, the Morill Land-Grant College Act of 1862, the acts of 1862–4 to establish transcontinental railways with heavy subsidies from the federal government, and the Homestead Act of 1862. But all these merely extended numerous earlier precedents, and the latter three dealt with disposal of the public domain, land owned by the federal government, which had from the beginning been exclusively within its jurisdiction.

The National Banking Acts altered things more profoundly. Before 1863, banks had been chartered and regulated by each state separately, with variable results in terms of soundness; thereafter many banks, especially those that wished to issue bank notes, took charters from the federal government and submitted to comparatively rigorous supervision by the Comptroller of the Currency. This signal, though partial, transfer of function from state governments to the federal government carried out a purpose partly and temporarily served by the second Bank of the United States (1816–36), and was in large measure passed to solve financial problems thrown up by the Civil War rather than deliberately to strengthen the federal government relative to state governments. In any event, this measure was certainly the greatest innovation in American economic policy during the 1860s – leaving aside only the abolition of slavery, an event too wide-reaching to be classified under *economic policy* – and no other change at that time approached it in long-term effect. A survey of American economic policy at the end of the Civil War reveals no great transformation, though many piecemeal changes of degree, emphasis, and style.

C.   THE THRESHOLD OF 1890

There are somewhat sounder reasons for treating 1890 as the approximate date of a great divide.

Two substantial innovations took place about then in federal legislation, both involving an effective transfer of power from state to federal government, both recognizing that markets which had been local enough to fit within the jurisdiction of one state or another had since widened, because of improved transport and because of changes in scale of production after the introduction of steam power, not to the extent of becoming literally national in scope yet sufficiently to bring them within the federal government's exclusive authority over interstate commerce.

Of these innovations the first was the Interstate Commerce Act of 1887, which established federal regulation of railways and provided a powerful precedent for federal regulation of other industries. Before this moment, railways had been subject to laws of the states, generally enforced by suits before the courts. After this, many railways were subjected to steady scrutiny by the federal Interstate Commerce Commission, a standing body, presumed to consist of experts, empowered to supervise all aspects of railway business.

Next came the Sherman Anti-trust Act of 1890, which prohibited monopolies and combinations so far as they arose in the course of interstate commerce. It established no regulatory commission to carry on the work of enforcement (the Federal Trade Commission was created in 1914 partly for this reason), but charged the Department of Justice with this task as well as authorizing private persons to initiate suits. For the first time the federal government thus undertook to enforce competition, in some degree, as a basic standard for the American economy – and it might be thought, therefore, that Darwin, Herbert Spencer, and many American 'social Darwinists' were closer kin to American economic policy than was Adam Smith.

These statutes are significant not only in themselves but as harbingers. Before 1890, the great tendency of economic policy was to encourage development: of agriculture, by selling public land cheaply and quickly; of manufacturing, by protecting it against foreign competitors; of transportation, by subsidies and direct investment; and of various other activities by one means or another. After 1890, the tendency of economic policy was to control, conserve, redistribute, and insure.

Why should this change have centred on 1890? It would not be altogether implausible to relate the timing to the spread of socialist ideas. Socialism as a distinct political movement aiming to abolish private ownership of the means of production never made substantial headway in the United States, but 'sewer socialism' – an insistence on honest, democratic, and efficient government, which would act to diminish economic inequality and to relieve the needy – underlay many of the attitudes brought into American politics by Populists and Progressives between 1890 and 1914.

Another reason why 1890 is a plausible divide is that the frontier was supposed to have closed in that year, or so said the Director of the Census. Many interpreted and still interpret this ostensible fact as meaning that by 1890 the land of the United States was fully peopled. As a result, so many suppose, the previous project of fostering economic development, having succeeded, ceased to be pertinent; and, in an instantaneous display of good sense, the American people, acting through congress, turned to the new business of putting a crowded house in order. But this explanation, appealing as it may seem, rests on a fiction. The most important sense in which the frontier vanished by 1890 is that the line westward of which the federal government declined to sell any of its land, a line which had been moved westward repeatedly, finally reached the Pacific Ocean by 1890. This does not mean that no public land was left for sale but, on the contrary, that for the first time the federal government stood ready to sell land from the public domain wherever it was located. In the broader sense of isolated and relatively uncivilized zones of settlement, the frontier persisted after 1890, and in the specifically economic sense of areas whose productive potential is sharply underdeveloped, the frontier is still open in many parts of the United States, as the dramatic growth of California since 1945 amply demonstrates.

In any event, the notion that the land of the United States was fully occupied in 1890 can easily be shown to be false. For one thing, the public domain still contained in 1890 nearly 700 million acres, or one-third of all land in the country. During the decade after 1890, some 200,000 homestead farmers acquired some 30 million of these acres, and about 20 million acres more were sold to other private persons; and this process continued at a similar pace until 1920. Moreover, if one considers that the population of the country increased during the 30 years after 1890 by over 40 million people – each of whom on the average enjoyed in 1920 a real income over 50 per cent higher than 1890 – then it becomes clear that only persons who registered too sensitively the heat of current affairs could reasonably have supposed in 1890 that their country was already 'fully peopled'.

The End of the Frontier, fiction though it was, quite possibly had as much effect in some quarters as if it had been fact. For instance, its announcement was closely followed by an increasingly intense desire for conservation, which led Congress to pass the Forest Reserve Act in 1891 and subsequent statutes which eventually insulated about one-quarter of the country's area against economic development.

Yet after all that can be said in favour of 1890 as the turning-point, there remains much to the contrary. For instance, although immigration was brought within the ambit of active federal power as early as 1865, it was not restricted in quantity until as late as 1921. Again if one surveys the situation from the standpoint of attitudes reflected in decisions by the

Supreme Court of the United States, 1890 loses all significance as a turning-point. Between 1873 and 1898, the Supreme Court frequently upheld economic regulations imposed by state governments; between 1905 and 1937 it displayed a tendency (but no more than that) in the opposite direction. After 1937, the court dedicated itself to the view that economic regulation by states, and also by the federal government, should be regarded as prima facie valid. But even so modest an effort to detect a pattern overstates the changes that took place. A closer approximation to the truth is that from 1865 to 1939 the court generally approved economic regulations, and only occasionally invalidated some for specific constitutional faults. A more definite drift has been ascribed to the court's views chiefly because after 1937 the court announced that it would act on the presumption that property rights do not deserve a large measure of constitutional protection from government regulation; so that if a great turn took place in the court's views on economic policy, it would be more properly dated at 1937 than 1890.

D. THE SUPPOSED REVOLUTION OF THE NEW DEAL

It remains to consider the claims of the most widely favoured candidate, the New Deal, to be regarded as the great turning-point in American economic policy.

The claims rest on certain obvious facts. By 1933, the country had sunk into the deepest economic depression ever known, which was thought by many to mark the final breakdown of a free economic order. Coming into office in that year, supported by overwhelming Democratic majorities in both houses of congress, Franklin D. Roosevelt pledged – as no president ever had – to concentrate the efforts of his administration on relieving at least the symptoms of the disorder.

At once, during the 'hundred days' of spring 1933, the compliant Congress enacted a large package of emergency measures, many drafted by officials of Administration (contrary to former practice whereby the main initiative for legislation came from congress), and many of a quite unprecedented character. Some of the principal pieces were the Emergency Banking Relief Act, the Civilian Conservation Corps Act (which created a quasi-military corps of men between 18 and 25 to work on public projects), the Federal Emergency Relief Act (to provide grants-in-aid to state relief programmes), the Agricultural Adjustment Act (to subsidize the incomes of farmers), the Tennessee Valley Authority Act, the Home Owners Refinancing Act (to provide easier loans for mortgage holders), the Glass–Steagall Act (which established a federal corporation to insure depositors in national banks), and, most prominent of all, the National Industrial Recovery Act (authorizing industries to adopt the so-called Blue Eagle codes, amounting to cartel agreements, which upon approval by the federal administrator acquired the full force of law). And during the next two years, further measures of this sort poured forth, creating a host of new schemes and organizations known as the 'alphabet soup' agencies because they were so numerous and their names so cumbersome that Americans fell into the habit of calling them CCC, FERA, AAA, TVA, NIRA, and the like.

The vigour or enthusiasm with which the Administration and Congress went ahead is, however, difficult to assess precisely. Statistics do not bear out the idea that the New Deal brought forth a tidal wave of legislation. The number of public acts passed in any two-year session of congress, which never reached 200 before the Civil War, rose more or less steadily to a peak of over 1,000 in the session 1927–9, which closed six months before the stock market crash, and the Congress of 1929–31 passed 869; by contrast Roosevelt's first Congress, the seventy-third, passed only 486 bills and the seventy-fourth only 851. Such statistics are of course crude; one law of a sweeping sort may affect the way people live much more than dozens of laws that fidget with superficial details. Nevertheless these statistics do cast some doubt on Roosevelt's allegation that Herbert Hoover's Administration met the crisis with lackadaisical and callous optimism. Whatever the truth is, the popular impression at the time that Roosevelt's Administration was meeting the crisis with unparalleled promptness and vigour, which historians have tended to take at face value, was largely produced by Roosevelt's own skills as a publicist.

Other statistics tend to confirm scepticism about the degree to which the New Deal revolutionized public policy. Civilian employees of the federal government increased in number by over 40 per cent between 1933 and 1937 – but this amounted in absolute terms to only about 300,000 persons, or 3 per cent of the number of unemployed. And in broader terms the expansion of federal government activity during Roosevelt's first Administration seems to have been far less remarkable than is supposed. Federal expenditures, after allowing for changes in the price level, were raised during Hoover's Administration (1929–33) by 100 per cent; and during Roosevelt's first term (1933–7) by about 50 per cent or less. Put another way, federal expenditures as a fraction of Gross National Product more than doubled during the Hoover years of 1929–32 and then rose from 8 per cent to 10 per cent between 1932 and 1936, after which date they remained fairly stable in the vicinity of 9 per cent until the Second World War set in. These statistics too are indecisive because the laws may fundamentally change the character of economic life without radically altering levels of public expenditure, or may result in higher levels of public spending without having fundamentally altered the general tenor of economic policy. In any event, it is interesting to note that between 1932, Hoover's last year in office, and 1940, the purchases of all governments remained surprisingly stable at about one-sixth of Gross National Product, though the federal government's share increased from one-fifth to two-fifths of the total. So although federal spending just took up the slack in spending by state and local governments, the New Deal did not extend federal spending at a more rapid rate than did Hoover's Administration.

Another ground for regarding the 1930s as a grand climacteric in American economic policy is the supposed introduction of the Keynesian policy of deficit finance. What has given rise to the supposition is that, in response to a sharp recession that began in the third quarter of 1937, Roosevelt advocated and Congress enacted a 'pump-priming' programme, designed to inject some $5 billion worth of spending into the economy. But to interpret this as Keynesian or to suppose that Roosevelt and congress had become converts to Keynes is totally implausible. In 1937 only a few professional economists in America knew what Keynes was advocating, and fewer were persuaded. To suppose that busy politicians would have seized the difficult and heterodox teaching before anyone else is to suppose a great deal. In any event, it seems clear that Roosevelt himself shared rather the opposite view, that in times of crisis the government should make especially determined efforts to balance the budget. Although the Revenue Act of 1932, passed under Hoover, had substantially raised levels of taxation, Roosevelt made no effort to reduce them. At the beginning of 1937, when the economic emergency seemed to be nearing an end, Roosevelt's budget message recommended that federal expenditure be sharply reduced in order to achieve once again a balanced budget. The pump-priming scheme of 1938 sounds Keynesian only in retrospect; its true tone is well represented by its title, the Emergency Relief Appropriation Act (21 June 1938), for what it did in large part was to renew earlier relief programmes, increase the number of jobs offered by the Works Progress Administration (a work-relief programme first established in 1935), and to ease credit. Again, when congressional opponents of the New Deal passed the Revenue Act of 1938, which reduced corporate income taxes, Roosevelt refused to sign it. It is pure irony that during Roosevelt's 12 years in office the federal budget was always in deficit, so that when he died the national debt stood at $260 billion, ten times larger than when he entered. Depression and war accounted for that, not Keynes, and certainly not Roosevelt's deliberate will.

Many other changes could be explored. The social security programme – providing unemployment insurance, compulsory retirement insurance, and similar benefits – which was the kernel of the 'second New

Deal', after 1935; a new group of commissions to regulate labour relations, the power industry, communications industry, stock exchanges, and air transport; the extension on a large scale of federal grants-in-aid to states, as a means of inducing them to undertake activities that the federal government lacked constitutional authority to undertake directly – all these were among the New Deal's innovations. Yet to counter these numerous claims to fundamental upheaval is less difficult than it might seem.

One large segment of all New Deal measures, especially those initiated before 1936, were emergency schemes. Of these, perhaps the most important, the National Industrial Recovery Act, was invalidated by the Supreme Court in 1935. Others, like the Works Progress Administration, Civilian Conservation Corps, and National Youth Administration, expired naturally when the onset of war transformed unemployment into labour shortages. Not only did these emergency schemes leave no permanent residue in American economic policy, but some of these were so reviled because of their similarity to corporatism under Mussolini that they have become a model for many Americans of techniques to be avoided.

Another large segment of New Deal measures consisted of previously unfinished business. The new regulatory commissions and the host of laws to regulate banking and finance echoed the strategy of Progressives during the first decade of the century. They might well have been put into practice under Woodrow Wilson's first administration, had the World War not intervened. That they were effected by Roosevelt is not surprising. The great depression made many feel that business and especially banks, blamed for the breakdown, ought to be bridled once and for all; and Roosevelt had learned his political programme at the feet of Wilson, under whom he had long served as Assistant Secretary of the Navy. Neither is it surprising, one might add, that this lineage was continued by Lyndon Johnson, whose vision was shaped during his early years in Roosevelt's congresses and who carried still further, during his years in office, the sorts of federal intervention characteristic of the Wilsonian Progressives.

To sum up, the permanent economic policies of the United States, which certainly did alter during the New Deal, altered far less dramatically than is usually thought. Many of the innovations, like the farm price-support programme, were the completion of actions repeatedly attempted and narrowly defeated in the past, completion made possible because the fears engendered by the depression overruled caution. And many other changes, rather than reflecting the intrusion of new principles, were merely corollaries of principles which had been assimilated into American economic policy one or two generations earlier. Economic policy, like many other aspects of American life, was closer in 1939 to that of 1900 than to that of 1960.

II. Branches of American economic policy

A. GENERALLY

The preceding account, which traces the general spirit of American economic policy through time, showing what persisted and what altered, is one way to present an account of the history. Quite a different way to recount the same history is to explore various particular branches of policy in order to explain their separate making, remaking, or unmaking. The first way tends to overstate the coherence of economic policy at any given moment, treating it as though policy were an organic whole rather than what it really is, the collective rubric for many policies. The second way corrects this defect at some risk of suggesting that each of the separate policies was conceived and executed in total isolation from all others. This implication is not wholly misleading. Each particular field of policy is a relatively closed environment, peopled by official and private specialists, who work with recondite information and esoteric routines, habits, and precedents which can only be dislodged against considerable opposition and at the cost of upsetting time-hallowed expectations. Each field of policy therefore runs on with a momentum of its own which persists even while the ensemble of policies is changing its shape. A drift of the whole does not imply that each part is drifting to the same extent or even in the same direction.

There is another reason for presenting the history of economic policy in terms of what happened to its parts. In America, more than in most nations, policies are formed not by the government but by a large number of relatively independent institutions. Within the federal government, each of the coordinate arms, the executive, congress, and the courts, makes policy more or less autonomously, as does also a fourth branch, superadded to the Constitution in fact though not in terms, the quasi-executive, quasi-legislative, and quasi-judicial administrative agencies. In order that a federal policy should become effective, the branches must normally concur; but this does not alter the fact that certain fields of policy have effectively been controlled, for a time, by one branch. Besides, much of American economic policy is made by states and municipalities and by thousands of other local authorities. The specific roles of these various actors are illustrated in what follows. Tariff policy was long a congressional preserve. Public policy about railways was largely made, after 1887, by a regulatory commission. Much of American labour law before 1935 consisted of laws of the states, though the evolution of this body of law was closely supervised by the federal courts. And finally, much of that amorphous collection of policies known as social policy was made and administered by local governments.

To show the interplay of various parts of American government in the making of economic policy is to illustrate one of its dominant features: the extent to which the Constitution, rather than any explicit economic doctrine, has limited and so shaped its contents.

B.   TARIFF POLICY

1. *Before 1861*

American tariff policy was in large measure intended to promote manufacture, and was indeed the most general encouragement to this end offered by the federal government. Yet tariffs were intended also to serve as a principal source of federal revenue, especially before the Civil War, and were often used besides to protect particular branches of farming, mining, and manufacture which, far from being infants, were adults in temporary distress. It is accordingly difficult to say just how much any tariff act aimed at fostering economic development by protecting various industries against foreign competition, especially as each act levied different rates of duty on thousands of distinct commodities, rates calculated on bases which make comparison uncertain. Moreover, statistics are not sufficiently full or precise, nor are methods of economic analysis powerful enough, to authorize any confident judgment about the extent to which tariff protection accounted for the development of American industry.

The importance of revenue considerations in the making of tariff policy before the Civil War is apparent from the fact that customs receipts provided 85 per cent and more of federal revenues in all but a few years. But despite this heavy dependence on customs receipts, considerations of revenue had variable effects on the policy of tariff protection. The federal budget tended to be in surplus chronically (during two of every three years between 1791 and 1861), an embarrassment which could not easily be covered up by increasing expenditures, as many Americans favoured inexpensive government in general and resisted, in particular, any expansion of federal spending relative to that of state and local governments. Persistent surpluses often therefore compelled reduction in the rates of duty, although ardent protectionists tried to evade this remedy by ingenious manoeuvres, such as the Surplus Revenue Act of 1836, devised by Henry Clay, father of the 'American System' (a set of policies aimed at making the US more self-sufficient economically), and the Distribution-Preemption Act of 1841, whereby surplus federal revenues were distributed to the states. Conversely, protectionists were able more easily to gain their objectives during periods of budget deficits.

In any event, the protective elements of American tariffs, high and wide as they frequently were, did not generally rise enough to diminish customs revenues. Purely prohibitive tariffs would of course have totally extinguished customs revenues by totally excluding imports. But because even during the heyday of protectionism, from 1865 to 1909, customs revenues generally rose and fell with the level of duties, it follows that the level of duties in general never reached even approximately prohibitive levels. This conclusion is vital in forming an accurate appraisal of American tariff policy.

Protection, inherited as an idea and practice from the colonial period (1620–1776), was thought especially appropriate for a young nation, beset by perennial deficits in foreign trade and fearful for its economic as well as political independence. Thus the tariff of 1816, for instance, sought to insulate native industries – textiles, iron, and other lesser ones – which had expanded while foreign trade was diminished before and during the war of 1812, and were exposed after the restoration of peace to more efficient foreign competitors. On these favoured objects, Congress set rates of duty at 25 per cent or more, and the 'apparent average rate of duty' – the ratio of customs receipts to value of imports – came to slightly more than 20 per cent. This average rate was almost doubled by the act of 1824 and the 'Tariff of Abominations' of 1828, a political stratagem that miscarried. In reaction to the latter and the South Carolina Nullification Crisis which it occasioned, duties were reduced to their former scale of about 20 per cent overall, a level at which they were kept with surprising uniformity during most years between 1832 and 1862.

2. 1861–1913

Like all wars the Civil War brought with it a fiscal crisis, in this case the sharpest of American history; and, as often happens, expedients adopted to deal with an emergency became consolidated afterwards into long-term policy. During the four years of the war (1861–5), federal expenditures rose twentyfold in nominal terms, or between ten- and fifteenfold in real terms. To provide for these expenditures, the government launched a series of innovations, installing an income tax, estate and gift taxes, a licence tax on all businesses, excise taxes on manufacturers, and an issue of inconvertible paper money, the famous 'greenbacks'. Additional revenue was also wrung from familiar sources, especially customs duties. Rates of duty were more than doubled, in response to a variety of urgings: the obvious need to curb runaway deficits in the federal budget;

the claim in equity that, as domestic producers had been subjected to heavy internal taxes, foreign producers should pay equivalently higher duties on imports; enduring pressure by those who favoured protection in principle; and special pleading by various American producers who saw an easy opportunity to feather their own nests.

After the Civil War, the advocates and beneficiaries of protection resisted all efforts to revert to pre-war levels. And because the Republican Party, the party of protection, retained control of the executive and congress for most of the next 47 years, duties of the protective sort were not only maintained but raised. At times to be sure, some were lowered, but generally these applied either to goods like coffee and tea which could not be produced in the United States, or to goods like pig-iron which enjoyed more protection than necessary to prohibit all imports. Such were the reductions in the Tariff Act of 1870, which lowered the average rate of duty – though at the same time it raised certain protective duties.

Again in 1872, when federal revenues had risen enough to generate large fiscal surpluses, another measure for tariff reduction was brought in. Gustavus A. Finkelnburg, a Republican from Missouri who managed the bill on the floor of the House, said that it was intended among other things to 'divest some industries of the superabundant protection which smells of monopoly and which it was never intended they should enjoy after the war'. In the act which emerged, Congress sharply reduced some non-protective duties, but declining to bring down the particular protective duties which were complained of as excessive, decided instead to lower all protective duties by 10 per cent. This cut was restored two years later, after a decline in imports due to the depression of 1873 led to a sharp fall in customs receipts.

A further general revision of tariffs took place in 1883. Notable changes were the raising of rates on the most heavily imported classes of woollen and cotton textiles; the lowering of the rate on steel rails from $28 to $17 per ton, which was still quite sufficient to exclude practically all imports thereafter; and the retention of duties on beef, pork, cheese, wheat, corn, and the like, in order, said Taussig, 'to maintain the fiction that the agricultural population secured through them a share of the benefits of protection'. Yet the overall effect of these changes was visible neither in the apparent average rate of duty on all imports, which hovered very close to 30 per cent, as it had since 1873 and continued to do until 1891, nor in the average rate on dutiable imports which fluctuated no more than three points to either side of 45 per cent between 1876 and 1891. This is not to deny that the volume and composition of imports, and the value of customs receipts, swung quickly from year to year and grew strongly over the years. There is nevertheless room for surprise that the overall rates – which depend exclusively on weighted averages of each particular rate – should have been kept so nearly constant by successive congresses which tampered enthusiastically with the myriad bits that made up the complex whole. It is surprising, also, that successive tariffs between 1865 and 1909, hailed and decried as 'extremely' protectionist, hardly raised the apparent average rate on dutiable imports above the rate it had reached by 1865. That rate, 48 per cent, was high enough; but all the efforts of congresses bent on protection did not make it more protective as a whole.

The peaks of protection were scaled by two tariffs during the last decade of the century. During the election of 1888, the only one in American history in which the tariff was the leading issue, the Republican platform declared that the party was 'uncompromisingly in favor of the American system of protection' and that whereas the incumbent Democratic administration and Party 'serve the interests of Europe, we will support the interests of America'. They made their promise good with the McKinley tariff of 1890. It raised rates on various sorts of textiles, lowered the rate on steel rails, though this change was largely ceremonial since the new rate was more than adequate to exclude imports, and raised the rates on wheat and corn, an exercise in futility as American farmers needed no protection against foreign grain, having long exported large amounts. Its most emphatically protective feature was a sharp rise in duty on tin-plated iron and steel. Between 1862 and 1890, tin plate had been subject to duties between 15 and 30 per cent, despite which none had been produced in America. The tariff of 1890 raised the rate of duty to 70 per cent; by 1894 domestic production had reached 73 million tons, or one-quarter of American consumption; and by 1897, when the rate of duty was down to about 40 per cent, American production had risen to 257 million tons, or three-quarters of American consumption. It was the instance *par excellence* of protection giving birth to an infant industry, although the American iron and steel industry was now so flourishing a giant that to speak of any of its subsidiary parts as an infant is to strain the metaphor.

The other high tariff of this decade was the Dingley Act of 1897. Historians are fond of saying that it established an average rate of duty at 57 per cent and was thus the most protective tariff up to that time. But the official statistics do not bear out this view. Average rates of duty on dutiable imports were 49 per cent in 1898, 52 per cent in 1899, and 49 per cent in 1900. At no time did the rates resulting from the Dingley tariff reach 57 per cent or, for that matter, perceptibly exceed those under the McKinley tariff.

After about 1902, the more extreme rates of protection began to be whittled down, either (as in the case of tin plate) because the protected

domestic industry improved its efficiency to the point where imports
were not in the same degree as before being excluded by duties, or
because congress reduced the rates, as it did in the Payne–Aldrich tariff of
1909 and the Underwood tariff of 1913.

3. 1913–39

Though the determination to protect American producers abated somewhat between 1903 and 1920, a time when domestic growth and then the
war made them and kept them unusually prosperous, circumstances
prompting a return to protection arose shortly after the war. The
problem now had to do with farmers. Although their average real
incomes had doubled from 1910 to 1919, after the war they fell steeply, so
that by 1921 farmers were earning only about three-quarters as much as
in 1910. To meet this crisis the Emergency tariff of 1921 raised duties on
agricultural products, and the Fordney–McCumber tariff of 1922 and
the Hawley–Smoot tariff of 1931 raised them further. To carry such
measures through congress, it was necessary of course to make concessions to groups other than farmers; the Hawley–Smoot Act, passed as the
great depression deepened, offered whatever aid protective duties could
afford to many parts of the American economy. It was indeed the most
protective tariff in American history, at least as judged by the average
rate on dutiable goods, which reached about 60 per cent in 1932.

Yet at this very moment, when the traditional policy of protection
seemed to be pursued more energetically than ever, it was being undermined by a number of quiet changes. One was the transfer from congress
to the executive of delegated responsibility for determining rates of duty.
This transfer had much to recommend it. Since the Civil War, congress,
when making tariff acts – as when deciding other large questions of
economic policy – had responded too sensitively, sympathetically, readily to the wants of any strident claimant. In effect, the eighteenth-century
notion, reflected in the *Federalist Papers*, that governments exist to serve
the 'public interest', was superseded by the notion pertinent to what has
come to be called a pluralist democracy, that the public interest means
nothing other than a compilation of private interests, that is, of the special
interests of all perceptible groups into which 'the public' might be
thought to divide. As President Hoover put it, the processes of making
tariffs in congress, with all their 'necessary collateral surroundings in
lobbies, logrolling, and the activities of group interests, are disturbing to
public confidence'. Yet if justice could authorize any one group of
Americans to benefit from protection, then it must surely authorize all
other groups to benefit alike; from which it follows that congress, when

making tariffs in the way it did, was acting out the prevailing political philosophy.

Nevertheless, because of the multitude of claimants for protection, the need somehow to reconcile their often contradictory claims, and the effort to make the whole package yield a revenue neither wildly low nor high, the technical task of tariff-making had become slow and painful. Senator Arthur Vandenburg, a staunch protectionist in his day, called the process an 'atrocity' lacking 'any element of economic science or validity', and said that after having spent eleven months in constructing the Hawley–Smoot Act he would rather resign than face such agony again.

For these reasons it was believed, by members of congress as well as many others, that the detailed work of tariff-making should be turned over to the executive branch. The president, following the recommendations of an administrative commission, and acting within broad lines of policy laid down by congress, could adjust the rate of duty for any commodity as soon as need arose, and could administer the policy in a comparatively detached manner. In all this, expertise would play a larger part, and special pleading a correspondingly smaller part, than when congress had been the arena.

The notion that an expert body could usefully contribute to the making of tariff policy first made itself heard in about 1865, the moment when the general notion began to appear that experts were needed in government to serve at the side of, though not yet above, politicians, who were common men, sometimes gifted common men, amateurs chosen to represent their common, amateur constituents. A number of councils of tariff experts were created temporarily, and finally a permanent Tariff Commission was established in 1916. Then in the Tariff Act of 1922, Congress authorized the president, should the Tariff Commission so recommend, to raise or lower the rates of duty set out in the act by as much as 50 per cent – not least because President Warren Gamaliel Harding had urged that flexibility be introduced 'so that rates may be adjusted to meet unusual and changing conditions'; and that the Tariff Commission be strengthened 'so that it can adapt itself to a scientific and wholly just administration of the law'. In fact, as might have been foreseen, most commissioners were appointed not for any scientific knowledge they might have but rather because their views about the desirability of protection corresponded to those of the administration and were acceptable to senators controlling confirmation.

A second basic change in policy came with the adoption in 1923 of the 'unconditional most-favoured-nation' principle, the rule that in making tariff treaties the United States would undertake that if it made concessions to any one nation it would grant the same concessions to all its treaty partners. This had the effect of assuring that American tariffs would not discriminate among various nations (at least among those with whom treaties existed), thus strengthening and making more automatic the principle of non-discrimination which had generally typified American tariff policy throughout.

The third basic change was in a sense a combination of the former two. The Trade Agreements Act of 1934, the chief New Deal measure on foreign trade, authorized the president to make agreements with other nations reciprocally to reduce tariffs and import quotas (which latter the United States had never used), such agreements to include the unconditional most-favoured-nation clause. Moreover, Congress gave its consent in advance to executive agreements that the president might make in pursuance of the act. From the constitutional standpoint this created a substantial delegation of power to the president. From the substantive economic standpoint, it recognized fundamental facts of the prevailing situation. During the course of the First World War the United States had become the world's principal creditor, and during the next two decades accumulated the great bulk of the world's monetary gold. To maintain a protective policy under such circumstances made it difficult for other nations to export sufficiently to the United States to repay war loans or even to avoid current deficits; foreign governments responded by erecting various barriers against free international trade, which tended to deepen the depression everywhere.

The Trade Agreements Act of 1934 – which established the basis for later liberalization of American commercial policy and of world trade generally – was thus partly a typical New Deal measure to deal with the economic emergency of that moment. Partly, also, it made a belated adjustment of American trade policy to the fact that by 1900 the United States had obviously been transformed from a beleaguered, underdeveloped economy into the richest and most highly developed economy in the world, one which in protecting its domestic industries must inevitably depress production everywhere. As is often the case, a policy continued long after its rationale had been vitiated by a slow change in circumstances, and whose abandonment had long been urged by some, was finally dismissed because of the intrusion of a temporary and irrelevant crisis. Relatively unimportant reasons prevailed where deep ones alone had failed.

4. Economic effects of tariff protection

In assessing the economic effects of protectionism, two questions present themselves at once. How much did the protected industry gain? How much did this cost American customers of the protected industry?

Answers to these questions would not tell the whole story, since protection has more remote consequences, encouraging the producers' suppliers and transferring burdens forward to the customers' customers, and so on; but these secondary effects are usually too involved to disentangle, and we should be content if we could estimate the immediate primary effects with any precision.

Economic theory offers clear guidance as to the general tendencies. Suppose that some commodity is imported from abroad and also produced at home, in both instances under competitive conditions. If customs duties are imposed on the imports, these will raise the effective supply costs of the foreign producers. In the short run the price of the goods will rise, though by less than the rate of duty (unless demand is absolutely inelastic); total consumption of the good will decline; the physical volume of imports will decline more sharply, and the physical volume of home production will rise. So the total earnings of domestic producers will rise, partly because the price has risen, partly because their output has risen – and this increase in the total revenues and in the rate of profit earned by domestic producers is, of course, the whole point of the exercise.

As the earnings of the domestic producers are identical with the spending of their customers, it is clear that the advantage to the domestic producers is exactly counterbalanced by a burden loaded on the domestic consumers. But the burden does not stop there, for the consumer pays a higher price not only for the home product but also for the imported product. The latter increment is, of course, paid over to the Treasury, though another part of the customs revenue is paid for by the foreign producers, who as a result end with lower profits than before.

Turning to the long run, and assuming that foreign producers and domestic producers all operate under constant returns to scale but that the costs of foreign producers are lower on the average than those of domestic producers, then the effects of protection will vary according to its weight relative to the cost differential. If the tariff is high enough, it will exclude all imports. Under these circumstances, again, domestic consumption will be reduced (assuming some price-elasticity of demand), and the price will rise exactly in proportion to the rate of duty. So the total burden on consumers will exceed the total gain realized by domestic producers, as they must pay a higher price for the output they buy and besides they lose the value of the volume of goods which they no longer buy because of the increased price. The total burden on customers, in these particular circumstances, consists of an enforced transfer of money income from them to domestic producers and, in addition, a 'deadweight loss' of real income.

How could an enforced transfer of income from customers to producers be justified in terms of equity, especially when the benefit received by the one group is less than the sacrifice imposed on the other? One answer might be that the transfer is justified as a means of creating employment – but this could have little pertinence to the American economy, which was typified by long-run shortages rather than surpluses of labour. Another answer, the most plausible used, was that protection would enable the domestic industry to achieve economies of scale in the long run, so that the temporary burden imposed on customers would yield them permanent benefits by way of reduced prices. And still another answer might have been, though not very plausibly, that if the tariff protected *all* branches of American production, then the distinction between producers and customers would disappear, since those who gained from protection and those burdened by it would be the very same people. Many other reasons could be conjured up to justify protective duties from the standpoint of distributive ethics, but all of them leave a doubt.

These abstract considerations can be seen at work practically when we examine the history of steel rails in America. Before 1867, railways had used wrought-iron rails. Steel rails, which became available on the introduction of the Bessemer process, proved superior; though they cost more, they could carry heavier, faster locomotives and would last five or ten times longer. As a result, they totally displaced iron rails within less than twenty years, not least because though in 1867 they cost twice as much as iron rails, by 1883 they cost no more.

Now the cost of producing steel rails in the United States was higher than in Britain at all times until 1896, though the difference diminished in absolute terms. During the early years of American steel production, from 1867 through 1873, British imports supplied about one-third of all rails used in the United States, or about 300,000 tons per year. Thereafter imports of English rails dropped off to negligible quantities or none, except for four boom years during the 1880s. This exclusion is traceable to import duties which had the effect of raising the price of English imports up to or above the price of the American product. For instance in 1887, when the price of American steel rails at works in Philadelphia was $46 while the price in England was about $30, the duty applicable was $28; in order to meet the American price, English exporters would have had to content themselves with less than $18 per ton; and it is not surprising that under that conjunction of costs and prices, no rails were imported into the United States. Nor is it surprising that the tariff succeeded in excluding virtually all English rails from the American market after 1890, even though they continued to be cheaper in Britain than were the American ones until about 1900 and as cheap until at least 1910. There can be no doubt that the tariff fostered the growth of steel-rail manufacturing, which incidentally accounted for far the larger part of all American steel products during the 1870s and 1880s.

The cost of achieving this result can be illustrated by considering the situation in 1881. Philadelphia mills quoted about $60 per ton for steel rails and English mills about $30 per ton; the duty stood at $28 per ton; so that relatively efficient English mills could and did sell their products in the United States. In fact, 345,000 tons were imported, which yielded customs revenues of nearly $10 million. The American output was 1,210,000 tons. Now assuming that in the absence of the tariff Americans could have bought this additional amount at the English price (and ignoring transportation costs), then the subsidy which American buyers were forced to pay to American producers amounted to some $30 million. In addition there was the 'deadweight loss', the additional value that American users would have enjoyed had rails sold at the lower price and assuming that they would therefore have bought more than the 1,550,000 tons which they did buy at the actual prevailing price of $60 per ton. To evaluate the deadweight loss we would need to know the elasticity of demand in relation to price. Making the very conservative assumption that at a price of $30 rather than $60, the users would have bought 10 per cent more rails, then the deadweight loss would have been $2,250,000. In short, in 1881, something more than half (and perhaps substantially more than half) of the total price that Americans paid for steel rails was accounted for by tariff effects. It seems a heavy price to pay for fostering domestic manufacture; but we are not able to say whether in truth it was or was not finally too heavy a price. It may be that if one could take into account all the direct and remote effects of promoting steel manufacture in the United States, tariff protection would turn out to have been a great bargain, or just as conceivably, a terrible waste. In a deeper sense the question is unanswerable because the distant beneficiaries of an investment project value its fruits differently (and on the whole more highly) than those who paid the costs; so that those who look back now at American economic development after 1865 might be expected to assess far more favourably its benefits relative to its costs than did their ancestors who bore the burdens of bringing it about.

We do not and cannot know enough to say whether American protection was beneficial. We do know that free international trade now commands the approval of many economists and, at least during prosperous times, of many governments.

C.   REGULATION OF RAILWAYS

Promoting economic development was a central objective of railway policies as of tariff policies. However, many other objectives entered into consideration, not only as usual in any broad field of policy but particularly so in this instance, because American railway policy was made not only by the federal government but also independently by governments of states, counties, and towns, each pursuing its special local interests. And besides, as often happens, the relative weights attached to various objectives were reshuffled from time to time.

At the outset, between 1825 and 1860, deliberations within the federal government were heavily influenced by the established practice of granting public subsidies and privileges to 'internal improvements', chiefly canals and roads. These were understood to constitute public benefits on the grounds that improved facilities for transportation served not only the direct users, passengers and shippers, but producers and consumers in all parts of the country. Railways, like their canal and road predecessors, would improve the national economy by easing transportation to remoter areas. This economic unification was thought to have a political counterpart. As they witnessed the territorial expansion of the United States, with new states being added regularly at the receding periphery, and observed the continuing discord between North and South, patched rather than healed by the Missouri Compromise, Americans feared that the Union was increasingly threatened by dissolution or violent rupture. Many hoped that railways would cement national unity by connecting not only the homes of the citizens but also their hearts. Again, fearing that the nation's existence might be destroyed by foreign enemies (had not British troops captured and destroyed the national capital in 1814?), Americans wanted railways to help move soldiers to the country's distant and sparsely settled borders. Then there were lesser economic goals. By making it easier for migrants to reach the western land, railways would increase its value, a public good inasmuch as the federal government owned most of it. Then again, by providing a land route from Atlantic to Pacific, the transcontinental lines that began to be discussed in the 1850s would put the United States in a position to dominate trade between the Western world and the Far East. This objective, which offended some Americans by the suggestion of an imperial design, was applauded by many others as a means of counteracting the economic hegemony at which they believed Britain to be aiming and which they feared would destroy America's economic, if not political, independence. All these large considerations of economic progress and nation-building were interwoven in the making of federal railway policy before and during the Civil War.

The chief instrument of federal policy during this time was grants of land from the public domain to railway companies, given sometimes directly, sometimes indirectly via governments of the states. The first such grant was made in 1850 to Illinois, Mississippi, and Alabama so that they might aid construction of the Illinois Central Railroad and the Mobile and Ohio Railroad; in the end these railways received subsidies to the extent of nearly 4 million acres. During the 1850s the federal government allocated to other railways 20 million acres more. In the next decade the federal government gave about 125 million acres to the various railways building the transcontinental network. And then in 1871 all gifts ceased, because – as Congressman James Abram Garfield, later president, said – of a 'general sentiment in the country that we ought to put a speedy and effective end to the policy of granting public lands to railway corporations'.

In the meanwhile, state and local governments had been pursuing similar policies of encouragement to railways – though to be precise, they started as early as the 1830s and continued into the 1880s or later. Their objectives were rather less lofty than those of the federal government. From the standpoint of any particular town what mattered was that the main line of a railway, preferably more than one, should connect it with the great ports and hubs, while bypassing and so isolating its competing neighbours or imposing on them the position of satellites. A great scramble resulted, in which localities tried to outbid each other for the favour of railway promoters. Local governments used public funds or public credit to buy stocks, lend money, or make outright gifts in cash, kind, or land. All in all they gave railways some hundreds of millions of dollars worth of aid, or roughly as much as the federal government gave; and although they supplied only a small fraction of all the capital invested in railways, it served as an important symbol of public approval and stimulus to private investors.

Because units of local government were creatures and agents of the sovereign states, acquiring powers only as state governments saw fit to grant them, any proposal by a local government to aid a railway needed to be legitimized by statute. The record of such legislation by the states – at first in the form of special acts authorizing particular subsidies and later of general enabling acts – enables us to trace the timing of local aid. The first great burst came in the 1850s. A far larger one followed immediately after the Civil War ended – apparently the expression of demand pent up during the war as well as a need to make good war damage, especially in the Old South. And then many states began to tighten the reins; and at least seven prohibited further aid. Beginning about 1870, state and local governments abandoned their previous practices of encouragement, though not as abruptly as did the federal government, and turned their attention to a purpose which had not hitherto much preoccupied them, to regulate railways and most particularly the prices that they charged.

This fairly abrupt shift from subsidy to regulation was impelled partly by the success of the earlier policy. By 1870 some 40,000 miles of rail had been brought into service. In communities well provided (at least for the time being), citizens now began to feel that they were paying too much; and recalling their generosity in advancing aid at an earlier stage, they felt justified in demanding that governments should now restrict rates to generally moderate levels and do away with differentials among different customers. Communities still lacking railway service objected that any effective regulation must diminish profitability and so discourage investment in new lines. In each state, and in the nation as a whole, the relative weights of these opposed groups influenced decisions as to whether to regulate, and how, and when. But as time went on and railways kept expanding their coverage, more and more people moved out of the group who were dissatisfied because they had no railway facilities and into the group dissatisfied with the price they had to pay.

That shippers should have wished for cheaper rates is easy to understand. Why they should have supposed, as many did, that railway charges were outrageously high is more difficult to make out. It was not as though railways were earning spectacular profits or ever had. On the average the rate of return on their capital investment hovered near 5 per cent during the 1870s as it had during the 1850s, although some particular railways earned 10 per cent or more, while others, of course, lost money, and to such an extent that by 1877 almost one-fifth of the nation's track was in the hands of receivers. But the notorious success of a few – exaggerated by promoters seeking to attract investors and also, no doubt, by optimistic investors – obscured the fact that the average rate of return in railways was not higher than normal.

Neither was complaint justified on the score that railway rates were rising. On the contrary they fell steadily from the end of the Civil War through the 1870s, and fell faster than prices in general – so at least the scrappy statistics suggest. But those who complained at the time were not aware of those statistics and the inferences that might be drawn from them. As to farmers, it may be that their attention was fixed on the nominal price of wheat, a symbol of remarkable force. If a bushel of wheat sold at $2, then all was thought to be well; if for less, then the fault was ascribed to malign influence, of unfair competition by depressed foreign peasant labour, grasping American middlemen, or greedy railway magnates. Now, whereas during the Civil War wheat had risen to the blissful level of nearly $3, by 1870 it had plummeted below $1.50. Compared to this fall, freight rates had declined little. Because the price of wheat dropped more than the cost of freight, midwestern farmers shipping wheat to the eastern seaboard found that an increasing fraction of the price they received – tending towards half, some said – went to pay freight charges. And this undoubtedly painful fact farmers blamed not on the precipitous fall in wheat prices but rather on monopolistic exactions of railway owners. Although this effect may have been felt more strongly by farmers and especially by growers of grain, it undoubtedly impressed the shippers of other products as well. Certainly protest against railways was not in any sense exclusively agrarian, although it was made to seem so by the undue prominence achieved by the Grangers, a national organization of farmers, founded in 1867, which on achieving great political success during the early 1870s in a number of agricultural states, proceeded to install laws and administrative agencies that would regulate railways.

The sense that railways ought to be regulated was fed further by evidence that railway owners had been engaged in corruption. Most notorious and best documented of instances was the scandal which broke out in 1872 with accusations that the Credit Mobilier company, engaged in building the Union Pacific Railroad, had promoted friendly relations with congressmen by giving them gifts of its stock. This charge, well documented, echoed many others that were alleged if not proven. It was in any event likely that corruption had been taking place. During the 30 or 40 years when railways could get subsidies and exclusive privileges from governments, it must naturally have occurred to some promoters that the surest way to win against contending promoters was to exercise immediate influence on public officials. Just as communities wanting the railways to come their way offered monetary inducements to promoters, so promoters wanting to acquire charters and grants offered monetary inducements to legislators, not being overimpressed always by the fact that the second sort was unlawful. Worse, the activities of railways in trying to influence legislation in their favour, even when pursued by the perfectly lawful means of mustering public opinion and contributing to election funds of well-disposed candidates, came to be widely interpreted as an assault on democracy. The solution proposed by many was that the operations of railway executives should be brought under the steady supervision of government – though it is not clear why those who proposed this solution should have overlooked the possibility that as long as government agencies could heavily influence the fortune of railway companies, the owners and managers of the companies would have powerful incentives to influence the decisions of those agencies.

Another element in mustering public support for regulation was the deep and durable American aversion to monopolies, coupled with the widespread conviction that railways were monopolies. If railways were monopolies, then naturally they would be overcharging. Moreover, if they were monopolies, then it was quite proper that government should supervise them, despite the strong general objection to limiting the freedom of private enterprises.

But in fact the railway industry was much more complicated than the public imagined. Seen as a whole it looked like a textbook case of competition. Entry was fairly easy. Mileage and total investment roughly doubled in each decade from 1850 to 1890. By 1890, over 1,000 separate companies operated railways, and the number kept growing until it reached a peak of 1,500 in 1907. In the meanwhile, numbers of unsuccessful firms failed and otiose mileage was abandoned – as befit a competitive industry.

Competition prevailed also in the substantial sense that railways tried to lure each other's customers by offering bargain rates. Shippers, especially those located in railway hubs like Chicago, often had a choice among several routes to their destination. In such places competing railways were prepared to cut prices to the bone, a practice often sensible from their standpoint because filling a train, even at low rates, might be more profitable than running it partly empty; in the lexicon of journalists and of managers who disliked price competition, episodes of this sort figured as 'rate wars'. Moreover, shippers in many places had the further option to send goods by water – indeed about one-third of all domestic freight travelled by water in 1890 – and in those places as well railways were forced to offer attractive terms.

On the other hand, there certainly were monopolistic elements in the industry. Least important, though frequently alluded to, was the technical legal fact that each railway enjoyed by its charter of incorporation an exclusive right to operate its own tracks, although this was in effect little more than the normal right of private property. More important was the fact that along certain stretches of its line, almost any railway enjoyed a real economic monopoly, for want of any parallel railway nearby, competing waterway, or feasible road connections. Along such privileged stretches, railways could and did charge rates substantially higher than they could command for journeys between points served by competitors. It is therefore impossible to say that the industry as a whole was either competitive or monopolistic; the truth is that almost any railway could charge monopolistic rates for some traffic and was forced to charge competitive rates for other traffic.

Beyond this, there were railway men who wished to eliminate competition among themselves or at least to limit its rigours. Sometimes it was possible simply to buy up one's competitors. Often it was more practical to achieve non-competitive pricing by forming some sort of combination. One sort, frequent after 1870, 'pooled' the profits of all the railways serving a given area and distributed the profits to each member firm on some pre-arranged basis. Since the profits received by any member of a pool were thereby made independent of how much traffic it carried, members had little incentive to bid down prices; rate wars were averted; and these exercises in 'industrial statesmanship' improved the profitability of railways by denying shippers the advantages of competition. Many other forms of cartelization were devised, ranging from loose 'gentlemen's agreements' and 'communities of interest' to joint ownership by competing roads of feeder lines and other facilities.

What made combination feasible was that although there were many hundreds of separate companies, all belonging to what was, from various points of view, one single industry, only a few of them offered service between any two given points on the map. Unlike wheat farmers, each of whom grows a product more or less identical with that of the rest, a railway connecting Omaha with St Louis renders a service not practically substitutable for the service of a railway connecting Pittsburgh with Nashville; though both are railways, both cannot serve the same need. In short, from the standpoint of most customers the railway industry was not one industry but many industries, each serving a relatively small region.

What made combinations specially desirable for railways was their special susceptibility to cut-throat competition. This resulted from the fact that the industry suffered at various times and places from overcapacity; so do other industries, though railways more than many, because in laying a track from one place to another a company commits itself to a large capacity and cost, unlike, for instance, many sorts of manufacturing firms which can choose whether to start with a small plant or a large one. This 'lumpiness of investment' is, however, a characteristic of the track and other fixed installations rather than of the rolling-stock, for an operating company could easily guard against overcapacity by restricting its investment in locomotives and wagons. Indeed the whole problem of lumpiness would have been less intense but for a peculiarity of law. Had privately owned railway tracks been regarded as public thoroughfares, along which anyone was entitled to move his own trains on payment of a reasonable charge – as indeed was the case in the beginning, by analogy with privately owned toll-roads and canals – then railway operating companies would have had a somewhat easier time in adjusting capacity to demand. Here, as so often, a small legal arrangement had large economic consequences, unintended and unforeseen.

An industry, then, prone to cartelization, thought to be overcharging and at times known to be, whose members had enjoyed heavy subsidies and special privileges from governments which they sometimes influenced indelicately or even illegally, whose promoters and executives had in some instances enriched themselves illicitly at the expense of trustful small investors, and whose services were consumed directly or nearly directly by almost every citizen – was an industry which required, more than almost any other, to be controlled for the public benefit. Such was the view which many Americans had reached in 1870.

The bare notion that railways should be regulated was not in 1870 totally novel. Railway companies were corporations which with few exceptions owed their existence to charters issued by state governments. These charters conferred limited liability and perpetual life – then still regarded as special privileges – not to mention the very particular power to seize private land by exercise of eminent domain and unusual immunity from certain sorts of suit. In exchange for these gifts, the state typically imposed conditions in the charter, as for instance to the frequency of service which the company must provide and the maximum price it could charge. Besides, the common law in many states still included rules of early vintage imposing obligations on common carriers to provide reasonable rates. Such provisions in charters or in common law had to be enforced by suit, and although suits were brought and won, they do seem to have been infrequent: the damages recoverable in a case of overcharging would seldom repay the trouble and cost incurred by a private person going to court, and public prosecutors, tending in America then to be overworked, did not seem to regard such actions as their most useful contributions to law and order.

Regulation, as demanded in the 1870s, accordingly meant that the rules should be made more stern and precise and that they should be enforced vigorously, by officials and, as some urged, by experts specially charged to do this and nothing else.

Steady and sharp regulation of railways began with laws passed by several midwestern legislatures between 1870 and 1874. These were labelled Granger Laws on the supposition that they were initiated by the National Grange, a farmers' organization. Historians have emphasized recently, as is hardly surprising, that manufacturers, merchants, and shippers of all sorts pressed as eagerly as farmers for regulation. As the main complaint of shippers was that freight rates were too high, the main thing that the Granger Laws did was to set absolute limits on how much railways could charge. Railway companies, and the warehouse owners coupled with them in the Granger Laws, responded in the first place by challenging the constitutional validity of statutory price-fixing. A number of the resulting cases were decided by the Supreme Court in 1877. In the leading opinion, on *Munn* v. *Illinois*, Chief Justice Waite expressed the view that despite the rule in the Fourteenth Amendment that no state could deprive a person of property without due process of law, it was quite constitutional for a state government to regulate the prices of such private firms as were 'affected with a public interest'. Precedents on which he relied concerned, in large measure, transportation routes that had traditionally been regarded as 'public thoroughfares' or their appurtenances – navigable waterways, above all, and also ferries, wharfs, coaches, and inns. The Chicago grain elevators, the specific subjects of regulation in the Munn case, were owned by private companies which certainly served the public; but the chief justice was unable to distinguish sharply between the way they served the public and the way any producer whatever served the public to whom he sold his product. Yet it was unthinkable, at that time, that American governments enjoyed any constitutional power to regulate the prices of all commodities and services: the farmers, who insisted that railway prices be restrained, would have rebelled had legislatures sought to restrain the price of wheat. The Supreme Court was therefore obliged to rest its decision on a novel and quite shadowy category: 'business affected with the public interest and consequently subject to regulation'.

During the 1870s and 1880s, as more states moved into regulation of railways, various inconveniences became apparent. The efforts of one state to regulate the conditions of traffic originating in or passing through its jurisdiction could not fail to collide with the efforts of adjoining states to impose different regulations on that same traffic. If, for example, one state prohibited the carrying of explosives through its territory while the adjoining state permitted it, which rule was to dominate a railway whose line crossed both states? In view of this, congress began to consider at least as early as 1874 how it should use its plenary power to regulate interstate commerce. For years it could do nothing because a deadlock developed between two opposed views. One group believed that a federal statute should prohibit railways from charging 'unreasonable' rates or engaging in 'unreasonable' practices, leaving it for federal courts to determine whether any contested terms of service were reasonable or not and to devise an appropriate remedy – a procedure which would have forced interstate railways to comply with general rules of common law, rules which in the absence of declaratory legislation were not part of the corpus of *federal* law. The opposing group in congress, believing that because this procedure, depending on the initiative of private litigants, would leave many injuries uncorrected, proposed that railways be regulated positively and continuously by an administrative commission.

This deadlock was finally broken in 1887. The immediate impetus to settle seems to have been a decision handed down by the Supreme Court in 1886. The Wabash Railway case arose from an order issued by the government of Illinois requiring the railway to stop charging more for shipping goods from Gilman, Illinois, to New York than from Peoria,

Illinois, to New York, even though the trip from Gilman was almost 100 miles shorter. In economic terms the railway could try to justify this differential (of a sort regularly condemned at this time as 'long-haul–short-haul discrimination') on grounds that while it charged a reasonable rate for shipping from Gilman it was forced to offer an unreasonably low rate to Peoria shippers in order to meet competition from other railways and waterway-carriers serving Peoria – an explanation which would not satisfy short-haul shippers, who felt that distance ought largely or solely to dictate the relative prices of transportation. But the main thrust of the railway's attack was that, in presuming to set rates for services to New York, the state of Illinois was overstepping the boundary of its power to regulate commerce within the state. This argument prevailed on the Supreme Court, who by invalidating the action of Illinois emphasized that if interstate traffic were to be regulated, the federal government alone could do it.

Within a few months Congress passed the Interstate Commerce Act, by the simple stratagem of conflating in it the two radically opposed views. The act therefore specifically prohibited any unjust or unreasonable charge, any undue or unreasonable discrimination in rates, any discrimination between long hauls and short hauls, any pooling of earnings, and the charging of any rates other than those stated on published schedules. At the same time it established the Interstate Commerce Commission, which it endowed with executive power to enforce these provisions as well as with quasi-judicial power to interpret them in specific cases. These powers were reinforced later, especially by the Hepburn Act of 1906 and the Mann–Elkins Act of 1910, so as to give the commission positive power to set railway rates on its own initiative instead of merely approving or disapproving those proposed by railways.

Although the detailed effects of the Interstate Commerce Commission on railways between 1887 and 1916 are not easy to identify, it is clear that the commission did little to resolve the uneasy tension between competition and monopoly in the industry as a whole. To be sure, the Interstate Commerce Act prohibited profit-sharing pools. Railways accommodated by turning to freight associations, price-fixing cartels against which the act said nothing. However, the Supreme Court held during the 1890s that freight associations violated the Sherman Anti-trust Act, despite the view of some judges in lower federal courts that, as the freight associations were combinations to prevent 'unhealthy competition' only, they were therefore both lawful and meritorious. Following the Supreme Court's decisions in the Trans-Missouri Freight Association and Joint Traffic Association cases (1897–8), railways turned to yet another method of rationalizing the industry in accordance with their own ends.

This was consolidation, a single name for two things with very different economic consequences. One was a manoeuvre to bring together independent railways whose tracks joined at a common terminus, so that, for instance, separate links joining Boston to New York and New York to Philadelphia would be welded into a single through-line connecting Boston with Philadelphia. Since the links in such end-to-end consolidations could never have competed with each other, and since linking them would eliminate the costs of transferring goods at their common terminal as well as of maintaining duplicate facilities there, the railways and their customers alike stood to benefit. The other kind of consolidation meant unifying under a single management two or more railways offering competing services between two termini, say Chicago and New York. In this case, the single owner would have every incentive to eliminate competition among his several lines; in this case the railways' gains would be matched more or less by shippers' losses. Such are the two polar cases of consolidation. In fact, the networks of each of the larger railways were sufficiently complex so that even a consolidation whose main effect was end-to-end would inevitably also cartelize previously competing feeder lines. In short, consolidation, which had been going on ever since 1870, and which intensified after pools and associations were outlawed, generally implied a decrease in competition and increase in cartelization.

But it soon turned out that consolidation was not entirely safe either. In the first place, certain states had begun to prohibit any outright and visible move of this sort. A Minnesota law, for instance, declared that 'no railroad corporation shall consolidate with, lease or purchase, or in any way become owner of, or control any other railroad corporation, or any stock, franchise, or rights of property thereof, which owns or controls a competing railroad'; on the strength of which the courts in 1896 invalidated an agreement between the Northern Pacific and the Great Northern Railroads, holding that the latter, being incorporated in Minnesota, was subject to its laws. Presently the Northern Pacific and Great Northern collaborated in buying the Burlington Road so as to connect their terminals in Minnesota with Chicago and other principal centres in the Mississippi Valley.

To pacify the great many-sided battle which resulted, J. P. Morgan set up a holding company to buy the whole capital stock of the Northern Pacific and Great Northern. This holding company, the Northern Securities Company, specifically authorized by the laws of New Jersey, was believed by Morgan's lawyers to offend against neither the Interstate Commerce Act nor the Sherman Anti-trust Act. In 1904, nevertheless, the Supreme Court ruled that such a consolidation did violate the Sherman Act. The avenue to consolidation was blocked still further by a section of the Clayton Anti-trust Act (1914) prohibiting all corporate mergers whose effect would be to lessen competition. So stood the legal circumstances of railways at the outset of the First World War. Those who had interpreted relations between railways and their customers as a running battle could now draw pleasure from the thought that 'the public' had won a conclusive victory over those 'malefactors of great wealth'.

But the economic effects of federal regulation down to 1916 did not justify that assessment. Some shippers, to be sure, benefited when discriminatory rates were evened out and rebates suppressed; but other shippers, who had enjoyed cheaper rates, warranted in many instances by their particular economic circumstances, were penalized when those rates were raised in the name of equity; and as for the railways, it is uncertain whether their earnings were lowered or raised by these effects of regulation. Again, between 1910 and 1915, when the Interstate Commerce Commission repeatedly refused the railways' applications for general increases in rates, all shippers benefited, at least for the time being. As a result of the commission's action, the overall level of rates was no higher in 1915 than it had been in 1906, even though the general price level had risen by 10 per cent or more. As a further result, the profits of railways were low and declining between 1908 and 1915, and – so it has been forcefully argued – railways responded by investing far less than would have been needed to keep capacity growing at the same pace as demand. If this analysis is correct, then the upshot of the commission's determination to benefit shippers by keeping rates down was to impose on these beneficiaries a longer-term shortage of railway services.

During the First World War, American production increased dramatically, first to supply goods no longer being produced by the belligerents (by 1916 the quantity of American exports stood some 60 per cent above the level of 1913), and later to supply the American armed forces as well as the domestic demand stoked by wartime boom. By 1916 railways were carrying tonnages about one-third greater than in 1913; the strain showed in shortages of goods wagons and in congestion, especially at eastern rail termini. These difficulties many people attributed to the atomistic, uncoordinated structure of the railway industry – rather than to the after-effects of rate regulation. So, shortly after American entry to the war in April 1917, a member of the Council of National Defense, the official mobilizing authority, urged on railway executives 'the necessity of tying together all of the railroads within one unit and making a single operating system of the 250,000 [miles]'. In response, the managers set up the Railroads' War Board, in which they vested authority to control and coordinate all railway corporations, an authority which however the board was not always able to exercise in practice. The Interstate Commerce Commission strongly endorsed this arrangement – even though it might be thought to be the greatest pool ever, and therefore contrary to the Interstate Commerce Act. The Attorney General certainly thought as much, for he kept warning that war or no war the board and the industry were probably violating the anti-trust laws; but Senator Francis G. Newlands, an expert on railways, said, 'We are somewhat shattering our old views regarding antitrust laws . . . I believe that we will enter upon an evolutional condition of mind that will make a great many beneficial changes in our economic systems.'

In the meanwhile, though railways were moving more freight than ever before, they were unable to meet the demand. In the autumn of 1917, for want of transport, mines were closing down, steel mills were curtailing output, and the harvest lay stranded on farms. Under pressure from public officials to expand their services faster, railway executives argued that they could do it if congress would exempt them from the anti-trust laws, make it possible for them to incorporate under federal laws so as to avoid regulation by the states – the 'forty-eight monsters' in their vocabulary – and if the Interstate Commerce Commission would allow them a large increase in rates. But, they added, if these aids were not forthcoming, and as they were unable to borrow or sell stock in the open market, the only way they could raise capital for expansion was to get it from the government. In December 1917, after long hearings, the Interstate Commerce Commission refused a rate increase, and reported to Congress that the entire network ought to be unified, under private control if the anti-trust laws were amended to permit it, or under direct public control. At the close of the year, using powers conferred by the Army Appropriations Act of 1916 and later expanded by the Federal Control Act, the president put railways in the charge of a federal agency, the United States Railroad Administration. Naturally enough, almost inescapably, the Railroad Administration was staffed by experienced railway executives, so that while some regarded federal operation of railways as a 'mild revolution', others interpreted it as a mere temporary donning of federal garb by men who had run the industry before and would run it again.

It had been stipulated from the beginning that the railways would revert to control by their owners after the war ended. When the time came, a few officials, publicists, and especially union leaders proposed that operation by a public authority be continued, perhaps indefinitely, mainly because they believed that operation by a single management would make the system work more efficiently than it could under many separate managements. But the great majority of officials and interested persons, including shippers, wanted to return to private control supervised by a federal commission. Accordingly the railways were returned to their owners in 1920. The pre-war regulatory regime was restored as well, in broad outline, but changed in certain interesting particulars by the Transportation Act of 1920. All the changes have a common character: the Interstate Commerce Commission was given additional powers, so that it could reduce 'wasteful competition' and promote the 'scientific efficiency' and 'rationalization of industry' of which many Americans became enamoured during the war.

Accordingly the commission was instructed to draw up a masterplan for consolidating railways, which was intended to make the whole system neater and trimmer, while drawing on the strong companies to shore up the weak ones; thereafter consolidations proposed by railways would be approved only if they accorded with the plan. As a corollary, railways were authorized to join in pools once again, if in the commission's view these did not 'unduly restrain competition'. In addition to its former rate-making powers, the commission could now set minimum rates, evidently to stop 'undesirable' competition. And finally the commission was given powers to control the industry's overall capacity. In short, the whole thrust of the act was to promote a gradual move away from competition, in the name of competition.

Charged with the duty of drawing up a masterplan for consolidation, the commission mapped out a tentative scheme, which it published in 1921 and about which it held extensive hearings during 1922 and 1923. But misgivings set in, and in 1925 the commission asked Congress to be relieved of the task, apparently believing that no such plan would have any practical effect. As Congress failed to act, the commission did finally report a plan in 1929, which instantly provoked torrents of objections from railway companies. With the onset of the depression, any thought of major consolidation along the lines of the scheme evaporated.

As railway companies failed or approached failure, the commission approved applications to sell their property or to merge with other railways. By the end of 1936, nearly 500 such applications had been granted, which affected one-fifth or more of total mileage; but many of these were *ad hoc* alliances not conforming to the commission's great plan of consolidation. To be sure, the number of separate companies was dwindling, but so was the railway system as a whole. Its capacity and output fell off between 1929 and 1939; the depression played some part in this no doubt, but the railways' new competitors, road haulage companies and intercity buslines, grew steadily throughout the depression.

For the ailing railway industry, as for all others, the managers of the New Deal felt compelled to prescribe immediate treatment. But their Emergency Railroad Transportation Act (1933) had more ritual to it than substance. It closed a loophole when it included railway holding companies among firms subject to the commission; it created a temporary office, the Coordinator of Transportation, whose functions were advisory. In fact the Coordinator proposed moves in the direction of enforced consolidation, while recognizing that any substantial step in that direction created an additional threat of monopoly. His suggestions were not acted on.

In 1939 the railway industry presented as complicated and puzzling a picture as ever before. It is remarkable that not until the 1960s did many disinterested experts begin seriously to consider the possibility that the railways and surface transport generally might function better, from everyone's standpoint, if regulation were drastically reduced or virtually abolished – and the corollary that the long-term decline of railways was hastened because regulators aimed to satisfy criteria other than general economic efficiency.

D. LABOUR LAW

In the course of industrialization, an increasing number of Americans became employees, and though little disposed to regard themselves as members of a peculiar class, even less a permanently oppressed class, some came to believe that they could improve their situation by joining labour unions. They aimed in this way to improve pay and conditions of work by collective bargaining, enforced by strike and boycott. More, they expected labour unions to press for legislation favourable to their interests. Like many other particular groups – farmers, manufacturers, railway owners, shippers – they believed it to be both possible and fitting to have the laws cater to their own advantage.

One large part of policy-making in the field of industrial relations bore on the desire of labour unions for a stable footing guaranteed by law.

When unions first began to be noticed on the American scene at the beginning of the nineteenth century, their legal status was confused and precarious. At common law, which continued largely to govern the field during the nineteenth century, a union was as free to exist as any other private association formed for innocent purposes, free though enjoying no privileges or special immunities. But insofar as the members of a union agreed to concert their action when dealing with an employer, agreed not to work for an employer who hired anyone but a member of the union, or not to buy goods from a recalcitrant employer, they might well offend the common-law rule against combinations in restraint of trade and might be sued for damages; if in the course of a dispute they did anything violent, they might find themselves accused of criminal conspiracy.

These legal risks were materially abated when, in 1842, the authoritative chief justice of Massachusetts handed down his opinion in the case of

Commonwealth v. *Hunt*. He held that a labour union was not in itself illegal, nor were its activities to secure objectives such as a closed shop, provided always that those activities were conducted peaceably.

In view of this powerful precedent and the rapid growth of manufacturing, unions increased considerably in number, began to form local councils and eventually national associations. In addition to their direct efforts to improve wages and other conditions of work by bargaining with employers, they began also to press for favourable legislation. From time to time they succeeded in procuring statutes concerning hours and conditions of work, but they quite failed to achieve a firm legal foundation for their existence, for their ultimate tactics of strikes and boycotts, and for their claimed role as authorized bargaining agents. Thus the American Federation of Labor, founded in 1886, emphasized in its legislative programmes that the conspiracy laws must be repealed (rather than slowly ameliorated by case law), that unions must be afforded official recognition, perhaps by formal incorporation, that they must be granted explicit rights to bargain on behalf of their members (an empty right, they said, unless reinforced by a legal duty of employers to bargain with unions), and that the right to strike must be confirmed by law.

Legislation was forthcoming, indeed towards the end of the century the states were passing more laws about labour than about any other subject with the exception of liquor. Many of these, regulating the conditions of work and methods of pay, were what unions wanted. Some, from the standpoint of unions, were mixed blessings – particularly the laws passed by industrialized states after 1878 to establish procedures for collective bargaining and compulsory arbitration, which latter solution unions totally rejected. And still other results of legislation the unions regarded as entirely inimical. Chief among these was an upshot of the Interstate Commerce Act (1887) and Sherman Anti-trust Law (1890): on the grounds that certain strikes and boycotts interfered with the courts' guardianship over railways in receivership or illegally interfered with interstate commerce, the courts began to issue injunctions to stop strikes and boycotts.

Labour injunctions, the greatest legal obstacle to union activity, seemed for a moment to be outlawed – at least as to federal courts – by the Clayton Anti-trust Act (1914). After declaring that the existence of unions and the pursuit of their aims by peaceable action were entirely compatible with the objectives of anti-trust law, the act prohibited federal courts from issuing injunctions in labour disputes affecting interstate commerce, except where such injunctions were essential 'to prevent irreparable injury to property . . . for which injury there is no adequate remedy at law'. Samuel Gompers, president of the American Federation of Labor, greeted these provisions as the 'Magna Carta of labor', but it soon turned out that the exception as to irreparable damage (which merely restated the previous common-law rule) allowed for renewed and intensive use of injunctions to stop strikes – unchecked until the Norris–La Guardia Act was adopted in 1932.

Some further steps towards institutionalizing collective bargaining were taken during the First World War. Various federal agencies established to prevent interruption of the war effort – the US Commission on Industrial Relations, the War Labor Conference Board, and the War Labor Board – proposed one way and another that the rights to join unions and of unions to bargain collectively be affirmed and enforced by federal law. But the return of peace, prosperity and Republican majorities abruptly halted these stirrings.

Victory, though not precisely the victory desired, was achieved by legislation of the New Deal. First, because the unions agreed to support the industry codes of fair competition authorized by the National Industrial Recovery Act (1933), the act gave them a lavish quid pro quo: employers, when drawing up a code, must include a guarantee that they would honour the employee's right to join a union of his choice and that they would recognize it as his bargaining agent. This provision proved less fruitful in practice than it promised on paper, because many large firms took to bargaining not with 'normal' national unions but with independent 'company' unions, so that by 1935 about two of every five unionists belonged to a company union. In any event, the little remaining hope that regular unions might benefit from the Recovery Act ended when the Supreme Court annulled it in 1935.

Congress immediately provided a more than satisfactory substitute in the National Labor Relations Act or 'Wagner Act' (1935), which reasserted the rights of organization and collective bargaining. It went far toward destroying company unions by declaring it improper for any employer to 'dominate or interfere with the formation or administration of any labor organization or contribute financial or other support to it'. Above all it created the National Labor Relations Board to serve as a rule-maker and referee for collective bargaining agreements. Soon the act survived a test of its constitutionality and was complemented by 'little Wagner Acts' passed by various states. After over a century of living uneasily within the law but without express warrant of law – a condition, it should be noted, not peculiar to themselves but shared by many other private associations including the political parties – unions finally reached the haven of official legitimacy.

But in an important sense, the efforts of unions to win objectives by enlisting the coercive powers of government had begun to succeed much earlier.

One of their particular goals after the Civil War was the eight-hour day. What they meant by the eight-hour day was not what it has come to mean since, that any work beyond eight hours must be paid for at higher overtime rates, but that the working day should be absolutely limited to eight hours by laws carrying criminal penalties. Obviously employees who in 1867 averaged 65 hours per week would welcome the leisure of 48, and they believed somehow that when the law reduced their daily hours, employers would be unable to reduce their daily wage; there was an idea besides that a shorter day for all would eliminate unemployment for some. In any event, several state governments did enact eight-hour laws in 1867, which however had little effect. In 1868, congress followed suit regarding certain workers employed by the federal government. Little by little, as the membership of unions grew and as, especially after the foundation of the American Federation of Labor, most unions shed any suggestion of anarchist or socialist leaning, they were able to prevail on governments of the states to adopt more of these laws. A well-known instance was a statute passed by Utah in 1896, which restricted work in mines and smelting-works to eight hours per day.

That statute is well known because it gave rise to the case of *Holden* v. *Hardy* (1898), the point from which the Supreme Court embarked on a 40-year trek through a thicket of constitutional law. The difficulty was to make out just how the Fourteenth Amendment bore on maximum-hours laws. Central to the Amendment is a clause proscribing any action whereby a state deprives a person of 'life, liberty, or property, without due process of law'. It might seem that any labour law, duly passed by a duly elected government, would satisfy the due-process test, even though it did deprive persons of liberty or property. It might seem, equally, that a law depriving competent persons of the liberty of making voluntary contracts to work as hard as they chose could not be a law conforming to 'due process' but must be the opposite, 'an arbitrary, capricious, or discriminatory' law. In trying to resolve this dilemma, the court therefore kept inquiring between 1898 and 1937 whether labour laws coming before it were reasonably adapted to serve objectives within the constitutional powers of the states.

In *Holden* v. *Hardy* the court held that the legislature of Utah had restricted hours of work in mines and smelters quite reasonably, having satisfied itself that long hours spent in such places would injure the worker's health. In support of its view, the court pointed out that the laws limiting the hours of work of women and children had previously been sustained as constitutional, presumably also on the grounds that they guarded the health of employees. And it carefully circumscribed its decision by suggesting that a law to limit the hours of work of all employees – whether male or female, adult or child, employed in safe and healthful work or otherwise – might exceed the limits on reasonable deprivation of liberty.

A result far less encouraging to unions emerged in the case of *Lochner* v. *New York* (1905), which arose from a statute limiting the hours of bakery workers to ten a day. Here the majority of the Supreme Court, while following the precedent of *Holden* v. *Hardy*, invalidated the act as unreasonable, and thus contrary to due process, because baking (unlike mining and smelting) was not a particularly dangerous or unhealthful occupation. Underlying the decision were two principles: one accepted by all judges at the time, that a state government had undoubted constitutional power to regulate private activities insofar as might be necessary to ensure public safety, health, and order; the other accepted by a majority, that state governments lacked constitutional power to interfere with voluntary contracts between competent adult males. Their decision thus pivoted on whether the act should be construed as labour legislation or health legislation; if the former, it could not be constitutional, if the latter, it could not be constitutional unless there was a clearly demonstrable and unusual hazard to health. While explicitly invalidating the act for want of sufficient justification on grounds of health, the majority delicately suggested that they might have invalidated it as a labour law, for so the New York legislature had labelled it, not least because they passed it on persistent urging of the New York bakers' union.

Interpretations of the Lochner decision then and since have been unduly influenced by a caustic quip in Justice Oliver Wendell Holmes' dissenting opinion. He said in effect that the majority of the court were guided not by the Fourteenth Amendment but by the *Social Statics* of Herbert Spencer. It was an undeserved rebuke. They acknowledged, as Holmes did and the court always had, the state's authority to protect any of its citizens who could not look after themselves; but they held that as to persons of adequate intelligence and ability the state's proper function is to serve as umpire, a responsibility betrayed if it uses its power to better the lot of some citizens to the detriment of others. Hence the majority's objection to comprehensive hours legislation, which unions wanted precisely in order to benefit workers at the expense (as they imagined) of employers. In contrast, Holmes' view, shared by many and by more as time went on, was that a democratically elected legislature does not exceed its constitutional power when it prefers the interests of one group of citizens to those of another, even though this preference result in a deliberate redistribution of income.

Given the Holden and Lochner decisions, it seemed evident that laws to limit hours stood the best chance of surviving if they applied to natural wards of the state, women, children, and the like. By 1908 at least 20 states had passed such laws, and the constitutionality of some had been upheld by state courts. The first to be tested by the Supreme Court was unanimously upheld in *Muller* v. *Oregon* (1908), the court taking notice of 'a widespread belief' that women are physically weaker than men, therefore 'needing especial care'.

Encouraged by their success, partial at least, in bringing law to their aid in the matter of hours, unions began early in the twentieth century to press for statutes to establish minimum wages. Massachusetts was the first state to respond favourably with a law in 1912 setting minimum wages for women and children. Several other states followed. And in 1918 Congress, acting in its capacity as municipal legislature of the District of Columbia, established a wage board with power to fix rates of pay for women and children. But this act the Supreme Court invalidated in *Adkins* v. *Children's Hospital* (1923), largely on the grounds that though maximum hours might, at least in some instances, be reasonably related to government's proper jurisdiction over health, minimum wages are not. Despite this setback, many states passed minimum wage laws, usually for women and children, especially after the great depression set in. And when next the issue came before the Supreme Court, in *West Coast Hotel* v. *Parrish* (1937), a majority of the justices upheld the statute in a manner which obliterated the older constraint on the states' powers by adding to the former categories of health, safety, good order, and morals, the portmanteau term 'welfare'.

All previous efforts were crowned in 1938 when Congress passed the Fair Labor Standards Act, which set minimum wages and maximum hours for most persons employed in 'interstate commerce', a term which had steadily been broadened by judicial interpretation until by 1938 it included a large part of all economic activity in the nation.

In the field of labour law, as in most branches of economic policy, what happened during the New Deal years was anything but a revolutionary transformation. Rather, tendencies which had been making themselves visible during fifty years or more were officially confirmed, tidied up in expansive pieces of federal legislation, and given special emphasis by pomposity of phrasing. Moreover, what was done about labour in the course of the New Deal years was in no sense final. That legal status which the Wagner Act gave to unions was, so unions have maintained, severely undermined by the Taft–Hartley Act in 1947. That guarantee of minimum wages given by the Fair Labor Standards Act was not a guarantee that jobs would be available at the minimum wage, and American government began to assume responsibility for assuring jobs to all only with the passage of the Employment Act in 1946.

E. SOCIAL POLICY

The limits of social policy are vague and as difficult to define as those of welfare. Its ambit presumably coincides with social services and raises the same questions of definition. Are these regarded as social because they pertain to the whole of society? But then all public policy would be social. Are these regarded as social because they are services rendered by governments and by private philanthropies rather than by business firms? 'Social' would seem then to be no more than an inflated synonym for 'non-profit'. Be this as it may, we may assume a loose consensus that when people speak of social policy they mean to refer to poor relief, pensions, unemployment insurance, health services, housing, sanitation, and also perhaps the services rendered by policemen, firemen, city planners, and the like.

In America, until 1939, social services were rendered mostly by families, friends, religious congregations, and specialized private organizations, of which Hull House, founded in Chicago in 1889, is a particularly famous example, celebrated beyond its significance among the multitude of similar activities. So far as such services were rendered by governments, a tendency that increased steadily after the Civil War, it was local governments that did the work. Not only were social services administered by cities, towns, counties, states, and the vast array of special districts that filled the crowded scene of American local government, but each largely determined its own policies.

Sometimes state governments superintended these activities of local governments, and sometimes subsidized them. This too made for a wide variety of solutions, with those of states like Massachusetts, Wisconsin, and Oregon occupying an end of the spectrum quite distant from those of Mississippi, Arkansas, and Oklahoma. The federal government, on the other hand, exercised virtually no control over the social policies of local authorities before 1939, only exceptionally subsidized the social services furnished by state and local governments, and furnished little or none itself; indeed there was general agreement before the great depression that the federal government was without constitutional power to enter these fields except slightly or circuitously.

American cities and towns owe their distinctive character to the fact that they did not evolve from a coordinating conception imposed by prince or lord or bishop. Palaces, castles, cathedrals did not define their centres, nor did walls form their outer contours. Rather they owed their shapes, so protean that one might better say shapelessness, to the uncoordinated, uninhibited efforts of their inhabitants. This accounts for the ugliness of many and also for their striking productivity as economic engines. In time purely private development was to some degree regulated by urban governments using devices such as zoning regulations, official maps, building codes, and overall city planning. But even then, because federalism excluded the central government from regulating the internal life of cities, and because state governments, though constitutionally empowered to regulate cities, shared a general conviction that they ought not to exercise this power in detail, American cities grew in a largely uncoordinated way. To put it briefly and bluntly, the United States until 1939 had no urban policy. More precisely, the life of American cities depended on the private activities of citizens and, in far smaller degree on their communal decisions, all of which differed widely from city to city.

American cities, at the outset, were founded and built up mainly by uncoordinated efforts of private persons. Occasionally a private entrepreneur deliberately laid out an urban development that successfully realized his intentions. More frequently, a projector publicized a dream that attracted no one; such was William Gilpin's scheme, in the 1850s, for an ideal city to be called Centropolis. Most often a city grew from the seeds of a settlement started by a few small men who set up shop at a likely place, built houses, sold land to newcomers, and saw other settlers arriving until, in due course, a city formed itself around them. In such a growth, no design was imposed. Streets were laid out as builders and home owners saw fit; a natural desire of each new inhabitant to be linked to the life of the place guaranteed that streets would make up some sort of pattern. Policing was provided by volunteer watches or by a sheriff and posse or by each man for himself. Fire protection was provided by volunteer companies which often doubled as dining clubs. Public transportation within the city was provided by competing private wagoners. Water supply, when not seen to separately by each householder, was the domain of street-merchants and small companies. Sewage and rubbish disposal was arranged by individuals for themselves or by commercial scavengers. Almost all of what are now thought of as essential public services were provided by each family, or by profit-making businesses, or by voluntary associations. And not only did this condition prevail in frontier settlements and small towns, but also more or less in the cities with over 100,000 inhabitants, of which by 1870 America had 14.

Sporadically after 1865 parts of this great mass of private activity came under regulation by local and state governments. In 1867 and 1879 the city of New York passed ordinances to impose minimum standards on tenement houses, such as that each room in the house must have a window. By 1880 Chicago had promulgated a general building code. As intra-urban transportation began to shift from coaches and horse-drawn trolleys to elevated or underground railways, which involved massive investment, private undertakers of such projects guarded their investments by applying for exclusive franchises. Licences, granted for as long as 50 or even 999 years to private utility companies of all varieties, coupled the award of a valuable monopoly with requirements supposed to assure good service at reasonable prices. But since statutory limitations could not easily be adjusted to changing circumstances, and were held by many, rightly or wrongly, to enable the companies to reap exorbitant profits, they were reinforced by agencies with discretionary powers of regulation. During the last quarter of the nineteenth century a few larger cities established special regulatory commissions, like the Rapid Transit Commission of New York City. The great surge in this direction came however about 1910, when some 15 states established public service commissions to regulate all public utility companies within their cities and towns.

During the same period, the more substantial cities began to municipalize certain services. Street-cleaning in New York City was handed over to uniformed public servants in the 1890s, and governments began to play a direct part in rubbish disposal, though most cities continued to have their streets cleaned by private contractors. In 1865 only eight cities maintained professional police forces; by the end of the century uniformed police and fire departments were commonplace among the larger cities. A movement for municipalization resulted in the establishment of many public water works and gas and electric plants and a few municipal transport ventures, though as proposals for forced municipalization of existing private ventures often met overwhelming opposition, public organizations usually filled gaps where private enterprise had not entered the field.

City governments often proved incapable of carrying out these new regulatory and service functions, because of the play of competing pressures from voters, or corruption, or want of constitutional power. This last arose because municipal governments, being then merely agents of a sovereign state, meant the state legislature was competent to rule cities by statute; and citizens dissatisfied for whatever reason with the conduct of local governments turned for relief to state legislatures. Beginning with Illinois in 1870, a few states adopted 'home-rule' amendments to their constitutions, which allocated to some cities greater if not full powers of self-government; but though such provisions were somewhat extended down to 1939, cities remained subject to the ultimate power of their states. The notorious corruptibility of municipal officials was met, with only qualified success, by measures to appoint officials by competitive examination, to establish independent fiscal control, to strengthen the powers of the mayor against the council, to install professional city-managers as chief executives, and to take politics out of city government by requiring elections to be non-partisan. Nevertheless, even though the purifying ambitions of reformers could not be achieved perfectly, the power and ability of city governments to regulate the housekeeping of cities increased during the early twentieth century, partly through improvement of their own machinery and personnel and partly thanks to supervisory control exercised by state governments, which were often more impartial, honest, and enlightened than city governments.

Increase of public control over civic life is vividly illustrated by the burst of regulations after 1900 concerning the uses of urban land. The method characteristically American is 'zoning': an official body draws a map dividing a city into pieces, usually quite small, each of which is thereafter confined to specified uses, such as commercial, industrial, single-family houses, apartment houses, or various detailed mixtures; on being adopted by the local council, the map becomes law. Fragmentary experiments in this direction were made by various local governments from 1900 onwards; the first comprehensive zoning ordinance was adopted in 1916 by New York City. A year later, 20 other municipalities were moving toward zoning laws; by 1922 it was reported that 'zoning has taken the country by storm', and by 1925 nineteen of the states had adopted enabling acts authorizing cities to proceed. This push was somewhat restrained by fear that zoning might be held to be an unconstitutional invasion of private rights without due process, but that obstacle was removed when the Supreme Court ruled to the contrary in *Euclid* v. *Ambler Realty Co.* (1926). Thereafter, zoning rapidly became standard practice and was moreover broadened into general city planning.

Private enterprise in housing markets was restricted, as to site, by zoning ordinances; as to format, by city planning; as to quality, by municipal building codes (often pressed for, in their own interest, by unions in the building trades); and for all these reasons housing was rather more expensive than it need have been. None of these regulations implied that governments should build housing on their own account. The first steps in that direction were taken as emergency measures during the great depression. By way of contributing to economic recovery, the federal government first adopted a policy, embodied in the National Housing Act of 1933, of offering easier credit to private builders; given the state of the housing market at the time, this scheme had a minute effect. The federal Public Works Administration then proceeded to build and operate some 50 federal housing projects in cities across the country. Further, the Federal Housing Act (1937) authorized federal loans to public housing authorities to be created by cities, subject to approval by state governments, for projects to be built, owned and managed by local public housing authorities in accordance with federal guidelines. By the end of 1939, public housing made up less than one in a thousand of the country's housing stock. Though public housing has grown in significance since then, it still is a small exception in a predominantly private market, an exception fairly tightly restricted to persons with low incomes.

It would be mistaken, however, to conclude that these shifts after 1900 towards public control over and direct public provision of certain services seriously reduced the diversity of objectives and methods which had traditionally typified American social policies. Evidence to the contrary is afforded by the American educational system.

State schools (public schools, as they are called in America) have always been operated by autonomous local school boards, whose members are elected by residents of the district. Even in 1939, after some consolidation had taken place, elementary and secondary schooling was still provided by over 100,000 independent authorities, entertaining different ideas about content, style, and standards. Pervading this diversity was a common view that education should be universal, free, and compulsory. Yet that view was not taken to imply that every child must attend a public school; even in 1939 about one in ten was enrolled in a private school.

In any event, the policy that every child should be required to attend school – because of the view that a republican form of government is rooted in an educated citizenry and that every child, however poor its parents, should be taught how to earn its own living – was not understood at first to imply free education, that is, education financed wholly by taxes. Indeed during the first half of the nineteenth century public (state) schools were financed partly by taxes (state as well as local, and sometimes augmented by gifts of land from the federal government), and partly by fees charged to parents. Under this dispensation, about 90 per cent of children between 5 and 16 years old attended school in New York State in 1820, and, it would seem, in other north-eastern states before the middle of the century. Thereafter pressure developed to do away with school fees, for a variety of reasons including dissatisfaction among teachers about delays in payment. Probably the most persuasive reason was that some parents could not afford fees, an unquestionable fact from which reformers drew the illogical conclusion that no parents should pay fees. So it came about that by the end of the century public schools were financed exclusively by tax revenues. In 1939, about 70 per cent of the cost of public schools was met by local governments (and this accounted for almost one-third of their total expenditures), about 30 per cent by state governments, and less than 2 per cent by the federal government.

In the field of higher education, however, the older pattern persisted.

Until the Civil War, most higher education was provided by private foundations, though 17 state governments had set up universities financed in part by taxes. After the Civil War, many more state colleges and universities were created, partly under stimulus supplied by the federal government, by grants of land from the public domain, especially under the Morrill Act (1862), and later by conditional grants of money. Such federal aid carried with it no assertion of federal power over the universities; on the other hand, the federal government specifically earmarked its grants for research and teaching in agriculture and industry, for practical rather than liberal arts, aimed in short at economic growth. Despite all this, American universities were in 1939 still largely private: taxes covered little over one-third of their costs, and the federal government paid only about 5 per cent, the large bulk being met by students' fees and by private gifts and endowments.

In short, though the educational system of the United States was by 1939 rather more centralized than it had once been, it still remained a bastion of local autonomy and, in its upper reaches, of voluntary private undertaking.

The single area of social policy most deeply altered during the 1930s was old age insurance and unemployment insurance. Previously these had chiefly been provided privately, by individual savings during times of plenty, by the support that extended families gave as a matter of course to unemployed members, by commercial insurance which paid annuities to the elderly, by a host of colourful fraternal orders such as the Eagles, Elks, and Shriners, by a plethora of private philanthropies, by firms which operated pension schemes for employees, and only in slight degree by local and state governments. All of these sources, of course, came under increasing strain as the depression continued and deepened. Even before, various reformers had been urging that the United States should imitate various European schemes for public aid to the unemployed and unemployable.

In 1934 President Roosevelt announced his intention to introduce a comprehensive scheme of social insurance. Eighteen months of drafting by the administration and consideration by congress produced the Social Security Act of 1935. In its main features it reflected the traditional ethos underlying American economic policy all along. Its insurance schemes were financed largely by contributions levied on the prospective beneficiaries and on their employers, and were thus chiefly organized on a self-supporting basis; they differed little from commercial insurance other than in being uniform and compulsory. As to its unemployment insurance scheme, the act left each state to decide for itself whether it would or would not participate, while offering certain fiscal inducements to participate, and left each state to devise its own detailed scheme, subject to broad rules laid down in the act. What the Social Security Act did, therefore, was to shift the basic part, a relatively small part, of income insurance further into the public sector and into the federal domain, though in a manner most congenial to persistent principles of American economic policy. To herald a change of this degree and character, even when associated with other similar changes, as the beginning of a welfare state is to indulge in melodrama.

III. *Conclusion*

Any account of policy, which is an altogether practical effort to achieve some sort of result, must be unsatisfactory if it fails to assess the success or failure of that policy. Yet to make that assessment loosely is equally unsatisfactory.

The goals of policies are never stated in a dependably authoritative, precise, and complete way. We can be sure that any single participant in the making of policy would be as baffled as any other human being when asked to rehearse all the considerations which moved him to a decision and to evaluate the relative weight of each. Since, moreover, public policy in a representative democracy is always made by many men, their individual views, conflicting or contradictory on many points, must somehow be transformed – by a process which nobody can specify or justifiably prescribe – into 'the' aims inherent in the act of policy. We may imitate a wise rule of judicial interpretation, which is to infer the policy of a written instrument by asking how reasonable ordinary men at that time would have understood its purposes. Proceeding in this manner, we may say that American economic policies aimed at increasing the earnings of Americans, at bringing their economic relations into more equitable order, at suppressing instability in the economy as a whole, at preserving free enterprise in general while overruling its operation in many particular instances, and at maintaining a constitutional balance between the central government and state governments even while bringing additional public business under the aegis of the central government.

Even if we knew the objectives of policies quite precisely, we could only measure their success by knowing what would have happened in the absence of those policies. Tariff protection was supposed to hasten industrialization, among other things. In fact manufacturing output did expand very quickly, yet there is good reason to deduce from general principles of economics that it might well have expanded more quickly had protective duties not induced overinvestment (if it did) in the protected industries. Railway regulation was supposed, among other things, to improve the supply of transportation. In fact transportation supply did grow at a rapid rate, though unevenly, yet there is no doubt that it grew faster in those parts of the transportation industry that remained exempt from regulation, and little reason to doubt that regulation itself was very costly. Labour law was supposed to improve the lot of employees. In fact, the average income of employees rose remarkably; but it is arguable that restrictions on hours and wages, while benefiting some or many employees, have been paid for by others in the form of unemployment, low incomes, reduced opportunities, and work less satisfying because more mechanized. Social policy might be said, by vigorous stretching of facts, to have aimed at making people's lives safer, healthier, more comfortable. In fact, so far as statistical indices measure, and making allowance for the accident of depression, Americans lived more safely and healthily in 1939 than in 1865; certainly they lived much longer. But it would be extravagant to attribute the whole result to public policy and excessively imaginative to allocate specific fractions of the whole improvement to various elements of public policy.

Lacking finer tools of analysis, we might content ourselves with the knowledge that policies of wide scope which aim at broad and distant results are always steps taken in the dark. Darkness is always an argument against walking, though not always an overwhelming argument; knowing that policy moves in darkness is a powerful argument against bold adventures. The history of American economic policy, in any event, is made up of small steps rather than great leaps.

CHAPTER X

Economic and social policy in France

I. *Introduction*

Two traditions, apparently conflicting but having more in common than appears on the surface, have operated to make up the social and economic policy of the French state since the eighteenth century. The older one expresses the need for greater centralization and control of economic and social life inherent in the creation and consolidation of the modern state manifested first of all by the monarchy of the old regime. The other emphasizes the objective character of economic laws and demands maximum freedom for the individual, conceived as a property owner, to do what he likes with his own. Ostensibly it is the revolution of 1789 which swings the balance from the one to the other and establishes the necessary juridical bases for the full development of the free market economy. But the earlier tradition was by no means dead. The revolutionary, and more especially the Napoleonic, regimes continued the centralizing mission of the monarchy and carried it out more successfully. The theoretical basis for the exercise of state power changed from divine right to the general will; the privileges of the nobility gave way to the rights of property; but in the new system of law the state had rights superior to those of the ordinary citizen. The centralization of power in the state, the establishment of bureaucratic agencies of control having interests of their own, were characteristic of the new order. During the nineteenth century and after the attitude of the bourgeoisie to the state remained ambivalent. The state was necessary to regulate the economic liberties regarded as sacrosanct. At the same time it was expected to carry out tasks in the economic and social spheres which were not profitable for the private entrepreneur. It was regarded with suspicion whenever it transgressed on the liberty of the individual property owner; at the same time its support was indispensable for carrying out these tasks, and in doing so it had favours to dispense. Powerful interests therefore courted the state whenever its support or protection was necessary to realize their projects.

In practice the sphere of state action proved to be a fluctuating one. The policy of the monarchy, formalized and extended by Louis XIV's minister, Jean-Baptiste Colbert (1619–83), gave it a very wide-ranging role, but decades before its downfall, paradoxically, the very officials charged with the administration of economic regulations had come to accept the need for greater freedom for the capitalist entrepreneur and property owner. Although it appeared that the revolution stood for economic liberalism, the exigencies of the time and particularly the imperatives of war, made its full application impossible. Successive regimes swung from more to less state intervention and control and back again. The two Napoleons left a powerful impress in the former sense. But while regimes and governments came and went the whole economic and social structure was being reshaped by industrial change. As industrialization took hold, bringing with it new class structures and styles of social living, new departures in policy became inevitable. The growing urban proletariat gave rise to new problems of poverty, housing, education, and factory legislation. The need for infrastructural support imposed on the state a greater role in both traditional and new spheres. Political factors, the growth of nationalism and economic rivalry between states, required new policies in the fiscal field and in the regulation of foreign trade. This was no straight-line development but was a product of many conflicting forces and cross-currents. The old centralizing policy, never dislodged by the revolution, indeed promoted by it, held out the prospect of extended intervention by the state. The Colbertian tradition was never extinguished; indeed, it was revived with a new content as industrialization proceeded.

In the course of the nineteenth century, too, other factors came to influence policy. The pressure of the working class for social reforms manifested itself in the 1840s and came to the surface in 1848. Subsequent regimes and governments had to take increasing note of the special problems constituted by the existence of a large, urban, wage-earning, and propertyless class. Moreover, critics of the unregulated market economy became more articulate and various schools of social reform and socialism appeared. In one way or another all called upon the state, either in its existing or in some new form, to charge itself with the solution of social problems and the promotion of improvement for the mass of the people. This was something which the *ancien régime* naturally had not had to contend with; it was common to all advanced societies and the French response to the challenge, as will be seen, was in no way exceptional or outstanding. Indeed, in some fields, such as social insurance, it was positively belated despite the role played by the state in other directions. An attempt will be made to explain the specific characteristics of French economic and social policy with reference to the nature of the economy and its development – including especially the preservation of a large agrarian sector – and the peculiar relationship between the bourgeoisie and the state in the post-revolutionary period. At the same time, the continuity with the state-making role of the old regime will be pointed out as well as the need for new policies as industrialization created new pressures and problems.

II. *The legacy of the old regime*

Under the old regime it can be said that the state entered the field of economic and social policy mainly through the fisc. It was concern with the taxable capacity of the population which led to a search for means of increasing production. However, such an aim was not consistently carried out, if only because the dominating need to find extra resources to finance state expenditure prevented it. The policy of Colbert was principally designed to manage the royal estate more efficiently, but it also became an aspect of the transformation of French society through the strengthening of the powers of the central government.[1] Thus state-building rather than a strategy of economic development was the basis of Colbertism. Fiscal and economic policy was of the type defined as 'mercantilist'. Its emphasis was upon pushing the export of manufactured goods and discouraging unnecessary imports to ensure a favourable balance of trade. By the Pacte Coloniale overseas territories were to depend upon France for manufactured goods and to supply her with colonial staples. This trade was to move freely, without duties, and be conducted in ships belonging to French shipowners and merchants. While the state was being more sharply defined in relation to its rivals, it was also to take steps to stimulate the economy. Solicitude for industry was expressed in the encouragement of technical improvement and investment and in measures intended to widen markets and open up opportunities for trade. However, in line with existing practice, inherited from the Middle Ages, it was believed that the promotion of industry required a minute system of regulation to be enforced by a corps of government officials, the *inspecteurs des manufactures*.

The strength of Colbertism lay in the fact that it embraced the country as a whole and elaborated policy on the national scale. It was in line with the state-building tendencies of the monarchy and contained the germs of economic nationalism. Its object was not rapid growth or the trans-

---

[1] Martin Wolfe, 'French Views on Wealth and Taxes from the Middle Ages to the Old Regime', *Journal of Economic History*, vol. XXVI, no. 4 (December 1966), pp. 471–2, identifies Colbertism with mercantilism and expresses its essence as follows: '(1) improvement in the structure of taxes, in fiscal administration, or in the burden of taxes can enhance the nation's wealth; (2) of all the devices for increasing royal revenues in the king's fiscal arsenal, the best by far, and the only one not self-defeating, is to improve trade and industry.' For a recent brief overview see C. Keyder, 'Industrial Policy in France: State and Industry in France, 1750–1914', *The American Economic Review*, vol LXXV, no. 2 (May 1985).

formation of the economy, but rather an ordered progress under state direction. The state was prepared to invest in industry or to grant tax concessions and other privileges to private businessmen ready to promote new enterprises. On the whole, however, the Colbertian system of industrial regulation was devised with the old-style small-scale or artisan industry in mind and so far as it was applied it put enterprise into a rigid strait-jacket.

The main lines of policy during the eighteenth century followed those traced by Colbert, with the state impinging on the economy at many points. Throughout this period the permanently distressed state of the Royal Treasury contrasted with the evident signs of economic growth in foreign trade and some sections of industry in particular. Successive wars aggravated the crisis in state finances. The industrial model of the old regime was one of ordered growth combining private initiative with overall state regulation of a corporate society. In practice the model did not work well and had already been undermined before the revolution. The reasons for this were several. The apparatus of the state was not adequate to administer the laws which it proposed. Powerful interests arose seeking greater freedom and were articulated in the doctrines of economic liberalism. Specifically there was a demand for freedom of rural industries, freedom to employ cheaper labour, freedom to produce goods acceptable to market demand but not necessarily to government norms. The state officials charged with administering the regulations were themselves becoming convinced that the manufacturers needed less regulation and more liberty. In an atmosphere of economic expansion after the middle of the eighteenth century the demand for economic liberty became more conscious. With the English example, and competition, the state made efforts to promote industrialization. The upshot was that the old regulative system was in decay but the new expedients, empirical in their origin, were of limited effect. The problem of the monarchy was that it was unable to align itself on the side of the new economic order which was appearing. Its budget was in disorder; it was unable to carry through necessary reforms in the tax system and even less to reconstruct the agrarian sector. Incessant wars worsened the financial position while private interests enriched themselves at the expense of the state.

Not only did the tax privileges of the nobility and clergy lead to intolerable inequities, but dependence on tax-farmers levying indirect taxes on the mass of the people aggravated the burden.[2] It was the very opposite of taxation by consent. If the tax system had worked there

---

[2] George T. Matthews, *The Royal General Farms in Eighteenth Century France* (New York, 1958).

might have been some justification for it. As it was, the state finances fell into increasing disorder. The sale of offices, the piling up of debt and the operations of the tax-farmers still left the state poised on the brink of bankruptcy until disaster finally struck. Chaotic fiscal practices helped to counteract any stimulating results from state policy in other directions. From about the 1730s the economy entered into a long period of expansion over which some recent historians have waxed enthusiastic to the extent of describing France at this time as 'the leading industrial power in the world'.[3] It is admitted, however, that French industry did not experience the structural transformation taking place on the other side of the English Channel. The growth in output was obtained mainly through the old forms of industry, from a growth in production rather than from a growth in productivity. What needs to be emphasized is that economic growth was taking place at a steady rate. More germane to our purpose is to ask: was this growth a result of the economic policies of the old regime or did it take place despite them?

The simultaneous presence of fiscal disorder and imminent state bankruptcy with evidence of economic activity promoted by private entrepreneurs would seem to suggest, a priori, that the latter was true. Indeed, there seems to be little evidence that the policy of the state contributed in any positive way to the economic expansion of the period. On the contrary, it was accompanied by a growing demand for economic freedom voiced, among others, by the Physiocrats, and by the awareness, even on the part of officials of the administration, that growth would be more likely to be promoted by less rather than more regulation. Now that the economy was on the move industry was pressing against the restraints of the old system of industrial regulation. Manufacturers saw that goods had to be made according to the needs of the market and not to norms laid down by the state. The whole system of regulation inherited from Colbert became an encumbrance in a dynamic market situation. Industries moved to the countryside in search of cheaper labour. Guild regulations were felt to be an obstacle in the competitive race for profits. Subtly the attitude of the government's own agents, the *intendants*, the *inspecteurs des manufactures*, and the more recently appointed *corps des ingénieurs* of the mines administration, began to change. Influenced by the current for economic freedom, they advocated the removal of barriers to enterprise and tended to become

---

[3] The term is from Tihomir J. Markovitch, 'La révolution Industrielle: le cas de la France', *Revue d'histoire économique et sociale*, vol. LII, no. 1 (1974). See also his 'L'évolution industrielle de la France au XVIIIe. siècle', *Revue d'histoire économique et sociale*, vol. LIII, no. 2–3 (1975), and 'La croissance industrielle sous l'ancien régime', in *Annales: Économies, Sociétés, Civilisations*, vol. XXXI, no. 3 (May–June 1976).

counsellors and guides for industry and mere collectors of statistics and other information for the government.[4] At the same time, as technical change quickened in Britain government agents became conduits for the passage of information about the new techniques to French manufacturers. The government also took the initiative in inviting English inventors and entrepreneurs to settle in France.

Despite the signs of an important shift in the policy of the state, it does not follow that its overall influence on economic development was positive. Although welcomed by the more progressive entrepreneurs it was opposed by others who preferred routine ways and a sheltered existence. Turgot (1727–81) succeeded in abolishing guild privileges in 1776 but they were restored under pressure within a short time. However, by then a large measure of industrial liberty undoubtedly existed. What was restrictive was the agrarian structure upon which the privileges of the ruling class of the old regime were based and the regressive and chaotic fiscal system that successive finance ministers had been powerless to reform precisely in the face of these entrenched privileges. It was not only, therefore, that at this stage, in a period of economic expansion, continued growth was conditional upon greater economic freedom as demanded by the Physiocrats and the political economists. It was also that the institutions of the old regime and the social relations it preserved had become an obstacle to the full development of industrial freedom and the realization of its benefits. The old regime was unable to provide a more equitable tax structure or to limit the size of the surplus going to the mainly non-investing privileged orders.

At the heart of this development was a further contradiction. The agents of the administration had themselves to a large extent become convinced both of the need for greater economic freedom and for tax reforms to realize the possibilities of economic growth. In fact, the last decade or two of the old regime sees a silent surrender to the new doctrines expressing the needs of merchants and manufacturers. Nowhere was this clearer than in the liberalization of the grain trade, including in 1764 and 1787 the export of grain as long as the home price was below a certain level. In the important sphere of *subsistence* the old regime was now ready to allow the laws of the market to operate.[5]

In the closing phase of the old regime, therefore, statist action in the economy was in full retreat before the doctrines of economic liberalism

[4] 'Simples surveillants à l'origine, les inspecteurs se transforment en agents de renseignements; on leur réclame des mémoires et des statistiques, on les envoie en mission. Ils tendent à devenir les conseillers économiques du gouvernement et les guides des fabricants, les agents d'un progrès voulu et dirigé par l'Etat', Pierre Léon and Charle Carrère, *Histoire économique et sociale de la France*, directed by Fernand Braudel and Ernest Labrousse, vol. II (Paris, 1970), p. 222.
[5] *Ibid.*, pp. 380–3.

and physiocracy. It had virtually abandoned its pretensions to control and regulate industry and taken on instead the role of assisting private investment. Restrictions and regulations resented by businessmen still had force. There were privileged concerns backed by the state and the crown itself. At least on paper a complex system of control still remained for the cloth industry. The internal tariff barriers operated to limit the free flow of goods. The privileges of the guilds and corporations had been restored. The ideal of the old regime was still an ordered society while the monarchy depended for its existence on the support of the nobility whose very privileges were the main barrier to a rational fiscal and economic policy. The monarchy's policy was characterized by indecision. It appeared on the one hand to sympathize with and foster the new forces of economic change and growth. Its influence here, however, tended to strengthen those forces which were to challenge and destroy it in and after 1789. On the other hand, it could not break decisively with the privileged orders and align itself with those forces its revised policies had tended to foster in the 1770s and 1780s. Its most abysmal failure lay in the fiscal field, where those best able to pay paid practically nothing, leaving the tax burden to be borne by those least able to do so. It was not so much that the system failed to raise revenue, simply that it never raised enough and did so by means which alienated wide sections of the population from the regime and implanted a hostility to taxation and a determination to avoid it wherever possible which has blocked tax reform even down to the present day.[6] The old regime paid for its financial laxity with its very existence; any industrial 'successes' it achieved were bought also at that price. In any case, the old regime was incapable of carrying out the necessary reforms in the agrarian sector either by favouring a system of enclosure and capitalist farming or by promoting peasant farming at the expense of the nobility. Meanwhile, despite the economic expansion the great fortunes were being made not by industrialists or even by merchants but by tax-farmers and bankers whose wealth derived from the financial embarrassment of the state. But that was nothing new; it went back to Colbert's day. If successful state financing depended upon a healthy economy, events showed that growing prosperity could not solve the problems of the fisc if the will and means for tax reform were not present. Moreover, the old regime showed itself to be congenitally incapable of avoiding the vice of all ambitious monarchical states, involvement in war. It was this extravagance which crippled the finances of the state and opened the floodgates of revolution, leaving to its successor all its unresolved problems.

[6] Jean Bouvier, 'Sur "L'immobilisme" du système fiscal français au XIXe siècle', *Revue d'histoire économique et sociale*, vol. L, no. 4 (October–December 1972).

III. *Economic and social policy in the revolutionary decade*

When the States General, called to extricate the monarchy from its financial crisis, declared itself in June 1789 to be a law-making body, an assembly representing the general will, it rapidly began to enact the programme of economic liberalism, the basis of French social and economic policy for the next century and more. With greater decisiveness and singleness of purpose, therefore, it continued a process which had begun in the last decades of the old regime. It translated into practice the principles of the Enlightenment and of the political economists in particular and expressed the aspirations of the bulk of the non-privileged and educated property owners making up the class conveniently described as the *bourgeoisie*. Economic development had not yet brought onto the scene a powerful nucleus of industrial capitalists and many of those in existence were to suffer a decline in their fortunes in the coming years. The revolutionaries represented a much broader, property-owning class with its basis in trade, landowning, and the professions and including some of the office-holders of the old regime. It was not a homogeneous class, as the internecine struggles of the revolutionary period were to show, and it was still very much in formation with new men pressing forward, avidly seizing the opportunities for accumulating wealth presented by the revolution itself. The policy-makers of the Constituent Assembly and its successors reflected the interests of this class and its different factions even in such abstract documents as the Declaration of the Rights of Man. A keen sense of the importance of property rights permeated all their policies.

It was first necessary, of course, to clear the ground of all the inherited lumber of the old regime, but equally to do so without threatening property rights *per se*. This clearing of the ground was carried out methodically during the life of the Constituent Assembly. It brought an end to feudal privilege in landowning and in other spheres and disposed of the special position of the church. It abolished the corporate order of the old regime, swept away the old restrictions on trade and the system of industrial regulation established by Colbert. It changed the basis of state finance, sweeping away the obnoxious taxes of the monarchy. It legislated for a free labour market and generally laid the juridical basis for the full development of capitalist relations. There is no doubt that this represented a permanent and revolutionary change in the economic policy of the state. In the social field, too, the policy of the Constituent Assembly and its successors, especially the Convention, marked a break with the past. In such fields as education and social welfare, however, the intentions expressed to provide for the illiterate, poor, and needy remained largely words on paper. It was in the economic sphere, in opening the way for the enrichment of the bourgeoisie, not in the social sphere, in improving the conditions of the masses, that the revolutionary assemblies achieved their most memorable successes.[7]

The importance assumed by agrarian questions in the revolution flowed from the fact that the privileges and position of the nobility were bound up with the surplus it exacted by various means from the rural sector in which lived over three-quarters of the population.[8] In many parts of the country the peasantry rose in revolt, refused to meet their obligations, and attacked the châteaux in order to destroy the documents in which they were inscribed. Continued rural violence forced the hand of the Assembly and the dismantling of the feudal land system began. The changes introduced in the next few years are well enough known not to need a lengthy description. What is apparent is that the peasant revolution was an autonomous movement with its own momentum and different aims to those of the urban revolutionaries. In August 1789, the Assembly abolished those feudal burdens based on compulsion and for which the peasants received no counterpart but left others, taken to have a contractual origin, to be re-purchased. It was a distinction perceptible to the legal mind but not to the peasant whose only desire was to obtain ownership of the land free of all payments. Moreover, while the revolutionary assemblies favoured a free market in land and a more individualist type of agriculture requiring the abolition of the open fields and other traditional practices, such changes were anathema to large sections of the peasantry, though not to all. Neither the Constituent Assembly nor its successor, the Legislative Assembly, assuaged the peasants' appetite for land or brought the rural discontent to an end. The latter body, in June 1792, laid on the landowner the onus of proof that the customary payments were legitimate but left an element of re-purchase still unacceptable to the mass of the peasants. It was left to the Convention, even more anxious to win peasant support, finally to sweep away, in February 1794, all payments having the least tinge of feudal origin. The assemblies moved circumspectly for fear that the kind of change demanded by the peasants would undermine the rights of private property

---

[7] Jacques Godechot, Les institutions de la France sous la Révolution et l'Empire, 2nd edn (Paris, 1968), provides the fullest and most systematic account of the social and economic changes of the period consecrated by legislative and administrative measures. The institutional structure established during these years has endured to the present day and there can, of course, be considerable debate about how far it provided a suitable framework for economic growth.

[8] Georges Lefebvre, Études sur la Révolution française (Paris, 1954); and Les paysans du Nord pendant la Révolution francqise (rep. Bari, 1959). Brief accounts in English in Alan Milward and S. B. Saul, The Economic Development of Continental Europe (London, 1973); and Tom Kemp, Economic Forces in French History (London, 1971). Social aspects of the revolutionary period are dealt with in Norman Hampson, A Social History of the French Revolution (London, 1963).

they were so anxious to safeguard. In the end the Convention had to endorse and give legal sanction to what much of the peasantry had succeeded in doing for itself.

Meanwhile, the confiscation of church land and the estates of the *emigré* nobles and their sale as *biens nationaux* in an effort to overcome the state's budgetary problems brought about a considerable transfer of landed property. The main beneficiaries were the urban bourgeois and richer peasants. Speculation in the vast amounts of land and property thus cast onto the market made possible the aggrandizement of some existing fortunes and the establishment of new ones. Although a large section of the peasantry benefited from the abolition of feudal dues and services the laws of the revolutionary assemblies did little or nothing for those rural dwellers, more numerous in some places than in others, who had insufficient land for the support of their families or none at all. On the other hand, by confirming the land-holding peasantry in the possession of its land, no longer encumbered by feudal obligations, with little inclination to abandon the traditional practices of husbandry, it undoubtedly reinforced the barriers to change in the rural areas and slowed down industrialization.

When the Constituent Assembly turned to the commercial and industrial legacy of the old regime it swept most of it away in the name of individual freedom. Here there was less sense of urgency, the main legislation coming in 1791. The guilds and corporations were abolished by the D'Allarde law of March 1791; in principle this threw all occupations and professions open to those able and qualified to perform them and thus realized one of the basic aims of the advocates of economic liberty. A few months later, following the outbreak of strikes for higher wages among some sections of workers, the Assembly passed the Le Chapelier law in June 1791. This effectively outlawed workers' combinations and trade unions and survived as a fundamental legal principle until 1864 through several changes of regime. Together these laws established a free market for labour greatly to the advantage of employers and the investors of capital. They were complemented by other laws passed in the autumn of the same year sweeping away the whole system of industrial regulation and the offices associated with it as well as the privileged factories or workshops. At the same time a patent law was adopted to protect inventions.

Various other measures passed in 1790 and 1791 abolished the old tax system, the *octrois* levied at the gates of towns, internal tariff barriers, and tolls. The *corvées* for the maintenance of highways and bridges were also abolished and henceforth responsibility for them was to lie with the newly established departments aided by a subsidy from the central government. Regulations concerning fairs and markets were also ended. A new mining law reversed that of the monarchy, passed in 1744, which had made the state proprietor of the subsoil, and returned the ownership of mineral rights to the landowner. All such measures were part of the liberal economic programme and satisfied the claims of the urban middle-class property owners for freedom to do what they liked with their own. In matters concerning external trade, however, the Assembly was less liberal. While the internal trade in grain was declared to be completely free as early as August 1789, protective tariffs and prohibitions were maintained, as were the regulations touching colonial trade. Merchants and traders, as well as much of the bourgeoisie as a whole, saw an interest in the free circulation of goods in the internal market but were equally afraid of a free influx of competitive goods from abroad. They had bitterly opposed the commercial treaty of 1786 with England, held responsible by some for the economic difficulties preceding the revolution. For the most part, through the subsequent changes in regime, business interests generally favoured free trade at home but remained protectionist in foreign trade policy.[9]

The rapid movement of revolutionary events during 1792, the internal divisions, the internecine struggle between political factions, the outbreak of war, the fall of the monarchy, the election of the Convention, and the period of Jacobin dictatorship in 1793–4, saw the temporary abrogation of the policy of economic liberalism. This retreat was carried out reluctantly, created new divisions and dissensions, and was of short duration. It was imposed principally, like the revolutionary dictatorship of Robespierre and the Committee of Public Safety, by the near desperate position on the battlefronts and the serious threat from armed uprisings inside the country. It was in fact a war policy, an attempt to impose a siege economy. But it was also, in part, a response to the pressure from the popular masses for a more equitable distribution of goods and control over profiteers and hoarders and all those who increased their wealth at the expense of the Republic. The system of wartime controls was supported by that section of the Committee of Public Safety like Lazare Carnot (1753–1823) and Pierre Joseph Cambon (1756–1826) who could be described as 'technocrats' rather than doctrinaires like their Jacobin colleagues. They saw controls as necessary for practical reasons and were no less liberals for that. The main, or only, commitment to a controlled economy came from the radicals outside the Convention, upon whom the Jacobin dictatorship depended for a short but critical period but from which it became separated in the months preceding Robespierre's fall on 9th Thermidor, 1794.

Although the state had already taken steps, such as the setting up of

[9] As Godechot puts it in *Les institutions*, pp. 232–3, 'Alors qu'en matière de commerce intérieur le libéralisme économique triomphe, dans le commerce extérieur, la réglementation est no seulement maintenue mais même renforcée. Ce libéralisme de la bourgeoisie n'était pas doctrinal, il n'était que l'expression de ses intérêts matériels et s'arrêtait avec eux.'

arms factories, to intervene in the economy under the pressure of war, it was the growing shortage of food and other goods in 1793 which forced it to go further. The shortages aggravated the popular ferment, especially in Paris, which characterized the early years of the revolution. It was under pressure from the masses against the background of the war emergency that the Convention voted to control prices. By a law passed on 4 May the authorities in each department were to fix maximum prices for grain and enforce them by administrative means including requisitioning. It proved impossible to apply this measure and during the summer the supply situation worsened. It was either necessary to attempt to relieve the shortages by returning to a free market, allowing prices to rise at will, or to impose still more stringent controls extending to other necessary goods. Intimidated by the Parisian masses the Convention decided on the latter. On 24 September the general law of the Maximum was passed, but without enthusiasm, by the reluctant Jacobin leaders. Enforcement, backed by the death penalty for hoarders, was left to the local authorities, most of whom were equally half-hearted. Some steps were also taken to establish municipal granaries and bakeries. Producers and traders were increasingly hostile to this interference with the market and goods simply disappeared to be sold at black market prices to those who could afford them. The Convention was unwilling to establish rationing and probably would not in any case have been able to operate an effective machinery, though some towns did issue ration cards. All in all, the experiment was a failure. It further embittered the urban artisans and workers, the most fervent supporters hitherto of the revolutionary government, as well as antagonizing producers and traders. Carried out with insufficient vigour, the attempt to impose economic controls prepared the way for the downfall of Robespierre and the Jacobins and a return to the policy of a free market economy by their successors.

With the overthrow of Robespierre, the moderate wing of the Convention, known as the Thermidoreans, took power, bent on a rapid dismantling of the apparatus of government control of the economy. The laws of the Maximum were repealed, though for a time war industries were still subject to state control. By the end of 1794 prices were freed to find their own level, with the result that they shot up at an alarming rate. Chronic supply shortages and the depreciation of the *assignats* meant that for the next three years France experienced an inflation of a classic type, only eclipsed in the twentieth century. The Convention continued to resort to the printing press to resolve its pressing financial problems.

Under the new constitution which came into operation in 1795 executive power was held by five Directors appointed by a lower house elected on a limited suffrage. The new government had to face a situation of financial chaos, scarcity, and continued war. The battle against inflation lasted until 1796 when paper money ceased to be legal tender, but the lack of specie produced a sharp fall in prices and a deflationary crisis. Lacking means of payment the state was forced back on coercive measures, forced loans, payments in kind, and other expedients. To reduce the public debt to manageable proportions two-thirds was repaid in bearer bonds which fell to 1 per cent of their value by 1799. This partial state bankruptcy was coupled with other measures to improve the revenue by tax reforms and a more rational administrative apparatus for the levying and collection of taxes. New indirect taxes were introduced, some becoming a permanent part of the tax system. Nevertheless, the financial policy of the Directory contributed to its downfall. It had to call upon the army to supplement its revenue with booty from the conquered countries. It became increasingly dependent upon bankers for loans. It forfeited the support of some sections of the property-owning class upon which it was most dependent. However, applying the principles of economic liberalism wherever possible, the Directory saw a business recovery with new opportunities for profit-making and accumulation. Sea-borne trade remained in a state of collapse, though markets for some French goods were extended overland in the wake of the conquering armies. While the economy of the west coast ports languished, internal trade also suffered. Roads deteriorated partly through lack of funds to pay for work to be carried out since the abolition of the *corvée*. Falling prices and shortage of money contributed to the decline of some forms of internal trade, although by the end of the Directory there had probably been some recovery compared with the worst years.

Economic policy was an integral part of the changes brought about by the revolution. It reshaped French laws and institutions in a way favourable to the bourgeoisie and to capitalist dealings. But although the way was now clear for the free and unfettered operation of the laws of the market, the revolution and its consequences slowed down economic growth and blighted sectors, especially foreign trade, which had been in the vanguard of the upsurge of the period from the 1740s. A considerable redistribution of wealth and income had taken place, but it was mainly within the propertied classes; those tied closely to the old regime mostly suffered (most of the tax-farmers were guillotined) while new fortunes were made and new dynasties of wealth established. The revolution was tender of property, but it tried to distinguish between different kinds of property rights; the upshot was that all property was assimilated to the one form: free, individual, and absolute. War conditions imposed some qualifications to this and others were added in time. What the revolution did not do was to redistribute property to the benefit of those possessing little or nothing. As for social policy, the revolution contributed little but good intentions and its influence may well have been negative as far as concerned the poor and needy.

The establishment of a free market for labour, the economic liberties and the rights of private property were the main aims of the revolutionary assemblies. That they claimed to speak in the name of the Nation, or even of Humanity, and that lip-service was paid to equality was only natural. The bourgeoisie was a minority in the nation but it had to mobilize the support of large masses if its projects, political and economic, were to be realized. No doubt the members of the revolutionary assemblies were not all hypocrites, but when it came to improving the conditions of the masses they were freer with words than with the material means to implement their good intentions.

The record of the revolution in social policy, at least in practice, is meagre. Care of the poor and the sick, under the old regime, had been mainly in the hands of religious institutions and congregations. The expropriation of church lands and the dissolution of the religious orders thus left serious gaps in what might be called the social services, if that term is not anachronistic in the circumstances. From the time of the National Assembly measures were passed aimed at ending private charity and providing assistance to the needy as a matter of right. The Comité de mendicité set up in 1790 declared that the relief of poverty by assisting the unemployed to find work and the provision of maintenance for the aged, sick, and needy were functions of the state. While carefully distinguishing the different categories of poor and prescribing for their plight, the committee suggested that funds should be provided nationally and that property belonging to the church and the hospitals should be sold and the money raised used for this purpose. These proposals had little practical effect either under the Constituent Assembly or the Legislative Assembly. During the period of the Convention Robespierre expressed similar good intentions and a law passed in March 1793 provided for the public support of the poor. Charity was forbidden, so was begging. Beggars were liable to be imprisoned for one or two years and repeated offenders could be deported to Guyana. In March 1794 provision was to be made for the support of a limited number of worthy aged and infirm people, mothers and widows in each department whose names were to be inscribed in the *Grand livre de la bienfaisance nationale*. The Convention also aspired to abolish the existing hospitals, mostly in the hands of religious orders, and to substitute a public system of domiciliary medical care. Apart from assistance given to dependents of members of the armed forces and victims of the war and demagogic emergency measures taken to appease popular discontent, these projects remained on paper. The same fate awaited the proposals for a national system of primary education. With the war absorbing energies and financial resources this was not a propitious time for wide-ranging social reforms requiring substantial outlays as well as trained personnel and buildings which were simply not available. Local authorities were lethargic in the face of the obligations thrust upon them and once the revolutionary fervour had subsided and the Thermidoreans were in the saddle little more was to be heard of such expensive schemes of social policy. Indeed, hospital care in many towns deteriorated, while inflation and food shortages aggravated the problems of poverty and destitution.

It can be said, however, that the other measures taken by the revolutionary assemblies from which a large section of the rural population gained made less urgent the relief of poverty, schemes for the aged, abandoned mothers, and orphans. In a peasant society such problems were customarily dealt with in the family and so far as family incomes were raised by the abolition of feudal dues and a reduced tax burden there was a less pressing need for public assistance. There is little question, however, that in the main the revolution was no better able than the old regime to deal with poverty, ill health, and unemployment. Indeed, so far as it undermined the old institutions and promoted the extension of market relations, it may have aggravated these problems. In any case, despite declarations of support for the poor and needy and paper plans for the organization of public welfare, these were the product of a particular situation: one in which the popular masses were pressing hard on the legislators and politicians. They were scarcely among the major preoccupations of the revolutionary bourgeoisie even in its most radical phase. All sections of it were firmly committed to economic individualism and the virtues of the free market.

However, it was a paradox of the situation that in establishing the conditions for the more effective operation of market forces the revolutionary assemblies also greatly enhanced the powers of the state. The ending of aristocratic and clerical privilege and the break up of the corporate order of the old regime left no intermediary between the individual and the state. The power of the state was now all the weightier because it claimed to represent the general will and not merely the head of the ruling dynasty claiming divine right. Clearly, therefore, the state could claim powers superior to those of the ordinary citizen. Conditions of revolution and war reinforced this claim. Even the proponents of economic liberalism did not desire *laissez-faire* in the literal sense. It was assumed that the state would continue to exercise functions which had been its responsibility under the old regime: those, for example, in connection with the 'infrastructure' which individual enterprise was unable or unwilling to undertake. The sphere of state action was to be determined pragmatically and the older tradition of interventionism, or statism, did not die out. The more powerful and centralized state, calling on the active or passive support of a much wider section of the population, could be more effective in imposing its policies in the economic and social spheres. The question was, therefore, who manned the state apparatus and in whose interests would it be operated. The revolution answered this question by bringing the bourgeoisie to power. The property owners as a whole, or the dominant faction at any one time, under the pressure of the prevailing social forces, determined the policy of the state. The number of offices available multiplied greatly; they were open to the talents, meaning the educated sons of the property owners. These offices were sought after because they gave security and influence. The attitude of the bourgeoisie towards the state, and its policies, was therefore ambivalent. It built itself into the state, as its private property, no longer alienated from it as had been the case under the old regime. The state was expected to protect property rights, provide the conditions necessary for the operation of a free market but also, where appropriate, to open up conditions for lucrative investment or widen the opportunities for profit-making. It had, moreover, to defend the national industry and agriculture from foreign rivals and assist maritime and colonial enterprise. A new class was in control, but what was expected of the state was not very different from what it had been doing under the old regime. On the other hand, the powers concentrated in the state were regarded with suspicion. If it could assist in the making of profits it could also, by its actions, block avenues of investment, confine them to privileged groups, or expropriate wealth and infringe property rights. The ruler therefore had to be suspiciously watched and if necessary opposed to ensure that he was using the state machinery in the way that the property owners desired, bearing in mind, of course, that they were themselves not of one mind about the policy which the state should pursue. The range and character of state action in the social and political spheres were, therefore, to be the subject of burning controversy. They contributed to and were reflected in the changes of regime which France experienced in the century and a half after 1789.

IV. The Napoleonic imprint

The policy of Napoleon Bonaparte, as Consul and as Emperor, completed the centralizing trend of the monarchy, consolidated the changes made to the advantage of the bourgeois property owners during the revolutionary period while, by its interventionism, it harked back to the methods of Colbert.[10] In practice, it proved above all to be a series of expedients required by the war situation. Napoleon's view of the econ-

[10] For a recent survey, Louis Bergeron, 'Problèmes économiques de la France Napoléonienne', *Revue d'histoire moderne et contemporaine*, vol. XVII (July–September 1970).

omy was very much that of a military overlord. He wanted a strong industry and a healthy agriculture as the basis for his strategic aim: to establish French hegemony over the European continent. It was this association of economic policy with state power which places Napoleon in the mercantilist tradition. At the same time he was a respecter of wealth and fortune and he knew well enough that his regime depended upon an alliance of his supporters, political and military, with the established bankers and industrialists. The latter were, for the most part, convinced adherents of the doctrines of economic liberalism and this limited Napoleon's capacity to intervene directly in the economy.

From the beginning Napoleon showed that he was not willing to confine his role to military matters and foreign relations. He insisted on intervening personally in all matters of policy. He appreciated in particular the need to establish stability and order and to restore confidence; he thought this could be done by showing that there was a firm hand on the tiller. At the same time, he remained suspicious of bankers and businessmen, or at least of certain of their practices. There was agreement, however, that the country's finances had to be placed on a sound basis while providing the state adequate means for its military and other needs. This required a stable monetary system and an efficient financial administration. The Consulate, basing itself on the work already carried out by the Directory, was able within the limits set by the war economy to satisfy these demands. One of its first economic measures was the foundation of the Banque de France in January 1800. It had the form of a private joint-stock company, governed by regents, and its list of shareholders reflected the alliance between the political backers of Bonaparte and the Parisian banking fraternity. While its independence from the state was emphasized, it was Napoleon who forced other banks to cease note-issuing and, after a serious run in 1805, saw to it that the governor was appointed by the government. The Banque de France was intended to fulfil the functions of a central bank as then understood and it worked closely with the Treasury in satisfying the financial needs of the state. Napoleon did not risk floating public loans to finance the deficit, but preferred instead to obtain credit from the Banque or to make special arrangements with banking groups. In March 1803 a new money, linked to silver, was adopted, the *franc germinal*; it was to last until 1928. The new money proved to be a success, assisting internal transactions and placing government finance upon more solid foundations. Specie was to form a high proportion of the circulating medium throughout the nineteenth century and the authorities were wary of permitting the expansion of paper credit. French banking certainly lagged behind and the banking habit spread slowly. Whether this was a factor in the retardation of the economy or merely reflected needs and preferences is a matter of doubt:

it depends upon whether banking is seen as playing an active role in growth or as mainly reflecting the degree of development of the economy.[11]

Napoleon entrusted the management of public finance to an expert, Mortin Gaudin, duc de Gaëte (1756–1841), who had served under the monarchy and the revolutionary regimes. He carried out a systematic reform of the administration, abolished methods of compulsion like forced loans and reduced the weight of direct compared with indirect taxes as means of raising revenue. New indirect taxes were introduced both for national government finance and to meet the needs of departments and communes. These taxes, some identical with, others recalling, those of the old regime were far from popular, but Napoleon and his advisers worked on the principle that they were less perceptible and thus less resented than taxes on incomes and property. His regime established a durable tax structure and a corps of officials, modern and efficient, which would have been the envy of the old regime and provided the foundation for the public finances of the nineteenth and twentieth centuries. With the enormous cost of war in treasure as well as lives the budget of the Consulate and Empire could not be balanced without resorting to loans from bankers and above all by the proceeds of the plunder of occupied countries and war indemnities. But with the campaigns in Spain and Russia war ceased to be a paying proposition.

Although the Napoleonic regime desired faster industrial growth it was scarcely in a position to promote it directly. What it did do was to lend an ear to the voice of producers rather than consumers or workers by excluding imports as far as possible, assisting invention and innovation, and providing education and technical training. The loss of colonies and the decline of overseas trade were not, however, easily compensated for and the few attempts at import substitution were not fully successful. In any case, it is difficult to disentangle the positive contribution of the state from the negative effects of incessant war and the continental system.[12] Economic warfare between France and Britain had begun with the opening hostilities in 1793. With the conquest of most of Europe, Napoleon hoped to be able to force Britain to accept French hegemony by bringing about her economic collapse by depriving her of markets for her exports. When the treaty of Amiens broke down and war was resumed in 1802, both sides declared a blockade of the other. Neutral

[11] See Rondo Cameron, *France and the Economic Development of Europe 1800–1914* (Princeton, 1962), and his chapter on France in the book he edited, *Banking in the Early Stages of Industrialization* (New York and London, 1967). For a comment see Jean Bouvier, 'Systèmes bancaires et entreprises industrielles dans la croissance européene au XIXe, siècle', in *Annales: Economies, Sociétes, Civilisations*, vol. XXVII, no. 1 (January–February 1972).

[12] On the continental system, Franççois Crouzet, 'Wars, Blockades and Economic Change in Europe, 1792–1815', *Journal of Economic History*, vol. XXIV, no. 4 (December 1964).

trade was not at first interfered with but British goods were as far as possible excluded from the markets of France and conquered territories. The measures became increasingly severe after the defeat of Prussia and the promulgation of the Berlin Decrees, November 1806. All trade with Britain was prohibited as was trade in British products or those deemed to be such. Neutral ships coming from Britain or her colonies or having called at a British port were refused entry. The British government replied with the Orders in Council, the first issued in November 1807. These imposed a blockade and called on neutral ships trading with the continent to call at British ports for the examination of their cargo. It proved impossible to exclude British goods from Europe and, indeed, Napoleon had to issue licences permitting the import of certain British goods while allowing the continued supply to Britain of French products under similar conditions. In this trial of strength Britain had the advantage of command of the seas, and thus of colonial products greatly in demand in Europe, as well as of a superior manufacturing industry producing at lower cost.

The Continental System acted as a protective forcing house for some French industries and enabled markets to be found on the continent to compensate for those lost overseas. If parts of eastern France benefited this was of no consolation to the west coast ports which continued to languish. Napoleon's strategic-military conceptions prevented the continental system from being used consistently to promote industrialization. Thus, while the prohibition of the import of cotton manufactures from 1806 and the encouragement given to innovators in the cotton industry stimulated the industry which was in the forefront of change, the prohibition of the import of raw cotton four years later threw it into a crisis. The weakening of the industry, as shown by the difficulties encountered by the leading firms, placed it at a serious disadvantage in the forthcoming competition with the Lancashire industry. Any incidental gains made by the other sections of French industry must be set against the incoherence of the policy as a whole. Contraband, official corruption, popular opposition, and the ingenuity of British exporters and smugglers largely defeated its ends. However, it must be said that historians are divided in their balance sheet of the Continental System and more work needs to be done on the question.

Undoubtedly, during the Napoleonic period, despite ups and downs, French industry revived and the more advanced sectors underwent important structural changes. But again, whether or not this was a result of Napoleon's policy remains uncertain. Interested as he was in promoting industrial power, the specific measures taken by his regime could have only had a marginal influence. They appear more impressive on paper than they were in reality. Assistance was given to industries in difficulties by the buying up of stocks. A new mining law, of 1810, gave the state the power to grant concessions for the mining of minerals and set up a corps of officials to administer the law. Subsidies were paid to a number of new enterprises and an attempt was made to develop substitutes for imports, notably cane sugar and indigo. Exhibitions were organized to encourage industrial efficiency. Efforts were made to improve the roads and inland waterways, the state of which had deteriorated since 1789. Such examples of state intervention were indicative of Napoleon's aims but could scarcely have had a major influence on the rate of economic growth.

During the Empire the French administrative system took on its modern form: highly centralized, it was managed by a trained bureaucratic elite. This training was imparted through a higher educational system partly inherited from the monarchy, partly established during the revolutionary period, and now itself incorporated into the general administration. The revolution had deprived the universities of autonomy and under Napoleon they were brought under centralized control. Alongside and separate from them existed other specialized institutions known as *les grandes écoles*. The most prestigious was the Ecole Polytechnique founded in 1794, the emphasis of which was upon science, and especially mathematics, required for the training of military engineers. Its products went on also to the other schools preparing civil engineers and scientists. However, there was a serious gap between the high quality of the instruction and the brilliance of some of the research at these institutions and the technical needs of industry which was never successfully bridged during the nineteenth century.[13]

Business organization was governed by the commercial code of 1807.[14] Joint-stock companies were associated with privilege during the revolution and this disapproval was echoed in the code. Companies with full limited liability, *sociétés anonymes*, required special government authorization including the signature of the Emperor himself. The code provided for two forms of partnership: one, the *société en nom collectif* in which the liability of all partners, presumed to be active, was unlimited and the *société en commandite* in which the 'sleeping' partners were granted limited liability. The latter form proved to be a flexible enough instru-

---

[13] On higher education, apart from Godechot, *Les institutions*, see, for example, Frederick B. Artz, *The Development of Technical Education in France* (Cambridge, Mass. and London, 1966), and the more critical study by Robert Gilpin, *France in the Age of the Scientific State* (Princeton, 1968), ch. 4; also Charles Kindleberger, 'Technical Education and the French Entrepreneur', in Edward Carter et al., (eds.), *Enterprise and Entrepreneurs in Nineteenth- and Twentieth-Century France* (Baltimore, Md., and London, 1976).

[14] See Charles Freedeman, 'Joint-Stock Business Organisation in France 1807–1867', *Business History Review*, vol. XXXIX, no. 2 (Summer 1965), and *idem, Joint Stock Enterprise in France 1807–1867* (Chapel Hill, NC, 1979).

ment to be adopted by many firms, even large ones, until the *société anonyme* ceased to be subject to government authorization in 1862. Until the 1850s the French law was no more restrictive than that in other European countries including England. In fact, French shareholders had the advantage that they all enjoyed limited liability.

Although no general labour code was promulgated, the law of April 1803 maintained the prohibition of combinations established in 1791. The same year saw the institution of the *livret*, held by the employer and giving details of each worker's qualifications and previous jobs.[15] A worker wishing to settle in another district was supposed to have an internal passport. Both documents were issued by the police and, so far as the laws were applied, brought the workers under continuous surveillance. The intention clearly was to provide employers with a disciplined labour force and to forestall working-class discontent. Other provisions in the legal codes established the inferior position of the worker in the contract of employment. The voracious demands of the war machine meant that there was a general labour scarcity, which helps to explain this legislation. The financial burdens of the war also limited the credits available for financing social and economic projects. War was, after all, the Emperor's first priority.

V. Liberalism, protection, and state intervention, 1815–50

The government of the restored Bourbons had no capacity for looking at the economy in an overall way, as Napoleon had tried or pretended to do. Dominated by the large landed proprietors and their allies in industry and business, it sought stability and order above all. Implicitly accepting the changes in French society brought about since 1789, it made only ineffective and unpopular attempts to restore elements of the corporative order of the old regime. Its policy was one which became typical of all the regimes which were to follow it: a compromise between the application of the principles of economic liberalism and state intervention continuing the Colbertian tradition. It had neither the will nor the financial resources to stimulate industrialization by state spending, but it was accepted that there were functions which only the state could perform and it kept in existence the bureaucratic apparatus it had inherited from the Empire. It was obsessed with the desire to establish the financial probity of the state and pressed by its supporters into a policy of high

---

[15] On the *livret* see, for example, Godechot, *Les institutions*, p. 668 and, for French labour legislation generally, François Bédarida and Claude Fohlen (eds.), *Histoire générale du travail*, vol. III: *'L'Ere des révolutions'* (Paris, 1964), pp. 46ff.

tariffs. The need for economy on the part of the state and the continuation of protection were in accord with the thinking of the bureaucracy. There was little support for free trade but rather an exaggerated, almost hysterical, demand for tariffs.

Anglo-Saxon economic historians of the previous and of the present generation have tended to deal unkindly with France's protectionist policies in the first half of the nineteenth century.[16] It is true that the tariffs were imposed at a high, even prohibitive, level and the claim that cheap wheat was piling up in Odessa ready to flood the market was a figment of the imagination. Distance from such sources of supply provided a natural protection for French producers. On the other hand, there could be little doubt that for the industrialists the call for tariffs was a rational response to the threat from English and other foreign competition.[17] Who can say whether their fears were exaggerated? They were high-cost producers, having to pay more for their fuel and raw materials, with a less well-equipped industry and in some fields a less well-qualified work-force. Events in 1814–16 showed that they could be undercut in their own home market, especially in a period of depression. There can be little doubt that the less progressive manufacturers continued with their old routine ways behind tariff walls which kept up prices and profits. Family businesses, self-financing and catering for a fairly stable home demand, were especially prone to accept the protectionist argument and perhaps to slide into complacency. But without the opportunity to make profits the more progressive firms could not grow and might be driven to the wall by foreign competition in the absence of the tariff. Only a detailed examination of industrial development after 1815 can show what use industry made of protection. At this stage it may be that high tariffs were a condition not only for continued industrialization but to prevent the deindustrialization of the less competitive industries and areas.[18]

Certainly industrialists were convinced that their survival depended upon protection. Every attempt of the government to lower tariffs was

[16] On the rationale of French tariffs in this and subsequent periods see Shephard B. Clough, *France: A History of National Economics 1789–1939* (New York, 1939, rep. 1964). Critics of French tariff policy include Arthur L. Dunham, Rondo Cameron, Alexander Gerschenkron and John Habakkuk.

[17] 'The obvious necessity in such a situation was complete tariff protection. French industrialists were virtually unanimous in desiring high tariffs and even actual prohibitions on imports within their branch of production; they were naturally less concerned with protection for goods other than their own. Almost always, the principal rival cited in demands for protection was Great Britain.' Peter Stearns, 'British Industry Through the Eyes of French Industrialists (1820–1948)', *Journal of Modern History*, vol. XXXVII, no. 1 (March 1965).

[18] On the adaptive strategies adopted by French business see Maurice Lévy-Leboyer, *Les banques Européenes et l'industrialisation internationale dans la première moitié du XIXe siècle* (Paris, 1964). State action takes up very little in a book of over 700 pages.

greeted with an outcry. Although the bourgeoisie broadly accepted the creed of economic liberalism it was no less devoutly wedded to a nationalist policy in the sphere of maritime, colonial, and foreign trade. At home the government was expected to uphold the rights of private property, to maintain a climate favourable for investment, and ensure a supply of docile labour. This was done mainly through applying the law as hammered out by the revolutionary assemblies and the Napoleonic regime. But the restoration also inherited the *grandes écoles*, the Ecoles des Mines, the mining department, the Ponts et Chaussées, and the specialized corps of engineers whose admirers claimed they were the finest in the world. It was perhaps in this period that these institutions began to yield their fruits. There was no doubt about the competence of French mining and civil engineers; a number of them made important scientific and technical contributions. The law gave them wide, even overriding powers, in the case, for example, of the exploitation of minerals. They gave advice to industrial firms and passed on technical knowledge. They were one of the vehicles through which the British techniques of iron-making with coke were passed on to French industry. They could even be seconded to private firms.[19] Outside mining and metallurgy, however, the role of the state was hardly significant and even in them it was markedly less than under the old regime (when, for example, it had holdings in Le Creusot). Indeed, it was generally in an indirect way that the state assisted industry throughout the nineteenth century. Apart from its continuous responsibilities for the infrastructure, it was chiefly in providing training for leading personnel, giving advice and encouragement (for example, by organizing exhibitions), and collecting and disseminating information. Even the *enquêtes* (government enquiries into economic problems) organized from time to time depended a good deal upon information provided by industrialists and officials rather than carrying out a thorough and independent investigation. Although the state thus seemed to be omnipresent, at least compared with the situation in Britain, its activities can hardly have been on a sufficient scale to have given a major impulse to industrialization – or to have caused the damage which some critics alleged. What was notable was the relatively small extent of state intervention; French industrialization came about mainly through the market mechanism and the profit-seeking drives of private entrepreneurs. Indeed, some of the latter criticized the Restoration governments for neglecting industrial interests. Certainly their passion for balanced budgets limited spending on canals, roads, and other public works and they were ideologically committed to assist the landed proprietors rather than the business community. Dissatisfaction on this

[19] Examples in Jean Vial, *L'industrialisation de la sidérurgie française, 1814-1864* (Paris and The Hague, 1967), pp. 128-32.

score may have had something to do with the ready acceptance of the new regime after the July revolution of 1830.[20]

Whatever the exact class basis of the July monarchy, there can be no doubt that it was responsive to pressures from the bankers, financiers, and industrialists and pursued policies in their interests. In the troubled period following the revolution the government gave emergency credits to business and concentrated on providing the climate of order and confidence which it required. Once popular discontent had been brought under control the regime showed itself somewhat more ready than its predecessor to loosen the public purse strings and embark upon a public works programme of the kind desired by business. The most important of these works concerned transport facilities – the essential infrastructure for an industrializing economy. There is no doubt here that, while continuing an old tradition, the state was also accepting what was widely held to be an essential responsibility. Private business neither had the resources nor did it have the desire to undertake the heavy outlays required without state aid and a large measure of state initiative. Increased expenditure on roads, river improvement, and canals improved the facilities that private industry needed to open up the internal market and thus make possible new opportunities for profitable investment. The same considerations applied to the major innovation of the time, the railway. Requiring considerable outlays both for the acquisition of land and the building and equipping of the lines, needing the backing of an advanced industry and comporting special risks, there were few countries in which a railway system could be built without the assistance of the state and France was not one of them. The debate which began once the railway became a practicable proposition was not about whether the government should intervene but about the nature and extent of its intervention. This brought into play a multiplicity of interests in national politics, at the regional and local level, in rivalry between financial groups as well as those represented in the bureaucracy, especially the engineers of the Ponts et Chaussées. The battles that were joined from 1833 over the law regarding the compulsory acquisition of land no doubt slowed down the rate at which concessions were made and construction began. The building of two competing lines from Paris to Versailles showed the need for a coordinated national development plan to avoid overlapping and waste and speed construction. Not until 1842 was such a project accepted and in the meantime France had fallen behind, no doubt as much because of scarcity of investment capital and the effect of the depression after 1837 as from the absence of a determined policy.

The act of 11 July 1842 ended 12 years of indecision with a compro-

20 Christopher H. Johnson, 'The Revolution of 1830 in French Economic History', in John M. Merriman (ed.), *1830 in France* (New York and London, 1973).

mise: the state was to acquire the land, laying out the route and building bridges and tunnels, and companies were to provide the track, the rolling stock, and station buildings.[21] The lines were to be leased to the companies without charge and for no definite term of years. A number of main lines, mostly radiating from Paris, were put in hand with the financial backing of *la haute banque* (the big Parisian private bankers, mostly Protestant at this time, who were powerful figures) and by 1848 the mileage of track had tripled, but it was still small compared with the needs of the country and amounted to less than one-third of that in Britain. The state, including the departments and communes through which the lines ran, contributed 1,051 million francs out of a total outlay of 2,270 million francs. A start had been made in endowing France with the infrastructure necessary to carry industrialization forward. The state had, to be sure, to play a prominent role, inevitable in the circumstances, but a more massive effort would be necessary before the railway network was at all adequate for the needs of the economy.

In general the July monarchy showed itself more responsive to the needs of business than its predecessor.[22] State outlays increased in various directions, including the setting up of state shipping lines in the Mediterranean and the subsidizing of others. The tariff laws of 1836 and 1841 removed some prohibitions but left the protectionist system basically intact. Free trade propaganda carried on in imitation of the Anti-Corn Law League in England found only a limited echo and practically no support from the main industries. Some manufacturers wanted duties reduced on raw materials, machinery, and semi-finished goods. The iron-master, Charles de Wendel, became a free-trader hoping in that way to drive the backward firms out of business. A plan to buy out the sugar industry with government money was withdrawn and in 1843 an internal-revenue tax equal to the duty on cane sugar was imposed. Attempts to lower duties on a reciprocal basis with particular countries, notably the south German states and Belgium, were defeated by heavy opposition from producers who feared competition from cheaper imports. The crisis and depression from 1846 took what little wind there was out of the free-traders' sails.

In the wake of industrialization French society began to undergo more

---

[21] Arthur L. Dunham, *The Industrial Revolution in France 1815–1848* (New York, 1955), ch. IV; George Lefranc, 'The French Railroads, 1823–1842', *The Journal of Economic and Business History*, vol. II, no. 2 (February 1930); Roger Price, *The Economic Modernisation of France* (London, 1975) tends to overstress the role of railways.

[22] Johnson, 'Revolution of 1830', sees the balance sheet of state action during the July monarchy as positive but adds 'much more could have been done to improve banking facilities, to ease the financing of business, and to rationalize the tariff system, although the situation was not as bad as is often claimed. The law nevertheless largely favoured business and left it free to exploit its labour resources virtually at will', p. 168.

rapid change. Against the background of a still predominantly rural and largely peasant society the overcrowding in the populous quarters of the larger towns and the growth of new towns into industrial centres with a large proletarian population incited interest and concern. A number of important studies of working-class conditions were published by Comte Christophe Villeneuve-Bargemont (1834), Louis Villermé (1840), Eugène Buret (1841) and Dr Thouvenin (1846). Missing were the official enquiries of the type undertaken by royal commissions and parliamentary committees in England. Correspondingly, there was little in the way of legislation. The *notables* and urban bourgeoisie evidently accepted that poverty could be dealt with by charity rather than public action. Previous legislation against mendicity had done nothing to stop begging and periods of high food prices and economic crisis saw the old problem become acute. There was a tradition of trying to make work during such periods, with little effect. Some employers, the Protestants of Alsace were in the lead, adopted paternalistic policies towards their workpeople. A law of 1841 prohibited the employment of children below 8 years old in factories employing more than 20 workers and regulated the hours to be worked by those up to 16.[23] Children between 8 and 12 were supposed to attend a public or private school in the locality. However, the arrangements for enforcing the act proved to be inadequate. As for schools, although an act had again been passed in 1833, it placed the onus on the communes and progress in providing schools and qualified teachers was slow. In 1855 32 per cent of bridegrooms were unable to sign the marriage register and 38.9 per cent of conscripts were classed as illiterate. In the field of social policy, between 1830 and 1848 little more was done than to identify problems; the short-run results of the attempts to deal with them were still minimal.

Structural changes in the economy were beginning to create new areas of tension and opening up the possibility of a widening range of state action. Besides the growth of an industrial proletariat, the position of artisans and craftsmen in some of the traditional trades was being undermined by new methods of control and finance. Large-scale production in the hands of merchants could bring a worsening in the position of many workers and it was among them that the main audience for utopian socialism, cooperative workshops and trade unionism was found.[24] The popular discontent of 1830–2 had brought little positive response, except, perhaps, François Guizot's education law, nor did the regime have an answer to the ferment beneath the surface in the

---

[23] Text of the law in *Documents of European Economic History*, ed. Sidney Pollard and Colin Holmes, 3 vols. (London, 1968), vol. I, pp. 538–40.

[24] See for example the contributions by Bernard H. Moss and Christopher H. Johnson in Roger Price (ed.), *Revolution and Reaction: 1848 and the Second French Republic* (London, 1975).

working-class quarters of the 1840s. The social polarization accompanying early industrialization was a major factor behind the February revolution of 1848.

The favourable economic climate of the early 1840s redounded to the credit of the regime of Louis-Philippe and helped conceal its underlying weaknesses.[25] The crisis which began in 1846, compounding food shortage following a bad harvest with an industrial slump and the reaction to a spell of hectic speculation, stripped it bare, leaving it with no policy to meet the situation. Discontent was widespread among many sections of the population affected by one or another aspect of the crisis. The regime had lost confidence in itself and few were prepared to fight for it; it fell virtually without a struggle. While in Paris and a few provincial towns the working classes had come on the scene with demands of their own and there was a challenge to the former power-holders, over much of the country there was no basic change. In Paris and in some other towns the small traders, artisans, and wage-earners who had taken to the streets in February expected the new government to carry out social changes; the revolution was not so much the end-product of a period of agitation and mass discontent as its starting point. The Provisional Government at first made concessions to the Parisian working class and to cope with an unemployment problem aggravated by the revolution by acceding to the demand for recognition of the right to work and set up national workshops.[26] At the same time employers and workers sent representatives to a commission of enquiry into the right to work and the other demands voiced by the working-class participants in the revolution. The national workshops were designed for failure and the commission was nothing but a talking shop. The crushing of the rising of the working-class quarters of Paris in June following the move to close the national workshops ended any hope that the Second Republic would initiate wholly new social policies.

There remained the question of reanimating the economy by reviving the confidence of the property-owning classes and the investors. This required both the restoration of public order and renewed state spending on railways and public works. The elections to the Legislative Assembly and the big vote for Louis-Napoleon Bonaparte for president reflected the conservative feeling in the provinces under the influence of the *notables* and the disillusionment of the workers. However, during 1849 and 1850 budgets were kept small and balanced, in an effort to restore public credit. While there was recovery from the trough of the depression it was limited by lack of internal demand and by the holding back of

[25] Ernest Labrousse, *Aspects de la crise et de la depression de l'économie française au milieu du XXe. siècle* (La Roch-sur-Yonne, 1956).
[26] Donald C. McKay, *The National Workshops* (Cambridge, Mass., 1933).

credit by the government and the Banque de France. There could be no sustained prosperity until new order flowed into heavy industry and the armies of unemployed in the towns could be set to work on building and construction. Increasingly discredited by its divisions and indecisiveness, the Second Republic was simply unable to project a policy in accord with the needs of the property owners and left open the threat of renewed revolution from below. Louis-Napoleon presented himself as the strong man able to use the authority of the state to guarantee the rights of property, launch a programme of recovery, and make good the losses of five years of crisis and revolution.

VI. *State intervention and free trade under the Second Empire*

The conditions under which Louis-Napoleon assumed authoritarian powers by the *coup d'état* of 2 December 1851 imposed on his regime the task of promoting economic recovery. His backers expected it and he was aware from the start that they looked to him to provide firm government and new opportunities for accumulation. This required that the state should play a promotional role in the great transformation which France was undergoing as a result of the building of railways and the spread of industrialization. Operating in a favourable international conjuncture the Second Empire was able, especially in its early years, to swing behind it the major part of the business and property-owning classes and gain a wide measure of popularity. The health of the regime depended upon the state of the economy and knowing this its agents worked closely with the leading economic interests to encourage investment and assist all the forces making for change and growth. It continued, in a more determined way, the policy of extensive public works initiated under the July monarchy, aimed to endow the country with a modern infrastructure of roads, waterways, ports and harbours, water and gas works, and above all railways. The Emperor was also well aware that the best way to keep the workers from the barricades was to provide jobs in plenty. His regime thus saw vast programmes of construction put in hand, speeding up the modernization of France and changing the face of its major cities.

The activities of the state were not guided by any plan nor by any clear theoretical conception of its role. Despite the influence of businessmen and public servants who had in their younger days been influenced by the doctrines of Saint-Simon, it is doubtful whether they can be considered a decisive or even a major influence on policy. Decisions were made from expediency and grew out of the situation, rather than being determined in advance. Without recovery and prosperity the regime could not expect to survive. After the crises and shocks of the years from 1846 until 1851 business confidence could not be restored and the conditions for renewed growth provided unless the state took a hand. Public works were already the established means for this; it was only necessary to launch them on a sufficiently audacious scale. This required a break with the parsimony of the past, new methods of finance, new financial institutions able to tap the savings of wider layers of the population, and the willingness to offer inducements and privileges to the powerful financial and business groups whose cooperation was indispensable for a successful policy of state action. There was no question of the state greatly extending its field of operation in the economic sphere. Indeed the doctrines of economic liberalism, far from losing their influence, were gaining ground both in business circles and in the administration throughout this period. The state did not substitute itself for the private entrepreneur nor did it intend to supply capital for new projects unless absolutely necessary. While providing a framework of security for property owners by its authoritarian political structure, the regime set out to use the state to open up new opportunities for profitable enterprise and investment. Otherwise business was to have the maximum scope for the management of its own affairs. In accord with liberal economic doctrine the state interfered as little as possible in the running of industry; it left public works to private contractors; it handed the railway system over to a few powerful companies, and dispensed concessions and privileges to favoured private interests. Now more than ever before businessmen, including industrialists like Eugene Schneider or the textile manufacturer Pouyer-Quartier, secured public recognition and political influence. The capitalists were seen as the recognized leaders of industry and the state gave them every support.[27] Perhaps Napoleon III's most controversial measure and certainly the one which was most unpopular among industrialists was the policy of commercial treaties inaugurated in 1860. But this policy, in line with the thinking of some of the big industrialists, was intended to give a new impulse to the economy and certainly not to harm the interests of private capital.

The *coup d'état* had an immediate effect on business confidence. From the early part of 1852 the effects were seen in the resumption of railway building, stock exchange speculation and freer spending on the part both of industry and municipal authorities. Particularly important was the change of policy towards the railway companies. Now companies were granted concessions for through-lines or a whole region. Decisions were taken promptly and the credit of the state was placed behind the

---

[27] Guy Palmade, *French Capitalism in the Nineteenth Century* (Newton Abbot, 1972), translated with an introduction by Graeme M. Holmes, pp. 152ff.

financing of new construction. As Blanchard puts it, 'from January 1852, lines whose construction had been suspended for five years were reactivated: the Avignon–Lyons contract was awarded on 3 January, the Paris–Lyons contract on 5 January. Such swift procedure was not to stop: during the next few years, while the French rail network doubled and tripled in size, decisions were arrived at elaborated by a few ministers, a few senior technicians and the great financiers.'[28] This was the new iron broom which the Bonapartist regime was wielding to clear a path for expanding capitalism. There was no longer any question of the state taking over the lines, or at least not for 99 years. The state placed its credit at the disposal of private interests, notably the few great companies henceforth to dominate the railway system. With state support they were able to raise the capital required, a growing proportion in the form of stock even before all the share capital was fully paid up.

Like the railways, the other projects put in hand and encouraged by the state involved borrowing on an extensive and unprecedented scale. In this process of credit creation, the expansion of banking and the foundation of new institutions, the most famous of which were the Crédit Mobilier and the Crédit Foncier, played a vital part.[29] Here again, the state did not directly control, it merely opened the way for private capital. It was interested in immediate results and was prepared, as long as it was possible, to go on opening an account upon the future to finance the infrastructure required for industrialization and the urban reconstruction with all its possibilities for private money-making and speculation.[30] Financing thus remained in private hands, sometimes with a formal state guarantee of interest, as with the railways, at other times without. This method of financing was always under strain and susceptible to shocks. By 1856 the initial boom fed largely by the railways and other public works had petered out. The most remunerative lines had been built or their concession granted, and to keep construction going the state was obliged to extend further guarantees by the Franqueville convention of 1859, again in 1863, and two years later with the offer of a subsidy for the building of railways of local interest. In the early 1850s the state had been guaranteeing interest on lines expected to be profitable as well as giving a much-desired boost to the economy. After the crisis of 1857 it was obliged to keep railway building going on the grounds of

---

[28] Maurice Blanchard, 'The Railway Policy of the Second Empire', in François Crouzet, W. H. Chaloner and W. H. Stern (eds.), *Essays in European Economic History, 1789–1914* (London, 1969), pp. 103–4.

[29] Rondo Cameron, *Economic Development*, and 'The *Crédit Mobilier* and the Economic Development of France', *The Journal of Political Economy*, vol. LXI, no. 6 (December 1953); Palmade, *French Capitalism*, pp. 138ff.

[30] For an account of these methods see Louis Girard, *La politique des travaux publics du Second Empire* (Paris, 1952); and David H. Pinkney, *Napoleon III and the Rebuilding of Paris* (Princeton, 1958).

public interest, despite the fact that many lines might not be remunerative. It was now having to launch loans to meet its obligations to the companies and, from 1864, pay out cash on bonds which it had guaranteed. These transactions, as well as those in other fields, did not mean an invasion of the private sphere by the state; on the contrary, they served to keep the field free for private capital, offer it opportunities it might not otherwise have had and provide facilities for transport in effect subsidized by state borrowing.

In a way the economic policy of the Second Empire can be seen as an attempt to restore the confidence of business after the blows it had received in the previous years and then to compensate for the weaknesses of French capitalism more rapidly than business unaided would have been able to do. France had fallen seriously behind in the provision of railways and other infrastructural facilities. By the end of the Empire there were 17,500 km in operation compared with less than 3,000 when Louis-Napoleon had taken over. With all the other building and constructional work stimulated by the state France had taken a giant stride towards modernization. With the friendly backing of the regime more adventurous financial methods had been adopted both by public and by private institutions. The Crédit Mobilier was ultimately defeated by its rivals, but they paid it the compliment of taking over its methods.[31] Deposit banking of a modern kind became established and a law recognizing the cheque was passed in 1865. Company law was modernized in the 1860s, notably by the law of 1867 making possible the formation of limited liability companies without government authorization as required under the commercial code of 1808, thus bringing the situation in line with that in Britain.[32] Such companies also acquired legal personality and were to play a growing part in the business structure in the following decades.

In relation to industry the state tended to reduce its powers – by now, in any case, very limited. Industrial opinion, while sometimes accusing the state of neglect, was generally in favour of ending the state's residual powers, now mainly confined to mining and metallurgy. By the law of 9 May 1866 landowners were free to dispose of iron ore under their land to whomever they pleased, but other mines could still be granted as concessions by the state to persons or companies other than the owner of the land, while giving the latter the right to force the concessionaire to buy the property under certain conditions as well as paying a royalty on the mineral extracted.[33] For some sections of heavy industry the state

---

[31] David S. Landes, 'The Old Bank and the New: The Financial Revolution of the Nineteenth Century,' in Crouzet, Chaloner and Stern (eds.), Essays.

[32] Freedeman, 'Business Organisation', pp. 197–8.

[33] Felix Ponteil, Les institutions de la France de 1814 à 1870 (Paris, 1966), pp. 422–3.

was an important client; technological changes in naval and land armaments underlined the point. During this period, however, this trend was still at an early stage; nevertheless, expenditure on naval armaments more than doubled between 1852 and 1869.[34] State demand was appreciated because it was steady and tended to expand as a result of the regime's foreign policy.

The most controversial innovation made by Napoleon III in economic policy came in 1860 with the signature of a commercial treaty with Britain followed by similar treaties with Belgium, the *Zollverein* (German customs union), Italy, Austria, and other countries.[35] These treaties provided for a substantial lowering in the traditional tariff wall protecting French industry and were generally unwelcome to the industrialists. The Emperor's policy was influenced by a number of convinced free-traders, notably the economist Michel Chevalier (1806–79) and possibly by Emile Pereire (1800–75) of the Crédit Mobilier.[36] Although Napoleon III may have had political reasons for improving relations with Britain, it seems probable that these advisers convinced him that a lowering of tariffs would be a means of reanimating the economy in much the same way as railway building had done from 1852. While industrial interests were mainly hostile to any lowering of tariffs and only the authoritarian nature of the regime permitted the treaties to be entered into, there were some signs that important industrialists like François de Wendel considered that they had nothing to fear from foreign competition. There were others, like Eugene Schneider, who, hostile at first to the treaty with Britain, revised his opinion within a few years and said in the *Corps Législatif* in 1864, 'Your Majesty was right to go on ahead of public opinion in the matter of industrial freedom . . . Our industrialists

[34] Franklin W. Wallin, 'French Naval Conversion and the Second Empire's Intervention in Industry', in F. J. Cox *et al.* (eds.), *Studies in Modern European History in Honour of Franklin Charles Palm* (New York, 1956). State orders were increased at the time of the 1857 depression, after the commercial treaty with Britain and during the 1867 recession. For a comprehensive enquiry into the role of armaments, see François Crouzet, 'Recherches sur la production d'armaments en France (1815–1913)' *Revue Historique*, vol. CCLI (January–March 1974), pp. 45–84; and *ibid.* (April–June), pp. 409–22.

[35] The literature on this matter is extensive and perhaps greater than its importance warrants. The main study is still Arthur Dunham's *The Anglo-French Treaty of Commerce and the Progress of the Industrial Revolution in France* (Ann Arbor, 1930). See also, Marcel Rist, 'Une expérience francaise de libération des échanges au dix-neuvième siècle: le traité de 1860', *Revue d'Economie Politique*, vol. LXVI (November–December 1956), in English in Rondo Cameron (ed.), *Essays in French Economic History* (Homewood, Ill., 1970); Jean Coussy, 'La politique commercial du Second Empire et la continuité de l'évolution structurelle française', *Cahiers de l'Institut de Science Economique Appliqué*, series P, no. 6 (December 1961). The recent *Tariff Reform in France 1860–1900* (Ithaca, NY, 1980) by M. S. Smith, stresses the support for free trade in some business circles and the accommodation of interests in later tariff legislation.

[36] Barry M. Ratcliffe, 'Napoleon III and the Anglo-French Commercial Treaty of 1860: A Reconsideration', *The Journal of European Economic History*, vol. II, no. 3 (Winter 1973). Incidentally, he concludes that 'the role Saint-Simonians are reputed to have played in the French economy as engineers, enterpreneurs, financiers, theorists' is 'mythical', pp. 512–13.

have been able, by their efforts and their sacrifices, to resist foreign competition'.[37] That the policy of lower tariffs was intended to speed up modernization was shown by the loans offered to industry for re-equipment (not unlike those made on previous occasions during slumps). The economic effects of the liberalization policy have been the subject of much debate among economic historians without very conclusive results. It is difficult if not impossible to separate the lowering of tariff barriers from the many other factors perturbing the economic conjuncture in the following decade or so. Gerschenkron's view that, 'Through a policy of reduction of tariff duties and elimination of import prohibitions, culminating in the Cobden–Chevalier treaty of 1860, the French government destroyed the hothouse in which French industry had been kept for decades and exposed it to the stimulating atmosphere of international competition' probably represents the view of a majority of economic historians.[38] However, there is no more real proof of this than of the view, almost equally widespread, that the lowering of tariffs adversely affected the performance of the economy in the following two decades. The statistics do, in fact, show a slowing down in industrial growth, but those produced by Crouzet indicate that the decline began before the lower tariffs became effective.[39] Likewise, the stronger growth recorded after the return to protection in the 1890s cannot be attributed entirely to the tariff. The evidence of industrial change and the growth rates in the more advanced industries suggest that the liberalization of the French tariff may have had a stimulating effect at least for a time. For example, the change-over to the use of modern methods in the iron industry speeded up and the death knell of the archaic, charcoal-using sections sounded as a result of the treaty of 1860s. While protection may have been a rational policy if French industry was to survive in the face of British competition after the Napoleonic wars, by the 1850s it can be argued that the progressive sectors of French industry no longer required the prop of tariffs, at least at the high and prohibitive level at

[37] Cited in Vial, *L'industrialisation*, p. 433. The effect of the treaty was to favour the large-scale enterprises and sign the death warrant of the archaic, small-scale forges. According to Vial, the most important iron-masters of the period were conservative in politics and liberal in economics: 'Ils se sentent maintenant assez puissants pour secouer une tutelle qui les avait beaucoup servis, qui ne pouvait maintenant que prolonger l'existence des concurrents archaïques ou gêner l'essor des grandes entreprises industrialisées', pp. 433–4.

[38] Alexander Gerschenkron, *Economic Backwardness*, p. 11.

[39] Francois Crouzet, 'An Annual Index of French Industrial Production in the 19th Century' in Cameron (ed.), *Essays*. The view that the treaty was responsible for the slowing down of industrial growth is argued by Paul Bairoch in 'Commerce extérieur et développement économique: quelques enseignements de l'expérience libre-échangiste de la France au XIXe siècle', *Revue économique*, vol. XXI, no. 1 (January 1970), and more recently in *Commerce extérieur et développement économique de l'Europe au XIXe siècle* (Paris and The Hague, 1976). Coussy, 'La politique commercial', had already noted that 'l'hypothèse d'une accélération de la croissance française par les traités de commerce est contraire à toutes les statistiques observables', p. 44.

which they then stood. The infant industries had grown up. The Emperor's advisers perceived this if industrialists, many of them understandably, did not.

The circumstances under which the Bonapartist regime had come to power and its commitment to the defence of property rights and the creation of favourable conditions for the accumulation of capital hardly permitted it to embark upon far-reaching programmes of social reform. When in exile Louis-Napoleon had pondered on the social effects of industrialism and had written a book on the *Extinction of Pauperism* – a plan to set the unemployed to work in agricultural colonies. He may well have had a social conscience, but even those in the middle class who shared it looked more to private charity, self-help, and employer paternalism than to the state for the relief of poverty and distress. The memory of the 'socialist' projects of the early days of the Second Republic was still fresh. The Empire could claim that it had provided work for the unemployed on the railways and urban construction sites, but it did little to deal with the social problems accumulating in the wake of the more rapid industrialization now taking place. As far as relations between employers and workers were concerned the initial tendency of the regime was to strengthen the powers of the former. The workers' *livret* which had tended to fall into disuse was re-established by the law of 22 June 1854 and was to be kept by the worker himself. However, the law appears to have had little effect.[40] Some workers were proud to possess a *livret* in good and due form but the majority disregarded it and employers did not insist – it was not legally abolished until 1890. The law against combinations going back to 1791 was not modified until 1864 when combinations ceased to be illegal. In principle a strike in itself was not punishable but the text of the law left little scope either for trade unions or for effective strike action in practice. Workers' grievances could find proper legal expression only through the *conseils des prud'hommes* (instituted by the law of March 1806), consisting of elected representatives of masters and workers, a system which may have worked well enough in a stable society of small workshop industry but was ill adapted to the labour problems of large-scale capitalism.[41] Not until the law of 2 August 1868 was the word of a worker equal to that of his employer in a dispute over wage payment; until then the employer's word was accepted on his affirmation. But on worker–employer relations local custom and practice were probably at least as important as the letter of the law. Local trade societies, ostensibly for mutual aid, existed despite legal bans.

---

[40] This is the view of Georges Duveau, whose *La vie ouvrière en France sous le Second Empire* (Paris, 1946), gives the most complete view of social conditions during the period. The minimal character of state intervention can be judged from the little attention Duveau needs to give it.

[41] *Ibid.*, pp. 281–2.

Once the fear of insurgency still present in the early 1860s had worn off, the regime became more tolerant or took the view that it was best to allow openly what would in any case take place illegally and underground. Hence, during the period of the 'liberal Empire' a certain amount of open working-class activity – *syndicats* and cooperatives – was permitted.

Audacious in its economic policy by giving free rein to the creation of credit and encouraging grandiose enterprises, the Second Empire was timid in its social policy. It did little more than carry on the very inadequate services it had inherited from its predecessors.[42] The Emperor was ready to impose his fiat when it came to commercial policy, but his regime was tender to the property owners and employers in other matters. The omnipresent activity of the state was hardly the product of a comprehensive economic and social policy. The state did not plan or do things; it merely cleared the way and gave its backing to private interests. Private investors found most of the capital; the state's guarantee was more of a moral factor than a token of its intervention. The budget was used to raise loans for public works which enriched contractors, financiers, and speculators. The increasing wealth of those who participated in *la fête impériale* was scarcely touched by taxation, still mainly levied on consumption and therefore regressive in character. The regime shared the faith of the bourgeoisie in economic liberalism and concentrated on providing a framework within which market forces could operate to the advantage of the possessing classes. The wage-earners were still legally inferior and suffered limitations on their freedom to associate or hold meetings or to bargain collectively over wages and conditions. During the 1860s, it is true, the regime became more liberal and some worker grievances were partially rectified. There was still a distinct lag in factory legislation, in social welfare, health, and education. Where the state financed services and facilities it was mainly to provide for the training of the cadres of the middle class or to assist industry in some way. Despite the growth of towns and an increase in the size of the factory labour force, the peasantry made up the preponderant part of the population and many of the wage-earners were employed in small-scale and artisan production. In a still largely rural country, therefore, the need for a social policy was not yet pressing or at least had not yet impressed itself upon politicians and administrators still imbibing the undiluted doctrines of economic liberalism.

---

[42] Ponteil lists the appointment of thirteen spectators by a decree of January 1852, for prisons, asylums and poorhouses; the appointment of a committee of 23 members and four vice-presidents concerned with hygiene and medical services in hospitals; a decree to encourage the formation of mutual aid societies; and the attempts of the regime to maintain surveillance over private charitable foundations. The state also sponsored, by a law of July 1868, a scheme for voluntary life and accident insurance. The emphasis was upon encouraging private thrift and the existing charitable organisations – and also keeping them under control for political reasons.

VII. *The apogee of economic liberalism,*
1870–1914

Economic liberalism emerged stronger than ever from the trials of the military defeat of 1870–1, the downfall of the Empire and the fears generated by the Paris Commune. Social reform was under a cloud and the repressive measures taken in 1871 restricted labour organisations more severely than under Napoleon III. The emphasis was on conservation and stability: the defence of property and of *situations acquises*. The liberal dogmas were accepted by the business world, held sway in the faculties, and even governed the thinking of the civil service. It was noticeable that from the 1890s the influential officials of the Ministry of Finance were addicted to economic liberalism and opposed to state intervention. In these circumstances it is not surprising that the Third Republic until the outbreak of war in 1914 saw France move as close to a *laissez-faire* policy as was practically possible.[43] The public sector of the economy, inherited from the past, was kept deliberately small. Neither the government nor the Banque de France, still a privately owned corporation, accepted any responsibility for the guidance of the economy. There was no commitment to the use of the state to propel industrialization forward or to modernize the archaic agrarian structure. Where the state intervened it did so on a pragmatic basis, to deal with a problem insoluble through market forces alone, to back up acquired positions or to protect the status quo. It is difficult to find examples of

---

[43] From the time of the revolution there was a contradiction in the French conception of 'economic liberalism'. As Godechot, *Les institutions*, notes, speaking of the policies of the Constituent and Legislative Assemblies, their members were not theoreticians lost in the clouds. 'Ils n'ont pas hésité à transgresser les principes du libéralisme pour sauvegarder les intérêts de leur classe, qu'ils confondaient d'ailleurs avec ceux de la France entière, à laquelle ils s'identifiaient', p. 236. A similar point is made by Claude Fohlen in his article 'Bourgeoisie française, liberté économique et l'intervention de l'état', *Revue économique*, vol. VII, no. 3 (May 1956), and he concludes: 'Le libéralisme économique de la bourgeoisie au XIXe siècle ne serait-il qu'un mythe? Non, pas exactement, mais le concept est si souple qu'il peut toujours s'adapter à des situations changeantes. Ce libéralisme est d'abord à sens unique: du fait qu'il est entre les mains d'une bourgeoisie dominante et d'un gouvernement bourgeois, il sert leurs intérêts et se retourne contre ceux de leurs adversaires. Deux poids, deux mesures. Ce libéralisme se mue facilement en interventionnisme lorsque le profit est en cause: en temps de guerre, de crise ou de transformation, il appartient à l'Etat d'assumer les risques que les enterprises ne veulent pas affronter. Finalement, cette conception bourgeoise écarte le sense du risque et le goût de l'aventure que le législateur révolutionnaire avait cru bon susciter', p. 428. More recently, in a study of 'Technocrats and Public Economic Policy: from the Third to the Fourth Republic', *The Journal of European Economic History*, vol. II, no. 1 (Spring 1973), Richard Kuisel writes 'Under the Third Republic public policy was what the French called economic liberalism. The non-interventionist state, the free market, and individual entrepreneurship were all ideals. Indeed the state had little influence on private economic behaviour given the minuscule public sector and its restrained use of fiscal and monetary controls. Yet in practice the state intervened. Its actions were normally to protect the status quo, however, and rarely, if ever, to promote industrialisation or economic

state action deliberately taken to promote economic growth or structural change. But the ideology of non-interference was not consistently held; businessmen and agrarian interests were ever ready to request state aid when their interests were at stake.[44] Their professed belief in the virtues of a free market economy did not prevent them associating together to regulate prices or to put pressure on the legislature to preserve their profits. The most outstanding example, of course, was the return to protection, the reversal of the Emperor's most hated policy, the liberalization of foreign trade. Under the Third Republic, therefore, the maximum economic liberalism at home was combined with mercantilist, or Colbertian, policies regarding foreign trade, shipping, and colonies. The state was expected to exclude foreign competition from the home market but otherwise to leave the field as open as possible to the free operation of market forces. Continued industrialization and urbanization pushed the state, however reluctantly, into accepting wider responsibilities than before in the social sphere. Without much coherence, and generally behind comparable countries, a social policy to deal with education, factory conditions, health, housing, and other aspects of social welfare began to take shape.

After 1871, with the heavy financial legacy of the war indemnity, there could be no return to the spendthrift habits of the Empire. The response to the loan raised to satisfy German demands exceeded expectations and the new regime settled down to establish budgetary orthodoxy. Revenue was raised by increasing the old taxes; part of the orthodoxy of economic liberalism was steadfast opposition to an income tax or new property taxes. As a consequence indirect taxes accounted for

expansion. The state restrained rapid economic change, especially industrialisation, because it would have harmed established interests, like a backward or timid branch of industry, or a powerful social stratum, like the farm vote . . . Restriction and protection were essential to the functioning of French liberalism', pp. 54–5. See also his important study, *Capitalism and the State in Modern France* (Cambridge, 1981) for the twentieth century. Influential economists, like Clément Colson, taught the doctrine of economic liberalism in the elite institutions of higher learning from which came the top administrators, notably those in the Ministry of Finance. Even more dogmatic were the *laissez-faire* opinions expressed in the press and in parliamentary debates. It is easy to understand why French industrialists, confronting powerful competitors on the world market, first and foremost Britain, should have been predominantly protectionist, and with good cause. In the past, economic historians, especially the Anglo-Saxons, have been hypercritical of French protectionism; at times it may have been excessive but a case can be made for it and Paul Bairoch, notably, has argued that it was necessary to promote economic growth and, with some exaggeration, has claimed that growth lagged after 1860 as a result of freer trade, see his *Commerce extérieur et développement économique de l'Europe au XIXe siècle* (Paris and The Hague, 1976).

44 'In the nineteenth century, in France as in other countries, *the bourgeoisie knew how much its profits were dependent on the management of the state.* They wanted their share in investments, canals, railways and mines. They wanted to be heard when tariffs were fixed or treaties of commerce negotiated' (emphasis in the original), Gabriel Ardant, 'Financial Policy and Economic Infrastructure of Modern States and Nations', in C. Tilly (ed.), *The Formation of National States in Western Europe* (Princeton, 1975), ch. 3, p. 231.

an increasing proportion of revenue, rising to 80 per cent by 1900. The tax system corresponded to an economic structure still largely made up of peasants and small businessmen, highly individualist and particularly unwilling to declare their incomes to a government official.[45] Favourable to profits and private accumulation, it also limited what the government could do, even in the traditional field of public works, without raising loans. Government expenses in the 1880s and 1890s rose steadily, partly because of the increased costs of armaments, partly because of the growing responsibilities of the state in such fields as education. Part of these increased expenses was met from the extraordinary budget, that is by increasing the public debt. An income tax law was not passed until June 1914, did not come into effect until 1917, and proved to be unsatisfactory in large part because of the difficulty of obtaining accurate information about the income of those liable to the tax.

The French state contrived to give the impression of being omnipresent and that is perhaps the reason why its role has been exaggerated as far as the economy is concerned. To be sure, it had a large number of employees and their ranks were swollen by the growth of the postal service (the telegraph was also taken over by the state in the 1890s) and of primary education. Some 315,000 state employees were entitled to pensions on their retirement. Apart from the policemen, postmen, and teachers, most of the civil servants were carrying out the routine tasks of government. No doubt these had an economic side, concerned as they were with the raising and disbursing of tax revenue and the upkeep of the various services of government, including the armed forces. But in this respect the state's role was mainly passive; its influence on economic life was an unintentional result of the pursuit of other goals, principally those approved by economic liberals: the upholding of the rights of property and the sanctity of contracts, defence against external enemies and, more controversially, the acquisition and administration of colonial territories. It was an *état gendarme*, not a welfare state. Even armaments spending, while rising, remained relatively modest. France had a conscript army (men served for five years until 1889 when the term was reduced to two and raised to three in 1913) and this no doubt affected economic life and perhaps even the demographic trends which were giving cause for concern. However, in the last quarter of the century technological developments in warfare continued to raise the cost of armaments and their proportion of state spending rose from 3.55 per cent in the period 1875–84 to 4.50 per cent for the period 1905–13.[46] The arms race pushed up expenditure rapidly in the closing years of peace. Arms spending may have had some countercyclical effect in the stagnation following the

45 Bouvier, 'Sur "l'immobilisme"'.
46 Crouzet, 'Recherches'. This was, of course, a modest proportion.

financial crash of 1882 – again, presumably unintended – especially in the metallurgical and engineering industries. Even these industries did not depend upon state orders; but they received more because state ordnance factories failed to keep pace with the demand for more sophisticated weaponry. In fact, the private arms industry was largely a creation of this period and its need for heavy artillery, armour-plating, and ever larger warships. Dominated by an oligopoly of large concerns, it profited exceedingly from government orders, and exports, in the pre-1914 decade.

Apart from these activities, the state's main sphere continued to be that of the infrastructure: undertaking projects that private enterprise was unable or unwilling to promote and finance or assisting it to do so. In this sphere, too, the state was expected to provide a safety net; in effect, to nationalize losses in the public (and private) interest. The special relationship thus cemented between the railway companies and the state was again to be illustrated under the Third Republic. Industry was interested in efficient transport facilities; financiers saw in the promotion and running of railways a legitimate source of profits. Neither favoured a state takeover of railways but their interests were liable to conflict. The grouping of the companies into six major networks raised fears of monopoly. Moreover, in the provinces small and medium-sized businessmen complained that services were still inadequate and sought further construction in areas unlikely to yield paying traffic on a strictly commercial basis. Such factors as these made for continued state intervention to arbitrate between conflicting interests and try to satisfy all sides. The economic difficulties of the 1870s underlined the need for more public works and indicated that the state should once again take the lead. It did so in the shape of the so-called *plan Freycinet*, proposed by the Minister of Public Works (Charles-Louis Freycinet, 1828–1923) in January 1878 and placed before parliament in July of that year.[47] It called for the building of 10,000 km of new railway lines as well as additional government expenditure on waterways and ports. As voted a year later the project comprised the completion of lines already in hand, together with 8,848 km of lines of general interest and other lines of local interest to be decided by the ministry. In all the plan involved some 28,800 km of railway, most of which were of secondary importance or branch lines in various parts of the country, the cost of which was to be borne by the state.

Intended to counter an industrial depression, by the time it made itself effective industry was beginning to recover. A central purchasing agency was established to negotiate with the main producers for the supply of rails and other materials. Two loans, one of 600 million francs floated in

[47] 'Le "plan Freycinet", 1878–1882: un aspect de la "grande dépression" économique de la France', by Yasuo Gonjo, *Revue Historique*, vol. CCCXLVIII, no. 1 (January–March 1972).

1878 and another for twice that sum in 1881, were expected to meet the cost of the plan. It no doubt contributed to the boom which ended in the following year with the collapse of the Union Générale. The new turn in the financial situation forced the government to change its policy; by an agreement reached with the companies in 1883 they undertook to construct the regional lines in return for advances and subsidies from the state and a guarantee of interest on the operation of the lines. It was hoped in this way both to prevent a further financial involvement which could be damaging to the credit of the state and to ensure the continuation of the public works programme without the necessity for nationalization. The distinction between the old and new networks was to be abolished; the companies obtained greater financial security and for them, at least in the short run, it was a victory. As an experiment in state intervention the *plan Freycinet*, confined as it was to the extension of the infrastructure in response to the demands of business, was well within the liberal canon as understood in France at this time.[48] It carefully ruled out nationalization as an immediate prospect and offered very considerable advantages in its original, and still more in its revised form, to the railway companies, the railmakers, the bankers, and investors. In the years which followed the funds received from the public Treasury saved the companies from serious financial embarrassment, if not the bankruptcy of the weaker networks. Indeed one, the Ouest, reached this unfortunate position and in 1908 it was duly nationalized, as a few smaller lines in the region it served had earlier been. By this time, the political complexion of the parliament had changed, reflecting some weakening of the hold of economic liberalism in its purer form.

The conjunctural background already sketched in can serve to explain the trend back to protectionism, beginning almost immediately after the downfall of the Empire. No doubt protectionism was not simply a depression phenomenon, but might be called a visceral tendency on the part of many French manufacturers as well as those offended by Napoleon III's *coup d'état industriel* of 1860. The attempt by Adolphe Thiers (1797–1877) to restore protection and abrogate the commercial treaties in 1871–2 falls under the latter heading and failed in the face of divisions between industrial and agrarian interests in a period of general prosperity. After 1873, in a different climate, protectionism gained ground. By the end of the decade agricultural prices were sliding downwards and opinion was impressed by Bismarck's tariff law of 1879. Some tariff rates were raised in 1881, then came the financial crash of 1882 followed by

[48] Gonjo sees the 'plan' as a new stage in the relationship between industrial and railway capital and concludes 'Le principe financier du plan resta *libéral* malgré le caractère tout spécial de l'intervention de l'Etat. On peut donc dire du plan qu'il fut *un remède libéral à la dépression économique*; et que, par conséquent, l'effrondrement du plan rend sensibles *a posteriori* les limites de la politique libérale de cette période' (emphasis in the original).

general business stagnation. Although the French market was not flooded by cheap grain, the low prevailing world price bore down upon home producers and prevented them from raising prices to compensate for bad harvests. In addition sugar beet farmers were suffering from overproduction and the phylloxera epidemic drove the wine-growers into the protectionist camp. The main new factor in the 1880s was the protectionist trend in the agrarian community spearheaded by the big landowners, concerned about their rents, and the larger peasant propri-etors and tenant farmers who marketed a considerable proportion of their output. They found their champion in Félix Jules Méline (1838–1925), Minister of Agriculture 1883–5; the drift back to protection was completed in 1892 with the tariff law which bears his name, since he, as secretary-general of the tariff commission which recommended it, was its strongest advocate.[49] This law introduced a double tariff, the lower one to be applied to imports from countries offering French goods corresponding advantages, and applied to agricultural as well as indus-trial products.

Despite his interest in rural questions Méline's constituency in the Vosges was an industrial one; his claim that the tariff law which bears his name was the salvation of agriculture deserves to be treated with scepticism. That it represented a conservative aim, however, seems undoubted: it was intended to ensure to industry the command of its home market and to hold up the drift from the land by preserving a large and prosperous peasantry. As with all such policy measures it is difficult to disentangle its effects from those of the multitude of other interacting factors which shaped the structure of the economy and determined its growth path.[50] Insofar as its protection of agriculture was effective, by

[49] The standard work is still Eugene O. Golob, *The Méline Tariff: French Agriculture and Nationalist Economic Policy* (New York, 1944). Like the treaty of 1860 the return to high protection in 1892 has resulted in a good deal of controversy. See, for example, Michel Augé-Laribé, *La politique agricole de la France de 1880 à 1940* (Paris, 1950); Charles Kindleberger, *Economic Growth in France and Britain 1851–1950* (London, 1964); Clough, *France*; Bairoch, *Commerce extérieur*; Jean Lhomme, 'La crise agricole à la fin du XIXe. siècle en France', *Revue économique*, vol. XXI, no. 4 (July 1970); and Daniel Salem, 'Sur quelques conséquences du retour de la France au protectionnisme à la fin du XIXe. siecle', *Revue d'histoire économique et sociale*, vol. XLV, no. 3 (1967), for a detailed critique with the emphasis heavily on the negative aspects of the tariff.

[50] Kindleberger, *Economic Growth*, p. 281, sees the tariff as stemming the deflationary tide but adds, 'The side effects, limiting transformation, were harmful to French growth. But some action was inescapable if growth was to be resumed. The mistake was to continue and extend the range of protection. On the other hand, Bairoch, *Commerce extérieur*, pp. 232–3, claims it kept up rural income and aided recovery, with the protectionist years 1892–1914 showing a more rapid rate of growth than the period of low duties after 1860. Jan Marczewski, 'Histoire quantitative de l'économie française', *Cahiers de l'ISEA*, no. 163 (July 1965), p. cxxii sees the Méline tariff as giving extremely positive results in the short run, averting the disappearance of many peasant holdings, but he goes on to add: 'Ce point admis, on peut se demander si, à plus long terme, l'option protectionniste était vraiment opportune. Elle a empêché la France d'adapter ses structures agricoles et industrielles aux besoins de l'économie moderne et l'a condamnée de ce fait à une croissance modeste jusqu'à la seconde guerre mondiale', p. cxxii.

keeping up prices, it held back structural change. But the tariff could do little for the peasants, a substantial part of the rural population, who sold little and frequently continued to cultivate wheat and other cereals on land not well suited for them. In the absence of other, more specific, policy measures it could only confirm the archaisms of the rural sector. The state was not able to contemplate a wholesale reorganization of the land. For the more dynamic sectors of industry the tariff may have provided an impulse for modernization to meet the growing demands of the home market for steel, machinery, and other engineering products. For the older industries, growing more slowly, it may have acted as a cushion against foreign competition and encouraged the routinism and conservatism for which the smaller, family firms in the textile and consumer goods sector have been blamed. It tended to uphold the old habits and patterns of trade while it was unable to prevent German and American penetration of the home market and even encouraged, unwittingly, the establishment of foreign-owned factories in France. In any case, after 1892 the tariff resumed its place as part of the institutional structure of French capitalism, as means whereby it asserted its national identity. It appeared to be a defensive weapon in a rapidly changing world of aggressive economic rivals. It was increasingly difficult in the period after 1892 for its free-trade critics to make out a case for the lowering of tariffs able to win significant support. On the contrary, increasingly well-organized industrial groups campaigned for higher protection with some success, especially as they could point to the constantly rising tariff walls of other countries. The hardening of protectionist sentiment was reflected in the new tariff law of 1910. While retaining the double tariff permitting the making of commercial agreements with other countries, rates were again raised and an armoury of administrative measures included to deal with dumping and other practices of foreign countries considered unfair to French trade. During this period, too, a large part of the colonial Empire was brought within the tariff system of the metropolis: this meant free trade within the Empire and high tariffs against foreign goods. The weakness of the French mercantile marine made it impossible to confine the colonial carrying trade to French ships, though this was done in the case of Algeria by a law of 1889. Subsidies were extended to shipbuilders and shipowners by a law of 1881, including sailing ships, which the other maritime nations were giving up. There were other subsidy laws in 1902 and 1906, the latter intended to compensate shipbuilders for the difference between their own and British constructional costs. Direct subsidies were also paid to the shipping lines.[51] Nevertheless, these state payments

---

[51] Clough, *France*, pp. 239–43.

did little to strengthen France's maritime position. The improvement of the principal ports and the construction of new docks under the various public works schemes, including the *plan Freycinet*, should also be noted.

Taken as a whole the economic policy of the Third Republic in this period, while not markedly different from that of previous regimes, certainly lacked the innovating quality of that of the Second Empire. It was wholly in keeping with the prevailing economic liberalism while retaining and even reinstating, as far as foreign trade and colonial policies were concerned, something of the Colbertian approach. State intervention in the economy remained minimal and was undertaken on pragmatic grounds and, in the case of the return to protection and the *plan Freycinet*, clearly in response to cyclical trends.

Social policy was equally unsystematic and uninspiring and was distinctly an empirical response to changing conditions. Right through until 1914 the rural sector retained its predominance and the peasantry continued to make up the majority of the population. For reasons already explained, a peasant population does not make great demands on the state; the family, the local community, and the church take care of many of those afflicted by misfortune. Even in the towns, hospitals, asylums, old people's homes, care of orphans, the blind, the deaf, and the lame fell largely in the province of private or religious charity with some support from local authorities on an *ad hoc* basis. These services therefore varied very greatly in quality and in extent but did not generally give rise to much state activity and then only in a supporting role. What changed particularly was the growth of a mainly urban working class, more or less cut off from peasant roots, liable to the hazards of the business cycle, working in factories, mines, and workshops with dangers to health and welfare, and unable to provide from their wages for adequate housing or to make proper provision for incapacity and old age. Only the state could deal with the new kinds of social problems inseparable from the growth of a capitalist market economy, by virtue of its sovereign powers and its financial capacity; it alone could define and establish social minima for all members of society. However, in a climate of economic liberalism and individualism such propositions do not find ready acceptance.[52] Intervention is generally forced on an unwilling legislature by pressing needs, flagrant abuses, or the threat of discontent on the part of the working classes. Where there is a wide or universal suffrage, moreover, these needs and demands can find expression through the ballot box and politicians have to take heed of them. Moreover, the rise of a labour and socialist movement brings them to public notice and may challenge the existing basis of the state. All these factors contributed to the develop-

[52] For liberal objections to any kind of interventionism in the social field and their theoretical basis see especially Henri Hatzfeld, *Du pauperisme à la sécurité sociale, 1850–1940* (Paris, 1971).

ment of social policy in all the advanced countries in the second half of the
nineteenth century. France was no exception, nor was it a pioneer. It
lagged behind Britain in factory legislation and behind Germany in the
development of social insurance. Its record on education, apart perhaps
from some branches of higher education, was no more than average and
despite Louis Pasteur its health record was not outstanding. Governments committed to financial orthodoxy and balanced budgets could not
afford to be open-handed in laying on such provisions, all of which had
the disadvantage of being costly and, as we have seen, French property
owners had a deep aversion to paying taxes. Even when laws were passed
they might be indifferently carried out for lack of funds or of zeal on the
part of those supposed to implement them. The brief survey which
follows will attempt an assessment of performance in some of the main
fields of social policy.

Concern with higher and secondary education goes back to the old
regime and was heightened in the revolutionary and Napoleonic period.
While the state paid part of the cost schools and universities remained fee-
paying institutions, thus effectively confining them to the children of
comfortably off or middle-class families. The defeat by Prussia in 1871
and the cracking pace imposed by German industry increased the demand for efficient professional training and high-level research. A basic
reform was made in 1896 as a result of which existing faculties in the
provinces became the basis for new universities. Subsequently they
contributed to the training of recruits to the 'new professions' of the late
nineteenth century and helped link research to social and industrial needs.
Educational policy was more concerned with the production of an elite
than with education for the masses, at least during the nineteenth
century.[53]

State provision for primary education following Guizot's law of 1833
took the form of a financial contribution, but the major part of the costs
was borne by the communes and the families of the pupils. Primary
education was closely linked with the question of child labour; until laws
were passed excluding children below a certain age from the labour
market its impact was bound to be limited. Moreover, until it was both
free and compulsory many children would not attend school at all or
only for brief and irregular periods. As industry and society generally
required at least some degree of literacy for everyday purposes an
impulse was given to the spread of primary education. In the countries of
Western Europe this stage was reached in the last quarter of the nineteenth century. In France it was signalized by the laws of 1881 and 1882
making primary education free and compulsory between the ages of

[53] See G. Weisz, *The Emergence of Modern Universities in France 1863–1914* (Princeton, 1983).

seven and thirteen.[54] These laws were accompanied by an expansion in teacher training and thus an increased supply of trained teachers who, from 1889, were paid and appointed by the state. By 1913 the state had assumed the major share of the expenditure on primary education which accounted for about three-quarters of total state expenditure on education. At the same time, the state and local government bodies had assumed a growing share of the cost of most other forms of education. Access to the secondary schools, whether run by the state or by the church, was still mainly confined to fee-paying children. The universities and *grandes écoles* also remained the preserves of the educated elite, drawn from the middle class, though the development of education itself, and the opportunities it provided for teachers, opened the way for those *nouvelles couches sociales* whose rise was characteristic of the Third Republic. In this area the state was financing, as it had been since the First Empire or even before, the formation of the administrators, technicians, managers, lawyers, doctors, teachers, and other professional people required in increasing numbers in an advanced, industrializing society. As a result, and under the pressure of international competition, the state and local authorities had to bear a greater share of steadily rising costs. There was as yet, however, little sign of a democratization of higher education; the growth in the middle classes generated the demand while children of peasants and workers had little opportunity of rising into a higher class through the educational ladder.

A corollary of the extension of primary education by the laws of the 1880s was a more comprehensive and effective system of factory legislation. During the period of intensive industrialization between the law of 1841 and until 1874 nothing was done to limit child labour.[55] In the latter year children under 12 were excluded from factory work, with certain exceptions when the hours worked were not to exceed 6 per day. Boys between twelve and sixteen years were not to work more than twelve hours per day and not for a continuous period. For the first time, under this law, a corps of inspectors was appointed. The law of 1892 applied to women as well as children, laying down that 'Girls under 18 and women may not be employed for more than 11 hours a day.'[56] The law regulated the hours of work in all kinds of employment, including educational and charitable institutions. With some exceptions children

---

[54] These laws could be described as the pride of the Third Republic, establishing a nationwide system of *secular* education. However, the church continued to occupy a strong position at both the primary and the secondary levels and in strongly Catholic areas had the support of the majority of families so that the schoolmaster might find himself a social pariah.

[55] For industrial conditions during this period see the recently reprinted work by Fernaud and Maurice Pelloutier, *La vie ouvrière en France* (Paris, 1900; rep. 1975).

[56] Text of the law in Pollard and Holmes, *Documents of European Economic History* (New York, 1968), vol. II, pp. 412–19.

under thirteen were excluded from the labour market; those between thirteen and sixteen were not to be employed in actual work for more than 10 hours a day; for young people up to 18 a work week of 60 hours was laid down as the maximum with not more than twelve hours to be worked in any one day. Women were also excluded from underground work and girls under 21 and women as well as children under eighteen were excluded from night work. During the 1890s there was further legislation on hygiene and safety at work. Employers' liability for accidents was established by the compensation law of 1898. The law of 1900 provided for a 10-hour day to become fully operative in 1904. In the following years there was a growth in administrative intervention in various directions, reflecting the growing pressure from the political and industrial wings of the labour movement and also the fact that only the state could impose the minimum standards considered to be socially desirable and check the excesses and abuses resulting from a competitive market economy.[57] More importance was given by the government to the Conseil Supérieur du Travail, an advisory body now to include elected representatives of labour; it enquired into and reported upon such matters as hours of work, a weekly rest day, trade training, and various aspects of industrial relations, and evidently exerted some influence on legislation. The growth of administrative business in this sphere led to the establishment of a new Ministry of Labour in 1906. The mass of legislation which had accumulated since the 1890s was codified between 1910 and 1912 into a comprehensive *Code du Travail*. Despite differences in detail and effectiveness this reflected the fact that the state in France was obliged to extend its role in the same way as was happening in all the advanced industrial countries.[58]

In some fields, however, France was definitely lagging behind. There was nothing comparable, for example, to the German system of social insurance but some steps were taken in that direction.[59] There was no general right to assistance under the French law; relief of the poor was left to public and private charity on a local basis. In 1893, however, the poor became entitled to free medical attention. About 45 per cent of the cost of succouring the two million or so beneficiaries was met by the state before 1914. Laws passed in 1904 and 1905 extended assistance as a right to indigent children, to the old, infirm, and incurably ill, mostly through institutional care. This was still provided through the existing channels, mixing private, religious, and local charity with financial aid from the communes, departments, and the state. It was a case of palliatives rather

---

[57] Charles W. Pipkin, *The Idea of Social Justice* (New York, 1927), ch. IX, for details. This was a pioneer study, on a comparative basis, of French and British social legislation.

[58] See, for example, Patrice Grevet, *Besoins populaires et financement public* (Paris, 1976).

[59] Hatzfeld, *Du pauperisme*.

than a systematic approach to the social problems of an advanced society. From the middle of the century the state had encouraged private saving and provision for old age, but only limited numbers took advantage of these facilities. With a growing wage-earning class the problem of providing for support in retirement became of more importance in the latter part of the century. State employees and members of the armed forces were already pensionable. Special schemes were also introduced into some industries, employing the insurance principle; miners' pensions were provided for under a law of 1894 and railwaymen (some of whom had been entitled to pensions before) were dealt with in laws passed in 1890 and 1909. A compulsory pension scheme for workers earning below a certain amount was not introduced until 1910, following much discussion and opposition. The weaknesses of the scheme and the smallness of the pension even for those who had paid in contributions for the full 30 years means that it can only be regarded as the first halting step towards the establishment of a general system of social insurance. In 1913 3,437,000 workers were covered by the law.

The rapid growth of towns from about 1890 posed more sharply the old question of working-class housing; pressure on housing space produced the familiar problem of overcrowding and the creation of slums. The difficulty which some, mostly the larger, enterprises found in recruiting a labour force because of the lack of low-rent housing in the vicinity led to the construction of factory villages or towns as an adjunct to factories and mines. This solution was not open to those firms which had of necessity to be located in or near existing centres of population and whose very presence tended to force up rents and create overcrowding. Here was a sphere, therefore, for intervention by the local authorities or the state by providing subsidized housing which wage-earners could afford. However, believers in economic individualism were reluctant to accept such a conclusion, some hoping that workers could be 'deproletarianized' by enabling them to buy their own homes. This proved to be a vain hope. Housing provided to rent by private enterprise remained far from adequate in extent or quality and it was impossible to build houses for sale within the reach of most wage-earners. By the end of the century it was conceded that a limited amount of state intervention might be necessary to bridge the gap between housing needs and the supply of cheap accommodation. The first step came with the law of 1894 which created a Conseil Supérieur des Habitations à Bon Marché (HBM) and similar bodies in the departments to encourage the building of low-cost housing, mainly by tax exemptions.[60] An addition to the law in 1906 enabled local authorities to make loans to societies set up to build HBM

---

[60] Grevet, *Besoins populaires.*

and in 1908 another law made it possible for the state to make loans at 2 per cent. Up to the outbreak of the war there were only about 40,000 housing units made available under this legislation so that it had made virtually no contribution to the housing problem and could have exerted no effect on the general level of rents. An enquiry at the time of the 1911 census suggested extensive overcrowding; for example, of the population of Paris 43 per cent lived in accommodation with less than one room per person. Many workers' dwellings lacked running water and lavatories (three-quarters according to one enquiry). In short, then, the state proved helpless in the face of one of the major social problems of the period mainly because of its reluctance to interfere with the rights of property and the laws of the market. It was a problem which was to be greatly aggravated by the war and hung heavily over the following decades.

VIII. *War, instability, and crisis, 1914–39*

The war of 1914 brought to an end a long period of relative stability in which the role of the state had been essentially to allow market forces to operate as freely as possible according to the canons of economic liberalism. True, there had been a steady extension of its functions into the social sphere to deal with particular problems and protectionism had hardened into a system of national policy. But the working of the economy was believed to be no concern of the state and it only influenced it indirectly, and not by intention. Despite the division of Europe into two armed camps and a series of diplomatic crises, adequate preparations had not been made for the war when it came on the assumption that industrial economies could not support a lengthy war. The nature of total war between advanced countries with considerable industrial potential had not been envisaged on either side and only became clear in the course of the conflict. In the early stages policy-makers were reluctant to intervene in the economy and it was only in the course of 1915 that an apparatus of controls and administrative intervention was built up. Policy-makers were forced by the implacable demands of the war machine to mobilize the entire economy and assume direct control over it.[61] Even so, the intervention of the state, continuing to grow throughout the war, was a pragmatic response to a series of exigencies imposed by the situation and not a conscious or systematic process. It was seen, moreover, as alto-

---

[61] Social and economic policy in the war period is covered in detail in the studies published under the auspices of the Carnegie Endowment for International Peace. Some of the volumes for France were published in English translation. A summary will be found in Tom Kemp, *The French Economy, 1913–39* (London, 1972); Pierre Renouvin, *The Forms of War Government in France* (New Haven, 1927), deals with the response of government.

gether exceptional and abnormal and thus to have no lessons for the post-war economy.

The involvement of the state with the economy began with the mobilization itself. It was assumed that the war would be short and the first steps were intended to facilitate the task of the military command and deal with the impact the war had made on the financial system and the families of those who had departed to the front. It was soon clear, however, that the resulting industrial chaos could not be tolerated. There had to be an organization of production to meet the needs of the armed forces and ensure civilian supplies. The market was not only inadequate under such conditions but it operated in contradiction with the aims of policy: it had to be superseded or held in check by administrative means. The state was driven inexorably to extend its powers regardless of the sacrosanct principles of liberal political economy and even the rights of private property.[62] As the war went on the state's involvement became deeper and more all-encompassing, but it remained pragmatic in its essence. Government demand on behalf of the armed forces and to ensure the maintenance of necessary supplies to the home front became paramount. It took whatever steps were required to control and allocate supplies of raw materials, direct and distribute the labour force, make available transport facilities, and fix prices and wages.[63] Most of the apparatus of production continued to be in private hands; the market was not abrogated completely. Although final output was largely deter-mined by the government in the last three years or so of the war it still had to be paid for at prices which included an often generous profit for the entrepreneur. In the mapping out of industrial policies and the allocation of materials representatives of the firms concerned were drawn into the administrative apparatus. Likewise, in dealing with labour the govern-ment went out of its way to win the cooperation of the trade unions without which it could not have carried out the mobilization of indus-trial labour, including that of many women, foreigners, and other newcomers.[64]

Unavoidably, in an atmosphere of war fever and desire to meet the imperative needs of the battle front, there was much improvization and the inevitable extravagances and mistakes. Costing was often over-

---

[62] Renouvin, *War Government*, pp. 53–4.

[63] See the Carnegie volumes, Arthur Fontaine, '*L'industrie française pendant la guerre* (Paris, 1924); Andre Créhange, *Chômage et placement*, (Paris, 1924); Marcel Peschaud, *Politique et fonctionnement des transports par chemin de fer* (Paris, 1926); and Pierre Pinot, *Le contrôle du ravitaillement de la population civile* (Paris, 1925).

[64] Roger Picard, *Le mouvement syndical devant la guerre* (Paris, 1927); William Oualid and Charles Piquenard, *Salaires et tariffs, conventions collectives et grèves* (Paris, 1928); Bertrand Nogaro and Lucien Weil, *La main d'oeuvre étrangère et coloniale* (Paris, 1926); and Marcel Frois, *La Santé et le travail des femmes pendant la guerre* (Paris, 1926).

generous; there was room for profiteering and outright fraud. Above all, the methods chosen to finance war spending proved to be excessively costly, divisive, and destabilizing. By choosing what appeared to be the easiest way out of budgetary difficulties while the war was on, wartime governments stored up enormous problems for the future. According to Jèze, the historian of wartime expenditure, 'The financial policy of France during the Great War of 1914–18 will remain a model of what *should not be done*. A worse financial administration it would be difficult to conceive.'[65] At the outbreak of the war the country's tax system remained archaic: the majority of taxes were indirect and although an income tax was passed on the eve of the war it did not go into operation until 1916 and was not really effective until after the war. Lack of an accepted system of assessment for income and property taxes was a serious handicap in financing the war. As direct taxes could not be increased the government resorted to borrowing from the banks and the public as the main source of war finance. While government expenditure rose ninefold during the war, receipts from taxation increased by only about 50 per cent. This policy brought an inevitable inflationary pressure, only held in check by wartime controls. Meanwhile some parts of foreign investments were sold off and debts were contracted with allied countries, notably the United States: storing up more trouble for the future.

Wartime controls became more complete as the war proceeded and the techniques of administration became more efficient. The state had to undertake more direct intervention in industry, encouraging large-scale production, concentration, and the application of new techniques and itself becoming an entrepreneur through the setting up of new munitions plants. However, it would be an exaggeration to speak of a 'planned' economy, although it was certainly a statist one. There was no overall plan, but rather a series of authorities and measures growing up in an empirical way to meet particular problems. Intervention on this scale had never been required in previous wars, but it was regarded as a distasteful necessity to be brought to an end as soon as the emergency was over; only a few individuals considered that there were any enduring lessons to be drawn from the experience. The overwhelming preference was for a return to a free market system as soon as possible after the war was over. Although business had been brought together into trade associations and similar organizations with government encouragement and the trade unions had assumed a more important role as part of wartime industrial mobilization, neither organized business nor labour were to exercise as

---

[65] Gaston Jèze and Henri Truchy, *The War Finances of France* (New Haven, 1927), pp. 119ff.

much influence in post-war France as they did in Germany and some other countries.[66]

The war had been a tremendous traumatic experience for France. The loss of manpower, the devastation of the occupied departments, and the disruption of established social and economic relations over four long years brought a desperate longing for a return to stability. For the upper and middle classes that meant an end to state intervention, the restoration of the franc to its pre-war gold value and the re-establishment of the pre-war social hierarchy. Unlike the defeated countries, and despite the terrible human and material costs of the war, post-war France did not face the threat of revolution. The services of organized labour were recognized by the passage of legislation providing for an eight-hour day in industry, but the new-found power of the unions was short-lived. The solidarity strike for the railwaymen in 1920 was a complete failure.[67] The split in the trade-union movement following the formation of the Communist Party at the end of 1920 weakened the labour movement still further as a bargaining force. Throughout the 1920s it hardly entered the arena as a serious factor and it won no other major concessions until 1936. The post-war problems of economic and social policy did not arise, therefore, out of a powerful challenge from labour but were the outcome of the war, aggravated by the ineptitude of bourgeois politicians both during and after the conflict. Divisions within the propertied classes rather than the class struggle of workers against employers governed the politics of the period.

Post-war financial policy, until 1924, was based on the illusion that the costs of the war and reconstruction would be met out of the reparations payments imposed upon Germany by the treaty of Versailles. Indeed, early in 1920 a special budget was established in which these costs, which it was hoped would be recovered, were inscribed. In the meantime they were to be met by an increase in the floating debt, in other words, by the same inflationary methods adopted during the war. While reconstruction went ahead in the former occupied territories, French statesmen, in an increasingly unsympathetic international atmosphere, tried to impose payment on Germany without avail.[68] As a consequence, confidence in the franc was further undermined especially when it was clear that there were no means of making Germany pay and that the United States was not willing to scale down the debts owing from its wartime ally. The problem of the franc cannot, however, be separated from the overall economic policy of the post-war years. Almost as soon as the war had

[66] Charles S. Maier, *Recasting Bourgeois Europe* (Princeton, 1975), especially pp. 70–6.
[67] Annie Kriegel, *Aux origines du communisme français* (Paris and The Hague, 1964), vol. I, part 2.
[68] Maier, *Bourgeois Europe*.

ended, and officially that was on 24 October 1919, the cry went up from the press and business circles for the ending of controls and the return to the pre-war free market economy. More or less rapidly this was done, demobilization steadily took place, refugees returned to their former homes in the northern and eastern departments, and government-financed rebuilding began. In contrast with most of Europe, and with the exception of the abortive rail strike of May 1920, relative social peace prevailed. Foreign workers, or many of them, went home, while the tasks of reconstruction provided work and prevented the appearance of an unemployment problem. At government expense, new factories, mines, means of communication, towns and villages were brought into being in the devastated regions. French industry entered on a period of expansion and modernization; there was a contrast throughout the 1920s between this industrial growth and the financial turmoil. Yet the troubles of the franc represented an unwillingness of the state to intervene with positive measures: higher direct taxes, control of the money markets, the restructuring of the economy.[69]

Despite continued faith in economic liberalism, however, state involvement with the economy had increased as a result of the war. Besides the costs of reconstruction, the budget now had to provide for the many millions of war victims and their dependants. Government tax revenues as a proportion of national income rose from about 10 to 12 per cent pre-war to between 15 and 18 per cent by 1924. Taxation had become slightly more progressive but the new income tax did not operate fairly and evasion was, and continued to be, widespread. Socialist advocacy of a capital gains tax went unheard, or rather only frightened owners of wealth during the years when confidence in the franc was falling. Neither the right-wing government elected in 1919, nor the Cartel des Gauches elected in 1924, had any grasp of the situation and both stood firm by liberal remedies. The monetary crisis had contributed to the downfall of the government in 1924, but it only worsened under a government regarded with suspicion and disapproval by much of the business and financial world. The question at issue was simple but crucial: was the franc to be stabilized at its pre-war gold parity? A positive answer was ruled out when it became obvious that reparations from Germany would not be forthcoming. The question therefore took on a different aspect: at what rate should it be stabilized? While these questions were being debated budgetary mismanagement and the collapse of public confidence drove the franc down and ruled out a high rate without an intolerably drastic deflationary policy requiring massive government

[69] On this question see Kemp, *French Economy*, and the literature cited. New light is cast on the debate in government and business circles by Jean-Noel Jeanneney, *Francoise de Wendel en Republique: l'argent et le pouvoir, 1914–40* (Paris, 1976).

intervention in the economy. The question was resolved on an emergency basis when, in July, Raymond Poincaré (1860–1934) was called upon to form a government of National Union. The return of a prestigious conservative leader helped restore confidence, but Poincaré was obliged to recognize the inevitable, however distasteful: the franc had lost four-fifths of its pre-war value. In fact, the *de facto* stabilization of 1926 and the *de jure* stabilization of 1928 slightly undervalued the franc and thus offered a premium to French exports in the closing stages of the boom and helped initially to shelter the economy against the first signs of depression.

During this period, then, the struggle for the franc overshadowed all other issues of economic policy. As long as prosperity continued there was no demand from industry for government assistance, apart from the by-now customary protective tariffs. There were a number of tariff laws in the 1920s, with comprehensive and detailed rates, opening the way for commercial bargaining with other countries. Taking into account international agreements the average rate of protection was 12 per cent by 1930.[70] The state had kept control of the railways and the potash mines recovered from Germany in Alsace-Lorraine, but the coal mines were handed over to private companies. 'Mixed' companies were formed in Alsace in 1924, the Compagnie de Navigation du Rhin and the Chantiers et Ateliers du Rhin, but this did not create an immediate precedent for similar forms of mixed enterprise. It was not until the economic crisis began to strike home that, with few exceptions outside the Left parties, there was serious pressure for a more positive state policy. Although the depression when it came struck with less force than in some other countries, its effects were more prolonged: for this the policy of successive governments of varying political complexions was in part responsible. While other countries left the gold standard and devalued their currencies from 1931, the franc was maintained at the parity established by Poincaré until 1936. This meant that French exports were priced out of many markets, the industrial expansion came to an end, and new investment was halted. The opposition to devaluation left the government with no alternative but deflation, thus aggravating the contraction in the home market. Confronted with shrinking markets industry adopted a defensive stance and turned increasingly to the state to uphold established positions, notably by assisting it to adapt production to the lower demand. Malthusianism of this kind permeated most aspects of policy during the depression.[71]

[70] Alfred Sauvy with the collaboration of Anita Hirsch and others, *Histoire économique de la France entre les deux guerres*, 4 vols. (Paris, 1975), vol. IV, ch. I, 'La politique commerciale' by Anita Hirsch reviews tariff policy from 1892.
[71] 'Malthusianism' is applied to policies designed to limit and restrict production whether promoted by the state or by private business, thus aggravating stagnation in the economy.

The first concern was to protect the home market more securely. Tariff rates were increased in 1931 and laws passed in 1934 gave the government powers to raise tariffs administratively subject to subsequent ratification. Surtaxes were imposed to compensate for lower prices prevailing in countries from which imports came; thus British goods became subject to a 15 per cent *ad valorem* surcharge. Quotas had already been provided for in a law of 1929 and were frequently made use of from 1931, applying to most agricultural products and then to many industrial goods. Administrative control of import trade became increasingly complex. Clearing agreements were made with a number of trading partners. The powers of the state became even wider in the late 1930s; although by then the average duty was 19 per cent, many commodities were, in practice, subject to quotas which had taken over from tariffs as the main protectionist weapon.[72]

A series of measures was taken to deal with the agricultural depression. In the case of cereals imports were prohibited, minimum prices were established, and in 1934 producers who rendered wheat unfit for human consumption were paid a premium. A number of laws regulated wine production, notably by prohibiting the planting of new vineyards, payment to wine-growers who reduced the number of their vines, and the compulsory distillation of a certain proportion of the vintage. These measures did not arrest the decline in peasants' income or assuage their discontent and were an open invitation to abuse and evasion. Part of the sugar beet crop was purchased by the Service des Alcools at a fixed price for distillation.

Industry was more capable of taking its own restrictive measures through cartels and inter-firm agreements. Organized business then sought the aid of the state to buttress *situations acquises* by tariff protection, the blocking of new entrants, and keeping up prices. While in the immediate post-war period French industry had been slow to organize on corporate lines, during the depression it began to make up for lost time. In coal, steel, chemicals, and other industries price-fixing agreements and quotas disposed of free competition under the benevolent eye of the state. The president of the employers' association the Confédération Générale de la Production Français called on the state to compel firms to adhere to cartel agreements and to assist in the organization of the economy, meaning the limitation of production to the capacity of the market. Under the impact of the depression the idea of an organized or regulated capitalism was taking over from the old doctrines of economic liberalism. Among intellectuals, industrial managers, and civil servants there was growing support for state intervention and a 'technocratic'

[72] Sauvy, *Histoire économique*, vol. IV.

policy to meet the crisis. The legislatures continued with an entirely haphazard and illogical policy of intervention, highly restrictive in nature. For example, no new plants were to be established in the sugar industry by a law of August 1935. By a law of March 1936 no new plant was permitted in the shoe industry and no expansion of an existing plant was to take place without authorization from the Ministry of Commerce; this was later extended to prevent the opening of new repair shops for a period of five years. A law of October 1935 prohibited the putting into service of new mobile shops. In March 1936 no new fixed-price shops were to be opened and in March 1937 a law gave legal backing to the limitation of the number of taxis by the trade.[73]

The Popular Front government of 1936–7 made some important changes in economic policy but did not represent a sharp break with these industrial policies. More from force of circumstances than from intention, however, it did abandon the attempt to hold the franc at its 1928 value and end the deflationary policies of previous governments. The policy of the Popular Front government differed somewhat from the programme on which it had been elected, but in neither one was the nationalization of basic industries, banks, or transport envisaged. The aim was an expansion of the economy within the framework of capitalist property relations by raising the purchasing power of the mass of the population. The policy actually carried out was determined by the pressure of the strike movement which heralded its arrival in power, and the constraints imposed on a reforming government opposed by those who controlled the levers of economic power and subject to the overriding laws of the market economy. The government was thus obliged to start with social reforms envisaged in the Matignon agreement which brought the strikes to an end. The wage increases, holidays with pay, and above all the forty-hour week raised industrial costs, passed on as higher prices.

It is worth mentioning that the cost of these reforms fell on private industry, not on the state budget, except insofar as the state was an employer. The only major increase in public expenditure (which opponents of the Popular Front could also accept) was a massive rearmament programme. There was no intention of embarking on a Keynesian-style policy of deficit spending; Keynes' ideas on this matter were little known in France. There were, however, advocates of a 'technocratic' style of interventionism and economic 'planning'; their ideas came into their own after 1945.[74]

---

[73] See especially Kuisel, *Capitalism and the State* and Frankenstein, *Réarmament*.

[74] See J. J. Clarke, 'The Nationalization of War Industries in France, 1936–37; a Case Study', *Journal of Modern History*, 49 (September 1977); R. Frankenstein, *Le prix du réarmament français, 1938–39* (Paris, 1982), and his 'Intervention étatique et réarmement en France, 1935–1939, *Revue économique*, no. 4 (July 1980).

The socialist Prime Minister Léon Blum (1872–1950) held that he had no mandate for making inroads into capitalist property. A long-time advocate of a tax on wealth, his government was too dependent on attempting to revive the confidence of investors to impose it when he had the opportunity. His theory that the crisis resulted from inadequate purchasing power led him to believe that he could count on the goodwill of employers and investors in an expansionist policy by raising wages without reducing the incomes of the better off. Blum failed to revive the economy; he neither satisfied the demands of the working class nor won the confidence of the bourgeoisie.

The only proposal for nationalization in the Popular Front programme was that of the armaments industry, a traditional demand of some Radicals as well as of the Socialists and Communists committed to the nationalization of industry as a whole. The intention was to take the profits out of war contracts; there had been much talk in the 1930s about 'the merchants of death'. It was also expected that state ownership would improve the efficiency of supply of modern weapons in accordance with the needs of the armed forces. In July and August 1936 a measure for the selective nationalization of the armaments industries in accordance with the needs of the service chiefs was introduced by the Radical Minister of War, Eduard Daladier. Although no doubt approved by those who had voted for the parties of the Popular Front, the measure was strongly opposed, not only by the firms concerned but also by business as a whole. It fitted in with the rearmament programme of the Popular Front which was handicapped by the inadequacies of the factories producing modern weapons and the unwillingness of private producers to commit themselves to producing long runs of such weapons. Such benefits as the nationalization conferred, however, were not to be seen for several years when plants had been re-equipped and decisions had been taken about which prototypes should be developed for large-scale production.[75]

Notwithstanding the prevailing Malthusianism and the failure of the Popular Front government, the 1930s can be said to have experienced a slow change in economic policy towards a more active intervention by the state.[76] The Popular Front government increased the state's powers over the Banque de France and nationalized part of the armaments and aeronautical industries on grounds of national defence. The law of August 1937 united the railways into a single system, the Société Nationale des Chemins de Fer, in which the state had a 51 per cent holding. It also took a share of shipping companies and airlines and was represented by minority holdings in the strategically important oil

[75] On these policies see Sauvy, *Histoire économique*, vol. II.
[76] Kemp, *French Economy*. Good factual coverage of the 1930s can be found in Sauvy, *Histoire économique*.

industry. From the 1920s the state had helped to develop hydroelectric power and participated in the Compagnie Nationale du Rhône founded in 1933. It continued to operate the old tobacco monopoly (1810) and the more recent match monopoly, for revenue purposes. It conserved its traditional concern with public works, seen as one of the ways to overcome the depression. The establishment of the Office Nationale du Blé represented a new attempt by the state to bring order into the cereals market. The bill bringing it into existence had a difficult passage through parliament (one speaker described it as 'the handsomest Marxist monument known to legislation anywhere') largely because it granted the new authority price-fixing powers. It had a monopoly of foreign trade and bought up the entire marketable surplus at a fixed price. Surplus grain could be exported, if necessarily at a loss. The main problem of the Office lay in determining the price: the different parties represented on the central council of the Office – producers, millers, civil servants – inevitably differed about what would be the most appropriate price. According to the law this had to be endorsed by three-quarters of those eligible to vote. By 1938 good harvests had complicated the Office's task: it was threatened with unsaleable surpluses and inadequate resources to buy them up. The wheat problem had evidently not been solved when the war began, but the experience of the Office suggested that government intervention in the market might serve peasant interests better than dependence upon the laws of supply and demand dear to the economic liberals.

The breakup of the Popular Front in 1937 and 1938 left little room for new policy measures. The government of Edouard Daladier (1884–1970) came to power in April 1938 claiming to be the 'last experiment in liberalism'. It aimed at a balanced budget, the restoration of confidence, and an expansionist programme to include the increased arms production called for by the rapidly deteriorating international situation. The government sought a confrontation with the unions, confident that it would win, as it did, and was then able to impose a longer working week in the factories. War overtook this government before it could begin to tackle the more deep-rooted problems of the French economy. It did, however, pass in July 1938, a comprehensive law for the organization of the nation in time of war.[77] Inspired largely by the experience of 1914–18, it provided for the transformation of the administrative apparatus and endowed it with far-reaching powers over the economy and the individual enterprise, powers which were virtually unlimited. Each type of resource was to be placed under a special ministry responsible for its allocation among users: transport, industrial production, food distribu-

[77] Text in Bernard Chenot, *Organisation économique de l'état* (Paris, 1965).

tion, manpower, and so on were each to be controlled in this way. The government also assumed powers over industrial and commercial enterprises as well as to set up new plants of its own. It was to have the power to control foreign trade, to fix prices, and to ration scarce supplies. This law became the basis of the war economy in September 1939.

While some reference has been made to social policy, from the eight-hour day of 1919 to the social reforms of the Popular Front, in dealing with economic developments it is necessary to review the field in more detail to reveal the significant changes it underwent. At the outbreak of war in 1914 France was far from being in the forefront, among European countries, in social legislation. Even the exigencies of war did not lead to a more comprehensive programme. There was state aid for those who lost their homes or who were dependants of those called up and pensions were provided for war victims and their families, but not until 1921 was a law proposed for the introduction of a comprehensive system of social insurance. One factor behind this measure was the return to France of Alsace-Lorraine which had benefited from the German social security system. To counter autonomist agitation Paris decreed that this system should remain in force. The question then arose of the differential treatment of the regained provinces compared with the rest of France or whether workers moving to other parts of the country would lose their rights. The German model, as well as other foreign examples, exercised a good deal of influence on the debates on social insurance during the 1920s.[78] However, it was not until 1928 that the national insurance scheme was adopted and not until after the law of April 1930 that it began to come into effect. Clearly, the legislature dealt with the question in a half-hearted manner and it was noticeable that its interest revived with the approach of elections; the result was a weak law, leaving France still behind the major countries. As passed, compulsory insurance was only to apply to wage-earners below a certain level of income (higher in urban areas and related to family size). By the outbreak of war a little more than one-third of the population was covered by the law. Contributions were paid by workers and employers; the existing state pension scheme was embodied in the new system together with the subsidy it had received. The sorry state of agriculture when the law came into effect meant that contributions paid in by workers and employers had to be reduced and the state made up the difference. However, the proportion of the cost borne by the state between 1930 and 1936 was only about 15 per cent, falling to 5 per cent by 1939. The benefits comprised sickness pay after

---

[78] But association of social insurance with Germany was far from being a recommendation either before the First World War or after it; it smacked of *caporalisme*. One doctor, cited by a deputy during the debate in 1930, attributed Germany's defeat to the damage done to its nervous system by social insurance, Hatzfeld, *Du pauperisme*, p. 90.

five (later three) days for a period not exceeding six months representing half of the basic wage when employed. In case of death the family of the deceased was entitled to a benefit amounting to 20 per cent of the annual basic wage. Subject to various restrictions the insurance covered the family of the insured and provided for medical and hospital care, but usually the cash benefits did not meet the whole cost; in practice the scheme tended to discriminate against the lower paid workers covered by the scheme. There was also provision for pensions to those incapacitated or retiring from work after the age of 60; in principle these pensions amounted to about 40 per cent of the average wage, but in practice could amount to less. Their real value tended to be undermined by the rising prices of the 1930s. The social insurance system established by the laws of 1928–30 utilized the existing friendly societies and assimilated certain private schemes administered by industrial firms. Coupled with the social insurance system was the payment of family allowances, perhaps France's only distinctive contribution to social policy in this period. Originally instituted by some paternalistic employers, a general system of family allowances seemed to offer one way of combating France's demographic decline which had been accentuated by war losses.

Under the family allowance law of 1932 employers paid contributions into a central fund for the industry and payments were made from the fund according to the number of children of workers in each enterprise. Thus a worker with children was not handicapped in the labour market as against a childless worker and was not a higher charge on the individual employer. By 1939 some 5.4 million workers were covered by family allowance schemes. In that year, too, the *Code de famille* was promulgated by the decree-law of 29 July; it dealt with a wide range of matters such as inheritance and measures against abortion and included the extension of family allowances to all wage-earners, independent workers and peasants for the second child. It was an indication that, at a late hour, the government had become conscious of the population crisis and intended to do something about it with a comprehensive demographic policy.

Another important field of state action was that of housing. The housing situation was already serious in the large towns and industrial areas before 1914 despite some subsidized housing and the provision of houses by some industrial concerns. The war resulted in the destruction of 350,000 houses and brought new house building to a standstill. The state also established a system of rent control during the war. After the war the state financed rebuilding in the devastated areas. Continued urbanization increased the pressure on housing accommodation while private capital was deterred from providing an adequate supply of homes by the low rate of return expected on the capital investment, for which rent restriction is frequently blamed. This is only a partial explanation; the gaps left by the wartime building standstill and low wages making it difficult for workers to afford adequate accommodation were also important. However, in the period between the wars rents rose less than other prices and the proportion of working-class income spent on housing tended to fall. In terms of overcrowding and the adequacy of dwellings, improvement was slow and helps to explain France's poor health record and high incidence of tuberculosis and alcoholism. The law of 1928, named after the responsible minister, Louis Loucheur (1872–1936), aimed to speed up building by loans and advances from the state at a 2 per cent interest rate to the organizations responsible for building *Habitations à Bon Marché*. The law also made it easier for intending purchasers to buy their own homes, especially for certain categories such as war pensioners, invalids, large families, and war widows. The programme, although embodying some new principles, was modest considering the housing needs of the country and it was soon overtaken by the economic crisis. Public outlays on housing, after rising to a peak in 1931–2 then fell abruptly in real terms; the HBMs thus became victims of the deflationary policy. New house building as a whole fell seriously during the depression and thus aggravated it; on the other hand, the industrial slow-down somewhat reduced the pressure on urban housing. Surprisingly, the Popular Front did not make the housing crisis an important issue or do anything to remedy it.

France's lag in social policy can be attributed to the indifference or determined opposition of a substantial part of the electorate: the peasantry, the self-employed middle class, and the small and medium-sized businessmen. Their weight in society reflected the incomplete character of French industrialization. At the same time, this meant that the need for social insurance was less pressing than in the more heavily industrialized countries. Moreover, the labour organizations were not enthusiastic for compulsory insurance requiring deductions from wages. Large-scale industry ran its own schemes and feared losing control of them to the state. The opposition to any extension of the state's responsibilities also raised the spectre of increased taxation and a growth in its power. The advocates of social insurance and, indeed, any extension of social policy, had to meet the tenacious resistance of the upholders of the liberal doctrines, often expressed in the press and in the parliament in an extreme form. But serious economic opinion was also largely opposed to any extension of the state's activities. Jacques Rueff, for example, argued that unemployment in Britain was caused by unemployment insurance and warned his countrymen not to follow such a dangerous example. The financial upheavals of the 1920s, followed by the depression of the 1930s, hardly created propitious conditions for measures likely to raise government expenditure. At a time when security based upon the ownership of property (whether real estate or the *rentes*) had collapsed, the middle classes were confirmed in their hostility to state action. Yet it was precisely at that time that France took the first halting step on the road to social security backed by the state.

Down to the Second World War no coherent policy had been developed to overcome the crisis or to deal with the long-term structural problems of the French economy. The state had responded to particular pressures and group interests and had come to the defence of *situations acquises* to produce a tangle of interventionist measures completely inadequate to meet the needs of the situation. Although there were signs of a change at the very end, politicians appear to have understood only dimly how the economy worked and feared to make any departure from the well-tried orthodox path. Policy tended therefore to be restrictionist and only aggravated the prevailing stagnation and pessimism. Likewise, social policy remained backward compared with comparable countries in Europe. It had taken ten years of debate to pass a very inadequate social insurance law. Under the pressure of the strike wave in 1936 it is true that a law was passed granting wage-earners fifteen days' paid holiday annually and that a forty-hour week was prescribed for industry. These measures met with much opposition from employers, the press, and economic opinion and have often been regarded as untimely. Perhaps they were burdensome in view of France's economic predicament but in themselves they hardly represented a massive concession to a working class ill provided for in social insurance, housing, and health services. Only in the field of encouragement and support for large families did policy-makers display any innovating ability and this policy came belatedly to meet an ominous demographic trend seemingly threatening the country with 'depopulation' at a time when other nations continued to grow in numbers and dynamism. Reflection on these shortcomings and dangers was to be high among the factors bringing big changes in both economic and social policy in the post-war era.

CHAPTER XI

German economic and social policy, 1815–1939

I. Introduction: principles of economic structure, theory, and policy in Germany, 1815–1939

Profound changes in manifestation and intensity have taken place in the relations between state and economy in Germany during the nineteenth and twentieth centuries. It could not have been otherwise in an age during which Germany passed through a violent and permanent upheaval of its economic and social structures and traditions, and repeatedly and fundamentally recast its political constitution. These upheavals had profound effects on the future development of economic and social policy. It would be unprofitable to consider at length whether it was economic change, sometimes more, sometimes less dynamic, or political decisions and turning-points which constituted the outstanding signposts marking off stages of development. There is no common denominator by which to measure one against the other. Undoubtedly many threads of development have stretched almost without interruption across political turning-points; equally indisputably, others have thereat gained new importance and orientation. Changes of direction in economic and social development have had similar effects. Where one period ends and another begins depends on individual evaluation and presentation; there are no objectively compelling divisions.

This was the case particularly since at no moment of time between 1815 and 1930 was there an all-embracing, purposive, and decisive determination of economic and socio-political principles, means, and objectives. A gradual increase and strengthening of the arsenal of economic and social policy and an extension of its range are characterized by a high degree of continuity in development. This is a manifestation and a consequence of an even more marked and striking continuity of economic and social history throughout this period: the continuity, the almost unchanging nature, of the economic structure. Throughout the 115 years, the principle and manner of functioning of the German economy has been that of a liberal competitive economy, pursued to begin with by an agrarian middle class, but increasingly by industrial capitalists. Within certain limits, this remained true even in the 1930s.

The history of the economic and social order and policy since the establishment of the German Federation is not the record of gradual, but all-embracing change from free competition, uninfluenced by the state, to a number of oligopolies in the field of production and sales, deliberately brought about by government planning, as has recently been suggested. As little as the state in Germany ever left the economy entirely to its own devices, along the lines of a misunderstood *laissez-faire*, as little has it ever deliberately and purposefully manipulated it. The relationship between state and economy in Germany between 1815 and 1939 was always close, but never close enough to speak of an 'interventionist state' – provided this signifies more than the commonplace that in the course of the nineteenth century the economy became a force shaping historical development, hence demanding from the state by the end of the century greater consideration, resourcefulness, ability to act and decide flexibly than at the beginning. This much is beyond doubt.

It is another question whether such consideration amounted to large-scale subjection of state policy to economic requirements and interests, whether resourcefulness managed to keep step with the increasing complexity of economic and social problems, whether actions and decisions reflected an adequate understanding of empirical situations, and hence proved capable of controlling and manipulating economy and society in a rational and purposeful manner. Nothing of the kind was the case. From beginning to end, practically all important and wide-ranging measures in the field of economic and social policy resulted from decisions taken for a multiplicity of motives, mostly determined by political considerations. The arsenal of means and measures employed, particularly in the pursuit of economic policy, remained throughout a limited one – never quite adequate to cope effectively with problems novel in structure, development, and economic constellation. Nor was it even meant to do so. At least up to 1930, German policy was never and nowhere designed to influence economic structure, growth, or employment; nor could it be so designed, because the idea of deliberately steering an economy towards structural growth and employment targets entered economic theory only hesitantly in the 1920s. Nor did the theoretical concept imply ability to implement it; this presupposed a knowledge of macro-economic relationships. This is quite apart from the fact that for a long time strong doubts, widely held and based on theory, persisted whether – even provided such steering of the economy could be done – it should be done.

The development and study of the science of economics has, paradoxically, provided more scholarly justification and support for the claim of the state to intervene in the free market economy for reasons of economic and social policy in Germany than elsewhere in the industrialized world;

at the same time, it has slowed down or impeded the development and use of a range of weapons of economic policy – weapons adequate to deal with problems as they arose, if flexibly applied. Academic economics, significantly described as the 'science of the state' in university syllabuses, from the beginning of the 1860s and substantially throughout the imperial era, bore the stamp of the so-called 'historical-ethical school', which tended to 'evaporate the substance of economics in a solution of economic history',[1] and based its presuppositions – respectable in themselves, but theoretically rather amorphous. This pushed Germany, earlier than all other industrial nations, in the last quarter of the nineteenth century, powerfully towards effective social reform, undertaken by the state, but economic scholarship at the same time lagged considerably behind that of contemporary science. Germany had not the intellectual stature to initiate an up-to-date economic policy, assured in its methods and objectives, nor did it do so. That remained true even when the historical school gradually lost its predominance and economics recovered its theoretical foothold, with Germany being at the receiving end. The theoretical paradigms dominating the first third of this century were theories of utility, particularly marginal utility as developed by the Austrian school, and of micro-economic theory of value and price. These were 'pure' theories, unrelated to social realities, and hence without guidelines for an effective practical economic policy. Thus until 1933, particularly during the fateful years from 1930 to 1932, Friedrich von Wieser's statement of 1924 remained true, 'Much is yet missing before the theoretical principles of a modern economic policy are fully clarified ... hence policy is left to its own devices in justifying the line it takes; the harmful consequences are apparent in the hesitant touch when it comes to limits and means.'[2] During the years of the Third Reich, the sole principle guiding economic and social policy, in patent disregard of all theory, was its serviceability in implementing the demands and aims of the National Socialist leadership.

In short, economic and social policy in Germany between 1815 and 1939 from beginning to end was not a continuous, rationally conceived, and adaptable policy of order and due progress towards predictable aims which would have social value; but a policy of arbitrary measures lacking theoretical foundations and adequate certainty of success.

As regards number, kind, intensity, and effectiveness of such measures, a good deal did change. Permanent emphasis, because of fiscal interests,

---

[1] Adolph Wagner, Berlin political scientist, on his colleague, the influential grand old man of the historical school, Gustav Schmoller, quoted from Heinrich Rubner (ed.), *Adolph Wagner: Briefe, Dokumente, Augenzeugenberichte 1851–1917* (Berlin, 1978), p. 257.

[2] Friedrich F. von Wieser, 'Theorie der gesellschaftlichen Wirtschaft', in *Grundriss der Sozialökonomik* (Tübingen, 1924), section 1, part 2, p. 287.

rested on commercial and financial policy, especially with regard to tariffs and taxation. To this was added in the early stage of industrialization – as if to give a particularly German flavour to the historical model of an industrial revolution – a variety of devices to promote crafts and industry. Public social policy at a period when the German Federation was split into many states played a very small part. That changed fundamentally in the Empire. Not only were foundations of a much praised and widely imitated policy of social insurance laid – broad, sound, and valid up to the present day, though they have become something of an embarrassment by now – but also the roots of an effective policy of workers' protection and of a socially conceived labour legislation, though not fully developed until the Weimar Republic, reach back into that period. Given the spontaneous expansion of industry, the policy of industrial promotion, on the other hand, lapsed into insignificance and was only revived, it could be argued, after 1949 in the guise of an infrastructural policy. At the latest from the 1880s onwards, the prime task of the state no longer consisted of helping industry to establish itself, but of counteracting its damaging social side-effects. Monetary policy and beginnings of market regulation remained at a rudimentary stage, following rather than inaugurating developments, both during the Empire and the Weimar Republic.

Details, illustrations, and causation to fill in the outlines of this brief sketch, will be the subject of four sections following in chronological order, each subdivided by topic. These sections cover two very long and two very short periods. There are good reasons for this. The first period comprises the years between the foundation of the German Federation and the German Reich. There can be no question of an essentially 'German' economic and social policy, during these 55 years (1815–70). Germany was splintered into 41 sovereign territorial and political units which pursued at the time above all Prussian, Saxon, Mecklenburg-Strelitz, Schwarzenburg-Sonderhausen and so on economic and social policies: as regards commercial policies, not only co-existing, but at times and in some respects, conflicting.

That the foundation of the German Reich was no turning-point in the economic and social development of Germany has by now been accepted as a historical commonplace. Yet, of course, it created institutional foundations for economic and social policy which were largely new in principle, and burdened it with novel and peculiar problems. Hence the foundation of the Reich is an appropriate landmark in this respect.

All this does not apply to the undoubtedly more dramatic political upheaval of the years 1918 and 1919. Looked at through spectacles of economic and social policy, the Empire and the pre-crisis period of the

Weimar Republic form a single era. It is not the case that everything remained as before. Much changed; undoubtedly transition from authoritarian monarchy to democratic republic provided directional impulses, but nowhere to the extent of a break in structure and development, and everywhere as an organic continuation from traditional beginnings, models, and tendencies – a continuation in part timely, in part anachronistic.

Not all continuity was interrupted in 1930 and 1933. Rather it is astonishing how slowly and gradually economic and social history changed from the democratic Weimar Republic through the semi-dictatorial crisis-Republic to the National Socialist dictatorship and eventually to the war. However, the crisis policies of the Brüning, Papen, and Schleicher governments, the creation of employment and economic armament programmes, each in its own way, were so different from traditional German economic and social policy as to deserve and demand separate discussion.

II.   Economic and social policy in the states of the German Federation

An essentially 'German' economic and social policy – we said above – certainly did not exist in the German Federation split into states. But this does not mean that the economic and social policy of that period can only be appropriately described by detailing the multiplicity of policies of 30 or 40 states, large and small. This would certainly not be the case for commercial policy which, amounting in practice to an embryo national economic policy, resulted eventually in creating a nation; nor would it be the case even for policy relating to industry and finance. Of course, there were everywhere regional peculiarities and deviations from the prototype – which amounted to reductions, increases, adaptations to situations and purposes; but there was a prototype which it is not difficult to discern and that is what concerns us. The multiple empiricism of individual states is used only by way of illustrating and clarifying examples.

A.   FINANCIAL POLICY

We suffer from a painful lack of even approximately reliable and continuous statistics which would disclose the background behind a facade, often unrevealing, of laws and decrees in the field of economic policy. This greatly impedes detailed and differentiated research, especially in the realm of financial policy. We simply do not know the actual amount of public expenditure before 1850. Only the south German states, where constitutions at the time of entry into the German Federation already regulated finance and secured their parliaments the right to approve budgets, published continuous public revenue and expenditure accounts from 1820. In Prussia and most north German states, such constitutions and legislation on the approval of government expenditure, and hence also continuous information regarding public finance, had to wait until 1850. Furthermore, the inclination of these states up to that date not only to manipulate such statistics as they published from time to time, but also to maintain secret accounts,[3] did not fool even contemporaries. We can therefore say with certainty for all of Germany that the public share of the Gross National Product rose a little, but we can quantify that rise only with reservations'. In the half century from 1815 to 1866, the Gross National Product may have increased by about 80 per cent, government consumption perhaps by 120 per cent. In Prussia for instance public expenditure grew between 1820 and 1866 from about 190 to 470 million marks.[4] In spite of this rise, as a share of Gross National Product it remained minimal; a figure of upward of 4 to perhaps 6 per cent would probably come close to the truth.

The functional divisions of public expenditure considerably changed the whole. No basically new tasks requiring finance were added to the range of state administrative activities. State construction and operation of railways in south German countries undoubtedly very different from the scope, aims, and character of usual promotional activities – required additional public expenditure only at their beginning, financed mostly by loans,[5] but then turned – contrary – into a profitable activity. Two different phenomena were responsible for the change, the first in the field of financial policy. In all the larger states, including Austria, serious and in general successful efforts were made after the wars of liberation to reform the system of public revenue, particularly to consolidate and reduce the public debt. The proportion of public expenditure servicing

[3] Karl Borchard, 'Staatsverbrauch und öffentliche Investitionen in Deutschland 1780–1850', dissertation, Göttingen University, 1968, pp. 27f.

[4] Fritz Terhalle, 'Geschichte der deutschen öffentlichen Finanzwirtschaft vom Beginn des 19. Jahrhunderts bis zum Schluss des Zweiten Weltkriegs', in Handbuch der Finanzwissenschaft (Tübingen, 1929), vol. I, p. 276.

[5] Incidentally, the original complete and only gradually abandoned abstinence from railway construction on the part of the Prussian state was largely a consequence of the state debt law of 1820, by which the state had undertaken to increase its debt only with the assent of an 'assembly of Reich estates'. Nothing was further from the minds of Prussian kings than to call a parliamentary diet for the whole state; hence the public debt up to 1847 not merely remained constant, but was even reduced from 232 to 158 million talers. Subsequently, the first united diet was called for the express purpose of granting a loan to enable the state to participate in the project of an eastern railway to Königsberg. The assembly refused, not considering itself to be the repeatedly promised and properly constituted assembly of Reich estates and was thereupon dissolved. For the first time, economic progress and political backwardness had come into harsh conflict.

Table 102. *Public expenditure in Prussia*

	1821		1849		1866	
	Million marks	%	Million marks	%	Million marks	%
Military	68.4	45.0	81.6	38.0	137.8	43.0
Debt service	42.0	28.0	22.8	11.0	49.7	16.0
Civil administration of which	39.6	27.0	109.3	51.0	131.5	41.0
Trade and industry	(4.7)	(3.1)	(27.8)	(12.9)	(20.8)	(6.5)
Judiciary	(5.1)	(3.4)	(22.8)	(10.6)	(38.5)	(12.1)
Culture and education	(6.0)	(4.0)	(10.5)	(4.9)	(14.2)	(4.5)
	150.0		214.0		319.0	

Sources: Calculated from Wilhelm Gerloff, 'Der Staatshaushalt und das Finanzsystem Deutschlands', in *Handbuch der Finanzwissenschaft*, 1st edn (1929); Otto Schwarz, *Der Staatshaushalt und die Finanzen Preussens*, vol. III (Berlin, 1904), Appendix XIII.

the public debt, substantial at the beginning, noticeably diminished in consequence. Secondly, there was the gradual elaboration of a bourgeois concept of law and administration that required increasing public funds. Expenditure on civil administration expanded out of all proportion, whereas military expenditure did not even increase in the same proportion as total expenditure. This was true even of the Prussian 'military state' (Table 102), far more of the small and medium states. However, we cannot trace an unambiguous trend without occasional deviations.[6]

From beginning to end, by far the largest contribution to public revenue to defray growing expenditure came from taxes.[7] Public income earned from postal and telegraph services, railways, mines, smelters, etc., grew in importance in the course of industrialization, but did

---

[6] See Borchard, 'Staatsverbrauch', especially pp. 112, 123–4, 136, 145–6, 158–58a, 169–70, 183–5, 200ff.

[7] The sketch by Wilhelm Gerloff, 'Der Staatshaushalt und das Finanzsystem Deutschlands', in *Handbuch der Finanzwissenschaft*, vol. III (Tübingen, 1929), pp. 7–13, still does service as a first quick survey (excluding Austria). The most important states are treated exhaustively in O. Schwarz and E. Strutz, *Der Staatshaushalt und die Finanzen Preussens*, vol. I, section 4: 'Die direkten und indirekten Steuern' (Berlin, 1902); Adolf Beer, *Die Finanzen Österreichs im 19. Jahrhundert* (Prague, 1877); A. Buchenberger, *Finanzpolitik und Staatshaushalt im Grossherzogtum Baden in den Jahren 1850–1890* (Karlsruhe, 1902); Hans von Nostitz, *Grundzüge der Staatssteuern im Königreich Sachsen* (Jena, 1903); von Riecke, *Verfassung, Verwaltung und Staatshaushalt des Königreichs Württemberg* (1887); J. Kock, *Handbuch der gesamten Finanzverwaltung im Königreich Bayern*, 4 vols. (Munich, 1881–7); F. von Reden, *Allgemeine vergleichende Finanzstatistik* (Darmstadt, 1851–2) vol. I, section 1: 'Staatshaushalt und Abgabewesen des Königreichs Bayern, des Königreichs Württemberg und des Grossherzogtums Baden', section 2: 'Staatshaushalt und Abgabewesen des Königreichs Sachsen'; A. Siebert, 'Die Entwicklung der direkten Besteuerung in den süddeutschen Staaten im letzten Jahrhundert', *Zeitschrift für die gesamte Staatswissenschaft*, vol. LXVIII (1912), pp. 1–52; Ernst Klein, *Geschichte der öffentlichen Finanzen in Deutschland 1500–1870* (Wiesbaden, 1974), pp. 90–125 (Austria and Prussia only).

not change the pattern. Nowhere and at no time did tax yields (inclusive of customs duties) ever fall below 60 per cent of public revenue.[8]

Numerous German states, Prussia, Bavaria, and Baden among them, entered the German Federation with a system of public finance which had been reorganized a decade earlier, in which the main weight of revenue had moved from rents paid for public land and mining royalties to taxes. The chief guidelines and pattern of that system were maintained throughout the nineteenth century, albeit occasionally adapted in practice to economic and social development. Other states, such as Austria (1817–35), Württemberg (1821), and Saxony (1830s), reformed their out-of-date revenue systems only after entry, along lines pioneered by Prussia and Bavaria.

The taxation system of all the larger states in the German Federation consisted of, or developed into, a trinity of direct taxes levied on the yield of real estate, buildings, and industrial establishments (the latter not in Austria), a rudimentary income tax – introduced everywhere as an emergency or subsidiary measure and eventually everywhere rendered permanent – and a multiplicity, varying in individual scope, of indirect consumption taxes (partly government monopoly revenues) on spirits, ale, wine, tobacco, salt, and sugar,[9] plus an increasing number of taxes, not yielding much, on turnover of goods and capital, usually designated 'stamp duties'. The yield of indirect revenues exceeded that of direct revenues slightly at the beginning, but tended to increase more quickly and more markedly; the gap between the two therefore widened over time. In the 1860s, the ratio of indirect to direct taxes in the area of the later Empire was 60:40 – a ratio which, with minor divergences, probably held good for the individual states.[10] Contemporaries concerned with economic principles greatly deplored this as a 'faulty' relationship.

This differential growth of tax yields had several causes. The most trivial and obvious, voiced at the time, is still proclaimed: social groups whose representatives in parliaments and administrations decide on increases in rate and number of direct taxes are liable to suffer most from

---

[8] In Prussia, for instance, direct income from state property increased from 6.8 million marks in 1849 to 43.4 million marks in 1866, its proportion in covering expenditure from 3 to 14 per cent; the proportion of taxes fell only from 69 to 65 per cent. The difference was accounted for by the relative decrease of new debts.

[9] Saxony added a tax on meat, Prussia for urban dwellers (one-sixth of its population) a levy on bakery goods and meat – a milling and slaughtering tax. In return Prussian urban dwellers were exempt from the direct classified tax. Separation of town and countryside based on a tax levied on estates was not removed in Prussia until 1873, when the milling and slaughtering tax was abolished and a classified income tax introduced for all inhabitants.

[10] Borchard, 'Staatsverbrauch', pp. 42ff. If one adds customs duties, the proportion amounts to 30 : 70. Owing to the considerable yield of beer and wine taxes, indirect taxes in south Germany bore an increasingly higher proportion.

them, hence desist from doing so and resort to consumption taxes. Whether this is true or not, simple technical aspects of taxation played a larger part in this differential growth. Yields of indirect taxes always tend to grow with the national income; direct taxes in Germany until well into the imperial era did not have that tendency, owing to the fact that the so-called revenue taxes were taxes on goods (*Objektsteuern*), whereas the rudimentary income tax was essentially a tax on people and anyhow of only minimal incidence. Principle and formulation suggested that revenue taxes be levied on annual yield arising from cultivation of land, annual rents of houses and dwellings, and annual yield of industrial activity. However, in the practice of levying them, there was an assumption of fixed characteristics which adhered without change to the sources of taxation for much longer periods. At long intervals, measured usually in decades, land was reregistered, buildings and industrial establishments were reclassified by objective standards,[11] and charged with a tax determined by such registration and classification, immutable up to the next period of reregistration and reclassification. Tax was levied, not on the variable output, but on a constant input.

Two consequences ensued:

1.   The tax levy, determined by what were meant to be objective criteria, frequently diverged widely from the subjective ability to pay, as justified by actual yield, soon after tax redetermination.
2.   Total revenue derived from land and building taxes remained completely immutable for decades, while in the course of industrialization the yield of industrial taxation lagged ever more obviously behind the community's industrial income. Hence the share of direct taxes in the increasing national income fell.

The effect of the rudimentary income tax, which at the beginning was usually designed as a personal (Prussia, Saxony, Baden) or family (Bavaria) tax, was similar. The tax was to be borne by income from industry or employment (variously determined and defined from country to country); but the determinants of the tax were subjective

[11] Saxony, for instance, from 1834 onwards had the following main classifications – subdivided in themselves – of revenue:
1. Merchants (including chemists)
2. Traders who were not merchants
3. Manufacturers
4. Restaurant keepers and publicans
5. Butchers, bakers, distillers, beer brewers
6. Millers
7. Elbe boatmen
8. Carters, horse hirers, transport businesses
9. Farmers
10. Craftsmen
11. Itinerant trades
Von Nostitz, *Grundzüge*, pp. 12ff.

conditions of life – status, occupation, wealth – which could only be assumed to constitute an indicator income, but which nevertheless assigned the taxpayer to income-tax classes with a standardized liability to fixed sums. Around the middle of the century, this type of classified tax was replaced in the three south German states by a 'special' income tax, consisting of a tax on the yields of capital and employent, at a slightly progressive rate, while Prussia and Saxony, at least for high incomes, changed to a so-called 'classified' income tax:[12] incomes in excess of 3,000 marks suffered 3 per cent rate of income tax, irrespective of the taxpayer's economic or social status. The amount of income-tax revenue thus obtained at least increased in proportion to total taxable income. Prussia did not adopt moderately progressive rates of taxation until the imperial era.

The continuing ineptitude of the levying and assessment of direct taxes which arose from the contemporary ideals of tax policy, that is, avoidance as far as possible of all tedious state enquiry into personal conditions, income, and wealth, had two further effects which did not relate to the yield, but to the equity of taxation and to economic development. Though the principle of tax equality was generally recognized and sought, it was substantially infringed, even after the widespread removal of tax privileges for particular social groups during the 'bourgeois' reforms of the first third of the century.[13] Large, but above all growing, incomes and wealth enjoyed favourable tax treatment; these were largely industrial incomes and wealth. Such a tax policy was likely to promote investment and growth in the early phase of German industrialization.[14] This cannot be proved, and in view of the extremely small burden represented by direct taxation, it cannot have had substantial impor-

[12] In Prussia, for instance, there were four main classes up to 1851, each with three sub-groups. Taxpayers in the highest main class then became liable to income tax. Tax yield immediately increased by one-third, while in the previous 30 years it had grown by only 20 per cent, as against a 60 per cent increase in population. Assignment to the three other main classes of the classified tax was ruled by the following criteria:

1st class: Small landowners and traders who, owing to the size of their estates or trades, depended on part-time earnings, also ordinary wage-earners, journeymen, servants, and day labourers (1.50–9 marks)

2nd class: Medium estate owners and traders who could make a living from the revenues of their estates or trades, and those who approximately equalled them in their incomes and other circumstances affecting ability to pay (12–30 marks)

3rd class: Well-to-do people whose income did not exceed 3,000 marks (37–72 marks)
Schwarz and Strutz, Der Staatshaushalt, p. 1092.

[13] However, in Prussia the exemption of aristocratic estates from land tax was not abolished until 1861.

[14] See Eckart Schremmer, 'Zusammenhänge zwischen Katastersteuersystem, Wirtschaftswachstum und Wirtschaftsstruktur im 19. Jahrhundert: Das Beispiel Württembergs 1821–187/ 1903', in Ingomar Bog Günther Franz, Karl Heinrich Kaubhold, Hermann Kellerbenz and Wolfgang Zorn (eds.), Wirtschaftliche und soziale Strukturen im säkularen Wandel, Festschrift für Wilhelm Abel zum 70. Geburtstag, vol. III (Hanover, 1974), pp. 679–706; W. R. Lee, 'Tax Structure and Economic Growth in Germany, 1750–1850', Journal of European Economic History, vol. IV (1975).

tance. It would not have made much difference to the propensity to invest whether the tax on yield or income amounted to 1 or to 3 per cent.

B.   COMMERCIAL AND TARIFF POLICY

The establishment and policy of the German customs union (*Zollverein*) was undoubtedly of much greater importance for the progress of industry and economy in Germany, though we cannot convincingly quantify its results as reflected in structure and growth. Counterfactual analysis – the only possible method – would be frustrated by the practically irremediable lack of appropriate data, quite apart from the well-known, serious objections to this method.

An enquiry of this kind would have to throw light on three questions:

1. How far did the rapid alliance in the field of commercial policy of most states in the German Federation change the volume and direction of currents of domestic trade across state frontiers after 1833?
2. For the first 45 years of its existence, the customs union tariff was a low tariff – often controversial, repeatedly strongly opposed. What was its effect on foreign trade currents across the boundaries of the customs union?
3. How did the presumable effects and changes influence the behaviour of entrepreneurs regarding establishment of and investment in enterprises?

There are no sources or analytical means available to answer these questions – particularly since the establishment of the customs union coincided almost precisely with the beginning of railway construction in Germany, which generated a tendency to the same impulses and effects on structure and growth: widening of markets and consumption areas, increase of demand, levelling out of regional cost and price differences, removal of local monopoly situations, etc. In short, railway construction and the customs union are inextricably linked in their effect on output, sales, commerce, investment, structure, and growth. Rational study can do no more than establish plausible hypotheses on the basis of recently gained theoretical insights.

Contrary to what has been customary for a long time, recent research has tended not to overestimate the effect of the customs union on stimulating the industrial revolution in Germany. Railway construction, not the customs union, was a continuing source of widespread and increasing demand, a constituent of a unified market area which set in motion and subsequently maintained the industrial breakthrough. This breakthrough would have been set in motion and continued, even if no customs union had been established in 1834. Persisting internal tariff

THE STATES OF THE GERMAN FEDERATION 763

boundaries could have no more stopped it than the actually persisting and resurrected occupational prohibitions and guild privileges. It would have been more laborious, beset by more obstacles, subject to more friction, and it could well, and probably would, have led to a different spatial distribution of production and sales. Hence, the importance of the customs union for the welfare and industrial development of the German economy, once adjusted to it, must not be underestimated, especially in its importance for the smaller states. In 1835, Bavaria, Baden, Württemburg, Saxony, and Hesse could have done without trade and tariff unification with Prussia and its north German satellites without suffering substantial obstacles to their development, such as they did indeed experience during the following 10 to 20 years. Once adapted to the customs union for 15 years or even 25 years, in 1850 and 1860, they could no longer do without it; the costs in terms of development drives would have been too heavy.[15] They knew this and Prussia knew it as well; hence the commercial policy of the customs union after the revolution of 1848 and the re-establishment, against Prussia's wish, of the German Federation largely and predominantly subserved Prussian state and power hegemony, camouflaged as economic policy.

Commercial policy in Germany during the period of the German Federation therefore falls into three phases of equal length: the proto- and establishment phase of the customs union (1818–33); the formative phase of conditions of output, trade, and exchange typical and determined by the customs union (1834–50); and finally the phase of Austria's elimination from Germany (1850–65), which proved to be the formative overture to political unification under Prussian leadership.[16]

---

[15] Without wanting to deprecate it altogether, I am inclined – contrary to the views expressed by Henderson and Fischer – to attribute little significance to the loss of customs receipts which had substantially risen in the customs union, owing to the lower expenses of administration, compared to the likely general economic disadvantages. Bavaria, for instance, by joining the customs union gained an amount equivalent to approximately 5 per cent of its public expenditure.

[16] Carl Krökel, *Das preussisch-deutsche Zolltarifsystem in seiner historischen Entwicklung seit 1818* (Jena, 1881); Alfred Zimmerman, *Geschichte der preussisch-deutschen Handelspolitik, aktenmässig dargestellt* (Oldenburg and Leipzig, 1892); W. O. Henderson, *The Zollverein* (London and Chicago, 1959–60); Wolfram Fischer, 'Der deutsche Zollverein. Fallstudie die einer Zollunion' and 'Der deutsche Zollverein, die europäische Wirtschaftsgemeinschaft und die Freihandelszone', in Wolfram Fischer, *Wirtschact und Gesellschaft im Zeitalter der Industrialisierung: Aufsätze, Studien, Vorträge* (Göttingen, 1972), pp. 110–38. For the first phase in addition W. von Eisenhart-Rothe and A. Ritthaler, *Vorgeschichte und Begründung des deutschen Zollvereins 1815–1834*, 3 vols. (Berlin, 1934); Carl Brinkmann, *Die preussische Handelspolitik vor dem Zollverein und der Wiederaufbau* (Jena, 1922); T. Ohnishi, *Zolltarifpolitik Preussens bis zur Gründung des deutschen Zollvereins* (Göttingen, 1973); A. H. Price, *The Evolution of the Zollverein* (Ann Arbor, 1949). For the third phase, Eugen Franz, 'Die Entstehungsgeschichte des preussisch–französischen Handelsvertrages vom 29.3.1862', *Vierteljahrschrift Für Sozial- und Wirtschaftsgeschichte (VSWG)*, vol. xxv (1932), pp. 1–37, 105–29; Eugen Franz, *Der Entscheidungskampf um die wirtschaftspolitische Führung Deutschlands* (Munich, 1933); Helmut Böhme, *Deutschlands Weg zur Grossmacht. Studien zum Verhältnis von Wirtschaft und Staat während der Reichsgrundungszeit 1848–1881* (Cologne, 1966).

However, Prussia set the scene and called the tune from the beginning. Its persistently liberal economic bureaucracy in 1815 pushed open, so to speak, the door to a Germany modern in its policy regarding trade and tariffs. Up to that date, Germany had not only some 40 state boundaries, but a multiplicity of internal tariff boundaries. The incomplete political reconstruction of Germany in Vienna in 1814/15 had not even attempted a new economic order, even though its necessity was universally admitted, but had merely inserted it as an urgent desideratum on the agenda of the new German Federation. Article 19 of the Act of Federation stipulated that the Federal Assembly immediately at its first meeting was to discuss how to facilitate and standardize trade and traffic in the federal territory. Neither at its first nor at any future meeting did this happen, because Austria, the presiding power, did not even remotely envisage abandoning its protectionist isolation and the numerous internal customs duties extant in that multinational monarchy. After many futile initiatives, Prussia therefore resolved in 1818 to wait no longer for a reform of the Federation, which it anyhow did not particularly desire, but to start on a Prussian reform. The Customs Law of 26 May[17] removed a multitude of the virtually innumerable, irrational, and dysfunctional embargoes on exports, imports, and transit of goods, town dues, road and river tolls, declared the state frontier to be the only customs frontier, and introduced a low customs tariff tending towards free trade. Raw materials, apart from a few irrelevant exceptions, were completely exempt from import duties; manufactured goods were charged at a rate determined by weight which amounted to about 10 per cent *ad valorem*. For fiscal reasons, high duties were levied on luxury goods, such as coffee, tea, beer, wine, tobacco, and groceries. Strictly agricultural duties, on the other hand, were of no significance because there was no need to import agricultural commodities.

On the contrary: for the next half century Prussia was and remained an exporter of cereals. Hence, not only did its economic bureaucracy believe in free trade on principle, but in addition the group of aristocratic landlords who dominated politics and society pursued free trade for reasons of self-interest. Prussia therefore persisted steadily and emphatically with its policy of low tariffs well into the Empire period. How far this benefited its economy remains uncertain; as a weapon of economic policy directed against an equally consistently protectionist Austria it was unfailingly effective, once the Prussian tariff in 1833 had been imposed upon the south German states in the form of the customs union tariff.

---

[17] See Gustav Schmoller, *Das preussische Handels- und Zollgesetz vom 26.5.1818 in Zusammenhang mit der Geschichte der Zeit, ihrer Kämpfe und Ideen* (Berlin, 1898).

Though the southern states, in those early years somewhat more pro-free trade in their attitude than Prussia, had combined in violent opposition to the latter's out-of-date 'protectionist particularism', their lengthy and laborious attempts to associate in an anti-Prussian trade association had largely failed. Not until ten years later had Bavaria and Württemberg concluded a customs union, but this achievement, in any case very limited, had immediately been curtailed by Prussia when it succeeded in the same year in enticing the Grand Duchy of Hesse-Darmstadt,[18] and three years later the Electorate of Hesse-Kassel, into a Prussian–Hessian customs union based on the Prussian tariff, thus linking the eastern and western parts of the monarchy from the point of view of economic geography. The south German states, and also Saxony which had meanwhile concluded a third German loose commercial alliance with Hanover, soon abandoned their resistance, so far as it was founded on commercial principles, and agreed to negotiations for an all-embracing customs union with Prussia. As their objections to the Prussian tariff had not similarly been waived, the somewhat controversial negotiations dragged on for two years. In the end, Prussian tariff policy carried the day. To the disgust of southern Germany, mollified a little, however, by favourable treatment in the allocation of customs revenues among members, the Prussian–Hessian tariff became the tariff of the German customs union[19] which came into existence on 1 January 1834, consisting at the time of 18 German states comprising a population of 23 million. Thus it remained, with occasional minor increases and decreases, until 1865. With it remained the grievance of the southern states which, however, soon ceased to be a grievance about the high level of tariffs. In the 1840s southern Germany turned protectionist.

Incisive and far-reaching tariff changes were inhibited by the rule that resolutions in the so-called General Tariff Conference – incidentally the only common institution of the union – had to be taken unanimously, not by majority vote. Hence, the only economically significant external change to the tariff system up to 1865 consisted of the introduction of a 10 marks per tonne duty on pig iron, hitherto import duty free, and of a moderate increase in the duties on wrought iron in 1844. This was designed to counteract dumping at low prices of English pig iron and wrought iron, a threat apparent after the English iron industry at the beginning of the 1840s had suffered a domestic market crisis. For a country with a developing industry, just about to establish itself and not within the foreseeable future able to supply its demand for iron from its own sources, such a policy was a two-edged sword; the iron tariffs, adopted explicitly for protectionist motives, remained in force, but in

[18] H. Schmidt, *Die Begründung des preussisch-hessischen Zollvereins von 1828* (Giessen, 1926).
[19] See Krökel, *Zolltarifsystem*, statistical section.

view of the considerably greater English cost advantage their effects were less to prevent imports than to raise prices.

Unchanging specific tariffs anyhow did not signify unchanging incidence of customs duty. The prices of the main goods imported between 1818 and 1865 fell considerably on average, thus imparting to a tariff policy originally free trade in nature increasingly a moderately protectionist character. As little as 10 or 15 years after the foundation of the customs union, tariffs were no longer inspired by any principles of commercial, far less of economic, policy.

Hence Prussia did not put the customs union on a new, but rather reverted, as it were, to the old, basis of tariff policy, when it insisted between 1862 and 1865 on turning a treaty on trade and tariffs previously concluded with France into a union tariff, in the face of loud protests from the central states. This was a tariff which reduced practically all important duties substantially, rarely to less than one-half, frequently to one-third, one-quarter or less.[20]

It would be a mistake to underestimate or ignore the economic motives of this decision, authoritatively enforced. The Prussian economic bureaucracy, as ever, was convinced that free trade was the policy which the hour demanded, thus remaining in general accord with the country's governing circles, with economic scholarship, and with economically enlightened public opinion; given the stage of development of the German economy, they were right. However, the renewal of the customs union treaty in 1865 represented less a practical return to the ideals of old-fashioned liberal trade policy current at the time of Prussian reform, but rather a spectacular culmination of the gradual metamorphosis from commercial to state and power politics.

This metamorphosis had begun after one-and-a-half comparatively quiescent decades of commercial policy during which a large number of initially undecided states had joined the customs union – among them Baden, Hesse-Nassau, Luxemburg – thus increasing the proportion of non-Austrian population among that part of the German Federation which had a common tariff to approximately nine-tenths. Of the countries that mattered in the German Federation, only Hanover, until 1837 still linked in personal union to England, remained aloof. Metternich's Austria had watched this development from a distance with astonishing indifference. Metternich fell in 1848, replaced by Prince Schwarzenberg; Baron von Bruck became his Minister of Commerce. Neither was inclined to continue as an indifferent spectator. They pushed into the customs union because the economically dominant and guiding part played in it by Prussia appeared to them increasingly irreconcilable with

---

[20] *Ibid.*, and summary in his text, pp. 47f.

Austria's political interests and demands. When Prussia – as was to be expected – offered decisive resistance to this push, all the more positively, having once again, in November 1850 at Olmütz, taken second place to Austria politically, they aimed to transform the customs union with or without Prussia into a Central European customs union dominated by Austria and protectionist in policy.

The concept of a Central Europe gave birth to a splendid idea, so enticing that it has never since disappeared, but has found practical expression only in the form of the European Economic Community. Prussia succeeded in 1852 – in quasi-revenge for humiliation at Olmütz – in excluding Austria from the customs union and in keeping the latter alive on the old terms, even in extending its scope; this was the most important precondition for making possible the establishment of a Prusso–German Reich, even though nobody at the time thought along these lines.

To begin with, the southern states were eager to listen to Austrian blandishments. A committee had been established in the Federal Parliament charged with preparing a standardization of tariffs with Austria to form the nucleus of a Central European customs union, when generous concessions on Prussia's part brought to a successful conclusion negotiations for accession, secretly conducted for a long time with the so-called 'tax association' of Hanover, Oldenburg, and Schaumburg-Lippe. This enabled Prussia to challenge the southern states to secede from the customs union and to find economic salvation henceforth as allies of an economically retarded Austria in conflict with a north German customs union. The prospect was frightening. An expansion of the customs union by the inclusion of Austria represented to the south German states a highly desirable alternative to a customs union dominated by Prussia; a customs alliance with Austria without, or even in opposition to, Prussia was no longer an alternative at all. The customs union treaty was renewed on the old basis on 8 April 1853. Hanover and Oldenburg, which had recently joined, increased the north German weighting; south Germany received a token of reconciliation and goodwill in the form of a promise on Prussia's part to enter into serious negotiations with Austria on custom unification in 1860.

It was no more than a promise. When 1860 dawned, Prussia, economically further strengthened and politically ever more self-confident, was less than ever inclined to relinquish the lever which could help substantially in the move towards ousting Austria from Germany to Prussia's advantage. Instead of yielding to south German demands for negotiations with Austria, Prussia complied after a brief hesitation with Napoleon III's suggestion to confer with France regarding a commercial free-trade treaty, such as France had just concluded with England (the

Cobden treaty). Economically, this was a rational decision which promised to integrate the customs union into a large-scale Western and Central European free-trade zone. But it was also a politically purposeful decision in that it promised once and for all to frustrate the undesirable customs unification with Austria. This is why the decision antagonized south Germany and Saxony to the point of opposing it; but they got no farther. The course of events was strongly reminiscent of 1852/3, except that Prussia, conscious of its economic indispensability and with Bismarck taking up office in September 1862, became even more imperious. On 2 August 1862 the commercial treaty with France was signed over the protests of Bavaria, Württemberg, Hesse, Saxony, even Hanover. That the rates of duty fell well below the traditional union tariffs and would, via France, also benefit England was bad enough. Worse still, the treaty included in article 31 a most-favoured-nation clause which henceforth excluded any preferential tariff treatment of Austria. For two years, there was vehement controversy regarding the ratification of the treaty and the renewal of the customs union on the basis of its tariffs. On 17 December 1863 Bismarck, following Manteuffel's precedent of 12 years earlier, took recourse to the ultimately effective resort of giving notice of termination of all customs union treaties. It had already for some time been agreed with France that the treaty should take effect even with a somewhat reduced customs union.

The first to yield was Saxony, whose extensive industrial sector could least do without the large contiguous Prussian market. That was in May 1864, and made so large a breach in the defensive front that it took only until October before everybody accepted the treaty. This reduced Austria to one among many trading partners with whom new commercial treaties were concluded in the following year.

These treaties were new, not only in time, but also in character. Not only had the customs union been put on to a different tariff basis by the Franco-German treaty, it had also adopted a different line of trade and tariff policy *vis-à-vis* third countries. Though it had been established 30 years earlier with a view to the principle of applying a standard system of tariffs to all imports without regard to origin, in practice commercial treaties had gradually introduced a multiplicity of differential tariffs favouring some countries more than others. This now ceased because most-favoured-nation treaties were rapidly concluded with all of the more important trading partners,[21] entitling each of them automatically to the lowest rate of duty conceded to any one.

With the Cobden treaty, the economically developed world had set sail towards free trade, and Germany appeared determined to allow herself to be blown in the same direction. This resolution did not last. A

[21] For the policy of trade treaties, see Gerhard Bondi, *Deutschlands Aussenhandel 1815-1870* (Berlin, 1958), pp. 73ff., 120ff.

mere 14 years later, Bismarck began to set course in the opposite direction.

C. PROMOTION OF INDUSTRY AND BEGINNINGS OF SOCIAL POLICY

Up to 1870 (and beyond) economic policy had primarily been financial policy and commercial policy with a strong fiscal flavour. This becomes apparent from the fact that after 1815 all the larger states invariably had ministries of finance, many of them later also ministries of commerce,[22] but nowhere were there ministries of economics, let alone ministries of social welfare or of labour.

However, even in the days of the German Federation there existed economic and social policies that were not financial and commercial policies. But these were rudimentary, neither generous nor far-seeing, unplanned, and subordinate in concept. They were either a sideline dealt with by ministries of the interior or entrusted to semi-official industrial institutes. Owing to a wealth of ideas of practical value exhibited by their managers, some of these institutes achieved a degree of fame, notably the Prussian Technical Commission for Industry and the private, though government-sponsored, Association for the Promotion of Diligence in Industry (established 1821) under the secretary of the Department of Trade and Industry and in the Ministry of the Interior, Peter Christian Wilhelm Beuth,[23] as well as the Württemberg Central Office for Trade and Industry (established 1848) under Ferdinand Steinbeis.[24] Excellent

---

[22] Friedrich Facius, *Wirtschaft und Staat. Die Entstehung der staatlichen Wirtschaftsverwaltung in Deutschland vom 17. Jahrhundert bis 1945* (Boppard, 1959). Prussia had its first ministry of commerce from 1817, Hanover from 1832, Austria and Bavaria from 1848, and Baden from 1860. The commerce ministries of Austria and Prussia were repeatedly dissolved and their departments reassigned to the ministries of finance and interior.

[23] For Prussian industrial promotion, see above all C. Matschosz, *Preussens Gewerbeförderung und ihre grossen Männer. Dargestellt im Rahmen der Geschichte des Vereins zur Beförderung des Gewerbefleisses in Preussen 1821–1921* (Berlin, 1921); Hans Joachim Straube, 'Die Gewerbeförderung Preussens in der ersten Hälfte des 19. Jahrhunderts mit besonderer Berücksichtigung der Regierungsmassnahmen zur Förderung der Industrie', dissertation, TU Berlin, 1933; Wilhelm Treue, *Wirtschaftszustände und Wirtschaftspolitik in Preussen, 1815–1825* (Stuttgart, 1937); W. O. Henderson, *The State and the Industrial Revolution in Prussia, 1740–1870* (Liverpool, 1958), pp. 96–118; Ulrich Peter Ritter, *Die Rolle des Staates in den Frühstadien der Industrialisierung. Die preussische Industrieförderung in der ersten Hälfte des 19. Jahrhunderts* (Berlin, 1961); Ilja Mieck, *Preussische Gewerbepolitik in Berlin 1806–1844: Staatshilfe und Privatinitiative zwischen Merkantilismus und Liberalismus* (Berlin, 1965).

[24] Paul Siebertz, *Ferdinand von Steinbeis. Ein Wegbereiter der Wirtschaft* (Stuttgart, 1952). For the earlier period see Franz Wauschkuhn, 'Die Anfänge der württembergischen Textilindustrie im Rahmen der staatlichen Gewerbepolitik 1806–1848', dissertation, Hamburg University, 1974, pp. 236–377; Franz Wauschkuhn, 'Staatliche Gewerbepolitik und frühindustrielles Unternehmertum in Württemberg von 1806 bis 1848', in Erich Maschke and J. Sydow (eds.), *Zur Geschichte der Industrialisierung in den südwestdeutschen Städten* (Sigmaringen, 1977); Frank Haverkamp, *Staatliche Gewerbeförderung im Grossherzogtum Baden. Unter bes. Berücksichtigung der Entwicklung des gewerblichen Bildungswesens im 19. Jahrhundert* (Freiburg and Munich, 1979), pp. 129–39.

work was done in ministries here and there by individual officials, for instance Johann Gottfried Tulla and Carl Friedrich Nebenius in Baden[25] and Albert Christian Weinling[26] in Saxony. However, their devotion and efforts did not greatly affect the principle of the German state leaving economic development well alone.

As far as it went, these policies constituted a step forwards, by no means self-evident after a century of tying economic efforts to the state's apron strings. Only in Prussia had general free choice of occupation been conceded during the first half of the century for a period between 1811 and 1845–9.[27] All other states had retained guild regulation of occupations until the 1860s, when the movement towards freedom of trade swept them away everywhere within a short decade.[28] Though overdue, this did not give economic development any great fillip. Craft guild regulations had never impeded the evolution of modern industries. It was a characteristic of manufacture that it did not generally grow out of guild crafts, but developed alongside them as a licensed trade. All states generously granted applications for manufacturing licences, without decisively influencing the process of industrialization by stimulus and promotion, guidance and formation of structure, provision of finance and direction. Conscious industrialization policy on the part of the state did not exist in Germany any more than in England or elsewhere, except for participation in the construction of various railways.[29] Funds for industrial promotion set aside in state budgets were never particularly ample.

Government departments, commissions, and institutes for industry pursued aims beneficial in detail, if modest on the whole – aims designed more to maintain a middle class than to expand the scope of economic modernization. These applied to all three important sectors of state industrial policy: acquisition of technical–organizational know-how and of machinery from abroad (especially from England, as long as that country maintained an embargo on the export of machinery), often

25 Wolfram Fischer, Der Staat und die Anfänge der Industrialisierung in Baden 1800–1850 (Berlin, 1962), pp. 139ff.; Wolfram Fischer, 'Planerische Gesichtspunkte bei der Industrialisierung in Baden', in Fischer, Wirtschaft und Gesellschaft, pp. 75–84; Haverkamp, Staatliche Gewerbeförderung.

26 Siegfried Moltke and Wilhelm Stieda, Albert Christian Weinling in Briefen von ihm und an ihn (Leipzig, 1931); J. Bode, 'Die Staatliche Gewerbeförderung im Königreich Sachsen', dissertation, Erlangen University, 1914.

27 Ernst Klein, Von der Reform zur Restauration. Finanzpolitik und Reformgesetzgebung des preussischen Staatskanzlers Karl August von Hardenberg (Berlin, 1965), pp. 100ff.; Reinhard Koselleck, Preussen zwischen Reform und Revolution. Allgemeines Landrecht, Verwaltung und soziale Bewegung von 1791 bis 1848 (Stuttgart, 1967), pp. 588–609.

28 See in general K. von Rohrscheid, Vom Zunftzwang zur Gewerbefreiheit (Berlin, 1898); and as a case study P. Horster, 'Die Entwicklung der sächsischen Gewerbefreiheit (1730–1861)', dissertation, Heidelberg University, 1908.

29 Even such laws were not predominantly designed to promote industry or based on a policy of infrastructure, but pursued fiscal ends, explicitly so in Bavaria, Baden and Württemberg, where the state from the outset took exclusive charge of railway construction and operation, and it still applied to the purchase of Prussian railways by the state at the beginning of the 1880s.

bordering on industrial espionage and smuggling; establishment of a system of industrial and technical training and advice; and occasional subventions, loans, subsidies to, and guarantees of, interest payments, remission of customs duties payable on machinery imports, and on rare occasions the setting up of industries and factories. This applied to all states in the German Federation, differences of scope and intensity being trivial. It will therefore suffice to describe in more detail the Prussian example to clarify this policy.

Apart from the employment of local agents to ascertain technical progress and transmit the knowledge to Berlin, Beuth himself from 1814 onwards undertook extensive journeys of technical exploration to England, France, Belgium, Holland, and Sweden and, at the expense of the Department of Industry and later of the Technical Commission, sent young technicians and manufacturers abroad, some even as far as America. The knowledge, skills, plans, and machine components brought back were communicated to interested craftsmen and manufacturers in the form of published transactions of the semi-official Industrial Association; they were also used by the Technical Commission for demonstration purposes, were reproduced in pamphlets and yearbooks and passed to a rapidly increasing number of students at the Berlin Industrial Institute, established in 1826, where the seeds fell on the most fertile soil. Some of those who were later to become prominent entrepreneurs in Prussia and elsewhere received their basic training there: for instance August Borsig and Wöhlert, Hermann Jaques Gruson and Emil Kessler, also later Gottfried Daimler. It was the origin of the Technical University of Berlin (Technische Hochschule).

Research on, and dissemination of, technical knowledge and skills, methods of production, and principles of operation were continuous and purposeful pursuits. Direct practical promotion of industry, on the other hand, remained unsystematic and unplanned, though neither unintentional nor accidental. The guiding principle was not a purposive concept of systematic industrial development, but a short-term plan to create and maintain employment and earnings for a small part of the poverty-stricken surplus population,[30] as, for instance, when the Prussian state after 1818 gave mules away several times free of charge to the hopelessly uncompetitive Silesian linen-spinning mills and provided them with working capital, when it permitted the duty-free import of steam and other engines, when it persuaded foreign entrepreneurs, such as the famous English industrialists, the Cockerill brothers, to establish factories in Prussia, and when it used Christian Rother's Königliche Seehandlung (a kind of state bank) to refloat or buy up bankrupt enterprises and especially to establish factories in the impoverished and overpopulated

---

[30] For Baden see Fischer, *Staat*, pp. 209ff.; 'Planerische Gesichtspunkte', pp. 78ff.; Haverkamp, *Staatliche Gewerbeförderung*, pp. 117ff.

area of Lower Silesia.[31] These activities were not particularly wide-ranging or effective and suffered many failures. Some acquisitions had to be resold after years of losses, as in the case of the subsequently flourishing Moabit machine-building complex sold to Borsig; many foundations proved to be still-born, but expensive, infants. It cannot be documented that the state, by promotion of industry, at times prevented or crowded out private initiative and damaged economic progress in this direction, but it is not inconceivable that this was so.

Indisputably helpful to economic progress was state development of the communications network. The Prussian allocation for road building increased between 1821 and 1841 from 1.6 to 9 million marks, the network of metalled roads from 420 to 1,573 miles.[32] Railway construction would undoubtedly have proceeded more slowly and would not have opened up the more remote areas, such as the extreme east, at all, had not the Prussian economic bureaucracy overcome initial doubts and assisted, hesitatingly from 1842, powerfully from 1850, by participating in capital investment and guaranteeing interest.

As the policy of direct promotion of industry had been largely designed for the purpose of creating and maintaining employment, it had implications not only of economic, but also of social objectives.[33] Yet the principles and practice of a public social policy before the establishment of the Reich could hardly be identified, let alone effectively developed. Modern social policy came into being explicitly as a policy of workers' protection and insurance. Not until the 1850s and the 1860s did the condition of the workers (*Arbeiterfrage*) figure as central in social problems (*soziale Frage*). It took another two decades of prevailing socio-economic liberalism before it was realized that the problem concerned the state.

The guiding motivation of both these embryonic developments which existed nevertheless had their roots largely outside the novel contemporary social problems. Early Prussian factory legislation[34] derived its origin from the social responsibility – no longer recognized as a principle – of a pre-modern authoritarian and welfare state, supplemented by fears regarding fitness for military service. Several ineffec-

---

[31] In addition to Henderson, *The State*, pp. 119–47; Ritter, *Die Rolle*, pp. 78ff.; Mieck, *Preussische Gewerbepolitik*, pp. 161–206; Koselleck, *Preussen*, pp. 612ff.; also Hermann Schleutker, *Die volkswirtschaftliche Bedeutung der königlichen Seehandlung* (Tübingen, 1920).

[32] Koselleck, *Preussen*, p. 615; Borchard, 'Staatsverbrauch', pp. 223ff., 263.

[33] See also Hans-Joachim Henning, 'Preussische Sozialpolitik im Vor-März? Ein Beitrag zu den arbeiterfreundlichen Bestrebungen in Unternehmen der Seehandlung', *VSWG*, vol. LII (1965), pp. 485–539.

[34] Günther K. Anton, *Geschichte der preussischen Fabrikgesetzgebung bis zu ihrer Aufnahme durch die Reichsgewerbeordnung* (Leipzig, 1891; rep. Berlin, 1953); Friedrich Syrup and Otto Neuloh, *Hundert Jahre staatliche Sozialpolitik, 1839–1939* (Stuttgart, 1957), pp. 58ff.; Wolfgang Köllmann, 'Die Anfänge der staatlichen Sozialpolitik in Preussen bis 1869', *VSWG*, vol. LIII (1966), pp. 28–52; Koselleck, *Preussen*, pp. 624ff.

tive attempts from 1817 onwards were followed in 1839 by a regulation 'for the protection of workers' children who were themselves child labourers' (Koselleck), prohibiting employment of children below the age of 9 and night work by juveniles, and limiting the daily hours of work to 10 up to the age of 16.[35] It was not policed. Not until 1853, in a period of deepest political reaction, was a factory inspectorate set up. At that time the prohibitions and limitations of 1839 were rendered more precise and extensive. Children below the age of 12 were not henceforth allowed to work in factories, below the age 14 for 6 hours only. In addition, factory owners were prohibited from paying workers in unsaleable goods in lieu of money. The state did not regulate the working conditions of adult factory operatives.

It took a long time before adult workers at least gained the right to use their own strength to improve their conditions by combination. This was the second start, motivated less by economic and social considerations than by constitutional law: legal exemptions and the implied inequality before the law were to be eliminated. Saxony pioneered in 1861; in Prussia, several bills promoted for this purpose between 1862 and 1865 by the Liberal Party in both houses of parliament were aborted.[36] It was not until the liberal Industrial Law for the North German Federation had been passed in 1869 and adopted two years later by the German Reich that article 52 came into force, which contained the principle of freedom to combine, though this was ominously limited in practice by article 53. Anybody attempting to coerce others into participating in a strike by force, threats, or social ostracism (boycott) committed a criminal offence. This not only detracted largely from the practical value of freedom to combine, it reintroduced through the back door exceptions to the law as far as it applied to workers; it became the bone of contention in a long-drawn-out and embittered battle of the working-class movement for labour legislation in the Empire.

III. Economic and social policy during the Empire and the Weimar Republic until 1930

The constitution of the German Reich of 16 April 1871 by article 4 assigned the principal responsibility for economic and social policy to imperial legislation. From that date onwards, there existed a German

---

[35] Bavaria and Baden followed in 1840 with corresponding laws, Austria in 1842, Saxony and Württemberg not until 1861.

[36] See Karl-Erich Born, 'Sozialpolitische Probleme und Bestrebungen in Deutschland von 1848 bis zur Bismarckschen Sozialgesetzgebung', *VSWG*, vol. XLIV (1959), pp. 29–44; Volker Hentschel, *Die deutschen Freihändler und der volkswirtschaftliche Kongress 1858–1885* (Stuttgart, 1975), pp. 188–92; Ulrich Engelhardt, *Nur vereinigt sind wir stark: Die Anfänge der deutschen Arbeiterbewegung, 1862/63–1869/70*, vol. I (Stuttgart, 1977), pp. 200f.

economic and social policy, merely supplemented by state policies. States were concerned with measures directly promoting and structuring the economy, but everywhere their scope and intensity diminished considerably. More importantly, states retained their own financial administrations and the right to levy taxes. Continuous conflicts of financial policy were among the most important inconveniences from the federal structure of the Empire.

'Reich responsibility for matters of economic and social policy' did not necessarily signify uniformity of motives and consequences of measures, untrammelled or unmodified by consideration of the wishes of individual states. The decisive body for Reich legislation was not the democratically elected Reichstag, but the Federal Council, a conference of delegates from state governments, which made the decision on which bills would be submitted to the Reichstag for its deliberation and in what form. The Reichstag itself had no right to initiate legislation. In addition, laws passed by the Reichstag required the assent of the Federal Council before attaining validity. Bills had therefore generally been widely discussed and harmonized; by the time they reached parliament, they represented a mutual adjustment of state interests. But they did not represent state interests alone: mediated by the latter, the economic and social interests of pressure groups often exercised a distorting and fragmenting influence on Reich legislation. Given that Prussia uninterruptedly dominated the Federal Council from beginning to end, it is indisputable that these interests were not exclusively, but predominantly, those of the landowning nobility and of large-scale industry. By this statement we do not contribute to the recently resurrected, loud and monotonous chant that economic and social legislation in the Empire amounted to hardly more than a satisfaction of demands put forward by agrarians and large-scale industry, in the interest – also from the point of view of public policy – of the growth of the economy as a whole, of private profits, and of social peace which would safeguard the preservation of pre-modern social structures and pre-democratic methods of domination. That is nonsense. Quite apart from the fact that economic and social policy was repeatedly pursued in opposition to the demands of such pressure groups, the mechanism of decision-making in the Empire – multi-dimensional, exposed to the influence of multiple interests, hence necessitating the reconciliation of many different interests – in fact prevented the effective and straight-forward pursuit of clear and consistently formulated aims by appropriate and rational measures. This cannot be discussed in detail here,[37] but it has to remain a guiding consideration

---

[37] There are plentiful recent and some older materials amply utilized, other older records but little used. As there are hardly any summaries of long-period trends, but only monographs on conditions affecting detailed decisions, they are mentioned in their appropriate places.

Table 103. *Share of public expenditure in Net National Product at market prices, 1875–1930*

	NNP (million marks)	Public expenditure (million marks)	Share (%)
1881	17.3	1.8	10.4
1891	22.6	2.7	11.9
1913	52.4	8.1	15.4
1925	67.3	14.5	21.5
1929	79.5	20.9	26.3

Sources: Net Social Product, Hoffmann, pp. 825f. Public Expenditure: 1881–1913, Weitzel, Tables 1, 26; 1925, 1929, *Statistisches Jahrbuch für das Deutschen Reich*, 1928, pp. 530, 539ff., 1932, pp. 450f.

Table 104. *Functional subdivision of public expenditure, 1875–1930 (percentage)*

	Administration	Armaments	Social	Education and training	Economy	Debt service
1881	25.5	24.8	7.7	17.7	13.7	10.6
1891	22.9	25.7	11.3	17.1	13.1	9.9
1913	20.4	21.0	15.9	19.1	12.0	10.7
1925	15.2	15.9	37.4	16.5	9.8	1.4
1929	15.4	14.6	35.1	16.0	14.3	5.0

Sources: As Table 103.

in reviewing the main path-breaking decisions, events, and inter-relationships which are here presented.

A.   FINANCIAL AND MONETARY POLICY

Statistical data improve in the period after the establishment of the Reich, but are still far from perfect. Primary sources for the financial administration of the Empire are in addition inconveniently diffuse, owing to the federalist nature of the financial constitution. We are indebted to some laborious research in the field of historical statistics or adequate and comprehensive information on public expenditure and its functional subdivision.[38]

[38] Especially Suphan Andic and J. Veverka, 'The Growth of Government Expenditure in Germany', in *Finanzarchiv*, vol. xxiii (1963); Otto Weitzel, 'Die Entwicklung der Staatsausgaben in Deutschland', dissertation, Nuremberg University, 1967; see also the ambitiously titled essay by Peter Christian Witt, 'Finanzpolitik und sozialer Wandel. Wachstum und Funktionswandel der Staatsausgaben in Deutschland 1871–1933', in Hans Ulrich Wehler (ed.), *Sozialgeschichte heute. Festschrift für Fritz Neumark* (Gottingen, 1974), pp. 565–74.

The share of public expenditure (excluding so-called parafiscal items, such as, for instance, social insurance) in Net National Product at market prices trebled in the 60 years under discussion. The increase was continuous. The First World War and its consequences accelerated it, though not to the extent of causing a break in continuity.[39] Parallel to a growth of public expenditure considerably more rapid than in the days of the German Federation was a more thorough-going and unambiguous re-examination of state functions. The three classic fields of public expenditure, that is administration and judicature, education and training, armaments and defence, were substantial losers, whereas social welfare – and above all and from the outset – and in the Weimar Republic also, support for and regulation of the economy and communications, gained in importance.[40] State payments accruing only to certain limited groups within the population (merit wants) grew faster than general payments accruing without reference to groups (social wants).

It is just as legitimate and reasonable for the period of the Empire and the Republic, as for the years from 1815 to 1866, to narrow down the description of revenue policy to cover increasing expenditure as a description of taxation policy. It cannot be exactly determined at what moment the gradual increase in the share of receipts from administrative and commercial services in total government revenue, which had begun half a century earlier, turned into an equally gradual decrease, but it was at the latest around 1890. The share in the Gross National Product taken by taxation therefore grew visibly faster than the share allocated to public funds, from hardly more than 5 per cent in the 1870s to approximately 20 per cent around 1930.

To collect this sharply and continuously increasing share posed a fiscal problem. Its solution was rendered more difficult by the political problem already indicated, which required a reconciliation of claims – for which invariably different reasons were advanced – from the Reich, states, and communes on sources of, and shares in, taxes. All tax reforms of any importance were also reforms of collection and allocation. In addition, after 1890 attempts – some more successful than others – were made to make tax policy reflect principles of social policy, especially those of taxable capacity and demands for a moderate redistribution of

---

[39] On the principle explaining the secular and world-wide rise in the share of the state, Horst C. Recktenwald, 'Staatsausgaben in säkularer Sicht', in Heinz Haller (ed.), *Theorie und Praxis des finanzpolitischen Interventionismus. Festschrift für Fritz Neumark* (Tübingen, 1970); Konrad Littmann, *Definition und Entwicklung der Staatsquote – Begrenzung, Aussagekraft und Anwendungsbereiche unterschiedlicher Typen von Staatsquoten* (Göttingen, 1975); C. B. Blankart, 'Neuere Ansätze aur Erklärung des Wachstums der Staatsausgaben', *Hamburger Jahrbuch für Wirtschafts- und Gesellschaftspolitik*, vol. XXII (1977), pp. 73–92.

[40] This would be even clearer in Table 103 if it took compulsory social insurance into account.

private incomes. Only after 1930 were objectives of growth and employment policy superadded. But even without them, there was no lack of conflict regarding objectives and measures of tax policy.

Such conflicts were, so to speak, immanent in the tax constitution of the Reich. The states in 1867–71 successfully insisted on reserving to themselves direct taxation of property, revenues, and incomes, conceding to the Reich customs, consumption, and stamp duties. If these proved insufficient, the Reich could levy 'matricular' contributions on the states, pursuant to a resolution passed by the Reichstag. No Reich finance administration was set up; the states also administered the customs and Reich taxes.

Though, contrary to occasional assertions, this was not a rule laid down by the constitution, this system lasted until 1919. Not the least of the reasons why states succeeded in defending their tax privileges until then was their ability to rely throughout on support from changing majority votes in the Reichstag. The – overwhelmingly Prussian – Conservatives supported these privileges as property owners, the Centre Party, the Liberals, and the Social Democrats as a matter of principle. The Conservatives preferred decisions on revenue and income taxes to be taken in the Prussian Lower House where nothing could be done against their wishes. The Centre Party, the Liberals, and the Social Democrats were concerned to keep the Reich short of funds and dependent on matricular contributions. As the military budget, which accounted for about 90 per cent of the Reich budget, was fixed for five or even seven years at a time, the annual parliamentary decision on the level of matricular contributions was the last remnant, more symbolic than effective, of the constitutional right to approve the budget.[41]

Between the millstones of state particularism, property owners' defence of privilege, and the preservation of a pretence of a constitutional right to approve the budget, all Reich tax reforms were ground to nought. Wide-ranging bills embodying principles were implemented piecemeal in a manner which achieved nothing. This is as true of the tariff and tax legislation of 1879 – which we shall discuss in connection with commercial policy – as for the chaotic reforms of 1906 and 1909.[42]

A heavier levy on property – whether by way of a continuous and

---

[41] Matricular contributions supplied in 1876 11 per cent, in 1910 no more than 2.5 per cent of revenue required by the Reich; Terhallle, 'Geschichte', p. 279.

[42] Albert Hesse, 'Die Reichsfinanzreform von 1909', *Jahrbücher für Nationalökonomie und Statistik*, vol. XXXVII (1909), pp. 721–70; Wilhelm Gerloff, *Die Finanz- und Zollpolitik des deutschen Reiches nebst ihrer Beziehungen zu Landes- und Gemeindefinanzen von der Gründung des Norddeutschen Bundes bis zur Gegenwart* (Jena, 1913), pp. 424–75; Terhalle, 'Geschichte', pp. 284ff.; Peter Christian Witt, *Die Finanzpolitik des Deutschen Reichs von 1903 bis 1913* (Lübeck and Hamburg, 1970); Volker Hentschel, *Wirtschaft und Wirtschaftspolitik im wilhelminschen Deutschland. Organisierter Kapitalismus und Interventionsstaat?* (Stuttgart, 1978), pp. 164ff.

moderate property tax or of an occasional substantial estate and inheritance duty – was thus in the long run prevented. For it was substituted a · conglomerate of taxes of low yield,[43] levied on consumption, turnover, capital transfers, and expenditure, in part unsoundly motivated and detrimental both to taxation and to private and economic welfare, expensive to collect and administer. They are still with us.

The only modern and pioneering model tax reform during the imperial period was not a Reich reform at all, but that of the Prussian tax system in 1891–4.[44] In essence it was a deliberate adaptation of financial policy to Germany's transition from an agrarian and craft society to a modern industrial state. Taxes based on revenue from occupation and property as defined by status lost in significance as against the general income tax.) This was equally true qualitatively, though not quantitatively, for the south German states which up to the war followed the Prussian example explicitly.[45] In addition, modern income tax introduced two effective principles of lasting value to the German system of taxation: the principle of social policy that taxation should be determined by ability to pay, and the linkage of tax revenue to the growth of the Gross National Product.

The Prussian Income Tax Law of 1891, inextricably linked with the name of the Finance Minister, Johannes von Miquel, removed the obsolete differentiation between class-determined and classified income taxes, while introducing a new differentiation at the 3,000 marks limit: incomes below this level continued to be assessed by the authorities, those above it had to be declared by the taxpayer. The rate was proportional to income throughout and moderately progressive (0.6–4 per cent) for incomes between 900 and 100,000 marks. Incomes below 900 marks were no longer liable to tax, whereas incomes above 100,000 marks bore tax at the 4 per cent rate. The principle of ability to pay found expression, besides the progressive rate and the exemption from tax at the minimum standard of living level, also in the consideration given to family com-

---

[43] Taxes were introduced on sparkling wine, matches, lighting materials, playing cards, acetic acid, sweepstake tickets, cheques, bills of exchange, dividend coupons, land transfers, bills of lading, passenger tickets, commissions and articles of association. A few more were added in the Weimar Republic. Their share in total tax revenue in 1913 amounted to 8, in 1929 to 9 per cent.

[44] Adolph Wagner, 'Die Reform der direkten Staatsbesteuerung in Preussen im Jahre 1891', *Finanzarchiv*, vol. VIII (1891), pp. 551–810; Schwarz and Strutz, *Der Staatshaushalt*, pp. 1134–91; Hans Herzfeld, *Johannes von Miquel*, vol. II (Berlin, 1938–9); Hentschel, *Wirtschaft*, pp. 157ff.

[45] In the last years of the peace, the percentage which income tax formed of total state tax revenue amounted to 76 in Saxony, 72 in Prussia, 60 in Hesse, 46 in Württemberg, 45 in Baden, 40 in Bavaria: Wilhelm Gerloff, *Die Steuerliche Belastung in Deutschland während der letzten Friedensjahre* (Berlin, 1916), pp. 62ff. See also Georg Schanz, 'Übersicht über die zur Zeit (1914) in den deutschen Bundesstaaten und Gemeinden geltenden direkten Steuersysteme', *Finanzarchiv*, vol. XXXI (1914), pp. 236ff.; Siegfried Strauss, 'Die Subjektivierung der direkten Steuersysteme in den deutschen Staaten durch Beseitigung der Ertragssteuern', dissertation, Würzburg University, 1926.

mitments and to particular economic and social circumstances. These principles have remained unchanged, though stressed more heavily and with multivarious differentiations. What has also remained unchanged is the frustration, to a large extent, of the achievement of tax justice by the differentiation between assessed and declared incomes. Miquel's idea, sound at first sight, was to use the obligation to declare income in order to do away with widespread tax evasion by the wealthy in Prussia. In fact, revenue from income tax from one year to the next rose by 39 per cent being accounted for by incomes exceeding 3,000 marks.[46] However, recipients of large incomes soon displayed much ingenuity in exploring new methods and achieving their former extent of tax evasion.[47]

Opportunities for fraudulent tax evasion were diminished markedly by the reform of assessment methods at the beginning of the Weimar Republic, whereas simultaneously opportunities for legal tax avoidance by those declaring their incomes were immeasurably increased. The 3,000 marks limit, representing the water-shed between those who declared and those who were assessed, was at that time removed; differentiation thereafter depended on the mode of income accrual. Gradually two classes of taxpayer emerged: income from employment was no longer assessed at all, but tax withheld at source from wages and salaries. This provided little opportunity for manipulation. All other incomes continued to be 'declared' – and, owing to increasingly numerous opportunities for deductions within the framework of a lenient tax law which allowed much scope for ingenuity, led to a discretionary figure determined almost arbitrarily. What were lost were the principles of ability to pay and tax justice.

Tax discrimination in respect of earned income became an unintended by-product of the most thorough reform of the German financial system after 1815. Its intellectual and practical progenitor was the Reich Minister of Finance, Matthias Erzberger, in 1919;[48] it received its enduring shape after his death at the hands of Johannes Popitz in 1925.[49] When Erzberger assumed the portfolio of finance in July 1919, budget revenue

---

[46] *Statistisches Jahrbuch für den Preussischen Staat* (1908), p. 232; Schwarz and Strutz, *Der Staatshaushalt*, p. 1212.

[47] F. Meisel, 'Moral und Technik bei der Veranlagung der preussischen Einkommenssteuer', *Schmollers Jahrbuch*, vol. XXXV (1911), pp. 285–373; F. Meisel, 'Wahrheit und Fiskalismus bei der Veranlagung der modernen Einkommenssteuer', *Finanzarchiv*, vol. XXXI, no. 2 (1914), pp. 144–68; Peter Christian Witt, 'Der preussische Landrat also Steuerbeamter 1891–1918', in I. Geiss and B. J. Wendt (eds.), *Deutschland in der Weltpolitik des 19. und 20. Jahrhunderts: Festschrift für Fritz Fischer zum 65. Geburtstag* (Düsseldorf, 1974), pp. 205–19.

[48] Paul Beusch, *Die Neuordnung des deutschen Finanzwesens* (Mönchengladbach, 1919); K. Bräuer, *Die Neuordnung der deutschen Finanzwirtschaft und das neue Steuersystem* (Stuttgart, 1920); Klaus Eppstein, *Matthias Erzberger und das Dilemma der deutschen Demokratie* (Munich, 1976), pp. 376ff.

[49] Fritz Terhalle, 'Zur Reichsfinanzreform von 1925', *Zeitschrift für die gesamte Staatswissenschaft*, vol. LXXIX (1925–6).

fell short of expenditure by 57 per cent, owing to the enormous burdens created by the war and the desperate state of the economy. Erzberger resolved not to adopt the most obvious solution, which would have been to declare the Reich bankrupt, but to close the gap by partially confiscatory taxation. In spite of very popular once-and-for-all levies on wealth and war profits which bordered on expropriation, and of drastic increases in rates of tax on incomes and turnover, success was incomplete, but the Erzberger solution did leave a permanent imprint on the system and the rates of taxation, which affected tax principles and administration, and the financial adjustment between Reich and states. The following list summarizes Erzberger's measures.

1. Turnover tax, introduced in 1916 in the guise of an emergency and crisis tax for the benefit of the Reich and regarded as unsuitable as a permanent tax because of defects inherent in assessment and of asocial regressive effects, was anchored in the German tax system as the ultimate substantial tax which constituted the 'backbone of the whole budget'.[50]

2. Rates of income and turnover tax were raised to a level unimaginable before 1919. Erzberger at the time made income tax progressive from 10 to 90 per cent – of course, a rate untenable once the political and social disturbance of the period had abated; Popitz subsequently stabilized the upper limit at 35 per cent. At the same time, the rate of turnover tax, raised in 1919/20 from 0.5 to 2.5 per cent, was halved and soon afterwards further lowered to 1 per cent.

3. The Reich Revenue Law of 13 December 1919 did away with the financial authority of the states: the Reich assumed sole authority for levying and administering taxes.[51] On the one hand, this was necessary for successfully balancing the Reich budget, but it also corresponded to the change in political constitution.[52] Instead of pensioners being dependent on the states, the Reich became their source of finance. By a legally fixed financial adjustment, the Reich henceforth put the larger part of income-tax and the smaller part of turnover-tax revenue at the states' disposal, with profit taxes accruing to the local authorities.[53]

4. Popitz' 'rule of the power of attraction of the superior budget' was decisively applied. The Reich's share of total public revenues had

[50] Hildemarie Dieckmann, *Johannes Popitz. Entwicklung und Wirksamkeit in der Weimarer Republik* (Berlin, 1960), pp. 29f.

[51] *Reichsgesetzblatt* (1919), p. 1993, arts. 8 and 11. See also H. Leidel, *Die Begründung der Reichsfinanzverwaltung* (Bonn, 1964).

[52] G. Hölfler, 'Erzbergers Finanzreform und ihre Rückwirkungen auf die bundesstaatliche Struktur des Reiches', dissertation, Freiburg University, 1955.

[53] *Einzelschrift zur Statistik des Deutschen Reiches, No. 6: Verwaltungsaufbau, Steuerverteilung und Lastenverteilung im Deutschen Reich* (Berlin, 1929).

already risen from 17.5 to 29.7 per cent between 1885 and 1913; up to 1925, it increased further to 37.6 per cent. Correspondingly, the share of the states fell from 57.1 per cent at first to 29.5, then further to 26 per cent. Local authorities had made considerable gains during the Empire: their share had gone up from 25.4 to 40.8 per cent. By 1925 it had lapsed to 23.4 per cent.[54]

The years between Erzberger's heroic achievements in the field of financial policy and their consolidation were full of innumerable hectic crises and bridging measures,[55] provoked by reparation payments, by the social consequences of the war, and by galloping inflation. Fiscal peace followed, but only for a short period, violently terminated when the great crisis broke in Germany in 1930.[56]

Even the reforms of 1919 and 1925 did not turn taxation into an instrument for countercyclical policy or income redistribution, though this possibility inhered in the German taxation system from that time onwards. A progressive income-tax rate contained within itself both the principle of 'in-built stability' and idea of a moderate income redistribution in favour of poorer people. As things turned out, neither could develop.

Redistribution effects were frustrated because a tax rate large enough to be effective only began at comparatively high levels, that is, exceeding 25,000 Reichsmark; hence the aggregate available for distribution remained small; hardly more than 5 per cent of all taxable incomes was likely to be subject to tax rates resulting in a palpable redistribution. And such results were largely neutralized by the regressive effects of turnover and consumption taxes. Owing to the progressive nature of income-tax rates, about 30 per cent of the incidence of income tax differed from what it would have been under strictly proportional taxation, but this affected no more than 6 per cent of total tax revenue and less than 1 per cent of national income.[57]

[54] Willi Albers, 'Finanzausgleich III', in *Handwörterbuch des Sozialwissenschaften* (Stuttgart, 1961), vol. III, pp. 556ff.

[55] G. Strutz, 'Die Reichssteuerpolitik der Nachkriegszeit', *Zeitschrift für die gesamte Staatswissenschaft*, vol. LXXVIII (1924); Johannes Popitz, 'Die deutschen Finanzen 1918–1928', in *Zehn Jahre deutscher Geschichte* (Berlin, 1928); K. B. Netzband and H. P. Widmaier, *Währungs- und Finanzpolitik der Ära Luther 1923–1925* (Berlin, 1964); C. D. Krohn, *Stabilisierung und ökonomische Interessen. Die Finanzpolitik des Deutschen Reiches* (Bonn, 1974); Peter Christian Witt, 'Reichsfinanzminister und Reichsfinanzverwaltung 1918/19–1924', *Vierteljahrshefte für Zeitgeschichte (VfZ)*, vol. XXIII (1975).

[56] Dietrich Baumgarten, *Deutsche Finanzpolitik 1924–1928* (Berlin, 1965); Ilse Maurer, *Reichsfinanzen und grosse Koalition. Zur Geschichte des Reichskabinetts Müller (1928–1930)* (Frankfurt and Bern, 1973).

[57] Problems and detailed results of the calculation from Volker Hentschel, 'Steuersystem und Steuerpolitik in Deutschland 1890–1970', in Rainer Lepsius (ed.), *Historische Grundlagen der Bundesrepublik Deutschland* (Stuttgart, 1980). The formulae used are in Willie Albers' 'Umverteilungswirkungen der Einkommenssteuer', in Willi Albers, *Öffentliche Finanzwirtschaft und Verteilung II, Schriften des Vereins für Sozialpolitik*, NS, vol. LXXV, no. 2 (Berlin, 1974).

A progressive rate could not properly achieve in-built stability during the Weimar Republic because income-tax revenue accounted only for about 4 per cent of national income, the elasticity of its incidence rising only just above unity – rates far too low to be effective. In addition, the effects of inbuilt stability were not known, and finance ministers naturally did not refrain from expending additional public revenue during a boom. Without such a policy, no results could follow.

Hence financial policy did not guide the state of the economy automatically, let alone try to do so consciously. Nor was there ever an attempt to use monetary policy as a guide. The idea that this was possible did not remain completely foreign to leading Reichsbank officials, who incidentally were subject to instructions from the Reich government, but they understood it only in one direction. Never would they have suggested a Bank Rate policy – the only instrument at their disposal – to originate and support a boom, but they were aware that an excessive boom should be headed off by a high rate of interest.[58] Yet, as far as can be ascertained, they never put such a policy to the test. Irrespective of the economic situation, their major endeavour remained the attempt to keep the circulation of banknotes within the limits prescribed by the Reichsbank Law of 14 March 1875. Admittedly, the limits were flexible. Circulation of banknotes was not to exceed cash holdings, foreign gold coins and notes, and Reich Treasury bills by more than 250 million up to 1899, 450 million from 1899 to 1909, thereafter up to the outbreak of the war 550 million marks. Any issue in excess of these limits had to bear a 5 per cent tax. As soon as banknote circulation approached or even exceeded this taxation limit, the Reichsbank raised its discount rate; as soon as it dropped below, it lowered it. In principle, this behaviour corresponded to business cycles. But acting simultaneously in its capacity as guarantor of adequate liquidity in the economy, the Reichsbank turned the discount screw only cautiously and often put up with being heavily 'caught in the tax trap'. Moreover, commercial interest rates were determined by the growing financial strength of the German universal banks and their diminishing demand for credit, mostly only short term and of not much importance in calculating costs. Thus

[58] See Karl von Lumm, member of the governing body of the Reichsbank, 'Diskontpolitik', *Bank-Archiv*, vol. XI (Berlin, 1911–12); in addition the volumes published by the Reichsbank, *Die Reichsbank, 1876–1900* (Berlin, 1901); and *Die Reichsbank, 1900–1925* (Berlin, 1925). For descriptive accounts, see above all Gert von Eyern, *Die Reichsbank. Problems des deutschen zentralen Noteninstituts in geschichtlicher Darstellung* (Jena, 1928); Josef Lienhart, *Die Reichsbank von 1876 bis 1933 aufgrund ihrer Bilanzen und Erlofgsrechungen* (Würzburg, 1936); K. R. Bott, 'Die Tätigkeit der Reichsbank 1876–1914', *Weltwirtschaftliches Archiv*, vol. LXXII, no. 1 (1954), pp. 34–59, pp. 179ff.; Jürgen Friedhofen, 'Die Diskontpolitik der Deutschen Reichsbank', dissertation, Berlin University, 1963; Knut Borchardt, 'Währung und Wirtschaft', in Deutsche Bundesbank, *Währung und Wirtschaft in Deutschland, 1876–1975* (Frankfurt am Main, 1976), pp. 3–53; Hentschel, *Wirtschaft*, pp. 136ff.

commercial rates usually did not even rise in response to Bank Rate, so that the Reichsbank policy did not in practice affect cyclical conditions at all. We cannot establish effectual correlation between Bank Rate, quantity of money, and price level, such as would suggest a successful trade cycle policy for the period up to 1914.[59]

Stabilization of the external value of the currency according to the rules of the gold standard, so as to keep foreign receipts and payments in balance, would not have impeded a monetary policy influencing cyclical fluctuations. Contrary to accepted theory and common belief, that fabulous mechanism possessed comparatively little practical importance. Between 1892 and 1911, Bank Rate was raised explicitly only on three occasions to counteract a deterioration in the rate of exchange lowering the value of the mark beneath the 'gold point',[60] the latter depending more on what happened to political than to economic relations with other countries.[61]

The state of German monetary policy on the eve of the First World War was succinctly expressed by Havenstein, president of the Reichsbank, in 1908, 'The central bank can . . . only follow the rate of interest ruling in the money market; it can take note of it, but it cannot set it'.[62] On good, if controversial grounds, the political scientist Johannes Plenge made the demand expressed by the title of his book, published in 1912, that the step *From a Bank Rate Policy to the Domination of the Money Market* ought to be taken.

Even if this was seriously considered, there could at the time be no question of it. After 1914, there was no longer any monetary policy. The credit of the Reichsbank was pressed into the service of financing the war and its consequences, with well-known inflationary effects. Already during the war, the public debt in Reich and state budgets had increased from 22,000 (financial year 1 April 1913 to 31 March 1914) to 179,000 million marks (1918/19), short-term debt alone from 1,500 to 80,600 million. Cash in circulation rose from 6,500 million (1913) to

---

[59] Willi Prion, *Das deutsche Wechseldiskontgeschäft mit besonderer Berücksichtigung des Berliner Geldmarktes* (Leipzig, 1907); Heinrich Ullmann, 'Die Stellung der Reichsbank auf dem Geldmarkt vor und mach dem Kriege', dissertation, Freiburg University, 1931; Klaus Werling, 'Der Preis- und Einkommensmechanismus der Goldwährung. Untersuchung am Beispiel Englands und Deutschlands zwischen 1880 und 1914', dissertation, Hamburg University, 1962, especially pp. 41f., 45f.

[60] On the principle, Arthur I. Bloomfield, *Short-Term Capital Movements under the Pre-1914 Gold Standard* (Princeton, 1963); contemporary, Lumm, 'Diskontpolitik', p. 33; see also more recent writings by Manfred Seeger, *Die Politik der Reichsbank von 1876 bis 1914 im Lichte der Spielregeln der Goldwährung* (Berlin, 1968); Ursula Fechter, *Schutzzoll und Goldstandard im Deutschen Reich (1879–1914). Der Einfluss der Schutzzollpolitik auf den international Goldwährungsmechanismus* (Cologne and Vienna, 1974).   [61] See Hentschel, *Wirtschaft*, pp. 139–42.

[62] Quoted from Borchard, 'Währung und Wirtschaft', p. 52.

50,100 million (1919).[63] Up to that time, the full extent of the resulting inflationary effects had found nowhere near complete expression in about a 100 per cent rise of the price level, owing to deficient, even catastrophic, supplies for the civilian population and the high rate of private saving. The full effects only appeared in the course of return to economic normality after the war, when the cessation of hoarding released a flow of money completely out of proportion to the reduced productive capacity which it encountered. Two further factors drove inflation beyond the level necessary to adapt to purchasing power and productive capacity:

1. The continued need for credit on the Reich's part to finance reparations, the social burdens arising from the war, and the service of the public debt;
2. Pressure for wage increases by workers whose pay had fallen behind.

The Reich government could cope with and correct the inflationary tendency in one of two ways. It could declare the Reich bankrupt and suspend payments, or it could pursue an unremitting policy of deflation: increased taxes, reduced social welfare payments, strict limits to credit, a standstill of prices and remunerations which would remove the recently conceded freedom of bargaining (see p. 799). The consequences from the first alternative would have been political sanctions on the part of the victorious powers, from the second symptoms of a serious economic and social crisis, and in both cases riots, *coups d'état*, overthrow of the government from the Right and the Left. The risk appeared too great. Hence the government permitted inflation to gather speed until currency and economy collapsed in the summer of 1923.[64]

The collapse made stabilization inevitable.[65] On 15 November 1923, the value of the mark was fixed at US $4.20, the Reichsbank note issue for

---

[63] Deutsches Bundesbank, *Deutsches Gold- und Bankwesen in Zahlen 1876–1975* (Frankfurt am Main, 1976), pp. 2, 313. See Walter Lotz, *Die deutsche Staatsfinanzwirtschaft im Kriege* (Stuttgart, 1927); K. Roesler, *Die Finanzpolitik des Deutschen Reiches im Ersten Weltkrieg* (Berlin, 1967); Heinz Haller, 'Die Rolle der Staatsfinanzen für den Inflationsprozess', in *Währung und Wirtschaft*, pp. 115–56.

[64] Statistisches Reichsamt, *Währung und Finanzen* (Berlin, 1924); Statistisches Reichsamt, *Zahlen zur Geldentwertung in Deutschland 1914–1923*, supplement to *Wirtschaft und Statistik*, vol. v (Berlin, 1925); J. Pedersen and K. Lauersen, *The German Inflation 1918–1923* (Amsterdam, 1964); Peter Czada, 'Ursachen und Folgen der grossen Inflation', in Harald Winkel (ed.), *Finanz- und wirtschaftspolitische Fragen der Zwischenkriegszeit*, *Schriften des Vereins für Sozialpolitik*, NS, vol. LXXIII (Berlin, 1973), pp. 9–42.

[65] Rolf E. Lüke, *Von der Stabilisierung zur Krise* (Zürich, 1958); Rudolf Stucken, *Deutsche Geld- und Kreditpolitik 1914–1963* (Tübingen, 1964); Rudolf Stucken, 'Schaffung der Reichsmark, Reparationsregelungen und Auslandsanleihen, Konjunkturen', in *Währung und Wirtschaft*, pp. 249–81; Gerd Hardach, 'Reichsbankpolitik und wirtschaftliche Entwicklung 1924–1931', *Schmollers Jahrbuch*, vol. XC (1970), pp. 563ff.; Gerd Hardach, 'Die beiden Reichsbanken:

the time being strictly limited, later restricted to a 40 per cent cover by gold, foreign currency, and commercial bills of exchange; the credit obtainable by the Reich from the Reichsbank was limited firmly to a comparatively small amount, the subordination of the Reichsbank to the government removed. When acceptance of the Dawes Plan, which rearranged Germany's reparations repayments, on 30 August 1924 had created the most important precondition for an orderly and rational management of the public finances, Germany returned to the gold standard.

In principle, the step from a Bank Rate policy to the domination of the money market could now have been taken. In practice, it failed again, in particular because the Reichsbank had, as before, no means other than a Bank Rate policy at its disposal: only after 1933 was it allowed to pursue an open-market policy, a policy of minimum reserves not at all until 1945. However, a Bank Rate policy remained quite insufficient at a period of easy international money, other countries displaying a wide readiness to invest in Germany, which was so short of capital, so much in need of investment, and paying such a high rate of interest. In the years of the short boom from 1926 to 1928, whatever the Reichsbank did was wrong: if it tried to throttle domestic credit demand by increasing interest rates, it encouraged a corresponding flow of foreign credit; if, on the other hand, it endeavoured to prevent, by a low rate of interest, the rather unsound indebtedness of private and public investors to foreign creditors, demand for accommodation became excessive and, given the permanently negative balance of trade, soon reduced gold and foreign currency reserves to their legal limits. For this reason, Reichsbank Rate and with it the money market rate remained almost throughout above the level of international interest rates, attracting from abroad those substantial credits – overwhelmingly short term – which, when invested overwhelmingly long term, turned into an additional disaster for the German economy in 1931.

B.   COMMERCIAL POLICY

Financial and monetary policy undoubtedly gained weight and importance in the Weimar Republic, compared with the Empire, within the framework of Reich economic policy and as a creative force in economic life. Equally without doubt, commercial and tariff policy lost weight and importance, both in historical fact and in contemporary opinion. No-

Internationales Währungssystem und nationale Währungspolitik 1924–1931', in Hans Mommsen, Dietmar Petzina and Bernd Weisbrad (eds.), *Industrielles System und politische Entwicklung in der Weimarer Republik* (Düsseldorf, 1974), pp. 375–86; H. Müller, *Die Zentralbank – Eine Nebenregierung. Reichsbankpräsident Schacht als Politiker der Weimarer Republik* (Opladen, 1973).

body in the 1920s would any longer have thought of raising tariff policy decisions to the importance of principles fundamental to the economic, social, and political nature and future of the Reich – a concept which in the Empire had seemed impossible to avoid. Curiously enough, though it ought to have been noticed long ago that all the horrors and the miracle cures expected from tariff increases and decreases, from the conclusion and repeal of trade treaties never happened and never could have happened, many historians have recently revived the traditional view. Commercial policy has become a kind of touchstone for the theory that the state in the Prusso-German Empire pursued its own advantage in acting as agent for the Conservative landowners and entrepreneurs in heavy industry collected under its unifying administration (*Sammlungspolitik*, joint rule of rye and iron, protectionism born of solidarity). Let us consider this view.

Three extremely controversial, fundamental and comprehensive trade proposals became law under the Empire: in 1879, 1891–4, and 1902, interspersed by numerous individual measures without significant consequences.

In 1879 Germany initiated the gradual conversion of European trade policy to protective duties by the introduction of iron and cereal tariffs and the return to an autonomous tariff. In 1891–4, Germany attempted to avert the acute threat of a European system of high protective tariffs emanating from expensive conflicts in the field of commercial policy by a policy of extensive trade treaties. This change of direction in tariff policy was reversed in 1902 without any far-reaching international objectives or consequences.

The acts of 1879 and 1902 arose from the same thinking concerning tariff policy, whereas the acts of 1891–4 represented a reaction against it, which dominated the principles and efforts of the Reich authorities for a bare 5 years, but – as is seldom realized – remained effective in practice for 15 years. However, the eventual ruling tariff policy of the Empire was a protectionist one. Were therefore both its aims and its results necessarily and entirely a policy of arbitrary favouritism?

In 1879, tariff policy represented above all a means, discretionary in principle, which Bismarck employed in the unsuccessful attempt to free the Reich from its burdensome financial dependence on the states, without interfering with their reserved powers in the field of financial policy. 'Discretionary in principle' does not signify an absence of clear practical preference for a protective tariff solution on Bismarck's part; he made serious efforts to impose such a solution. Economic development in the last few years and the novel organization and pronouncements of pressure groups which it created, pointed this way. Moreover, tariff protection had a side-effect very desirable to Bismarck. In common with the entire industrialized world, the industrial sector in Germany had by

1873 slid into a deep crisis, heavy industry being worst hit. Soon afterwards a kind of world-wide transport revolution put an end once and for all to the certainty of effortless sales at high prices at home and abroad – a certainty accepted with unquestioning lassitude by Germans, above all by the aristocratic cereal producers east of the Elbe. Cheaper wheat from overseas and Russian rye, both of high quality and no longer excluded by excessive transport costs, forcefully invaded European and west German markets, threatening the comparatively inefficient and high-cost cereal growers east of the Elbe with inability to compete. Tariff protection was then, and for a long time continued to remain, the first and practically the only remedy industry and agriculture could think of to deal with problems of outlet and revenue, even if their causes were to be found in a different direction. Protection was therefore demanded promptly and vociferously. The first industrial and agrarian pressure groups (Central Association of German Industrialists, and Association of German Tax and Economic Reformers) were established to agitate and exert pressure. Bismarck's instinct quickly divined that here was a soil on which *his* wheat would flourish. Just as he had assumed the role of a convinced free trader in 1862–5 for reasons of power politics, so he now played the part of a convert to protectionism to forward his financial policy, especially as the change of direction promised another bonus. An alliance with Conservative agrarians and conservatively minded industrialists enabled Bismarck to dispense with consideration for the Liberals, which he had long found painfully nerve-wracking. Thus, as Bamberger, inspired by the just wrath of the defeated, put it, 'Bismarck's lust for power coincided with all mean and selfish instincts in Germany.'[66]

Early in 1878, Liberal free traders still held it impossible that agrarians and industrialists, each coveting protective tariffs for themselves, should abandon their energetic resistance to protective tariffs for the other and make common cause. Under Bismarck's direction, it had become possible within the course of one year. On 15 December, Bismarck in his famous 'Christmas message' announced to the Federal Council that he would promote in the coming year a comprehensive new tax law, the core of which would be a general *ad valorem* tariff 'for the protection of national labour', in addition to making taxes on beer and tobacco more productive.[67] Seven months later, the tariff was in fact passed by a broad majority in the Reichstag. It agreed on a basis of mutual interests, barely held together, to a new pig-iron tariff of 10 marks per tonne, to moderate

---

[66] To Stauffenberg on 13 August 1878, quoted from Paul Wentzcke, *Deutscher Liberalismus im Zeitalter Bismarcks. Eine politische Briefsammlung*, vol. II (Bonn and Leipzig, 1926), p. 216.

[67] Reprinted in Heinrich Poschinger, *Bismarck also Volkswirt*, vol. I: *Biz zur übernahme des Handelsministeriums 1880* (Berlin, 1889), pp. 170–7.

rises in the rates on semi-finished and finished products of heavy industry, and to the introduction of cereal tariffs (10 marks per tonne on wheat, rye, and oats). The excise on beer was postponed, that on tobacco reorganized and increased.[68]

The real gains of this operation accrued to entrepreneurs in heavy industry. They retained their tariffs permanently, even when, as the result of an upswing beginning in the following year and progressing with unexpected speed in 1894, they no longer needed them. The tariffs yielded them a pleasant differential profit. A similar gain accrued to the agriculturists from the cereal tariffs, but though wheat and rye tariffs by 1887 had been pushed up to 50 marks per tonne, even this did not suffice to compensate for the increasing losses of income brought about by the continuing fall in the world level of agricultural prices.

Bismarck, on the other hand, was the loser. As a quid pro quo for the assent of the Centre Party, he had had to concede the transfer to the states of the revenue from customs duties and from the tobacco excise, exceeding 130 million marks, to be reclaimed, if required, via the Reichstag in the form of matricular contributions (Franckenstein's clause). This signified the failure of Bismarck's original schemes.

There was another loser: the peaceable European free-trade system of trade treaties. For almost two decades, European tariff policy had been determined by reciprocal international treaties rather than unilateral national edicts. The autonomous German tariff law sounded the death-knell for this brief reign of free trade. Article 5, which authorized the Reich government arbitrarily to introduce retaliatory tariffs, showed that Bismarck was preparing for battle on the field of commercial policy. This corresponded to his concept of international trade politics which he summarized in the Reichstag debate on the tariff by the brief phrase that there was only one question at issue, '*Qui trompe t'on?*'

Europe did not switch to a protectionist and trade-war policy immediately. Above all France attempted to continue on the former lines, in the 1880s becoming the focal point of a ramified and complicated network of most-favoured-nation treaties based on comparatively low tariffs. When in 1890 even France made ready to introduce highly protective

---

[68] A prolific literature has grown up on the reversal of commercial policy and its signficance in political policy, overinterpreted as a 'conservative re-establishment of German Reich'. See particularly the relevant passages in the following: Alfred Zimmermann, *Geschichte der preussisch-deutschen Handelspolitik aktenmässig dargestellt* (Oldenburg and Leipzig, 1892); M. Nitzsche, *Die handelspolitische Reaktion in Deutschland* (Stuttgart and Berlin, 1905); Wilhelm Gerloff, *Die Finanz- und Zollpolitik des Deutschen Reiches* (Jena, 1913); Karl Hardach, *Die Bedeutung wirtschaftlicher Faktoren bei der Wiedereinführung der Eisen- und Getreidezölle in Deutschland 1879* (Berlin, 1967); Ivo N. Lambi, *Free Trade and Protection in Germany 1868–1879* (Wiesbaden, 1963); Helmut Böhme, *Deutschlands Weg zur Grossmacht* (Cologne, 1966); Michael Stürmer, *Regierung und Reichstag im Bismarkstaat 1871–1880. Caesarismus oder Parlamentarismus* (Düsseldorf, 1974); Hentschel, *Die deutschen Freihändler*.

minimum and maximum tariffs and to destroy that network, a period of costly wars of all against all in the field of trade policy seemed to threaten, from which no country stood to lose more than Germany, which could hardly have done without about 70 per cent of her imports (40 per cent industrial raw materials, 30 per cent foodstuffs), whereas 70 per cent of her exports consisted of commodities not difficult to substitute and highly price-elastic.[69] The deficit in the balance of trade, hitherto inconsiderable, was threatened with limitless expansion.

It was the economic aim of the policy of trade treaties which the new Reich Chancellor Caprivi initiated to take timely action to avert these dangers by lowering duties, especially agricultural duties. But the treaties served even more comprehensive objectives. A peaceable policy of European trade treaties was to be resurrected, possibly even a wide-ranging Central European customs union. These were to serve as land-marks on the route to a European system of political peace. In the course of three comprehensive and intensive rounds of negotiations with Austria-Hungary, Belgium, Italy, and Switzerland (1890), Spain, Romania, and Serbia (1892) and Russia (1894), Caprivi 'sacrificed' a fair volume of customs duties on the altar of this somewhat idealist plan, unimpressed and uninfluenced by particular economic pressure groups and in the face of ultimately malicious resistance on the part of Conservative agrarian circles.[70] Nevertheless, his policy failed in its objectives: it merely created an imperfect system of bilateral treaties providing for a multitude of differential tariffs, not a lasting multilateral basis for a European commercial union. This system could not serve as a focus for farther-reaching political links. Nevertheless, it created order which prevailed until 1906 and undoubtedly did no harm to the industrial upswing from 1894 onwards. Friendly foreign countries celebrated Caprivi's commercial policy as a 'rescue action, preventing general economic anarchy in Europe'. The French newspaper Le Temps referred to it as an 'industrial Sedan'.[71]

But the policy cost Caprivi his office. Agrarians greatly resented the

---

[69] Walther G. Hoffmann, Das Wachstum der deutschen Wirtschaft seit der Mitte des 19. Jahrhunderts (Berlin, Heidelberg and New York, 1965), pp. 520, 534.

[70] For commercial policy in 1890–4, there are still the earlier works by Ernst Suter, 'Die handelspolitische Kooperation des Deutschen Reiches und der Donaumonarchie 1890–94', dissertation, Marburg University, 1930; Horst Öhlmann, 'Studien zur Innenpolitik des Reichskanzlers von Caprivi', dissertation, Freiburg University, 1953; Hans Christian Sievers, 'Die Innenpolitik des Reichskanzlers Caprivi', dissertation, Kiel University, 1953; of more recent work, J. Alden Nichols, Germany after Bismarck: The Controversy over German Industrialization 1890–1902 (Chicago, 1970); Peter Leibenguth, 'Modernisierungskrisis des Kaiserreichs an der Schweller zum wilhelminischen Imperialiasmus. Politische Probleme der Ära Caprivi 1890–1894', dissertation, Cologne University, 1975; Rolf Weitwitz, Deutsche Politik und Handelspolitik unter Reichskanzler Leo von Caprivi, 1890–1894 (Düsseldorf, 1978).

[71] Quoted from Suter, 'Die handelspolitische Kooperation', pp. 81f. (Sedan was a German military victory in 1870. Translator's note.)

policy, but no part of it as much as the lowering of cereal tariffs from 50 to 35 marks while industrial tariffs remained untouched. They did not rest until the Chancellor was toppled in 1894.[72] Only three years later, a revision of Caprivi's tariff and principles of commercial policy took place. No general considerations of public, power, or treaty policy were taken into account, as they had been in 1879 and 1890. A Committee for the Drafting of Trade Treaties, formed in the Reich Ministry of the Interior by its minister, Posadowski, and his colleague Miquel from the Prussian Ministry of Finance, was given the brief to deliberate a tariff which would increase protection – a tariff which could be passed in the shape of an autonomous law and would provide a basis for new negotiations when the Caprivi treaties, concluded for 12 years, had expired. Above all, agricultural duties were to be raised.

Having been entrusted with proposing a tariff along protectionist lines, the committee was understandably staffed by men of a protectionist turn of mind, most of them members of the Central Association of German Industrialists and the German Agricultural Council, or those close to them. This committee concerned with trade policy has been described as almost a kind of symbol for the intertwining of private and public interests and power, and for the increasing influence of economic pressure groups on decisions of public policy in an era of combination policy (*Sammlungspolitik*).[73] This description ignores two points: that the 'combined' industrialists and agriculturists remained irretrievably at loggerheads during the committee's deliberations; and that the Reich government was far from adopting the outcome of the committee's deliberations, but with great determination and in the face of resolute resistance on the part of the committee's majority in the end forced on the Reichstag the adoption of that tariff which the government had wanted from the outset.

In June 1901, Reich Chancellor Bülow publicized the government's

[72] See Hans-Jurgen Pühle, *Agrarische Interessenpolitik und preussischer Konservatismus im wilhelminischen Reich 1893–1914* (Hanover, 1966).

[73] See for instance Dirk Stegmann, *Die Erben Bismarcks. Parteien und Verbände in der Spätphase des wilhelminischen Deutschland, Sammlungspolitik 1897–1918* (Cologne, 1970); Peter Christian Witt, *Die Finanzpolitik des Deutschen Reiches von 1903 bis 1913* (Lübeck and Hamburg, 1970), pp. 66, 71; Hans-Peter Ulmann, *Der Bund der Industriellen. Organisation, Einfluss und Politik klein- und mittelbetrieblicher Industrieller im deutschen Kaiserreich 1895–1914* (Göttingen, 1976), pp. 107ff.; opposite views in Geoff Eley, 'Sammlungspolitik, Social Imperialism and the Navy Law of 1891', *Militärgeschichtliche Mitteilungen*, vol. xv (1974), pp. 29–63; Hentschel, *Wirtschaft*, pp. 183ff. In addition, the writings of Franz W. Bidler, 'Der Kampf um den Zolltarif im Reichstag 1902', dissertation, Berlin University, 1929; Gerhard Schöne, 'Die Verflechtung wirtschaftlicher und politischer Motive in der Haltung der Parteien zum Bülowschen Zolltarif (1901/02)', dissertation, Halle University, 1934; Hartmut Kaelble, *Industrielle Interessenpolitik in der wilhelminischen Gesellschaft: Zentralverband deutscher Industrieller 1895–1914* (Berlin, 1967); Ekkehard Boehm, *Überseehandel und Flottenbau. Hanseatische Kaufmannschaft und deutsche Seerüstung 1879–1902* (Düsseldorf, 1972).

bill by a deliberate leak. Its rates of duty remained throughout substantially below those recommended by the committee. The agrarians especially protested immediately and vociferously, as a result of which the committee was no longer convened. There is nothing to suggest that the Tariff Law passed by the Reichstag on 13–14 December 1902 would have looked any different had there been no advisory committee or an active association lobby. Duties on wheat and rye were raised to 55 marks, all other agricultural duties being also increased – far too little for the liking of organized agriculturists. Industrial duties by and large remained at traditional levels. Entrepreneurs in the industries concerned were satisfied.[74]

None of the statements and apprehensions voiced at the time regarding the new tariff proved correct in the long run.

1. The customs tariff neither impeded the continuation of a policy of trade treaties nor did it damage exports. Up to 1906, new treaties on the basis of this tariff were concluded with all important trading partners. The German export volume during the 8 years leading up to the war grew proportionately as fast as it had done in the preceding 12 years (1894–1906) when the Caprivi treaties were in operation.[75]

2. The customs tariff did not secure an economic basis for the social preponderance and the political domination by east Elbian agriculturists.[76] For one thing, the social and political situation of Junkers would have been eroded in the 12–14 years while the Caprivi treaties remained in force if it had depended on 10 or 15 marks of duty per tonne of cereals, given the miserably low world market prices and a duty which raised internal prices by far less than the full amount above world market prices. For another, from the turn of the century agriculturists gradually did better, after 1905 obviously so, some even splendidly, but this was due less to the customs tariff than to a vigorous and permanent rise in world market prices. After 1905 prices of rye and wheat on average reached a level about 25 per cent above the mean of the

[74] Reich Ministry of the Interior, *Systematische Zusammenstellung der Zolltarife des In- und Auslandes* (Berlin, 1898); Reich Ministry of the Interior, *Der Zolltarif vom 25.12.1902 mit den auf den Handelsverträgen beruhenden Bestimmungen* (Berlin, 1911).

[75] Hoffmann, *Wachstum*, p. 531.

[76] Witt, 'Finanzpolitik', p. 302; similar is Alexander Gerschenkron, *Bread and Democracy in Germany* (New York, 1966), pp. 56, 67; Dirk Stegmann, 'Wirtschaft und Politik nach Bismarcks Sturz. Zur Genesis der Miquelschen Sammlungspolitik 1890–1897', in Geiss and Wendt (eds.), *Deutschland in der Weltpolitik*, p. 182. Detailed arguments to the contrary, taking full account of the notorious system of import certificates, in Hentschel, *Wirtschaft*, pp. 195ff. See in addition Manfred Günther Plachetka, 'Die Getreideausfuhrpolitik Bismarcks und seiner Nachfolger im Reichskanzleramt. Darstellung und Auswirkungen insbesondere während des Ersten Weltkreigs', dissertation, Bonn University, 1969.

previous decade. Duties contributed over one-quarter of the rise or 6 to 8 per cent of selling prices.

3. The customs tariff represented no intolerable burden on consumers' cost of living. A family of four with a low household income around 1,200 marks per annum would have to spend an additional 1 per cent on bread because of the duty; as income rose, the percentage fell.[77]

Though vigorously contested and abused, the Tariff Law of 1902 remained the basis of German trade policy from 1906 to the war. After the outbreak of war, there was no longer a freely decided trade policy, but a dirigiste fight against the blockade to secure Germany's military and essential supplies. Most agricultural and raw materials duties were removed and a multiplicity of import and export embargoes imposed.

At the behest of the victorious powers, foreign trade in 1919 subserved entirely the reparations policy.[78] Only on 10 January 1925, after currency stabilization and the passing of the Dawes Plan, did the German Reich recover control over its own trade policy. For the time being, the Reich continued its pre-war policy. The so-called 'little customs duty law' (*kleine Zolltarifvortage*), discussed hurriedly and taking effect on 1 October 1925, showed a marked resemblance to the Bülow tariff. Agricultural and iron duties were reintroduced, while many more radical representations on the part of agrarian pressure groups again fell victim to resistance from industry, parliament, and government. However, the revived agricultural protectionism may have put a brake on necessary and slowly progressing change-over in the agricultural structure east of the Elbe from extensive wheat cultivation to intensive livestock breeding and the production of higher-quality output. During the next two years, the moderately protectionist autonomous tariff served as a basis for the negotiation of a large number of most-favoured-nation treaties with Germany's more important trading partners. Stresemann's scheme as Minister of Foreign Affairs to back foreign and power politics by use of 'the only Great Power attribute left to us, our economic power',[79] had no effects which can be traced or proved. The scheme probably represen-

---

[77] Paul Mombert, *Die Belastung des Arbeitereinkommens durch die Kornzölle* (Jena, 1901); Wilhelm Gerloff, 'Verbrauch und Verbrauchsbelastung kleiner und mittlerer Einkommen in Deutschland um die Wende des 19. Jahrhunderts', *Jahrbücher für Nationalökonomie und Statistik*, vol. XXXV (1908), pp. 1–44, 145–72.

[78] G. Baum, *Die Gesetzegebung über Ein- und Ausfuhr* (Stuttgart, 1922); G. Haberland, *11 Jahre staatlicher Regelung der Ein- und Ausfuhr* (Leipzig, 1927); 'Neue Grundlagen der Handelspolitik. Wissenschaftliche Gutachten', *Schriften des Vereins für Sozialpolitik*, vol. CLXXI, part 1 (Munich and Leipzig, 1925).

[79] Quoted from Henry A. Turner, 'Eine Rede Stresemanns über seine Locarno-Politik', *VfZ*, vol. XV (1967), pp. 416f.

ted that extravagant overestimate of the political and social potential of a
tariff and commercial policy, at home and abroad, which had been a
German tradition from 1870 onwards.

C. SOCIAL POLICY: SYSTEM OF SOCIAL INSURANCE AND THE RIGHT OF COLLECTIVE BARGAINING

The beginnings of a systematic and continuous social policy in Germany
are to be found in the field of social insurance. This was neither inevitable
nor without significance for its further development. When in 1881
Bismarck set in motion a policy of working men's compulsory insurance
in his famous imperial proclamation, this represented a conscious preference against an expansion of workers' protection and the right of
collective negotiation which some, for instance Theodor Lohmann,
Bismarck's closest collaborator in the field of social policy, considered to
have at least as great, if not a greater urgency and importance.[80] It gave
precedence in time and institutional emphasis to the insurance concept
within the framework of total state social policy; after which it was very
difficult for other problems and attempted solutions in the field of social
policy to secure similar attention in theory or practice.

More seriously, the main inspiration for social insurance legislation
was not so much contemporary social problems in themselves, attached
as the form in which they were perceived. Bismarck's social policy was
designed only in a superficial sense to help needy groups and classes;
essentially it sought to maintain the Prusso-German state, as visualized by
Bismarck, against the burgeoning working-class movement – a social
policy born in fact not of love, but of fear.[81] Such fear was misconceived:
Social Democrats had neither the strength nor the desire to unhinge the
German Reich, and the hope of mollifying them by a system of state
social insurance was misconceived because workers would not be paci-
fied by sick pay and pensions, nor would they desert the working-class
movement. It said much for the essential value and substance of the
concept that it nevertheless gave birth to an effective social security
system, capable of further development and for a long time considered as

---

[80] The argument derives support from my essay 'Das System der sozialen Sicherung in historischer Sicht 1880–1975', *Archiv für Sozialgeschichte*, vol. XVIII (1978), pp. 310ff.

[81] Theodor Lohmann on 22 April 1889 adapted from Walter Volgel, *Bismarcks Arbeiterversicherung – Ihre Entstehung im Kräftespiel der Zeit* (Brunswick, 1951), p. 185. Fundamental to this topic, Hans Rothfels, *Theodor Lohmann und die Kampfjahre der staatlichen Sozialpolitik (1871–1905)* (Berlin, 1927); Hans Rothfels, 'Prinzipienfragen der Bismarckschen Sozialpolitik', in his *Bismarck, der Osten und das Reich* (Darmstadt, 1962), pp. 165–81; Friedrich Lütge, 'Die Grundprinzipien der Bismarckschen Sozialpolitik', *Jahrbücher für Nationalökonomie und Statistik*, vol. CXXXIV (1931), pp. 580–96; Carl Jantke, *Der Vierte Stand* (Freiburg, 1955).

a model.[82] This was at least in part due to a series of modifications which the Reichstag inserted in Bismarck's bill. At least three important social insurance principles were at that time introduced which ran counter to Bismarck's original intentions:[83]

1. The principle of insurance rather than of public welfare and maintenance;
2. A decentralized system of independent administration rather than a centrally administered Reich institution;
3. Participation by the insured in the provision of funds (establishing a right to benefit) rather than exclusive finance by employers and state which would create a mentality of dependency among recipients of welfare.

Three different basic concepts, on the other hand, became elements of the permanent structure of German social insurance policy as conceived by Bismarck:

1. The compulsory nature of insurance;
2. The network character, which found its expression in the common origins and functional relationships of the different insurance branches;
3. The unilateral character of the beginnings, conceptually and in practice.

The insurance legislation of the 1880s included at that time only industrial workers, as individuals without regard to their families, and entitled them to benefit only after they had lost the ability to earn. On these assumptions and for this purpose, three branches of insurance were created and put on a single legal basis by the Reich Insurance Law of 1911, but their organization remained independent: health insurance (1883), accident insurance (1884), and disability and old age insurance (1889).

The official *health insurance* consolidated in a single measure a haphazardly accrued conglomerate of friendly societies of craftsmen, voluntary organizations, trade unions, guilds, and similar bodies, including in compulsory insurance also workers who had not hitherto been members of any society at all. The insured paid for two-thirds of the contributions,

---

[82] Heinrich Rubner, 'Das kaiserliche Deutschland also Ausgangspunkt für den modernen Wohlfahrtsstaat', paper prepared for the International Economic History Congress, Edinburgh, 1978; Peter Flora et al., 'Zur Entwicklung der westeuropäischen Wohlfahrtsstaaten', *Politische Vierteljahrsschrift*, vol. xviii (1977), pp. 707-72; Gaston V. Rimlinger, *Welfare Policy and Industrialization in Europe, America and Russia* (New York, 1971).

[83] While Bismarck's part in the genesis of social insurance must not, of course, be underestimated, it should also not be emphasized to the complete exclusion of all others, as has long been the case. At last a wider view in Michael Stolleis, 'Die Sozialversicherung Bismarcks. Politisch-institutionelle Bedingungen ihrer Entstehung', in Hans F. Zacher (ed.), *Bedingingen für die Entstehung und Entwicklung von Sozialversicherungen* (Berlin, 1979), pp. 387-411.

the employer added one-third, this proportion also determining their share in the administration of the funds. In the beginning most of the funds were organized within one firm (or company) only. Gradually, local insurance offices, originally set up to cater for workers in places of work without an insurance office, gained in importance. In 1919 the establishment of new insurance offices at places of work was prohibited.

Accident insurance held employers liable for all accidents at work which occurred on their premises, and not only for those for which their guilt could be proved, as under the Employers' Liability Law of 1871. Accordingly, the insurance was financed exclusively from employers' contributions, but was also exclusively administered by employers. The scheme was organized by trade associations (*Berufsgenossenschaften*). The Reich functioned merely as a subsidiary guarantor of their ability to pay, contrary to what Bismarck had intended; in actual insurance practice, the Reich did not come into the picture at all.

Only *disability* and *old age insurance* were financially based from the outset on public subsidies, in addition to equal contributions from the insured and their employers, and administered by Reich civil servants through corporations subject to public law. The subsidy accounted for approximately one-third of the funds. Committees consisting of equal numbers of workers and employers assisted civil servants in control of the funds.

Social insurance came into being as an unmistakeable political reaction to industrialization, to working-class problems, and to the workers' movement. Up to the turn of the century, it retained this exclusive frame of reference. Thereafter, compulsory participation was extended to white-collar employees earning less than 2,000 marks, for pensions in 1900, for health insurance in 1903. An institutionally separate white-collar employees' insurance, paying higher benefits, was introduced in 1911.

In another respect too, 1911 was a key date for the development of German social policy. In that year, not only was the Reich Insurance Law passed, but for the first time all those not self-employed, especially agricultural labourers, were included in health insurance; also, welfare for insured members' dependants was added to disability and old age pensions. This ended the exclusive link of social insurance with industrial activity and the principle of individual insurance, pointing instead the way to a general and family insurance.

The Weimar Republic travelled farther along this route.[84] However,

---

[84] For the social policy of the Weimar Republic, still above all Ludwig Preller, *Sozialpolitik der Weimarer Republik* (Stuttgart, 1949, rep. Düsseldorf, 1978). See in addition Syrup and Neuloh, *Hundert Jahre*; Florian Tennstedt, 'Sozialgeschichte der Sozialversicherung', *Handbuch der Sozialmedizin* (Stuttgart, 1976), vol. III, pp. 385–492.

the social security system as it had emerged from the Empire was not greatly improved and reformed until well into the 1930s. Unemployment insurance was added in 1927. The law regarding employment exchanges and unemployment insurance[85] owed its main inspiration and principles of operation to the trade unions. It had originally been regarded by them, as also by the employers, as the instrument and legal basis of an organized labour market policy rather than as a pillar of the social security system; it was to remove the causes of unemployment and thereby obviate the need for insurance. That law and the Reich institution for labour exchanges and unemployment insurance, established to put it into effect and jointly and independently administered by trade unions and employers' organizations, were, as it were, consequences of two decisions of principle, taken with constitutional sanction in the field of social policy. Article 163 of the Reich constitution secured to everybody at all times a right to work and to the receipt of income; article 165 conceded to parties in the labour market independent administration of substantial sectors of social policy, confining official bodies to regulatory and conciliatory tasks (see pp. 799f.). One-half the funds for unemployment insurance were raised from employees, one-half from employers; the state by an unlimited loan ensured ability to pay at all times.

Ability to pay, however, proved the Achilles' heel of the entire German social insurance system as much during the Empire as in the Weimar Republic. The system of social insurance was not a system of social security. Benefits did not even reach a subsistence minimum. During the Empire, health insurance offices, in addition to free medical treatment, paid benefits at first for no more than 13, from 1903 onwards for 26 weeks at the rate of half the average wage of the insured, up to a maximum of 12 marks a week. Around 1907, two-thirds of the insured drew less than 8.50 marks.[86] A family of four could hardly manage to exist on three times that amount.

Even less adequate were the payments made by the *pensions insurance* which from the outset had been regarded only as an addition to income from other sources. Moreover, it was difficult to become qualified for it. The claim to disability pension was established by paying contributions for at least 4 years and by no longer being able to earn one-third of a healthy person's income in relevant employment, the claim to old age pension by 20 years of contributions and an age of 70; that age limit was

[85] *Reichsgesetzblatt*, no. 32 (1927), pp. 187ff. See also Bernhard Lehfeld, 'Das Gesetz über Arbeitsvermittlung under Arbeitslosenversicherung', *Jahrbücher für Nationalökonomie und Statistik*, vol. CXXVII (1927), pp. 932ff.

[86] *Handwörterbuch der Staatswissenschaften*, 3rd edn (1920), vol. V, pp. 677ff., vol. VI, p. 202.

lowered to 65 in 1916. The average disability pension in 1911 amounted to 187 marks, the maximum to 450 marks a year, the old age pension, for which hardly more than 100,000 people qualified because of the high age limit and comparatively low life expectancy, amounted to an average of 166 marks and a maximum of 230 marks.

Those who did best were the recipients of *accident pensions*; if fully disabled, they were entitled to two-thirds of their last wages. If they died, the widow and every child below 15 years of age received 20 per cent each, but in aggregate no more than 60 per cent.

Benefits increased substantially during the Weimar Republic. At 4.2 per cent, their share in national income at market prices in 1927 was twice that of 1913; the share of all public social payments (that is, adding social welfare, unemployment insurance, and maintenance of war victims) had risen from 3.3 to 10.1 per cent. Even so, these payments did not amount to a subsistence minimum. The rate of health insurance remained unchanged; benefits disbursed were higher on average because the level of wages had risen. Rather more important were noticeable improvements and extensions of medical welfare, though these had only indirect pecuniary effects.

Average pensions had substantially increased, especially because for many the period of benefit became longer; but they still did not constitute a subsistence minimum. Between 1925 and 1930, pensions grew from approximately 400 to barely 450 marks, with another 120 marks added for every dependent child below 18 years of age. Mean annual income at the time amounted from 1,200 to 1,500 marks. It is therefore not surprising that 70 per cent of all recipients of social pensions also drew supplementary welfare payments.

Lack of data prevents us from ascertaining whether social insurance in the Empire and in the Weimar Republic achieved any redistribution of income, but as not even the much more extensive and adequate network of social security of the Federal Republic changed the distribution of incomes,[87] the possibility can be excluded.

Causes for the very limited reforms and developments of the social security system under the Weimar Republic included the deep-seated financial problems associated with and consequent upon inflation, but even more significantly the 'change of model' in the practice of social policy which had taken place in 1918/19. The concept of social insurance as the 'main impulse' of social policy yielded pride of place to the

---

[87] See Klaus Dieter Schmidt, W. Schwarz and G. Thiebach, *Die Umverteilung des Volkseinkommens in der Bundesrepublik Deutschland 1955 and 1960* (Tübingen, 1967); M. Heilmann, *Dei Umverteilung des Einkommens durch den Staat in der Bundesrepublik Deutschland 1960–1972* (Göttingen, 1976); Hentschel 'Das System', pp. 338ff.

collective settlement of the employment contract. Theodor Lohmann came, so to speak, into his own 40 years later.[88]

The roots of an effective labour law are embedded in the Empire, but are difficult to recognize and do not lie predominantly in the public domain. Article 153 of the Industrial Law of 21 June 1869 had ceased to legally sanction the right to combine. What was legally protected was the right not to combine. This was an almost inevitable consequence of the rigid Liberal spirit which had inspired the Industrial Law. But a rigid Liberal spirit could not do justice to this problem.

Throughout the imperial period, trade unions had to grow in the shadow of article 153 which presented a formidable obstacle to any form of effective organization and discipline on their part. The article was never repealed or relaxed. The most that happened was that attempts in the course of a comprehensive reform of industrial legislation in 1891 – which increased protection for women and juvenile workers – to formulate it more rigidly still miscarried, and the so-called House of Correction Bill put forward by the Reich government seven years later was defeated: this had proposed the punishment of certain cases of incitement to strike by hard labour.[89] But similarly defeated was a bill on occupational associations nine years later, which would at least have given trade unions legal status.[90] Up to the First World War, the organization, articulation and achievement of collective working-class interests remained subject to legal and administrative discrimination.

The origins of the subsequent emergence of collective labour legislation must be sought elsewhere. The industrial law reform of 1891 had made it compulsory for entrepreneurs who employed more than 19 workers to issue and publish legally binding working conditions. Though workers had no right to participate in their formulation, factory owners could not change them arbitrarily or unilaterally. This formed the first 'step on the path of establishing rules, in lieu of an employer's unfettered decision'.[91]

---

[88] Reich Minister of Labour, Heinrich Brauns, in *Deutsche Sozialpolitik 1918–1928. Erinnerungsschrift des Reichsarbeitsministeriums* (Berlin, 1929); p. 3; Eduard Heimann, speech in Verein für Sozialpolitik in *Schriften des Vereins für Sozialpolitik*, vol. CLXXXII (Munich and Leipzig, 1931), pp. 58ff.

[89] For reform of the occupation law and the hard-labour bill, Karl Erich Born, *Staat und Sozialpolitik seit Bismarcks Sturz* (Wiesbaden, 1957), pp. 84–135, 142–66. For the subsequent inconclusive discussion on the combination law prior to a political decision, Klaus Saal, *Staat, Industrie, Arbeiterbewegung im Kaiserreich. Zur Innen- und Sozialpolitik des wilhelminischen Deutschland 1903–1914* (Düsseldorf, 1974), pp. 283ff.

[90] Chronology of the 'bill on the legal situation of occupational associations', in Peter Rassow and Karl Erich Born, *Akten zur staatlichen Sozialpolitik in Deutschland 1890–1914* (Wiesbaden, 1959), pp. 150ff.

[91] Hugo Sinzheimer, *Der korporative Arbeitsnormenvertrag*, 2nd edn (Berlin, 1977), p. 20. See also Hans-Jürgen Teuteberg, *Geschichte der Industriellen Mitbestimmung in Deutschland* (Tübingen, 1961), pp. 380ff.

The second step was taken by the state after another quarter of a century. The so-called Law of Auxiliary Service to the Fatherland of 5 December 1916 made German people liable to conscription for any work imposed by the third supreme command of armed forces. To persuade the Reichstag to pass it, Reich authorities accompanied this grave limitation of personal freedom by a series of positive measures of social law. For the first time, trade unions were recognized as legitimate organizations representing working men's interests and as equal partners with employers in the determination of wages and working conditions. All places of work of more than 49 employees had to form workers' committees, though these were not at the time endowed with particularly wide-reaching rights of co-determination.[92] Conciliation offices, headed by civil servants, with equal numbers of representatives from trade unions and industrial employers' associations, were made responsible for mediation in disputes concerning wages and conditions of work. The hated and obsolete article 153 of the Industrial Law was inconspicuously repealed.

Common experience in conciliation offices helped in various ways in the establishment of a central working party of trade unions and employers on 15 November 1918, which was most important in setting a course for further development of collective labour law.[93] Articles 159 and 165 of the Weimar constitution, passed subsequently, represented, as it were, the constitutional ratification of working party agreements by conceding an unrestricted right to combine, by treating compulsory works committees in establishments of more than 19 workers as legal representatives of social and economic interests of workers and employees, and by calling upon workers' and employers' organizations to undertake on terms of equality the autonomous regulation of wages and conditions of work and the planning of overall economic development.[94] What did not attain constitutional sanction was a general introduction of the eight-hour day.

[92] On the minimal importance of the optional workers' committees recommended in 1891 and the beginnings of a movement for collective wage agreements up to the war, see Teuteberg, *Geschichte*, pp. 490ff.; *Handwörterbuch der Staatswissenschaften*, 3rd edn (1911), vol. VII, pp. 1103f., 4th edn (1927), vol. VIII, p. 23; E. Lederer and I. Marschak, 'Die Klassen auf dem Arbeitsmarkt und ihre Organisationen', in *Grundriss der Sozialökonomik (GdS)*, section IX: *Das soziale System des Kapitalismus* (Tübingen, 1927); Martin Martini, *Integration oder Konfrontation* (Bonn, 1976).

[93] For the emergence, intentions, and practice, see above all Gerald Feldman, 'German Business between War and Revolution: The Origins of the Stinnes–Legien Agreement', in G. A. Ritter (ed.), *Entstehung und Wandel der modernen Gesellschaft. Festschrift für Hans Rosenberg zum 65. Geburtstag* (Berlin, 1970); Friedrich Zunkel, *Industrie und Staatssozialismus. Der Kampf um die Wirtschaftsordnung in Deutschland 1914–1918* (Düsseldorf, 1974), pp. 188ff.

[94] E. Tartarin-Tarnhayden, 'Rechte der Berufsverbände und Wirtschaftsdemonkratie. Kommentar zu Artikel 165 W.R.', in C. Nipperdey (ed.), *Die Grundrechte und Gundpflichten der Reichsverfassung. Kommentar zum zweiten Teil der Reichsverfassung* (Berlin, 1930).

The most important decrees and laws to implement these principles had either preceded the constitution or followed soon afterwards. On 23 December 1918, a 'decree regarding collective wage agreements, workers' and employees' committees and conciliation in industrial disputes'[95] made collective wage agreements henceforth legally binding and enforceable in the courts; contracting out was not permitted. The technical legal basis for the future practice of co-determination within establishments was laid by a Law on Works Committees on 4 February 1920. The state's own readiness to participate was emphasized in 1923 by legislation modifying the Conciliation Law of December 1918: this enabled the state, or, strictly speaking, the newly created Reich Ministry of Labour to impose collective agreements contrary to the wishes of one negotiating party and, if the interests of general economic and social policy required it, even contrary to the wishes of both negotiating parties.[96]

This indicated to some extent a retrogression in social law, because neither the autonomy of collective agreements nor works committees during the Weimar Republic came up to the expectations which had accompanied them at the outset. They did not become solid pillars supporting the socio-economic and socio-political order. The enthusiasm at the inauguration of the central working party was not sustained. Harmony between trade unions and employers, born of the emergency, soon evaporated; their ability to arrive at collective wage agreements by consensus declined visibly. Thus they, so to speak, handed back the opportunity for autonomously shaping social policy to the state which gladly resumed it by way of reforming the Conciliation Law. Already in 1925/6, one-third of all wage settlements were decided by state. By 1928, 7.8 million workers were involved in state conciliation proceedings; 6.5 million of them ended up with state arbitration awards and application of compulsion.[97] It might well be argued that this enabled the state to pursue a kind of minimum wage policy in the workers' interest.

There were three reasons why works committees were prevented from engaging in activities which would have turned them into pillars of increasing works democracy:

1.   The Compromise Law of 1920 changed their legal character from that of unilateral representatives of workers' interests, prepared to fight if necessary, by calling upon them to promote harmony between workers and employers and to support employers in fulfilling production targets.

[95] *Reichsgesetzblatt*, 1918, no. 287, p. 1456.
[96] *Reichsgesetzblatt*, 1923, vol. I, p. 1043. For the judicial development, see *Soziale Praxis*, vol. XXXVII (1928), pp. 858ff.
[97] *Soziale Praxis*, vol. XXV (1926), cols. 118f., vol. XXXVIII (1929), cols. 980ff., vol. XXIX (1930), col. 377; *Reichsarbeits-Blatt*, 1930, part 2, pp. 572ff., part 3, pp. 372ff.; Werner Bohnstedt, 'Schlichtungswesen', in *Internationales Handwörterbuch des Gewerkschaftswesens*, vol. II (Berlin, 1932); Hans-Hermann Hartwich, *Arbeitsmarkt, Verbände, Staat 1918–1933* (Berlin, 1967).

THE CRISIS OF 1930-3

2. By invoking the law, employers had no difficulty in denying to works committees insight into, and control of, the conduct of business within the establishment.

3. Trade unions endeavoured, with a large degree of success, to limit independent activities of works committees to measures of social welfare within individual establishments, downgrading them otherwise to executive bodies implementing collective wage agreements in accordance with instructions.[98]

Hence they neither were nor became more than the traditional optional workers' committees of imperial times.

IV. *Economic and social policy during the crisis of 1930–3*

The last democratically legitimate government of the Weimar Republic was wrecked on the rocks of controversy over social policy, more precisely, over rates of contribution and benefits of unemployment insurance in March 1930[99] – at least this is how it appeared superficially; the real reasons were more far-reaching.

Up until Hitler's seizure of power on 30 January 1933, there had been four authoritarian emergency and emergency-decree cabinets (two headed by Brüning, one each headed by von Papen and von Schleicher as Chancellor) which pursued an authoritarian interventionist economic and social policy[100] under the impact of the world economic crisis, which – paradoxical as it may sound – on the one hand fitted seamlessly into the tradition of German economic and social policy, and on the other hand signified a sharp break with it. It fitted because it was primarily designed to employ measures of economic policy for non-economic ends; it signified a break because for the first time it represented a consistent plan, deliberately seeking to influence the macro-economic process. It was fatal that the macro-economic process was inadequately comprehended, and therefore the plan misconceived.

However, this assertion is not entirely correct. The plan was miscon-

---

[98] Kurt Brigl-Matthiass, *Das Betriebsräteproblem* (Berlin and Leipzig, 1926); *Jahrbuch der ADGB* (1930), p. 150; *GdS*, vol. IX, part 2, p. 248; Preller, *Sozialpolitik*, p. 265.

[99] Helga Timm, *Die deutsche Sozialpolitik und der Bruch der Grossen Koalition im März 1930* (Düsseldorf, 1952).

[100] The most important investigations, especially concerning the economic policy of the Brüning government, are Wilhelm Grotkopp, *Die grosse Krise* (Düsseldorf, 1954); René Erbe, *Die nationalsozialistische Wirtschaftspolitik 1933–1939 im Lichte der modernen Theorie* (Zürich, 1958); Lüke, *Von der Stabilisierung*; Gerhard Koll, *Von der Weltwirtschaftskrise zur Staatskonjunktur* (Berlin, 1958); Wolfgang J. Helbich, *Die Reparationen in der Ära Brüning* (Berlin, 1962); Horst Sanmann, 'Daten und Alternativen der deutschen Wirtschafts- und Finanzpolitik in der Ära Brüning', *Hamburger Jahrbuch für Wirtschafts- und Gesellschaftspolitik* (1965), pp. 109–35.

ceived only on the assumption that the Brüning government had also intended to lift the German economy out of the crisis. In that case, a successful policy would have required countercyclical expansive monetary and fiscal measures, in contrast to the sharply cyclical and deflationary policy pursued. This was not necessarily wrong, provided it had been decided to give priority to the pursuit of political objectives without regard to the state and development of the economy and social structure. These political objectives consisted in Germany's deliverance from reparations as a precondition for the re-establishment of equal political and military rights.[101] The means employed to gain these ends was good conduct in the field of economic policy which would prove both willingness and inability to pay. Such economic good conduct had two components: balancing the state budget, irrespective of the aggregate amount, to pay homage to the principle and to manifest an anti-inflationary attitude; and maintaining or, better still, improving the international competitiveness of German industry as a means of earning some – even though not enough – foreign currency for the transfer of reparations payments. Brüning succeeded in both these respects and eventually even in the abolition of reparations. However, it must remain questionable – to put it no stronger – whether such success came about in the way which Brüning himself imagined. Reparations payments were postponed (and never restored) by the victorious powers when they could no longer be certain whether the system of international payments and credits could be saved from collapse by such measures or whether it had already broken down. German economic policy bore the chief responsibility for this state of affairs, less because of its actual economic effects than because of its psychological consequences at home and abroad.[102] A – somewhat remote – connection between Brüning's

[101] There is unlikely to be a conclusive answer to the question whether Brüning was aware that his economic policy was faced with a conflict of objectives (effective measures to fight the crisis versus success in foreign and reparations policy) and whether he consciously opted for the political aim, regardless of economic and social costs, or whether he believed he could kill the economic and the political birds with the same stone. Brüning's memoirs, suggesting clarity of vision and conscious decision, but deriving no support from contemporary sources, have rendered the enquiry more difficult rather than easier. The literature quoted contains contradictory views.

[102] Two points deserve emphasis: the negotiations regarding a customs union with Austria, which could be regarded as violating the Versailles treaty and presumably provoked France in March and April 1931 to sanctions in the realm of currency, above all against Austria, and the preamble of an emergency decree on economic and social policy of 5 June 1931, designed to enable the German population to stomach more easily the burdens newly imposed upon it. It contained the following sentences: 'The commitment of the last resources and reserves of all sections of the population entitles the German government, indeed makes it a duty towards its own people, to proclaim to the world that we have reached the limit of deprivations that we can impose on our people ... The government is conscious that the extremely precarious economic and financial situation of the Reich imperatively requires Germany's delivery from insupportable reparation obligations.' These sounded like declarations of bankruptcy and of war in the same breath,

deflationary policy and the renunciation of further reparations is therefore undeniable, but not the particular connection which Brüning had in mind.

According to the point of view adopted, Brüning's economic policy, to be outlined below both as regards overall concept and some essential individual measures, can therefore be appraised as right or wrong, enforced or voluntary, theoretically misconceived or negligently designed, in disregard of better and accessible theoretical insights. This has been done many times and need not be done here once more. But however the policy is interpreted and evaluated, one has to avoid – though writers often fail to do so – giving the impression that a purposeful and efficacious economic policy within the scope of practical possibilities at the time could have stopped the crisis and thereby prevented the consequences leading to Hitler. Expansive deficit spending might at best have mitigated, up to a point, a fall in industrial output amounting in three successive years to 18, 26, and 24 per cent and of Gross National Product amounting to 7, 17, and 18 per cent;[103] it could not have stopped it entirely.

The legal framework of Brüning's economic policy consisted above all of four 'emergency decrees for safeguarding the economy and finances' of 1 December 1930, 5 June 1931, 6 October 1931 (with the addition of 'and for combating political excesses') and 8 December 1931 (with the addition of 'and for protecting domestic peace'), in addition to three laws and decrees on agricultural policy of 31 March 1931, 17 November 1931 and February 1932.

The emergency decrees lowered wages and prices at an increasingly rapid rate (putting the main emphasis on civil servants' salaries and cartel prices which hardly responded even to a violent downswing), raised taxes and customs duties, lowered pensions and social insurance subsidies, raised rates of interest and lowered rents – the intention being to adapt prices to the world market level and to balance the budget; but the effects were sagging demand, production, and incomes, and therefore a continuous contraction of economic activities. On the other hand, Germany did not associate herself with the devaluation of the pound sterling in September 1931, though that would have promised the desired effect on

though not designed as such, but were so understood and caused that rush on foreign credits (including massive capital flight) which ruined first the German banks and then completely unhinged the international payment system.

[103] Dietmar Petzina Werner Abelshauser and Anselm Faust, *Sozialgeschichtliches Arbeitsbuch III. Materialien zur Geschichte des Deutschen Reiches 1914–1945* (Munich, 1978), p. 61; Dietmar Keese, 'Die volkswirtschaftlichen Gesamtgrössen für das Deutsche Reich in den Jahren 1925–1936', in Werner Conze and Hans Raupach (eds.), *Die Staats- und Wirtschaftskrise des Deutschen Reichs, 1929/1933* (Stuttgart, 1967), p. 43; Knut Borchardt, 'Wachstum und Wechsellagen, 1914–1970', in Hermann Aubin and Wolfgang Zorn (eds.), *Handbuch der deutschen Wirtschafts- und Sozialgeschichte* (Stuttgart, 1976), vol. II, p. 709.

foreign trade without the need for domestic contraction. Instead, Brüning persisted in maintaining the gold standard, and hence strict control of foreign currency, which had been introduced after the banking breakdown and the currency crisis in early August 1931. He has been frequently and emphatically accused of that omission. However, one has to be careful. Everything suggests that the reparations creditors would not have tolerated a devaluation of the Reichsmark; there is little to suggest that it would have appreciably affected the course of the crisis. It did not have an appreciable effect in England. Once half the world devalues, devaluation loses much of its economic sense.

Deflation and the parallel policy of balancing the budget were interrelated and compatible – agricultural policy ran diametrically counter to both. Brüning had not inaugurated the policy, but took it over, expanded it regionally and intensified it under pressure from the Reich president on whom he was dependent. The policy consisted of lowering the burdens, increasing the yield and removing the debts in the first instance of east Prussian, but eventually east Elbian, farms and aristocratic estates by raising tariff protection, providing finance at favourable rates of interest, facilitating credits, and supplying public funds for debt reduction. In Brüning's day, the later was the chief preoccupation. While the Reich budget effected savings in all other directions, it poured out 2,000 million Reichsmark for agrarian debt reduction alone between 1930 and 1932, representing 8 per cent of Reich expenditure. Brüning linked to the policy of debt reduction a plan and scheme of purchasing on the state's behalf lands which could not be rendered solvent, so as to make them available for peasant settlement. This met with violent and ultimately successful resistance from the influential landowning aristocracy and from Reichspräsident Hindenburg. The first of Brüning's important laws in the field of agricultural policy concerned 'measures of assistance for the distressed areas in the East' and 'promotion of agricultural settlement'. Both the following laws mentioned only 'safeguards of agricultural debt reduction' and 'accelerated achievement of agricultural debt reduction'. When Brüning attempted by a further decree to make a serious start on settlement activities, he was overthrown because of this, and other measures, on 29 May 1932.[104]

---

[104] Werner Conze, 'Zum Sturz Brünings', in VfZ, vol. I (1953); Bruno Buchta, Die Junker und die Weimarer Republik. Charakter und Bedeutung der Osthilfe in den Jahren 1928–1933 (Berlin, 1959); Heinrich Muth, 'Zum Sturz Brünings. Der agrarpolitische Hintergrund', Geschichte in Wissenschaft und Unterricht, vol. XVI (1965); Heinrich Muth, 'Agrarpolitik im Frühjahr 1932', in F. A. Hermens and T. Schieder (eds.), Staat, Wirtschaft und Politik in der Weimarer Republik. Festschrift für Heinrich Brüning (Berlin, 1967); F. M. Fiederlein, 'Der deutsche Osten und die Regierungen Brüning, Papen, Schleicher', dissertation, Würzburg University, 1967, pp. 363–74; Dieter Gessner, Agrarverbände in der Weimarer Republik. Wirtschaftliche und soziale Voraussetzungen ararkonservativer Politik vor 1933 (Düsseldorf, 1976).

Papen's and Schleicher's short-lived regimes did not fundamentally change Brüning's economic and social policies, but merely supplemented them by efforts to create employment, whose order of magnitude proved inadequate to stimulate economic life permanently, but which contributed further to the destruction of social policy.[105] The stress was to be on indirect measures which would not call for funds from the public budget. Both the emergency decrees 'for the stimulation of the economy' and 'for the increase and maintenance of employment opportunities' of 4 and 5 September 1932, however, quickly proved almost complete failures. In compensation for turnover and profit taxes payable in the following year, taxpayers were to receive so-called tax credits which could be used instead of cash to pay taxes from 1934. This did nothing to increase immediately effective purchasing power. Tax credits could be used as collateral for loans, but the German economy's principal complaint was not lack of investment or working capital which could have been cured by enlarging credit facilities; it suffered from lack of demand, in the light of which credits in order to promote investment or employment made no sense, nor did anybody take them up. Similarly – with a few exceptions – there was no employment of additional labour into which entrepreneurs were also to be beguiled by the prospect of tax credits. Tax credits to the value of 700 million marks and 1.75 million workers newly engaged had been envisaged; three months later, a mere 75,000 more had been employed. It can be surmised that these had been engaged not mainly because of tax credits, however willingly employers pocketed these, but because the nadir of the crisis had clearly passed. To what extent employers made use of the opportunity for employing additional workers, in return for reducing up to 50 per cent the wage rates of the entire workforce in respect of any weekly working hours between 30 and 40 without having to secure the agreement of the trade unions, is unknown and uncertain; but there is no doubt that this part of the decree represented the most dramatic retrograde intervention in the policy of social regulation which occurred in the terminal phase of the Weimar Republic.

On 14 December the decree was countermanded by Schleicher who was concerned to secure cooperation from the trade unions. Schleicher relied on direct creation of employment through public works which previously with a mere 300 million marks budget had remained in the shadow of the, by now abortive, tax credit scheme. On the day of his appointment as Reich Chancellor, 3 December 1932, a Reich Com-

---

[105] In addition to works quoted in n. 100, see Dieter Petzina, 'Hauptprobleme der deutschen Wirtschaftspolitik 1932/33', *VfZ* (1967), pp. 18–55; Helmut Marcon, *Arbeitsbeschaftfungspolitik der Regierungen Papen und Schleicher. Grundsteinlegung für die Beschäftigungspolitik im Dritten Reich* (Frankfurt, 1974).

missar for Employment Creation was appointed. On the day on which his 500 million marks programme was accepted by the cabinet, 28 January 1933, he was dismissed. Two days later Adolf Hitler became German Reich Chancellor.

V.   Economic and social policy during the Third Reich: continuities and new beginnings

The National Socialists assumed power without preconceived or thought-through plans or rules regarding economic and social policy, nor did they develop them subsequently. Economic and social policy concerned them only to the extent to which it served the consolidation of their power, the elimination of their opponents, the realization of their ideology, and especially their schemes of war and conquest. To these purposes they disciplined and subordinated the economy, not so much in the form of a decisive total subjugation to state planning, but rather by gradual and partial adaptation and instrumentation which afforded to non-governmental elements much scope for activity and decision – at least until 1939. The German economy and society did not undergo at National Socialist hands a change of structure and functions as basic and pervasive as the theory of 'Hitler's social revolution'[106] would indicate. Nowhere in the history of the Nazi regime is there as much continuity, as much fluidity in transition, from the Weimar Republic as in the fields of economic and social regulation and policy.

A 'free market economy' never characterized the economic order of the Weimar Republic; no more does the description of 'state-directed or command economy' fit the Third Reich. Both are instances of mixture and half-measures.[107]

The wages block and price control introduced in the first months of the Nazi regime were not as fundamental a change in the policy of

---

[106] Its founder is probably Talcot Parsons. It has been popularized by Ralph Dahrendorf, *Gesellschaft und Demokratie in Deutschland* (Munich, 1968), pp. 431ff.; detailed description, but no convincing documentation, in David Schoenbaum, *Die braune Revolution. Eine Sozialgeschichte des Dirtten Reichs* (Cologne and Berlin, 1968). To prevent misunderstanding: the book is nevertheless a very valuable piece of work. An opposite, though rather narrow view, expressed vehemently, somewhat monomaniac and brief, in Eike Hennig, *Thesen zur deutschen Sozial- und Wirtschaftsgeschichte 1933–1938* (Frankfurt, 1973).

[107] On the economic system in the Third Reich, Hans-Heinrich Rubbert, 'Die "gelenkte Marktwirtschaft" des Nationalsozialismus. Ein Literaturbericht', *Hamburger Jahrbuch für Wirtschafts- und Gesellschaftspolitik*, vol. VIII (1963), pp. 215–34; Arthur Schweitzer, 'Der organisierte Kapitalismus. Wirtschaftsordnung in der ersten Phase der nationalsozialistischen Herrschaft', *Hamburger Jahrbuch für Wirtschafts- und Gesellschaftspolitik*, vol. VII (1962), pp. 32–47; Fritz Blaich, 'Wirtschaftspolitik und Wirtschaftsverfassung im Dritten Reich', in *Aus Politik und Zeitgeschichte*, B8/71, pp. 3–18; A. Barkai, *Das Wirtschaftsystem des Nationalsozialismus. Der historische und ideologische Hintergrund 1933–1936* (Cologne, 1977).

economic control as might at first sight appear. For one thing, much fixing of wages and prices had been assigned to the state already under Brüning's and Papen's governments; for another, the wages block and price control did not signify that wages and prices thenceforth became immutable or that they were settled by the state in pursuit of a regulatory policy. Purposeful planning of wages and prices cannot be detected at all. On the same day, 19 May 1933, which saw the wages block, 'labour trustees' were appointed, who were Reich civil servants entrusted with ultimate decisions regarding wages and employment conditions. But they hardly intervened at all in wage settlements, changes in which henceforth found their expression not in wage rates, but in fringe benefits, bonuses, or upgrading. Hence nominal wage rates remained stable up to 1939, while the hourly level of real remuneration rose considerably after 1936. During 1936/7, unemployment[108] which had persisted until then on a large scale, though to a diminishing extent, turned within a short period into an acute and urgent shortage of workers which employers tried to overcome by competitive bids for hands. Wage control notwithstanding, in these circumstances the level of hourly wages for skilled workers up to the beginning of the war increased by 10 per cent.[109]

Prices had never been stabilized from the outset, but merely submitted to control by a 'price commissar'. There had already been one since 1931 – it was in fact the same man, Karl Goerdeler, Lord Mayor of Leipzig. He discharged his newly constituted duty in the same manner and with the same degree of success or failure as previously. For non-cartelized commodities, he left price determination to the market; his attempts to 'loosen' the ties of cartel pricing suffered defeat. The artificially high prices of cartelized capital goods stayed firm, whereas prices of industrial consumer goods rose 20 per cent by 1937, wholesale prices 16 per cent.[110]

No more than this lax price control on the part of the state did the cartel decree of 15 July 1933, passed for ideological rather than rational motives of market control, affect market price formation substantially. The opaque slogan of the 'organic growth of economy' allowed a vigorous and compulsive growth in the number of cartels, but growth without plan, without sense, without effect on market regulation. The

---

[108] The average for the year 1935 still amounted to 2 million = 10 per cent of potentially occupied population, even in 1936 to 1 million.

[109] Council of States in the American Zone of Occupation, *Statistical Handbook of Germany 1928–1944* (Munich, 1949), pp. 470ff. See also Gerhard Bry, *Wages in Germany 1871–1945* (Princeton, 1960), pp. 233–65; Tim Mason, *Sozialpolitik im Dritten Reich. Arbeiterklasse und Volksgemeinschaft* (Opladen, 1977), pp. 147ff., 215ff.

[110] Erbe, *Die nationalsozialistische Wirtschaftspolitik*, p. 87. For price control, Barkai, *Das Wirtschaftssystem*, pp. 147f.

controlling power and economic strength of cartels in any case almost of necessity diminishes rather than increases as cartels multiply.

The first comprehensive and methodical intervention in the economy did not occur until 1936 with the second Four Year Plan.[111] It was caused by the threat of a shortage of raw materials and foreign currency, attributable partly to a striking deterioration in the terms of trade since 1933, partly to the almost archaic bilateralization of German foreign trade.[112] From this, three consequences relevant to regulation policy resulted:

1. Allocation of important raw materials;
2. Planning and direction of labour;
3. Control of industrial investment in capital goods industry.

The effects on market relations however remained less incisive than intentions and decrees would lead us to believe. From the outset, no consistent system of state direction towards identifiable and predictable aims was designed. This poorly conceived attempt at overall planning was sacrificed in 1938 when general plenipotentiaries – soon to compete with one another – were appointed to look after sectors of the Four Year Plan. Their occasional and divisive interventions were mainly frustrated by the stronger forces of the market.

Allocation of raw materials according to urgency miscarried in the absence of an overall plan of priorities and needs. Mobilization of labour potential and regulation of the utilization of the work-force miscarried because of a flood of decrees regulating consequences and practical applications, which in absence of competent implementing authorities were consigned to the wastepaper basket as they appeared.[113]

Redirection of investment funds into special capital goods industries was not a complete failure. It is questionable, however, whether it was entirely in accordance with National Socialist interests and wishes that it occurred at the expense of other capital goods industries and not at the expense of consumer goods industries. In any case, investment up to the war remained at a level of 40 per cent below the sums envisaged by the Four Year Plan.

All in all, the parameters set by the regime for planning the economy

[111] Wolfgang Birkenfeld, *Der synthetische Treibstoff 1933–1945. Ein Beitrag zur national-sozialistischen Wirtschafts- und Rüstungspolitik* (Göttingen, Berlin and Frankfurt, 1964); Dieter Petzina, *Autarkiepolitik im Dritten Reich. Der nationalsozialistische Vierjahresplan* (Stuttgart, 1968); Johann Sebastian Geer, *Der Markt der geschlossenen Nachfrage. Eine morphologische Studie über die Eisenkontingentierung in Deutschland 1937–1945* (Berlin, 1961).

[112] Jörg Johannes Jäger, *Die wirtschaftliche Abhängigkeit des Dritten Reiches vom Ausland dargestellt am Beispiel der Stahlindustrie* (Berlin, 1969); Dörte Doering, 'Deutsche Aussenwirtschaftspolitik 1933–35', dissertation, FU Berlin, 1969.

[113] Especially Mason, *Sozialpolitik*, pp. 271ff.

were so elastic, either deliberately or in the absence of theoretical and practical capacity to plan, that they did not, either before or after 1936, drastically curtail the entrepreneurs' freedom to pursue their private interests. The struggle for scarce commodities and means of production continued to take place mainly on the lines of a market economy.

The National Socialists might have been more effective and successful in their policy of economic regulation had not this yielding to private interests held out hopes of achieving their objectives, rapid, comprehensive rearmament and readiness for war, faster, more surely, and more flexibly. As long as the regime could rely on its always superior purchasing power, thanks to an effective tax and monetary policy, it could afford to remain comparatively indifferent to the success of planning measures. A private capitalist market economy, quick to respond and indirectly steered by a policy of unconstrained public expenditure, was likely to serve its purposes better than a cumbersome planned command economy.

The financial and monetary policies pursued during the years of peace of the Third Reich successfully aimed at the continuous increase of state purchasing power, but not at continuous intervention in the process and structure of the economy. Even the direct and indirect policies of employment creation[114]. of the first two years, which incidentally already in part benefited rearmament, qualify for that description only with considerable reservations. Their psychological and political effect was – entirely in keeping with Nazi intentions – certainly much greater than their results in promoting growth and employment. To 'remove from the streets' unemployed workers by relief work at, so to speak, symbolic wages differs from the use of long-term public stimuli to growth to secure permanent productive employment. The National Socialist work creation programme did not suffice to do this. 1,000–2,000 million Reichsmark were expended in 1933/4 on direct measures of work creation; in addition, there were tax reliefs inspired by a policy of enhancing employment which, in contrast to Papen's ineffable tax credits, immediately produced a gain in purchasing power on the part of entrepreneurs and consumers, amounting in years from 1933 to 1935 to about 1,600 million marks: 8 per cent of potential tax revenue, about 1 per cent of national income. Given a Gross National Product which effectively fell by 25,000 to 30,000 million marks (= 30 per cent) below potential Gross National Product at full employment, and an extraordinarily low multiplier, perhaps 1.75, even both together could not have had substantial effects on growth and employment, all the less so because

---

[114] Karl Schiller, *Arbeitsbeschaffung und Finanzordnung in Deutschland* (Heidelberg, 1935); Petzina, *Autarkiepolitik*, pp. 43ff.; Michael Wolfsohn, 'Arbeitsbeschaffung und Rüstung im national-sozialistischen Deutschland: 1933', *Militärgeschichtliche Mitteilungen*, vol. XXI (1977), pp. 9–21.

the percentage of tax and social insurance contributions in Gross National Product for the years from 1933 to 1935 at 25.8 remained exactly the same as in the years from 1930 to 1932.[115]

Up to 1938 that percentage rose by almost one-third. Tax remissions soon gave way to substantial additional tax burdens. The taxation system of the Weimar Republic was retained unchanged, but more fully utilized by assessing and levying consumers more heavily.[116]

Meanwhile, public expenditure grew faster – from about 20 per cent of Gross National Product at market prices in the Republic years before the crisis to about 35 per cent in 1938, armament expenditure alone growing from less than 1 to more than 15 per cent. The National Socialists financed a large part of this by incurring extensive public debts, along with an extraordinary increase in total money supply. National Socialist financial and monetary policy was never determined by fear of inflation. In the six years of peace, the public debt rose from 7,000 to 36,000 million marks, from 12 per cent to 35 per cent of Gross National Product. Of that increase 60 per cent represented a growth in short-term debt. The tools employed in the policy of debt creation were an ostensible procedure of pre-financing Reich expenditure on the part of the Reichsbank by means of 'MEFO bills' and the far-reaching closure of the capital market to private entrepreneurs seeking funds.

MEFO bills derived their name from the Metallurgische Forschungsgesellschaft (Metallurgical Research Company) instituted by the state, but privately financed, which accepted Reich Treasury bills, thus rendering them discountable at the Reichsbank. Up to 1935, this kind of inconspicuous creation of money may have been a sensible instrument of countercyclical deficit spending; thereafter it was merely a convenient pro-cyclical means of supplying the state with cash. Never was there the slightest suggestion of funding the debt. Money in circulation in the economy between 1933 and 1939 increased by 80 per cent. The money market lost all sensitivity to respond to economic events and monetary measures.[117]

---

[115] Erbe, *Die nationalsozialistische Wirtschaftspolitik*, pp. 28ff.; Keese, 'Die volkswirtschaftlichen Gesamtgrossen', pp. 43, 47; B. Ries, 'Die Finanzpolitik im Deutschen Reich vom 1933–1935', dissertation, Freiburg University, 1964.

[116] Lutz Graf Schwerin von Krosigk, 'Wirtschaftspolitische und sozialpolitische Grundsätze der deutschen Steuergesetzgebung', *Zeitschrift der Akademie für deutsches Recht* (1937), pp. 611ff.; Fritz Blaich, 'Die "Grundsätze nationalsozialistischer Steuerpolitik" und ihre Verwirklichung', in Friedrich-Wilhelm Henning (ed.), *Problems der nationalsozialistischen Wirtschaftspolitik*, *Schriften des Vereins für Sozialpolitik*, NS, vol. LXXXIX (Berlin, 1976), pp. 99–117; M. Landscheid, 'Die Beteiligung der "breiten Massen" am deutschen Steueraufkommin in Mass und Methode in der Zeit von 1928–1946', dissertation, Munich, 1950; Barkai, *Das Wirtschaftssystem*, pp. 143ff.

[117] Erbe, *Der nationalsozialistische Wirtschaftspolitik*, pp. 42ff., 54, 63, 121ff.; J. J. Klein, 'German Money and Prices, 1932–44', in Milton Friedman (ed.), *Studies in the Quantity Theory of Money* (Chicago, 1956), pp. 121–59.

The capital market was placed entirely at the service of the Reich. Already in 1933, a prohibition of new issues for non-public purposes had been imposed, supplemented in December 1934 by a loan stock law, which prohibited companies from distributing dividends in excess of 6 per cent. Part of the undistributed profits was to be used for self-financing investments in the enterprise, the remainder channelled into a loan stock placed at the state's disposal. Private savings were anyhow inconspicuously put at the Reich's disposal by drawing on bank deposits.

Even the policy of social insurance was eventually prostituted to the financing of armament expenditures.[118] National Socialists took over the Republic's system of social security, as they did its taxation system, and left it almost unimpaired. Autonomous administration was replaced by the ubiquitous leader principle, but the separation of the four branches of insurance was maintained in principle, notwithstanding some organizational links and the collective title of Reich insurance. An ephemeral scheme of replacing social insurance by a general provision for all citizens was quickly dropped. Only one further step in the direction of a comprehensive insurance of the population was taken: at the end of 1937, independent craftsmen as a body became subject to compulsory pension insurance, while all other Germans below 40 years of age not hitherto insured became entitled to join the pension insurance scheme.

None of this interested the Nazis very much. Of more relevance was that unemployment insurance from 1936 onwards, owing to the state of full employment, could be explicitly turned into a means of financing armaments by marked rises in contributions and reductions in benefits. From 1933 to 1939, 8,800 million marks were collected by way of contributions, but only 3,100 million marks expended in benefits.[119] In 1938, the proportion which total public social payments constituted of national income at market prices at 7 per cent was 2 per cent lower than in 1928, but the share which social contributions from insured persons constituted of gross remuneration at 10.5 per cent was 1.75 per cent higher.

To judge by the ideology and propaganda of the National Socialists, the most incisive and lasting economic and social interventions after 30 January 1933 should have been in favour of independent peasants and in the interest of middle-class traders and craftsmen, but most expectations which sprang from National Socialist ideology and propaganda were

[118] Walter Schumann and Ludwig Brucker, *Sozialpolitik im neuen Staat* (Berlin and Charlottenburg, 1934); Johannes Krohn, 'Der Umbau der deutschen Sozialversicherung', *Zeitschrift für das gesamte Versicherungswissenschaft*, vol. XXXIV (1934), pp. 201–97; Wolfgang Scheur, 'Einrichtungen und Massnahmen der sozialen Sicherheit in der Zeit des Nationalsozialismus', dissertation, Cologne University, 1967; Karl Teppe, 'Zur Sozialpolitik des Dritten Reichs am Beispiel der Sozialversicherung', *Archiv für Sozialgeschichte*, vol. XXVII (1977), pp. 195–250.
[119] Hennig, *Thesen*, p. 203.

disappointed. Thus, middle-class and peasant protection policy[120] disappeared almost completely from the economic policy programme after 1935 because it was inconsistent with the Nazis' armament and war plans. Up to that date, peasants did not do badly, whereas the industrial middle class was sent away with placebos. The fundamental wish and hope of the industrial middle class to be relieved of market risks and to be guaranteed secure outlets and revenues by way of controlled prices and markets remained a dream. The anachronistic reintroduction of compulsory guilds and of licensing by competence, the embargo on the establishment of new and expansion of existing department stores were mere palliatives which could not safeguard this occupational group as a whole – and were probably never meant to do so. National Socialist policy regarding the middle class accelerated rather than inhibited the loss of economic independence by about 200,000 (= 13 per cent) not very efficient craftsmen and individual traders.

Agriculture, on the other hand, was taken out of the market system. In September 1933, the compulsory organization of *Reichsnährstand* was established, comprising producers, processors of, and traders in, agricultural produce, and allowing regional marketing boards to regulate prices, transport costs, outlets, and eventually even soil cultivation, in the interest of a futile effort at self-sufficiency. Prices paid to agricultural producers were raised by 25 per cent. All this rebounded, however, more to the benefit of owners of large estates, eloquent in pleading their case and providing a large proportion of the produce coming to the market, than to the benefit of middle peasants. This was equally true of the increased drive to debt reduction. Just as before 1933, roughly half the

---

[120] See the following, especially Schoenbaum, *Dei braune Revolution*, pp. 170ff.; Arthur Schweitzer, *Die Nazifizierung des Mittelstandes* (Stuttgart, 1970); Heinrich-August Winkler, 'Der entbehrliche Stand. Zur Mittelstandspolitik im "Dritten Reich" ', *Archiv für Sozialgeschichte*, vol. XVII (1977), pp. 1–40; Adelheid von Saldern, *Mittelstand im 'Dritten Reich'. Handwerker–Einzelhändler–Bauern* (Frankfurt and New York, 1979); Valentin Chesi, *Struktur und Funktion der Handwerksorganisation in Deutschland seit 1933* (Berlin, 1966); Hans-Jürgen Puhle, *Politische Agrarbewegung en in kapitalistischen Industriegesellschaften. Deutschland, USA und Frankreich im 20. Jahrhundert* (Göttingen, 1975), pp. 94–103; Frieda Wunderlich, *Farm Labour in Germany 1810–1945* (Princeton, 1961), pp. 160ff., 222ff.; Horst Gies, 'Der Reichsnährstand – Organ berufsständischer Selbstverwaltung oder Instrument staatlicher Wirtschaftslenkung?', *Zeitschrift für Agrargeschichte und Agrarsoziologie*, vol. XXI (1973), pp. 216–33; Jürgen von Krüdener, 'Zielkonflikt in der nationalsozialistischen Agrarpolitik', *Zeitschrift für Wirtschafts- und Sozialwissenschaft*, vol. IV (1974), pp. 335–61; Max Rolfes, 'Landwirtschaft 1914–1945', in Aubin und Zorn, *Handbuch*, pp. 755ff.; Karl-Rolf Schulz-Klinken, 'Preussische und deutsche Ostsiedlungspolitik von 1886–1945', *Zeitschrift für Agrargeschichte und Agrarsoziologie*, vol. XXI (1973), pp. 198–214; W. Tornow, *Chronik der Agrarpolitik und Agrarwirtschaft des Deutschen Reichs 1933–1945* (Stuttgart, 1972); Wilhelm Bauer and Peter Dehem, 'Landwirtschaft und Volkseinkommen', *Vierteljahrhefte zur Konjunkturforschung* (1938–9), pp. 411–32; John E. Farquarson, *The Plough and the Swastika: The NSDAP and Agriculture in Germany 1928–1945* (London, 1976); statistics from *Statistisches Handbuch von Deutschland 1928–1944* (Munich, 1949), pp. 32f.

finance employed in debt reduction benefited estate owners. Peasant land settlement, which Schleicher had tried to link more firmly with the policy of debt reduction, dried up almost completely. Between 1925 and 1932 470,000 ha were settled by peasants, between 1933 and 1939, only 350,000 ha.

Even the Reich Law on Hereditary Farms, propounded with a great deal of propaganda, proved an illusory success for the peasantry, accompanied by painful side-effects. Farms between 7.5 and 125 ha were elevated to the status of hereditary farms, provided their occupants satisfied certain, mainly racial, conditions of Nazi ideology. Only a man who managed a hereditary farm was entitled to the honorific title of 'peasant'. It applied to about 700,000 who farmed around 40 per cent of agriculturally cultivated land. All others engaged in arable or livestock farming were mere 'husbandmen'. The hereditary farm was property secured to the family, a kind of middle-class entail. But this meant that the farm could be neither sold nor mortgaged. On account of these considerable restrictions on their ability to raise funds, hereditary peasants soon ceased to value the law on hereditary farms, though its initial effects had been purely protection and guarantee in their favour. The disenchantment increased, since their need for credit increased when output and marginal costs grew. The effect of the single price rise of September 1933 was soon spent. In the long run, agriculture in the Third Reich was less affected by legal regulation of the organization of *Reichnährstand* than by the law of diminishing returns. By 1935, the growth of agricultural income again fell markedly below the growth of national income. Thus, National Socialist agricultural policy ultimately made no difference to the undervaluation of agricultural work, to the gap in remuneration between agriculture on the one hand, industry and the tertiary sector on the other, and – contrary to the romantic concepts of agriculture, feeding on an ideology of blood and soil – to the continuous reduction of land surface under agricultural cultivation and the migration of men from agriculture into towns (1933–9: 640,000 = 10 per cent).

CHAPTER XII

Economic policy and economic development in Austria–Hungary, 1867–1913[1]

I. *Introduction*

The Emperor of Austria, Franz Joseph I of the House of Habsburg-Lothringen, had every right to be pleased as he stood in the Hungarian capital city of Buda, atop a mound of earth gathered from every part of the country, to be crowned I. Ferencz József, King of Hungary, on 8 June 1867. Ten days earlier, the Hungarian parliament had passed the acts constituting the Compromise of 1867 which, with their counterpart laws in Austria,[2] formally established the Austro-Hungarian monarchy as of 1 January 1868. Very largely the personal work of the Kaiser himself, the Compromise regulated the political relations between the two constituent parts of his Empire, at one and the same time stabilizing both the internal conditions and the international position of the Habsburg lands. Franz Joseph had rightly seen that the position of Hungary was the key both to the internal cohesion of the Empire and to the arrest and reversal of the decline of Austria as a major power, which defeat in the war with Prussia in 1866 had exposed so clearly. Under the Compromise, Hungary regained full internal autonomy and most of the status of an independent country, but remained united with Austria in the person of the common monarch and in the conduct of foreign affairs.

The Compromise established two classes of relations between the

---

[1] I am particularly grateful to the following colleagues for perceptive criticism of an earlier draft of this paper: Iván Berend, Karl Helleiner, László Katus, Herbert Matis, György Ránki, and Roman Sandgruber. The errors and defects which remain are solely the responsibility of the author. Manuscript submitted in final form in February 1979.

[2] Names vex any study of Austria–Hungary. 'Austria' was not a defined political unit, despite there being an Emperor of Austria (who also held, among other titles, that of King of Illyria). Austria or Cisleithania – the latter a reference to the Leitha River, the then border between the two countries on the road from Vienna to Budapest – was the popular name for The Kingdoms and Lands Represented in the Reichsrat. Hungary, or Transleithania, was officially known as The Lands of the Holy Crown of St Stephen. Towns and cities, or regions, may have had as many as four names: a German and a Hungarian designation in addition to a name in one or two of the locally common languages. I have adopted the convention of referring to places by their English names, if one is in common use – e.g., Vienna, Prague, Galicia – or otherwise by the name that is official in the country in which the place is currently located. In the latter case, I have added the German and/or Hungarian appellation for further identification – e.g., Bratislava (Pressburg, Pozsony) or Cluj (Klausenburg, Kolozsvár).

partners in the new Austria–Hungary: 'Common affairs' embraced the army and navy, and all aspects of international relations including the diplomatic service; a common ministry was set up to handle the financial side of these matters. 'Dualistic affairs' were to be regulated by identical laws passed in each state separately after prior agreement. Such agreement was required in respect of commercial policy (most particularly tariff legislation), indirect taxes, the monetary system, the central bank, the state debt, and railway matters which touched upon the interest of both states. Quite naturally, the accords reached on these issues were popularly known as the 'economic compromise'.

Officially designated a 'tariff and trade agreement', the economic compromise provided for a common tariff and continuation of the customs union which had been in force since 1850, for a common currency and a single bank of issue, and for free movement of labour and capital: a citizen of Austria had the right to set up a business in Hungary on a basis of strict equality with a Hungarian citizen, and vice versa. The agreement also required identity of the major consumption taxes – on beer, wine, spirits, sugar, meat, and later petroleum – in both Austria and Hungary, and established the rules by which the existing imperial debt and the expenses for common affairs were to be shared.

Tariff revenue was earmarked for common expenditures; any shortfall had to be covered by the two partners in a ratio specified by the *quota*, initially set at 70 per cent for Austria and 30 per cent for Hungary. Austria agreed to pay the first 25 million florins (about £2.1 million) of interest on the imperial debt; the rest was shared according to the same 70:30 quota ratio.

The quota ratio was to have been established according to the taxpaying capacity of the two countries, but agreement could never be reached on a suitable formula by which this ability-to-pay principle could be implemented. Each partner thought the other had received undue advantage in the initial 70:30 shares, and the quota, along with the tariff and customs union, was a constant irritant in Austrian–Hungarian relations. The required decennial renewal or renegotiation of the economic compromise virtually guaranteed a major political crisis at 10-year intervals, as the quota and other contentious issues boiled back up to the surface. Franz Joseph was forced on more than one occasion to use his residual powers to extend the tariff and trade agreements when the delegations from the two countries could not find common ground by the expiry date.

Despite these inherent strains, the agreements were in fact renewed, and without major change in the actual economic relations between the two states. The quota was modified, raising Hungary's share[3] in return

---

[3] Her share stood at 36.4 per cent after the 1907 renewal.

for political concessions from Austria, but the common customs territory, a uniform tariff, one currency, and a single central bank were retained throughout the period. Certainly more far reaching than the effects of any of the minor changes in the structure of these institutional arrangements were the consequences of the uncertainty and atmosphere of crisis that attended all but the very first renewal.

Because the quantitative economic history of the Dual Monarchy is still in its infancy, especially for the Austrian half, it is difficult to draw a picture of even the broad outlines of economic growth during the period under review. Some estimates, of varying degrees of speculativeness, exist, and in Table 105 I have tried to summarize the available results for gross output, agriculture, and industry. If there is any consensus at all among scholars of this period, it is that industrialization was rather a long drawn-out process in Austria-Hungary, and that the process of economic development – at least in the Austrian half – could be described as a case of 'leisurely' economic growth.[4] Such notions are sharpened because both the contemporary and historical comparison is to Prussia or Germany, whose growth in industrial and political power was not only rapid, but often directly at Habsburg expense. It is interesting to note, however, that if Bairoch's calculations have produced a reasonably correct relative ranking of growth rates of Gross National Product among the major European powers, then Austria-Hungary's performance appears in a more favourable light: among the 'great powers', *only* Germany shows rates of increase in total and per capita product which exceed those of the Dual Monarchy.[5]

The effect of revisions in earlier estimates for the major sectors has generally been to reduce the implied rates of growth of output. This has been most evident in industry, where the most recent research both de-emphasizes the importance of certain spectacular, but short, boom periods such as 1867-73, and pushes further back the beginnings of a substantial industrial sector in Austria, into the 1820s and 1830s at least.[6] The industrial sector of Hungary was of much more recent vintage, and much smaller, than that of Austria. It is unlikely that Hungarian industry produced even one-third as much as its Austrian counterpart in 1913; in 1913 Hungarian industry had reached an output level which the Cisleithanian sector had already passed by 1870.[7]

[4] The term is from Richard Rudolph, 'Austrian Industrialization: A Case Study in Leisurely Economic Growth', in *Sozialismus, Geschichte und Wirtschaft: Festschrift für Eduard März* (Vienna, 1973).

[5] Rates of growth calculated from the data in Paul Bairoch, 'Europe's Gross National Product', give the following results from GNP and per capita GNP respectively in the 1870-1913 period: Germany, 2.5 (1.3); Russia, 1.9 (0.6); UK, 1.9 (1.0); France, 1.1 (1.1); Italy, 1.5 (0.8). It is very difficult to assess the reliability of Bairoch's data, since the discussion of sources and methodology is incomplete.   [6] Reference mainly to the work of Komlos and Rudolph. See Table 105.

[7] Based on Komlos' data ('The Habsburg Monarchy', Appendix B) which are the most complete and accessible.

Austria was the richer half of the monarchy, as Table 106 shows. The average Cisleithanian income was, according to the data in the table, about 24 per cent higher than that in Transleithania, considering that the average for Hungary proper and Croatia-Slavonia comes to about 417 crowns, using 1910 population weights. There may be a relative under-statement of Austrian income which tends to minimize the difference between the income levels of the two countries; the best contemporary estimates put the disparity at about 35 per cent.[8]

Whichever figure may be more accurate, a striking feature of the table is the large regional disparities within Austria. The contrast with Hungary would be even more pronounced if Budapest were considered separately: Budapest contained 12 per cent of the population of the 1920 territory of Hungary in 1910, but a far higher proportion of her total industry.[9] Alpine Austria and the Czech crownlands, where the Cisleithanian industry was concentrated, enjoyed levels of income per person which were a multiple of those of some of the other provinces, despite the central government's efforts to reduce regional disparities.

In the 'Multinational Empire', regional disparity meant national disparity as well. The more prosperous areas of Austria were home to Germans, Italians, and Czechs; the other Slavs and the Romanians found themselves living in vastly poorer areas. The situation was not so clear-cut in Hungary, where in many areas the various nationalities lived in a more mixed settlement pattern and where the cities often exhibited a radically different ethnic composition from the surrounding country-side. The differences in political and economic power were great in both halves of the Empire, and the failure of the two governments to find a solution to the 'nationality problem' doomed the Dual Monarchy to extinction.

From the weight of literature alone, both scholarly and propagandistic, the nationality problem was and is the primary question in Austro-Hungarian history. Neither the scope of this chapter nor the competence of the author would permit a definitive treatment of the issue, but its main economic dimensions must be sketched out, since nationality considerations impinged on economic policy in every area with which we are here concerned.

Eleven major national groups inhabited Austria–Hungary: Germans, Magyars, Czechs, Poles, Italians, Croats, Serbs, Slovaks, Slovenes, Romanians, and Ruthenians. Each had a large majority in a clearly identifi-able area, although in some important regions populations were mixed

[8] Friedrich von Fellner, 'Die Verteilung des Volksvermögens und Volkseinkommens der Länder der ungarischen heiligen Krone zwischen dem heutigen Ungarn und den Successions-Staaten', *Metron*, vol. III, no. 2 (September 1923) and *idem*, 'Das Volkseinkommen Oesterreichs und Ungarns', *Statistische Monatschrift*, 21 (September–October 1917).

[9] Budapest accounted for only 5 per cent of the population of the 1910 territory, but for fully 28 per cent of the factory labour force. Katus, 'Die Magyaren'.

Table 105. *Comparison of rates of growth of real output (per cent per annum, continuously compounded)*

Period	Country	Output measure	Bairoch[1]	Gross[2]	Katus[3]	Komlos[4]	Rudolph[5]	Sandgruber[6]
	A–H	GNP (per capita)	1.9(1.1)[a]					
	A	GDMP[b] (per capita)			2.3(1.5)			
	H	GDMP[b] (per capita)			2.4(1.7)			
	A	Mfg., mining & constr.				3.1		
c.1867 to c.1913	A	Mfg. industry		3.9^f		3.4[c]	3.5^{a,g}	
	H	Mfg., mining & constr.			4.2	3.2		
	H	Mfg. industry				3.3[c]		
	A	Agriculture			1.3			
	A	Agriculture						1.2[d],1.6[d]
	H	Agriculture			1.7[e]			
1865–1885	A	Mfg. industry		4.1^f		3.7	3.1^g	
	H	Mfg. industry				3.1		
1880–1911	A	Mfg. industry		4.2^f		3.3	3.7^g	
	H	Mfg. industry				4.3	3.6	
1880–1913	A	Mfg., mining, constr.				3.3		
	H	Mfg., mining, constr.				4.1		

Notes:

A = Austria

H = Hungary

A–H = Austria–Hungary

[a] 1870–1913

[b] Gross domestic material product

[c] 1865–1911

[d] 1868/75–1904/13; gross value of output and gross value added, respectively.

[e] 1865/69–1911/13

[f] Gross emphasizes (p. 61) that his data give *upper limits* to growth rates.

[g] Includes mining

Sources:

1 Paul Bairoch, 'Europe's Gross National Product: 1800–1975', *Journal of European Economic History*, vol. v, no. 2. (Autumn 1976), pp. 281 and 286.

2 Nachum T. Gross, 'Industrialization in Austria in the Nineteenth Century' (unpublished Ph.D. dissertation, Department of Economics, University of California, Berkeley, 1966). p. 62.

3 Lázló Katus, 'Economic Growth in Hungary during the Age of Dualism (1867–1913): A Quantitative Analysis', *Studia Historica Academiae Scientiarum Hungaricae*, vol. LXII (Budapest, 1970), pp. 108–9, 112–13.

4 John Komlos, 'The Habsburg Monarchy as a Customs Union: Economic Development in Austria–Hungary in the Nineteenth Century' (unpublished Ph.D. dissertation, Department of History, University of Chicago, 1978), pp. 239–40.

5 Richard Rudolph, 'Quantitative Aspekte der Industrialisierung in Cisleithanien 1848–1914', in Adam Wandruszka and Peter Urbanitsch (eds.), *Die Habsburgermonarchie 1848–1918*, vol. I (Vienna, 1973), p. 243.
Richard Rudolph, 'The Pattern of Austrian Industrial Growth from the Eighteenth to the Early Twentieth Century', *Austrian History Yearbook*, XI (1975), Table I.

6 Roman Sandgruber, *Österreichische Agrarstatistik 1750–1918*, Materialien zur Wirtschafts– und Sozialgeschichte, vol. III (Vienna, 1978), p. 109.

Table 106. *Net domestic product per capita (by region, 1913, in crowns)*

Austria		516
Alpine provinces	790	
Bohemia, Moravia, Silesia	630	
South Tyrol, Trieste, Istria	450	
Slovenia, Dalmatia, Bukovina	300	
Galicia	250	
Hungary		435
Territory of 1920	521	
Territory of 'successor states'	374	
Croatia-Slavonia		295
Habsburg monarchy		475

Sources: László Katus, 'Die Magyaren', in Adam Wandruszka and Peter Urbanitsch (eds.), *Die Habsburgermonarchie 1848–1918*, vol. III: *Die Völker der Monarchie* (Vienna, in press). Katus takes his Austrian data from Ernst Waizner, 'Das Volkseinkommen Alt-Österreichs und seine Verteilung auf die Nachfolgestaaten', *Metron*, vol. VII, no. 4 (1928) and Anton Kausel, Nándor Németh, and Hans Seidel, 'Österreichs Volkseinkommen 1913 bis 1963', *Monatsberichte des österreichischen Instituts für Wirtschaftsforschung*, Sonderheft 14 (1965).

to the extent that no nationality occupied a majority position. Neither the Germans in Cisleithania nor the Magyars in Transleithania had an absolute majority in their half of the monarchy, although they were the dominant nations. The other nationalities[10] had – depending on place, time, and their own development – widely varying degrees of political influence or economic strength. Among these peoples the Czechs were economically by far the most fortunate group, although the Poles exercised greater political power. Romanians and Ruthenians, on the other hand, lived in poverty in both Austria and Hungary, and were virtually shut out of politics in both places. Austria and Hungary adopted very divergent general methods of dealing with the issue of nationality. The Hungarian concept was both simpler and more straightforward; let us deal with it first.

Upon the establishment of the Dual Monarchy, Hungary took two

[10] I am using the words 'nation' and 'nationality' interchangeably. It should be noted that a clear distinction between these two terms existed in both German and Hungarian, and was pejorative: 'nationality', in both languages, carried the connotation of referring to a lesser or inferior ethnic group.

immediate steps to regulate her nationality problem: a 'compromise' with Croatia-Slavonia in 1868 granted local autonomy in internal administration, justice, religion, and education. Defence, finance, and the economy were to remain within the competence of the central government in Budapest, but special Croatian-Slavonian departments were created within the ministries of finance, commerce, industry, transport, and defence. Croatia-Slavonia also received specific representation in the Hungarian parliament, and one cabinet minister (without portfolio).

More important perhaps, and certainly more revealing of the philosophy of the Magyars, was the Nationalities Act of 1868. This act affirmed the equality of all nationalities before the law, and assured them fundamental rights in the use of their own language, including in education; it also expressly declared Hungary to be a unitary and Magyar state. There was therefore no ambiguity whatever concerning which was to be the leading nation, and in practice the dominance in political life exceeded anything which might be inferred from the language of the act: limited franchise with a relatively high property qualification, and an open ballot, kept 'representative' organs of government firmly in Magyar hands. Despite the guarantees of the act, educational policy was employed throughout most of the Dual Monarchy period much more as an instrument of magyarization than as one of sustenance of minority cultures. Hegemony certainly, assimilation if possible, would describe the main thrust of the Magyar politicians' policy toward Hungary's non-Magyar inhabitants.

In Austria, both the dimensions of the problem and the manner of dealing with it were different. The provinces, or crownlands, had historic identities (there was no counterpart at all to these lands in the system of political administration in the Kingdom of Hungary, except for Croatia-Slavonia), and were often home to one or more nationalities living in a compact block and increasingly conscious of their national identity. The *curia* system of election provided a form of 'electoral geometry' (to use the contemporary term) which ensured German majorities in the Reichsrat until later in the period when the franchise was broadened. The Emperor appointed the members of the Upper House but the members of the Lower House were elected by four *curiae*: the great landowners, members of the chambers of commerce and industry, urban males aged over 24 who paid at least 10 florins (about 16s. 8d.) of direct taxes annually, and rural males over 24 who met the same tax criterion.[11]

Gradually the franchise for election to the Lower House was extended

---

[11] In 1879 this system produced one deputy per 63 great landlords, one for every 27 chamber of commerce members, and one for 1,600 urban, or 7,900 rural voters, respectively. William Jenks, *The Austrian Electoral Reform of 1907* (New York, 1950), p. 17.

- finally to universal male suffrage in 1907 – and the Germans found it increasingly difficult, and finally impossible, to govern without forming a coalition with one of the other national groups. The Poles from Galicia were the most frequent allies, and the Czechs the most troublesome foes. The Austrian government relied on a combination of pork-barrel legislation, limited increases in provincial autonomy and the concept of *Kaisertreue* (loyalty to the Emperor) to placate their nationalities, although – in the case of the Czechs – they sometimes had to resort to martial law. Thus Austrian economic policy came more and more to be dictated by the exigencies of the nationality question.

Comprehensive statistics in sufficient detail to allow a thorough assessment of the economic dimensions of the nationality problem do not exist for either Austria or Hungary. Contemporary and most historical sources, in so far as they rely on quantitative information at all, typically demonstrate the numbers of German-speaking and Magyar-speaking persons in politics, education, professions, upper levels of business and industry, banking, publishing, and land ownership significantly surpassed their proportion in the general population. Tax data reveal that Germans paid a nearly double share of direct taxes, compared to their share in the population, and that direct tax collections from the city of Budapest alone exceeded those from Transylvania and the Slovak-Ruthenian territory combined. Ignoring for the moment later developments in the Czech lands, we find that except for the position of the Serbs in large-scale farming, and of the Poles and Italians in some categories of official and economic positions, these data uniformly support the impression that the two politically dominant nations were in firm control of the economic life as well.

The banking system was one of the main pillars supporting this system of control. The Viennese great banks and the cartels they supported exerted a powerful influence on nearly every industry, and much of agriculture, over the entire territory of the Dual Monarchy. To overcome this influence and to establish a greater degree of national economic independence, many ethnic groups founded their own banks, credit societies, and other financial institutions. The most conspicuous success among these was the Živnostenská Banka in Bohemia, but it was not an isolated phenomenon. Even in the poorer regions of Transylvania, against the opposition of the Magyar landlords, Romanian and other 'nationality' financial institutions mushroomed from the 1890s onwards.

The growth of these institutions was in part connected to the inflow of money from emigrant remittances, which was particularly important to Hungary, where much of the money was destined for land purchase or other investment in the non-Magyar regions. Emigrants had been concentrated among the nationalities: even as late as the 1899–1913 period, therefore after the major waves of Slovaks and Ruthenians had already left, official statistics show that two-thirds of the emigrants from Hungary were of non-Magyar mother tongue. The expansion of the network of financial institutions and the inflow of funds were two of the main ingredients in the powerful economic upsurge which gripped the non-Magyar areas at the beginning of the twentieth century.[12]

Apart from some minor individual instances, the Hungarian government did not have an explicit policy of direct economic aid or stimulation to either Magyar or non-Magyar regions. The primary aims were to build up the infrastructure – especially railways – and to develop Hungarian industrial productive capacity, although assistance to agriculture was certainly not ignored. Sectorally oriented government help flowed to wherever the productive units were located; in particular, industrial subventions after 1907 were directed in disproportionate measure into non-Magyar areas simply because the resources of timber, ore, coal and water power were typically located near the periphery of the country, in those areas. But there was no 'pro-nationalities' cast to this action; it was done because it served the interests of the unitary Hungarian state.

In Austria, on the other hand, government policies often had to be based on explicit considerations of nationality issues. The construction of railway lines was frequently a regional quid pro quo for political support on some legislation in the Reichsrat. The Koerber plan was a grand scheme for building canals and other transport links to improve the economic position of the nationalities and to reduce some of the enormous disparities in standards of living among the people of Austria.[13] The Austrian state budget acted as a major vehicle for interregional (and therefore inter-nationality) redistribution of wealth. The richer German, Czech, and Italian provinces paid far more in taxes than they received in government expenditures, while the opposite was true for the eastern and southern Slavic lands. Galicia was especially favoured in this regard, not only because its poverty meant low tax collections, but no doubt also because of the support of the 'Polish Club' (the Polish representatives from Galicia in the Reichsrat) for the Germans.

In the end, neither the Hungarian nor the Austrian policy succeeded in preventing the parcellization of the Habsburg Empire among its constituent nationality groups. The Hungarians had failed to learn the

---

[12] The ideas in this paragraph are derived from László Katus, 'Über die wirtschaftlichen und gesellschaftlichen Grundlagen der Nationalitätenfrage in Ungarn vor dem ersten Weltkrieg', in Peter Hanák (ed.), *Die nationale Frage in der österreichisch-ungarischen Monarchie 1900–1918* (Budapest, 1966).

[13] Although passed by the Austrian parliament, the plan was scuttled from within by officials in the Ministry of Finance, according to Alexander Gerschenkron (*An Economic Spurt That Failed: Four Lectures in Austrian History* (Princeton, 1977)).

lessons of the failure of germanization and centralization in their own land, first under Joseph II (1780–90) and later under the 'Bach system' of military rule after 1849 following the defeated insurrection. Austria's policy of appeasement also failed, although we cannot know whether it was inherently ineffective, or merely too feeble.[14] Whether, indeed, *any* government policy could have prevented the breakup of the Habsburg Empire is still a matter for serious debate among historians.

There is less debate over the importance of the Compromise of 1867 as an economic dividing line, especially in the Austrian-oriented literature. The standard periodization (1848–73, 1873–96, and 1896–1913) passes over the founding of the Dual Monarchy on 1 January 1868 almost as if the date had not existed, and focuses on the Crash of 1873 as marking the end of one era and the beginning of another.[15] While I have no wish to quarrel with the choice of 1873 as a major turning point – indeed, one of the main themes of what is to follow is that 1873 marks a watershed in many economic areas, although more so for Austria than for the monarchy as a whole – the signing of the Compromise also significantly altered the economic future of the Habsburg Empire, perhaps in more profound ways than did the events of 1873. With the establishment of the Dual Monarchy, the central direction of Hungarian state economic policy passed from the control of Viennese bureaucrats and Austrian generals into the hands of an independent, chauvinistic, and development-oriented Magyar government which gave far lower priority to being a great power than did the Austrians. The new system also imposed a rigid discipline on the monetary system of the Habsburg Empire, which had hitherto had a history of fiscal mismanagement, monetary manipulation, periodic crises, and general financial disorder. The final exclusion of Austria from any influential role in Germany carried with it, from within and from without, forces which changed fundamentally some of Austria–Hungary's most important political and economic circumstances. These themes will be elaborated in the succeeding sections, which deal with trade and tariffs, government finances, industrial promotion, agricultural policy, and the state role in railway transport.

II.   *Trade and tariff policy*

Austria–Hungary entered the Age of Dualism with the most liberal tariff structure in the history of the Habsburg dominions. Striving for hegemony in Germany, Austria prepared to enter the German customs union

---

[14] Gerschenkron (in *An Economic Spurt that Failed*) strongly suggests that a wilful, fiscally overcautious bureaucracy deliberately enfeebled such policies.

[15] An excellent work espousing this view is Herbert Matis, *Österreichs Wirtschaft 1848–1913: Konjunkturelle Dynamik und gesellschaftlicher Wandel im Zeitalter Franz Josephs I* (Berlin, 1972).

by lowering her import duties towards the *Zollverein* levels. Towards this end she legislated reductions and simplifications of her tariffs in 1851, 1853, and 1865, and concluded a series of relatively liberal trade treaties during the 1850s and 1860s. The British treaty of 1865, with its Supplementary Convention of 1869, represented the apex of this liberalizing process.

Retreat from the unaccustomed position of liberality began even before the negotiations for the agreements with the British were complete.[16] Under great pressure from her industrialists and pleading unforeseen difficulties in foreign affairs, Austria successfully prevented implementation of the clause that would have required her specific duties not to exceed certain *ad valorem* levels (generally 25 per cent, to be lowered to 20 per cent in 1870). Following this victory for their cause, Austrian manufacturing interests fought with renewed vigour for a return to protection after the Crash of 1873; in consequence, the Reichsrat demanded in 1874 that notice be given on the British treaty, which then expired at the end of 1876.

As the terminal dates of other trade agreements approached, Austria–Hungary – along with most of the rest of Europe – entered a new phase of 'autonomous' tariff policy (that is, not bound by treaty provisions). When Prussia, Austria's rival for leadership in Germany, refused either to modify or to renew their treaty before its expiry at the end of 1877, Austria–Hungary prepared and passed the Autonomous Tariff of 1878, the first legislative step away from the direction of freer trade. While still largely a liberal document based primarily on the principles of a 'revenue tariff', it contained definitely protectionist duties on cotton and woollen textiles although nearly all raw products and semi-manufactures could still be imported duty free. (A requirement to pay the customs in gold amounted to a further increase of perhaps 25 per cent in all existing duties.) In 1882, industrial goods' tariffs were raised to the levels of the German tariff of 1881, and some agricultural duties were introduced. The most important of these amounted to 50 *kreuzer* (about 10*d.*) per 100 kg of wheat. The tariff of 1887, which with some modifications remained in force until the major revision of 1906, raised grain tariffs to the German levels of 1885, pushed textile duties still higher, and extended and increased imposts on other industrial items, most importantly iron and steel.

The dozen years or so of mutually antagonistic exercises of autonomous tariff policy by the major continental powers ended as the 'Caprivi network' of treaties (signed mostly between 1891 and 1894) ushered in a

---

[16] See Karl F. Helleiner, *Free Trade and Frustration: Anglo-Austrian Negotiations, 1860–70* (Toronto, 1973).

third phase of trade policy in Europe. Trade was once again regulated by an interlocking set of explicit agreements, but tariffs were higher, as the forces of protectionism had reconquered the continent.

Austria-Hungary's tariffs and trade agreements formed an integral part, of course, of her overall foreign relations. The era of the Dual Monarchy opened with a fundamental reorientation of Habsburg foreign policy; indeed, the very structure of Dualism itself was part and parcel of this new direction.

The reduction of tariffs which began in 1851 did not result from the conversion of a protectionist dynasty to the principles of free trade, but was rather an economic expedient undertaken for a political end: in order to realize her ambition of hegemony in Germany, Austria had to overcome the influence of Prussia in other German states. Prussian ascendancy could not be successfully combated from without, so Austria's joining the *Zollverein* became a necessary first step in achieving her goal, and she commenced the series of moves which was to result in her becoming a member of the German customs union.

Prussia resisted, and undertook counter-efforts to keep Austria out; the conflict was finally resolved by the Seven Weeks' War in 1866, which culminated in a decisive Prussian victory at Sadowa (Königgrätz). Permanently deprived of any future chance to assume leadership in Germany, the Habsburgs were forced to seek a new direction in foreign affairs, and they turned towards the south-east, to the Balkans. In order to pursue this and other goals, the Emperor had first to consolidate his domestic position, and from this necessity – as we have seen – was born the Compromise with the Hungarians and the Dual Monarchy.

Austria–Hungary strove to avoid confrontation with Russia in the Balkans, an endeavour which was by and large successful at first. Near the end of the century, however, the growing power of a united Germany under Prussian leadership drove both Great Britain and France to woo Russia as a counterweight to Germany. Unable to count on the support of the other great powers for many of her aims in the Balkans, Austria–Hungary saw her position there begin to deteriorate. The beginning of a new series of disasters was heralded by the overthrow of the Obrenović dynasty in 1903 in Serbia, which was the linchpin of the Habsburgs' Balkan position.

Austro-Hungarian domination of Serbia was also critical to the internal affairs of the Dual Monarchy. A subservient Serbia automatically deprived southern Slav nationalism of an external focus or pole of attraction, and therefore constituted a key element in preserving the integrity of the Habsburg Empire. Thus the independence of Serbia, born in the 1903 revolution and developed during the tariff war which began in 1906, weakened Austria–Hungary both externally and internally.[17]

The connection between internal and external policy was no less marked in the economic sphere, and inherent in the complementarity between the Austrian and Hungarian economies was a potentially catastrophic policy dilemma: in order to be a 'great power', Austria–Hungary had to have both industrial strength and a sphere of influence beyond her own borders. A secure influence would have to be based on a strong trade position, but the exports of the Balkan countries competed directly with those of Hungary. Austria's major export industries, on the other hand, were heavily dependent on the Hungarian market, and the prosperity of that market could be seriously undermined by an expansion of imports from the Balkans. A strain in the Dualist relationship was therefore inevitable with each treaty negotiated; concessions on Balkan imports came mainly at Hungarian expense; the gains from increased exports accrued mainly to Austria (whereas with industrial countries, particularly Germany, the pattern of gains and losses was just the reverse – but either way, tension between Austria and Hungary was unavoidable).

The Dual Monarchy's opening to the Balkans depended in large measure on maintaining access to the German market for her own agricultural exports, but Bismarck and his successors restricted this access through veterinary prohibitions, discriminatory railway rate policy, and tariffs. Hungary was far less committed than Austria to the endeavour to become a major political power in Europe; she was more interested in her own internal development. Hungarian intransigence in protecting her traditional economic interests led directly to a tariff war with Romania (1886–91), and delayed settlement of the tariff war with Serbia (1906–10[18]).

The tariff wars severely crippled Austria–Hungary's trade position with these two countries, and Germany exploited the opportunity to increase her influence at Habsburg expense. In 1884, Austria–Hungary accounted for 44 per cent of Romania's imports, to Germany's 15 per cent. A decade later, after Austria–Hungary and Romania had concluded a most-favoured-nation treaty to end their customs war, the respective figures stood at 27 and 28 per cent. The Dual Monarchy was unable even to retain that share of the market, and by 1910 supplied less than 24 per cent of Romanian imports, whereas Germany provided nearly 34 per cent.

[17] The ideas in this and the preceding paragraph are taken mainly from Solomon Wank, 'Foreign Policy and the Nationality Problem in Austria–Hungary, 1867–1914', *Austrian History Yearbook*, vol. III, part 3 (1967), pp. 37–56.   [18] It actually terminated in January 1911.

The relative loss of position in the Serbian market was even more dramatic: Austria–Hungary was a virtual monopsony buyer, purchasing 90 per cent of Serbian exports in 1905,[19] a share which dropped to 42 per cent in 1906 and a mere 15 per cent in 1907, as Serbia energetically sought new outlets for her produce. Germany moved in to take up most of the slack (her purchases rose from 3 to 27 to 40 per cent in the same three years), while Belgium and Great Britain also proved to be significant new markets. Austria–Hungary had been supplying about three-fifths of Serbian imports before the tariff war, a proportion which was cut to less than one-fifth as the conflict deepened. Germany, for whom Serbia purchased only 11 or 12 per cent of her import requirements in the years immediately preceding the tariff war, increased her share to 30 and then 40 per cent of the Serbian market.[20]

Because of the outbreak of the Balkan Wars soon after the termination of the Austro-Hungarian customs war with Serbia, trade in this area could not be said to have returned to 'normal' in any year before the First World War. Austria–Hungary did regain a portion of her lost markets in Serbia, accounting for 41 per cent of both imports and exports in 1911, and for about 45 per cent of Serbian imports and 43 per cent of her exports in 1912. Germany's share of Serbian imports was about 27 per cent in 1911 and 29 per cent in 1912, and of exports 25 and 21 per cent, respectively.[21] Thus, although Austria–Hungary became once again Serbia's principal trading partner, the former dominance was irretrievably broken. Economically and politically, Serbia had declared her independence from Austria–Hungary.

Table 107 summarizes Austria–Hungary's export position compared to the other European powers. The relative deterioration of the Dual Monarchy's standing, especially with respect to that of her greatest rival – but still, however, her most important trading partner – is particularly striking. Low levels of income and relatively slow economic growth can account for some of the sluggishness in Austro-Hungarian foreign trade, and rising protectionism – at home and abroad – for some more. But, shortly before the outbreak of the First World War, Austria–Hungary probably exported a smaller proportion of its Gross National Product

[19] The 90 per cent is surely an exaggeration, since an indeterminate – but perhaps significant – amount of these shipments were throughput, i.e., for re-export from Austria–Hungary.

[20] The data in this and the previous paragraph are derived from statistics appearing in Dimitrije Djordjević, Carinski rat Austro-ugarske i Srbije, 1906–1911 [The Customs War of Austria–Hungary and Serbia, 1906–1911] (Belgrade, 1962); Austria, k.k.Handelsministerium, Statistische Materialien über den Aussenhandel Rumäniens in den Jahren 1890–1901 (Vienna, 1903); idem, Statistische Materialien über den Aussenhandel Serbiens in den Jahren 1892–1903 (Vienna, 1905); and József Szterényi, 'Kereskedelempolitikai szemlélődések' [Reflections on Commercial Policy], Közgazdasági Szemle [Economic Review], vol. xxxviii, issue 51 (1914).

[21] Data from B. R. Mitchell, European Historical Statistics, 1750–1970 (New York, 1976), Tables F1 and F2.

Table 107. *Share of various countries in total European exports (per cent)*

Country	1860	1880	1900	1910
Austria–Hungary	5.8	7.4	7.0	5.6
[4, 6]	(5.4)	(7.2)		
Germany	18.4	18.2	19.6	20.4
[3, 2]	(16.8)	(15.4)		
France	19.2	16.3	14.4	13.4
[2, 3]	(17.5)	(17.6)		
Italy	5.1	5.3	4.9	4.5
[6, 7]	(4.8)	(4.8)		
Russia	5.6	6.7	6.6	8.9
[5, 4]	(4.8)	(5.1)		
United Kingdom	29.8	26.0	24.7	23.7
[1, 1]	(33.4)	(30.4)		

Note:
[ ] = Rank among European exporters, 1860 and 1910, resp.
Sources: Paul Bairoch, *Commerce extérieur et développement économique de l'Europe au XIXe siècle* (Paris and The Hague, 1976), p. 74; *idem*, 'European Foreign Trade in the XIX Century: The Development of the Value and Volume of Exports (Preliminary Results)', *Journal of European Economic History*, vol. II, no. 1 (Spring 1973), p. 15; figures in parentheses for 1860 and 1880 from Nachum T. Gross, 'Die Stellung der Habsburgermonarchie in der Weltwirtschaft', in Adam Wandruszka and Peter Urbanitsch (eds.), *Die Habsburgermonarchie 1848–1918*, vol. I: *Die Wirtschaftliche Entwicklung* (Vienna, 1973), p. 19.

than any other European country save Russia. Bairoch's rough estimate puts this proportion at approximately 7 per cent of Austro-Hungarian Gross National Product, well below the continental European average (12.3 per cent), or that of such countries as Germany (14.6 per cent), France (15.3 per cent), and even Italy (11.0 per cent).[22] Countries which were poorer or more protectionist, or both (Spain, for example) were relatively more active in the international market place than was Austria–Hungary. Although a low percentage of exports in Gross National Product is not by itself an indicator of weak economic performance (the example of the USA easily confirms this statement), and if we take into account other possible reasons such as low aggregate levels of income, 'leisurely' rates of economic growth, the size and extent of the domestic market (along with the Habsburgs' historical inclination towards self-sufficiency), and geographical disadvantages such as difficult access to the sea, in making comparisons to other countries of Europe, one remains with the distinct impression that there existed a symbiotic relationship between foreign policy failures and a relatively weak international trade

[22] Paul Bairoch, *Commerce extérieur*, pp. 79–80.

Table 108. *Austria–Hungary's treaty relations with her major European trading partners*

	Germany	Italy	Romania	Serbia	Britain	Russia	France
1868		Treaty (with concession on textiles, cheese, olive oil) signed 1867	Regulated by 1862 treaty with Turkey	Regulated by treaty with Turkey; no treaty after independence until 1881	1865 treaty	Treaty of trade and navigation from 1860	Treaty from 1866 with MFN and tariff concession
1869	Treaty with MFN and other special concessions (extended 1 year beyond expiry)						
1870							
1871							
1872							
1873					New treaty deleting *ad valorem* duties (never implemented under 1865 treaty)		
1874							
1875			MFN treaty including duty-free import of Romanian grain and reduced duties on Romanian wine				
1876							
1877							
1878					MFN agreement only		
1879							MFN agreement several times renewed
1880	1-year MFN agreements only	Treaty with mutual concessions (textiles, duty-free horse and wood import to Italy)					
1881				Treaty with mutual concessions including special 'border trade' concessions (1882 levels of grain tariffs held for Serbia)			
1882							
1883	MFN treaty several times renewed						
1884		Trade agreement					
1885							
1886			Tariff war				
1887							Trade agreement with MFN; prohibition of embargo on animal imports by France and
1888							
1889							
1890							
1891							

			Treatyless status			
Year	(Caprivi network)	(Italy)	(MFN only)	(Serbia)	(Russia)	(champagne)
1892	12-year treaty as part of Caprivi network; included some reduction in grain and flour duties; extended	12-year treaty with important concession on imports of Italian wine	Trade agreement with MFN only	Treaty with significant tariff reductions to Serbia; Serbia gave only MFN to Austria–Hungary	Trade agreement with binding concessions Austria–Hungary to Russia; German–Russian MFN assured to Austria–Hungary	reduction of champagne duty in Austria–Hungary
1893						
1894						
1895						
1896						
1897						
1898						
1899						
1900						
1901						
1902						
1903						
1904		Provisorium to extend treaty				
1905						
1906				Tariff war (with brief respite)	New treaty with tariff clauses	
1907	New treaty with mutual tariff reduction and a new veterinary convention	New treaty with some concessions to Italy, mostly on strictly Italian goods				
1908						
1909						
1910						
1911			New supplementary treaty with concessions	New treaty with tariff concessions		
1912						
1913						

Note:

MFN = most favoured nation

Sources: Ludwig Lang, *Hundert Jahre Zollpolitik* (Vienna and Leipzig, 1906); Sándor Matlekovits, *A vámpolitika mai helyzete* [The Current Situation in Tariff Policy] (Budapest, 1905); *idem, Vám és kereskedelmi politika* [Tariff and Trade Policy], (Budapest, 1914); *idem, Magyarország Közgazdasági és közmüvelödési állapota ezeréves fennállásakor* [Hungary's Economic and Education Situation at the Millenium of Her Existence] (2 vols., Budapest, 1898).

position.[23] The new, Balkan version of the Habsburg dream of greatness foundered on its own contradictions.

The three sections of Table 109 summarize the structure of the trade of the Austro-Hungarian customs union. Three points must be emphasized before using the table. (1) Because so little systematic quantitative work has been done on Austria–Hungary's trade, the data must be understood as provisional only. They are derived from summary figures for the 49 (later 50) tariff categories (exclusive of precious metals and coin) used in official statistics. (2) Austria did not publish separate data on her own international trade until after 1900; accordingly, the 'Austria' numbers are calculated by subtracting Hungarian from monarchy totals. This procedure restricts the starting point to the 1880s, when reliable Hungarian data became available. (3) An indeterminate amount of throughput may show up as, for example, an export from Hungary to Austria and then as an export from Austria to somewhere else. Since both exported and imported over the territory of the other, the data probably exaggerate the importance of each partner as a market and supplier for the other. This is most obvious in the first category, which includes tropical fruit, spices, and other goods not produced in either half of the monarchy.

Even making generous allowance for such problems, certain patterns still emerge clearly from the table. Most striking, perhaps, is Austria's overwhelming dominance, not only for Hungary's trade, but in the monarchy's commerce with the outside world as well. Only in the group 'industrial raw materials and fuels' can we find any figures less than 50 per cent for Austrian purchases of Hungarian exports, and only in animals and animal products did Austria supply less than 50 per cent of Hungary's imports. Austria accounted for three-quarters or more of the monarchy's imports and exports for virtually every category in nearly all years, and for more than four-fifths of the total exports and imports throughout the period.

Data from the Habsburg Empire as a whole show nearly continuous export surpluses in merchandise trade from 1860 until the last half-dozen years before the First World War, broken only by a seven-year series of import surpluses beginning with 1870. For the years in which the two partners' contributions to this pattern can be separately assessed (1882–1913), Austria's paramountcy showed up as a sequence of surpluses and deficits on merchandise account with the outside world which is exactly the same as that for the whole monarchy. Austrian export surpluses in extra-monarchy trade were normally augmented by further surpluses in her commerce with Hungary (only for a short half-decade immediately

---

[23] 'In the final analysis, her economic strength was insufficient to support her foreign policy, whereas the setbacks in external and internal politics on their part contributed to the relative backwardness of the economy', Nachum T. Gross, 'Die Stellung', p. 14 (my translation).

Table 109. *Structure of Austro-Hungarian trade (provisional data)*

A. *Net exports (million crowns)*

Goods categories	Five-year average	Austria to Hungary	Austria to non-Hungary	Hungary to non–Austria	Monarchy total
Coffee, tea, cocoa, spices, and tropical fruit	1884–1888	17.7	−77.2	−2.0	−79.1
	1889–1893	17.2	−97.9	−3.8	−101.7
	1894–1898	13.2	−83.0	−8.6	−91.6
	1899–1903	11.9	−66.6	−12.1	−78.6
	1904–1908	15.1	−87.0	−15.2	−102.2
	1909–1913	19.7	−130.0	−23.9	−154.0
Field crops, sugar and flour	1884–1888	−196.6	158.6	59.0	217.7
	1889–1893	−280.8	219.5	75.0	294.5
	1894–1898	−320.0	121.3	17.4	138.7
	1899–1903	−363.7	147.3	65.5	212.8
	1904–1908	−454.8	135.7	48.5	184.2
	1909–1913	−560.0	40.9	23.1	64.0
Animals and animal products	1884–1888	−138.3	54.4	5.5	59.9
	1889–1893	−193.5	96.1	12.4	108.5
	1894–1898	−186.0	120.2	28.5	148.7
	1899–1903	−220.2	136.1	43.9	180.0
	1904–1908	−242.7	87.4	48.3	135.7
	1909–1913	−328.2	32.1	64.9	97.0
Foods and beverages	1884–1888	1.1	33.5	7.8	41.4
	1889–1893	0.7	28.4	4.1	32.5
	1894–1898	−12.3	2.2	−11.0	−8.8
	1899–1903	−15.0	0.3	−6.3	−5.9
	1904–1908	−14.5	8.1	2.6	10.7
	1909–1913	−27.2	−0.1	−2.3	−2.4
Industrial raw materials and fuels	1884–1888	−6.9	65.2	20.9	86.0
	1889–1893	−3.8	76.6	21.2	97.9
	1894–1898	−0.9	91.3	21.1	112.4
	1899–1903	1.7	154.1	39.1	193.2
	1904–1908	14.3	161.6	17.6	179.2
	1909–1913	40.5	106.2	−11.5	94.7
Fibres and textiles	1884–1888	296.3	−178.8	0.9	−177.9
	1889–1893	314.3	−195.7	−0.8	−196.5
	1894–1898	348.3	−209.1	−3.3	−212.4
	1899–1903	370.9	−248.6	−4.3	−252.9
	1904–1908	449.0	−321.3	−16.4	−337.7
	1909–1913	537.6	−389.0	−32.0	−421.0
Iron and metals	1884–1888	27.7	−5.0	0.7	−4.3
	1889–1893	36.3	−4.1	−0.3	−4.4
	1894–1898	54.1	−16.0	−5.8	−21.8
	1899–1903	42.3	−7.5	−3.2	−10.7
	1904–1908	66.9	−10.5	−14.1	−24.6
	1909–1913	105.1	−4.6	−26.9	−31.5

Table 109. (cont.)

A. Net exports (million crowns)

Goods categories	Five-year average	Austria to Hungary	Austria to non-Hungary	Hungary to non-Austria	Monarchy total
Salt, chemicals and fertilizer	1884–1888	5.9	5.7	4.2	10.0
	1889–1893	7.7	6.9	6.7	13.6
	1894–1898	9.5	−5.5	5.4	−0.1
	1899–1903	8.5	−10.8	9.4	−1.5
	1904–1908	13.2	−19.6	7.9	−11.7
	1909–1913	23.8	−31.9	1.0	−30.9
Machinery and engineering	1884–1888	28.7	52.7	−4.2	48.5
	1889–1893	36.2	7.8	−3.1	4.7
	1894–1898	38.5	−8.3	−4.8	−13.1
	1899–1903	40.1	−2.1	−1.9	−4.0
	1904–1908	61.4	−47.4	−12.2	−59.6
	1909–1913	87.2	−90.8	−36.5	−127.3
Other manufactures	1884–1888	101.6	59.1	0.1	59.3
	1889–1893	103.4	66.6	−0.9	65.7
	1894–1898	115.3	63.7	−4.6	59.1
	1899–1903	103.3	55.5	−2.3	53.1
	1904–1908	131.5	96.1	−3.0	93.0
	1909–1913	183.4	54.7	−18.2	36.5
Total exports	1884–1888	137.1	168.4	93.1	261.3
	1889–1893	37.7	204.3	110.6	314.9
	1894–1898	59.9	76.8	34.4	111.1
	1899–1903	−20.2	157.8	127.7	285.6
	1904–1908	39.5	3.1	67.8	71.0
	1909–1913	82.1	−412.5	−62.5	−475.0

B. Shares in total monarchy exports and imports (per cent)

Goods categories	Five-year average	Share of category in total value of		Austrian share in total value of category[a]	
		Exports	Imports	Exports	Imports
Coffee, tea, cocoa, spices, and tropical fruit	1884–1888	0.1	6.5	8.2	95.2
	1889–1893	0.1	8.2	50.9	95.2
	1894–1898	0.3	7.4	74.9	89.9
	1899–1903	0.2	4.9	85.5	84.7
	1904–1908	0.2	4.6	90.3	85.3
	1909–1913	0.2	4.8	81.3	84.4
Field crops, sugar and flour	1884–1888	28.8	16.0	72.9	73.0
	1889–1893	28.2	11.4	74.8	75.2
	1894–1898	25.3	12.9	74.8	67.3
	1899–1903	21.6	14.8	71.0	72.7
	1904–1908	19.6	12.6	71.7	70.2
	1909–1913	18.3	12.5	69.4	70.2

Table 109. *(cont.)*

B. Shares in total monarchy exports and imports (per cent)

Goods categories	Five-year average	Share of category in total value of		Austrian share in total value of category[a]	
		Exports	Imports	Exports	Imports
Animals and	1884–1888	12.9	9.6	81.1	75.4
animal	1889–1893	12.2	8.9	77.4	66.7
products	1894–1898	17.5	9.1	79.6	78.4
	1899–1903	16.1	9.6	75.2	74.7
	1904–1908	17.6	11.1	76.0	82.6
	1909–1913	14.7	8.8	75.1	89.2
Foods and	1884–1888	4.2	1.9	81.3	81.6
beverages	1889–1893	4.7	1.9	77.6	67.5
	1894–1898	2.8	3.2	76.4	59.6
	1899–1903	2.6	3.5	78.1	69.3
	1904–1908	2.4	2.5	79.1	80.0
	1909–1913	2.0	1.7	77.7	74.5
Industrial raw	1884–1888	13.0	9.3	81.8	86.9
materials and	1889–1893	14.6	10.4	81.0	83.0
fuels	1894–1898	14.4	10.3	81.7	82.0
	1899–1903	19.5	10.8	82.8	85.7
	1904–1908	18.5	10.5	85.1	81.6
	1909–1913	18.2	12.1	86.0	79.7
Fibres and	1884–1888	14.8	33.8	90.6	95.1
textiles	1889–1893	14.8	34.7	92.5	95.8
	1894–1898	13.6	30.6	93.0	95.7
	1899–1903	13.3	27.9	92.4	95.2
	1904–1908	14.6	30.8	91.2	93.6
	1909–1913	17.7	30.5	91.1	91.7
Iron and metals	1884–1888	2.7	4.2	90.3	92.9
	1889–1893	3.3	4.1	91.7	91.7
	1894–1898	3.4	5.1	92.3	87.5
	1899–1903	4.7	6.4	90.2	88.2
	1904–1908	5.1	5.9	90.1	82.7
	1909–1913	6.6	7.2	92.3	81.1
Salt, chemicals	1884–1888	3.0	2.9	84.7	92.9
and fertilizer	1889–1893	3.4	2.9	82.3	92.7
	1894–1898	3.3	3.5	78.5	88.5
	1899–1903	3.3	3.8	71.6	85.3
	1904–1908	3.8	4.4	72.3	83.1
	1909–1913	4.0	4.1	77.1	82.8
Machinery and	1884–1888	7.8	4.8	96.8	85.6
engineering	1889–1893	5.0	5.1	92.2	87.0
	1894–1898	4.3	5.6	88.7	84.7
	1899–1903	4.9	5.6	82.7	81.6
	1904–1908	3.9	5.8	75.3	77.1
	1909–1913	3.5	6.9	79.0	74.7

Table 109. *(cont.)*

B. *Shares in total monarchy exports and imports (per cent)*

Goods categories	Five-year average	Share of category in total value of		Austrian share in total value of category[a]	
		Exports	Imports	Exports	Imports
Other	1884–1888	12.8	11.1	93.1	90.0
manufactures	1889–1893	13.6	12.1	94.4	91.5
	1894–1898	15.2	12.4	95.2	91.2
	1899–1903	13.9	12.4	94.4	92.0
	1904–1908	14.4	12.0	92.4	88.4
	1909–1913	14.5	11.3	91.9	86.1
Total exports	1884–1888	100.0	100.0	83.4	87.9
or imports	1889–1893	100.0	100.0	83.0	87.5
	1894–1898	100.0	100.0	83.7	84.8
	1899–1903	100.0	100.0	81.7	86.0
	1904–1908	100.0	100.0	82.7	84.9
	1909–1913	100.0	100.0	82.8	83.4

Note:

[a] Based on point of exit or entry of goods. Actual country of destination or origin of goods is not revealed in the statistics. The Austrian share is likely overstated for both exports and imports as a result.

C. *Partners' shares in each other's trade (per cent)*

Goods categories	Five-year average	Austrian share in value of		Hungarian share in value of	
		Hungarian exports	Hungarian imports	Austrian exports	Austrian imports
Coffee, tea,	1884–1888	42.2	83.1	99.1	1.8
cocoa, spices,	1889–1893	51.8	78.8	93.6	1.3
and tropical	1894–1898	75.0	63.1	83.3	3.7
fruit	1899–1903	77.4	52.7	77.8	3.2
	1904–1908	82.7	52.0	82.3	2.0
	1909–1913	68.7	46.6	84.5	1.5
Field crops, sugar	1884–1888	70.1	50.9	14.2	67.0
and flour	1889–1893	74.6	56.2	12.5	74.5
	1894–1898	79.4	35.5	13.1	69.8
	1899–1903	76.2	39.4	11.2	71.6
	1904–1908	79.8	33.0	10.7	73.2
	1909–1913	80.0	28.5	13.0	66.7
Animals and	1884–1888	83.0	33.9	9.0	65.9
animal	1889–1893	80.9	31.8	9.2	73.8
products	1894–1898	77.5	41.6	8.8	64.3
	1899–1903	73.6	35.5	8.3	65.5
	1904–1908	75.4	44.1	10.3	58.3
	1909–1913	79.3	55.9	12.1	58.8

Table 109. *(cont.)*

C. *Partners' shares in each other's trade (per cent)*

Goods categories	Five-year average	Austrian share in value of		Hungarian share in value of	
		Hungarian exports	Hungarian imports	Austrian exports	Austrian imports
Foods and beverages	1884–1888	76.0	90.4	42.9	67.2
	1889–1893	78.3	83.8	51.3	71.0
	1894–1898	84.2	67.0	56.3	63.8
	1899–1903	83.0	69.2	49.7	58.0
	1904–1908	85.2	85.4	54.1	65.1
	1909–1913	88.9	82.6	62.1	69.7
Industrial raw materials and fuels	1884–1888	50.2	66.7	15.3	27.3
	1889–1893	47.6	61.3	16.2	26.3
	1894–1898	46.8	60.0	16.2	25.1
	1899–1903	40.4	62.7	12.8	21.3
	1904–1908	42.9	56.8	14.5	18.7
	1909–1913	43.7	54.1	18.3	14.5
Fibres and textiles	1884–1888	75.5	94.9	65.0	14.3
	1889–1893	78.0	95.4	64.0	13.0
	1894–1898	79.2	95.7	66.7	12.3
	1899–1903	73.5	94.4	62.4	10.4
	1904–1908	68.2	91.9	60.2	9.7
	1909–1913	67.1	89.3	58.7	9.6
Iron and metals	1884–1888	72.7	92.6	52.1	20.0
	1889–1893	77.4	91.4	51.0	22.3
	1894–1898	79.3	87.2	55.5	20.1
	1899–1903	76.0	85.0	45.1	24.1
	1904–1908	69.5	78.0	44.5	18.8
	1909–1913	67.9	76.7	44.1	14.6
Salt, chemicals and fertilizer	1884–1888	69.7	89.9	36.6	33.1
	1889–1893	64.3	89.3	35.8	31.4
	1894–1898	65.0	83.3	42.2	31.0
	1899–1903	57.6	77.2	41.5	30.7
	1904–1908	55.2	71.8	40.2	26.7
	1909–1913	57.4	70.4	40.5	22.6
Machinery and engineering	1884–1888	60.6	81.9	25.7	10.1
	1889–1893	43.0	82.2	37.7	6.7
	1894–1898	52.3	78.6	42.8	11.0
	1899–1903	42.4	73.3	38.9	13.0
	1904–1908	39.6	69.9	552.	10.7
	1909–1913	40.2	63.8	56.3	7.6
Other manufactures	1884–1888	62.3	90.5	41.2	15.6
	1889–1893	65.0	90.4	37.5	13.9
	1894–1898	70.6	89.7	38.0	14.2
	1899–1903	69.1	88.5	34.6	14.5
	1904–1908	65.5	86.1	36.3	18.3
	1909–1913	65.7	83.0	40.1	16.5

Table 109. *(cont.)*

C. *Partners' shares in each other's trade (per cent)*

		Austrian share in value of		Hungarian share in value of	
Goods categories	Five-year average	Hungarian exports	Hungarian imports	Austrian exports	Austrian imports
Total exports	1884–1888	71.7	84.0	38.3	37.0
or imports	1889–1893	73.6	83.1	37.4	40.2
	1894–1898	75.2	78.9	38.7	38.4
	1899–1903	70.9	78.3	34.7	37.5
	1904–1908	72.4	76.5	36.6	35.9
	1909–1913	74.11	73.2	39.1	33.8

Source: Magyar Statisztikai Közlemények [Hungarian Statistical Reports], új sorozat (new series), vol. LXIII (Budapest, 1923).

following the turn of the century did Hungary ever have an export surplus in her Austrian trade), and when just before the First World War import surpluses came to characterize Austrian trade outside the customs union, they were partially offset by continuing export surpluses with Hungary. Until 1909 – except for one year – Hungary, too, had a persistent export surplus in her non-Austrian trade; these surpluses offset her deficits with Austria, resulting in a roughly equal number of deficit and surplus years in Hungary's overall merchandise trade before 1908. From 1909 on, her balances became sharply negative with both Austria and the rest of the world.

In trade between the partners in the customs union, the exchange of Hungarian agricultural products for Austrian industrial goods shows up very clearly: Austria had an export surplus in her trade with Hungary in each of the groups of manufactures shown in section A. For no group is the importance of the Hungarian market clearer than for 'fibres and textiles'. The monarchy's striking import surplus – the result of massive Austrian imports of raw cotton and wool, plus yarn and thread – never attained the absolute size of Austria's export surplus of textile goods in her trade with Hungary. Great as these export surpluses were, by the last few years before the First World War they ultimately became insufficient to pay for Austria's net imports of field crops – primarily wheat and other bread grains – and flour (Austria exported sugar net to Hungary). The pattern observed for fibres and textiles was repeated on a smaller scale for the iron and metal industries and, after the mid-1890s for machinery and engineering as well. The complementarity and interdependence of the two partners' economies, the result of both natural endowments and the Hasburgs' long-standing deliberate promotion of regional specialization within their Empire, are clearly evident.

The monarchy's trade with the outside world shows net exports of primary products and of the products of certain 'light' industries (paper, leather, wood, glass, and pottery in particular). Austria had a substantial import surplus in agricultural goods, but Hungarian production was sufficient to satisfy the Austrian excess demand and provide for export beyond the monarchy's frontiers as well. The gross level of exports and imports of agricultural goods (including sugar and flour) was considerable, making up one-third to two-fifths of all exports and one-fifth to one-quarter of all imports.

Some of the changes evident in the table are also revealing. The dramatic shifts seen under 'Foods and beverages' in section A were first and foremost the results of a single treaty: after an agreement was signed with Italy in 1891 as part of the Caprivi network, Italian wine began almost literally to flood the Austro-Hungarian market. While vintners in both halves of the monarchy suffered, the Austrians appeared to have borne the larger burden of the sudden and massive inflow of Italian wine. Austrian wine exports to Hungary dropped 30 per cent immediately (1892–4 average compared to 1888–90 average), at the same time that total Hungarian imports of wine increased by 24 per cent. Imports of Italian wine into Hungary were negligible before the signing of the treaty, but averaged nearly 13.9 million crowns (about £576,000) annually in 1892–4. Total Hungarian imports of wine in the same period increased by about 5.8 million crowns, but imports from Austria dropped by 6.8 million, accounting for nearly 12.7 of the 13.7 million increase in imports from Italian sources. Even after the expiry of the treaty and the virtual disappearance of Italian wine from the monarchy, only in 1912 could Austrian sales of wine to Hungary regain even the low post-treaty level of 1894. On the other hand, Hungarian exports of wine to Austria declined much more gradually. In the years immediately following the signing of the treaty (1892–4), sales to Austria were still nearly 95 per cent of what they had been on average in 1888–90, and they never fell below two-thirds of that level. Indeed, the peak level of exports of wine to Austria in 1912 (65.5 million crowns, about £2.7 million) was nearly double the 1888–90 average.

Other shifts noticeable in the summary data of the table occurred mainly as a result of trends in the economic development of the two halves of the monarchy. This is perhaps most obvious in industrial raw materials and fuels, where the industrialization of Hungary, the rapid development of the Galician oil fields, and the growing Austrian imports of metal ores account for most of the observed changes. Hungary's burgeoning imports of hard coal from Austria and Germany, and of coking coal and crude oil from Austria give eloquent testimony to the process of industrialization underway there. Impressive growth in net exports from Austria to both Hungary and to the outside world were in both cases the product not only of increased exports as the petroleum reserves of Galicia were exploited, but also of the near-total replacement of imports, which previously had come primarily from the Russian Empire. Russia saw its former market in Hungary virtually disappear by the turn of the century, while the Austrian market shrank to a fraction of its former size.

Examining section C briefly, we can note that the decline in Austria's importance as a supplier of field crops is almost entirely a consequence of Turkey's replacing Austria as the primary source of tobacco imports into Hungary, beginning in the mid-1890s. Hungary's increasing importance as a market for the products of the Austrian machinery industry rests primarily on the growth of imports of agricultural machinery of all kinds, of motor vehicles, of tools, and of musical instruments. All but the last of these demands are directly derived from the growth of industrial activity in Hungary, which fortunately for Austrian manufacturers took place at the same time that it became increasingly difficult for the machinery and engineering branches to export abroad because of tariff and other barriers.

It would seem safe to conclude, based on the provisional but nevertheless revealing data of Table 108, that not only was the complementarity between the Austrian and Hungarian economies striking, but that this interdependence appeared to be increasing. Hungary's attempts to industrialize did not decrease, and Austria-Hungary's tariff policies served to emphasize, the two partners' mutual dependence.

We have seen above that two principal forces determined the direction of Austro-Hungarian tariff policy: the degree of complementarity between the Austrian and Hungarian economies, and reaction to German initiatives in tariff legislation and treaty negotiations. The liberal trend with which the era of Dualism opened was much favoured by the Hungarians, who found ready markets for their grain exports and who saw in free trade great advantages for keeping down the cost of imports necessary to their programme of infrastructural and industrial development. The tariff of 1878, introduced as it was because of Prussian refusal to renew or renegotiate their trade treaty, nevertheless remained a liberal document because the Hungarians refused to go along very far with Austrian efforts for high protective tariffs. Hungarian attitudes began to change as the price of grains began to fall. As a result, the 1882 and 1887 tariff laws were essentially carbon copies of the German tariffs of 1881 and 1885, particularly in the duties they levied on agricultural products.

Germany, as the Caprivi treaties began to expire, passed a new and much higher tariff in 1902 in order to have a strong bargaining position in the new round of negotiations. Austria-Hungary thereupon introduced her own draft tariff in 1903 which, however, did not pass until 1906. The delay came partly because the Hungarian parliament gave its assent only in 1904, but more importantly because the 'obstruction' (physical interference) by the Czech delegates to the Reichsrat completely disrupted that body and paralyzed the legislative process. Thus did the nationality problem impinge directly on tariff policy.

The 1906 tariff reveals – in its higher duties, vastly elaborated category structure, and statutory minima below which no treaty could allow any further reduction – the general advance of protectionist influence. It also shows, in its much-increased duties on grain and flour, how far the traditional Hungarian export group had come to make common cause with their former opponents, the protectionist captains of Austrian industry. The Hungarian response to falling farm prices in the 1880s and 1890s was an attempt to reserve the Austrian market for Hungarian foodstuffs, just as the Hungarian market had been earlier reserved for Austrian textiles.

Just because the cause was common, it was not necessarily equal. To illustrate, the 1906 tariff specified a minimum duty of 6.30 crowns (slightly in excess of 5s.) per 100 kilograms of wheat, the great traditional crop of Hungary. This new minimum duty, about double the former maximum level, in the absence of a quota would determine how far the domestic price could rise. It amounted to 33 per cent of the average Vienna wholesale price of 1902–6 (pre-tariff), and represented 24 per cent of the post-tariff wholesale average for 1907–11. Therefore only with the major increase of 1906 did Hungarian wheat producers achieve *ad valorem* levels of protection which Austrian industrialists – especially the textile manufacturers – had successfully fought, in the negotiations with the British in the late 1860s, as being ruinously low. Not only had industry received several tariff increases and extensions since that time, an adjustment to examine the degree of protection on value added – since most raw materials and other goods for further processing still entered duty free – would show even larger discrepancies in favour of Austrian industry than does the simple comparison of nominal tariff rates.

These discrepancies notwithstanding, the relative prices at which Hungary carried on her trade with Austria improved throughout the Dual Monarchy period. Only a part of this gain could be traced to the general movement in favour of agriculture in the world market from about the turn of the century onwards. The Hungarian latecomers to the protectionist alliance managed to make the improvement in the terms of their trade with Austria exceed that which was occurring in the world, and the relative increase is most marked for grains and flour, Hungary's traditional exports.

The gain for grain farmers and flour millers was so strong, in fact, that even taking into account the protection on imports which competed with Austrian manufactures, their terms of trade within the customs

Table 110. *Comparison of tariff levels, 1913 (per cent)*

| | | Average *ad valorem* tariff rates | |
| | (1) | (2) | (3) |
Country	Tariff revenue ÷ value of all imports	European produce overall[a]	European manufactured goods[a]
Austria–Hungary	6.5[b]	18	18
Germany	8.2	12	13
France	8.8	18	20
Italy	9.6	17	18
Russia	n.a.	n.a.	n.a.
United Kingdom	5.4	0	0

Notes:
[a] From a sample of 278 goods representing the principal export items of 14 European countries.
[b] My calculation from official statistics.
Source: League of Nations, Economic and Financial Section, International Economic Conference (Geneva, May 1927), *Tariff Level Indices* (Geneva, 1927), pp. 15, 21.

union were subsidy prices during the last few years of the Dual Monarchy. Overall, however, for Hungarian export goods as a whole, the relative gain which their improving terms of trade represented was still – even by 1913 – insufficient to offset the great initial advantage which Austria had achieved through the structure of the tariff system. Although its effects were ameliorated as time passed, the set of relative prices produced by the system of tariffs in Austria–Hungary 'taxed' Hungary and resulted in a net transfer of income to Austria.[24]

Non-traditional producers and peasant producers of traditional exports – livestock in particular – were not similarly advantaged. Tariff policy was used for the benefit of traditional producer interests in both halves of the Dual Monarchy. When the Hungarian agrarians joined the Austrian industrialists and their fiscal allies in support of protective tariffs, they formed a triumvirate against which the consumers and the merchants could mount no really effective opposition.

It would be easy, however, to exaggerate both the level of protectionism and the degree of its increase, in Europe as well as in Austria–Hungary. Table 110 shows a comparison, by two different methods, of Austro-Hungarian tariff levels in 1913 with those of the other major

[24] Scott M. Eddie, 'The Terms of Trade as a Tax on Agriculture: Hungary's Trade with Austria, 1883–1913', *Journal of Economic History*, vol. XXXII (1972). The argument is further developed, and the data refined, in *idem*, 'Cui Bono? Magyarország és a Dualista Monarchia védővámpolitikája' [Cui Bono? Hungary and Protectionism in the Dual Monarchy], *Történelmi Szemle* [Historical Review], vol. XIX (1976).

European countries. By the standards of the time, Austro-Hungarian tariffs appear to be high – about on a par with those of France and Italy, and significantly above the German levels.[25] By modern standards, of course, such tariffs are still relatively modest. The lower yield of Austro-Hungarian tariffs, compared to those of the other continental countries, is probably explained by the concentration of imports in the low-duty and duty-free goods, including the substantial 'border traffic' with Serbia and Italy, a provision which allowed certain goods to enter Austria–Hungary from these two neighbours at rates well below the statutory minima that applied to every other country.

Tariff receipts in Austria–Hungary, as a proportion of total value of merchandise imports exclusive of precious metals and coin, increased by more than 70 per cent as a result of the various tariff laws since 1878. If we divide the period under review each time a major act was passed, the average yield of the customs revenue appears as follows:

1863–67 (pre-Dual Monarchy)	4.70 per cent
1868–78	4.11
1879–82	4.63
1883–87	6.99
1888–1906	6.60
1907–13	7.09

The lowest yield was 3.98 per cent in 1877, the highest 8.29 per cent in 1909, according to official data. Comparing the revenue from import duties to the value of imports is at best an imperfect guide to the degree of protection in a country's tariff structure.[26] It is still clear, however, that the tariff levels of the later years are significantly higher than those of the earlier 'liberal' period.

The income from tariffs was a very important component of the Dualist financial system. After rebate of consumption taxes paid on goods exported, the net tariff revenue was earmarked for expenditure on common affairs. Hungary objected to this system – which one year (1881) actually caused net tariff revenue to be negative – because while she accounted for only about 15 per cent of imports and tariff receipts, her quota towards common expenses not covered by net tariff revenue

[25] Columns (2) and (3) of the table are unweighted averages, and therefore useful only for very rough comparison among countries. For 1925 averages weighted by the share of imports in each category were made; the differences between the two calculations were generally small. We can therefore probably use the unweighted averages, with caution. See League of Nations, Economic and Financial Section, International Economic Conference (Geneva, May 1927), *Tariff Level Indices* (Geneva, 1927), esp. pp. 11–20.

[26] An extreme example may be used to make the point clear. If a country had tariffs so high that they completely shut out imports of goods which competed with local manufactures, and the country only imported – but duty free – what it could not produce itself, then the yield calculated as above would be zero, even though the tariff system was prohibitive.

was never less than 30 per cent. Refunds of consumption taxes out of tariffs were shared in a ratio usually exceeding 80:20 in favour of Austrian producers, but the resulting revenue shortfall was shared in the quota ratio of 70:30. Eventually the economic compromise was changed to stipulate that the rebates would come directly from the revenue of the consumption taxes themselves.

The Austrians, of course, complained that using customs revenue to finance common expenditures burdened them in a measure exceeding that set by the quota. About 85 per cent of imports entered the monarchy at Austrian border stations,[27] but the quota only required her to pay 70 per cent of expenses not covered by customs duties. She therefore resisted Hungarian efforts to raise the relatively low duties on 'colonial wares' – coffee was by far the most important – which provided a major portion of customs revenue (between 25 and 40 per cent, depending on the year) and of which Austria consumed the overwhelming proportion. Although these positions of the two partners rest on discrepancies away from the quota ratio, that ratio itself was a constant item of dispute, and neither the contemporary negotiators nor modern analysts could agree on a basis for deriving a 'fair' proportion.

Tariffs were also a prop supporting cartels, but whether the cartelization of industry was more costly to Austria or to Hungary cannot be determined. Other contentious issues existed concerning whether one or another provision benefited one partner more than the other, but even taken in the aggregate they are insignificant when compared to the impact of the tariff itself on the internal economic structure and income distribution, or to the consequences of the striving for great power status for both the political and economic life of the entire Habsburg Empire.

III. *Financial policy*

Austrian imperial finances suffered from frequent crises, usually resulting from wars, throughout most of the middle part of the nineteenth century. Recurring deficits in the state budget were covered in various ways, but most often by resorting to money creation. The near-chronic deficits of the two decades preceding the Compromise saw the government resorting not only to longer-term borrowing and money creation, but also to the sale of state property: between 1854 and 1859 all the state railways were sold off (actually leased for 90 years for a lump-sum amount) in an attempt to put the imperial accounts in order. Just as success seemed to be at hand, war in the Italian provinces upset the

---

[27] What proportion of these were destined for customers in Hungary is unknown, although it may be likely that more imports to Hungary entered via Austria than vice versa.

precarious financial equilibrium, as the war with Prussia was to do a scant seven years later. Austria–Hungary moved into the era of the Dual Monarchy with a rather sorry record of financial disarray and a widely fluctuating currency (the so-called *Agio*, the premium one had to pay for silver, was widely reported and became the popular measure of the health of the Austrian florin). It is therefore easily understandable that the questions of the service of the imperial debt and of the quota ratio by which the two states would cover common expenditures were two of the most contentious issues in the negotiations which established the Dualist system.

Hungary, faced after the Compromise of 1867 with the task of setting up a state apparatus, filling an empty treasury, and building its own separate bureaucracy, quite naturally was content at first to take over the Austrian tax system virtually intact. The compromise left both governments not only an essentially free hand on the expenditure side, but a great deal of latitude in revenue collection as well. The principal consumption taxes were designated a 'dualistic' item, to be assessed and collected according to identical laws and regulations; aside from this restriction, the two partners were by and large free to tax as they wished. The pressures to coordinate tax structures were still very strong, of course, and the vagueness of that part of the Compromise was soon replaced by a number of specific supplementary agreements on taxation.

The existing Austrian tax system drew its revenue from four main sources: direct taxes, indirect taxes, stamp and documentation fees, and income from state monopolies. Direct taxes fell on land, on houses and buildings (with rates and exemptions very much favouring rural and village properties at the expense of urban real estate), on interest income, on personal incomes, and on 'earnings'. The earnings tax (*Erwerbsteuer*) attempted to tax earning capacity from incorporated and unincorporated businesses and professions. Indirect taxes consisted of a set of consumption levies on beer, wine, spirits, sugar, and meat, to which a petroleum tax was added in 1882. Tariff income does not figure in the yield of indirect taxes in either Austria or Hungary because all customs revenue, net of refunds of consumption taxes on exported items, was earmarked for financing of the common affairs of the Dual Monarchy. Stamp and documentation fees were a major source of revenue, as was the income from the state monopolies – salt, tobacco, and the lottery. The net income from state enterprises (chiefly mines, forests, the post and telegraph, and later the railways) formed a relatively small, but considerably fluctuating, component of government revenue in both partner states.

That the revenue patterns of Austria and Hungary did not differ significantly, and that these two patterns exhibited a very similar, parallel

Table 111. *Distribution of central government income by source (per cent of total ordinary income)*

Five-year average	Direct taxes		Indirect taxes, fees and monopolies		Net income of state enterprises		Sale of state property		Other		Total Austria ÷ Hungary per cent
	Austria	Hungary	Austria	Hungary	Austria	Hungary	Austria	Hungary	Austria	Hungary	
1869–73[a]	32.2	[42.4]	58.0	[53.8]	1.6	[2.8]	2.5	n.a.	5.8	[0.9]	[193]
1874–78	31.9	[43.8]	58.2	[45.5]	—[b]	[9.5]	0.4	n.a.	9.5	[1.3]	[166]
1879–83	30.7	37.1	63.3	42.2	—[b]	1.0	0.1	1.5	5.9	18.2	130
1884–88	31.8	33.5	63.8	41.3	—[b]	2.2	0.1	2.1	4.2	20.9	111
1889–93	29.8	31.1	64.5	50.3	2.2	8.0	0.2	1.0	3.4	9.6	112
1894–98	28.1	29.1	63.9	52.0	4.6	8.4	0.0	0.6	3.3	10.0	114
1899–1903	29.1	27.9	64.8	52.1	4.2	10.1	0.1	0.1	1.8	9.9	125
1904–08	27.5	28.1	66.6	54.3	4.4	7.5	0.1	0.3	1.4	9.8	129
1909–13	24.8	28.5	70.4	61.1	3.5	1.5	0.1	0.1	1.2	8.8	151

Notes:

[a] 1871–3 for Hungary.

[b] Loss; entered in Table 112.

Sources: Austria: *Zentralrechnungsabschluss über den Staatshaushalt der im Reichsrate vertretenen Königreiche und Länder für das Jahr ...; Der österreichische Staatshaushalt in dem Jahrzehnt 1903 bis 1912* ("Österreichische Statistik", N.F. 12, Band 1. Heft, Vienna, 1915). Hungary: *Magyar Statisztikai Évkönyv* [Hungarian Statistical Yearbook], various years.

FINANCIAL POLICY 847

development during the period of the Dual Monarchy, can quickly be confirmed by an examination of Table 111. The Hungarian figures for the first two periods have been placed in brackets to indicate that they are not complete, and not strictly comparable with either the Austrian data or the later statistics for Hungary. For the period in which comparable data are available (1879–1913), the total revenues of the Austrian government as defined in the table grew slightly faster than those of Hungary (3.2 per cent annual rate versus a 2.7 per cent yearly average). 'Gross' revenues – including the gross receipts from state enterprises but excluding borrowed funds – increased at about a 3.5 per cent annual rate for Austria, compared to 3.3 per cent for Hungary, during the same interval. Over the entire period (1869–73 average compared to 1909–13 average) Austrian net revenues showed a slower rate of increase, about 2.2 per cent per annum.

The Austrian Empire had collected about 31.5 per cent of its total revenue from direct taxes in 1847,[28] and this proportion had not materially changed in the two decades preceding the signing of the Compromise. Despite the introduction of the income tax into imperial Austria in 1849, the reform of the direct taxes in Hungary in 1875 and in Austria in the 1890s, the share of direct taxes in the state revenues of both partner countries declined gradually but steadily through the Dual Monarchy period. On the other hand, the yield of indirect taxes and similar imposts (the fees and the income of state monopolies) increased both absolutely and relatively. The differences in the observed shares of these indirect revenue sources in Austria and in Hungary were largely accounted for by the vastly greater income which Austria enjoyed from the beer and sugar taxes: in the mid-1890s, for example, while the spirits and wine taxes brought in very similar sums in the two countries, beer-tax receipts in Austria were about 12 times what they were in Hungary, and sugar-tax receipts about 6 times. The beer tax alone accounted for about 8 per cent of total Austrian government revenue at this time (down from 12 per cent around 1870). The differences were reflections both of dissimilar consumption preferences and of different levels of per capita income.

During the Dual Monarchy period, unlike in the 1850s, the sale of state properties was a negligible source of revenue; indeed, both central governments of Austria–Hungary added mightily to the amount of property which they owned. The net income of state enterprises appears to have been of greater importance in Hungarian than in Austrian revenues for most periods, but since so much of outlays on railway acquisition, construction, equipping, and the like was included in 'extra-ordinary expenditure', we cannot make any meaningful comparisons in

[28] Mihály Szepessy, *Ausztria birodalmi adórendszere* [Austria's Imperial Tax System] (Pest, 1867), p. 5.

this area. Finally, if most of the unidentified 'other income' for Hungary came from indirect-tax-like sources, any differences from the Austrian revenue pattern would disappear almost completely.

Within the general similarity of patterns, however, the two governments met their growing revenue needs in somewhat different ways. Over the period in Austria, the income from state monopolies and from the stamp and documentation fees increased more rapidly than the other income here considered, so that whereas they together had supplied under 40 per cent of tax revenue (exclusive of tariffs) in 1868, they accounted for almost half in 1913. Meanwhile, consumption taxes became relatively less important as a revenue source, while the indirect imposts in total were increasing. In Hungary, however, the increase in the relative share of total revenue collected from those indirect levies grew because the share of consumption taxes trebled (from less than 9 per cent in 1868/70 to over 26 per cent in 1911/13), while that of stamp and documentation fees nearly doubled (8.6 per cent to over 15 per cent). The state monopolies, on the other hand, declined in relative importance, as their share in total revenue collections fell from more than 27 per cent to less than 21 per cent.[29]

Both Austria and Hungary were involved throughout nearly the entire Dual Monarchy epoch in a protracted process of 'tax reform'. The indirect taxes underwent considerable modification in both countries throughout the 1880s. One of the most important of these modifications was a great increase in the tax on alcoholic spirits (the 'brandy tax'): in Austria its revenue tripled from 8.7 million florins in 1887 to 29.2 million in 1889; in Hungary the increase in the spirits tax served as the very cornerstone of Premier Kálmán Tisza's three-year plan (introduced 1887) to bring balance to the Hungarian budget. Changing the sugar tax from a tax on input (beets) to output (sugar produced) proved a particular boon to the Hungarian sugar industry, which processed beets of lower sugar content than did the Bohemian mills. Along with a boom in production came, of course, a flood of revenue: the Hungarian government's income from this source multiplied tenfold by 1913, compared to the levels of the middle 1880s. At the same time, the absolutely much larger Austrian sugar-tax revenues became relatively less important. The third principal change in the indirect taxes, the introduction of the petroleum tax in 1882, has already been mentioned.

[29] Alois Gratz, 'Die österreichische Finanzpolitik von 1848–1948', in Hans Meyer (ed.), *Hundert Jahre österreichischer Wirtschaftspolitik, 1848–1948* (Vienna, 1949), p. 228; László Katus, 'A tőkés gazdaság és a gazdasági növekedés megalapozása' [The Capitalist Economy and the Basis of Economic Growth], in *Magyarország Története* [History of Hungary], vol. VI, ch. 3 (Budapest, forthcoming); László Katus, 'Magyarország gazdasági fejlödése, 1890–1914' [The Economic Development of Hungary, 1890–1914], in *ibid.*, vol. VII, ch. 4.

The reforms of the 1880s meant more to Hungary than to Austria, as the following figures clearly demonstrate:

Revenues from consumption taxes (1887 = 100)

Year	Austria	Hungary
1889	114	127
1890	121	138
1891	120	147
1892	129	159
1893	133	188

Hungarian revenues from the consumption taxes, having been only 45 per cent of Austrian revenues in 1887, reached 63 per cent in 1893, and amounted to fully 80 per cent of the Austrian total in 1913. We may note additionally that after 1888, the rebate of consumption taxes on exports was paid from consumption tax revenue, rather than from tariff revenue. Since 80 per cent or more of these rebates went to Austrian producers, but common expenditures not covered by tariff revenue were shared roughly 70:30 between Austria and Hungary, this change in the source of rebates was to Hungary's advantage. Finally, the 1899 renewal of the economic compromise contained a provision, long sought by the Hungarians because in their favour, that consumption taxes, collected at point of production, would henceforth flow into the Treasury of the country in which the items were consumed.

The direct taxes, which had already assumed their essential form in the 1820s, continued nearly unchanged – except for the introduction of the income tax in 1849 – until the 'reforms' which began in 1896. These reforms, still incomplete when the war broke out, were designed to reduce the taxes on real property and to compensate for this reduction by increasing the income tax. The earnings tax already discriminated very strongly against limited corporations (with rates two to four times as high as those for unincorporated businesses); this discrimination was further intensified in the tax reform by the addition of a transitional surcharge on the earnings tax for joint-stock companies. In all, the 1896 reform in Austria had been labelled 'a signal triumph for the agrarian interests' and a manifestation of 'the prevailing bitterness against large-scale enterprise'.[30]

As a result both of the reforms and of growing incomes, income-tax receipts in Austria increased from about 35 million crowns (roughly £1.25 million) in 1898 to 101 million (about £4.2 million) in 1913, but even the latter figure represented less than 5 per cent of total ordinary

[30] John V. Van Sickle, *Direct Taxation in Austria*, Harvard Economic Studies, vol. XXXV (Cambridge, Mass., 1931), pp. 28, 34.

Table 112. *Distribution of central government expenditure (per cent of total ordinary expenditure)*

Five-year average	Common affairs		Home defence corps		Debt service		Parliament		Internal governments; subsidies		Net loss on state enterprises		Pensions		Other		Total A÷H per cent
	Austria	Hungary	Austria	Hungary	Austria	Hungary	Austria	Hungary	Austria	Hungary	Austria	Hungary	Austria	Hungary	Austria	Hungary	
1869–73[a]	27.5	[16.4]	2.6	[2.8]	36.5	[29.1]	0.2	[0.6]	27.7	[45.3]	[b]	[b]	4.5	[1.2]	1.0	[4.6]	[128]
1874–78	28.9	[18.6]	2.7	[2.7]	33.0	[33.9]	0.4	[0.5]	30.5	[38.9]	0.1	[b]	4.1	[1.4]	0.2	[3.9]	[135]
1879–83	27.4	15.8	2.6	2.5	36.4	49.4	0.5	0.5	27.6	18.9	1.3	[b]	4.3	1.5	—	11.5	123
1884–88	25.5	15.0	3.4	3.1	36.7	46.1	0.3	0.4	25.7	21.2	3.6	[b]	4.7	1.8	—	12.4	121
1889–93	20.4	11.8	4.8	5.1	41.9	46.0	0.3	0.5	27.4	24.4	[b]	[b]	5.0	2.3	0.3	9.9	118
1894–98	19.6	10.5	5.3	5.1	40.9	40.7	0.3	0.5	28.7	27.5	[b]	[b]	5.2	2.2	—	13.4	110
1899–1903	17.2	11.9	5.9	5.1	36.4	36.7[c]	0.3	0.5	34.2	34.1	[b]	[b]	6.0	2.5	—	9.3	120
1904–08	17.4	12.2	6.3	4.6	33.8	31.5	0.3	0.4	35.5	46.0	[b]	[b]	6.7	2.8	—	2.5	118
1909–13	19.7	14.3	7.5	5.9	32.5	26.0[c]	0.3	0.3	32.7	41.0	[b]	[b]	7.2	2.8	—	9.6	119

Notes:
[a] 1871–3 for Hungary.
[b] Net income; entered in Table 111.
[c] Four-year average.
— = Less than 0.05%.
Sources: See Table 111.

revenue for the Austrian government. The Hungarian income tax, despite its nominally wider range and somewhat more progressive structure, was an even less important revenue source than its Austrian counterpart. A further reform to add both more 'bite' and more progressivity to the Hungarian income tax was introduced in 1909, but implementation was postponed, and then the war intervened.

While the sums collected from the direct taxes increased steadily, the indirect forms of extracting revenue from the public gained in relative importance as the period progressed. Given the structure of the increase, it is likely that both countries' taxation systems became more regressive in the process. This would seem to be particularly true for Hungary: total revenue from the consumption excises expanded to more than 11 times its initial level and the stamps and fees income more than sextupled (this latter is probably an index of increased bureaucratization as well). Income from direct tax collections, on the other hand, grew at a slower-than-average rate, so that these revenues reached only $2\frac{2}{3}$ times their 1868–70 levels by 1911–13, whereas the total non-tariff, non-enterprise revenue expanded to $3\frac{2}{3}$ times its initial level over the same period. Since customs revenues nearly sextupled, that is, increased more rapidly than total internal tax collections in either Austria or Hungary, we can conclude that the consumers of the Habsburg Empire were in this fashion yet further burdened by the weight of indirect taxation.

While the structure of revenues for Austria and Hungary appeared very similar, more divergence can be noted in their patterns of expenditure (see Table 112. As in Table 111, the Hungarian figures for the first two periods are bracketed to indicate that they are incomplete and not comparable with the Austrian data or the later Hungarian data.). Because the quota ratio (63.6:36.4 in the 1907 agreement) was much larger than the ratio of the two governments' expenditures, common affairs account for a significantly larger share of Austrian than of Hungarian outlays. Relatively small, and essentially similar, shares of total expenditure were devoted to the home defence corps and the parliaments of the two states; and while pensions absorbed a considerably larger share of the Austrian budget, they were growing more rapidly as a proportion of Hungarian government outlays. It is in the two largest expenditure categories, debt service and the cost of internal government, where the principal differences emerge.

Servicing her accumulated debt took nearly half of Hungary's budget in the early 1880s, and it still claimed over 40 per cent in the late nineties. The reduction in this share which began in the 1890s continued until only a little over one-quarter of the total budget had to be set aside for debt service by the end of the period. While over the same time span Table 111 reveals some slight reduction in the proportion of debt service in the Austrian budget, the change is not nearly so dramatic, and the debt service component is virtually the same size relative to the total budget as it was in the late 1870s. The explanation for these dissimilar trends is to be found primarily in the Hungarian government's greater involvement in infrastructure investment, in the different timing of railway nationalization in the two countries, and in the phasing of capital flow between Austria and Hungary. Each of these will be treated in some detail in sections v and vi.

The costs of internal government include the outlays of the various ministries of the two states (except that the railway department, elevated to ministry status in Austria in 1890, is included with state enterprises) and such subsidies (other than to state-owned enterprises) as were specifically reported in the accounting summaries. Once the critical first needs had been met, and Hungarian finances had achieved a certain order, the activities of the government in this 'internal' sphere quickly began to grow. While the counterpart share in the Austrian government's outlays grew as well, the more rapid increase in this category of expenditure for Hungary is explained mainly by the faster growth of the interior and finance ministries in Hungary, and the even more rapid increase in expenditure on education (from less than 3 per cent of the budget in the late 1880s and early 1890s, to just over 9 per cent by 1913). The 'other expenditures', substantial in most periods for Hungary, are not further identified, but there is some likelihood that they might fall under the 'internal government and subsidies' rubric, further sharpening the contrast between the Hungarian and Austrian patterns.

Using the same periods of comparison as earlier for revenues, we find that net ordinary expenditure of the Hungarian government increased at an average annual rate slightly in excess of 2.7 per cent, while in Austria the growth rate was just over 2.6 per cent (2.1 per cent 1869/73–1909/13). In gross terms, that is including the gross outlays reported for all state enterprises, the rates of increase for Austria and Hungary in the 1881/3–1911/13 period were 3.2 per cent and 3.7 per cent, respectively.

The simple comparison of revenue and expenditure growth of the two central governments can be very misleading, however, since the importance of the Austrian provinces (Länder), for which there was no counterpart at all in Hungary, increased very sharply. The expenditures of Austrian provincial governments were a trivial fraction of total government outlays at the beginning of the Dual Monarchy (1.25 million florins in total in 1870, only a little more than £100,000), but they had grown to quite significant size by the end (196 million crowns in 1910, well over £8 million, and therefore of the order of 13 per cent of the 1909–13 average net outlays of the Austrian government used in the calculations for Table 111).[31] The absence of any studies of the expenditures of the provincial governments changes analysis to speculation, but we can presume that by far the overwhelming share of their outlays would have occurred in the areas covered under 'internal government and subsidies'. Were we able to include the provincial with the central government totals for Austria, the likely effect would be to increase the share of 'internal government', and to reduce all others (except perhaps debt service), thus producing a pattern more similar to the Hungarian than appears from the comparison of the two national governments' budgets alone. Since the provincial governments' revenues came largely from surtaxes on both direct and indirect taxes, and since the 1896 tax reform increasingly turned over the real estate taxes to the jurisdiction of the provinces, including these totals on the revenue side would in all probability make little or no difference in the relative shares of revenue discussed above.

Combining expenditures and revenues, we find that there are some variations in the sequence of deficits and surpluses on ordinary account for the two governments. Austria's financial recovery from the war with Prussia was remarkably rapid, buoyed by the 'wonder harvests' and good agricultural prices of 1867 and 1868 and by the business boom (the so-called *Gründerzeit* or *Gründerboom*) based mainly on railways and banking investments during 1867–73. The Austrian state budget showed either a balance or a small surplus in each of the eight years 1868–75. The Hungarians, on the other hand, suffered from a number of very serious initial difficulties. Aside from the empty treasury and personnel problems already mentioned, the inflow of tax money dwindled markedly: voluntary taxpaying had not been part of the public ethos – indeed, refusal to remit taxes had been a part of the campaign of passive resistance to Austrian rule – and receipts from direct taxes nearly dried up during the first few weeks of the new 'independence'. The 1868 budget nevertheless appears to have showed a slight surplus, but deficits appeared in the next year and grew, and soon the government found its borrowing power to be strained. By 1873–4, it was able to obtain credit only on a relatively short-term basis (five years' repayment period), and only by offering state property as collateral.

The year 1873 marked a turning point in Austrian government finance. The surpluses of the early years disappeared, and the precarious balance achieved in each of the years 1873–5 was followed by significant deficits. These deficits persisted and averaged just under 7 per cent of outlays from 1876 to 1888 (the 1878 deficit exceeded 19 per cent), with a

[31] Data taken from Josef Wysocki, 'Die österreichische Finanzpolitik', in Adam Wandruszka and Peter Urbanitsch (eds.), *Die Habsburgermonarchie, 1848–1918*, vol. 1: *Die wirtschaftliche Entwicklung* (Vienna, 1973), p. 74.

tiny surplus in only one year, 1886. After recording the largest deficit since 1878 in 1888, the Austrian government managed to achieve a budget surplus in every year but one between 1889 and 1908. Three of the last five years then produced deficits.[32]

During the same time, the Hungarian budget was in deficit through 1881, then in surplus from 1882 through 1900, except for a deficit in 1884 and a balance in 1885. Every year from 1901 to 1913 showed a deficit except 1906. It is therefore during the first and last years of the Dual Monarchy that the variations in budget patterns primarily occurred.

While the difficulties of financing her deficits weighed heavily on Hungary during the early years of the Dual Monarchy, her problem was rather paradoxically eased by the consequences of the Crash of 1873. The excesses of the pre-1873 boom in Austria produced both a public and an official reaction; the former manifested itself in a general reluctance to invest in private bonds and shares, the latter in legislation more strictly regulating and circumscribing such investment. A large pool of savings sought other, safer outlets, and Hungarian government securities appealed to an increasing number of Austrian investors.

The flow of Austrian savings into Hungarian government debt had reached significant size already by the end of the 1870s, and became a veritable flood in the 1880s: by 1878 more than one-seventh of all outstanding Hungarian government securities were held by Austrians, and in 1893 in excess of three-fifths. Austrian capital allowed the Hungarian government to proceed with its infrastructure programme, and especially with the great push to nationalize the railways in the 1880s, without having to resort to crushing taxation. This had favourable implications for the development of Hungary's industrial sector, just as the withdrawal of Austrian funds which began in 1894 was perhaps the principal underlying factor in the relatively slow growth of Hungarian industry between 1896 and 1907.[33]

Capital-market conditions turned increasingly favourable for both governments as the 1880s progressed. As a result it became feasible to

---

[32] It would be preferable, of course, to include all income and outlays, ordinary and extraordinary, and thus to examine the overall deficit or surplus in government operations. Josef Wysocki, in his *Infrastruktur und wachsende Staatsausgaben: Das Fallbeispiel Österreich, 1868–1913* (Stuttgart, 1975), presents a table (Table 40, p. 136) which appears to provide these more ideal data. Unfortunately, the deficit or surplus shown in his table is – except for two years – exactly equal to that reported for ordinary income and expenditure in the *Zentralrechnungsabschluss* up to 1899. For the rest of the years until 1913 it differs markedly, but since it agrees neither with the 'ordinary' budget result, nor with the results including extraordinary expenditure available from the official accounts for the years 1903–12 (*Der österreichische Staatshaushalt in dem Jahrzehnt 1930–1912*), it cannot be used. Making a comparison based on all government income and outlays must thus await further research.

[33] See John Komlos, 'The Habsburg Monarchy as a Customs Union: Economic Development in Austria–Hungary in the 19th Century' (unpublished Ph.D. dissertation, University of Chicago, 1977), especially pp. 150–5.

think of implementing article XII of the 'Tariff and Trade Agreement' – the so-called economic compromise – which bound the two partners to set up a commission to recommend measures by which specie payment could be reinstituted. Nominally on a silver standard, but with specie payment having been suspended since well before the formation of the Dual Monarchy, Austria–Hungary faced the prospect of conforming to the now-general (for Europe at least) gold standard. This was clearly recognized when the two finance ministers met in 1889 to start the process in motion, and shortly thereafter two commissions of experts began their deliberations separately in Vienna and Budapest.

The principal debate concerned the value of the new currency, and the limits of discussion ranged between 2.0 and 2.5 gold francs per florin. A Hungarian compromise pegging the new florin at its average market value over the 1879–91 period was finally accepted. This put the florin at 2.1 francs, very close to the current exchange value, and therefore a most fortunate choice. The official transition to the gold standard in 1892 included a monetary reform which introduced a new basic unit, the crown (2 crowns = 1 florin), which was to circulate alongside the florin until the crown became sole legal tender on 1 January 1900. The cost of exchanging the old coins and of minting new coins was shared by Austria and Hungary in the 70:30 quota ratio, as was the cost of retiring the old common debt of some 312 million florins.

Austria–Hungary, in fact, never went fully onto the gold standard. Specie payments were not resumed: the Austro-Hungarian Bank was ordered to buy gold, but it was not obligated to sell. The time of conversion was so propitious, however, that the requirement to buy kept the new currency from *appreciating* against gold.[34]

Not only the abundance of loanable funds in the capital market eased the transition to gold; the completely fortuitous monetary events in the USA played a major part as well. With the Americans selling gold to promote their silver interests, the bank consortium responsible for acquiring reserves for Austria–Hungary stepped in to take advantage of this policy, so that in one three-month period of 1892 alone, 40 million florins in gold bars and coins flowed into the Austro-Hungarian Bank, mostly from the USA. The Bank, charged with holding the foreign exchange rate within a band of 1.5 per cent, pursued its policy by dealing in foreign bills rather than in gold, thereby earning interest on part of its reserve. All in all, the transition was made so smoothly as hardly to cause a ripple in the international money market.

---

[34] Ludwig von Mises, 'The Foreign Exchange Policy of the Austro-Hungarian Bank', *Economic Journal*, vol. XIX, no. 2 (June 1909), p. 201. According to von Mises, the Austro-Hungarian Bank had more reserves of gold at the end of 1908 than any other central bank save the Bank of France and the Russian State Bank (p. 202).

Even prior to the quasi-adoption of the gold standard, the Austro-Hungarian florin had enjoyed quite stable and orderly foreign exchange value, contrary to the claims of the contemporary financial press in Vienna. During the 1879–91 period from which the average of the gold price of the florin was chosen, despite being *de facto* on a strictly paper standard and in the absence of any official efforts at stabilizing intervention, the florin fluctuated only slightly against sterling.[35]

The stability of the Austro-Hungarian currency could be traced directly to the establishment of the Dual Monarchy system. The very first economic compromise imposed a much-needed discipline on the monetary system of the Habsburg Empire: the Austrian National Bank remained the sole bank of issue for the new Austria–Hungary, but the amount that either country could borrow from it was strictly limited, and could not be changed without the assent of both parliaments. Because so severely circumscribed, the traditional all-purpose panacea for financial ills, money creation, was effectively closed off. Both governments were free to issue their own debt, but they were forced to borrow from the public, and could not turn willy-nilly to the Bank. The soundness of the common currency was a particular advantage for Hungary, who came to depend heavily on foreign capital both for government finance and for industrial investment. Austria, too, was a capital importer, but towards the end of the period about 80 per cent of the capital inflows were re-exported, primarily to Hungary. The importance of these capital flows is more thoroughly discussed in the concluding section of this chapter.

Capital flows into (and occasionally out of) Austria–Hungary were a primary determinant of changes in the money supply, the more so because the growth of the monetary stock of the Habsburg lands was almost entirely 'organic': the Austro-Hungarian Bank did not engage in the modern sort of purposeful manipulation of bank reserves, and the law specified strict limits to its note issue and its lendings to the two central governments. Changes in the money supply therefore depended closely on private economic decisions and movements in the balance of payments.

Because the frenetic boom of the first years of the Dual Monarchy ended in the spectacular Crash of 1873, with large inflows and then outflows of foreign funds augmenting domestic expansion and contraction, the money supply also increased rapidly, and then declined. It peaked in 1872 at a figure approximately 88 per cent above its 1867 position, implying an average growth rate in excess of 12.6 per cent per

[35] Leland B. Yeager, 'Fluctuating Exchange Rates in the Nineteenth Century: The Experiences of Austria and Russia', in Robert A. Mundell and Alexander K. Swoboda (eds.), *Monetary Problems of the International Economy* (Chicago and London, 1969), especially p. 67.

annum.[36] Only in 1881 did the Austro-Hungarian money supply surpass its 1872 level, but already from about 1875 an orderly growth had begun, showing remarkably little year-to-year fluctuation. The rate of growth averaged slightly above 5 per cent per annum (5.3 per cent 1879–1913) during this time, which can conveniently be divided into three subperiods. Over the interval from which the exchange value of the florin was chosen for the new monetary reform (1879–91), annual growth of the money stock averaged 5.0 per cent; the tempo then slowed after the reform to 4.3 per cent per annum, 1892–1902. An acceleration of the pace to a 6.6 per cent annual average for the years 1903–13 brought the overall post-reform rate of increase of the money supply (5.4 per cent per annum, 1892–1913) remarkably close to that of the pre-reform period.[37]

Although Austria–Hungary simultaneously 'reformed' her currency and adopted the gold standard *de jure* if not completely *de facto*, the smoothness and ease of this double transition were testimony not only to the skill of those who carried it out, but also to the fundamental soundness of the currency to begin with. In the 1879–91 period, prices generally were falling, as they were also in Austria–Hungary, yet the Dual Monarchy was able to combine an increase of more than 80 per cent in the stock of money over only a dozen years with a remarkably stable foreign exchange rate. When the changeover to the gold standard began, the failure to resume specie payments was of no real consequence for a currency that threatened to appreciate against gold.

Particularly after 1873 we will look in vain – whether in the fiscal or in the monetary arena – for spectacular, or even striking, developments. Indeed, the really remarkable feature of government finance during the Dual Monarchy was its pervasive normality – a sharp and welcome contrast to the recurrent chaos of the decades preceding the Compromise of 1867. The major reason for this normality, of course, was Austria–Hungary's successful avoidance of involvement in shooting wars. Although military preparations briefly caused the budget to bulge, as during the 'annexation crisis' in 1908 over the occupation of Bosnia-Herzegovina, or the build-up of the last two or three years before the First World War, deficits normally resulted from more productive

---

[36] These and the immediately subsequent estimates are based on unpublished data for currency plus private bank deposits, very closely approximating the modern 'M$_2$' definition of the money supply, kindly put at my disposal by Professor John Komlos.

[37] Lacking any price index for Austria–Hungary, we cannot reach any conclusion about the increase for the 'real' money supply. David Good's preliminary cost-of-living index for Austria (*Journal of European Economic History*, vol. v, no. 2 (Autumn 1976)) probably overstates both the upswings and downswings of the 'true' price level because of the overwhelming weight of food items in the index; if we use his index to deflate the nominal money supply data, we would derive speculative rates of growth of the real purchasing power of the money stock of 5.8, 4.4, and 4.0 per cent respectively during the three subperiods cited above.

outlays. Both governments borrowed quite heavily, but both were forced to adapt the needs of the state to the public's willingness to finance those needs. For most of the half-century of the Dual Monarchy's existence, capital-market conditions at home and in the rest of Europe were favourable, and domestic and foreign savers were prepared to absorb the debt. Neither government faced many serious disruptions to its financial plans.

IV. *Agricultural policy*

When the Austro-Hungarian Dual Monarchy officially came into existence on 1 January 1868, economic conditions were unusually auspicious. A railway and banking boom – the previously mentioned *Gründerzeit* – which had begun in 1867 was reinforced by unprecedented prosperity in the agricultural sector as a result of the 'wonder harvests' of 1867 and 1868. At the same time, crops in much of the rest of Europe were poor, so this vast output of grain found a ready export market at good prices. These years were so exceptional, in fact, that the monarchy never again experienced two successive years in which the quantity of grain exports attained the levels of 1867 and 1868.

Because of the policies and events of the previous decades, both Austria and Hungary were in a good position to take advantage of the opportunities to profit from the favourable developments of the late 1860s. From at least the reigns of Maria Theresa (1740–80) and her son Joseph II (1780–90), the Habsburg Empire had pursued a clear-cut programme of regional specialization in production. The direct pressure of this deliberate policy, and of the market forces which it and other phenomena – notably population growth – created, caused the growing industrial sector to concentrate in Austria, while Hungary increasingly became the granary of the Empire. Although political motives perhaps formed the fundament of this programme, a recognition of natural endowments of productive resources clearly shaped its broad economic outlines. As a result, the liberal reforms following 1849 neither reversed nor arrested the trends already set in motion under a mercantilist system. Indeed, available evidence tends to confirm the view that specialization intensified during the era of liberal economic policy preceding the establishment of the Dual Monarchy.[38]

[38] The following table clearly indicates increasing specialization in grain production (growth rates in per cent per annum):

Period	Production			Production per capita		
	Austria	Hungary	Monarchy	Austria	Hungary	Monarchy
1789–1841	0.55	1.2	0.93	−0.1	0.7	0.3
1850–1868/70	0.40	1.4	0.90	−0.4	0.6	0.1

Source: John Komlos, 'The Habsburg Monarchy', p. 88.

The conventional interpretation of the results of the agrarian reforms of 1848–9 in both Austria and Hungary regards the freeing of the peasants as the catalyst that permitted the pent-up forces contained in earlier trends to erupt into a grain boom in Hungary in the 1850s. Recent research casts considerable doubt on this long-accepted thesis. Following more than a half-century of steady growth in grain output, and an expansion of grain exports in the 1840s at a rate exceeding 5 per cent per annum, the 1850s now appear to have been more a time of relative stagnation than of acceleration in grain production. Indeed, there was even famine in the northern counties in 1852, and only in 1858–9 did grain exports from Hungary once again reach the levels already attained in the 1840s.[39]

Under this new interpretation, the 1860s emerge as a really remarkable period in the growth of Hungarian grain exports. The fabulous harvests of 1861 and 1862 followed immediately upon a near-tripling of the length of track in service in Hungary by the railway construction boom of 1857–61. Lines were extended farther into the fertile grain-growing regions of the east, south-east, and south, providing larger areas with easier access to markets. Exports of grain grew at twice or more the rate of growth of agricultural exports in general. A subsequent decline in grain exports in the mid-1860s was only short-lived, as both the harvest and foreign shipments reached record levels beginning in 1867.

We see therefore that agriculture had, even before the agrarian reforms, expanded and specialized, and that this process was still continuing when the era of Dualism began. The serfs had been emancipated, the Hungarian nobility stripped of its tax-exempt status, internal free trade established for the entire monarchy (except for the retention of traditional rights to levy grain duties in the Tyrol and Dalmatia), and the main agricultural regions provided with transport connections to the principal internal and external markets. Thus all the principal policy steps determining the subsequent agricultural development had already been taken, save one: the only major change in policy to occur during the Dual Monarchy and which significantly affected agriculture was the return to protectionism after the brief liberal interlude which had begun at mid-century.

Ivan Berend and György Ránki, in their *Economic Development in East-Central Europe in the 19th and 20th Centuries* (New York and London, 1974), tell us that 'according to some estimates, agricultural production in the Austrian provinces increased by approximately 70 per cent between 1789 and 1847' (p. 31). This would imply a growth rate of 0.9% per annum. They do not cite the source of their statement, and the recent estimates by Roman Sandgruber for Austria, in his 'Die Agrarrevolution in Österreich: Ertragssteigerung und Kommerzialisierung der landwirtschaftlichen Produktion im 18. und 19. Jahrhundert', in Alfred Hoffman (ed.), *Österreich-Ungarn also Agrarstaat*, Sozial- und wirtschaftshistorische Studien, vol. x (Vienna, 1978) imply growth rates of grain production of 0.63 and 0.25 per cent per annum respectively in the two time periods. If these be closer to the 'true' rate, they only intensify the impression gained from Komlos' data.

[39] Komlos, 'The Habsburg Monarchy', pp. 93–5.

Within the confines of the monarchy after 1867, Hungary retained a comparative advantage in agricultural production; in consequence, her farm output grew more rapidly than that of Austria, especially in the early years of the dualist period (3.4 per cent per annum in the years 1868/70–1881/3, compared to a rate of 1.6 per cent in Austria; between 1881/3 and 1911/13, Hungary's rate dropped to 1.6 per cent, and Austria's to 1.2 per cent.[40]) These overall figures conceal, however, a vast diversity in conditions, techniques, and organization of agriculture in the two countries. The differences were particularly extreme in Austria, where the agricultural population ranged from 20 per cent of the total in Lower Austria (the region around Vienna) to more than 83 per cent in Dalmatia, according to the census of 1900.

The Austro-Hungarian monarchy could be divided roughly into four zones according to the predominant form of agricultural organization and technique used. The northern area comprising the Czech crownlands (Bohemia, Moravia, Silesia) was characterized by a highly developed, relatively capital-intensive agriculture in which large estates predominated, whereas the eastern areas of large estates (Hungary, Galicia, Bukovina) were technically less advanced and much more dependent on extensive grain cultivation. The west and the south were the main regions of peasant farming, but while Alpine Austria (Upper and Lower Austria, Tyrol, Salzburg, Vorarlberg, Carinthia, and Styria) featured highly developed dairying and other 'intensive' forms of agriculture, the south Slav areas (Slovenia, Dalmatia, and the 'Coastal Provinces') adhered to much more traditional methods of farming and institutions of land tenure. In this last region the *Zadruga*, a communal form based on the extended family, still held sway.[41]

Within each of the four zones, there was also great variety; when conditions of agriculture were so varied, a uniform approach to its problems was essentially impossible. In any case, agricultural policy never enjoyed first priority in Austria, and her policy was characterised by the same sort of *ad hoc*, non-systematic measures so common in other areas of government concern. Overall, large estates (properties in excess of 500 ha) accounted for as large a share of total land in Austria as they did in Hungary, and their owners were a mighty political force, even if their power did not approach the near-total domination by the landed interests in Hungary. While they often differed sharply on political issues, the

---

[40] Komlos, 'The Habsburg Monarchy', p. 88. Komlos uses Sandgruber's index to calculate the Austrian rates.

[41] This typology is taken from Tibor Kolossa, 'Beiträge zur Verteilung und Zusammensetzung des Agrarproletäriats in der österreichisch-ungarischen Monarchie', in V. Sándor and P. Hanák (eds.), *Studien zur Geschichte der österreichisch-ungarischen Monarchie*, (Budapest, 1961).

great landlords in both halves of the monarchy usually formed a united front in the defence of the economic position and privileges of large estates. Given these conditions, it is hardly surprising that the two governments' policies served primarily the interests of the larger landowners.

In Hungary, this tendency was particularly obvious. An 1869 government order permitted the recrudescence of entail, and the territory of entailed estates more than quintupled between 1870 and the turn of the century, from 463,000 to 2,369,000 cadastral *hold* (about 660,000 acres to nearly 3,400,000 acres). Not only did the expansion of entail shrink the area of land potentially available for subdivision and sale in smaller parcels, the Minister of Agriculture later intervened directly in the land market to stop the 'exploitation' of the peasants by middlemen who bought up debt-ridden properties for subsequent sale in smaller lots at higher prices. During the Dual Monarchy period the latifundia (taken to be estates over 10,000 *hold* – about 14,300 acres) came to possess one-fifth of Hungary, although they comprised a mere 321 properties. The share of land owned by the *latifundistas* more than doubled, chiefly at the expense of properties in the 1,000–10,000 *hold* range.[42]

The state intervened in the labour market as well: Hungarian Law XIII of 1876 regulated the conditions of domestics, agricultural servants, and day labourers, making it more difficult for such persons to leave their employment, and empowering the authorities to return them against their will to fulfil an employment contract. The government even sent in troops to put down the harvest strikes of 1897 and 1906.

One of the very few programmes to benefit primarily the peasantry was the Hungarian government's active assistance in the improvement of cattle herds. Support for cattle breeding, begun modestly in 1867 and extended in 1878 and 1880, expanded rapidly in the 1890s and led to a complete transformation in the breed composition of Hungarian herds. The native gray Hungarian stock virtually disappeared, replaced by Western roan breeds which gave both more meat and more milk. Agricultural specialization within Hungary saw grain production concentrate on the larger estate, and animal husbandry on peasant properties; it was therefore clearly the peasantry who gained most from the programme to improve cattle breeding.

Despite Austria's efforts to develop her agriculture, and Hungary's promotion of industrial expansion, the already long-established regional concentration of production predetermined concomitant national concentration of economic interests. Consequently, in matters agricultural, Hungary's wishes usually dominated in the Dual Monarchy's external

[42] See my 'The Changing Pattern of Landownership in Hungary, 1867–1914', *Economic History Review*, 2nd series, vol. XX, no. 2 (August 1967), especially p. 296.

policy, as did Austria's interests in matters industrial. We have seen in an earlier section how Germany's stance with respect to Hungarian agricultural exports was a primary, if indirect, determinant of Austria–Hungary's foreign-policy difficulties in the Balkans. As export opportunities for Hungarian agricultural products became increasingly restricted both by higher relative costs of production and by rising tariff walls around Germany and other countries, the conflict between the two partners' interests assumed larger dimensions as an internal problem as well.

Population growth and her own tariffs made the Austro-Hungarian market increasingly the nearly exclusive preserve of the Hungarian grain producers. The Dual Monarchy was transformed from a grain-surplus to a grain-deficit area, which Oscar Jászi contends was the consequence of a deliberate effort of the Hungarian estate owners to limit production in order to enjoy the full price-raising effect of the tariff.[43] The grain deficit is certainly no prima facie evidence of combination in restraint of trade, since a profit-maximizing monopoly would practise price discrimination – selling to the home market as much as it would take at the world price plus the tariff, and 'dumping' additional output elsewhere so long as the world price exceeded marginal cost of production (as the German steel cartel did, for example, in those very years). The absence of such 'dumped' exports from Hungary is very damaging to Jászi's interpretation, and is much more in line with both contemporary and historical evidence of high cost rather than of monopoly power. The Hungarian estate owners used their *political* power to provide sufficient tariffs so that they would not have to change over from the cultivation of the traditional crops. The failure to transform their agriculture may show lack of long-range foresight, but the Magyar magnates were certainly not maladept in recognizing their short-run self-interest. Thus, had they in fact acted like a vast agricultural cartel, we would have expected to find evidence of this behaviour in the external, as well as in the monarchy, market.

Agricultural policy was not a common affair, nor even a dualistic matter under the Compromise, and each country followed its own independent path. While these paths differed in detail, they ran essentially parallel, since neither country wished to alter substantially the course already charted between 1848 and 1867. Thus two primary elements comprised the agricultural policies of the two countries: a legislative 'filling in' of the areas left ambiguous or unregulated by the laws of 1848–9, and various measures to facilitate productivity-raising activities in agriculture.

---

[43] Oscar Jászi, *The Dissolution of the Habsburg Monarchy* (Chicago and London, 1929), pp. 197–200.

Austria removed the prohibition on division of peasant properties without official permission in 1868, and Hungary finally removed all restrictions on peasant land sales 10 years later. Much of the estate land in Austria remained encumbered with residual peasant rights to wood, straw, and pasturage long after the reform; although these rights were gradually extinguished by a series of legal measures, there were still about 1.5 million ha so burdened as late as 1890. The problem of consolidation of scattered plots was a vexing one in both countries, but neither ever took effective legislative steps to deal with the issue. Austria passed a law to regulate the usage of common property (which comprised about one-seventh of the total taxable acreage) in 1883; this was merely enabling legislation, and by 1896 only five provincial diets had passed implementation laws, and less than 20,000 ha had actually been either distributed or regulated under these measures. Austria re-established an independent Ministry of Agriculture in 1868; Hungary, curiously, did not take the same step until 1889. Perhaps the single most important programme of the Hungarian government in the agricultural field was the regulation of the Tisza River, which not only materially reduced the danger of periodic flooding of vast fertile areas, but also shortened the course of the river substantially and brought under cultivation thousands of hectares of previously unusable land.

Both countries engaged in measures to try to stimulate productivity growth. Investment was encouraged as estate owners, and later smallholders, received state help in obtaining credit and in founding credit societies. The first two agricultural colleges, founded in 1797 and 1818, were both on Hungarian territory (but the language of instruction was German until late in the nineteenth century); upon foundation of the College of Agriculture (*Hochschule für Bodenkultur*) in 1872, Vienna became the principal centre for agricultural education.

In the 1880s and 1890s, as the distress of low prices and high taxes strengthened the anti-liberal forces in both Austrian and Hungarian agriculture, a new political orientation emerged. The Hungarian parliament, alarmed at the speed with which the countryside was changing, passed a law in 1894 forbidding any further ploughing up of pasture. Austria, under pressure of rural agitation, inaugurated a policy of 'small steps' to assist agriculture which included not only favourable credit regulations, expansion of agricultural education, and encouragement of cooperatives, but also help with the establishment of political organizations and a promise to take account of agriculture as an integral part of the economy when making external trade policy. To implement this new policy, the budget of the Ministry of Agriculture more than doubled in the decade following 1898, and agriculture-related outlays of the other ministries increased as well. Hungarian grain farmers and Austrian

Table 113. *Grain imports into Austria–Hungary for milling traffic*
(thousands of metric tons)

Year	Total	From Russia	From Romania	From Serbia
1891	98.6	27.1	24.6	45.0
1892	139.8	6.2	70.9	55.4
1893	216.6	17.9	95.5	97.8
1894	193.0	21.5	115.5	47.6
1895	118.6	35.6	34.4	44.9
1896	122.6	12.5	18.9	89.3
1897	162.4	61.2	55.2	43.3
1898	196.3	46.2	101.8	37.7
1899	179.4	16.7	72.4	83.2
1900	(0.4)	0	0	0

Source: *Österreichisches statistisches Handbuch.*

millers united in opposition to Hungary's 'milling turnover' – duty-free import of cheap Balkan grain to be milled for export, including export to Austria – and succeeded in having this measure limited in 1896 and repealed altogether in 1900.

The abolition of the milling turnover drove yet another wedge between Austria–Hungary and her Balkan neighbours, exacerbating the difficulties described in the previous section on trade and tariff policy. The milling traffic had accounted for a substantial volume of imports (see Table 113), especially from Serbia and Romania. This milling traffic constituted a significant proportion of the monarchy's gross imports of grains – typically between one-fifth and one-third of 'general trade', that is, all imports for whatever purpose, including re-export. During the years shown in the table, the milling traffic ranged between a high of 61 per cent of 'general trade' imports of grain (1893) to a low of 14 per cent (1898). The 14 per cent was an unusually low proportion because total grain imports were abnormally large that year, as buyers quickly rebuilt inventories depleted as a result of the harvest strike of 1897.

Other than in the issue of the milling turnover, the independence of the two partners' agricultural policies did not lead to serious friction. Problems and differences within each country in agriculture overshadowed the differences between them. The really contentious issues between the partners lay outside the sphere of agricultural policy, in the areas of tariffs, the quota, railway freight rates, industrial promotion, and the military. While particularly the tariff question and the question of freight rates had strong agricultural overtones, they – and the conflicts they engendered – properly belong to the consideration of other sections of this chapter.

V. *Industrial promotion*

Fundamental differences in the economic situations of Austria and Hungary resulted in markedly contrasting positions regarding industrial promotion; basic differences in their political conditions helped to sharpen these contrasts as time passed. Conflict was inherent in the two postures, as each country saw herself bearing the major share of the cost of gains made by her partner. Four principal reasons underlay this divergence in the two countries' efforts in aid of industry:

1. Austrian industry was more highly developed and produced much more than did Hungarian industry; the structure of the two sectors also varied significantly.
2. Although both governments eschewed *laissez-faire*, their interventions in this area proceeded from fundamentally opposed basic premises. Austria aimed to preserve its large industrial sector and to expand it, if possible, via exports. Hungary, embarking on a belated programme of industrial development after the formation of the Dual Monarchy, sought to encourage development of her nascent industry chiefly on the basis of import substitution.
3. The nationality question had a much stronger direct impact on Austrian than on Hungarian industrial policies.
4. The common customs tariffs had different implications for the two economies.

Let us consider each of these issues in turn.

Tables 114–17 provide a summary of the present state of knowledge about the growth, structure, and relative size of the industry of the two partners in the Dual Monarchy.[44] As is evident immediately from Table 114, the two most detailed sets of estimates agree neither in their concept of dividing the era into subperiods, nor in their estimates of growth rates. Both within industries as well as within the time periods, major variations appear between the Komlos and Rudolph indices. Each has its own strengths and weaknesses; without further detailed research it is impossible to judge fairly the relative accuracy of the two sets of estimates. Consequently, for Tables 115–17, I have chosen to use Komlos' data because he provides far more of the detail necessary for further calculation[45] than does Rudolph.

---

[44] I have unfortunately had to omit a comparison of Katus' and Komlos' estimates for Hungarian industrial expansion, because Katus' tables do not include any of the details necessary for comparisons such as those of Table 113.

[45] Some of the detail is still lacking, however: in particular, Komlos omits his series on Austrian mining output, which would have been useful in permitting a more nearly direct comparison with Rudolph's indices.

Table 114. *Growth rates of Austrian industrial output, according to Komlos (K) and Rudolph (R)*

	Mining		Metals		Foodstuffs		Textiles		Total	
	K	R	K[a]	R	K[b]	R[c]	K	R	K	R
Rudolph's periodization										
1830–1855	n.a.	6.4	5.0	4.6	0.7	2.3	2.8	2.0	2.5[d]	2.4
1855–1890	n.a.	4.8	3.9	3.5	2.0	1.5	2.0	1.9	2.3[d]	2.1
1890–1913	n.a.	2.7	4.7	5.8	2.1	2.2	1.5	2.4	2.7[d]	3.1
1830–1913	n.a.	4.7	4.4	4.4	1.6	1.9	2.1	1.9	2.5[d]	2.5
Komlos' periodization*										
1830–1846	n.a.	6.7	4.9	4.9	0.9	1.6	3.1	3.9	2.6[d]	3.6
1846–1871	n.a.	4.5	5.6	1.6	1.1	−0.2	2.7	0.3	3.4[e]	0.0
1871–1898	n.a.	4.6	10.3	5.9	1.8	4.2	1.3	2.7	2.6[d]	4.0
1898–1912	n.a.	2.7	3.5	5.7	2.2	1.5	2.7	1.9	3.0[e]	2.7
1867–1913	n.a.	3.8	4.7	5.8	2.5	3.1	1.9	2.4	3.2[e]	3.5[f]

Notes:

*I have amalgamated some periods. Komlos measures peak to peak over a business cycle; his cycles are 1830–46, 1846–61, 1861–71, 1871–84, 1884–98, 1898–1907, 1907–12. Rudolph's index is available only at five-year intervals. For his index, the periods chosen are 1830–45, 1845–70, 1870–95, 1895–1913.

[a] Iron only.
[b] Flour and sugar.
[c] Flour, sugar, beer and spirits.
[d] Manufacturing only.
[e] Manufacturing and mining.
[f] 1870–1913.
n.a. = Not available.

Sources: John Komlos, 'The Habsburg Monarchy', pp. 161, 239–43; Richard Rudolph, 'The Pattern of Austrian Industrial Growth from the Eighteenth to the Early Twentieth Century', *Austrian History Yearbook*, XI (1975), Tables 1–3.

Hungary produced only a fraction of Austrian output, as Table 115 shows. Whether the proportion varied as much as appears in the table is problematical – the earliest figures must be regarded as more highly conjectural than the later data, especially for Hungary. At least for the Dual Monarchy period, it is also likely that the table overstates somewhat the relative size of Hungarian industry, because the coverage of the Hungarian data is probably more complete than that of the Austrian. As a result of differences in policy as well as in historical development, large-scale units (which are more easily captured in the collection of statistics) were relatively more important in Hungarian industry, and smaller units – including 'backyard industry' (*Hinterhofindustrie*) – were more characteristic of the Austrian sector. The extent of this putative bias is impossible to determine.

Table 115. *Hungarian industrial production as proportion of Austrian industrial production (per cent)*

	Manufacturing, mining and construction	Manufacturing alone
1830–34	39.5	29.3
1840–44	34.4	25.9
1850–54	28.4	20.8
1860–64	33.2	27.2
1870–74	28.1	18.2
1880–84	28.4	24.5
1890–94	29.3	29.3
1900–04	30.5	29.2
1910–13	32.7	30.9

Source: John Komlos, 'The Habsburg Monarchy', Appendix B, Table 58, pp. 239–40. All figures are value added, calculated using 1913 prices.

By comparing the relative sizes of major industrial groups within the manufacturing sector, we can gain an impression of the variations in the structure of production in the two countries. Table 116 highlights the great but declining dominance of flour milling in Hungary, and the relative unimportance of the textile industry there. By the end of the period, the Austrian flour industry was relatively no more important than Hungarian textiles, while Austrian textiles came to account for a larger share of the value added in the selection group in Austria than flour did in Hungary.[46] The similarities which emerge from the data of Table 116 are also worth noting – the rapidly and continuously increasing importance of the iron industry and the even more rapid growth, again in both countries, of the sugar industry.

The underlying principles of Habsburg government policy toward industry went through several phases. Following the active promotion, including import prohibitions and direct subsidies, engaged in by the Empress Maria Theresa and her son Joseph II, the period from the end of the Napoleonic Wars to 1848 bore the stamp of Metternich – continuation of autarky, but a distaste for innovation and progress. After 1849, as we have seen, the spirit of economic liberalism penetrated even the

[46] This is a manifestation of Hanák's view of Hungarian industry as a 'negative copy' of its Austrian counterpart. Péter Hanák, 'Hungary in the Austro-Hungarian Monarchy: Preponderancy or Dependency?', *Austrian History Yearbook*, III (1967), part I, p. 279.

Table 116. Structure of production of five major industries in Austria and Hungary (per cent of total value added in the group, calculated at 1913 prices)

Year	Iron		Cotton textiles		Woollen textiles		Sugar		Flour	
	Austria	Hungary	Austria	Hungary	Austria	Hungary	Austria	Hungary	Austria	Hungary
1846	9.9	6.0	27.0	4.0	38.6	—	0.6	0.8	23.8	89.9
1867	10.4	17.2	30.8	6.4	37.4	—	1.3	0.7	16.5	77.9
1883	22.0	22.3	37.7	1.6	22.0	—	4.4	2.6	13.9	63.4
1896	29.5	32.2	34.6	9.7	19.5	—	4.3	3.9	12.0	54.1
1913	36.1	38.7	33.0	10.9	14.4	0.9	5.6	8.7	10.9	32.8

Note:
— = Not given in the source.
Source: John Komlos, 'The Habsburg Monarchy', Appendix B, Tables 59 and 60, pp. 242–5.

Table 117. *Comparative growth rates of Austrian and Hungarian manufacturing*

Cycle	Dates	Rate A	Rate H
1	1830–46 Austria 1830–47 Hungary	2.6	1.3
2	1846–61 Austria 1847–64 Hungary	2.6	2.2
3	1861–71 Austria 1864–74 Hungary	3.2	1.4
4	1871–84 Austria 1874–83 Hungary	1.8	5.5
5	1884–98 Austria 1883–96 Hungary	2.2	3.4
6	1898–1907 Austria 1896–1906 Hungary	3.9	2.2
7	1907–12 Austria 1906–12 Hungary	1.7	5.9
	1867–1913	2.8	3.2

Source: John Komlos, 'The Habsburg Monarchy', pp. 160–2.

Austrian Empire, but during the great depression following the Crash of 1873 a return to state intervention, guidance, and protection became ever more evident.

Hungary, after regaining internal autonomy with the Compromise, at first concentrated strongly on infrastructure – in particular on railways, canals, and the massive Tisza River regulation project. Only in 1881 did Hungary begin to enact legislation for the direct promotion of industry. Since Hungary's industrial promotion was based primarily on import substitution in the home market, it came into direct conflict with the interest of Austrian manufacturers, who found their greatest export market in Hungary.

The nationality question impinged on Austrian policy more than on Hungarian efforts. Because of the historical geographic concentrations of industry, and the growing assertiveness of the various nationality groups, Austrian aid to a particular industry was always closely identified – even if falsely – with concession to a given ethnic group. Austrian economic policy exhibited a generally much more *ad hoc* character than that of Hungary; the constant necessity to balance regional and national interests when making policy intensified that tendency. For a time, the Reichsrat lost all real control of government policy, when the Czech 'obstruction' over language rights completely paralysed the legislative process. As a result, from 1898 to the end of 1904, Franz Joseph and his ministers virtually ruled by decree, invoking the 'section 14' provisions which allowed the Emperor to give orders with the force of law if the Reichsrat was not in session. The 'obstruction' made it impossible for the Reichsrat to exercise its veto power over these orders.

The tariff structure also led Austria and Hungary to follow non-parallel paths in industrial promotion. Put crudely, Austria had the industry, and industry had the tariff. Hungary could not erect its own separate tariff wall[47] and therefore sought other means to reduce Austrian competition against budding Hungarian manufacturers. Moreover, tariffs protect vested interests, and the politically dominant Austrian manufacturers and Hungarian landlords seldom allowed their respective minority interests – Austrian agriculture and Hungarian industry – any effective influence in tariff negotiations.

Lacking the weapon of an independent tariff, Hungary sought to provide substitute measures of aid, and even became somewhat of a pioneer in devising and implementing non-tariff measures of industrial promotion. Despite the considerable public attention paid to the Hungarian programme in both halves of the monarchy, the direct expenditures of the Hungarian government to promote industry were modest, even trifling. During the first 13 years of the Dual Monarchy, direct support for cottage and small industry (there was as yet no programme to aid factory industry) averaged a mere 32,000 crowns (slightly over £1,300) annually. Laws for the promotion of factory industry were passed in 1881, 1890, 1899, and 1907. The annual average outlays, including direct subsidies, under these laws were respectively 126,000 crowns (just over £5,200); 487,000 crowns (about £20,000); 2,300,000 crowns (approximately £96,000); and 6,800,000 crowns (about £283,000; data are for the years 1907-14).[48] Roughly 10 per cent of the new factories founded from the turn of the century to the outbreak of the First World War received state subsidies. The 47 million crowns (somewhat under £2 million) of subsidies paid out 1900-14 could account, by the most recent modern estimates, for only 5.9 per cent of the total investment that flowed into joint-stock industrial companies alone during those years.[49]

47 In the 1907 economic compromise, Hungary traded an increase in her quota ratio for the *right* to an independent customs territory. She never exercised that right.
48 László Katus, 'Magyarország gazdasági fejlődése (1890-1914)' [Economic Development of Hungary (1890-1914)], in Péter Hanák (ed.), *Magyarország Története*, vol. VII (Budapest, 1978), p. 347.
49 Iván Berend and Miklós Szuhay, *A tőkés gazdaság története Magyarországon 1848-1944* [The History of the Capitalist Economy in Hungary 1848-1944] (Budapest, 1973), p. 96.

Austrian fears of the success of the Hungarian industrial promotion programme, if based solely on the effects of such relatively insignificant direct expenditures as summarized above, would surely have been grossly exaggerated. Indeed, quantitative evidence of success is difficult to find. Of 843 enterprises other than agricultural distilleries (of which there were 627) to receive concessions under the various laws between 1881 and 1912, 158 – nearly 19 per cent – had suspended operations by the end of 1912.[50] The rates of growth of output in Table 116 do not correlate at all with the passage of the laws to promote industry; they depend, as a subsequent section points out, more strongly on international capital flows than they do on government expenditures in aid of industry.

Indirect help to industry, though impossible to quantify, was seen from both halves of the monarchy to have been much more important than direct assistance or subsidy. The various promotion acts provided a multiplicity of these indirect favours: tax and fee holidays (typically for 15 years), provision of materials and supplies to building sites at cost, subsidized supplies of industrial salt from the state monopoly, cheap loans, tariff concessions on imports of certain vital machinery, and the like. The most important indirect aid was likely the Hungarian government's 'buy at home' policy regarding public contracts. Government purchases of industrial products amounted to about 33 million crowns in 1887 and had grown to about 204 million by 1907 (so about £1.4 million to £10 million).[51] Contemporary industrialists clearly recognized the importance of government purchases in Hungary, reporting that 'in no country of Western Europe do government purchases, in proportion to the quantity of industrial production, assume so much significance as here'.[52]

It has been claimed, however, that Hungarian industry did not take full advantage of government purchases, because it often lacked the productive capacity to fulfil its share of orders from the common army, which was supposed to buy from the two countries according to their quota ratio.[53] Even before the 1907 act had had much time to take effect, Hungarian industry in fact appeared to be able quickly to meet very large increases in military orders. The crisis over annexation of Bosnia-Herzegovina caused military expenditures to rise quickly: compared to

---

[50] Josef Szterényi, 'Die ungarische Industriepolitik', *Zeitschrift für Volkswirtschaft, Sozialpolitik, und Verwaltung* (1913), p. 24.

[51] Hungary. Kereskedelmi m. kir. Miniszterium [Royal Hungarian Ministry of Commerce], *Emlékirat a hazai kis- és gyáripar fejlesztéséről* [Memorandum Concerning the Promotion of Domestic Small and Factory Industry] (Budapest, 1909), pp. 45–56.

[52] Magyar Gyáriparosok Országos Szövetsége [Hungarian National Factory Industrialists' Association], *Közlemények* [Reports], 30 May 1908, as quoted in László Katus, 'Magyarország gazdasági fejlődése', p. 348 (my translation).

[53] Ákos Paulinyi, 'Die sogenannte gemeinsame Wirtschaftspolitik in Österreich–Ungarn', in Wandruszka and Urbanitsch (eds.), *Die Habsburgermonarchie*, vol. I, p. 581.

the 1904–5 level of purchases of industrial goods, the military bought 1.8 times as much in 1906, 3 times as much in 1907, and 3.8 times as much in 1908. Hungary's deliveries went up even more; the respective figures are 1.9, 3.3, and 4.4 times the 1904–5 average. In 1908 she supplied 35.8 per cent of these greatly expanded military requirements;[54] the quota ratio had been raised in the 1907 tariff and trade agreement to 36.4 per cent.

Since Austria had a similar programme of state purchases, the Hungarian outlays in this area evoked little protest from Cisleithania. Sharp Austrian criticism was directed much more at the system of railway freight rates, discussed in the next section, which quite frankly discriminated in favour of Hungarian producers. Railway rates were another of the weapons used to ameliorate the disadvantage of not having an independent customs tariff. The tax concessions and other indirect inducements offered by the Hungarian government also drew the fire of Austrian critics.

There seems little doubt that indirect assistance benefited Hungarian industry more than did the direct expenditure on industrial promotion, including subsidies. Yet neither the effectiveness of these measures nor their cost to Austria should be overestimated. Hungarian foreign trade statistics do not support an hypothesis of either successful import substitution or export promotion in manufactures.[55] The textile industry received special attention, particularly when the largest programme of industrial promotion began under the 1907 law. In the years 1907–9 alone, 57 per cent of all state help to industry was directed into the textile branch,[56] yet textiles appeared unable to gain in relative importance – indeed, among the major industries in Table 116, its relative position in 1913 was worse than that of 30 years earlier. Apparently most important to Hungary was the 'climate'[57] of government encouragement to industrial development, which was so clearly evident in Hungary and which played an important role in attracting the foreign and domestic capital which flowed into the industrial sector.

After the demise of liberalism, the policy of the Austrian government did not provide the same sort of congenial 'climate', at least to large enterprise. Joint-stock companies were taxed more heavily than noncorporate forms of enterprise,[58] and the founding of corporations was made more difficult in an attempt to prevent recurrence of the excesses which led to 'Black Friday' on the Vienna Stock Exchange in 1873. As a

---

[54] Calculated from data in Royal Hungarian Ministry of Commerce, *Emlékirat*, 1909, p. 49.
[55] Scott M. Eddie, 'The Terms and Patterns', pp. 352–3.
[56] Berend and Szuhay, *A tőkés gazdaság*, p. 46.
[57] The term is taken from *ibid.*, pp. 96–7.
[58] Taxes on a corporation typically were two to four times higher than they would have been on an equivalent single proprietorship. Herbert Matis, 'Leitlinien der österreichischen Wirtschaftspolitik', in Wandruszka and Urbanitsch (eds.), *Die Habsburgermonarchie*, vol. I, p. 58.

result, there were 490 industrial corporations in Austria in 1910, but 756 in the much smaller Hungarian sector. A mere 0.3 per cent of all establishments (*Betriebe*) covered by the Austrian industrial census of 1920 were joint-stock corporations, as against 18.8 per cent in Hungary in 1899.[59]

Under the leadership of Count Eduard Taaffe, the 'Iron Ring' coalition of great landowners, farmers, craftsmen and small merchants controlled the Austrian government from 1879 to 1893. While the autonomous tariff policy which was almost identically coterminous with the Iron Ring's rule conferred benefits on large industry, the domestic policy very much favoured smaller enterprises. Besides the previously mentioned discrimination against corporations, an 1883 law repealed the freedom of occupation (*Gewerbefreiheit*) which had been in existence since 1859, and reinstituted a guild-like system which required a 'certificate of competence' (*Befähigungsnachweis*). This and other legislation contributed to a 'petrification' of Austrian industry which limited both its scale and its growth.[60]

None of the foregoing should be interpreted, however, to imply that the Austrian state spent nothing to help its industry. While it budgeted little for direct promotion, and while Hungary's outlays in this area were increasing at a faster rate than Austria's, the Austrian expenditures for industrial instruction alone were, even in 1901, still more than twice the Hungarian spending for industrial promotion and industrial education combined. Unfortunately published data do not allow us to carry this comparison beyond the turn of the century, after which the Hungarian programme continued to expand, but Table 118 illustrates the trend up to that time. There seems little doubt that the trend continued, perhaps even accelerated, in the decade and a half before the outbreak of the First World War.[61] Over the period 1868–1900, as the table shows, Austria spent not only *absolutely*, but also *relatively* more than Hungary on industrial promotion, since we have seen from Table 115 that Austrian industry was likely rather less than 4.3 times the size of its Hungarian counterpart.

Neither Austrian nor Hungarian outlays represent large sums of money, and the promotion of industrial development through direct government expenditures in both halves of the monarchy was also as limited in scope as it was in financing. The Austrian assistance was almost

[59] Herbert Matis, *Osterreichs Wirtschaft*, p. 327.
[60] *Ibid.*, p. 328.
[61] In 1911, the Austrian Ministry for Industry, Trade and Commerce reported an outlay of nearly 18 million crowns for specialist training (*Fachunterricht*). The Hungarian government outlays for industrial instruction were 4.2 million crowns in the same year. See Albert Vig, *Magyarország iparoktatásának története az utolsó száz évben* [History of Hungary's Industrial Education in the Last Hundred Years] (Budapest, 1932), Table II.

Table 118. *Annual average spent on direct industrial promotion and industrial education (thousands of crowns, 24.06 crowns = £1)*

	Austria	Hungary	Ratio, $\dfrac{\text{Austrian}}{\text{Hungarian}}$ exp.
1868–72	543	40	26.7
1873–77	1,240	46	27.2
1878–82	1,589	206	7.7
1883–87	2,972	561	5.3
1888–92	4,264	578	7.4
1893–97	5,657	1,559	3.6
[1898–1900]	7,724	2,961	2.6
1868–80	1,029	62	16.7
1881–90	3,059	506	6.0
1891–99	5,758	1,580	3.6
1868–1900	3,166	739	4.3

Source: Calculated from data appearing in Hungary, Ministry of Commerce, *A Magyar korona országainak gyáripara az 1898 évben* [The Factory Industry of the Lands of the Hungarian Crown in 1898] (20 vols., Budapest, 1901), vol. i, pp. 7–10.

entirely for the training of industrial workers; the Hungarian outlays were more varied, but until the passage of Act iii of 1907 these and the indirect concessions contained in the various laws for industrial assistance would be extended only to industries specifically enumerated or to those proposing to produce something not hitherto manufactured in Hungary. The 1907 act finally allowed the Minister of Commerce to use his discretion in making awards which he deemed to be in the national interest.

The discretion to act in the 'national interest' again emphasizes the two principal dissimilarities in Austrian and Hungarian policy to promote industry: Austria relied on the overall security of a protective tariff and tried to preserve traditional forms and regional balances; Hungary encouraged new industries in the interests of the entire state, using measures devised as substitutes for tariff protection.

Of course, with a common tariff, Hungarian manufacturers could avail themselves of exactly the same protection that the Austrians enjoyed. With the Hungarian industrial promotion programme's early emphasis on technological modernity, it is difficult to understand why potential Hungarian firms apparently had such difficulty in competing with Austrian firms in the Hungarian market. An Austrian firm could freely found a branch plant in Hungary, where both wages *and taxes* were lower, thereby enjoying a cost advantage in production over a 'home' plant using identical production techniques. Closer proximity to the market should have produced a further advantage in lower cost of transport and distribution.

There are at least three possible reasons for this apparent paradox. The modern technology so favoured by the Ministry of Commerce may have been inappropriate to Hungarian factor endowments and prices, and industries in which Hungary had a comparative disadvantage may have been precisely the ones chosen for assistance. Economies of scale may have been so large in some lines that, given the small size of the Hungarian market, the established Austrian firms possessed an insurmountable advantage. A third set of explanations may be found in market structure and the behaviour of firms: in some instances cartels clearly divided production and assigned markets.[62] The textile industry, however, was never successfully cartelized, and Hungary had particular difficulty in textiles. It may be that Austrian firms were not so inefficient, relative to 'world' cost levels, as is commonly assumed. They could have practised or threatened price discrimination in the Hungarian market to discourage potential competitors. Whether this last or one of the other reasons accounts for the difficulties of Hungarian industry, especially in textiles, cannot be answered, given the present state of empirical research into this set of questions for Austria–Hungary.

It seems safe to conclude that while Hungary's industrial encouragement programme was innovative, clear in intent, and attention getting, it was also small, limited in effectiveness, and late – no match for the tariff under fair rules or foul. Although the Hungarian programme by itself had little short-run economic disadvantage for Austria, the Austrians were probably nevertheless right in regarding their partner's measures with apprehension because of the political implications. Viewed against the backdrop of Austrian political drift, the purposeful policies of Hungary could be seen as eroding Austrian hegemony and leadership in the Empire; beyond that, these policies – when taken together with other economic and political measures of the Hungarian government – could easily be interpreted to be part of a larger plan to achieve complete political independence from Austria. Whether Hungary ever would or could have attempted to break away is now a moot point, since the First World War intervened to alter radically the course of history.

[62] Cartelization is the primary reason offered by Berend and Ránki (see I. T. Berend and G. Ránki, *Magyarország gyáripara az imperializmus első világháború előtti időszakában 1900–1914* [The Factory Industry of Hungary during the Imperialistic Period before the First World War] (Budapest, 1955), p. 88). The advance of cartels was quite limited, however, before the turn of the century. In an Austrian survey of cartels from 1910, four-fifths of the 120 cartels mentioned had been founded in the 1904–9 period. See Eduard März and Karl Socher, 'Währung und Banken in Cisleithania', in Wandruszka and Urbanitsch (eds.), *Die Habsburgermonarchie*, p. 359.

VI. *Railway policy*

Although the very first railways in Austria–Hungary were privately owned, the state began its own building and acquisition programme in the early 1840s, so that by the end of 1853 more than two-thirds of the railway trackage in Austria, and over 90 per cent in Hungary, were state owned. Although the Austrian Empire maintained an armed neutrality during the Crimean War, the financial difficulties resulting from mobilization led to a decision to sell off[63] the state railways to private interests. Austria–Hungary entered the age of Dualism with a completely privately owned network, except for two short stretches totalling some 13 km which remained in government hands. The state lines were sold at bargain prices, and various estimates have put the loss at between 136 million and 223.5 million florins (approximately £13–22 million sterling).[64]

A system of interest guarantees on railway indebtedness replaced direct state involvement, with two detrimental consequences. At first, the private lines often charged monopoly rates, choking off traffic. As more companies were given charters to operate lines and the network expanded, a series of rate wars broke out in the 1860s. While advantageous for the customers, they put a burden on state finances, for the government – through its interest guarantees on railway bonds and the *profit* guarantees it had extended in concessioning some lines – had to pick up much of the tab for losses caused by the rate wars. Although already in the late 1860s some lines came to separate agreements to end cut-throat competition, it was not until 1873 that the Austrian government was able to secure a uniform rate structure for the private railways.

A boom in railway construction had begun just before the signing of the Compromise of 1867, and the first years of Dualism witnessed a great expansion in the networks of both halves of the monarchy: Austria's operating railways more than doubled in length, from 4,145 km at the end of 1866 to 9,344 by the end of 1873, while Hungary's network nearly tripled, from 2,160 to 6,233 km, in the same period. The boom came to an abrupt end with the Crash of 1873, and private capital pulled out of railway building, particularly from Hungary, where not a single new kilometre was opened to traffic in 1875. Between 1874 and 1877, an average of 429 km per annum was added to the Austrian railway network (as against an average of 743 per annum, 1867–73), while in Hungary the figure fell to 128 km (from 582 per year, 1867–73). The slump in private construction, and the weight of interest guaran-

---

[63] They were actually leased for 90 years for a lump-sum payment.
[64] Karl Bachinger, 'Das Verkehrswesen', in Wandruszka and Ubanitsch (eds.), *Die Habsburgermonarchie*, vol. I, p. 285.

Table 119. *Expansion of railway network in Austria–Hungary (kilometres in operation at year-end)*

	Austria			Hungary		
	(1) Total	(2) State railways^a	(2) ÷ (1) (per cent)	(4) Total	(5) State railways^a	(5) ÷ (4) (per cent)
1848	1,071	487	45	178	—	0.0
1853	1,392	953	68	414	408	99
1858	2,401	13	0.6	1,252	—	0.0
1863	3,316	13	0.4	1,945	—	0.0
1868	4,533	13	0.3	2,633	125	4.7
1873	9,344	13	0.1	6,253	947	15
1878	11,302	876	7.8	6,904	1,702	25
1883	12,240	3,214	26	8,339	3,259	39
1888	14,810	5,529	37	10,395	5,281	51
1893	15,927	7,776	49	12,573	10,266	82
1898	18,124	10,171	56	16,362	13,297	81
1903	20,369	12,144	60	17,703	14,732	83
1908	21,921	17,822	81	19,634	16,400	84
1913	22,981	18,859	82	21,997	18,413	84

Note:
^{a} State-owned or state-operated railways.
Sources: Austria: Aloys von Czedik, *Der Weg von und zu den österreichischen Staatsbahnen* (Vienna and Leipzig, 1913); k.k. Statistische Zentralkommission, *Österreichisches Statistisches Jahrbuch.*
Hungary: József Tominác, *A magyar szent korona országainak vasútjai, 1845–1904* [The Railways of the Lands of the Holy Hungarian Crown, 1845–1904] (Budapest, 1905); Magyar Királyi Központi Statisztikai Hivatal [Royal Hungarian Central Statistical Bureau], *Magyar Statisztikai Évkönyv* [Hungarian Statistical Yearbook].

tees borne by the state in the aftermath of the Crash, led to the decision to re-nationalize the rail lines. Austria legislated first, passing a Sequestration Act in 1877 giving the government the right to assume administration of any line which showed an operating deficit that the state must pay, or of any one which had claimed more than half its interest guarantee in a five-year period. While the initial tempo of nationalization in Austria was quite rapid, resulting in the takeover of more than one-third of the total network by 1884, the pace then slowed. Significant efforts at nationalization began again in 1890, and reached a peak in the 1905–8 period, resulting in state control of more than four-fifths of all the lines in Austria (see Table 119).

Although both Hungary and Austria authorized loans to raise funds for railways immediately after legislating the Compromise, Hungarian railway policy began immediately to diverge from that of Austria. Through her own programme of construction and the purchase of the bankrupt Budapest–Salgótarján line in 1868, the new Hungarian government inaugurated a 'mixed' policy towards railways. Other lines were either purchased or built after 1868, so that Hungary's own Sequestration Act of 1883, while similar to that of Austria, did not represent nearly so significant a departure from previous policy. In 1883, a larger share of total railway network was already in the hands of the state in Hungary than in Austria (see Table 119), despite Austria's six-year lead in passing a sequestration act.

Some of the results of the policy divergence can be found in the data presented in Table 119, where the year 1873 marks a clear dividing line in the pattern of expansion of the railway networks of Austria and Hungary. Taking the increments to the rail systems in each five-year period as our data, we find the correlation between additions to Hungary's network and additions to that of Austria is 0.996 between 1849–53 and 1869–73, but this correlation drops dramatically to only 0.125 in the interval 1874–8 to 1909–13. There are three primary reasons behind this change in relationships. (1) Austria, the more developed half of the monarchy, had an earlier start in building railways and had completed her main trunk lines already by the 1870s; after that, the emphasis was on such things as double-tracking and 'filling in'. (2) Much of the speculation and scandal which accompanied the pre-1873 boom centred on railway finance; investors were understandably wary of private shares after the Crash, while the Hungarian government began actively to engage itself in the construction of state rail lines. (3) Large amounts of capital flowed from Austria to Hungary after 1873, as investors sought safer havens for their savings; the Dual Monarchy arrangement, with a common currency and stable government finances, lent an aura of attractiveness to Hungarian government securities for many Austrian investors. The inflow of funds grew steadily, and kept up until the mid-1890s,[65] allowing the Hungarian government to proceed on its programmes of infrastructural investment, in which railways were a centrepiece.

Hungary began vigorously to undertake nationalization of existing lines in 1886. Within five years more than 80 per cent of the railways were state owned or operated, a proportion which then remained relatively stable until the outbreak of the war. Austrian nationalization proceeded more steadily and slowly, until the great drive of 1905–8 brought the Austrian State Railways to the same relative position their Hungarian counterpart had been in nearly two decades earlier.

The two states' divergent approaches to the nationality question and Austria's lead in building her main trunk lines resulted in differing uses of

[65] See John Komlos, 'The Habsburg Monarchy' (especially Ch. 4) for a more thorough quantitative assessment of this process.

the railways as an instrument of 'national policy'. National policy in Austria meant concessions to the various nationalities, resulting – especially after 1800 – in a diffusion of investments in railways based more on the regional claims of different nationalities for a quid pro quo in political bargaining than they were on either economic or military considerations.[66] In Hungary, on the other hand, the Magyar-dominated government paid far less attention to the desires of minority populations and much more to the economic development of the country as a whole. The political debate over whether to join with Austria in the Dualist system had centred on whether independence had to precede economic development, or vice versa, but both sides recognized the primacy of the goal of economic development and the critical role which the provision of social overhead capital, particularly railways, would play in the attaining of that goal. National policy in this context meant both the provision of a railway network that should serve the economic interests of the unitary state proclaimed in the Nationalities Act of 1868, and that the government should assume the lead in directing the location and operation of that network. Hungarian policy was perhaps no more consistent than that of Austria, but it was much more single-minded and served a more clear-cut long-term goal. For this reason it is likely that Hungarian railways contributed relatively more to overall economic development in Transleithania than did the Austrian network in Cisleithania.

Neither this speculation about the relative efficacy of railway policy nor the contrasts should be carried too far, however. In neither half of the Dual Monarchy is there strong evidence of the railways as a leading sector,[67] except perhaps in the 1867–73 boom, when the rate of expansion of the length of track actually exceeded even the increase in ton-kilometres of freight traffic.[68] After 1873, during any sustained period covered by the Rudolph or Komlos estimates (see Table 104), the Austrian railway network expanded more slowly than did industrial output. The major sustained period of railway growth began in Hungary in 1881 and continued until 1899, adding about 4.5 per cent to the network each year. This is very little different from the rate of growth of

---

[66] Josef Wysocki, *Infrastruktur und wachsende Staatsausgaben: Das Fallbeispiel Österreich 1868–1913* (Stuttgart, 1975), pp. 192, 212–13. See also Karl Bachinger, 'Das Verkehrswesen', p. 321.

[67] Karl Bachinger ('Das Verkehrswesen', pp. 320–1) takes a more aggressive position: railways were established on the basis of the traditional economic structure, and did not alter that structure very much; furthermore, they did little to expand foreign trade and generated little internal demand for iron and steel. This argument may perhaps be overdrawn, but in any case is much less applicable to Hungary than to Austria.

[68] The rates were 13.9 per cent and 13.0 per cent per annum on average, for length of track and ton-kilmetres of freight, respectively, for the entire monarchy. Rates calculated from data appearing in Albert Pauer, 'Frachten-Tarife', in Hermann Strach (ed.), *Geschichte der Eisenbahnen der österreichisch-ungarischen Monarchie* (Vienna, Teschen and Leipzig, 1898), vol. III, p. 235.

industrial production implied by Komlos' estimates (4.3 per cent) and substantially below that calculated by Katus (see Table 105). This is by no means conclusive, especially if railway development in one period makes possible industrial development in a later period, but the evidence does suggest that railways may have played a more passive role, responding to opportunities rather than creating them.

Moreover, many uneconomic lines were built, and they became a real burden on the finances of both Austria and Hungary. The interest guarantees, which were routinely awarded on request, effectively removed the risk to the private entrepreneur in constructing a line, and even in operating it. Ignoring entirely the numerous bankruptcies precipitated by the Crash of 1873, there were legions of unprofitable railways in Austria–Hungary even in prosperous times. At the passage of the Sequestration Act in 1883 in Hungary, any guaranteed railway which failed to meet interest payments on its 'priority debts' (preferred shares) out of earnings could be taken over by the state. Nationalization could then have been effected *en masse*, since all but one of the guaranteed lines found themselves in this position. The bungling and mismanagement (sometimes even corruption) which were part and parcel of government railway policy in Austria–Hungary certainly served to blunt, if not nullify, much of the positive economic impact that railways did have, in whatever period we consider.

Besides the policies with respect to capital outlays and current purchases referred to in earlier sections on state finances and industrial promotion, both governments employed railway freight rates to serve domestic policy purposes, often at the expense of the other partner. They competed with each other to direct export traffic to, and import traffic from, the ports of Trieste (Austria) and Fiume (Hungary).[69] Discounts designed to favour local production at the expense of production abroad or in the partner country were freely instituted, as the provisions of the Compromise for equal treatment on lines affecting the interests of both states was very narrowly interpreted. In Austria, rate concessions usually took the form of special low freight charges for certain typically Austrian products (petroleum, sugar, glassware, spirits, malt, and timber, for example).

Hungary copied the Austrian system of generally favouring certain major export products (grain, wood), but also tried to promote less-important exports in particular directions (coal to the Balkans, petroleum and sugar to the Mediterranean). She also granted concessionary rates to certain desired imports such as wool and yarn. Hungary further

[69] Now Rijeka, in Yugoslavia.

discriminated against foreign – including Austrian – suppliers and in favour of local producers by granting low rates for shipments originating from certain *stations*. In this way she quite deliberately used freight-rate policy as a partial substitute for customs duties which could not be levied against Austrian goods. Even the concessions on rates *to* certain stations, given on coal and coke, sometimes put Austrian producers at a competitive disadvantage with respect to suppliers from outside the monarchy (in this example in Prussian Silesia). Though both partners practised discrimination against the other, the Austrians probably had stronger grounds for complaint than did the Hungarians.

In applying their freight-rate policies, the Hungarian State Railways (MÁV) were also not above engaging in rate wars with private lines in order to bend them to the will of the government. In this way they forced the powerful Austrian State Railway Corporation (despite its name, a private company controlled by the Rothschilds) to sign a comprehensive rate agreement with the MÁV in 1882. Then, as nationalization proceeded,[70] both Austria and Hungary used it as a vehicle to unify and stabilize freight and passenger charges. The rate structures which emerged in both countries were characterized by generally relatively low long-haul rates, and relatively expensive short- and medium-distance charges, when compared to other European countries.

It is evident, then, that both countries used the railways and their freight rates to promote primarily the interest only of their own half of the Dual Monarchy. Austria's goals were generally more political and more diffuse in nature, whereas Hungary's were more economic and more sharply focused. At the present stage of research in the field, it is impossible to assess the quantitative importance of the two governments' railway policies. Rail transport was obviously absolutely very important to both economies, although it was perhaps relatively more important to Hungary, which had fewer navigable rivers and a poorer road system than did Austria.[71] It is obvious that Austria's use of railway construction as a tool of its nationalities policy did not prevent the break-up of the Habsburg Empire; whether the economic outcome of Austrian railway policy was either more or less favourable than that of Hungary cannot be known with certainty. It is my guess that by almost any standard of relative importance, the impact on Hungary of her government's action with respect to railways would be greater than the corresponding measure for Austria.

[70] The Austrian State Railway Corporation itself was nationalized in 1891.

[71] For example, in 1911 79 per cent of Hungary's imports by weight came from Austria and Germany; of this amount, 92 per cent arrived by rail. For exports, the corresponding figures were 83 per cent and 81 per cent respectively. Calculated from data appearing in Wilhelm Offergeld, *Grundlagen und Ursachen der industriellen Entwicklung Ungarns* (Jena, 1914), p. 167.

VII. Summary and speculations

Four primary influences can be seen to have shaped most of the principal themes of the preceding sections, and I should like to group my concluding considerations of economic policy in the Habsburg monarchy according to those four influences:

2. The structure of the dualist system (i.e., its institutional arrangements).
3. The financial operations of the two governments.
4. The goals and intentions of the two governments.

The establishment of the Dual Monarchy appeared to interrupt the 'unitary monarchy' policy which had endeavoured, since at least the time of Maria Theresa, to promote both regional specialization and as much self-sufficiency as possible within the confines of the Habsburg lands. The strivings of the Hungarians towards greater economic autonomy seemed to have had only marginal effect on the long-term trends, and may have served to emphasize in the public mind the complementarity and interdependence with Austria. The traditional economic interests in Austria (industry, especially textiles and iron) and in Hungary (mainly grain farms and flour-millers) maintained political control, and overall economic policy strongly reflected their influence. While these interests were able to make common cause, at least from the 1880s, in advancing protectionism in the Dual Monarchy's tariff structure, the economic conflict inherent in the process of treaty negotiations with other countries and in the Hungarian domestic programme of import substitution, was never successfully resolved. It may be that two so complementary economic units cannot join together on a basis of political equality precisely because so many domestic policies, treaty provisions, or other dealings can be seen to confer a benefit on one country at the expense of the other. Perhaps sovereignty and complementarity of the Austro-Hungarian type are basically incompatible; the apparent paradox of a very centralized political structure successfully implementing a liberal economic programme – as happened in the neo-Absolutist period preceding the Dual Monarchy – is no paradox at all. Rather than having too much in common, it has been suggested that the Dual Monarchy had too little.[72] While a tempting thesis, a supergovernment – able to take a holistic outlook and act in the best interests of the monarchy considered as a single unit – was politically completely out of the question at the time

[72] See for example, Ákos Paulinyi, 'Die sogenannte gemeinsame Wirtschaftspolitik', p. 604.

the Dual Monarchy came into existence. Franz Joseph made about the best bargain he could have made, given the circumstances.

The institutional arrangements which put economic flesh on the political bones of the Compromise of 1867 profoundly influenced the course of development of the two economies and the economic policies of the two governments, as we have seen at many points in the preceding sections. The continuation of the common customs territory ensured both the essential maintenance of the powerful economic forces for specialization and interdependence, and the establishment of policies – particularly by the Hungarian government – to try to circumvent these forces. The common tariffs benefited Austria more than they did Hungary, but the consistent trend throughout the period of the Dual Monarchy was toward the alleviation of this bias.

The monetary discipline enforced by the prohibition on further borrowing from the central bank by either government without the agreement of both finance ministers and the assent of both parliaments, was absolutely salutary.[73] The stability in public finance – shorn of the former all-purpose solution to financial crisis, money creation – permitted (or forced) both governments to put their finances in order, and to benefit fully and easily from the favourable conditions in the European capital market. Vienna became a great financial centre, channelling funds to Hungary and to the Balkans and elsewhere, but we should not forget that even though the benefits were probably greater for Hungary, Austria also was a net importer of capital, and thus she, too, reaped a direct benefit from the stability of the common currency.

The greater the influence which one feels the dualist structure gave Hungary in the affairs of the monarchy, the more important the year 1867 becomes as a dividing line between epochs in Habsburg economic history. While we have seen that the Crash of 1873 reversed the liberal direction in trade policy, inaugurated a long depression, forced a turnaround in government policy towards railways, and led to the establishment of a regime which discriminated against large enterprise, these were all Austrian phenomena. Hungarian economic policy after 1873 continued along the same lines established earlier, emphasizing infrastructural development and the promotion of local production. It did not restrict enterprise in the way the Austrian government did, and it even benefited from Austrian savers' post-1873 aversion to investment in the shares of private companies, as it attracted their funds into Hungarian government securities.

The requirement that the trade and tariff agreement be renegotiated

---

[73] When the absolute restriction was relaxed in 1887, it did not lead back down the road towards monetary excess. The two governments had learned their lessons; but in any case the relaxation was only partial.

every 10 years was, as we have seen, a built-in guarantee of crisis. These periodic negotiations afforded Hungary repeated opportunities to indulge her passion for trading economic concessions for symbolic political gains, although she did manage to win advantageous changes in the refund of consumption taxes on exported goods. The revenue implications of these changes were rather marginal, and likely more than offset by the increase in the quota ratio which political provisions had cost her. The basic provisions of the 'economic compromise' remained essentially intact, and the gains or losses from the modifications mentioned must have been small when compared to the cost of uncertainty which the renewals engendered. A market economy can adapt to almost any set of rules; it is uncertainty about what the rules will be, or unpredictable changes in the rules, which disrupt the functioning of markets and increase the costs of doing business.

Starting from a common system of revenue-raising under the neo-Absolutist government, the tax and expenditure patterns of the two central governments exhibited developments similar in both structure and size. Although the cost of common affairs (of which 95 per cent or more were military outlays) nearly quadrupled during the era of the Dual Monarchy, this category of expenditure in fact grew more slowly than either country's 'domestic' budget. The relative burden of supporting the structure of Dualism thus declined, and the relative importance of internal matters increased for both Austria and Hungary. This latter trend was further emphasized in Austria by the growth of the provincial governments, for which there was no counterpart in Hungary.

In both countries, the taxation system appeared to have become more regressive, as the share of total revenue derived from consumption taxes, service fees, and income from state monopolies, all of which bore heavily on the lower-income strata, increased. Those aspects of government expenditure on which we have concentrated here seemed to confer their benefits largely on the upper-income groups of the society in both countries, and the tariff system exhibited a double tendency for income redistribution. Not only were vested interests advantaged at the expense of consumers in both halves of the monarchy, but also the structure of the tariff transferred income from Hungary (poorer) to Austria (richer). On the basis of the preceding considerations, it would be tempting to speculate that the overall effect of the fiscal operations of the two governments was to make the income distribution more unequal than it otherwise would have been both within and between the two partners of the Dual Monarchy. While one may rather confidently venture this conjecture with respect to the Hungarian budget, the Austrian case, and the influence of the outlays for common affairs, are much less clear.

The budget of the Cisleithanian government consistently showed receipts in excess of expenditures in the richer provinces, and the opposite pattern in the poorer provinces. The substantial interprovincial income redistribution could well have offset the effects of redistribution between economic classes which was contained in the fiscal system. The size of the Hungarian population was two-thirds or more that of Austria, and per capita income, as we have seen, was perhaps two-thirds to three-quarters of the Austrian level. If the per capita income difference was of this order of magnitude it suggests that the quota ratio near the end of the period (63.6:36.4), because it was supposed to be based on taxpaying capacity, probably favoured Austria over Hungary, since the population and per capita income figures suggest a total income in Hungary around half (or somewhat less) that of Austria. The redistributional effects of the common expenditures would on this basis appear to be approximately neutral.[74]

The considerations of the nationality question, which was at the root of the Austrian government's conscious attempts at regional income redistribution, were a major characteristic of overall economic policy in Cisleithania. The drift, irresolution, and tendency toward *ad hoc* measures which were features of Austrian policy were part of the legacy of former dominance which the German Austrians had enjoyed in the monarchy. As a group, they were typically either a-nationalistic or still pursuing the shattered dream of hegemony in a greater Germany. It was natural, then, to run the country as a collection of nationalities, with all that implied about operating on the basis of 'the demands of day-to-day politics and proportionality considerations'.[75]

The Hungarians, on the other hand, have appeared throughout to have engaged in a resolute and purposeful pursuit of clearly seen objectives. We have traced this to the different concepts of the two states: Austria, which never even had an official name as a country, was an historical collection of individual crownlands with separate identities, while the Hungarian concept was clearly spelled out in the Nationalities Act of 1868 – 'a unitary and Magyar state'. Such a concept gave a clearness and direction to Hungarian policy which Austrian policy lacked, but which in the end proved to be at least as misguided as the less clearly articulated approach. Only Franz Joseph, and some of his leading statesmen, genuinely thought in terms of the entire monarchy; everyone else was either an Austrian, or a Hungarian, or identified himself with an even smaller group. In the end, such particularism destroyed the Empire.

[74] That the Hungarian government in fact collected about the same absolute amount of tax per capita as the Austrian government does not enter this discussion, since it is not tax effort, but rather ability to pay, that is under consideration. If we consider that the presumption behind progressive taxation is that ability to pay increases more than in proportion to income per capita, then Hungary's quota could clearly be seen as too high.

[75] Herbert Matis, 'Leitlinien', p. 65 (my translation).

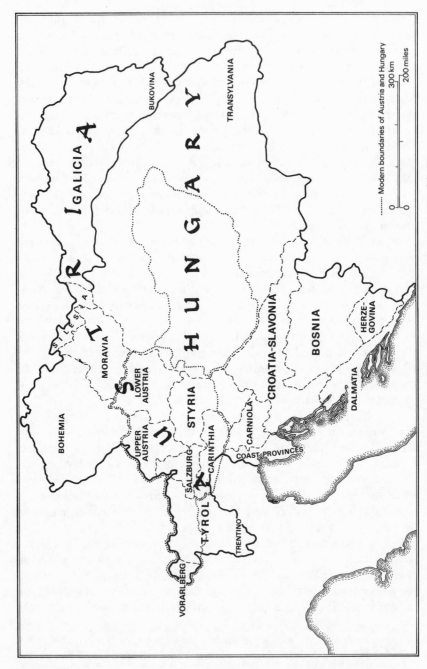

Fig. 10. The Habsburg monarchy on the eve of the First World War

CHAPTER XIII

East-central and south-east Europe, 1919–39[1]

I. Introduction

This chapter is concerned with the economic history of the countries east of the Elbe and along the Danube (Poland, Czechoslovakia, Hungary, Romania, Yugoslavia, and Bulgaria) with special consideration of the social and economic policies of their states. Their different levels of industrialization show a marked west to east–south-east gradient. Only Czechoslovakia's development did not conform to that of the other relatively economically backward Central and south-east European countries but progressed on a pattern similar to Western European economies. Under the Habsburg monarchy the western regions of Czechoslovakia – Bohemia and Moravia – had already undergone an industrial revolution essentially of the nineteenth-century type, starting with the textile industry, then penetrating to the agricultural industries (sugar, brewing, distilling), to heavy industry (iron and steel, coal), and to engineering (agricultural and textile machinery). In all its phases the industrialization of the Czech Lands was supported by a continuous inflow of labour and by a fairly substantial level of domestic capital accumulation derived mainly from a relatively advanced agriculture which had developed simultaneously.[2] Such a gradual rise of industrial development permeating the whole economy was largely bypassed in the other countries as they were faced with the need to industrialize in

---

[1] This chapter draws upon materials collected during two research undertakings for which thanks are due to the Social Science Research Council (UK) for their financial support: the East European Economic History Project in which I conducted research with the Investigator Michael C. Kaser at St Anthony's College, Oxford, and my research on Multinational Companies in Central East Europe at the University of East Anglia, Norwich. My participation in an international research project on 'Inflation and reconstruction in Europe 1914–1924' enabled me to substantiate certain parts of this chapter with archival evidence, for which I am indebted to the Stiftung Volkswagenwerk.

[2] Jaroslav Purš, *Průmyslová revoluce v českých zemích* (The Industrial Revolution in the Czech Lands) (Prague, 1960), pp. 9–16; a shortened English version by Purš in *Historica*, vol. II (1960), pp. 183–272. Slovakia's level of industrialization was lower than that of the Czech Lands, but in the Transleithanian half of the Habsburg monarchy it belonged to the relatively most industrialized regions. Slovakia had produced about 20 per cent of the total Hungarian industrial output before the First World War, which included more than half of the paper and cellulose industry and more than a quarter of the iron industry of the eastern part of the Austro-Hungarian Empire.

twentieth-century conditions alongside and in unequal competition with high-powered industrial nations.

The main obstacle to modern economic development remained the overwhelming weight of agriculture in the economies of that region, and any assessment of economic growth can only be made by taking into account the basic relationship between agriculture and industry. Under the prevailing political and socio-economic conditions between the two world wars it was impossible to overcome effectively the enormous differences between the advanced agriculture of Western Europe and its relatively backward state in Eastern Europe. Agricultural reforms had become a political necessity but they were neither incisively carried through nor economically sound; modernization and capitalization of agriculture, particularly in the Balkan area, were frustrated both by fragmentation of land and relative rural overpopulation. The only viable solution to economic backwardness lay in industrialization. However, its pace and extent were impaired by the stagnant conditions in agriculture which tended to emphasize rather than redress the imbalance in the economies of Central and south-east Europe. Notwithstanding, industry was the crucial sector which contributed most to any economic growth registered in this area.

Whilst before the First World War the nations living in the Central and south-east European region formed an economic unity within precariously held together empires – most of them belonging to the Habsburg monarchy but also to tsarist Russia and Wilhelmine Germany – the Versailles peace settlement of 1919 so changed the political map of Central and south-east Europe that not only frontiers but also economic contours had to be redrawn. Despite this abrupt break with the past, strong forces of continuity remained such as historical ties, geographical proximity, as well as common post-war problems which affected the economies of the region similarly during a clearly defined period flanked by the end of one and the beginning of another world war. The newly established group of states entered the inter-war phase of the process of industrialization with the disadvantages of latecomers and with the heritage of war, revolution, and counter-revolution. Those states belonging to the defeated nations emerged with smaller areas (Bulgaria and Hungary), those belonging to the victorious camp enlarged their territory (Yugoslavia and Romania) or were resurrected after centuries of political dependence (Czechoslovakia and Poland); but all alike were marked by various degrees of dislocation, destruction, inflation, misery, and want in the aftermath of war.

After territories had been allocated and all frontier disputes in Europe had been settled either by treaty or by force of arms, the countries which form the centre of interest in this chapter took up about one-third of the area of Europe and represented just under one-quarter of Europe's population. They had to adapt themselves to new conditions; their economic life had been orientated towards Vienna and Budapest, and in the case of Poland her component parts had even been tied to three centres: St Petersburg, Berlin, and Vienna. Thus, initially, they did not form individual economic units and recovery and reconstruction was a long-drawn-out and painful process. Czechoslovakia alone escaped the worst economic upheavals by an early currency reform and a complete separation from the Austrian monetary and banking system. She was first to succeed in stabilizing her economy.

The different points in time of stabilization in the social, political, and monetary spheres diminished the generally weak opportunities for domestic capital formation and lessened the chances of sufficiently large inflows of foreign long-term investment into the capital-starved industries of Central and south-east Europe. Constant lack of capital and dependence on foreign loans and investments were in a varied measure common to all.

Closely related to this phenomenon was another common feature which consisted of a chronically insufficient demand on the domestic market. When the Czechoslovak Republic was established it acquired like all successor states part.of the Dual Monarchy's uneven distribution of resources and levels of industrialization. Overall, Czechoslovakia comprised 21 per cent of the territory, 26 per cent of the population but no less than about 70 per cent of the industrial capacity[3] and also 44 per cent of the entire labour force[4] of the Austro-Hungarian Empire. The widespread areas of the Habsburg monarchy had provided a convenient outlet for the industries of the Czech Lands and until 1918 had been their home market; after 1918 the relatively highly developed Czechoslovak industry was faced with an immensely diminished new home market which was unable to absorb its products. This so-called Austro-Hungarian structure of Czechoslovak industry emphasized the problem of foreign trade, for the country had to export at least 30 per cent of its total output in order to survive.

From the point of view of a drastically shrunken domestic market and, as a result of this, a relative over-capacity of industrial production, postwar Hungary had to grapple with similar problems, but in most other aspects her situation was very different from that of Czechoslovakia. Within her new boundaries Hungary retained only 32.7 per cent of her

[3] Rudolf Olšovský Václav Průcha, Hana Gebauerová, Antonín Pražský, Anatol Dobrý and Josef Faltus (eds.), *Přehled hospodářského vývoje Československa v letech 1918–1945* (Outline of Economic Development in Czechoslovakia 1918–1945) (Prague, 1963), p. 24.

[4] Zora P. Pryor, 'Czechoslovak Economic Development in the Interwar Period', in Victor S. Mamatey and Radomir Luža (eds.), *A History of the Czechoslovak Republic* (Princeton, 1973), p. 190.

Table 120. *National income per head (in 1937 US dollars)*

	1920	1929	1937
Czechoslovakia	115	181	170
Hungary	79	115	120
Poland	—	108	100
Romania	—	—	81
Yugoslavia	66	86	80
Bulgaria	—	60	75
United Kingdom	329	372	440
Germany	—	304	340
France	196	312	265

Note:
— = Not known.
Source: E. Ehrlich, 'Infrastructure and an International Comparison of Relationships with Indicators of Development in Eastern Europe 1920–1950', *Papers in East European Economics*, no. 33 (August 1973).

pre-war areas and 41.6 per cent of her former population; 47 per cent of her industrial enterprises had remained on her territory producing about 55 per cent of her former value of production. As well as being separated like the territory of Czechoslovakia from the monarchy's nearly self-sufficient trade network her industries were largely cut off from essential raw materials which now lay beyond her frontiers and became increasingly surrounded by tariff walls. Thus imports of raw materials became essential to keep the wheels of the relatively expanded iron works, engineering factories, spinning and weaving mills turning. Even the strongest branch of industry, flour milling, was unable to utilize its capacity, for domestic supplies of grain on the diminished territory could not reach more than between one-third and one-half of available capacity at the best of harvests. As a result of the territorial changes of 1919–20 Hungary was transformed into a more industrial country, but the domestic market was unable to absorb the produce of Hungarian industry and agriculture in sufficient quantities; therefore, securing export markets became of critical importance.[5] Fundamentally, the persistently low level of incomes, descending from west to east–south-east, could not generate any buoyant demand on domestic markets throughout the entire region over the whole inter-war period (see Table 120). This problem was most pressing in the predominantly agricultural countries,

[5] See Ivan T. Berend and Görgy Ránki, *Hungary: A Century of Economic Development* (Newton Abbot, 1974), pp. 94–8; also K. Fink, 'Spezielle Aspekte der Wirtschafts- und Sozialentwicklung seit der Jahrhundertwende in Ungarn', *Südosteuropa Jahrbuch*, vol. IX (1969), p. 128.

Table 121. *Percentage distribution of the gainfully occupied population in six European countries*

	Year	Agriculture and fishing	Mining	Manufacture and handicraft	Commerce and transport	Administration, domestic service, etc.
1. Among typically industrialized countries:						
Czechoslovakia	1930	28	2	40	14	16
2. Among less industrialized countries:						
Hungary	1930	54	1	23	10	12
Poland	1931	65	1	16	8	10
3. Countries lagging in industrial development:						
Romania	1930	78	—	7	5	10
Yugoslavia	1931	79	—	11	4	6
Bulgaria	1934	80	—	8	4	8

Source: League of Nations, *Industrialization and Foreign Trade* (Geneva, 1945), pp. 26–7.

that is, Yugoslavia, Bulgaria, and Romania where more than 70 per cent, and in Poland and Hungary more than 50 per cent of the population were dependent on agriculture.

The comparative economic structure of the six Central and south-east European countries shown in Table 121 clearly divides them into three categories. Czechoslovakia alone belonged to the typically industrialized countries of the inter-war years, Hungary and Poland fall into the category of less industrialized countries, and Romania, Yugoslavia, and Bulgaria range themselves with the countries lagging behind in industrial development. Their combined contribution to Europe's industrial production amounted to no more than 7 or 8 per cent whilst the three leading industrial powers alone (Britain, France, and Germany) produced 67 per cent of the total industrial output of Europe.[6] The great disparities existing in the inter-war period strongly influenced economic and social policies of Central and south-east European governments in their pursuit of industrialization. They were particularly powerfully affected by the expansive financial and business operations of the world's most advanced economies of Britain, France and the United States of

[6] Ivan T. Berend and György Ránki, *Economic Development in East Central Europe in the 19th and 20th Centuries* (New York, 1974), pp. 303–4.

America with whom they found themselves in imminent contact after having attained formal political independence.

In the immediate post-war years the new states sought the support of the Western powers in their efforts to stabilize their political and economic systems, and later they leant heavily financially on the West in their endeavour to arm and to industrialize. In this way they became increasingly dependent on the capital mainly of France, Britain and the United States, although the degree of dependency varied in the different countries according to the strength or weakness of industrial development in their economies. Through their greater dependence on the international capital market and on foreign trade, the Central and south-east European countries were drawn more closely into the international economy and were caught up in the competitive struggles of the great industrial powers.

During the two decades bounded by the two world wars, economic and social policies were influenced decisively by factors impinging upon the states situated in the region between Germany and the Soviet Union from outside. Whilst in the first decade government policies were dominated essentially by the repercussions of the October revolution of 1917 in Russia and the outcome of the First World War and governed by the terms and conditions of the Versailles peace treaties, state policies in the second decade of the inter-war period were largely shaped by the world economic crisis and the rise of Fascism in Europe.

Within the scope of this chapter it would be foolhardy to plunge into an account of the role of the state in economic development in the whole Central and south-east European area by dealing with each country in turn. Historical accounts of the individual states' economic growth taking cognizance of the specific, widely differing economic systems, indeed of the regional uneven economic development within each state, are accessible.[7] So are assessments of economic growth in east-central and south-east Europe using a chronological structure with a mixture between a country-by-country and a problem-area approach.[8] The only viable approach for a chapter on a comparatively large number of dissimilar small national, partly multinational states (see Table 122) is through their international economic relationships: their policies in the context of international capital movements, of foreign trade, and of their place in the capitalist inter-war world.

[7] Berend and Ránki, *Hungary*; Olšovský *et al.*, *Přehled*; Zbigniew Landau and Jerzy Tomaszewski, *Gospodarka Polski miedzywojennej* (The Interwar Economy of Poland) (Warsaw, 1967); J. Natan, V. Khadzhinikolov, L. Berov (eds.), *Ikonomikata na Bulgaryа do socialisticheskata revoluciya* (The Economic Development of Bulgaria until the Socialist Revolution) (Sofia, 1969); R. Davidović, 'Die Industrialisierung Jugoslawiens', *Südosteuropa Jahrbuch*, vol. 1 (1957).

[8] For example, Wolfgang Piper, *Grundprobleme des wirtschaftlichen Wachstums in einigen südosteuropäischen Ländern in der Zwischenweltkriegszeit* (Berlin, 1961); more recent and wider in scope is Berend and Ránki, *Economic Development*.

II. *State policies: continuity and discontinuity*

In the period under discussion the state played an increasing part in all spheres of economic life. *Laissez-faire* has never been the basis of policies in Central and south-east Europe, neither of imperial cabinets nor of the successor states' governments, though liberal economics tempered with Listian ideas were, in theory, accepted as desirable. Whilst the phenomenon of state intervention in the economy is not specific to the history of East European industrialization, since it was symptomatic also of early industrialization in Western Europe, the role of the state in the Central and south-east European economies grew stronger under the particular conditions of the inter-war years.[9] In addition to long historical experience of state activity in the life of the region, economic nationalism became official policy as a reaction to formal political independence. As the respective governments used their legislative powers to consolidate their national and political position they endeavoured to build a viable capitalist economy. In the course of these efforts they had to take account of the relative backwardness of their economies as a whole and had to step into the breach left by the lag in industrialization, by insufficient domestic capital accumulation, and by a severe lack of entrepreneurship.

However, more immediately, governments were forced to intervene by the sheer necessity of coping with the enormous post-war problems which their states had inherited and the consequences of which threw their shadows over the whole inter-war period. As a result of the First World War the existing chronic deficiency in domestic capital supply deteriorated further, above all caused by the physical destruction of fixed capital, the transfer of national minorities and repatriation of refugees, the burden of war debts and reparation payments, and also due to the capital required, however scantily, to finance the post-war land reforms.

Every country in the area, whether victorious or vanquished, suffered from severe economic exhaustion. The greatest damage was done to Poland not only by belligerent armies advancing and retreating over her territory but also by deliberate devastation and dismantling conducted by the occupying powers of Russia, Germany, and Austria. As a result, at the beginning of 1919 the volume of industrial production within her new boundaries had fallen to about 15 per cent and at the end of 1919 it had recovered to about 30 per cent of the 1913 level.[10] Only Yugoslavia can bear comparison with Poland in scale of devastation, pillage, and

---

[9] Jerzy Tomaszewski points out the crucial difference in time since 'Western countries had built their industrial strength in an agricultural world. East-Central Europe had to find its place among the industrial powers', in 'Some Problems of the Capital Formation and Investment in the Capitalist Societies of East-Central Europe', *Acta Poloniae Historica*, vol. xxv (1977), p. 159.

[10] Landau and Tomaszewski, *Gospodarka Polski*, p. 64.

Table 122. *Ethnic distribution and religious affiliation around 1930*

	Albania (1930)* Thousands	%	Bulgaria (1934)* Thousands	%	Czechoslovakia (1930)* Thousands	%	Hungary (1931)* Thousands	%	Poland (1931)* Thousands	%	Romania (1930)* Thousands	%	Yugoslavia (1931)* Thousands	%
Ethnic distribution														
Albanians	926	92.3											342[a]	2.5
Bulgarians			5,275	86.8							361	2	176	1.3
Czechs and					7,426[a]	50.5			30	0.1				
Slovaks					2,295	15.6	105	1.2						
Germans					3,318	22.5	479	5.5	1,700[a]	5.2	740	4.2	499	3.6
Greeks	50	5.6												
Gypsies			81	1.3	135						278	1.6		
Hungarians					720	4.9	7,556	87			1,426	8	468	3.4
Jews			28	0.5	205	1.4	445	5.1	2,700	8.3	725	4.1	77	0.6
Poles					100	0.7			22,208	67.9				
Romanians							16	0.2			12,980	72.9	230	1.6
Russians									56	0.2	415	2.3		
Ruthenians/Ukrainians					569[b]	3.9			4,200[b]	12.8	578	3.3		
Turks			618	10.2							289	1.6	132	0.9
White Russians									1,500[b]	4.6				
Serbs / Croats / Slovenes (Yugoslavs)	7	0.7					34	0.4					11,565[b]	83
Others	20	2	76	1.2	61	0.2	49	0.6		1.7			444	3.1
Total	1,003	100	6,078	100	14,729	100	8,684	100	32,394	100	17,793	100	13,934	100
Religious affiliation														
Roman Catholic		10.1	46	0.8	10,831	73.5	5,634	64.9	20,670	64.8	1,200		5,218	37.4
Uniate and Greek (and Armenian) Catholic		19.7	5,130	84.4	584	4	201	2.3	3,336	10.4	1,426		45	0.3
Orthodox					146		40	0.5	3,762	11.8	13,200		6,785	48.7

*Year of census.

Protestant		8	0.1	1,130^c	3.7	2,347	27	835	2.6	1,295	231	1.6
Jewish		48	0.8	357	2.4	445	5.1	3,114	11.8	1,500	68	0.4
Moslem	70.2	821^a	13.5	800^d	55	21	0.2	198	0.6	260	1,561	11.2
Others		25^b	0.4							140	18	0.1

Sources: Compiled from J. Robinson et al., *Were the Minorities Treaties a Failure?* (New York, 1943); H. Seton-Watson, *Eastern Europe Between the Wars 1918–1941* (Cambridge, 1945), pp. 430–3; *Annuaire Statistique du Royaume de Bulgarie 1938*; *Mały rocznik statystyczny*; *Annuarul Statistic al Rômaniei 1939/40*, pp. 58–9, 62. Ethnic statistics on Albania are taken from Robinson; religious percentage referring to 1945 from S. Skendi's handbook *Albania* (New York, 1958), p. 57.

Figures on Bulgaria are based on official statistics of the 1934 census contained in *Annuaire Statistique du Royaume de Bulgarie 1938*.
a Including the Pomaks, ethnic Bulgarians of Moslem faith, numbering 134,125 (1934); 615,000 were Turks, 67,000 gypsies and about 5,000 Tartars.
b Mainly Armenians numbering 23,000 in 1934.

Ethnic and religious statistics on Czechoslovakia based on census of 1 December 1930; religious statistics on *Annuaire Statistique de la Republique Tchecoslovaque 1938* and on Seton-Watson.
a *The Czechoslovak Statistical Abstract of 1958*, p. 39, gives the proportions of Czechs and Slovaks as 53% and 16.4% respectively (7,426,000 and 2,295,000).
b Includes Russians as well.
c Protestant churches include the Evangelical Church of Czech Brethren and the Lutherans.
d Mainly members of the 'Czechoslovak Church'. About 855,000 Czechoslovak citizens declared 'without denomination'.

Ethnic statistics on Hungary based on Robinson; religious statistics on E. C. Helmreich's handbook *Hungary* (New York, 1956), p. 66 (*Magyar Statisztikai Zsenkonyr*, vol. XIII, pp. 1446; *Annuaire Statistique Hongrois* (1939), p. 17).

Ethnic statistics on Poland based on Robinson; religious figures on Seton-Watson, and the *Osteurope-Handbuch-Polen*, ed. W. Markert, (Cologne, 1959), pp. 37–42.
a Polish official statistics put the total number of Germans at 741,000, or 2.3 per cent of total population (1931) (see *Concise Statistical Yearbook of Poland 1938*).
b Due to the biased Polish official census, it is estimated that the number of Ukrainians and White Russians put together was between 6 and 7 million (see Halecki's handbook *Poland*, pp. 49–69, *Polen*).

Ethnic statistics on Romania based on Robinson roughly correspond to the official census of 29 December 1930, as published in the *Annuarul Statistic al Rômaniei*, 1939/40, pp. 58, 62–9, 84. Religious statistics are based on Seton-Watson.

Ethnic statistics on Yugoslavia are taken from Robinson; religious figures from Seton-Watson, *Osteuropa-Handbuch Jugoslawicy*, ed. W. Markert (Cologne, 1954), pp. 16–17.
a The number of Albanians is obviously underestimated – rough estimates put it between 500,000 and 700,000.
b This rubric includes also Bulgarians and Macedonians, estimated at over 700,000, who, according to official census figures, did not exist. Rough estimates of 'Yugoslavs' (Seton-Watson)

Serbs	5,953,000
'Bosnian Moslems'	729,000
Croats	3,221,000
Slovenes	1,134,000

Source: Milan Hauner, 'Demographic Structure of Eastern Europe between the Two Wars', *Papers in East European Economics*, no. 40 (Oxford, January 1974), pp. 4–5.

disruption due to war and in magnitude of post-war difficulties; destruction was particularly severe in Serbia which had become the first battlefield of the war. A similar fate was shared by certain areas in Romania where also part of the existing industrial plant and equipment was dismantled or requisitioned by the German occupation administration, and the all-important oil output fell by more than half between 1912 and 1918.[11]

Industry and agriculture on the territory of Czechoslovakia escaped physical destruction. However, since the main armaments works were situated in the Czech Lands they became the arsenal of the Austro-Hungarian Empire. By the end of the war plant and equipment were severely run down and total production fell by half at the beginning of 1919 in comparison with 1913. Exhaustion from war affected also the relatively advanced Czech agriculture and the needs of war had particularly decimated livestock in the country. This applied to an even greater extent to the Hungarian economy where industry and agriculture were virtually paralysed by war and revolution. Also Bulgaria's economy was hit hard, since Bulgaria had already been involved in the Balkan wars and had sided with the central powers in the First World War. As a result she lost part of her territory and emerged with a decrease of more than 50 per cent in her agricultural output, whilst her industry had only begun to take its first steps.

In the overwhelmingly agricultural countries crops and livestock suffered most. Disruption was aggravated by the devastation of the railway network, as much of the East European states' efforts in reconstructing their economies depended on their capability of transporting agricultural produce and raw materials in bulk. Thus in most countries of the region decreased agricultural production paralysed their crucial exports and a vicious cycle was created in the post-war years in which they could not export enough to reconstruct the heavily damaged agriculture nor accumulate sufficient capital in agriculture as a basis for transfers into industrial investment.

The dismal situation in agriculture was exacerbated by territorial changes which highlighted the great differences in land tenure within the newly drawn borders of the individual states, ranging from the latifundia system in the Balkans, over-large aristocratic landed estates in east-central Europe, to semi-feudal tenancies and dwarf peasant holdings everywhere – most numerous in Bulgaria – to viable peasant farms and

---

[11] According to the requirements of the Anglo–French–Romanian Treaty of 1916 the Romanian government organized the destruction of 800,000 tons of oil by fire, buried 1,500 oilwells and shut down the majority of oil refineries to prevent their falling into the hands of the invading armies of the Central Powers. See G. C. Adams, 'Die rumänische Staatsanleihepolitik' (dissertation, University of Hamburg, 1939), p. 60.

agricultural enterprises in the Czech Lands. Greater awareness of the gross inequalities emphasized social tensions which were enhanced by national enmities since peasants, as a rule belonging to the nationalities who recently had become the decisive element in government (Poles, Czechs and Slovaks, Romanians, Serbs and Croats), were faced with alien landlords (mainly of Russian, German, Austrian, Hungarian, or Turkish origin) who had been part of the former ruling elites. Concurrently with the decline in agriculture existing social problems were accentuated, above all, land-hunger, landlessness, and pauperism. The war had strengthened the peasants' consciousness as well as their political parties and the Bolshevik revolution had deeply influenced the peasantry's urgent demand for radical redistribution of the land.

III. *Land reforms*

These pressing circumstances made land reforms inevitable, quite apart from the economic necessity of changing land distribution to try to achieve greater efficiency in agricultural production as a vital background to industrialization. The very first step in state intervention taken by all new governments in Central and south-east Europe consisted of land reforms which received legislative priority.[12]

Earliest in timing and relatively most radical in application were the land reforms in the kingdoms of Yugoslavia and Romania. Parallel with the proclamation of her independence in December 1918 Yugoslavia declared her intent to introduce a land reform and to abolish feudal privileges. This policy was enacted in the Land Reform Bill of 25 February 1919 and extended after 1930 by further regulations to Dalmatia. The administration and execution of the law was in February 1920 entrusted to a Ministry of Land Reform which functioned throughout the whole inter-war period and redistributed about 2.5 million ha by liquidating all estates larger than 50–300 hectares. About one-half of this area passed into legal ownership of liberated serfs, one-quarter consisting of forests was nationalized and the remaining cultivable land was allocated to peasant families. Between 1920 and 1938 about one-quarter of all peasant families (about 650,000) received land. As a result large estates entirely disappeared (after 1931 holdings over 50 ha accounted for 0.4 per cent of the total number of holdings on about 10 per cent of total

---

[12] This section draws mainly from the following publications: Milan Otáhal, *Zápas o pozemkovou reformu v ČSR* (Struggle for Land Reform in ČSR) (Prague, 1963); David Mitrany, *The Land and the Peasant in Rumania: The War and Agrarian Reform* (London, 1930); J. Tomasevich, *Peasants, Politics and Economic Change in Yugoslavia* (Stanford, 1955); Roger Munting, 'A Comparative Study of Land Reform after the First World War', *Papers in East European Economics*, no. 18 (Oxford, 1972); Ivan T. Berend, 'Agriculture in Eastern Europe 1919–1939', *Papers in East European Economics*, no. 35 (Oxford, 1973).

cultivated land) and the overwhelming number of peasant holdings (67.8 per cent) were no larger than 5 ha on which about 7 million peasants tried to eke out a precarious subsistence on 28 per cent of total land. From the point of view of social policy the land reform achieved greater legal equality in property relations, although not in property holding, by abolishing serfdom in the south and ending semi-feudal tenancies in the north, thus staving off peasant revolts. In national policy greater Slav consolidation was attained by dispossessing foreign landlords. However, the great increase in small and dwarf holdings coupled with relative overpopulation created serious problems in the economy of Yugoslavia and her agrarian structure became very similar to the fragmented agriculture of Bulgaria: in both countries a reflection of the strength of peasant parties in government.

Romania announced her land reform on 1 December 1918 and passed the first law on the 15th of the same month which was later (July 1921) expanded. Emphasis was laid on the socio-political character of the reform since Romania, a country of large aristocratic estates, had witnessed recent peasant revolts (1907) and the potential of a peasant revolution seemed more imminent since Bessarabia, which had undergone a Bolshevik revolution in 1917, was incorporated into the Romanian state. This explains also the more radical measures of the reform applied to Bessarabia, where estates exceeding 100 ha were expropriated, in comparison with other parts of the country, where the legal limit ranged from 100 to 500 ha. Social policy was backed up with radical nationalism as the reform announced the expropriation of all land occupied by non-Romanian citizens – particularly directed against Hungarian landlords in Transylvania – and by absentee landlords. Regarding the extent and effect on the agrarian structure the Romanian reform was the most incisive as the area earmarked for redistribution amounted to more than 6 million ha, that is, about 30 per cent of total cultivable land, and from this almost two-thirds were allocated to 1.4 million peasant families whilst the rest was as a state reserve consecutively used for further settlement. In spite of the substantial transformation in ownership there remained a sizeable area in the hands of large farms and estates (0.8 per cent of the total number of holdings on 27.7 per cent of total agricultural land) whilst 75 per cent of the total number of holdings at 28 per cent of total cultivated land consisted of no more than 5 ha. The Romanian land reform did not liquidate large estates altogether and in this respect it was not completed at the end of the 1930s, having left many landowners (according to official figures 3,900) eligible for expropriation in possession, but it extended owner occupation considerably creating in the process a sharp increase in very small and dwarf holdings. Whilst in the short term greater equality was obtained by emphasizing the social and national aspect of the reform, the economic necessity to provide adequate state aid to newly established farms was essentially neglected and thus any possible initial economic advantage was lost.

Chronologically, Czechoslovakia followed Yugoslavia and Romania in implementing her land reform and, although in social and national aims there was little difference and also in intensity of structural change it was similar, it differed greatly in its economic effect. Its realization became one of the most significant actions of the Czechoslovak state which was compelled to introduce a reform programme not only because of the revolutionary movement and the existence of an acute land hunger but also because of the need for further modernization, for supporting and increasing capitalist production and marketing methods in agriculture to provide, at the same time, more favourable economic conditions for further industrial growth. Striking structural changes resulted from the implementation of three main laws: the Land Confiscation Bill of 16 April 1919 concerning all landowners with holdings over 150 ha arable and over 250 ha non-arable land; then the Land Allocation Bill of 30 January 1920 by which smallholders were to be satisfied prior to all other claimants, and the land which was left over was to be divided up into 'residual estates' (holdings of substantial size averaging 80–100 ha) – the actual procedure was mainly the other way round; and lastly, the Compensation Bill of 8 April 1920 regulated the prices to be paid to owners of the confiscated land. The results of the Land Reform of 1919 as summed up by the administrative centre created by the state, the Czechoslovak Land Office, at the end of 1937 were that 29 per cent of all the land in the country (4 million ha) of which 16 per cent was arable (1.3 million ha) came under the Confiscation Act. However, 57 per cent of the confiscated land was in the course of time returned to the original owners and another 34 per cent was eventually exempted from confiscation, thus altogether 1,800,782 ha were actually redistributed. The most marked and thus structurally most important new element consisted of 2,291 residual estates taking up 226,306 ha with an average holding of 100 ha (85 ha of which was, as a rule, arable land) which increased the number of capitalist agricultural enterprises. The socio-political aspect of the land reform emerges in the allocation of 789,803 ha to 638,182 peasants whose average holding was about 1.2 ha. These holdings were insufficient for economic farming and the indebtedness of small peasant holdings rose steadily. On the one hand, the land reform created a large number of new small and medium holdings, many of which went under fairly soon. On the other hand, the last vestiges of feudal survivals definitely disappeared and the agrarian bourgeoisie was substantially strengthened. The changes in the structure of agricultural holdings show a decisive increase in the share of arable land for the medium and larger farms which were run on a strict profit basis. Czechoslovak agriculture was thus enabled to accumulate capital and transfer part of it into industry.

The Polish, Hungarian, and Bulgarian land reforms did not pave the way to any significant changes in the countries' agrarian structure and were, essentially, ineffective in producing a sounder basis for industrialization.

In Poland the immediate fear of peasant revolts strongly influenced the timing of the enactment of the land reform on 10 July 1919 which came into force at the height of the Soviet-Russo–Polish war on 15 July 1920. Yet, the pace of its implementation was so slack, particularly after political stabilization of the Polish regime, that new legislation had to be passed on 28 December 1925 and an annual target for land allocation of 200,000 ha was set. But in the early 1930s the administration of the law practically ground to a halt. Altogether 2.65 million ha, that is, about 10 per cent of total agricultural land, was distributed in diminutive parcels to landless peasants between 1919 and 1938, whilst 5.4 million ha were allocated to peasants to increase the size of their holdings. Thus the reform reduced the number of dwarf holdings and increased the category of holdings between 2 and 10 ha. However, neither were the large estates broken up, nor land fragmentation stopped, nor landlessness removed. The slowness of redistribution which averaged 133,000 ha annually could not keep up with the fast-growing population amounting to 250,000 annually in rural areas and, in this sense, the nature of the land reform in Poland even aggravated the problem of landlessness, rural unemployment, and inefficiency of agricultural production. In fact, the great noble families remained a powerful political force.

Similarly, and even more urgently, political and social motives rather than economic policy were decisive in the land reform in Hungary. In the revolutionary wave of 1918 and 1919, first the democratic government of Count Mihály Károly promised the peasants land, but was quickly superseded by the short-lived Communist regime of Béla Kun who had visions of collectivized agriculture. When the counter-revolution brought Admiral Horthy into power a Land Reform Bill was passed in 1920 to avoid further unrest and a Land Reform Court was established to regulate distribution. This most moderate reform of the region resulted in an even more unfavourable agrarian structure in Trianon Hungary than in the pre-1914 period, mainly because of the dominant political influence of the landed aristocracy. At the end of the inter-war period about 1,500 large estates amounting to 0.1 per cent of the total number of holdings occupied 23.5 per cent of total cultivated land, whilst 99.9 per cent of holdings between 1 and 50 ha owned 53.6 per cent of agricultural land. Hungary's land reform created the largest rural proletariat in south-east Europe; that is, agricultural labourers' and peasants' holdings less than 1 ha accounted for 52.3 per cent of all active persons in agriculture as against 15.7 per cent in Romania, 15.2 per cent in Yugoslavia and 9.1 per cent in Bulgaria.

Under the influence of the radical peasant leader Alexander Stamboliski Bulgaria also introduced a land reform in 1921 which only strengthened the small-scale agriculture that had resulted from previous reforms. The enactment to limit the maximum size of holdings to 30 ha and to redistribute 6 per cent of the country's agricultural land served also to settle refugees from Thrace and Macedonia in the early 1920s. Measures connected with the land reform could not stop the continuous process of fragmentation and redivision of land which accompanied the fast-growing population in all east-central and south-east European countries, except Czechoslovakia. The process of subdivision of land as a corollary to government policy and rapid population growth was strongest in Bulgaria. This was a serious obstacle to efforts aimed at raising the level of efficiency of farming. Agriculture was thus unable to make any worthwhile contribution to investment in industry.

The implementation, administration, and execution of land reforms, generally entrusted to special government institutions, became an integral part of social and economic policies of the Central and south-east European states during the 1920s and continued to do so practically throughout the whole inter-war period. Government acts to redistribute land were initiated mainly for political reasons to meet, at least formally, the peasants' revolutionary demands, but in the course of their fulfilment legal, social, national, and economic aspects came into play. In the legal sphere the abolition of the last feudal remnants strengthened individual/private ownership and the marketability of land. In the social sphere some of the most obvious inequalities were removed; war veterans, orphans and widows, and refugees were settled on allotted land, their claims receiving priority. At the same time national sentiments were rewarded by transfers of landed property from alien owners into indigenous hands; loyal citizens were settled in strategically sensitive frontier districts. However, compensation to former owners had to be paid in every country. Undoubtedly, the social cause and effect of land reforms can be regarded as paramount, but their economic significance cannot be underrated. Through them the structure of land ownership was changed to a greater or lesser extent in every country by state intervention. Although such shifts in property relations made hardly any net contribution to total gross capital formation they were part of a restructuring process in the region's economies with widely varying results. On the one side, the medium-size unit in agricultural holdings in Czechoslovakia was strengthened which increased efficiency in producing for the market, whilst in other countries this category of holdings remained of little economic significance. On the other side, especially in Yugoslavia and Bulgaria, by increasing subsistence agriculture on small and dwarf holdings the non-market sector of those economies tended to grow.[13]

On the whole, state policy connected with land reforms failed to stimulate technical improvements and the growth of agricultural production sufficiently. It failed to create agricultural credit for productive investment and thus failed to give aid in closing the gap between agriculture and industry.

Thus as an instrument of policy to promote investment the land reforms fell short of providing a basis for eventual transfers of capital and labour into industry, except in Czechoslovakia. There, above all, the cooperative movement emanating from the development of Czech capitalism traditionally has been performing an effective economic function by concentrating the widely scattered financial resources of the countryside and creating a basis for the accumulation of capital for agrarian credit, as well as providing a channel for the transfer of agrarian capital to industry. The Czech agricultural cooperatives established a central organ as early as 1921 at the initiative of the Ministry of Agriculture and by 1924 the German and Slovak cooperatives affiliated with it. Its top organization became the Centrokooperativ which controlled about 90 per cent of all existing agricultural cooperatives and acted as an auditing centre; it also decided centrally on marketing and credit conditions and represented the Czechoslovak agricultural cooperatives at home and abroad.[14]

In the centralized federative organs of the agricultural cooperatives agrarian capital was concentrated, and this enabled them to control credit and trade with agricultural products and investment into agricultural industry and into the great joint-stock companies of the chemical and armaments industries. The cooperatives became powerful partners of industrialists and bankers and by controlling the Agrarian Party (Republikánská strana malorolnického lidu – Republican Party of Smallholders), the strongest political party in the country, their representatives belonged to the leading politicians and took up important government posts (for example, prime ministers, ministers of agriculture, interior and defence). Due to the cooperative movement, its ability to organize the bulk of the agricultural population (of a population of 15

[13] Jerzy Tomaszewski, 'Some Problems of the Capital Formation', p. 150. In addition, hoarding served to extend the non-market character of agriculture in many areas in the Danubian region. In the Balkan countries the amount of hoards were estimated at almost one-quarter of total money in circulation. See *Economic Development in South-Eastern Europe*, PEP (London, 1945), p. 114.

[14] Ladislav K. Feierabend, *Agricultural Cooperatives in Czechoslovakia 1918–1938* (New York, 1952).

million in Czechoslovakia 6 million were associated with the cooperative movement), its tradition in gathering up the peasants' savings, its monopolistic practices, and its political power and influence on state policy, Czechoslovak agriculture became more intertwined with industry than that of any other Central and south-east European country.

However, the organizational framework for gathering up potential capital from agriculture was not lacking in the other countries either as there existed various and numerous cooperatives of agricultural producers, consumers, and savers which could have become a wide-flung basis for agricultural credit and capital accumulation. Indeed, any advance in financing agriculture in the region was primarily due to a combination of cooperative activity and state intervention. In Hungary agricultural credit was encouraged by the state and was given to farmers through the banking system but used chiefly to buy more land and buildings and very little was applied to raising productivity. Poland possessed a relatively well-organized system of credit cooperatives which were centralized with state aid to form the Centralna Kasa Spółek Rolniczych in 1924, but its interest rates of 36–180 per cent served to contract rather than expand credit. Ruinous interest rates were quite usual in the Balkan countries and due to the backward credit and banking systems the burden of indebtedness in agriculture could not be lightened perceivably through state policy.[15] For instance new banks were founded in Bulgaria with state aid, such as the Bulgarian Agrarian Bank and the Bulgarian Central Cooperative Bank and the Bulgarian Mortgage Bank, with the express aim to finance agriculture, and also the Bulgarian National Bank was empowered to provide loans to peasants. But the bulk of agricultural credit came from private merchants, publicans, and moneylenders. This was the case also in Romania and Yugoslavia; the more backward the area the higher and the more usurous were interest rates. In order to lessen the hardships of procuring credit the Bulgarian government spent 50 million leva on agricultural machines which were sold to peasants on hire purchase below purchasing prices; the Yugoslav government legislated in June 1925 to establish the Privilegovana Agrarna Banka which was to provide credit at 5 per cent interest especially to new farms, but it started to function only on 16 April 1929. Most of these administrative steps were taken by states in the more favourable economic conditions of the second half of the 1920s when agricultural world prices were rising. This proved to be too little and too late, for any noticeable productive use of credit was frustrated by the impact of the world economic crisis.

Thus as a domestic source of capital accumulation the agricultural sector proved largely futile. Agriculture was neither able to contribute

[15] Piper, *Grundprobleme*, p. 78.

significantly to domestic capital formation nor to induce an expansion of purchasing power for industrial goods on the home market and thus could not play the same role as it had played in nineteenth-century industrialization in Western European countries when part of the fast-growing population on the land was transferred into industry. In Central and south-east Europe, except Czechoslovakia, the rapidly increasing rural population could not be adequately absorbed into industry because industrial growth, being hindered by backward conditions in agriculture, was not large and rapid enough to do so. The vital relationship between agriculture and industry was caught up in this vicious circle and without breaking out of it no significant advance in economic development could be expected.

IV. *Promotion of investment and industry*

Since, after the ravages of war, over the major part of the region production had fallen to less than half in comparison with 1913 and continued to decline during 1919, which in turn accelerated the war-induced inflationary development, the ever-present need for capital became acutely urgent. In order to realize the transition to peace production in the newly established national states and in order to stabilize their economies and thus their regimes, the successor governments' uppermost concern was to procure capital. The immediate problem on their markets was not a lack of demand. Quite the contrary, as they faced an excess demand inflation. The phenomenon of an insufficient home market and the need for remedial state intervention occurred later, soon after stabilization in the second half of the 1920s; whilst in the first post-war years there existed a dearth in supplies of producer and consumer goods. Indeed, how to acquire capital for industrial production was one of the crucial economic questions in inter-war east-central and south-east Europe.

Factors which had necessitated swift government action in the agricultural sector demanded state intervention in the industrial field. Most immediately, as a result of civil wars and uprisings in Eastern Europe, strong pressures urging the socialization, that is, the abolition, of private ownership of large factories and big banks endured. Each new government on taking power had declared all existing laws and ordinances of the old empires as remaining in force to give the successor states a still-functioning legal apparatus as an instrument of social control until they were able to create their own police force and equip and train a new national army. Another powerful factor was nationalism which played an equally important part in state intervention in industry as it did in the concept of land reforms. Indeed, government policy in all states under discussion here was successful in replacing socialization with nationalization by legally enforcing the transfer of foreign- (former enemy-) owned property wherever possible into domestic ownership, preferably into the hands of the ethnic majority whose interests the state chiefly represented. This was to be realized by the purchase of shares in enterprises and banks from their foreign owners under the legislative process known as *Nostrification*.

The possibility of such transfers was given to the successor states belonging to the victorious camp, Czechoslovakia, Poland, Romania, and Yugoslavia, by article 297 of the Versailles peace treaty concerning property of German nationals, by article 249 of the treaty of St Germain and by article 232 of the Trianon treaty with regards to Austrian and Hungarian nationals respectively. Thus *Nostrification* became an expression of national economic policy in the first phase of those states' existence. The Czechoslovak government passed a *Nostrification* Act at the end of 1919 which enforced the transfer of managements and central offices of joint-stock companies, mainly from Vienna and Budapest, to the new state where their factories and works were situated. This was reinforced by a further act of parliament which required that at least half of the members of boards of directors of joint-stock companies and the general director had to be Czechoslovak citizens and the latter's domicile had to be on the territory of the new republic. With substantial government aid Czechoslovak banks and enterprises acquired Austrian-owned shares. These purchases could be made on very favourable terms as inflation spiralled in Austria and the Czechoslovak crown remained relatively strong. But also assets in other neighbouring countries where inflation rates were high were acquired by Czechoslovak entrepreneurs and Czechoslovak capital in many cases replaced Austrian and Hungarian controlling participations in Romanian and Yugoslav industrial companies.[16] *Nostrification* was most intensive in Czechoslovakia during 1921 and 1922 and was completed by the end of the 1920s. It affected 235 industrial companies and all the big banks exept the Živnostenská banka which had been purely Czech from its foundation. Part of the process included disinvestment in Slovakia's heavy industry and the concentration of large industrial capacities in the Czech Lands.

Romania took *Nostrification* in hand by a government order of 25 May 1919 requiring all German, Austrian, and Hungarian shares to be deposited for stamping, so that at a later date they could be purchased by Romanians. German interests were reduced chiefly in Romanian banking and in the oil industry, not so much by transfers to national Romanian capital but to Western European groups. A large part of Hungarian

[16] See Alice Teichova, *An Economic Background to Munich International Business and Czechoslovakia 1918–1938* (Cambridge, 1974), p. 98.

possessions on the ceded territory of Transylvania was transferred to the leading Romanian bank, the Banca Marmorosch Blank & Co., and industrial plant in the coal, cement, and engineering industries passed from Hungarian to Romanian management. Ownership relations, however, remained opaque. Most important for Romania's natural wealth was the section in her Constitution of 1923 which transferred the entire mining rights to the state; thus all natural resources underground were to be exploited either by government enterprise or by concessions granted by the state. This was followed by the Mining Law of 1925 which empowered the state to give concessions to Romanian joint-stock companies only in which at least 60 per cent of the shares, the president, and two-thirds of the board of directors were Romanian citizens. However, existing firms were given ten years' time to reach the legally required national company organization.[17]

Yugoslav nationalization and her use of *Nostrification* was much more moderate, but its effects in both countries, in Romania and Yugoslavia, was that state property increased. Also the Polish government attempted with meagre success to dislodge German ownership in the large companies of heavy industry in Silesia which had become part of the new Polish territory. Equally unsuccessful were the Polish government's endeavours to persuade its own national entrepreneurs to acquire majority control, or shares, in former enemy-owned companies. Only the property of the German and Austrian states was taken over by the Polish government, thus increasing state-ownership in Poland. In the process of nationalizing south-Polish resources the big bank, Bank Gospodarstwa Krajowego (1925), became an influential state-owned institution.[18] But, unlike in Czechoslovakia, Romania, and Yugoslavia, *Nostrification* did not constitute a consistent government policy in Poland.

The instrument of *Nostrification* was primarily resorted to in order to break the umbilical cord with Vienna and Budapest and, in Poland's case, also with Berlin. It could not solve the capital shortage in the successor states because it did not at first produce new funds; on the contrary, compensation had to be paid for shares. It did, however, strengthen domestic capital in the long run. Yet, because of the general lack of capital, not even the strongest domestic financial groups possessed sufficient financial resources to obtain majority holdings in the nationalization process, and, therefore, not only shifts from foreign to domestic entrepreneurs but also from former enemy alien to contemporary

---

[17] G. Ránki, 'The Role of the State in the Economy in the Interwar Period – Hungary, Yugoslavia, Bulgaria, Romania', *Papers in East European Economics*, no. 29 (Oxford, 1973); Nicolas Spulber, *The State and Economic Development in Eastern Europe* (New York, 1966).

[18] Zbigniew Landau and Jerzy Tomaszewski, *Zarys historii gospodarczej Polski 1918–1939* (Outline of an Economic History of Poland 1918–1939) (Warsaw, 1971).

friendly foreign investors took place. Thus shifts in ownership relations in industry and banking occurred on a similar national principle as in agriculture, but unlike the redivision of land in agricultural policy no social redistribution of property was included in industrial policy.

A. LEGISLATION FAVOURING INDUSTRIAL DEVELOPMENT

Due to the severe lack of domestic capital resources in the countries under discussion and their industries' dependence for a large part of capital supplies either on direct or indirect state intervention, of which the procurement of foreign investment was a vital part, governments introduced and extended legislation in furtherance of industrialization.

Continuing a well-established pre-war practice the east-central and south-east European states pursued policies of direct encouragement of industry from which both domestic and foreign investors were able to benefit. It was directed largely to those industries connected with army requirements (iron and steel, engineering, chemicals, textiles) and, in general, governments – not unlike the big banks and foreign investors – supported the relatively financially strongest and commercially soundest enterprises, thus enhancing the process of concentration.

All successor governments proffered preferential treatment to industrial companies mainly through their budgetary mechanism, such as duty-free imports of machinery and raw materials, substantial freight reductions and tax allowances, gifts or rent-free use of state-owned land for factory buildings, long-term tax exemptions and high tariff barriers for the manufacture of goods which hitherto had not been produced in the country, and many other externalities. At the same time the states themselves, frequently by necessity, assumed the role of entrepreneur and of customer. They enforced national monopolies in the manufacture of products which could comparatively easily be controlled like tobacco, salt, explosives, saccharine, matches, and playing cards. Such monopolies were either effectively administered by the states themselves or concessions were granted to domestic and often to foreign entrepreneurs.

Although state monopolies (e.g., tobacco, saccharine, explosives) also existed in Czechoslovakia and her government imposed one of the strictest systems of controls in Europe, the state itself did not, as a rule, invest directly in industry or administer state enterprises. Private investment expanded in the Czechoslovak economy within a favourable legal climate created by the state. From 1924 the government abstained from major internal borrowings, thus keeping the level of domestic public indebtedness comparatively low and releasing sources of savings to investors. Legislation to encourage private investment in industry was much more pronounced in other Eastern European states than in

Czechoslovakia but they could neither objectively nor subjectively obtain similar results.

Hungary's post-war economic collapse had led to a conscious policy of her government to finance and reorganize the national economy, which was pursued with uneven intensity and varying success during the 1920s when government financing of domestic needs was largely derived from the money printing presses and from foreign loans. During the inflationary years the Hungarian government supported company financing by granting frequent new share issues which each time increased in volume; it also exempted company reserves which were not used for dividend payment from taxation. Such funds, if quickly invested, could be employed for productive purposes, or, under conditions of a rapidly depreciating currency, be used to rid enterprises of their debts. In 1920 a State Credit Issuing Office (Országos Központi Hitelszövetkezet) was established in Budapest which granted unvalorized credits to industrial establishments.[19] As these loans were repayable at face value, the debtor who had purchased land, buildings and machinery or goods gained productive capacity under very favourable conditions. In general, large enterprises benefited most. Thus, to a certain extent, inflationary government policies aided the conversion of war to peace production in Hungary.[20] The same effect was achieved in other successor states, which were experiencing inflationary booms of varying intensity and length; but in the process many European states ended up holding substantial amounts of industrial shares. This was not so much the case in Hungary where direct government enterprise amounted to only slightly more than 5 per cent of total joint-stock capital, whereas over 70 per cent was in the hands of domestic owners, predominantly in conjunction with the seven largest commercial banks, and about 25 per cent of total shares were held by foreign investors.[21] However, the proportions of shareholdings between domestic and foreign capitalists in Hungary can only be regarded as fairly vague approximations, for in Hungarian commerical practice shares were mainly issued to 'bearer' and not to 'name'. Thus it is difficult to distinguish between domestic and foreign capital in public companies.[22]

Following a tradition from the end of the nineteenth century, the post-1918 Hungarian government added further enactments favouring indus-

---

[19] Országos Központi Hitelszövetkezet was established by amendment xxx/1920 of the act of 1898/xxiii.

[20] Elizabeth A. Boross, 'The Role of the State Issuing Bank in the Course of Inflation in Hungary between 1918 and 1924', in Gerald D. Feldman, Carl-Ludwig Holtfrerich, Gerhard A. Ritter, Peter-Christian Witt (eds.), *The Experience of the Inflation: International and Comparative Studies* (Berlin and New York, 1984), pp. 188–227.

[21] I. T. Berend and G. Ránki, *Magyarország gyáripara a második világháború elött és a háború időszakávan (1933–1944)* (The Hungarian Manufacturing Industry before and during the Second World War 1933–1944) (Budapest, 1958), p. 132.

[22] Public Record Office, London, Board of Trade Report 11/40/C.R.T. 3492/29.

trialization to its bill of 1907 relating to the development of home industry. All regulations issued for the purpose of encouraging investment in Hungary referred both to national and foreign capital. Neither was there any legal provision about the nationality of members of boards of directors as, for instance, in Czechoslovakia and Romania, although in judicial practice it was desirable that such boards should not be composed entirely of foreigners. In practice Hungarian legislation greatly favoured its own industrialists and provided every encouragement to attract foreign capital.

Similar, even more strenuous, endeavours by the government in Poland to encourage private investment in industry resulted in a complete reversal of roles in which the state became the main investor not only in industry but in all walks of life. The inability, inertia, cautiousness, and reluctance of the generally weak strata of Polish entrepreneurs forced the government into an increasing investment activity which is associated with etatism in Poland during the inter-war period. Poland's economy found itself in even greater straits than Hungary's with regards to capital accumulation, and – although the weight of her agriculture was similar to the Hungarian economy – she resembled in her low level of savings and investments the predominantly agricultural economies of south-east Europe.

In the early stage of the Polish independent state, government programmes of industrial policy were influenced by liberal ideas but realities proved to be inconsistent with such theoretical tendencies. In spite of the great number of extraordinary privileges offered by the Polish government to potential investors, whether private individuals, firms, or foreign states, capital could not be attracted in sufficient amounts to infuse significant industrialization. By the mid-twenties active capital had sunk to below 25 per cent of the pre-war level and total deposits in banks on the territories within the boundaries of the inter-war Polish state amounted to about 11 per cent of those in 1913.[23]

Investment in industry was not only encouraged by legislation but conducted increasingly by the state itself which had to function as an entrepreneur and engage in industrial activity. As a result nearly one-third of Poland's entire joint-stock capital in industry was held by the state, just under one-half was in foreign hands, leaving hardly one-quarter in the ownership of domestic private enterprise.[24] Most conspicuous of all state enterprises were the undertaking in connection with the building of the port of Gdynia in the 1920s and the establishment of

[23] Z. Landau and J. Tomaszewski, *Bank Handlowy w Warszawie S.A. History and Development 1870–1970* (Warsaw, 1970), pp. 45–6.

[24] M. Drozdowski, *Polityka Gospodarca Rządu Polskiego* (Economic Policy of the Polish State 1936–1939) (Warsaw, 1963), p. 21.

the Central Industrial Region (Centralny Okreg Przemysłowy – COP) for defence reasons at the end of the 1930s. By that time etatism was established in Poland.

The system of state intervention in industry is in no other south-east European country so well documented as in Bulgaria, but in Romania and Yugoslavia also industrial policy of the state had in principle the same aims and tended to have similar results. Industrial enterprise in the whole south-eastern region suffered from a chronically low level of savings and inefficiency of the credit system.

In inter-war Bulgaria the entire state-encouraged sector of industry comprised just under one-third of the total number of enterprises including some of the largest, employed just under one-half of all persons active in industry, and produced two-thirds of the total value of the country's total industrial output.[25] State encouragement provided these favoured enterprises with opportunities to accumulate and invest capital, although these were sparingly realized, and enhanced their chances to attract foreign capital investment. Accordingly, by 1929 foreigners held well over two-thirds of total Bulgarian share capital and by the end of the inter-war period, when the proportion of domestic capital had increased, foreign investors still owned more than half of Bulgaria's total joint-stock capital.[26] State encouragement gave the same and in many cases even more privileges to foreign-owned as to domestic industrial enterprises.

As to state encouragement of industrial investment in Romania, a special institution was set up in 1923, the Societatea Nationala de Credit Industrial (SNCI), which advanced credits at 10 per cent to enterprises owned by Romanians or with Romanian interests. Those credits amounted to about 2 milliard lei annually on the average, of which 40 per cent was granted to the textile industry. Although the activities of the SNCI contributed to investment in Romania's industry, the capital it provided covered approximately 5 per cent of the total annual demand for investments. In its policy the SNCI gave preference to large existing companies wishing to extend their production base or to the establishment of new large-scale production lines. In addition to far-reaching legislation favouring industrial development the Romanian state aided private enterprise in self-financing by placing large orders and paying advances on them which reached up to 40 per cent of the value of the orders. By the end of the inter-war period the state bought about 70 per cent of the entire coal output and 80 per cent of the total output of the

[25] Calculated from *Staticheski Godishnik na Bulgarskoto Tsarstvo* (1938, 1939, 1940).

[26] Calculated from Peter Aladjoff, 'Das Auslandskapital in Bulgarien' (dissertation, University of Berlin, 1942); and L. Berov, 'The Withdrawing of Western Capitals from Bulgaria on the Eve of the Second World War', *Studia Balcanica*, no. 1 (1969).

metallurgy industry of Romania. The biggest companies in these branches of heavy industry reaped state support and in them foreign capital substantially participated.[27]

Yugoslavia's records do not allow an assessment in greater detail. However, since entrepreneurship was lacking, the state had taken over mines and industrial enterprises in the metal, wood, chemical, and textile industries, mainly from the comparatively most industrially advanced former Austro-Hungarian territory (Slovenia). Yugoslav government legislation in furtherance of industry began in 1919 and was maintained and enlarged during the whole period. In the first inter-war decade 28–39 per cent of Yugoslavia's budget expenditure was allotted to state enterprises.[28]

Just as Poland's etatism arose out of the necessity of state direction of industry because of the deficiencies in domestic capital accumulation and entrepreneurship, the weakness of private enterprise in Bulgaria led to a comprehensive policy of state encouragement of industry, and almost identical conditions evoked far-reaching economic legislation, state enterprises, and state direction of industry in Romania and Yugoslavia. Hungary's laws for the development of home industry particularly favoured those wishing to invest in industrial activity irrespective of their nationality. Still, the fundamental problem remained the lack of capital for investment. All the east-central and south-east European states recognized the continuing inadequacy of native capital. Therefore, in their legislation for the furtherance of industry, substantial favours, privileges, concessions, licences, various safeguards, and every possible encouragement was offered to attract foreign capital.

V. The quest for capital

One of the main outside influences affecting economic policies of the east-central and south-east European states was the peace settlement as its consequences could aid or impair industrial reconstruction.

The Versailles peace treaties, by which Germany and her allies formally accepted responsibility for causing the First World War and, consequently, undertook to make compensation for all damages, created legal conditions by means of their financial and economic clauses in favour of the victorious economies and to the detriment of the defeated states. Thus, at the same time as the treaties of 1919 and 1920 codified the

---

[27] Figures on Romania calculated from *Anuarul Statistic al României* (1938–9); *Statistisches Taschenbuch von Rumänien* (1941); *Statistica Soc. An.*, vol. xx (1938); see also V. G. Axenciuc, 'Les monopoles dans l'industrie de la Roumaine', *Revue Roumaine d'Histoire*, vol. iv, no. 1 (1965).

[28] Sergije Dimitrijević, *Das ausländische Kapital in Jugoslawien vor dem Zweiten Weltkrieg* (Berlin, 1962), p. 14.

changes in the balance of power which had arisen as a result of the outcome of the war they provided a legal framework within which economic relationships were substantially altered.[29] International trade and investment, above all, offered the victors advantageous opportunities since the allied and associated powers were granted most-favoured-nation treatment on the territory of the central powers for the first five post-war years, whilst the German, Austrian, Hungarian, and Bulgarian governments were to give up all rights, privileges, and immunities of sovereignty in international trade; only concessions to former inter-Habsburg monarchy commercial relations were granted. During the same period of five years after signing the peace treaties Germany and her allies were to modify their laws to protect the property rights of the Entente and Associated nations and afford their nationals the same legal position, protection, and privileges as enjoyed by indigenous nationals. This was to facilitate any takeover bids or the acquisition of direct participating capital investment by businessmen and -groups of the victorious nations in banks, commercial, and industrial companies belonging to nationals of the defeated countries at home or abroad. In addition, the position of creditors from the Entente and Associated countries was greatly strengthened in relation to debtors from the states of the central powers by the treaty provision that each of the Allied and Associated states could dispose of enemy assets and property within its jurisdiction.[30]

It has been assumed that the east-central and south-east European region was – due to the break-up of the Austro-Hungarian monarchy – virtually paralysed economically and thus offered little attraction to prospective investors from the Western democracies, and that urgent pleas for aid from the new governments met with little response.[31] Statistics published by the League of Nations – which are, however, only available from 1923 onwards – seem to back up the assumption that foreign investment was obtained by the successor states to a larger extent only later in the 1920s after they had stabilized their political systems and their currencies.[32] However, this view needs to be revised, for it applies primarily to public loans. In the immediate post-First World War years

---

[29] *The Treaty of Peace between the Allied and Associated Powers and Germany* (further German Treaty) (London, 1919), arts. 231 and 232, pp. 101–2; *The Treaty of Peace between the Allied and Associated Powers and Austria* (further Austrian Treaty) (London, 1921), arts. 177 and 178, pp. 63–4; especially parts IX and X in both treaties.

[30] *Ibid.*, German Treaty, arts. 252, 264–7, 276–7, 281; Austrian Treaty, arts. 201, 217–20, 228–9, 233.

[31] Ivan T. Berend, 'Investment Strategy in East-Central Europe' in H. Daems and H. van der Wee (eds.), *The Rise of Managerial Capitalism* (Louvain, 1974), p. 185; also Rudolf Nötel, 'International Capital Movements and Finance in Eastern Europe 1919–1949', *Vierteljahrschrift für Sozial- und Wirtschaftsgeschichte*, vol. LXI, no. 1 (1975), pp. 79ff.

[32] League of Nations, *Statistical Yearbook* (Geneva, 1928, 1929), Balances of Payments.

there existed objective economic and specific political conditions which were more conducive to participation of foreign capital in the Danubian region – especially in the three main successor states, Austria, Hungary, and Czechoslovakia – than has been supposed. The new governments sought political and financial support from leading European Entente powers, as they were convinced that their economies would not be viable without foreign aid and they considered Western capital as essential for their own economic development; but also, and more immediately, as a safeguard against uncontrollable inflation and as a means of meeting their rising budget deficits.

Thus the main engineers of the Versailles system decisively influenced – for better or for worse – the path and methods of economic reconstruction in the lands between Germany and Russia. On the supply side funds were available for investment as they had accumulated during the war years in the economies of the great powers and were seeking profitable outlets, whilst the direction and amount of their deployment remained essentially under government controls. On the demand side throughout Europe, but particularly in the east-central and south-east European area, there were desperate shortages of capital; these were enhanced by the great demand for imports of raw materials to keep the industries going and by the constant shrinking of the value of money during rising inflations. Prospective investors were indeed encouraged to take advantage of the inflationary situation by bankers and industrialists and, above all, by politicians of the east-central European countries.[33] In this way a buyer's market arose which was reinforced by sharp competition amongst the successor states for capital imports from the Entente powers. In striving for foreign loans and investments the governments, particularly of the defeated states, hoped that, in return for favourable treatment of Western, above all British and French investors, certain advantages would accrue to them by mitigating the rigorous conditions of the Versailles treaties, or by alleviating the expected burdens under consideration by the Reparation Commission, and by gaining assistance in the procurement of state loans.

The strenuous efforts of the successor states to attract capital did not remain without success. There is ample evidence that there existed an active interest in business circles of the Allied states to acquire assets either in return for their exports (by accepting shares in the industrial enterprises of the importing countries with an unfavourable exchange rate in payment for raw materials or goods) or to purchase shares in reputable banks, industrial and transport companies in the countries of east-central

[33] Alice Teichova, 'Versailles and the Expansion of the Bank of England into Central Europe', in Norbert Horn and Jürgen Kocka (eds.), *Recht und Entwicklung der Grossunternehmen im 19. und frühen 20. Jahrhundert* (Göttingen, 1979), pp. 370–1.

Europe much below their real value because their currencies were inflated out of all proportions.[34]

The shift of interest towards east-central and south-east Europe was connected with the defeat of the central powers and also with the loss of the Russian market after the Soviet government had nationalized and confiscated foreign holdings at the end of 1917. Since the greater part of French long-term investment in Europe and half of British capital export to Europe had been placed in tsarist Russia, the newly established states in east-central and south-east Europe were to provide a field for capital investment which would substitute to some extent for the losses suffered in Russia. Although the Western powers accepted the political reality of the successor states and regarded them as a belt (or cordon sanitaire) which was to immunize Poland and the Danubian Basin, on the one hand, against infiltration of Bolshevism from Soviet Russia and, on the other, against renewed German Mitteleuropa aspirations, they regarded the area as a single unit with relation to their economic interests.[35] Yet, within this general context the successor states were able either individually to pursue their own national aims against each other or in changing combinations to further their own interests.

In the immediate post-war years France and Britain alike aimed at eliminating Germany as a serious rival in international trade. Thus there existed a community of interests in both countries between the policy-makers at their ministries of foreign affairs and economic ministries, as well as their banking and industrial circles, about the necessity to penetrate into former German markets and thus prevent a revival of Germany's pre-war economic, financial, and diplomatic positions.[36] Considerations such as these influenced the direction and composition of French and British capital exports into the east-central and south-east European countries. However similar the aims of France's and Britain's economic diplomacy may have been, their motivations in channelling investments to the successor states through their systems of capital export controls differed fairly substantially.[37]

France's preoccupation with security and military prestige in Europe intensified her awareness that her economic position was substantially weaker than that of her Anglo-American allies, particularly in the area of international investment. Therefore, her capital export aimed to close

[34] See Philip L. Cottrell, 'Aspects of Western Equity Investment in the Banking Systems of East Central Europe', in Alice Teichova and Philip L. Cottrell (eds.), *International Business and Central Europe 1919–1939* (Leicester and New York, 1983).
[35] Teichova, *An Economic Background*, pp. 14–16, 378.
[36] *Ibid.*; concerning Britain, see Marie-Luise Recker, *England und der Donauraum 1919–1929* (Stuttgart, 1979).
[37] Alice Teichova and Penelope Ratcliffe, 'British Interests in Danube Navigation after 1918', *Business History*, vol. XXVII, no. 3 (November 1985), p. 284.

any permanent ties of the receiving countries with her own economy. Between 1919 and 1921 the French government encouraged leading business groups to obtain strong positions in those east-central European countries which were traditionally francophile by securing permanent participations of French concerns in enterprises which dominated the economy of these countries. Thus France's endeavours to acquire key positions in banking and heavy industry of the successor economies and to strengthen her hold over these states by military alliances arose out of her comparatively weak position among the victorious powers and were not only directed against potential German but also actual allied, particularly British competition in this area.

Britain's increased economic interest in east-central and south-east Europe also emanated from her generally changed position in the world economy, but her priorities differed from those of France. British capital export to this region was intended to open up or expand formerly neglected markets for British goods. The British government and its diplomats extended active political support to those businessmen and bankers who were interested in investment in the Danubian Basin, for they considered capital injections from Britain necessary in order to help rebuild trade connections. From the point of view of global economic policy Britain's interest in east-central and south-east Europe was a post-war addition to the areas of her main concern, the British Empire and Latin America; and yet, from the very beginning of the inter-war period she played a leading role in the economic life of the region.

The period from 1919 to 1923/4 is decisive for changes in the structure and the importance of international investments in the east-central and south-east European area, for in those years the inter-war contours were drawn. Instead of the traditional form of capital export which before 1914 consisted mainly of foreign loans, in the immediate post-war period influential financial and business groups from the Western democracies, strongly encouraged and urged by the east-central and south-east European governments, acquired direct participating shares in the joint-stock capital of the largest commercial banks and industrial companies of the successor states and, at the same time, decisive influence in their business strategy. Governments on both sides of the spectrum not only supported these shifts in ownership relations but their presidents, prime ministers, foreign and finance ministers were actively engaged in their realization, in the process of which German, Austrian, and also Hungarian interests were largely ousted from key positions in the east-central and south-east European economies by French, British, Belgian, Swiss, and Italian groups.

The most direct and effective access to the economic life of the east-central and south-east European countries led through the great Viennese commercial banks which historically – under conditions of relative economic backwardness – have tended to replace the capital market and have channelled funds into industry.[38] After 1918 they were the best assets the Austrian state, hovering on the brink of bankruptcy, and its indebted bankers had to offer in their quest for capital; and the Entente governments regarded them as such. The big banks of Vienna had secured strategic positions in almost all branches of industry, and the war years had accelerated further concentration and strengthened their economic power. Numerous industrial companies clustered round them either through direct participating investments or through credits. In this way the large joint-stock banks had thrown a net of relationships of various degrees of dependency over virtually every field of production and reached from Vienna to all territories of the former monarchy and the Balkans. As the Austro-Hungarian Empire disintegrated the leading Viennese banks found themselves suddenly at the head of multinational, diversified combines. But due to serious reductions in their liquidity their ability to provide credits to the economy generally, and to their own subsidiaries in particular, steadily weakened. Centripetal efforts by the other successor economies to cut loose from Vienna, as well as inflation, exacerbated their instability. In order to rescue their position and, where possible, their influence the Viennese joint-stock banks solicited foreign direct participation in their capital. They could offer their foreign investors, who penetrated into their concerns from above, influence in their subsidiary companies, which in turn could expect new supplies of credit from their new, mainly Western European, shareholders.

Within a surprisingly short space of time, between 1919 and 1922, the eight greatest Viennese banks were internationalized.[39] Two were fully incorporated into Western institutions. The one, the Anglo-Austrian Bank, moved its headquarters to London as a subsidiary of the Bank of England which prevented the dissipation of its assets in the Danubian region and thus it could deal with Central and Eastern Europe through its former branches in the capitals of the successor states. After the absorp-

---

[38] Eduard März, *Österreichische Industrie- und Bankpolitik in der Zeit Franz Josephs I* (Vienna, 1968); Richard Rudolph, *Banking and Industrialization in Austria–Hungary* (Cambridge, 1976).

[39] See Cottrell, 'Aspects of Western Equity Investment'; Teichova, 'Versailles and the Expansion of the Bank of England'. It has been suggested by Herbert Matis, 'Disintegration and Multinational Enterprises in Central Europe during the Postwar Years (1918–1923)' in A. Teichova and P. L. Cottrell (eds.), *International Business and Central Europe 1918–1939* (Leicester and New York, 1983), that Western capital acted mostly as a cloak for Austrian and also Hungarian interests. Evidence from national and company archives leaves little doubt about the effective, controlling direct participation by foreign investors in the most important enterprises in that period. See, for example, report of the British ambassador, Lindley, dated 23 June 1921, Public Records Office, London, FO371/4645; or case studies in Teichova, *An Economic Background*, and Teichova and Cottrell, *International Business*.

tion of the Viennese branch of the Anglo-Austrian Bank into the Österreichische Kreditanstalt für Handel und Gewerbe (Austrian Credit-Anstalt) in 1926, the subsidiary in Prague, the Anglo-Czechoslovak Bank, formed a point of intersection for British capital in the whole area throughout the inter-war period. The other, the Österreichische Länderbank, became a branch of the Paris headquartered Banque des Pays de l'Europe Centrale, as did its former branches in the Danubian countries, 'in order to carry on . . . and assist the economic development of Central Europe and support international trade and commerce'.[40] This diversified banking–industrial structure, which similarly to the Anglo-Austrian Bank had its most valuable subsidiary industrial enterprises in Czechoslovakia, survived until the Anschluss in 1938 and the dismemberment of Czechoslovakia in 1939.

The remaining great banks of Vienna were not wholly taken over by Western banking and business groups, but either a majority or a large packet of their shares were acquired by them, and it soon became evident that Austrian capital lost its former importance in the economies of the successor states as the intermediary function of the big Viennese commercial banks between Western European finance and the Eastern European countries receded considerably and was primarily replaced by British, French, Belgian, Swiss, and Czechoslovak financial institutions. The only and biggest bank in Vienna which still held the two parts of the former Dual Monarchy together was the Österreichische Kreditanstalt für Handel und Gewerbe through its holdings in the Hungarian General Credit Bank (Magyar Általános Hitelbank), although international groups also participated in its capital.

Among the largest joint-stock banks in east-central European capital cities, the Živnostenská banka in Prague was a conspicuous exception, since no foreign capital participated in it; on the contrary, it penetrated through shareholdings, often together with Western business groups, into the south-east European banking and industrial system. But in the other six out of a total of eight largest commercial banks in Czechoslovakia substantial equity capital was owned by Western European and American financial groups, whereas before 1918 all these banks had been branches of Viennese banks.[41]

Backed by the monetary measures of their government the Czechoslovak banks had severed their ties with Vienna immediately after the break-up of the Austro-Hungarian Empire and through the Czechoslovak *Nostrification* Law they tried to acquire as many bank and industrial

---

[40] Finanzarchiv, Vienna–6574/21, Länderbankeingabe, 22 March 1921.
[41] Teichova, *An Economic Background*, p. 340.

shares on the territory of the new state as possible from Viennese financial institutions. Thus, the main feature of the Czechoslovak banking system between the two wars was the function of the financially strongest joint-stock banks as important centres of complicated and widespread holding companies which tied almost the whole structure of Czechoslovak industry together with the banks. Through equity holdings in the capital of these leading banks foreign investors indirectly participated in their industrial subsidiaries.

The historical experience of the Czechoslovak banks faced with competition and domination from Vienna was, to a certain extent, shared by the Hungarian banking system. Like the Prague banks, the great banks in Budapest either by shareholdings or credit ties wielded their influence over about 60 per cent of Hungary's industrial capital. The two largest joint-stock banks – the Hungarian General Credit Bank and the Pesti Magyar Kereskedelmi Bank (Hungarian Commercial Bank of Pest) – were able effectively to influence one-third of the capital of the whole Hungarian credit system. Foreign capital participated substantially by purchases of shares and taking up large parts of new issues in all important commercial banks in Budapest. However, the capacity of these financial institutions to accumulate capital, in spite of massive state support, greatly deteriorated after 1918 until it was virtually halted in 1930.[42]

In all countries of the area international investors were officially encouraged to participate direct in the equity capital of the leading banks and thus to penetrate into the network of links between banks and industrial enterprises, such as the Hungarian General Credit Bank in Budapest, the Bank Handłowy in Warsaw, the Banca Marmorosch, Blank and Co. in Bucharest, the Bulgarian General Credit Bank in Sofia.

Thus the successor state governments' efforts to procure capital aided the internationalization of the east-central and south-east European banking system. Concurrently it reopened a channel through which capital could reach industry, for through the commercial banks the creditor economies continued to use methods of financial penetration similar to the pre-war investment patterns in Austria–Hungary and in Russia.

Another problem facing the new states was the acute want of capital to maintain the chiefly state-owned passenger and goods traffic. The railway system which had been a crucial factor in pre-war economic growth of the region could serve the immediate post-war needs of the individual countries only perfunctorily, as it had to be reconstructed, re-directed and unified within the new borders of each state. Large parts of it, mainly

[42] Berend and Ránki, *Hungary*, pp. 148–9.

in the eastern territory, had been destroyed and the tracks and equipment which remained in service needed repairs and renewal urgently (see p. 964).

In this situation the significance of the great historical shipping trade routes along the Danube grew. Instead of the former three countries, its river transport could after 1918 potentially serve seven states. Also the transport costs of shipping were lower than of railways as less coal was needed at a time of acute energy shortages, but also less materials and personnel were required. Also, under the treaty of Versailles the Danube was internationalized from Ulm to the Black Sea which broke the monopoly of the First Danube Steamship Company (Erste Donaudampfschiffahrtsgesellschaft – 1.DDSG), founded in 1830 in Vienna, which had dominated shipping from Regensburg to Sulina. The same applied to the Royal Hungarian River and Ocean Shipping Company Ltd (Magyar Királyi Folyam-és tengerhajózási Részvérzytársaság – MFTR) in Budapest which was closely intertwined with the 1.DDSG through bank connections and mutual shareholdings.[43]

Since British policy intended to aid the reorganization and reconstruction of a Central European transport network as a precondition of the expansion of British trade interests, British entrepreneurs' efforts to gain a dominant position in the Danube shipping companies received effective diplomatic support from their government. In autumn 1919 one of the most influential British groups in shipbuilding, insurance and banking, The River Syndicate Ltd, began negotiations first with the Austrian Federal Chancellor, Dr Renner, and the influential banker, Dr Sieghart, then with the Hungarian and later Romanian and Yugoslav governments and banks, and in March 1920 it founded the Danube Navigation Company Ltd with a capital of £1,200,000 in London which held the shares acquired from the shipping companies in Regensburg, Vienna, and Budapest together with their interests in the other south-east European Danube shipping enterprises. The inflow of British capital led to increases in the transport of cereals, flour, and oil and profits rose during the inflationary period. In the later years, however, the shipping companies received continuously substantial government subsidies. Although, in general, insufficient funds were available for the necessary improvements in the transport system, the capital imported from Britain also found employment in other infrastructural projects mainly through loans to municipalities in the east-central and south-east European region.

France felt that she had suffered a setback in her competition with

---

[43] The account of capital transfers and the role of the state in Danube shipping is based on Teichova and Ratcliffe, 'British Interests in Danube Navigation'.

Britain who had gained control over shipping on the Danube, and in July 1920 the Quai d'Orsay launched negotiations with the Hungarian government about a stake in Hungary's railways. But these failed, on the one hand, because of strong British objections, and on the other, because Hungary's price included the revision of the Trianon treaty which France was unwilling to pay. Her economic policy in the area was concentrated increasingly on the countries of the Little Entente, particularly on Czechoslovakia.

France succeeded as the first of the Entente powers to invest capital in the producer goods industries of the newly established Czechoslovak Republic where, in the Bohemian and Moravian industrial regions almost 70 per cent of the former Austro-Hungarian iron and steel and engineering production was concentrated. In spite of its comparative industrial strength the Czechoslovak economy alone could not overcome the prevalent shortages of capital. While peace was still being negotiated at Versailles, Dr Eduard Beneš, the Czechoslovak Minister of Foreign Affairs, was attempting to attract Western European investment, especially in those enterprises which had been dominated by German and Austrian shareholders. During his stay in Paris he was actively engaged in discussions with the French Ministers of Foreign Affairs and Finance and with representatives from Schneider et Cie, Creusot, the leading iron and steel producer in France, which led to the latter's 73 per cent participation in the capital of the Škoda-Works in Plzeň in September 1919, followed very soon (Spring 1920) by the purchase of a majority holding in the second largest iron and steel combine in Czechoslovakia, the Baňská a hutní společnost (Mining and Metallurgy Company) in Třinec. This provided Czechoslovak heavy industry, particularly the Škoda-Works, with urgently needed capital and with the first impulse to post-war reconstruction and expansion. For the French majority shareholder the Czechoslovak works were to take over the role of the Petrograd (Leningrad) Putilov Works on the Eastern European market.

The incorporation of the largest engineering and armaments works in east-central and south-east Europe into the Schneider combine corresponded with the intentions of French power politics and, at the same time, constituted a decisive step towards implementing the political conception of the most influential Czechoslovak governing circles around the President, T. G. Masaryk, and his Foreign Minister, Eduard Beneš. Its wider implications were, however, that the great trust of Schneider–Creusot, aided by the Czechoslovak government, gained a foothold in Central Europe for further expansion into Eastern and south-eastern Europe, into the iron and steel and engineering industries of Poland, Romania, Yugoslavia, and Bulgaria and into the magnesite industry in Slovakia and in Austria. In April 1920 the Union Européenne Industrielle et Financière was founded by Schneider together with the Banque l'Union Parisienne as a holding company in Paris in which the financing and administration of all Schneider's direct participating investments in east-central and south-east European enterprises were concentrated. A network of financial, trading and technical relations was created which was headquartered in Paris and which remained intact until the outbreak of the Second World War.[44] For France's economic policy the direct capital participations acquired between 1919 and 1921 remained her most valuable possessions in east-central and south-east Europe throughout the inter-war period.

However, the realization of French economic policy was limited by Anglo-American competition in the states of the Little Entente and by revisionist claims of the defeated successor states. Whilst France maintained her leadership in the armaments production of the Danubian region, British and also renewed German groups penetrated into the iron and steel industry, and American groups into the magnesite mining industry; whilst French petroleum interests were substantial in the richest oil-producing country, Romania, but also in Austria, Poland and Czechoslovakia, British groups attained foremost importance, followed by American and German oil interests. Concurrently, the east-central and south-east European chemical industry was, to a large extent, penetrated by Western participating capital. The Czechoslovak government transferred its state monopoly in the production of explosives for industrial and military purposes to a joint-stock company (Explosia, a.s. pro průmysl výbušnín) in 1921. At its foundation Anglo-French interests participated directly through acquiring one-third of its capital in equal parts by the Société Centrale Dynamite, Paris, and Nobel Industries Ltd, London – later (from 1926) Imperial Chemical Industries; yet, in the course of the inter-war period the British company wielded significantly greater influence in the technical and financial policy of the Czechoslovak explosives industry. Neither French nor British groups succeeded in gaining a similar monopoly position in the chemical industry of the other successor states, for their endeavours were curbed by strong German competition already in the early 1920s.[45]

At this point account must be taken of Czechoslovakia's role in the inter-war period as a jumping-off point for foreign investment and as an intermediary between Western, above all British and French economic interests in the east-central and south-east European capital market at the same time as the Viennese banks failed to hold on to their former

[44] See Teichova, *An Economic Background*, pp. 92–118, 193–217.
[45] Alice Teichova, 'Internationale Kartelle und die chemische Industrie der Vormünchener Tschechoslowakei', *Tradition*, vol. XVII (1972).

positions. Through its significant participation in the iron and steel and engineering industries, the chemical industry and the large joint-stock banks of Czechoslovakia, Western capital gained immediate access to enterprises and banks in south-east European economies, and in the course of the 1920s branched out further in these countries' industries. For the pyramidical organization of the strongly concentrated industry and banking system of Czechoslovakia provided favourable opportunities for far-reaching connections of direct foreign participating capital investment in the economy of Czechoslovakia herself and for further expansion through subsidiaries of Czechoslovak banks and industrial combines into the economies of Eastern and south-east European countries.[46] On the one hand, the Czechoslovak government, more than any other successor state, paved the way for Entente economic interests into the Danubian region; on the other hand, Western business and banking groups received diplomatic assistance from their own governments. Thus banks like the Anglo-Austrian Bank, the Banque des Pays de l'Europe Centrale or companies like Solvay, Schneider–Creusot, Nobel Industries, the Société financière de Paris as a holding company of French oil interests in east-central and south-east Europe, and other groups, regarded the territory of the region even more consistently than the governments of the great industrial nations as a compact whole for their economic activities, with Prague often functioning as a nodal point.

Capital export to east-central and south-east Europe was not a minor part but an integral part of the world-wide operations of international business and finance, and constituted after the British Empire and Latin America the third most important area for international investment after the First World War. Particularly from the viewpoint of the east-central and south-east European countries and their economic development these connections were supremely important.

A. THE SIGNIFICANCE OF DIRECT FOREIGN INVESTMENT IN INDUSTRY

International investment, so coveted by the capital-starved successor states, reached the peak of the inter-war period in 1930. After that the world economic crisis halted investment activity and the total sum of foreign investment fell somewhat. But since the dramatic shifts resulting from the First World War no striking structural changes in the distribution of direct long-term participating investment had occurred in the countries under discussion, except in Czechoslovakia *after* the Munich Agreement in September 1938 and her dismemberment in March 1939.

---

[46] Teichova, *An Economic Background.*

Table 123. *Origin of foreign investments in joint-stock capital of Czechoslovakia, Poland, Bulgaria, and Yugoslavia, 1937 (percentages)*

Country of origin of foreign investment	Czechoslovakia[a]	Poland[b]	Bulgaria[c]	Yugoslavia[d]
Great Britain	30.8	5.5	1.1	17.3
France	21.4	27.1	9.2	27.5
Austria	13.1	3.5	—	—
Holland	8.8	3.5	0.4	2.1
Germany	7.2	13.8	9.3	6.2[e]
Belgium	7.1	12.5	20.5	5.3
Switzerland	4.5	7.2	25.1	7.3
United States	3.5	19.2	11.1	12.0
Italy	2.2	—	13.2	3.1
Sweden	0.9	2.7	—	1.2
Hungary	0.5	—	2.3	2.0
Czechoslovakia	—	1.6	7.4	8.5
Other countries	—	3.4	0.4	—
Monaco				2.9
Poland				0.3
Liechtenstein				0.3
Luxemburg				0.5
Swiss mixed capital				2.6
Anglo-Dutch capital				0.8
USA–French capital				0.1
Total	100.0	100.0	100.0	100.0

Notes:
[a] Industry and banking.
[b] Industry and trade.
[c] All joint-stock companies in private enterprise.
[d] Industry in private enterprise.
[e] Includes Austria.
Sources: Calculated from A. Teichova, *Economic Background to Munich, International Business and Czechoslovakia* (Cambridge, 1974), pp. 48–9; L. Wellisz, *Foreign Capital in Poland* (London, 1938), p. 151; B. Jurković, *Auslandskapital in Jugoslawien* (Berlin, 1941), p. 441; P. Aladjoff, 'Das Auslandskapital in Bulgarien' (dissertation, Berlin University, 1941), p. 55.

Table 123 contains a quantitative assessment of direct foreign participating investment in industrial and commercial joint-stock companies and banks in the individual countries in 1937, the last 'normal' pre-war year for which statistical data were available. The figures demonstrate the priority of Western investment gained at the beginning and maintained to the end of the inter-war period which amounted for the whole area on the average from 70 to 75 per cent of total direct foreign investment (including Britain, France, the United States, Belgium, Holland, and

Table 124. *Comparative data of long-term foreign investment in six east-central and south-east European countries, 1937*

	Foreign debt of government in % of total public debt	Direct foreign participation in industrial companies, banks and insurance companies, in percent of total capital			
		Joint-stock companies	Limited companies	Banks	Insurance companies
Romania	89.2[a]	83	—	75	70
Yugoslavia	82.5[a]	61	—	75	52[b]
Hungary	81.1[a]	c.25	—	—	—
Bulgaria	72.3[a]	48	—	31	30
Poland (1936)	63.0	44.2	89.7	29	65[c]
Czechoslovakia[d]	17.5	29	3	15	26

Notes:
[a] 1931–2.
[b] 1936.
[c] 1935.
[d] Czechoslovakia was the only country in this area which also exported capital.
— = Date not known.
Sources: Compiled from: H. Gross, *Südosteuropa, Bau und Entwicklung der Wirtschaft* (Leipzig, 1939); Ivan T. Berend and György Ránki, 'Capital Accumulation and the Participation of Foreign Capital in Hungarian Economy after the First World War', *Nouvelles Études Historiques* (1965); B. Jurković, *Auslandskapital in Jugoslawien* (Berlin, 1941); V. Rozenberg, *Inostrani kapital v jugoslavenskoj privredi* (Belgrade, 1937); P. Aladjoff, 'Das Auslandskapital in Bulgarien' (dissertation, Berlin University, 1942); A. Teichova, *An Economic Background to Munich, International Business and Czechoslovakia* (Cambridge, 1974); L. Wellisz, *Foreign Capital in Poland* (London, 1938); *Anuarul Statistical Rômaniei* (1938, 39); *Statistisches Taschenbuch v. Rumänien* (1941).

Switzerland and excluding Germany). Britain and France took up either first or second place in the rank order of international investors whilst Germany, which was leading before 1914, held on the average fifth or sixth place.

The total amount of foreign investment in the individual economies varied from country to country; but its composition in east-central and south-east European industry profoundly influenced its structure and performance. Table 124 illustrates the different levels by comparing figures of foreign public loans and direct foreign participating investment as a percentage of total public indebtedness and total capital of six countries in this region. It is obvious that, if mere percentages are compared, foreign capital had a much stronger hold over the industry and banking of the predominantly agrarian economies than over the industrially relatively advanced economies of Czechoslovakia and Hungary. Figures in aggregate are usually deceptive and a further breakdown

shows that foreign direct investment was decisive in the largest companies of the leading industries and in the most powerful banks in all these
economies. Disaggregating total distribution of foreign investment further among the branches of industry an identical pattern emerges in all
invested-in economies, which is reflected in the rank order of industries
in the list below, arranged according to the magnitude of foreign direct
participation in the total joint-stock capital of each branch: the highest
proportion of foreign shares was found to be in mining and metallurgy,
then in chemicals, followed by engineering and by stone, glass, ceramics,
wood, textiles, paper, and printing in descending order.

*Rank order of industries (according to amount of foreign participation in
total joint-stock capital)*

1. Mining and metallurgy (including petroleum)
2. Chemicals
3. Metalworking (engineering and power)
4. Stone, glass, ceramics
5. Wood
6. Textiles
7. Paper
8. Printing

Source: A. Teichova, 'Konzentrationstendenzen in der Industrie Mittelost- und
Südosteuropas nach dem Ersten Weltkrieg', in H. Mommsen, D. Petzina and B.
Weisbrod (eds.), *Industrielles System und politische Entwicklung in der Weimarer Republik*
(Düsseldorf, 1974), p. 147.

Foreign participating capital inputs were the most direct way into the
productive process. How did this crucial development, encouraged by
policies of the capital-seeking east-central and south-east European states,
promote industrial development? This can be summarized in the following points: first, foreign capital usually held the predominant share of the
extracting and capital goods industries; for example, in Poland over 70
per cent and in Czechoslovakia over 60 per cent and in Yugoslavia over
80 per cent of the total capital in mining and metallurgy, in Romania
over 90 per cent of the total capital in the oil industry; secondly, foreign
capital almost invariably participated in the more concentrated section of
each branch of industry, that is, in the minority of joint-stock companies
in which, however, the majority of the industry's capital and productive
capacity was concentrated; thirdly, by flowing into the strongest and to a
large extent already concentrated industries, or by initiating or by taking
part in the establishment of large combines, direct foreign investment
emphasized and accelerated tendencies towards large-scale enterprise in
the receiving countries' economies; fourthly, foreign capital was invested mostly in those branches of industry which were interwoven with

Table 125. *Credit financing of aid deliveries 31 December, 1918–31 December, 1923 (million gold dollars old parity)*

	Amount of credits received		Total	Distribution according to creditor countries		
	31 December, 1918 to 30 July, 1919	7 January, 1919 to 31 December, 1923		USA	United Kingdom	Canada and Newfoundland
Czechoslovakia	77.2	3.8	81.0	78.5	2.5	—
Hungary	—	2.3	2.3	1.7	0.6	—
Poland	119.1	32.5	151.5	135.8	15.8	—
Romania	51.9	—	51.9	36.5	10.0	5.4
Yugoslavia	43.3	—	43.3	33.7	9.6	—
Total	291.5	38.6	330.1	286.2	38.5	5.4

Source: League of Nations, *Relief Deliveries and Relief Loans, 1919–1923* (Geneva, 1943) cited by R. Nötel, 'Capital Movements and Finance in Eastern Europe 1919–1949', *Vierteljahrschrift für Sozial- und Wirtschaftsgeschichte*, vol. LXI (1974), p. 69.

the international business interests of the investors, and although playing a positive role in encouraging industrialization, the investment was directed to serve the interests of the capital-exporting economies rather than those of the receiving countries. This created isles of comparatively high-powered industrial complexes among a sea of small-scale and dwarf enterprises which continued to perform an important economic function on the home market in all Eastern European countries; fifthly, foreign capital investment was initially essential to the receiving countries' economic progress, but in the long term its activities produced serious disproportions in those countries' economic development.

Assessing the inter-war period as a whole, on the one hand, foreign participating investment from the Western creditor nations in east-central and south-east European industries satisfied to a certain extent their urgent need for capital, which provided benefits also from the scientific experience and technological know-how of the advanced industrial economies and brought higher forms of business organization into some sections of their relatively less developed economies. On the other hand, the operations of foreign capital aggravated the disproportions in their economies as the gap between agriculture and industry widened; they also emphasized disproportions in their industrial development as they affected substantially those spheres of industrial activity which offered investors the most economic advantage. As a result labour, modern technology, and capital were concentrated in those branches and more precisely in the largest enterprises of those branches where foreign capital participated. Basically, the input of directly participating foreign capital into industry was neither sufficient to generate sustained economic growth nor did its presence provide a viable and secure home and export market for any of the countries in the long run. Therefore, industrialization was slow and tariff walls grew higher.

VI. *The quest for credits*

Whilst capital imports as direct participating investment contributed relatively most to capital accumulation and thus influenced the course of industrialization the loans which were requested with great urgency from the very inception of the east-central and south-east European states in their search for capital had comparatively less positive effects on industrial development.

Most urgently and immediately the successor states needed import-finance for food supplies. Credit-financing of aid deliveries from the end of 1918 to the end of 1923 came to 86.7 per cent from the United States, 11.7 per cent from Britain and 1.6 per cent from Canada (see Table 125). Such aid – except for gifts which financed 13 per cent of all food relief in the region – was provided on a strictly commercial basis. Whereas over 90 per cent of all food deliveries to Romania and Yugoslavia, and over 70 per cent of food imports to Poland and Czechoslovakia were supplied on credit, Hungary paid for over 40 per cent and Bulgaria for all relief deliveries in cash.[47] These credits must be considered lost for productive purposes.

In addition to the absolute necessity of subsidizing food supplies for the restive, undernourished, and in many areas starving populations, large state expenditure was required for the successor governments' policies of pacification. For, under conditions of political and social turmoil, only great concessions, such as the eight-hour day and comparatively far-reaching social and land reforms, were able to restore government control. Inevitably, war-induced budget deficits grew and the printing of banknotes to cover them added fuel to already existing inflated currencies.

As one of its bequests the Habsburg monarchy had left the successor states, whether victorious or defeated, with the most depreciated currency of post-war Europe outside Russia. Since, initially, currency unity was retained on the territory of the former Dual Monarchy, inflation spread from Vienna where the Austro-Hungarian Bank printed notes under the strong influence of the Austrian government. Money circulation in Poland did not only consist of Austrian crowns (kronen) but also of a number of other highly inflated currencies (such as roubles, marks, various emergency currencies). The influx of paper money from neighbouring successor states into each other's economies exacerbated difficulties of controlling the money supply within the individual states. By March 1919 it was estimated that, whereas one-fifth of total Austro-Hungarian notes circulated in Austria, another one-fifth in Hungary, and about one-tenth in Yugoslavia, almost one-third had found its way into Czechoslovakia where the value of the crown was higher.[48] At this point the Czechoslovak government, and also the Yugoslav regime, took the first significant step towards extricating their economies from the old Austro-Hungarian unit through currency separation. The Yugoslav dinar established itself in the new frontiers of the kingdom, and the monetary reform of the Czechoslovak government of March and April 1919 launched the Czechoslovak crown (Kč) on its independent career.

However, currency separation did not stop inflation. The new Kč kept on falling until October 1921 when it reached its lowest value of one-sixteenth of the old crown. Also the Yugoslav dinar continued its downward slide until by 1923 it was worth one-eighteenth of the old

[47] League of Nations, *Relief Deliveries and Relief Loans 1919–1923* (Geneva, 1943); see also Nötel, 'International Capital Movements'.

[48] J. van Walré de Bordes, *The Austrian Crown* (London, 1924), pp. 42, 46–7.

parity. But in Yugoslavia as in Romania, where the lei fell to 2 per cent of its value by 1924, inflation remained moderate. Bulgaria's inflation began during the Balkan wars in 1912 and took a gradual but persistent course until in 1925 the leva reached its lowest value at one-thirteenth of its pre-1914 level. In Czechoslovakia monetary reform undoubtedly lessened the impact of imported inflation and was one of the factors which prevented a headlong descent into hyperinflation. In Hungary and Poland currency separation did not bring the same results. When the Hungarian crown and the Polish mark were introduced in 1920 they continued to depreciate into galloping inflation which culminated in 1924. Whilst the conversion of the crown into the pengö in 1927 reflected stabilization in Hungary, a second attempt in Poland to introduce a new currency, the złoty, led to a further inflationary run in 1927.[49] These differentiated experiences show that inflation is only outwardly a monetary phenomenon but underlying it are economic disturbances, inability of production to satisfy consumption, and deep political and social conflicts.

Czechoslovakia's monetary policy was not primarily deflationary. Its main purpose was to sever direct financial ties with the other successor states, above all with Austria and Hungary, to create a separate banking system, and to provide a monetary framework for an independent national economy. To this end the Bankovní úřad ministerstva financí – BÚMF (Banking Office of the Ministry of Finance) was established and received the state's monopoly of banknote issue as a forerunner of the National Bank of the Czechoslovak Republic. Thus the main thrust of the monetary reform was directed against Austrian economic dominance. Further, the Czechoslovak government aimed at coping with inflation without outside aid, for it wished to convince its Western Allies and potential business partners of the preparedness of its people to help themselves and of the creditworthiness of the new state. For these reasons budget deficits in Czechoslovakia were covered through government borrowing from domestic banks and public subscriptions to internal loans, such as the 'loan of national liberation', followed by a wealth levy and a succession of further internal loans. Consequently, from the outset Czechoslovakia's internal indebtedness exceeded her external public debt in contradistinction to all other Eastern European states. Also, in spite of her harsh tax policy, particularly in the field of indirect taxation including a stiff coal tax, her tax receipts were consistently higher than government estimates anticipated.[50] Government policies met with a more favourable response because the industrial potential was greater

---

[49] On Poland's inflations see Landau and Tomaszewski, *Gospodarska Polski*; on Hungary's inflation see Berend and Ránki, *Hungary*.

[50] Alois Rašín, *Financial Policy of Czechoslovakia During the First Year of its History* (Oxford, 1923).

and the social and business climate was more optimistic in Czechoslovakia than in most other successor states.

In Czechoslovakia stabilization and revaluation of the currency occurred predominantly through forces within the economy. It did not exclusively follow upon deflationary policies, as is generally believed, but economic conditions created by falling prices and recession in 1921 made deflationary intervention possible.[51] Deflation became official policy only during 1922. It succeeded then because political stability had been achieved, production exceeded consumption, and favourable trade balances had been reached since 1920 under stringent exchange controls and protective tariffs. In purely monetary terms the value of the Kč on foreign exchanges was raised artificially by open market operations of the Minister of Finance, Dr Alois Rašín, and also aided by the first instalment of the British investment credit to Czechoslovakia in 1922. This led to the relative overvaluation of the Czechoslovak currency which erased the price advantages of Czechoslovak exports. Rašín's monetarism negatively influenced output and employment at a time when the Czechoslovak economy suffered from recession. However, much of the adverse effect was blunted by the flight from the German mark into safer currencies which strengthened the Czechoslovak crown. Similarly, the French occupation of the Ruhr, which brought orders to Czechoslovak industries, mitigated the rigours imposed on exports by the overvalued Kč. But full recovery of the economy came only with the re-imposition of controls which had been loosened in 1921 and the general upswing from 1924.[52]

At the time when Czechoslovakia stabilized her economy the other successor states were still in the grip of inflation. Indeed, hyperinflation had engulfed Austria, Hungary, and Poland. Before the drastic depreciation of these currencies could be halted the value of the Austrian gold crown equalled 14,000 paper crowns, the price level in Austria had risen 15,500 times and wages had on average increased 9,000 times in Autumn 1922; in Hungary one gold crown was worth 17,000 paper crowns in June 1924, in aggregate prices had risen 8,000 times and wages only 3,500 times; and about the same time the Polish mark hit rock bottom at 9.3 million marks to one US dollar. Currency stabilization in Poland, Romania, and Bulgaria came about only in the second half of the 1920s.

In all those countries government policies were geared almost exclusively to the procurement of foreign loans as the only remedy to stop inflation. Certain attempts were made by ministers of finance to put

---

[51] Jozef Faltus, *Povojnová hospodárka kríza v Československu v rokoch 1921–3 – priemysel a peňažníctvo* (The Postwar Economic Crisis 1921–3 in Czechoslovakia – Industry and Finance) (Bratislava, 1966), pp. 67, 71.

[52] See Pryor, 'Czechoslovak Economic Development', pp. 195–7.

forward reform policies designed to balance their budgets primarily from domestic sources and to rely on foreign loans only in the second place. But unlike the Rašín monetary reform in Czechoslovakia, such efforts were wrecked even before being implemented, as the Schumpeter Finance Plan of 1919 in Austria, or they miscarried after some initial success, as the reform programme of the Finance Minister Hegedüs in Hungary and that of the Polish Premier and Finance Minister W. Grabski in 1923. In the latter two cases they were able to break into the international credit market but this source was too meagre and covered only a fraction of state expenditure. At home they were unable to raise the required financial means since revenue from taxation was negligible, wealth levies were made ineffective by obstruction from the propertied classes, mainly landowners and banks, and internal government loans failed to get sufficient public support.

Therefore, governments reached continuously for the printing presses as the policy of least resistance and thus kept enlarging their budget deficits. In the early stages this triggered off an inflationary boom, stimulated investment, accelerated renewal and replacement in industry, and increased exports. For a limited time inflationary policies bridged economic and social difficulties and served post-war reconstruction. But inflation as an instrument of recovery was delusory. Not only did speculation soon become rampant but sales of assets abroad and the export of goods far below cost prices sapped the national wealth: a development which the east-central and south-east European states could ill afford. Their experience of the 1920s shows a complicated pattern where different types of inflations intertwined, such as excess demand inflation, conflict inflation, anticipated inflation until in a number of countries self-propelled inflation became hyperinflation.[53]

International financial aid was seen as the only possible solution to save the post-war system of governments in the region. Whilst Hungary wished to demonstrate economic stability to potential foreign creditors and Poland offered them excessive economic and financial advantages, Austria based her case for outside aid on claiming non-viability of her shrunken economy. She was first to stabilize her currency successfully and surprisingly quickly with a League of Nations loan granted in 1922. Its method of organization and control became the model for League stabilization loans to Hungary in 1924 and to Bulgaria between 1926 and

---

[53] The comparative assessment of the inflations in east-central Europe is based on Alice Teichova, 'The Inflations of the 1920s in Austria and Czechoslovakia – A Comparative View', in Nathan Schmukler and Edward Marcus (eds.), *Inflations Through the Ages: Economic, Social, Psychological and Historical Aspects* (New York, 1983). See also Peter-Robert Berger, *Der Donauraum im wirtschaftlichen Umbruch nach dem ersten Weltkrieg Währung und Finanzen in den Nachfolgestaaten Österreich, Ungarn und Tschechoslowakei 1918–1929* (Vienna, 1982).

1928. Among the creditors were Britain, the United States, France, Italy, Sweden, Holland, Belgium, Switzerland, and Czechoslovakia.[54]

In the process of initiating, organizing, and providing League of Nations loans which were administered by the League's Financial Committee, Britain's policy played a decisive role, specifically the leadership of Montagu Norman, the Governor of the Bank of England. According to his concept European stabilization was to be achieved by re-establishing 'normal' pre-war conditions; above all, the return to the gold standard, the construction of a network of central banks so that free trade on the basis of comparative costs could take place and the exchange between agriculture and industry furthered. Thus in return for financial aid the League of Nations schemes singlemindedly pursued the foundation of national banks with a monopoly of note issue, the attainment of balanced budgets, and – to avoid further inflation – the granting of loans to reconstruct the currencies. As securities the debtor countries had to pledge their state property, their monopolies and their revenues. These measures were controlled by a Commissioner General appointed by the League of Nations on whom executive powers were conferred by the receiving countries' parliaments and who was to reside in the respective capitals until budgetary equilibrium was reached and the servicing of the stabilization loans secured.

Consequently, for a number of years all their incomes were pawned and commissioners general carefully scrutinized each item of state expenditure before giving their approval. By this procedure independent government action was severely curtailed since monetary and fiscal policies were subordinated to Western, mainly Anglo-American, guidance. Neither were conditions of repayment mild. Hungary's reconstruction loan (1924–44) amounted nominally to US $68.8 million, and the Bulgarian loans to US $43.1 million, consisting of a refugee loan of US $16.2 million (1926–66) and a stabilization loan of US $26.9 million (1928–48). But prices of issue received by these governments averaged at about 88.5 per cent of the nominal total with an interest rate of about 8.5 per cent.

Poland did not quite fall into line as in 1924 she accepted a French bridging loan which was offered to forestall British penetration. When the Polish government got into renewed difficulties during her second inflation it was Montagu Norman's opinion that no credits should be given to Poland as long as she did not ask the League of Nations to order her finances. But with the support of the Governor of the Bank of France, Emile Moreau, and the Governor of the Federal Reserve Bank of the USA, Benjamin Strong, an international consortium of banks extended

[54] League of Nations, *The League of Nations Reconstruction Schemes in the Interwar Period*, part II (Geneva, 1945), pp. 35–73.

Table 126. *Total foreign debt and its distribution in six east-central and south-east European countries, 1931/2*

	Total debt	Pre-1918 debt	Post-war debt	Pre-1918 debt	Post-war debt
	(Millions of gold dollars)			(Percentages)	
Bulgaria	138.9	90.1	48.8	64.5	35.5
Czechoslovakia	395.6	281.4	114.2	70.1	28.9
Hungary	732.9	249.5	483.4	34.0	66.0
Poland	865.5	-359.3	506.2	41.5	58.5
Romania	1,022.7	649.9	372.8	63.5	36.5
Yugoslavia	634.8	460.9	173.9	72.6	27.4
Total of six countries	3,790.4	2,091.1	1,699.3	55.2	44.8

Source: R. Nötel, 'International Capital Movements and Finance in Eastern Europe 1919–1949', *Vierteljahrschrift für Sozial- und Wirtschaftsgeschichte*, vol. LXI (1974), p. 84.

a stabilization loan of US $62 million to Poland in 1927. At the same time an American Controller, Charles Dewey, was appointed to reside in Warsaw for three years and observe the fulfilment of the loan's stringent conditions.[55]

The background to the stabilization loans of the 1920s provides a pattern of competition among the creditors for economic and political influence in the countries between Germany and the Soviet Union.

Since stabilization loans were almost entirely exhausted in the exercise of balancing budgets they had little direct effect on industrial development. Indirectly, however, they were designed to integrate the economies of the new states into the world currency system and thus into international finance and trade. An essential part of this process of adaptation was the far-reaching arrangements concerning the repayment of pre-war loans which were made concurrently with the provision of stabilization loans (see Table 126). For the east-central and south-east European state stabilization of currencies, the establishment of a chain of national banks linked to London, New York, and Paris, replacing the previous links with Vienna and Berlin, together with the war debt settlement, created the basis for a further influx of loans.

But endeavours to restore the pre-war credit mechanism were doomed to failure. Against a single gold standard in the pre-1914 period the east-central and south-east European countries were faced with a gold exchange standard based on London and Washington whose rates

[55] Z. Landau, 'Polskie zagraniczne pozyczki panstwowe 1918–1926' (Foreign loans of the Polish State 1918–1926), in *Gospodarka Polski 1918–1939* (The Economy of Poland) (Warsaw, 1961).

often differed. Because of the greater risks involved in continuing unstable circumstances credits could not be taken up by governments of the region below an interest rate of 7.5–8 per cent as against a pre-war rate of 3.5–4 per cent; in addition, the prices received by borrowers were very low (between 80 and 88 per cent of nominal totals) and the guarantees demanded by the lenders much more burdensome. However, the interest rates of long-term bank credits to industrial enterprises in the Eastern and south-east European region varied between 15 and 30 per cent from the mid-1920s.

The main input of foreign loans into east-central and south-east Europe was limited to a comparatively short period which began with the League of Nations stabilization loans followed by a veritable flood of credits between 1924 and 1928. This stream practically ended with the world economic crisis. During 1929–33 capital import had turned into a trickle and by 1934–8 had on balance changed into an outflow of sorely needed resources from the countries investigated here (see Table 127).

From the viewpoint of the most pressing needs of industrialization the question arises how far foreign loans, obtained during the period of credit expansion, 1924–8, were utilized for productive purposes. The balances of international payments (see Table 127) indicate a differentiated distribution of funds in the receiving countries. Again here Czechoslovakia takes up an exceptional position as – at the time – a creditor country, which enabled her to export capital, partly for direct investment in the south-east European economies and partly for granting credits to trade partners. The other countries mentioned in Table 127 fall into two groups. The first is Bulgaria and Yugoslavia, where the inflow of not very substantial amounts almost entirely went out again as interest and dividend payments. The second group is Hungary and Poland, where larger loans were received with which these countries were able to finance not only outgoings in interest and dividends but also a sizeable import surplus. However, the loans were used only to a very modest extent for investment purposes. In Hungary about 50 per cent of the long-term loans was used to pay off old debts, 25 per cent to cover the government's budget deficits, a further part to expand the state's bureaucracy and at the most 20 per cent found its way into productive industrial investment. Of the short-term loans to Hungary about 40 per cent consisted of commercial credit and the rest was too short term to be utilized for industrial development.[56] An even bleaker picture is presented by Poland where in the early years of independence loans were used to almost 90 per cent for food and arms purchases and no more than 9 per cent remained for the needs of industry;[57] whilst later in the period

[56] Berend and Ránki, *Hungary*, pp. 107–8.
[57] Landau, 'Polskie zagraniczne pozyczki panstwowe 1918–1926', p. 284.

of credit expansion Poland had to stabilize her currency and balance her budget with the aid of foreign loans, leaving very little for productive purposes after the needs for commodity imports and military expenditure had been satisfied. Thus Poland, and to a large extent also Hungary, were servicing debts which in the first place had not been used to provide the countries with the means to increase their incomes sufficiently.

In spite of their policies to advance their national economic interests the successor governments neither grasped the opportunities during relatively favourable conditions created by inflation nor did they utilize stabilization loans to initiate a conscious policy of adapting their adverse industrial structure to the post-1918 economic realities. In the short run favourable market conditions for agricultural products in the second half of the 1920s aided the Eastern and south-east European countries to consolidate their economies; in the long run the only solution was seen – in addition to financial backing from foreign investors – in an all-out export drive supported by protectionist tariffs and government subsidies to industry which perpetuated the structural weaknesses in their economies. In this sense Czechoslovakia was no exception, although in her successful export-led development investments flowed into protected industries and doubtlessly contributed to the remarkable growth of aggregate production until 1929.[58] This, however, at the same time concealed the structural inadequacies in the first decade of Czechoslovakia's existence.

At the peak of European indebtedness in 1931–2 over one-half of the total external debt of the six east-central and south-east European countries in Table 126 consisted of pre-1918 loans. These included pre-war debts of the Austro-Hungarian monarchy and of the pre-war regimes of Romania, Yugoslavia, and Bulgaria, as well as debts contracted during the war period, and to this were added commitments arising out of the peace treaties such as reparations from the defeated countries (Hungary and Bulgaria) and a 'liberation contribution' from the Associated to the Allied states (that is, from Czechoslovakia, Poland, Romania, and Yugoslavia). In the course of the 1930s total foreign indebtedness declined as demonstrated in Table 128. This was partly due to repayments, partly to the devaluation of creditor countries' currencies, and partly to agreements on reductions of interest rates. Yet, capital starvation continued, because at the same time capital was withdrawn from the east-central and south-east European countries, and no substantial new credits were forthcoming. This can be demonstrated by the capital movements

[58] See Zora P. Pryor and Frederic L. Pryor, 'Foreign Trade and Interwar Czechoslovak Economic Development, 1918–1938', *Vierteljahrschrift für Sozial – und Wirtschaftsgeschichte*, vol. LXII, no. 4 (1975), pp. 500–33.

Table 127. *Excerpts from balances of international payments (League of Nations) (millions of US dollars of old parity)*

	Bulgaria	Hungary	Poland	Yugoslavia	Total of 4 countries	Czechoslovakia	Total of 5 countries
1924–8							
1. Capital movements							
Long-term capital	32.4	130.5	154.0	49.7	366.6	−103.1	263.5
Short-term capital	−6.7	86.3	152.7	5.7	238.0	−71.5	166.5
Total	25.7	216.8	306.7	55.4	604.6	−174.6	430.0
2. Goods and services							
Goods (gold excluded)	5.2	−172.6	−242.3	−83.0	−492.7	236.4	−256.3
Services	−6.1	6.1	118.2	81.2	199.4	41.4	240.8
Total	−0.9	−166.5	−124.1	−1.8	−293.3	277.8	−15.5
3. Interest and dividends	−24.3	−64.5	−102.6	−56.4	−247.8	−83.5	−331.3
1929–33 (Period of credit contraction and crisis)							
1. Capital movements							
Long-term capital	15.7	34.2	21.7	31.9	103.5	−4.5	99.0
Short-term capital	11.0	90.2	−14.7	1.5	88.0	13.7	101.7
Total	26.7	124.4	7.0	33.4	191.5	9.2	200.7

2. Goods and services							
Goods (gold excluded)	6.2	21.4	8.8	−29.2	7.2	105.1	112.3
Services	−3.3	−6.0	132.1	82.8	205.6	49.0	254.6
Total	2.9	15.4	140.9	53.6	212.8	154.1	366.9
3. Interest and dividends	−29.1	−105.5	−195.9	−82.8	−413.3	−56.3	−469.6
1934–7 (Period of recovery)							
1. Capital movements							
Long-term capital	−2.1	−0.3	−11.8	10.2	−3.4	−21.9	−25.3
Short-term capital	−9.3	−18.4	−7.3	−5.2	−40.2	−9.2	−49.4
Total	−11.4	−18.7	−19.1	5.0	−43.6	−31.1	−74.7
2. Goods and services							
Goods (gold excluded)	14.8	33.9	22.8	6.3	77.8	62.5	140.3
Services	1.4	7.0	62.7	20.8	91.9	2.0	93.9
Total	16.2	40.9	85.5	27.1	169.7	64.5	234.2
3. Interest and dividends	−4.8	−16.8	−62.7	−29.7	−114.0	−43.8	−157.8

Source: As Table 125, pp. 102–7.

Table 128. *Changes in totals and per capita amounts of foreign debt between 1931-2 and 1937[a]*

	Total (in million gold dollars[b])			Per capita (in gold dollars[b])	
	1931-2	1937	Change	1931-2	1937
Bulgaria	138.9	92.1	− 46.8	23	15
Czechoslovakia	395.6	243.4	− 152.2	27	16
Hungary	732.9	308.0	− 424.9	84	34
Poland	865.5	449.0	− 416.5	—	—
Romania	1,022.7	571.8	− 450.9	57	29
Yugoslavia	634.8	338.8	− 296.0	46	22
Total of six countries	3,790.4	2,003.1	− 1,787.3	—	—

Note:
[a] Public indebtedness only.
[b] Of old parity.
—— = Date not known.
Source: As Table 125.

in the period for credit contraction during the world economic crisis and also during the period of recovery from 1934 to 1937, as shown in the excerpts of balances of international payments in Table 127.

It is evident that from 1929 onwards international capital movements practically ceased to contribute to these countries' domestic resources. Where there had been a certain marginal surplus, or at least a balancing of flows before 1929, outgoing interest and dividend payments exceeded capital inflows in the subsequent years, and from 1932 capital moved out absolutely from all these countries. None of them was able to cover their outgoings with export surpluses, except Czechoslovakia, but she had to reduce her capital exports simultaneously. Although massive state intervention, particularly exchange controls and strict foreign trade regulations, did lead to export surpluses, these proved to be insufficient fully to meet capital claims and commitments for interest and dividend payments.

Under the prevailing economic and political conditions in east-central and south-east European countries very little of this type of capital import contributed to their industrial development because – with the exception of Czechoslovakia – roughly more than three-quarters of the total foreign loans contracted in the inter-war period were put either to cover budget deficits, consumption uses, or prestige spending, including excessive military expenditure, as well as to convert old debts repeatedly into new ones. Perhaps the most positive feature of Eastern European government borrowing was, on the one hand, that some part of these public loans was used for infrastructural investment and, on the other hand, that some of the funds used for state expenditure trickled into industry. But this investment activity did not absorb the major part of inter-war loans.

VII. *The quest for markets*

A. THE IMPACT OF THE CRISIS

The all-pervading crisis of 1929–33 was the decisive turning point in inter-war economic development. It constituted a watershed between the remnants of a free market economy and a system of regulated and administered production and marketing. It shook the foundations on which all international agreements were built and, in Europe, the system of Versailles began to crumble rapidly. World prices, industrial output, and foreign trade plummeted whilst unemployment soared and international capital movements were virtually halted. As an immediate result the big creditor nations, the United States foremost, withdrew short-term loans from everywhere in Europe. However, in east-central and south-east Europe the rush to withdraw short-term credits started in earnest after the collapse of the most influential bank in the region, the Austrian Credit-Anstalt, in May 1931. Repercussions were all the more calamitous because, due to the lack of domestic capital formation, a large proportion of short-term money had been channelled into long-term loans through the interlocking banking–industry mechanism. In the wake of the world financial crisis practically all capital imports dried up which exacerbated the chronic shortage of capital in east-central and south-east Europe. At the same time the competitive struggle between the great European powers intensified and Germany redoubled her efforts to gain greater influence in the economies of the countries east of her borders.

As no more foreign credits were forthcoming the east-central and south-east European debtor states could not rely any more on credits to pay for imports, or to balance their budgets, or to convert old debts into new ones. Their economic problems could not be bridged by further credits, they could only begin to be solved by intensifying their endeavours to achieve a favourable balance of trade by boosting exports and curbing imports. Consequently, as credits ceased, the search for markets became a priority in their economic policies.[59]

Through the narrowing of foreign markets (see size of trade decline

---

[59] Györgi Ránki, *Economy and Foreign Policy: The Struggle of the Great Powers for Hegemony in the Danube Valley, 1919–1939* (Boulder, Col., and New York, 1983), pp. 42–3.

Table 129. *Size of trade decline during the crisis*

	1933 as % of 1929		Maximum decline during crisis		1938 as % of 1929	
	Imports	Exports	Imports	Exports	Imports	Exports
Albania	58.7	40.4	68.3	70.8	59.5	66.7
Bulgaria	75.5	55.4	73.5	60.3	59.4	87.4
Czechoslovakia	71.0	71.5	72.8	71.5	38.1[a]	40.7[a]
Hungary	70.8	62.6	70.8	67.8	38.7	50.4
Poland	73.3	65.8	76.2	67.0	41.9	42.2
Romania	60.2	50.9	69.3	52.7	45.3	53.4
Yugoslavia	70.4	66.8	70.4	66.8	50.9	49.3
World	65.0	64.5	66.3	65.7	40.2	40.7
Europe	62.0	63.0	64.7	65.5	42.3	39.2

Note:
[a] January–September 1938.
Source: Z. Drábek, 'Trade Performance of East European Countries 1919–1939', *Papers in East European Economics*, no. 37 (October 1973).

during the crisis in Table 129), autarchic endeavours were greatly enhanced by militant nationalism and dictatorial regimes in Central and south-east Europe. Indeed, the comparatively free market economy of Czechoslovakia, the only remaining democratic state of a Western type in this area, was one of the hardest hit by the world economic crisis and recovery was a slower process than in the predominantly agricultural economies of south-east Europe. Czechoslovakia's manufacturing production decreased by one-half between 1929 and 1933 and recovery began later and progressed more sluggishly elsewhere in the area (see Fig. 11). Her vital export trade dropped to almost one-third of the 1929 level in 1932. Although she met the situation with an economic policy of protective tariffs and devaluations not dissimilar to other industrial countries her recovery had only reached two-thirds of the 1929 level by 1937.[60]

Poland experienced a crisis of similar severity in 1930 and 1935. Its ruinous effect on industry and the inability of domestic private enterprise[61] to extricate itself from the slump unaided led to the massive and direct state intervention which ushered in the climax of etatism in Poland between 1936 and 1939 together with an upswing in industrial produc-

[60] Zora P. Pryor, 'Czechoslovak Fiscal Policies in the Great Depression', *Economic History Review*, 2nd series, vol. XXXII (May 1976), pp. 228, 232; also see I. Svennilson, *Growth and Stagnation in the European Economy* (Geneva, 1954), pp. 312–13.

[61] Private investment turned into disinvestment when the index of new investments fell from 100 in 1928 to −11 in 1933 and still showed no significant improvement by 1936. See *Materiały do badán*, p. 170.

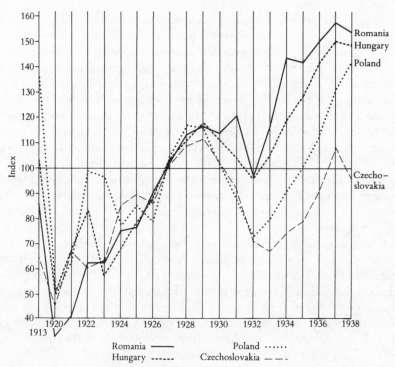

Fig. 11. Annual manufacturing production in Romania, Hungary, Poland, and Czechoslovakia, 1913–38
Source: I. Svennilson, *Growth and Stagnation in the European Economy* (Geneva, 1954), pp. 304–5.

tion (see Fig. 11). There were differences in timing and intensity of the crisis in the individual south-east European countries: Hungary's industrial production attained its peak in 1929, Yugoslavia's in 1930, and Romania's in 1931, but all of them reached the lowest volume of output in 1932. Yet, in comparison, industrial output declined considerably less than in Czechoslovakia and Poland. There were remarkable similarities in the relatively quick and sustained recovery of industrial production in all the agrarian south-east European countries (see Fig. 11). These figures do not substantiate the widespread assumption that the agrarian countries of Eastern Europe were damaged most by the crisis.[62] Indeed, specific factors such as a large non-market sector in the relatively most backward economies and the high degree of state direction, of which more will be said later, contributed to cushion the impact of the crisis.

[62] Generally held views, recently expounded by Eckhard Weber, *Stadien der Aussenhandelsverflechtung Ostmittel- und Südosteuropas* (Stuttgart, 1971), p. 19.

In the second half of the 1920s recovery had been supported largely by comparatively favourable prices for their agricultural produce on world markets and by imports of foreign capital. When the crisis brought about a reversal of the terms of trade, income from agricultural exports fell substantially. Most of the south-east European countries were able to compensate for the decline in world prices in part only by increasing the volume of exports which grew at a faster rate than that of falling prices: the volume of exports of cereals from Bulgaria, Hungary, Poland, Romania, and Yugoslavia trebled on average between 1928 and 1933, whilst prices fell by about 75 per cent in the same period.[63]

Export surpluses were achieved at the cost of reduced living standards, since the volume of output did not increase in the same proportion as the volume of exports. However, both per capita consumption and export surpluses declined between 1928 and 1934. Shares of exports in the national income of the east-central and south-east European agrarian economies had remained on a low level of about 2–6 per cent (in Czechoslovakia it amounted to 24 per cent and in Hungary to 16 per cent in 1929 but fell to 9 per cent in the crisis years),[64] but the continuing existence of export surpluses was vital to enable them to meet repatriation of profits, servicing of debts, and to pay for essential imports of machinery and finished manufacturing products which they needed to encourage their own industrialization.

At the end of the 1920s the share of agricultural produce in total exports amounted to 80 per cent in Bulgaria, 60 per cent in Hungary and over 50 per cent in Poland and Romania. In the 1930s the composition of exports did not change significantly[65] and access to markets for their main export commodities became tantamount to economic survival for these countries.

The shift in emphasis of economic policy from credits to markets during the world economic crisis brought about a definite change in the intensity and character of state intervention in the economy, especially from 1931. One by one the east-central and south-east European debtor states created agrarian monopoly organizations through which they managed agricultural credits and exports; international payments came under total state control to prevent the depreciation of the currency and the flight of capital; and foreign trade was subordinated to complete state supervision through exchange controls to further exports and to keep imports within the limits of a system of priorities.

Similarly, intensive state intervention was to meet problems of shrinking demand on the home market by cartel legislation, forced syndicalization, and direct state entrepreneurship. Economic activity of

---

[63] Calculated from Zdeněk Drábek, 'Trade Performance of East European Countries 1919–1939', *Papers in East European Economics*, no. 37 (October 1973), Table III–7 on p. 54.

[64] *Ibid.*, p. 27.   [65] *Ibid.*, estimated from Tables A–5 to A–11, pp. 76–82.

Table 130. *General tariff levels in Europe, 1913–31*

	Absolute height			1927 as % of	1931 as % of
	1913	1927	1931	1913	1913
Germany	16.7	20.4	40.7	122.0	244
France	23.6	23.0	38.0	97.5	160
Austria[a]	(22.8)	17.5	36.0	77.0	158
Czechoslovakia[b]		31.3	50.0	137.0	220
Poland[c]	72.5	53.5	67.5	74.0	93
Romania	30.3	42.3	63.0	140.0	207
Hungary[d]	(22.8)	30.0	46.0	144.0	207
Yugoslavia[e]	22.2	32.0	46.0	144.0	207
Bulgaria	22.8	67.5	96.5	296.0	420

Notes:
[a] Austria, 1913 = Austria–Hungary 1913.
[b] Czechoslovakia, 1913 = Austria–Hungary 1913.
[c] Poland, 1913 = Russia 1913.
[d] Hungary, 1913 = Austria–Hungary 1913.
[e] Yugoslavia, 1913 = Serbia 1913.
Source: M. Liepmann, *Tariff Levels and the Economic Unity of Europe* (Philadelphia, 1938), p. 415.

the state was not seen any more as a temporary measure to bridge over disturbances until things returned to 'normal' but became accepted practically and theoretically as a political necessity.

B.   TRADE POLICY

Under extremely unfavourable conditions of the world depression, foreign trade became the chief concern of policy makers. A succession of heavy protectionist blows began with the Hawley–Smoot tariffs in May 1930, the highest tariff wall in United States history up to that time; followed by the devaluation of the pound sterling in 1931 and the protectionist measures of the Ottawa Conference in 1932 which practically severed the British Commonwealth from the rest of the world; whilst France intensified her agrarian protectionism and developed preferential arrangements within her colonial empire. Germany strengthened exchange controls to maintain an artificial parity.[66] As retaliatory measures agricultural tariffs were imposed – or increased as in the case of Czechoslovakia – by industrial states, and industrial duties were raised prohibitively by agrarian countries and tariff levels doubled, trebled, and in Bulgaria's case even more than quadrupled (see Table 130).

[66] League of Nations, *Commercial Policy in the Postwar World*, Off.no.C.31.M.1945.IIA (Geneva, 1945), p. 16.

Where were the agrarian economies of east-central and south-east Europe to find markets for their main export commodities? Their chief creditors and investors restricted access to their own home, colonial, and dependent markets even further in the 1930s than in the 1920s; the east-central and south-east European share in total foreign trade of Britain and France rarely reached 10 per cent in the 1920s and fell to about 3 per cent in the early 1930s only barely to recover its former level in the later 1930s (see Table 131). This was a crucial handicap for the small and weaker east-central and south-east European states, since the possibilities of paying their debts with commodity exports to the creditor states remained severely limited. Therefore, the spectre of default loomed large until it became a reality when budgets slid back into deficits and income from exports failed to cover annual interest and amortization of their foreign debts by 1931 (see Table 132). Whilst Czechoslovakia serviced her debt uninterruptedly at full contractual rates and Poland honoured her external debt regularly, all other south-east European governments suspended transfers of payments for varying periods at different times after 1931.

Theoretically another possibility for extending trade relations between industrial and agricultural countries offered itself in the east-central and south-east European region, which before 1918 had been part of a single, largely complementary home market. In the early 1920s the Danubian successor states still conducted more than half of their foreign trade with each other. Already from the mid-twenties discriminatory tariffs weakened mutual trade links between the industrial states, Austria and Czechoslovakia, and the agrarian countries of the Danube region. By 1929 only about one-third of total foreign trade of the successor states remained inter-area trade. Prospects for its revival did not look promising. In spite of efforts of the countries of the agrarian bloc to devise a common trade policy, fear of losing any of their real or supposed individual advantages was stronger than solidarity among them. Also, diverging economic interests, differing political systems, and their division into revisionist (defeated) and non-revisionist (victorious) states rendered agreement difficult. Furthermore, competition over who was to be the regional leader in any economic and political combination obstructed progress.[67]

Similarly, the great powers – although aware of the distressing market problems of the east-central and south-east European states – were unable and unwilling to agree on a common approach to alleviate the situation. Britain and France recognized the need to establish inter-Danubian economic cooperation. At that time, in 1931, they were not

[67] Holm Sundhaussen, 'Die Weltwirtschaftskrise im Donau–Balkan-Raum und ihre Bedeutung für den Wandel der deutschen Aussenpolitik unter Brüning', in Wolfgang Benz and Hermann Graml (eds.), *Aspekte deutscher Aussenpolitik im 20. Jahrhundert* (Stuttgart, 1976), p. 134.

prepared to tolerate Germany's move towards a customs union with Austria, which not only looked like a step in the direction of an Anschluss but would have broken all the political, financial, and business ties built up within the Versailles system. Whilst Britain consistently asserted her most-favoured-nation status in the area she was ready to grant certain concessions to trade among the successor states themselves as long as other great powers, especially Germany, remained excluded from these advantages.[68] A British proposal of a customs union among the Danubian states existed in 1932, but it never emerged from the preliminary stage of debate in the Foreign Office.[69] She preferred to extend comparatively greater support to the revisionist states such as Austria and Hungary in order to prevent French domination of the area. France's efforts at stabilizing the Danubian economies centred on the states of the Little Entente, Czechoslovakia, Romania, and Yugoslavia, who like her were interested in preserving as much of the Versailles system as possible. The nearest that any of her proposals came to the needs of the Danubian region was the Tardieu Plan in 1932, which joined the question of credits with that of the market but it, as well as the idea of the Stresa Conference in the same year to create a fund from which industrial nations would support agricultural countries, was scuttled by opposition from Germany and Italy and disinterestedness from Britain.[70]

The result was that mutual trade among the seven successor states, including Austria, shrank further from 36 per cent of their total foreign trade in 1929 to 23 per cent by 1937[71] – a steady decline through the years of crisis as well as of recovery. Even had any of the proposals of inter-Danubian economic cooperation succeeded, the market of the predominantly industrial states of Austria and Czechoslovakia could only have absorbed a limited amount of agricultural produce from south-east European countries. This was, among others, also one of the reasons why the attempt at organizing an 'Economic Little Entente' failed in the 1930s. The dilemma of the east-central European agrarian states necessarily continued as long as large industrial cereal-importing nations did not open their markets to them. However, competition among the great powers prevented any viable commonly agreed solution to the debt and export problems of east-central and south-east Europe.

[68] Public Records Office, London, FO 371/21139 – *Southern (Danubian States)*, contains material on Danubian Basin from 1932 to 1937.

[69] F. G. Stambrook, 'A British Proposal for the Danubian States: The Customs Union Project of 1932', *The Slavonic and East European Review*, vol. XLII, no. 98 (December 1963).

[70] Sundhaussen, 'Die Weltwirtschaftskrise im Donau–Balkan-Raum'.

[71] League of Nations, 'Trade and Production in the Danubian States', Appendix I in *The League of Nations Reconstruction Schemes in the Inter-War Period*, Off.no.C.59.M.59.1945.IIA (Geneva, 1945), p. 140. The seven states are: Austria, Bulgaria, Czechoslovakia, Hungary, Poland, Romania, Yugoslavia. Although severely diminished, not even on the eve of the Second World War were inter-Danubian economic ties utterly destroyed.

Table 131. *Trade of the area with Germany, France, Italy, United Kingdom, United States, and Czechoslovakia, 1922, 1929, 1933, 1937 (percentage of total)*

	Albania		Bulgaria		Czechoslovakia		Hungary		Poland		Romania		Yugoslavia	
	EX	IM	EX	IM	EX	IM	EX	IM	EX	IM	EX	IM	EX	IM
Germany														
1922	0.0	0.8	16.5	21.5	18.8	27.9	9.1	16.6	49.5	37.0	5.9	19.7	8.4	7.2
1929	0.0	4.9	29.9	22.2	19.4	25.0	11.7	20.0	31.2	27.3	27.6	24.1	8.5	15.6
1933	0.0	6.3	36.0	38.2	17.8	20.7	11.2	19.7	17.5	17.6	10.6	18.6	13.9	13.2
1937	0.0	5.1	47.1	62.2	13.7	15.5	24.0	25.9	14.5	14.5	18.9	28.7	21.7	32.4
France														
1922	3.3	0.0	7.1	6.0	4.8	3.5	1.1	2.6	1.8	4.3	9.6	5.9	5.8	3.0
1929	0.0	2.1	5.1	8.2	1.6	3.8	1.2	2.3	2.2	6.9	4.5	5.5	4.0	4.0
1933	1.8	3.1	3.3	4.4	5.1	5.8	4.5	5.6	5.5	6.8	12.4	10.5	2.2	4.2
1937	0.0	2.0	1.6	1.1	3.8	5.3	2.0	0.9	4.1	3.2	5.8	6.2	5.4	1.7
Italy														
1922	66.7	69.4	12.1	12.3	3.7	2.3	4.3	2.8	0.3	1.8	8.0	5.9	28.1	15.3
1929	60.5	46.1	11.0	10.7	2.7	2.3	6.9	4.4	1.4	2.7	7.7	6.9	24.9	10.8
1933	80.7	42.1	9.1	12.7	2.8	4.1	8.6	7.4	2.6	4.6	9.2	10.5	23.1	20.4
1937	78.4	24.7	4.2	5.3	3.0	2.3	12.3	7.0	4.5	2.6	6.6	4.4	9.4	8.2

United Kingdom

1922	0.0	3.3	0.7	15.0	7.4	5.1	1.8	3.1	4.1	7.0	2.4	8.9	1.9	7.1
1929	0.7	7.0	1.6	8.9	6.9	4.1	3.6	2.8	10.2	8.5	6.4	7.3	1.6	5.6
1933	0.0	8.8	1.8	6.9	6.2	4.2	8.0	4.4	19.2	10.0	15.4	14.9	2.7	9.7
1937	1.0	5.1	13.8	5.0	8.7	6.3	7.2	5.3	18.3	11.9	8.7	9.5	7.4	7.8

USA

1922	3.3	1.7	2.4	1.9	5.2	18.0	0.2	2.1	0.9	0.3	0.2	3.3	0.5	3.4
1929	15.6	10.1	1.7	3.3	7.2	5.4	1.1	4.6	1.1	1.8	0.2	6.1	1.6	4.7
1933	8.8	6.3	1.1	2.2	7.3	4.2	1.5	6.6	1.7	2.5	0.2	3.0	1.9	5.1
1937	8.8	4.5	3.8	2.2	9.3	8.8	2.9	4.7	8.4	1.5	1.7	3.9	4.8	6.0

Czechoslovakia

1922	0.0	0.0	2.4	3.8	—	—	15.0	23.8	4.8	6.5	8.0	9.4	8.1	19.8
1929	0.0	6.2	4.8	9.0	—	—	16.4	21.5	10.5	7.3	6.2	13.6	5.4	17.5
1933	0.0	6.9	3.5	4.8	—	—	7.3	10.1	5.0	4.3	6.9	9.8	10.8	12.1
1937	0.0	7.1	5.6	5.3	—	—	3.5	6.3	4.3	3.5	8.3	16.2	7.9	11.1

Note:
IM = imports   EX = exports.
Source: Z. Drábek, 'Trade Performance of East European Countries 1919–1939', *Papers in East European Economics*, no. 37 (October 1973).

948   EAST-CENTRAL AND SOUTH-EAST EUROPE, 1919-39

Table 132. *Discrepancy between debt service and income from foreign trade in east-central and south-east Europe, 1931 (millions of Swiss francs)*

	Amount of debt service for 1931	Total debt service as % of exports	Balance of trade
Austria	214	22	− 622
Bulgaria	35	16	+ 47
Czechoslovakia	105	5	+ 213
Hungary	248	48	+ 16
Romania	203	28	+ 192
Yugoslavia	124	29	− 15

Source: G. Ránki, *Economy and Foreign Policy: The Struggle of the Great Powers for Hegemony in the Danube Valley, 1919–1939* (New York, 1983), p. 121.

It was in Germany's interest to prevent any plan of furthering mutual trade preferences among the Danubian states where her economic influence had had to retreat. Therefore German foreign policy aimed at undermining the French security system and at isolating Czechoslovakia which from its very establishment as an independent state was considered to represent an obstacle to Germany's economic advance in the area. Although Germany had ceased to be the main investor she had remained the largest trading partner of her Eastern neighbours (see Table 131); yet her trade with the successor states had been declining and reached its deepest point in 1934 (see Table 133a and b). For one thing, because of her tariff policy, Germany, like Austria and Czechoslovakia, imposed import duties on agricultural produce from south-east Europe and her trade relations with Poland had deteriorated into a tariff war between 1925 and 1931 from which German–Polish trade never fully recovered in the inter-war period. For another thing, Germany's trade with the Danubian area declined because of the general contraction of foreign trade during the world economic crisis (see Tables 129 and 131). Indeed, Germany as the most indebted nation of the post-war world and a large trading country needed markets for her industrial goods as badly as the agrarian states of the Danubian Basin for their agricultural products, but both sides needed foreign exchange just as badly.

When Germany's proposal for a customs union with Austria had to be withdrawn in 1931,[72] because of resistance from France and the Little Entente, the first tentative steps were taken by the German government in the spring of 1931 towards a trade drive into south-east Europe. It

---

[72] F. G. Stambrook, 'The German–Austrian Customs Union Project of 1931', *Journal of Central European Affairs*, vol. XXI (1961).

Table 133a. *Germany's trade with seven east-central and south-east European states as percentages of her total imports and exports*

	Imports				Exports			
	1924	1929	1934	1937	1924	1929	1934	1937
Austria	1.5	1.5	1.5	1.7	4.8	3.3	2.6	2.1
Bulgaria	*a*	*a*	*a*	*a*	*a*	*a*	*a*	*a*
Czechoslovakia	4.8	3.6	3.6	2.6	5.9	4.9	3.6	2.6
Hungary	0.5	0.7	1.4	2.1	1.2	1.1	1.0	1.9
Poland	4.4	2.5	1.2	1.2	4.6	2.5	0.9	1.2
Romania	*a*	1.6	1.3	3.3	*a*	1.2	1.2	2.2
Yugoslavia	*a*	0.4	0.8	2.4	*a*	1.1	0.8	2.3
Percentages of Germany's total trade done with above seven states	11.2	10.3	9.8	13.3	16.5	14.1	10.1	12.3
Percentages of the total trade of the above seven states transacted with Germany	21.5	22.3	19.5	26.7	19.9	22.0	21.8	23.0

Note:
a Not specified: insignificant amounts (Bulgaria's share in total German imports: 0.4 per cent in 1924; 0.4 per cent in 1929; 0.8 per cent in 1934; 1.3 per cent in 1937). *Statistisches Jahrbuch des Deutschen Reichs*, relevant years.

Table 133b. *Percentages of total foreign trade of the above seven states transacted in 1929 and 1937*

	With						
	Germany	Each other	United Kingdom	Italy	United States	France	Other continents
1929	22.2	36.5	5.7	8.0	4.1	4.2	19.3
1937	24.9	24.5	8.4	6.2	5.5	3.9	26.6

Sources for Tables 133a and b: League of Nations, *The League of Nations Reconstruction Schemes in the Inter-War Period* (Geneva, 1945), Appendix 1, pp. 142–4.

began with an offer by the German Foreign Ministry of generous preferences to Romania and Hungary for imports of their agricultural produce to Germany.[73] This was a policy which initially encountered opposition as it violated Germany's most-favoured-nation commercial treaty with the United States as well as similar treaties between the Danubian and Entente governments, but in spite of this government regulated foreign trade came to fruition in the following years.

As the slump turned into a prolonged depression between 1931 and 1933, bilateral trade and tight exchange controls marked the end of multilateral trade in Europe. Payments and compensation agreements between debtor and creditor countries increased in foreign trade mainly to find a way to settle debts and resume their servicing rather than to provide a market for the produce of the east-central and south-east European countries. It was initially also Germany's aim to recover outstanding payments from her Danubian trading partners who had fallen into arrears. But at the same time no other industrial nation except Germany could absorb primary products in large quantities from south-east Europe; yet, she was neither able nor willing to pay in free exchange. During the financial and political crisis of the summer of 1931 the government of the Weimar Republic by emergency measures had pioneered the introduction of exchange controls which developed through economic necessity and political expediency into a conscious instrument of commercial and foreign policy and continued to be used as such more intensively in the era of National Socialist Germany.[74]

As far as east-central and south-east Europe were concerned Germany embarked upon a policy of bilateral trade agreements with the weaker agrarian Danubian countries who were attracted by her guarantees to purchase agricultural commodities they could not have expected to market. Bilateralism succeeded more immediately with Hungary and Yugoslavia, later with Bulgaria and Romania. With the advent of the Hitler government in Germany and the implementation of his Minister of Economics, Hjalmar Schacht's, autarchic New Plan in 1934 the Danubian region was to be drawn more effectively into the German sphere of influence as part of the concept of *Grossraumwirtschaft*. German

---

[73] Sundhaussen, 'Die Weltwirtschaftskrise', p. 157.

[74] There is overwhelming evidence in the German political and business archives to this effect. A great number of publications deal with the synchronization of foreign trade and foreign policy. For example, on the continuity between Weimar Germany and National Socialist Germany: Sundhaussen, 'Die Weltwirtschaftskrise', pp. 121–64; Dirk Stegmann, ' "Mitteleuropa" 1925–1934. Zum Problem der Kontinuität deutscher Aussenpolitik von Stresemann bis Hitler', in D. Stegmann, B. J. Bernd-Jürgen Wendt and Peter-Christian Witt (eds.), *Industrielle Gesellschaft und politisches System* (Bonn, 1978), pp. 203–21. On the National Socialist period see, for example, Hans-Erich Volkmann, 'Aussen Handel und Aufrüstung in Deutschland 1933 bis 1939', in Friedrich Forstmeier and Hans-Erich Volkmann (eds.), *Wirtschaft und Rüstung am Vorabend des Zweiten Weltkrieges* (Düsseldorf, 1975), pp. 81–131.

business welcomed this as a revival of the Mitteleuropa idea which had never been entirely abandoned.[75]

By that time most of the east-central and south-east European governments, except Austria, Czechoslovakia, and Poland, had subordinated their foreign trade to the clearing system generally and to bilateral trade with Germany in particular. Yugoslavia's foreign trade took place almost wholly within clearing by 1932/3, also about 70 per cent of the total foreign trade of Bulgaria and Hungary and 50 per cent of that of Romania which kept on rising to reach 80 per cent by 1937.[76] As they traded more and more with Germany they traded less and less with the industrial Danubian countries, especially with Czechoslovakia (see Table 131). As they traded increasingly with Germany they were piling up credit balances in Sperrmarks at specially agreed rates of exchange because their exports to Germany on average exceeded their imports from Germany between 1930 and 1938.[77] Published export and import figures are misleading as they are not identical with clearing figures, but even according to official trade statistics the south-east European region's share in Germany's total imports was higher than in her total exports by 1937 (see Table 133).

Thus flows of trade revived under stringent government controls but not flows of capital. Bilateralism in foreign trade obviously did not contribute to solving the problem of capital and trade flows, since the exchange control states of east-central and south-east Europe were neither able to get sufficient payments in free exchange nor to attract new capital in loans from abroad but still had to meet their foreign debt commitments.[78] For this reason the governments of Bulgaria, Hungary, and Poland, but also of Germany, did not follow those who devalued their currencies because their debt burden would have become greater. However, this meant that the economically weak exchange control countries were caught in the foreign trade price shears by having to accept low prices for exports and to pay high prices for imports. Since governments carried the expense, taxpayers but mainly consumers had to foot the bill.

C.   CONSEQUENCES OF BILATERAL TRADE

How successful was the search for markets under these constraints? Bilateralism between the weak agrarian economies and the crisis-ridden German economy seemed the only way out of the trough of the depression. But soon the expectations of both sides were disappointed as

[75] Wolfgang Schumann (ed.), *Griff nach Südosteuropa* (Berlin, 1973).
[76] Drábek, 'Trade Performance', p. 59.   [77] Weber, *Stadien*, p. 27.
[78] See League of Nations, *Balances of Payments 1937* (Geneva, 1938), p. 27.

disadvantages began to outweigh the advantages of such arrangements. Contemporary debates about the economic viability of bilateral trade between National Socialist Germany and the Danubian Basin never quite subsided and have recently been revived among economic historians.[79] In the heat of the arguments either Germany's advantageous economic and political penetration[80] and her subjugation of south-east Europe,[81] or the beneficial effects of her policy on her trade partners[82] and her sacrifices in her relations with the Danubian economies were stressed.[83] Particularly, the view that Germany had already achieved economic domination of south-east Europe before 1939 has been overstated,[84] although she doubtlessly aimed to achieve this.

Important advantages in her bilateral trade relations with the weaker agrarian countries did, of course, exist for Germany. By holding credit balances in blocked accounts for imports from south-east Europe, Germany was, in effect, able to draw upon interest-free loans for increasingly long periods and solve part of her debt and foreign exchange problems. In addition, she was able to gain free exchange by re-exporting agricultural produce, thus selling as yet unpaid goods, and finding a way into world markets over the relatively less developed Danubian countries. There can be little doubt that it was Germany's deliberate aim after 1934 to purchase as much as possible over the clearings obliging the governments of the capital-starved exporting countries to become involuntary exporters of capital as well, as they were credit-financing Germany's imports.[85] A further important advantage accrued to Germany through supplies of primary products from the Danubian states, which alleviated

[79] Paul Einzig, *Bloodless Invasion: German Economic Penetration into the Danubian States and the Balkans* (London, 1938); Antonin Basch, *The Danube Basin and the German Economic Sphere* (London, 1944); Howard S. Ellis, *Exchange Controls in Central Europe* (Westport, Conn., 1941, rep. 1971), pp. 257-70; Hermann Gross, *Südosteuropa. Bau und Entwicklung der Wirtschaft* (Leipzig, 1937).

[80] Dörte Doering, 'Deutsch-österreichische Aussenhandelsverflechtungen während der Weltwirtschaftskrise', in Hans Mommsen, Dietmar Petzina and Bernd Weisbrod (eds.), *Industrielles System und politische Entwicklung in der Weimarer Republik* (Düsseldorf, 1974), pp. 514-30.

[81] Charles P. Kindleberger, *Foreign Trade and the National Economy* (New Haven and London, 1962), p. 143; Holm Sundhaussen, 'Südosteuropa in der nationalsozialistischen Kriegswirtschaft am Beispiel des "Unabhängigen Staates Kroatiens" ', *Südostforschungen*, vol. XXXII (1973), pp. 233-8.

[82] Weber, *Stadien*, pp. 32-3; Piper, *Grundprobleme*, p. 146.

[83] Alan S. Milward, 'The Reichsmark Bloc and the International Economy', in Gerhard Hirschfeld and Lothar Kettenacker (eds.), *Der 'Führerstaat'. Mythos und Realität* (Stuttgart, 1981), pp. 377-413.

[84] Hans-Jürgen Schröder, 'Südosteuropa als "Informal Empire" Deutschlands 1933-1939. Das Beispiel Jugoslawiens', *Jahrbücher für die Geschichte Osteuropas*, 23 (1975), pp. 70-96; Berend and Ránki, *Economic Development*, pp. 278-80.

[85] Thus, for instance, the secret Yugoslav-German trade agreement of 1 May 1934 resulted in large import surpluses of Yugoslavia in Germany amounting to 5 million Reichsmark in 1934, 10 million in 1935 and 20 million in 1936; and although by resisting Germany's demands for more

the problems of bottlenecks in her domestic economy created by her public works and rearmament programmes under Schacht's New Plan and from 1936 under Goering's Four Year Plan. Whilst this did not solve Germany's food and raw material shortages, bilateral trade with south-east European countries eased the supply situation on her domestic market and to a certain extent enabled her to pursue a discriminating policy against imports.[86]

Until the very eve of the Second World War, however, National Socialist Germany's economic policy towards the east-central and south-east European states, in spite of cajoling, pressurizing, blackmailing, and threatening, rendered disappointing results. In the first place, trade with the region did not grow enough. Germany's total trade transacted with the seven successor states had by 1937 not risen above the highest share reached in the 1920s (see Table 133a). Her foreign trade turnover exceeded the 1929 level only with Bulgaria in 1937; no other south-east European country had attained the 1929 volume of trade with Germany.[87] A further problem was that trade, contrary to the belief of many commentators and historians, was not sufficiently complementary.[88] Only three Danubian countries were truly complementary to industrial Germany: Bulgaria and Yugoslavia, and to a lesser extent Romania, who were net exporters of food and raw materials and net importers of manufactured goods.[89] Therefore, the region as a whole could not satisfy Germany's steeply rising demand for strategic raw materials.

In the second place, Germany used the accumulated clearing balances and tried to coerce her partners to expand their imports to the German market within bilateral trade. In practice she was able to alter the composition of German imports – in violation of agreements – away from agricultural products to raw materials, such as Romanian oil.[90] But the supplier states wanting to reduce their blocked credit balances tried to evade deliveries of commodities which they were able to sell for free exchange under improving terms of trade during the general recovery on world markets as the trade cycle moved from depression to revival. In the second half of the 1930s Germany stepped up her demands on

deliveries her credit balance was reduced during 1937, it rose to almost double again in 1938 (see Schröder, 'Südosteuropa', pp. 79–80.) Similarly Hungary's credit balance in Germany was 15 million pengö in 1934 and rose to 46 million in 1936 (see Ellis, *Exchange Controls*, p. 264). Romania's and Bulgaria's balances tended to move in the same direction.

[86] Bernd-Jürgen Wendt, 'Südosteuropa in der nationalsozialistischen Grossraumwirtschaft. Eine Antwort auf Alan S. Milward', in Gerhard Hirschfeld and Lothar Kettenacker (eds.), *Der 'Führerstaat'. Mythos and Realität* (Stuttgart, 1981), pp. 426–7. See also Holm Sundhaussen, *Wirtschaftsgeschichte Kroatiens im nationalsozialistischen Grossraum 1941–1945* (Stuttgart), 1983), p. 36.   [87] Weber, *Stadien*, p. 27.   [88] See n. 81.
[89] Cleona Lewis, *Nazi Europe and World Trade* (Washington, DC, 1941), p. 11.
[90] See William S. Grenzebach, 'German Economic Policy in Rumania 1933–1939', paper given at conference on *Südosteuropa im Spannungsfeld der Grossmächte 1919–1939* in Mainz, 1979.

Bulgaria and Hungary, and in Bulgaria's case partially succeeded in influencing the government to change some of the country's crops from grain to oil seeds. But in the case of Yugoslavia, and even more so in the case of Romania, her urgent demands for larger deliveries met with resistance and she had to compromise because of the progressive weakening of the Reichsmark between 1933 and 1939 in relation to the currencies – particularly the pound sterling – of the main Western European foreign investors in these countries.[91] Yugoslavia and especially Romania were able to demand armaments and investment goods from Germany for greater wheat deliveries in 1937. Their bargaining power increased as their monetary policies followed more closely those of Britain, France, and Czechoslovakia because of their mutual financial and capital ties. At that time Britain – alerted by German advances – began to show increasing interest in the area[92] and Germany thus came under pressure to export more as she needed to import massively. This produced serious obstacles to Germany's trade and payments transfers by 1938 and the resistance of the south-east European countries to bilateralism was broken only after Austria fell into Germany's hands and when Czechoslovakia was dismembered between autumn 1938 and spring 1939.

In the third place, whilst trade figures developed in Germany's favour in relation to the relatively weakest agrarian economies, the balance of foreign investments in the east-central and south-east European area remained heavily weighted towards the financially stronger Western European powers. Germany had made hardly any headway at all in changing the distribution of foreign investments in her favour before 1938.[93]

As Germany encountered difficulties in her economic policy aims in relation to states of the Danubian region, the effect of economic collaboration with Germany was even more disappointing to them. The advantages that accrued to the agrarian south-east European economies from German–Danubian bilateral trade have been exaggerated. It was repeatedly pointed out that these states benefited from Germany's purchases of

91 Philippe Marguerat, 'Le protectionnisme financier allemand et le bassin danubien à la veille de la seconde guerre mondiale: l'example de la Romanie', *Relations internationales*, vol. XVI (1978), pp. 351–64.

92 A great number of memoranda, correspondence and reports in the Public Record Office, London, deal with the Danubian and Balkan trade question in relation to Germany's penetration. That they reached the cabinet see, for example, CAB 27/627, British influence in Central and South-east Europe, circulated by Halifax to cabinet (report by Leith Ross, 26 October 1938); also Bernd-Jürgen Wendt, *Economic Appeasement. Handel und Finanz in der britischen Deutschland Politik 1933–1939* (Düsseldorf, 1971).

93 Alice Teichova, 'Die deutsch–britischen Wirtschaftsinteressen in Mittelost- und Südosteuropa am Vorabend des Zweiten Weltkrieges', in F. Forstmeier and H. E. Volkmann (eds.), *Wirtschaft und Rüstung am Vorabend des Zweiten Weltkrieges* (Düsseldorf, 1975), p. 285.

their agricultural produce for higher than world prices, and that their industrialization was aided by the trade links with Germany.[94] Most recently this argument was carried to extremes by a statement that the weak agrarian economies of the Danubian Basin exploited Germany rather than the other way around.[95]

Doubtless, the economies caught in the breakdown of multilateral trade and starved of capital benefited from the revival of any kind of trade and there was only Germany to turn to when agricultural prices hit rock bottom. However, taking the decade 1928–38 as a whole, the expectations of the east-central and south-east European countries of exchanging their agricultural products for imports which would assist in their industrialization were not fulfilled. Until the eve of the Second World War the 1929 volume of their foreign trade had not been regained, but the direction of trade flows changed as trade of the whole region with Germany markedly expanded in the 1930s. Only Hungary and Bulgaria were drawn entirely into the German orbit, to a lesser extent Yugoslavia and Romania, whilst Czechoslovakia and Poland reduced their trade with Germany (see Table 131).

As it became more obvious that bilateralism with Germany ever more limited the economic moving space of the south-east European states they tried to extricate themselves from the German trade ensnarement and to develop their commerce with countries in which they could freely dispose of the proceeds of their exports, in order to obtain raw materials in which they were deficient. This became more possible as the bargaining position of the south-east European states was strengthened by the revival of world trade. Table 131 shows an improvement in trade beween Britain, France and the United States and the Danubian countries, who thus managed to reach favourable trade balances with their most important creditors and investors. This was, however, only partially conducive to purchasing raw materials and machinery with foreign exchange surpluses as large shares of export proceeds were used for liquidating old debts. But the new element in the geographical distribution of east-central and south-east European trade as compared with the previous decade was the trend away from Germany to export to free exchange countries in other continents where export surpluses could be used to purchase capital goods for their industrialization (see Table 133b). This was possible for, on balance, exports exceeded imports from overseas countries by 1938;[96] in the same year German exports and

[94] Weber, Stadien, p. 32; Piper, Grundprobleme, p. 285.
[95] Milward, 'Reichsmark Bloc', p. 411. See my brief reaction to Milward's thesis: A. Teichova and R. Waller, 'Der tschechoslowakische Unternehmer am Vorabend und zu Beginn des Zweiten Weltkrieges', in Waclaw Długoborski (ed.), Zweiter Weltkrieg und sozialer Wandel (Göttingen, 1981), pp. 291–2.
[96] League of Nations, Europe's Trade, II. Economic and Financial (Geneva, 1941), p. 51.

imports in the region as a whole practically cancelled each other out (see Table 133a).

Whilst trade flows changed direction, no significant change took place in the commodity composition of exports of the agrarian countries under discussion. As Germany insisted on increased deliveries of grain and foodstuffs, the comparatively least developed countries, Bulgaria, Yugoslavia, and Romania, showed the highest concentration of exports of primary products. Exports of the comparatively more industrialized countries became more diversified with manufactured commodities rising proportionately in total Czechoslovak and Hungarian and raw materials in Polish exports. Initially, Germany offered the agrarian countries incentives of higher than world prices for their agricultural products and raw materials but when they were forced deeper into the channels of bilateralism and the levels of their domestic prices had risen as a result, German export prices rose, or Germany reduced the quality and quantity of her exports, or delayed deliveries to her Danubian trade partners. In order to get more adequate returns from Germany the governments of south-east Europe had little choice but to accept manufactured goods. Such exchanges hampered rather than furthered these countries' endeavours to industrialize.

Bilateral trade with Germany did not aid industrialization of the less developed south-east European countries or accelerate their economic growth to a remarkable extent as has been claimed. On the contrary, the larger Germany's share in Danubian foreign trade on a bilateral basis grew, the more the industrialization of the region was threatened.

D. INDUSTRIALIZATION POLICY

However, the industrialization policies of the east-central and south-east European states did have a vital connection with their exchange controls and their trade policies. Complete government control of foreign trade intensified the previously existing development towards autarchy. Whilst there was little change in the composition of exports the structure of imports changed significantly. Overall, the volume of imports fell absolutely but most remarkable was the fall in the share of consumer goods in total imports of the area's agricultural countries (see Table 134). At the same time as the proportion of finished products declined, the share of industrial raw materials and semi-finished goods increased. These had mainly to be acquired from outside the German trading sphere and the governments of the agrarian states had to make free exchange available for these purchases in order to continue the state encouragement of the growing industrialization which had to a certain extent been aided by capital imports in the 1920s (see p. 925).

Table 134. *Shares of consumer goods in
total imports (per cent)*

	Average 1922–4	Average 1937–8
Bulgaria	46.2	20.4
Hungary	48.9	26.5
Poland	25.8	11.0
Romania	51.1	25.0
Yugoslavia	49.7	37.4

Source: Drábek, 'Trade Performance of East European Countries 1919–1939', *Papers in East European
Economics*, no. 37 (October 1973), p. 41.

As industrial production rose in the course of the 1930s, consumer
goods industries expanded absolutely and relatively more than producer
goods industries,[97] especially after the fast and sustained recovery of the
volume of industrial output since the crisis (see Fig. 11). This specific
development was not significantly stimulated by trade with Germany as
was shown above. Neither was the increase in industrial output accompanied by an expansion of consumer demand despite the rapid population growth in the region.[98] Because of the low level of purchasing
power of the mass of the population effective demand on domestic
markets outside state purchases consisted mainly of the needs of essentials
of life such as food and clothing. Therefore, home markets offered
greater opportunities for the development of consumer goods industries,
especially for textiles. But domestic industrial production of the relatively most backward economies could not have grown at a higher rate than
the average for Europe in the inter-war period (in Bulgaria an annual rate
of over 6 per cent and in Romania over 4 per cent against a European

[97] These historical facts do not confirm the theory of Alexander Gerschenkron regarding the
industrialization of economically backward countries in twentieth-century conditions. According to this theory, late-industrializing economies benefit from the advanced technology
reached by the leading industrial nations and development is heavily weighted towards the
producer goods sector which, as a rule, becomes the leading force, in the twentieth-century
process of industrialization. The east-central and south-east European agrarian economies
evidently could not exploit the theoretically advantageous position of latecomers as they had
not built up a modern structure and were unable to apply the best developed technology. For
Gerschenkron's theory see Alexander Gerschenkron, *Economic Backwardness in Historical Perspective* (New York, 1962), pp. 8–10, 26, 26–7, 50, 362–3.

[98] League of Nations, *Industrialization and Foreign Trade*, II. Economic and Financial (Geneva,
1945), p. 65. In Europe the total growth of population between 1920 and 1940 was 20 per cent, in
Yugoslavia 35 per cent, in Bulgaria 32 per cent, in Romania 30 per cent, and Poland 27 per cent
(Hungary remained on the European average and Czechoslovakia below it).

average of 1.4 per cent),[99] had it not been for the constantly increasing restrictions on imports of manufactured commodities to the east-central and south-east European countries and for the state encouragement of their industries.

Thus growth of state-encouraged branches of industry, especially of the textile industry whose output rose fastest, was not primarily induced by linkages between capital goods and consumption goods industries and a growing population entering an expanding market, but above all by import substitution. Under these circumstances objective limits were imposed by this type of industrialization of the less developed east-central and south-east European states in the inter-war period as it was not sufficiently stimulated by domestic or foreign capital investment, as there was no commensurate tendency of demand on domestic markets to grow and because of the historical fact that it was primarily based on the states' policy of import substitution.[100]

E.   CARTEL POLICY

The enduring narrowness of domestic markets in the successor states was conducive to cartelization, which had been a characteristic feature of the region since the turn of the century. Cartels became a component part of government economic policy in all the east-central and south-east European countries during the economic crisis of the early 1930s when their formation was greatly enhanced. Their impact on industrial development reinforced the existing tendencies to concentration in their economies. In the wake of the crisis many firms were either closed down altogether or their production was concentrated in more efficient or often financially more powerful enterprises as a result of the intervention of state-supported cartels. The cartelized sector of the successor state economies benefited most from exchange controls, as they defied price reductions throughout the depression; they also suffered least from raw materials scarcities, for as large producers they had priority access to allocations of free exchange,[101] and they enjoyed the concessions of the legislation in furtherance of domestic industries as well as guaranteed state orders (see p. 907).

Hungary was the first country of the region to introduce a Cartel Law in 1931. From that year until 1936 the number of registered cartels rose

[99] Alice Teichova, 'Besonderheiten im Strukturwandel der mittelost- und südosteuropäischen Industrie in der Zwischenkriegszeit', in D. Stegmann, B. J. Wendt and P. C. Witt (eds.), *Industrielle Gesellschaft und politisches System* (Bonn, 1978), p. 137.

[100] Alice Teichova, 'Structural Change and Industrialization in Inter-war Central-East Europe', in Paul Bairoch and Maurice Lévy-Leboyer (eds.), *Disparities in Economic Development since the Industrial Revolution* (London, 1981), pp. 175–86.

[101] Ellis, *Exchange Controls*, pp. 108, 110.

from 256 to 357, and one-third of these were concluded with international partners. Over one-half of Hungary's industrial production was cartelized by the second half of the 1930s.[102]

The crisis years also brought about a marked rise in the cartels in Poland where a Cartel Law was passed in 1933. Whereas during 1926 and 1929 24 cartels were founded annually, the annual average of new cartel agreements rose to twice that number between 1930 and 1934. In the same period international cartels with Polish participation increased from 32 in 1929 to 164 in 1935. More than half of the total number were international cartels. It may safely be assumed that at least two-thirds of Polish industrial production was cartelized.[103]

In the case of Czechoslovakia it was estimated that already in the initial phase of the economic crisis about 70 per cent of her industry was linked with cartels.[104] During the crisis and in the immediately following years the Czechoslovak state legally enforced cartelization of those branches of industry that to some extent had still been competitive. 'Forced syndicalization' was enacted by law in a certain industry at the request of those who commanded a decisive proportion of production in their field. In those state-enforced cartels modelled on private cartel agreements no outsiders were permitted to exist nor could there be any newcomers to the industry without special permission from the authorities. Czechoslovak cartels were an integral part of the country's economic structure and they were legally recognized and supported by the Cartel Bill of 1933 which required the registration of all existing cartel agreements. In 1933 the total number was 538 and by 30 September 1938, the last date of the life of the First Republic, it had risen to 1,152, of which 212 were concluded with foreign partners.[105] The Czechoslovak economy became practically fully cartelized in the 1930s by the usual process of cartel formation or by government intervention.

As in the other countries the role of cartels in Bulgaria, Romania, and Yugoslavia remained important throughout the inter-war period. There was public pressure for their abolition in Yugoslavia and Bulgaria followed by legislative attempts to prohibit them in Romania in 1934 and to curb and regulate their activities in Bulgaria in 1936, but these laws were never fully put into effect. Romania's 94 cartels were absorbed into state protection in 1937. The national cartels of the south-east European economies were mainly allocated to Central European market-sharing

---

[102] T. I. Berend and G. Ránki, *Mágyarorszag gyáripara a második világhábaru elött és a háború idöszakában (1933–1944)*, p. 99.

[103] I. Kostrowicka, Z. Landau and J. Tomaszewski, *Historia gospodarcza Polski XIX i XX wieku* (Economic History of Poland: XIX and XX centuries) (Warsaw, 1966), p. 313.

[104] E. Hexner, *Československé kartely* (Czechoslovak Cartels) (Prague, 1935), p. 5.

[105] Teichova, *An Economic Background*, pp. 56–7.

agreements based on Czechoslovakia. For these cartels south-east Europe, often named the 'original territory' in memory of the Habsburg monarchy, represented one of their most important markets for semi-finished and finished industrial products in Europe.

In the depressed conditions of the 1930s the aim of national and international cartelization was to curtail free competition, to distribute quotas of production among the members of cartels, to control prices, and regulate supply and demand generally in a contracting market. The study of the contents of cartel agreements leaves little doubt that in the conditions of the world economic crisis cartel policy significantly influenced the rigidity of prices, enhanced the concentration process in industry, and contributed notably to the reduction as well as the reorientation of foreign trade. The foremost concern of international cartel agreements was the division of markets. Whilst the common interest of national cartels entering into an international agreement is invariably directed toward an effective control of the market of their products, each international cartel can be regarded as an expression of the existing balance of economic forces between its partners. In this sense cartel policy provided an insight into one of the aspects of the economic relations between European states in the 1930s.

Within the chain of cartel relations from the west to the south-east of Europe a special link was formed by Czechoslovak producers as partners of British and French industrial combines which decisively participated in the leading enterprises of the country (see p. 922). As Germany's efforts of economic expansion and political revision in the countries of east-central and south-east Europe intensified in the 1930s Czechoslovakia became an area of complicated competitive struggles in international business in which the competition between Czechoslovak and German groups took place within the framework of Western European and German competition. In the sphere of international investment German companies and banks were unable to dislodge Britain and France, and with them Czechoslovakia, from key positions in east-central and the south-east European economies even in the decade after 1929 when Germany regained her economic strength. She was therefore obliged to try to satisfy her economic demands on Central and south-east Europe in ways other than through direct capital investment.[106]

As shown in the previous pages, Hitler Germany's trade offensive into south-east Europe aimed at undermining the capital structure and the political alliances which rested on a line from Britain and France in the West to Czechoslovakia as the centre point linking them to south-east Europe. Concurrent and closely intertwined with the German trade drive into the Danubian Basin, the Hitler regime with the cooperation of

---

[106] *Ibid., passim.* This topic is analysed in detail.

German business used the cartel system as an instrument of furthering its trade expansion.

Since in the most important international cartel agreements either the whole or part of the south-east European market had been allocated to Czechoslovak companies, German cartel partners tried to get Czechoslovak cartels to agree to revise conditions in a way that would enable them to gain bigger shares of the traditional Czechoslovak export markets as well as, wherever possible, a stake in the domestic market of Czechoslovakia. The most numerous and influential German cartels were able to make inroads into the trade of those industries, such as iron and steel, chemicals, engineering, and electrical products, in which British and French capital was strongly represented. Also through cartels, German business groups attempted to gain greater influence in the economic life and the trade connections of Czechoslovakia and thus weaken the position of their British and French competitors. The gradual advance of German manufacturing products into the east-central and south-east European market reflected in foreign trade statistics can largely be traced to new cartel agreements and contractual additions to existing ones negotiated and concluded in the 1930s. This added to sharpening the contrast between the origins of capital investments and credit, on the one hand, and the direction of foreign trade in the Danubian Basin, on the other.[107]

However, even in the field of international cartels German expansion was kept in limits because the Czechoslovak firms were often a go-between and behind them stood their stronger partners from Britain and France. Within the cartel mechanism Germany competed for higher production quotas and a larger share in the Central and south-east European markets, but her demands were not met to her satisfaction before 1938, particularly before the Munich Agreements of 30 September 1938.

Until that time no substantial changes had occurred within the inter-war framework of the international cartel structure. After Munich, negotiations were to take place between the two most influential associations of industrialists in Europe, the Reichsgruppe Industrie and the Federation of British Industries, which indeed began in mid-March 1939, to adjust the cartel system to the new balance of power in which German industries, having gained the Austrian and Czechoslovak quotas, were holding out for larger possibilities in east-central and south-east Europe. These endeavours were, however, interrupted by the outbreak of the Second World War.

---

[107] Bernd-Jürgen Wendt, 'England und der deutsche "Drang nach Südosten". Kapitalbeziehungen und Warenverkehr in Südosteuropa zwischen den Weltkriegen', in Imanuel Geiss and Bernd-Jürgen Wendt (eds.), *Deutschland in der Weltpolitik des 19. und 20. Jahrhunderts* (Düsseldorf, 1974), p. 496.

VIII. *Economic and social policies and infrastructures* [108]

Within the limits of the post-war system of international treaties and the new balance of economic power in Europe the east-central and south-east European governments' policies fundamentally aimed at consolidating their national and political position. Accordingly, the infrastructure of their states had to evolve alongside their armed forces and their security and bureaucratic state apparatus. In their endeavour to narrow the gap between economically advanced Western nations and their own relative economic backwardness the development of infrastructure played an important role. However, the implementation of their policy aims encountered complex and contradictory realities.

In general, the governments of the area were aware of the need to equip their economies with the necessary infrastructure as part of their policy for furthering domestic industry. Thus one of the urgent requirements was to rebuild, extend, and modernize the transport system which had developed fast since the 1870s but the progress of which was halted by the First World War. In that period the transport infrastructure was essentially determined by the railway network. Between 1885 and 1905 the Austro-Hungarian Empire held the ninth and Romania the twelfth place in the rank order of transport systems of 13 European countries; this changed with the new territorial division of Europe and in 1920 out of 28 European states Czechoslovakia ranked eighth, Hungary seventeenth, Poland nineteenth, Yugoslavia twenty-fourth, Bulgaria twenty-fifth and Romania twenty-sixth. Except for Czechoslovakia, which met Western European standards, the east-central and south-east European countries lagged far behind (Switzerland occupied first, Denmark second, and Britain third place in 1920).[109]

A further infrastructural requirement of industrialization and modernization was an educational system able to prepare an effective, literate labour force with an adequate number of skilled workers and technicians. However, for most countries in the area the essential problem remained a vast illiterate peasantry. In 1920 well over 50 per cent of the population (of 10 years old and over) in Bulgaria, Romania, and Yugoslavia was illiterate, in Poland it was 33 per cent, whilst the illiterate population (of those more than 10 years old) in Hungary amounted to 13

---

[108] This section on infrastructural policies is based mainly on the research of Dr Eva Ehrlich and Dr Milan Hauner to whom my sincerest thanks are due for giving me permission to draw from their results. For the interpretation of the material and for any errors or omissions I take full responsibility.

[109] Eva Ehrlich, *Infrastruktura, korok es országok* (Infrastructure, Periods and Countries), (Budapest, 1975), pp. 101-3; David Turnock, *Eastern Europe* (Folkestone, 1978).

per cent and in Czechoslovakia only to 5 per cent. Also in this case the gap between the Western level reached by Czechoslovakia and the high illiteracy of the other investigated countries was indeed enormous.

A corollary to an educated labour force is a sufficient supply of healthy workers which presented a problem in countries having to grapple with undernourishment, epidemics, and shortages of hospitals and physicians. However, the provision of health care and social security was not only a requirement of the region's economy but became, not unlike the land reforms, a political necessity. Like aspirations of democratic liberties, pluralistic government, the right to organize trade unions and to collective bargaining, social welfare also appeared as one of the persistent demands for social reform.

With regards to the development of infrastructure, government policy was in no country of the area guided by a conscious, comprehensive concept of providing either a public consumer service or a long-term social investment in order to meet the objective demands of economic growth and social improvement. It consisted rather of rescue actions, emergency measures, and concessions in the face of strong popular pressure and mass support for certain social welfare amenities. This can mainly be attributed to the intransigent policy of ruling elites governing in autocratic monarchies and military dictatorships and also to the strong conservative influence of agrarian elites in parliamentary governments. In addition, the want of capital largely prevented far-reaching social reforms.

The successor states laboured under the conflict between competing demands on scarce funds and the inflexibility of social budgets. Since military spending was by all states considered an absolute priority and, only second to it, the state-owned transport system was regarded as a necessary externality to industry and trade, social budgets consisting of education, health, and social security were held to an irreducible amount.

In east-central and south-east Europe the standard and composition of the inter-war infrastructure has historically been connected with the various empires to which the individual states had belonged before 1918. Taking transport, communications, housing, education, and health as indicators and assuming that economic growth and infrastructural development move together, three different levels can be distinguished. Those countries emerging from the industrialized regions of the Austro-Hungarian Empire – Bohemia and Moravia in Czechoslovakia, also parts of Hungary and Poland – approached the level of infrastructure in Western Europe; less developed in the sphere of infrastructure were the countries which had belonged to the Hungarian territories of the Habsburg monarchy, to Wilhelmine Germany, and to tsarist Russia – such as parts of Poland, Romania, and Hungary; whilst hardly any major infrastructural development had taken place in the Balkan countries – parts of Romania, Yugoslavia, and Bulgaria – under Turkish rule. For example, any railway building in this latter region not only began with a 30–40 years' delay compared to the Central European areas but the lines only accidentally linked agricultural provinces with urban centres or mining areas with industries because the direction and destination of railway construction were totally subordinated to foreign strategic objectives.

A.   TRANSPORT AND COMMUNICATION

As a result of the historical role of the state in the economies of east-central and south-east Europe, the overwhelming part of the transport system (roads, railways, river shipping, and navigation) and of the communication network (post, telegraph, and telephone) was owned and administered by the governments on their post-1918 territories. However, neither public nor private finance in any of the east-central and south-east European countries could without outside aid muster sufficient resources to reconstruct the partially destroyed and seriously run-down transport system (see the financial reconstruction of Danube shipping, p. 918). Yet all the national governments endeavoured to adapt the system as quickly as possible to the new geographical shapes of their states.

The traditionally most important transport system, the railway network, had in wartime been strained beyond its limits, its upkeep had been neglected, and the further east the greater was the destruction of its lines, stations, locomotives, wagons, and equipment. Moreover, due to the new west–east orientation in Europe the successor states inherited a derouted railway system whose mainlines converged on Vienna and Budapest and were largely directed to the Mediterranean and Danube ports, whilst Poland's lines led to Berlin, Vienna, or Petrograd. Thus almost every country in the region was compelled to adjust its transport system to the new economic units or spheres of political influence. Therefore, whilst in Western Europe railway building practically ceased, the east-central and south-east European countries were involved in unifying their network and building a few new railway lines. In contrast to Western countries where inter-war railway development concentrated on modernization and technical improvements rather than lengthening of lines, there was some increase in density of the railway network in the discussed area. When, however, railway building ceased also in east-central and south-east Europe, it did so at a much lower density than in Western European countries and it had failed to modernize the railway system (see Table 135).

Throughout the inter-war period, therefore, these economies largely

Table 135. *Length of railway lines per 100 km² and rolling stock per 1,000 head of population between 1921 and 1936*

	Railway lines			Rolling stock[a]
	1921	1928	1936	1921–36
Czechoslovakia	9.7	9.8	9.8	7.46
Hungary	8.8	9.2	9.3	5.63
Poland	4.4	5.0	5.0	5.45
Yugoslavia	3.7	4.0	3.8	4.15
Romania	3.6	3.7	3.8	3.31
Bulgaria	2.5	2.8	3.2	1.92
	1921	1929	1936	
United Kingdom	13.38	13.44	13.44	
France	7.79	7.90	7.90	
Germany	12.35	12.45	12.45	

Note:
[a] Rolling stock consists of locomotives, passenger carriages, goods trucks, other wagons and mail wagons.
Sources: Compiled from Eva Ehrlich, 'Infrastructure and an International Comparison of Relationships with Indicators of Development in Eastern Europe 1920–1950', *Papers in East European Economics*, no. 34 (Oxford, July 1973), and Eva Ehrlich, *Infrastruktura, korok és országok* (Budapest, 1975), p. 103.

consumed the stock produced in earlier periods. Only in Czechoslovakia and Hungary were the cosseted iron and steel and engineering industries able to supply a substantial part of locomotives, carriages, and wagons from their own production whilst the other countries had to rely on imports. After a small increase in railway construction in all the investigated countries between 1921 and 1928 the system stagnated (see Table 135), but this was not accompanied by faster growth of road transport as was the case in Western Europe and the United States in the inter-war period.

According to available statistics road density in Europe had remained fairly stable for almost one hundred years since the middle of the nineteenth century; at least, no significant change had taken place between the groups of countries with developed and less developed road networks. In 1937 the length of roads in km per 1,000 km² was in Czechoslovakia 500, in Romania 367, in Hungary 326, in Poland 312, in Bulgaria 299, and in Yugoslavia 170, as against Britain's figure of 1,200, France's 1,300 and Germany's 520.[110] Although informative, these figures give no evidence of the quality of these roads' surfaces or widths.

[110] Calculated from Eva Ehrlich, 'Infrastructure and an International Comparison of Relationships with Indicators of Development in Eastern Europe 1920–1950', *Papers in East European Economics*, no. 34 (Oxford, July 1973), hereafter cited as Ehrlich, *Paper 34*.

Table 136. *Passenger cars, buses, lorries, and tractor trailers per 1,000 inhabitants, 1929 and 1937*

	Passenger cars		Buses, lorries, tractor trailers	
	1929	1937	1929	1937
Czechoslovakia	1.8	6.3	0.8	2.2
Hungary	2.3	2.84	0.48	0.45
Romania	0.7	1.23	0.78	0.22
Yugoslavia	0.6	0.72	0.43	0.26
Poland	0.5	0.6	0.16	0.24
Bulgaria	0.3	0.4	0.19	2.42
United Kingdom	21.85	38.7	10.09	12.65
France	23.33	37.7	8.20	10.2
Germany	7.63	16.9	3.11	4.78

Source: As Table 135.

However, the virtual absence of motorization leaves little doubt about the generally poor state of roads if the east-central and south-east European areas as a whole is considered. In the absence of financial resources items for infrastructure were continuously reduced in national and local budgets.

Whilst in Western Europe the stagnation in railway building was outweighed by the expansion of motor and later air traffic, no such buoyant development took place in Eastern Europe with the exception of Czechoslovakia (see Table 136).

Telecommunications had from the outset been state initiated and administered in all east-central and south-east European regions. As the first and most important instrument of telecommunication, the building of the telegraph system coincided with that of the railways and its density resembled the progress or stagnation of the density of the railway network. Thus it was part of the infrastructural stock inherited by the successor states. Similarly, telephone lines were created by the state as a component of the postal system on the territory of the Habsburg Empire almost simultaneously with the leading industrial countries in the 1880s and growing annually between 5 and 7 per cent. But between the two world wars the number of telephones per 1,000 inhabitants increased more rapidly in Western European countries than in east-central and south-east Europe. From 1929 to 1937 the increase amounted to 78 per cent in Western Europe as against 45 per cent in Eastern Europe (see Table 137).[111] Thus also in the field of telecommunications the gap widened.

[111] See Ehrlich, *Infrastruktura*, pp. 111–12.

Table 137. *Telephone*
extensions per 1,000
inhabitants, 1928 and 1937

	1928	1937
Hungary	10.9	16.4
Czechoslovakia	10.7	15.3
Poland	6.0	8.6
Romania	2.93	4.14
Yugoslavia	2.6	3.7
Bulgaria	3.04	3.5
United Kingdom	38.6	64.0
France	23.6	37.8
Germany	46.0	94.5

Source: Eva Ehrlich, 'Infrastructure and an International Comparison of Relationships with Indicators of Development in Eastern Europe 1920–1950', *Papers in East European Economics*, no. 4 (Oxford, July 1973).

B.   HOUSING

Since almost everywhere in Europe population growth accelerated after the First World War and the drift of the rural population to cities continued, although at an uneven pace, governments were faced with an increasing need for housing. On the whole, the urban population during the inter-war years in the countries of east-central and south-east Europe grew faster than the rural population, though the overwhelmingly rural character of most of the region prevailed (see Table 138). The tendency of urban growth was also reflected in rising industrial relative to agricultural employment. In Poland and Hungary there was an absolute drift away from agriculture (− 518,000 and − 96,000 respectively), whilst non-agricultural employment grew (2,001,000 and 272,000 respectively), between 1921 and 1931; in Yugoslavia during the same period the volume of agricultural employment rose by 259,000 persons but the flow into other occupations was greater, amounting to 320,000; yet in Bulgaria by far the larger part of the increase of gainfully occupied persons was absorbed by agriculture, although non-agricultural employment grew as well: 602,000 as against 231,000 between 1920 and 1934.[112] During the

[112] League of Nations, *Industrialization and Foreign Trade*, p. 65. For figures on comparative population growth, see n. 98.

Table 138. *Rural/urban distribution of population in Eastern Europe (thousands)*

Country, census year	Population				
	Rural	%	Urban	%	Total
Europe (excluding USSR)	185,034	47.8	201,835	52.2	386,869
Bulgaria, 1934	4,775	78.6	1,303	21.4	6,078
Czechoslovakia, 1930	7,688	52.2	7,042	47.8	14,730
Hungary, 1930	4,997	57.5	3,691	42.5	8,688
Poland, 1931	23,227	72.8	8,689	27.2	31,916
Romania, 1930	14,406	79.8	3,651	20.2	18,057
Yugoslavia, 1931	10,825	77.7	3,109	22.3	13,934
	(millions)	%	(millions)	%	(millions)
United Kingdom	11.9	24.5	37	75.5	49
France, 1936	19.9	47.6	21.9	52.4	41
Germany, 1939	20.8	30.1	48.4	69.9	69.3

Notes:
For (France), Hungary and Yugoslavia places of 10,000 or more inhabitants classified as urban, the remainder as rural.
For Bulgaria and Romania, administrative definition is used.
For Czechoslovakia (Germany) places of 2,000 or more inhabitants classified as urban, the remainder as rural.
For Poland administrative definition is used but excluding 191,500 soldiers in barracks.
Source: Compiled by M. Hauner, 'Demographic Structure of Eastern Europe between the two Wars', *Papers in East European Economics*, no. 40 (Oxford, January 1974), based on D. Kirk, *Europe's Population in the Interwar Years* (League of Nations, Geneva, 1946), pp. 30–1.

severest crisis years there was a movement back to the land but the trend towards the cities reasserted itself in the later 1930s.

In the inter-war period the housing shortage was exacerbated in east-central and south-east Europe because, initially, available housing had been damaged by the war; later, between 1920 and 1940, the rise in population significantly exceeded the European average.

In the 1920s large-scale house building began with a high degree of state participation which was withdrawn for a time during the world economic crisis but was revived after it. With this development the installation of water mains and electricity services by the state and municipalities gradually spread to dwellings, although almost exclusively urban areas benefited from this development. In spite of the rich potential resources of electric power in the region they remained essentially unused.

Throughout east-central and south-east Europe the urban housing situation doubtlessly improved supported by legislative measures and direct involvement of the state. In this respect, however, there were large differences between countries and various regions within the individual countries. Thus in parts of Czechoslovakia – Bohemia and Moravia – with a high density of urban settlements, practically every built-up area gained from the development of housing. In Hungary and Poland villages and relatively large rural settlements were bypassed and only the housing situation in cities improved; whilst construction of new housing and qualitative improvement of existing dwellings proceeded on a very small scale in the south-east area where primarily capital cities made certain headway.

In the field of housing as a component of the infrastructure the west to east–south-east gradient of development shown in other indicators is repeated if consumption of cement and production of bricks per inhabitant are applied as a measure.[113] A more direct indicator of standards is the size of dwellings, on which some figures relating to certain years in the inter-war period are available and these confirm the declining standards from Northern to east-central Europe: the overwhelming proportion of dwellings in towns and villages like in Northern Europe had four or five rooms, in Western Europe three rooms; but in east-central Europe the majority of dwellings in towns consisted only of one or two rooms, whilst the situation in villages was worse.[114] But it is impossible to ascertain how much of total building activity went into industrial projects and how much was applied to housing. It is even more difficult to quantify the exact role of the state providing public housing except that it can fairly safely be assumed that direct or indirect state intervention was substantial.

C. EDUCATION, HEALTH, AND SOCIAL SECURITY

In the introduction of this section on infrastructural policies priorities in government spending, especially the over-riding importance of military budgets as well as the downward inflexibility of social budgets, were mentioned (pp. 962–4). To illustrate this point Table 139 shows the comparative expenditure on public health and education, on the one hand, and defence spending, on the other, as a percentage of total

---

[113] See Svennilson, *Growth and Stagnation*, pp. 307–9; and Ehrlich, *Paper 34*.

[114] One- and two-room dwellings in Czechoslovakia amounted to 65 per cent as a national average in 1921; in Hungary it was 76 per cent in provincial towns and 54 per cent in Budapest in 1930; in Poland, also in 1930, in towns with a population of more than 20,000 such dwellings accounted for 65 per cent and in smaller towns for 89 per cent. See Ehrlich, *Infrastruktura*, p. 118.

Table 139. *Comparative expenditure on public health, education and defence, 1928/9–1938/9 (millions of national currencies and percent)*

	Years	A Total expenditure	B Public health and education	C Defence	B as % of A	C as % of A
Bulgaria	1928/9	8,254	1,293	1,039	15.7	12.2
(leva)	1935	6,074	1,072	1,047	17.5	18.0
	1938	7,217	1,390	1,792	19.3	24.7
Czechoslovakia^a	1929	10,275	2,412	1,792	23.4	17.0
(koruna)	1936	12,433	3,110	3,761	25.1	30.0
	1938	10,117	3,164	4,499	31.3	40.4
Hungary	1928/9	1,473	210	111	14.0	7.5
(pengö)	1935/6	1,230	115^b	97.8	9.5^b	7.9
	1938/9	1,723	116^b	155.1^c	6.8^b	9.0^c
Poland	1928/9	2,841	788	870.3	28.1	30.6
(złoty)	1935/6	2,228	667	768	30.7	34.4
	1938/9	2,475	725	800	29.0	32.3
Romania	1928/9^d	35,223	7,785	7,589	22.4	21.5
(lei)	1935/6^e	22,623	4,903	10,665	21.6	43.1
	1938/9	33,104	5,781	10.750	17.5	32.3
Yugoslavia	1928/9	7,301	955	2,429	13.0	33.1
(dinar)	1935/6	6,319	1,016	2,000	16.1	31.6
	1938/9	11,814	1,272	2,772	10.7	23.5

Notes:
^{a} Frontier guard and gendarmerie included in defence budget.
^{b} Data for education only.
^{c} Actual military expenditure was much higher by calculations of G. Ránki and I. Berend: 618.9 million pengö for 1938/9, or 35 per cent of total (see *The Hungarian Economy in the Twentieth Century* (London and Sydney, 1985), pp. 155–6).
^{d} Financial year of 1928/9 was 18 months.
^{e} In Romania's defence budget the National Fund was included from 1935/6 onwards.
Sources: Calculated from League of Nations, *Public Finance 1928–1935* (Geneva, 1936); *Armaments Year Book 1924–1939/40; International Statistical Yearbook 1926–1940/41.* These were used by M. Hauner as the basis of the above calculations in: 'Comparative Social Infrastructure and Education in Eastern Europe', and 'Military Budgets and the Armaments Industry', *Papers in East European Economics*, nos. 26 and 36 (Oxford, 1973).

expenditure in ordinary budgets between 1928 and 1938.[115] Military expenditure was roughly equal or higher than spending on education and social services in the majority of the countries listed in Table 139 by the end of the 1920s. But during the 1930s the share of defence in total budget expenditure exceeded absolutely and proportionately the outlay on public health and education. Published figures in ordinary budgets

[115] The composition of col. B in Table 139 under the heading 'Public health and education' include the budget expenditure of the relevant ministries. In the case of Bulgaria this comprises the

are, however, misleadingly low with regard to defence. Military expenditure soared after the breakdown of the disarmament conference of the League of Nations which further weakened the Versailles system. Revisionist countries were able to rearm openly without fear of retaliation, particularly with the backing of Fascist Italy. Non-revisionist countries accelerated their armaments drive to meet the growing threat from National Socialist Germany. Poland's and Romania's military spending had been continuously crippling based mainly on their mutual assistance agreement against the USSR.

Domestic funds were diverted in all countries to military spending rather than to social purposes which made shortages in this sphere more acute in times of greater social need. From 1935/6 onwards, Romania created special funds for national defence in her extraordinary budget which rose year by year.[116] Poland channelled 36 per cent of total public investment as part of her extraordinary budget to military purposes between 1936 and 1939.[117] Also Czechoslovakia is a case in point where in 1936 an extraordinary budget was introduced specifically to alleviate the financial consequences of the crisis and to spend through the Ministry of Public Works on the relief of unemployment, on road works, melioration, and water board needs. However, five-sixths of the total allocated to these tasks were siphoned off for rearmament between 1936 and 1938.[118] Absolute amounts allocated to social spending remained in most east-central and south-east European countries fairly stable throughout the whole period, except for Poland and Romania where the sum total declined absolutely and relatively in the second half of the 1930s (see Table 139).

D. EDUCATION

In all walks of life in Central and south-east Europe the heritage of the former empires affected the starting point of the states which superseded

spending of the Ministry of Interior and Public Health whose spending amounted on average to 6 per cent, and of the Ministry of Education whose spending amounted on average to 12 per cent of total budget expenditure. Since the share of the expenditure for the resort of the Interior cannot be ascertained, obviously, considerably less than 6 per cent must have gone into public health. The role of the church is emphasized in Hungary and Yugoslavia as education was part of the total expenditure of the Ministry of Church and Education and in Romania education comes under the combined item for the Ministry of Education and the Ministry of Church and Arts. Also in these cases the share of education cannot be disaggregated from that used for church affairs.

[116] Romania's extraordinary budget contained the following item:

Special funds for national defence (in million lei)

	1935/6	1936/7	1938/9
Extraordinary budget	2,000	2,600	4,000

See Milan Hauner, 'Military Budgets and the Armaments Industry', *Papers in East European Economics*, no. 36 (Oxford, October 1973), p. 49. [117] *Ibid.*, p. 69. [118] *Ibid.*, p. 45.

them; it specifically influenced the level and organization of their differing inter-war educational structures.

The beginning of a modern education system in the western half of the Habsburg monarchy can be traced to Maria Theresa who on 6 December 1774 ordered the establishment of village schools (*Trivialschule*).[119] Yet the legal foundation for free and compulsory education of the age group from 6 to 14 was laid in 1869. From it arose a graduated system of education linking primary with secondary schools and universities. As a result illiteracy was practically wiped out in the western territories of the Dual Monarchy; particularly Bohemia and Austria had reached the highest levels of education in Europe by the turn of the century. Although illiteracy fell to one-third also in the eastern provinces of Cisleithania during the same period, they lagged behind the western regions. This applies also to the Hungarian half of the Habsburg Empire which, whilst following the steps of the Austrian regions, went at a slower pace in education after the Compromise of 1867.

In the Russian and Turkish provinces the educational level was much lower. The shortfall of primary schools was so severe that 70–80 per cent of seven year olds and over were still illiterate at the beginning of the twentieth century. Similarly backward was the situation in Romania and Bulgaria, where – after they had shaken off Ottoman rule – free and compulsory education was adopted in principle in 1864 and 1878 respectively, but no effective measures were taken to enable children to benefit from it.[120]

Advances in the field of educational policy in the inter-war period have to be measured against this historical background. The successor states (except Romania where the example of the French educational system was followed) retained the basic Austro-Hungarian pattern of state-supported schooling. Each regime in the area legally reaffirmed its policy of free, universal, and compulsory education and expanded its scope. In general, the educational framework consisted of a primary school level from 6–11 to 7–14 years of age encompassing all children. With the second educational level equal and comprehensive schooling ended, as no more than 20 per cent of primary school leavers were channelled into a 3 or 4 year upper primary or middle-level school, whilst another smaller stream, at the most about 6 per cent of them, went into 8 years of secondary schooling which gave pupils an opportunity to prepare for university studies. At each stage the number of entrants far exceeded the number of those completing its full cycle. In addition, the

---

[119] The population of Bohemia and Moravia had traditionally been aware of the importance of education. This goes back to the Hussite period in the fifteenth century and is later connected with the great influence of Jan Amos Komenský (Comenius) (1592–1670).

[120] Berend and Ránki, *Economic Development*, pp. 24–6.

policies of the individual states implementing and pursuing these goals and the degree of achieving them differed widely.

The most immediate and thorough education reform in the area took place in the Czechoslovak Republic. Since in her western territory she could build upon one of the most advanced educational levels in Europe and her national income per head was the highest in the region investigated here, she was able to meet the more urgent needs of the backward eastern territories of Slovakia and Ruthenia. Her programme of reconstruction succeeded in achieving practically full school attendance and in largely equalizing the educational level throughout the country. In its education drive the Czechoslovak state initially used Czech teachers also in the non-Czech speaking eastern region where illiteracy was very high. At the same time, in accordance with its nationality policy, this was followed up by providing adequate educational facilities for the nationalities living within its borders. Thus by the end of the first inter-war decade 96 per cent of Czechs, Slovaks, and Romanians, 97 per cent of Germans, 93 per cent of Hungarians, 91 per cent of Ruthenians and 88 per cent of Poles were instructed in their mother tongues.[121] This policy was carried through also with regard to universities. As in the other countries their number was increased. To the German and Czech universities in Prague, whose origins go back to the foundation of Charles University in 1348, a further Czech university in Brno and a Slovak university in Bratislava were added in 1919, where also students of oppressed nationalities or of persecuted religious faiths from neighbouring countries found opportunities to pursue their academic studies.

Czechoslovakia's comparatively wide network of higher vocational schools greatly differed from the poor picture presented by the area as a whole (see Table 140). It catered for a whole range of trades and professions and pupils could continue to study arts, humanities, science, or technology at traditional or technical universities. Throughout the school system many denominational and private educational institutions existed but the state's policy was decisive.

None of the other countries in east-central and south-east Europe had reached Czechoslovak standards by the end of the inter-war years. As governments increasingly put into practice the legal requirements of primary education they succeeded in reducing illiteracy by about half between 1920 and 1940 (see Table 141). Nevertheless, full school attendance was not achieved despite growing enrolment at primary schools (see Table 140).

---

[121] *Aperçu Statistique de la République Tchécoslovaqie* (1930), p. 244. Cited by Milan Hauner, 'Comparative Social Infrastructure and Education in Eastern Europe', *Papers in East European Economics*, no. 26 (January 1973), p. 13 (hereafter cited as Hauner, *Paper 26*).

Table 140. *Types and numbers of schools in six east-central and south-east European countries between the wars*

Country (millions of school age/ number enrolled)	Year	Infant schools	Primary schools	Secondary schools	Technical and special schools	higher education and universities
Bulgaria	1920/1	36	6,042	68[a]	127	2 (+3)
(1.9/1.08)	1938/9	252	7,229	137[a]	379	2 (+4)
Czechoslovakia	1924/5	1,416	15,713	357[a]	3,130[b]	8 (+9)
(2.8/2.8)	1935/6	2,670	17,335	354[a]	3,760[b]	8 (+8)
Hungary	1920/1	780	6,470	239[a]	239	5
(1.35/n.k.)	1937/8	1,140	7,296	285[a]		5 (+16)
Poland	1925/6	—	27,431	1,000[a]	1,600	(18)
(7.97/5.03)	1937/8	1,659	28,778	851[a]	1,489	10 (+17)
Romania	1930/1	2,080	16,207	1,031[c]		
(4.56/1.78)	1938/9	1,577	13,654	266[c]		4 (+33)
Yugoslavia	1928/9	357	10,246	279[d]	602[e]	3 (+25)
(2.5/1.69)	1937/8	434	9,341	283[d]	431[e]	3 (+29)

Notes:
[a] Includes teacher training colleges.
[b] Includes supplementary agricultural, and vocational courses.
[c] Includes industrial and trade gymnasia, and lycea with teacher training colleges, leaving no separate vocational school figures.
[d] Includes teacher training colleges, theological seminaries, and special arts schools.
[e] Includes commercial, agricultural, vocational, girls, and railway transport schools, and mercantile naval academies.
Millions of school age includes for Bulgaria 5–19 years of age, for Czechoslovakia 5–14, for Hungary 6–14, for Poland 7–17, for Romania 5–18, for Yugoslavia 6–14; number enrolled refers to these ages at primary and secondary level, both figures for later year shown.
n.k. = not known.
Parenthetical figures in the last column give the number of independent establishments of higher learning.
Sources: Compiled from M. Hauner, 'Comparative Social Infrastructure and Education in Eastern Europe', *Papers in East European Economics*, no. 26 (Oxford, 1973), and Eva Ehrlich, 'Infrastructure and an International Comparison of Relationships with Indicators of Development in Eastern Europe 1920–1950', *Papers in East European Economics*, no. 34 (Oxford, July 1973).

In defeating illiteracy Hungary had progressed relatively the most. Since she lost some of the more backward territories due to the peace settlement, she had a comparative advantage from the outset. She also introduced only six years of compulsory elementary school in her education legislation of 1923, which was lower than in the other states, and raised it to 8 years as late as 1940. Poland's situation was less advantageous as she had gained territories of various degrees of back-wardness. She set to work unifying a maze of different systems by making 7 years of school attendance compulsory from the age of 7 in her

Table 141. *Illiterate population, 10 years and over, both sexes (percentage)*

	1920	1929	1937
Bulgaria	50.3	36.5	29.0
Czechoslovakia	5.5	4.1	3.0
Hungary	13.0	9.3	7.0
Poland	32.7	24.6	18.5
Romania	58.0	42.0	—
Yugoslavia			
(11 years and over)	62.0	48.0	39.0
United Kingdom	—	0	0
France	—	5.9	3.8
Germany	—	0	0

Sources: Compiled from Ehrlich and Hauner, as Table 140.

National School Act of 1922. However, the absence of funds and the rapid growth of the population of school age prevented effective advancement in schooling. Aggregate figures on illiteracy (see Table 141) gloss over the enormous regional disproportions in Poland; these are highlighted in the census of 1931 when illiteracy in Silesia was a mere 1.5 per cent and in Polesia it was still 48.4 per cent.

According to the census of 1934 enrolment in Bulgaria was 83 per cent of the total school population, yet no information is available on how many completed the 7 years of compulsory attendance. In Romania, 75 per cent of 7 to 14 year olds attended school in 1939/40 and less than 50 per cent of primary pupils completed their seven years' course between 1929 and 1938. In the heterogeneous Kingdom of Yugoslavia coordination of the school system came latest with the Education Law of 1929 which was to enforce 8 years' attendance at primary and complementary schools. However, school attendance of children between 7 and 14 years of age had barely reached 50 per cent of the eligible total by 1939. Yugoslavia also furnished the most glaring examples of unequal distribution of resources and the resulting discrepancies within the country which is illustrated by the 1931 census: illiteracy in Slovenia was 5.5 per cent but in Bosnia–Herzegovina, Vardavska and Vrbska it was over 70 per cent.[122]

These large regional discrepancies were not merely the result of uneven objective social and economic conditions. Since all states considered in this chapter were to a lesser or greater extent multinational units (for distribution of nationalities Table 122 should be consulted), their

[122] Hauner, *Paper* 26.

educational policies invariably tended to extend greater benefits to the ruling nationality than to their citizens of other nationalities, although this violated the Statute of Minority Rights they all had accepted as members of the League of Nations. Progress in education was hampered by discriminatory policies of states towards national and religious minorities. Thus Hungary's School Law of 1923 made provision for minority schools but their number was negligible and not a single secondary school existed for the non-Magyar speaking population. As to the religious field the Hungarian Catholic Church strongly influenced education. Whilst a large total number of denominational schools functioned in Hungary's education system the overwhelming majority was Catholic. Indeed, the number of Catholic lower elementary schools (2,848) exceeded that of state and communal schools (2,104). Also the majority of teacher training colleges was maintained by the Roman Catholic Church.

In Poland's education institutions also the Roman Catholic Church was powerful. However, the state determined overall educational policy and its nationalistic and anti-Semitic content accompanied the implementation of the compulsory school system. This was most conspicuously applied to the polonization of Ukrainians and White Russians, together with using schools as an instrument of enforcing Roman rites on the Greek Catholic population. Also at university level the proportion of non-Polish students declined steadily. Discrimination was likewise officially practised in Yugoslavia in contradiction to her School Law of 1929 where instructions in the languages of minorities were to be provided; but only Yugoslav teachers were permitted to give them. This was especially directed against Turks, Albanians, Bulgarians, and Macedonians who had not a single school in their languages. Discriminatory funding was a corollary to this policy resulting in such great differences as 84.3 per cent school attendance and 51 pupils per classroom in Slovenia, but 21 per cent school attendance and 219 pupils per classroom in Bosnia–Herzegovina.[123] Any pretence to take minority rights into consideration was dropped in Romania's educational legislation and policies. Schools of national minorities, especially in former Hungarian territory in Transylvania and the Banat, and former Russian territory in the Ukraine and Bessarabia, were taken over by the government and romanized or closed down. This was confirmed in the so-called Anghelescu Education Law of 1925 in which nationalistic policies were strengthened. At Romanian universities – as in Hungary and Poland – the *numerus clausus* was introduced discriminating, above all, against Jews. A significant number of denominational and some private schools also existed in Romania but the state controlled at least 80 per cent of the educational system.

---

[123] The average number of pupils per class was 109. *Ibid.*, p. 51.

In the context of assessing policies on infrastructural development this cursory illustrative account of educational structures presents a certain picture of the scale of the problem but also tries to give reasons for the uneven and slow pace of progress. To conclude, as this section was begun, on a more general note, state policies and strong state participation in education led to an increase in schools of all types except in Romania and Yugoslavia (see Table 140), and a rise in literacy (see Table 141). Available statistical data confirm that, excepting the Czechoslovak school system, conditions were severely overcrowded in the primary level, secondary schools remained limited to small numbers and vocational training schemes were scarce. In this latter sphere the system had been caught in a vicious circle in the predominantly agricultural countries: because of the low level of industrialization there was little demand for trained and educated labour, but neither did the school system supply enough skilled people who could initiate and further industrial development to a significant extent. Even more serious was the lack of care and forethought given to agricultural schools. In sharp distinction to the high level of agricultural training schemes in Czechoslovakia, the states with a crushing majority of their populations occupied in agriculture hardly provided any opportunities for peasants to improve their farming methods. For instance, Yugoslavia had over 70 per cent of her population active in agriculture but only 25 lower and three higher agricultural schools with less than 900 students in 1929; even though the number of these schools doubled and that of students trebled by 1938, training in this important field was still insignificant. Education above elementary level remained inaccessible to peasants in Romania and less than 1 per cent participated in secondary and higher schools.

As in vocational training, the policies of the national states neglected to encourage the study of science and technology at universities, although high national and social prestige was attached to academic studies in general. Consequently, the majority of students graduated in the humanities, in law, in medicine, and to a lesser extent in engineering, which more than satisfied the small demand for secondary school teachers or for the civil service as well as the effective demand for physicians. Indeed, in the years of the economic crisis graduate unemployment was exceptionally high. Government education policies failed to anticipate the potential demand of a modernizing economy for technicians, scientists, and experts in agriculture.

Principally, because of lack of funds the school systems could not muster sufficient teachers, school buildings, or text-books to satisfy the demands of a relatively backward economy and a fast-growing population. At the same time the educational system lent itself conveniently to the pursuance of nationalistic policies which tended to exacerbate the unevenness in the distribution of funds and resulted in stressing the

Table 142. *Infant mortality rate, hospital beds, and physicians per 1,000 inhabitants in six east-central and south-east European countries, 1921 and 1937*

	Deaths of infants under 1 year of age per 1,000 live births		Hospital beds		Physicians	
	1921	1937	1921	1937	1921	1937
Bulgaria	183	150	1.40[a]	1.9[b]	0.33	0.47
Czechoslovakia	173	122	4.02	5.4	0.66[c]	0.74
Hungary	193	134	4.38	5.25	0.90	1.14
Poland	160	136	1.98	2.11	0.31	0.37
Romania	215	178	n.k.	2.08	—	0.425
Yugoslavia	155	141	n.k.	1.83	—	0.31[d]

Notes:
[a] 1930.
[b] 1936, *United Nations Statistical Yearbook* (1951).
[c] 1932.
[d] I. Tomasevich, *Yugoslavia*, United Nations Series (Stanford, 1949).
— = Data not known.
Sources: Compiled from Ehrlich and Hauner, as Table 140.

economic, social, and cultural differences between the ruling and ruled nationalities and religions.

E. HEALTH AND SOCIAL WELFARE

Perennial lack of funds and their unequal distribution also characterized government policies in health care and social security. And yet, progress was relatively more significant than in other fields of infrastructural development. Table 142 compares infant mortality rates, provision of hospital beds, and services of physicians in the six countries between 1921 and 1937, which gives a certain measure of the steady advance made in the inter-war period. Whilst one cannot speak of striking achievements, steps taken by ministries of public health and social welfare in controlling drinking water, extending drainage, and canalization succeeded in reducing epidemics, especially of malaria, typhoid, and dysentery in south-east Europe. Tuberculosis was still rampant and remained the cause of the highest number of deaths – in Yugoslavia it was responsible for every eighth death.

Among the countries listed in Table 142, Hungary's system of medical care belonged to the relatively most advanced. It was centralized in the National Hygiene Institute which supplied vaccines and equipment to communal and district medical officers engaged in preventive medicine. There also existed a network of health advice centres in the countryside. After the severe repressions of the post-revolutionary years had slackened, a compulsory insurance system for workers in industry and commerce was introduced covering accident, sickness, invalidity, old age, and death. It was administered by the National Social Insurance Institute established in 1928 and financed by a 13 per cent levy on all wages, divided into equal contributions from employers and employees. Workmen's compensation was met entirely by employers' funding and the state contributed toward old age pensions. Only in 1938 were agricultural labourers and persons in domestic service included in compulsory social insurance.

Whilst these welfare provisions were made by the Hungarian state as a concession to social peace, labour legislation lagged behind. Thus, for instance, the eight-hour working day and paid statutory holidays were introduced by law only in 1937. Also, as an outcome of revolution and counter-revolution between 1918 and 1921, trade-union membership had fallen from 721,000 in 1918 to 164,000 by 1933 and never recovered its strength during the clerical-Fascist regime in the 1930s.

As to comprehensiveness of modern social security systems, Bulgaria and Poland led the world together with New Zealand. Not only did their welfare legislation follow the standard of international conventions approved by the International Labour Office, but they often preceded them. Bulgaria first introduced compulsory insurance for workers in 1905 followed by insuring civil servants. This was extended in 1924–5 to include, besides health, accident, and old age, also unemployment insurance. The whole system was run by the state through autonomous institutions which were funded separately. Admittedly, the working class in Bulgaria was small and politically subdued after having been put down in 1923. It is, most probably, no accident that improvements in social security, particularly in unemployment benefits, were enacted soon after the revolutionary uprising in 1923. But the majority of the active population, accounting for 80 per cent occupied in agriculture, did not benefit from the government's social welfare policy.

Poland's central administration of health and social security was to apply universally throughout the country, but funds were highly unequally distributed to different regions. Under the direction of the Institute of Hygiene in Warsaw health inspection was carried out over the whole territory of Poland, which slowly but steadily improved the quantity and quality of medical services.

Also in the field of social security successive laws enacted improvements. In the early 1920s this was undoubtedly to a significant extent connected with workers and peasant unrest, with the Polish–Soviet war and with the close proximity of Soviet Russia. In 1918 the 46-hour working week was made law, and only in 1933 was it increased again to 48 hours. This was followed in 1922 by the enactment of two weeks' paid annual holiday for salaried employees rising to one full month after one year of employment, and 15 days for workers after three years of employment. As early as 1919 a compulsory insurance system covering sickness and maternity was started, later in 1927 it included workmen's compensation, old age, disability, and widows' and orphans' insurance. By the act of 1933 this was extended to all salaried and wage-earners and their families as well as to agricultural workers. Poland, like Bulgaria – as the only countries in Europe – introduced compulsory unemployment insurance for blue-collar workers in 1924 and for white-collar workers in 1927 which provided benefits for thirteen weeks and nine months respectively amounting on average to 30 per cent of earnings. In 1934 the entire system came under the administration of the Central Social Insurance Institute in cooperation with the Ministry of Labour and Social Welfare. It was financed from contributions by employers, employees, and the state.

Labour organizations had been comparatively strong and they were centred on the industrial regions of Poland. During the whole inter-war period trade-union membership continued to be relatively large (945,000 in 1935/6) and the labour history of Poland is crowded with confrontations between workers, on the one side, and employers and the power of the state, on the other. Poland's Constitution of 1921 guaranteed the right to strike, but as the military elite gained strength this was eroded. After Piłsudski's *coup d'état* labour inspectorates were set up in 1927 to supervise collective agreements and differences were to be settled in industrial courts. As labour unrest and consistently high unemployment continued throughout the 1930s the Polish state intervened with schemes of public works which alleviated some of the pressures, but these uncoordinated rescue actions were unable to solve the chronic unemployment in the inter-war economy of Poland.

The Czechoslovak compulsory social insurance system resumed the thread of the Austro-Hungarian schemes introduced in Bohemia and Moravia in 1888 and in Slovakia in 1907. Thus legislation in Czechoslovakia provided assistance for workers and their families in old age, disability, sickness, maternity, and death. However, the administration of social security and health was greatly dispersed among many institutions, and contributions and benefits differed widely. In the 1930s the various bodies were unified under the Central Social Insurance Institute concentrating mainly upon health, and the General Pensions Institute which administered old age pensions. But the Czechoslovak state did not provide unemployment insurance. The test came during the world economic crisis when almost one million people were registered as unemployed in February 1933, but the state supported only one-quarter of a million through the 'Ghent' system of unemployment relief administered by the trade unions. Czechoslovakia, as the most industrialized country in the region and as a pluralistic democracy, had the largest organized trade-union movement whose membership consisted of 1,994,000 blue- and white-collar workers in 1934.

Most hardships were suffered by the populations in Romania and Yugoslavia. In both countries there were Central Institutes of Hygiene and National Health which dealt with the prevention of epidemics and with fighting against venereal diseases. Because of the acute shortage of physicians, who were mainly concentrated in the capital cities, and because of the lack of hospitals and pharmacies little could be achieved until the late 1930s. Romania established a Central Social Insurance Fund in 1933 to provide insurance for the lowest paid workers – with a monthly income under 8,000 lei – and covered sickness, accidents, maternity, disability, old age, and death, but agricultural workers remained unprotected. Similarly, in Yugoslavia the principle of a compulsory state insurance scheme was introduced in 1922 but it did not become effective over the whole country before 1937. In both countries trade unions, just as all labour organizations which did not conform, were persecuted. Romania's labour legislation in 1921 forbade strikes in state-owned enterprises and introduced compulsory arbitration. Additional laws of 1924 contained strong nationalistic tendencies which were also part of Romanian educational policies. State employees became insured in 1925 and workers in 1927, and in 1928 certain improvements in labour legislation followed, such as the 48-hour working week and 7–14 days' paid annual holidays. But there was no unemployment insurance scheme; on the contrary from 1933 labour courts settled disputes and compulsory labour service was imposed on young people as part of pre-military training in 1937. In Yugoslavia, on the other hand, conditions somewhat relaxed in the later 1930s, when minimum wages were legally enforced from 1937, labour exchanges were established in 1938, and the state assisted with unemployment relief.[124]

In concluding the assessment of state policies concerning the development of infrastructure there can be little doubt that in conditions of scarce resources outlay on social services was kept to an essential minimum whilst military spending was excessive. Of the mutual relationship between social and defence spending inter-war Romania and Yugoslavia

---

[124] Factual information on social welfare schemes is based on Hauner, *Paper* 26 and M. C. Kaser, *Health Care in the Soviet Union and Eastern Europe* (Boulder, Col., 1976).

are a particularly blatant example, when – even in their ordinary budgets – twice as much was spent on armaments in the 1930s than on the elementary needs of these states in public health and education. If, however, all aspects of the inter-war development of infrastructure in east-central and south-east Europe are weighed, then the less capital-intensive fields of education, health, and social welfare advanced more than the capital-intensive areas of transport and communications. The latter remained the most backward sphere of infrastructure in the region between the wars and qualitatively lagged most significantly behind Western Europe.

IX. *Conclusion*

The economic and social policies of the east-central and south-east European states in the inter-war period evolved in the context of international capital, credit, and trade movements dominated by the leading industrial powers of Europe. Only within this objective framework were the small and, except for industrial Czechoslovakia, mainly agrarian economies able to pursue their own economic interests.

In the first decade of the successor states' independent political existence their economic policies were adjusted to the realities of the Versailles system. East-central and south-east Europe, formerly the main area of German and Austrian economic influence, was drawn into the financial and capital orbit of the Entente powers. With the shock of the world economic crisis followed by the rise of National Socialist Germany in the 1930s the gradual disintegration of the economic structure which had been built up in the 1920s began.

East-central and south-east Europe became an area of sharpening competition between the great powers as Germany's Hitler regime claimed it as its sphere of interest. By 1938 a wide gap had developed between the dominance of Western finance and industry in the field of capital investment, on the one side, and the rising share of German trade in the Danubian states, on the other. This development crucially affected the economic policies of the successor states which had been geared to the relations with the Western European industrial states. Britain and France had backed the successor states with capital and credits in the 1920s but, when from 1931, they stopped capital flows to the area they did not provide these economies with access to markets to enable them to meet their commitments and to continue their policy of industrialization. Thus they were forced into largely unequal trade with Germany. The uneven relationship of the weaker agrarian south-east European countries with Hitler Germany prevented a solution of their market and credit problems, neither did it assist their endeavour to industrialize. In due course the economic policies of the east-central and south-east European states were directed toward resisting the disadvantages of the German advance into their economic life and they increasingly appealed, above all, to Britain for assistance. Although Britain's trade and also investment in the area rose somewhat and although certain steps were taken to assess the possibilities of greater British economic involvement, Britain had comparatively less interest in the Central–south-east European countries than in the areas of her main concern, in the British Empire and Latin America. Therefore, she was ready to make concessions to Germany. In pursuit of her policy of appeasement Britain did not object to a certain strengthening of German economic influence in south-east Europe, but she insisted on safeguards of her own interests there.

Neither France nor Britain voluntarily withdrew their capital investments or trade interests to make room for the German economic advance into east-central and south-east Europe. Until the Munich Conference and the resulting dismemberment of Czechoslovakia, Germany had not been able to change the relations of forces between Western and German capital in Central and south-east Europe. Neither were Germany's demands fully satisfied in cartel arrangements concerning the Danubian area. But also Germany's trade offensive in south-east Europe got into an impasse by 1938. That there was no deliberate economic retreat by the Western democracies before the political Munich Pact is essential for an understanding of the disastrous political and economic impact of the Munich Agreement. The consequences of it broke all European political treaties, disrupted all economic links, opened the Danubian Basin and Poland to German aggression, and thus ushered in the prelude to the Second World War.

The manuscript of this chapter was submitted in 1980, revised in 1981, and footnotes and bibliography were brought up to date in 1986.

CHAPTER XIV

Economic and social policy in the USSR, 1917–41[1]

I. *The background: objectives and environment*

Soviet policy throughout the inter-war years was dominated by the unprecedented endeavour to construct a radically new social and economic order, using the economic and political power of the state and the authority of the Bolshevik, or Communist, Party. Soviet economic and social policy – in the sense of the management and allocation of resources by government for economic and social purposes – was subordinate to the wider goal of establishing and consolidating a new type of society. By 1936, with the adoption of the Stalin constitution, this task had been accomplished. But the outcome was ambiguous: the new society was in many respects radically different from the vague and optimistic notions about the socialist future held by Marx and Engels and by their Russian successor Lenin.

Soviet policy is discussed in this chapter against this background. The main issues examined are the successes and difficulties of Soviet policy in attempting to reach the long-term objectives, and the modifications of objectives and policy which resulted from the mutual impact of policy and economic environment. Special attention is devoted to those 'moments of choice', or of apparent choice, when the course of policy changed substantially.

Marx and Engels, in their scattered comments on the nature of the society which would be established after the conquest of political power by the proletariat (the wage-earning working class), anticipated that the factories, the land, and the other means of production would be transferred into social ownership. Production and distribution would be managed by the direct and conscious control of the community. A planned economy would replace commodity circulation, and money, the medium for this circulation, would cease to exist. During the first, or socialist, phase of Communism, the social product would be distributed according to the work done by each individual. The immense expansion

---

[1] This chapter was submitted to the editors in March 1978 and slightly revised in December 1985 to take some account of publications in the intervening period. The author is grateful to Drs E. Mawdsley, R. Service and S. G. Wheatcroft for their comments on the draft. A few passages in this chapter have already appeared in the author's *The Socialist Offensive: The Collectivisation of Soviet Agriculture, 1929–1930* (Cambridge, 1980).

of production which would occur during this socialist phase would lead to an economy of abundance, a prerequisite for the higher phase of Communism, in which the social product would be distributed according to need.

This would not be a mere economic transformation. In socialist society, classes would disappear, and with them the state: 'administration over persons would be replaced by the administration of things'. National barriers would be eliminated. The bourgeois family would be superseded, and a new form of education would be established in which productive labour was combined both with instruction and with physical training. In the higher phase of Communism, the distinctions between town and country, and between intellectual and manual labour, would also disappear.

In *Anti-Dühring* (1878) Engels summed up the prospects for mankind in ringing phrases which have inspired the Marxist wing of the European socialist movement for a century:

Anarchy in social production is replaced by conscious organisation on a planned basis. The struggle for individual existence comes to an end. And at this point, in a certain sense, man finally cuts himself off from the animal world, leaves the conditions of animal existence behind him and enters conditions which are really human . . . Men's own social organisation which has hitherto stood in opposition to them as if arbitrarily decreed by Nature and history will then become the voluntary act of men themselves . . . It is only from this point that men, with full consciousness, will fashion their own history; it is only from this point that the social causes set in motion by men will have, predominantly and in constantly increasing measure, the effects willed by men. It is humanity's leap from the realm of necessity into the realm of freedom.

To carry through this world-emancipating act is the historical mission of the modern proletariat.

Important aspects of Soviet economic history remain incomprehensible if it is not realized that Lenin and the Bolsheviks were fully committed to the whole of Marx's programme. Though they rarely discussed these matters in print before the revolution except in the vaguest of terms, their vision of the communist future, together with their hatred of the capitalist present, were mainsprings of their political activity.

The first successful proletarian revolution took place in unpropitious circumstances, or rather in an unpropitious country. For Marx, the establishment of a communist society was only possible because of the immense economic development which had already resulted from the socialization of production within individual capitalist firms, and which would be followed by much greater development after modern industry was taken into social ownership. The proletariat, Marx therefore believed, would come to power not in an agrarian country like Russia but in the advanced capitalist countries – Britain, France, Germany or the United States. Marx devoted much attention to Russia in his later years and in 1882, the year before his death, the last joint statement by Marx and Engels on Russian affairs eventually concluded that Russia might depart from the classical pattern of Western European capitalist development and evolve a communist society based on the rural commune; but it cautiously added that this could take place only 'if the Russian revolution serves as a signal for a workers' revolution in the West, so that the two complement each other'.

Between this statement by Marx and Engels in 1882, and the Bolshevik revolution of November 1917, the structure of the Russian economy changed considerably. According to recent estimates, between 1891 and 1912 capital stock increased by 181 per cent in industry and only 23 per cent in agriculture.[2] A modern iron and steel industry, and some important branches of engineering, were established during this period; by 1914 some $2\frac{1}{2}$ million workers (in a population of 147 millions) were employed in factory industry, many of them in large units. After 1900 several producer goods' industries came under the control of powerful 'syndicates', the Russian equivalent of cartels. In his famous pamphlet *Imperialism: The Highest Stage of Capitalism*, written in 1916, Lenin argued that the organization of large-scale industrial production in Russia was similar to that in the advanced capitalist powers.[3] In some respects Russian industry appeared at its strongest during the first two years of the war. By 1916 total output of large-scale industry was 20 per cent higher than in 1913, and in the engineering and metalworking industries, including armaments, output trebled.[4] In 1915 and 1916 central planning of production and distribution for military purposes was established in rudimentary form by the tsarist state.

But Russia remained economically much less developed than the other major European powers. By the eve of the First World War, industrial output per head of population was still much smaller in Russia than in Britain, France and Germany. Many modern industries, especially engineering industries, simply did not exist at all.[5] Moreover, as Dobb succinctly put it, 'the patches of factory industry in the Leningrad and

[2] A. Kahan, 'The Growth of Capital during the Period of Early Industrialization in Russia (1890–1918)', in P. Mathias and M. M. Postan (eds.), *Cambridge Economic History of Europe*, vol. VII (Cambridge, 1978), pp. 301, 303; the figures are three-year moving averages, in 1913 prices. No precise sources or methods of estimation are provided.

[3] V. I. Lenin, *Selected Works*, vol. V (London, 1936–8), p. 47.

[4] A. L. Sidorov, *Ekonomicheskoe polozhenie Rossii v gody pervoi mirovoi voiny* (Moscow, 1973), p. 350, reproducing data provided by N. Y. Vorob'ev in *Vestnik statistiki*, vol. XIV (1923), pp. 152–3.

[5] See J. M. Cooper, 'The Development of the Soviet Machine Tool Industry, 1917–1941', unpublished Ph.D. thesis, University of Birmingham, 1975, pp. 8, 10–12.

Moscow districts and in the south were no more than industrial "islands" in a vast agricultural area'.[6] By 1914 only one-sixth of the population lived in the towns; and much industrial production, one-quarter or one-third of the total, came from artisan workshops and small factories, most of them owned by peasants and active only in the winter months.[7]

Above all, Russia remained an overwhelmingly peasant country. Only about one-tenth of the sown area on the eve of the First World War was cultivated as part of the private estates of landowners; the remainder was cultivated by over 20 million peasant households. Most peasant households belonged to 'repartitional communes' in which the land, divided into strips, was periodically redistributed among the members. Although the use of horse-drawn machinery greatly increased in the last quarter of a century before 1914, most land was still cultivated by simple metal-tipped ploughs or wooden *sokhas* (ards) and almost everywhere either a three-field system or even forms of shifting cultivation still prevailed. Over 90 per cent of the cultivated land was sown to grain. Moreover, industrialization had failed to withdraw from the countryside as much as two-thirds of the rapid natural increase in the population since the middle of the nineteenth century. The average size of holdings fell; and over a large part of European Russia there was considerable underemployment in the villages. Estimates of the rate of growth of agricultural production in the last quarter of a century before the revolution vary considerably. Certainly both output per person employed in agriculture, and the grain yield per hectare, remained far lower on the eve of the revolution than in Britain, France or Germany.[8]

Straddling Europe and Asia, Russia thus presented a dual face to the world: a colonial power and a semi-colony, the most backward of the European powers, the most advanced of the great peasant countries. It should not be forgotten that Russia in 1917 was far more advanced than unindustrialized Asia, in terms of agricultural as well as industrial output. Output per head of population was higher in Russia in 1913 than in Communist China in 1952 (see Table 143), and a comparison with India before the Second World War would yield a similar result. Russia's dual position in the world was well understood by Lenin and the Bolsheviks; here they were more far-sighted than the other revolutionary parties. For

---

[6] M. H. Dobb, *Soviet Economic Development since 1917* (London, 1948), pp. 35–6.

[7] For artisan production see *Ekonomicheskoe obozrenie* (Moscow), no. 9, 1929, p. 114.

[8] Alternative estimates may be found in R. W. Goldsmith, 'The Economic Growth of Tsarist Russia, 1860–1913', *Economic Development and Cultural Change*, vol. IX (1961), pp. 443–54, and P. Gregory, *Russian National Income, 1885–1913* (Cambridge, 1982), pp. 70–8. See also P. P. Bairoch, 'Agriculture and the Industrial Revolution', in C. M. Cipolla (ed.), *The Fontana Economic History of Europe: The Industrial Revolution* (London, 1973), p. 472; T. Shanin, *The Awkward Class: Political Sociology of Peasantry in a Developing Society, 1910–1925* (Oxford, 1972), p. 21.

Table 143. *Production per capita in the Russian Empire in 1913 and China in 1952*

	Absolute figures			Production per head of population		Russia : Chinese production per head of population (Chinese production per head = 100)
	Russia, 1913[a]	China, 1952		Russia, 1913[a]	China, 1952	
Electric power (milliard kWh)	1.95	7.3	(kWh)	14.0	12.4	113
Crude steel (million tons)	4.23	1.3	(kg)	30.4	2.21	1,376
Coal (million tons)	29.11	66.5	(kg)	209	113	185
Chemical fertilizers (thousand tons)	13.1	194	(g)	94	330	28
Cotton cloth (million linear metres)	2,582	3,829	(linear metres)	18.5	6.51	284
Grain (million tons)[b]	65.2[c]	154	(kg)	468	262	179
Population (millions)	139.3	588[d]				—

Notes:

[a] Pre-17 September, 1939, frontiers of USSR.

[b] Chinese figure includes rice.

[c] This is the present-day official figure for 1909–13 (average); it is likely to be an underestimate (see S. G. Wheatcroft, 'The Reliability of Prewar Grain Statistics', *Soviet Studies*, vol. XXVI (1974), pp. 157–80).

[d] 1954.

Sources: Chinese data from *China: A Reassessment of the Economy* (Washington, DC, 1975), pp. 77, 166–8. Soviet data from *Promyshlennost' SSSR: statisticheskii sbornik* (Moscow, 1964), pp. 142, 163, 192, 231, 364 (industrial products); *Sotsialisticheskoe stroitel'stvo SSSR* (Moscow, 1935), p. 139 (population); *Sel'skoe khozyaistvo SSSR: statisticheskii sbornik* (Moscow, 1960), p. 196 (grain).

the Bolsheviks, as for other parties, Russia was certainly part of Europe: 'we must remember that we are not living in the wilds of Africa, but in Europe, where news can spread quickly', Lenin remarked on 7 November 1917.[9] But at the same time, from the point of view of revolutionary possibilities, as well as in her economic development, Lenin saw Russia as the weakest link in the imperialist chain. Her ambiguous position had prepared Russia for revolution. In view of the development of Russian industry, this would now be not merely a peasant revolution, as Marx and Engels anticipated in 1882, but a revolution led by the industrial proletariat in alliance with the peasantry.

Lenin and his colleagues agreed with Marx, however, that while the proletarian revolution might well begin in Russia it could not be completed there: 'Russia is a peasant country, one of the most backward of European countries', Lenin wrote in April 1917, 'Socialism *cannot triumph there directly at once*. But [its peasant character] *may* make our revolution a *prelude* to a *step* towards the world socialist revolution.'[10] After the revolutionary overthrow of the tsarist regime and its replacement by a Provisional Government in March 1917 the Bolshevik Party, while advocating a further revolution which would bring the proletariat to power, did not call for the establishment of a fully socialist economy in Russia in advance of the revolutions in the West. Instead, its immediate aims were to end the war and bring economic chaos to an end by ceasing military production and taking the economy under strict control and partial state ownership. According to a resolution of the sixth congress of the Bolshevik Party, which was convened in August 1917, three months before the Bolshevik revolution:

It is necessary to intervene in the sphere of production in order to bring about the planned control (*uregulirovanie*) of production and distribution, and it is also necessary to nationalize and centralize banking, and to nationalize a number of the enterprises which belong to syndicates (for example, oil, coal, sugar, iron and steel, and also transport).

This would not be a fully socialist economy. The abolition of money was not even considered: instead, the financial crisis would be dealt with by 'the immediate cessation of further issues of paper money', the repudiation of the national debt and a large increase in direct taxation, and the taxation of luxuries. While the economy could not be fully socialist, control over it would be revolutionary and democratic in form. According to the sixth congress, elected supervisory agencies should be established, including representatives of trade unions, soviets, factory committees and technical personnel, and this 'workers' supervision' (*rabochii kontrol'*) should be 'developed by a gradual series of measures

---

[9] Lenin, *Selected Works*, vol IV, p. 405.   [10] *Ibid.*, p. 17.

into the full control (*regulirovanie*) of production'.[11] This revolutionary approach sharply distinguished the Bolsheviks from those socialist parties which supported the Provisional Government, which also aimed at some kind of planned economy, but assumed that the Russian proletariat was not mature enough to take power. Lenin posed the issue squarely three weeks before the Bolshevik revolution in a dispute with the ex-Bolshevik economist Bazarov:

We are in favour of centralism and of a 'plan', but it must be the centralism and the plan of a proletarian state – it must be a proletarian regulation of production and distribution in the interests of the poor, the toilers, the exploited, *against* the interests of the exploiters.[12]

The Bolsheviks also supported revolutionary action in the countryside. They wholeheartedly endorsed peasant demands for the confiscation of privately owned land, while expressing the hope that the commercial estates would not be broken up. Confiscation of the private estates by the peasants, together with the nationalization of all land, was seen, like partial nationalization in industry, as a step towards socialism. In the long run the peasants would be encouraged to go over to socialist mechanized agriculture. But in the immediate future:

The peasants want to retain their small-holdings, to equalize them according to standards [i.e. on the basis of fixed norms], and to re-equalize them periodically. Let them. No intelligent socialist will quarrel with the poor peasants on this score.[13]

II. First steps to socialism, November 1917– March 1918

The first five months after the Bolshevik revolution were a time of rapid reorganization and precipitate change. The new Soviet government, backed by its supporters in the local soviets, took over from the Provisional Government and from individual capitalists what Lenin later called the 'commanding heights' of the economy, and broke the active resistance of its opponents in government service. The State Bank was seized and the main private banks were nationalized, the national debt was annulled. Trade in foodstuffs and the principal consumer goods was declared to be a state monopoly, and foreign trade was first taken under strict control, and then (April 1918) also declared a state monopoly. A Supreme Council of the National Economy (*Vysshii Sovet Narodnogo*

---

[11] *Kommunisticheskaya partiya Sovetskogo Soyuza v rezolyutsiyakh i resheniyakh s"ezdov konferentisii i plenumov TsK*, vol. I (Moscow, 1954), pp. 376–9 (referred to below as *KPSS v rezolyutsiyakh*).

[12] Lenin, *Selected Works*, vol. VI, p. 278; Bazarov's article appeared in *Novaya zhizn'*, no. 138, 10 October 1917, and Lenin's reply was completed on 14 October.

[13] Lenin, *Selected Works*, vol. VI, pp. 380–90 (article dated September and October 1917).

Khozyaistva, or Vesenkha) was established (December 1917) as part of the Council of People's Commissars (Sovnarkom) (People's Commissars was the new name for Ministries). Vesenkha, nominally responsible for the whole economy, was in practice concerned almost exclusively with industry. It took over and reorganized the various wartime planning and distribution committees, and the headquarters of the major private syndicates; on this basis it established centralized departments for the major industries at a national level (these departments soon became known as chief committees, *glavki*). Between November 1917 and March 1918 a substantial number of individual factories were nationalized, partly by the decision of the central authorities, partly on the initiative of local soviets or of the workers in particular factories. Factory committees elected by the workers extensively practised 'workers' supervision' in private industry, often indistinguishable from management by the workers, and factory or trade-union committees were prominent in the management of nationalized enterprises. In the countryside, the 'Decree on Land' approved by the Congress of Soviets on the first day after the revolution (8 November 1917) legalized the spontaneous agrarian revolution which was already taking place. Within a few weeks the property and land of the private estates were divided among the peasants.

How democratic control over the Soviet economy should be exercised in practice was the subject of fierce controversy during the first few months of Soviet power. The debate turned on two issues. First, should the elected representatives of particular industries, organized into trade unions, play a role in general policy making at the top level, or should such major decisions be the responsibility solely of the elected government, which was effectively under the control of the Bolshevik party? Secondly, should the trade unions administer their own industries?

These problems were central to a dramatic clash between the Soviet government and the executive committee of the railwaymen's union, Vikzhel, in which the Bolsheviks were a small minority. On 8 November 1917, Vikzhel declared its opposition to one-party rule and took over the management of the railways, threatening a general railway strike unless the Bolsheviks formed a coalition with other socialist parties. The campaign by Vikzhel played an important part in the formation of a temporary coalition between Bolsheviks and Left Socialist Revolutionaries (the left wing of the peasant revolutionary party). But a few weeks later the Bolshevik minority at a railwaymen's congress seceded and formed their own trade union. This new trade union was recognized by the Soviet government, and made directly responsible, both locally and nationally, for administering the railways.[14] This solution also proved

[14] This account is based on E. H. Carr, *The Bolshevik Revolution, 1917–1923*, vol. II (London, 1952), pp. 394–7.

temporary. On 23 March 1918, on the grounds or pretext that the railways were being destroyed, a decree of the Council of People's Commissars granted dictatorial powers to the People's Commissar for Transport, establishing 'strict centralization, one-man management and discipline'.[15] The decree of 23 March was a crucial event in the evolution of Soviet economic management. No national organization representing a section of the Soviet working class ever again challenged the political authority of the Soviet government. The decree, which aroused the bitter hostility of the Left Communists within the Bolshevik party, also marked the beginning of the end of the participation of national trade unions in the management of their industry. The cause was not yet lost: the decree of 23 March established a 'collegium', or committee, attached to the People's Commissariat for Transport, which included trade-union representatives, and had the right of appeal to the Council of People's Commissars. Meanwhile 'collegia' had already been established in each of the *glavki* of Vsenkha; the largest group of members in each collegium were the representatives from the trade unions. The collegia of the industrial *glavki* were assigned much greater powers than the collegium attached to the People's Commissariat for Transport. They were at least formally, and to some extent in practice, fully responsible for managing the *glavki*. This situation continued until the spring of 1920.[16]

At the regional level, practices varied. In Petrograd the interests of the regional organizations of the factory committees were fused with those of the regional economic administration by the simple device of transforming the regional factory committee organizations into regional economic councils. Elsewhere regional economic councils developed separately from the factory committees. In all the economic councils, which were local agencies of Vesenkha attached to the local soviets, the principle of committee management operated no less than in the *glavki*.[17]

In the factories themselves, no clear solution was reached. In January 1918, it was resolved that the elected factory committee should be combined with the factory trade-union organization into a single committee. In March 1918, a decree of the production organization department of Vesenkha insisted that factory directors should not be elected but appointed by the *glavki*, though they should be subject to the decisions of a representative 'economic administrative council'. But this decree, like so many others at this time, appears not to have been put into effect.[18]

---

[15] *Dekrety Sovetskoi vlasti*, vol. II (Moscow, 1959), pp. 12–21; for the alleged disorganization of the railways, see V. Serge, *Year One* (London, 1972), p. 241.

[16] See A. V. Venediktov, *Organizatsiya gosudarstvennoi promyshlennosti v SSSR*, vol. I (Leningrad, 1957), pp. 292–303, 530–41.   [17] *Ibid.*, pp. 100, 304–14.

[18] See Carr, *The Bolshevik Revolution*, vol. II, pp. 86–7; Venediktov, *Organizatsiya*, vol. I, pp. 317–27.

Table 144. *State grain collections in 1916/17–1922/23 (thousand tons)*

	From whole territory[a]	From territory mainly not occupied during civil war[b]
1916/17	8,323	3,225
1917/18	1,202	347
1918/19[c]	1,768	1,736
1919/20[c]	3,480	2,501
1920/21[c]	6,012	2,037
1921/22[d]	3,814	1,339
1922/23[d]	5,916	2,600

Notes:

These figures refer to agricultural years (1 July–30 June).

[a] Russian Empire in 1916/17; Soviet territory from 1917/18 onwards.

[b] Grain-deficit area of European Russia; Central Black-Earth region; Volga-Kama, Central Volga and Lower Volga areas.

[c] Requisitionings (*prodrazverstka*).

[d] Tax in kind and return of seed loan.

Source: Calculated from data in *Itogi desyatiletiya sovetskoi vlasti v tsifrakh, 1917–1927* (Moscow, n.d. [?1928]), p. 379.

By the spring of 1918, the economic crisis, already serious under the Provisional Government, was much graver. The railways were in chaos; industrial production was rapidly declining. The disorder has frequently been attributed largely to the effects of workers' control, and many anecdotes have been told of the consequences of the inexperience of the new masters of the railways and the factories. But raw material shortages and general economic disorder, in the context of military defeat at the hands of the central powers, contributed much to the troubles of industry. The previous acceleration of the rate of issue of paper money continued: currency in circulation rose by 62 per cent in the course of 1916, under the tsarist regime, by 71 per cent in the seven months 1 March–1 October 1917, under the Provisional Government, and by 74 per cent in the five months 1 November 1917 to 1 April 1918, under the Bolsheviks. Retail prices doubled in January–March 1918, and doubled again in April–June.[19] The gravest problem of all was the inability of the government to secure food supplies. The grain collection machinery established in 1915–17 had virtually collapsed; and state grain collections of a mere 1,200,000 tons were recorded after the 1917 harvest, as compared with 8.3 million tons after the 1916 harvest (see Table 144). Private trade, and the personal interests of the peasants, had temporarily triumphed; the big towns were on the verge of starvation.

[19] See R. W. Davies, *The Development of the Soviet Budgetary System* (Cambridge, 1958), p. 31.

III. *The attempt to consolidate, March–April 1918*

The respite or 'breathing space' provided by the signing of the peace treaty with Germany on 3 March 1918 was followed in March and April by a far-reaching reconsideration of economic policy. The new watchwords were consolidation and discipline. Lenin concluded, in his programmatic article of April 1918, *The Next Tasks of Soviet Power*, that the offensive against private capital must be temporarily halted. Instead attention should be directed towards 'nation-wide accounting and supervision of production and distribution', including 'the strict nation-wide, all-embracing accounting and control of *grain and the production of grain*' (this was almost the only reference by Lenin to relations with the peasantry in the article). Lenin insisted that the guidance of bourgeois specialists must be accepted throughout the economic administration. The mass democracy of workers' meetings, 'turbulent, surging, overflowing its banks like a spring flood' must henceforth be combined 'with *iron* discipline while at work, with *unquestioning obedience* to the will of a single person'. In industry, labour discipline must be greatly improved, and piecework and the Taylor system must be experimented with in order to improve labour productivity: 'the possibility of building socialism will be determined precisely by our success in combining the soviet government and the soviet organization of administration with the modern achievements of capitalism'. 'We must learn socialism from the organizers of trusts.'[20]

A few weeks later he turned his attention to financial policy, and his proposals were a model of financial orthodoxy. Inflation must be dealt with by introducing an income and property tax and by a currency reform. The use of the printing press could be justified 'only as a temporary expedient' and, in order to remove from circulation currency which was in the hands of kulaks (richer peasants) and speculators, the present currency should be withdrawn and a new currency issued.[21]

Lenin's economic policy in the spring of 1918 suffered from a major defect and a major omission. The major defect was the lack of realism of its financial proposals. Given the decline in the income of the propertied classes since the revolution, and the difficulty of collecting direct taxes from peasants and petty traders, the proposed income and property tax could not have raised substantial revenues. Without a fundamental change in tax policy, further budget deficits, the issue of paper money and further large increases in prices were bound to continue. Yet Lenin

[20] Lenin, *Selected Works*, vol. VII, pp. 313–35; *Sochineniya*, 4th edn, vol. XXVII, p. 263; the Taylor system was an American method of work intensification.
[21] Lenin, *Selected Works*, vol. VII, pp. 380–3 (speech of 18 May 1918).

still rejected indirect taxes as regressive, insisting that 'all socialists are opposed to indirect taxation, because the only proper system of taxation from the Socialist point of view is the graduated income and property tax'.[22] The major omission in Lenin's new policy was its failure to discuss how the 'nation-wide, all-embracing accounting and control of *grain and the production of grain*' was actually to be brought about. Lenin said nothing about how, in the absence of adequate economic incentives, the peasants were to be persuaded to surrender their grain to the authorities for distribution to the army and the urban population.

IV. *War Communism, 1918–19*

The brief interval in March and April 1918 was brought to an end by foreign intervention and civil war. At the end of May 1918 the Czech legions and the Don Cossacks revolted; by the end of June intervention by the Allied powers was well under way; in July uprisings of Socialist Revolutionaries took place in Moscow and in several other towns. For the next two years the Soviet government was engaged in a desperate battle for survival; for part of this time the territory it controlled was no more extensive than sixteenth-century Muscovy.

A.   MAIN FEATURES

Within a few months of the outbreak of civil war, the characteristic features of the system which was later described as 'War Communism' were firmly established. The core of the system was the compulsory acquisition of grain from the peasants, using armed force when necessary. In the summer of 1918 grain surpluses were seized in a more or less *ad hoc* way. From the end of 1918 onwards, systematic grain requisitioning (*prodrazverstka*) was introduced. Requisitioning was at first supposedly directed at the 'surpluses' of the peasant, particularly of the so-called kulak, but often all grain stocks were seized. This policy soon gave way to an attempt to secure definite quotas of grain from each village. In 1920 a revealing directive of the central committee of the Communist Party told local committees that 'the quota required from a rural district (*volost'*) is to be taken as in itself a definition of the surplus, and is to be fulfilled by the population on their collective responsibility'.[23] The available information about the amount of grain

---

[22] *Ibid*, vol. VII, p. 380.

[23] *Direktivy KPSS i sovetskogo pravitel'stva po khozyaistvennym voprosam: sbornik dokumentov*, vol. I (Moscow, 1957), p. 179 (a letter from the party central committee first published on 4 September 1920); for a useful brief account of the main stages in grain requisitioning, see the extracts from A. M. Bol'shakov, 'The Soviet Countryside, 1917–1924', in R. E. F. Smith (ed.), *The Russian Peasant, 1920 and 1984* (London, 1977), pp. 46–8.

collected is not very reliable, but the impression provided by Table 144 that it increased from harvest to harvest is undoubtedly correct. The requisitioned foodstuffs were distributed in the towns by an elaborate rationing system, the most unusual feature of which was that the amount of the ration depended on the social class or occupation of the recipient. Industrial consumer goods were also brought under close central control, and elaborate and usually futile efforts were made to distribute them to the peasants in such a way as to compensate them, in small part, for the requisitioning of their grain.[24] The aim of War Communism in respect of food and consumer goods was thus to secure their physical distribution by the state; and no private trade was officially permitted.

In industry, all firms of a substantial size were nationalized by the summer of 1918. During the summer and autumn of 1918 an elaborate central apparatus, with special powers, was established with the purpose of regulating industrial production and allocating it to military needs. A similar centralized organization regulated movements on the railways. Centralized direction of labour, and compulsory labour service, were introduced more cautiously, and were apparently not very effective until control over industrial labour was transferred from the trade unions to the People's Commissariat for Labour at the end of 1919.[25]

The issue of paper money continued throughout the civil war. After a brief improvement in the second half of 1918 associated with an emergency taxation campaign (see p. 999), the rate of issue accelerated. The percentage increase in currency in circulation was as follows:

1 Jan.– 1 July 1918	1 July 1918– 1 Jan. 1919	1 Jan.– 1 July 1919	1 July 1919– 1 Jan. 1920	1 Jan.– 30 June 1920	1 July 1920– 1 Jan. 1921
58	40	65	123	127	128

In each period of six months, the real value to the government of the new issue, in terms of the resources it could command, was less than in the previous six months; the real value of currency in circulation is estimated to have declined from some 1,300 million gold rubles on 1 January 1918, to only 70 million on 1 January 1921. Attempts to collect budgetary revenue were gradually abandoned; the official economy was gradually transformed into an economy in kind, in which decisions were taken in physical terms.[26]

The official, centrally planned economy, intended to embrace all

[24] See Carr, *The Bolshevik Revolution*, vol. II, pp. 232–5.
[25] For the centralized organizations to control the economy, see Venediktov, *Organizatsiya*, vol. I, pp. 477–511; for the control of labour, see Carr, *The Bolshevik Revolution*, vol. II, pp. 198–211.
[26] See Davies, *Development of the Soviet Budgetary System*, pp. 26–45.

economic activity, was supplemented by numerous illegal and semi-legal free markets. It was estimated that at the end of 1919 even workers' families in provincial capitals received less than half of their grain, flour and potatoes from their official ration, the rest being purchased direct from peasants or from private traders. State enterprises and organizations also used the private market for much of their essential supplies. According to another estimate, referring to three provinces, peasants obtained only 11 per cent of their purchases at fixed prices. And, with the decline in the value of the currency, the use of money as a medium of exchange on the private market was increasingly replaced by barter.[27] In personal consumption, the unofficial economy was thus much more important than the official economy.

The economy as a whole was in decline. According to official estimates, the production of 'census' (large-scale) industry in 1919 was only 48 per cent of 1918, and only 15 per cent of 1913.[28] Agricultural production also declined substantially, perhaps by a quarter or a third: no reliable figures are available.[29]

B. IMPROVISATION AND IDEOLOGY IN SOVIET POLICY

Historians continue to debate whether War Communism was, in the words of an American economist, a 'product of marxian ideas', developed in conformity with the aim of abolishing commodity production,[30] or, in Dobb's well-known phrase, 'an improvisation in face of economic scarcity and military urgency in conditions of exhausting civil war'.[31] The truth seems to be that it was certainly a response to the emergency of civil war, but a response influenced by Bolshevik assumptions and predilections. As Nove put it, 'there was a process of *interaction* between circumstances and ideas'.[32] The nature of this interaction will now be considered.

Each major step towards War Communism was undoubtedly a

---

[27] See L. Szamuely, *First Models of the Socialist Economic Systems: Principles and Theories* (Budapest, 1974), pp. 18–19; Y. G. Gimpel'son, *'Voennyi kommunizm': politika, praktika, ideologiya* (Moscow, 1973), pp. 158–62.

[28] Calculated from data in *Itogi desyatiletiya sovetskoi vlasti v tsifrakh, 1917–1927* (Moscow, n.d. [?1928]), pp. 4, 230, and in *Ekonomicheskoe obozrenie* (Moscow), no. 9 (1929), p. 114. These figures include territory occupied by anti-Soviet regimes.

[29] According to a recent Soviet source, total agricultural production in 1920 was 67 per cent of that in 1913 (*Sel'skoe khozyaistvo SSSR* (Moscow, 1960), p. 79).

[30] P. C. Roberts, *Alienation and the Soviet Economy* (Albuquerque, 1971), pp. 20–47.

[31] Dobb, *Soviet Economic Development since 1917*, p. 122.

[32] A. Nove, *An Economic History of the USSR* (London, 1969), p. 48; the recent discussions of War Communism by Szamuely and Gimpel'son (see note 27 above) respectively stress its ideological and its emergency aspects. The different assessments of War Communism are discussed, and the economic system carefully analysed, in S. Malle, *The Economic Organisation of War Communism, 1918–1921* (Cambridge, 1985), which was published after this chapter was concluded.

response to an emergency. The decree of 28 June 1918, which nationalized virtually all large enterprises, was prompted by fear that the German
government was about to lodge an immediate claim that important
Russian firms should be permanently exempted from nationalization, on
the grounds that they had been acquired by German citizens.[33] The
establishment of elaborate centralized agencies to manage state industry
in the six months after this general nationalization decree was undoubtedly inspired by urgent military need. The grain requisitioning policy,
the central feature of War Communism, cannot, it is true, be attributed
to the civil war as such: it was first introduced systematically by a decree
of 9 May 1918, when the clouds of civil war were gathering, but the
storm had not yet burst. But it was certainly a response to an emergency
of unparalleled gravity. The grain crisis was already severe in the spring
and summer of 1917: the Provisional Government introduced a state
grain monopoly in April 1917, and its later legislation, though little used
in practice, provided for the confiscation of concealed stocks, banned all
transport by rail or water of any grain except the official deliveries, and
permitted the use of armed force for the seizure of grain.[34] By May 1918,
with stocks exhausted and no grain forthcoming from the peasants,
famine was imminent. On 9 May, the same day as the grain decree, food
riots in Kolpino near Petrograd led to the introduction of martial law.[35]
The decision to send armed detachments of workers and conscripts to the
villages to acquire grain was unambiguously attributed by Lenin to the
emergency. Thus on 22 May he wrote of 'hundreds of thousands and
millions of people who suffer from hunger (in Petrograd, in the non-
agricultural provinces, and in Moscow)' and warned that 'catastrophe
faces us, it has moved very, very close'.[36] Some means must be found of
holding out till the new harvest: 'time will not wait: after an incomparably difficult May will come an even more difficult June and July, and
perhaps also part of August'.[37] It seemed clear to Lenin, and this was no
doubt right in the circumstances of 1918, that the cities could not be fed
through the market without enormous profits being made by kulaks and
speculators; hence there was no alternative to the seizure of grain. He
pointed out that when the Ukrainian nationalist government under
Skoropadskij abolished the grain monopoly, in which the fixed state
price was 6 rubles a pood, the price rose to 200 rubles a pood, compelling
them to contemplate the reintroduction of the monopoly.[38]

[33] M. H. Dobb, *Russian Economic Development since the Revolution* (London, 1928), pp. 59–60.
[34] N. Kondrat'ev, *Rynok khleba i ego regulirovanie v gody voiny i revolyutsii* (Moscow, 1922),
pp. 115–16.
[35] D. Mandel, *The Petrograd Workers and the Soviet Seizure of Power: From the July Days 1917 to July
1918* (London and Basingstoke, 1984), p. 398.
[36] Lenin, *Soch.*, vol. XXVII, pp. 356–7 (written on 22 May).
[37] *Ibid.*, vol. XXVII, p. 354 (draft telegram to Petrograd workers, 21 May).
[38] Lenin, *Selected Works*, vol. VII, p. 403 (speech of 27 June 1918); a pood is 16.38 kg.

The continuous issue of large quantities of depreciating currency was also due to the emergency, rather than to a policy favouring a moneyless economy, at least during the first year of Soviet power. In the spring and summer of 1918, the Soviet government and the People's Commissariat for Finance (Narkomfin) made valiant efforts to collect existing taxes and to establish new ones, even moving some distance towards the introduction of the hated indirect taxation. A powerful campaign was conducted in the winter of 1918–19 to collect in cash hoards of urban and rural property owners by means of an Extraordinary Revolutionary Tax. Preparations were made for a currency reform, including the printing of new notes.[39]

Thus the main features of War Communism – wholesale nationalization, centralized governmental control of the economy, grain requisitioning, massive currency issues – were all a response to emergency; they did not form part of a comprehensive and deliberate policy, planned in advance. But this is not the whole story. The progress of nationalization and the methods of grain requisitioning in 1918 were undoubtedly influenced by Bolshevik ideology. Even during the 'breathing space', several weeks before the outbreak of civil war, active preparations were being made for further, more systematic nationalization. In April 1918 the Soviet government rejected a proposal from a private trust to form a mixed engineering trust jointly owned by the state and by private capitalists, and resolved to embark on the complete nationalization of the metal industry. The whole sugar industry was nationalized in May and the whole oil industry in June; the latter decision had been in preparation since the beginning of 1918.[40] The influential first congress of economic councils, which met in May and June 1918, resolved that the chemical and textile industries should also be nationalized.[41] Even if the 'breathing space' had continued, there seems little doubt that most large-scale industry would have been nationalized in the space of a few months.

Although grain requisitioning was a direct consequence of a grave emergency, its form was shaped by the assumptions, or prejudices, of Lenin and the other Bolshevik leaders. They firmly believed that any sale of grain on the market involved profiteering; the only permissible transactions with the peasants must be carried on by the state and its agencies, and must be conducted either at fixed prices, or by the direct exchange of industrial for agricultural products ('product exchange', or barter). This assumption naturally drove the Soviet authorities faster and more completely towards a socialist economy, by which they meant a non-market moneyless economy. Lenin rejected out of hand a proposal

[39] See Davies, *Development of the Soviet Budgetary System*, pp. 21–3, 26–8.
[40] Venediktov, *Organizatsiya*, vol. I, pp. 184–6, 195–6; *Sobranie uzakonenii i rasporyazhenii rabochego i krest'yanskogo pravitel'stva* (Petrograd and Moscow, 1917–18), arts. 457, 546.
[41] Carr, *Bolshevik Revolution*, vol. II, pp. 97–8.

from the Menshevik economist Groman that grain prices should be increased and a bonus paid for delivering grain on time. In this connection Lenin complained that 'one has to hear more and more frequently from the intelligentsia that the bag-traders are doing them a service, and feeding them all':

When people talked to us about other solutions, we replied: 'Go to Skoropadskij, go to the bourgeoisie.' Go and teach them such methods as increasing grain prices and making an alliance with the kulaks – you will find willing ears to listen to you there.[42]

The shape of requisitioning policy was also influenced by the Bolshevik assumption that successful relations with the mass of the peasantry could be achieved by inflaming the class struggle between poor peasants and kulaks. The decree of 9 May 1918 assumed that grain was 'in the hands of the rural kulaks and the rich'.[43] Committees of poor peasants were formed in the villages, and poor peasants were offered a share of the grain collected from the kulaks. Before the end of 1918 the committees were dissolved, and it was henceforth admitted that grain must be taken from all the peasants. But in their requisitioning policy the Soviet authorities continued to place great hopes on class divisions in the countryside. The effectiveness of this policy is a matter of dispute among historians; but it is clear that it owed its origins not only to the emergency situation, but also to Bolshevik social policy.

In the course of the civil war, ideological considerations also came into play in another important respect. Although the main features of War Communism were forced upon the Soviet government by emergency, the Soviet leaders soon began to see them as essential and irreversible steps on the road to socialism or communism. In the spring of 1918, as has been shown, Lenin justified the grain campaign as a response to a dire emergency. But at the same time he treated it as a step towards socialism. As early as 22 May 1918, he referred to the acquisition and distribution of grain and fuel on a national scale by the state as a 'real and chief prelude to socialism' and a '*communist* task'.[44] A month later, on 27 June 1918, he sent a telegram to a provincial soviet congress which described the grain monopoly as 'one of the most important methods of gradual transition from capitalist commodity exchange to socialist product exchange', that is, to exchange in which money was not involved.[45] By the end of 1918, the People's Commissar for Finance, while still endeavouring to limit currency issues, assumed that a moneyless economy was rapidly coming

---

[42] Lenin, *Soch.*, vol. XXVII, pp. 393–7 (report of 4 June 1918); the Mensheviks were the more moderate wing of the Russian Social Democratic Labour Party to which both Bolsheviks and Mensheviks formally belonged until 1917.   [43] *Direktivy KPSS*, vol. I, p. 52.
[44] Lenin, *Soch.*, vol. XXVII, p. 360.   [45] *Ibid.*, vol. XXVII, p. 417.

into being: 'When the cycle of economic measures is completed, money
will be abolished and replaced by exchange in kind . . . It is important for
us to hold out until that time.'[46] In March 1919, the programme of the
Communist Party while insisting that 'the abolition of money is impossible in the first period of transition from capitalism to communism', also
reported that the party 'is endeavouring to carry out a number of
measures extending the sphere of moneyless accounting and preparing
the abolition of money'.[47]

Large-scale currency issues, undertaken in the first months after the
October revolution as an emergency measure, were now seen as a
necessary step towards a moneyless economy; it was taken for granted
that victory in the civil war would not be followed by a return to the
money economy; the moneyless economy in which product exchange
replaced commodity circulation would, once introduced, be permanent.

The rival claims of efficiency and ideology clamoured for priority in the
protracted disputes about how the workers' state should be governed.
The outcome remained confused and ambiguous throughout the civil
war. The need for efficient administration, a central theme of Lenin's
proposals during the breathing space of the spring of 1918, haunted the
Soviet authorities. While the ultimate goal was that all should share in
administration, the immediate need was to manage the workers' state
competently. Yet the Bolshevik party consisted largely of industrial
workers plus a sprinkling of intellectuals, few of whom had any technical
training, and most of the established administrators and engineers – the
so-called 'bourgeois specialists' – at every level were undoubtedly hostile
to the new regime and its objectives. Lenin soon became passionately
convinced that the expertise of the bourgeois specialists was essential to
efficiency. Against strong opposition, Trotsky employed former tsarist
officers in the Red Army and Lenin encouraged the use of specialists in
industrial administration, closely supervised by loyal Bolsheviks.

But enthusiastic support from the industrial workers was also essential
if victory was to be achieved, and the notion that in some substantial sense
workers should manage their own industry – immediately, rather than
after a long period of training and experience – was strengthened in the
revolutionary climate of War Communism. It is not generally appreciated that during the civil war efforts by the central authorities to establish
the practice that officials and managers in nationalized industry should be
appointed, not elected, were much weaker than during the first few
months of 1918. Legislation and practice varied greatly from industry to
industry, and frequent changes took place. But throughout the civil war

---

[46] *Ekonomicheskaya zhizn'* (Moscow), no. 40 (1918) (speech of 17 December 1918, by N.
Krestinsky).   [47] *KPSS v rezolyutsiakh*, vol. 1 (Moscow, 1957), pp. 426–7.

most industries were apparently managed by collegia working collectively rather than by the methods of 'one-man management' advocated by Lenin. Moreover, a Vesenkha questionnaire showed that 35.2 per cent of the members of the collegia of the *glavki* were representatives of the trade unions, 9.1 per cent were representatives of the factory committees, and 8 per cent of various congresses and conferences. Even as late as the end of 1920 most trade unions appointed their own candidates to the collegia rather than simply accepting the names of trade unionists suggested by Vesenkha.[48] Thus the trade unions of each industry played an important part in its administration. How this worked in practice has not been studied in detail; it is not clear how far the representatives of trade unions and other organizations were genuinely representative of the rank and file. Only 23.3 per cent of the members of the collegia of *glavki* were workers, according to the survey of 1 August 1919; 29.6 per cent were 'higher administrative and technical personnel'; 22.6 per cent middle administrative and technical staff, and office workers; the remaining 24.5 per cent included former officials of central and local government, cooperative officials and academics.[49] Thus many of the representatives put forward by trade unions were not themselves workers. Moreover the powers of the collegia of the *glavki* were greatly restricted by powerful planning and coordinating organizations appointed by and entirely responsible to the central government, notably by Chusosnabarm, the Extraordinary Commission for the Supply of the Red Army.

In the factories, the form of management did not conform to a single pattern. While in some factories the director was entrusted with considerable powers, as a general rule the board of management, including representatives of the factory committee, was directly responsible for running the factory.[50] In 1919 only 10.8 per cent of 831 enterprises investigated by Vesenkha had introduced one-man management.[51] The names of the members of the board, however, had to be approved by the local economic council, or sometimes by Vesenkha itself, and local plenipotentiaries of Chusosnabarm were given extensive powers over factories.[52] But by and large, the declaration in the party programme approved by the eighth party congress in March 1919 that 'the organizational machinery of socialized industry must rely in the first place on the trade unions'[53] retained some reality throughout the civil war.

[48] See Venediktov, *Organizatsiya*, vol. I, pp. 530–40.
[49] See *ibid.*, vol. I, p. 538.   [50] *Ibid.*, vol. I, pp. 591–612.
[51] V. Z. Drobizhev, *Glavnyi shtab sotsialisticheskoi promyshlennosti (ocherki istorii VSNKh, 1917–1932 gg.)* (Moscow, 1966), pp. 120–1, citing the archives.
[52] Venediktov, *Organizatsiya*, vol. I, pp. 592–3.
[53] *KPSS v rezolyutsiyakh*, vol. I, p. 422.

C.   SOCIAL POLICY

The revolutionary impetus strongly affected social as well as economic policy, in intention if not always in practice. Some of the dramatic measures adopted by the Soviet government in 1918–20 were considered by them, reasonably enough, as completing the 'bourgeois–democratic revolution' rather than as steps from a capitalist to a socialist society. Labour legislation provided for an eight-hour day, almost immediately put into practice, and for a comprehensive social insurance scheme, which in contrast had little practical outcome owing to inflation.[54] Other measures provided equal rights for women; these included the right to vote and to be elected in all types of election, equal pay, and equal status in the family. Legislation on the family made abortion legal and provided that divorce must be automatic if desired by one of the parties.[55] The labour legislation established in Russia rights and conditions which already existed in several other European capitalist countries, and the legislation on women provided rights which women in Western Europe hoped to achieve within the framework of capitalism. But owing to its speed and comprehensiveness the revolutionary character of this legislation was perhaps more noticeable than its bourgeois content. And it was associated with much more democracy in the factory, and much more freedom in sexual activity (for those who cared to avail themselves of it), than were to be found in any capitalist country.

In education policy the Soviet authorities moved farther and faster towards a socialist transformation of the institutions of tsarism than in any other sphere of social activity. After much controversy the Council of People's Commissars approved on 30 September 1918, the establishment of a Unified Labour School, intended to cover the whole of normal education. The school was to be secularized, coeducational and comprehensive, and no fees were to be charged. Schools were to be self-governing, with a considerable amount of power for the pupils: the teacher was to be the 'elder brother in a family of various ages', and homework and examinations were abolished. In its curriculum, the school was to be based on free activity, on the model of the American educationalist Dewey, but at the same time was to be polytechnic, acquainting pupils with industrial and agricultural labour in all its forms.[56]

[54] See Carr, *Bolshevik Revolution*, vol. II, pp. 104, 198–9.
[55] See Carr, *Socialism in One Country, 1924–1926*, vol. I (London, 1958), pp. 27–9.
[56] S. Fitzpatrick, *The Commissariat of Enlightenment: Soviet Education and the Arts under Lunacharsky, October 1917–1921* (Cambridge, 1970), pp. 31–4; N. J. Dunstan, 'Making Soviet Man: Education', in R. W. Davies (ed.), *The Soviet Union* (London, 1978), pp. 92–5.

Little of the proposed transformation of education was accomplished in practice, not merely because resources were scarce but also because most teachers opposed or were indifferent to the new school system – a variant on the general problem of the 'bourgeois specialists'. But in spite of great shortages, some expansion took place in the number of pupils attending school: according to official figures, the number of pupils in general education schools rose from 7,801,000 in 1914/15 to 9,781,000 in 1920/21. In addition, over 1 million illiterate or semi-literate adults were receiving some kind of instruction at special institutions. But the greatest expansion took place in higher education, mainly because admission procedures were greatly simplified: the number of students rose from 125,000 to 207,000.[57] Against the grim background of war and economic decline, these figures show the seriousness with which mass education was regarded by central, and still more by local, soviet authorities.

V.   The false start, 1920

By the beginning of 1920, the major part of the territory of the former Russian Empire was in the hands of the Soviet government. The war with Poland was resumed between May and September 1920, but attention turned increasingly throughout 1920 to the task of peaceful reconstruction. It was universally assumed within the Bolshevik Party that the methods successful in war should be continued – with certain modifications – during peace. In February Lenin described reconstruction as 'war without bloodshed', and at the ninth party congress in March 1920 he insisted that for 'the peaceful tasks of economic construction and the restoration of our disrupted industry . . . we need the iron discipline, the iron system without which we could not have held on for two months, let alone for over two years'.[58] The congress approved the use of 'labour armies' formed from military units, together with the mass mobilization of civilian labour and the strict allocation of skilled workers as if they were army officers. 'Labour desertion' was to be dealt with 'by publishing punishment lists of deserters, by organizing deserters into workers' punishment battalions and, finally, by confining them in a concentration camp'.[59] The congress also, on Lenin's insistence, reaffirmed the support of the party for 'one-man management', already approved in principle in the spring of 1918 but not put into effect in 1918 and 1919. The resolution, drafted by Trotsky, was strongly resisted by the trade unions, by Vesenkha and by the opposition group in the party known as the 'democratic centralists'. In face of this resistance, its

[57] *Statisticheskii spravochnik SSSR za 1928* (Moscow, 1929), pp. 878–9.
[58] Lenin, *Soch.*, vol. xxx, pp. 322–3; *Selected Works*, vol. viii, p. 88.
[59] *KPSS v rezolyutsiyakh*, vol. i, pp. 479–80, 487–8.

wording was cautious: 'congress considers it necessary to approximate the administration of industry to one-man management, that is – establish full and unconditional one-man management in workshops and factory departments, move towards one-man management in factory administrations and to smaller collegia in the middle and higher levels of administration and production management'. A further resolution was poised delicately between the recognition that trade unions 'participate from bottom to top in the organization of production' and the warning that they 'shall not interfere directly in the operation (*khod*) of enterprises'. In the factories themselves, while trade unions were to participate in deciding the composition of the management, 'the principle of election must be replaced by the principle of selection on the basis of the length of practical experience, and of the technical competence, firmness, organizational ability and business-like approach of the candidates'.[60] In spite of their cautious wording, the congress resolutions undoubtedly greatly assisted the general trend towards the control of the economy by appointed administrators rather than elected committees. By December 1920, in 2,183 out of 2,483 enterprises one-man management had already replaced collective management.[61] These important developments could be justified at the time on the grounds that they were made necessary by the immaturity and inexperience of the Soviet worker. The failure to modify them in the ensuing decades was certainly contrary to the original Marxist notions about the organization of a socialist society.

Peace did not bring the abolition of the requisitioning of grain and other agricultural products. On 2 February 1920, Lenin unequivocally praised the system developed since the spring of 1918:

We collected by means of the apparatus of our food commissariat, we collected by the socialist and not the capitalist method, at fixed prices, by allocation among the peasants and not by sale on the free market – that is, we found the road for ourselves. We are convinced it is correct and will provide the possibility of obtaining results which would secure tremendous economic construction.[62]

A proposal from Trotsky that requisitioning should be replaced by a tax in kind in certain areas was rejected by the party central committee in the same month by eleven votes to four.[63] With the consolidation of the main grain regions under Soviet control, the plan for the harvest of 1920 envisaged a substantial increase in grain requisitions;[64] and in the autumn

---

[60] *Ibid.*, vol. I, pp. 482–3, 492.   [61] Venediktov, *Organizatsiya*, vol. I, p. 600.

[62] Lenin, *Soch.*, vol. XXX, pp. 308–9.

[63] *Odinnadtsatyi s"ezd RKP(b): mart–aprel' 1922 goda: stenograficheskii otchet* (Moscow, 1961), p. 270; Trotsky's proposal, as printed in L. Trotsky, *The New Course* (London, 1956), pp. 60–1, was abbreviated by Trotsky, and its significance thereby somewhat exaggerated (see F. Benvenuti, 'Dal communismo di guerra alla NEP; il dibattite sui sindicati', in *Pensiero e azione politica di Lev Trockij* (Florence, 1982), vol. I, pp. 287–8).

[64] Lenin, *Soch.*, vol. XXXI, p. 388.

of 1920 requisitions were pressed vigorously ahead in spite of the bad harvest (see Table 144). At the eighth congress of soviets in December 1920, Osinsky, a leading party member in the People's Commissariat for Food, Narkomprod, insisted against the opposition of a small Menshevik and Left Socialist-Revolutionary group that it was impossible to replace requisitioning by a fixed tax in kind:

Just open this little door, and at once there will be no grain; and he who opens this little door to free trade will lead us to the crash of our food policy and the destruction of our economy.[65]

At the congress Lenin defended grain requisitioning and supported a resolution on agriculture, passed by the congress, calling for the establishment of sowing committees in every rural district; these would impose a national obligatory sowing plan in the spring of 1921.[66]

It would be wrong to suppose that no rethinking of economic policy took place before the crisis of the spring of 1921. During 1920, while the main features of War Communism remained intact, or were even strengthened, some attempt was made to relax the rigidities of central control. At the ninth party congress in March 1920, Lenin successfully prevented a resolution being carried which proposed to nationalize the agricultural cooperatives and make them part of soviet local government; the draft resolution objected to the cooperatives on the grounds that they were dominated by the richer peasants. Lenin attacked those who supported the nationalization proposal as 'animated by a Chekist [political police] spirit, wrongly introduced into an economic question':

Have you not shaken your fists at the peasants enough? . . . We are dealing with a class which is less accessible to us and which under no circumstances is amenable to nationalization.[67]

The alternative resolution supported by Lenin, which was approved by the congress, called for the subordination of agricultural cooperatives not to the state direct but to the consumer cooperatives, and expressed the hope that 'the initiative and independent activity of peasant producers who belong to or are joining these cooperatives should not be curbed'.[68]

The same congress, while approving the draconic measures to control the labour force already described, sought more flexible means of using conscript labour armies to restore the economy. As soon as an army did not need to be kept together for military purposes, 'its large staff and administration should be disbanded and the best elements of the skilled workers should be used as small shock-labour detachments at major

[65] *Vos'moi Vserossiiskii s"ezd Sovetov: stenograficheskii otchet* (Moscow, 1921), pp. 146–7.
[66] Lenin, *Soch.*, vol. XXXI, pp. 471–7, 490–1, 492–8; *Direktivy*, vol. I, pp. 191–6.
[67] Lenin, *Selected Works*, vol. VIII, pp. 226–30, 429–30.
[68] *KPSS v rezolyutsiyakh*, vol. I, p. 496.

industrial enterprises'.[69] Later in the year, simultaneously with the nationalization of a large number of small enterprises, the eighth congress of soviets resolved that the administration of all except the largest and most important enterprises should be transferred to the provincial councils of national economy from the central agencies of Vesenkha, which should confine their activities to planning and guidance. According to one report, 1,800 industrial enterprises were so transferred.[70] Efforts were also made from September 1920 onwards to abandon the priority or shock system of planning, in which resources were concentrated on key or crisis sectors of the economy such as transport or fuel, and replace it by smoother and more rationally based arrangements for the allocation of resources.[71]

Even more significant than these endeavours to reduce detailed central control of the economy was the series of measures introducing or extending material incentives which would partly replace or supplement coercion and administrative control. In industry from June 1920 onwards the importance of bonuses for improved productivity was increasingly stressed; and in view of the depreciation of the currency, particular attention was paid to bonuses in kind. Piecework was favoured in preference to time work.[72] And the resolution of the eighth congress of soviets in December cautiously announced that village communes and peasant households which achieved success in sowing and cultivating their land in 1921 would be given priority in implements and consumer goods, and allowed to retain more of their own agricultural production for their own consumption.[73]

But the balance was clearly tilted towards the continuation of the old policy. The policy of requisitioning foodstuffs from the peasantry continued unabated in the spring and autumn of 1920. At the soviet congress in December 1920 prevailing attitudes were reflected in the decision of a meeting of the communist delegates to the congress to omit the clause offering bonuses to individual peasant households. The clause eventually remained in the resolution only because the central committee of the party overruled the delegates, and even so an amendment suggested by the central committee stressed that bonuses given collectively to village communes were to have top priority.[74] Nor was there any suggestion in

[69] *Ibid.*, vol. I, pp. 487–8.
[70] *Direktivy*, vol. I, pp. 188–90; Lenin, *Selected Works*, vol. VIII, p. 424.
[71] See Lenin's speech of 30 December 1920, in his *Selected Works*, vol. IX, pp. 12–14; Lenin contrasted '*udarnost'*' (the 'shock', or priority, principle) with '*uravnitel'nost'*' (the principle of equal treatment).
[72] *Direktivy*, vol. I, pp. 176–7 (decree of 8 June 1920); *Sobranie uzakonenii*, 1920, art. 276 (decree of 17 June 1920); Gimpel'son, '*Voennyi kommunizm*', pp. 177–80.
[73] *Direktivy*, vol. I, pp. 195–6.
[74] Y. A. Polyakov, *Perekhod k nepu i sovetskoe krest'yanstvo* (Moscow, 1967), pp. 254–5.

1920 that the money economy and commodity production could be restored. It was rather that one trend within economic policy sought a system in which product exchange with the peasantry rather than outright seizure of grain, together with payments in kind to the industrial workers proportionate to their production, would play some role, and local as against central powers would be increased. These modifications were seen as entirely compatible with the introduction of the compulsory planning of peasant production, the continued compulsory acquisition of peasant products according to a central plan, and the compulsory direction of urban labour.

During 1920 and the first few months of 1921, in accordance with this scheme, the moneyless economy was further extended. Payments were abolished for many goods and services: the economist Strumilin wrote in the middle of 1920 that 'the unsuitability of money accounting for the planned control of the state economy of Soviet Russia in present conditions is so evident that no one doubts it'. Proposals were approved for drawing up a budget of state income and expenditure in kind (the 'material budget'), and much discussion took place about the appropriate accounting unit which would replace money.[75] The edifice was crowned with the Goelro ten–fifteen year plan for the electrification of Russia, approved in principle by the eighth congress of soviets in December 1920.[76]

VI.   The introduction of the New Economic Policy, 1921–4

In retrospect, the economic system of the New Economic Policy (NEP), which continued throughout the 1920s, seems logical and coherent; in 1920–1, the political leaders groped hesitatingly towards it under the impact of economic and social crisis. From the summer of 1920 onwards, peasant disturbances were widespread.[77] But the apparent success of the grain campaign in September–December 1920 after a reasonably good harvest encouraged the authorities in their expectations that the policies of the civil war could be continued in time of peace. These expectations were also fostered by the revival of the production of fuel, metal, and textiles in the last few months of 1920.[78] But this optimism proved illusory. From the beginning of 1921, the country plunged into a disastrous fuel, transport and food crisis. Both the fuel and the food crises

[75] Davies, *Development of the Soviet Budgetary System*, pp. 38–45.
[76] *Direktivy*, vol. I, pp. 200–1.   [77] Carr, *Bolshevik Revolution*, vol. II, pp. 169–70, 271.
[78] E. B. Genkina, *Gosudarstvennaya deyatel'nost' V. I. Lenina, 1921–1923 gg.* (Moscow, 1969), pp. 61–2.

were particularly severe as a result of the over-optimism of the authorities, who distributed available supplies at the end of 1920 in anticipation of more to come.[79] Thus the bread ration was substantially increased in the autumn of 1920, but grain requisitions declined drastically at the beginning of 1921.[80] In January 1921 large numbers of Petrograd workers went on strike, and according to Lenin a mood of hostility to Bolshevik dictatorship 'widely affected the proletariat . . . in the Moscow factories, and in the factories in a number of places in the provinces'.[81] At the same time, peasant disturbances continued, and spread to all the major grain areas, including Siberia, where rail communication with the centre was temporarily cut off.[82]

Against this disturbed background the tenth party congress, meeting from 8 to 16 March 1921, agreed to depart in two major respects from the prevailing principles of economic management. First, after a stormy debate which began as early as the ninth party conference in September 1920, the tenth congress resolved, against the opposition of Trotsky, that 'the rapid conversion of the trade unions into state agencies (*ogosudarstvlenie profsoyuzov*) would be a major political mistake'; the 'main method of the trade unions should not be the method of compulsion but the method of conviction'. The militarization of labour was no longer treated as a permanent feature of the Soviet system; instead, it was described as 'a result of necessity'. The congress also repeated the earlier decision that the trade unions should 'directly participate in the organization of production'.[83] But at the same time it firmly rejected the proposal of the 'Workers' Opposition' that the Soviet economy should be managed by a central agency elected by a 'producers' congress' based on the trade unions. This was denounced as 'a syndicalist and anarchist deviation', which would deprive the Communist Party of its leading role in relation to the trade unions. Only the political party of the working class could withstand the petty-bourgeois vacillations of the mass of the population, and the craft prejudices of trade-union members, and act on behalf of the proletarian movement as a whole.[84] Thus the tenth congress agreed to a departure from War Communism in the direction of great flexibility in trade union organization, but within very strict limits.

Secondly, the tenth party congress decided to replace requisitioning by a food tax in kind. Lenin played a crucial role in this decision. Although he curtly rejected a similar proposal from Menshevik and

---

[79] Lenin, *Selected Works*, vol. IX, pp. 84–9 (report to tenth party congress in March 1921); Genkina, *Gosudarstvennaya deyatel'nost'*, pp. 62–7.

[80] *Ibid.*, p. 61; Polyakov, *Perekhod*, p. 231; Lenin, *Selected Works*, vol. IX, p. 209.

[81] *Ibid.*, vol. IX, p. 98.   [82] Genkina, *Gosudarstvennaya deyatel'nost'*, pp. 38, 65.

[83] *KPSS v rezolyutsiyakh*, vol. I, pp. 539–40, 537.

[84] *Ibid.*, vol. I, pp. 530–3; for this controversy, see Carr, *Bolshevik Revolution*, vol. II, pp. 219–27.

Socialist-Revolutionary delegates at the congress of soviets in December 1920, he privately began to investigate the need for a fundamental change as early as November 1920. While grain requisitions after the 1920 harvest greatly exceeded those in the previous year, this was due to the reincorporation of the Ukraine and other rich grain areas into Soviet Russia. In the autumn and winter of 1920–1, before the crisis of February–March 1921, the government was impelled to reduce or even cancel requisition quotas in a number of major provinces. Simultaneously Lenin sought out peasant opinion about requisitioning in conversation with local officials and the peasants themselves.[85] As early as 30 November 1920, he suggested to a government commission that they should investigate 'the transformation of food requisitioning into a tax in kind'.[86] Soviet historians have argued that Lenin delayed any revision of policy until after the main period of grain requisitioning from the 1920 harvest; but direct evidence that this was a major reason for delay is lacking. On 2 February 1921, he received the grain plenipotentiary for Siberia of the People's Commissariat for Agriculture, V. M. Sokolov, who strongly argued that for the 1921 harvest a tax in kind, fixed in advance, should replace requisitioning in Siberia in order to provide the peasants with an adequate incentive to sow grain in the spring of 1921.[87] Six days later, on 8 February 1921, Lenin wrote a 'preliminary rough draft of theses concerning the peasants' which contained all the ingredients of a fundamental change in policy:

1.   Satisfy the desire of the non-party peasantry that requisitioning (in the sense of removing surpluses) shall be replaced by a grain tax;
2.   Reduce the amount of this tax in comparison with last year's requisition;
3.   Approve the principle that the amount of tax shall correspond to the effort of the farmer (*zemledelets*), in the sense that the percentage of tax shall be reduced when the effort of the farmer increases;
4.   Extend the freedom of the farmer to use his surpluses, in excess of the tax, in local economic turnover, provided that the tax is handed over quickly and in full.[88]

Sokolov's similar proposals were dismissed by a Siberian party conference as involving 'kulak–Socialist-Revolutionary incentives', and met with little sympathy in the People's Commissariats for Agriculture and Food in Moscow.[89] Local party conferences preceding the tenth party

[85] See Polyakov, *Perekhod*, pp. 237–9.
[86] Lenin, *Polnoe sobranie sochinenii*, vol. XLII (Moscow, 1958–65), p. 51.
[87] Genkina, *Gosudarstvennaya deyatel'nost'*, pp. 77–80.
[88] Lenin, *Polnoe sobranie*, vol. XLII, p. 333.
[89] Genkina, *Gosudarstvennaya deyatel'nost'*, pp. 78, 80.

congress took it for granted that requisitioning would continue; and great efforts were required on Lenin's part to persuade the party central committee and the People's Commissar for Agriculture, Tsyurupa, that the peasants should be permitted to dispose freely of grain in excess of the tax.[90] These hesitations and resistance reveal the strength of the assumption in the Communist Party that the direct Communist approach attempted during the civil war would continue permanently. The resolution on the tax in kind adopted by the tenth party congress in March 1921 involved only a limited reform. It assumed that the peasant would dispose of his surpluses through 'exchange of products' (that is, barter) either with other individuals locally, or with state agencies for other foodstuffs, consumer goods and agricultural implements. The money economy, and trade on a national scale, would not be resumed: Lenin still argued at the tenth congress that 'free trade will lead to the rule of the White Guards'.[91] And Lenin's original proposal that tax should be reduced in proportion to effort was toned down in the congress resolution, and ambiguously supplemented by a firm declaration that middle and 'economically weak' peasants should pay a lower rate of tax.[92]

This partial retreat did not prove viable. By May 1921 a leading economic official acknowledged that the introduction of the tax in kind 'meant, in essence, the development of the free market and the initiative of the small producer'.[93] In October 1921, Lenin frankly admitted at a Moscow party conference that the further retreat was an unplanned response to the pressure of events:

It was intended to exchange the products of industry for the products of agriculture in a more or less socialist way throughout the state, and, by means of this commodity exchange, to restore large-scale industry, as the only foundation of socialist organization. What in fact happened? What happened, as you now know very well from experience, but it can also be seen throughout our press, was that commodity exchange broke down . . . We must recognize that the retreat was insufficient, that an additional retreat must be carried out, a further retreat in which we go over from state capitalism to the establishment of state control of purchase and sale and of currency circulation. Nothing came of commodity exchange; the private market proved stronger than us, and instead of commodity exchange what resulted was normal purchase and sale, or trade.[94]

No detailed examination has yet been undertaken of the mechanism of the retreat. Were the proposed intermediate stages between War Com-

---

[90] Ibid., pp. 91-3.   [91] Lenin, Selected Works, vol. VIII, p. 98.

[92] KPSS v rezolyutsiyakh, vol. I, pp. 563-4.

[93] Trudy IV Vserossiiskogo S"ezda Sovetov Narodnogo Khozyaistva (18 maya–24 maya 1921 g.) (Moscow, 1921), p. 26 (Milyutin).

[94] Lenin, Soch., vol. XXXIII, p. 72; it will be noted that Lenin by this time was using the term 'commodity exchange' rather than 'product exchange', even though this 'commodity exchange' had been intended as a kind of barter.

munism and full NEP inherently unstable, or was the inexperience of the Soviet leaders at managing such a transition primarily responsible for the drift? We do not know.

The retreat to a market relationship between the peasant and the state soon transformed the organization of the whole Soviet economy, a transformation which was completed in the spring of 1924 with the stabilization and reform of the currency and the conversion of the whole of the tax in kind into a tax in money (the agricultural tax). The NEP economy was a mixed economy, in which state industry traded with individual peasant agriculture through a market which was partly in private and partly in state hands. The transition to socialism was to be undertaken not by direct Communist methods, but by establishing an alliance between industrial workers and peasants, the so-called 'link' (*smychka*), based on economic incentives for the peasants. The individual peasant was permitted almost complete freedom to sell his products, locally or nationally, to private traders, direct to other individuals or to state agencies. Trade was resumed on a national scale, with most retail trade in private ownership.

In industry, while artisan workshops and some small factories were rented or sold by the state to individual owners, all the major factories and most of the minor ones remained in state ownership. But NEP overturned the principles on which industry was organized. The decision to return to a money economy required the stabilization of the currency, and this in turn required the gradual reduction of the inflationary currency issues which financed state expenditure. Nationalized industry was deprived of most of the subsidies it received during the civil war and instructed to operate on principles of profit-and-loss accounting (*khozraschet*), and to adapt itself to the needs of the market. Consequently, the wage system was restored, and enterprises were permitted to hire and fire labour in accordance with their needs. For the worker all restrictions on changing jobs, and all direction of labour, were removed; but at the same time substantial urban unemployment re-emerged. Trade unions now became voluntary organizations, as proposed by the tenth party congress, and membership fell drastically between 1921 and 1923. But in the new atmosphere of efficient production for the market much of the resolution on the trade unions approved by the tenth party congress no longer seemed relevant. The functions of the trade unions and their representatives in the management of the economy were whittled away, both at the centre and in the factories, though 'one-man management' was not completely established at any time in the 1920s. The trade unions under NEP exercised a certain amount of autonomy. While their leading personnel were brought under closer party control, and they were expected to assist in the promotion of production, they at the same time retained substantial bargaining powers, at both central and factory level. Their voice was muted, but they still continued, albeit fitfully, to speak for the immediate interests of the workers they claimed to represent.

The effort to balance the budget carried with it other important changes. All kinds of state expenditure in kind and money were drastically reduced. Education expenditure, most of which was transferred to local budgets, particularly suffered, in spite of the temporary introduction of school fees.[95] The number of pupils declined from 9,781,000 in 1920/21 to 7,334,000 in 1922/23, less than in 1914/15; and the number of literate and semi-literate adults receiving instruction fell from 1,158,000 to a mere 111,000.[96] At the same time, the taxation system was restored, and relied heavily on the previously condemned indirect taxes. The reintroduction of the vodka monopoly and the tax on vodka, abolished by the tsarist government in 1914, aroused strong but ineffective opposition as an indirect tax based on mass drunkenness.

These were years in which many high ideals were relinquished – sometimes only temporarily – in order to cope with grim economic reality. But limits were firmly set to the retreat. The establishment, in February 1921, more or less simultaneously with the introduction of the tax in kind, of Gosplan, the 'State General Planning Commission', headed by Krzhizhanovsky, the Bolshevik engineer in charge of Goelro, emphasized that the long-term objective of constructing a socialist planned economy had not been forgotten. Major industrial enterprises were not denationalized, only minor private credit institutions were permitted, and stringent conditions were imposed on foreign firms seeking to invest in the USSR. In March 1922, a year after the introduction of the tax in kind, Lenin announced in his report to the eleventh party congress that the retreat had gone far enough, and mocked at Mensheviks and Socialist-Revolutionaries, who argued that the retreat should go further towards capitalism in view of the immaturity of the Soviet proletariat:

Allow us to put you against the wall for that. Either you must make the effort to refrain from expressing such views in the present situation, when we are in far more difficult conditions than when the Whites directly attacked us, or we are sorry to say we shall treat you like the worst and most harmful Whiteguard elements.[97]

Throughout 1922, Lenin struggled stubbornly and successfully, in spite of severe illness, to prevent a substantial modification in the monopoly of

[95] See Fitzpatrick, *Commissariat of Enlightenment*, pp. 277–88.
[96] *Statisticheskii spravochnik* (1929), pp. 878–9.   [97] Lenin, *Soch.*, vol. XXXIII, p. 253.

foreign trade by the state, arguing that the industrial proletariat would be 'completely unable to restore its industry and make Russia an industrial country without the protection of industry not merely by a customs policy, but solely and exclusively by the monopoly of foreign trade'.[98]

The economic retreat was conducted within a strictly controlled political framework. Much freedom of discussion was permitted throughout the NEP years, and different schools of thought flourished even in such sensitive fields as economics. But Lenin frankly argued that the Bolshevik Party, in power in a country in which the majority of the population were peasants, and surrounded by rich, powerful and hostile capitalist states, could not permit freedom to other parties.[99] In the course of 1921–2, the one-party dictatorship was consolidated, and, following the ban on 'fractions and groupings' in March 1921, discipline within the single party was tightened up. Early in 1922, the elaborate system of preliminary censorship of all publications, which still continued 60 years later, was formally established.

With all the main features of NEP already agreed, Lenin insisted in his last speeches and articles at the end of 1922 and the beginning of 1923 that 'not tomorrow, but in a few years . . . socialist Russia will emerge from NEP Russia'.[100] The state was controlled by the proletariat and owned the means of production, and on this basis the peasants could be educated by means of a 'cultural revolution' and brought towards socialism through participation in the cooperatives, which offered 'everything essential for the construction of a full socialist society'.[101] Lenin freely admitted that in Soviet Russia, contrary to earlier expectations, the political and social revolution had taken place before the material and cultural prerequisites existed for the creation of socialism. He argued, however, that this had not changed the 'general line of development of world history'. 'On the basis of workers' and peasants' power and the Soviet system, we shall move forward and catch up other nations.'[102] These developments in Russia would be a step towards the final victory of world socialism, the inevitability of which was assured by the fact that 'Russia, India, China, etc. constitute the overwhelming majority of the population', and were rapidly being drawn into the struggle for their own emancipation.[103] In his last writings Lenin did not relinquish the

[98] Lenin, *Soch.*, vol. xxxiii, pp. 417–20; according to Lenin, tariff protection of Soviet industry would be inadequate because any of the rich industrial countries might offer bonuses on exports to Russia of the protected commodities (p. 419). For this controversy see M. Lewin, *Lenin's Last Struggle* (London, 1969), pp. 35–42, Genkina, *Gosudarstvennaya deyatel'nost'*, pp. 352–64.

[99] Lenin, *Soch.*, vol. xxxii, pp. 479–83 (letter to Myasnikov, 8 August 1921).

[100] *Ibid.*, vol. xxxiii, p. 405 (speech of 20 November 1922).

[101] *Ibid.*, vol. xxxiii, pp. 427–35 (articles of 4 and 6 January 1923); see E. H. Carr and R. W. Davies, *Foundations of a Planned Economy, 1926–1929*, vol. i (London, 1969), pp. 920–4.

[102] Lenin, *Soch.*, vol. xxxiii, pp. 435 (6 January), 438 (16 January 1923).

[103] *Ibid.*, vol. xxxiii, p. 458; this article, dated 2 March 1923, is translated in *Selected Works*, vol. ix, pp. 387–401, and in Lewin, *Lenin's Last Struggle*, pp. 156–74.

notion that a socialist economy would be based on product exchange, though he did not specifically refer to it.[104] Nor did he ever specifically reject the view that the successful construction of socialism in Russia would require the victory of the proletarian revolution in one of the advanced countries. But the principles of NEP which were developed between 1921 and 1923 offered a new path to the construction of an industrialized and cultured socialist society in isolated peasant Russia.

VII. *Planning and the market, 1921–6*

A.   ECONOMIC RECOVERY

By the economic year 1926/27 both agricultural and industrial production had approximately regained their pre-war level.[105] As in other parts of war-devastated Europe, the rate of recovery to pre-war capacity was much faster than both politicians and economists anticipated. As a result of the recovery of agriculture, food consumption per head of population, in terms of both calories and proteins, also regained approximately the pre-war level.[106] Social and cultural services shared in the general revival. The number of pupils at primary and secondary schools increased from 7,395,000 in the school year 1922/23, the lowest figure in the Soviet period, to 10,716,000 in 1926/27, which exceeded both the pre-war figure and the very high level reached in 1920. The number of adult illiterates and semi-literates under instruction rose from 111,000 to 1,554,000.[107] Reliable comparisons of pre- and post-revolutionary expenditure on health, urban housing and social insurance are not available, but there is abundant evidence that expenditure on these purposes increased rapidly in real terms from 1924/25 onwards.[108]

During the years of recovery the Soviet authorities established an

[104] His last reference to product exchange as the basis of a socialist economy appeared in a draft article of February 1922 (Lenin, *Polnoe sobranie*, vol. XLIV, pp. 502–3; Genkina, *Gosudarstvennaya deyatel'nost'*, p. 156).

[105] See Carr and Davies, *Foundations*, vol. I, p. 977; it was three more years, however, before the engineering and chemical industries reached the peak level of 1916. For a discussion of the extent of the recovery, see Gregory, *Russian National Income*, pp. 112–13, and S. G. Wheatcroft, R. W. Davies and J. M. Cooper, 'Soviet Industrialization Reconsidered: Some Preliminary Conclusions about Economic Development between 1926 and 1941', *Economic History Review*, vol. XXXIX (1986), pp. 267–70. From 1922 to 1930, the economic year was from 1 October–30 September, after which it coincided with the calendar year.

[106] S. G. Wheatcroft, 'The Population Dynamic and Factors Affecting it in the Soviet Union in the 1920s and 1930s', unpublished Discussion Papers, CREES, University of Birmingham, SIPS Nos. 1–2 (1976), p. 97a; the pre-war figure is an average for 1900–13, and so may underestimate food consumption on the eve of the First World War.

[107] *Statisticheskii spravochnik* (1929), pp. 878–9.

[108] See *Kontrol'nye tsifry narodnogo khozyaistva SSSR na 1927/1928 god* (Moscow, 1928), pp. 532–3, 587; Carr, *Socialism in One Country*, vol. I, pp. 402–9. Expenditure on housing construction and repair did not exceed the estimated level of depreciation until 1925/26.

effective machinery for planning the mixed market economy. In the state sector, the central economic agencies provided finance and exercised control over wholesale prices, tariffs and wages; and some physical controls were retained from the previous period – over iron and steel, for example, and over all imports. The fiscal, credit and price policies of the state also strongly influenced the private sector, including the peasantry. This was primarily planning through and not against the market.

Substantial resources were directed into industrial investment by the state. In 1926/27 gross capital investment in industry, purely from internal resources, was at least as large as in 1912/13, when a substantial part of industrial investment came from abroad. In 1926/27 it amounted to some 1,200 million rubles in current prices, 715 million rubles in pre-war prices; the highest estimate for 1912/13, 700 million rubles in 1913 prices, is almost certainly exaggerated.[109] This achievement casts doubt on Gerschenkron's assertion that, towards the end of the 1920s, 'barring further fundamental changes in the economic structure of the country, the conditions for resumption of industrial growth would seem to have been rather unfavorable'.[110] This increase in industrial investment from internal resources in 1926/27 as compared with 1913 was apparently obtained at the expense of other sectors of the economy. From the partial figures which are available, it appears that net investment in both railways and housing was substantially lower than in 1913. Net investment in education, health, and municipal services in 1926/27 was also low.[111]

The state monopoly of foreign trade was also used to assist the development of industry. In 1926/27 imports were less than 50 per cent of the 1913 level in real terms, but the proportion of consumer goods and foods in total imports was reduced from 27 to 10 per cent, and the proportion of industrial raw materials and capital equipment increased from 73 to 90 per cent. In 1926/27, the import of machine-tools equalled, and the import of mining and lifting equipment considerably exceeded, the 1913 level.[112]

B.   THE PROBLEM OF AGRICULTURAL MARKETINGS

Much less agricultural production was marketed in the 1920s than before the First World War. Sales on the extra-peasant market, on a conserva-

---

[109] See M. Barun in *Puti industrializatsii* (Moscow), no. 16, 31 August 1929, pp. 28–9, 31–2; the figures for the previous two years 1910/11 and 1911/12 were only 405 and 362 million rubles.
[110] A. Gerschenkron, *Economic Backwardness in Historical Perspective* (New York, 1962), p. 145.
[111] See estimates in Wheatcroft, Davies and Cooper, 'Soviet Industrialization Reconsidered', pp. 268–70, 275; these estimates are in turn based on Gregory, *Russian National Income*, pp. 109–11; *Kontrol'nye tsifry narodnogo khozyaistva SSSR na 1929/30 god* (Moscow, 1930), pp. 446–59.
[112] *Vneshnyaya torgovlya SSSR za 1918–1940 gg.* (Moscow, 1960), pp. 13, 17, 204–10, 269–74.

tive estimate, amounted to only 16.3 per cent of all agricultural production in 1926/27, as compared with 22.2 per cent in 1913.[113] All groups of
products were affected, but the decline in marketed grain crops was
particularly steep.[114] This decline was primarily responsible for the
decline in foreign trade, in which grain exports were by far the largest
single item before the revolution; even in the good harvest year of
1926/27, only 2 million tons of grain were exported as compared with
over 9 million tons in 1913. The authorities were constantly preoccupied
in the 1920s with the danger that supplies of food to the towns and the
army would be inadequate.

The reasons for the decline are not entirely clear. Two main factors
appear to have been at work. First, the terms of trade for agricultural
products in the mid-1920s were much less favourable than immediately
before the war. The ratio of retail prices of industrial goods to the prices
for agricultural products received by the producer was calculated at
140.6 for 1926/27 (1911–14 (average) = 100).[115] Until recently students
of the period all agreed that the shift in the terms of trade against the
peasants led them to reduce their supply of products to the market
and 'retreat into self-sufficiency'. The American economist James
Millar argues, however, that peasant demand for industrial goods is
inelastic, and that family labour on the peasant farm is treated as an
overhead. If this is true, the peasants would be likely to put *more* products
on sale at the lower prices when the terms of trade turned against them.
Little evidence is so far available to test these rival assumptions.[116] In
addition to the unfavourable price-ratios for his products, the peasant
also had less easy access to industrial goods than before the war.
Throughout most of the 1920s, industrial goods were scarce; and the
number of trading outlets in rural areas had substantially declined.[117]

The second major reason for the decline in agricultural marketings
was the changed social and economic organization of the countryside
after the revolution. The large estates, which had higher yields and
produced primarily for the market, were seized and divided up among

[113] See *Ekonomicheskii byulleten' Kon"yunkturnogo Instituta* (Moscow), no. 11–12, 1927, p. 52;
Byulleten' Ekonomicheskogo Kabineta prof. S. N. Prokopovicha (Prague), no. 49 (May 1929), p. 7.

[114] For a discussion of the level of marketings see J. Karcz, 'Thoughts on the Grain Problem', *Soviet
Studies*, vol. XVIII (1966–7), pp. 399–434; R. W. Davies, 'A Note on Grain Statistics', *ibid.*, vol.
XXI (1969–70), pp. 314–29; J. Karcz, 'Back on the Grain Front', *ibid.*, vol. XXII (1970–1), pp.
262–94. Grain production and its distribution before 1914 and in the 1920s are examined in
detail in S. G. Wheatcroft, 'Grain Production and Utilisation in Russia and the USSR before
Collectivisation', unpublished Ph.D. thesis, University of Birmingham (1980).

[115] *Kontrol'nye tsifry na 1929/30 g.* (Moscow, 1930), p. 579; this ratio was known as the 'scissors',
from the shape of the graph comparing industrial and agricultural prices.

[116] The discussion is reviewed in R. M. Harrison, 'Soviet Peasants and Soviet Price Policy in the
1920s', unpublished Discussion Papers, CREES, University of Birmingham, SIPS No. 10
(1977).

[117] *Materialy po istorii sovetskogo obshchestva* (Moscow), vol. VII (1959), pp. 121–5.

the peasants during the revolution; there was only a small number of large state farms in the 1920s. More prosperous peasants, who marketed a higher proportion of their production than the average peasant, were weakened by the equalization of land holdings during the civil war, and in the 1920s the growth of 'rural capitalism' was deliberately restricted by the Soviet government. In 1918–20 some landless labourers received land previously cultivated by prosperous peasants or by landowners, and in the 1920s they grew food for themselves but took little or no produce to market. Grain marketing from two major grain regions, the North Caucasus and the Lower Volga, declined particularly drastically; in these regions farming had been gravely damaged during the civil war.[118]

Agricultural marketings were unstable as well as insufficient. This was partly due to Russian climatic conditions which resulted in great variations in the harvest. But policy failures were also important. Maintenance of equilibrium on the market between a relatively small number of state-owned industrial enterprises and over 20 million individual peasant households proved a delicate task, and only two harvests – those of 1922 and 1926 – escaped serious economic difficulties resulting in a policy crisis. But the problem was not only one of the delicate adjustment of supply and demand in an imperfect market. Behind all the successive crises lurked the incompatibility between the ambitious goals of the Soviet government and the inadequate resources available to achieve them. The urgent desire to increase the share of resources available for industry and for all kinds of urban development constantly threatened the economic basis of the 'link' between the regime and the peasantry.

C.   THE INDUSTRIALIZATION DEBATE

As soon as economic recovery gained momentum, divergent views about the future paths of development for the Soviet economy, and for the Soviet system, emerged within the ruling party. Three interrelated issues were at the heart of the debate: growing centralization and the emergence of a ruling group in the party; the pace and methods of future industrial development, now that the pre-war level of output was being approached; and policy towards agriculture and the peasantry. The majority of the Politburo, in which Bukharin and Stalin were most prominent in the mid-1920s, naturally supported both the political regime in the party and its economic policies. From the beginning of 1925 onwards, they firmly asserted that the construction of socialism could be successfully undertaken and completed in the USSR, even if a successful proletarian revolution did not occur in an advanced capitalist

---

[118] See R. W. Davies, *The Socialist Offensive: The Collectivisation of Soviet Agriculture, 1929–1930* (London and Cambridge, Mass., 1980), pp. 21–8.

country. The basis for this achievement would be a firm link with the peasantry. Industrialization could be achieved only by developing the internal market, by improving the standard of living of both workers and peasants, and by 'smoothing and overcoming internal contradictions, not sharpening them'; resources would be accumulated for industrialization primarily from within the state sector itself.[119] In agriculture gradualness must remain the watchword. The technical level of individual peasant agriculture must be steadily raised, and simultaneously cooperation among individual peasant households would be encouraged.[120]

Within the Politburo majority, different shades of opinion can be detected, which were to be of major importance within a couple of years. Bukharin enthusiastically and passionately stressed the importance of moving towards socialism via market relations;[121] in two famous phrases in 1925 he called upon 'all the peasants', including the well-to-do and kulak peasants, to '*enrich yourselves*', and admitted that 'we shall move forward at a snail's pace'.[122] Stalin in a letter unpublished at the time declared that the slogan 'enrich yourselves' 'is not ours, it is wrong . . . Our slogan is socialist accumulation'.[123] In his writings and speeches of 1925 and 1926, Stalin paid less attention to the market relationship with the peasantry, and displayed less understanding of it, than Bukharin. But all the Politburo majority shared a confidence – or a complacency – about the present and future course of economic policy which was reinforced by the healthy economic climate after the 1926 harvest.

The minority in the party – the Left Opposition headed by Trotsky in 1923–4, the Leningrad Opposition of Zinoviev and Kamenev at the end of 1925, and the United Opposition of both groups in 1926–7 – rejected the optimistic diagnoses of the majority. They shared a common conviction that the party was suffering from 'bureaucratic degeneration', and that the confidence of the leaders in the possibility of completing the construction of a socialist society in the isolated Soviet Union was leading them to adapt their policies to the petty-bourgeois environment in which they were located. The Left held that in economic policy the party was making dangerous concessions to the private traders, and above all to the kulaks. Much more emphasis must be placed on the development of industry; even the transformation of agriculture itself required the prior development of industry, which would supply farm

---

[119] I. V. Stalin, *Sochineniya* (Moscow), vol. VIII, pp. 286–7 (November 1926), pp. 122–9 (April 1926).   [120] Stalin, *Soch.*, vol. VIII, pp. 315–16, 339–40 (December 1925).

[121] See, for example, N. Bukharin, *Put' k sotsializmu v Rossii* (New York, 1967), pp. 288–90 (written 1925).

[122] See Carr, *Socialism in One Country*, vol. I, pp 260, 352 (speeches of April and December 1925).

[123] Stalin, *Soch.*, vol. VII, p. 153 (dated 2 June 1925).

machinery and consumer goods to the peasants. But a policy of industrialization could not succeed without the restoration of party, workers' and soviet democracy, and the construction of socialism could not be completed without the support of successful revolution in an advanced country.

The 'bourgeois specialists' associated with Bukharin, and the party economists associated with the Left Opposition, took more extreme positions than the political leaders. Kondratiev, the most influential economist in the People's Commissariats for Agriculture and Finance, called for a reduction in the '*insupportable rate* of development of industry', a wage-freeze in industry, a switch of resources from producer goods' to consumer goods' industries, a reduction in the 'excessively heavy burden' of taxation on the 'developing strata of peasant farms', and an increase in imports of consumer goods to meet peasant demand.[124]

In contrast to Kondratiev, Chayanov, the head of the 'organization and production school' of agricultural economists, the so-called 'neo-narodniks' (neo-populists), which was the main focus of 'bourgeois' economic influence in the People's Commissariat for Agriculture, attached little significance to economic differentiation in the countryside. According to Chayanov, the way forward to socialism was to develop 'vertical cooperatives', first in marketing and then in agricultural processing; collective farms, which he called 'horizontal' producer cooperatives, should not be established immediately.[125] If Kondratiev and his colleagues provided the Soviet authorities in 1925 with the arguments which led them to relax the restrictions on the hiring of labour and renting of land in the countryside, Chayanov bolstered Bukharin's view, expressed in February 1925, that 'the high road leads along the cooperative line'; 'collective farms are not the main line, not the high road, not the chief path by which the peasant will come to socialism'.[126]

No 'bourgeois' economists provided such direct inspiration for Trotsky. But Preobrazhensky, a prominent member of the Left Opposition, was an outstanding economist. In his famous work *New Economics* he declared that the Soviet Union must pass through a stage of 'primitive socialist accumulation', analogous to the 'primitive accumulation' postulated by Marx in his analysis of the rise of capitalism. According to

[124] Kondratiev's theses on agriculture and industrialization are extensively cited by Zinoviev in *Bol'shevik* (Moscow), no. 13, 15 July 1927, pp. 33–47.

[125] A. V. Chayanov, *On the Theory of Peasant Economy* (Homewood, Ill., 1966), ed. D. Thorner, B. Kerblay and R. E. F. Smith, pp. 264–9 (first published in 1925).

[126] See Carr, *Socialism in One Country*, vol. 1, pp. 220–1; Carr and Davies, *Foundations*, vol. 1, pp. 921–2; for passages in Bukharin which directly echo Chayanov's approach to the agricultural cooperatives see Bukharin, *Put' k sotsializmu* (1967), pp. 266–7 (written in 1925).

Preobrazhensky, industry could not rely only or mainly on 'socialist accumulation', i.e. accumulation within the state sector, for its expansion, both because the state sector was too small and because of the political and social necessity, neglected by the Politburo majority, to pay high wages to the industrial workers. Instead, the peasant economy must play a role analogous to that played by the exploitation of pre-capitalist forms of production, including the colonies, in primitive capitalist accumulation: part of the product or incomes of the small-scale peasant economies, and particularly of the kulaks, must be exploited or 'alienated' by the state.[127] Preobrazhensky, like Trotsky, firmly insisted that this activity would remain within the framework of the market economy: the peasants' product would be obtained through taxation or price policy, not by the forcible methods of War Communism or by the plunder characteristic of primitive capitalist accumulation. And neither Preobrazhensky nor Trotsky envisaged the collectivization of agriculture as anything but a remote prospect.

But a significant disagreement about the role of the market between Preobrazhensky and his opponents in the party majority appeared in a doctrinal dispute about the operation of the NEP economy. Preobrazhensky argued that two laws or regulators of the economy, the 'law of value' (roughly equivalent to the law of supply and demand) and the 'law of socialist accumulation', were in conflict, and could be resolved only by the victory of one regulator over the other. His opponents, including Bukharin, argued that while two 'principles' existed, the 'principle of spontaneity' and the 'planning principle', these principles struggled and cooperated within the framework of the law of value, which would be gradually transformed into a 'law of labour outlays' as planning became predominant.[128] The significance of the dispute was that Preobrazhensky did not treat the regulatory power of the state as operating only through the market. Instead the law of socialist accumulation was in principle independent of the market forces exercised through the law of value.

Preobrazhensky was not alone in seeing the market as secondary to the larger goals of state planning. In 1924, Krzhizhanovsky, chief author of the Goelro plan and chairman of Gosplan for most of the 1920s, stressed that commodity exchange and currency circulation must be subordinate to the plan.[129] In 1925 Strumilin, a leading economist in Gosplan, insisted on the need 'to *adapt* the market environment consciously to our

---

[127] See E. Preobrazhensky, *The New Economics* (Oxford, 1965), *passim* (first published in Moscow in 1924 to 1926).

[128] See the long discussion in *Vestnik Kommunisticheskoi Akademii* (Moscow), vol. XIV (1926), pp. 3–254, and in Preobrazhensky, *New Economics*, pp. 8–41, 224–67.

[129] *Ekonomicheskaya zhizn'* (Moscow), 13 January 1924.

planning efforts', and at the beginning of 1927 he argued, in an introduction to the draft five-year plan of Gosplan, that 'as the initial coordinates in constructing our plans we can and must take not what can be forecast by a prognosis but what can be programmed by positing it as a goal'.[130] Strumilin was in effect refusing to think within the terms of the market economy. The plan targets he advocated at this time were only loosely tied in with any possibility of equilibrium on the market, and were correctly castigated by the People's Commissariat for Finance as risking 'a break in the link with the peasantry'.[131]

Several other events in the course of the economic year 1926/27 revealed the spread of the tendency to relax the axiom that planning should take place through and not against the market. In February 1927, the party central committee ordered that retail prices of industrial consumer goods should be reduced by 10 per cent. In the middle-1920s, all schools of thought, among both economists and politicians, were passionately convinced that even the mildest increase in the level of prices would be intolerable; the effects of inflation during the civil war and in Germany in 1928 were fresh in everyone's memory, and the influence of pre-Keynesian Western economics was pervasive. Given both their monetary orthodoxy, and their equally firm conviction that the terms of trade of the peasantry should not deteriorate, the decision to reduce industrial prices was a logical consequence of the reduction in official grain prices which had taken place in the summer of 1926.[132] Logical but not sensible: the price reduction campaign was carried out at a time when purchasing power was rising rapidly owing to the further expansion of capital investment in the course of 1927, and the success of the campaign brought prices below the equilibrium position. From the autumn of 1927 onwards, serious shortages of industrial goods resulted. A substantial number of private shops were forcibly closed and some private traders were arrested for speculation. Kuibyshev, chairman of Vesenkha, declared in August 1927 that 'to reduce prices when there is a goods shortage' was 'a very great achievement of the planning principle'.[133] In the same month Vesenkha successfully put great pressure on the Politburo to increase the already substantial capital investment plan for industry for the economic year 1927/28; on 25 August, the Politburo increased the planned allocation to capital investment from the state budget.[134] Thus at the time of the 1927 harvest, an influential group in the party and in the economic agencies of the state secured the adoption

[130] S. G. Strumilin, *Na planovom fronte* (Moscow, 1958), p. 225; *Planovoe khozyaistvo* (Moscow), no. 7–8, 1927, p. 14.   [131] See Carr and Davies, *Foundations*, vol. 1, pp. 856–61.

[132] On 16 September 1926, the Politburo resolved that the reduction of grain prices made it necessary to reduce industrial prices (*Industrializatsiya SSSR, 1926–1928 gg.* (Moscow, 1969), p. 510).   [133] *Torgovo-promyshlennaya gazeta*, 14 August 1927.

[134] *Industrializatsiya SSSR, 1926–1928 gg.*, p. 510.

of plans for industrialization which were incompatible with market equilibrium and involved overcoming the market by administrative instructions of a kind which had been absent since the end of War Communism.

This fundamental shift in approach was veiled by loud denials that the framework of policy had changed. Strumilin insisted that his five-year plan targets were compatible with financial stability and would not put a strain on relations with the peasantry. Mikoyan, who was in charge of the price reduction campaign, declared that price reduction had strengthened the ruble and provided 'a powerful lever for increasing the agricultural surplus disposed of by the peasantry'.[135] The increases in investment in industry and in other state expenditure in 1927/28 were implausibly planned to take place without currency inflation.[136] Wishful thinking – sometimes amounting to deliberate deception – was much more prominent in Soviet plans and policies than in the immediate past.

To examine the causes of these shifts in approach in 1927 lies beyond the scope of this chapter, and beyond the scope of economic history as such. Part of the explanation certainly lies in the intractability of the obstacles in the way of raising resources for industrialization in a predominantly peasant country. But other factors than the needs of industrialization as such pressed the leaders towards using administrative measures to achieve a quick solution to their difficulties. The hopes for a rapid transformation of society which are inherent in revolutionary Marxism led the section of the party majority headed by Stalin to be impatient with the results achieved by the cautious policies of 1925–6. This section of the party leadership was certainly influenced in a radical direction by the repeatedly stated fears of the United Opposition that current moderate policies were endangering the very basis of the gains achieved by the revolution; it was in October 1926 that Trotsky called Stalin at a Politburo meeting 'the grave-digger of the revolution'.[137] Further, the one-party system, and the monolithic regime within the party which was being consolidated by 1927, encouraged administrative solutions, as did the outlook and methods of work of a large number of party members, acquired in the civil war and not entirely abandoned afterwards (the apparatus and methods of grain requisition, for example, ceased to be used only in the spring of 1924). Finally, the defeat of the Chinese Communist revolution and the breaking-off of diplomatic relations with the USSR by the British Conservative government both occurred in the spring of 1927, and revealed the extreme isolation of the USSR; this gave an added sense of urgency to plans for industrialization.

[135] A. Mikoyan, *Rezul'taty kampanii po snizheniyu tsen* (Moscow, 1927), p. 3.
[136] *Kontrol'nye tsifry na 1927/1928 god*, pp. 326–7.
[137] See Carr, *Foundations*, vol. II, pp. 16–17.

Paradoxically, it was just at the moment of the greatest practical success of the efforts to guide the peasant economy through the market that the pressures towards administrative methods proved sufficiently strong to overthrow the previously firm commitment to the market relationship with the peasantry.

VIII. *The grain crisis, 1927–8*

The conflict between the rival approaches of 'planning through the market' and 'planning by overcoming the market' was soon put to a decisive test. In October–December 1927, peasants sold the official collection agencies only half as much grain as in the same months of 1926. With this amount of grain the towns and the army could not be fed.

The peasants were reluctant to sell grain to the official agencies for several reasons. First, the grain harvest in 1927 was several million tons lower than in the previous year, when the weather was more favourable and the yield was high. Hence the peasants had less grain at their disposal. Secondly, the price offered for grain by the official agencies was low relative to those of industrial crops and meat and dairy products, so it was more advantageous for the peasants to acquire the cash they needed by selling these other products. Moreover, in view of the rapid growth of the urban economy they also had more opportunity to earn money on seasonal work in the towns. Thirdly, many industrial consumer goods were in short supply, so the peasants were reluctant to convert their grain, which could easily be stored, into cash which they could not use to buy the goods they wanted. Finally, the peasants were in a stronger position than in previous years to resist changes in the terms of trade which were to their disadvantage. Their stocks of cash were higher, and by 1927 they had acquired sufficient basic consumer goods to be prepared to wait for the variety or quality they preferred.[138]

The crisis could have been mitigated if the Soviet leaders and their immediate advisers had been more perceptive in the months before the harvest. It is true that consumer goods were in short supply partly because they were bought up and hoarded during the war scare of the spring and summer of 1927, and partly because, as in 1925, the expansion of industry and of capital construction generally led to an increase in purchasing power. But the shortage was also due to the substantial reduction in prices in the spring of 1927 (see p. 1022), without which the supply of consumer goods would have been much closer to demand. Other remedies were also available: an increase in agricultural taxation in 1927 would have compelled the peasants to seek more cash by selling more products.

---

[138] See Carr and Davies, *Foundations*, vol. 1, pp. 44–6, which also discusses some secondary factors omitted above.

In other respects the state had much less freedom of manoeuvre. According to a contemporary survey, the most important factor in peasant reluctance to sell grain was its price relative to those of other agricultural products.[139] This was also the most intractable problem for the authorities. A complicated story lies behind the low official price of grain. In 1925, the official agencies increased the price of grain when peasants were reluctant to sell it; while this solved the grain crisis, it also led in the following year to a disastrous decline in the production of industrial crops such as cotton and flax, the prices of which were also controlled by the state. In 1926, the official agencies therefore again reduced the price offered for grain. During the course of these manipulations the prices of meat and dairy products rose steadily – meat and dairy products were mainly sold on the free market and their prices were therefore outside state control. By 1927 it was clearly to the advantage of the peasants to concentrate on the production and sale of livestock products. A less crude price policy in 1926 might have avoided these difficulties. But at the end of 1927 the only way in which the state could hope to persuade the peasants to sell more grain to the official agencies was by substantially increasing its official price.

This course was rejected. During the similar crisis in the autumn of 1925 the Soviet authorities increased the price of grain and cut their plans for industrialization; now they kept the price of grain stable and pressed ahead with industrialization. At the beginning of 1928, compulsion was used to obtain grain from the peasants for the first time since 1924, and on a greater scale. Grain was seized with the aid of the so-called 'extraordinary measures' and, as in 1918–20, the authorities unsuccessfully endeavoured to win the support of the mass of the peasantry against the more prosperous peasants, many of whom were put on trial for hoarding grain and profiteering from its sale.

This was the beginning of the end of NEP. The 'Right wing' of the party headed by Bukharin, leading political thinker and editor of *Pravda*, Rykov, chairman of the Council of People's Commissars, and Tomsky, head of the trade unions, and supported by all the bourgeois economists, drew the lesson from the grain crisis that the policy errors which led to it must be avoided at all costs in the future; equilibrium on the market must be restored and industrialization must again fit into the NEP framework. But other party leaders, such as Kuibyshev, Politburo member in charge of industry, and Kaganovich, a close associate of Stalin at party head-

[139] In a survey of 800 voluntary correspondents in the grain regions of the RSFSR, the main factors mentioned as hindering the grain collections were as follows (percentage of correspondents mentioning the factor in brackets): low yield in 1927 (54), low grain collection price (57), more profitable to sell livestock (51), shortage of industrial goods (25), rumours of war and famine (23), unpreparedness of grain collection agencies (21), growth of non-agricultural work (11) (*Statistika i narodnoe khozyaistvo* (Moscow), no. 2, 1928, p. 146). I am indebted to Dr S. G. Wheatcroft for drawing my attention to this source.

quarters, took an entirely different view. For them the policies of 1927 which preceded the grain crisis were not errors but bold attempts to subordinate market forces to the will of the state, the grain crisis occurred because controls over market spontaneity were not yet adequate, and the 'extraordinary measures' were not a regrettable temporary necessity but a convincing demonstration of the efficacy of 'administrative methods'. 'The will of the state opposed itself to the *Konjunktur* [i.e. to market trends]', Kuibyshev declared, 'and thanks to *all* the levers at the disposal of the proletarian state, this *Konjunktur* was broken.'[140] From 1928 onwards, industrialization proceeded at a pace entirely incompatible with a market relationship with the peasantry; and coercion of the peasantry became a permanent feature of Soviet policy. In the course of 1929, the old leadership of the trade unions, headed by Tomsky, was removed, and the trade unions, while continuing to retain some influence at factory level, in practice lost all bargaining power at the national level. In September 1929 a party resolution again insisted on the importance of one-man management, 'the concentration of all the threads of the administration of the economic life of the enterprises in the hands of their managers'.[141] In the machinery of government, the balance of forces which existed until 1926 was reversed; henceforth bold administrative decisions took precedence over delicate adjustments in financial and price policy. In the course of 1928–9 the trend within the party represented by Kuibyshev and Kaganovich, with Stalin at its head, broke the resistance of the Right wing and emerged triumphant.

IX. *Forced industrialization, 1928–41*

A. OBJECTIVES

By 1928 the protagonists of rapid industrialization in the Politburo and in the party at large were in general agreement on their major objectives for industry.[142] The construction of socialism in a single country, surrounded by a hostile capitalist world, imperatively required that Soviet industry – and the Soviet economy at large – must become 'self-sufficient', in the sense that they should not depend on the capitalist countries for any major type of product. This did not imply immediate autarky: on the contrary, the Soviet leaders insisted, in opposition to some Russian engineers, that foreign technology should be fully utilized in order to pull Soviet industry forward. But it did require the establish-

---

[140] See Carr and Davies, *Foundations*, vol. I, pp. 307–10; this statement was made on 2 February 1928.   [141] *Direktivy*, vol. II, p. 121.

[142] On this topic generally see Carr and Davies, *Foundations*, vol. I, pp. 401–52.

ment of a capacity to produce capital equipment, chemicals, and other advanced products which were lacking in the industry inherited from the tsarist period. Closely associated with the principle of self-sufficiency was the further requirement that Soviet industry should be based on the most advanced technology. Some influential economists argued that capital-intensive production would be uneconomical in view of the backwardness of the economy and the abundance of unskilled labour, but the Soviet leaders, encouraged by Krzhizhanovsky and other leading planners, held that in the course of the technological revolution labour would soon cease to be cheap. Moreover, in order to reach an advanced level of technology new up-to-date enterprises must be introduced intact into the existing economy; these would act as an example to the rest of industry and enable Soviet engineers and workers to acquire the latest skills.

The further principle that the output of producer goods, 'means of production' in Marxist terminology, must expand more rapidly than the output of consumer goods, 'means of consumption', was a corollary of the drive for self-sufficiency and advanced technology. Lenin had already detected the operation of this principle in expanding capitalist economies, and the backwardness or absence of many producer goods industries in the USSR served to reinforce the general case for priority for producer goods. Special emphasis was placed on the importance of acquiring a capacity to produce capital equipment, 'means of production for producing means of production'.

After much controversy, it was also agreed that a substantial proportion of the new factories should be located not in the traditional centres of modern industry in north-west and central European Russia and in the Ukraine, but in the Urals and Siberia, and in backward Central Asia. The economic development of the former 'colonial' areas of Central Asia was imperatively required by Soviet social policy. In the Urals and Siberia, vast unused, and largely unexplored, mineral resources would provide the basis for cheap production. Above all, the needs of defence required the construction of iron and steel, engineering, and armaments industries in relatively inaccessible areas of the Soviet Union.[143]

The need to catch up with Western defence technology in view of the likelihood of armed attack was a constant preoccupation of the Soviet authorities, and powerfully reinforced their commitment to construction of a self-sufficient industry based on advanced technology. It also provided a persuasive argument for accelerating the pace of industrialization. Technology in the advanced capitalist countries was 'simply racing

[143] See R. W. Davies, 'A Note on Defence Aspects of the Ural–Kuznetsk Combine', *Soviet Studies*, vol. XXVI (1974), pp. 272–4.

ahead', Stalin warned a party central committee plenum in November 1928: 'it is necessary to catch up and surpass these countries technologically and economically; either we achieve this, or they will destroy us'.[144]

Soviet plans for industrial expansion were not restricted to the producer goods industries. The promises held out to the Soviet consumer contained, it is true, a strong propaganda element, and cannot be assumed to reflect the genuine expectations of the political leaders. But they certainly believed that the industrialization of agriculture would enable an immediate increase in the supply of industrial crops as raw materials for industry and, after at most a few years of restriction, a vast expansion of agricultural production generally. This would provide the basis for the development of modern consumer goods and food industries and for a rapid improvement in the standard of living of the whole population.

A vast programme of social development accompanied the industrial and agricultural plans. The education of the mass of the population and the training of large numbers of people for employment in the new factories were a condition of successful industrialization: as the plenum of the party central committee put it in November 1929, 'the scale on which cadres are trained, from the engineer to the skilled worker, must correspond to the general scale of socialist construction'.[145] The technological revolution required a cultural revolution.

Above all, Soviet industrialization was to form part of the advance of Soviet society to socialism and communism. In spite of their enthusiasm for rapid economic development, the Soviet leaders rejected the notion that the supreme criterion of economic policy should be the development of production. 'We do not need just *any* growth of the productivity of the labour of the people,' Stalin told the central committee plenum in April 1929, 'We need a *particular kind* of growth of productivity, *which ensures a systematic preponderance of the socialist sector of the economy over the capitalist sector*.'[146]

B.   RESULTS

In the decade after 1928, Soviet industry developed at a rate and on a scale entirely without precedent in world economic history. Industrial production in 1937 reached 446 per cent of the 1928 level according to Soviet official figures, and 249 per cent according to the most conservative

144 Stalin, *Soch.*, vol. XI, p. 248.   145 *KPSS v rezolyutsiyakh*, vol. II, p. 642.
146 Stalin, *Soch.*, vol. XII, pp. 79–80.

Western estimate; the corresponding annual rates of growth are 18 and 10.5 per cent. Soviet industry became large-scale industry: while one-third of industrial production came from small-scale industry in 1913, by 1937 the proportion had fallen to a mere 6 per cent.[147] Major new industries were established with the assistance of substantial imports of machinery and know-how from the West. By 1937 the Soviet Union could produce in substantial quantities its own iron and steel-making and electric power equipment, tractors, combine-harvesters, tanks and metal aircraft, as well as almost all types of machine tools; and the level of technology rose throughout industry. But the policy of concentrating investment in new capital-intensive factories was only partially achieved in practice. The pressures for more output and lower costs partly diverted reserves into the expansion of existing factories and into projects yielding immediate results. As has been clearly shown in an American study of the Soviet tractor industry, these pressures, and the abundant availability of unskilled labour, resulted in the employment of much more labour per unit of output, particularly in auxiliary processes, than in equivalent United States factories.[148] The rate of utilization of industrial capital was also higher in the USSR than in Western countries: more shifts were worked per day, and the average percentage of capacity in use also tended to be higher. The outcome has been well described as 'a labour-intensive variant of capital-intensive technology'.

Location policy was similarly modified in practice under the impact of short-term pressures. A major new industrial complex was established in the Urals and beyond, and this formed the basis of the Soviet armaments industry in the darkest period of the Second World War, when much of the European USSR was occupied by the enemy. The foundations of modern industry were also established in some of the most backward republics. The industrial output of the eastern areas of the USSR (the Urals and beyond) rose from 11–12 per cent of all Soviet output in 1928 to over 16 per cent in 1940.[149] But re-location of industry was less extensive than originally planned, owing to the pressure for immediate output; in the last years before the war, complacency about Soviet ability

---

[147] *Promyshlennost' SSSR: statisticheskii sbornik* (Moscow, 1964), p. 34; G. W. Nutter, *The Growth of Industrial Production in the Soviet Union* (Princeton, NJ, 1962), p. 155; N. M. Kaplan and R. H. Moorsteen, *Indexes of Soviet Industrial Output*, RAND Research Memorandum RM-2495 (Santa Monica, 1960), p. 226; A. Kaufman, *Small-Scale Industry in the Soviet Union* (Washington, DC, 1962), p. 58. The various production series are examined in R. W. Davies, 'Soviet Industrial Production, 1928–1937: The Rival Estimates', unpublished CREES Discussion Papers, University of Birmingham, SIPS No. 18 (1978).

[148] N. T. Dodge, 'Trends in Labor Productivity in the Soviet Tractor Industry: A Case Study in Industrial Development', unpublished Ph.D. thesis, Harvard University (1960).

[149] H. Hunter, *Soviet Transportation Policy* (Cambridge, Mass., 1957), p. 32.

to halt the enemy at the frontiers also encouraged the construction of armaments factories in the European USSR.[150]

Thus the development of the producer goods industries in the 1930s very broadly corresponded to the objectives proclaimed by the party leaders at the end of the 1920s. Agricultural production, on the other hand, declined considerably in 1929–33; the fall in the number of livestock was catastrophic. In 1932–3, there was famine in large areas of the countryside and hunger in the towns. Even in 1937, the year of the best inter-war harvest, gross agricultural production exceeded that of 1928 by only 8.1 per cent, according to official figures; and in the three years 1937–9 it was on average only 2.5 per cent higher than in 1927–9.[151] In the same period, the population increased by about 12 per cent, so agricultural production per capita did not recover to the level of the later 1920s at any time before the Second World War. Within this total the production of industrial crops increased substantially, and this enabled an increase in the production of consumer goods based on agricultural raw materials. The production of other consumer goods also increased. But, taking both food and industrial consumer goods together, total private consumption per capita in 1937 is estimated by Western economists to have fallen by between 3 and 8 per cent as compared with 1928; consumption declined further in the years immediately before the Second World War.[152]

This ruthless industrialization drive resulted in much human suffering through hunger and malnutrition, and was accompanied by the rapid expansion of the use of forced labour. Among widely divergent estimates, Lorimer's calculation in 1946 that the unexpected excess mortality between 1926 and 1939 was about $5\frac{1}{2}$ million persons still seems to be the most reliable; this population loss was primarily due to the famine of 1932–3 and to excess deaths in labour camps.[153] No official statement has ever been made about the number of people incarcerated in labour camps in the 1930s; according to Wheatcroft's careful estimate, 'the maximum number of concentration camp labourers', excluding those who were

[150] On Soviet location policy generally, see I.S. Koropeckyj, 'The Development of Soviet Location Theory before the Second World War', *Soviet Studies*, vol. xix (1967–8), pp. 1–28, 232–4; on the construction of iron and steel and armaments factories in the traditional industrial areas immediately before the Second World War, see M. G. Clark, *The Economics of Soviet Steel* (Cambridge, Mass., 1956), pp. 229–34; A. Yakovlev, *Tsel' zhizni* (Moscow, 1967), pp. 254–7, 262.

[151] *Sel'skoe khozyaistvo SSSR*, p. 97. For a somewhat higher estimate by Wheatcroft, see Wheatcroft, Davies, and Cooper, 'Soviet Industrialization Reconsidered', pp. 280–4, especially Tables 3 and 4.

[152] See P. Hanson, *The Consumer in the Soviet Economy* (London, 1968), pp. 31–7.

[153] See F. Lorimer, *The Population of the Soviet Union: History and Prospects* (Geneva, 1946), pp. 133–4; for a discussion, see S. G. Wheatcroft, 'A Note on Seven Rosefielde's Calculations of Excess Mortality in the USSR, 1929–1949', *Soviet Studies*, (vol, xxxvi (1984), pp. 277–81.

exiled but not incarcerated in camps, was 'some four to five million' at the time of the 1939 census.[154]

While the standard of living of the consumer deteriorated during the industrialization drive, state expenditure on social and cultural services increased rapidly. The number of persons employed in education increased more rapidly than the industrial labour force (see Table 145). The number of pupils at all kinds of schools increased from 12 million in 1928/29 to 33 million in 1939/40; four-year education became almost universal during the first five-year plan, and by 1939 seven-year education (from 7 + to 14 +) was almost universal in the towns, and nearly one-third of all urban children were attending the 8–10 year school (from 14 + to 17 +). The number of students in higher and secondary specialized education increased even more rapidly, and the total number of specialists in the state and cooperative sector rose from 4.6 to 7.1 per cent of all employed persons.[155] Adult education was also a major feature of the 1930s – from mass literacy campaigns to special academies for the higher education of industrial managers. According to the population censuses the percentage of illiterates in the age-group 9–49 fell from 43.4 per cent in 1926 to 12.6 per cent in 1939;[156] this was due partly to the higher proportion of children attending school, partly to the success of the literacy campaign.

The social security provisions for the employed population, introduced during the course of the 1920s, largely remained in force, for a vastly increased labour force, throughout most of the 1930s. Expenditure on social insurance, social security and labour protection, about half of which consisted of sickness and pregnancy benefits and pensions, amounted in 1930 to about 10 per cent of the total wage bill, and in 1938 was still in excess of 8 per cent.[157] Old age pensions were provided only for people who had been in employment for a definite period, so collective farmers (who counted as self-employed) and housewives received no pension: there were only 4 million pensioners at the beginning of 1941.[158]

---

[154] See S. G. Wheatcroft, 'On Assessing the Size of Forced Concentration Camp Labour in the Soviet Union, 1929–56', *Soviet Studies*, vol. XXXIII (1981), pp. 265–95; R. Conquest, 'Forced Labour Statistics: Some Comments', *Soviet Studies*, vol. XXXIV (1982), pp. 434–9; S. G. Wheatcroft, 'Towards a Thorough Analysis of Soviet Forced Labour Statistics', *Soviet Studies*, vol. XXXV (1983), pp. 223–37.

[155] *Kul'turnoe stroitel'stvo SSSR: statisticheskii sbornik* (Moscow, 1956), pp. 122–3, 204; *Trud v SSSR: statisticheskii sbornik* (Moscow, 1968), p. 251.

[156] *Strana sovetov za 50 let: sbornik statisticheskikh materialov* (Moscow, 1967), p. 271.

[157] Calculated from data in Davies, *Development of the Soviet Budgetary System*, pp. 254, 296; on the eve of the Second World War, stricter arrangements for the payment of benefits were introduced (*ibid.*, p. 252). Social insurance grants and pensions are estimated to have declined from 5.7 per cent of the wage bill in 1928 to 4.3 per cent in 1937 and 3.4 per cent in 1940 (J. Chapman, *Real Wages in the Soviet Union since 1928* (Cambridge, Mass., 1963), p. 126).

[158] *Strana sovetov*, p. 267.

Table 145. *Number of persons employed in selected sectors of the Soviet economy (annual average, thousands)*

	1928		1932		1937		1940	
	Number	%	Number	%	Number	%	Number	%
Industrial production	4,339	59.7	9,374	62.1	11,641	63.8	13,079	62.2
Building	749	10.3	2,313	15.3	1,604	8.8	1,620	7.7
Railway transport	971	13.4	1,297	8.6	1,512	8.3	1,767	8.4
Health	399	5.5	669	4.4	1,127	6.2	1,512	7.2
Education	725	10.0	1,292	8.6	2,088	11.4	2,678	12.7
Science and scientific services	82	1.1	145	1.0	279	1.5	362	1.7
Total for these sectors	7,265	100.0	15,090	100.0	18,251	100.0	21,018	100.0

Note:
These figures refer to the territory of the USSR in the year concerned. The figures for 1940 may therefore be somewhat too high in comparison with those for previous years; for the whole of 1940 Western Byelorussia and Western Ukraine were incorporated into the USSR, and the three Baltic republics were incorporated in June 1940. The additional population of the territories increased the total population of the USSR by 17 million persons, or 9.8 per cent. The figures for 1940 may not, however, fully include persons employed on the newly incorporated territories: the percentage increases in the employed population in 1940 as compared with 1928 given in *Trud v SSSR*, pp. 30–1, differ only slightly from the percentages which can be calculated from the above table, and these percentage increases are said to refer to 'the territory within the frontiers of the USSR in 1928' (*Trud v SSSR*, p. 16).

Source: Calculated from *Trud v SSSR: statisticheskii sbornik* (Moscow, 1968), pp. 24–5.

Employment in the health services increased rapidly (see Table 145), and so did many health facilities: the number of hospital beds, for example, rose from 250,000 in 1928 to 790,000 in 1940.[159] But severe malnutrition in the early 1930s and poor conditions of life in the rapidly developing towns resulted in the spread of malaria and other diseases:[160] infant mortality actually rose from 174 per 1,000 births in 1926 to 182 in 1940, and mortality also increased in the 1–5 age group.[161]

Employment elsewhere in the services sector, particularly in trade and in general administration, increased much more slowly than urban employment as a whole.[162] In spite of substantial state investment, the urban housing stock increased more slowly than the urban population, and urban housing per head fell from 8.3 m² in 1926 to a mere 6.7 m² in 1940.[163] In the same period, urban employment increased more rapidly than the urban population, owing to the recruitment of a higher proportion of women into the labour-force.[164] Expenditure on all aspects of the urban infrastructure, apart from the education and health services, was thus kept relatively small.[165] Resources were also saved by the intensive exploitation of the railways and their labour force, though at the cost of frequent transport crises.

C.   FACTORS CONTRIBUTING TO GROWTH[166]

The enormous increase in industrial production in 1928–37 in turn involved very large increases in the input of both labour and capital into industry. By 1937, the number of employed persons in industry reached 273 per cent of the 1928 level (see Table 145), so the labour force increased less rapidly than industrial production, except on the most conservative estimate of the latter. Capital stock expanded much more rapidly than the labour force: fixed production capital in industry in 1937 reached 534 per cent of the 1928 level, according to official figures.[167] Thus according to official statistics the capital–labour ratio in industry doubled

---

[159] *Statisticheskii spravochnik* (1929), pp. 932–3; *Strana sovetov*, p. 255.

[160] See S. G. Wheatcroft, 'Population Dynamic', pp. 14–28, 106.

[161] *Strana sovetov*, p. 257; Wheatcroft, 'Population Dynamic', p. 15; infant mortality substantially declined in the first years after the revolution, from 273 in 1913.

[162] See *Trud v SSSR*, p. 20.

[163] Calculated from data in *Narodnoe khozyaistvo SSSR v 1958 godu: statisticheskii ezhegodnik* (Moscow, 1959), p. 541.

[164] The proportion of women in the employed (mainly urban) population rose from 24 per cent in 1928 to 39 per cent in 1940 (*Trud v SSSR*, p. 76).

[165] The comparative size of the Soviet services sector is examined, but with only a brief consideration of the inter-war period, in G. Ofer, *The Service Sector in Soviet Economic Growth: A Comparative Study* (Cambridge, Mass., 1973).

[166] For further discussion of changes in employment and investment in this period, see Wheatcroft, Davies and Cooper, 'Soviet Industrialization Reconsidered', pp. 273–7.

[167] *Promyshlennost' SSSR*, p. 68.

during this period (part of this increase was, however, a result of the more rapid expansion of the more capital-intensive industries). Estimates of the increase in labour productivity (output per person employed) depend directly on the estimate used for the increase in industrial output: according to Soviet official figures, labour productivity was 244 per cent of the 1928 level in 1937; according to an American estimate, based on a selected group of industries, it was 174–177 per cent of the 1928 level.[168] Even the lower figure implies that labour productivity increased on average by 6 per cent per annum, much more rapidly than in Britain or the United States at any time in the nineteenth century. However, labour productivity failed to increase in this period according to the most conservative Western estimate of Soviet industrial production.

Some attempts have been made to assess the share of the principal factors of production in Soviet industrial growth, and the efficiency with which they were utilized. All estimates, not surprisingly, show that both the increase in the labour force and the increase in capital stock made a major contribution to growth. Estimates of efficiency are much less reliable. According to one estimate, 'technical progress' (the residual left after capital and labour have been allowed for), or total factor productivity, accounted for between 13 and 15 per cent of all industrial growth between 1926 and 1937; almost all the increase in production attributed to technical progress occurred after 1933.[169] An alternative estimate of technical progress in 1928–40 gives an even lower figure.[170] While these results are inconclusive, it is tempting to argue that they confirm the commonsense view that substantial increases in the efficiency with which resources were used are unlikely to have occurred in a period of rapid economic change and considerable social disorder.

In agriculture, the increase in production was small, but a major change occurred in the factors responsible for that production. The annual number of days devoted to agriculture is estimated to have increased by a total of 4 per cent between 1928 and 1936–9 (average); this is mainly a result of the greater involvement of peasant women in agricultural work. But the agricultural labour force in terms of physical persons is estimated to have fallen from 71 million in 1928 to 57 million in 1937.[171] Thus far more than the natural increase in the rural population

[168] *Ibid.*, p. 56; W. Galenson, *Labor Productivity in Soviet and American Industry* (New York, 1955), p. 236.

[169] F. Seton, 'Soviet Economic Trends and Prospects – Production Functions in Soviet Industry', *The American Economic Review*, vol. LXIX (1959), pp. 1–14.

[170] L. A. Neale, 'The Production-function and Industrial Growth in the Soviet Union', unpublished Discussion Papers, CREES, University of Birmingham, Series RC/A, No. 1 (1965), p. 14.

[171] N. Nimitz, *Farm Employment in the Soviet Union, 1928–1963*, RAND Memorandum RM-4623-PR (Santa Monica, 1965), Table 1; W. W. Eason, 'Labor Force', in A. Bergson and S. Kuznets (eds.), *Economic Trends in the Soviet Union* (Cambridge, Mass., 1963), pp. 77, 88–95.

left the countryside for urban occupations. The decline in agricultural personnel was accompanied by an even more serious decline in a major item of agricultural capital: owing to the death of large numbers of horses during the collectivization drive, a major unintended consequence of Soviet policy, animal draught-power declined from 29 million hp in 1929 to 15 million in 1934, and hardly increased in the later 1930s. This loss was gradually replaced by a large inflow of tractors, combine-harvesters and lorries. Total animal and mechanical hp is estimated to have recovered to the 1929 level by 1938; mechanical power rose from 2 per cent of total hp in 1929 to 57 per cent in 1938.[172] It should be added that the increase in mechanized hp was much slower than had been planned in 1929–30. Thus the losses in animal power and the failure to achieve completely the over-optimistic plans for industry together disrupted Soviet plans for a major increase in the capital–labour ratio in agriculture, and in agricultural production.

D.   THE ECONOMIC SYSTEM: A MECHANISM FOR GROWTH

While the ambitious objectives of the industrialization drive were clearly stated by the Soviet leaders in the late 1920s, they offered no realistic programme for the provision of the immense resources which would be needed. The myth that neither the peasant nor the worker would be required to make sacrifices was sedulously propagated. All official documents, including the various versions of the first five-year plan, stipulated that both urban and rural living standards would increase even during the initial years of rapid industrialization. According to the first five-year plan, labour productivity in industry would more than double in the course of the plan; this would make it possible to increase wages and reduce costs simultaneously. The reduction in costs would be used partly to provide profits from which industry would finance its own expansion, and partly to reduce retail prices of industrial goods, so that the whole population, including the peasants, would benefit. This was a pipe-dream and a smoke-screen. At closed sessions of the party central committee Stalin referred more realistically to the 'tribute' which the state was compelled to exact from the peasantry in the interests of industrialization, while Bukharin even more realistically complained that the exaction of such 'tribute' meant the 'military–feudal exploita-

---

[172] N. Jasny, *The Socialized Agriculture of the USSR: Plans and Performance* (Stanford, 1949), p. 458. Jasny assumes that 1 animal hp = 0.75 tractor hp; according to an alternative estimate in which 1 animal hp = 0.5 tractor hp, the 1928 level of draught-power was reached by 1936 (S. G. Wheatcroft, 'The Soviet Economic Crisis of 1932: The Crisis in Agriculture', unpublished paper presented to the Annual Conference of the National Association of Soviet and East European Studies, 23–25 March 1985, pp. 9, 18).

tion of the peasantry'.[173] But even at closed party meetings Stalin did not admit that the standard of living of either peasants or workers would decline.

When the first five-year plan was approved in the spring of 1929, its assumptions about the provision of resources for industrialization had already been tacitly abandoned. The use of coercion by the state to collect grain from the peasants had replaced the market relationship in 1928 and 1929, and during the next few years the collectivization of peasant agriculture strengthened state control over agricultural output. Twenty-five million individual peasant farms were combined into 250,000 collective farms (*kolkhozy*), one or several to each village. The centres of economic and political resistance in the rural commune were destroyed. The old boundaries between the strips of peasant land were removed, and most land was pooled and worked in common. Agricultural machinery was gradually made available from several thousand state-owned Machine–Tractor Stations (MTS). The substantial proportion of *kolkhoz* output which was supplied to the collection agencies at low fixed prices was used by the state to make available a minimum amount of foodstuffs to the growing urban population; in 1930–2 grain was also exported to pay for equipment and industrial materials.

During 1928–32 inflation was permitted to develop: the wages of the expanding industrial and building labour force were partly met by increasing the flow of paper money. Prices began to rise, but the inflation was partly repressed through price control in both the producer goods and retail markets; private shops and trading agencies were taken over by the state to facilitate this. Between 1929 and 1935 a rationing system existed in the towns, with rations differentiated by social class and by occupation as during the civil war. Rations were supplemented by state sales of goods above the ration at high prices. Foodstuffs were also sold extensively by the peasants at high prices on the free market. In this way, the available supply of consumer goods and food was distributed over the old and the new urban population, and consumption per head in the towns was forced down.

Within industry, the system of physical controls which already existed during the 1920s was greatly extended. Prices were fixed, and there was no market for producer goods; instead, materials and equipment were distributed to existing factories and new building sites through a system of priorities, which enabled new key factories to be built and bottlenecks in existing industries to be widened. The plan set targets for the output of major intermediate and final products, and the physical allocation system

[173] Stalin, *Soch.*, vol. XI, p. 19 (speech of 11 July 1928), vol. XII, pp. 49–56 (speech of April 1929); these passages were first published in 1949; for Bukharin's phrase see *KPSS v rezolyutsiyakh*, vol. II, p. 558.

was designed to ensure that these were reached. These methods of obtaining forced savings through physical controls resembled both War Communism and the wartime planning controls used in capitalist economies to shift resources towards armaments and the maintenance of the armed forces. In Soviet industrialization, the 'end-product' to which resources were shifted was the producer goods industries and the maintenance of the workers employed in building and operating them: but in both the war economies and the Soviet economy of the 1930s a shift in the allocation of resources which could not easily be achieved through manipulating the market mechanism was achieved through direct controls.

This was not simply a system of physical controls. Between 1930 and 1935 several important elements were incorporated into the physical planning system so far described. First, each peasant household was permitted to work a personal plot, and to own its own cow and poultry. From 1932 onwards, after obligations to the state had been met, the separate households and the *kolkhoz* as a unit were permitted to sell their produce on the free market ('*kolkhoz* market'), on which prices were reached by supply and demand. Here an important part of all marketed foodstuffs was bought and sold. The large flow of money to the peasants through these sales compensated them for the low prices they received for their compulsory deliveries to the state. Secondly, rationing of food and consumer goods was abolished in 1935, and an attempt was made to balance supply and demand on the consumer market, as a whole and for individual goods, through fiscal measures, particularly by large increases in the 'turnover tax', which was a sales tax differentiated according to commodity. At the same time, employees continued, with some important exceptions, to remain free to change their jobs. A market for labour existed, if a very imperfect one, and wage-levels were formed partly in response to supply and demand. A corollary of this was that costs controls and profit-and-loss accounting were introduced in industry, to supplement the physical controls. Thus a money economy, with recognized market elements, coexisted with the physical planning system. Moreover, a large variety of unplanned and illegal activities between firms supplemented and made feasible the rather crude controls of the central plan, and must be considered as part of the logic of the system. Black and 'grey' markets for consumer goods emerged as a result of the widespread shortages which were prevalent throughout the 1930s.

How effective was the economic system which emerged in the 1930s as a mechanism for providing the resources for economic growth? It undoubtedly has several major achievements to its credit. It succeeded in enforcing the allocation of a very high proportion of Gross National Product to capital investment in general and to the producer goods

industries in particular. Owing to central control of the capital investment programme, advanced technology was diffused rapidly throughout the USSR in certain key industries. By planning industries on a
national scale, considerable economies of scale, including economies
from standardization of products, were also achieved. The production
drive from above successfully induced management and workers to
exert great efforts to fulfil the plan.

The unintended consequences of the system were, however, considerable, and the cost was high. Centralized administrative planning is
inherently clumsy in its effects at the point of production. If success
indicators are very detailed, initiative and innovation at the factory level
are prevented. But if they are not very detailed, factories produce what it
is easier to produce rather than what is wanted. Control of quality
through centrally determined indicators is also very difficult. And it was
already becoming apparent by the end of the 1930s that a mechanism
which brought about technological revolution from above inherently
tended to restrict, and was incapable of encouraging, technological
innovation from below, unless it was drastically modified.[174]

The sellers' market which was associated with Soviet administrative
planning reinforced these difficulties. At the same time it led to the
tendency for each industrial ministry to become a self-contained 'Empire' carrying out wasteful backward integration in order to control its
supplies. If advertising and inflated sales organizations are a high cost of
modern capitalism, inflated supplies organizations were a high cost of
Soviet central planning.

In recent discussion, fundamental questions have been raised about the
effectiveness of the collectivization of agriculture, which was a major
feature of the Soviet economic mechanism, in providing resources for
industrialization. Until recently all Western scholars assumed that agriculture was in a substantial sense the major source of the large inputs of
labour and capital into industry and the associated urban sectors of the
economy and that collectivization was the crucial mechanism by which
this was achieved. Most of the increase in urban labour certainly came
from the agricultural sector. Net rural immigration into the towns
increased rapidly, rising from 1.4 million persons in the last pre-collec-
tivization year, 1929, to a maximum of 4.1 million in 1931. Between the
censuses of 1926 and 1939, the urban population rose by 29.6 million, and

---

[174] See the striking account by Academician Kapitsa of his efforts immediately before the Second
World War to obtain development facilities for a liquid oxygen process (P. L. Kapitsa, *Teoriya,*
eksperiment, praktika (Moscow, 1966), pp. 42-4).

some 23 million of this increase was a result of net migration from rural to urban areas.[175] This huge migration was not, however, an intended consequence of Soviet policy, nor did it result directly from the economical use of labour in *kolkhozy* as compared with individual peasant households. It was rather an unintended consequence of the pressure exercised by the state on well-to-do peasants in 1928–30, the dissatisfaction of the peasants with conditions in the countryside during collectivization, and the lure of ample employment in the towns. It was thus a mechanism which emerged from the priorities of the central authorities rather than a planned strategy.

The sources of industrial capital accumulation are much more difficult to determine. The classical view that agriculture was the main source of capital for Soviet industrialization was summed up by the Russian *emigré* economist Jasny: 'even non-economists realize that collectivization of peasant farming is a means of industrialization by way of obtaining farm products from the producers without adequate pay'.[176] The increase in the compulsory delivery of grain to the state provided the most striking proof that the peasants paid 'tribute' to industrialization: in 1938–40, average annual deliveries were 30 million tons out of an average harvest of some 77 million tons, as compared with 10.7 out of 73 million tons in 1928.[177] Similarly the increased production of cotton and other products which were previously imported enabled foreign currency to be diverted to the purchase of capital equipment.

Recent work by the Soviet economic historian Barsov, using previously unpublished data, has strongly and explicitly challenged this Western view. Barsov claims that the terms of trade for agriculture did not deteriorate in 1928–32, and improved in 1933–7. While some agricultural commodities were sold to the state at low prices, others were sold on the free market at high prices, and in physical terms the increased flow of grain to the towns was accompanied by a decline in the flow of meat and dairy products: thus peasants' money incomes were higher and their supplies to the towns lower than previously believed. The higher money earnings of the peasants enabled them to buy substantial quantities of industrial consumer goods, and agriculture (mainly the Machine–Tractor Stations) received greatly increased supplies of machinery from industry at low prices: thus the flow of industrial products to the

[175] Eason, 'Labor Force', p. 74; 4.5 of the 23 million migrated to places whose status changed from rural to urban between 1926 and 1939; the total population of these areas in 1939 was 5.8 million.

[176] N. Jasny, *Soviet Industrialization, 1928–1952* (Chicago, 1961), p. 95.

[177] Calculated from M. Vyltsan, *Sovetskaya derevnya nakanune Velikoi Otechestvennoi voiny (1938–1941 gg.)* (Moscow, 1970), p. 103; *Sel'skoe khozyaistvo SSSR*, pp. 90, 196.

countryside was higher than previously believed.[178] The correct interpretation of these findings is hotly disputed. The American economist
Millar, unlike Barsov, draws the conclusion that 'economically no one
gained from collectivization, including those promoting rapid industrial
development'. The British economist Nove argues that in the circumstances of 1928–32, in which all goods were scarce, the state could not
have obtained increased supplies of grain voluntarily from the peasant
without a drastic and unacceptable increase in the price paid for grain
(this links up with the argument about terms of trade on p. 1017 above).
He also points out that food consumption in the villages declined more
drastically than in the towns, so that the peasants in some sense made a
major sacrifice for industrialization.[179] All contributors to the discussion
agree that the urban as well as the rural population suffered from the
impact of industrialization. But this is a case where rapid structural
change makes unambiguous conclusions impossible. As we have seen,
some 23 million of the 56 million people living in the towns in 1939 were
peasants who had migrated in the previous 13 years: their shift from a
peasant to an urban way of life makes it very difficult to decide whether
their standard of living rose or fell.

Whatever the outcome of this controversy, it seems clear that the
collectivization of agriculture, the prevention of autonomous working-
class activity in industry, and the subordination of the professional classes
to the will of the party together provided a framework in which, in spite
of certain major unintended and costly consequences, the economic
priorities of the party leaders were imposed on the economy. In this
process the standard of living of nearly all those peasants who remained
in the countryside, and of most workers and intellectuals, declined, and
to maintain even this lower standard of living the average number of
working members in each peasant and worker household increased
substantially. Collectivization thus formed part of a general system of
economic, social and political control which placed, in the words of
the Gosplan journal in 1929, 'a steel hoop around consumption'.[180] It

---

[178] A. Barsov, *Balans stoimostnykh obmenov mezhdu gorodom i derevnei* (Moscow, 1969), *passim*, and
'Nep i vyravnivanie ekonomicheskikh otnoshenii mezhdu gorodom i derevnei', in M. P. Kim
(ed.), *Novaya ekonomicheskaya politika: voprosy teorii i istorii* (Moscow, 1974), pp. 93–105;
Barsov's work is summarized in M. Ellman, 'Did the Agricultural Surplus Provide the
Resources for the Increase in Investment in the USSR during the First Five-Year Plan?',
Economic Journal, vol. LXXXV (1975), pp. 844–63.

[179] J. R. Millar and Alec Nove, 'A Debate on Collectivization: Was Stalin Really Necessary?',
Problems of Communism, vol. XXV (1976), pp. 49–62; see also D. Morrison, 'A Critical
Examination of A. A. Barsov's Empirical Work on the Balance of Value Exchanges between the
Town and the Country', *Soviet Studies*, vol. XXXIV (1982), pp. 570–84; and S. G. Wheatcroft
and R. W. Davies (eds.), *Materials for a Balance of the Soviet National Economy, 1928–1930*
(Cambridge, 1985), pp. 23–32.   [180] *Planovoe khozyaistvo*, no. 3, 1929, p. 283.

thus formed part, though a costly part, of the mechanism for industrialization.

E.   THE MAIN STAGES IN POLICY AND ORGANIZATION

In the course of the 1930s Soviet policy went through many vicissitudes. Five main phases may be distinguished.

(1) Until the summer of 1930 the succeeding drafts of the five-year and annual plans for economic and social development became increasingly ambitious. The climax was reached with the approval by the sixteenth party congress in July 1930 of revised five-year plan targets for major producer goods industries which were not eventually achieved until after the Second World War.

Over-ambitious plans were accompanied by even more ambitious attempts to transform the social and economic system. In October 1929, Pyatakov, former Left Opposition leader, enthusiastically declared that '*the heroic period of our socialist construction has arrived*', echoing the title of a famous Soviet book on War Communism;[181] Stalin more prosaically characterized the period as 'the expanded socialist offensive along the whole front'. In agriculture, the all-out collectivization drive brought 55 per cent of peasant households into the *kolkhozy*, at least nominally, by the beginning of March 1930, and attempts were made to socialize all peasant livestock and close down peasant markets. The expansion of the urban labour force was financed by large currency issues and, as in the days of War Communism, the prevailing view at the beginning of 1930 was that the transition to socialism, with its moneyless system of product exchange, would soon be completed. In industry, 'production communes' in which wages were earned in common by teams of workers received some official approval; and it was generally expected that workers would participate more creatively in decision-making and move towards more collective forms of production, and of life. Far-reaching plans were prepared for the construction of entirely new kinds of socialist towns in which the monogamous family would no longer exist; and the dominant group of educationalists proclaimed that schools, and all formal education, must be replaced by merging education and production for children and adults alike. Symbolically, an authoritative government commission decided that the year should be divided into 72 five-day weeks plus 5 holidays, and that the years should in future be

[181] *Torgovo-promyshlennaya gazeta*, 5 October 1929; the book was L. Kritsman, *Geroicheskii period velikoi russkoi revolyutsii* (Moscow, n.d. [?1924]).

numbered not from the birth of Christ but from the October 1917 revolution.[182]

While these optimistic programmes for social transformation were being elaborated, increasingly brutal measures of repression were used against the enemies and alleged enemies of industrialization. Collectivization was accompanied by the mass deportation of hundreds of thousands of kulak families; those heads of kulak households believed to be most dangerous were summarily executed. In the towns bourgeois engineers, economists, and other specialists were arrested and put on trial for alleged sabotage.

(2) Between the spring of 1930 and the end of 1932, the ambitious plans for social transformation were gradually abandoned. Serious unrest among the peasants in key grain areas in February 1930 led Stalin to call a halt to the collectivization drive, to the socialization of livestock, and to attempts to completely eliminate the peasant market. The relentless collectivization drive was resumed at the end of 1930, but collective farmers were now permitted to retain their own livestock and their personal plot; and from May 1932 onwards the free peasant markets (the so-called 'kolkhoz markets') were legalized. The flirtation with the moneyless economy was abandoned in the autumn of 1930 in favour of a policy of strengthening the ruble and strict financial discipline; attempts to introduce product exchange soon gave way to insistence on the importance of 'Soviet trade'. In the course of 1930 and 1931, the attempts to establish production communes in the factories were denounced in favour of providing higher wage differentials for skill and effort to individual workers, and considerable efforts were made to tighten up labour discipline. The schemes to construct socialist towns and abolish schools were abandoned in favour of a more conventional approach. No more was heard of the proposed reform of the calendar. In the spring of 1931, with their resistance broken, the pressure against the bourgeois specialists was relaxed, though never entirely removed. The outlines of the Soviet economic mechanism described on pp. 1036–7 emerged.

The over-ambitious industrial production plans approved in 1930 were not so easily discarded; while plans were not further increased, the feverish attempt to achieve the impossible continued throughout 1931 and 1932.[183] After a short moratorium on the issue of new currency between the autumn of 1930 and the middle of 1931, large currency issues were again resumed and continued till the end of 1932. While the

---

[182] *Za industrializatsiyu* (Moscow), 25 February, 1930; the chairman of the commission was Rudzutak, a member of the Politburo and deputy chairman of Sovnarkom.

[183] On the changing targets in these years, see E. Zaleski, *Planning for Economic Growth in the Soviet Union, 1918–1932* (Chapel Hill, 1971), *passim*.

industrial plans were not achieved, an unprecedented increase took place in industrial investment: gross capital investment in socialized industry more than quadrupled in the four years 1928–32.[184] Even according to Soviet official calculations, *'all the increase in the national income went to accumulation'* in 1931, and the 'consumption fund' declined.[185] In agriculture, the state continued to compel the peasants to surrender very large quantities of grain and other products, and virtually no economic inducement was offered to the collective farmer to work on the collectively cultivated *kolkhoz* land.

(3) During 1932, a grave economic crisis ensued, culminating in the famine of 1932–3. Internal economic difficulties were coupled with a serious shortage of foreign currency.[186] Confronted with these difficulties, the authorities shifted to a policy of consolidation. Much more modest production targets were set for 1933 than for any other year since the industrialization drive began; and the level of investment was reduced in absolute terms. The plan for 1933, and the draft of the second five-year plan (1933–7) compiled in that year, stressed the importance of completing the construction of factories already started during the first five-year plan, and assimilating them into production. The rate of increase in state budgetary expenditure was greatly reduced. In consequence the amount of currency in circulation actually declined in 1933.

Consolidation was combined with further repression. The exaction of grain from the peasants was pursued with particular brutality in 1932–3; many peasants starved, and others were exiled. To reduce migration from the countryside into the overcrowded towns, the tsarist internal passport system was reintroduced for urban inhabitants in December 1932; henceforth peasants could not live in towns legally without permission of the authorities (peasants remained passportless second-class citizens until the late 1970s). Further groups of specialists were put on trial.

(4) In the years 1934–6, no major change was made in Soviet economic organization; in social policy these were years of an increasing conservatism, reflected most dramatically in the abolition of legal abortion in 1936. This was a period of spectacular economic development: the factories started during the first five-year plan were brought into operation and agriculture began to recover from crisis. The gross production of all industry increased in the three years 1934–6 by 88 per cent

---

[184] See J. M. Cooper's index (in 1928 prices) in J. M. Cooper, R. W. Davies and S. G. Wheatcroft, 'Contradictions in Soviet Industrialisation' (unpublished seminar paper, 1977), Tables 1 and 2.

[185] *Materialy po balansu narodnogo khozyaistva SSSR za 1928, 1929 i 1930 gg.* (Moscow, 1932), pp. 52–4.

[186] See R. W. Davies, 'The Soviet Economic Crisis of 1931–1933', unpublished Discussion Papers, CREES, University of Birmingham, SIPS No. 4 (1976), *passim*.

according to Soviet official figures, and by nearly 80 per cent according to the estimates of the American economist Holzman.[187] Output per person in industry rose rapidly, and costs fell. The standard of living also improved very substantially, from the very low level of 1933.

Prosperity did not carry with it a fundamental relaxation of the system of repression. The assassination of Kirov, a prominent member of the Politburo, was followed by numerous arrests which included leading party members; the Zinoviev–Kamenev trial, the first major public trial of Old Bolsheviks, took place in August 1936. The danger of aggression against the Soviet Union, following the seizure of power by the Nazis in Germany in January 1933, increasingly dominated Soviet internal affairs: the Spanish civil war began in August 1936, the month of the Zinoviev–Kamenev trial, after Franco attempted to overthrow the republican government in Spain with the connivance of the Fascist powers.

(5) The remaining years before the German invasion of the Soviet Union on 22 June 1941, were a period of political purges and war preparation. The growth of industry slowed down considerably. The mass arrests of leading economic officials and industrial managers in 1936–8 and their replacement by recently trained and less experienced engineers undoubtedly harmed economic performance. The transfer of engineering and other producer goods industries to the production of armaments was also a major factor in this deceleration, especially in 1939–41.[188] The large increases in direct defence expenditure in 1937–41 had repercussions throughout the economy. Purchasing power rose much more rapidly than state and cooperative retail sales, and in consequence prices and sales on the kolkhoz market increased substantially; in 1940 and 1941 some official retail prices were also increased. Numerous austerity measures were introduced to restrict budget expenditure. Social insurance benefits were cut. Charges were introduced for crèches and kindergartens, and for tuition in the senior forms of secondary schools and in universities; all these costs were previously borne by the state budget. These measures tended to discriminate against the lower-paid and their children, and both reflected and encouraged a certain consolidation of the social structure.

X.   Soviet socialism in perspective

The dominant objective of the Bolshevik revolution and of the Soviet regime was to establish a socialist society, and all aspects of economic and

---

[187] D. R. Hodgman, *Soviet Industrial Production, 1928–1951* (Cambridge, Mass., 1954), p. 89. Hodgman's estimates refer to large-scale industry.

[188] See J. M. Cooper, 'Defence Production and the Soviet Economy, 1929–1941', unpublished Discussion Papers, CREES, University of Birmingham, SIPS No. 3 (1976), *passim*.

social policy were supposed to be directed towards achieving this object-ive. This final section reviews the extent to which this objective was achieved in the first 23 years of Soviet power, and examines the changes made in the definition of the objective.

During the first seven or eight years after 1917 the Bolsheviks con-tinued to accept the classical Marxist standpoint that the full establish-ment of a socialist society in Soviet Russia must await a proletarian revolution in one or more industrialized capitalist countries. By 1925, a new perspective had become orthodox: the construction of socialism could be successfully completed in the Soviet Union without a successful revolution elsewhere. The political power of the proletariat, supported by the peasantry, would itself create the prerequisites for socialism by carrying through an industrial and cultural revolution; throughout a long transition period, the economic foundation for peasant support would be the market relationship between individual peasant agriculture and state industry. In 1928–30, this programme of constructing a socialist economy through the market was abandoned: market relations with the peasant were replaced by so-called 'product exchange'; and the structure of agriculture was transformed through collectivization.

Throughout these vicissitudes much of the original concept of what constitutes a socialist society remained intact. Under socialism, the means of production would all be in public ownership. Socialist society would be classless: the exploitation of man by man would no longer exist. While different kinds of labour would still be remunerated unequally, on the basis of their contribution to society, the socialist economy would be a moneyless economy based on product exchange and not commodity circulation. And in a fully socialist society, the state, an instrument of class coercion, would have withered away.

When the new Soviet constitution was adopted in 1936 Stalin pro-claimed that 'in principle we have already achieved socialism, the first phase of Communism'. With the predominance in the Soviet economy of a powerful state industry, collectivized agriculture, and socialist trade, socialist ownership of the means of production had been established; capitalist relations, based on the exploitation of man by man, had been eliminated.[189] It was officially recognized that the designation of the USSR of the late 1930s as a socialist society involved several substantial modifications of the concept of socialism which prevailed until the early 1930s. First, although the means of production of the *kolkhoz*, except the land, were not owned by society as a whole but jointly by its members, it was treated as 'one of the forms of socialist economy'; the personal plot of the collective farmer was also treated, not without some backsliding, as part of the socialist economy, and trade on the free market by *kolkhozy*

---

[189] Stalin, *Soch.*, vol. I(XIV), pp. 138–46, 149–50 (report of 25 November 1936).

and their members was described as 'kolkhoz trade'. The kolkhoz was thus fully incorporated into the concept of socialism.[190] Socialist society was therefore not a classless society, but one based on the cooperation of two non-antagonistic classes, the workers and the peasants.[191] The second major modification in the original definition concerned exchange relationships in a socialist economy. Socialism was no longer a moneyless economy based on product exchange; this would come only with the higher stage of Communism; instead it was a money economy involving a socialist form of trade: 'money will still remain with us for a long time, until the completion of the first stage of Communism – the socialist stage . . . Money is an instrument of bourgeois economy which Soviet power has taken into its own hands and adapted to the interests of socialism so as to develop Soviet trade to the utmost.'[192] Thirdly, it was recognized that the state as an organ of repression would not wither away under socialism. In official Soviet doctrine, the repressive power of the state was attributed primarily to the continued capitalist encirclement of the USSR: 'the main task of our state within the country is the peaceful work of economic organization and cultural education; the cutting edge of our army, punitive agencies and intelligence services is no longer turned towards the interior of the country but to the exterior, against the external enemies'.[193]

Stalin's attribution of the role of the state in Soviet socialist society solely to the external situation was quite inadequate. The increasing concentration of political and repressive power in the USSR in the 1920s and 1930s stood in bleak contrast to the programme of liberation set out by Lenin in State and Revolution in 1917, with its famous dream that every cook would learn to govern.[194] Such an outcome was certainly not anticipated by Lenin when he insisted in 1920 that the immaturity of the Soviet working class made one-man management and the appointment of leading officials essential in the interests of efficiency. Moreover, economic and social differentiation in the Soviet Union in the 1930s were far more extensive than in the socialist society envisaged by all Marxists before 1930.

These developments proved difficult to accommodate within a Marxist framework. It was not until the end of the 1920s that any Soviet Marxists, even those in opposition, recognized, and then only half-heartedly, the autonomous power acquired by what they dubbed the

---

190 See R. W. Davies, 'The Emergence of the Soviet Economic System, 1927–1934', unpublished Discussion Papers, CREES, University of Birmingham, SIPS No. 9 (1977), pp. 6–9.
191 Stalin, Soch., vol. 1(XIV), pp. 142–6, 170 (report of 25 November 1936).
192 Ibid., vol. XIII, pp. 342–4 (report to seventeenth party congress, January 1934).
193 Ibid., vol. 1(XIV), pp. 384–95 (report to eighteenth party congress, March 1939).
194 See M. Lewin, 'The Communist Party, Yesterday and Today', in R. W. Davies (ed.), The Soviet Union (London, 1978), pp. 67–8.

'bureaucracy'.[195] During the 1930s, this power, and the social privileges associated with it, were much augmented. Marxists critical of the Soviet Union feverishly sought to find an explanation of the Soviet system in terms of socio-economic class. For Trotsky the USSR remained a 'workers' state', because the main means of production were owned by society as a whole and hence by the working class; but it was a 'workers' state with bureaucratic distortions', in which a privileged bureaucratic caste controlled the levers of power.[196] To some of Trotsky's followers, Soviet society in the 1930s seemed already to be a new variety of class society based on exploitation by a ruling class. To other Marxists the description of the leading groups in Soviet society as a caste or a class seemed forced. The system offered a very high degree of upward social mobility for millions whose parents had lived without hope in the lower depths of pre-revolutionary society. The membership of the leading groups of Soviet society was very unstable. The stratification of income was not straightforward: a skilled 'Stakhanovite' worker at the bench could earn more than a factory director. And above all Soviet society continued to be dominated by its original dynamic policies of economic expansion and social and cultural construction. Perhaps, then, when the external dangers from the aggressive fascist powers were removed, Soviet society would move closer towards its ultimate communist objectives? If this optimism proved justified, then, in spite of the primitive features in Soviet society resulting from the unfortunate circumstance that it was still dominated numerically and culturally by the peasantry, perhaps Stalin was right in describing it as a socialist society 'in principle'?[197] Developments in Soviet society between the Second World War and 1985 did not provide much favourable evidence for this optimistic assessment, but the Gorbachev period has revived hopes of a return to the principles of 1917.

To recapitulate, the Bolshevik Party, led by Lenin, seized political and economic power in an isolated, partly industrialized, but largely peasant country, and Lenin's successors subsequently augmented this power and used it in a feverish endeavour to create the economic basis for establishing socialism in the USSR, and for its military protection. In the course of these developments, by 1941 a new political, economic and social order emerged, which in part corresponded to the original concept of socialism, and in part operated by its own laws, with its own power structure, its own hierarchy of status and privilege, its own vested interests, its own ideology.

[195] See the extracts from Rakovsky's letter to Valentinov dated August 1928, in Carr, *Foundations*, vol. II, pp. 432–4.

[196] L. Trotsky, *The Revolution Betrayed: What is the Soviet Union and Where is it Going?* (New York, 1970, first published 1937), *passim*.

[197] This approach, supported by Otto Bauer, is exemplified by R. Schlesinger, *The Spirit of Post-War Russia: Soviet Ideology, 1917–1946* (London, 1947).

CHAPTER XV

Economic and social policy in Sweden, 1850–1939

I. *Introduction*

The ends and means of Swedish economic policy have changed over the years. When analysing this economic policy, however, it is difficult to determine the exact nature of these ends and means. What during one phase was an end could in others become a means. As long as the economy was tied to the gold standard, operations in the open market were a means of changing Bank Rate and controlling the money supply. And these latter can, in turn, be seen as a means of influencing investments and consumption as, for example, during the 1930s. Bank Rate and money supply, too, can be a means of influencing overall demand for commodities, thus influencing production, employment, and prices.

Clearly, too, the goals of Swedish economic policy, after having become increasingly generalized during the *laissez-faire* period, became steadily more specific. As for the means applied, these can be largely divided into two categories: on the one hand, those, like monetary, currency and financial policy, have a general effect; on the other, such specific means of intervention as regulatory measures, for example, as applied to prices and imports. During the period under consideration economic growth was not a goal of policy; nor did it become so until the 1950s. As long as Sweden was on the gold standard, the aim of policy was a fixed rate of exchange, which was regarded as means of supporting industry and the economy, and therefore as beneficial to the population as a whole. All manner of regulations and controls, reduced during the first half of the nineteenth century, were virtually abolished in the 1860s, and economic policy came to operate within a decentralized market system of private concerns and market prices. Politicians, it was assumed, should not intervene to bring about changes in relative prices, for example, by selective customs tariffs, taxes, or subsidies. This doctrine, it was felt, could legitimately be set aside in what were regarded by certain groups as crises situations in favour of more specific aims. Differences in view on the interrelationships between various economic factors gave rise to differences of opinion concerning the appropriate means to be adopted, these being based on whatever economic theory was regarded as 'correct'. Thus the means adopted cannot be explained exclusively in terms of the ends to be achieved.

The politicians' preferences and their level of ambition must also be related to changing political constellations and power distributions, as well as to the extent of the electorate's ability to act, either as a whole or as pressure groups.

A social group whose interests are affected by some change in economic policy can be in varying degrees politically aggressive and eloquent. The more the group is clearly defined and important, the more easily it will usually make its voice heard, and the greater its chances of gaining a hearing – more so if the group that is to be the loser by such a change happens to be more diffuse, or merely 'society' in general. An instance of this is the free trade issue of the 1880s. Among other things it was a struggle over differing political goals. Should Swedish farmers get more income? Or should the urban, non-agricultural population get cheaper food? Politicians, furthermore though loath to actually take any steps to bring about a change affecting certain groups (for example, greater profits for export firms), may well have accepted the idea passively.

Thus, to analyse economic policy, we must first familiarize ourselves with the socio-economic structure. Most nineteenth-century Swedes were occupied in agriculture. Questions of economic policy therefore tended rather to hinge more on agricultural problems than they were to do afterwards, when urbanization had thrust other branches of the economy into the forefront. Similarly, with the decline in the agricultural labour force and the steady growth in the numbers of industrial workers, numerical relationships between employees and employers changed. Trade unions, employers' organizations, farming cooperatives all began to become active pressure groups. The population's as well as the politicians' level of ambition also gradually changed.

II. *Economic growth and fluctuations*

It is easier to analyse economic and social policy if our period is divided into sub-periods. Since economic policy must be seen against a background of real economic changes, one condition for our analysis is that these sub-periods should have been economically fairly homogeneous.

Fluctuations in economic growth for the whole 1861–1970 period can be seen in Table 146. The two series, one for the Gross National Product by destination, and one for total consumption, are volume series per capita. During this time, the country's per capita Gross National Product grew enormously, 10 or 11 times, whilst consumption increased 8 or 9

Table 146. *Annual percentual per capita growth in Gross National Product and total consumption (volume)*

	GNP	Total consumption
1861–75	2.2 } 1.4	1.7 } 1.4
1875–90	0.8	1.1
1890–1907	2.5 } 2.0	2.2 } 1.9
1907–30	1.8	1.7
1930–51	2.6 } 2.8	2.3 } 2.4
1951–70	3.0	2.6

Source: O. Krantz and C. A. Nilsson, *Swedish National Product 1861–1970* (Lund, 1975), p. 183.

times. The latter's slower growth indicates an increase in the investment share of Gross National Product. These figures show an increase in the growth rate for the 1861–1970 period as a whole. Three 'levels' can be discerned: namely, 1861–90, 1890–1930 and 1930–70.

There were also short-term fluctuations, whose strength varied. These were at their most extreme during the period of the two world wars and the great depressions of the twenties and thirties. From the earlier part of the fifties, on the other hand, the trade cycle was comparatively weak. Short-term fluctuations were on the whole smaller for consumption than for Gross National Product, and therefore for investment.

Throughout the period the investment ratio at fixed prices grew, though not evenly. Both in the 1860s, especially the latter half, and in the early 1870s there was a very sharp rise, followed by a period up to the early 1890s when the investment ratio showed a downward trend. At about that time, however, the tide began to turn, and the period up to about the middle of the first decade of the twentieth century was characterized by a swift rise. The period following – up to the early 1930s – was a phase of slower growth. During and immediately after the First World War, however, there was again a fall, with subsequent recovery. From the beginning of the thirties up to the late forties or early fifties the rate of increase of the investment ratio is sharper, yet the period of the Second World War, too, is marked by a certain stagnation. Thereafter, during the fifties and sixties, the rise again accelerates, until, at the end of this period, it once more tends to slow down. We encounter here much the same limits for our various sub-periods as those shown in Table 146.

So far we have only considered the Gross National Product by destination, that is, quantity of goods and services, whether produced in Sweden or imported, utilized for consumption or investment. But we touch on its sources, namely, the total net output of the various sectors, either for domestic consumption or export.

Changes in the composition of total output have been found to follow a similar pattern. In all industrialized countries the agricultural share has fallen, often strikingly, and the industrial has increased. In many cases, however, the service sector's share has developed less clearly, a circumstance usually regarded as connected with the fact that this sector contains both old and retardatory branches, for example, domestic services, as well as new and expanding ones. A similar pattern has been found in the employment shares, albeit with one difference: after a certain limit has been reached, industrial growth slackens off and the service sector grows more steadily than the production share. That this pattern is by and large also characteristic of Sweden can be seen from Fig. 12. Agriculture's share of production falls, and industry's rises, notably from the early 1890s onwards. Further, the service sector's share shows no definite trend, a certain falling off perhaps being discernible during the 1930s and 1940s. But trends for employment are quite clear. In the agricultural sector there is a massive and striking drop. Equally striking is the way in which, during our period's final phase, industry, having grown more or less uninterruptedly, falls off, whilst at the same time there is a striking growth in the service sector share. These different developments for the shares of production, on the one hand, and employment, on the other, indicate crucial differences in the way in which the productivity of the three sectors developed.

The development of foreign trade in relation to production can be seen from the changes in the export ratio – the export volume expressed as a percentage of production in those sectors of the economy producing goods and services saleable on the international market: agriculture, industry, and transport. Exports in relation to the total output of these three sectors are shown in Fig. 13. The data on which this figure is based are not altogether satisfactory, one reason being that the volume calculations for the various variables have been made by different methods. Certain tendencies are nevertheless quite clear. Short-term fluctuations – in certain cases, strong ones – occurred throughout the period. Further, an overall long-term pattern can be discerned (the division into sub-periods has been made clearer by inserting the trends).

Between the 1850s and the end of the 1880s the export ratio almost doubled. Yet since Swedish exports were dominated by raw materials

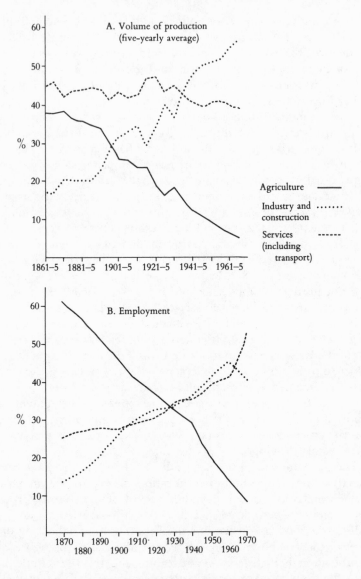

Fig. 12. Shares (by sector) of total production in Sweden, in fixed prices (A)
and of employment (B), 1861–1970
Up to 1940 only the total population is given, distributed into sectors of the
economy. Here it is assumed that the ratio employment share:population
share in 1940 is also valid for other census years.
Sources: A: O. Krantz and C. A. Nilsson, *Swedish National Product*
(Lund, 1975), Tab. 2.2.3, pp. 163ff.
B: Census data from *Historisk statistik för Sverige*, vol. 1; and *Statistisk årsbok*

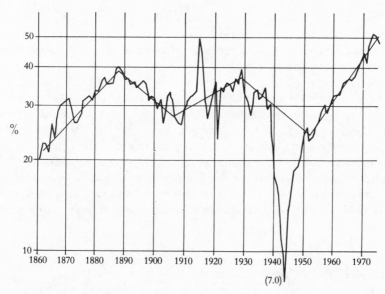

Fig. 13. Export ratio in fixed prices in Sweden (export volume in
percentage of total production volume in industry, agriculture, and
transport sectors together), 1861–1975 (base period 1908/9)
Sources: Exports, 1861–1950: G. Fridlizius, 'Sweden's Exports 1850–1960',
Economy and History, vol. VI (1963); 1950–65: L. Ohlsson, *Utrikeshandeln och
den ekonomiska tillväxten i Sverige 1871–1966* (Uppsala, 1969); *Statistisk
årsbok*; and *Konjunkturläget*.
Production volume: O. Krantz and C. A. Nilsson, *Swedish National Product*
(Lund 1975); and O. Krantz and C. A. Nilsson, 'Om strukturgränser i
svensk ekonomi 1861–1975', *Meddelande från Ekonomisk-historiska
institutionen*, Lunds universitet, no. 2 (1978).

and semi-manufactured goods, the export structure was *not* characteristic
of an industrialized country. From the end of the 1880s up to the middle
or later part of the new century's first decade the trend was downwards.
In other words, an increased share of production was going to the
domestic market. This phase saw a striking change in the composition of
exports, and a striking rise in industrial products.

In the second and third decades of the new century the export ratio
showed a steady upward trend, whilst a rising share of production
consumed domestically was characteristic of the 1930s and 1940s. The
turn of the tide can be located at the very end of the 1920s. In the early
1950s the trend again changed: the export ratio grew more swiftly than
during any earlier sub-period.

In periods with a rising export ratio there was negative import
substitution, by which is meant that a growing share of the many

industrial products consumed domestically was being imported. The opposite occurred during periods with a dwindling export ratio. That is to say, a rising ratio coincides with growing foreign competition for Sweden's industries.

For a great number of variables crucial to Sweden's economic development a fairly clear periodic pattern can be discerned. One such period limit can be set in the 1890s or around 1900, another around the year 1930. These distinguishable periods have, in various respects, the characteristic homogeneity necessary for this analysis. This does not mean, of course, that the economy was not dynamic during these years: rather, that there is some specific homogeneity in the pattern of change for any given sub-period. From this it follows that any analysis of economic and social policy must take these sub-periods strongly into account.

III.   Pre-1870

A.   POLITICAL CHANGES

In economic policy, as in other economic and social fields, the nineteenth century was a period of striking change and renewal. Socially this transformation is usually regarded as being the final collapse of the old estates society, and its replacement by modern classes. The former was a system of privileges, based on rules established and enforced by the estates of the realm, these being in their turn based on the social power structure.

Up until 1866, the Swedish parliament (Riksdag) was divided into four estates: nobility, clergy, burghers, and peasants. Since the last of these groups, constituting the majority of the population, had only one-quarter of the votes, their interests could never dominate politically. In the new two-chamber Riksdag the interests of the peasants – or more precisely, the agriculturalists – were better satisfied, since during the first two decades after 1866 they enjoyed an absolute parliamentary majority, whilst in the indirectly elected First Chamber the estate-owners held more than one-third of the total seats.

This parliamentary reform, however, had a somewhat paradoxical result. It reduced the influence of liberal and reformist groups. In the old Riksdag the nobility had felt itself under some pressure to go along with reforms, if it was to retain its privileges. Even if their reformism was often directed at aspects of society which did not affect their own privileges, many members of the old estate Riksdag had been far-sighted and radical-minded men. What they wanted was freer trade, better conditions for manufacturing industry, and a land reform policy from which they themselves, as great landowners, would also have something to gain. In cultural affairs, too, they were liberal.

The new Riksdag was more conservative; socially, it was even reactionary, particularly the Second Chamber which, as we have seen, was dominated by the peasants. But the franchise was restricted, and largely excluded the growing class of industrial workers and the agricultural proletariat. That is to say, at the very moment when Sweden was rapidly becoming industrialized, her economic policy came to be dominated by her peasantry. The middle class, too, was over-represented; legislators more or less coincided with employers or groups with similar interests. So the new and thrusting working class was worse off, politically speaking, than the peasantry had been before.

In modern class societies social groupings are chiefly determined by economic differences, that is, by differences in wealth and income. Not that economic differences had not been important in the old estates society too; yet its privileges, while contributing to economically favour the already privileged, had endowed the social grouping with a certain stability. The old society of privilege did dissolve, however, if only slowly. The commercialization of the economy, the expansion of foreign trade, the development of an industrial base prior to what has been called the industrial breakthrough during the latter half of the nineteenth century, the transformation of agriculture by technical and organizational changes, as well as the swift population growth, accelerating during the century's first half – all these factors together transformed Sweden, both socially and economically.

B. ECONOMIC POLICY

Nineteenth-century economic policy had no ambitions to stabilize the economy by political means, in the modern sense. Politics was only one stage in the process giving rise to a society where the market system was omnipotent.

1. Agricultural policy

In pre-industrial society the state had tried to protect the peasants' economy by establishing guarantees to enable them to pay their taxes, primarily in order to finance itself. Rigorous landownership regulations had been introduced to ensure that the peasantry's ability to pay taxes did not dwindle. Even so, the legal obstacles to splitting up farms into ever smaller units were circumvented, particularly at times when population growth had resulted in pressure to obtain available land. Inheritance laws, too, were designed to preserve the peasant class, land being traditionally regarded as the property not of the individual but of his family. Various legal institutions existed to protect the family's interests. So that his land should not be excessively burdened with debt, a new landowner could borrow money on favourable terms and thus buy out his co-heirs. In the upshot this restrictive agricultural policy had split the agricultural population into two social layers; on the one hand, the landowners; on the other, the landless workers and outcroppers, etc. This was a policy, however, which had been abandoned even before the abolition of the four estate Riksdag. Against the will of the peasant estate, changes, mainly in the interest of the agricultural lower classes, were forced through; reforms only possible because of the Riksdag's undemocratic composition, and which must be seen against the background of overall mid-century liberal trends.

2. Industrial policy

Other branches of the economy also liberalized. Various bans were removed, among them restrictions on the right to establish businesses and utilize raw materials, finished, or half-finished products. In the first half of the nineteenth century, for instance, there had been numerous state restrictions on Sweden's iron industry. One of the motivations of these restrictions was to prevent a shortage of timber by controlling the establishment of new concerns, to assure the ironworks an adequate supply of charcoal by regulating the charcoal trade, by imposing bans on exports of iron ore and of pig-iron to secure the necessary semi-manufactures required by the iron industry, and restricting the manufacture of pig-iron and bar iron in order to keep down charcoal consumption.

Other laws, poorly though they seem to have been obeyed, regulated the erection of new sawmills. Urban crafts had been regulated by a guild system. Rules had defined the qualifications of master and apprentice, and competition between the craftsmen of different cities had been forbidden. The whole of this system assumed a static economy. It did not aim at economic expansion. True, besides the guilds there had been so-called 'manufactories' which were not subject to guild regulations; so that, in reality, anyone could establish a new one. More expansive than the guilds, most of those branches of production which were in the van of Western European industrial developments fell within this special branch of legislation.

But the swift growth of the population, combined with economic and social change, had removed the bases for these restrictions and undermined the prevailing system. In 1846, the guilds were abolished; and in 1864 the last of these old barriers disappeared, together with all restrictions on entry into trades and professions. The gist of these new reforms was to permit the rural population to engage in any activity they liked and put an end to the old 'urban policy' which had tried to restrict all industry and commerce to the towns. If Swedish towns had developed very slowly, these restrictions may have to some extent been responsible. Up to the mid-nineteenth century only about 10 per cent of the population had lived in towns. At the same time, the regulations, as the Board of Commerce declared as late as the 1830s, had been consciously designed to prevent capitalist development.[1] Opposing this, others maintained that the population increase was threatening to create a proletariat unable to support itself, whilst the agricultural sector could not be expected to absorb an increasing share of landless population groups.

3. Commercial policy

Liberalization also occurred in the field of commercial policy. During the first decades of the nineteenth century, customs policy had been entirely protectionist. The customs regulations for 1816 list more than 300 commodities which might not be imported, as well as forbidding the export of some 50 others. The so-called Navigation Acts hindered free competition in shipping – a policy based on the assumption that there was only a fixed and given amount of international trade, and the desirability of a maximum share of it being carried in Swedish ships. To some extent the restrictions were a consequence of internal regulation, since it was not thought possible at one and the same time to permit free international competition and to govern domestic trade by regulations.

From the 1820s onwards these restrictions on shipping had been reduced by treaties with other countries. And indeed the arguments in favour of a restrictive or protectionist tariff policy, based as they were on a concern to support the population, were becoming less and less realistic. Agriculture was developing, and was well able to support the country's population. Agricultural produce, indeed, came to be one of Sweden's largest export items and agricultural interests in the Riksdag came to see less and less benefit to be gained from protective tariffs.

The effects of the Anglo-French free trade agreement of 1860 were strongly felt all over Europe, not least in Sweden. In 1865, Sweden signed a free trade agreement with France, the inclusion of a most-favoured-nation clause meaning that Sweden now had in practice adopted free trade doctrines by radically lowering her industrial tariffs and abolishing import and export bans. The only trade of any importance still to enjoy protection was textiles. The tariffs, being specific, were not influenced by price changes; this meant that they became more efficient as prices fell, and less so as they rose.

[1] H. Lindström, *Näringsfrihetens utveckling i Sverige*, vol. I: *1809–36* (Gothenberg, 1923), pp. 337–48.

4. *Monetary policy*

In the field of monetary policy, too, there were changes in a liberal direction. In the mid-nineteenth century the Riksbank was not a central bank, in the modern sense of the term. It competed with the commercial banks then appearing, and made considerable loans to the public. Loans to agriculture and industry were often subsidized by a lower rate of interest than was demanded by the commercial banks. Loans against securities and mortgages could run at 2–3 per cent, considerably under the 6 per cent interest maximum permitted by the bank's statutes right up to 1864, when this regulation was removed. These subsidized loans, however, were limited to a fixed ratio above the bank's so-called 'metal reserve'. Between 1834 and 1875 Sweden was on the silver standard; therefore a fall in the metal reserve resulted in a credit squeeze, since any rise in exchange rates caused silver to pour out of the country. This system, known as 'direct deflation', prevailed right up to the 1870s, discount policy still being virtually unknown.[2] This meant that the Riksbank's influence on credit was extremely limited. Even after 1864, when the restrictions were lifted, it still did not influence interest rates. This automatic link between domestic credit and currency reserve came to an end in the early 1870s, however, when a separate reserve for foreign currency was established, and the bank was permitted to buy foreign bonds and even take up loans abroad.

The Manufactory Discount, a state-owned industrial bank founded as early as 1756, but which reached the height of its importance in the mid-nineteenth century, enjoyed a peculiar status in Swedish industrial finance. Offering loans at a low rate of interest against securities in kind, it seems to have played an important part in financing industry, the iron and timber industries excepted, which had no rights to borrow from the bank. The bank was also prepared to take considerable risks in supporting new concerns unable to obtain ordinary bank loans. Up to the 1860s the Manufactory Discount was Sweden's leading industrial financier, whose loans for a long while amounted to more than those issued by the combined commercial banks together.

C.   SOCIAL REFORM POLICY

As we have seen, Swedish social reform policy had been more comprehensive and progressive during the decades before the parliamentary reform of 1866 than it was afterwards. In 1847, the Poor Law was reformed. In 1864, a new and more liberal penal law was introduced, and

---

[2] S. Brisman, *Sveriges Riksbank* (Stockholm, 1931), part 4, pp. 87–9.

the prison system became more humane. In 1842, universal elementary education was introduced and, in 1860, freedom of religion: a great number of restrictions which hitherto had made Sweden one of the most reactionary and doctrinaire countries in Europe then being abolished. Unmarried women became legally capable, and in 1862 extensive local self-government was reintroduced.

A retrograde step in social matters was taken in 1871 with a new Poor Law Reform Act. The rural communes, dominated by the peasants, were now allowed to decide the organization of social welfare, and the regulations which until then had permitted anyone who felt himself hard done by to appeal to the government were abrogated.[3] At the same time as the economic policy intention was to facilitate population movements into new industries and – in agriculture – from areas with a labour surplus to others where there was a shortage – the Poor Law regulations against vagrancy and its insistence on a legal place of abode, which discouraged many communes from accepting new immigrants, made it difficult for people to move from one part of the country to another.

IV.   1870–1900

A.   ECONOMIC POLICY

By about 1870 virtually all the restrictions that had existed in the earlier periods of the nineteenth century, and which had had their roots in eighteenth-century economic policy, had been abolished. Liberal doctrine had become an accepted principle, and the choice seemed justified by the swift developments during the latter part of the century. A positive effect was ascribed to the absence of state intervention; the massive transformation of Swedish society was accepted as inevitable, and the conclusion was drawn that, if Sweden had been able to profit from international economic expansion, it had above all been thanks to the removal of all these regulations.

In 1887, the prime minister formulated this principle in the Riksdag:

The state wishes to leave production *free*, and not intervene in these fields by supervising conditions for production and labour. No doubt the state has certain tasks to perform within these fields, e.g., in what concerns technical training, the supervision of security measures, and so forth. But for the state to *directly* collaborate by supporting production is, in my opinion, wholly out of the question.[4]

Yet even in the 1880s, with international economic conditions becoming less favourable, especially for agriculture, and protectionist tenden-

---

[3] A. Montgomery, *Svensk socialpolitik under 1800-talet* (Stockholm, 1934), p. 115.
[4] Olle Gellerman, *Staten och jordbruket 1867–1918* (Uppsala, 1958), p. 15.

cies beginning to develop on the continent, Swedish politicians were prepared to renounce liberal ideas, above all in commerce.

1. Monetary policy

Like Denmark and Norway, Sweden went onto the gold standard in the 1870s. This made her economic trade cycles extremely sensitive to international developments, if only because most of her trading partners were – or became – linked with gold. The system's advantages were thought to lie in the ease with which disturbances in balance of payments could be evened out by small measures and adjustments. But if international payments relations were to be modified according to the rules of the game, the central banks would have to implement an active monetary policy. The gold standard's whole manner of functioning assumed the existence of a simple connection between the quantity of money and price levels. Throughout the pre-1914 period Sweden imported considerable quantities of capital. Both the state and various private institutions, such as mortgage companies, made loans to finance domestic investments, notably to build railways. This import of capital, like the increased money supply during boom periods, contributed to keep down the interest rate, hasten economic growth by augmenting investment capacity, and ease the country's balance of payments problem. According to gold standard theory, Sweden's strained balance of payments situation should have forced her to export gold and follow a deflationary monetary policy. As we have seen, the opposite happened: capital was imported, and economic policy became expansive.

The reason why, in spite of everything, the gold standard may have functioned efficiently and given rise to no major disturbances may have been that the central banks only needed rather a small flow of gold in order to extend or reduce their economic activity. One indication of the extent to which the central banks followed the rules of the game would be a connection between gold inflow and increases in domestic money supply. No such connection has been found.[5] One reason for this may be that the mere risk of arbitrage sufficed to level out prices and interest rates between one country and another, as the obviously parallel price developments in the trading nations proves. For Sweden, this parallel can be shown to have existed even before she went on the gold standard, or even as far back as the eighteenth century.[6] In the nineteenth century, the parallel became dominant, above all in what concerned prices for agricultural products, though wholesale prices, too, responded rapidly, both

[5] D. N. McCloskey and R. J. Zeches, 'How the Gold Standard Worked 1880–1913', in J. A. Frenkel and H. G. Johnson (eds.), *The Monetary Approach to the Balance of Payments* (London, 1976).   [6] L. Jörberg, *History of Prices in Sweden 1732–1914* (Lund, 1972), vol. II.

upwards and downwards. If the gold standard seems to have functioned satisfactorily, therefore, it is not because the central banks were obeying the rules of the game, but because they were operating within a situation where the markets were clearly united by the flow of commodities, of which gold was only one. In fact, as soon as serious disturbances did occur within the system, the gold standard collapsed.

2. Commercial policy

As noted, the changed agricultural situation of the 1880s gradually caused Swedish economic policy to become protectionist. Prices fell, above all for grain, a fall which was seen as a threat to the profitability of agriculture. Today we see that this so-called agricultural crisis was to a high degree structural. Swedish farmers were switching to livestock production, and even if grain-growers found themselves in a more exposed situation than previously,[7] agricultural prices did not, as a whole, deteriorate in relation to prices for industrial products. But no general overproduction was needed for a producer to feel threatened. Supply and demand only had to get out of balance for producers to begin to worry, particularly as the commercialization of agriculture had led to a growth in investment and greater indebtedness among farmers. With industry already enjoying some degree of protection against imports, Swedish farmers felt they were being discriminated against; what they demanded was, not that import duties on industrial goods should be removed, but that other tariffs should be introduced to protect agriculture.

However, the situation was complicated by the fact that various agricultural interest groups were not, economically speaking, in one and the same position. Most small farmers, having no grain surplus to sell, had little to gain from tariffs. On the contrary; they were themselves buyers, particularly in the north, where on the whole the peasantry had to purchase their grain. To give their demands more impact, the protectionists also wanted to raise the industrial import tariffs. Everyone ought to show solidarity with everyone else, and everybody should benefit from these new import restrictions. The tariffs debate of the 1880s made politics more interesting, and polling participation at Riksdag elections rose sharply.

At the 1887 elections the protectionists won, and in the following year import tariffs were introduced for grain. Industrial tariffs, too, were raised, and again in 1892, on the expiry of Sweden's trade agreement with France. Free trade thus proved to be a brief parenthesis in Swedish

[7] Jörberg, History of Prices, ch. 18.

economic policy. Thereafter, up to the First World War, Sweden's trade policy was to bear the hallmark of her relations with Germany. As Germany became increasingly protectionist, Sweden felt herself obliged to reply with higher tariffs, so as to give herself a better bargaining position at the 1906 and 1911 negotiations.

It has been calculated that, for 1913, industrial import duties amounted to an average of between 15 per cent and 20 per cent of product value, whilst agricultural tariffs, being specific and not having been raised to keep pace with rising prices, had fallen.[8] There are also indications that Swedish farmers were unable to benefit to the full extent of the tariff: domestic production and competition were too great.[9]

Even if agricultural interests came to dominate the public debate, and Swedish farmers, to gain support, also demanded the imposition of industrial tariffs, justifying such a measure by appealing to social solidarity, the real purpose behind the introduction of these levies can hardly be said to have been an attempt to level income distribution. What was being discussed at the time, at least as much as changes in production, was the distribution of income between various branches of the economy. The goal was to lock relationships between one branch and another by means of import tariffs. Consumers, too, it was pointed out, could gain from such a policy; yet it was clearly producer interests that were mainly involved in this struggle. The state's policy was to satisfy these interests. The large group of citizens, above all small peasants and industrial workers, on whom lay the onus of paying for this producer protection, were not consulted. Most of them lacked the vote.

3. Railway policy

One of the few fields in which the state did try to some extent to plan economic development was the building of railways. Here the basic idea was that the state should lay down and operate a mainline network, after which branch lines would be built by private interests, which would have to adapt themselves to the state's norms, and thus complement – not compete with – the state railways. It was in the 1850s that these matters began to be discussed and it was stressed that, since the gain to society as a whole was a more important consideration than the railways companies' profits, the state should do the building work. Nor did government policy yield to demands for railways always to be built where the demand for transport was greatest. Railway lines were also laid through economically weak parts of the country, to whose development they were expected to contribute. The idea of railways only being a

---

[8] A. Montgomery, *Svensk tullpolitik 1816–1911* (SOU 1924:37), pp. 9, 38, 44.
[9] Jörberg, *History of Prices*, p. 319.

complement to other means of transport, notably shipping, was also abandoned. Instead, the railways were laid as the backbone of Sweden's communications.

This plan was implemented by the very people who were urging the country's liberalization. There was something pragmatic, too, about the way in which the railways were financed, the state being regarded as in a better position than private concerns to obtain advantageous foreign loans. True, as a first step the state issued domestic bonds, but since these were far from fully subscribed foreign loans became crucial, until by 1913 the state had borrowed more than 500 million crowns for railways out of a total of 900 million. After 1880, almost all these loans, earlier placed in Germany and Britain, were placed in France. Such foreign borrowings also eased the Swedish loan market for industry, and brought down interest rates. The planned development of the railways also had indirect consequences: it contributed to preventing the growth of large continental-type conurbations. The iron and sawmills industries, as well as many others, were located far out in the countryside. This may have had social advantages. Its disadvantages lay above all in the consequent high cost of the infrastructure – water, drainage, schools, hospitals, etc.

B.   SOCIAL REFORM POLICY

If industrial expansion provided the necessary conditions for improving workers' standard of living, it may also have led to a deterioration in their working conditions and to a more disciplined and demanding rate of work. Though the general rise in standard of living (measured as total per capita consumption) opened up new possibilities in the economic and social fields, the means available proved hard to mobilize. Taxation was not yet an instrument for the levelling of incomes or the political implementation of social reforms.

Up to 1910, total taxation, chiefly derived from customs and excise, tended if anything to be regressive. The 1910 fiscal reform introduced a mildly progressive annual income and wealth tax; but if indirect taxation is taken into account, total taxation tended to be proportional rather than progressive. Low taxes may have stimulated industrial expansion by preserving a lop-sided distribution of income and wealth; but they were also an obstacle to the state taking initiatives in the economic and social fields. At the same time there was, of course, a clear connection between social developments and their ever more tangible effects: urbanization, industrial fluctuations, leading to varying levels of unemployment, perhaps to greater accident risks, and to more occupational diseases.

The old guild regulations had prescribed, in detail, the time an apprentice had to serve. They had, however, little to say about the length of the working day. Nor was this fixed for the new factory industries. A normal working day seems to have been 12 hours for adults and almost as much for factory-employed children. In 1852, certain prohibitions were introduced against children working at night, and the regulations were steadily sharpened during the 1880s. Not until 1900, however, did they become subjected to effective state supervision.

The introduction of compulsory education (1842) had gradually put an end to the worst abuses of child labour, and since the workers' standard of living was rising, child labour declined even more sharply than the law demanded. In the 1890s, when the trade-union movement became a factor to reckon with, one of its first goals was to shorten working hours. These were gradually reduced, until on the eve of the First World War they stood at about 10 hours. In 1918, the 8-hour working day was introduced. But in all these developments the state had played no very tangible part. Before the nineteenth century had come to an end, preventative social policy had been dismantled and replaced by agreements between more or less equal parties in the labour market,

The Swedish state's old attitude towards its citizens had been authoritarian. Among other things it required of every individual evidence of gainful employment. Lack of employment had been regarded as evidence of having no place of abode, and this law prevailed formally right up to 1885. The aim of this old law – directed, naturally, at unpropertied groups – was to 'correct' anyone who refused to take a job by forcing him to work either for the state or for the local authorities. As industrialism made its inroads, it became more difficult to distinguish between those who were unemployed through no fault of their own and other categories of the workless. Repeated attempts were made to find a solution to this problem, but it remained unsolved.

This law clearly gave employers the upper hand, originally justifying itself in terms of mercantilist notions of a low-wage economy. But now the law became useful as a means of bringing pressure to bear in labour conflicts. The last time this happened was in 1879, when there was a widespread strike in the north Swedish sawmills district – the strikers being threatened with forced labour if they refused to return to work. Though this legislation became obsolete long before it was annulled, its history shows what huge transformations of society had occurred before it was deemed necessary to change the law.

In agrarian society unemployment had been due to population pressure and failed harvests. With the advent of industrialism its character changed. Fewer and fewer employees now belonged to their employers' household, or possessed their own plot of land. Another aim behind the legal obligation to be in gainful employment had been to reduce the costs of poor relief. As the country became industrialized and urbanized, and also more sensitive to foreign trade fluctuations, the situation changed.

Nineteenth-century economic policy shows two tendencies, to some extent successive, but also intricately linked in point of time, namely, *laissez-faire* and interventionism. The period up to the 1870s was characterized by the state authorities' attempts to get rid of the laws and regulations which had formerly regulated the country's economic life. The great exception to this trend towards reducing goverment interference in the economy was the state's involvement in railway construction. If this very important national investment was to some extent planned, it was because the state both financed the mainlines and built them, and thus obliged private railway companies to adapt. Another state activity which flouted *laissez-faire* doctrine was the introduction, in 1842, of compulsory schooling. Although implemented by central regulations, this measure was mostly financed by local government.

The 1870–1900 period saw a certain reaction to the once-so-popular *laissez-faire* doctrine, even though groups which stood to benefit by it continued to invoke it wherever suitable, notably in what concerned tariffs. One reason given for the reintroduction of tariffs was that the German tariff system obliged Sweden to protect herself in the same way in order to be in a position to negotiate more favourable conditions for her exports. The so-called agricultural crisis of the 1880s, which brought grain prices, more especially, under pressure, provided a further protectionist argument.

Industrial expansion also gave rise to social problems for which the state felt it should assume responsibility. The 1871 Poor Law was a good deal more severe than the earlier more liberal legislation, and reduced the rights of the needy. Various laws were introduced in the 1870s and 1880s to regulate child labour and job safety in industry. About unemployment on the other hand, the state, committed as it was to remain neutral on the labour market, felt it could do nothing. One reason why unemployment was not even regarded as a major problem – apart from the notion that all unemployment was self-imposed – was emigration. In the latter part of the nineteenth century hundreds of thousands of Swedes had left the country and this, so it was thought, helped to reduce unemployment. In the end, such vast numbers emigrated, however, that the authorities took fright, and tried to reduce emigration by various measures, one being subsidies for the cultivation of virgin soil. A major commission was appointed, whose labours resulted in a great number of volumes about the Swedish economy and demography which have afterwards been of great value to economic historians. But in the upshot the measures it proposed for reducing such emigration never had to be implemented, as the numbers of emigrants began to fall off anyway.

These changed attitudes, and the measures taken during this period to give effect to them, mirror a changed view of poverty and economic insecurity. From having regarded the poor as a threat to state and local government finances – indeed, as a danger to established society – other attitudes began to dominate as the century drew to a close. The best means of improving the economic circumstances of the individual were now seen to lie in positive supportive measures, no longer by state coercion.

In 1909, universal male suffrage was introduced, and the fierce struggles around this reform may also have done something to awaken the authorities to social reform as a means of abating revolutionary tendencies among the working class. The reform of the franchise made the Social Democratic Party a power factor in Swedish politics, thus putting an end to the domination of the old political constellations in the Riksdag. A new force appeared. It was to provide a counterpoise to the former agrarian and middle-class interests and set its stamp on Swedish politics throughout the next period.

V.   1900–30

A.   POLITICAL CHANGES

It was during this period that the modern party system established itself, the franchise was extended to become universal, and full parliamentary government achieved. Earlier, political groupings in the Riksdag had appeared as more or less firmly organized parliamentary parties. Not until the beginning of the present century, however, did national parties with complete political programmes and organized methods for agitating for their views come into existence.

In 1902, The Frisinnaade Landsföreningen, a national liberal organization, was formed; and in 1904 the Allmänna Valmansförbundet, the Conservatives' national organization. Unlike the Social Democratic Party, both of these organizations attached themselves to existing parliamentary parties. The Social Democratic Party was formed in the 1880s, and by 1896, when its first representative (elected on a liberal vote) took his seat, it had become a fully organized national party. Not until 1906 was a Social Democratic parliamentary group constituted; and not until the 1909 franchise reform, which as mentioned gave the vote to all men, did the party become a big one.

Already a parliamentary party existed to represent farmers, and now it, together with other groups, began to support Conservatives' national organization. But gradually it came to be felt that agriculture needed its own nationally organized party to represent its interests, and during the century's second decade two such parties came into existence. After a few years they merged into one, the Bondeförbundet (Farmers' Party). In 1917, a left-wing faction broke away from the Social Democrats and formed its own party. Known after a while as the Communist Party, it has always remained very small. Since that break there have been no major changes in the party pattern.

Sweden's political parties fell into a 'bourgeois' or non-socialist group – Liberals, Conservatives, and Farmers – and a socialist group, dominated by the Social Democrats. The former, however, have never been homogeneous in their views, and especially during the century's first two decades were clearly opposed on basic general issues. The Liberals' aim was universal equal franchise, instead of the existing kind, graded by income. They were also in favour of pure parliamentary government. The Conservatives opposed this.

The great economic changes, notably from the latter part of the nineteenth century onwards, brought into existence new groups of electors, whose sympathies were for the most part clearly liberal. This led to a growth, both absolute and relative, in the size of the Liberal Party. The Social Democrats, too, increased their share of the electorate, and for the same reasons. If their share grew more slowly, it was chiefly because of the income limit, which was in force up to 1909. On major constitutional questions, however, these two parties were largely in agreement.

Because of the changed composition of the electorate the Conservatives' resistance to demands for democracy – a struggle which often allied them with the throne, whose power would have vanished if the parliamentarians had prevailed – gradually became a rearguard action. Although forced to make concessions, it was not until the difficult economic situation which arose towards the end of the century's second decade that the Conservatives were routed. In 1918, universal and equal suffrage was introduced in both national and local elections.

Politically, this reform largely removed the basis for further collaboration between Liberals and Social Democrats. Instead, after the shift in the political system, the 1920s saw a certain rapprochement between Liberals and Conservatives, the latter having swiftly accepted the new situation. The kind of conservatism which had idealized the conditions prevailing in the pre-capitalist era vanished swiftly as a political power factor, and was replaced by a Conservative Party that was strongly linked with major finance, and in whose fundamental views economic liberalism was a crucial ingredient.

Though this rallying of Liberals and Conservatives did not lead them to form any coalition government during the 1920s, they did form a common front against the Social Democrats, who had gained enormously in strength as a result of the franchise reform. However, they were not, in the twenties, strong enough to come anywhere near achieving a parliamentary majority. Neither, on the other hand, could the non-socialist parties achieve a stable majority at that time. Sweden's first decade of purely parliamentary government was therefore also an era of parliamentary weakness. In the absence of strong majorities there was a series of minority cabinets: between 1920 and 1932 no fewer than eight – three Social Democrat, two Conservative, two Liberal, and one caretaker ministry. Since these supported themselves on 'floating majorities', questions were often settled within the parliamentary commissions only after protracted negotiations.

Generally speaking, the 1900–30 period can be described as one in which non-socialist ideas, and thus economic liberalism, still had the upper hand. Nor is this overall picture affected by the few short-lived Social Democratic governments which, during the 1920s, were unable to implement any socialist policies. Virtually throughout the whole period, indeed, politics were dominated by other than economic questions. It is symptomatic that, with certain characteristic exceptions, the economy remained, in true liberal spirit, undisturbed by political measures.

B.   ECONOMIC POLICY

As during the previous period, economic policy between 1900 and 1930 bore the hallmark of the gold standard. Admittedly, it was suspended during the First World War and the years immediately following. Yet if gold, with the possible exception of the actual war years, played such a leading role both economically and politically, it was because of the discussion concerning, and the measures taken for, its reintroduction. This occurred formally in 1924. Gold being so central during this period, economic policy was dominated by monetary policy. In accordance with the prevailing doctrine and the rules of the gold standard, almost no financial policy was possible.

1. *Pre-war policies*

This hegemony of the gold standard, demanding as it did a rather passive economic policy, set a low level of ambition. As earlier, stabilization measures were sharply restricted to currency matters, the most important weapon being Bank Rate policy.

According to the accepted theory, Bank Rate had to be regulated according to the note reserve at the Riksbank, which constituted the difference between the Bank's note-issuing privilege and its gold reserve. In a situation where, for instance, note circulation rose or the gold reserve fell, it was for the Riksbank to raise Bank Rate; in other words, to

Table 147. *Net balance on current account in crowns and in per cent of Gross National Product, 1871–1910 (current prices)*

	Deficit, million crowns	Percentage of GNP
1871–5	20.0	1.6
1876–80	36.2	2.7
1881–5	63.6	4.5
1886–90	59.2	4.2
1891–5	14.4	0.9
1896–1900	39.2	1.9
1901–5	80.6	3.3
1906–10	71.0	2.2

Sources: Balance on current account: L. Ohlsson, *Utrikeshandeln och den ekonomiska tillväxten i Sverige 1871–1966* (Uppsala, 1969), Tab. B:1, pp. 123ff.
Gross National Product: O. Krantz and C. A. Nilsson, *Swedish National Product 1861–1970* (Lund, 1975), Kap 8, tab. 1.

implement a restrictive policy of deflation. This made Bank Rate dependent on the balance of payments situation.

Even so it must be emphasized that the Riksbank had been in no position fully to control monetary policy until around the turn of the century. Not until 1903 did it have an exclusive right to issue notes. Sharing this right with the private banks, it had been unable to fill all the functions of a central bank in the modern sense.

In the previous period, as already seen, policy had not entirely accorded with the model. Rather, it had been a period of easy, expansive monetary policy and capital imports. The new century's first decade, too, saw considerable imports of capital, and thus a deficit in the balance on current account. As can be seen from Table 147, these deficits were larger, absolutely speaking, than they had been at any time during the previous period. But since foreign trade and production were both growing, their relative extent was somewhat different.

Expressed as a percentage of Gross National Product, these deficits grew during the 1870s, reaching their peak values during the 1880s, and thereafter fell. Afterwards, during the 1900–10 period, they were relatively greater than during the 1890s, though considerably smaller than in the 1880s, when capital imports had been at their maximum. For the 1871–1900 period as a whole the deficits, expressed as a percentage of Gross National Product, averaged about the same as during the 1901–10 period.

Monetary policy during the new century's first decade can best be described as expansive. Up to 1913, apart from the years around the turn of the century and the two years 1907 and 1908, Bank Rate was under or

Fig. 14. Balance on current account and average Bank Rate in Sweden,
1900–31
Sources: L. Ohlsson, *Utrikeshandeln och den ekonomiska tillväxten i Sverige
1871–1966* (Uppsala, 1969), Tab B:1, pp. 123ff.; *Statistisk årsbok.*

around 5 per cent, as can be seen in Fig. 14. There seems to be no
covariation with the net balance of payments. Instead, the curve for
changes in Bank Rate reveal the clear influence of the trade cycle during
the period's first decade. After 1912, international political disturbances
began to affect developments.

2. *The war years*

The system functioned more or less without friction up to the First
World War, but then it was subjected to such stresses and strains that it
quickly collapsed. Most countries suspended the gold standard. The
period was characterized by major price rises and altered exchange rates.

Immediately upon the declaration of war, Sweden went off the gold
standard, and the crown devalued against the dollar and sterling. But
very soon there was a swing in the opposite direction, and the crown

began to rise. For a short while the gold standard was reintroduced; but soon afterwards gold was blocked, and likewise the public's right to demand minting of gold. For a couple of years this caused an appreciation of the crown, whose value in relation to the old parities, even though prices seem to have risen more in Sweden than they did in the major Western countries, was the highest in the world.[10] This appreciation, however, did not prevent massive export surpluses, one reason for these being that other countries were urgently demanding Swedish goods at a time when there was very little for them to export in exchange.

All this enabled Sweden to repay large parts of her earlier borrowings in inflated currency. Seen only from this point of view this was an extraordinarily advantageous development. Seen from others – the commodities available, high cost of living and falling real wages – the situation for the nation as a whole was far from favourable.

3. The post-war years

As transpires from Fig. 14, Sweden's balance of current account showed massive surpluses for the years 1919–20. Therefore the demand for foreign currency, above all for dollars, was extremely high. As for sterling, the crown depreciated heavily against the dollar. The dollar reached its highest quotation in early 1920, when the crown had sunk to 65 per cent of its old gold value. Even so, the crown held its own better than did most European currencies.[11] Towards the end of 1920 it began to rise against the dollar, and in the course of 1922 again more or less reached par. Not until 1 April 1924, however, did Sweden formally return to the gold standard.

During the rest of the 1920s the currency system, as far as Sweden was concerned, functioned fairly smoothly, as it had in the pre-war period. From the end of the war up to 1922 Bank Rate had been high (see Fig. 14). This was due, first, to the inflationary development which had increased the need for cash and, later, to the deflationary policy whose goal was a return to gold at pre-war parity. Further, as we have seen, Sweden had a large balance on current account deficit, but upon this being liquidated and the crown again reaching pre-war parity it became possible to reduce Bank Rate.

This eased the credit market, and from this point onwards it is possible to trace a covariation between balance on current account and Bank Rate, the latter showing a tendency to fall as the former rose. Symptomatic of this is that when, in 1928, the situation deteriorated, Bank Rate went up,

[10] A. Östlind, *Svensk samhällsekonomi 1914–1922. Med särskild hänsyn till industri, banker och penningväsen* (Stockholm, 1945), pp. 23ff.

[11] *Ibid*, pp. 309ff.

though this is not discernible in the average rate. In 1929, however, at the same time as Britain put up her Bank Rate, even the average rate rose.

In 1931, Sweden began to be seriously affected by the depression then sweeping the world. The banks began to call in their overseas assets, and exchange rates came under pressure. There was a negative balance on current account, and foreign loans became unobtainable. By clinging to the gold standard Sweden had obliged herself to put a sharp brake on credits, deflate heavily, and suffer massive unemployment. This was why, one week after England had suspended the gold standard (in September 1931), Sweden too abandoned it.

4. Return to gold in the early 1920s

The gold standard period was not an era of stable prices; nor indeed were they one of the system's conditions. Taking a long-term view, prices cannot be said to have changed very greatly, certainly not in comparison with what happened in the 1940s and afterwards. During 1875/9–1891/3 the price index for total consumption had fallen by 0.8 per cent per annum, and between the mid-1890s and the early part of the new century's second decade it had risen by 1.7 per cent per annum.[12]

Against this background the 25 per cent annual changes for the 1914–18 period seemed unacceptable; and upon the rise continuing – by 18 per cent in 1919 – it is not surprising if, in retrospect, the pre-war situation should have come to seem a highly desirable state of affairs. Further, the crown, as we have seen, had depreciated against the dollar, a currency which had retained its gold parity.

Monetary policy became a topic of very lively discussion and a strong body of opinion grew up which desired the crown's return to its pre-war gold parity. With few exceptions economists were in favour of deflation – a policy theoretically justified by Gustav Cassel, (see p. 1091) whose theory of purchasing power parity hinged upon the connection between a currency's external and its internal values, between its rate of exchange, on the one hand, and the country's price level, on the other.

That this policy seemed to have so much to recommend it was due, one could say, to a longing to return to a stable state of affairs, of which the pre-war period was the ideal. But these were not the reasons put forward. The commonest argument seems to have been the one based on 'honesty'. It was pointed out that inflation had brought about a massive redistribution of the country's resources, that some individuals had made undeserved profits, whilst others had suffered losses, and that only a policy of deflation would set all this to rights. The extremist among

---

[12] O. Krantz and C. A. Nilsson, *Swedish National Product 1861–1970* (Lund, 1975).

economists was Knut Wicksell, who favoured a complete return to the 1914 price level, an idea which, however, did not gain much acceptance among his colleagues.

If economists were so strongly in favour of deflation it was because they were thinking in terms of static neo-classical theory, a theory which assumed among other things that the economy must be able to adapt smoothly to changing conditions.[13] The notion that deflation could be carried out without excessive sacrifices was rooted in this idea.

Most politicians took the same line as the economists. Only certain Conservative Members of Parliament uttered warnings. As we have seen, the Conservatives had abandoned a 'pre-capitalist' for a 'capitalist' conservatism, the interests they represented largely coinciding with those of industrialists and businessmen. Their representatives, too – for example, the well-known financier Ivar Kreuger – warned against a deflationary policy. One reason they gave was that, with the trade unions now so powerful, wages could only be lowered gradually. Crucial to businessmen was that production, employment, and profits would all be maintained. The gold standard was less important.[14] But their opposition to a deflationary policy made no headway. A compact majority of politicians and economists were in favour of it.

The Social Democrats' attitude toward economic policy during the beginning of the 1920s is of interest, since it is connected with an issue much discussed in Swedish economic history, namely, unemployment policy. Were the Social Democrats' policies during the 1920s mostly passive, thereafter to become intensely active in the 1930s? Or can some continuity be discerned? In the thirties, unemployment policy became expansionist; and it was a Social Democratic government which introduced it. Was this something new for the party? Or can ideas of applying an activist policy be traced further back in the party's history? And if the latter be the case, then why did the Social Democrats not apply – or at least agitate for – such a policy in the twenties?

They, too, supported deflation and a return to pre-war gold parity. Indeed, the crucial decisions to do this were taken during the first purely Social Democratic government period. From this it would seem to follow that, in all crucial respects, the Social Democrats also accepted the neo-classical viewpoint, whose desideratum was a situation with largely built-in self-regulating economic mechanisms. This in the current situation, with the crown depreciated *vis-à-vis* the dollar (thus also gold), meant lowering production costs, including wages, in order to be able to compete internationally after appreciation. The neo-classical theorists' view of unemployment was largely similar here. Since it was excessively

[13] Östlind, *Svensk samhällsekonomi*, p. 365.   [14] *Ibid.*, pp. 364ff. and 380.

high wages that caused unemployment, the remedy was clear: lower wages. That the Social Democrats accepted such a viewpoint without jibbing is, however, unlikely.

Their alternative could have been to recommend that gold parity be adapted to the *de facto* currency market. Production costs would then not have had to be lowered, nor, consequently, would there have been any need to depress wages. In this way the idea need never have arisen that the Social Democrats accepted lower wages as the only cure for unemployment. This brings us to ask why they did, in fact, accept a return to earlier gold parity.

The following factors were probably decisive. Before 1914, real wages had been rising, but during the war years and the years immediately following wages had failed to keep pace with rising prices. This caused people to associate inflation with a fall in real wages, whence it was a short step to associate a *rise* in real wages with deflation. Probably the eight-hour working day, introduced in 1919 on condition that there should be no reduction in real wages – as indeed there was not; in fact, hourly earning rose – here played an important part. The Social Democrats perfectly understood that this reform would aggravate Swedish industry's cost situation; and a reduction in nominal wages and prices, and therewith a retention of real wage levels, should not have been difficult for them to accept.

A third factor was the party's attitude to foreign trade. Traditionally, the Social Democrats had been in favour of free trade, even if the party had to relinquish some part of this demand in connection with the introduction of the eight-hour day. If it favoured free trade, it was in order to keep down prices of commodities that loomed large in the working-class family budget. But free trade requires that one's own competitive position *vis-à-vis* foreign producers – and therewith one's own production costs – should also be taken into account.

Finally, we should note the party's attitude to unemployment. Immediately after the war unemployment, in comparison with the pre-war period, was not particularly high (see p. 1077). The Social Democrats seem to have regarded the low level as mainly due to the trade cycle. Admittedly, there were individuals in the party who were not unaware of the unemployment problems that would follow in the wake of deflation; but these troubles were regarded as small compared with the long-term gains to be expected from stable prices and currency. What could *not* have reasonably been foreseen was that, in the years following, the problems of unemployment would become massive, not merely as a result of domestic deflation but above all as a result of the downward trend in the international trade cycle.

In a word, the Social Democratic Party thought the gains to the working class from a return to gold at pre-war parity would more than outweigh other drawbacks which they regarded as merely temporary.

C.   SOCIAL REFORM POLICY

In contrast to economic policy, where the level of ambition was low, social reform during part of this period became rather prominent. Like the Social Democrats, the Liberals were in favour of reforms; nor were the Conservatives opposed to them.

The background to all this reformist activity was the swift industrialization which had taken place in the 1890s and after. On the one hand, this had drawn attention to problems arising from sickness, poverty, accidents, etc., and therewith to the need for social reforms; and on the other, to the labour–capital antagonism, which emerged more sharply than before – and found expression partly in the workers' struggle for the right to form unions and to strike, etc., and partly in the unemployment problems which arose as the chances of earning a living in this new industrial society became more uncertain.

Reform seems to have had various motivations. The Liberals were essentially philanthropic: a general demand for justice and equality. The Social Democrats, of course, called for reforms that would secure working-class interests, seeing them as part and parcel of a fundamental transformation of society in the direction of socialism. Finally, the Conservatives had been influenced by the social conservatism of Bismarck's Germany. They regarded the working-class movement as a threat, best staved off by reform.

1. *Unemployment policy*

In principle, at least, unemployment policy seems to have been the most important field for reform. Much attention was devoted to it, particularly in the 1920s, when there was a sharp parting of the ideological ways.

As already seen, industrial production and its share both of total production and of total employment rose sharply from the 1890s onwards. Therefore this expansive sector and those parts of the economy associated with it were demanding more and more labour. But with productivity rising, this increased demand was naturally not so great as the growth in output. Output per working hour rose more sharply during this period than it had done either in the pre-1890 period or was afterwards to do in the 1930s and 1940s. In the 1920s the rise was not least precipitous. Partly this was due to rationalization and partly to the greater efficiency accruing from the introduction of the eight-hour working day, in 1919.

Table 148. *Average annual increase
in the total population of Sweden and
in the age-group 15–64, 1890–1950*

	a Total	b Ages 15–64	$\frac{b}{a}$
1890–1900	35,146	21,637	0.62
1900–10	38,596	26,488	0.69
1910–20	37,552	35,365	0.94
1920–30	23,028	35,687	1.55
1930–40	22,726	40,508	1.78
1940–50	63,174	19,673	0.31

Source: *Historisk statistik för Sverige*, Del 1,
Befolkning (Stockholm, 1969).

At the same time changes occurred in the labour supply. Here we note
only two. One of these has to do with changes in the agrarian sector,
whose productivity development, combined with a shortage of outlets
for expansion, reduced the need for labour. As already seen, one expression of this was that between 1890 and 1930, the agricultural share of
employment fell by about 22 percentage points, 13 of these falling in the
1890–1910 period.

Since the last phase of the nineteenth century, markets for Swedish
agriculture had been largely domestic. This prevented any appreciable
rise in production over and above what was motivated by population
growth and rising incomes. But income elasticity for agricultural products is low, albeit in different degrees for different commodities; and
this is why redistribution effects within production probably outweighed the growth of total production.

Notwithstanding a certain amount of protection from tariffs, foreign
competition, together with a strong internal competition, was constantly putting pressure on prices. Means of countering it were found in
rationalization and higher productivity, thus releasing labour for other
sectors of the economy.

The second element in the altered supply situation is connected with
changes in the population's age distribution. Some data concerning this
can be seen in Table 148. From the beginning of the century there had
been a sharp rise in active population – that is, generally speaking, those
aged 15–64 – a rise both absolute and relative. It reached its peak in the
1930s, to fall swiftly again the next decade. For the 1900–40 period this
meant that, whilst for every individual of working age there were fewer
and fewer children and old people to support, the labour market came

Fig. 15. Percentage of unemployment in Sweden, 1911–75
Note: The series have been linked 1956 and 1971. The data being of
different kinds, the long series is obviously not wholly consistent.
Sources: 1911–56: Number of unemployed in percentage of number of trade
unions' reported membership, according to *Statistik årsbok.*
1956–71: Number of unemployed in percentage of unemployment relief
funds, according to *Statistisk årsbok.*
1971–5: Number of unemployed according to the Labour Force Surveys
published in *Statistiska Meddelanden,* various numbers.

under pressure. More and more people were competing for the available
jobs.

These trends led to changes in the relationship between demand and
supply for labour, and therewith to changes in unemployment, as can be
seen in Fig. 15. The unemployment figures, comprising as they do only
the figures for industrial trade unions, are probably too high.[15] But in all
probability they give a clear enough picture of the variations.

Up to and including the year 1920, the figures are rather low; but with
the crisis of the twenties they rise swiftly to reach a level of around 25 per
cent. This crisis once overcome, they remain at around 10–12 per cent for
the rest of the twenties, considerably above pre-war level. The depression of the thirties caused them to rise again, this time to over 20 per cent.
Thereafter they show a downwards trend; but not until the mid-forties
do they fall below 5 per cent, thereafter to fall steadily to the low levels of
the fifties and sixties.

[15] E. Lundberg, *Instability and Economic Growth* (New Haven, 1968), p. 31.

It is customary to distinguish between various types of unemployment. Turnover unemployment, also called frictional unemployment, is due to a lack of new jobs easily available when short-term jobs, for example, housing construction, come to an end – a type seemingly more or less inevitable in all economies. So, to some extent, is seasonal unemployment, which is due to certain jobs being impossible, or anyway not customary, on a year-round basis. The third type is the unemployment which arises during downward turns of the trade cycle.[16]

The existence of these three types of unemployment is recognized by most theoretical schools, including the neo-classical, which has Say's law as a basic element. This theoretical view was dominant up to the Keynesian revolution of the 1930s.

According to the neo-classical economists, the rise in unemployment at the trough of the trade cycle was to be explained in terms of lack of equilibrium in the labour market, that is, to a situation dominated neither by over- nor underemployment. Instead, the price of labour, i.e., wages, was said to be too high. If wages were lowered, so the theory went, more people would find employment, and unemployment would come to an end. Trade-cycle unemployment, that is to say, could be seen as a result of sluggish price adaptation within the economy.

Another type of unemployment, which could not reasonably be recognized by the neo-classical economists, was so-called 'permanent unemployment'. This type can, however, be perceived in a Keynesian perspective. According to Keynes, there were situations in which equilibrium could be reached but without full employment ensuing. Nor need there be any mechanisms within the economy itself capable of putting an end to this kind of unemployment. Not until the end of the 1920s did it become a topic of debate. If the concept of permanent unemployment had previously been used in the Swedish discussion of these matters, it had been as a name for what might be called the 'structural' kind.

There are two kinds of measure which can be applied in periods of unemployment: on the one hand, cash support to the unemployed; on the other, public works. The latter can in turn be divided into three categories.[17] The first of these is 'charitable' works, on the whole identical with poor relief, but where the provision of work takes the place of cash assistance. In Sweden this was the category that became dominant during the 1920s. The work to be done fell outside the framework of regular state investments, and should be adapted, so it was

---

[16] A modern explanation of unemployment is that there is no homogenous labour market; instead it is divided up into sub-markets; and one of its effects is problems of information.

[17] K. G. Landgren, *Den 'nya ekonomin' i Sverige* (Uppsala, 1960), pp. 56ff.

thought, to the labour market's ordinary demand for labour.

The second category is 'redistribution' works, that is, the kind of work normally carried out by the state and by the local authorities, though timed as far as possible to coincide with troughs in the trade cycle.

A third category is expansionist measures: works which can be carried on both in booms and recessions. Such works are motivated by the theoretical view that, though there can be a state of equilibrium without full employment, political measures must be taken in order to break down this state of equilibrium. In other words, such works are theoretically motivated by a Keynesian multiplier reasoning. It is likely that expansionistic works were not argued for before the late 1920s; or anyway, if they were, their supporters would have found themselves involved in mutliplier-like motivations, that is, a Keynesian line of reasoning.

Earlier, it had been the first two categories that had been in question; namely, the charitable and the redistributive. When people, a decade or so before the First World War, had begun to become aware of unemployment as a problem, it was mainly redistributive works they had discussed. And it had been chiefly the Social Democrats who had urged their implementation – a demand which can be traced back to the end of the previous century.

At first, the Social Democrats saw emergency works as primarily the corner of local government. The party's first local government programme (1905) had included a demand that such works should be set in motion, and the demand was repeated in the revised programmes for 1908 and 1911. According to the Social Democratic programme, it was the duty of the communes (municipalities or local government districts) to plan works aimed at reducing unemployment. In times of crisis, every measure should be resorted to that could provide jobs. This, it was claimed, would not damage the general conditions of work (nor, of course, wages) obtaining in society at large.[18]

As industrialism progressed and unemployment became an ever more obvious element in trade recessions, the state, too, began to interest itself in this question. In 1906, for instance, it decided to contribute to the cost of local labour exchanges and on several occasions thereafter made contributions to anti-unemployment measures.

In 1910, the Social Democrats, who were keen that the state should implement measures, introduced a bill to set up a commission to enquire into job redistribution possibilities. Though supported by the Liberals, the bill was rejected. Again, in 1912, there was a Social Democrat motion

[18] J. Lindhagen, *Socialdemokratins program, part 1, 1890–1930* (Karlskrona, 1972), p. 178.

on this subject. On the one hand, it proposed that the state redistribute its works in such a fashion as to counteract unemployment, on the other, that special works be put in hand to counter unemployment due to the flight of labour from certain branches of the economy, notably agriculture. The bill called this latter type of unemployment 'permanent', an expression seemingly having nothing to do with any Keynesian definition of the concept. What the Social Democrats, who had been influenced by the British Minority Report (to the Poor Law Commission, 1909), were referring to in using it – not only here, but also in other sections of their bill – was an imbalance due to certain branches' sluggishness in absorbing the labour made available by others, that is, what was really in question was structural unemployment.

This 1912 bill has been much discussed. According to one view, it is here we find the earliest roots of the Social Demoratic policy of the early 1930s.[19] That is to say (see pp. 1098–100), it sprang more or less directly from an old Social Democratic tradition of ideas. To this it has been objected that the 1912 bill's ideas refer only to redistributive works; there is no idea of a multiplier factor.[20] As we have seen above, the latter view seems the more reasonable. Yet it could be asserted that the Social Democrats' fundamental attitude towards public works, as expressed in their local government programme and parliamentary bills, must have exerted a good deal of influence on their new policy of the 1930s, even if only by making the party receptive to expansionist ideas. This time the Riksdag, though it accepted the bill's demand for a commission on redistributive works, rejected the demand for extra works designed to reduce permanent unemployment.

Then came 1914 and a swift change in the whole situation. The outbreak of war led to a disturbed labour market, to a fall in output, to attempts to depress wages, and so forth. Among the several commissions then appointed was the Unemployment Commission, (Arbetslöshetskommissionen). Initially intended to be only consultative, its powers were subsequently extended.

The war once over, the various wartime organs were dismantled. So should the Unemployment Commission have been, too. But the massive unemployment which began to make itself felt in 1920 made it a permanency. It survived for two decades. Indeed, during the 1920s the commission came to acquire a status unique among Swedish organizations and commissions, and enjoyed an autonomy and a power capable of overthrowing cabinets. During the 1920s two Social Democratic

[19] O. Steiger, *Studien zur Entstehung der Neuen Wirtschaftslehre in Schweden* (Berlin, 1971); and O. Steiger, 'Bakgrunden till 30-talets socialdemokratiska krispolitik', *Arkiv*, no. 1 (1972).
[20] K. G. Landgren, 'Socialdemokratisk krispolitik och engelsk liberalism – ett genmäle till Otto Steiger', *Arkiv*, no. 2 (1972).

governments had to resign after being voted down in the Riksdag on matters touching directives to the Unemployment Commission. Obviously, however, such a powerful position could not have been reached unless the commission had been backed up by a political majority.

At first there was nothing controversial about its activities. Its unemployment policies took the form either of cash support or providing jobs on emergency or – as they later came to be called – 'reserve' works. These were to be paid for at market wages, usually (since the works were of that nature) equivalent to an unskilled labourer's. But in 1922 the principles were altered; and the works took on a notably charitable quality, with sub-market wage levels.

This crisis of the 1920s led to a rapid expansion in the commission's activities. Some very incomplete data for 1921 indicate a sharp rise in the number of persons applying to the commission for jobs during that year, the top level being higher than the average for 1922. But the commission's distribution of social benefits was less extensive. Data for 1922–38 can be seen in Table 149. They show that it was already during the first year that social benefits reached their maximum. Thereafter, the commission's assistance activities dwindled swiftly, not merely because the unemployment figures began to fall (see Fig. 15), but above all because the commission itself had gradually come to withdraw its assistance from more and more groups, beginning with women and unmarried men. Two other striking features are the sharp drop in the numbers of unemployed receiving cash benefits as the decade wore on, and the high level of the share receiving no help at all.

Sweden's solution to the unemployment problem, that is to say, differed from most other countries'. Above all she saw it as lying in the provision of work – a circumstance probably connected with the fact that, internationally speaking, Sweden was very late in introducing any general unemployment insurance. No such scheme became law until 1934.

Typical of the emergency jobs, as has been said, was that they were badly paid. Wages were below market levels. One reason for this was a concern not to upset the policy of deflation and thus damage the country's foreign trade prospects at the desired dollar and gold parity (see pp. 1072–5). Further, it was argued that these emergency works were not to compete with private enterprise. A theoretical justification was found in the neo-classical argument that unemployment is due to wages having risen above equilibrium and, that if they were lowered, more people could be employed, thus terminating the unemployment.

As we have also seen, introduction of universal franchise and parliamentary government at the close of the century's second decade had radically changed the parliamentary power structure. The Conservative

Table 149. *Assistance given to unemployed according to the Unemployment Commission and occupied in public works (annual averages from monthly figures, 1922–38)*

| | Total applying for assistance (AK) | Of these | | | | | | Employed in public works | |
| | | Engaged in emergency works[a] | | Receiving cash assistance[b] | | Not assisted | | | Of these, formerly unemployed[c] |
		Number	%	Number	%	Number	%	Number	
1922[d]	80,500	27,476	34.2	24,749	30.7	28,275	35.1	—	—
1923	26,400	13,198	50.0	2,574	9.8	10,628	40.2	—	—
1924	9,200	3,583	38.9	305	3.3	5,312	57.8	—	—
1925	14,900	4,776	32.1	416	2.8	9,700	65.1	—	—
1926	16,800	5,116	30.5	885	5.1	10,829	64.4	—	—
1927	19,200	6,116	31.8	1,959	10.2	11,125	58.0	—	—
1928	16,700	5,173	30.9	2,013	12.1	9,514	57.0	—	—
1929	10,200	3,687	36.1	1,101	10.8	5,412	53.1	—	—
1930	13,723	4,150	30.3	1,615	11.8	7,958	57.9	—	—
1931	46,540	12,832	27.6	7,074	15.2	26,634	57.2	—	—
1932	113,907	31,539	27.7	28,378	24.9	53,990	47.4	—	—
1933	164,054	44,494	27.1	60,623	37.0	58,937	35.9	4,808	3,221
1934	114,802	44,208	38.5	35,426	30.9	35,168	30.6	24,085	11,802
1935	61,581	29,781	48.4	11,852	20.0	20,218	32.8	30,559	14,974
1936	35,601	16,065	45.1	8,842	24.8	10,694	30.1	23,252	11,394
1937	18,213	7,829	43.0	4,971	27.3	5,413	29.7	16,651	8,159
1938	14,927	4,776	32.0	4,886	32.7	5,265	35.3	12,916	6,329

Notes:

[a] These were later on called 'reserve works'.

[b] From 1934 onwards so-called 'youth assistance', i.e., special measures against unemployment among the young, included among those assisted with cash.

[c] In accordance with Gustafsson, the figures have been calculated on the basis of the known ratio for 1934 between the number of formerly unemployed and the total number in public works for the 1935–8 period.

[d] The figures for October–December 1921 were: 119,767 seeking assistance. Of these, 28,928 (24.2 per cent) were found employment in emergency works, 35,098 (29.3 per cent) received cash assistance, and 55,721 (46.5 per cent) were not given any assistance.

Sources: 1921–9: SOU 1931:20, *Arbetslöshetsutredningens betänkande I*, Tabellbilaga A, pp. 507ff.

1930–8: AK-statistiken, *Sociala meddelanden*, 1935:3, p. 168; 1937:3, p. 170; and 1939:3, p. 206.

Public works: B. Öhman, *Svensk arbetsmarknadspolitik 1900–1947*, p. 114; B. Gustafsson, 'Perspektiv på den offentliga sektorn under 1930–talet', in *Kriser och krispolitik i Norden under mellankrigstiden*, p. 129.

Party's altered attitudes powerfully reinforced those of the protagonists of economic liberalism; this had created a political watershed between a non-socialist majority block and a socialist minority. The former whole-heartedly supported the Unemployment Commission's principles. Not that the Social Democrats immediately rejected the commission's overall low-wage principle, either. The party had accepted a policy of deflation, that is a return to the gold standard at pre-war parity,[21] and, as noted, probably underestimated the amount of unemployment imminent, and therefore thought the prevailing policy's advantages outweighted its short-term drawbacks.

The Social Democrats were also probably influenced by the belief built into prevailing economic theory of adaptive processes within the economy. At that time, no other fundamental theoretical view of the economic questions of the day than the neo-classical as yet existed. Economic theorists, furthermore, were largely agreed on questions of monetary policy. Neither was Marxism, or any theoretical elements derived from it, a theory which directly offered any practical help or recommendations when it came to economic policy. It was hardly surprising, then, if the neo-classical theory enjoyed such wide support that it even influenced the reformist Social Democrats.

But though the commission's policy prevailed during the 1920s, among the workers themselves it gave rise to ever greater dissatisfaction. Opposition from the Swedish Confederation of Trade Unions became steadily stronger, and the Social Democrats, too, modified their attitudes – attitudes they did not altogether abandon, however, until the end of the decade, when they began to call for an entirely novel unemployment policy. This alternative, too, had its theoretical impetus, and was ex-pressed in a parliamentary bill of 1930.

To sum up, we can say that up to 1914, that is as long as there was no great degree of unemployment, opinions did not differ greatly on unemployment policy. Redistributive works – naturally at market wages – were regarded as the cure. This was therefore the policy pursued during the war years; it continued until charitable works, motivated on the basis of prevailing economic theory, ousted the other categories in the early 1920s. Once having accepted deflation, the Social Democrats could not oppose an unemployment policy that was logically in line with it. But dissatisfaction spread, and by and by they changed their policy. These problems, however, were not to be solved until the early 1930s.

[21] L. Jörberg and O. Krantz, *The Fontana Economic History of Europe*, vol. VI: *Scandinavia 1914–1970*, p. 64; and P.G. Edebalk, *Arbetslöshetsförsäkringsdebatten. En studie i svensk socialpolitik 1892–1934* (Lund, 1975), p. 218.

2. Social policy

In earlier times, many tasks of socio-political nature had been solved within an institutional framework consisting basically of the family, the farm, the village council, the parish or the typical Swedish *bruk*. But as industrialism spread, the older type of working organization either changed character or was dissolved, and with it the means of ensuring a livelihood for everyone. Some new system of support had to be found to replace the old one, and the responsibility of organizing and paying for it became less localized. The tasks of the commune became more extensive, and the state was obliged to adopt a more active policy than hitherto. In other words, certain functions had to be transferred from the private to the public sector.

As in other countries, laws against employing child labour in industry had been passed in the latter part of the nineteenth century. Special child welfare legislation, introduced in 1902, was improved in 1918 and 1924, when local child welfare boards were set up.

Like child welfare, care of the aged had earlier fallen under the Poor Law authorities and had had an element of – and was often regarded as – charity. At the end of the nineteenth century, however, the idea of special old age insurance had been mooted, and in 1907 the question began to be looked into. The upshot was a law concerning pensions, which came into force in 1914. Though of no very great practical importance – the sums paid out were very small – it was nevertheless important in principle. The pension scheme comprised the entire nation, and this was a novelty; in other countries insurance was mainly restricted to industrial workers or less highly paid employees.

Health insurance through private associations began to become common in the last phase of the nineteenth century, and in 1891 the state began to contribute to these. In 1910 state contributions were increased, the associations being placed under a certain degree of public control. Health insurance nevertheless remained voluntary, and it was not until the 1930s that it began to become obligatory.

Social policy, too, began to concern itself more actively with trades and occupations. Workers' protection acts were passed, and, in 1901, an act making it mandatory for employers to compensate industrial workers for injuries suffered at work. At the same time, employers were permitted to insure workers on a voluntary basis and thus disburden themselves of compensation. In 1916 such insurance was made obligatory.

From this brief survey of some of the social reforms, the two first decades of this period – not least the first – may seem to have witnessed a

Table 150. State and municipal (commune) expenditure on health and medical care and social services, in percentage of Gross National Product, 1904–58 (current prices)

	Health and medical care		Social services		Total	
	Average	Year with lowest and highest value	Average	Year with lowest and highest value	Average	Year with lowest and highest value
1904–20	0.9	1904, 1906: 0.6 / 1918: 1.1	1.0	1910, 1914: 0.8 / 1918: 1.3	1.9	1906, 1910: 1.5 / 1918: 2.4
1922–30	1.4	1926, 1928, 1930: 1.4 / 1922, 1924: 1.5	2.0	1924: 1.6 / 1922: 2.7	3.4	1924: 3.1 / 1922: 4.2
1933–46	1.8	1934, 1936, 1942: 1.7 / 1932, 1946: 1.9	3.1	1934, 1936, 1940: 2.9 / 1944: 3.5	4.9	1934, 1936: 4.6
1948–58	2.7	1948: 2.3 / 1958: 3.1	5.9	1952: 5.2 / 1958: 6.7	8.6	1952: 7.8 / 1958: 9.8

Note:
Data for health and medical care and social services for the 1914–58 period are only available for even-numbered years, 1914, 1916, 1918, etc. Throughout these figures refer only to such years. Data for the 1904–12 period are approximate.
Sources: Health and medical and social services: 1904–12 estimated on basis of available data in Statistisk tidskrift (1904–13) and Statistisk årsbok (1915); 1914–58: Höök, Den offentliga sektornas expansion, pp. 464ff; Gross National Product: O. Krantz and C. A. Nilsson, Swedish National Product 1861–1970 (Lund, 1975), ch. 8, Table 1.

great deal of activity, compared with the 1920s when reform stagnated. And, indeed, this seems to have been the case, as can be clearly seen by a comparison with the post-1930 period, when social policy entered into a new and intensely active phase.

The parliamentary situation of the 1920s had given rise to many minority governments. Though some of these had been reformist, they had hardly been in a position to implement their ideas, for lack of a majority. Further, the age's basic economic ideas aimed at thrift. Yet this did not prevent certain reforms being carried through, concerning the care of the poor, of children, and the sick. Most of these measures, however, were only minor additions to those already in force.

Up to the 1930s social policy can be said to have been still regarded, on the whole, as an affair for local government. Often it was viewed as a kind of poor relief, and had definitely philanthropic and patriarchal undertones. Naturally, social reform – including political measures to reduce unemployment – entailed economic consequences in the shape of rising costs both for state and local authorities. Table 150 gives some data. The costs for public health services and social security in percentage of Gross National Product have been calculated for the 1904–58 period (with approximate values for 1904–12). The series of percentages fall very clearly into periods, as can be seen from the table's data on minimum and maximum values for each. In no case does the highest value for one period reach the lowest for those following. Nor is there any steady annual increment.

The first period in this table comprises the time up to and including 1920; a period of intensely active social policy. The values here are definitely below those for the following period, 1922–30. That is, the earliest reform activity clearly assumes quantitative expression. To this must be added some rise in costs for unemployment policy, reaching their maximum in 1922 – the value of this latter year, even so, not being so great as to fall outside the framework for the period as a whole.

From the early 1930s onwards reform policy came much more to the fore, as can be seen from increased costs, both absolute and relative. The policy initiated at that time gradually led to fresh reforms and, as a consequence in the late 1940s, to a new rise in cost levels relative to the Gross National Product.

VI. *Post-1930*

A.   POLITICAL CHANGES

During the 1920s Social Democratic and non-socialist ideologies diverged sharply on a number of crucial points. The Social Democrats were forced to retreat for lack of any clear day-to-day programme.

Looking back over the decade, one of their leading representatives, Ernst Wigforss, said the party had two sources of inspiration: Marxism and Liberalism. Both had had the effect of making its policies more passive. Marxism did not provide any concrete measures in order to deal with economic crises and liberalism blocked every attempt to create a positive economic policy.[22]

But as the decade came to an end, the Social Democrats became more active and radical. Opposition to the non-socialist parties' labour market policy was, for instance, a theme of the 1928 elections. A socialist bill for higher death duties was violently attacked by the Right. Opposition between the socialist and non-socialist parties which had existed throughout the decade became more acute. The 1928 elections were among the most passionate ever fought in Swedish politics. The Social Democrats lost heavily, a defeat which committed them to still greater efforts to renew themselves as a party. This renewal is discernible, for instance, in their parliamentary bills of 1930 and 1932, proposing new-style unemployment programmes and measures against economic crises. In the 1932 elections the Social Democratic offensive celebrated a great success, leading to the formation of a purely Social Democratic government.

Yet the Riksdag still had a non-socialist majority. Some form of agreement with one or another non-socialist group was therefore necessary if the government was to implement its crisis programme. Negotiations began with the Farmers' Party whose members had been hard hit by the depression. Prices for agricultural products having fallen heavily, they were demanding an active agricultural policy. In 1933, the two parties reached an agreement, known as the 'cow deal'. Under its terms the Farmers' Party were to support the Social Democratic crisis programme in the Riksdag, in exchange for Social Democratic acceptance of an extensive support programme for agriculture.

This agreement gave the government a sufficient parliamentary majority for them to pursue an active policy. Admittedly, the alliance between Farmers and Social Democrats had its stresses and strains. A break between them even led to the resignation of the Social Democratic government, and for a short while (in 1936) the Farmers formed their own. But the elections of that year returned the Social Democrats to power, this time with a firm basis in their coalition with the Farmers' Party, thus enabling them to pursue their activist policy.

In politics, as in economics, the 1930s saw the beginnings of a period differing in crucial respects from the one that had preceded it. Govern-

---

22 B. Södersten, 'Per Albin och den socialistiska reformismen', in *Per Albin linjen* (Stockholm, 1970), p. 108.

ments enjoyed a stable majority in the Riksdag and could therefore implement their policies.

B. ECONOMIC POLICY

Economic policy in the previous period had really only had one goal: to keep Sweden on the gold standard. The means for doing this were changes in the Bank Rate. Post-war policy had aimed at re-establishing the gold standard at pre-war parity by following a policy of deflation.

One of the state's norms – which can also be said to have been a goal of financial policy – was the sanctity of its wealth. This meant balancing its budget from year to year. The International Financial Conference at Brussels in 1920 had formulated this latter rule as follows, 'The country whose financial policies accept a policy of budget deficits enters on a slippery slope, which leads to disaster. No sacrifice is too great to escape this danger.'[23] Not that Swedish economic policy ever achieved this norm in the 1920s.

Nor did the gold standard system stand up to the stresses and strains the depression of the early thirties exposed it to. After 1929, international payments became extremely unstable. Sweden had an inflow of short-term capital in 1930 and early 1931; partly balanced by long-term capital exports, thus continuing a trend from the twenties. In the later part of 1931, after bank and currency crises in Germany and Austria, the capital tide turned and began seeking other shores of refuge. This precipitated a currency crisis; and on 27 September 1931, Sweden was forced off the gold standard, one week after Britain had done the same after an even heavier capital outflow. To have tried to stay on the gold standard in such a situation would have entailed grievous consequences for the country's domestic economy and led infallibly to a credit squeeze and massive deflation.

1. Monetary policy

In 1931 the old rates of exchange were abandoned and Sweden devalued heavily. But no new rates were immediately fixed. Instead, the crown fluctuated considerably against dollar and pound, among other currencies. Not until 1933 was a new sterling parity established, and for a couple of years the crown continued to fluctuate in relation to other currencies. By 1935, some degree of stability had been achieved. The crown was devalued by about 45 per cent against gold and those currencies which

---

[23] This statement attached to the 1921 budget plan is quoted after V. Bergström, *Den ekonomiska politiken i Sverige och dess verkningar* (Uppsala, 1970), p. 29.

were still tied to it, and by about 25 per cent against the major currencies.[24]

This devaluation powerfully reinforced the domestic market for industry against foreign competition, and also eased exports. Indeed, the measure went so far that for the rest of the decade the crown was somewhat undervalued and Swedish exports became extremely competitive. The suspension of the gold standard made possible an active monetary policy, and international elbow-room was created for financial policy to become expansive. In both cases a new era can be said to have started with the thirties.

The new monetary policy's goal was to stabilize the Swedish crown's domestic purchasing power. Now, for the first time, price stabilization was openly declared a superordinate goal for a central bank. Thus a norm which Wiksell had proposed 30 years earlier had become the new basis of policy.[25] The means for achieving such price stability were to be Bank Rate policy and adjustments in the rates of exchange. But since no major interventions became necessary during the thirties, it is impossible to judge how far the authorities would have gone in implementing the new doctrine. For most of the decade both prices and exchange rates remained fairly stable.

The goal of monetary policy can be explained in terms of fears of the inflation that might follow on devaluation. This was why Bank Rate was raised so high. Its fluctuations, around 17 September 1931, the time when Sweden went off the gold standard, can be seen from the following:[26]

		Per cent			Per cent
1931	31/7	4	1932	19/2	5.5
	21/9	5		3/3	5
	25/9	6		17/5	4.5
	28/9	8		3/6	4
	8/10	7		1/9	3.5
	19/10	6			

Soon it was realized that there was in fact no danger of inflation, and Bank Rate was lowered, gradually settling at around 3 per cent, the level it stayed at until the mid-1950s. In other respects, too, monetary policy during the 1930s was expansive, making possible a great increase in production and employment.

[24] E. Lundberg, *Konjunkturer och ekonomisk politik* (Stockholm, 1953), p. 65. (Published as *Business Cycles and Economic Policy* (London, 1957.)

[25] L. Jonung, 'Knut Wicksells prisstabiliseringsnorm och penningpolitiken på 1930-talet', in J. Herin and L. Werin (eds.), *Ekonomisk debatt och ekonomisk politik* (Lund, 1977), p. 41.

[26] *Riksbaukens årsbok*, 1931 and 1932.

2. Financial policy

For a good many years Wigforss had been advancing a new view of financial policy. This view was both political and, to some extent, theoretical. Where theory was concerned, a number of young Swedish political economists had also begun to plead for new ways of seeing these matters. One of these innovators was Gunnar Myrdal who treated these problems in an appendix to the 1933 budget proposals.[27] Yet his recommendations were cautious; he saw monetary policy as central, financial policy as a complement to it. The budget, instead of being balanced annually, should be balanced over the whole trade cycle. The motivation for this new departure was that the state's finances must be healthy, and its wealth grow in the long run. Here, then, was a limit to freedom of movement in financial policy.

It was in this document that the view of the trade cycle on which this new financial policy was based was first presented. A recession, it declared, was characterized by insufficient demand for consumer goods and services, investments, and activity in the public sector, thus reducing expenditure. The cure was therefore obvious. Greater state expenditure, primarily in the form of public works, must stimulate demand by raising incomes in one part of the economy and thus generating further expenditure – and thus new income – in some other part. In other words, a multiplier process was set in motion which helped to trigger off an upswing in the trade cycle. The new government's programme was a practical expression of these ideas.

Both the new policy and the theory behind it broke with neo-classical macro-theory. Those who held with the older theory would not admit that, whilst a lowering of wages during a recession must entail a fall in total demand, any increase in state expenditure would stimulate greater activity throughout the economy. Among the new theory's opponents was Gustav Cassel. During the 1920s at least Cassel was perhaps the internationally best-known and influential of Swedish economists.

Just why Cassel rejected the new theory so categorically is not altogether easy to understand. Even before the First World War he had developed a theory of economic growth, or, as he called it in his book *Teoretisk socialekonomi,* 'uniformly progressive economy'.[28]

He defined 'monetary income' as the 'value, expressed in money, of the commodities utilized for consumption within the economy over any

[27] G. Myrdal, 'PM ang. verkningarna på den ekonomiska konjunkturutvecklingen i Sverige av olika åtgärder inom den offentliga hushållningens område', *1933 års statsverksproposition, bilaga III.*

[28] See also E. Lundberg, 'Gustav Cassels insatser som nationalekonom', *Skandinaviska Banken Kvartalsskrift,* no. 1 (1967).

given period, plus any increase in that economy's capital for the same period, less any reduction in capital'.[29] Here Cassel is speaking, of course, of Gross National Product (or national income) all the while in net terms. Further, he conceives of it as being distributed in constant proportions as between savings and consumption. Thus the 'degree of society's saving', that is, the savings ratio, remains constant. The latter he signifies by $1/s$, and total income by I. Thus, saving is I/s, and is used in order to increase 'society's stock of real capital'. In other words, total savings equal total investments. Cassel used the letter K to stand for society's total real capital. A uniform progress presupposes that K shall increase by the same percentage as I, a percentage he indicates by $p/100$. This gives Cassel the equation

$$\frac{I}{s} = \frac{p}{100} \times K$$

which he develops into

$$I = \frac{ps}{100} \times K$$

Since p and s are constants, I constitutes a constant share of K. Cassel concludes 'that in a uniformly progressive economy both *income* and its two components *consumption* and *capital formation* will grow by the same constant percentage as *capital*' (Cassel's italics).[30]

Developed in another way, the first equation becomes

$$\frac{p}{100} = \frac{I}{s} \times \frac{1}{K}$$

If S stands for saving, the 'degree of saving', $1/s$, is the same as S/I. Consequently

$$\frac{p}{100} = \frac{S/I}{K/I}$$

or, put in words: growth is equal to savings ratio divided by the capital output ratio, this being the simplest variant of what later was to be known as the Harrod–Domar theory. According to Cassel, uniform progress is an average, with which *de facto* developments can be compared, the latter being a series of fluctuations above and below the curve of uniform development.[31] And this brings us to Cassel's discussion of movements of the trade cycle.

[29] G. Cassel, *Teoretisk socialekonomi* (Stockholm, 1938 edn), p. 81.
[30] *Ibid.*, p. 86.   [31] *Ibid.*, p. 507.

In italics he states that 'in its innermost nature the fluctuation between periods of upswing and recession is a variation in the production of fixed capital, but is not immediately connected with the rest of production'.[32] Here Cassel could be said to touch on an accelerator theory. This is more clearly expressed in the following: we can 'distinguish between the durable means of production, which work directly for consumers, and those which are used up in order to produce new durable means of production'. For the second group to find itself idle does not necessarily mean that there must be a falling off in consumer demand. It suffices for it to rise 'a little more slowly than normal' for the second group of means of production to be exposed to a certain degree of inactivity.[33]

From all this the conclusion could reasonably have been drawn that to stimulate demand might be the cure for a depression. It should also have been possible to conclude that public works at market wages, apart from stimulating demand, would also produce something to be included in capital formation, for example, roads. Cassel, however, drew no such conclusions. Instead, he stressed the need for thrift and lower wages in periods of depression, in order to achieve balance on the labour market and thus, in accordance with neo-classical macro-theory, achieve full employment.

Two possible causes why Cassel failed to grasp the new policy's theoretical foundations may be touched on. One may have been psychological: the new theories had been launched by other economists, and so Cassel simply did not want to understand them. Or again, the reason may have lay in his deeply rooted 'ultra-liberal' sense of values.

Differences in definitions, too, may have prevented Cassel from grasping certain distinctions on the basis of his own theoretical assumptions. This, for instance, could be true of saving. By 'saving' Cassel clearly understood what has afterwards come to be called saving *ex post*, which of course (in a close economy) equals investments *ex post*. Naturally, this does not also imply a similarity *ex ante*. If planned saving is greater than planned investments, there will be a reduction in demand, and thus in national income. This again means that any rise in saving *ex ante* during a depression will tend rather to make the crisis more acute, for lack of readiness to invest. Cassel thought, on the contrary, that saving must be increased in order to make room for investments; or, in other words, if 'the degree of saving' rises, then, according to the above equation, so too must growth. But if, instead, Cassel had seen the problem *ex ante*, surely he could equally have maintained that a planned increase in investment, if implemented, would have meant a growth in saving *ex post*.

[32] *Ibid.*, p. 525.   [33] *Ibid.*, p. 559.

3. Results of economic policy

As we have seen, the early 1930s were a structural limit for the Swedish economy. One element in the new pattern of developments that emerged at that time was the new economic policy, already sketched, which immediately made monetary policy into a matter of great practical importance, whilst it was only in the long term that financial policy played a crucial role.

The monetary measures were important because of the expansion they permitted. By going off the gold standard in 1931, Sweden was able to extricate herself from her international ties. To begin with, at least, monetary policy became autonomous; exchange rates were to be adapted to the Swedish crown's domestic purchasing power. Afterwards, the link with sterling led to the krona being undervalued, giving Sweden a favourable balance of payments.

Another implication of the expansionist monetary policies of the thirties was generally low interest rates, contrasting with the high rates charged during the previous decade. The credit situation, too, improved considerably compared with what it had been in the twenties, when investment, particularly in buildings, had been restrictive. Between 1921–25 and 1926–30, total investment in buildings grew in real terms by about 24 per cent, and between 1931–5 and 1936–40 by 43 per cent. The figures for investment in machinery were 65 per cent and 97 per cent respectively. If we only look at investment in industrial building we find that, whilst the rise during the twenties was 8 per cent, in the thirties it was 76 per cent. The corresponding figures for investment in industrial machinery were 89 per cent and 82 per cent respectively.[34] From this it is also possible to conclude that the great rationalization of the 1920s had produced a higher degree of mechanization and greater efficiency within the prevailing industrial structure. In the 1930s, on the other hand, the structure changed, a development facilitated by the generous monetary policy.

Within the field of financial policy, by contrast, the direct effects were modest. In practice, the new principle of methodically underbalancing the budget in times of recession was no new departure. Expenditure is dictated less by political decisions, whilst income derived as it is mainly from taxation, tends to vary with the trade cycle.

Budget deficits were bigger during the crisis of the 1920s than during that of the 1930s; and during the latter they had already begun to grow even before the Social Democrats came into power in 1933. Thereafter these deficits fell swiftly, and in 1936–8 there was a surplus. Not until the

[34] Krantz and Nilsson, *Swedish National Product*, ch. 8.

Second World War did the deficits again become really large.[35] That is to say, the underbalancing of the budget in the early 1930s had hardly any effect on the trade cycle; nor were the new financial measures applied until after the beginning of the upswing. Only in the long run did the new principle come to have any practical importance. What *did* to some extent affect stability, even in the thirties, was the relatively higher level of state expenditure than in the previous decade. Shown as a share of Gross National Product, and with the exception of the years 1921–2, state expenditure for the 1920–31 period had been 2 to 3 percentage points lower than during the 1932–9 period, when the share was 10–11 per cent, except for the last year, when it rose to 15 per cent.[36]

There was a similar change in the state's total income from taxation, expressed as a percentage of Gross National Product. During the twenties this percentage remained fairly stable, at around 6 per cent; of this something over 2 per cent came from income, wealth, and company taxes. During the first half of the thirties the level was somewhat higher, and state taxes as a whole rose steadily, from just over 7 per cent in 1935 to just over 9 per cent in 1939. Of this 2.4 and 3.6 percentage points respectively were income tax, wealth tax, and company tax.[37]

Psychologically, the expansionist policy and the changed attitudes towards both economic and social policy would seem to have meant a great deal during the thirties. Confidence grew and people felt more optimistic. Seeing the government take many measures they felt to be positive (see also pp. 1096–103), people dared to make long-term plans. In the business community confidence seems to have expressed itself in the form of positive expectations. The role of expectations also came to be an element in economic theory. As we have seen above, investments *ex ante*, and therewith the propensity to invest, began to be discussed at a theoretical level. Factors determining investment can thus contain expectations for the future, whether pessimistic or optimistic.

C. SOCIAL REFORM POLICY

The 1930s were the beginning of a reform period of a different kind from previously. Social reform policy began to be generally regarded less in the older 'patriarchal' fashion than in one which regarded social security as the right of every citizen. To a considerably greater degree than before, underprivileged groups were to be given a share of steadily improving standards, by means of social reform. In other words, it was in the thirties that the Swedish 'welfare state' began to assume shape.

[35] Bergström, *Den ekonomiska politiken*, Table A:10.
[36] *Ibid.*, Table A:5; Krantz and Nilsson, *Swedish National Product*, ch. 8.
[37] *Riksräkenskapsverkets årsbok*; and Krantz and Nilsson, *Swedish National Product*.

Three particularly important factors lay behind the decade's new perspective. The first was economic. Up to about 1930 production had grown swiftly, and it grew even more swiftly in the years following. This economic growth provided steadily more elbow-room for reforms. The second factor derived from economic theory. The theoretical view of how unemployment could be abolished changed. It was realized that the effective policy for abolishing unemployment was to strengthen the unemployed's purchasing power – instead of, as before, lowering wages. One implication of this was that other aspects of social policy could now be regarded as a means of strengthening purchasing power, and thus stabilizing the economy. This meant, further, that social policy was no longer regarded merely as a burden on the economy. The third factor was political. Minority governments were followed by majority reformist governments.

We could also adduce one further factor. For a long while the birth rate had been falling until in the early 1930s it reached a level so low that there was even talk of a nativity crisis. To this crisis an active social policy was regarded as one possible solution.

1. Unemployment policy

Most striking, in principle, in this reorientation during the thirties was the new unemployment policy, on which we have touched before, in connection with, for example, financial policy. Here the general background was, on the one hand, widespread dissatisfaction with the older policy the Unemployment Commission stood for; on the other, the strength which the advocates of change could derive from the new theoretical motivations. These were provided both by Liberals and Social Democrats, but it was primarily the latter who stood for the new policy and therefore it is only natural to associate its implementation with the Social Democrats' accession to power after their 1932 victory at the polls.[38]

From the beginning of the 1930s production in industry, manufacturing, building, and construction grew as much as, or even more than, before. Industrial output per working hour, on the other hand, grew more slowly than during the previous period. This gave rise to a greater demand during the thirties for labour, and to greater growth of the share in the industrial building and construction sector than during the twenties. There was also a sharp increase in the labour force. The number

---

[38] Steiger, *Studien*; see also B. Öhman, *Svensk arbetsmarknadspolitik 1900–1947* (Halmstad, 1970).

of persons of working age (15–64) grew more than during the previous decade (see Table 148). At the same time, there was a sharp fall in the agrarian population.

In the 1920s economic conditions for agriculture had been a good deal worse than they now became in the 1930s. One reason for the improvement was the agreement between Social Democrats and Farmers that had been forced on by the crisis. Even so, the fall in the agrarian population was greater during the thirties than it had been in the twenties. Probably this development was due primarily to an expansion in the domestic sector of industry and in building and construction, their increased demand for labour precipitating a flight from agriculture; more especially, it seems, from very small farms, whose numbers fell during the thirties, after having risen during the previous decade.

In the thirties, however, the supply of labour exceeded demand, as can be seen from the continuing high rate of unemployment (Fig. 15). Unemployment, of course, had risen sharply during the depression, and thereafter only fell gradually; so that it was not until the late 1940s onwards that unemployment was reduced to a very much lower level than before.

The figures for unemployed persons seeking help show a similar pattern (Table 149). The share of those receiving no help reached a maximum in 1930–1, and thereafter fell off. During and after the depression, that is to say, society made great efforts to provide some assistance for the unemployed.

Up to mid-1933 this assistance work had been given along the old lines; above all, as we have seen, by providing jobs. The unemployed were occupied with reserve works (earlier called 'emergency assistance works') where wage levels were lower than for equivalent jobs in the open markets. This method proving inadequate, large-scale cash assistance was arranged. But from mid-1933 onwards the new principles of unemployment policy, implemented by the Social Democrats after their crisis agreement with the Farmers' Party, began to be applied. For several reasons the older system of reserve works was now regarded as untenable – partly in view of the wages paid, and for organizational reasons; and partly because of this system's 'passivity' as a stimulus to the trade cycle. According to the new principles, the state itself should operate large-scale and 'meaningful' undertakings, producing various kinds of durables. This was a more efficient work policy than before, and it did not have the earlier goal of tending to depress wages. Now the same wages were to be paid as on the open market. Further, the works would be financed by deficit spending and by loans, pumping out purchasing power into the economy and thus stimulating an upswing in the trade cycle.

As we have seen, this new policy's contribution to ending the depression was in fact minimal. Where it *was* crucial – together with the change in official attitudes towards unemployment – was socially. As can be seen from Table 149, the number of unemployed seeking assistance was greater during the 1930s than in the 1920s, but the share of those who failed to receive it was considerably greater in the twenties and up to and including 1930–1. A further factor in the 1930s was employment in public works, not included in the Unemployment Commission figures. Comparison between the numbers of persons assisted by the commission and the numbers employed in public works – once the latter had got going, from the mid-1930s onwards – reveals that the latter figure was the greater (Table 149). This is true even if we only look at the number of ex-unemployed occupied in such public works. That is to say, the numbers of unemployed helped by political anti-unemployment measures were considerably greater after the new unemployment policy had come into force than they had been before.

We have earlier touched on the history of the ideas lying behind this new Social Democratic unemployment policy, and therefore also behind financial policy. This history has been much discussed, and three main lines of thought are clearly discernible. The first sets most store by the party's own indigenous tradition of ideas, pointing to what have come to be called 'the ideas of 1912'. In our section on unemployment policy up to 1930, however, we have maintained that these ideas cannot be regarded as having had the same theoretical background as that of the crisis policy. What was important, of course, was the party's long-standing reformist tradition. This disposed it to try, as quickly as possible, to carry out far-reaching reforms in the interests of the working class. One implication of this is that it is not possible, as certain researchers have maintained, to explain Social Democratic policy during the 1920s – when very little reform could be successfully implemented – in terms of the Social Democrats' will to action being paralysed by 'Marxist fatalism'.[39] As seen, the causes of their passivity must be sought elsewhere: in the deflationary policy, in the parliamentary situation, etc.

The second main interpretation stresses the domestic theoretical influence. Here a leading group of young Swedish economists, Myrdal and Bertil Ohlin being among the most prominent, are regarded as having exerted a crucial influence. These economists derived their new theoretical attitudes from a Swedish tradition (that of Wicksell) which, in their eyes, made the new theory seem quite natural. Together with Wigforss – the Social Democrats' protagonist in these questions and the Social Democrats' government's Minister of Finance after their 1932 election

[39] H. Tingsten, *Den svenska socialdemokratins idéutveckling I* (Stockholm, 1941); see also L. Lewin, *Planhushållningsdebatten* (Uppsala, 1967).

victory – these economists are claimed to have been the new policy's designers.

Wigforss was a member of the state Unemployment Commission, appointed in 1927. A number of other younger Swedish economists had also been attached to this commission, and had thus an opportunity to develop their ideas in special reports. This collaboration continued even after the Social Democrats had come to power. Myrdal, for instance, was the author of the aforementioned appendix to the 1933 budget proposals, a task with which he had been entrusted by Wigforss. Ohlin, too, was a member of the special committees on economic issues.[40]

If we look at the practical form taken by government policy, we can hardly doubt the crucial role played by the new government's collaboration with these younger economists. From this it does not necessarily follow, however, that it was they who, in the late 1920s, actually inspired the Social Democrats or, more especially, Wigforss, to adopt their new theoretical attitudes. Rather, the economists' contribution seems to have been to legitimize the new policy at scientific level.

The third view of the historical background to Wigforss' and the Social Democrats' new line mainly stressed the influence of British liberals, not least of Keynes. This line of argument starts with the fact that Wigforss had been following British liberal debate in the twenties, both in *The Nation and the Atheneum* and in books and pamphlets. Notable among the latter was one called *Britain's Industrial Future*, known as the Yellow Book. These writings contained ideas concerning expansionistic economic policies which, at many points, showed the way to the Swedish Social Democrats.[41]

The Swedish Social Democrats, therefore, inherited a tradition of thinking which had among other things manifested itself in their pre-1914 anti-unemployment initiatives. Here we should add the important effect of Marxist theory on the party's attitude. Wigforss, himself an eminent Marxist theorist, must have been impressed to find certain tangible points of similarity between the Marxist and Keynesian analyses. Simultaneously the domestic theoretical tradition comprised a line derived from Wicksell which, if followed up, could help to legitimize the new ideas. Wigforss' main direct inspiration for these ideas was derived from the British liberal debate.

Here we are stressing Wigforss' role; and indeed there seems to be no question but that, even if other individuals also made important contributions, it was his signature the party's policy bore in these respects. One researcher has even gone so far as to suggest that it was Wigforss who

[40] C. G. Uhr, 'Economists and Policy Making 1930–1936: Sweden's Experience', *History of Political Economy*, vol. IX, no. 1 (Spring 1977), pp. 89–121.
[41] Landgren, *Den 'nya ekonomin' i Sverige*, pp. 288ff.

influenced the younger economists into accepting the state's expansionist policies in the early thirties. This would make an amateur in economics these economists' herald and forerunner.[42] Even if there is something to be said for this assumption, it is doubtful whether Wigforss here played any great role. Swedish economists, at least the younger among them, cannot have been ignorant of what was being discussed on the other side of the North Sea. Ohlin, for example, made more than one contribution to the above-mentioned journal.

A question within the field of unemployment policy was unemployment insurance. As has already been pointed out, Sweden was one of the last industrial countries to introduce this reform. France had carried out hers in 1905, Norway in 1906, and Denmark in 1907. Like Sweden afterwards, these countries had adopted the so-called Ghent System, under which the state contributed to the trade unions' unemployment funds.

Ever since the beginning of the century, the Social Democrats had been more or less loudly demanding a state-supported scheme. Successive commissions were set up to look into the matter, and various possibilities were considered. In the twenties, more especially, the Social Democrats were active; and indeed the party's cautious attitude towards overall unemployment policy can to a certain extent be said to have been offset by its activity in the insurance issue.

But resistance from the non-socialist parties was strong. In their view, unemployment insurance favoured the workers; and they adduced the principle of the state's neutrality in labour conflicts. By now the Liberals, too, had joined the opposition. Up to 1914 they had been in favour of unemployment insurance.

Not until 1934 could a reform be implemented. The rules were anything but generous, and the immediate effects therefore limited. Even so, it was a victory for an important principle, and the Social Democrats entertained hopes of gradually being able to get rid of the restrictions imposed on them by their political compromise with the Liberals. The first step in this direction was taken in 1941, when the conditions of unemployment were greatly improved.[43]

2. Social policy

Political reform in the social field had been in the forefront during the first decades of the century. During the 1930s the earlier reforms continued to be extended and complemented, and many important new measures were taken. Fields where reforms were complemented in-

---

[42] Ibid., pp. 288ff.   [43] Edebalk, Arbetslöshetsförsäkringsdebatten.

cluded accident insurance at work, retirement pensions, and health insurance. There were new developments in family and housing policy, etc.

The population question and thus also population policy as a whole had an important bearing on several social reforms. The Swedish birth rate had been falling since the end of the nineteenth century. It dropped from 25–30 pro mille to an average of just over 14 in the early part of the 1930s, the years showing the lowest values (14.7 pro mille) being 1933 and 1934. The mortality rate, on the other hand, changed much less. The result was a sharp drop in natural increase,[44] and a relative rise in the population of working age (Table 148).

The population problem had long been under debate, both in Sweden and internationally.[45] Not least important in this issue, particularly around the turn of the century, was the neo-Malthusian movement. The neo-Malthusians had urged people to have fewer children and thus check the rise in the population, so fighting the miseries of poverty. Neo-Malthusian views were based on a pessimistic idea of the economy's potential, and thus of the possibilities of improving living conditions for the broad mass of the population. In other words, this movement were doubtful as to whether long-term economic growth could be combined with a rise in population. One Swedish protagonist of neo-Malthusian ideas was Wicksell.

This birth-control propaganda aroused moral indignation in Conservative circles which, as a counter-measure, passed the so-called Contraceptive Law of 1910. It forbade demonstrations and sales of contraceptives, as well as information about them. Another reason why the anti-contraception bill became law was indeed the concern about the falling birth rate and dwindling population figures.

Nevertheless, the birth rate continued to fall, and this – for various reasons, among them defence and racial–biological considerations – was something that mainly troubled the Conservatives. Indeed, it was these aspects, not neo-Malthusian ones, which dominated the debate on population during the century's second and third decades.

In 1934, two Social Democrats, Alva and Gunnar Myrdal, published *Kris i befolkningsfrågan* (Crisis in the Population Question). The book's starting point was the prospect of the Swedish population dwindling, unless the birth rate should soon begin to rise again. The Myrdals urged a number of social reforms aimed at bringing about such a rise. Demands were made for a radical policy of income redistribution.

One result of this book, and of the discussion it unleashed, was the

---

[44] *Historisk statistik för Sverige*, vol. 1.
[45] Concerning the population debate, see among others A. K. Hatje, *Befolkningsfrågan och välfärden* (Stockholm, 1974).

appointment of a major Population Commission in 1935. This commission looked into many matters and made many proposals. Its directives stressed, among other things, the need to bring down the individual's costs for supporting his children. These, it recommended, should be reduced by a social security policy that guaranteed a certain standard of living. Among the various measures the commission regarded as feasible were maternity support, housing loans, day nurseries, and free school meals.

In 1937, maternity and child care were introduced: among other reforms were free natal care, assistance to nursing mothers (subject to means test), special child allowances for certain children, and an improved maternity insurance. The 1940s saw the introduction of such reforms as free school meals, first for the children of the poor and afterwards for all children, and free school books. But the most important of all these reforms was the general child allowance (1948), a grant which has since been successively increased.

One field of reform partly connected with the population question was housing policy. There was also a connection with labour market policy, the changes in housing policy being motivated by the very bad housing conditions of the less well off.

In the thirties, improvements in housing began to be implemented with the aid of loans and grants. To bring down the housing costs of families with many children, in addition to family allowances, state concessions were granted in the form of reduced rents for poor families with three or more children. In the long term these investments in housing policy were extended to include, among other things, housing allowances subject to means test.

Whether all this reformist activity had any demographic effect is doubtful. After 1934 the birth rate rose more or less continuously up to the mid-1940s, when it stood at just over 20 pro mille. Thereafter it fell again. Other demographic variables, significant in this context, show a similar development. The inceptuality rate, for instance, began to rise sharply in 1934. That is to say, the trend changed before the reforms had time to take effect or were even decided on. Where the population question did play a crucial role was in reducing the non-socialist parties' resistance to social reform – a resistance stronger in some parties than in others. The Liberals, for instance, had a long-standing tradition of social policy, and this made them more favourably disposed to reforms than the other non-socialist parties.

But what gradually and in ever higher degree came to worry the non-socialists, and more especially the Conservatives, was that this social policy meant a redistribution of income by means of steeply progressive taxation. The Conservatives saw in the ever-rising transfers via the state budget and a consequently expanding public sector, a step towards a planned economy. In their view, a 'free society' could better provide for its citizens.

Evidence of the new reform epoch which began in the 1930s can also be seen in the different data for the public sector. As noted, taxes were growing relative to Gross National Product, and so was total state expenditure. As can be seen from Table 150, the early thirties saw a rise in level of expenditure on health and medical care and – even more sharply – in the social budget's share of the total production. Expenditure on unemployment had proved crucial in the decade's earlier years; and it subsequently came to lend added significance to other elements in social policy. The next rise in levels occurred at the end of the forties, as a result of new reforms, not least the introduction of the child allowance. This steady rise can thus be seen as a long-term effect of the policy first implemented in the thirties.

VII. *Concluding remarks*

In the latter part of the nineteenth century Swedish economic policy was based on liberal ideas. Economic liberalism, described as a generalized doctrine of business economics, regarded the rationally managed firm as the economy's most important component which, it thought, should in principle be allowed to operate unhindered. According to this view, it was the state's business to remove all obstacles to free competition. Yet the state's role could also be 'positive', in the sense of operating concerns which had the character of natural monopolies and demanded a great deal of capital. Swedish railway policy, for instance, had been based on this idea.

This liberal doctrine prevailed in more or less modified forms in most industrialized countries, or in countries going through industrialization:

Thanks to a temporary harmony between technical development, population increase and emigration to countries whose national resources were still unexploited, and due to the stimulus given to society by political reforms, the successful strivings to achieve national independence and the extension of the franchise – progress is regarded as a natural law, which does not clash with the principles of equality in what concerns income distribution.[46]

At the same time, it was considered society's duty to protect people against the most malign consequences of industrialization. At first, this protection took the form of measures to assist the sick and the poor. Poor law administration was the object of the first conscious measure of social policy. Gradually, these measures spread over an ever wider field.

---

[46] J. Åkerman, *Nationalekonomins utveckling* (Lund, 1951), p. 170.

Recourse was made open to them in order to cure various troubles arising in the wake of industrialization. These measures included, among other things, worker protection acts, including the regulation of – and, in due course, bans on – the employment of child labour. Another social field was sickness insurance.

Liberal economic policy continued to dominate the first three decades of the twentieth century. Admittedly, the periodically recurring crises did not escape attention. But here a rational monetary policy was regarded as the cure. Above all, it was a question of observing the rules imposed by the international gold standard. The economic policy system could not function during the economic turmoil of the First World War. The gold standard was suspended and the period was characterized by heavy inflation of different order in different countries. After the war a general endeavour to return to pre-war policy was manifested in trying to reestablish the gold standard at the old parity.

But it soon turned out that various tendencies within the economy – trends toward concentration in industry, problems arising out of the excessive size of the agricultural sector, persistent high unemployment, etc. – rendered a *laissez-faire* economic policy inadequate. The depression of the 1930s marks the limit of the *laissez-faire* phase and the beginning of a new one, both economically and politically, with an obviously much higher level of ambition in economic policy than before.

Thus the economic policies of the 1920s were largely restricted, first, to reintroducing the gold standard and, thereafter, maintaining it. Compared with later periods, not least the 1950s and 1960s, economic policy can be seen as having 'either intermediate, secondary, irrelevant, or irrational targets, such as restoration or preservation of a specific exchange rate, the annual balancing of the government budget, and the stability of the price level at a prevailing or a previously reached level'.[47]

In these circumstances social policy remained on the whole a continuation of what had been begun in the last phase of the nineteenth century. It was still a question – most political groups agreed, albeit on different ideological grounds – of curing social ills. Thus health insurance, for instance, was extended, and old age pensions introduced. Reforms were also implemented in such fields as child welfare.

The period which began in the early 1930s was generally characterized by an increase in state intervention in the economy. An active economic policy aimed at stabilizing economic developments and creating more and – later – even full employment. Trade-cycle policy, too, was linked with social reform policy, for example, by increasing purchasing power by means of an active unemployment policy.

[47] Lundberg, *Instability*, pp. 37–8.

The goal of social reform policy was broad, and 'its basis should be a *systematic reshaping* of the whole of society in accordance with a properly worked out social programme'.[48] In other words, the 1930s can be seen as an introductory phase in the development of the welfare state. No longer was it a question of applying more or less limited measures in order to counteract certain troubles. Instead, the welfare state bore the hallmark of the view that everyone has a social right to feel – and be – basically secure.

[48] Åkerman, *Nationalekonomins utveckling*, p. 162 (italics original).

CHAPTER XVI

Aspects of economic and social policy in Japan, 1868–1945

I. Introduction

Japan entered a new era in its economic history in 1868, when the Tokugawa regime ended and the Emperor Meiji was installed as the head of state. This is not to say that the Tokugawa period (1603–1868) was one lacking in economic and social change. There had been substantial population growth in the seventeenth century, considerable urban development, growth in agricultural productivity, industrial growth on a domestic system basis, and, most spectacular of all, the rise of the merchant class, whose economic power had increased greatly relative to that of the samurai and the peasants. At the end of the Tokugawa period, from the 1840s, there had also been efforts to introduce modern naval armaments industries, and also, after Perry forced Japan open to international intercourse in 1853–4, negotiations to conclude commercial treaties with the great powers, treaties which from 1858, brought Japan into the network of foreign trade. But Japan remained in 1868 an economically and politically backward nation compared with the industrial nations of Europe.

What was needed was a new government determined to introduce modern economic and political structures; this government was provided by the lower and middle samurai of, principally, the Choshu and Satsuma *han*, or domains, which had led the fight to overthrow the Tokugawa regime. These domains had already made substantial progress in reforming their own financial and economic organization and in introducing new strategic industries for their military and naval forces. These policies were now to be pursued on a national scale, although few had envisaged, during the civil wars of the 1860s, the lengths to which the new leaders would be driven in the destruction of the old order and the creation of a modern state. In fact, in summarising government policy it is easy to overlook the disputes which occurred within the post-1868 administrations, which were sometimes split and occasionally lost important members, over crises such as Japan's foreign policies and their effect on domestic economic development. One such conflict was over policy to Taiwan in the early 1870s, where the issue was the decision to send a military expedition. This was regarded by some as very harmful to the immediate aims of domestic development and protection of Japan from outside pressures. The dispute was one of many to follow, and echoes, as we shall see, arguments of modern historians about the impact of militarism on Japan's economic development.

The first tasks, over which there was no disagreement, were the pacification and unification of the country, which involved, in 1868 and 1869, the crushing of the anti-imperial forces. Gradually, the leaders of the Meiji government came to believe in the necessity of strengthening the imperial regime by the abolition of the feudal structure, which would involve the surrender of feudal forces and revenues to the central government, and the dismantling of the 250 or so feudal domains which currently existed. The abolition of this feudal structure took several years to accomplish and it was achieved by the Meiji government in 1871, when the domains were replaced by prefectures, governed by nominees of the central government. Soon after, military conscription was introduced, thus abolishing the exclusive right of the samurai to carry arms. A steady erosion of the old class structure took place up to 1876, by which date feudalism, with all its artificial restraints on the individual's freedom of action, can be said to have disappeared. The samurai, in particular, lost their privileges. Voluntary commutation of their stipends was introduced in 1873 and compulsory commutation in 1876.

II.   Economic modernization, 1868–1914

While this process of dissolving feudalism was going on the government embarked on a series of economic and social measures designed to create a modern structure. Machinery was imported and model factories were established: the famous Tomioka silk-spinning mill, the Aichi cotton-spinning factory, the Mombetsu sugar refinery, the Fukugawa cement and brick factories, the Shinagawa glass factory and the Akabane machine-making plant. The Tokugawa-founded Yokosuka naval yard was brought into operation, the Osaka and Nagasaki yards continued to function, while the government created the Kobe yard. In 1872 the first railway, from Tokyo to Yokohama, was completed, the national Post Office was created, a network of National Banks was started and systems of universal compulsory education and conscription were introduced. Experimental farms and agricultural colleges were established, and many students and officials were sent abroad to study, and foreign experts brought in. The telegraph was an early import, and spread, especially with the government railways in the 1870s. Efforts were made to create a modern mercantile marine: ships were bought and handed over to Iwasaki, who later founded the Mitsubishi zaibatsu. Additional railways were built in later years, such as the Osaka–Kobe line, opened in 1874, and it was to take a long time before private enterprise entered this sphere.

This extensive programme necessitated financial reorganization. At the time of the Meiji Restoration of 1868 there was no single, unified, national currency. Each of the hundreds of domains had issued its own *hansatsu*, or domain paper currency, and there were many other kinds of notes, in addition to coinage. It was now necessary to replace this chaos with a single, acceptable note issue. An attempt was made in May 1868 with the issue of the *dajokansatsu*, or cabinet notes, but the notes were distrusted and confusion still prevailed. Nevertheless, domain notes were gradually withdrawn in the 1870s and with the establishment of the Bank of Japan in 1882 the final effort to provide a single note issue was made. By 1885 the Bank of Japan had an effective monopoly of the note issue.

Meanwhile, notes had also been issued by the various banking institutions that developed after 1868. The first embryo banks were the exchange companies, formed under government stimulus in 1869, which were designed to provide funds for the trading companies, established at the same time. These trading companies would, it was hoped, carry on the foreign trade of Japan, which was at that time, and for many decades after, dominated by foreign merchants. Neither the exchange companies nor the trading companies were successful and in 1872 the government made a second attempt to introduce banks when it passed the National Bank Regulations which provided for the creation of National Banks on the American model. The rules governing the conduct of the banks' operations were so stringent, however, that very few were set up between 1872 and 1876, when the rules were relaxed and the bonds issued to samurai in commutation of their stipends, were allowed as the initial capitalization of the banks. They mushroomed between 1876 and 1878 – some 150 in all – but, as will be seen, they were accompanied by considerable financial difficulty.

At the same time that the government was endeavouring to set up an extensive and sound banking system, it attempted to deal with its own financial problem of the gap between revenue and expenditure. Between 1868 and 1872 public expenditure exceeded revenues by almost ¥100 million and the government issued inconvertible notes to cover the deficit. Loans were raised from merchants but there was hardly any import of foreign capital beyond a loan raised in London to finance the Tokyo–Yokohama railway. There were no income or business taxes and reliance was wholly upon the excise, the land tax, and domestic borrowing. The traditional land tax yield was erratic, based as it was on the physical yield of the land and in 1873 the government launched its Land Tax Reform to stabilize its revenues. The reform took a long time to accomplish and the process was only completed in 1881. The main features of the Land Tax Revision Act were the substitution of a money payment in kind, and the substitution of a tax based on the value of the land for a tax as a proportion of the harvest. The tax rate was initially to be 3 per cent of land value, so all land had to be valued, which explains why the reform took so long. But the new tax brought stable revenues and constituted some 80 per cent of all the income of the government right into the 1880s.

On the other hand, it was of dubious benefit to the government to have stable revenues during a period of rapid inflation, and rapid inflation was what Japan suffered after 1876. This was largely the result of the rebellion of disaffected samurai, sparked off by the compulsory commutation of stipends and the ban on samurai wearing swords which was imposed in 1876. The rebellion, known as the Satsuma rebellion because it occurred in the old Satsuma domain in southern Kyushu, was crushed by government forces. This major rebellion came on top of almost constant peasant uprisings during the first decade of the Meiji period, and was by no means even the first samurai rebellion. These pressures led to very rapid inflation as government expenditure soared and deficits mounted. Government paper money increased from ¥105 million in 1876 to ¥139 in 1878, and the government also borrowed heavily from the new National Banks, established during the rebellion period. Their note issues increased from about ¥2 million in 1876 to ¥26 million in 1878. So total note issues rose some 60 per cent between 1876 and 1878, from ¥107 million to ¥166 million.

By 1881 wholesale prices had risen by 64 per cent over 1877, and some individual price increases were even greater: rice doubled in price between 1877 and 1881. Since the land tax was now based on a percentage of the value of land, government revenues did not increase along with the price rise, with the benefits of the increase in the price of rice and other provisions falling into the landowners' hands. Non-military government investment fell drastically and the whole modernization programme seemed in danger of collapsing. Gloomy predictions for the future of Japan were rife. Then came the Matsukata deflation of 1881 to 1885. Henry Rosovsky has written:

A country is fortunate when in times of emergency a capable leader is waiting in the wings ... In October 1881 a most remarkable man became Finance Minister of Japan. He combined firmness and wisdom with a strong belief in financial orthodoxy, and succeeded by 1885 in regaining control of the economic situation. He cleared the decks, and made it possible for modern economic growth to begin.[1]

[1] Henry Rosovsky, 'Japan's Transition to Modern Economic Growth, 1868–1885', in H. Rosovsky (ed.), *Industrialization in Two Systems* (New York, 1966), p. 132.

Matsukata slashed expenditure and raised revenues. Investment in model factories was stopped and government enterprises were sold to private buyers. The land tax became more valuable in real terms as deflation developed, and in addition other taxes were increased and new indirect taxes were introduced. An extra ¥20 million of tax receipts were added to revenues in 1884 compared with 1877 and surpluses in the budgets averaged ¥13 million in the period 1881–5. During this same period the quantity of money dropped by 20 per cent, wholesale prices by 25 per cent, and the price of rice was halved.

Another plank in Matsukata's efforts to build a sound financial system was the creation of the Bank of Japan in 1882. This was to function like the Bank of England in holding the national reserves and in monopolizing the convertible note issue. By 1885 its notes were circulating freely and the discount on them had disappeared by 1886. Confidence in the currency was fully established, therefore, by the mid-1880s. The deflation had also had a remarkably beneficial effect on the balance of trade, which showed a sustained surplus in the period 1882–9, the only period of sustained surplus between the Restoration and the First World War.

The successful conclusion of the deflationary policy in 1886 is seen by Rosovsky as the beginning of modern economic growth in Japan. But there were other consequences of the policies of the deflationary period which were, perhaps, not so favourable. The first of these is the rise of the zaibatsu, some of whose nuclei benefited from the sale of government enterprise in the 1880s and 1890s. Mitsubishi acquired the Takashima coal-mine in 1881 and the Nagasaki shipyard, first on lease in 1884, and then outright in 1887. Mitsui took over the Shinmachi spinning concern in 1887, the Miike coal-mine in 1890, and the Timioka silk mill in 1893; and other examples could be cited. The deflationary period can therefore be viewed as one in which the domination of the Japanese economy by a few huge combines was inaugurated. It is possible that these combines were an engine of growth, but the concentration of economic power was for long regarded as excessive. Some historians have regarded the sale of government enterprises as a hand-out to private capitalists, but others have pointed out that those enterprises were operating at a loss, and that the government's motive was to cut expenditure. Certainly, that was Matsukata's aim. Another unfavourable consequence was the growth in tenancy. Deflation hit the small landowners, who either sold their land or were dispossessed: between 1883 and 1890 some 368,000 peasants were dispossessed for failure to pay taxes. So one of the major problems of Japanese agriculture in the inter-war period is often traced back to the Matsukata deflation.

In addition to these criticisms of the economic policy of the 1880s, are the doubts cast by Kozo Yamamura on the efficacy of state support for industrial development in the years after the Meiji Restoration.[2] According to Yamamura, officials in charge of state industrial establishments did not welcome visits by entrepreneurs and were very secretive about their operations. If this is true then the commonly accepted view of the government's role in pioneering new industries would have to be modified. It may be instructive to take some specific examples. In the shipbuilding industry both domain and central governments had set up yards in the closing years of the Tokugawa regime to build naval ships. But it is certainly true that in the early Meiji years modern commercial shipbuilding, like most other new technologies, did not flourish.

To highlight the embryonic stage of shipbuilding in Japan one has only to contrast her total output in 1870 with British production. Japan built only two steamships in 1870 with a combined tonnage of 57 tons; Britain launched 382 iron steamships totalling over 220,000 tons for British owners alone. Japanese shipbuilders were quite unable to match foreign suppliers in capital supplies, equipment, technology or labour, and although a part of the traditional industry attempted to modernize, the mass had neither the confidence nor the ability to compete with foreign industrialists even if they could have launched large amounts of capital in risky ventures. So in such conditions, and with such an unstable demand, conventional shipbuilding retained much of its appeal for the general run of producers.

Between 1879 and 1896 Japanese yards built only 3 ships of over 700 gross tons, totalling 3,626 tons, compared with an import of 174 ships of over 700 tons, totalling 337,236 tons, so imports were almost 100 times domestic production of this class of larger ship. As late as the mid-1890s Japanese yards were totally incapable of competing with foreign producers. There were two major obstacles: the total lack of domestically produced steel, and the almost total absence of an engineering industry, which was the result of the lack of mechanization of Japanese industry in general, which in turn was partly the result of Japan's factor proportions. The engineering that did exist was very largely associated with the shipbuilding industry and was concentrated in the yards. There was a correspondingly vastly increased need for capital to provide engineering and machine works. In later years yards even turned to steel production, as did Kawasaki in 1907.

But Yamamura's strictures should not be taken to apply to the whole of the Meiji period; the government did step in again after the hiatus of the 1880s and early 1890s. The Sino-Japanese war of 1894–5 highlighted the deficiencies in the country's industrial structure and resulted in a series of measures designed to stimulate heavy industry, and thus to eliminate

[2] In his book, *A Study of Samurai Income and Entrepreneurship* (Cambridge, Mass., 1974).

Japan's heavy dependence on imports of capital goods. The government announced its plans for a state-controlled steel industry in April 1896, construction was started in June 1897, and the Yawata works, with an annual capacity of 90,000 tons, commenced operating in November 1901. From this grew the present huge complex of Nippon Steel in northern Kyushu.

Also in 1896 the government passed laws to promote the development of the shipping and shipbuilding industries. Subsidies were granted to make up the difference between the English and the Japanese prices of steel materials used in shipbuilding, taking into account, in the case of imports from England, the cost of freight, insurance and custom duties. The results of the new legislation were significant. More tonnage of the larger ships was built by Japanese yards in 1898 alone than in the whole of the previous 29 years; and within 5 years of the act annual production was topping 20,000 tons. It will be remembered that the entire output of the 18 years from 1879 to 1896 was less than 4,000 tons. Technological progress was rapid and quite large ships were turned out. By 1907 Mitsubishi were capable of producing the 13,444 gross ton *Tenyō-maru*, a 20.6 knot turbine liner.

However the need for imports remained overwhelmingly important for most of the remainder of the Meiji period, and the crisis of the Russo-Japanese War again showed that the domestic industry was seriously under-equipped to deal with extraordinary demand. In 1904 and 1905 imports totalled 143 ships of over 700 tons, a combined tonnage of 314,000 tons, contrasting with only 21 domestically built ships of under 25,000 tons. Even in peacetime, imports could be three to four times domestic production, as in 1906 and 1907. Japan also remained heavily dependent on imports of steel and machinery.

To sum up, then, the position at the end of the Meiji period, it can be said that the production of Japanese shipbuilding, steel and machinery had made considerable progress with government stimulation since 1896, after some 25 years or so of very little achievement. But in spite of subsidies many Japanese shipowners had to buy foreign-built ships and as late as 1913 imports equalled domestic production. The industry still relied on foreign steel for much of its requirements (in 1914 34,000 tons of steel out of a total requirement of 44,000 tons were imported), and the difficulties of obtaining these and other supplies were often great and involved expenditure of time as well as money.

Other industries which were regarded as important for Japan's economic growth and independence were chemicals and textiles. In these sectors there is a mixture of private enterprise and state help and there has been controversy over the relative importance of the two kinds of initiative. Cotton and silk became vital for Japan's international balance of payments, both as import substitutes and as foreign earners (and were even regarded as important as job-creators). In both industries the government provided investment in technological progress and quality control, and established pilot plants, but private entrepreneurship was extremely important. Silk was developed by many minor rural capitalists and became a principal source of foreign exchange until the 1930s. Until the 1880s both government and private cotton-spinning mills were on a small scale but cotton spinning expanded rapidly from the mid-1880s (particularly with the emergence of the Osaka Spinning Company, largely the creation of one of the leading private entrepreneurs of the Meiji period, Shibusawa Eiichi) and by the 1890s yarn was being exported. By the 1900s imports of yarn were insignificant. It has been said that the growth of the Japanese textile industries illustrates both the leading sector hypothesis of industrialization, and the export-led growth hypothesis. What is pretty certain is that Japan had an almost continuous balance of payments problem and both import substitution and foreign earnings were imperative. Japan was virtually unprotected by tariff or other obstacles to imports for most of the Meiji period – a lack of protection imposed on her by the 'unequal treaties' of the 1850s and 1860s – and this was a great spur to improve efficiency and competitiveness.

One area of obvious importance was the chemical industry, the industrial linkages of which were numerous.[3] Flows of personnel and technical knowledge between government and private enterprises were important, while links between academic chemists in Japan and Europe, and between Japanese universities and government and private firms, helped to diffuse Western technology around the turn of the century. Like the shipbuilding, steel and cotton industries, the heavy chemical industry illustrates the many problems that faced Japan in the adoption of modern industry in the late nineteenth century: import substitution was important but domestic markets were, paradoxically, often too small to support local production on an efficient scale. Export markets were therefore an important potential supplement enabling larger-scale and economical production, but were extremely difficult to break into, because Japanese units of production were seldom initially producing at a competitive cost level. Moreover, they could not adopt a discriminatory pricing policy.

Another serious problem was the existence of numerous alternative technologies available from outside, and the consequent difficulty of an immature industrial nation and its entrepreneurs, engineers and chemists

---

[3] A useful study is M. Tanaka, 'Industrialisation on the Basis of Imported Technology: A Case-Study of the Japanese Heavy Chemical Industry, 1870–1939', unpublished M.Phil. thesis, University of Sussex, 1978.

in deciding which was an appropriate technology to adopt: appropriate not only for existing resource endowments but also for quality and for future competitiveness. The controversies over British industrial development in the late nineteenth century should convince anyone of the anguish of Japanese industrialists over their decision-making. If Britain should have adopted the ring in spinning, Solvay in chemicals, new steel processes, electrification, new precision tool processes – the list of accusations and criticisms is almost endless – then how much more difficult was the set of problems facing Japan? In any case, there are plenty of economic historians who argue that Britain's pattern of resource endowments, markets and social and educational structures made it sensible for her to pursue the technological path she actually followed.

Japan, it is often said, mixed her styles of capital formation, and used her resources, in a beautifully appropriate manner. Japan was, in the long run, successful. Therein lies a problem: most of her policies can be judged to be successful because she succeeded. Frequently too little is said of her industrial problems, setbacks, failures and occasional salvation by fortuitous events like the First World War.

What is important in this context is to stress that government and private industry may have sometimes been in conflict, may occasionally have been less than cooperative, may have been less than successful at times, but the thrust of policy after 1868 was to encourage the emergence of Japan as a strong, independent industrial state. To this end, government and private enterprise worked mostly together, and one does not have to assume away the self-interests of entrepreneurs and bureaucrats to believe this. The entrepreneurs may well have been profit-maximizers to a degree comparable to those of the Western world, but they were also community centred to the extent that their activities integrated into a generally accepted policy of development. This last point may not lend much support to those who view Japan's leading entrepreneurs as unselfish patriots, but it does argue that in the conditions of the Meiji period self-interest and national aims could fairly easily be reconciled.

It should also be stressed that a great deal of economic development occurred outside these major industrial sectors from the late nineteenth century, and that many industries, indeed, many traditional industrial pursuits such as pottery and dolls, as well as small-scale production of new Western-developed products, contributed greatly both to the rise of the Gross National Product and to the export sector. In spite of considerable government assistance, industries such as heavy chemicals and commercial shipbuilding did not become competitive until the special circumstances of the First World War, and even after 1918 found it difficult to survive.

The account of the shipbuilding and other industries in the Meiji period illustrates the point that the state did sometimes intervene effectively although it also emphasizes that reliance on outside sources of supply remained heavy, and that private entrepreneurship was also vitally important.

III. *Foreign economic relations and their consequences, 1896–1914*

There is the wider question of the extent to which economic policy was successful in avoiding excessive reliance on foreign assistance in the process of economic development. It is often said that Japan is the classic, if not the unique example of a developing nation that managed to pull itself up by its own sandal-thongs; that it financed its own development from domestic sources of capital and therefore managed to avoid the fate of Egypt and other countries. David Landes insists that

Japan accomplished [her] gains largely on her own; certainly she relied far less on outside help than did the follower countries of Continental Europe . . . The initial Japanese advances – in textiles, metallurgy, even railways – were accomplished with domestic savings almost exclusively . . . This largely independent achievement is the more surprising because one would have expected just the reverse. The usual experience has been that, the poorer an economy and the more backward its technology, the greater its dependence on outside aid.[4]

It is true that capital imports into Japan were very low indeed between 1868 and 1896. Two loans amounting to some ¥14.5 million were raised in 1868 and 1872 in London, the first, of ¥3.75 million, to finance the Tokyo–Yokohama railway. These loans were paid off quickly and, according to Landes, total foreign indebtedness up to 1896 never exceeded ¥30 million, and was negligible on the eve of the Sino–Japanese War. Edwin Reubens estimates the *net* inflow of capital into Japan between 1868 and 1895 at a tiny ¥2.4 million.[5] Since these years span the very difficult period from 1868 to 1885, a period of government deficits, rebellion, inflation and deflation, and also part of the initial period of modern economic growth from 1886, it can be agreed that initial reliance on foreign capital was negligible. With the exception of the Takashima coal mine, founded by British capital and operated by British management, direct foreign investment was confined to a few minor undertakings, the most important of which were factories for curing tea. Some attempt was made to spread the benefits of Western

[4] David S. Landes, 'Japan and Europe: Contrasts in Industrialization', in William W. Lockwood (ed.), *The State and Economic Enterprise in Japan* (Princeton, NJ, 1965), pp. 93, 96, 99.
[5] Edwin P. Reubens, 'Foreign Capital and Domestic Development in Japan', in S. Kuznets (ed.), *Economic Growth: Brazil, India, Japan* (Durham, NC, 1955), p. 181

civilization when a foreign tooth-brush factory was set up, but none of this was vital, and even the Takashima mining company was taken over by the Japanese government in 1874.

However, the picture changes considerably from the later years of the 1890s, and more particularly from 1904. Industrialization accelerated under government stimulus after the deficiencies of Japanese heavy industry were revealed by the Sino-Japanese War. Greater investment in iron and steel, shipbuilding, shipping, railways, electricity and armaments was required, and the demand for capital generally exceeded domestic capital formation. The gold standard was adopted in 1897, thus making Japan more attractive to the foreign investor. But investment in Japan in these years was not the result of foreign initiative; it was firmly controlled by government agencies which directed investment into the desired sectors. The central government began borrowing in 1897, and prefectural and municipal governments started raising loans in 1899. The result was a substantial increase in the import of capital – almost ¥200 million between 1897 and 1903 – compared with previous decades. The national debt doubled in these years, in spite of increases in taxation, particularly indirect taxation, as government expenditure rose sharply, trebling between the early 1890s and the early 1900s.

There had been a substantial increase in capital imports between 1897 and 1903, but this increase was dwarfed by the upsurge in foreign borrowing after 1903. During the period 1904–13 capital imports increased tenfold compared with 1897–1903, yielding almost ¥2,000 million. The greatest single cause was the need to finance war preparations and then the actual war with Russia in 1904–5. The political and financial foundations for the war were provided by the Anglo-Japanese Alliance of 1902, which was directed against Russia, and which helped the Japanese to raise loans in the London capital market. Naturally enough the overwhelming proportion of the ¥2,000 million was raised by means of imperial Japanese government bonds, and was used mainly for military purposes – over one-half of the foreign debt was incurred for war and armament, and almost one-third for railways and other public works. It was in this period between the Russo-Japanese War and the First World War that Japan became self-sufficient in naval shipbuilding and laid the foundations of the mightiest navy in the Far East.

So it could be argued that capital imports in this period were of critical economic and strategic importance. They enabled Japan to expand her economic and military power at a far greater rate than could have been financed by domestic supplies of capital alone. They secured her position in Manchuria and Korea, placing her in a much more powerful position vis-à-vis China and Russia, and did much to ensure her long-lived hegemony in East Asia. The period from 1897 to 1914 was crucial in the build-up of heavy industry, which depended heavily on the development of the armament industries and which could not have been financed without this foreign help. Total foreign borrowing between 1904 and 1914 provided about one-sixth of total government revenues, and probably provided about one-fifth of productive capital formation. All in all, about 2–3 per cent of Japan's national income was derived from foreign borrowing in this period.

It has been suggested, once again by Kozo Yamamura,[6] that Japanese militarism, which was partly financed by this import of capital, made a positive contribution to technological progress and the industrialization of the country. This contribution was, he maintains, far greater than that made by direct government efforts to establish modern industrial concerns, efforts which, in any case, he feels were less than successful, a view we have already cited above. Interpretation of the Meiji governments' economic and military policies will probably always be controversial: Harry Oshima, as we shall see, has argued the opposite to Yamamura's thesis: Oshima believes that militarism retarded Japan's economic development.

There are other aspects of economic policy to be considered as qualifying the argument that there was little dependence on outside help, even in the period up to the mid-1890s when, we have argued, the contribution of foreign capital was negligible. If foreign trade and intercourse made a vital contribution to Japan's economic and political development, then dependence on foreigners remained crucial throughout the Meiji period in one form or another.

First of all there was the dependence on foreign technical expertise. Landes tends to minimize this also. He quotes a peak estimate of 213 foreign experts employed by the Japanese government and says that the number declined to 56 in 1887. This, he maintains, shows that Japan relied far less on foreign technical assistance than did nineteenth-century European industrializing nations. But there is dispute about the extent of government employment, and Landes himself mentions the employment of foreigners by private concerns. The great Mitsubishi shipping company NYK (Nippon Yūsen Kaisha) employed no fewer than 224 foreigners during the Sino-Japanese War. Koichi Emi gives more detailed statistics of the employment of foreigners.[7] In contrast to Landes' figure of 213 in 1874 he gives a total of 385 employed by both central and local governments in 1872. Between 1876 and 1895, just under 4,000 foreign employees were used, and their salaries were a heavy burden on

[6] K. Yamamura, 'Success Illbegotten? The Role of Meiji Militarism in Japan's Technological Progress', Journal of Economic History, vol. XXXVII, no. 1 (March 1977).
[7] Koichi Emi, Government Fiscal Activity and Economic Growth in Japan, 1868–1960 (Tokyo, 1963), especially pp. 114–19.

government revenues. Emi estimates that the cost of employing foreigners averaged 42 per cent of the Ministry of Industry's entire budget
between 1870, when the Ministry was established, and 1885. The Ministry set up a School of Technology in 1871 and by the later 1870s
expenditure on foreign instructors was comparable to expenditure on
mining and telegraphic experts, although the railways accounted for the
largest expenditure on foreign technicians.

So it is clear that dependence on foreign technicians was more substantial than Landes has argued, and, moreover, the measure of Japan's
dependence on foreign technology and other expertise must include the
large number of Japanese sent abroad to study foreign methods, and who
replaced foreigners when they returned. Between 1868 and 1895,
125,000 Japanese went abroad to study and to engage in diplomacy and
business. All this was of immense advantage to Japanese modernization,
but it was very costly, and the Japanese made intensive efforts to cut
down the cost by replacing foreigners with Japanese as quickly as
possible, so that by the mid-1880s the proportion of the Ministry of
Industry's budget spent on foreigners had dropped from two-thirds to
less than one-fifth.

There were other areas of strategic dependence on foreigners that
government economic policy had to cope with. Until the establishment
of the Yokohama Specie Bank in 1880, the financing of Japan's foreign
trade was entirely in the hands of foreigners, and despite the rise of
Mitsubishi's NYK in the 1880s (with substantial government subsidy),
over 90 per cent of Japan's foreign trade was carried in foreign ships, and
90 per cent of trade was handled by foreign merchants in 1885. By 1900
the Japanese had made considerable progress in developing mercantile
firms and overseas shipping lines, but were still dependent on foreign
firms and ships for the handling of the bulk of their trade: in 1900 60 per
cent of trade was still handled by merchants and 70 per cent of trade went
in foreign bottoms. After 1900 the rise of the giant zaibatsu trading
companies such as Mitsui Bussan and Mitsubishi Shoji completely altered
this part of the picture and by 1913 the bulk of foreign trade was handled
by Japanese firms. However, the expansion of Japan's mercantile marine,
though rapid, was not rapid enough to wrest supremacy from foreign
carriers, and in 1913 over 50 per cent of Japan's foreign trade was still
carried in foreign bottoms.

One of the problems of developing the native mercantile marine was
that before the First World War the Japanese shipbuilding industry was
still not big enough – or competitive enough – to meet the demands of
Japanese shipowners. Japan was still importing one-half of her shipping
requirements in 1913. The expansion of the shipbuilding industry was, as
we have seen, hampered by the slow development of the Japanese iron

and steel and engineering industries. It is true that progress had been made since 1900, when, from the strategic and balance of payments points of view, Japan was dangerously dependent on foreign sources for 99 per cent of her total steel consumption. But in 1914 the Yawata steel works was still only capable of supplying rather less than one-quarter of the shipbuilding industry's steel requirements.

All in all, then, the Japanese were, in fact, quite dangerously dependent on many forms of foreign aid and trade in the period up to 1914. Moreover, the uses to which capital imports were put, and the general pattern of government expenditure – in fact, virtually the whole of the government's economic policy – have been severely criticised. Professor Harry Oshima is one of the foremost critics of fiscal policy in the Meiji era.[8] He insists that agriculture was overburdened with taxation to such an extent that progress in the sector was hampered. Over the whole of the Meiji period the land taxes supplied at least two-fifths of the combined revenues of both central and local governments. Earlier in the period it was even more important; probably three-quarters of all revenue came from the land in the 1870s, while central government revenues alone depended upon the land to the extent of four-fifths. And very little of this money was ploughed back into agricultural improvement.

Oshima maintains that the land tax bore particularly heavily on agriculture because the Meiji economy was basically a subsistence economy. Taxes probably constituted some 10 per cent or more of income and this was a serious matter for many peasants, who had little, if any, income surplus to subsistence requirements, and consequently found it all but impossible to make improvements in farm productivity.

... the frequency of disputes, uprisings and riots, the rise in unpaid taxes and land confiscated in lieu of tax payments, the increase in debts and mortgage foreclosures, and the rapid rise in the amount of tenanted land (from around 30 per-cent of the total cultivated land to 45 per-cent by the end of the Meiji period) were clear signs of the difficulties experienced by the majority of agriculturists in the period.[9]

This drain on farm income had adverse effects far beyond the retardation of the agricultural sector. Low rural incomes and low urban wages restricted the domestic market for manufactured goods, and so the development of the whole economy was also retarded, or only stimulated by an aggressive drive for colonies and bigger export markets. It would not necessarily have been retrograde to tax the agricultural sector if a large proportion of the revenue received had been returned to agriculture and industry. But this, Oshima says, did not happen.

[8] Harry T. Oshima, 'Meiji Fiscal Policy and Agricultural Progress', in William W. Lockwood (ed.), *The State and Economic Enterprise in Japan* (Princeton, NJ, 1965).   [9] *Ibid.*, p. 364.

Table 151a. *Percentage of
government expenditure on the
military*

	1880	1890	1900	1910
Military	13	20.5	31	42

Table 151b. *Percentage distribution of government expenditure
(selected items)*

	1880	1890	1900	1910
Military	13	20.5	31	42
All state services	71	67	57	62
Primary industry	4	4	4	3.5
Secondary industry	1.5	0.4	2	1
Transport and communications	9	15	18	11
Education and research	7.5	8	10	11
Health and welfare	2.5	1	2	1

Source: Harry T. Oshima in William W. Lockwood (ed.), *The State and Economic
Enterprise* (Princeton, NJ, 1965), p. 370.

It did not happen because an increasing proportion of government
revenue was spent on the military (Table 151a). Contrast these figures
with expenditure on other sectors – particularly primary and secondary
industry, education and research, and health and welfare (Table 151b).
The massive expenditure on defence and war caused inflationary pressures. It diverted investment funds and demand into almost totally
unproductive channels, and produced little or nothing for the purposes
of useful consumption. Naturally the Japanese needed some military
establishment but they provoked war with China and Russia, and if
expenditure on these wars is excluded, defence expenditure is halved. If
this reduction had been applied to land taxes the burden on agriculture
could also have been halved. A less regressive structure of indirect taxes,
upon which the government came to rely heavily in the later years of the
Meiji period, would also have been beneficial to economic and social
development.

So Oshima concludes that the fiscal and economic policies of the Meiji
governments had pernicious short-term effects. If we add to these
strictures the undoubted fact that much of the capital imported between
1897 and 1914 went on defence and war, the economic policies of the
later Meiji governments seem on reflection, to some historians at least, to

have been less than sublimely successful, contrary to what is often said. Since the Japanese economy was running into serious difficulties on the eve of the First World War, as a result of borrowing heavily on the international capital market, these criticisms of economic policy seem to be reinforced.

During the years from 1904 to 1913 serious deficits on both invisible and visible accounts of the balance of payments developed. The visible deficit exactly doubled, from ¥350 million in the period 1896–1903 to ¥700 million. Almost as serious was the huge rise in the invisible deficit, which reached over ¥400 million between 1904 and 1913. So Japan imported a massive ¥1,100 million in excess of her exports of goods and services. The deficit on invisible account was almost entirely due to the cost of servicing the foreign debt which had been incurred, because net freight receipts had become positive from 1905. Moreover the deficit on merchandise account about equalled the total imports of capital goods in the period, so one can realize the importance of the capital imports that financed these deficits. Japan was going all out for economic growth and military expansion and to hell with the balance of payments. But the situation was becoming critical. By 1913 more than half, 55 per cent, of the loans raised by the government had gone into war and armament, and this could not be said to help the balance of payments. Nearly half of the government's entire budget in 1913 was devoted to the military services and war debt interest, and over half the greatly increased national debt was foreign held.

The inflow of foreign capital was inflationary because it was used to increase gold reserves, against which the Bank of Japan increased its note issues substantially: its note circulation doubled between 1900 and 1913, forcing prices up. William Lockwood sums up the process:

Expanding money incomes and rising prices tended to make the trade deficit even larger. This necessitated still more loans to support the exchange, and these in turn further increased service charges on the mounting debt.

Once this inflationary cycle got under way it was difficult to check. The Bank of Japan had no effective control over the money market. In any case its policy was subordinated to the fiscal requirements of the Treasury. Expenditures for the production of armaments and other strategic undertakings expressed a national policy inflexibly pursued, and amounted to a fixed charge on the economy. From 1910 to 1913 Japan lost over 20% of her gold holdings, despite continued borrowing abroad. A financial crisis was approaching.[10]

Japan was already in an economic crisis: Gross Domestic Product dropped in 1913, and grew again only very slowly in 1914 and 1915. She was rescued from this financial and economic crisis, not by any

---

[10] William W. Lockwood, *The Economic Development of Japan: Growth and Structural Change, 1868–1938* (Princeton, NJ, 1954), p. 37.

acts of government economic policy, but by a completely fortuitous event – the outbreak of the First World War. The war made a tremendous impact on the Japanese economy after 1915, and Japan became a vital source of supply for the Allies and for the many markets previously supplied by the belligerents. Many sectors of industry, trade and commerce enjoyed rapid expansion, and exports grew so quickly that even rising imports were outstripped. The volume of cotton piece goods exported quadrupled, and their value sextupled between 1913 and 1918. Iron and steel production, the generation of electricity, and the mercantile marine all more than doubled. The balance of payments deficits were wiped out and foreign balances accumulated abroad probably exceeded ¥2,000 million. The deficit on current account of ¥1,100 million between 1904 and 1913 was converted into a surplus of over ¥2,400 million between 1914 and 1919.

IV. *Social policy*

It is convenient to pause at this point in the account of economic policy in order to consider in more detail some aspects of social policy in Japan. Japanese social history has not attracted very much attention from Western historians and economists, who have often been preoccupied with the 'lessons' to be learned from the analysis of Japan's economic development, lessons for such varying economies as those of the less-developed nations and that of the United Kingdom.

Over the past couple of decades there has, it is true, been much interest in the development of education in both 'pre-modern' Tokugawa, and post-Restoration Japan. R. P. Dore led the way among non-Japanese historians and sociologists in highlighting the considerable development of formal education in Tokugawa Japan, although he shocked his followers in 1972 by questioning his own earlier estimates of the extent of schooling before 1868, suggesting that perhaps quality, not quantity, was the relevant variable.[11]

The Meiji governments built upon the foundations of formal education laid before 1868 and this educational tradition, and structure, which were unique to Japan among non-Western nations in the nineteenth century, and were a contrast to the situation in the less-developed countries after the Second World War, has led to much speculation on the importance of literacy and general educational attainment as a contributory factor in economic development.

From 1872, when the government announced the introduction of a universal and compulsory system of elementary education (a system

---

[11] See Dore's *Education in Tokugawa Japan* (London, 1965), and his article 'The Importance of Educational Traditions: Japan and Elsewhere', *Pacific Affairs*, vol. XLV, no. 4 (Winter 1972–3).

which incorporated, for instance, the *terakoya*, which supplied the kind of tuition suitable for ordinary, non-aristocratic children, who would be the future entrepreneurs, artisans, factory workers, clerks and farmers) to the early 1900s, the elementary education sector grew and flourished. Eventually Japan was to become what is perhaps the most literate and education-conscious nation in the world, generating all its virtues and vices (for instance, the diploma-diseased society, in Dore's words, with a disturbing rate of juvenile suicide).

As in other diverse fields like banking and constitutional development the Japanese ranged widely, from France to United States, in their search for appropriate educational techniques, expertise and systems. The government founded a large variety of educational and quasi-educational institutions – once again, often building on pre-modern foundations: after all, it was under the Tokugawa that the Bureau for the Translation of Barbarian Books had been established. Universities, high schools and agricultural research centres were among its creations. But it should be remembered that Japan then, as now, offered scope also for a huge amount of private enterprise in this as in other areas of human activity; private universities and other establishments flourished. In fact, the first Japanese university, Keio, was a private foundation, the creation of Fukuzawa Yukichi in the 1860s.

The government imported teachers as well as systems, and the Japanese educational system offered scope for foreigners, many of whom brought alien concepts and useful expertise; some of whom used Japan for their own cultural as well as academic and material development.

The government also endeavoured – not uniquely, surely – to impose its own views of ethics on its educational system. In conjunction with universal conscription, also introduced in 1872, the state, it has been forcibly argued, created a population and workforce characterized by unquestioning obedience, work-discipline, group- and state-orientated service, and Emperor-worship. Shinto became a state religion and, reinforced by the Imperial Rescript on Education of 1890, was an instrument for inculcating traditions of loyalty and filial piety. Schools had morals courses based on the oligarchy's views of desirable personal and social qualities. But at least one authority has argued that the oligarchs were 'pragmatists, not ideologists'.[12] This may be true, but it is also believed by many that, just as in the agricultural and industrial sectors, the 1880s and 1890s saw the seeds of future serious troubles sown, so in the political and social spheres were the catastrophes of the twentieth century germinated by educational, social and political attitudes fostered by Meiji oligarchs.

[12] Herbert Passin, *Society and Education in Japan* (New York, 1966), p. 81. This book gives a valuable account of educational developments in Japan from the Tokugawa era to the post-Second World War period.

On a more mundane level, the Meiji period witnessed the familiar, perennial debate over vocational versus cultural training. The debate, then, as now, was inconclusive. Education in Japan provided both job-preparation and general education. Whether the reputation of the Japanese worker for intelligent, skilled and arduous work singled – and singles – him or her out from others is, of course, also debateable. T.C. Smith once wrote, 'It is easy to overlook the significance of labour in Japanese industrialization because it posed no major problem.'[13]

This remark should imply that our next important sphere of social policy is either one that requires little treatment, or one that requires a great deal of sociological, political and economic analysis to explain the alleged docility of Japanese labour. The government's attitude towards labour was, quite simply, repressive whenever signs of trouble appeared. Yet unionism, and politically motivated unionism particularly, was scanty compared with European and North American countries. Some industrial unions – like the seamen's – did emerge in the twentieth century, but it is well known that, even in the post-Second World War period, enterprise-based unions are the more common form of association. To read Ayusawa's book is to be impressed by the odd eruptions of labour discontent: the rickshaw men, for example.[14] Japan had its quota of socialists, anarchists and so on, and there were dissident political movements, but these were all small groups, not comparable to the social democratic movements of Europe in the second half of the nineteenth century, let alone to the early efforts at unionization in Britain in the first half of the century.

Even more recent works than Ayusawa's, works such as Hugh Patrick's *Japanese Industrialization and its Social Consequences*,[15] are characterized by very brief remarks on labour movements and labour conditions in Meiji Japan. One reads of exploitation of young dormitory-housed females, of appalling conditions in ships, factories and workshops, of long hours and poor pay. But measuring-sticks for comparison are notoriously unreliable and it is far from clear that in these respects Japan was very different from most countries even in the same time-span, as well as in comparable stages of the industrialization process. She certainly lacked the mass of master–servant, union, and factory legislation that Britain enjoyed, the social insurance of Germany in Bismarck's time, or the alliance of labour and politicians of many countries. She equally certainly lacked neither repressive legislation nor

---

[13] T. C. Smith, *The Agrarian Origins of Modern Japan* (Stanford, 1959), p. 212.
[14] I. F. Ayusawa, *A History of Labor in Modern Japan* (Honolulu, 1966).
[15] Hugh Patrick (ed.) (Berkeley, 1976). An exception is Koji Taira's contribution on labour to vol. VII of the *Cambridge Economic History of Europe* (Cambridge, 1978), in which he explains the small extent of unionism.

punitive police action. The Public Peace Police Act of 1900 was neither the first, nor the last, law aimed at repressing unwanted political and labour movements, but it is regarded as a particularly effective and harmful assault on democratic aims as well as on incipient socialist or union associations. Under this and other laws the government imprisoned and silenced opponents both of the state and of the employers. The one law designed to protect certain classes of workers – the Factory Law of 1911 – took 30 years to come to pass and further years before even its limited sanctions against the employment of women and juveniles on, for example, night shifts were implemented in the 1920s. By this time the Meiji era had long since ended, and so early Japanese industrialization – even relatively mature industrial change also – took place with none of even the limited government constraints that characterized Britain before 1850. The employers and the state always argued that (a) since paternalism was prevalent, the workers did not need Western-style legislative protection and (b) contradictorily, that the imposition of Western-style conditions of work would cripple Japan in its struggle to be competitive and achieve its place in the sun.[16]

On a par with legislative neglect of labour conditions was the serious neglect of social infrastructure over the entire century from 1868. Yet mortality rates declined – as far as the deficient demographic statistics can indicate this – during even the Meiji period, and certainly more substantially in the 1920s. Irene Taeuber's invaluable study of Japan's population trends points out that Japan provided the first proof that mortality was susceptible to cheap and elementary improvements in water supply and basic disease-prevention measures in a physical and nutritional environment that was far from good.[17] Japan remained a country of high mortality rates relative to the other industrial nations until the late 1940s, suffering from the killing diseases, such as tuberculosis, associated with poor sanitation, poor living and working conditions, and poor nutrition. But other diseases, such as cholera, which attacked millions in the nineteenth century, were eliminated by the application of relatively simple medical and sanitary methods fostered by the government in the Meiji period. The traditionally excellent personal hygiene of the Japanese also contributed to the health of the population. Nevertheless, the strictures on official attitudes towards public health must stand. According to Oshima's figures, cited on p. 1120, government expenditure on health and welfare was only 1 per cent of the total in 1910. While first the Education Department, and then the Home Department, had a Sanitary Bureau, from 1873, it was not until 1937 that a Ministry of Health and

[16] See Byron K. Marshall, *Capitalism and Nationalism in Prewar Japan: The Ideology of the Business Elite, 1868–1941* (Stanford, 1967).
[17] Irene B. Taeuber, *The Population of Japan* (Princeton, NJ, 1958).

Welfare was established. The average expectation of life in Japan remained low by European standards until after the Second World War. Most Japanese have always used such comparisons in their self-critical way, but it is worth noting that by Asian standards Japan was doing well, in this as in other respects, before the end of the nineteenth century. She was feeding and employing one of the world's bigger populations, and her neglect of many of the basic amenities – like sewers – was the other side of her single-minded pursuit of economic growth and great power status. Her people were poor, but better off than most of the world's population, and this pursuit (later, after 1950, the phrase 'economic animal' was to be coined) solved many of her problems. It created others, of course, but Japan has, since as far back as the 1780s, when she first began to feel serious Russian pressure, long been faced with difficult choices.

The possibilities of redistributing income and wealth, for instance, may not have been considered very seriously anywhere in the world before 1914, and therefore one should not condemn the Japanese government for its patterns of taxation. But these patterns persisted throughout the inter-war period and even reappeared after the early 1950s. Initially, in the Meiji period, the structure of taxation may well have been conducive to economic growth, just as the British structure was from the eighteenth century to the First World War, and most comment on the very slight burdens imposed on larger personal incomes, corporate incomes, and inheritances, has been concerned with the relationship these have had to the need to foster the development of the economy. But government taxation policies also had social results. Japan relied heavily on land taxes at first and then, increasingly, on indirect taxes and revenues from state enterprises or monopolies; these two categories included railways, post office, salt and tobacco (long a wise and lucrative monopoly) and 'essentials' such as soy sauce, sugar, medicines and textiles.

The finance of health and welfare services was, therefore, doubly hampered for a very long time after the era in which these services were not well developed in most industrial nations, and, in the case of Japan, in which a mounting relative burden of defence expenditure cut back the amount available for transfers. By the end of the Meiji period the revenue from direct taxes, other than land taxes, only just about equalled the latter, and by this time commodity taxes surpassed either of these two categories of direct taxes, and non-tax revenues surpassed any other source of government income. The incidence of this structure on the poorer people, including the urban workers but more particularly the farm population, was very heavy.

To this day the provision of state social services remains, in Japan, comparatively underdeveloped. In the past this has been explained by the substitution of family, village and enterprise services, and by the high personal savings level. The offset of high personal standards of cleanliness in the sphere of health and hygiene is an analogy: the Japanese learned to substitute their own efforts for the comparative absence of the state in these fields. There were some promising signs of progress in the 1920s: the creation of the Social Affairs Department of the Ministry for Home Affairs (1921) and the Health Insurance Law (1922) were all part of not only a Japanese reform movement but of an international trend. Legislative changes continued along these lines into the 1930s, but their effectiveness, as well as their coverage, was often very limited. In Japan, as in other countries, more comprehensive reforms had to await the post-1945 world, and even these reforms were to leave Japan far behind Europe in social security provision.

V. The First World War and its aftermath, 1914–32

The Japanese have led a very precarious existence in many respects, and this precariousness was particularly apparent in Japan's fortunes, in both the economic and social spheres, during and after the First World War. The wartime boom was heady stuff, with impressive advances in shipbuilding, steel, textiles, engineering, electricity generation and application, and in many other branches of manufacturing.

One of the most spectacular gains was in the shipbuilding industry. Annual launchings increased from 55,000 gross tons in 1913 to a peak of 636,000 gross tons in 1919 (a peak not surpassed till the Second World War), while imports of ships virtually disappeared by the end of the war. All this was not achieved without difficulties. Japan was dependent on imports for many supplies and these gradually ceased as the war spread. With the steep rise in price of ships home manufacture of the necessary machinery outside the yards got under way for the first time. By the end of the war Japanese yards and machine-producers had made tremendous technological progress, particularly in reciprocal engine, turbine and boiler construction, and could at last supply the needs of the industry. Especially rapid progress had been made in naval ship technology, which always led the private sector, as the construction in 1920 of two 33,800 ton warships in the Yokusuka and Kura naval yards illustrates. By July 1917, it no longer seemed necessary to provide government aid, and the laws of 1896 were suspended; in December 1919, they were abolished.

Of even greater significance for the 1920s – although not for the post-Second World War era – than the expansion of the shipbuilding sector was the remarkable boom in Japan's textile industries. Woollen production almost trebled. Cotton and silk were launched on an upward path that continued, in the case of silk, until the crash of 1930–2, and in the case of cotton, until the Second World War. Cotton yarn production doubled, and raw silk output more than doubled, between 1913 and 1929.

In the cotton industry, the increase in yarn production was overshadowed by an important structural change. Japan became a serious competitor in the world's piece-goods markets. The expansion of both silk and cotton was to lay up severe but different problems for the 1930s. Japan entered markets for cottons previously dominated by European countries, and was therefore to antagonize them in the 1930s, while the collapse of the American demand for silk was to produce a particular strain for the long-suffering rural sector. It was in the years after 1914 that the value of cotton exports began to approach more closely the value of those of silk goods, although it did not surpass silk until the mid-1930s. During the war the number of factory operatives increased by more than 650,000, and almost half this increase was in textile factories.

The government did not intervene very actively in this period before the 1930s. Even after 1900 when the government was able to act more independently in tariff policy, it refrained from imposing any serious obstacles, and the tariff revisions of 1911 and after were usually very moderate. Policy to manufacturing industry was to encourage cooperation, and to stimulate and improve the quality of exports, but generally there was little direct intervention except during crisis periods such as after the great Kanto earthquake of 1923. It was not until the 1930s that direct government intervention in industry returned.

As in other advanced industrial economies the end of the war was soon followed by recession; as elsewhere, the boom broke in 1920. In Japan over-expansion of capacity had led to labour shortages and excess demand had caused hyperinflation. Deflation followed and the old pattern of labour surplus re-emerged. International productive capacity was far larger in many sectors than total demand warranted, and competition became severe. Japanese exports fell off sharply from the inflated wartime levels, export surpluses were soon replaced by import surpluses, and the surplus on invisibles also dropped.

The 1920s saw severe retrenchment and a marked increase in the tempo of industrial concentration and rationalization. There was a keener awareness of the need for higher levels of efficiency, and the drive to adopt better technology meant a strengthening of the oligopolistic structure of industry, since the groups with adequate resources were those like the zaibatsu which had been gaining in power since before the First World War. Labour productivity rose sharply and greatly outstripped the increase in wages. Bank rationalization – aided by state intervention – helped to enhance the financial power of the zaibatsu. After the financial crisis of 1927, new banking legislation in January 1928 doubled the capital requirements of banks. The number of ordinary banks, which had been 2,285 in 1918, dropped to 1,359 in early 1927, 1,030 at the end of 1929, and further slid to 913 in 1930. The average capital per bank increased from ¥430,000 in 1918 to ¥1.5 million in 1928, and although banking remained unitary, the number of branches per bank did increase from two in 1918 to five in 1928.

Rationalization did not, however, extend to the traditional economy. So productivity differentials and wage differentials grew, and while the traditional economy maintained a large share of the labour force, the modern sector produced a larger share of total output. The cleavage between the rural population and the urbanized industrial population became more marked, and was later to feed the trend towards militaristic authoritarianism. But the 1920s was the period in which parliamentary democracy and liberal economic policy were more dominant than at any other time between 1868 and 1945. Until the great depression the state did not furnish all the trappings of economic nationalism: foreign trade was still comparatively liberalized, Japan was striving to resume the gold standard, state support for industry was much less than it was to be after 1930, and liberal parliamentarians did not sympathize with a military build-up.

The comparative lack of state support for industry in the 1920s may be illustrated by the way in which the shipbuilding industry was allowed to slide into depression from the dizzy heights attained during the war and the short-lived boom that followed it. Shipbuilding production held up well in 1920, but in each of the years 1921 and 1922 it was more than halved. The nadir of the industry was reached in the mid-1920s: in the five years from 1924 to 1928 only 330,000 gross tons were launched, with an inter-war low of 48,000 tons – one-tenth of the 1920 figure – reached in 1925. Once again imports outstripped domestic production: 486,000 tons against 330,000 tons in the five years. The government did very little to help, and the policies of the 1920s and the liberal groups that espoused them were to be discredited by the end of the decade, which was one of great difficulties caused by the slower rate of economic growth, the economic policies of the governments of the time, and by rural distress underpinned by increased population pressure.

The population of Japan almost doubled in the 60 years from the mid-1870s to the mid-1930s, rising from 36 million to 71 million. Moreover, the *rate* of growth of population showed a steady tendency to rise, from under 1 per cent per annum before 1900, to 1.25 per cent between 1900 and 1920, and to 1.5 per cent per annum in the 1920s. Over 2.25 million workers were added to the labour force in the 1920s and a major problem of the period was where to place them. A poverty-stricken agriculture could not absorb them; indeed, it needed to lose labour itself, yet the number employed in it was virtually the same in 1930 as it had been in 1920. Agriculture, including other primary industries, was still huge in 1930, employing exactly one-half of the working population, yet only contributing just under one-fifth of the national income. It suffered enormously in the 1920s and 1930s and its suffering and unrest contributed significantly to the rise of militarism and foreign expansionism after 1930.

Nor could manufacturing industry absorb the additional workers, let alone relieve agriculture of its underemployed. One problem was that the rate of economic growth and of industrial expansion was, in the 1920s, the lowest since 1890. Net Domestic Product probably rose at no more than 3 per cent per annum, and with a population growth rate of 1.5 per cent per annum, per capita incomes rose by a mere 1.5 per cent per annum, and by no means all of this was enjoyed in rising consumption standards. The result was that employment in manufacturing and construction rose very slowly between 1920 and 1930: only 500,000 of the 2.25 million went into these sectors, and in 1930 employment in them was only 5,876,000 compared with over 14 million in agriculture alone. The problem was exacerbated by the movement towards industrial rationalization, which was emphasizing capital intensity rather than labour intensity in industry.

A number of factors combined to induce an attitude of pessimism about the population problem in the 1920s. The birth-rate appeared to soar in the early years of the decade, while the need for rice imports grew drastically: imports of rice quintupled between 1917 and 1927. During the war and up to the mid-1920s the price of rice increased dramatically and the cost of living index much more than doubled between 1914 and 1924. The Tokyo–Yokohama earthquake of 1923 was another blow to confidence, and then the US Immigration Law of 1924 seemed the final straw. The Japanese bitterly resented the total exclusion of Orientals, while quotas were imposed on most other nationalities. They already felt themselves discriminated against by the White Australia policy, and it is sobering to reflect that if the Americans had allowed a Japanese quota on the same basis as for others, fewer than 300 Japanese would have been admitted. It was for this that yet another step on the way to the disasters of 1941 was taken.

All these circumstances began to make some inroads into the hitherto prevailing government and military attitudes toward population growth. Right through the Meiji and Taisho periods the attitude had generally been quite sanguine: more numbers meant greater economic and military strength, and it was accepted that a great power would have to have a population of some 80–100 million by the later twentieth century. But by the later 1920s even the government and the military had to acknowledge the strength of the arguments over overpopulation. In 1927 the Tanaka government set up a Commission for the Study of the Problems of Population and Food Supply, and also established a Department of Overseas Affairs to encourage emigration and colonization. Nevertheless, the attitudes of many officials, including the prime minister himself, remained ambiguous: Tanaka stated before the commission that an increasing population was one symbol of expanding national strength. He was an army general. The commission, however, in its reports in 1930, emphasized the limits of emigration and colonization, and urged population control. Even in the 1930s the views of the military and other nationalists did not entirely swamp enlightened opinion, for there was increased advocacy of birth control by some authorities, including a minister of education. But in general, long-term industrialization combined with expansion overseas were the accepted solutions in the 1930s, and even before then great efforts were made to increase food supplies from the colonies of Chosen (Korea) and Taiwan. In 1912 rice imports from the two colonies had totalled under 1.25 million *koku*,[18] with Taiwan supplying by far the greater amount – just under 1 million *koku*. In the later 1920s they were supplying 8 million *koku*, or 12 per cent of Japan's annual supply of rice. By now Chosen was contributing well over twice the amount coming from Taiwan. However, by the late 1920s colonial rice was seriously depressing the Japanese farmer's market, especially when there were good harvests in Japan, as in 1930, when many farmers were virtually ruined.

Colonial competition is one explanation of the extremely poor record of Japanese farming in the 1920s. Farm prices halved between 1925 and 1930 and so there was no price incentive for the Japanese farmer to increase production. Costs of production were one-third lower in Chosen, from which ever-increasing quantities of food were coming. When, on top of this, the silk boom burst in 1930 – with the catastrophic drop in American demand during the great depression – disaster came to Japanese agriculture. It was greatly overpopulated, resulting in extremely small-scale farming. The average size of a farm in Japan excluding Hokkaido was one *chō*, or 2.5 acres; the average in south-west Japan was even smaller, around 2 acres. In 1930, 56 per cent of all farms were in the size range 0.5–2 *chō*, and this percentage had been steadily increasing. The survival of small units was ensured by the prohibition of the sale of land, the confining of the oldest son to the land, and the persistence of

---

[18] A *koku* is approximately five bushels.

paddy rice cultivation in a mountainous country. Farming was not only grossly overpopulated, it was also grossly unprofitable. If wages are attributed to family labour, and interest allowed on capital invested, most Japanese farms were in deficit. With the average farm size standing at 1 *chō*, the Japanese Bureau of Statistics estimated that farms of less than 1.2 *chō* were in deficit, and that a reasonable standard of life could not be achieved on farms of less than 2.5 *chō*. The maintenance of production was requiring massive inputs of labour and fertilizer.

Tenancy was a serious problem of low living standards in rural Japan. The proportion of agricultural land let out to tenants in 1868 has been estimated at 20 per cent; by 1930 it was 48 per cent. The Bureau of Agriculture estimated that rents of ricefields varied from 25 per cent to over 80 per cent of the value of their produce, with average rents above 50 per cent. It was reckoned that rents in Japan were seven times the English level, and much higher than European rents. Ryoichi Ishii commented in 1937, 'It is rather surprising that the vast and ever-increasing population of tenants and part-tenants have silently endured, until quite recently, the feudal heritage of such exorbitant rents.'[19]

The tenants were beginning to rebel in the 1920s. The number of tenancy disputes was only 85 in 1917, but had jumped to 2,206 in 1925 and by 1934 was 5,828. By 1930 over 4,000 peasants' unions had been formed. The cause of disputes was shifting from, for example, rent rebates after bad harvests, to the problem of security of tenure, which had always been very slight, but was becoming ever more precarious as landlords demanded the termination of leases as a counter to tenants' protest movements. New tax measures which allowed relief on owner-cultivated land worsened the situation for the tenants. Termination of leases sometimes resulted in the amalgamation of fields and more extensive farming – even occasionally in mechanization – resulting in the displacement of labour.

The government responded in a very half-hearted fashion to the problem. There was a Tenancy Conciliation Law in 1924, and in 1926 the Regulations for the Establishment of Owner-Farmers were promulgated, but these measures barely touched the problem. It was generally agreed that a thoroughgoing land reform which would confirm to tenants the titles of their land was politically and financially impossible. Yet it would be such a land reform, combined with rapid industrialization to siphon off the surplus labour, which would be the salvation of Japanese agriculture after the Second World War.

The problems of the 1920s were, of course, much wider than population pressure and rural distress, and some historians have argued that they

---

[19] Ryoichi Ishii, *Population Pressure and Economic Life in Japan* (London, 1937), p. 155.

embraced misguided economic policies amidst generally very difficult international economic conditions. However, not every writer on Japan would subscribe to the view that government economic policies worsened the situation. G. C. Allen has argued that the 1920s saw a familiar kind of episode in Japanese economic history.[20] They were an example of the pattern of boom and bust which he believes characterizes the economic development of Japan: a period of deflation, retrenchment in government expenditure, and of rationalization of industry, during which the inefficient firms were weeded out and industrial concentration increased, strengthening groups like the zaibatsu. A period, in other words, like the first half of the 1880s, the late 1940s, and the mid-1960s. Such periods followed phases of rapid expansion, inflation, and the proliferation of business concerns and were, Allen argues, essential episodes in the creation of a dynamic, efficient industrial economy.

Hugh Patrick adopts a different view of the decade.[21] He does not deny the rationalization and streamlining that took place in various economic sectors, particularly banking, but he does argue that monetary policies retarded growth, thus making conditions in agriculture, and general social and political trends, worse than they might have been. The government thinking of the 1920s was dominated by typical liberal doctrines of financial orthodoxy. Like the British governments of the same period, Japanese administrations were committed to a return to the gold standard at a parity with the dollar which seriously overvalued the domestic currency. To maintain the high exchange rate of the yen would be very difficult if domestic prices were not brought down substantially so as to make Japan's exports more competitive and to discourage imports, thus correcting the growing import surpluses of the period, which put pressure on the exchange value of the yen. But during the war prices in Japan had risen faster than those of her major competitors on the world's markets, and domestic prices did not fall as rapidly as did prices in other major countries in the recession of 1920–2. This recession lasted longer in countries like Britain and the United States, and prices and wages there fell faster. The Japanese government persisted in supporting the yen at about the pre-war rate, which meant that export prices were too high and import prices were too low. The result was current account deficits which had to be cured.

The only policy instrument that financial orthodoxy could contemplate at the time was deflation, even if this meant restricting industrial growth and producing unemployment, although there were short

[20] G. C. Allen, 'Factors in Japan's Economic Growth', in C. D. Cowan (ed.), *The Economic Development of China and Japan* (London, 1964).

[21] Hugh T. Patrick, 'The Economic Muddle of the 1920's', in James W. Morley (ed.), *Dilemmas of Growth in Prewar Japan* (Princeton, NJ, 1971).

periods during which circumstances forced the government to try other methods, such as allowing the exchange rate to depreciate in the face of rapidly rising imports after the 1923 earthquake. But it was deflation that triumphed, in spite of the fact that this periodically hit the unstable banking system very hard. It was this effect on the banking system that, Patrick says, was to inhibit the government from going for a short but savage deflation that may have solved the problem. It was spasmodic deflation throughout the 1920s that was so debilitating. It is not surprising that the government hesitated: the number of banks was very large and on the average they were very small, weak unit banks – the branch system, prevalent in Britain, was very undeveloped – which were undercapitalized and overconcentrated in landing policies. Many failed even before the 1927 crisis, but in that year a severe panic gripped the banking world, and even major banks like the Bank of Taiwan and the Fifteenth Bank (the old 15th National Bank of the 1870s) failed. The government passed a new Banking Law in 1927 which came into operation in January 1928, and enforced a doubling of the capitalization of a bank. The result was that by 1929 the average net worth of a bank was double that of the 1922 level.

With such an unstable banking system, the dangers of deflation and credit restriction were obviously great, but the government, though inhibited, nevertheless plumped for these measures in order to return to the gold standard at the pre-war parity of approximately 50 US cents to the yen. It reinforced its deflationary monetary policies in the 1920s by a deflationary fiscal policy: except for 1927 and 1928, the policy was to have budget surpluses between 1921 and 1931. The ratio of government expenditure to Net Domestic Product declined particularly sharply between 1921 and 1925, and again in 1929 and 1930. This may have been deflationary but at least it was now more useful government expenditure – military expenditure dropped sharply. However, some might argue that this also validates the arguments of those who believe that Japanese economic growth traditionally depended on a strong military stimulus.

According to Patrick:

the Japanese government's muddled objective to return to the gold standard at pre-World War I par, and the attendant deflationary fiscal and monetary policies taken in the 1920s, were responsible for much of the retardation of growth in that decade. At fault was not the gold standard itself, but the decision to compete internationally by pushing down the domestic price level and returning to gold at the old par, rather than depreciating the yen and establishing a new, lower yen parity with gold. Deflation slowed growth. Slower growth caused, or at least exacerbated, the stresses of industrialization and the social and political conditions which put the militarists in power.[22]

---

[22] Hugh T. Patrick, *Japanese Industrialization*, p. 213.

There were a number of immediate pressures to return to the gold standard at the very end of the 1920s, quite apart from the long-standing desire to return to financial orthodoxy and the pre-First World War state of affairs. The United States had been on gold standard throughout the 1920s, the United Kingdom had returned in 1925, and most of the major Western European powers had quickly followed suit. Of the major trading nations Japan remained an isolated exception. Fluctuating exchange rates were reckoned to increase business uncertainty, especially in the field of foreign trade; they made the risks of transferring funds between the international financial centres of the world much greater, and with the rise of interest rates in the United States in 1928 and 1929, America became a profitable place to send money, and the big Japanese banks were very liquid in the aftermath of the financial panic of 1927: the failure of many small banks had pushed up the deposits of the big, stable banks. These banks wanted a return to a fixed parity to protect them from the possible losses of exchange rate fluctuation. In addition, there was a large amount, ¥230 million, of sterling debt falling due between July 1930 and January 1931, and it was going to be very difficult to refund it by a new issue, unless British and American underwriters could be convinced that the Japanese government was pursuing financially orthodox and sound policies, which would include a gold standard fixed exchange rate. Eventually, in January, 1930, Japan returned to the gold standard at approximately 50 US cents to the yen. The immediate decision was reinforced by the American boom up to late 1929: there was a large demand for silk and export demand was generally buoyant in 1928 and 1929. The Stock Exchange crash in the United States in October 1929 was regarded as only a temporary setback. But Japan's new exchange policy coincided with the onset of the great depression, and authorities like Allen and Patrick are agreed that return could not have come at a worse time: in fact, Patrick, who argues that it would have been a fundamental mistake to return to gold at pre-war parity at any time in the 1920s, calls the new policy 'disastrous'.

The yen was now seriously overvalued and exports would have suffered even if the depression had not slashed them. Silk prices slumped as a result of the enormous drop in the American market, Indian tariffs were raised, hitting Japan's cotton textile industry, and the Chinese initiated a boycott of Japanese goods. No one believed Japan could maintain the new parity, and capital rushed out of the country both for legitimate interest differentials, and for less legitimate speculation. It would obviously pay to buy foreign exchange while the yen was high and repurchase yen when it was devalued. The financiers' speculation was to increase the violence of the right-wing nationalists' antagonism towards liberals, zaibatsu, and high-finance capitalism in general. The zaibatsu particularly came under fire for what was called their disloyal and unpatriotic actions. Gold poured out of the country in 1931, particularly after Britain abandoned the gold standard in the September. It followed the capital outflow, and was also caused by the mounting deficits in the balance of payments. According to Patrick, Japan lost some 58 per cent of its gold reserves while it was on the gold standard. By the end of 1931 the liberal government of the Mineseito party under Prime Minister Hamaguchi had fallen, and in December 1931 Japan too abandoned the gold standard. It had been a traumatic experience.

VI. *Economic policy, 1932–45: the struggle for power*

There was a complete change in economic policy in 1932. Korekiyo Takahashi became Finance Minister and initiated an intriguingly Keynesian policy in a pre-General Theory era. The government ran budget deficits, drastically increasing government borrowing and expenditure without compensating increases in taxation. An easy money policy was inaugurated. The yen was allowed to depreciate after Japan abandoned the gold standard and during 1932 sank from 50 US cents to 21 cents to the yen. There was some recovery in 1933 and 1934 as Japanese exports boomed and the average rates were 25 cents and 29 cents respectively. The military approved of these policies as military expenditures shot up after the Manchurian Incident of 1931: before 1937 some 60 per cent of increased government expenditure was for military purposes. Takahashi met with army approval only until 1936, when he tried to call a halt to reflation through fear of inflation. He was promptly assassinated.

Industrial expansion was increasingly based on military demand, new industries were expanded, and a series of government measures supporting industrial development, particularly in steel, shipping, shipbuilding, and in newer industries such as motor cars and aircraft, were taken. Imports of ships were forbidden for a while, and there was a dramatic recovery of shipbuilding production under these measures, which included familiar Scrap and Build schemes, as well as the laws of 1932 and 1937 designed to improve quality of shipping, and as a result of the quasi-war footing on which Japan was placed from 1937 onwards. Production soared to over 400,000 tons in 1938. Output in 1932 had been only 53,000 tons. By 1937 and 1938 Japan was producing on a par with Germany; that is, second only to the United Kingdom. The combined output of Germany and Japan almost equalled British production.

Other industries expanded rapidly with the policy of reflation. For the first time the Japanese crude steel industry, now largely state owned, approached great-power levels of production: output more than trebled to over 6 million tons in the decade after 1929. This did not, however, mean anything like self-sufficiency, particularly for an economy that was increasingly on a war-footing: Japan still had to import large quantities of scrap and raw materials (it was a bitter joke among Allied servicemen after 1941 that the missiles hurtling towards them were merely on their way back to the original sources of supply).

In more sophisticated areas of production – machine tools, motor vehicles, aircraft, radios, synthetics – Japan again made great strides. Some of these items may be classed as part of the military build-up which was widely supposed to be creating an artificial, brittle, industrial state. Japan was, to use some famous words of the mid-1930s, an industrial pygmy brandishing a big sword. She had, economically, feet of clay. But in radios, motor vehicles, aircraft, and even more in textiles, Japan was also participating in a world-wide industrial expansion, even in the provision of consumer durables, much of it less than directly associated with militarism. Famous names such as Matsushita (National Panasonic), and Nissan (Datsun) were on their way to eventual world prominence at this time, some of them, like Nissan, directly fostered by government and military, it is true.

There was, with the depreciation of the yen and with full government backing for the zaibatsu-based trading companies, a huge increase in the volume of Japanese exports, an increase which raised Japan's percentage of world exports. An increasing amount – relative as well as absolute – was in goods, such as metal and machinery, that had previously hardly touched the world's markets. In the international political and economic atmosphere of the time, which we shall now consider, Japan seemed increasingly dangerous to virtually every country in East Asia and the Pacific. Its government was now engaging in economic policies and political manoeuvres that threatened too many interests and suscepti-bilities, as well as the national integrity of countries like China.

As in many other countries, such as Germany, Italy and Spain, the trend in the 1930s in Japan was away from democracy and free enterprise capitalism to dictatorship and totalitarianism, away from free trade and international economic interdependence to economic nationalism and economic autarchy. This process was cumulative, and even in those countries, like Britain, where totalitarianism was not the solution, econ-omic nationalism intensified. Often the measures were taken in self-defence as other nations imposed tariffs, quotas and outright prohibition of imports or exports. In this atmosphere it came to be regarded as dangerous not to possess supplies of strategic raw materials, strategic for either industrial or military purposes, and the impulse to aggression to

Table 152a. *Index of industrial production (1929 = 100)*

	Japan	USA	Germany	France	UK
1929	100	100	100	100	100
1934	129	66	80	75	98
1938	173	72	126	76	115

Table 152b. *Index of employment (1929 = 100)*

	Japan	USA	Germany	France	UK
1929	100	100	100	100	100
1934	109	81	83	77	94
1938	154	82	117	81	104

Source: E. B. Schumpeter *et al., The Industrialization of Japan and Manchukuo, 1930–1940* (New York, 1940), p. 27.

secure those supplies was strengthened. Thus Japan took over Manchuria in 1931, creating the puppet state of Manchukuo, intensified pressure on, and finally invaded China in 1937, and then set out at the end of 1941 to break the power of the Western colonial nations, and to secure oil, rubber, tin and iron-ore in Malaya, the Dutch East Indies, and the Philippines.

All this time the power of the military had been increasing steadily in Japan. The reaction against parliamentary liberalism in the early 1930s had resulted in a series of assassinations – the former Finance Minister, Inouye, the head of Mitsui, Baron Dan, and Prime Minister Inukai in the spring of 1932 – and the complete breakdown of party government. Each cabinet had to contain a war minister, who had to be a general on the active list, and a navy minister, who had to be an admiral on the active list. Since these had to be approved by the Army and Navy Councils, the military were given an effective veto over any cabinet, which was an extraordinarily powerful position to be in. The military used their power to increase government expenditure on armaments, which helped to stimulate heavy industry, and aided the economic recovery of Japan from the great depression. This was, as we have seen, backed by the deficit spending indulged in by the government from 1932 onwards. Between 1931 and 1936, about 30 per cent of government expenditure was financed by borrowing, and the national debt rose from ¥6,000 million to over ¥10,000 million. This was not inflationary because, firstly, of the slack in the economy in 1932, and secondly, of the steady fall in the costs of production in industry as a result of rationalization and increased efficiency. The fall in costs was also due to simple cuts in wages, although later on labour costs were kept down through increased productivity. Taxes, particularly on incomes and business profits, were kept low.

Japan therefore recovered from the depression much faster than did the other industrial nations, as can be seen from the indices of industrial production and employment in Japan, the United States, Germany, France and the United Kingdom. This recovery was achieved with the help of government fiscal and monetary policies, and of specific measures designed to stimulate particular industries, as in the shipbuilding industry, and in the steel industry, where the Japan Iron Manufacturing Company, which was state owned, was established in January 1934. So there was increased state intervention, but in the recovery period up to the outbreak of war with China in 1937, Japan was by no means a fully fledged totalitarian state. There was little economic regimentation, no control of consumption, and little control of domestic investment, though some measures were passed to control the export of capital. Nor was there any government control of prices, wages or profits, nor any central direction of labour. The military were increasingly powerful, especially after war with China broke out, but big business, the bureaucracy, and the court were still far from impotent.

The situation changed from 1937, with the move towards a more intensive war-footing in Japan. Groups of extreme nationalists joined with the military in presenting anti-democratic and anti-capitalist programmes, in demanding ever-increasing state control of economic life. They were opposed to the major political parties, to the old zaibatsu, and to capital in general, but supported the farmers and the small entrepreneurs, and wanted more assistance for strategic industries. They advocated a yen bloc of economic self-sufficiency, a bloc which would include China, Manchukuo, Taiwan and Chosen, as well as Japan. Even before the outbreak of war with China in July 1937 special measures had been taken affecting vital sectors like iron and steel, shipbuilding, the mercantile marine and the engineering industry, while other strategic sectors like petroleum (1934) and automobiles and chemical fertilizers (both in 1936), had become controlled industries, subject to government licensing and assistance. From the outbreak of war with China there was enormously increased military and industrial expenditure, so that, in order to avoid inflation, the government was forced to regulate investment, production and consumption, and also to intervene in foreign trade to ensure supplies of vital raw materials.

Government licensing and control of industries was extended after 1936. In return for special privileges in capital supply and the import of raw materials free of duty, these industries were subjected to increased governmental supervision of production and prices. Between 1937 and 1940 11 laws were passed under this system, covering such sectors as airplanes, machine tools, synthetic chemicals, minerals, and electric power. National Policy Companies were set up to develop these industries with government financial assistance and guarantees. Authorized firms were to be exempt from income and profits taxes for five years. Great industrial progress was made between 1937 and 1940 in many sectors; for instance, Japan became a net exporter instead of a net importer of motor vehicles. Airplane manufacture also increased substantially.

With war, the need for more centralized control of resources was recognized, and in 1937 the Prime Minister, Prince Konoye, created a Cabinet Advisory Council and a Planning Board, which was to coordinate plans for the mobilization and expansion of national resources, and also to coordinate the work of the various government ministries, making recommendations to the Advisory Council. It was the Planning Board which was responsible for the National General Mobilization Law of 1938, which provided for the control and utilization of all human and commodity resources for the purposes of national defence; in other words, for the control of labour, raw materials, equipment, business, investment, prices and so on. Civilian consumption of a wide range of industrial and raw materials was placed under restriction from 1938. Under the General Mobilization Law wages and dividends were controlled from April 1939 and then, when war broke out in Europe, all prices, wages, rents and other costs were frozen. Consumer rationing was introduced in the summer of 1940, and the government subsidized the producers of such items as coal, iron and steel, and fertilizers in order to keep prices down. So even before war broke out with the Western powers in December 1941, much of the economy of Japan was on a war basis.

There are three distinct theories about the origins of Japan's involvement in the Second World War, so far as the apportionment of blame among the Japanese is concerned. First, there is David Bergamini's thesis that it was the Emperor and the court clique that conspired to involve Japan in an aggressive war against China and the Western imperial powers. His thesis is summed up in the title and subtitle of his book: *Japan's Imperial Conspiracy. How Emperor Hirohito led Japan into War against the West.* No major historian of Japan subscribes to this view. Secondly, there is the view that the Emperor and the civilian Japanese, including the businessmen, were largely innocent, and that it was the generals who were responsible for leading Japan to war right from the Manchurian Incident of 1931, through the war in China from 1937, to the attack on Pearl Harbour in December 1941. After all, it is said, General Tojo became Prime Minister in October 1941, and this was the

final surrender to the military. Moreover, the old zaibatsu were hated by
the military, who encouraged new combines under their influence, the
shinzaibatsu, or new zaibatsu.

Thirdly, there is the argument that agrees that the Emperor can be
exonerated, that he was dragged most reluctantly into the war, but insists
that to lay all the blame on the military is grossly to oversimplify the
pressures making for an aggressive Japan in the 1930s and 1940s. This
argument lays an equal, if not greater, share of blame on the zaibatsu,
which, it is said, benefited enormously from Japan's economic and
military policies, and which came to exert a decisive influence in Japan
during the late thirties and early forties.[23] It is this third thesis that is
considered here in relation to economic policy and its direction.

Prince Konoye, who was Prime Minister of Japan during most of the
pre-Second World War involvement in hostilities with China (he was
Prime Minister from 5 June 1937 to 5 January 1939, and from 17 July
1940 to 18 October 1941) re-formed his Cabinet in May 1938 in such a
way as to lend a good deal of support to the thesis that it was the military
that dominated affairs. General Ugaki was Foreign Minister and Minister of Overseas Affairs, General Itagaki was War Minister, General Araki
was Education Minister, Admiral Suetsugu was Home Minister and
Admiral Yonai was Navy Minister. It is therefore all the more remarkable that a man from a zaibatsu, which the generals bitterly opposed,
should have been included in the Cabinet. Seihin Ikeda, former chairman
of the Mitsui Bank, former managing director of Mitsui Gōmei Kaisha,
and former governor of the Bank of Japan, was appointed to the posts of
Finance Minister and Minister of Commerce and Industry. Elizabeth
Schumpeter wrote, 'The Army had come to feel the necessity of com-
promising and of co-operating with leaders of business and finance in
order that the war and the program of industrial expansion might be
carried on simultaneously.'[24] In other words, the conduct of the war and
the growth of Japan's military and industrial potential depended upon
the zaibatsu's full involvement, but it should be noted at once that both
Ikeda and Ugaki were in favour of a settlement with China. So the
presence of zaibatsu and other businessmen in wartime cabinets is a
complex matter. It may be that they cooperated fully in the war effort,
but really they saw their functions as restraining the military, and
protecting the interests of big business. The employers were anxious to
avoid army and government control, and proposed their own plans for
the organization of industry.

Thus the Japan Economic Federation in May 1940 advocated

[23] See T. A. Bisson, *Japan's War Economy* (New York, 1945), from which much of the material in
this chapter on economic policy in the 1930s and early 1940s is drawn.
[24] E. B. Schumpeter, 'Industrial Development and Government Policy', in E. B. Schumpeter *et al.*,
Industrialization of Japan and Manchukuo, 1930–1940 (New York, 1940), pp. 819–20.

cartelization in all the major industrial sectors, leaving the industries themselves to control production and prices. The employers argued that they had plenty of experience in these matters since the passing of the Major Industries Control Law of 1931, which had made private cartel agreements legally enforceable. Hundreds of cartels were formed in the 1930s, and the process was speeded up after 1937. Some members of the government wanted to bring these cartels under government control but they were defeated. For example, Hoshino, head of the Planning Board, who had advocated such control, was dropped from the cabinet in the spring of 1941, and Ogura of the Sumitomo zaibatsu entered the cabinet to handle economic affairs. Success for the Japan Economic Federation came in August 1941, when the Major Industries Association Ordinance was promulgated. This provided for Control Associations, or cartels, in all major sectors of industry, finance, trade and communications. The cartels had control of production and distribution, control over the supply of factors of production, and official recognition by the government to the extent that they could participate in planning the development of their industries.

General Tojo's Cabinet of 18 October 1941 is usually cited as the victory of the military: a hawkish general became prime minister and the businessmen lost their ministerial posts, and, of course, the decision for war was taken. But cartelization under the control of business itself continued. Throughout 1942 mergers and enforced absorptions of businesses – often hitting the smaller concerns – went on, and this was intensified after May 1942, when the Renovation of Enterprises Ordinance gave ministries the power to order the sale, transfer or lease of industrial and other facilities.

Tojo has been called the dictator of Japan in this period – apart from being Prime Minister he was also War Minister and Home Minister – but his ministers were not directly responsible to him, only to the Emperor, and each ministry jealously guarded its prerogatives. It is true that Tojo obtained wider formal powers. Economic conditions in Japan were becoming increasingly difficult towards the end of 1942. The Japanese had lost command of the high seas and critical bottlenecks in raw materials supplies were developing. Tojo sought wider powers to control industrial production, and in February 1943 ordinances were passed empowering the Prime Minister to give direct instructions to ministries and to industry concerning the use of key raw materials. Nevertheless, this increased power was counterbalanced immediately by the simultaneous creation of a Cabinet Advisers Council, which consisted of seven prominent businessmen, each of whom was a president of a control association. These businessmen formed in joint session with the cabinet a Supreme Economic Council. So businessmen were now right at the centre, and Tojo was in no sense in a dictatorial position. The position of the military leaders was further eroded in the spring of 1943, when former despised political leaders were appointed to cabinet posts, including the economic ministries and the Foreign Office, which went to Shigemitsu.

The struggle for control of Japan's war economy continued throughout 1943. In November of that year a new Ministry of Munitions was created to try to solve, among other problems, the critical issue of the supply of airplanes. Tojo became Minister of Munitions but he was, apparently, merely a titular head. Effective control was exercised by Kishi, the Vice-Minister, who was a career bureaucrat. A further attempt was made in February 1944 to give Tojo more power, when he became Chief of the Army Staff, in addition to being Prime Minister, War Minister and Munitions Minister. But this, in fact, only increased his political vulnerability as the war went badly for Japan. In April 1944 Saipan was lost and B29s started to bomb Japan. In July 1944 Tojo fell from power. General Koiso became Prime Minister – and only Prime Minister. Shigemitsu's position was enhanced by his appointment to the Great East Asia Ministry as well as the Foreign Office. And Fujihara of Mitsui took over the Munitions Ministry. It has been said of Fujihara that

He was in himself a living refutation of the dangerous myth that Japan's business leaders were unwilling to carve out an empire with the sword. His outspokenly expansionist views . . . were fully shared by the other members of his class. Since the twenties this class, and not the military, had been the dominant political force in Japan.[25]

Fujihara had published a book in 1936 called *The Spirit of Japanese Industry*, in which he had argued that armament was a form of investment in national political and economic expansion. 'Diplomacy', he said, 'without force is of no value.'[26] It was businessmen like Fujihara who, as Arthur Tiedemann says,

by their presence in the government . . . were able to resist bureaucratic and military attempts to take away from big business control of the management of its organizations.

The end result was that the industrial combines came through the destruction of war intact and arose phoenix-like to even greater heights in the postwar period. For them the Occupation reforms proved but a passing phase, except in so far as the efficiency of combines may actually have been improved by the stripping away of the irrational impediments which had lingered from the days of their origin as family businessess. The industrial combines had successfully preserved their organisation, built up their technical skills, and were ready to

[25] T. A. Bisson, *Japan's War Economy*, p. 143.
[26] Ginjiro Fujihara, *The Spirit of Japanese Industry* (Tokyo, 1936), p. 134.

take advantage of the opportunities for growth presented in the 1950's and 1960's. They and the bureaucracy have survived war and defeat to become, for the present at least, the dominating elements on the Japanese scene.[27]

VII. *Conclusion and epilogue*

Historians have apportioned blame for the Second World War in Asia among the various powerful groups in Japan: the court, the bureaucracy, the military and the zaibatsu. The policies of the entire period from 1868 to 1945 have been condemned as a cumulative build-up to a situation in which the Japanese economy was dualistic: the structural maladjustment where agriculture suffered while industry grew, and where, even within the industrial sector, the combines exploited the rest. They were thus responsible for political intolerance and extremism, aggressive external policies, and domestic indifference to poverty. The roots of the 1930s and 1940s are said to have been established in the 1880s, when such political and economic problems as tenancy, agricultural distress, lack of political democracy and Emperor-worship were generated, and when social, moral and political indoctrination were built into the educational system. Japan did degenerate into political extremism in the 1930s, and it adopted distressing attitudes towards its neighbours (both indigenous and colonial powers). But, when its leaders have been accused of lack of perception of the correct paths to follow after 1931, one should also ask: which leaders of which countries displayed perception during that decade? In the 1930s G. C. Allen pointed out that Japan was a 'hungry guest',[28] and he and others, while acknowledging the existence of her sins, suggest that she was also much sinned against. Even the criticisms of her economic policies in the 1920s must be tempered by the reflection that other countries' policies were also misguided. Since 1945 much of Japan's power-complex has remained the same, as Tiedemann has insisted, but there have also been remarkable and deep-rooted changes. In the current economic situation of the late 1970s, Japan's leaders must make the difficult effort of understanding European and American problems – as well as those of the Third World – but they have also to generate solutions to their own country's serious economic and social maladjustments. These include a massive industrial capacity in sectors such as shipbuilding, steel and motor cars, a capacity which at present is grossly excessive. Once again, their economic policies since 1950 may have often been mistaken, but they are not alone in this, and not only they have an effort to make; the political leaders, industrialists, and workers of Europe

---

[27] Arthur E. Tiedemann, 'Big Business and Politics in Prewar Japan', in James W. Morley (ed.), *Dilemmas of Growth in Prewar Japan* (Princeton, NJ, 1971), pp. 315–16. Tiedemann renders Fujihara's name as Fujiwara.   [28] G. C. Allen, *Japan: The Hungry Guest* (London, 1938).

and North America particularly must also try to appreciate Japan's difficulties. Current analyses of Japan's trading position are reminiscent of the 1930s, when her share of world trade also increased, and, perhaps more important, its composition also changed. In contrast to the 1930s, Japan's share is now large, but even now (in 1978), her exports per capita are *less* than the United Kingdom's figure. Her industrialization policies have borne fruit, as they did before 1945; but some of the peaches remain sour.

Writers such as Koji Taira,[29] Kozo Yamamura,[30] and Chitoshi Yanaga,[31] have severely criticized the lack of economic democracy since 1952. Yamamura pointed to the taxation changes unfavourable to the lower income groups; Yanaga to the alliance of the bureaucracy, big business, and the government. Both postulated the conflict between rapid economic growth and democracy. The continued absence of real interest in social infrastructure and pollution in the two decades after 1952, an absence acknowledged by Japan's leaders to be the result of their pursuit of economic growth, has left Japan in a situation in which there is now a serious combination of economic and social difficulties; a combination which may be even more intractable than the problem of non-existent industrial growth in the United Kingdom. For all this her leaders may have been culpable. But in 1945 few would have imagined the real benefits that would also accrue to the Japanese people – now numbering 114 million – who were psychologically, physically, politically and economically devastated. The mistakes of Japan's leaders over the past century have not been unique, however serious, and even tragic, those mistakes may have been, and there is reason for congratulation as well as condemnation. As late as the mid-1950s there was no lack of extremely gloomy forecasts by responsible and reputable economic and social analysts, who believed that even the mere employment of Japan's increasing millions would be virtually impossible. The Japanese worker or peasant is now one of the most productive in the world. No one would have predicted this 30 years ago.[31]

[29] Koji Taira, *Economic Development and the Labor Market in Japan* (New York, 1970).
[30] Kozo Yamamura, *Economic Policy in Postwar Japan: Growth versus Economic Democracy* (Berkeley, 1967). [31] This conclusion was written in 1978.

BIBLIOGRAPHIES

CHAPTER I

European trade policy, 1815–1914

This bibliography can be divided into two main groups. The first is devoted to basic data and general literature together with the literature on three specific sections of this study: institutions for the promotion of foreign trade; colonial trade policies; and labour movements and trade policies. The second group is devoted to countries or regions. The small share of recent titles in this bibliography is due to the fact that there is very little recent literature on the subject.

1 BIBLIOGRAPHIES OF TARIFF LITERATURE

Martinstetter, H. *Internationale Bibliographie des Zollwesens*. Konstanz, 1954.
US Department of Commerce, Bureau of Foreign and Domestic Commerce, *Bibliography of Barriers to Trade*. Washington, DC, 1942.
US Tariff Commission. *Handbook of Commercial Treaties; Digest of Commercial Treaties, Conventions and Other Agreements of Commercial Interest between all Nations*, Washington, DC, 1922.
—— *Reciprocal Trade: A Current Bibliography*, 3rd edn, Washington, DC, 1937. Supplement, Washington, DC, 1940.
—— *The Tariff: A Bibliography, a Select List of References*. Washington, DC, 1934.

2 GENERAL EVOLUTION OF TRADE POLICIES

Ashley, P. *Modern Tariff History: Germany–United States–France*, 3rd edn. London, 1920.
Bastable, C. F. *The Commerce of Nations*, 9th edn (revised by T. E. G. Gregory). London, 1923.
Boiteau, P. *Les traités de commerce: textes de tous les traités en vigueur . . .* Paris, 1863.
Corden, W. M. *Trade Policy and Economic Welfare*, Oxford, 1974.
Cuddington, J. T. and McKinnon, R. I. 'Free Trade Versus Protection: A Perspective', in: W. Adams *et al.*, *Tariffs and Quotas and Trade: The Polities of Protection*. San Francisco, 1978, pp. 3–23.
Culbertson, W. S. *International Economic Policies: A Survey of the Economics of Diplomacy*. New York, 1925.
Dawson, W. H. (ed.) *Protection in Various Countries*. London, 1904.
Dietzel, H. *Retaliatory Duties*. London, 1906.
Ebner, J. *La clause de la nation la plus favorisée en droit international public*. Paris, 1931.
Fisk, G. M. and Peirce, P. S. *International Commercial Policies with Special Reference to the United States*. New York, 1923.
Graf, K. *Die Zollpolitischen Zielsetzungen im Wandel der Geschichte*. St Gallen, 1970.
Great Britain Parliamentary Papers. *Report on Tariff Wars between Certain European States*. Parliamentary paper by command, Cd 1938, London, 1904.
Green, J. L. *Agriculture and Tariff Reform*. London, 1904.
Gregory, T. E. G. *Tariffs: A Study in Method*. London, 1921.
Henderson, W. O. *Studies in British Influence on the Industrial Revolution in Western Europe*. Liverpool, 1954.
Hirst, M. *Life of Friedrich List and Selections from his Writings*. London, 1909.
Holland, B. *The Fall of Protection, 1840–1850*. London, 1913.
Hornbeck, S. K. *The Most Favored Clause in Commercial Treaties: its Function in Theory and in Practice and its Relation to Tariff Policies*. Madison, Wis., 1910.
Illasu, A. A. 'The Cobden Chevalier Commercial Treaty of 1860', *The Historical Journal*, vol. XIV (March 1971), pp. 67–98.

Kindleberger, C. P. 'The Rise of Free Trade in Western Europe, 1820–1875', *Journal of Economic History*, vol. XXXV, no. 1 (March 1975), pp. 20–55.
League of Nations. *Tariff Level Indices*. International Economic Conference, Geneva (May 1927). Geneva, 1927.
Liepmann, H. *Tariff Levels and the Economic Unity of Europe*. London, 1938.
Mackeown, T. J. 'Hegemonic Stability Theory and 19th Century Tariff Levels in Europe', *International Organization 37*, no. 1 (Winter 1983), pp. 73–91.
Pollard, S. *The Integration of the European Economy since 1815*. London, 1981.
Poznanski, C. *La clause de la nation la plus favorisée: Etude historique et théorique*. Bern, 1917.
Schnerb, R. *Libre-échange et protectionnisme*. Paris, 1963.
Semmel, B. *The Rise of Free Trade Imperialism: Classical Political Economy, the Empire of Free Trade and Imperialism 1750–1850*. Cambridge, 1970.
Tarbell, I. M. *The Tariff in Our Times*. New York, 1911.
Turner, B. *Free Trade and Protection*. London, 1971.
US Tariff Commission. *Reciprocity and Commercial Treaties*. Washington, DC, 1919.
—— *Dictionary of Tariff Information*, Washington, DC, 1934.
—— *The Tariff and its History*. Washington, DC, 1934.
Vaughan, R. *Twentieth-Century Europe: Paths to Unity*. London, 1979.
Vereins für Socialpolitik (Schriften Des). *Die Handelspolitik der wichtigeren kulturstaaten in den letzten Jahrzehnten*, 4 vols: vols. XLIX, L, LI: Leipzig, 1892; vol. LVII: Leipzig, 1893.

3 BASIC DATA ON TARIFFS

Bernhardt, G., de. *Handbook of Commercial Treaties, etc., relating to Commerce and Navigation between Great Britain and Foreign Powers*. London, 1912.
Chisholm, G. C. *Handbook of Commercial Geography*, 7th edn. London and New York, 1908.
Eichmann, A. *Recueil des tarifs conventionnels des douanes de tous les pays et des traités de commerce suisses*. Bern, 1889.
Hubner, O. *A Collection of the Customs Tariffs of all Nations*. London, 1855.
Kelly, S. *Customs Tariffs of the World*. London, 1904 and following years.
MacGregor, J. *The Commercial and Financial Legislation of Europe and America*. London, 1841.
Newdegate, C. N. *A Collection of the Customs' Tariffs of all Nations: Based upon a Translation of the Work of M. Hübner*. London, 1855.
Smart, W. *Economic Annals of the Nineteenth Century*. London, 1900–17.
United Kingdom. *Foreign Import Duties 1913*, Parliamentary papers by command, Cd 7180. London, 1913.

4 INSTITUTIONS FOR THE PROMOTION OF FOREIGN TRADE

Barker, E. R. N. *The Development of Public Services in Western Europe 1660–1930*. London and Oxford, 1944.
Caillez, M. *L'organisation du crédit au commerce extérieur en France et à l'étranger*. Paris, 1923.
Chauncey, D. S. *German Foreign Trade Organization*, US Department of Commerce, Bureau of Foreign and Domestic Commerce, Miscellaneous Series no. 57. Washington, DC, 1917.
Drossinis, C. G. *Les Chambres de commerce à l'étranger*. Paris, 1921.
Herscher, M. *Les Chambres de commerce*. Paris, 1937.
Huynem, J. M. H. *Trends in Trade Fairs*. Utrecht, 1973.
Isaac, M. *Les expositions internationales*. Paris, 1936.
Jaunin, V. *Foires et comptoirs d'échantillons*. Lausanne, 1919.
Keucher, J. *Gechichtliche Entwicklung und gegenwärtiger Stand des Kammer-Systems*. Weissenfels, 1931.
Luckhurst, K. W. *The Story of Exhibitions*. London and New York, 1951.

Poirier, R. *Des foires, des peuples, des expositions*. Paris, 1958.
Tamir, M. *Les expositions internationales à travers les âges*. Paris, 1939.
Wolfe, A. J. *Foreign Credits: A Study of the Foreign Credit Problem with a Review of European Methods of Financing Export Shipments*. US Bureau of Foreign and Domestic Commerce. Washington, DC, 1913.

5 COLONIAL TRADE POLICIES

Bell, K. N. and Morrell, W. P. (eds.) *Select Documents on British Colonial Policy, 1830–1860*. Oxford, 1928.
Fuchs, C. J. *The Trade Policy of Great Britain and her Colonies since 1860*. London, 1905.
Girault, A. *The Colonial Tariff Policy of France*. Washington, DC, 1916.
Harnetty, P. *Imperialism and Free Trade: Lancashire and India in the Mid Nineteenth Century*. Manchester, 1973.
Messersmitt, R. E. *Le régime douanier et le commerce extérieur de l'Algérie*. Alger, 1927.
Porritt, E. *The Fiscal and Diplomatic Freedom of the British Overseas Dominions*. Oxford, 1922.
Robinson, R. and Gallager, J. 'The Imperialism of Free Trade', *Economic History Review*, 2nd Series, vol. VI, no. 4 (August 1953), pp. 1–15.
Root, J. W. *Colonial Tariffs*. Liverpool, 1906.
Rutter, F. R. *Tariff Systems of South American Countries*. Tariff Series no. 34. Washington, DC, 1916.
Schuyler, R. L. *The Fall of the Old Colonial System: A Study in British Free Trade, 1770–1870*. New York, 1945.
Shan, N. J. *History of Indian Tariffs*. Bombay, 1924.
US Tariff Commission. *Colonial Tariff Policies*. Washington, DC, 1922.

6 LABOUR MOVEMENTS AND TRADE POLICIES

Buisson, E. *La politique douanière de la classe ouvrière*. Paris, 1909.
Erzberger, M. *Socialdemokratie und Zollpolitik*. Munich, 1908.
Gemahling, P. *Travailleurs au rabais, la lutte syndicale contre les sous-concurrences ouvrières*. Paris, 1910.
George, H. *Protection or Free Trade: An Examination of the Tariff Question with Special Regard to the Interests of Labor*. New York, 1886.
Hollande, M. *La défense ouvrière contre le travail étranger: Vers un protectionnisme ouvrier*. Paris, 1913.
Jay, R. 'Protection douanière et protection ouvrière', *Eveil démocratique*, 6 June 1909.
Lorenz, J. *La classe ouvrière et la politique douanière*. Fribourg, 1914.
MacNamara, T. J. *Tariff Reform and the Working Man*. London, 1910.
Penty, A. J. *Protection and the Social Problem*. London, 1926.
Prato, G. *Le protectionnisme ouvrier (l'exclusion des travailleurs étrangers)*. Paris, 1912.

7 EVOLUTION OF TRADE POLICIES BY COUNTRY OR REGION

Austria and Hungary

Beer, A. *Die österreichische Handelspolitik im neunzehnten Jahrhundert*. Vienna, 1891.
Helleiner, K. F. *Free Trade and Frustration: Anglo-Austrian Negotiation, 1860–70*. Toronto, 1973.
Korntheuer, H. *Zoll und Wirtschaftsgeschichte österreich: 100 Jahre österreichs Zollwache*. Vienna, 1933.
Matlekovits, A. von. *Die Zollpolitik der österreichisch-ungarischen Monarchie und des Deutschen Reiches seit 1868 und deren nächste Zukunft*. Leipzig, 1891.
Peez, A. 'Die österreichische Handelspolitik der letzten fünfundzwanzig Jahre', in *Schriften des Vereins für Soialpolitik* (Die Handelspolitik der wichtigeren Kulturstaaten in den letzten Jahrzehnten), vol. XLIX. Leipzig, 1892, pp. 167–94.

Balkan countries

Andreades, A. *Histoire des finances grecques depuis l'antiquité jusqu'à nos jours*. Athens, 1918.
Averoff, E. A. *Union douanière balkanique*. Paris, 1933.
Baicoiano, C. L. *Geschichte der rumänischen Zollpolitik seit dem 14. Jahrhundert bis 1874*. Stuttgart, 1896.
Cioriceanu, G. D. *La Roumanie économique et ses rapports avec l'étranger de 1860 à 1915*. Paris, 1928.
Faust, C. B. *La politique douanière de la Roumanie des débuts jusqu'à nos jours*. Neuchâtel, 1934.
Jordachescou, V. T. *L'evolution de la politique douanière de la Roumanie de l'époque Dacie-Trajane à nos jours*. Paris, 1925.
Stroll, M. 'Die Handelspolitik der Balkanstaaten Rümanien, Serbien u. Bulgarien', in *Schriften des Vereins für Socialpolitik* (Die Handelspolitik der wichtigeren Kulturstaaten in den letzten Jahrzehnten), vol. LI. Leipzig, 1892, pp. 1–65.

Belgium and The Netherlands

Heringa, A. *Freetrade and Protectionism in Holland*. Haarlem, 1914.
Loridan, W. 'Esquisse de la politique douanière de la Belgique (1830 à 1844)', *Revue Economique Internationale*, vol. IV, 30e année (November 1938), pp. 313–49.
Mahaim, E. 'La politique commerciale de la Belgique', in *Schriften des Vereins für Socialpolitik* (Die Handelspolitik der wichtigeren Kulturstaaten in den letzten Jahrzehnten), vol. XLIX. Leipzig, 1892, pp. 195–238.
Reus, H. (de) 'Die Handelspolitik der Niederlande in den letzten Jahrzehnten', in *Schriften des Vereins für Socialpolitik* (Die Handelspolitik der wichtigeren Kulturstaaten in den letzten Jahrzehnten), vol. XLIX. Leipzig, 1892, pp. 239–71.
Steels, J. *La politique commerciale extérieure de la Belgique*. Brussels, 1945.
Suetens, M. *Histoire de la politique commerciale de la Belgique depuis 1830 à nos jours*. Brussels, 1955.
Wright, H. R. C. *Free Trade and Protectionism in the Netherlands, 1816–30: A Study of the First Benelux*. Cambridge, Mass., 1955.

France

Amé, L. *Etude sur les tarifs de douane et les traités de commerce*, vol. II. Paris, 1876.
Arnauné, A. *Le commerce extérieur et les tarifs de douane*. Paris, 1911.
Augier, C. and Marvaud, A. *La politique douanière de la France dans ses rapports avec celle des autres états*. Paris, 1911.
Devers, A. 'La politique commerciale de la France depuis 1860', in *Schriften des Vereins für Socialpolitik* (Die Handelspolitik der wichtigeren Kulturstaaten in den letzten Jahrzehnten), vol. LI. Leipzig, 1892, pp. 125–208.
Dunham, A. L. *The Anglo-French Treaty of Commerce of 1860 and the Progress of Industrial Revolution in France*. Ann Arbor, 1930.
Golob, E. O. *The Meline Tariff: French Agriculture and Nationalist Economic Policy*. New York, 1944 (rep. New York, 1968).
Heywood, C. 'The Launching of an "Infant Industry"? The Cotton Industry of Troyes under Protectionism, 1793–1860', *The Journal of European Economic History*, vol. X, no. 3 (Winter 1981), pp. 53–81.
Levasseur, E. *Histoire du commerce de la France*, vol. II: *De 1789 à nos jours* Paris, 1912.
Lutfalla, M. 'Aux origines du libéralisme économique en France. Le "Journal des Economistes". Analyse du contenu de la première série, 1841–1853', *Revue d'Histoire Economique et Sociale*, vol. L, no. 4 (1972), pp. 494–517.
Moye, M. and Nogaro, B. *Les régimes douaniers, législation douanière et traités de commerce*. Paris, 1910.
Nogaro, B. and Moye, M. *Le régime douanier de la France*. Paris, 1931.

Germany

Dawson, W. H. *Protection in Germany: A History of German Fiscal Policy during the Nineteenth Century.* London, 1904.

Fort, J. *Das Zollwesen im Getreideverkehr.* Vienna, 1899.

Gerber, U. *Deutschlands Zoll-und Handelspolitik seit Einleitung de Schutzzollpolitik durch Bismark im Jahre 1879.* Berlin, 1924.

Hahn, H. W. *Geschichte des deutschen Zollvereins.* Göttingen, 1984.

Hardach, K. W. *Die Bedeutung wirtschaftlicher Factoren bei der Widereinführung der Eisen- und Getreidezölle in Deutschland 1879.* Berlin, 1967.

Henderson, W. O. *The Zollverein.* Cambridge, 1939.

—— 'Prince Smith and the Free Trade in Germany', *Economic History Review*, vol. II, no. 3 (1950), pp. 295–302.

Lambi, I. N. *Free Trade and Protection in Germany 1868–1879.* Wiesbaden, 1963.

Price, A. H. *The Evolution of the Zollverein: A Study of the Ideas and Institutions Leading to the German Economic Unification between 1815 and 1833.* Ann Arbor, 1949.

Richelot, H. *L'Association douanière allemande ou le Zollverein.* Paris, 1859.

Robinet de Clery, A. *La politique douanière de l'Allemagne depuis l'avènement de Caprivi jusqu'à nos jours (1890–1925).* Paris, 1935.

Roepke, W. *German Commercial Policy.* Geneva, 1934.

Scheel, H. von. 'Der auswärtige Handel des Deutschen Zollgebiets im letzten Jahrzehnt', in *Schriften des Vereins für Socialpolitik* (Die Handelspolitik der wichtigeren Kulturstaaten in den letzten Jahrzehnten), vol. L. Leipzig, 1892, pp. 521–645.

Italy

Bresciani-Turroni, C. *La politica commercial dell'Italia.* Bologna, 1921.

Busino, G. *L'Italia di Vilfredo Pareto: Economia e Societa 1870–1923.* Milan, 1987.

Cardini, A. *Stato Liberale e Protezionismo in Italia (1870–1900).* Bologna, 1981.

Coppa, F. J. 'The Italian Tariff and the Conflict between Agriculture and Industry: The Commercial Policy of Liberal Italy, 1860–1922', *Journal of Economic History*, vol. XXX, no. 4 (December 1970), pp. 742–69.

Giretti, E. 'Nouveaux gestes du protectionnisme en Italie', *Journal des Economistes*, vol. XVII, no. 2 (February 1908), pp. 231–9.

Pareto, V. *Libre-échangisme, protectionnisme et socialisme.* Geneva, 1965.

Pedone, A. *La politica del commercio estere*, in G. Fua (ed.), *Le Sviluppo economico in Italia*, vol. II. Milan, 1969.

Prodi, R. 'Il protezionismo nella Politica e nell' industria italiana dall' unificaizione al 1886', *Nuova Revista Storica*, vol. L, fasc. I–II (1968), pp. 1–74.

Ricci, V. *Protezionisti e liberisti italiani.* Bari, 1920.

Sombart, W. 'Die Handelspolitik Italianes seit der Einigung des Königreichs', in *Schristen des Vereins für Socialpolitik* (Die Handelspolitik der wichtigeren Kulturstaaten in den letzten Jahrzehnten), vol. XLIX. Leipzig, 1892, pp. 75–116.

Stringher, B. 'Gli Scambii con l'estero e la politica commerciale italiana dal 1860 al 1910', in *Cinquata Anni di Storia italiana*, vol. III, part 3. Milan, 1911, pp. 1–183.

Portugal and Spain

Gwinner, A. 'Die Handelspolitik Spaniens in den letzten Jahrzehnten', in *Schriften des Vereins für Socialpolitik* (Die Handelspolitik der wichtigeren Kulturstaaten in den letzten Jahrzehnten), vol. LI. Leipzig, 1892, pp. 67–123.

Halpern-Pereira, M. *Livre Câmbio e Desenvolvimento Economico: Portugal na Segunda metade do seculo XIX.* Lisbon, 1971.

Huenlich, F. A. *Die Steuerverfassung Spaniens in Geschichte und Gegenwart.* Jena, 1932.

Pereira, J. C. *Para a Historia dal Alfandegag en Portugal Inicio do Seculo XVI.* Lisbon, 1983.

Puges, M. *Como triunfo el Proteccionismo en Espania.* Barcelona, 1931.

Sideri, S. *Trade and Power: Informal Colonialism in Anglo-Portuguese Relations.* Rotterdam, 1970.

Russia

Kirchner, W. 'Russian Tariffs and Foreign Industries before 1914: The German Entrepreneur's Perspective', *Journal of Economic History*, vol. XLI, no. 2 (June 1981), pp. 316–79.
Miller, M. S. *The Economic Development of Russia, 1905–1914, with Special Reference to Trade Industry and Finance*. 2nd edn, New York, 1967.
Wittschewski, V. *Russlands Handels, Zoll-und Industriepolitik von Peter dem Grossen bis aud die Gegenwart*. Berlin, 1905.
—— 'Die Zoll- und Handelspolitik Russlands während der letzten Jahrzehnte', in *Schriften des Vereins für Socialpolitik* (Die Handelspolitik der wichtigeren Kulturstaaten in den letzten Jahrzehnten), vol. XLIX. Leipzig, 1892, pp. 361–449.

Scandinavia

Drachmann, P. *The Industrial Development and Commercial Policies of the Three Scandinavian Countries*. Washington, DC, 1915.
Fahlbeck, P. E. 'Die Handelspolitik Schwedens und Norwegens', in *Schriften des Vereins für Socialpolitik* (Die Handelspolitik der wichtigeren Kulturstaaten in den letzten Jahrzehnten), vol. XLIX. Leipzig, 1892, pp. 303–60.
Finland: The Country, its People and Institutions. Helsinki, 1926.
Frederiksen, N. C. *La Finlande: Economie politique et privée*. Paris, 1902.
Gøtrik, H. P. *Danish Economic Policy 1931–1938*. Copenhagen, 1939.
Harmaja, L. *Svomen Tullipolitiikka venäjän vallan aikana*. Porvoo, 1920.
Scharling, W. 'Die Handelspolitik Dänemarks 1864–1891', in *Schriften des Vereins für Socialpolitik* (Die Handelspolitik der wichtigeren Kulturstaaten in den letzten Jarzehnten), vol. XLIX. Leipzig, 1892, pp. 273–301.

Switzerland

Bleuler, W. *Studien über Aussenhandel und Handelspolitik der Schweiz*. Zurich, 1929.
Derobert, E. *La politique douanière de la Confédération suisse*. Geneva, 1926.
Frey, E. 'Die Schweizerische Handelspolitik der letzten Jahrzehnte', in *Schriften des Vereins für Socialpolitik* (Die Handelspolitik der wichtigeren Kulturstaaten in den letzten Jahrzehnten), vol. LXIX. Leipzig, 1892, pp. 451–519.
Kupper, W. *Die Zollpolitik der schweizerischen Landwirtschaft seit 1848*. Bern, 1929.
Marx, P. *Répertoire systématique des traités en vigueur entre la Confédération Suisse ou les cantons et l'étranger*. Zurich, 1918.
Schmidt, P. H. *Die Schweiz und die Europäische Handelspolitik*. Zurich, 1914.
Steiger, C. von. *Die Schweizerische Zollpolitik von 1900 bis 1930*. Bern, 1933.
Vogel, R. M. W. *Politique commerciale de la Suisse*. Montreux, 1966.

United Kingdom

Amery, J. *Joseph Chamberlain and the Tariff Reform Campaign*, vols. V and VI: *The Life of Joseph Chamberlain*. London, 1969.
Barnes, D. G. *A History of the English Corn Laws from 1660 to 1846*. London, 1930.
Bell, K. N. and Morrell, W. P. (eds.) *Select Documents on British Colonial Policy 1830–1860*. Oxford, 1928.
Brown, B. H. *The Tariff Reform Movement in Great Britain, 1881–1895*. New York, 1943.
Brown, L. *The Board of Trade and the Free-Trade Movement, 1830–1842*. Oxford, 1958.
—— 'The Chartists and the Anti-corn Law League', in A. Briggs (ed.), *Chartist Studies*. London, 1959, pp. 342–71.
Crosby, T. L. *English Farmers and the Politics of Protection, 1815–1852*. Brighton, 1977.
Fairlie, S. 'The Corn Laws and British Wheat Production 1829–1876', *Economic History Review*, vol. XXXII, no. 1 (April 1969), pp. 88–116.
Free Trade Union Handbook of the Tariff Question. 4th edn, revised, London, 1908.
Grampp, W. D. 'Economic Opinion when Britain turned to Free Trade', *History of Political Economy*, vol. XIV, no. 4 (Winter 1982), pp. 496–520.

Henderson, W. O. 'The Anglo-French Commercial Treaty of 1786', *Economic History Review*, 2nd series, vol. x, no. 1 (1957), pp. 104–12.

Hoffman, R. J. S. *Great Britain and the German Trade Rivalry, 1875–1914*. Philadelphia, 1933.

McCord, N. *Free Trade: Theory and Practice from Adam Smith to Keynes*. London, 1970.

—— *The Anti-Corn Law League 1838–1846*. London, 1958.

Mongredien, A. *History of Free Trade Movement in England*. New York, 1881.

Morley, J. *The Life of Richard Cobden*. London, 1882.

Morrell, W. P. *British Colonial Policy in the Age of Peel and Russell*. Oxford, 1930.

—— *British Colonial Policy in the mid-Victorian Age: South Africa, New Zealand, the West Indies*. Oxford, 1969.

Prentice, A. *History of the Anti-Corn-Law League*, 2 vols. London, 1853.

Puryear, V. J. *International Economics and Diplomacy in the Near East: A Study of British Commercial Policy in the Levant, 1834–1853*. Stanford, 1935.

Williams, J. B. *British Commercial Policy and Trade Expansion, 1750–1850*. Oxford, 1972.

Wood, J. C. 'Alfred Marshall and the Tariff-Reform Campaign of 1903', *Journal of Law and Economics*, vol. XXIII, no. 2 (October 1980), pp. 481–95.

CHAPTER II

Commercial policy between the wars

For a useful, immediately post-war bibliography on international economics generally, with approximately seventeen pages on commercial policy, see American Economic Association (H. S. Ellis and L. Metzler), *Readings in the Theory of International Trade*, Homewood, Ill., 1950, pp. 555ff. and especially pp. 608–25.

Andersen, F. Nyboe. *Bilateral Exchange Clearing Policy*. Copenhagen, 1946.

Arndt, H. W. *The Economic Lessons of the Nineteen-Thirties*. London, 1944.

Australia: Committee on Economics (Brigden, J. B.) *The Australian Tariff, An Economic Enquiry*. Melbourne, Melbourne University Press, 1929.

Benham, Frederic C. *Great Britain under Protection*. New York, 1941.

Bergsten, C. Fred. *Completing the GATT: Toward New International Rules to Govern Export Controls*. No place stated, British–North-American Committee, 1974.

Beveridge, William H. *Tariffs, The Case Examined by a Committee of Economists under the Chairmanship of Sir William Beveridge*. New York, 1931.

Bidwell, Percy W. *The Invisible Tariff. A Study of Control of Imports into the United States*. New York, 1939.

—— *Raw Materials: A Study of American Policy*. New York, 1958.

Brigden, J. L. 'The Australian Tariff and the Standard of Living', *Economic Record*, vol. I, no. 1 (November 1925), pp. 29–46.

Brown, William Adams, Jr. *The United States and the Restoration of World Trade*. Washington, DC, 1950.

Childs, Frank C. *The Theory and Practice of Exchange Control in Germany*. The Hague, 1958.

Committee on Finance and Industry (United Kingdom, Macmillan Report, Cmd 3897), London, 1931.

Condliffe, J. B. *The Reconstruction of World Trade: A Survey of International Economic Relations*. New York, 1940.

Copland, Douglas B. and James, C. V. *Australian Tariff Policy: A Book of Documents, 1932–1937*. Melbourne, 1937.

Davis, Joseph S. *The World Between the Wars, 1919–1939: An Economist's View*. Baltimore, Md., 1975.

Dohan, Michael and Hewett, Edward. *Two Studies in Soviet Terms of Trade, 1918–1970*. Bloomington, Ind., 1973.

Drummond, Ian M. *British Economic Policy and the Empire, 1919–1939*. London, 1972.

—— *Imperial Economic Policy, 1917–1939: Studies in Expansion and Protection*. Toronto, 1975.

—— *Economist, The*.

Einzig, Paul J. *Bloodless Invasion: German Penetration into the Danube States and the Balkans*. London, 1938.

Elliott, William Y., May, Elizabeth S., Rowe, J. F. W., Skelton, Alex and Wallace, Donald H. *International Control in Non-ferrous Metals*. New York, 1937.

Federal Trade Commission. *The International Petroleum Cartel*, US Senate Select Committee on Small Business, 82nd Congress, Committee Print no. 6. Washington, DC, August 1952.

Feis, Herbert. *Three International Episodes seen from E.A.* New York, 1946.

—— *1933, Characters in Crisis*. Boston, 1966.

Friedman, Philip. *The Impact of Trade Destruction on National Income: A Study of Europe, 1924–38*. Gainesville, Fla., 1974.

Furnivall, J. S. *Netherlands India: A Study of Plural Economy*. Cambridge, 1939.

Gordon, Margaret S. *Barriers to World Trade: A Study of Recent Commercial Policy*. New York, 1941.

Haight, Frank Arnold. *A History of French Commercial Policies*. New York, 1941.

Hancock, W. Keith. *Survey of British Commonwealth Affairs*, vol. II: *Problems of Economic Policy*. London, 1940.

Hexner, Erwin. *International Cartels*. Durham, NC, 1946.
Hoover, Herbert. *The Memoirs of Herbert Hoover*, vol. III, *The Great Depression, 1929–1941*. New York, 1952.
Hull, Cordell. *The Memoirs of Cordell Hull*. New York, 1948.
Johnson, Alvin S. 'Protection and the Formation of Capital', *Political Science Quarterly*, vol. XXIII (June 1908), pp. 220–41.
Johnson, D. Gale. *Trade and Agriculture; A Study of Inconsistent Policies*. New York, 1950.
Jones, Joseph M., Jr. *Tariff Retaliation, Repercussions of the Hawley-Smoot Bill*. Philadelphia, 1934.
Kindleberger, Charles P. *The Terms of Trade: A European Case Study*. New York, 1956.
—— *The World in Depression, 1929–1939*. Berkeley, 1973; revised edn, 1986.
Knorr, Klaus E. *World Rubber and its Regulation*. Stanford, 1946.
Kreider, Carl. *The Anglo-American Trade Agreement: A Study of British and American Commercial Policies, 1934–39*. Princeton, 1943.
Lary, Hal B. (US Department of Commerce, Bureau of Foreign and Domestic Commerce). *The United States in the World Economy*, Economic Series, no. 23. Washington, DC, 1943.
League of Nations. *Enquiry into Clearing Agreements*. Geneva, 1935.
—— *Commercial Policy in the Interwar Period: International Proposals and National Policies*. Geneva, 1942.
—— Economic Committee. *Considerations on the Present Evolution of Agricultural Tariffs*. Geneva, 1935.
—— (Folke Hilgerdt). *Europe's Trade, A Study of the Trade of European Countries with Each Other and with the Rest of the World*. Geneva, 1941.
—— (Folke Hilgerdt). *The Network of World Trade, A Companion Volume to 'Europe's Trade'*. Geneva, 1942.
—— (James E. Meade). *World Economic Survey, 1937/38*. Geneva, 1938.
—— (James E. Meade). *World Economic Survey, 1938/39*. Geneva, 1939.
—— (W. T. Page). *Memorandum on European Bargaining Tariffs*. Geneva, 1927.
—— (Jacob Viner). *Trade Relations between Free-market and Controlled Economies*. Geneva, 1943.
Lewis, Cleona. *Nazi Europe and World Trade*. Washington, DC, 1941.
Lewis, W. Arthur. *Economic Survey, 1919–1939*. Philadelphia, 1950.
Liepmann, H. *Tariff Levels and the Economic Unity of Europe*. London, 1938.
McDiarmid, Orville J. *Commercial Policy in the Canadian Economy*. Cambridge, Mass., 1946.
Malenbaum, Wilfrid. *The World Wheat Economy, 1895–1939*. Cambridge, Mass., 1953.
Manoilesco, Mihail. *The Theory of Protection and International Trade*. London, 1931.
Mason, Edward S. *Controlling World Trade, Cartels and Commodity Agreements*. New York, 1946.
Office of the Chief Counsel for Prosecution of Nazi Criminality. *Nazi Conspiracy and Aggression*, vols. I and VII. Washington, DC, 1946.
Petzina, Dieter. *Autarkiepolitik im dritten Reich, Der national-sozialistiche Vierjahresplan*. Stuttgart, 1968.
Reitsama, A. J. 'Trade and Redistribution of Income: Is There Still an Australian Case?', *Economic Record*, vol. XXIV, no. 68 (August 1958), pp. 172–88.
Richardson, J. H. *British Economic Foreign Policy*. London, 1936.
Roepke, Wilhelm. *German Commercial Policy*. London, 1934.
—— *International Economic Disintegration*. London, 1942.
Rowe, J. W. F. *Markets and Men: A Study of Artificial Control Schemes*. New York, 1936.
Salter, Sir Arthur. *Recovery, the Second Effort*. London and New York, 1932.
Schacht, Hjalmar. 'Germany's Colonial Demand', *Foreign Affairs*, vol. XIV (January 1937), pp. 223–34.
Schattschneider, E. E. *Politics, Pressures and Tariffs: A Study of Free Private Enterprise in Pressure Politics as Shown by the 1929–30 Revision of the Tariff*. New York, 1935.
Schuker, Stephen A. *The End of French Predominance in Europe: The Financial Crisis of 1924 and the Adoption of the Dawes Plan*. Chapel Hill, NC, 1976.

Smith, Mark A. 'The United States Flexible Tariff', in *Explorations in Economics, Notes and Essays Contributed in Honor of F. W. Taussig*. New York, 1936.

Stolper, W. F. and Samuelson, P. A. 'Protection and Real Wages', *Review of Economic Studies*, vol. IX (November 1941), pp. 58–73.

Suetens, M. *Histoire de la politique commerciale de la Belgique jusqu'à nos jours*. Brussels, 1955.

Tasca, Henry J. *The Reciprocal Trade Agreement Policy of the United States: A Study in Trade Philosophy*. Philadelphia, 1938.

Thorbecke, Erik. *The Tendency toward Regionalization in International Trade, 1928–1956*. The Hague, 1960.

United Nations, Department of Economic Affairs. *Customs Union: A League of Nations Contribution to the Study of Custom Union Problems*. Lake Success, NY, 1947.

United States Department of State. *Foreign Relations of the United States*. Washington, DC, various years.

—— Tariff Commission. *Foreign Trade and Exchange Controls*, Report no. 150. Washington, DC, 1942.

Van Gelderen, J. *The Recent Development of Economic Foreign Policy in the Netherlands East Indies*. London, 1939.

Viner, Jacob. *The Customs Union Issue*. New York, 1950.

—— *Dumping: A Problem in International Trade*. 1923, rep. New York, 1966.

Winslow, E. M. 'Administrative Protection: A Problem in Commercial Policy', in *Explorations in Economics: Notes and Essays in Honor of F. W. Taussig*. New York, 1936.

World Trading Systems. Paris, 1939.

CHAPTER III

International financial policy and the gold standard, 1870–1914

Ashworth, W. *A Short History of the International Economy since 1850.* 3rd edn. London, 1975.

Beach, W. E. *British International Gold Movements and Banking Policy, 1881–1913.* Cambridge, Mass., 1935.

Bloomfield, A. I. *Monetary Policy under the International Gold Standard 1880–1914.* New York, 1959.

—— 'Short-term Capital Movements under the pre-1914 Gold Standard', *Princeton Studies in International Finance*, no. 11 (1963).

Bordo, M. D. and Schwartz, A. J. (eds.). *A Retrospective on the Classical Gold Standard, 1821–1931.* Chicago, 1984. (The contribution in vol. VIII was completed before this valuable work appeared.)

Brown, W. A., Jr. *The International Gold Standard Reinterpreted, 1914–34.* New York, 1940.

Cottrell, P. *British Overseas Investment in the Nineteenth Century.* London, 1975.

De Cecco, M. *Money and Empire.* Oxford, 1975.

Eichengreen, B. (ed.) *The Gold Standard in Theory and History.* London, 1985.

Einzig, P. *The History of Foreign Exchange.* London, 1962.

Ford, A. G. *The Gold Standard 1880–1914: Britain and Argentina.* Oxford, 1962.

—— 'Bank Rate, The British Balance of Payments, and the Burdens of Adjustment, 1870–1914', *Oxford Economic Papers*, vol. XVI, no. 1 (1964).

—— 'Overseas Lending and Internal Fluctuations 1870–1914', *Yorkshire Bulletin of Economic and Social Research*, vol. XVII, no. 1 (1965).

Friedman, M. and Schwartz, A. J. *Monetary Trends in the United States and the United Kingdom 1867–1975.* Chicago, 1982.

Goodhart, C. A. E. *The Business of Banking 1891–1914.* London, 1972.

Hawtrey, R. G. *The Gold Standard in Theory and in Practice.* 5th edn. London, 1947.

—— *A Century of Bank Rate.* London, 1938.

Keynes, J. M. *Indian Currency and Finance.* London, 1913.

Lindert, P. H. 'Key Currencies and Gold 1900–13', *Princeton Studies in International Finance*, no. 24 (August 1969).

McCloskey, D. N. and Zecher, J. R. 'How the Gold Standard Worked 1880–1913', in J. A. Frenkel and H. G. Johnson (eds.), *The Monetary Approach to the Balance of Payments.* London, 1976.

Michaely, M. *Balance of Payments Adjustment Policies.* New York, 1968.

Morgan, E. V. *The Theory and Practice of Central Banking 1797–1913.* rep. London, 1965.

Morgenstern, O. *International Financial Transactions and Business Cycles.* Princeton, 1959.

Narkse, R. *International Currency Experience.* League of Nations, Geneva, 1944.

Saul, S. B. *Studies in British Overseas Trade 1870–1914.* Liverpool, 1960.

Sayers, R. S. *Bank of England Operations 1890–1914.* London, 1936.

—— *Central Banking after Bagehot.* Oxford, 1957.

—— *The Bank of England 1891–1944.* Cambridge, 1976.

Scammell, W. M. 'The Working of the Gold Standard', *Yorkshire Bulletin of Economic and Social Research*, no. 17 (1965).

Simkin, C. G. F. *The Instability of a Dependent Economy.* Oxford, 1951.

Triffin, R. 'National Central Banking and the International Monetary System', *Review of Economic Studies*, vol. XIV (1946–7).

—— 'The Evolution of the International Monetary System', *Princeton Studies in International Finance*, no. 12 (1964).

United Kingdom, Parliament. *First Interim Report of the Committee on Currency and Foreign Exchange after the War*, Cmnd 9182 (The Cunliffe Report). 1918.

—— *Report of the Committee on Finance and Industry*, Cmd 3897 (The Macmillan Report). 1931.

Viner, J. *Canada's Balance of International Indebtedness, 1900–1913*. Cambridge, Mass., 1924.

—— *Studies in the Theory of International Trade*. London, 1937.

Whale, P. Barrett. 'The Working of the Pre-War Gold Standard', *Economica*, NS, vol. IV (1937).

White, H. D. *The French International Accounts, 1880–1914*. Cambridge, Mass., 1933.

CHAPTER IV

The gold standard and national financial policies, 1919–39

As well as the works cited below which have proved useful in preparing this chapter, readers should remember that there is a wide range of autobiographical and biographical material concerning many of the main participants in the events discussed, such as Hjamar Schacht of the Reichsbank, Henry Mogenthau of the United States Treasury, Sir Frederick Leith Ross of the British Treasury, and Jacques Rueff who held various important French positions during the period.

Aldcroft, Derek H. *The Inter-War Economy: Britain 1919–1939.* London, 1970.
—— *From Versailles to Wall Street 1919–1929.* London, 1977.
Alford, B. W. E. *Depression and Recovery? British Economic Growth 1918–1939.* London, 1972.
Aliber, Robert Z. 'Speculation in the Foreign Exchanges: The European Experience, 1919–1926', *Yale Economic Essays,* vol. II, part 1 (Spring 1966), pp. 171–245.
Anderson, Benjamin M. *Economics and the Public Welfare: Financial and Economic History of the United States, 1914–1946.* New York, 1949.
Arndt, H. W. *The Economic Lessons of the Nineteen-Thirties.* London, 1944.
Atkin, J. M. 'Official Regulation of British Overseas Investment, 1914–1931', *Economic History Review,* 2nd series, vol. XXIII, part 2 (August 1970), pp. 324–35.
Balderston, T. 'The German Business Cycle in the 1920s: A Comment', *Economic History Review,* 2nd series, vol. XXX, part 1 (February 1977), pp. 159–61.
Balogh, Thomas. 'The Import of Gold into France: An Analysis of the Technical Position', *Economic Journal,* vol. XL, no. 159 (September 1930), pp. 441–60.
—— *Studies in Financial Organisation,* National Institute of Economic and Social Research, Economic and Social Studies, VI. Cambridge, 1947.
Bank for International Settlements. *Annual Reports,* various years.
—— *The Sterling Area.* Basle, 1953.
Benham, Frederick. *British Monetary Policy.* London, 1932.
Bennett, Edward W. *Germany and the Diplomacy of the Financial Crisis, 1931.* Cambridge, Mass., 1962.
Beyen, J. W. *Money in Maelstrom.* London, 1951.
Bloomfield, Arthur I. 'Rules of the Game of International Adjustment', in C. R. Whittlesey and J. S. G. Wilson (eds.), *Essays in Money and Banking in Honour of R. S. Sayers.* Oxford, 1968, pp. 26–46.
Bonn, M. J. *Wandering Scholar.* New York, 1948.
Boyle, Andrew. *Montagu Norman: A Biography.* London, 1967.
Bresciani-Turroni, Constantino. *The Economics of Inflation: A Study of Currency Depreciation in Post-War Germany, 1914–1923* (trans. M. E. Sayers). London, 1937.
Brown, A. J. *The Framework of Regional Economics in the United Kingdom.* National Institute of Economic and Social Research, Economic and Social Studies, XXVII. Cambridge, 1972.
Brown, William Adams, Jr. *The International Gold Standard Reinterpreted, 1914–1934.* 2 vols. New York, 1940.
Capie, F. 'The British Tariff and Industrial Protection in the 1930s', *Economic History Review,* 2nd series, vol. XXXI, part 3 (August 1978), pp. 399–409.
Cassel, Gustav. *Postwar Monetary Stabilization.* New York, 1928.
—— *The Downfall of the Gold Standard.* Oxford, 1936.
Chandler, Lester V. *Benjamin Strong: Central Banker.* Washington, DC, 1958.
—— *American Monetary Policy 1928–1941.* New York, 1971.
Child, Frank C. *The Theory and Practice of Exchange Control in Germany.* The Hague, 1958.
Clarke, Stephen V. O. *Central Bank Cooperation 1924–1931.* New York, 1967.
—— 'The Reconstruction of the International Monetary System: The Attempts of 1922 and 1933', *Princeton Studies in International Finance,* no. 33 (November 1973).
—— 'Exchange-Rate Stabilization in the Mid-1930s: Negotiating the Tripartite Agreement', *Princeton Studies in International Finance,* no. 41 (September 1977).

Clauson, G. L. M. 'The British Colonial Currency System', *Economic Journal*, vol. LIV, no. 213 (April 1944), pp. 1–25.

Clay, Sir Henry. *Lord Norman*. London, 1957.

Cohen, Benjamin J. 'International Reserves and Liquidity', in Peter B. Kennen (ed.), *International Trade and Finance: Frontiers for Research*. Cambridge, 1975, pp. 411–51.

Cohen, Jon S. 'The 1927 Revaluation of the Lira: A Study in Political Economy', *Economic History Review*, 2nd series, vol. XXV, part 4 (November 1972), pp. 642–54.

Cooper, Richard N. 'International Liquidity and Balance of Payments Adjustment', in International Monetary Fund, *International Reserves: Needs and Availability*. Washington, DC, 1970, pp. 125–45.

Copland, D. B. *Australia in the World Crisis 1929–1933*. Cambridge, 1934.

Costigliola, Frank C. 'Anglo-American Financial Rivalry in the 1920s', *Journal of Economic History*, vol. XXXVII, part 4 (December 1977), pp. 911–34.

Davis, Joseph S. *The World between the Wars, 1919–39: An Economist's View*. Baltimore, 1975.

Dulles, Eleanor Lansing. *The French Franc, 1914–1928: The Facts and their Interpretation*. New York, 1929.

Eastman, Harry C. 'French and Canadian Exchange Rate Policy', *Journal of Economic History*, vol. XV, no. 4 (December 1955), pp. 403–10.

Ellis, Howard S. *Exchange Control in Central Europe*, Harvard Economic Studies, vol. LXIX. Cambridge, Mass., 1941.

Falkus, M. E. 'The German Business Cycle in the 1920s', *Economic History Review*, 2nd series, vol. XVIII, part 3 (August 1975), pp. 451–65.

—— 'The German Business Cycle in the 1920s: A Reply', *Economic History Review*, 2nd series, vol. XXX, no. 1 (February 1977), p. 165.

Feis, H. *1933: Characters in Crisis*. Boston, 1966.

Fleisig, Heywood. 'The United States and the Non-European Periphery during the Early Years of the Great Depression', in H. van der Wee (ed.), *The Great Depression Revisited*. The Hague, 1972, pp. 145–81.

Frenkel, Jacob A. 'Purchasing Power Parity: Doctrinal Perspective and Evidence', *Journal of International Economics*, vol. VIII, part 2 (May 1978), pp. 169–92.

Friedman, Milton. *Essays in Positive Economics*. Chicago, 1953.

Friedman, Milton and Schwartz, Anna Jacobson. *A Monetary History of the United States, 1867–1960*. Princeton, 1963.

Gardner, Richard N. *Sterling–Dollar Diplomacy: The Origins and Prospects of our International Economic Order*. Rev. edn. New York, 1969.

Gayer, A. D. *Monetary Policy and Economic Stabilisation: A Study of the Gold Standard*. 2nd edn. London, 1937.

Gilbert, Milton. *Currency Depreciation and Monetary Policy*. Philadelphia, 1939.

Graham, Frank D. *Exchange, Prices and Production in Hyperinflation: Germany, 1920–1923*. Princeton, 1930.

—— 'Recent Movements in International Price Levels and the Doctrine of Purchasing Power Parity', *Journal of the American Statistical Association*, vol. XXX (1935), pp. 159–66.

Gregory, T. E. *The Return to Gold*. London, 1925.

—— *The First Year of the Gold Standard*. London, 1926.

—— 'The "Norman Conquest" Reconsidered', *Lloyds Bank Review*, October 1957, pp. 1–20.

—— 'Lord Norman: A New Interpretation', *Lloyds Bank Review* (April 1968), pp. 31–50.

Grubel, Herbert G. *The International Monetary System*. 3rd edn. Harmondsworth, Middx., 1977.

Harris, Seymour E. *Exchange Depreciation: Its Theory and History, 1931–35, with some Consideration of Related Domestic Policies*. Harvard Economic Studies, vol. LIII. Cambridge, Mass., 1936.

Hawke, G. R. 'New Zealand and the Return to Gold in 1925', *Australian Economic History Review*, vol. XI, no. 1 (March 1971), pp. 48–58.

Hawtrey, R. G. *Good and Bad Trade*. London, 1913.
—— *Currency and Credit*. London, 1919.
—— 'The Genoa Resolutions on Currency', *Economic Journal*, vol. XXXI, no. 127 (September 1922), pp. 290–304.
—— *The Art of Central Banking*. London, 1932.
—— *The Gold Standard in Theory and Practice*, 5th edn. London, 1947.
Hodgson, John S. 'An Analysis of Floating Exchange Rates: The Dollar–Sterling Rate, 1919–1925', *Southern Economic Journal*, vol. XXXIX, part 3 (October 1972), pp. 249–57.
Hoover, Calvin D. 'Old and New Issues in Regional Development', in E. A. G. Robinson (ed.), *Backward Areas in Advanced Countries*. London, 1969, pp. 343–57.
Howson, Susan. 'The Origins of Dear Money, 1919–20', *Economic History Review*, 2nd series, vol. XXVII, no. 1 (February 1974), pp. 88–107.
—— *Domestic Monetary Management in Britain 1919–38*. University of Cambridge, Department of Applied Economics, Occasional Paper 48. Cambridge, 1975.
—— 'The Managed Floating Pound 1932–9', *The Banker*, vol. CXXVI, no. 601 (March 1976), pp. 249–55.
—— 'Monetary Theory and Policy in the 20th Century: The Career of R. G. Hawtrey', in M. Flinn (ed.), *Proceedings of the Seventh International Economic History Congress*. Edinburgh, 1978, pp. 505–11.
Howson, Susan and Winch, Donald. *The Economic Advisory Council, 1930–1939: A Study of Economic Advice During Depression and Recovery*. Cambridge, 1977.
Hume, L. J. 'The Gold Standard and Deflation: Issues and Attitudes in the Nineteen Twenties', *Economica*, NS, vol. XXX, no. 119 (August 1963), pp. 222–42.
Hurst, Willard. 'Holland, Switzerland and Belgium, and the English Gold Crisis of 1931', *Journal of Political Economy*, vol. XL, no. 3 (October 1932), pp. 638–60.
Jacobsson, Per. *Some Monetary Problems, International and National*. London, 1958.
Kahn, Alfred E. *Great Britain in the World Economy*. New York, 1946.
Kemp, Tom. 'The French Economy under the Franc Poincaré', *Economic History Review*, 2nd series, vol. XXIV, part 1 (February 1971), pp. 82–99.
—— *The French Economy, 1919–39: The History of a Decline*. London, 1972.
Keynes, J. M. *The Economic Consequences of the Peace*. London, 1971 (first published 1919).
—— *A Revision of the Treaty: Being a Sequel to the Economic Consequences of the Peace*. London, 1972 (first published 1922).
—— *A Tract on Monetary Reform*. London, 1923.
—— *The Economic Consequences of Mr Churchill*. London, 1925.
—— 'The French Stabilisation Law', *Economic Journal*, vol. XXXVIII, no. 151 (September 1928), pp. 490–4.
—— *A Treatise on Money*. 2 vols. London, 1930.
Kindleberger, Charles P. *The Terms of Trade: A European Case Study*. New York, 1956.
—— *Economic Growth in France and Britain, 1851–1950*. Cambridge, Mass., 1964.
—— *The World in Depression 1929–1939*. London, 1973.
—— *Manias, Panics, and Crashes: A History of Financial Crises*. New York, 1978.
Landes, David M. *The Unbound Prometheus: Technological Change and Industrial Development in Western Europe from 1750 to the Present*. Cambridge, 1969.
Lary, H. B. and associates. *The United States in the World Economy: The International Transactions of the United States during the Interwar Period*. Washington, DC, 1943.
Laursen, K. and Pedersen, J. *The German Inflation, 1918–1923*. Amsterdam, 1964.
League of Nations, Gold Delegation of the Financial Committee. *First Interim Report*. Geneva, 1930.
—— *Second Interim Report*. Geneva, 1931.
—— *Select Documents on the Distribution of Gold*. Geneva, 1931.
—— *Final Report*. Geneva, 1932.
—— *The Course and Phases of the World Economic Depression*. Geneva, 1931.
—— *International Currency Experience: Lessons of the Inter-war Period*. Princeton, 1944.
—— *The Course and Control of Inflation: A Review of Monetary Experience in Europe after World War I*. New York, 1946.

Lester, Richard A. *Monetary Experiments: Early American and Recent Scandinavian.* Princeton, 1939.

Lewis, W. Arthur. *Economic Survey 1919–1939.* London, 1949.

Lindert, Peter H. 'Key Currencies and Gold 1900–1913', *Princeton Studies in International Finance*, no. 24 (August 1969).

McCloskey, Donald N. and Zecher, Richard J. 'How the Gold Standard Worked, 1880–1913', in Jacob A. Frenkel and Harry G. Johnson (eds.), *The Monetary Approach to the Balance of Payments.* Toronto, 1976, pp. 357–85.

Maddison, Angus. 'Growth and Fluctuations in the World Economy, 1870–1960', *Banca Nazionale del Lavoro Quarterly Review*, no. 61 (June 1962), pp. 127–95.

Maier, Charles S. *Recasting Bourgeois Europe: Stabilisation in France, Germany and Italy in the Decade after World War I.* Princeton, 1975.

Malach, Vernon W. *International Cycles and Canada's Balance of Payments 1921–33.* Toronto, 1954.

Marcus, Edward. *Canada and the International Business Cycle 1927–1939.* New York, 1954.

Meyer, Richard H. *Bankers' Diplomacy: Monetary Stabilisation in the Twenties.* New York, 1970.

Meyers, Margaret C. *Paris as a Financial Center.* New York, 1936.

Michaely, Michael. *Balance-of-Payments Adjustment Policies.* National Bureau of Economic Research Occasional Paper. New York, 1968.

Mitchell, B. R. *European Historical Statistics 1750–1970.* London, 1975.

Moggridge, D. E. *The Return to Gold, 1925: The Formulation of Economic Policy and its Critics.* University of Cambridge, Department of Applied Economics, Occasional Paper 19. Cambridge, 1969.

—— 'The 1931 Financial Crisis: A New View', *The Banker*, vol. CXX, no. 534 (August 1970), pp. 832–9.

—— *British Monetary Policy 1924–1931: The Norman Conquest of $4.86.* University of Cambridge, Department of Applied Economics Monograph 21. Cambridge, 1972.

Moggridge, D. E. (ed.) *The Collected Writings of John Maynard Keynes*, vol. XX: *Activities 1929–1931: Rethinking Employment and Unemployment Policies.* London and New York, 1981.

Moreau, Emile. *Souvenirs d'un Gouverneur de la Banque de France: Histoire de la Stabilisation du Franc (1926–1928).* Paris, 1954.

Morgan, E. Victor. *Studies in British Financial Policy 1914–1925.* London, 1952.

Morgenstern, Oscar. *International Financial Transactions and Business Cycles.* Princeton, 1959.

Nevin, Edward T. *The Mechanism of Cheap Money: A Study of British Monetary Policy 1931–1939.* Cardiff, 1955.

Niehans, Jürg. 'The Need for Reserves of a Single Country', in International Monetary Fund, *International Reserves: Needs and Availability.* Washington, DC, 1970, pp. 49–85.

Northrop, M. B. *The Control Policies of the Reichsbank, 1924–1933.* New York, 1938.

Officer, Lawrence E. 'The Purchasing-Power-Parity Theory of Exchange Rates: A Review Article', *International Monetary Fund Staff Papers*, vol. XXIII, no. 1 (March 1976), pp. 1–60.

Paish, F. W. *The Post-War Financial Problem.* London, 1950.

Palyi, Melchior. *The Twilight of Gold 1914–1936: Myths and Realities.* Chicago, 1972.

Perrot, M. *La Monnaie et l'Opinion Publique en France et en Angleterre (de 1924 a 1936).* Paris, 1955.

Phelps Brown, E. H. and Browne, M. H. *A Century of Pay: The Course of Pay and Production in France, Germany, Sweden, the United Kingdom and the United States of America 1860–1960.* London, 1968.

Pigou, A. C. *Aspects of British Economic History 1918–1925.* London, 1947.

Pollard, S. (ed.). *The Gold Standard and Employment Policies between the Wars.* London, 1970.

Poole, K. E. *German Financial Policies 1932–39.* Cambridge, Mass., 1939.

Pressnell, L.S. '1925: The Burden of Sterling', *Economic History Review*, 2nd series, vol. XXXI, part 1 (February 1978), pp. 67–88.

Richardson, H. W. *Economic Recovery in Britain 1932–39*. London, 1967.
Robbins, Lionel. *The Great Depression*. London, 1934.
Rowland, Benjamin M. (ed.). *Balance of Power or Hegemony: The Interwar Monetary System*. New York, 1976.
Royal Institute of International Affairs. *The International Gold Problem*. London, 1931.
—— *The Problem of International Investment*. London, 1937.
Safarian, A. E. *The Canadian Economy in the Great Depression*. Toronto, 1959.
Sarti, R. 'Mussolini and the Italian Industrial Leadership in the Battle of the Lira, 1925–1927', *Past and Present*, no. 47 (May 1970), pp. 97–112.
Sauvy, A. *Histoire économique de la France entre les deux guerres*, 4 vols. Paris, 1965–75.
Sayers, R. S. *Modern Banking*. 2nd edn. Oxford, 1947.
—— *Financial Policy 1939–1945*. London, 1956.
—— 'The Return to Gold, 1925', in S. Pollard (ed.), *The Gold Standard and Employment Policies between the Wars*. London, 1970, pp. 85–98.
—— *The Bank of England 1891–1944*. 3 vols. Cambridge, 1976.
Schedvin, C. B. *Australia and the Great Depression: A Study of Economic Development and Policy in the 1920s and 1930s*. Sydney, 1970.
Schuker, Stephen A. *The End of French Predominance in Europe: The Financial Crisis of 1924 and the Adoption of the Dawes Plan*. Chapel Hill, NC, 1976.
Schwartz, Anna Jacobson. 'Review of C. P. Kindleberger, *The World in Depression*', *Journal of Political Economy*, vol. LXXXVIII, part 2 (April 1975), pp. 231–7.
Shepherd, Harvey L. *The Monetary Experience of Belgium, 1914–1936*. Princeton, 1936.
Stewart, R. B. 'Great Britain's Foreign Loan Policy', *Economica*, NS, vol. V, no. 17 (February 1938), pp. 45–60.
Stolper, W. S. 'Purchasing Power Parity and the Pound Sterling from 1919–1925', *Kyklos*, vol. II, part 3 (1948), pp. 240–69.
Strange, Susan. *Sterling and British Policy: A Political Study of an International Currency in Decline*. London, 1971.
Svennilson, I. *Growth and Stagnation in the European Economy*. Geneva, 1954.
Temin, Peter. 'The Beginning of the Depression in Germany', *Economic History Review*, 2nd series, vol. XXIV, part 2 (May 1971), pp. 240–9.
—— 'The German Business Cycle in the 1920's: T. Balderston, A Comment; A Comment and Reply; M. E. Falkus, A Reply', *Economic History Review*, 2nd series, vol. XXX, part 1 (February 1977), pp. 162–4.
Triffin, Robert. 'The Evolution of the International Monetary System: Historical Reappraisal and Future Perspectives', *Princeton Studies in International Finance*, no. 12 (June 1964).
Tsiang, S. C. 'Fluctuating Exchange Rates in Countries with Relatively Stable Economies: Some European Experiences After World War I', *International Monetary Fund Staff Papers*, vol. VII, no. 3 (October 1959), pp. 244–73.
United Kingdom, Committee on Currency and Foreign Exchanges after the War. *First Interim Report*. Cd 9182. London, 1918.
—— Court of Inquiry Concerning the Coal Mining Dispute. *Report*. Cmd 2478. London, 1925.
—— Committee on Finance and Industry. *Report*. Cmd 3897. London, 1931.
—— Committee on Finance and Industry. *Minutes of Evidence*. Q.1595. London, 1931.
—— HM Treasury. *Reserves and Liabilities 1931 to 1945*. Cmd 8354. London, 1951.
United States, Board of Governors of the Federal Reserve System. *Banking and Monetary Statistics*. Washington, DC, 1943.
van der Wee, Herman (ed.). *The Great Depression Revisited: Essays on the Economics of the Thirties*. The Hague, 1972.
van der Wee, Herman and Tavernier, K. *La Banque Nationale de Belgique et l'Histoire Monetaire entre les Deux Guerres Mondiales*. Brussels, 1975.
Wicker, Elmus R. *Federal Reserve Monetary Policy, 1917–1933*. New York, 1966.
Williams, David. 'Montagu Norman and Banking Policy in the 1920s', *Yorkshire Bulletin of Economic and Social Research*, vol. XI, no. 1 (July 1959), pp. 38–55.
—— 'London and the 1931 Financial Crisis', *Economic History Review*, 2nd series, vol. XV, part 3 (April 1963), pp. 513–28.

—— 'The 1931 Financial Crisis', *Yorkshire Bulletin of Economic and Social Research*, vol. xv, no. 2 (November 1963), pp. 92–110.
—— 'The Evolution of the Sterling System', in C. R. Whittlesey and J. S. G. Wilson (eds.), *Essays in Money and Banking in Honour of R. S. Sayers*. Oxford, 1968, pp. 266–97.
Williamson, John. 'International Liquidity: A Survey', *Economic Journal*, vol. LXXXIII, no. 331 (September 1973), pp. 685–746.
Winch, Donald. *Economics and Policy: A Historical Study*. London, 1972.
Wolfe, Martin. *The French Franc between the Wars, 1919–1939*. New York, 1951.
Wonnacott, P. *The Canadian Dollar, 1948–1962*. Toronto, 1965.
Woytinsky, W. S. and Woytinsky, E. S. *World Commerce and Governments: Trends and Outlook*. New York, 1955.
Wynne, William H. 'The French Franc, June 1928–February 1937', *Journal of Political Economy*, vol. XLV, part 3 (August 1937), pp. 484–516.
Yeager, Leyland B. *International Monetary Relations: Theory, History and Policy*. 2nd edn. New York, 1976.

SUPPLEMENTARY BIBLIOGRAPHY

Balderston, T. 'The Beginnings of the Depression in Germany, 1927–1930: Investment and Capital Markets', *Economic History Review*, 2nd series, vol. XXXVI, part 3 (August 1983), pp. 395–415.
Bank of England Panel of Economic Consultants. 'The U.K. Economic Recovery in the 1930s', *Panel Paper*, no. 23 (April 1984).
Brunner, K. (ed.). *The Great Depression Revisited*. The Hague, 1981.
Cairncross, A. and Eichengreen, B. J. *Sterling in Decline: Three Devaluations of Sterling*. Oxford, 1983.
Dam, K. W. *The Rules of the Game: Reform and Evolution in the International Monetary System*. Chicago, 1982.
Deutsches Bundesbank. *Währung und Wirtschaft in Deutschland 1876–1976*. Frankfurt, 1976.
Dimsdale, N. H. 'British Monetary Policy and the Exchange Rate 1920–1938', in W. A. Eltis and P. J. N. Sinclair (eds.), *The Money Supply and the Exchange Rate*. Oxford, 1981.
Drummond, I. M. 'London, Washington and the Management of the Franc, 1935–1939', *Princeton Studies in International Finance*, no. 45 (November 1979).
—— *The Floating Pound and the Sterling Area 1931–1939*. Cambridge, 1981.
Eichengreen, B. J. 'Sterling and the Tariff, 1929–1932', *Princeton Studies in International Finance*, no. 48 (September 1981).
——'Central Bank Cooperation under the Interwar Gold Standard', *Explorations in Economic History*, vol. XXI, no. 1 (January 1984), pp. 64–87.
Feldman, G. D., Holtfereich, C. L., Ritter, G. A. and Witt, P. C. (eds.). *The Experience of Inflation*. Berlin, 1982.
—— *The German Inflation*. Berlin, 1982.
Fritsch, W. 'Aspects of Brazilian Economic Policy under the First Republic', unpublished PhD dissertation, University of Cambridge, 1983.
Holtfereich, C. L. *Die deutsche Inflation 1914–1923: Uraschen and Folgen in internationaler Perspektive*. Berlin, 1980.
Howson, Susan. 'Sterling's Managed Float: The Operation of the Exchange Equalisation Account, 1932–1939', *Princeton Studies in International Finance*, no. 46 (November 1980).
James, H. 'The Causes of the German Banking Crisis of 1931', *Economic History Review*, 2nd series, vol. XXXVII, part 1 (February 1984), pp. 68–87.
—— *The Reichsbank and Public Finance in Germany 1924–1933: A Study of the Politics of Economics during the Great Depression*. Frankfurt, 1985.
März, E. *Austrian Banking and Financial Policy: Creditanstalt at a Turning Point 1913–1923*. London, 1984.
Matthews, R. C. O., Feinstein, C. H. and Odling-Smee, J. C. *British Economic Growth 1856–1973*. Stanford, 1982.

Redmond, J. 'An Indicator of the Effective Exchange Rate of the Pound in the Nineteen-Thirties', *Economic History Review*, 2nd series, vol. XXXIII, part 1 (February 1980), pp. 83–91.
—— 'The Sterling Overvaluation in 1925: a Multilateral Approach', *Economic History Review*, 2nd series, vol. XXXVII, part 4 (November 1984), pp. 520–32.
Shearer, R. A. and Clark, C. 'Canada and the Interwar Gold Standard, 1920–1935: Monetary Policy without a Central Bank', in M. Bordo and A. J. Schwartz (eds.), *A Retrospective on the Classical Gold Standard 1821–1931*. Chicago, 1984.
Tomlinson, B. R. *The Political Economy of the Raj, 1914–1947: The Economics of Decolonization in India*. London, 1979.
Williamson, Philip. 'Financiers, the Gold Standard and British Politics 1925–1931', in J. Turner (ed.), *Businessmen and Politics 1900–1945*. London, 1984.
—— 'A "Bankers' Ramp"? Financiers and the British Political Crisis of August 1931', *English Historical Review*, vol. XCIX (October 1984), pp. 770–806.
Wright, J. F. 'Britain's Inter-War Experience', in W. A. Eltis and P. J. N. Sinclair (eds.), *The Money Supply and the Exchange Rate*. Oxford, 1981.

CHAPTER V

Taxation and public finance: Britain, France, and Germany

GREAT BRITAIN

Acworth, A. W. *Financial Reconstruction in England, 1815–1822.* London, 1925.
Baxter, R. D. *The Taxation of the United Kingdom.* London, 1869.
Binney, J. E. D. *British Public Finance and Administration, 1774–92.* Oxford, 1958.
Bowley, A. L. *The Change in the Distribution of National Income, 1880–1913.* Oxford, 1920.
Cannan, E. *The Paper Pound.* London, 1919.
Crouzet, François. *L'économie britannique et le blocus continental (1806–1813).* 2 vols. Paris, 1958.
Deane, P. and Cole, W. A. *British Economic Growth, 1688–1959.* 2nd edn. Cambridge, Mass., 1969.
Dickson, P. G. M. *The Financial Revolution in England: A Study in the Development of Public Credit, 1688–1756.* London, Melbourne and Toronto, 1967.
Dilling, Dolf. 'Entwicklung und Problematik der Einkommensbesteuerung in Grossbritannien bis zur Gegenwart'. Dissertation, Heidelberg University, 1950.
Dowell, S. *A History of Taxation and Taxes in England from the Earliest Times to the Present Day.* 4 vols. New York, 1883. 3rd edn 1965.
Feinstein, C. H. *National Income, Expenditure and Output of the United Kingdom, 1855–1965.* Cambridge, 1972.
Fetter, F. W. *Development of British Monetary Orthodoxy, 1797–1875.* Cambridge, Mass., 1965.
Gayer, A. D., Rostow, W. W. and Schwartz, A. J. *The Growth and Fluctuation of the British Economy, 1970–1850.* 2 vols. Oxford, 1953.
Grellier, J. J. *The History of the National Debt from the Revolution in 1688 to the Beginning of 1800, with a Preliminary Account of the Debts contracted previous to that Era.* 1810.
Harzendorf, F. *Die Einkommensteuer in England.* Tübingen, 1914.
Hicks, U. K. *Public Finance.* 2nd edn. London, 1955.
—— 'Die öffentliche Finanzwirtschaft Grossbritanniens, 1799–1949', in W. Gerloff and F. Neumark (eds.), *Handbuch der Finanzwissenschaft,* vol. I. 2nd edn. Tübingen, 1952.
—— *British Public Finances: Their Structure and Development, 1880–1952.* London, New York and Toronto, 1954.
Hoon, E. E. *The Organization of the English Customs System, 1696–1786.* Newton Abbot, 1968.
Hope-Jones, A. *Income Tax in the Napoleonic Wars.* Cambridge, 1939.
Keith, A. B. *The Constitution and Laws of the Empire: The British Empire.* 3rd edn ed. Hugh Gunn. London, 1924.
McCulloch, J. R. *A Treatise on the Principles and Practical Influences of Taxation and the Funding System.* London, 1845.
Madge, S. J. *The Domesday of Crown Lands: A Study of the Legislation, Surveys and Sales of the Royal Estates under the Commonwealth.* London, 1938.
Mallet, B. *British Budgets, 1887–88 to 1912–13.* London, 1913.
Mallet, B. and George, C. O. *British Budgets, 1913–14 to 1920–21.* London, 1929.
—— *British Budgets, 1921–22 to 1932–33.* London, 1933.
Manes, A. 'Die Einkommensteuer in der englischen Finanzpolitik und -literatur bis zu William Pitts Tode', in *Festschrift für W. Lexis.* Jena, 1907.
Mann, F. K. 'Geschichte der angelsächsischen Finanzwissenschaft', in W. Gerloff and F. Neumark (eds.), *Handbuch der Finanzwissenschaft,* vol. I. 2nd edn. Tübingen, 1952.
Mathias, P. *The First Industrial Nation: An Economic History of Britain, 1700–1914.* London, 1969.
Peacock, A. and Wiseman, J. *The Growth of Public Expenditure in the United Kingdom.* Princeton, 1961.
Pebrer, P. *Taxation, Expenditure, Power, Statistics and Debt of the whole British Empire.* 1833.

Pollard, S. and Crossley, D. W. *The Wealth of Britain, 1085–1966*. London, 1969.
Rees, J. F. *A Short Fiscal and Financial History of England, 1815–1918*. London, 1921.
Sabine, B. E. V. *A History of Income Tax*. London, 1966.
—— *Short History of Taxation*. London, 1980.
Seligman, E. R. *The Income Tax: A Study of the History, Theory and Practice of Income Taxation at Home and Abroad*. 2nd edn. London, 1921.
Silberling, N. J. 'British Financial Experience, 1790–1830', in *Review of Economic Statistics*. Cambridge, Mass., 1919.
Stamp, J. C. *British Incomes and Properties*. 1916.
The Statesman's Year Book: Statistical and Historical Annual of the States of The World. London, 1889 and various years.
Statistical Abstracts for the United Kingdom, no. 28 (*1866–1880*), 1881; no. 43 (*1881–1895*), 1896; no. 49 (*1887–1901*), 1902; no. 58 (*1896–1910*), 1911; no. 70 (*1911–1925*), 1927; all London.
Turner, S. H. *The History of the Local Taxation in Scotland*. London, 1908.
Veverka, J. 'The Growth of Government Expenditure in the United Kingdom since 1790', *Scottish Journal of Political Economy*, vol. x (1963).
Vocke, W. *Geschichte der Steuern des britischen Reiches*. Leipzig, 1866.
Ward, W. R. *The English Land Tax in the Eighteenth Century*. London, 1953.
Weise, H. *Die Steuern im Vereinigten Königreich; unter Berücksichtigung der Entwicklung seit dem Ersten Weltkrieg*. 2 vols. Kiel, 1957.
Wilson, C. *England's Apprenticeship, 1603–1763*. London, 1965.
Wright, R. S. and Hobhouse, H. *An Outline of Local Government and Local Taxation in England and Wales*. London, 1922.

SUPRA-NATIONAL AND GENERAL WORKS

Austin, O. P. *Colonial Administration: Methods of Government and Development adopted by the Principal Colonizing Nations*. Washington, DC, 1910.
Barker, E. *The Development of Public Services in Western Europe, 1660–1930*. London, 1944.
Baumstark, E. *Staatswissenschaftliche Versuche über Staatskredit, Staatschulden und Staatspapiere, nebst drei Anhängen*. Heidelberg, 1833.
Baxter, R. D. *National Debts*. London, 1871.
Blankart, C. B. 'Neuere Ansätze zur Erklärung des Wachstums der Staatsausgaben; ein interpretierender Überblick', in H. D. Ortlieb, B. Molitor and W. Krone (eds.), *Hamburger Jahrbuch fur Wirtschafts- und Gesellschafts- politik*, vol. XXII. Tübingen, 1977.
Bräuer, K. *Umrisse und Untersuchungen zur einer Lehre vom Steuer tarif*. Jena, 1931.
Braun, R. 'Taxation, Sociopolitical Structure and State Building: Great Britain and Brandenburg–Prussia', in C. Tilly (ed.), *The Formation of National States in Western Europe*. Princeton, 1975.
Büsch, O., Fischer, W. and Herzfeld, H. (eds.). *Industrialisierung und 'Europäische Wirtschaft' im 19. Jahrhundert*, conference report. Berlin and New York, 1976.
Cameron, R. *France and the Economic Development of Europe, 1800–1914*. 2nd edn. Chicago, 1961.
Cohen, B. *Compendium of Finance, containing an Account of . . . Public Debts, Revenue, Expenditure . . .* London, 1822.
Colm, G. 'Die methodischen Grundlagen der international-vergleichenden Finanzstatistik', *Weltwirtschaftliches Archiv*, vol. XXII (1925).
Crouzet, G. 'Angleterre et France au XVIIIe siecle. Essai d'analyse comparée de deux croissances économiques', *Annales*, vol. XXI (1966).
Czoernig, C. von. *Das österreichische Budget für 1862 in Vergleichung mit jenen der vorzüglicheren anderen europäischen Staaten*. 2 vols. Vienna, 1862.
—— *Darstellung der Einrichtungen über Budget, Staatsrechnung und Controlle in Österreich, Preussen, Sachsen, Bayern, Wurttemberg, Baden, Frankreich und Belgien*. Vienna, 1866.
Eheberg, K. T. von. 'Finanzen', in J. Conrad, L. Elster, W. Lexis and E. Toening (eds.), *Handwörterbuch der Staatswissenschaften*, vol. IIII. 3rd edn. Jena, 1892.

Elster, L. 'Der Bevölkerungsstand und die Bevölkerungsbewegung der neusten Zeit bis zum Ausbruch des Weltkrieges', in *Handwörterbuch der Staatswissenschaften*, vol. II. 4th edn. Jena, 1924.

Fabricant, S. *The Trend of Government Activity in the United States since 1900*. New York, 1952.

Feis, H. *Europe, the World's Banker, 1870–1914*. 2nd edn. New York, 1965.

Fournier de Flaix, E. *Traité de critique et de statistique comprée des institutions financières. Systèmes d'impôts et réformes fiscales des divers états au XIXe siècle*. Paris, 1889.

Franke, S. F. *Entwicklung und Begründung der Einkommensbesteuerung*. Darmstadt, 1981.

Gaettens, R. *Inflationen*. Munich, 1955.

Hartmann, P. C. *Das Steuersystem der europäischen Staaten am Ende des ancien régime. Eine offizielle französische Enquête (1763–1768). Dokumente, Analyse und Auswertung; England und die Staaten Nord- und Mitteleuropas*. Munich, 1979.

Hasbach, W. *Untersuchungen über Adam Smith und die Entwicklung der politischen Ökonomie*. Leipzig, 1891.

Heckel, M. von. *Lehrbuch der Finanzwissenschaft*. 2 vols. Leipzig, 1907, 1911.

Helleiner, K. F. *The Imperial Loans: A Study in Financial and Diplomatic History*. Oxford, 1965.

Henderson, W. O. *The Industrial Revolution in Europe: Germany, France, Russia, 1815–1914*. Chicago, 1968.

Jähnke, F. *Die deutsche und die englische Einkommensbesteuerung*. Berlin, 1935.

Jenetzky, J. *System und Entwicklung des materiellen Steuerrechts in der wissenschaftlichen Literatur des Kameralismus von 1680 bis 1804*. Berlin, 1978.

Justi, J. H. G. von. *System des Finanzwesens*. Halle, 1766.

Kaufman, R. von. *Die öffentlichen Ausgaben der grösseren europäischen Länder nach ihrer Zweckbestimmung*. 3rd edn. 1893.

Kindleberger, C. P. 'Foreign Trade and Economic Growth: Lessons from Britain and France, 1850–1913', *Economic History Review*, vol. XIV (1961–2), pp. 289–309.

—— *Economic Growth in France and Britain, 1851–1950*. Cambridge, Mass., 1964.

Kisselbach, W. *Die Kontinentalsperre in ihrer ökonomisch-politischen Bedeutung*. Stuttgart, 1850.

Klimpert, R. *Lexikon der Münzen, Masse, Gewichte, Zahlarten und Zeitgrössen aller Länder der Erde*. Berlin, 1896.

Knauss, R. *Die deutsche, englische und französische Kriegsfinanzierung*. Berlin and Leipzig, 1923.

Knowles, L. C. A. *Economic Development in the Nineteenth Century: France, Germany, Russia and the United States*. New York, 1967.

Kruedener, J. von. *Die Rolle des Hofes im Absolutismus*. Stuttgart, 1973.

Kuczynski, J. *Propheten der Wirtschaft*. Berlin, GDR, 1970.

Kuznets, S. *Modern Economic Growth: Rate, Structure and Spread*. New Haven and London, 1966.

Landmann, J. 'Geschichte des öffentlichen Kredits', in W. Gerloff and F. Neumark (eds.), *Handbuch der Finanzwissenschaft*, vol. III. 2nd edn. Tübingen, 1958.

Lee, R. W. (ed.). *European Demography and Economic Growth*. London, 1979.

Leroy-Beaulieu, P. *Les impôts et les revenues en France, en Angleterre et en Allemagne*. Paris, 1914.

Mann, F. K. *Steuerpolitische Ideale: vergleichende Studien zur Geschichte der ökonimischen und politischen Ideen und ihre Wirken in der öffentlichen Meinung, 1600–1935*. Jena, 1937.

Mayer, T. 'Geschichte der Finanzwirtschaft vom Mittelalter bis zum Ende des 18. Jahrhunderts', in W. Gerloff and F. Neumark (eds.), *Handbuch der Finanzwissenschaft*, vol. I. 2nd edn. Tübingen, 1952.

Meisel, F. *Britische und deutsche Einkommensteuer, ihre Moral und Technik*. Tübingen, 1925.

Mitchell, B. R. *European Historical Statistics, 1750–1970*. London and Basingstoke, 1975.

Musgrave, R. A. 'Theorie der öffentlichen Schuld', in W. Gerloff and F. Neumark (eds.), *Handbuch der Finanzwissenschaft*, vol. III. 2nd edn. Tübingen, 1958.

—— *Fiscal Systems*. New Haven and London, 1969.

Musgrave, R. A. and Culbertson, J. M. 'The Growth of Public Expenditures in the United States, 1890–1948', *National Tax Journal*, vol. VI (1953), pp. 97–115.

Neumark, F. 'Theorie und Praxis der Budgetgestaltung', in W. Gerloff and F. Neumark (eds.), *Handbuch der Finanzwissenschaft*, vol. I. 2nd edn. Tübingen, 1952.
—— 'Grundsätze und Arten der Haushaltführung und Finanzbedarfdeckung', in W. Gerloff and F. Neumark (eds.), *Handbuch der Finanzwissenschaft*, vol. I. 2nd edn. Tübingen, 1952.
O'Brien, P. and Keyder, C. *Economic Growth in Britain and France, 1780–1914: Two Paths to the Twentieth Century*. London, 1978.
—— 'Les voies de passage vers la société industrielle en Grande-Bretagne et en France', *Annales*, vol. XLIV (1979), pp. 1284–303.
Otsuka, H. *The Spirit of Capitalism: The Max Weber Thesis in an Economic Historical Perspective*. Tokyo, 1982.
Peacock, A. *The Economic Analysis of Government and Related Themes*. Oxford, 1979.
Pfeiffer, E. *Vergleichende Zusammenstellung der europäischen Staatsausgabern*. 1865 (2nd edn, 1877).
Plenge, J. 'Die Finanzen der Grossmächte. Eine Kritik neudeutscher Finanzstatistik', *Zeitschrift fur die gesamte Staatswissenschaft*, vol. LXIV (1908), pp. 713–75.
Pollard, S. 'Industrialization and the European Economy', *Economic History Review*, vol. XXVI (1973), pp. 636–48.
—— *European Economic Integration, 1815–1970*. London, 1974.
—— 'Industrialization and Integration of the European Economy', in O. Busch, W. Fischer and H. Hertsfeld (eds.), *Industrialisierung und 'Europäische Wirtschaft' im 19. Jahrhundert*. Berlin and New York, 1976.
—— *Peaceful Conquests: The Industrialisation of Europe, 1760–1970*. Oxford, 1981.
Popitz, J. 'Einkommensteuer', in L. Elster, A. Weber and F. Wieser (eds.), *Handwörterbuch der Staatswissenschaften*, vol. III. 4th edn. Jena, 1926.
Recktenwald, H. C. 'Umfang und Struktur der öffentlichen Ausgaben in säkularer Entwicklung', in F. Neumark (ed.), *Handbuch der Finanzwissenschaft*, vol. I. Tübingen, 1977.
Reden, F. W. von. *Deutschland und das übrige Europa*. Wiesbaden, 1854.
—— *Allgemeine vergleichende Finanz-Statistik. Vergleichende Darstellung des Haushalts, Abgabewesens und der Schulden Deutschlands and des übrigens Europas*. 2 vols. in 2 parts each vol. Vol. I, Darmstadt, 1851, vol. II, 1853, 1856.
Riecke, C. V. von. *Die internationale Finanzstatistik, ihre Ziele und ihre Grenzen*. Stuttgart, 1876.
Rostow, W. W. *Politics and the Stages of Growth*. Cambridge, Mass., 1961.
—— 'The Beginnings of Modern Growth in Europe: An Essay in Synthesis', *Journal of Economic History*, vol. XXXIII (1973), pp. 547–80.
—— *How It All Began: Origins of the Modern Economy*. London, 1975.
Schnabel, G. N. *General-Statistik der europäischen Staaten nebst einer theoretischen Einleitung*, 2 vols. Vienna, 1833.
Schremmer, E. 'Die Wirtschaftsordnungen, 1800–1970', in H. Aubin and W. Zorn (eds.), *Handbuch der deutschen Wirtschafts- und Sozialgeschichte*, vol. II. Stuttgart, 1976.
Schumpeter, J. A. *Kapitalismus, Sozialismus und Demokratie*. 2nd edn. Bern, 1950.
Shirras, G. F. *Volkseinkommen und Besteuerung*. Jena, 1926.
—— *The Science of Public Finance*. London, 1925.
Smith, Adam. *An Inquiry into the Nature and the Causes of the Wealth of Nations*. 1776. New York edn, 1937.
Spaulding, H. *The Income Tax in Great Britain and the United States*. London, 1927.
Stammhammer, J. *Bibliographie der Finanzwissenschaft*. Jena, 1903.
Statistisches Reichsamt (ed.). *Die Staatsausgaben von Grossbritannien, Frankreich, Belgien und Italien in der Vor- und Nachkriegszeit. Unterlagen zum internationalen Finanzvergleich*. Berlin, 1927.
Terhalle, F. *Finanzwissenschaft*. Jena, 1930.
Timm, H. 'Das Gesetz der wachsenden Staatsausgaben', *Finanzarchiv*, NS, vol. XXI (1961), pp. 201–47.
Wagner, A. 'Entwicklung der europäischen und deutschen Staatsgebiete', *Preussisches Jahrbuch*, vol. XIX (1867), vol. XXI (1868).

—— *Finanzwissenschaft*, part 1, 1883; part 2, 2nd edn, 1890; part 3, 1889; part 4, Leipzig, 1901.

—— *Steuergeschichte vom Altertum bis zur Gegenwart*. Leipzig, 1910, also 2nd edn of part 3 of *Finanzwissenschaft*, cited above.

Zahn, F. 'Finanzstatistik', in *Handworterbuch der Staatswissenschaften*, vol. IV. 4th edn. Jena, 1927.

—— *Die Finanzen der Grossmächte*. Berlin, 1908.

FRANCE

André, Christine and Delorme, Robert. 'L'évolution séculaire des dépenses publiques en France', *Annales*, vol. XXXIII (1978), pp. 255–78.

Ardant, G. 'Financial Policy and Economic Infrastructure of Modern States and Nations', in C. Tilly (ed.), *The Formation of National States in Western Europe*. Princeton, 1975.

Arnould, M. *Histoire générale des finances de la France, depuis le commencement de la monarchie; pour servir d'introduction à la loi annuelle ou budget de l'empire français*. Paris, 1806.

Arnoux, E. 'Cadastre', in Say (ed.), *Dictionnaire des finances*, vol. I, 1889, pp. 743ff.

—— 'Foncière (contribution)', in Say (ed.), *Dictionnaire des finances*, vol. II, 1894, pp. 1334ff.

—— 'Portes et fenêtres, contribution des', in Say (ed.), *Dictionnaire des finances*, vol. II, 1894, pp. 232ff.

d'Audifret, C. L. G. *Système financier de la France*, 6 vols. 3rd edn. Paris, 1863–70.

Bailly, A. *Histoire financière de la France, depuis l'origine de la monarchie jusqu'à la fin de 1786, avec un tableau général des anciennes impositions*, 2 vols. Paris, 1830.

Bergeson, L. 'Die "Receveurs Généraux" im Konsulat und Kaiserreich', *Geschichte und Gesellschaft*, vol. VI. 1980, pp. 484–9.

Boiteau, P. 'Budget général de l'état: budgets annexes rattachés pour ordre au budget général de l'état; budget sur ressources extraordinaires; budgets sur ressources spéciales', in Say, (ed.), *Dictionnaire des finances*, vol. I, 1889, pp. 501ff.

—— *Fortune publique et finances de la France*, 2 vols. Paris, 1866.

—— *Etat de la France in 1789*. Paris, 1861.

Bosher, John F. *French Finances: From Business to Bureaucracy*. Cambridge, 1970.

Bouvier, J. 'Histoire financière et problèmes d'analyse des dépenses publiques', *Annales*, vol. XXXIII (1978), pp. 207–15.

Bouvier, J. and Wolf, J. (eds.). *Deux siècles de fiscalité française, histoire, économie, politique; recueil d'articles en hommage à Robert Schnerb*. Paris, 1973.

Braesch, Fritz. *Finances et monnaie révolutionnaire*. Nancy, 1934.

Bray, E. de. 'Rentes sur l'état', in Say (ed.), *Dictionnaires des finances*, vol. II, 1894, p. 1051.

—— '*Indemnité de guerre*', in Say (ed.), *Dictionnaires des finances*, vol. II, 1894, pp. 378ff.

Bruguières, M. *La première restauration et son budget*. Geneva and Paris, 1969.

Cailloux, J., Touchard, A. and Privat-Deschanel, A. *Les impôts en France. Traité technique*, 2 vols. Paris, 1896, 1904.

Carvallo, M. E. 'Manufactures de l'état', in Say (ed.), *Dictionnaires des finances*, vol. II, 1894, pp. 517ff.

Charton, P. 'Algérie', in Say (ed.), *Dictionnaires des finances*, vol. I, 1889, pp. 98ff.

Chaumard, 'Domaine', in Say (ed.), *Dictionnaires des finances*, vol. I, 1889, pp. 1481ff.

Clamagérand, J. J. *Histoire de l'impôt en France*, 3 vols. Paris, 1867, 1873, 1876.

Cluseau, M. 'Die Geschichte der Finanzwissenschaft in Frankreich', in W. Gerloff and F. Neumark (eds.), *Handbuch der Finanzwissenschaft*, vol. I, Tübingen, 1952.

—— 'Geschichte der französischen Finanzwirtschaft vom 18. Jahrhundert bis zur Gegenwart', in W. Gerloff and F. Neumark (eds.), *Handbuch der Finanzwissenschaft*, vol. I. Tübingen, 1952.

Coulbois, F. 'Staatshaushalt und Finanzsystem Frankreichs', in W. Gerloff and F. Neumark (eds.), *Handbuch der Finanzwissenschaft*, vol. III. 2nd edn. Tübingen, 1958.

Crisenoy, J. de. 'Budget communal', in Say (ed.), *Dictionnaires des finances*, vol. I, 1889, pp. 467ff.
—— 'Budget départemental', in Say (ed.), *Dictionnaires des finances*, vol. I, 1889, pp. 467ff.
Crouzet, F. 'Essai de construction d'un indice annuel de la production industrielle française au XIXe siecle', *Annales*, vol. XXV (1970), pp. 56–99.
Dawison, W. 'Frankreichs Bank- und Finanzwirtschaft in der Kriegs- und Nachkriegszeit'. Unpublished dissertation. Heidelberg University, 1923.
Dreux, T. 'Le cadastre et l'impôt foncier', in L. Eyrolles (ed.), *Encyclopédie industrielle et commerciale*. Paris, 1933.
Dumaine, C. 'Enregistrement', in Say (ed.), *Dictionnaires des finances*, vol. II, 1894, pp. 88ff.
Dumaine, C., Neymarck, A. and Salefranque, L. 'Valeurs mobilières', in Say (ed.), *Dictionnaires des finances*, vol. II, 1894.
Durant de Saint-André, J. 'Protectorats', in Say (ed.), *Dictionnaire des finances*, vol. II, 1894, pp. 1007–11.
Fontaine, C. 'Instruction publique', in Say (ed.), *Dictionnaires des finances*, vol. II, 1894.
Fontvieille, L. 'Dépenses publiques et problématique de la dévalorisation du capital', *Annales*, vol. XXXIII (1978), pp. 240–78.
Formery, L. *Les impôts en France*, 2 vols. Paris, 1946.
Ganiage, J. *L'expansion coloniale de la France sous la troisième Republique 1871–1914*. Paris, 1968.
Goldscheider, E. 'Colonies', in Say (ed.), *Dictionnaire des finances*, vol. I, 1889, pp. 1,090ff.
Gomel, C. *Les causes financières de la Révolution française; les ministères Turgot et Necker; les dernier controleurs généraux*, 2 vols. Paris, 1892, 1893.
Guéry, A. 'Les finances de la monarchie française sous l'ancien régime', *Annales*, vol. XXXIII (1978), pp. 216–39.
Hennebique, 'Patentes (contribution des)', in Say (ed.), *Dictionnaire des finances*, vol. II, 1894, pp. 740ff.
—— 'Rôles', in Say (ed.), *Dictionnaire des finances*, vol. II, 1894, pp. 1116ff.
—— 'Personnelle-mobilière (contribution)', in Say (ed.), *Dictionnaire des finances*, vol. II, 1894, pp. 845ff.
Herbin, R. and Pebereau, A. *Le cadastre français*. Paris, 1956.
Hirschfeld, L. von. *Die Finanzen Frankreichs nach dem Kriege von 1870–71*. Berlin, 1875.
Hock, C. von. *Die Finanzverwaltung Frankreichs*. Stuttgart and Augsburg, 1857.
Jèze, G. *Cours élémentaire de science des finances et la législation financière française; théorie générale de budget*. 6th edn. Paris, 1922.
Kaufmann, R. von. *Die Finanzen Franckreichs*. Leipzig, 1882.
Kempter, E. 'Die finanzielle Lage Frankreichs von 1914 bis 1922'. Dissertation, Heidelberg University, 1924.
Köbner, O. *Die Methode der letzten französischen Bodenbewertung. Ein Beitrag zum Katasterproblem*. Jena, 1889.
Leroy-Beaulieu, P. *Traité de la science des finances*, 2 vols. Paris, 1877.
Lesourd, J. A. and Gérard, C. *Histoire économique XIXe et XX siècles*, 2 vols. Paris, 1963.
Lévy-Leboyer, M. 'Croissance économique en France au XIXe siecle', *Annales*, vol. XXIII (1968), pp. 788–807.
—— *La position internationale de la France. Aspects économiques et financiers XIXe et XX siècles*. Paris, 1977.
Mallez, P. *La restauration des finances françaises après 1814*. Paris, 1927.
Marczewski, J. 'Le produit physique de l'économie française de 1789 à 1913 – comparaison avec la Grande-Bretagne', in *Histoire quantitative de l'économie française (Cahiers de l'ISEA)*. Paris, 1965.
Marion, M. *La vente des biens nationaux sous la Révolution*. Paris, 1908.
—— *Les impôts directs sous l'ancien régime, principalement au XVIIIe siècle*. Paris, 1910.
—— *Histoire financière de la France depuis, 1715*, 6 vols. Paris, 1914–28.
Markovitch, T. J. 'L'industrie française de 1789 à 1964; conclusions generales', *Cahiers de l'ISEA*. Paris, 1966.
Martel, L. 'Octrois', in Say (ed.), *Dictionnaire des finances*, vol. II, 1894, pp. 663ff.

Matthews, G. T. *The Royal General Farms in 18th Century France.* New York, 1958.
Merly, C. M. *Le régime financier des colonies.* Paris, 1926.
Morrisson, C. and Goffin, R. *Questions financières au XVIIIe et XIXe siècle.* Paris, 1967.
Necker, M. *Compte rendu au Roi.* Paris, 1781.
Nervo, G. de. *L'administration des finances sous la restauration, 1814–1830.* Paris, 1865.
Neymarck, A. 'Dette publique', in Say (ed.), *Dictionnaire des finances,* vol. I, 1889, pp. 1418ff.
Nicolas, C. *Les budgets de la France depuis le commencement du XIXe siècle.* Paris, 1883.
Oualid, W. 'Das Budget und das Finanzwesen Frankreichs', in W. Gerloff and F. Meisel (eds.), *Handbuch der Finanzwissenschaft,* vol. III. Tübingen, 1929.
Parieu, M. L. P. F. de. *Traité des impôts, considérés sous le rapport historique, économique et politique en France et à l'étranger . . . ,* 4 vols. Paris, 1866–7.
Salefranque, L. 'Timbre', in Say (ed.), *Dictionnaire des finances,* vol. II, 1894, pp. 1390ff.
Say, M. L. (ed.). *Dictionnaire des finances,* 2 vols. Paris, 1889, 1894.
Sestier, L. 'Contributions indirectes', in Say (ed.), *Dictionnaire des finances,* vol. I, 1889, pp. 1226ff.
Stourm, R. *Le budget, son histoire et son mécanism.* Paris, 1889.
—— *Les finances de l'ancien régime et de la révolution: origines du système financier actuel,* 2 vols. Paris, 1885.
—— 'Boissons', in Say (ed.), *Dictionnaire des finances,* vol. I, 1889, pp. 416ff.
—— *Bibliographie historique des finances de la France au XVIIIe siècle.* Paris, 1895.
—— *Les Finances du Consulat.* Paris, 1902.
Swarte, V. de. 'Revenu (impôt sur le)', in Say (ed.), *Dictionnaire des Finances,* vol. II, 1894, pp. 1079ff.
Thiers, M. A. *Histoire de la révolution française,* 10 vols. Paris, 1828–9.
Trotabas, L. *Les finances publiques et les impôts de la France.* Paris, 1937.
Tulard, J. 'Der "Domaine extraordinaire" als Finanzierungsinstrument napoleonischer Expansion', *Geschichte und Gesellschaft,* vol. VI (1980), pp. 490–9.
Vignes, E. 'Contributions directes', in Say (ed.), *Dictionnaire des finances,* vol. I, 1889, pp. 1210ff.
Vuitry, M. A. *Etudes sur le régime financier de la France avant la révolution de 1789,* 2 vols. Paris, 1883.
Walle, E. van de. 'France', in R. Lee (ed.), *European Demography and Economic Growth.* London, 1979.
Wolfe, M. *The Fiscal System of Renaissance France.* New Haven, 1972.
Wolff, J. 'La conception des finances publiques en France au XIXe siècle: analyse de deux dictionnaires d'économie politique', *Revue de Science Financière,* vol. LXIX (1977), pp. 421–59.

PRUSSIA

Beckerath, Erwin von. *Die preussische Klassensteuer und die Geschichte ihrer Reform bis 1851.* Leipzig, 1912.
Behre, Otto. *Geschichte der Statistik in Brandenburg–Preussen bis zur Grundung des Königlichen Staatlichen Bureaus.* Berlin, 1905.
Benda, O. *Die Gewerbesteuerverfassung des Preussischen Staats, nach dem Edikt vom 2. Nov. 1810.* Breslau, 1817.
Benzenberg, J. F. *Über Preussens Geldhaushalt und neues Steuersystem.* Leipzig, 1820 (with postscript 1821).
Bergius, C. J. *Die Grundsteuer und die Mahl- und Schlachtsteuer.* Beslau, 1853.
Bergmann, R. *Geschichte der ostpreussischen Stände und Steuern von 1688 bis 1704.* Leipzig, 1901.
Boeckh, R. *Die geschichtliche Entwicklung der amtlichen Statistik des preussischen Staates.* Berlin, 1863.
Dieterici, Carl. *Zur Geschichte der Steuerreform in Preussen (1810–1820).* Berlin, 1875.
Dieterici, F. W. C. (ed.). *Mitteilungen des statischen Bureaus in Berlin.* Berlin, 1848 and various years.

Feldenkirchen, W. 'Staatliche Kuntsförderung im 19. Jahrhundert', in E. Mai, H. Pohl and S. Waetzold (eds.), *Kunstpolitik und Kunstförderung im Kaiserreich*. Berlin, 1892.

Fischer, O. *Die preussische Klassensteuner.* 3rd edn. Magdeburg, 1878.

Fuisting, B. *Das preussische Gewerbesteuergesetz vom 24. Juni 1891 und die Ausführungs-Anweisungen.* Berlin, 1893.

—— *Die geschichtliche Entwicklung des preussischen Steuersystems und systematische Darstellung der Einkommensteuer.* Berlin, 1894.

—— *Die preussischen direkten Steuern,* vol. I, ed. G. Strutz (1st half): *Income Tax Law,* 8th edn, Berlin, 1915; (2nd half): *Income Tax Law,* 8th edn, Berlin, 1916; vol. II, ed. G. Strutz: *Commentary on the Supplementary Tax Law,* 2nd edn, 1905; vol. III: *Commentary on the Business Tax Laws,* 3rd edn, 1906; vol. IV: *Two Principles of the Science of Taxation,* 1902.

Gerlach, O. *Die preussische Steuerreform in Staat und Gemeinde.* Jena, 1893.

Gesetz-Sammlung für die königlichen preussischen Staaten. Preussisches Staatsministerium. Berlin, 1829 and following years.

Grabower, R. *Preussens Steuern vor und nach den Befreiungskriegen.* Berlin, 1932.

Grätzer, R. *Zur Geschichte der preussischen Einkommen- und Klassensteuer, 1812–1851.* Berlin, 1884.

Helwing, E. von (ed.). *Mitteilungen des statistischen Bureaus in Berlin.* Berlin, 1860.

Herrfurth, G. *Das gesamte preussische Etats-, Kassen- und Rechnungswesen, einschliesslich der Rechtsverhältnisse der Staatsbeamten.* 4th edn. Berlin, 1881, 1905.

Hohorst, G. *Wirtschaftswachstum und Bevölkerungsentwicklung in Preussen 1816–1914.* New York, 1977.

Jahrbuch für die amtliche Statistik des preussischen Staates. Royal Statistical Office. Berlin, 1867.

Kanitz, K. C. F. and Schönbrodt, K. *Handbuch über die gesamten Zweige der indirekten Steuerverfassung in den preussischen Staaten,* 2 parts. Leipzig, 1822.

Kaufmann, R. von. 'Einige Bemerkungen zu den preussischen Budgets seit 1880', *Finanz-Archiv,* vol. XVII (1900), pp. 144–77.

Kautz, G. *Das preussische System der direkten Steuer.* Berlin, 1889.

Kletke, G. *Die Classen- und classifizierte Einkommensteuer im preussischen Staate.* Hamm, 1865.

—— *Die preussische Klassensteuer erläutert.* Berlin, 1877.

Krug, Leopold. *Geschichte der preussischen Staatsschulden.* Breslau, 1861.

—— *Betrachtungen über den Nationalreichtum des preussischen Staats und über den Wohlstand seiner Bewohner,* 2 parts. Berlin, 1805.

Lohmann, W. *Die besonderen direkten Gemeindesteuern in Preussen.* Jena, 1913.

Lundgreen, P. *Bildung und Wirtsschaftswachstum im Industrialisierungsprozess des 19. Jahrhunderts.* Berlin, 1973.

Mamroth, K. *Geschichte der preussischen Staatsbesteuerung 1806–1816.* Leipzig, 1890.

Mascher, H. A. *Die Grundsteuer-Regelung in Preussen auf Grund der Gesetze vom 21. Mai 1861: Dargestellt nach Geographie, Geschichte, Statistik und Recht.* Potsdam, 1862.

—— *Die Gewerbesteuer-Gesetzgebung Preussens in ihrer neuesten Gestalt.* Potsdam, 1868.

Mauz, F. 'Geschichte der preussischen Einkommensteuer bis zu ihrer Reform im Jahre 1891'. Dissertation, Tübingen University, 1935.

Oesfeld, M. von. *Die Gewerbesteuer-Verfassung des preussischen Staates in ihrer neuesten Gestalt.* Breslau, 1877.

Ohnishi, T. 'Die preussische Steuerreform nach dem Wiener Kongress', in B. Vogel (ed.), *Preussische Reformen, 1807–1870.* Königstein/Ts., 1980.

Riedel, A. F. *Der Brandenburgisch–Preussische Staatshaushalt in den beiden letzten Jahrhunderten.* Berlin, 1866.

Sattler, C. *Das Schuldenwesen des preussischen Staates und des Deutschen Reiches.* Stuttgart, 1893.

Schimmelpfennig, F. G. *Die preussischen direkten Steuern,* 2 parts. 3rd edn. Berlin, 1859.

—— *Die Kommunalabgaben in Städten und Landgemeinden der Preussischen Staaten.* Berlin, 1859.

Schmoller, G. 'Die Epochen der preussischen Finanzpolitik bis zur Gründung des deutschen Reiches', a modified and augmented version of the essay published in 1877 by G. Schmoller, *Umrisse und Untersuchungen zur Verfassungs-, Verwaltungs- und Wirtschaftsgeschichte besonders des preussischen Staates im 17. and 18. Jahrhundert.* Leipzig, 1898.

Schwarz, O. and Strutz, G. *Der Staatshaushalt und die Finanzen Preussens,* 3 vols. Berlin, vol. I in 4 parts 1900–2; vol. II in 9 parts, 1900–4; vol. III, 1904.

Statistical Handbook for the Prussian State, 3 vols. Royal Statistical Office. Berlin, 1888, 1893, 1898.

Statistical Yearbook for the Prussian State. Royal Prussian Statistical State Office. Berlin, 1903 and various years.

Statistics of the Prussian State. Berlin, 1845.

Strutz, G. *Die Neuordnung der direkten Staatssteuern in Preussen.* Berlin, 1902.

Teschemacher, H. *Die Einkommensteuer und die Revolution in Preussen.* Berlin, 1912.

Wagner, A. 'Die Reform der direkten Staatsbesteuerung in Preussen', *Finanz-Archiv,* vol. VIII (1891), pp. 71–300; vol. XI (1894), pp. 1–76.

Wagner, S. *Die staatliche Grund- und Gebäudesteuer in der preussischen Rheinprovinz von 1815 bis 1895.* Cologne, 1980.

GERMAN REICH, MEMBER STATES

Albers, W. 'Finanzausgleich (Deutschland)', in E. V. Beckerath *et al.* (eds.), *Handwörterbuch der Sozialwissenschaften,* vol. III. Stuttgart, Tübingen and Göttingen, 1961.

Andic, S. and Veverka, J. 'The Growth of Government Expenditure in Germany since the Unification', in *Finanzarchiv,* NS, vol. XXIII (1963), pp. 169–278.

Anon. (C. Schutz). *Handbuch der Steurgesetzgebung Württeembergs.* Stuttgart, 1835.

Aubin, H. and Zorn, W. (eds.). *Handbuch der deutschen Wirtschafts- und Sozialgeschichte,* vol. II. Stuttgart, 1976.

Beckerath, E. von. 'Die neuere Geschichte der deutschen Finanzwissenschaft seit 1800', in W. Gerloff and F. Neumark (eds.), *Handbuch der Finanzwissenschaft,* vol. I. Tübingen, 1952.

Beer, A. *Die Finanzen Österreichs im 19. Jahrhundert.* Prague, 1877.

—— *Die Staathaushalt Österreich-Ungarns seit 1868.* Prague, 1881.

—— *Die Staatschulden und die Ordnung des Staatshaushaltes unter Maria Theresia.* Vienna, 1895.

Biberger, R. 'Das österreichische Ertragsteuersystem und sein Einfluss auf die Industrialisierung im 19. Jahrhundert'. Dissertation, Hohenheim University, 1979.

Birnbaum, B. *Die gemeindlichen Steuersysteme in Deutschland.* Berlin, 1914.

Bolenz, J. 'Wachstum und Strukturwandlungen der kommunalen Abgaben in Deutschland 1849–1913'. Dissertation, Freiburg University, 1965.

Borchard, K. 'Staatsverbrauch und öffentliche Investitionen in Deutschland 1780–1850'. Dissertation Gottingen University, 1968.

Borght, R. van der. *Die Entwicklung der Reichsfinanzen.* Leipzig, 1908.

Caasen, H. G. 'Die Steuer- und Zolleinnahmen des Deutschen Reiches 1872–1944'. Dissertation, Bonn University, 1953.

Cohn, S. *Die Finanzen des Deutschen Reiches seit seiner Begründung.* Berlin, 1899.

Conrad, J. 'Die neueste Entwicklung der Steuergesetzgebung in Sachsen', in *Jahrbücher für Nationalökonomie und Statistik,* vol. XXXII (1879).

—— 'Zur Finanzreform in Deutschland', in *Jahrbücher für Nationalökonomie und Statistik,* vol. XXXVI (1908).

Denkschriftenband zur Begründung des Entwurfs eines Gesetzes betreffend Änderungen im Finanzwesen. Reichsschatzamt. Berlin, 1908.

Deutsche Bundesbank (ed.). *Währung und Wirtschaft in Deutschland 1876–1975.* Frankfurt am Main, 1976.

—— *Deutsches Geld- und Bankwesen in Zahlen, 1876–1975.* Frankfurt am Main, 1976.

Eheberg, K. T. von. *Das Reichsfinanzwesen, seine Entwicklung, sein heutiger Zustand, seine Ausgestaltung.* Bonn, 1908.
—— *Finanzwissenschaft.* 10th edn. Leipzig, 1909.
Forberger, R. *Industrielle Revolution in Sachsen,* vol. I: *Die Revolution der Produktivkräfte in Sachsen, 1800–1830.* Berlin (GDR), 1982.
Gerloff, W. 'Beitrage zur Reichsfinanzreform', in *Jahrbücher für Nationalökonomie und Statistik,* vol. XXXVII, 1909.
—— *Die Finanz- und Zollpolitik des Deutschen Reiches nebst ihren Beziehungen zu Landes- und Gemeindefinanzen von der Gründung des Norddeutschen Bundes bis zur Gegenwart.* Jena, 1913.
—— *Die steuerliche Belastung in Deutschland während der letzten Friedensjahre.* Berlin, 1926.
—— 'Die Staatshaushalt und das Finanzwesen Deutschlands', in W. Gerloff and F. Meisel (eds.), *Handbuch der Finanzwissenschaft,* vol. III. Tübingen, 1929.
Gerstfeld, P. *Beitrage zur Reichssteuerfrage auf Grund einer Vergleichung der Ausgabe- und Einnahmeverhältnisse im Deutschen Reich mit denen der grösseren Staaten Europas.* Leipzig, 1879.
Glässing, C. 'Die Neugestaltung der direkten Staatsbesteuerung im Grossherzogtum Hessen (1899)', *Finanzarchiv,* vol. XVII (1900), pp. 178–360.
Grotewold, C. *Das Finanzwesen des Deutschen Reiches.* Leipzig, 1906.
Henderson, W. O. *The Zollverein.* Chicago, 1959.
Hoffmann, W. G. *Das Wachstum der deutschen Wirtschaft seit der Mitte des 19. Jahrhunderts.* Heidelberg, Vienna and New York, 1965.
Hoffmann, W. G. and Müller, J. H. *Das deutschen Volkseinkommen, 1851–1957.* Tübingen, 1959.
Holtfrerich, C. L. *Die deutsche Inflation, 1914–1923: Ursachen und Folgen in internationaler Perspektive.* Berlin and New York, 1980.
Humpert, M. *Bibliographie der Kameralwissenschaften.* Cologne, 1937.
Klein, E. *Geschichte der öffentlichen Finanzen in Deutschland.* Wiesbaden, 1974.
Laufer, F. *Die deutschen Einkommensteuertarife unter berücksichtigung der englischen Income Tax.* Jena, 1911.
Leutwein, P. 'Kolonien und Kolonialpolitik', in *Handwörterbuch der Staatswissenschaften,* vol. V. 4th edn. Jena, 1923.
Linden, J. *Die Grundsteuerverfassung in den deutschen und italienischen Provinzen der österreichischen Monarchie.* Vienna, 1840.
Löbe, E. *Der Staatshaushalt des Königreichs Sachsen in seinen verfassungsrechtlichen Beziehungen und finanziellen Leistungen.* Leipzig, 1889.
Lohmann, W. *Die besonderen direkten Gemeindesteuern in Preussen.* Jena, 1913.
Mann, F. K. *Deutsche Finanzwirtschaft.* Jena, 1929.
Mensi, F. von. *Die Finanzen Österreichs von 1701 bis 1740.* Vienna, 1890.
Nostitz, H. von. *Grundzüge der Staatssteuern im Königreich Sachsen.* Jena, 1903.
Popitz, J. 'Finanzausgleich', in *Handwörterbuch der Staatswissenschaften,* vol. III. 4th edn. Jena, 1926.
—— 'Der Finanzausgleich', in W. Gerloff and F. Meisel (eds.), *Handbuch der Finanzwissenschaft,* vol. II. Tübingen, 1927.
Riecke, K. V. *Verfassung, Verwaltung und Staatshaushalt des Königreichs Württemberg.* 2nd edn. Stuttgart, 1887.
Schmoller, G. 'Historische Betrachtungen über Staatsbildung und Finanzentwicklung', in *Jahrbuch für Gesetzgebung, Verwaltung und Volkswirtschaft im Deutschen Reich,* vol. XXXIII (1909), pp. 1–64.
Schnee, H. (ed.). *Deutsches Kolonial-Lexikon,* 3 vols. Leipzig, 1920.
Schremmer, E. 'Die Steuerverfassung der vormals schwäbisch–österreichischen Landstände vom Jahr 1767', in *Zeitschrift fur Württembergische Landesgeschichte,* vol. XXV (1966).
—— 'Zusammenhänge zwischen Katastersteuersystem, Wirtschaftswachstum und Wirtschaftsstruktur im 19. Jahrhundert; das Beispiel Württembergs; 1821–1877/ 1903', in I. Bog, G. Franz, K. H. Kaufhold, H. Kellenbenz and W. Zorn (eds.), *Wirtschaftliche und soziale Strukturen im säkularen Wandel. Festschrift für Wilhelm Abel*

zum 70. Geburtstag. Schriftenreihe für ländliche Sozialfragen, Agrarsoziale Geseltschaft, Göttingen, vol. LXX. Hanover, 1974.

—— 'Föderativer Staatsverbund, öffentliche Finanzen und Industrialisierung in Deutschland', in H. Kiesewetter and R. Fremdling (eds.), *Staat, Region and Industrialisierung.* Ostfildern, 1985.

—— 'Die badische Gewerbasteuer und die Kapitalbildung in gewerblichen Anlagen und Vorräten in Baden und in Deutschland, 1815 bis 1913', *Vierteljahrschrift für Sozial- und Wirtschaftsgeschichte,* vol. LXXIV (Wiesbaden, 1987), pp. 18–61.

Statistical Yearbooks for the German Reich. Reich Statistical Office. Berlin, 1880 and various years.

Stein, L. von. *Lehrbuch der Finanzwissenschaft,* 4 vols. 5th edn. Leipzig, 1885, 1886.

Steitz, W. *Feudalwesen und Staatssteuersystem,* vol. I: *Die Realbesteuerung der Landwirtschaft in den süddeutschen Staaten im 19. Jahrhundert.* Göttingen, 1976.

Stiassny, P. *Der österreichische Staatsbankerott von 1811.* Vienna and Leipzig, 1912.

Stumpp, H. 'Die Entwicklung des Finanzausgleichs in Deutschland von 1871 bis zur Gegenwart'. Dissertation, Würzburg University, 1964.

Tautscher, A. 'Geschichte der deutschen Finanzwissenschaft bis zum Ausgang des 18. Jahrhunderts', in W. Gerloff and F. Neumark (eds.), *Handbuch der Finanzwissenschaft,* vol. I. Tübingen, 1952.

Terhalle, F. *Die Finanzwirtschaft des Staates und der Gemeinden.* Berlin, 1948.

Viebahn, G. von. *Statistik des zollvereinten und nördlichen Deutschlands.* 3 vols. Berlin, 1858–68.

Vierteljahrshefte zur Statistik des Deutschen Reichs, Reich Statistical Office. Berlin, 1892.

Weitzel, O. 'Die Entwicklung der Staatsausgaben in Deutschland. Eine Analyse der öffentlichen Aktivität in ihrer Abhängigkeit vom wirtschaftlichen Wachstum'. Dissertation, Erlangen-Nuremberg University, 1967.

Wiesinger, K. *Die Zölle und Steuern des Deutschen Reiches.* 6th edn. Munich and Berlin, 1912.

Wilke, G. 'Die Entwicklung der Theorie des staatlichen Steuersystems in der deutschen Finanzwissenschaft des 19. Jahrhunderts', *Finanzarchiv,* vol. XXXVIII (1921), pp. 1–108.

Witt, P. C. *Die Finanzpolitik des Deutschen Reiches von 1903 bis 1913.* Lübeck and Hamburg, 1970.

Wolf, J. *Die Reichsfinanzreform und ihr Zusammenhang mit Deutschlands Volks- und Weltwirtschaft.* Leipzig, 1909.

Zimmermann, F. W. R. *Die Finanzwirtschaft des Deutschen Reichs und der deutschen Bundesstaaten zu Kreigsausbruch 1914.* Berlin and Leipzig, 1916.

Zincke, G. H. *Cameralisten-Bibliothek,* 4 parts. Leipzig, 1751, 1752.

Zorn, W. 'Staatliche Wirtschafts- und Sozialpolitik und öffentliche Finanzen 1800–1970', in H. Aubin and W. Zorn (eds.), *Handbuch der deutschen Wirtschafts- und Sozialgeschichte,* vol. II. Stuttgart, 1976.

CHAPTER VI

State policy towards labour and labour organizations, 1830–1939: Anglo-American union movements

GENERAL AND COMPARATIVE

Books

Allen, H. C. *Bush and Backwoods, A Comparison of the Frontier in Australia and the United States*. East Lansing, Mich., 1959.

Bagwell, Philip S. and Mingay, G. E. *Britain and America 1850–1939: A Study of Economic Change*. London, 1970.

Cole, G. D. H. *History of Socialist Thought*, 7 vols. London, 1953–60.

Epstein, Leon D. *Political Parties in Western Democracies*. New York, 1967.

Feuer, Lewis S. *Marx and the Intellectuals: A Set of Post-ideological Essays*. Garden City, NJ, 1969.

Gollan, Robin. *The Coalminers of New South Wales: A History of the Union, 1860–1960*. Melbourne, 1963.

—— *Radical and Working Class Politics: A Study of Eastern Australia, 1850–1910*. Parkville, 1960.

Habakkuk, H. J. *American and British Technology in the Nineteenth Century: The Search for Labour-Saving Inventions*. Cambridge, 1962.

Harrison, John F. C. *Quest for the New Moral World: Robert Owen and the Owenites in Britain and America*. New York, 1969.

Hartz, Louis. *The Founding of New Societies: Studies in the History of the United States, Latin America, South Africa, Canada, and Australia*. New York, 1964.

Horowitz, Gad. *Canadian Labour in Politics*. Toronto, 1968.

Industrial Relations Research Association. *Interpreting the Labor Movement*. Madison, Wis., 1952.

Lipset, Seymour M. *The First New Nation: the United States in Historical and Comparative Perspective*. Garden City, NJ, 1967.

Logan, H. A. *Trade Unions in Canada: Their Development and Functioning*. Toronto, 1948.

Lorwin, Val R. (ed.). *Labor and Working Conditions in Modern Europe*. New York, 1967.

Lubasz, Heinz (ed.). *Revolutions in Modern European History*. New York, 1966.

Moore, R. Laurence. *European Socialists and the American Promised Land*. New York, 1970.

Pelling, Henry. *America and the British Left: From Bright to Bevan*. London, 1956.

Perlman, Mark. *Labor Unions Theories in America: Background and Development*. Evanston, Ill., 1958.

Perlman, Selig. *A Theory of the Labor Movement*. New York, 1928.

Stearns, Peter N. and Walkowitz, Daniel J. (eds.). *Workers in the Industrial Revolution: Recent Studies of Labor in the United States and Europe*. New Brunswick, NJ, 1974.

Sturmthal, Adolf F. *Unity and Diversity in European Labor: An Introduction to Contemporary Labor Movements*. Glencoe, Ill., 1953.

Trachtenberg, Alexander (ed.). *Letters to Americans 1848–1895, by Karl Marx and Frederick Engels*. New York, 1953.

Articles

Blumer, Herbert. 'Early Industrialization and the Labouring Class', *Sociological Quarterly*, vol. I, no. I (January 1960), pp. 5–14.

Fischer, Wolfram. 'Social Tension at Early Stages of Industrialization', *Comparative Studies in Society and History*, vol. IX, no. I (October 1966), pp. 64–83.

Gulick, Charles A. and Bers, Melvin K. 'Insight and Illusion in Perlman's Theory of the Labor Movement,' *Industrial and Labor Relations Review*, vol. VI, no. 4 (July 1953), pp. 510–31.

Pelling, Henry. 'The American Labour Movement: A British View', *Political Studies*, vol. II, no. 3 (October 1954), pp. 227–41.

Schiffrin, Harold and Pow-Key Sohn, 'Henry George on Two Continents: A Comparative Study in the Diffusion of Ideas', *Comparative Studies in Society and History*, vol. XI, no. 1 (October 1959), pp. 86–109.

Stearns, Peter N. 'National Character and European Labor History', *Journal of Social History*, vol. IV, no. 2 (Winter, 1970), pp. 95–124.

Sturmthal, Adolf. 'Comments on Selig Perlman's "A Theory of the Labor Movement" ', *Industrial and Labor Relations Review*, vol. IV, no. 4 (July 1951), pp. 483–96.

BRITISH MATERIALS

Books

Arnot, R. Page. *The Miners: A History of the Miners Federation of Great Britain*, 3 vols. London, 1949–53.

Bagwell, Philip S. *The Railwaymen: The History of the National Union of Railwaymen.* London, 1963.

Briggs, Asa (ed.). *Chartist Studies.* London, 1959.

Briggs, Asa and Saville, John (eds.). *Essays in Labor History*, 2 vols. London, 1960, 1971.

Cleggs, H. A., Fox, Alan and Thompson, A. F. *A History of British Trade Unions Since 1887*, vol. I: *1899–1910*. Oxford, 1964.

Cline, C. A. *Recruits to Labour: The British Labour Party, 1914–1931.* Syracuse, NY, 1963. [Catherine A. Cline]

Cole, G. D. H. *British Working Class Politics, 1832–1914.* London, 1941.

—— *A Short History of the British Working Class Movement, 1789–1947*, London, 1948.

Collins, Henry and Abramsky, Chimen. *Karl Marx and the British Labour Movement, Year of the First International.* London, 1965.

Dangerfield, G. *The Strange Death of Liberal England.* New York, 1935.

Dowse, Robert E. *Left in the Centre: The Independent Labour Party, 1893–1940.* London 1966.

Foster, John. *Class Struggle and the Industrial Revolution: Early Industrial Capitalism in Three English Towns.* London, 1974.

Fox, Alan. *A History of the National Union of Boot and Shoe Operatives, 1874–1957.* Oxford, 1958.

Gregory, Roy. *The Miners and British Politics, 1906–1914.* London, 1968.

Harrison, Royden. *Before the Socialists: Studies in Labour and Politics, 1861–1881.* London, 1965.

Hobsbawm, E. J. *Labouring Men: Studies in the History of Labour.* New York, 1964.

Hobsbawm, E. J. and Rudé, George. *Captain Swing.* London, 1969.

Hovell, Mark. *The Chartist Movement.* London, 1925.

Inglis, K. S. *Churches and the Working Classes in Victorian England.* London, 1963.

Jeffreys, J. B. *The Story of the Engineers.* London, 1945.

Kendall, Walter. *The Revolutionary Movement in Britain, 1900–1921: The Origins of British Communism.* London, 1969.

Klugmann, James. *History of the Communist Party of Great Britain*, 2 vols. London, 1968–9.

McKibbin, Ross. *The Evolution of the Labour Party, 1910–1924.* London, 1974.

Martin, Roderick. *Communism in the British Trade Unions, 1924–1933: A study of the National Minority Movement.* Oxford, 1969.

Milliband, Ralph. *Parliamentary Socialism: A Study in the Politics of Labour.* London, 1961.

Musson, A. E. *British Trade Unions, 1800–1875.* London, 1972.

Pelling, Henry. *A Short History of the Labour Party.* London, 1961, 4th edn, 1974.

—— *Origins of the Labour Party, 1880–1910.* London, 1954.

—— *A History of British Trade Unionism.* Harmondsworth, Middx., 1965.

—— *Social Geography of British Elections, 1885–1910.* London, 1967.

—— *Popular Politics and Society in Late Victorian Britain.* London, 1968.

Phelps Brown, E. H. *The Growth of British Industrial Relations: A Study from the Standpoint of 1906–14.* London, 1959.

Phillips, G. A. *The General Strike: The Politics of Industrial Conflict.* London, 1976.

Poirier, Philip P. *The Advent of the British Labour Party*. London, 1958.
Roberts, B. C. *The Trades Union Congress, 1868–1921*. London, 1958.
Stansky, P. *The Left and War: The British Labor Party and World War One*. New York, 1969.
Stedman-Jones, Gareth. *Outcast London: A Study in the Relationship between Classes in Victorian Society*. London, 1971.
Thompson, E. P. *The Making of the English Working Class*. London 1963.
Thompson, Paul R. *Socialists, Liberals and Labour: The Struggle for London, 1885–1914*. London, 1967.
Wearmouth, Robert F. *Methodism and the Struggle of the Working Classes, 1850–1900*. Leicester, 1954.
Webb, Sidney and Beatrice. *The History of Trade Unionism*. London, 1920.

Articles

Allen, V. L. 'A Century of the British T.U.C.', in Ralph Miliband and John Saville (eds.), *The Socialist Register*. London, 1968.
Bythel, Duncan. 'The Hand Loom Weavers in the English Cotton Industry during the Industrial Revolution: Some Problems', *Economic History Review*, 2nd series, vol. XVII, no. 2 (December 1964), pp. 339–53.
Cole, G. D. H. 'Some Notes on British Trade Unionism in the Third Quarter of the Nineteenth Century', *International Review of Social History*, vol. II (1937), pp. 1–22.
Duffy, A. E. P. 'New Unionism in Britain, 1889–1890: A Reappraisal', *Economic History Review*, 2nd series, vol. XIV, no. 2 (December 1961), pp. 306–19.
Marwick, Arthur. 'The Labour Party and the Welfare State in Britain, 1900–1948', *American Historical Review*, vol. XXIII, no. 2 (December 1967), pp. 380–403.
Meacham, Stanley. 'The Sense of Impending Clash: English Working Class Movement Before the First World War', *American Historical Review*, vol. LXXVII, no. 5 (December 1972), pp. 1,343–68.
Neale, R. S. 'Class and Class Consciousness in Early Nineteenth Century England, Three Classes or Five?', *Victorian Studies*, vol. XII, no. 1 (September 1968), pp. 5–32.
Oliver, W. H. 'The Consolidated Trades Union of 1834', *Economic History Review*, 2nd series, vol. XVII, no. 1 (August 1964), pp. 77–95.
Pollard, Sidney. 'Factory Discipline in the Industrial Revolution', *Economic History Review*, 2nd series, vol. XVI, no. 2 (December 1963), pp. 254–71.
Reid, Fred. 'Socialist Sunday Schools in Britain, 1892–1939', *International Review of Social History*, vol. XI (1966), pp. 18–47.
Saville, John. 'The Background to the Revival of Socialism in England', *Bulletin of the Society for the Study of Labour History*, no. 11 (Autumn 1965), pp. 13–17.
Thomas, Keith. 'Work and Leisure in Pre-Industrial Society', *Past and Present*, no. 29 (December 1964), pp. 50–62.

AMERICAN MATERIALS
Books

Bernstein, Irving. *The Lean Years: A History of the American Worker, 1920–1933*. Boston, 1970.
—— *The Turbulent Years: A History of the American Worker, 1933–1941*. Boston, 1970.
Berthoff, Rowland T. *British Immigrants in Industrial America, 1790–1950*. Cambridge, Mass., 1953.
Brody, David. *Steelworkers in America: The Nonunion Era*. Cambridge, Mass., 1960.
—— *Labor in Crisis: The Steel Strike of 1919*. Philadelphia, 1965.
Christie, Robert A. *Empire in Wood: A History of the Carpenters Union*. Ithaca, NY, 1956.
Commons, John R. *History of Labour in the United Sates*, 4 vols. New York, 1918–35.
Common, John R. *et al.* (eds.). *A Documentary History of American Industrial Society*, 11 vols. Cleveland, 1910–11.

Dawley, Alan. *Class and Community: The Industrial Revolution in Lyyn.* Cambridge, Mass., 1976.

Derber, Milton. *The American Idea of Industrial Democracy, 1865–1965.* Urbana, Ill., 1970.

Derber, Milton and Young, Edwin (eds.). *Labor and the New Deal.* Madison, Wis., 1957.

Dubofsky, Melvin. *We Shall Be All: A History of the Industrial Workers of the World.* Chicago, 1969.

Erickson, Charlotte. *American Industry and the European Immigrant, 1860–1885.* Cambridge, Mass., 1959.

Fine, Sidney. *Sit-down: The General Motors Strike of 1936–37.* Ann Arbor, 1969.

Fink, Leon. *Workingmen's Democracy. The Knights of Labor and American Politics.* Urbana, Ill., 1983.

Foner, Eric. *Free Soil, Free Labor, Free Men: The Ideology of the Republican Party Before the Civil War.* New York, 1970.

Foner, Philip S. *History of the Labor Movement of the United States,* 6 vols. New York, 1947–82.

—— *Organized Labor and the Black Worker, 1619–1973.* New York, 1974.

Green, Marguerite. *The National Civic Federation and the American Labor Movement 1900–1925.* Washington, DC, 1956.

Greene, Victor R. *The Slavic Community on Strike: Immigrant Labor in Pennsylvania Anthracite.* Notre Dame, 1968.

Grob, Gerald N. *Workers and Utopia: A Study of Ideological Conflict in the American Labor Movement, 1865–1900.* Evanston, Ill., 1961.

Gutman, Herbert G. *Culture and Society in Industrializing America; Essays in American Working-Class and Social History.* New York, 1976.

Hofstadter, R. and Lipset, S. N. (eds.). *Turner and the Sociology of the Frontier.* New York, 1968.

Howe, Irving and Coser, Lewis. *The American Communist Party: A Critical History.* New York, 1962.

Hugins, Walter. *Jacksonian Democracy and the Working Class: A Study of the New York Workingmen's Movement, 1829–1837.* Stanford, 1960.

Jacobson, Julius (ed.). *The Negro and the American Labor Movement.* Garden City, 1968.

Jernegan, M. W. *Laboring and Dependent Classes in Colonial America, 1607–1783.* Chicago, 1931.

Korman, Gerd. *Industrialization, Immigrants and Americanizers: The View from Milwaukee, 1866–1921.* Madison, 1967.

Laslett, John H. M. *The Workingman in American Life.* Boston, 1968.

—— *Labor and the Left: A Study of Socialist and Radical Influences in the American Labor Movement, 1881–1924.* New York, 1970.

Laslett, J. H. M. and Lipset, S. M. (eds.). *Failure of a Dream? Essays in the History of American Socialism.* New York, 1974.

Lipet, S. M. *Agrarian Socialism, The Cooperative Federation in Saskatchewan: A Study in Political Sociology.* Garden City, 1968.

Lorwin, Lewis. *The Women's Garment Workers: A History of the International Ladies Garment Workers' Union.* New York, 1924.

Montgomery, David. *Beyond Equality: Labor and the Radical Republicans, 1862–1872.* New York, 1967.

Pelling, Henry. *American Labor.* Chicago, 1960.

Pessen, Edward. *Most Uncommon Jacksonians: The Radical Leaders of the Early Labor Movement.* Albany, 1967.

Pope, Liston. *Millhands and Preachers: A Study of Gastonia.* New Haven, 1942.

Rayback, J. G. *A History of American Labour.* New York, 1966.

Rosenblum, Gerald. *Immigrant Workers: Their Impact on American Labor Radicalism.* New York, 1973.

Saxton, Alexander. *The Indispensable Enemy: Labor and The Anti-Chinese Movement in California.* Berkeley, 1971.

Shannon, David. *The Socialist Party of America: A History.* New York, 1955.

Smith, Henry N. *Virgin Land: The American West as Symbol and Myth.* Cambridge, Mass., 1950.

Spero, Sterling D. and Harris, Abram L. *The Black Worker, The Negro and the Labor Movement*. New York, 1931.
Taft, Philip. *The A. F. of L. in the Time of Gompers*. New York, 1957.
—— *The A. F. of L. From the Death of Gompers to the Merger*. New York, 1959.
Ware, Norman. *The Labor Movement in the United States, 1860–1895*. New York, 1929.
—— *The Industrial Worker, 1840–1860: The Reaction of American Industrial Society to the Advance of the Industrial Revolution*. New York, 1924.
Weinstein, James. *The Decline of American Socialism, 1912–1924*. New York, 1967.
Yearley, C. K. *Britons in American Labor: A History of the Influence of the United Kingdom Immigrants on American Labor, 1830–1914*. Baltimore, Md., 1957.
Young, Alfred F. *Dissent: Explorations in the History of American Radicalism*. DeKalb, Ill., 1968.
—— *Ambiguous Legacy: The Left in American Politics*. New York, 1975.

Articles

Auerbach, Jerold S. 'Southern Tenant Farmers, Socialist Critics of the New Deal', *Labor History*, vol. VII, no. 2 (Winter 1966), pp. 3–18.
Bernstein, Irving. 'John L. Lewis and the Voting Behavior of the CIO', *Public Opinion Quarterly*, vol. V, no. 2 (June 1941), pp. 233–49.
Bridsall, William C. 'The Problem of Structure in the Knights of Labor', *Industrial and Labor Relations Review*, vol. VI, no. 4 (July 1953), pp. 532–46.
Brody, David. 'Labor and the Great Depression: The Interpretative Prospects', *Labor History*, vol. XIII, no. 2 (Spring 1972), pp. 231–44.
Conlin, Joseph R. 'The IWW and the Question of Violence', *Wisconsin Magazine of History*, vol. LI, no. 4 (Summer 1968), pp. 316–26.
Dubofsky, Melvyn. 'The Origins of Western Working Class Radicalism, 1890–1905', *Labor History*, vol. VII, no. 2 (Spring 1966), pp. 131–54.
Gitelman, Howard M. 'The Waltham System and the Coming of the Irish', *Labor History*, vol. VIII, no. 3. (Autumn 1967), pp. 227–53.
Green, James. 'Working Class Militancy and the Great Depression', *Radical America*, vol. VI, no. 6 (November–December 1972), pp. 1–35.
Gutman, Herbert G. 'The Worker's Search for Power', in H. Wayne Morgan (ed.), *The Gilded Age. A Reappraisal*. Syracuse, NY, 1963, pp. 38–68.
Laslett, John H. M. 'Socialism and the American Labor Movement: Some New Reflections', *Labor History*, vol. VIII, no. 2 (Spring 1967), pp. 136–55.
McKirdy, R. A. 'Conflict of Loyalties: The Problem of Assimilating the Far West into the Canadian and Australian Federations', *Canadian Historical Review*, vol. XXXII (December 1951), pp. 337–55.
Montgomery, David. 'The "New Unionism" and the Transformation of the Workers' Consciousness in America 1909–1922', *Journal of Social History*, vol. VII, no. 4 (Summer 1974), pp. 509–30.
Seidman, J. 'Organized Labor in Political Campaigns', *Public Opinion Quarterly*, vol. III, no. 4 (October 1939), p. 648.
Shannon, F. A. 'A Post-Mortem on the Labour-Safety-Valve Theory', *Agricultural History*, vol. XIX (January 1945), pp. 31–7.
Taft, P. 'On the Origins of Business Unionism', *Industrial and Labor Relations Review*, vol. VII, no. 1 (October 1963), pp. 20–38.
Young, Alfred. 'The Mechanics and the Jeffersonians New York, 1789–1801', *Labor History*, vol. V, no. 3 (Autumn 1964), pp. 247–76.

CHAPTER VII

Labour and the state on the continent, 1800–1939

GENERAL

Galenson, Walter (ed.). *Comparative Labor Movements*. New York, 1952.

Lorwin, Val R. 'Working-Class Politics and Economic Development in Western Europe', *American Historical Review*, vol. LXIII, no. 2 (January 1958), pp. 338–51.

Lowe, Boutelle E. *The International Protection of Labor*. New York, 1935.

Magnier, André. *La participation du personnel à la gestion des entreprises*. Paris, 1946.

Marquand, H. A. (ed.). *Organized Labour in Four Continents*. London, 1939.

Rimlinger, Gaston V. *Welfare Policy and Industrialization in Europe, America, and Russia*. New York, 1971.

—— 'Welfare Policy and Economic Development: A Comparative Historical Perspective', *Journal of Economic History*, vol. XXI, no. 4 (July 1968), pp. 559–69.

—— 'The Legitimation of Protest: A Comparative Study in Labor History', *Comparative Studies in Society and History*, vol. II, no. 3 (April 1960), pp. 329–43.

Sturmthal, Adolf F. *Comparative Labor Movements: Ideological Roots and Institutional Development*. Belmont, Cal., 1972.

—— *Unity and Diversity in European Labor*. Glencoe, Ill., 1953.

US Department of Health, Education, and Welfare. *Social Security Programs Throughout the World, 1975*. Washington, DC, 1976.

Veditz, C. W. A. 'Child-Labor Legislation in Europe', *Bulletin of the Bureau of Labor*, vol. XXI, no. 89 (July 1910), pp. 1–413.

Willoughby, W. F. 'Foreign Labor Laws: Austria', *Bulletin of the Department of Labor*, no. 28 (May 1900), pp. 552–97.

—— 'Foreign Labor Laws: Belgium, Switzerland', *Bulletin of the Department of Labor*, no. 26 (January 1900), pp. 77–177.

FRANCE

Aguet, Jean-Pierre. *Les grèves sous la monarchie de Juillet 1830–1847*. Geneva, 1954.

Bourgin, Georges. 'Neutralité gouvernementale et conflits ouvriers à Lyon au début du Second Empire', *Revue d'histoire économique et sociale* (1921), pp. 92–102.

—— 'La législation ouvrière du Second Empire', *Revue des etudes napoléoniennes*, vol. IV, pp. 220–36.

Bouvier-Ajam, Maurice. *Histoire du travail en France des origines à la Révolution*. Paris, 1957.

—— *Histoire de travail en France depuis la Révolution*. Paris, 1969.

Bron, Jean. *Histoire du mouvement ouvrier français*, 3 vols. Paris, 1968–73.

Colton, Joel. *Compulsory Labor Arbitration in France 1936–1939*. New York, 1951.

Desmarest, Jacques. *La politique de la main-d'oeuvre en France*. Paris, 1946.

Dolléans, Edouard. *Histoire du mouvement ouvrier*, 3 vols. Paris, 1936, 1939, 1953.

Douglas, Paul H. 'The French Social Insurance Act', *Annals of the American Academy of Political and Social Science*, vol. CLXIV (November 1932), pp. 209–48.

Dunham, Arthur L. 'Unrest in France in 1848', *Journal of Economic History*, vol. VIII (1948 supplement), pp. 74–84.

—— 'Industrial Life and Labor in France 1815–1848', *Journal of Economic History*, vol. III (1943), pp. 117–51.

Duveau, Georges. *La vie ouvrière en France sous le Second Empire*. Paris, 1946.

Ehrmann, Henry W. *French Labor from Popular Front to Liberation*. New York, 1947.

Fasel, George. 'Urban Workers in Provincial France, February–June 1848', *International Review of Social History*, vol. XVII, part 3 (1972), pp. 661–74.

Galant, Henry C. *Histoire politique de la sécurité sociale française 1945–52*. Paris, 1955.

Halévy, David. *Essais sur le mouvement ouvrier en France*. Paris, 1901.

Hatzfeld, Henri. *Du paupérisme à la sécurité sociale*. Paris, 1971.

Jeanneney, J. M. and Perrot, M. *Textes de droit économique et social français*. Paris, 1957.
Kelso, Maxwell R. 'The Inception of the Modern French Labor Movement (1871–1879): a Reappraisal', *Journal of Modern History*, vol. VIII, no. 2 (June 1936), pp. 173–93.
—— 'The French Labor Movement during the Last Years of the Second Empire', in Donald C. McKay (ed.), *Essays in the History of Modern Europe*. New York, 1936, pp. 98–113.
Kulstein, David I. *Napoleon III and the Working Class: A Study of Government Propaganda under the Second Empire*. Sacramento, 1969.
Laroque, Pierre. *Les Relations entre patrons et ouvriers*. Paris, 1938.
Lefranc, Georges. *Histoire du mouvement syndical français*. Paris, 1937.
—— *Le mouvement socialiste sous la Troisième République (1875–1940)*. Paris, 1963.
Leroy-Beaulieu, Paul. *La question ouvrière au XIXe siècle*. Paris, 1871.
Levasseur, E. *Questions ouvrières et industrielles en France sous la Troisième République*. Paris, 1907.
—— *Histoire des classes ouvrières et de l'industrie en France de 1789 a 1870*, 2 vols. 2nd edn. Paris, 1903–4.
Lorwin, Val R. *The French Labor Movement*. Cambridge, Mass., 1954.
Louis, Paul. *Histoire du socialisme en France*. Paris, 1950.
—— *Histoire du mouvement syndical en France*, 2 vols. Paris, 1947–8.
McKay, Donald C. *The National Workshops*. Cambridge, Mass., 1933.
Montreuil, Jean (pseud.) *Histoire du mouvement ouvrier des origines à nos jours*. Paris, 1946.
Moss, Bernard H. *The Origins of the French Labor Movement 1830–1914*. Berkeley, 1976.
Perrot, Michelle. *Les ouvriers en grève. France 1871–1900*. Paris, 1974.
Price, Roger. *The French Second Republic*. Ithaca, NY, 1972.
Rigaudias-Weiss, Hilde. *Les enquêtes ouvrières en France entre 1830 et 1848*. Paris, 1936.
Rude, Fernand. *Le mouvement ouvrier à Lyon de 1827 a 1832*. Paris, 1944.
Saposs, David J. *The Labor Movement in Post-War France*. New York, 1931.
Scott, Joan W. *The Glassworkers of Carmaux*. Cambridge, Mass., 1974.
Stearns, Peter N. 'Against the Strike Threat: Employer Policy toward Labor Agitation in France, 1900–1914', *Journal of Modern History*, vol. XL, no. 4 (December 1968), pp. 474–500.
—— *Revolutionary Syndicalism and French Labor: A Cause without Rebels*. New Brunswick, NJ, 1971.
Tilly, Charles and Shorter, Edward. *Strikes in France 1830–1968*. Cambridge, 1974.
Virton, P. *Histoire et politique du droit du travail*. Paris, 1968.
Weill, Georges. *Histoire du mouvement social en France*. Paris, 1924.

GERMANY

Anton, Günther K. *Geschichte der preussischen Fabrikgesetzgebung bis zu ihrer Aufname durch die Reichsgewerbeordnung*. New edn. Berlin, 1953.
Balser, Frolinde. *Sozial-Demokratie 1848/49–1863*, 2 vols. Stuttgart, 1962.
Bergmann, Günther. *Das Sozialistengesetz im rechtsrheinischen Industriegebiet*. Hanover, 1970.
Berthelot, Marcel. *Works Council in Germany*. International Labour Office. Geneva, 1924.
von Bismarck, Otto Furst. *Die Gesammelten Werke*, 15 vols. Berlin, 1924–35.
Born, Karl E. 'Sozialpolitische Probleme und Bestremungen in Deutschland von 1848 bis zur Bismarkschen Sozialgesetzgeburg', *Vierteljahrschrift für Sozial- und Wirtschaftsgeschichte*, vol. XLV.
—— *Staat und Sozialpolitik seit Bismarcks Sturz*. Wiesbaden, 1957.
Born, Karl E. and Rassow, Peter (eds.). *Quellensammlung zur Geschichte der deutschen Sozialpolitik 1867 bis 1914*. Wiesbaden, 1966.
Conze, Werner (ed.). *Staat und Gesellschaft im deutschen Wormärz 1815–1848*. Stuttgart, 1962.
Dawson, W. D. *Bismarck and State Socialism*. London, 1890.

Dawson, W. H. *Social Insurance in Germany 1883–1911*. London, 1912.

Erdmann, Gerhard. *Die Entwicklung der deutschen Sozialgesetzgebung*, vol. x: *Quellensammlung zur Kulturgeschichte*. Göttingen, 1957.

Feldman, Gerald D. *Army Industry and Labor in Germany 1914–1918*. Princeton, 1966.

Fischer, Wolfram. 'Staat und Gesellschaft, Badens im Vormärz', in W. Conze (ed.), *Staat und Gesellschaft*, pp. 143–71.

Grebing, Helga. *Geschichte der deutschen Arbeiterbewegung*. Munich, 1973.

Grunberger, Richard. *The 12-Year Reich*. New York, 1971.

Guillebaud, C. W. *The Works Councils*. Cambridge, 1928.

—— *The Social Policy of Nazi Germany*. Cambridge, 1941.

Hamerow, Theodore S. *Restoration Revolution Reaction: Economics and Politics in Germany 1815–1871*. Princeton, 1968.

Hartwich, Hans H. *Arbeitsmarkt Verbände und Staat 1918–1933*. Berlin, 1967.

Heidegger, Hermann. *Die deutsche Sozialdemokratie und der nationale Staat 1870–1920*. Göttingen, 1956.

Henning, Hansjoachim. 'Preussische Sozialpolitik im Vormärz?', *Vierteljahrschrift fur Sozial- und Wirtschaftsgeschichte*, vol. LII, no. 4 (December 1965), pp. 485–539.

Höffner, Joseph. *Sozialpolitik im deutschen Bergbau*. Münster, 1956.

Hoppe, Ruth (ed.). *Geschichte der Kinderarbeit in Deutschland 1750–1939*. Document. Berlin, 1958.

Kolb, Eberhard. *Die Arbeiterräte in der deutschen Innenpolitik 1918–1919*, vol. XXIII: *Beiträge zur Geschichte des Parlamentarismus und der politischen Parteien*. Düsseldorf, 1962.

Köllman, Wolfgang. 'Politische und soziale Entwicklung der deutschen Arbeiterschaft 1850–1914', *Vierteljahrschrift für Sozial- und Wirtschaftsgeschichte*, vol. L, no. 4 (January 1964), pp. 480–504.

—— 'Die Anfänge der staatlichen Sozialpolitik in Preussen bis 1869', *Vierteljahrschrift fur Sozial- und Wirtschaftsgeschichte*, vol. LIII, no. 1 (March 1966), pp. 28–52.

Kuczynski, Jürgen. *Geschichte der Kinderarbeit in Deutschland 1750–1939*. Berlin, 1958.

—— *Germany: Economic and Labour Conditions under Fascism*. New York, 1945.

Lidtke, Vernon L. *The Outlawed Party: Social Democracy in Germany 1878–1890*. Princeton, 1966.

Ludwig, Karl-Heinz. 'Die Fabrikarbeit von Kindern im 19. Jahrhundert', *Vierteljahrschrift fur Sozial- und Wirtschaftsgeschichte*, vol. LII (April 1965), pp. 63–85.

Lütge, Friedrich. 'Die Grundprinzipien der Bismarckschen Sozialpolitik', *Jahrbücher für Nationalökonomie und Statistik*, vol. CXXXIV (1931).

Mason, T. W. 'Labour in the Third Reich, 1933–1939', *Past and Present*, no. 33 (April 1966), pp. 112–41.

Mehring, Franz. *Geschichte der deutschen Sozialdemokratie*, 2 vols. originally published 1897/8. Berlin, 1960.

Morgan, R. P. *The German Social Democrats 1864–72*. Cambridge, 1965.

Na'aman, S. (ed.). *Die Konstituierung der deutschen Arbeiterbewegung 1862/63*. Documents. Assen, The Netherlands, 1975.

Nathan, Otto. *The Nazi Economic System*. Durham, 1944.

Noakes, Jeremy and Pridham, Geoffrey (eds.). *Documents on Nazism, 1919–1945*. London, 1974.

Obermann, Karl. *Die deutschen Arbeiter in der Revolution von 1848*. 2nd edn. Berlin, 1953.

Pack, Wolfgang. *Das parlamentarische Ringen um das Sozialistengesetz Bismarcks 1878–1890*. Düsseldorf, 1961.

Peschke, Paul. *Geschichte der deutschen Sozialversicherung*. Berlin, 1962.

Pöls, Werner. *Sozialistenfrage und Revolutionsfurcht in ihrem Zusammenhang mit den angeblichen Staatsstreichplänen Bismarcks*. Historische Studien no. 377. Hamburg, 1960.

Preller, Ludwig. *Sozialpolitik in der Weimarer Republik*. Stuttgart, 1949.

Puppke, Ludwig. *Sozialpolitik und soziale Anschauungen Früindustrieller Unternehmer in Rheinland-Westphalen*. Cologne, 1966.

Quandt, Otto. *Die Anfänge der Bismarckschen Sozialgesetzgebung und die Haltung der Parteien*, Historische Studien no. 344. Berlin, 1938.

Quarck, Max. *Die erste deutsche Arbeiterbewegung Geschichte der Arbeiterverbrüderung 1848–49*. Originally published 1924. Glashütten im Taunus, 1970.

Rassow, Peter and Born, Karl E. (eds.). *Akten zur Sozialpolitik in Deutschland 1890–1914*. Wiesbaden, 1959.
Ritter, Gerhard A. *Die Arbeiterbewegung im Wilhelminischen Reich*. Berlin, 1959.
Roth, Günther. *The Social Democrats in Imperial Germany*. Totowa, NJ, 1913.
Rothfels, Hans. 'Bismarck's Social Policy and the Problem of State Socialism in Germany, Part II', *Sociological Review*, vol. xxx (1938), p. 291.
Schmierer, Wolfgang. *Von der Arbeiterbildung zur Arbeiterpolitik: Die Anfänge der Arbeiterbewegung in Württenberg 1862/63–1878*. Hanover, 1970.
Schmitz, Heinrich Karl. *Anfänge und Entwicklung der Arbeiterbewegung im Raum Düsseldorf*. Hanover, 1968.
Schraepler, Ernst. *Handwerkerbünde und Arbeitervereine 1830–1853*. Berlin, 1972.
Schulze, Wally. 'Kinderarbeit und Erziehungsfragen in Preussen zu Beginn des 19. Jahrhunderts', *Soziale Welt* (1958), pp. 299–309.
Schumann, Hans-Gerd. *Nationalsozialismus und Gewerkschaftsbewegung*. Hanover, 1958.
Stern, Leo (ed.). *Der Kampf der deutschen Sozialdemokratie in der Zeit des Sozialistengesetzes*, 2 vols. Archivalische Forschungen. Berlin, 1956.
Teuteberg, Hans Jürgen. *Geschichte der industriellen Mitbestimmung in Deutschland*. Tübingen, 1961.
Timm, Helga. *Die deutsche Sozialpolitik und der Bruch der grossen Koalition im März 1930*. Beiträge zur Geschichte des Parlamentarismus und der politischen Parteien, no. 1. Düsseldorf, 1952.
Todt, Elisabeth and Radant, Hans. *Zur Frühgeschichte der deutschen Gewerkschaftsbewegung 1800–1849*. Berlin, 1950.
Tormin, Walter. *Zwischen Rätediktatur und sozialer Demokratie*. Beiträge zur Geschichte des Parlamentarismus und der Parteien. Düsseldorf, 1954.
Vogel, Walter. *Bismarcks Arbeiterversicherung*. Braunschweig, 1951.
Wachenheim, Hedwig. *Die deutsche Arbeiterbewegung 1844 bis 1914*. Cologne, 1967.
Waline, Pierre. *Cinquante ans de rapports entre patrons et ouvriers en Allemagne*, vol. I: *1918–1945*. Paris, 1968–70.
Wehler, Hans-Ulrich (ed.). *Moderne deutsche Sozialgeschichte*. Cologne, 1966.
Wolff, Herta. *Die Stellung der Sozialdemokratie zur deutschen Arbeiterversicherungsgesetzgebung*. Dissertation. Freiburg University, 1933.
Wunderlich, Frieda. *German Labor Courts*. Chapel Hill, NC, 1946.
Zorn, Wolfgang. 'Gesellschaft und Staat im Bayern des Vormärz', in W. Conze (ed.), *Staat u. Gesellschaft*, pp. 113–42.

RUSSIA

Anweiler, Oskar. *The Soviets: The Russian Workers, Peasants, and Soldiers Councils, 1905–1921*. Translated from German (1958 edn.). New York, 1974.
Conquest, Robert. *Industrial Workers in the USSR*. New York, 1967.
Deutscher, Isaac. 'Russia', in Walter Galenson (ed.), *Comparative Labor Movements*. New York, 1952.
Dewar, Margaret. *Labour Policy in the USSR 1917–1928*. London, 1956.
Gordon, Manya. *Workers before and after Lenin*. New York, 1941.
Kaplan, Frederick I. *Bolshevik Ideology and the Ethics of Soviet Labor 1917–1920: The Formative Years*. New York, 1968.
Keep, J. L. H. *The Rise of Social Democracy in Russia*. Oxford, 1963.
Lenin, W. I. *Ueber die Arbeitsgesetzgebung*. Translated from Russian. Berlin, 1962.
Litvinov-Falinskii, F. P. *Fabrichnoe Zakonodatel' stvo i Fabrichnaia Inspektsia v Rosii* [Factory Legislation and Factory Inspection in Russia]. St Petersburg, 1900.
Madison, Bernice Q. *Social Welfare in the Soviet Union*. Stanford, 1968.
Mergner, Gottfried (ed.). *Die russische Arbeiteropposition: die Gewerkschaften in der Revolution*. Reinbeck, 1972.
Meschewetski, Peisach. *Die Fabrikgesetzgebung in Russland*. Tübingen, 1911.
Mikulin, A. A. *Ocherki iz Istorii Primeneniia Zakona 3-go Iiunia 1886 Goda o Naime Rabochikh* [Sketches from the Implementation of the Law of June Third 1886 on the Hiring of Workers]. Vladimir, 1893.

Nikitin, I. *Die ersten Arbeiterverbände und sozialdemokratischen Organisationen in Russland*. Berlin, 1954.
Ozerov, I. Kh. *Politika po Rabochemu Voprosu v Rossii za Poslednye Gody* [Labour Policy in Russia in Recent Years]. Moscow, 1906.
Pankratova, A. M. (ed.). *Rabochee Dvizhenie v Rossii v XIX Veke* [The Labour Movement in Russia in the Nineteenth Century], 4 vols. Moscow, 1950–5.
Pashitnow, K. *Die Lage der arbeitende Klasse in Russland*. Translated from Russian. Stuttgart, 1907.
Pipes, Richard. *Social Democracy and the St Petersburg Labor Movement 1885–1897*. Cambridge, Mass., 1963.
Pospielosky, Dimitry. *Russian Police Trade Unionism*. London, 1971.
Prokopovich, S. N. *K Rabochemu Voprosu v Rossii* [On the Labour Question in Russia]. St Petersburg, 1905.
Rimlinger, Gaston V. 'Social Security, Incentives, and Controls in the U.S. and U.S.S.R.', *Comparative Studies in Society and History*, vol. IV, no. 1 (November 1961), pp. 104–24.
—— 'The Trade Union in Soviet Insurance: Historical Development and Present Functions', *Industrial and Labor Relations Review*, vol. XIV, no. 3 (April 1961), pp. 397–418.
—— 'Autocracy and the Factory Order in Early Russian Industrialization', *Journal of Economic History*, vol. XX, no. 1 (March 1960), pp. 67–92.
—— 'The Management of Labor Protest in Tsarist Russia: 1870–1905', *International Review of Social History*, vol. V, part 2, pp. 226–48.
Schneiderman, Jeremiah. *Sergei Zubatov and Revolutionary Marxism*. Ithaca, NY, 1976.
Schwarz, Solomon M. *Labor in the Soviet Union*. New York, 1952.
—— *The Russian Revolution of 1905*. Trans. Gertrude Vakar. Chicago, 1967.
Shelymagin, I. I. *Fabrichno-Trudovoe Zakonodatel' stvo v Rossii* [Factory Labour Legislation in Russia]. Moscow, 1947.
Sorenson, Jay B. *The Life and Death of Soviet Trade Unionism 1917–1928*. New York, 1969.
Tugan-Baranovsky, M. I. *The Russian Factory in the 19th Century*. Translated from 3rd edn. (1907) by A. Levin and C. S. Levin. Homewood, Ill., 1970.
Turin, S. P. *From Peter the Great to Lenin*. Westminster, 1935.
von Laue, T. H. 'Tsarist Labor Policy, 1895–1903', *Journal of Modern History*, vol. XXXIV, no. 2 (June 1962), pp. 135–45.
—— 'Factory Inspection under the "Witte System": 1892–1903', *American Slavic and East European Review*, vol. XIX (1960), pp. 347–62.
—— 'Russian Peasants in the Factory 1892–1904', *Journal of Economic History*, vol. XXI, no. 1 (March 1961), pp. 61–80.
Voitinskii, Vladimir S. *Peterburgskii Soviet Bezrabotnykh 1906–1907* [The Petersburg Council of the Unemployed 1906–1907]. New York, 1969.
Walkin, J. 'The Attitude of the Tsarist Government Toward the Labor Problem', *American Slavic and East European Review*, vol. XIII (April 1954), pp. 163–84.
Wildman, Allan K. *The Making of a Workers' Revolution: Russian Social Democracy 1891–1903*. Chicago, 1967.
Zelnik, Reginald E. *Labor and Society in Tsarist Russia*. Stanford, 1971.

OTHER COUNTRIES

Dällenbach, Heinz. *Kantone, Bund und Fabrikgesetzgebung*. Zürich, 1961.
Garcia Venero, Maximiano. *Historia de los movimientos sindicalistas españoles 1840–1933*. Madrid, 1961.
Haider, Carmen. *Capital and Labor under Fascism*. New York, 1930.
Hautmann, Hans and Kropf, Rudolf. *Die Oesterreichische Arbeiterbewegung vom Vormärz bis 1945*. Vienna, 1974.
Henneaux-Depooter, Louise. *Misères et luttes dans le Hainaut*. Brussels, 1969.
Hirschberg-Neumeyer, Margherita. *Die italienischen Gewerkschaften*. Jena, 1928.
Horowitz, David L. *The Italian Labor Movement*. Cambridge, Mass., 1963.
LaPalombara, Joseph. *The Italian Labor Movement*. Ithaca, NY, 1957.

Neufeld, Maurice F. *Italian Unions and National Politics*. Ithaca, NY, 1954.
—— *Italy: School for Awakening Countries*. Ithaca, NY, 1961.
Rappard, William E. *La révolution industrielle et les origines de la protection légale du travail en Suisse*. Bern, 1914.
Rubinow, I. M. *Studies in Workmen's Insurance: Italy, Russia, Spain*. New York, 1911.
Sellin, Volker. *Die Anfänge staatlicher Sozialreform im liberalen Italien*. Stuttgart, 1971.
Steiner, Herbert. *Die Arbeiterbewegung Oesterreichs 1867–1889*. Vienna, 1964.
Tuñon de Lara, Manuel. *El movimieto obrero en la historia de España*. Madrid, 1972.

CHAPTER VIII

British public policy, 1776–1939

Checkland, S. G. *British Public Policy 1776–1939*. Cambridge, 1983, 1985.

Coats, A. W. (ed.) *The Classical Economists and Economic Policy*. London, 1971.

Flinn, M. W. *Public Health Reform in Great Britain*. London, 1968.

Fraser, D. *The Evolution of the British Welfare State*. Basingstoke, 1973.

Frazer, W. M. *A History of English Public Health 1839–1939*. 1950.

Gilbert, B. B. *The Evolution of National Insurance in Great Britain*. London, 1966.

—— *British Social Policy 1914–1939*. Ithaca, NY, 1970.

Glynn, S. and Oxborrow, J. *Interwar Britain: A Social and Economic History*. Hemel Hempstead, 1976.

Harris, J. *Unemployment and Politics: A Study of English Social Policy 1886–1914*. Oxford, 1972.

Howson, S. *Domestic Monetary Management in Britain 1919–1938*. Cambridge, 1975.

Hunt, E. H. *British Labour History, 1815–1914*. London, 1981 (especially part 2).

Hurt, J. S. *Elementary Schooling and the Working Classes 1860–1918*. Toronto, 1979.

Pelling, H. *A History of British Trade Unionism*. New York, 1963.

Roach, J. *Social Reform in England 1780–1880*. New York, 1978.

Rose, M. E. *The Relief of Poverty 1834–1914*. London, 1972.

Smith, A. *The Wealth of Nations*. 1776. New edn ed. R. H. Campbell and A. Skinner. Oxford, 1976.

Smith, F. B. *The People's Health 1830–1910*. New York, 1979.

Tomlinson, J. *Problems of British Economic Policy 1870–1945*. London, 1981.

Ward, J. T. *The Factory System*, 2 vols. Newton Abbot, 1970.

CHAPTER IX

American economic policy, 1865–1959

GENERAL ٠

Historical Statistics of the United States. Washington, DC, 1960.
Orsagh, Thomas (ed.). *The Economic History of the United States Prior to 1860: An Annotated Bibliography.* Santa Barbara, Cal., 1975.

Abrams, Richard (ed.). *The Issues of the Populist and Progressive Eras, 1892–1912.* Columbia, SC, 1970.
Andreano, Ralph (ed.). *New Views on American Economic Development.* New York, 1966.
Beth, Loren P. *The Development of the American Constitution, 1877–1917.* New York, 1971.
Braeman, John, Bremner, Robert H. and Brody, David (eds.) *The New Deal,* 2 vols. Columbus, Ohio, 1975.
Broude, Henry W. 'The Role of the State in American Economic Development, 1820–1890', in Hugh G. J. Aitken (ed.), *The State and Economic Growth,* pp. 4–25. New York, 1959.
Cochran, Thomas. *The American Business System.* Cambridge, Mass., 1957.
Davis, Lance E. and Legler, John. 'The Government in the American Economy, 1815–1902: A Quantitative Study', *Journal of Economic History,* vol. XXVI (1966), pp. 514–52.
Elazar, Daniel J. Comment on 'Government–Business Relations', in D. T. Gilchrist and W. D. Lewis (eds.), *Economic Change in the Civil War Era.* Greenville, Del., 1965.
Fabricant, Solomon. *The Trend of Government Activity in the United States since 1900.* New York, 1952.
Faulkner, Harold U. *Decline of Laissez Faire.* New York, 1951.
Fine, Sidney. *Laissez Faire and the General-Welfare State: A Study of Conflict in American Thought, 1865–1901.* Ann Arbor, 1956.
Fogel, Robert W. and Engerman, Stanley L. (eds.). *The Reinterpretation of American Economic History.* New York, 1971.
Friedman, Lawrence M. *A History of American Law.* New York, 1974.
Hammond, Bray. *Sovereignty and an Empty Purse: Banks and Politics in the Civil War.* Princeton, 1970.
Harris, Seymour E. (ed.). *American Economic History.* New York, 1961.
Hays, Samuel P. *The Response to Industrialism, 1885–1914.* Chicago, 1957.
Hurst, James W. *Law and the Conditions of Freedom in the Nineteenth-century United States.* Madison, 1956.
Keller, Morton. *Affairs of State: Public Life in Late Nineteenth Century America.* Cambridge, Mass., 1977.
Kendrick, M. Slade. *A Century and a Half of Federal Expenditure.* New York. 1955.
Kolko, Gabriel. *Main Currents in Modern American History.* New York, 1976.
Letwin, William. *A Documentary History of American Economic Policy Since 1789.* New York, 1961, 1972.
—— *Law and Economic Policy in America: The Evolution of the Sherman Antitrust Act.* New York, 1965.
McDonald, Forrest. *The Phaeton Ride.* New York, 1977.
Manning, Thomas G. and Potter, David M. *Government and the American Economy, 1870–present.* New York, 1950.
Mendelson, Wallace. *Capitalism, Democracy, and the Supreme Court.* New York, 1960.
Morgan, H. Wayne (ed.). *The Gilded Age.* Syracuse, NY, 1970.
North, Douglas C. *Growth and Welfare in the American Past.* Englewood Cliffs, NJ, 1966.
Redford, Emmette S. and Hagan, Charles B. *American Government and the Economy.* New York, 1965.
Stein, Herbert. *Fiscal Revolution in America.* Chicago, 1969.
Temin, Peter (ed.). *New Economic History.* Harmondsworth, Middx., 1973.

White, Leonard D. *The Republican Era, 1869–1901: A Study in Administrative History*. New State, 1958.
Wiebe, Robert H. *Businessmen and Reform: A Study of the Progressive Movement*. Cambridge, Mass., 1962.

TARIFFS

Crapol, Edward P. *America for Americans: Economic Nationalism and Anglophobia in the Late Nineteenth Century*. Westport, Conn., 1973.
Kelly, William B., Jr (ed.). *Studies in United States Commercial Policy*. Chapel Hill, NC, 1963.
Ratner, Sidney. *The Tariff in American History*. New York, 1972.
Schattschneider, E. E. *Politics, Pressures and the Tariff*. Englewood Cliffs, NJ, 1935.
Stanwood, Edward. *Tariff Controversies in the Nineteenth Century*. Boston, Mass., 1903.
Taussig, Frank W. *Some Aspects of the Tariff Question*. Cambridge, Mass., 1915.
—— *The Tariff History of the United States*. New York, various dates.
Temin, Peter. *Iron and Steel in Nineteenth-Century America*. Cambridge, Mass., 1964.
Terrill, Tom E. *The Tariff, Politics, and American Foreign Policy, 1874–1901*. Westport, Conn., 1973.

RAILWAYS

Berger, Harold. *The Transportation Industries, 1889–1946*. New York, 1951.
Fogel, Robert W. *Railroads and American Economic Growth*. Baltimore, Md., 1964.
—— *The Union Pacific Railroad: A Case Study in Premature Enterprise*. Baltimore, Md., 1960.
Goodrich, Carter. 'Local Government Planning of Internal Improvements', *Political Science Quarterly*, vol. LXVI (1951), pp. 411–45.
Haney, Lewis H. *A Congressional History of Railways in the United States to 1850*. Madison, 1908.
—— *A Congressional History of Railways in the United States, 1850–1887*. Madison, 1910.
Hines, Walker D. *War History of American Railroads*. New Haven, 1928.
Johnson, Emory R. *Government Regulation of Transportation*. New York, 1938.
Kerr, K. Austin. *American Railroad Politics, 1914–1920*. Pittsburgh, Pa., 1968.
Kolko, Gabriel. *Railroad and Regulation, 1877–1916*. Princeton, 1965.
McAfee, Ward. *California's Railroad Era, 1850–1911*. San Marino, Cal., 1973.
MacAvoy, Paul W. *The Economic Effects of Regulation: The Trunk-Line Railroad Cartels and the Interstate Commerce Commission before 1900*. Cambridge, Mass., 1965.
Martin, Albro. *Enterprise Denied: Origins of the Decline of American Railroads, 1897–1917*. New York, 1971.
Miller, James C., III (ed.). *Perspectives on Federal Transportation Policy*. Washington, DC, 1975.
Taylor, George Rogers, and Neu, Irene. *The American Railway Network 1861–1897*. Cambridge, Mass., 1956.

LABOUR

Dulles, Foster R. *Labor in America*. New York, 1966.
Gregory, Charles O. *Labor and the Law*. New York, 1949.
Kirkland, Edward C. *Industry Comes of Age: Business, Labor and Public Policy, 1860–1897*. New York, 1961.
Leek, John H. *Government and Labor in the United States*. New York, 1952.
Taft, Philip. *Organized Labor in American History*. New York, 1964.
Ulman, Lloyd. *The Rise of the National Trade Union*. 2nd edn. Cambridge, Mass., 1966.

SOCIAL POLICY

Brandes, Stuart D. *American Welfare Capitalism, 1880–1940*. Chicago, 1976.
Callow, Alexander B., Jr (ed.). *American Urban History*. New York, 1969.
Cremin, Lawrence A. *The American Common School*. New York, 1951.
Good, H. G. *A History of American Education*. New York, 1965.
Haar, Charles M. *Land-Use Planning*. Boston, 1959.
Leiby, James. *Charity and Correction in New Jersey*. New Brunswick, NJ, 1967.
McKelvey, Blake. *The Urbanization of America, 1860–1915*. New Brunswick, NJ, 1963.
Toll, S. *Zoned America*. New York, 1969.
West, Edwin George. 'The Political Economy of Public School Legislation', *Journal of Law and Economics*, vol. x (1967), pp. 101–28.
Witte, Edwin E. *The Development of the Social Security Act*. Madison, 1962.

CHAPTER X

Economic and social policy in France

ECONOMIC HISTORY: GENERAL

Asselin, J. C. *Histoire économique de la France*, 2 vols. Paris, 1984.
Braudel, F. and Labrousse, E. *Histoire économique et sociale de la France*. Vol. II, Paris, 1970; vol. III, Paris, 1976; vol. IV, Paris, 1979.
Caron, F. *An Economic History of Modern France*, translated by B. Bray. London, 1979.
Clapham, J. H. *Economic Development of France and Germany*. 4th edn. Cambridge, 1936.
Clough, S. B. *France: A History of National Economics 1789–1939*. New York, 1939, rep. 1964.
Dunham, A. L. *The Industrial Revolution in France 1815–1848*. New York, 1955.
Kemp, T. *Economic Forces in French History*. London, 1971.
Kindelberger, C. P. *Economic Growth in France and Britain 1851–1950*. London, 1964.
Labrousse, E. *Aspects de l'évolution économique et sociale de la France et du Royaume-uni de 1851–1880*, 3 vols. (duplicated) Paris, 1949.
Landes, D. S. *The Unbound Prometheus*. Cambridge, 1969.
Palmade, G. *Capitalisme et capitalistes française au 19e. siècle*. Paris, 1961. English translation by Graeme M. Holmes, *French Capitalism in the Nineteenth Century*. Newton Abbot, 1972.
Rowley, A. *Évolution économique de la France du milieu du XIX siècle à 1914*. Paris, 1982.
See, H. *Histoire économique de la France*, 2 vols. Paris, 1957.

SOCIAL HISTORY

Ariès, P. *Histoire des populations françaises*. 2nd edn. Paris, 1971.
Daumard, A. *La bourgeoisie parisienne de 1815 à 1848*. Paris, 1963.
—— 'L'évolution des structures sociales en France à l'époque de l'industrialisation', *Revue historique* (April–June 1972).
Dupeux, G. *La société française*. 6th edn. Paris, 1972. English translation, London, 1976.
Duveau, G. *La vie ouvrière en France sous le Second Empire*. Paris, 1946.
Levasseur, E. *Histoire des classes ouvrières et de l'industrie en France de 1789 à 1870*. Paris, 1903–4.
Lhomme, J. *La grande bourgeoisie au pouvoir (1830–1880): essai sur l'histoire sociale de la France*. Paris, 1960.
—— *Économie et histoire*. Geneva, 1967.
Magraw, R. *France 1815–1914: The Bourgeois Century*. London, 1983.
Morazé, C. *Les bourgeois conquérants*. Paris, 1957. English translation, *The Triumph of the Middle Classes*. London, 1966.
—— *La France bourgeoise*. Paris, 1946.

HISTORY OF INSTITUTIONS

Godechot, J. *Les institutions de la France sous la Révolution et l'Empire*. 2nd edn. Paris, 1968.
Ponteil, F. *Les institutions de la France de 1814 à 1870*. Paris, 1966.
Ripert, G. *Aspects juridiques du capitalisme moderne*. Paris, 1946.

LABOUR

Bedarida, F. and Fohlen, C. *Histoire générale du travail*, vol. III: *L'ère des révolutions, 1765–1914*. Paris, 1964.
Bouvier-Ajam, M. *Histoire du travail en France depuis la Révolution*. Paris, 1969.
Chevalier, L. *Classes laborieuses et classes dangereuses à Paris pendant la Première moitié du XIXe. siècle*. Paris, 1958. English translation, *Labouring Classes and Dangerous Classes*. London, 1973.

Dolléans, E. *Histoire du mouvement ouvrier*, 2 vols. Paris, 1946.
Gueneau, L. 'La législation restrictive du travail des enfants', *Revue d'histoire économique et sociale*, vol. xv (1927).
Lefranc, G. *Le mouvement syndical sous la troisième république*. Paris, 1967.
Perrot, M. *Les ouvriers en grève en France, 1871–1890*. Paris, 1974.
Shorter, E. and Tilly, C. *Strikes in France*. Cambridge, 1974.

TRANSPORT AND PUBLIC WORKS

Blanchard, M. 'The Railway Policy of the Second Empire', in F. Crouzet, W. H. Chaloner and W. H. Stern (eds.), *Essays in European Economic History, 1789–1914*. London, 1969.
Caron, F. *Histoire de l'exploitation d'un grand réseau. La compagnie du chemin de fer du Nord, 1846–1937*. Paris, 1973.
Cavailles, H. *La Route française*. Paris, 1946.
Girard, L. *La politique des travaux publics du second Empire*. Paris, 1952.
Gonjo, Y. 'Le "plan Freycinet", 1878–1882: un aspect de la "grande dépression" économique de la France', *Revue Historique*, vol. CCXLVIII, no. 1 (January–March 1972).
Jouffroy, L. M. *L'ère du rail*. Paris, 1953.
Lefranc, G. 'The French Railroads, 1823–1842', *The Journal of Economic and Business History*, vol. II, no. 2 (February 1930).
Pinkney, D. H. *Napoleon III and the Rebuilding of Paris*. Princeton, 1958.

BANKING AND FINANCE

Bouvier, J. 'The Banking Mechanism in France in the Late Nineteenth Century', in R. C. Cameron (ed.), *Essays in French Economic History*. Homewood, Ill., 1970.
—— 'Systèmes bancaires et entreprises industrielles dans la croissance européene au XIXe siècle', *Annales: Economies, Sociétés, Civilisations*, vol. XXVII (January–February 1972).
Cameron, R. C. *France and the Economic Development of Europe 1800–1914*. Princeton, 1961.
Cameron, R. C. (ed.) *Banking in the Early Stages of Industrialization*. New York and London, 1967.
Freedeman, C. 'Joint-Stock Business Organisation in France 1807–1867', *Business History Review*, vol. XXXIX (1965).
—— *Joint Stock Enterprise in France 1807–1867*. Chapel Hill, NC, 1979.
Gille, B. *La Banque et le credit en France de 1815 à 1848*. Paris, 1959.
Landes, D. S. 'The Old Bank and the New: The Financial Revolution of the Nineteenth Century', in F. Crouzet, W. H. Chaloner and W. H. Stern (eds.), *Essays in European Economic History, 1789–1914*. London, 1969.
Plessis, A. *La Banque de France et ses deux cent actionnaires*. Paris, 1982.

TARIFF AND FISCAL POLICIES

Ardant, G. 'Financial Policy and Economic Infrastructure of Modern States and Nations', in C. Tilly (ed.), *The Formation of National States in Western Europe*. Princeton, 1975, ch. 3.
Bairoch, P. 'Commerce extérieur et développement économique: quelques enseignements de l'expérience libre-echangiste de la France au XIXe siècle', *Revue economique*, vol. XXI, no. 1 (1970).
—— *Commerce extérieur et développement économique de l'Europe au XIXe siècle*. Paris and The Hague, 1976.
Bouvier, J. 'Sur "l'immobilisme" du système fiscal français au XIXe siècle', *Revue d'histoire économique et sociale*, vol. L, no. 4 (October–December 1972).
Cole, C. W. *Colbert and a Century of French Mercantilism*. New York, 1939.

Coussy, J. 'La politique commercial du Second Empire et la continuité de l'évolution structurelle française', *Cahiers de l'Institut de Science Économique Appliquée*, series P, no. 6 (December 1961).
Dunham, A. L. *The Anglo-French Treaty of Commerce of 1860 and the Progress of the Industrial Revolution in France*. Ann Arbor, 1930.
Golob, E. O. *The Méline Tariff: French Agriculture and Nationalist Economic Policy*. New York, 1944.
Haight, F. A. *A History of French Commercial Policies*. New York, 1941.
Kemp, T. 'Tariff Policy and French Economic Growth 1815–1914', *Revue Internationale d'Histoire de la Banque*, vol. XII (1976).
Matthews, G. T. *The Royal General Farms in Eighteenth Century France*. New York, 1958.
Meredith, H. O. *Protection in France*. London, 1904.
Rist, M. 'Une expérience française de liberation des échanges au dixneuvième siècle: le traité de 1860', *Revue d'Economie Politique*, vol. LXVI (November–December 1956). In English in R. C. Cameron (ed.), *Essays in French Economic History*. Homewood, Ill., 1970.
Schnerb, R. *Libre-échange et protectionnisme*. Paris, 1953.
Smith, M. S. *Tariff Reform in France 1860–1900*. Ithaca, NY, and London, 1980.
Wolfe, M. 'French Views on Wealth and Taxes from the Middle Ages to the Old Regime', *Journal of Economic History*, vol. XXVI, no. 4 (December 1966); rep. in D. C. Coleman (ed.), *Revisions in Mercantilism*. London, 1979.

INDUSTRIES

Fohlen, C. *L'industrie textile au temps du Second Empire*. Paris, 1956.
Leon, P. *La naissance de la grande industrie en Dauphiné*, 2 vols. Paris, 1954.
Vial, J. *L'industrialisation de la sidérurgie française, 1814–1864*. Paris and The Hague, 1967.

AGRICULTURE

Augé-Laribé, M. *La politique agricole de la France de 1880 à 1940*. Paris, 1950.
Barral, P. *Les agrairiens français de Méline à Pisani*. Paris, 1968.
Houssel, J. P. (ed.) *Histoire des paysans françias du XVIIIe siecle à nos jours*. Roanne, 1976.
Lefebvre, G. *Etudes sur la Révolution française*. Paris, 1954.
—— *Les paysans du Nord pendant la Révolution française*. Rep. Bari, 1959.
Lhomme, J. 'La crise agricole à la fin du XIXe siècle en France', *Revue économique*, vol. XXI, no. 4 (July 1970).
Weber, E. *Peasants into Frenchmen*. London, 1977.
Wright, G. *Rural Revolution in France*. Stanford, 1964.

EDUCATION AND SOCIAL POLICY

Artz, F. B. *The Development of Technical Education in France*. Cambridge, Mass., and London, 1966.
Fox, R. and Weisz, G. (eds.) *The Organisation of Science and Technology in France 1808–1914*. Cambridge, 1980.
Gilpin, R. *France in the Age of the Scientific State*. Princeton, 1968.
Grevet, P. *Besoins populaires et financement public*. Paris, 1976.
Hatzfeld, H. *Du pauperisme à la securité sociale, 1850–1940*. Paris, 1971.
Kindleberger, C. P. 'Technical Education and the French Entrepreneur', in Edward Carter, Robert Forster and Joseph Moody (eds.), *Enterprise and Entrepreneurs in Nineteenth- and Twentieth-Century France*. Baltimore, Md., and London, 1976.
Pipkin, C. W. *The Idea of Social Justice*. New York, 1927.
Ponteil, F. *Histoire de l'enseignement en France*. Paris, 1966.
Prost, A. *Histoire de l'enseignement en France, 1800–1967*. Paris, 1968.
Weisz, G. *The Emergence of Modern Universities in France 1863–1914*. Princeton, 1983.

ECONOMIC LIBERALISM

Fohlen, C. 'Bourgeoisie française, liberté économique et l'intervention de l'état', *Revue économique*, vol. VII, no. 3 (1956).

Girard, L. *Le Libéralisme en France de 1814 à 1848: doctrine et mouvement*. Paris, 1966.

Kuisel, R. 'Technocrats and Public Economic Policy: From the Third to the Fourth Republic', *The Journal of European Economic History*, vol. II no. 1 (spring 1973).

Raj, K. N. 'Poverty, Politics and Development', *Economic and Political Weekly* (Bombay), Annual Number (February 1977).

Sherman, D. 'The Meaning of Economic Liberalism in Mid-Nineteenth Century France', *History of Political Economy*, vol. VI, no. 2 (1974).

OTHER WORKS BY PERIOD

The Revolution and Napoleon I

Bergeron, L. 'Problèmes économiques de la France Napoléonienne', *Revue d'histoire moderne et contemporaine*, vol. XVII (July–September 1970).

Crouzet, F. 'Wars, Blockades and Economic Change in Europe, 1792–1815', *Journal of Economic History*, vol. XXIV, no. 4 (December 1964).

Hampson, N. *A Social History of the French Revolution*. London, 1963.

Jaurès, J. *Histoire socialiste de la Révolution française*, vol. II. Paris, 1922.

Lefebvre, G. *The French Revolution*. English translation in 2 vols. New York, 1962–4.

—— *Napoleon: From Eighteen Brumaire to Tilsit, 1799–1807*. English translation in 2 vols. New York, 1969.

Mathiez, A. *La vie chère et le mouvement social sous la Terreur*. Paris, 1927.

1815–71

Bertier de Sauvigny, G. de. *The Bourbon Restoration*. English translation. London, 1966.

Girard, L. *La IIe République*. Paris, 1968.

McKay, D. C. *The National Workshops*. Cambridge, Mass., 1933.

Merriman, J. M. *1830 in France*. New York and London, 1973.

Price, R. (ed.) *Revolution and Reactions: 1848 and the Second French Republic*. London, 1975.

Stearns, P. 'British Industry Through the Eyes of French Industrialists (1820–1948)', *Journal of Modern History*, vol. XXXVII, no. 1 (March 1965).

1871–1914

Chastenet, J. *Histoire de la troisième republique*. 3 vols. Paris, 1952, 1954, 1955.

Combe, P. *Niveau de vie et progrès technique en France (1860–1939)*. Paris, 1956.

Crouzet, F. 'Recherches sur la production d'armaments en France (1815–1913)', *Revue Historique*, vol. CCLI (January–March and April–June 1974).

Salem, D. 'Sur quelques conséquences du retour de la France au protectionnisme à la fin du XIXe siècle', *Revue d'histoire économique et sociale*, vol. XLV, no. 3 (1967).

1914–18

Augé-Laribé, M. and Pinot, P. *Agriculture and Food Supply in France During the War*. New Haven, 1927.

Crehange, A. *Chômage et placement*. Paris, 1924.

Fontaine, A. *L'industrie française pendant la guerre*. Paris, 1924.

Frois, M. *La santé et le travail des femmes pendant la guerre*. Paris, 1926.

Jèze, G. and Truchy, H. *The War Finances of France*. New Haven, 1927.

Nogaro, B. and Weil, L. *La main d'oeuvre étrangère et coloniale*. Paris, 1926.

Oualid, W. and Piquenard, C. *Salaires et tariffs, conventions collectives et grèves*. Paris, 1928.

Picard, R. *Le mouvement syndical devant la guerre*. Paris, 1927.

Pinot, P. *Le contrôle du ravitaillement de la population civile*. Paris, 1925.

Renouvin, P. *The Forms of War Government in France*. New Haven, 1927.

1918–40

Arndt, H. W. *Economic Lessons of the Nineteen Thirties*. 2nd edn. London, 1963.

Asselin, J. 'La semaine de 40 heures, le chômage et l'emploi', *Le Mouvement Social*, no. 54 (January–March 1966), pp. 184–204.

Aucy, M. 'Habitations et logement', *Revue d'économie politique*, vol. LVII (1947).

Fohlen, C. *La France de l'entre-deux-guerres*. Paris, 1966.

Jackson, J. *The Politics of Depression in France 1932–1936*. London, 1985.

Kemp, T. *The French Economy, 1913–39*. London, 1972.

Kriegel, A. *Aux origines du communisme français*. Paris and The Hague, 1964.

Kuisel, R. F. *Capitalism and the State in Modern France*. Cambridge, 1981.

Lefranc, G. *Histoire du Front Populaire*. Paris, 1964.

Maier, C. S. *Recasting Bourgeois Europe*. Princeton, 1975.

Ogburn, W. F. and Jaffe, W. *The Economic Development of Post-War France*. New York, 1929.

Sauvy, A. *Histoire économique de la France entre les deux guerres*. 4 vols. Paris, 1965–75.

CHAPTER XIII

East-central and south-east Europe, 1919–39

GENERAL ECONOMIC HISTORIES OF THE REGION

Berend, I. T. and Ránki, G. *Economic Development in East Central Europe in the 19th and 20th Centuries*. New York, 1974.

Kaser, M. C. and Radice, E. A. *The Economic History of Eastern Europe 1919–1975*, vols. I and II. Oxford, 1986.

Lampe, J. R. and Jackson, M. R. *Balkan Economic History 1550–1950: From Imperial Borderlands to Developing Nations*. Bloomington, 1982.

Moore, W. E. *Economic Demography of Eastern and Southern Europe*. Geneva, 1945.

Plaschka, R. and Mack, K. H. (eds.) *Die Auflösung des Habsburgerreiches*. Munich, 1970.

Raupach, H. 'The Impact of the Great Depression on Eastern Europe', *Journal of Contemporary History*, vol. IV (1969), pp. 75–86.

Seton-Watson, H. *Eastern Europe Between the Wars 1918–1945*. Hamden, 1962.

Spulber, N. *The State and Economic Development in Eastern Europe*. New York, 1966.

Teichova, A. and Cottrell, P. L. (eds.) *International Business and Central Europe 1918–1939*. Leicester and New York, 1983.

Warriner, D. *Economics of Peasant Farming*. New edn. New York, 1963.

Zagaroff, S. D., Vegh, J. and Bilimovich, A. D. (eds.) *The Agrarian Economy of the Danubian Countries 1933–1945*. Palo Alto, 1955.

Żarnowski, J. (ed.) *Dictatorships in East-Central Europe 1918–1939*. Warsaw, 1983.

ECONOMICS AND FOREIGN POLICY

Bandera, V. N. *Foreign Capital as an Instrument of Economic Policy*. The Hague, 1964.

Kaiser, D. E. *Economic Diplomacy and the Origins of the Second World War; Germany, Britain, France and Eastern Europe 1930–39*. Princeton, 1980.

Ránki, Gy. *Economy and Foreign Policy: The Struggle of the Great Powers for Hegemony in the Danube Valley, 1919–1939*. Boulder, Col., and New York, 1983.

Schröder, H. J. 'Deutsche Südosteuropapolitik 1929–1936. Zur Kontinuität deutscher Aussenpolitik in der Weltwirtschaftskrise', *Geschichte und Gesellschaft* vol. II (1976), pp. 5–32.

Stegmann, D. '"Mitteleuropa" 1925–1934. Zum Problem der Kontinuität deutscher Aussenpolitik von Stresemann bis Hitler', in D. Stegmann, B. J. Wendt and P. C. Witt, (eds.), *Industrielle Gesellschaft und politisches System*. Bonn, 1978.

Sundhaussen, H. 'Die Weltwirtschaftskrise im Donau–Balkan Raum und ihre Bedeutung für den Wandel der deutschen Aussenpolitik unter Brüning', in W. Benz and H. Graml (eds.), *Aspekte deutscher Aussenpolitik im 20. Jahrhundert*. Stuttgart, 1976.

Wendt B. J. 'England und der deutsche "Drang nach Südosten." Kapitalbeziehungen und Warenverkehr in Südosteuropa zwischen den Weltkriegen', in I. Geiss and B. J. Wendt (eds.), *Deutschland in der Weltpolitik des 19 und 20. Jahrhunderts*. Düsseldorf, 1974.

BULGARIA

Berov, L. 'The Withdrawing of Western Capitals from Bulgaria on the Eve of the Second World War', *Studia Balcanica* (1969).

Lampe, J. R. *Bulgarian Economic Development in the Twentieth Century*. London, 1985.

Natan, J., Khadzhinikolov, V., and Berov, L. (eds.) *Ikonomikata na Bulgarya do socialisticheskata revoluciya*. Sofia, 1969.

CZECHOSLOVAKIA

Bloomfield, J. 'Surviving in a Harsh World: Trade and Inflation in the Czechoslovak and Austrian Republics 1918–1925', in G. D. Feldman, C. L. Holtfrerich, G. A. Ritter and

P. C. Witt (eds.) *The Experience of the Inflation: International and Comparative Studies.* Berlin and New York, 1984.

Faltus, J. *Povojnová hospodárska kríza v Československu v rokoch 1921–23 – priemysel a peňažníctvo.* Bratislava, 1966.

Faltus, J. and Průcha, V. *Prehľad hospodárskeho vývoja na Slovensku v rokoch 1918–1945.* Bratislava, 1969.

Lacina, V. 'K dynamice hospodářského vývoje v předmnichovské ČSR', *Sborník historický*, vol. XXIII (1976), pp. 119–68.

—— *Velká hospodářská krize v Československu 1929–1934.* Prague, 1984.

Lipták, L. *Slovensko v 20. storočí.* Bratislava, 1968.

Průcha, V., et al. *Hospodářské dějiny Československenksa v 19. a 20. století.* Prague, 1974.

Pryor, Z. P. and Pryor, F. L. 'Foreign Trade and Interwar Czechoslovak Economic Development, 1918–1938', *Vierteljahrschrift für Sozial- und Wirtschaftsgeschichte*, vol. LXII, no. 4 (1975), pp. 500–33.

Pryor, Z. 'Czechoslovak Fiscal Policies in the Great Depression', *Economic History Review*, 2nd series, vol. XXXII, no. 2 (1976), pp. 228–40.

Teichova, A. 'The Inflations of the 1920s in Austria and Czechoslovakia – A Comparative View', in N. Schmukler and E. Marcus, (eds.), *Inflations through the Ages: Economic, Social, Psychological and Historical Aspects.* New York, 1983, pp. 531–67.

—— *An Economic Background to Munich, International Business and Czechoslovakia 1918–1938.* Cambridge, 1974.

HUNGARY

Berend, I. T. and Ránki, G. *The Hungarian Economy in the Twentieth Century.* London, 1986.

—— *Hungary: A Century of Economic Development.* Newton Abbot, 1974.

—— *Underdevelopment and Economic Growth Studies in Hungarian Economic and Social History.* Budapest, 1979.

Boross, E. A. 'The Role of the State Issuing Bank in the Course of Inflation in Hungary between 1918 and 1924', in G. D. Feldman, C. L. Holtfrerich, G. A. Ritter and P. C. Witt (eds.), *The Experience of the Inflation: International and Comparative Studies.* Berlin and New York, 1984.

—— 'The Effect of Inflation of the 1920s on the Hungarian Manufacturing Industry: Capital Accumulation in Large Enterprises', in G. D. Feldman, C. L. Holtfrerich, G. A. Ritter and P. C. Witt (eds.) *Inflation and Reconstruction in Germany and Europe 1914–1924.* Berlin and New York, forthcoming.

Ránki, G. 'Inflation in Hungary', in N. Schmukler and E. Marcus (eds.), *Inflations through the Ages: Economic, Social, Psychological and Historical Aspects.* New York, 1983.

POLAND

Kostrowicka, I., Landau, Z. and Tomaszewski, J. *Historia gospodarcza Polski XIX i XX wieku.* Warsaw, 1966.

Landau, Z. 'Inflation in Poland after World War I', in N. Schmukler and E. Marcus (eds.), *Inflations through the Ages: Economic, Social, Psychological and Historical Aspects.* New York, 1983.

Landau, Z. and Tomaszewski, J. *Polska W Europie i Swiecie 1918–1939.* Warsaw, 1980.

—— *Robotnicy Przemysłowi w Polsce 1918–1939.* Warsaw, 1971.

Tomaszewski, J. and Landau, Z. *The Polish Economy in the Twentieth Century.* London, 1985.

Zweig, F. *Poland Between the Two Wars.* London, 1964.

ROMANIA

Fischer-Galati, St. A. *Twentieth Century Rumania.* New York, 1970.

Mitrany, D. *The Land and the Peasant in Rumania: The War and Agrarian Reform.* London, 1930.

Pearton, M. *Oil and the Romanian State 1895–1948*. London, 1971.
Sundhaussen, H. 'Politisches und wirtschaftliches Kalkül in der Auseinandersetzung über die deutsch–rumänischen Präferenzverhandlungen von 1931', *Revue des Études Sud-Est Europeennes*, vol. XIV (1976), pp. 405–25.
Turnock, D. *The Romanian Economy in the Twentieth Century*. London, 1986.

YUGOSLAVIA

Dimitrijević, S. *Das ausländische Kapital in Jugoslawien vor dem Zweiten Weltkrieg*. Berlin, 1962.
Singleton, Carter B. *The Economy of Yugoslavia in the Twentieth Century*. London, 1984.
Tomasevich, J. *Peasants, Politics and Economic Change in Yugoslavia*. Stanford, 1955.
Vinski, J. 'National Product and Fixed Assets in the Territory of Yugoslavia 1909–1959', in P. Deane (ed.), *Studies in Social and Financial Accounting*. London, 1961.

CHAPTER XIV

Economic and social policy in the USSR, 1917–41

This bibliography is restricted to works cited in the text, with a few major authorities added.

Anweiler, O. *Geschichte der Schule und Pädagogik in Russland vom Ende des Zarenreiches bis zum Beginn der Stalin-Ära.* Berlin, 1964.
Bailes, K. E. 'The Politics of Technology – Stalin and Technocratic Thinking among Soviet Engineers', *American Historical Review*, vol. LXXIX (1974), pp. 445–69.
—— *Technology and Society under Lenin and Stalin: Origins of the Soviet Technical Intelligentsia, 1917–1941.* Princeton, NJ, 1978.
Bairoch, P. P. 'Agriculture and the Industrial Revolution', in C. M. Cipolla (ed.), *The Fontana Economic History of Europe: The Industrial Revolution.* London, 1973, pp. 452–506.
Barsov, A. *Balans stoimostnykh obmenov mezhdu gorodom i derevnei.* Moscow, 1969.
—— 'Nep i vyravnivanie ekonomicheskikh otnoshenii mezhdu gorodom i derevnei', in M. P. Kim (ed.), *Novaya ekonomicheskaya politika: voprosy teorii i istorii,* Moscow, 1974, pp. 93–105.
Baykov, A. *The Development of the Soviet Economic System.* Cambridge, 1946.
Benvenuti, F. 'Dal communismo di guerra alla NEP: il dibattito sui sindicati', in *Pensiero e azioni politica di Lev Trockij,* vol. I, pp. 261–88. Florence, 1982.
Bergson, A. *The Real National Income of Soviet Russia since 1928.* Cambridge, Mass., 1961.
Bol'shakov, A. M. 'The Soviet Countryside, 1917–1924', in R.E.F. Smith (ed.), *The Russian Peasant, 1920 and 1984.* London, 1977.
Bol'shevik. Journal. Moscow.
Bukharin, N. *Put' k sotsializmu v Rossii.* New York, 1967 (writings and speeches first published in Moscow in the 1920s).
Byulleten' Ekonomicheskogo Kabineta prof. S. N. Prokopovicha. Journal, Prague.
Carr, E. H. *The Bolshevik Revolution, 1917–1923,* vol. II. London, 1952.
—— *Socialism in One Country, 1924–1926,* vol. I. London, 1958.
—— *Foundations of a Planned Economy, 1926–1929,* vol. II. London, 1971.
Carr, E. H. and Davies, R. W. *Foundations of a Planned Economy, 1926–1929,* vol. I. London, 1969.
Chapman, J. *Real Wages in the Soviet Union since 1928.* Cambridge, Mass., 1963.
Chayanov, A. V. *On the Theory of Peasant Economy,* ed. D. Thorner, B. Kerblay and R. E. F. Smith. Homewood, Ill., 1966 (first published Moscow, 1925).
Clark, M. G. *The Economics of Soviet Steel.* Cambridge, Mass., 1956.
Clarke, R. A. *Soviet Economic Facts, 1917–1970.* London, 1972.
Conquest, R. 'Forced Labour Statistics: Some Comments', *Soviet Studies.* vol. XXXIV (1982), pp. 434–9.
Cooper, J. M. 'Defence Production and the Soviet Economy, 1929–1941'. Unpublished Discussion Papers, CREES, University of Birmingham, SIPS No. 3, 1976.
—— 'The Development of the Soviet Machine Tool Industry, 1917–1941'. Unpublished Ph.D. thesis, University of Birmingham, 1975.
Cooper, J. M., Davies, R. W. and Wheatcroft, S. G. 'Contradictions in Soviet Industrialisation'. Unpublished seminar paper, delivered at conference of National Association for Soviet and East European Studies, Cambridge, 1977.
Danilov, V. P. *Sozdanie material'no-tekhnicheskikh predposylok kollektivizatsii sel'skogo khozyaistva v SSSR.* Moscow, 1957.
—— 'Materialy o sostoyanii chastnogo kapitala v narodnom khozyaistve SSSR i merakh po ego vytesneniyu v 1926–1927 gg.', in *Materialy po istorii sovetskogo obshchestva,* vol. VII. Moscow, 1969, pp. 5–166.
—— *Sovetskaya dokolkhoznaya derevnya: naselenie, zemlepol'zovanie, khozyaistvo.* Moscow, 1977.
Davies, R. W. *The Development of the Soviet Budgetary System.* Cambridge, 1958.
—— 'A Note on Grain Statistics', *Soviet Studies,* vol. XXI (1969–70), pp. 314–29.

——— 'Economic and Non-Economic Factors in Soviet Industrialisation: 1927'. Unpublished seminar paper, CREES, University of Birmingham, 1970.
——— 'A Note on Defence Aspects of the Ural–Kuznetsk Combine', *Soviet Studies*, vol. XXVI (1974), pp. 272–4.
——— 'The Soviet Economic Crisis of 1931–1933'. Unpublished Discussion Papers, CREES, University of Birmingham, SIPS No. 4, 1976.
——— 'The Emergence of the Soviet Economic System, 1927–1934'. Unpublished Discussion Papers, CREES, University of Birmingham, SIPS No. 9, 1977.
——— 'Soviet Industrial Production, 1928–1937: The Rival Estimates'. Unpublished CREES Discussion Papers, University of Birmingham, SIPS No. 18, 1978.
——— *The Socialist Offensive: The Collectivisation of Soviet Agriculture, 1929–1930*. London and Cambridge, Mass., 1980.
Dekrety Sovetskoi vlasti. Vol. II, Moscow, 1959.
De Witt, N. *Education and Professional Employment in the USSR*. Washington, DC, 1961.
Direktivy KPSS i sovetskogo pravitel'stva po khozyaistvennym voprosam: sbornik dokumentov, vols. I–II. Moscow, 1957.
Dmitrenko, V. P. *Torgovaya politika sovetskogo gosudarstva posle perekhoda k nepu, 1921–1924 gg*. Moscow, 1971.
Dobb, M. H. *Russian Economic Development since the Revolution*. London, 1928.
——— *Soviet Economic Development since 1917*. London, 1948.
Dodge, N. T. 'Trends in Labor Productivity in the Soviet Tractor Industry: A Case Study in Industrial Development'. Unpublished Ph.D. thesis, Harvard University, 1960.
Dohan, M. R. 'The Economic Origins of Soviet Autarky, 1927/28–1934', *Slavic Review*, vol. XXXV (1976), pp. 603–35.
Drobizhev, V. Z. *Glavnyi shtab sotsialisticheskoi promyshlennosti (ocherki istorii VSNKh, 1917–1932 gg.)* Moscow, 1966.
Dunstan, N. J. 'Making Soviet Man: Education', in R. W. Davies (ed.), *The Soviet Union*. London, 1978, pp. 92–108.
Eason, W. W. *Soviet Manpower*. Princeton, NJ, 1959.
——— 'Labor Force', in A. Bergson and S. Kuznets (eds.), *Economic Trends in the Soviet Union*. Cambridge, Mass., 1963, pp. 38–95.
Ekonomicheskaya zhizn'. Newspaper. Moscow, 1918–37.
Ekonomicheskii byulleten' Kon"yunkturnogo Instituta. Journal. Moscow.
Ekonomicheskii vestnik. Journal. Berlin.
Ekonomicheskoe obozrenie. Journal. Moscow.
Ellman, M. 'Did the Agricultural Surplus Provide the Resources for the Increase in Investment in the USSR during the First Five Year Plan?', *Economic Journal*, vol. LXXXV (1975), pp. 844–63.
Engels, F. *Herr Eugen Dühring's Revolution in Science (Anti-Dühring)*. London, n.d. (first published 1878).
Erlich, A. *The Soviet Industrialization Debate, 1924–1928*. Harvard, 1960.
Fitzpatrick, S. *The Commissariat of Enlightenment: Soviet Education and the Arts under Lunacharsky, October 1917–1921*. Cambridge, 1970.
——— 'Cultural Revolution in Russia, 1928–1932', *Journal of Contemporary History*, vol. I (1974), pp. 33–52.
——— *Education and Social Mobility in the Soviet Union, 1921–1934*. Cambridge, 1979.
Galenson, W. *Labor Productivity in Soviet and American Industry*. New York, 1955.
Genkina, E. B. *Gosudarstvennaya deyatel'nost' V. I. Lenina, 1921–1923 gg*. Moscow, 1969.
Gerschenkron, A. *Economic Backwardness in Historical Perspective*. New York, 1962.
Gimpel'son, Ye. G. *'Voennyi kommunizm': politika, praktika, ideologiya*. Moscow, 1973.
Goldsmith, R. W. 'The Economic Growth of Tsarist Russia, 1860–1913', *Economic Development and Cultural Change*, vol. IX (1961), pp. 441–75.
Granick, D. *Soviet Metal-Fabricating and Economic Development: Practice versus Policy*. Madison, Milwaukee and London, 1967.
Gregory, P. *Russian National Income, 1885–1913*. Cambridge, 1982.
Hanson, P. *The Consumer in the Soviet Economy*. London, 1968.

Harrison, R. M. 'Soviet Peasants and Soviet Price Policy in the 1920s'. Unpublished Discussion Papers, CREES, University of Birmingham, SIPS No. 10, 1977.
Hodgman, D. R. *Soviet Industrial Production, 1928–1951*. Cambridge, Mass., 1954.
Hunter, H. *Soviet Transportation Policy*. Cambridge, Mass., 1957.
Industrializatsiya SSSR, 1926–1928 gg. Moscow, 1969 (contemporary documents).
Istoriya politicheskoi ekonomii sotsializma. Leningrad, 1972.
Itogi desyatiletiya sovetskoi vlasti v tsifrakh, 1917–1927. Moscow, n.d. [?1928].
Jasny, N. *The Socialized Agriculture of the USSR: Plans and Performance*. Stanford, 1949.
—— *Soviet Industrialization, 1928–1952*. Chicago, 1961.
Kahan, A. 'The Growth of Capital during the Period of Early Industrialization in Russia (1890–1913)', in P. Mathias and M. M. Postan (eds.), *Cambridge Economic History of Europe*, vol. VII. Cambridge, 1978, pp. 265–307.
Kapitsa, P. L. *Teoriya, eksperiment, praktika*. Moscow, 1966.
Kaplan, N. M. and Moorsteen, R. H. *Indexes of Soviet Industrial Output*, RAND Research Memorandum RM–2495. Santa Monica, 1960.
Karcz, J. 'Thoughts on the Grain Problem', *Soviet Studies*, vol. XVIII (1966–7), pp. 399–434.
—— 'Back on the Grain Front', *Soviet Studies*, vol. XXII (1970–1), pp. 262–94.
Kaufman, A. *Small-Scale Industry in the Soviet Union*. Washington, DC, 1962.
Kommunisticheskaya partiya Sovetskogo Soyuza v rezolyutsiyakh i resheniyakh s"ezdov, konferentsii i plenumov TsK, Vols. II–III. Moscow, 1954.
Kondratiev, N. *Rynok khleba i ego regulirovanie v gody voiny i revolyutsii*. Moscow, 1922.
Kontrol'nye tsifry narodnogo khozyaistva SSSR na 1927/1928 god. Moscow, 1928.
Kontrol'nye tsifry narodnogo khozyaistva SSSR na 1929/30 god. Moscow, 1930.
Koropeckyj, I. S. 'The Development of Soviet Location Theory before the Second World War', *Soviet Studies*, vol. XIX (1967–8), pp. 1–28, 232–44.
Kritsman, L. *Geroicheskii period velikoi russkoi revolyutsii*. Moscow, n.d. [?1924].
Kul'turnoe stroitel'stvo SSSR: statisticheskii sbornik. Moscow, 1956.
Lampert, N. 'The Technical Intelligentsia in the USSR, 1928–1935'. Unpublished Ph.D. thesis, University of Birmingham, 1976.
Lenin, V. I. *Selected Works*, 12 vols. London, 1936–8.
—— *Polnoe sobranie sochinenii*, 55 vols. Moscow, 1958–65.
—— *Sochineniya*, 40 vols, 4th edn. Moscow, 1941–62.
Lewin, M. *Russian Peasants and Soviet Power*. London, 1968.
—— *Lenin's Last Struggle*. London, 1969.
—— 'Society and the Stalinist State in the Period of the Five Year Plans', *Social History*, vol. I (1976), pp. 139–75.
—— 'The Communist Party, Yesterday and Today', in R. W. Davies (ed.), *The Soviet Union*. London, 1978, pp. 66–79.
Lorimer, F. *The Population of the Soviet Union: History and Prospects*. Geneva, 1946.
Malafeev, A. N. *Istoriya tsenoobrazovaniya v SSSR (1917–1963 gg.)*. Moscow, 1964.
Malle, S. *The Economic Organisation of War Communism, 1918–1921*. Cambridge, 1985.
Mandel, D. *The Petrograd Workers and the Soviet Seizure of Power: From the July Days 1917 to July 1918*. London and Basingstoke, 1984.
Materialy po balansu narodnogo khozyaistva SSSR za 1928, 1929 i 1930 gg. Moscow, 1932.
Materialy po istorii sovetskogo obshchestva. Moscow, 1959.
Mendel'son, A. S. (ed.) *Pokazateli kon"yunktury narodnogo khozyaistva SSSR za 1923/24–1928/29 gg.* Moscow, 1930.
Mikoyan, A. *Rezul'taty kampanii po snizheniyu tsen*. Moscow, 1927.
Millar, J. R. and Nove, A. 'A Debate on Collectivization: Was Stalin Really Necessary?', *Problems of Communism*, vol. XXV (1976), pp. 49–62.
Morrison, D. 'A Critical Examination of A. A. Barsov's Empirical Work on the Balance of Value Exchanges between the Town and the Country', *Soviet Studies*, vol. XXXIV (1982), pp. 570–84.
Moshkov, Yu. A. *Zernovaya problema v gody sploshnoi kollektivizatsii sel'skogo khozyaistva SSSR*. Moscow, 1966.
Narodnoe khozyaistva SSSR v 1958 godu: statisticheskii ezhegodnik. Moscow, 1959.

Neale, L. A. 'The Production-function and Industrial Growth in the Soviet Union'. Unpublished Discussion Papers, CREES, University of Birmingham, Series RC/A, No. 1, 1965.

Nimitz, N. *Farm Employment in the Soviet Union, 1928–1963.* RAND Memorandum RM–4623–PR. Santa Monica, 1965.

Nove, A. *An Economic History of the USSR.* London, 1969.

Nutter, G. W. *The Growth of Industrial Production in the Soviet Union.* Princeton, NJ, 1962.

Odinnadtsatyi s"ezd RKP(b): mart–aprel' 1922 goda: stenograficheskii otchet. Moscow, 1961.

Ofer, G. *The Service Sector in Soviet Economic Growth: A Comparative Study.* Cambridge, Mass., 1973.

Pethybridge, R. *The Social Prelude to Stalinism.* London, 1974.

Planovoe khozyaistvo. Journal. Moscow.

Polyakov, Yu. A. *Perekhod k nepu i sovetskoe krest'yanstvo.* Moscow, 1967.

Preobrazhensky, E. *The New Economics.* Oxford, 1965 (first published Moscow, 1924–6).

Promyshlennost' SSSR: statisticheskii sbornik. Moscow, 1964.

Puti industrializatsii. Journal. Moscow.

Roberts, P. C. *Alienation and the Soviet Economy.* Albuquerque, 1971.

Schlesinger, R. *The Spirit of Post-War Russia: Soviet Ideology, 1917–1946.* London, 1947.

Sel'skoe khozyaistvo SSSR: statisticheskii sbornik. Moscow, 1960.

Serge, V. *Year One of the Russian Revolution.* London, 1972.

Seton, F. 'Soviet Economic Trends and Prospects – Production Functions in Soviet Industry', *The American Economic Review*, vol. LXIX (1959), pp. 1–14.

Shanin, T. *The Awkward Class: Political Sociology of Peasantry in a Developing Society: Russia, 1910–1925.* Oxford, 1972.

Sidorov, A. L. *Ekonomicheskoe polozhenie Rossii v gody pervoi mirovoi voiny.* Moscow, 1973.

Smith, R. E. F. (ed.) *The Russian Peasant, 1920 and 1984.* London, 1977.

Sobranie uzakonenii i rasporyazhenii rabochego i krest'yanskogo pravitel'stva. Petrograd–Moscow, 1917–24. (The main series of government decrees published before the formation of the government of the USSR; continued as the decrees of the Russian Republic.)

Sobranie zakonov i rasporyazhenii SSSR. Moscow, 1924– . (The main series of government decrees published after the formation of the government of the USSR; regularly published in two parts – part two, not cited here, concerned personnel and institutional changes.)

Sotsialisticheskoe stroitel'svo SSSR. Moscow, 1935.

Spulber, N. (ed.) *Foundations of Soviet Strategy for Economic Growth: Selected Soviet Essays, 1924–1930.* Bloomington, Indiana, 1964.

Stalin, I. V. *Sochineniya*, 13 vols. Moscow, 1946–51.

—— *Sochineniya*, vols. I(XIV)–III(XVI), ed. R. H. McNeal. Stanford, Calif., 1967.

Statisticheskii spravochnik SSSR za 1928. Moscow, 1929.

Statistika i narodnoe khozyaistvo. Journal. Moscow.

Strana sovetov za 50 let: sbornik statisticheskikh materialov. Moscow, 1967.

Strumilin, S. G. *Na planovom fronte.* Moscow, 1958 (writings and speeches of the 1920s).

Sutton, A. C. *Western Technology and Soviet Economic Development, 1930 to 1945.* Stanford, Calif., 1971.

Swianiewicz, S. *Forced Labour and Economic Development: An Enquiry into the Experience of Soviet Industrialization.* London, 1965.

Szamuely, L. *First Models of the Socialist Economic Systems: Principles and Theories.* Budapest, 1974.

Torgovo-promyshlennaya gazeta (renamed *Za industrializatsiyu* from 1 January 1930). Newspaper. Moscow.

Trotsky, L. *The New Course.* London, 1956 (first published 1923).

—— *The Revolution Betrayed: What is the Soviet Union and Where is it Going?* New York, 1970 (first published 1937).

Trud v SSSR: statisticheskii sbornik. Moscow, 1968.

Trudy IV Vserossiiskogo S"ezda Sovetov Narodnogo Khozyaistva (18 maya–24 maya 1921 g.) Moscow, 1921.

Vainshtein, A. L. 'Itogi, osnovnye tendentsii i kon"yunktura narodnogo khozyaistva v 1923–1924 godu', in *Khozyaistvennye itogi v 1923–1924 g.* Moscow, 1925, pp. 7–51.

Valentinov, N. (Vol'sky). *Novaya ekonomicheskaya politika i krizis partii posle smerti Lenina: goda raboty v VSNKh vo vremya NEP: vospominaniya.* Stanford, Calif., 1971.

Venediktov, A. V. *Organizatsiya gosudarstvennoi promyshlennosti v SSSR*, 2 vols. Leningrad, 1957, 1961.

Vestnik Kommunisticheskoi Akademii. Journal. Moscow.

Vestnik statistiki. Journal. Moscow.

Vneshnyaya torgovlya SSSR za 1918–1940 gg: statisticheskii obzor. Moscow, 1960.

Vos'moi Vserossiiskii s"ezd Sovetov: stenograficheskii otchet. Moscow, 1921.

Vyltsan, M. *Sovetskaya derevnya nakunune Velikoi Otechestvennoi voiny (1938–1941 gg.)* Moscow, 1970.

Wheatcroft, S. G. 'The Reliability of Prewar Grain Statistics', *Soviet Studies*, vol. xxvi (1974), pp. 157–80.

—— 'The Population Dynamic and Factors Affecting it in the Soviet Union in the 1920s and 1930s'. Unpublished Discussion Papers, CREES, University of Birmingham, SIPS Nos. 1–2, 1976.

—— 'Grain Production and Utilisation in Russia and the USSR before Collectivisation'. Unpublished Ph.D. thesis, University of Birmingham, 1980.

—— 'On Assessing the Size of Forced Concentration Camp Labour in the Soviet Union, 1929–56', *Soviet Studies*, vol. xxxiii (1981), pp. 265–95.

—— 'Towards a Thorough Analysis of Soviet Forced Labour Statistics', *Soviet Studies*, vol. xxxv (1983), pp. 223–37.

—— 'A Note on Steven Rosefielde's Calculations of Excess Mortality in the USSR, 1929–1949', *Soviet Studies*, vol. xxxvi (1984), pp. 277–81.

—— 'The Soviet Economic Crisis of 1932: The Crisis in Agriculture'. Unpublished paper presented to the National Association of Soviet and East European Studies, 23–25 March 1985.

Wheatcroft, S. G. and Davies, R. W. (eds.) *Materials for a Balance of the Soviet National Economy, 1928–1930.* Cambridge, 1985.

Wheatcroft, S. G., Davies, R. W. and Cooper, J. M. 'Soviet Industrialization Reconsidered: Some Preliminary Conclusions about Economic Development between 1926 and 1941', *Economic History Review*, vol. xxxix (1986), pp. 264–94.

Wilber, C. K. *The Soviet Model and Underdeveloped Countries.* Chapel Hill, NC, 1969.

Yakovlev, A. *Tsel' zhizni.* Moscow, 1967.

Yurovskii, L. *Denezhnaya politika sovetskoi vlasti, 1917–1927.* Moscow, 1928.

Zagorskii, S. O. *K sotsializmu ili k kapitalizmu.* [Paris], 1927.

Za industrializatsiyu. Newspaper. Moscow.

Zaleski, E. *Planning for Economic Growth in the Soviet Union, 1918–1932.* Chapel Hill, NC, 1971.

CHAPTER XV

Economic and social policy in Sweden, 1850–1939

Akerman, J. *Ekonomisk teori*, vol. II. Lund, 1944.
—— *Nationalekonomins utveckling*. Lund, 1951.
Arbetslösutredningens betänkande I. Sou, 1931: 20.
Bäckström, K. *Arbetarrörelsen i Sverige*, vols. I and II. Surte, 1973.
Beckman, S. 'Ekonomisk politik och teori i Norden under mellankrigstiden', in *Kriser och krispolitik i Norden under mellankrigstiden*. Uppsala, 1974.
Bergström, V. *Den ekonomiska politiken i Sverige och dess verkningar*. Uppsala, 1970.
—— 'Nationalekonomerna och arbetarrörelsen', in J. Herin and L. Werin (eds.), *Ekonomisk debatt och ekonomisk politik*. Lund, 1977.
Brisman, S. *Sveriges Riksbank*, del IV. Stockholm, 1931.
Carlsson, S. *Bonden i svensk historia*, del III. Stockholm, 1956.
Cassel, G. *Socialpolitik*. Stockholm, 1902.
—— *Socialism eller framåeskridande*. Stockholm, 1928.
—— *Teoretisk socialekonomi*. Stockholm, 1938 edn.
Edebalk, P. G. *Arbetslöshetsförsäkringsdebatten. En studie i Svensk socialpolitik 1892–1934*. Lund, 1975.
Elmér, Å. *Svensk socialpolitik*. Malmö, 1958.
Från Palm till Palme, Den svenska socialdemokratins program 1882–1960. Stockholm, 1972.
Fredriksson, G., Strand, D. and Södersten, B. *Per Albin-linjen*. Stockholm, 1970.
Fridlizius, G. 'Sweden's Exports 1850–1960', *Economy and History*. vol. VI (1963).
Gårdlund, T. '1933 års svenska krispolitik – Marcus Wallenbergs brevvåxling med Strakosch och Keynes', in J. Herin and L. Werin (eds.), *Ekonomisk debatt och ekonomisk politik*. Lund, 1977.
Gellerman, Olle. *Staten och jordbruket 1867–1918*. Uppsala, 1958.
Gerdner, G. *Parlamentarismens kris i Sverige vid 1920-talets början*. Uppsala, 1954.
Gustafsson, B. 'A Perennial of Doctrinal History: Keynes and "the Stockholm school"', *Economy and History*, vol. XVI (1973).
—— 'Perspektiv på den offentliga sektorn under 1930-talet', in *Kriser och krispolitik i Norden under mellankrigstiden*. Uppsala, 1974.
Hadenius, S., Wieslander, H. and Molin, B. *Sverige efter 1900*. Stockholm, 1968.
Hammarskjöld, D. 'Den svenska diskussionen om penningpolitikens mål', in Eli Heckscher (ed.), *Studier i ekonomi och historia, tillägnad*. Uppsala 1944.
Hansson, S. *Arbetarrörelsen i Sverige*. Stockholm, 1938.
Heckscher, E. F. *Bidrag till Sveriges ekonomiska och sociala historia under och efter världskriget*. Stockholm, 1926.
—— *Svenskt arbete och liv*. Stockholm, 1965.
Historisk statistik för Sverige, vol. I: *Befolkning 1720–1967*. Stockholm, 1969.
Håstad, E. *Sveriges historia under 1900-talet*. Stockholm, 1958.
Hatje, A. K. *Befolkningsfrågan och välfärden*. Stockholm, 1974.
Höjer, K. J. *Svensk socialpolitisk historia*. Malmö, 1952.
Höök, E. *Den offentliga sektorns expansion*. Uppsala, 1962.
Hultén, G. *Arbetsrätt och klassherravälde. Kring strejklagarnas historia*. Halmstad, 1971.
Jonung, L. 'Knut Wicksells prisstabiliseringsnorm och penning-politiken på 1930-talet', in J. Herin and L. Werin (eds.), *Ekonomisk debatt och ekonomisk politik*. Lund, 1977.
Jörberg, L. 'The Industrial Revolution in the Nordic Countries', *The Fontana Economic History of Europe*, vol. IV, no. 2. London, 1973.
—— *A History of Prices in Sweden 1732–1914*, vols. I–II. Lund, 1972.
Jörberg, L. and Krantz, O. *Scandinavia 1914–1970*, *The Fontana Economic History of Europe*, vol. VI, no. 2. London, 1976.
Karleby, N. *Socialismen inför verkligheten*. Stockholm, 1926.
Kock, K. *Kreditmarknad och räntepolitik 1924–1958*, vols. I–II. Uppsala, 1961, 1962.
Kragh, B. *Konjunkturläget. Svensk penningpolitik 1914–1942*. Malmö, 1943.

—— 'Den penningpolitiska diskussionen i Sverige under och efter förra världskriget', *Ekonomisk tidskrift*, 1944.

Krantz, O. and Nilsson, C. A. *Swedish National Product 1861–1970*. Lund, 1975.

—— 'Om strukturgränser i svensk ekonomi 1861–1975', *Meddelande från Ekonomiskhistoriska institutionen, Lunds universitet*, no. 2 (1978).

Landgren, K. G. *Den 'nya ekonomin' i Sverige*. Uppsala, 1960.

—— 'Socialdemokratisk krispolitik och engelsk liberalism – ett genmäle till Otto Steiger', *Arkiv*, no. 2 (1972).

Lester, R. A. 'Sweden's Experience with "Managed Money"', *Supplement till Svenska Handelsbankens Index* (January 1937).

Lewin, L. *Planhushållningsdebatten*. Uppsala, 1967.

Lindeberg, S. O. *Nödhjälp och samhällsneutralitet. Svensk arbetslöshetspolitik*. Lund, 1968.

Lindhagen, J. *Socialdemokratins program, första delen, 1890–1930*. Karlskrona, 1972.

Lindström, H. *Näringsfrihetens utveckling i Sverige*: vol. I, *1809–1836*; vol. II, *1837–1864*. Gothenberg, 1923, 1929.

Lundberg, E. *Konjunkturer och ekonomisk politik*. Stockholm, 1953. (Published as *Business Cycles and Economic Policy*. London, 1957.)

—— 'Gustav Cassels insatser som nationalekonom', *Skandinaviska Banken Kvartalsskrift*, vol. I (1967).

—— *Instability and Economic Growth*. New Haven, 1968.

—— 'Ekonomernas debatt om ekonomisk politik. Strödda synpunkter', in J. Herin and L. Werin (eds.), *Ekonomisk debatt och ekonomisk politik*. Lund, 1977.

McCloskey, D. N. and Zecher, J. R. 'How the Gold Standard Worked 1880–1913', in J. A. Frenkel and H. G. Johnson (eds.), *The Monetary Approach to the Balance of Payments*. London, 1976.

Montgomery, A. *Svensk tullpolitik 1816–1911* (SOU 1924:37).

—— *Svensk Socialpolitik under 1800-talet*. Stockholm, 1934.

—— *How Sweden Overcame the Depression*. Stockholm, 1938.

—— *The Rise of Modern Industry in Sweden*. London, 1939.

—— *Svensk och internationell ekonomi 1913–1939*. Malmö, 1954.

Myrdal, A. and Myrdal, G. *Kris i befolkningsfrågan*. Stockholm, 1934.

Myrdal, G. 'PM ang. verkningarna på den ekonomiska konjunkturutvecklingen i Sverige av olika åtgärder inom den offentliga hushållningens område', *1933 års statsverksproposition, bilaga III*.

Nilsson, A. and Pettersson, L. 'Nationalekonomi och historia. Exemplet svenskt 1930-tal', *Meddelanden från Ekonomisk-historiska institutionen, Lunds universitet*, no. 5 (1979).

Nordström, H. *Svensk arbetslöshetspolitik 1914–1933*. Stockholm, 1934.

—— *Svensk arbetslöshetspolitik*. Stockholm, 1949.

Nyman, O. *Krisuppgörelsen mellan socialdemokraterna och bondeförbundet 1933*. Uppsala, 1944.

Ohlin, B. *Ung man blir politiker*. Stockholm, 1972.

—— 'Några intryck från Nationalekonomiska föreningen 1918–23', in J. Herin and L. Werin (eds.), *Ekonomisk debatt och ekonomisk politik*. Lund, 1977.

Ohlsson, L. *Utrikeshandeln och den ekonomiska tillväxten i Sverige 1871–1966*. Uppsala, 1969.

Öhman, B. 'Krispolitikens förhistoria', *Tiden* 1969.

—— *Svensk arbetsmarknadspolitik 1900–1947*. Halmstad, 1970.

Östlind, A. *Svensk samhällsekonomi 1914–1922. Med särskild hänsyn till industri, banker och penningväsen*. Stockholm, 1945.

Riksbankens årsbok. 1931 and 1932.

Riksräkenskapsverkets årsbok.

Sellberg, H. *Staten och arbetarskyddet 1850–1918*. Uppsala, 1950.

Silenstam, P. *Arbetskraftsutbudets utveckling i Sverige 1870–1965*. Uppsala, 1970.

Simonsson, K. 'Riksbanken som centralbank', *Sveriges Riksbank IV*. Stockholm, 1931.

Sociala meddelanden. 1935, no. 3.

Södersten, B. 'Per Albin och den socialistiska reformismen', in G. Fredriksson *et al.*, *Per Albin linjen*. Stockholm, 1970.

Steiger, O. *Studien zur Entstehung der Neuen Wirtschaftslehre in Schweden*. Berlin, 1971.

—— 'Bakgrunden till 30-talets socialdemokratiska krispolitik', *Arkiv*, no. 1 (1972).
Thomas, B. *Monetary Policy and Crises: A Study of Swedish Experience*. London, 1936.
Tingsten, H. *Den svenska socialdemokratins idéutveckling*, vol. 1. Stockholm, 1941.
Uhr, C. G. 'Economists and Policy Making 1930–1936: Sweden's Experience', *History of Political Economy*, vol. IX, no. 1 (Spring 1977), pp. 89–121.
Unga, N. *Socialdemokratien och arbetslöshetsfrågan 1912–34*. Stockholm, 1976.
Wigforss, E. *Den ekonomiska krisen*. Stockholm, 1931.
—— 'Den nya ekonomiska politiken', *Ekonomisk tidskrift*, no. 5 (1960).
—— *Från klasskamp till samverkan*. Stockholm, 1941.
—— *Krispolitik, miljonrullning och sparsamhet*. Stockholm, 1934.

CHAPTER XVI

Aspects of economic and social policy in Japan, 1868–1945

Akamatsu, Paul. *Meiji 1868: Revolution and Counter Revolution in Japan*. London, 1972.
Allen, G. C. *Modern Japan and Its Problems*. London, 1928.
—— *Japan: The Hungry Guest*. London, 1938.
—— *Japanese Industry: Its Recent Development and Present Condition*. New York, 1939.
—— *A Short Economic History of Modern Japan*. London, 1972.
—— 'Factors in Japan's Economic Growth', in C. D. Cowan (ed.), *The Economic Development of China and Japan*. London, 1964.
Asakawa, K. 'Characteristics of Finance in the Meiji Period', *Developing Economies*, vol. v, no. 2 (1967).
Ayusawa, I. F. *A History of Labor in Modern Japan*. Honolulu, 1966.
Beasley, W. G. *The Meiji Restoration*. London, 1973.
—— *The Modern History of Japan*. London, 1973.
Bergamini, David. *Japan's Imperial Conspiracy*. London, 1971.
Bisson, T. A. *Japan's War Economy*. New York, 1945.
Bolitho, Harold. *Treasures Among Men: The Fudai Daimyo in Tokugawa Japan*. New Haven, 1974.
Broadbridge, Seymour. *Industrial Dualism in Japan*. London, 1966.
—— 'Technological Progress and State Support in the Japanese Shipbuilding Industry', *Journal of Development Studies*, vol. i, no. 2 (January 1965).
—— 'Shipbuilding and the State in Japan since the 1850s', *Modern Asian Studies*, vol. xi, no. 4 (1977).
Cameron, Rondo (ed.) *Banking and Economic Development*. London, 1972.
Cameron, Rondo, Crisp, Olga, Patrick, Hugh T. and Tilly, Richard. *Banking in the Early Stages of Industrialization*. London, 1967.
Chambliss, William Jones. *Chiaraijima Village*. Tucson, 1965.
Cowan, C. D. (ed.) *The Economic Development of China and Japan*. London, 1964.
Craig, Albert M. *Choshu and the Meiji Restoration*. Cambridge, Mass., 1961.
Crawcour, E. Sydney. 'The Tokugawa Heritage', in William W. Lockwood (ed.), *The State and Economic Enterprise in Japan*. Princeton, NJ, 1965.
Crocker, W. R. *The Japanese Population Problem: The Coming Crisis*. London, 1931.
Crowley, James B. *Japan's Quest for Autonomy: National Security and Foreign Policy, 1930–1938*. Princeton, NJ, 1966.
Crowley, James B. (ed.) *Modern East Asia: Essays in Interpretation*. New York, 1970.
Dore, R. P. *Education in Tokugawa Japan*. London, 1965.
—— *Land Reform in Japan*. London, 1959.
—— 'Agricultural Improvement in Japan 1870–1900', in E. L. Jones and S. J. Woolf (eds.), *Agrarian Change and Economic Development*. London, 1969.
—— 'The Importance of Educational Traditions: Japan and Elsewhere', *Pacific Affairs*, vol. xlv, no. 4 (Winter 1972–3).
—— 'Japan as a Model of Economic Development', *Archives Europeennes de Sociologie*, vol. v (1964).
Dore, R. P. and Ōchi, Tsutomu. 'Rural Origins of Japanese Fascism', in James W. Morley (ed.), *Dilemmas of Growth in Prewar Japan*. Princeton, NJ, 1971.
Emi, Koichi. *Government Fiscal Activity and Economic Growth in Japan, 1868–1960*. Tokyo, 1963.
Frost, Peter. *The Bakumatsu Currency Crisis*. Cambridge, Mass., 1970.
Fuji Bank. *Banking in Modern Japan*. Tokyo, 1967.
Fujihara, Ginjiro. *The Spirit of Japanese Industry*. Tokyo, 1936.
Gleason, Alan H. 'Economic Growth and Consumption in Japan', in William W. Lockwood (ed.), *The State and Economic Enterprise in Japan*. Princeton, NJ, 1965.
Hackett, Roger F. *Yamagata Aritomo in the Rise of Modern Japan, 1838–1922*. Cambridge, Mass., 1971.

Hall, John W. 'The Tokugawa Bakufu and the Merchant Class', *University of Michigan Center for Japanese Studies, Occasional Papers*, no. 1 (1951).
Halliday, Jon. *A Political History of Japanese Capitalism*. New York, 1975.
Harootunian, H. 'The Economic Rehabilitation of the Samurai', *Journal of Asian Studies*, vol. XIX, no. 4 (1960).
Hauser, William B. *Economic Institutional Change in Tokugawa Japan: Osaka and the Kinai Cotton Trade*. Cambridge, 1974.
Havens, Thomas R. H. *Farm and Nation in Modern Japan: Agrarian Nationalism, 1870–1940*. Princeton, 1974.
Hirschmeier, Johannes. *The Origins of Entrepreneurship in Meiji Japan*. Cambridge, Mass., 1964.
Hirschmeier, Johannes and Yui, Tsunehiko. *The Development of Japanese Business, 1600–1973*. London, 1975.
Ishii, Ryoichi. *Population Pressure and Economic Life in Japan*. London, 1937.
Ishii, Ryosuku (ed.) *Japanese Legislation in the Meiji Era*. Tokyo, 1969.
Islam, Nurul. *Foreign Capital and Economic Development: Japan, India and Canada*. Tokyo, 1960.
Jansen, Marius B. *Sakamoto Tyoma and the Meiji Restoration*. Princeton, NJ, 1961.
Johnston, B. F. 'Agricultural Productivity and Economic Development in Japan', *Journal of Political Economy*, vol. LIX, no. 6 (1951).
Kelley, Allen C. and Williamson, Jeffrey G. *Lessons from Japanese Development*. Chicago, 1974.
Klein, Lawrence, and Ohkawa, Kazushi (eds.) *Economic Growth: The Japanese Experience since the Meiji Era*. Homewood, Ill., 1968.
Kuznets, S. *et al. Economic Growth: Brazil, India, Japan*. Durham, NC, 1955.
Landes, David S. 'Japan and Europe: Contrasts in Industrialization', in William W. Lockwood (ed.), *The State and Economic Enterprise in Japan*, Princeton, NJ, 1965.
Lockwood, William W. *The Economic Development of Japan: Growth and Structural Change, 1868–1938*. Princeton, NJ, 1954.
Lockwood, William W. (ed.) *The State and Economic Enterprise in Japan*. Princeton, NJ, 1965.
Maddison, Angus. *Economic Growth in Japan and the U.S.S.R.* London, 1969.
Marshall, Byron K. *Capitalism and Nationalism in Prewar Japan: The Ideology of the Business Elite, 1868–1941*. Stanford, 1967.
Mathias, Peter and Postan, M. M. (eds.) *The Cambridge Economic History of Europe*, vol. VII: *The Industrial Economies*. Cambridge, 1978.
Minami, Ryoshin. *The Turning Point in Economic Development: Japan's Experience*. Tokyo, 1973.
Mitsubishi Economic Research Bureau. *Japanese Trade and Industry: Present and Future*. London, 1936.
Morley, James W. (ed.) *Dilemmas of Growth in Prewar Japan*. Princeton, NJ, 1971.
Nakamura, James I. 'Growth of Japanese Agriculture, 1875–1920', in William W. Lockwood (ed.), *The State and Economic Enterprise in Japan*. Princeton, NJ, 1965.
—— *Agricultural Production and the Economic Development of Japan, 1873–1922*. Princeton, NJ, 1966.
—— 'The Meiji Land Reform', *Economic Development and Cultural Change*, vol. XIV, no. 4 (1966).
Ohkawa, Kazushi. *Differential Structure and Agriculture*. Tokyo, 1972.
Ohkawa, Kazushi, Johnston, Bruce F. and Kaneda, Hiromitsu (eds.) *Agricultural and Economic Growth: Japan's Experience*. Princeton, NJ, 1970.
Ohkawa, Kazushi and Rosovsky, Henry. 'A Century of Japanese Economic Growth', in William W. Lockwood (ed.), *The State and Economic Enterprise in Japan*. Princeton, NJ, 1965.
—— *Japanese Economic Growth*. Stanford, 1973.
—— 'The Role of Agriculture in Modern Japanese Development', *Economic Development and Cultural Change*, vol. IX, pt II (1960).
—— 'Recent Japanese Growth in Historical Perspective', *American Economic Review*, vol. LIII, no. 2 (May 1963).

Oshima, Harry T. 'Meiji Fiscal Policy and Agricultural Progress', in William W. Lockwood (ed.), *The State and Economic Enterprise in Japan*. Princeton, NJ, 1965.

Passin, Herbert. *Society and Education in Japan*. New York, 1966.

Patrick, Hugh T. 'The Economic Muddle of the 1920's', in James W. Mor'ey (ed.), *Dilemmas of Growth in Prewar Japan*. Princeton, NJ, 1971.

—— 'Japan 1868–1914', in Rondo Cameron (ed.), *Banking in the Early Stages of Industrialization*. London, 1967.

—— 'External Equilibrium and Internal Convertibility: Financial Policy in Meiji Japan', *Journal of Economic History*, vol. XXV, no. 2 (1965).

Patrick, Hugh T. (ed.) *Japanese Industrialization and its Social Consequences*. Berkeley, 1976.

Ranis, Gustav. 'Factor Proportions in Japanese Economic Development', *American Economic Review*, vol. XLVII (1957).

—— 'Capital–Output Ratio in Japanese Economic Development', *Review of Economic Studies*, vol. XXVI, no. 1 (1958).

—— 'The Financing of Japanese Economic Development', *Economic History Review*, 2nd series, vol. XI, no. 3 (1959).

Reubens, Edwin P. 'Foreign Capital and Domestic Development in Japan', in S. Kuznets (ed.), *Economic Growth: Brazil, India, Japan*. Durham, NC, 1955.

Roberts, John G. *Mitsui: Three Centuries of Japanese Business*. New York and Tokyo, 1973.

Rosovsky, Henry. *Capital Formation in Japan, 1868–1940*. New York, 1961.

—— 'Japan's Transition to Modern Economic Growth, 1868–1885', in Henry Rosovsky (ed.), *Industrialization in Two Systems*. New York, 1966.

Sansom, Sir George. *The Western World and Japan*. London, 1950.

—— *A History of Japan Vol. III, 1615–1867*. London, 1964.

Schumpeter, E. B. *et al. The Industrialization of Japan and Manchukuo, 1930–1940*. New York, 1940.

Sheldon, Charles David. *The Rise of the Merchant Class in Tokugawa Japan, 1600–1868*. Locust Valley, NY, 1958.

Shibagaki, K. 'The Early History of the Zaibatsu', *Developing Economies*, vol. IV, no. 4 (1966).

Shinohara, Miyohei. *Growth and Cycles in the Japanese Economy*. Tokyo, 1962.

—— *Structural Changes in Japan's Economic Development*. Tokyo, 1970.

Smith, Thomas C. *Political Change and Industrial Development in Japan: Government Enterprise, 1868–1880*. Stanford, 1955, 1965.

—— *The Agrarian Origins of Modern Japan*. Stanford, 1959.

—— 'The Land Tax in the Tokugawa Period', *Journal of Asian Studies*, vol. XVIII, no. 1 (1958).

Taeuber, Irene B. *The Population of Japan*. Princeton, NJ, 1958.

Taira, Koji. *Economic Development and the Labor Market in Japan*. New York, 1970.

—— 'Factory Labour and the Industrial Revolution in Japan', in Peter Mathias and M. M. Postan (eds.), *The Cambridge Economic History of Europe*. vol. VII, *The Industrial Economies*. Cambridge, 1978.

Takahashi, Kamekichi. *The Rise and Development of Japan's Modern Economy*. Tokyo, 1969.

Tanaka, M. 'Industrialisation on the Basis of Imported Technology: A Case-Study of the Japanese Heavy Chemical Industry, 1870–1939'. Unpublished M. Phil. thesis, University of Sussex, 1978.

Tanin, O. and Yohan, E. *Militarism and Fascism in Japan*. London, 1934.

Tiedemann, Arthur E. 'Big Business and Politics in Prewar Japan', in James W. Morley (ed.), *Dilemmas of Growth in Prewar Japan*. Princeton, NJ, 1971.

Totten, George O. *Democracy in Prewar Japan*. Lexington, Mass., 1965.

Tsukahira, Toshio G. *Feudal Control in Tokugawa Japan: The Sankin Kōtai System*. Cambridge, Mass., 1970.

Tsuru, Shigeto. *Essays on Japanese Economy*. Tokyo, 1958.

Utley, Freda. *Japan's Feet of Clay*. London, 1936.

Wilkinson, Thomas O. *The Urbanization of Japanese Labour, 1868–1955*. Amherst, Mass., 1965.
Yamamura, Kozo. *Economic Policy in Postwar Japan: Growth versus Economic Democracy*. Berkeley, 1967.
—— *A Study of Samurai Income and Entrepreneurship*. Cambridge, Mass., 1974
—— 'Japan, 1868–1930: A Revised View', in Rondo Cameron (ed.), *Banking and Economic Development*. London, 1972.
—— 'The Founding of Mitsubishi', *Business History Review*, vol. XLI, no. 2 (1967).
—— 'Zaibatsu Pre-War and Zaibatsu Post-War', *Journal of Asian Studies*, vol. XXIII, no. 4 (1964).
—— 'Success Illbegotten? The Role of Meiji Militarism in Japan's Technological Progress', *Journal of Economic History*, vol. XXXVII, no. 1 (March 1977).
Yanaga, Chitoshi. *Big Business in Japanese Politics*. New Haven, 1968.

INDEX